TO THE STUDENT: A study guide to accompany this textbook is available to you through your college bookstore. If the study guide is not in stock, ask your bookstore manager to order: Study Guide to Accompany Principles of Accounting by Helmkamp, Imdieke, and Smith prepared by Bruce A. Baldwin. The study guide will be a valuable study aid for your accounting course.

Ochenduski

Ochenduski

PRINCIPLES OF ACCOUNTING

ACCOUNTING TEXTBOOKS FROM JOHN WILEY & SONS

Arpan and Radebaugh: INTERNATIONAL ACCOUNTING AND MULTINATIONAL ENTERPRISES

Bedford, Perry and Wyatt: ADVANCED ACCOUNTING, 4th

Buckley, Buckley and Plank: SEC ACCOUNTING

Burch and Sardinas: COMPUTER CONTROL AND AUDIT

Burch, Strater, and Grudnitski: INFORMATION SYSTEMS: THEORY AND PRACTICE, 3rd

Copeland and Dascher: FINANCIAL ACCOUNTING

Copeland and Dascher: MANAGERIAL ACCOUNTING, 2nd

DeCoster, Ramanathan, and Sundem: ACCOUNTING: FOR MANAGERIAL DECISION MAKING, 2nd

DeCoster and Schafer: MANAGEMENT ACCOUNTING: A DECISION EMPHASIS, 3rd

Delaney and Gleim: CPA EXAMINATION REVIEW—AUDITING

Delaney and Gleim: CPA EXAMINATION REVIEW—BUSINESS LAW

Delaney and Gleim: CPA EXAMINATION REVIEW—THEORY AND PRACTICE

Delaney and Gleim: CPA EXAMINATION SOLUTIONS (Semiannually May and November)

Gleim and Delaney: CPA EXAMINATION REVIEW Volume I OUTLINES AND STUDY GUIDE

Gleim and Delaney: CPA EXAMINATION REVIEW Volume II PROBLEMS AND SOLUTIONS

Gross and Jablonsky: PRINCIPLES OF ACCOUNTING AND FINANCIAL REPORTING FOR NONPROFIT ORGANIZATIONS

Guy: STATISTICAL SAMPLING IN AUDITING

Haried, Imdieke and Smith: ADVANCED ACCOUNTING, 2nd

Helmkamp, Imdieke and Smith: PRINCIPLES OF ACCOUNTING

Kell and Ziegler: MODERN AUDITING, 2nd

Kieso and Weygandt: INTERMEDIATE ACCOUNTING, 4th

Loeb: ETHICS AND THE ACCOUNTING PROFESSION

McCullers and Schroeder: ACCOUNTING THEORY, 2nd

Mock and Grove: MEASUREMENT, ACCOUNTING, AND ORGANIZATIONAL INFORMATION

Moscove and Simkin: ACCOUNTING INFORMATION SYSTEMS

Ramanathan: MANAGEMENT CONTROL IN NONPROFIT ORGANIZATIONS. TEXT AND CASES

Ramanathan and Hegstad: READINGS IN MANAGEMENT CONTROL IN NONPROFIT ORGANIZATIONS

Sardinas, Burch and Asebrook: EDP AUDITING: A PRIMER

Stenzel: APPROACHING THE CPA EXAMINATION: A Personal Guide to Examination Preparation

Taylor and Glezen: AUDITING—INTEGRATED CONCEPTS AND PROCEDURES, 2nd

Taylor and Glezen: CASE STUDY IN AUDITING, 2nd

Wilkinson: ACCOUNTING AND INFORMATION SYSTEMS

PRINCIPLES OF ACCOUNTING

JOHN G. HELMKAMP
Indiana University

LEROY F. IMDIEKE
Arizona State University

RALPH E. SMITH
Arizona State University

JOHN WILEY & SONS
New York   Chichester   Brisbane   Toronto   Singapore

To our families—for their support and endurance

Cover photographer: ©Martin Bough 1982
Cover photograph retoucher: Béla Mandl

Library of Congress Cataloging in Publication Data:

Helmkamp, John G.
   Principles of accounting.

   Includes index.
   1. Accounting.   I. Imdieke, Leroy F.   II. Smith,
Ralph Eugene, 1941–   .   III. Title.
HF5635.H453   1983   657   82-20124
ISBN 0-471-08510-3

Printed in the United States of America

10 9 8 7 6 5 4 3

PREFACE

During the twentieth century, accounting has become essential to the needs of our society. Almost every person and organization use accounting information to make decisions. Many times, we use accounting concepts and procedures without even realizing it. Individuals maintain bank accounts, account for their income, and file income tax returns. Investors evaluate alternative investments such as bonds, stocks, money market funds, and real estate to decide how to invest their money. Often, people must prepare personal financial information that will support the application for an automobile loan or a home mortgage. A small business needs accounting information to determine if it is financially successful. Large corporations must have detailed records to allocate scarce resources among their various activities and to report financial results to their owners. Charitable organizations rely on accounting information to determine their sources and uses of funds. Governments use accounting procedures to plan and control the receipts and expenditures of public funds. In addition, much of the information needed by the federal government to plan and control our economy is prepared initially by accountants. The list of accounting applications is practically endless.

As we will see in Chapter 1, accounting can be described as the "language of business." Because of its essential role in our society, accounting as a means of communication must be continually modified to satisfy the changing needs of society. In a world of constant and rapid change, the one thing we can be certain of is that our lives and environment in the future will be vastly different from those of today. Accounting as a service activity must alter its structure to satisfy these societal changes. For example, inflationary pressures in recent years have raised questions about certain traditional accounting fundamentals and have forced the accounting profession to seek a better means of accounting. In addition, the severe squeeze on business profits in today's competitive economy has created the need for more effective managerial accounting techniques.

This textbook presents a comprehensive, straightforward description of a modern day version of the principles of accounting. It is a blend of the preparation and use of accounting data, designed primarily for students who have not studied accounting or business subjects before. Our primary objective has been to describe accounting fundamentals as they relate to today's world. Consequently, the coverage is relevant as an introduction to the subject for students interested in a career in accounting as well as for those who need a general understanding of how accounting information is used by businesses. The book is designed primarily for a two semester (two or three quarter) course at the undergraduate level.

ORGANIZATION

The textbook is organized into eight parts as a logical development of both financial and managerial accounting. Part One includes Chapters 1 to 5 and covers the Basic Accounting Process. Chapters 6 and 7 constitute Part Two and describe Accounting Systems and Controls. Part Three discusses Accounting for Assets and Liabilities in Chapters 8 to 13. Partnerships and Corporations are described in Part Four consisting of Chapters 14 to 16. The final coverage of financial accounting topics is presented in Part Five (Chapters 17 to 20) entitled Additional Financial Reporting Issues.

A transition is made from financial accounting to managerial accounting in Chapter 21 as an introduction to Part Six, Managerial Accounting Fundamentals (Chapters 21 to 23). Financial Planning and Controlling Operations makes up Part Seven and is discussed in Chapters 24 and 25. The final segment of the textbook (Part Eight, Chapters 26 to 28) is directed toward Business Decision-making. The 28 chapters represent a comprehensive, modern version of the principles of accounting.

BASIC FEATURES

1. Each chapter begins with a concise description of the coverage (overview) of the chapter and a list of the learning objectives involved. The learning objectives are keyed to specific pages in the chapter.
2. A glossary of key terms is presented at the end of each chapter. Each definition is keyed to a particular page within the chapter where the term is used.
3. Demonstration problems are used in certain early chapters wherever needed to reinforce understanding of the basic concepts and procedures.
4. Discussion questions are included in every chapter to emphasize major points.
5. Exercises related to the most important topics of the chapters are presented in a compact form.
6. Problems and alternative problems are included for more comprehensive homework assignments.
7. Each exercise and problem has a brief description of the topic covered.
8. Business decision cases are included as thought-provoking applications of accounting topics. Many of the cases require the student to refer to infor-

mation contained in the annual reports of three companies presented in the Appendix to the text.

9. Illustrations based on real world applications are presented throughout the textbook to strengthen understanding of the material.

10. Authoritative and informative references are made in nontechnical language wherever applicable to such sources as Accounting Principles Board, Financial Accounting Standards Board, Accounting Trends and Techniques, and specific corporate financial statements.

11. A comprehensive discussion of the time value of money is presented in an Appendix to Chapter 17.

SUPPLEMENTARY MATERIALS

A complete package of supplementary materials carefully designed to support the teaching and learning processes is available with this textbook.

FOR THE STUDENT

Study Guide

Written by Bruce Baldwin of Arizona State University, the Study Guide contains objectives, study tips, and a synopsis for each chapter as well as matching, true/false, completion, multiple-choice, and short answer exercises.

Practice Sets

Four practice sets related to specific chapters in the textbook are available to provide the student with opportunities to apply accounting concepts and procedures to specific situations.

Practice Set IA: Written by Gordon Pirrong of Boise State University, it is in narrative style and covers a small business. It is used after Chapter 6.

Practice Set IB: This is a business papers style version of Practice set 1A.

Practice Set II: It was written by Roselie E. Kenney of Pace University and deals with a corporation. It is to be used after Chapter 16.

Practice Set III: Written by John G. Helmkamp, this managerial practice set covers profit planning and control with a corporation. It is to be used after Chapter 26.

Computerized Practice Set: Prepared by Warren D. Stallings, it relates the accounting cycle to a microcomputer. Supporting software is included.

Workpapers I and II

Workpapers designed to minimize the "pencil pushing" aspect of accounting for the student are available for Chapters 1–14 and Chapters 14–28. The workpapers should assist students in learning proper formats and procedures.

FOR THE INSTRUCTOR

Solutions Manual:

It provides answers to all discussion questions, exercises, and problems in the textbook.

Instructor's Manual:

It identifies learning objectives, keys discussion questions, exercises, and problems to the learning objectives, gives time for completion and difficulty level of the problems, and contains chapter outlines.

Test Bank:

This consists of multiple-choice, true/false, and completion questions for each chapter; it is also available in computerized form.

Achievement Tests:

These are available in forms A and B in quantity to be used for the evaluation of student progress.

Checklist of Key Figures:

These are available in quantity for instructors to distribute as learning aids to students.

Transparencies:

They are available for solutions to all problems plus some of the illustrations in the text.

Solutions to Practice Sets:

These are available for practice sets IA, IB, II, and III as well as for the computerized practice set.

ACKNOWLEDGMENTS

Any textbook is the product of numerous efforts and contributions. We are indebted to many people for their assistance in helping us with this textbook. Early in the book's development, the following professors made valuable suggestions concerning the organization and content of the text: Hobart Adams, University of Akron; Robert Barnes, National College; Craig Christopherson, Richland Junior College; Edward Corcoran, Philadelphia Community College; Paul Herz, University of Illinois; Bill Magers, Tarrant County Junior College; and Earl Purkhiser, San Antonio College. As the project progressed, the following professors reviewed parts or all of the manuscript and helped us in many ways: Toby Atkinson, Brevard Community College; Gerald Axel, Nassau Community College; Bruce Baldwin, Arizona State University; Robert Barnes, National College; Henry Beck, Danville Community College; Pauline Corn, Virginia Polytechnic Institute; William Donahue, Jr., University of Maryland; David Hansen, State University of New York, Genesee; Clara LeLievre, University of Cincinnati; Gary Maydew, Iowa State University; Lois McClain, California State University; Alice Nichols, Florida State University; Lynn Paluska, Nassau Community College; Gordon Pirrong, Boise State University; David Schmedel, Amarillo Junior College; and William Welke, Western Michigan University.

We especially thank Professor David Schmedel who also read galley proofs for accuracy and Professors Arthur LaPorte and William Monagle of Salem State College who solved all the homework material in the text as an independent check on the authors. Professors Jane Burns of Indiana University and Bruce Baldwin of Arizona State University class tested the manuscript of the book and made many valuable suggestions. Thea Hare of Indiana University was instrumental in the development of exercises and problems for the managerial accounting segment. In addition, numerous students have played prominent roles in assisting us, especially Mark Sullivan, Kevin Arnold, and Sharon Johnson of Indiana University, and Karen Curosh, Don Frost, Bob Greenawalt, Steve Limberg, Lori Mann, Andrea Pietrenka, and Bernie Schmitz— all of Arizona State University. Ruby Haltom and Lynn Winkelman provided the essential typing services for the text.

Finally, we are especially grateful for the support and dedication of the Wiley staff members who were involved with the textbook in one way or another. Donald Ford initiated the project, and Lucille Sutton made it all happen. Of course, any errors or omissions are the sole responsibility of the authors.

John G. Helmkamp
Leroy F. Imdieke
Ralph E. Smith

ABOUT THE AUTHORS

John G. Helmkamp, DBA, CPA, is a Professor of Accounting at Indiana University. He received his doctorate in accounting from Indiana University and has published articles in such journals as the Accounting Review, Journal of Information Science, and Managerial Planning. He has taught undergraduate and graduate accounting courses at Arizona State University, Purdue University, and Indiana University during a fifteen year academic career. In addition, Professor Helmkamp has developed and taught a variety of managerial accounting courses offered both nationally and internationally in executive development programs. He is a member of the American Institute of Certified Public Accountants, American Accounting Association, Financial Executives Institute, and the Indiana CPA Society. Professor Helmkamp is also active as a consultant to business and government.

Leroy F. Imdieke, PhD, CPA, is Professor of Accounting at Arizona State University. He received his PhD in accounting from the University of Illinois. He has instructed graduate and undergraduate courses in financial accounting and reporting and has conducted many professional development seminars during his twenty-year career. Professor Imdieke's articles on financial accounting and reporting topics have appeared in *The Accounting Review*, the *Journal of Accountancy*, and other professional journals. He is a member of the American Accounting Association and the Arizona State Society of Certified Public Accountants. He has served on several committees of the American Accounting Association and is currently a member of the Financial Accounting Standards Committee of the Arizona Society of Certified Public Accountants. He has served as a consultant to a number of business firms and state agencies.

Ralph E. Smith, PhD, CPA, is Professor of Accounting at Arizona State University. He has instructed graduate and undergraduate courses and seminars in financial accounting theory and problems. He has also been active in developing and conducting a number of professional development seminars. Professor Smith received his PhD in accounting from the University of Kansas. He is a CPA in the State of Kansas and is a member of the American Accounting Association and the American Institute of Certified Public Accountants. He has served on several committees of the American Accounting Association and also holds membership in Beta Gamma Sigma and Beta Alpha Psi. He has written a number of articles that have appeared in *The Accounting Review*, the *Journal of Accountancy*, the *Journal of Financial and Quantitative Analysis*, and other professional and academic journals.

CONTENTS

PART ONE

THE BASIC ACCOUNTING PROCESS   1

CHAPTER 1
AN INTRODUCTION TO
ACCOUNTING AND ITS CONCEPTS   3
OVERVIEW AND OBJECTIVES   3
ACCOUNTING—THE LANGUAGE OF BUSINESS   4
CHARACTERISTICS OF ACCOUNTING
    INFORMATION   5
USING ACCOUNTING INFORMATION   6
RECORDING AND REPORTING ACCOUNTING
    INFORMATION   7
ACCOUNTING AS A PROFESSION   8
  PUBLIC ACCOUNTING   8
  PRIVATE ACCOUNTING   10
  GOVERNMENTAL ACCOUNTING   11
THE SOURCE OF ACCOUNTING PRINCIPLES
    AND PRACTICES   12
  THE AICPA   12
  THE FASB   12
  THE SEC   13
  THE AAA   13
  THE CASB   14
  THE NAA   14
FORMS OF BUSINESS ORGANIZATION   14
FINANCIAL STATEMENTS   15
  THE BALANCE SHEET   16
  THE INCOME STATEMENT   18
  THE CAPITAL STATEMENT   19
SOME UNDERLYING ACCOUNTING
    CONCEPTS, PRINCIPLES, AND
    ASSUMPTIONS   20
  THE BUSINESS ENTITY CONCEPT   20
  THE COST PRINCIPLE   20
  THE OBJECTIVITY PRINCIPLE   21
  THE GOING CONCERN ASSUMPTION   21
  THE STABLE-DOLLAR ASSUMPTION   21
THE EFFECT OF TRANSACTIONS ON THE
    ACCOUNTING EQUATION   22
GLOSSARY   27
DISCUSSION QUESTIONS   29
EXERCISES   30
PROBLEMS   33
ALTERNATE PROBLEMS   36

CASE FOR CHAPTER 1   39

CHAPTER 2
RECORDING BUSINESS
TRANSACTIONS   41
OVERVIEW AND OBJECTIVES   41
TRANSACTIONS   42
  TYPES OF TRANSACTIONS   42
  TYPICAL TRANSACTIONS OF A BUSINESS
    ENTITY   43
THE ACCOUNTING CYCLE   43
BUSINESS DOCUMENTS   44
RECORDING BUSINESS TRANSACTIONS—USE
    OF ACCOUNTS   45
  STANDARD ACCOUNT FORMS   46
  INDIVIDUAL ACCOUNTS COMMONLY USED   46
  BALANCE SHEET ACCOUNTS   47
GENERAL LEDGER   51
  SEQUENCE AND NUMBERING OF
    ACCOUNTS   51
TRANSACTION ANALYSIS   52
  DEBIT AND CREDIT RULES   52
  NORMAL ACCOUNT BALANCES   54
GENERAL JOURNAL   54
  RECORDING TRANSACTIONS IN A JOURNAL   55
TRANSFERRING INFORMATION FROM THE
    JOURNAL TO THE LEDGER ACCOUNTS   57
ILLUSTRATIVE PROBLEM   57
TRIAL BALANCE   70
DISCOVERY AND CORRECTION OF ERRORS   71
  CORRECTING ERRORS   72
DEMONSTRATION PROBLEM   73
GLOSSARY   76
DISCUSSION QUESTIONS   78
EXERCISES   79
PROBLEMS   83
ALTERNATE PROBLEMS   88

CHAPTER 3
ADJUSTING THE ACCOUNTS AND
PREPARING FINANCIAL STATEMENTS   93
OVERVIEW AND OBJECTIVES   93
MEASUREMENT OF NET INCOME   94
  CASH BASIS   94
  ACCRUAL BASIS   94

WHY ARE ADJUSTING ENTRIES NEEDED? 97
ADJUSTING ENTRIES 97
PREPAID EXPENSES 98
UNEARNED REVENUE (PRECOLLECTED REVENUE) 104
UNRECORDED EXPENSES 105
UNRECORDED REVENUE 109
ADJUSTED TRIAL BALANCE 109
PREPARATION OF FINANCIAL STATEMENTS 109
INCOME STATEMENT 112
BALANCE SHEET 115
DEMONSTRATION PROBLEM 121
GLOSSARY 123
DISCUSSION QUESTIONS 125
EXERCISES 126
PROBLEMS 132
ALTERNATE PROBLEMS 139
CASE FOR CHAPTER 3 146

CHAPTER 4
THE PREPARATION OF A WORKSHEET AND COMPLETION OF THE ACCOUNTING CYCLE 148
OVERVIEW AND OBJECTIVES 148
COMPLETION OF THE ACCOUNTING CYCLE 149
THE WORKSHEET 150
PREPARATION OF THE WORKSHEET 150
USING THE WORKSHEET TO COMPLETE THE ACCOUNTING CYCLE 156
PREPARATION OF FINANCIAL STATEMENTS 156
RECORDING ADJUSTING ENTRIES 157
CLOSING THE ACCOUNTS 160
ACCOUNT BALANCES AFTER COMPLETION OF THE CLOSING PROCESS 169
THE POST-CLOSING TRIAL BALANCE 174
PREPARING INTERIM STATEMENTS WITHOUT CLOSING THE ACCOUNTS 175
ENTRIES MADE IN SUBSEQUENT PERIODS RELATED TO ACCRUALS 176
ACCOUNTING PROCEDURES APPLICABLE TO A PARTNERSHIP OR A CORPORATION 177
ACCOUNTING FOR A PARTNERSHIP 178
ACCOUNTING FOR A CORPORATION 178
REVERSING ENTRIES 180
DEMONSTRATION PROBLEM 183
GLOSSARY 186
DISCUSSION QUESTIONS 186
EXERCISES 187
PROBLEMS 192
ALTERNATE PROBLEMS 198

CHAPTER 5
ACCOUNTING FOR MERCHANDISING OPERATIONS 204

OVERVIEW AND OBJECTIVES 204
MERCHANDISE INVENTORY 205
MERCHANDISING FIRM OPERATIONS 205
INCOME STATEMENT FOR A MERCHANDISING FIRM 206
ACCOUNTING FOR SALES TRANSACTIONS 206
SALES RETURNS AND ALLOWANCES 207
CASH DISCOUNTS 207
TRADE DISCOUNTS 209
FREIGHT-OUT 209
ACCOUNTING FOR INVENTORY AND COST OF GOODS SOLD 210
PERPETUAL INVENTORY SYSTEM 210
ILLUSTRATION OF A PERPETUAL INVENTORY SYSTEM 211
PERIODIC INVENTORY SYSTEM 215
ILLUSTRATION OF A PERIODIC INVENTORY SYSTEM 215
PERPETUAL AND PERIODIC INVENTORY SYSTEMS CONTRASTED 218
END OF PERIOD PROCESS 220
ILLUSTRATION OF WORKSHEETS FOR A MERCHANDISING FIRM 220
PERPETUAL INVENTORY SYSTEM 223
PERIODIC INVENTORY SYSTEM 223
INCOME STATEMENT OF A MERCHANDISING FIRM 225
NET INVOICE METHOD OF RECORDING PURCHASES AND SALES 227
GLOSSARY 228
DISCUSSION QUESTIONS 230
EXERCISES 231
PROBLEMS 235
ALTERNATE PROBLEMS 239
CASE FOR CHAPTER 5 243

PART TWO
ACCOUNTING SYSTEMS AND CONTROLS 245

CHAPTER 6
ACCOUNTING SYSTEMS 246
OVERVIEW AND OBJECTIVES 246
OPERATION OF AN ACCOUNTING SYSTEM 247
INTERNAL CONTROL 248
DEVELOPMENT OF AN ACCOUNTING SYSTEM 248
SYSTEMS ANALYSIS 249
SYSTEMS DESIGN 249
SYSTEMS IMPLEMENTATION 250
MANUAL ACCOUNTING SYSTEMS 250
CONTROL ACCOUNTS AND SUBSIDIARY LEDGERS 251

SPECIAL JOURNALS   252
SALES JOURNAL   253
ADVANTAGES-SALES JOURNAL   255
SUMMARY OF SALES JOURNAL PROCEDURES   255
PURCHASES JOURNAL   256
CASH RECEIPTS JOURNAL   259
SUMMARY OF POSTING PROCEDURES   261
CASH DISBURSEMENTS JOURNAL   262
SUMMARY OF POSTING PROCEDURES   264
USE OF GENERAL JOURNAL   265
REFINEMENTS OF AN ACCOUNTING SYSTEM   266
DATA-PROCESSING EQUIPMENT   267
ELECTRONIC DATA PROCESSING (EDP)   268
   WHAT IS A COMPUTER?   269
   HOW DOES A COMPUTER WORK?   270
COMPUTER ACCOUNTING SYSTEMS   271
GLOSSARY   272
DISCUSSION QUESTIONS   273
EXERCISES   274
PROBLEMS   277
ALTERNATE PROBLEMS   282
CASE FOR CHAPTER 6   288

CHAPTER 7
CASH AND CASH CONTROLS

CASH AND CASH CONTROLS   289
OVERVIEW AND OBJECTIVES   289
GENERAL INTERNAL CONTROL CONCEPTS   290
   ADMINISTRATIVE CONTROLS AND
      ACCOUNTING CONTROLS   290
   THE FOREIGN CORRUPT PRACTICES ACT   291
   CLEARLY ESTABLISHED LINES OF
      RESPONSIBILITY   292
   SEPARATION OF RECORDKEEPING AND
      CUSTODIANSHIP   292
   DIVISION OF RESPONSIBILITY FOR RELATED
      TRANSACTIONS   294
   MECHANICAL AND ELECTRONIC DEVICES   294
   ADEQUATE INSURANCE AND BONDING OF
      EMPLOYEES   294
   INTERNAL AUDITING   295
CONTROL OF CASH   295
   CONTROL OF CASH RECEIPTS   295
   CONTROL OF CASH DISBURSEMENTS   297
APPENDIX: CASH DISBURSEMENTS AND THE
      VOUCHER SYSTEM   308
   PLACING ORDERS   308
   RECEIPT OF GOODS   308
   VERIFICATION OF THE ACCURACY OF
      INVOICES AND APPROVAL OF PAYMENT   311
THE VOUCHER   312
THE VOUCHER REGISTER   313
UNPAID VOUCHERS FILE   314
THE CHECK REGISTER   315
MAKING PARTIAL PAYMENTS   316
RECORDING PURCHASE RETURNS AND
      ALLOWANCES   316

GLOSSARY   316
DISCUSSION QUESTIONS   317
EXERCISES   318
PROBLEMS   321
ALTERNATE PROBLEMS   325
CASE FOR CHAPTER 7   328

PART THREE
ACCOUNTING FOR ASSETS AND LIABILITIES

ACCOUNTING FOR ASSETS
AND LIABILITIES   331

CHAPTER 8
ACCOUNTING FOR RECEIVABLES AND PAYABLES

ACCOUNTING FOR RECEIVABLES
AND PAYABLES   332
OVERVIEW AND OBJECTIVES   332
RECEIVABLES   332
   CLASSIFICATION OF RECEIVABLES   333
   ACCOUNTS RECEIVABLE   333
   NOTES RECEIVABLE   341
PAYABLES   347
   CLASSIFICATION OF PAYABLES   348
GLOSSARY   351
DISCUSSION QUESTIONS   352
EXERCISES   354
PROBLEMS   355
ALTERNATE PROBLEMS   359
CASE FOR CHAPTER 8   362

CHAPTER 9
ACCOUNTING FOR INVENTORIES

ACCOUNTING FOR INVENTORIES   363
OVERVIEW AND OBJECTIVES   363
DETERMINING THE INVENTORY ON HAND   364
   TRANSFER OF OWNERSHIP   365
   GOODS ON CONSIGNMENT   365
DETERMINING THE COST OF INVENTORY   366
ASSIGNMENT OF COST TO ENDING
      INVENTORY AND COST OF GOODS SOLD   366
   PERIODIC INVENTORY SYSTEM   368
COMPARISON OF COSTING METHODS   371
   SPECIFIC IDENTIFICATION   373
   FIRST-IN, FIRST-OUT   373
   LAST-IN, LAST-OUT   374
   WEIGHTED AVERAGE   375
   WHICH METHOD TO SELECT?   375
CONSISTENCY IN USING A COSTING METHOD   375
THE LOWER OF COST OR MARKET RULE   376
NET REALIZABLE VALUE   379
PERPETUAL INVENTORY SYSTEM   380
   PERPETUAL INVENTORY SYSTEM ILLUSTRATED   380
COMPARISON OF INVENTORY SYSTEMS   383

INVENTORY ERRORS | 386
ESTIMATING INVENTORIES | 388
  RETAIL INVENTORY METHOD | 389
  GROSS PROFIT METHOD | 390
PRESENTATION IN FINANCIAL STATEMENTS | 391
GLOSSARY | 391
DISCUSSION QUESTIONS | 393
EXERCISES | 394
PROBLEMS | 398
ALTERNATE PROBLEMS | 404
CASE FOR CHAPTER 9 | 407

CHAPTER 10

PLANT AND EQUIPMENT: ACQUISITION AND ALLOCATION

PLANT AND EQUIPMENT: ACQUISITION AND ALLOCATION | 409
OVERVIEW AND OBJECTIVES | 409
DETERMINING THE COST OF PLANT ASSETS | 410
  APPORTIONING THE COST OF A LUMP-SUM ACQUISITION | 412
  EXCHANGING A NOTE FOR PLANT ASSETS | 412
THE NATURE OF DEPRECIATION | 414
  DETERMINING THE AMOUNT OF DEPRECIATION | 414
  COMPARISON OF DEPRECIATION METHODS | 420
  DEPRECIATION FOR INCOME TAX PURPOSES | 421
  REVISION OF DEPRECIATION RATES | 422
REPORTING DEPRECIATION IN THE FINANCIAL STATEMENTS | 423
  ACCUMULATED DEPRECIATION DOES NOT REPRESENT CASH | 423
CAPITAL AND REVENUE EXPENDITURES | 424
  ORDINARY REPAIRS AND MAINTENANCE | 425
  EXTRAORDINARY REPAIRS | 425
PLANT AND EQUIPMENT RECORDS | 426
GLOSSARY | 428
DISCUSSION QUESTIONS | 429
EXERCISES | 430
PROBLEMS | 433
ALTERNATE PROBLEMS | 437
CASE FOR CHAPTER 10 | 441

CHAPTER 11

PLANT AND EQUIPMENT DISPOSALS: NATURAL RESOURCES AND INTANGIBLES

PLANT AND EQUIPMENT DISPOSALS: NATURAL RESOURCES AND INTANGIBLES | 442
OVERVIEW AND OBJECTIVES | 442
DISCARDING PLANT ASSETS | 443
SALE OF PLANT ASSETS | 444
EXCHANGING PLANT ASSETS | 446
  EXCHANGING SIMILAR ASSETS | 446
  EXCHANGING DISSIMILAR ASSETS | 448
FEDERAL INCOME TAX RULES FOR
EXCHANGES OF PLANT ASSETS | 449
COMPOSITE-RATE DEPRECIATION | 449
NATURAL RESOURCES | 451
  DEPLETION | 451
  DEPRECIATION OF RELATED PLANT ASSETS | 452
INTANGIBLE ASSETS | 453
  AMORTIZATION | 454
  PATENTS | 454
  COPYRIGHTS | 455
  TRADEMARKS AND TRADE NAMES | 455
  LEASEHOLDS | 456
  LEASEHOLD IMPROVEMENTS | 457
  FRANCHISES | 457
  GOODWILL | 458
GLOSSARY | 460
DISCUSSION QUESTIONS | 460
EXERCISES | 461
PROBLEMS | 464
ALTERNATE PROBLEMS | 468
CASE FOR CHAPTER 11 | 471

CHAPTER 12

PAYROLL SYSTEMS

PAYROLL SYSTEMS | 472
OVERVIEW AND OBJECTIVES | 472
IMPORTANCE OF INTERNAL CONTROL | 473
EMPLOYER–EMPLOYEE RELATIONSHIP | 474
GROSS EARNINGS | 475
DEDUCTIONS FROM GROSS EARNINGS | 476
  FICA TAXES | 476
  FEDERAL INCOME TAXES | 477
  OTHER INCOME TAXES | 478
  OTHER DEDUCTIONS | 479
COMPUTATION OF NET EARNINGS | 479
EMPLOYER'S LIABILITY FOR WITHHOLDING | 480
EMPLOYER PAYROLL TAXES | 480
PAYROLL RECORDS AND PROCEDURES | 481
  INPUT DATA | 481
  PAYROLL REGISTER | 482
  EMPLOYEE EARNINGS RECORD | 483
  PAYMENT OF EMPLOYEES | 484
  WAGE AND TAX STATEMENT | 486
  PAYROLL TAX RETURNS | 486
  PAYROLL TAX PAYMENTS | 487
  PAYMENT OF OTHER WITHHOLDING | 487
  SUMMARY OF JOURNAL ENTRIES FOR PAYROLL ACCOUNTING | 487
GLOSSARY | 488
DISCUSSION QUESTIONS | 489
EXERCISES | 490
PROBLEMS | 492
ALTERNATE PROBLEMS | 495
CASE FOR CHAPTER 12 | 498

CHAPTER 13

ACCOUNTING CONCEPTS: EFFECTS
OF INFLATION   500
OVERVIEW AND OBJECTIVES   500
PART A: ACCOUNTING CONCEPTS   501
THE NEED FOR ACCOUNTING STANDARDS   501
GENERALLY ACCEPTED ACCOUNTING
   PRINCIPLES   501
   THE ENTITY CONCEPT   502
   THE GOING CONCERN ASSUMPTION   502
   THE TIME PERIOD ASSUMPTION   503
   THE MONETARY UNIT PRINCIPLE   504
   THE OBJECTIVITY PRINCIPLE   504
   THE COST PRINCIPLE   505
   THE REVENUE REALIZATION PRINCIPLE 505
   EXPENSE RECOGNITION—THE MATCHING
    PRINCIPLE   509
   THE PRINCIPLE OF CONSISTENCY   510
   THE FULL DISCLOSURE PRINCIPLE   511
   MATERIALITY   511
   CONSERVATISM   512
PART B: EFFECTS OF INFLATION   513
REPORTING THE EFFECTS OF INFLATION   514
   CONSTANT DOLLAR ACCOUNTING   515
   CURRENT VALUE ACCOUNTING   518
   FASB REQUIREMENTS   521
GLOSSARY   523
DISCUSSION QUESTIONS   525
EXERCISES   526
PROBLEMS   529
ALTERNATE PROBLEMS   533
CASE FOR CHAPTER 13   539

PART FOUR
PARTNERSHIP AND CORPORATIONS   541

CHAPTER 14

ACCOUNTING FOR A PARTNERSHIP   542
OVERVIEW AND OBJECTIVES   542
PARTNERSHIP DEFINED   543
REASONS FOR FORMING A PARTNERSHIP   543
CHARACTERISTICS OF A PARTNERSHIP   543
   UNLIMITED LIABILITY   544
   LIMITED LIFE   544
   MUTUAL AGENCY   544
   TRANSFER OF PARTNERSHIP INTEREST 544
PARTNERSHIP AGREEMENT   545
ACCOUNTING FOR A PARTNERSHIP   546
   RECORDING THE FORMATION OF A
    PARTNERSHIP   547
ALLOCATION OF PARTNERSHIP NET INCOME
   OR NET LOSS   548
   FIXED RATIO   549
   RATIO BASED ON CAPITAL BALANCES   549

   INTEREST, SALARIES, AND THE REMAINDER IN
    A FIXED RATIO   550
FINANCIAL STATEMENTS FOR A PARTNERSHIP   552
CHANGES IN THE MEMBERS OF A PARTNERSHIP   553
   ADMISSION OF A NEW PARTNER BY
    PURCHASING AN EXISTING INTEREST 553
   ADMISSION OF A NEW PARTNER BY
    CONTRIBUTING ASSETS   554
   WITHDRAWAL OF A PARTNER   556
PARTNERSHIP LIQUIDATION   559
   DISPOSAL OF NONCASH ASSETS—EACH
    PARTNER'S CAPITAL BALANCE SUFFICIENT
    TO ABSORB SHARE OF LOSSES   560
   A PARTNER WITH A DEBIT CAPITAL BALANCE 561
GLOSSARY   563
DISCUSSION QUESTIONS   563
EXERCISES   564
PROBLEMS   567
ALTERNATE PROBLEMS   571
CASE FOR CHAPTER 14   576

CHAPTER 15

CORPORATIONS: ORGANIZATION
AND OPERATION   576
OVERVIEW AND OBJECTIVES   576
THE CORPORATION   579
   ADVANTAGES OF THE CORPORATE FORM 579
   DISADVANTAGES OF THE CORPORATE FORM 581
   FORMING A CORPORATION   582
   MANAGING THE CORPORATION   583
CORPORATE CAPITAL   586
   AUTHORIZED CAPITAL STOCK   587
   OUTSTANDING STOCK   588
   THE ISSUE OF COMMON STOCK   588
   DONATED CAPITAL   590
   NO-PAR STOCK   590
   CASH DIVIDENDS   591
   PREFERRED STOCK   593
   CAPITAL STOCK SUBSCRIPTIONS   596
   BOOK VALUE PER SHARE OF COMMON
    STOCK   597
GLOSSARY   598
DISCUSSION QUESTIONS   600
EXERCISES   601
PROBLEMS   603
ALTERNATE PROBLEMS   607
CASE FOR CHAPTER 15   611

CHAPTER 16

CORPORATIONS: OTHER
TRANSACTIONS, INCOME AND
RETAINED EARNINGS   612
OVERVIEW AND OBJECTIVES   612
TREASURY STOCK   612

PURCHASE OF TREASURY STOCK   613
REISSUE OF TREASURY STOCK   614
RETIREMENT OF STOCK   615
STOCK DIVIDENDS   617
STOCK SPLITS   619
COMPARISON OF LARGE STOCK DIVIDENDS
AND STOCK SPLITS   620
RETAINED EARNINGS RESTRICTIONS   620
COMPREHENSIVE ILLUSTRATION OF
STOCKHOLDERS' EQUITY   621
SPECIAL INCOME STATEMENT ITEMS   621
DISCONTINUED OPERATIONS   622
EXTRAORDINARY ITEMS   624
CHANGE IN ACCOUNTING PRINCIPLE   626
EARNINGS PER SHARE   628
EARNINGS PER SHARE ON THE INCOME
STATEMENT   630
COMPREHENSIVE INCOME STATEMENT
ILLUSTRATED   630
PRIOR PERIOD ADJUSTMENTS   630
RETAINED EARNINGS STATEMENT   633
GLOSSARY   633
DISCUSSION QUESTIONS   633
EXERCISES   635
PROBLEMS   638
ALTERNATE PROBLEMS   641
CASE FOR CHAPTER 16   644

ADDITIONAL PROBLEMS RELATED TO
ACCOUNTING FOR BONDS PAYABLE   664
BONDS ISSUED BETWEEN INTEREST-PAYMENT
DATES   664
YEAR-END ADJUSTING ENTRY FOR BOND
INTEREST EXPENSE   665
RETIREMENT OF BONDS BEFORE MATURITY   667
CONVERSION OF BONDS INTO COMMON
STOCK   667
BOND SINKING FUND   668
EFFECTIVE INTEREST METHOD OF
AMORTIZATION   669
OTHER LONG-TERM LIABILITIES   672
MORTGAGE NOTES PAYABLE   673
LEASE OBLIGATIONS   673
PENSION PLANS   675
GLOSSARY   676
DISCUSSION QUESTIONS   677
EXERCISES   678
PROBLEMS   681
ALTERNATE PROBLEMS   685
CASES FOR CHAPTER 17   689
APPENDIX: TIME VALUE OF MONEY   690
OVERVIEW   690
SIMPLE AND COMPOUND INTEREST   690
FUTURE VALUE OF A SINGLE AMOUNT   691
FUTURE VALUE OF AN ORDINARY ANNUITY   694
PRESENT VALUE OF A SINGLE AMOUNT   696
PRESENT VALUE OF AN ORDINARY ANNUITY   699
EXERCISES   701

PART FIVE
ADDITIONAL FINANCIAL REPORTING ISSUES
647

CHAPTER 17
ACCOUNTING FOR LONG-TERM LIABILITIES
648

OVERVIEW AND OBJECTIVES   648
THE NATURE OF LONG-TERM
LIABILITIES   649
WHY FINANCE THROUGH LONG-TERM DEBT?   650
BONDS PAYABLE   652
CLASSIFICATION OF BONDS   653
ACCOUNTING FOR BONDS ISSUED AT PAR
VALUE   654
THE EFFECT OF MARKET INTEREST RATES ON
BOND PRICES   656
HOW IS THE ISSUE PRICE OF A BOND
DETERMINED?   657
ACCOUNTING FOR BONDS ISSUED AT A
DISCOUNT   658
AMORTIZING THE BOND DISCOUNT   659
ACCOUNTING FOR BONDS ISSUED AT A
PREMIUM   661
AMORTIZING THE BOND PREMIUM   662

CHAPTER 18
INTERCORPORATE INVESTMENTS AND CONSOLIDATED FINANCIAL STATEMENTS
703

OVERVIEW AND OBJECTIVES   703
CLASSIFICATION OF INVESTMENTS   704
TEMPORARY INVESTMENTS   704
LONG-TERM INVESTMENTS   706
ACCOUNTING FOR LONG-TERM INVESTMENTS
IN COMMON STOCK   707
THE COST METHOD   708
THE EQUITY METHOD   709
RECORDING THE SALE OF STOCK
INVESTMENTS   710
ACCOUNTING FOR LONG-TERM INVESTMENTS
IN BONDS   712
BONDS PURCHASED AT A PREMIUM   713
BONDS PURCHASED AT A DISCOUNT   715
RECORDING THE SALE OF BOND
INVESTMENTS   715
CONSOLIDATED FINANCIAL STATEMENTS   716
PRINCIPLES OF CONSOLIDATION   717
CONSOLIDATED BALANCE SHEET   718

PURCHASE OF LESS THAN 100% OF
  SUBSIDIARY STOCK 720
PURCHASE OF STOCK FOR MORE (OR LESS)
  THAN BOOK VALUE 723
CONSOLIDATED INCOME STATEMENT 725
PURCHASE VERSUS POOLING OF INTERESTS ... 726
CONDITIONS FOR THE PREPARATION OF
  CONSOLIDATED FINANCIAL STATEMENTS ... 729
LIMITATIONS OF CONSOLIDATED FINANCIAL
  STATEMENTS 730
GLOSSARY 731
DISCUSSION QUESTIONS 732
EXERCISES 733
PROBLEMS 736
ALTERNATE PROBLEMS 740
CASE FOR CHAPTER 18 745

CHAPTER 19
STATEMENT OF CHANGES
IN FINANCIAL POSITION 746
OVERVIEW AND OBJECTIVES 746
CONCEPTS OF FUNDS 747
SOURCES AND USES OF WORKING CAPITAL ... 748
TRANSACTIONS THAT DO NOT AFFECT
  WORKING CAPITAL 749
TRANSACTIONS THAT AFFECT WORKING
  CAPITAL 749
  SOURCES OF WORKING CAPITAL 750
  USES OF WORKING CAPITAL 752
  THE SPECIAL CASE OF EXCHANGE
    TRANSACTIONS 753
PREPARING THE STATEMENT OF CHANGES IN
  FINANCIAL POSITION—WORKING CAPITAL
  BASIS 754
CASH FLOW STATEMENTS 764
  CASH PROVIDED BY OPERATIONS 766
  PREPARATION OF THE CASH FLOW
    STATEMENT 769
GLOSSARY 770
DISCUSSION QUESTIONS 771
EXERCISES 772
PROBLEMS 776
ALTERNATE PROBLEMS 780
CASE FOR CHAPTER 19 784

CHAPTER 20
ANALYSIS OF FINANCIAL
STATEMENTS 785
OVERVIEW AND OBJECTIVES 785
SOURCES OF FINANCIAL INFORMATION 785
THE NEED FOR ANALYTICAL TECHNIQUES ... 786
OBJECTIVES OF FINANCIAL ANALYSIS 786
PERCENTAGE ANALYSIS 787
  HORIZONTAL ANALYSIS 787

TREND ANALYSIS 790
VERTICAL ANALYSIS 791
RATIO ANALYSIS 791
  RATIOS TO ANALYZE PROFITABILITY 792
  RATIOS TO ANALYZE LIQUIDITY 796
  RATIOS TO ANALYZE SOLVENCY 800
LIMITATIONS OF FINANCIAL ANALYSIS 801
GLOSSARY 802
DISCUSSION QUESTIONS 803
EXERCISES 804
PROBLEMS 808
ALTERNATE PROBLEMS 814
CASE FOR CHAPTER 20 819

PART SIX
MANAGEMENT ACCOUNTING
PRINCIPLES 821

CHAPTER 21
MANAGERIAL ACCOUNTING AND
BUSINESS SEGMENTS 822
OVERVIEW AND OBJECTIVES 822
ORGANIZATIONAL CONSIDERATIONS 823
ROLE OF MANAGEMENT 823
  PLANNING 824
  ORGANIZING 825
  DIRECTING 825
  CONTROLLING 825
  DECISION MAKING 825
DIFFERENT COST CLASSIFICATIONS 826
BUSINESS SEGMENTATION 826
RESPONSIBILITY ACCOUNTING 828
  FUNDAMENTALS OF RESPONSIBILITY
    ACCOUNTING 828
  CHOICE OF RESPONSIBILITY CENTERS ... 828
  MATCHING ACCOUNTING SYSTEM AND
    ORGANIZATION 828
  CONTROLLABILITY FOCUS 828
  PARTICIPATIVE MANAGEMENT 829
  PERFORMANCE REPORTING 829
  MANAGEMENT BY EXCEPTION 830
DEPARTMENTAL ACCOUNTING 830
DEPARTMENTAL GROSS PROFIT:
  MERCHANDISING FIRM 831
ELECTRONIC DATA PROCESSING 832
INCOME STATEMENT WITH DEPARTMENTAL
  GROSS PROFITS 833
DEPARTMENTAL NET INCOME 833
  DIRECT AND INDIRECT OPERATING
    EXPENSES 834
  BASES FOR ALLOCATING EXPENSES 836
  DEPARTMENTAL INCOME STATEMENT 840

DEPARTMENTAL CONTRIBUTION TO INDIRECT EXPENSES	840
FUNDAMENTALS OF BRANCH ACCOUNTING	843
CENTRALIZED VERSUS DECENTRALIZED ACCOUNTING	844
BRANCH ACCOUNTING ILLUSTRATION	845
GLOSSARY	847
DISCUSSION QUESTIONS	848
EXERCISES	849
PROBLEMS	852
ALTERNATE PROBLEMS	857
CASE FOR CHAPTER 21	862

CHAPTER 22
ACCOUNTING FOR A
MANUFACTURING FIRM

MANUFACTURING FIRM	864
OVERVIEW AND OBJECTIVES	864
MANUFACTURING VERSUS NONMANUFACTURING FIRMS	866
RAW MATERIALS	866
WORK IN PROCESS	867
FINISHED GOODS	867
PRODUCT AND PERIOD COSTS	867
MANUFACTURING COST ELEMENTS	869
DIRECT MATERIALS	869
DIRECT LABOR	870
MANUFACTURING OVERHEAD	870
BASIC COST BEHAVIOR CONSIDERATIONS	871
VARIABLE COST	872
FIXED COST	872
COST OF GOODS SOLD (MANUFACTURING VERSUS MERCHANDISING	873
COMPARISON OF INCOME STATEMENTS (MANUFACTURING VERSUS MERCHANDISING)	873
COST OF GOODS MANUFACTURED STATEMENT	873
ACCOUNTING SYSTEM CONSIDERATIONS	875
PERIODIC INVENTORY SYSTEM FOR MANUFACTURING	876
WORK SHEET FOR A MANUFACTURING FIRM	877
CLOSING ENTRIES FOR A MANUFACTURING FIRM	880
VALUATION OF INVENTORIES IN MANUFACTURING	883
LIMITATIONS OF A PERIODIC INVENTORY SYSTEM	886
GLOSSARY	887
DISCUSSION QUESTIONS	888
EXERCISES	890
PROBLEMS	893
ALTERNATE PROBLEMS	897
CASE FOR CHAPTER 22	901

CHAPTER 23
COST ACCOUNTING SYSTEMS

COST ACCOUNTING SYSTEMS	903
OVERVIEW AND OBJECTIVES	903
JOB ORDER COSTING	904
CONTROL DOCUMENT—JOB ORDER COST SHEET	905
ACCOUNTING FOR MATERIALS	906
ACCOUNTING FOR LABOR	909
ACCOUNTING FOR MANUFACTURING OVERHEAD	910
OVERAPPLIED AND UNDERAPPLIED MANUFACTURING OVERHEAD	912
ACCOUNTING FOR THE COMPLETION OF A JOB	913
ACCOUNTING FOR THE SALE OF A JOB	913
PROCESS COSTING	914
CONCEPT OF EQUIVALENT UNITS	914
CONTROL DOCUMENT—COST OF PRODUCTION REPORT	916
PROCESS COSTING PROCEDURES	917
ILLUSTRATION OF PROCESS COSTING	918
GLOSSARY	921
DISCUSSION QUESTIONS	922
EXERCISES	923
PROBLEMS	925
ALTERNATE PROBLEMS	929
CASE FOR CHAPTER 23	934

PART SEVEN
FINANCIAL PLANNING AND
CONTROLLING OPERATIONS

CONTROLLING OPERATIONS	935

CHAPTER 24
FINANCIAL PLANNING AND
CONTROL WITH BUDGETING

CONTROL WITH BUDGETING	936
OVERVIEW AND OBJECTIVES	936
IMPORTANCE OF GOAL CONGRUENCE	937
BENEFITS OF BUDGETING	938
FINANCIAL PLANNING WITH BUDGETING	940
SALES FORECAST	940
STRUCTURE OF THE MASTER BUDGET	941
MASTER BUDGET ILLUSTRATION	943
SALES BUDGET	943
PRODUCTION BUDGET	943
DIRECT MATERIALS BUDGET	944
DIRECT LABOR BUDGET	945
MANUFACTURING OVERHEAD BUDGET	946
COST OF GOODS SOLD BUDGET	948
SELLING EXPENSES BUDGET	949
ADMINISTRATIVE EXPENSES BUDGET	950
BUDGETED INCOME STATEMENT	950

CAPITAL EXPENDITURES BUDGET 952
CASH BUDGET 952
BUDGETED BALANCE SHEET 954
BUDGETED STATEMENT OF CHANGES IN
   FINANCIAL POSITION 955
FINANCIAL CONTROL WITH BUDGETING 955
GLOSSARY 957
DISCUSSION QUESTIONS 958
EXERCISES 959
PROBLEMS 962
ALTERNATE PROBLEMS 965
CASE FOR CHAPTER 24 969

CHAPTER 25
FLEXIBLE BUDGETS AND STANDARD
COSTS 971
OVERVIEW AND OBJECTIVES 971
PERFORMANCE EVALUATION WITH A FIXED
   BUDGET 972
PREPARATION OF A FLEXIBLE BUDGET 973
PERFORMANCE EVALUATION WITH FLEXIBLE
   BUDGET 974
USE OF STANDARD COSTS 976
BENEFITS OF STANDARD COSTS 977
ESTABLISHING STANDARD COSTS 978
STANDARD COST VARIANCES 979
MATERIAL VARIANCE ANALYSIS 981
   PRICE VARIANCE 981
   QUANTITY VARIANCE 981
LABOR VARIANCE ANALYSIS 982
   RATE VARIANCE 982
   EFFICIENCY VARIANCE 982
STANDARD APPLICATION OF
   MANUFACTURING OVERHEAD 983
FLEXIBLE BUDGET FOR MANUFACTURING
   OVERHEAD 983
UNDERAPPLIED AND OVERAPPLIED OVERHEAD 986
OVERHEAD VARIANCE ANALYSIS 987
   CONTROLLABLE VARIANCE 987
   CAPACITY VARIANCE 987
RECAP OF VARIANCES 988
DISPOSITION OF COST VARIANCES 989
GLOSSARY 990
DISCUSSION QUESTIONS 991
EXERCISES 992
PROBLEMS 994
ALTERNATE PROBLEMS 997
CASE FOR CHAPTER 25 1000

PART EIGHT
BUSINESS DECISION MAKING 1003

CHAPTER 26
COST-VOLUME-PROFIT
RELATIONSHIPS 1004
OVERVIEW AND OBJECTIVES 1004
COST BEHAVIORAL ANALYSIS REVISITED 1005
VARIABLE COST BEHAVIOR 1007
FIXED COST BEHAVIOR 1008
MIXED COST BEHAVIOR 1008
COST BEHAVIORAL ANALYSIS OF MIXED
   COSTS 1009
COST BEHAVIOR AND THE INCOME
   STATEMENT 1011
VARIABLE COSTING 1013
RECONCILING VARIABLE COSTING AND
   ABSORPTION COSTING 1014
   NET INCOME 000
ILLUSTRATION OF VARIABLE COSTING 1015
BENEFITS AND LIMITATIONS OF VARIABLE
   COSTING 1018
   BENEFITS 1018
   LIMITATIONS 1018
ASSUMPTIONS OF COST-VOLUME-PROFIT
   ANALYSIS 1018
PROFIT PLANNING WITH CVP ANALYSIS 1019
BREAK-EVEN ANALYSIS 1020
   BREAK-EVEN EQUATION 1020
   CONTRIBUTION MARGIN APPROACH 1021
   GRAPHIC APPROACH 1021
MARGIN OF SAFETY CONCEPT 1022
TARGET NET INCOME 1023
EVALUATING THE IMPACT OF CHANGE 1024
   CHANGE IN SELLING PRICE 1025
   CHANGE IN VARIABLE COSTS 1026
CHANGE IN FIXED AND VARIABLE COSTS 1026
CHANGE OF FIXED COSTS AND SALES
   VOLUME 1027
EXTENSION TO MULTIPLE PRODUCTS 1027
GLOSSARY 1028
DISCUSSION QUESTIONS 1029
EXERCISES 1031
PROBLEMS 1033
ALTERNATE PROBLEMS 1036
CASE FOR CHAPTER 26 1039

CHAPTER 27
MANAGERIAL ACCOUNTING AND
DECISION MAKING 1041
OVERVIEW AND OBJECTIVES 1041
BASICS OF MANAGERIAL DECISION MAKING 1042
DIFFERENTIAL ANALYSIS (INCREMENTAL
   ANALYSIS) 1043
   EVALUATION OF A SPECIAL ORDER 1045
   EVALUATION OF A MAKE OR BUY DECISION 1046
   TREATMENT OF JOINT PRODUCT COSTS 1047

PRODUCT-MIX DECISIONS 1049
RETURN ON INVESTMENT ANALYSIS 1050
RESIDUAL-INCOME ANALYSIS 1051
TRANSFER PRICING DECISIONS 1052
CONTRIBUTION MARGIN VARIANCE ANALYSIS 1053
   SELLING PRICE VARIANCE 1053
   SALES VOLUME VARIANCE 1054
   COST VARIANCE 1054
CAPITAL BUDGETING 1054
USE OF CASH FLOWS 1055
DEPRECIATION AS A TAX SHIELD 1056
PAYBACK PERIOD 1056
RETURN ON AVERAGE INVESTMENT 1057
DISCOUNTED CASH FLOWS 1058
GLOSSARY 1060
DISCUSSION QUESTIONS 1062
EXERCISES 1063
PROBLEMS 1066
ALTERNATE PROBLEMS 1068
CASE FOR CHAPTER 27 1071

CHAPTER 28
INCOME TAXES: AN OVERVIEW 1072
OVERVIEW AND OBJECTIVES 1072
A BRIEF HISTORY OF FEDERAL INCOME
   TAXATION 1073
SOME FEATURES OF THE FEDERAL INCOME TAX
   SYSTEM 1074
   CLASSIFICATIONS OF TAXABLE ENTITIES 1074
   RELATIONSHIP TO GENERALLY ACCEPTED
      ACCOUNTING PRINCIPLES 1074
   THE ROLE OF TAX PLANNING 1075
   CASH BASIS VERSUS ACCRUAL BASIS 1075
TAX CONSIDERATIONS FOR INDIVIDUALS 1076
   TOTAL INCOME, EXCLUSIONS, AND GROSS
      INCOME 1077
   DEDUCTIONS FROM GROSS INCOME 1080

   DEDUCTIONS FROM ADJUSTED GROSS
      INCOME 1081
   COMPUTING THE TAX LIABILITY 1083
   TAX CREDITS 1087
   THE IMPORTANCE OF THE MARGINAL TAX
      RATE 1088
COMPUTATION OF INCOME TAX FOR A JOINT
   RETURN ILLUSTRATED 1089
TAX CONSIDERATIONS FOR CORPORATIONS 1089
   TOTAL REVENUES AND EXCLUSIONS 1091
   DEDUCTIONS FROM GROSS INCOME 1091
   COMPUTING THE TAX LIABILITY 1093
TAX PLANNING AND BUSINESS DECISIONS 1093
   TAX IMPLICATIONS FOR THE CHOICE OF
      BUSINESS ORGANIZATION 1093
   CHOICE OF FINANCING METHODS 1095
   OPERATING THE BUSINESS 1097
REPORTING INCOME TAX EXPENSE 1097
GLOSSARY 1103
DISCUSSION QUESTIONS 1104
EXERCISES 1105
PROBLEMS 1107
ALTERNATE PROBLEMS 1110
CASE FOR CHAPTER 28 1112

APPENDIX
**CONSOLIDATED FINANCIAL
STATEMENTS** A1
GENERAL MOTORS CORPORATION A1
MODERN MERCHANDISING, INC. A12
MARY MOPPET'S DAY CARE SCHOOLS, INC. A25

INDEX I1

PART ONE
THE BASIC ACCOUNTING PROCESS

CHAPTER 1
AN INTRODUCTION
TO ACCOUNTING
AND ITS CONCEPTS

OVERVIEW AND OBJECTIVES

This chapter presents an overview of the purpose and nature of accounting. When you have completed the chapter, you should understand:

- What accounting information is (pp. 5–6).
- Uses of accounting information (pp. 6–7).
- The difference between recording and reporting accounting information (pp. 7–8).
- The main fields of accounting and the type of work involved in each (pp. 8–11).
- The purpose of the balance sheet, income statement, and capital statement (pp. 15–19).
- The meaning of the terms *asset, liability, owner's equity, revenue,* and *expense* (pp. 15–19).
- Some of the basic accounting principles (pp. 20–22).
- How to prepare simple financial statements (pp. 15–19).
- The effect of transactions on the accounting equation (pp. 22–27).

Accounting is a service activity. Its function is to provide financial information about economic activity that is intended to be useful in making economic decisions.[1] Business firms, governmental agencies, charitable foundations and nonprofit organizations, family units, and individuals all engage in economic

[1]Accounting Principles Board, "Basic Concepts and Accounting Principles Underlying Financial Statements of Business Enterprises," *APB Statement No. 4* (New York: AICPA, October, 1970), par. 9.

activity. Most economic activity involves decisions about how to allocate available resources effectively among alternative needs. People need relevant information to be able to make sound decisions. In a society as complex as ours, decision-makers rely on data supplied by specialists in various fields. For example, lawyers provide information about the ramifications of existing and changing legislation, and medical professionals offer advice about the possible effects of different health-care decisions. Accounting as a profession has evolved in response to society's need for economic information.

Decision-makers generally follow a five-step process in making and executing decisions:

1. Goals are established.
2. Various alternatives for reaching the goals are considered.
3. Decisions are made.
4. Decisions are implemented.
5. Results of decisions are evaluated and goals may be revised.

Thus, the decision-making process may be illustrated by the following system:

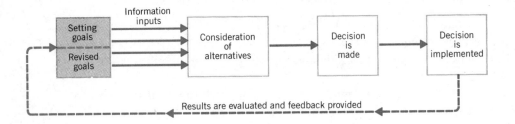

ACCOUNTING—THE LANGUAGE OF BUSINESS

Accounting is often called the "language of business." A language is a means of social communication and involves a flow of information from one person to one or more other persons. To be effective, the recipient of the information must understand the message that the sender intends to convey. Accounting uses words and symbols to communicate financial information that is intended to be useful for decisions made by managers, investors, creditors, and other parties.[2] The terminology and symbols of accounting were developed over a long time in an effort to communicate financial information effectively. As you study accounting, you must learn the meanings of the words and symbols

[2]*Ibid.*, par. 40.

used by accountants if you are to understand the messages contained in financial summaries and reports. Everyone involved in business, from the beginning employee to the top manager, eventually uses some accounting information.

The importance of understanding accounting information is not restricted to those engaged directly in business. Persons with little knowledge of accounting must interpret accounting data. For example, lawyers must often understand the meaning of accounting information if they are to represent their clients effectively, and engineers and architects must consider cost data when designing new technology and buildings. In fact, every adult engages in business transactions dealing with financial aspects of life. Thus, accounting plays a significant role in society and, in a broad sense, everyone is affected by accounting information.

Although accounting procedures and techniques can be used in accounting for all types of economic units, in this book we will concentrate on accounting for a business. Business managers need information provided by the accounting system to plan and control their business activities. In addition, investors, creditors, and governmental agencies need financial information to make investing, lending, regulatory, and tax related decisions.

CHARACTERISTICS OF ACCOUNTING INFORMATION

Accounting is the process of measuring, recording, classifying, and summarizing financial information that is used in making economic decisions. Accounting information is financial data about business transactions expressed in terms of money. **Business transactions** are the economic activities of a business. Accountants classify these business transactions into two types, external and internal. *External transactions* (often called *exchange transactions*) are those that involve economic events between one firm and another independent firm. When a business purchases merchandise from a supplier, borrows money from a bank, or sells merchandise to customers, it participates in an external or exchange transaction. *Internal transactions* are those economic events that take place entirely within one firm. The conversion of wheat into flour and the use over time of machinery and equipment are internal transactions. Accountants use the single term *transaction* to refer to both internal and external transactions, which constitute the inputs of the accounting information system. Recording these historical events is one important function of accounting.

Before the effects of transactions can be recorded, however, they must be *measured*. If accounting information is to be useful, it must be expressed in terms of a common denominator so the effects of transactions can be combined. We cannot add apples to oranges unless we express them in terms of a common measuring unit. In our economy, business activity is measured by prices expressed in terms of money. *Money* serves as both a medium of exchange and as a measure of value, allowing us to compare the value or worth of diverse objects and add and subtract the economic effects of various transactions.

Simply measuring and recording transactions, however, would provide information of limited use. The recorded data must be classified and summarized to be useful in making decisions. *Classification* permits reduction of the effects of thousands of transactions into useful groups or categories. All transactions involving the sale of merchandise, for example, can be grouped into one total sales figure and all transactions involving cash grouped to report a single net cash figure. *Summarization* of financial data is achieved by summaries, reports, and financial statements, which are provided for use by both internal management and outside users of accounting information. These reports usually summarize the effects of all business transactions occurring during some time period such as a month, a quarter, or a year.

USING ACCOUNTING INFORMATION

Accounting provides techniques and procedures for accumulating and reporting financial data. Although accountants are sometimes involved in the analysis and interpretation of accounting data when they serve as advisors to users of accounting information, the ultimate objective of accounting is to provide information usable to internal and external decision-makers. Managers (internal decision-makers) must have financial data for planning and controlling operations of the business. Managers need answers to such questions as: What resources are available to the firm? How much does the company owe to outsiders? How much income is being earned? What products should be produced? What is the most efficient production process? What will be the effect of increasing or decreasing selling prices? Will cash be available to pay debts as they come due? What is the comparative effect of owning and of leasing facilities? Providing data to help answer these and similar questions is an accounting function generally called *managerial accounting*. Chapters 21 through 27 are devoted to the preparation of reports and analyses for use by management.

External decision-makers such as creditors, stockholders, and governmental agencies need accounting information for making decisions concerning the granting of credit, the purchase of shares of stock, and compliance with tax laws and other regulatory standards. Questions raised by external users include: Will the business be able to repay money lent to it? What are the company's earnings prospects? Is the business financially sound? Reports prepared for external users are called *financial statements* and generally consist of a Balance Sheet (sometimes called a Statement of Financial Position), an Income Statement, a Statement of Changes in Financial Position, and a Capital Statement. These statements are often called *general purpose financial statements* because they provide general information for use by all external users. General purpose financial statements also are used, along with the various internal reports, by management. Figure 1-1 illustrates the relationship between accounting reports and users of accounting information.

RECORDING AND REPORTING ACCOUNTING INFORMATION

Many people with little knowledge of accounting tend to view accounting as being limited to the recording process and do not distinguish clearly between the recording and reporting of accounting data. The *recording* or *bookkeeping* process involves measuring and recording business transactions and may take one of several forms: handwritten records, mechanical or electronic devices, or simply punched holes or magnetic marks on cards or magnetic tape in a computerized system.

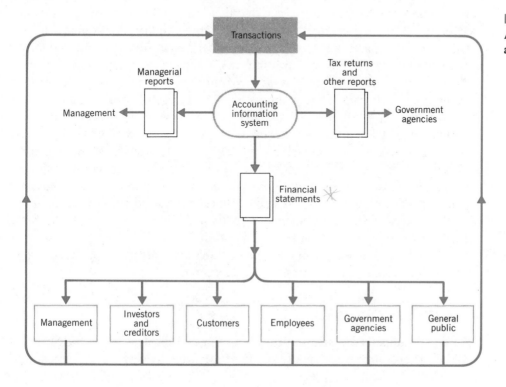

Figure 1-1
Accounting Reports
and Users

The *reporting* process is a much broader function of accounting. It consists of the classification and summarization of accounting data into financial statements as well as the preparation of other interpretive disclosures necessary to make the accounting data understandable. The process is highly technical, requiring extensive training, experience, and professional judgment by the accountant. In addition to recording and reporting, accounting includes such work as the design of accounting systems, the audit of financial statements, cost studies, and the preparation of various tax returns.

ACCOUNTING AS A PROFESSION

Accountancy has developed as a profession over the past century, attaining a status equivalent to that of law and medicine. Individual states license **Certified Public Accountants** (CPAs) just as they license lawyers and doctors. Only those accountants who have passed the CPA examination, met certain education and experience requirements, and received a license may use the designation of Certified Public Accountant.

Although requirements for the CPA license vary, all states require that the candidate pass a uniform examination. Most states require a college degree with a specified minimum number of college credits in accounting and business. The CPA examination is a rigorous, two-and-a-half-day examination covering accounting theory, accounting practice, auditing, and business law. The exam is prepared and graded by the American Institute of Certified Public Accountants, a national organization of CPAs, and is administered by each state on the same dates in May and November. A minimum grade of 75 is required on each part of the examination for successful completion.

Most states also require that a candidate have one or two years' experience working in a CPA office—or equivalent experience—before the license is issued. Because of the increasing complexity of business transactions and the related accounting requirements, many states have enacted continuing-education laws. These laws require CPAs to take a minimum number of hours of additional education periodically in order to retain their licenses. Students interested in the specific requirements of individual states can write to the State Board of Accountancy of the state in question.

Accountants generally work in one of three main areas: public accounting, private accounting, or governmental accounting.

PUBLIC ACCOUNTING

Public accountants practice in firms that offer their professional services to the public. These vary from small, single-office firms to very large international organizations with several thousand employees. Because of the complexity of today's business structure and increasing regulations by governmental agencies, members of public accounting firms tend to specialize in one of three general services: auditing, taxation, or management advisory services.

Auditing

Auditing is the primary service offered by most public accounting firms. An **audit** is an independent examination of a firm's financial statements, supporting documents, and records in order to give an opinion about the fairness and general reliability of the financial statements. Banks and other lending agencies frequently require an audit by an independent CPA before making a business loan. Companies that want to offer their securities for public sale must prepare a report that includes a set of audited financial statements, and annual audited statements must be presented thereafter if the securities are traded through national securities markets or exchanges. Creditors and investors who use financial statements in decision-making place considerable reliance on the CPA's audit report.

Tax Services

Another service offered by accountants is advice concerning the tax consequences of business decisions. Accountants are often engaged to aid in tax planning to minimize the tax liability of the business, consistent with the rules and regulations established by taxing agencies. Few business decisions are made without considering the tax consequences. Accountants are also often called upon to prepare the state and federal tax returns required by law. To offer such services, accountants must be thoroughly familiar with federal and state tax laws and regulations. They must also keep up-to-date on court decisions and changes in tax law, which occur frequently.

Management Advisory Services

Although audit and tax services have traditionally been the mainstay of public accountants, another area, generally called *management advisory services,* has become increasingly important in recent years. While performing an audit, accountants often discover defects or problems in the client's accounting system. It is natural for the accountant to advise the client on means of correcting defects and improving procedures for the purpose of producing more efficient operations and related cost savings. Clients expect these recommendations and often engage the accountant to undertake additional investigations to improve operations. Public accountants offer a wide range of advisory services, some with little relationship to accounting. Services provided include advice on such things as mergers with other companies; installation or modification of accounting systems; design or modification of pension plans; and advice regarding budgeting, forecasting, and general financial planning.

PRIVATE ACCOUNTING

An accountant working for a single industrial company is employed in private accounting. The firm's chief accounting officer, the **controller,** has overall responsibility for directing the activities of the accounting personnel. In a large company the controller may have several assistant controllers, each with assigned responsibility for various accounting functions. Private accountants may be CPAs and often specialize in a single phase of the accounting process.

General Accounting

One function of the private accountant is to record the transactions undertaken by the company and to prepare reports for use by management. The transaction data must also be classified and summarized for the preparation of financial statements for external distribution. It is difficult to draw a clear line of distinction between general accounting and the other phases of private accounting because the accounting data recorded from transactions forms the basic data base from which other phases draw relevant information.

Cost Accounting

Cost accounting deals with the collection, allocation, and control of the cost of producing specific products and services. Knowledge of the cost of each business operation and manufacturing process is important in making sound business decisions. If management wants to know whether the production and sale of a product is profitable, it must know that product's cost. Large manufacturing companies employ many accountants in their cost accounting departments.

Budgeting

Budgeting is the phase of accounting that deals with the preparation of a plan or forecast of future operations. Its primary function is to provide management with a projection of the activities necessary to reach established goals. Budgets are generally prepared for the business as a whole as well as for subunits.

They also serve as control devices and as a means of measuring the efficiency of operations.

Tax Accounting

Businesses are assessed a variety of taxes—including income tax, payroll tax, and excise tax—all of which require the preparation of periodic reports to taxing agencies. Tax effects must be considered in every investment and financing decision made by management. Although many businesses rely on public accountants for some tax-planning advice and tax-return preparation, most large companies also maintain a tax accounting department to deal with day-to-day tax problems.

Internal Auditing

To supplement the annual audit by a CPA, many companies also maintain an internal audit staff. Its primary function is to conduct ongoing reviews to make certain that established procedures and policies are being followed. Thus, any deficiencies can be identified and corrected quickly. An efficient internal audit process can also reduce the time required by the CPA firm in conducting its annual audit, often producing significant cost savings.

GOVERNMENTAL ACCOUNTING

Another area of activity employing many accountants is governmental accounting. Cities, counties, states, and the federal government collect and spend huge amounts of money annually. Elected and appointed officials have ultimate responsibility for the collection and efficient use of the resources placed under their control. Many of the problems and decisions faced by governmental officials are the same as those encountered in private industry, but governmental accounting requires a different approach in some respects because of the absence of a profit motive. Governmental accounting is concerned with the identification of the sources and uses of resources consistent with the provisions of city, county, state, and federal laws. Other not-for-profit organizations (churches, hospitals, charities, public educational institutions) follow accounting procedures similar to those used in governmental accounting.

  This chapter so far has presented a basic introduction to the nature of accounting, its purpose, and its fields of specialization. As indicated earlier, accounting is applicable to all types of economic entities, including governmental and nonprofit units. The rest of this book, however, will concentrate on accounting methods used in accounting for business entities that have a profit motive.

THE SOURCE OF ACCOUNTING PRINCIPLES AND PRACTICES

Accounting has evolved through time, changing with the changing needs of society. As new types of transactions evolved in trade and commerce, accountants developed rules and practices for recording them. These accounting practices have come to be known as *Generally Accepted Accounting Principles* (GAAP). GAAP consist of the rules, practices, and procedures, the authority of which stems from their general acceptance by the accounting profession. They have evolved from the experiences and thinking of the members of the accounting profession with the help of several formal accounting organizations. Six of these organizations—the American Institute of Certified Public Accountants (AICPA), the Financial Accounting Standards Board (FASB), the Securities and Exchange Commission (SEC), the American Accounting Association (AAA), the Cost Accounting Standards Board (CASB), and the National Association of Accountants (NAA)—predominate in the development of accounting practices and procedures. Knowledge of their historical and continuing roles in the development of accounting will help in understanding the overall accounting process.

THE AICPA

The AICPA is a national professional organization of certified public accountants that has been particularly active in describing and defining GAAP. Between 1939 and 1959, the AICPA's Committee on Accounting Procedure issued fifty-one *Accounting Research Bulletins* containing recommendations on a wide variety of accounting problems. These recommendations, however, were not mandatory in accounting. As a result, different companies often developed different practices for accounting and reporting identical transactions. In recognition of the need for a more formal process in the development of GAAP, in 1959 the AICPA replaced the Committee on Accounting Procedure with the Accounting Principles Board (APB). The APB was asked to establish principles that would narrow the areas of difference and inconsistency in accounting. Between 1959 and 1973 the APB issued thirty-one *APB Opinions* dealing with specific accounting problems. The AICPA publishes a monthly journal, *The Journal of Accountancy,* which serves as a medium by which accountants share their experiences and research results.

THE FASB

The Accounting Principles Board consisted of 18 part-time, nonsalaried members from accounting firms, industry, and universities, who maintained their affiliations with their respective firms or educational institutions. As a result, the APB was frequently charged with being unduly influenced by the wishes of clients and management. Because of the part-time nature of its members' appointments, the APB was also attacked for moving too slowly in solving accounting problems. To avoid such criticism as well as the possibility of having a governmental body take over the accounting rule-making activities, the APB was terminated in 1973 and a new board, the Financial Accounting Standards Board, was created by the leaders of the accounting profession.

The FASB has seven members, all of whom work full time, receive substantial salaries, and must sever their relationships with prior employers. It is an independent, autonomous body whose members are appointed by the Financial Accounting Foundation. The foundation receives its financial support from the private sector—from public accounting and industrial firms. The FASB is responsible for establishing accounting standards that will be responsive to the needs of the entire business community, not just the accounting profession. It provides a forum in open hearings, discussion memoranda, and exposure drafts through which all interested parties may express their views concerning proposed accounting standards. After considering the views of all parties, the FASB issues *Statements of Financial Accounting Standards* which, like APB Opinions, must be followed by accountants. Both APB Opinions and FASB Statements will be referred to frequently in this book.

THE SEC

The Securities and Exchange Commission is a regulatory agency established by Congress through the Securities Acts of 1933 and 1934. It has the authority to establish accounting standards for the financial reports required of corporations that list their securities for sale through one of the national securities exchanges. It has published Regulation S-X and other accounting guidelines that contain specific reporting standards for the financial statements that must be filed annually with the SEC. The SEC has played a significant role in accounting since its inception, not only through its published regulations but also by working closely with the APB and FASB in the development of accounting standards.

THE AAA

The American Accounting Association Membership consists mainly of accounting educators. It encourages the improvement of accounting instruction and sponsors various types of accounting research, the results of which are often published in its quarterly publication, *The Accounting Review*. Its committees work with the FASB on various accounting problems. Several of its members have served on the APB and FASB. The AAA has had a continuing significant effect on the development of accounting standards.

THE CASB

The Cost Accounting Standards Board played an important role in developing cost accounting standards. It was established in 1970 as an arm of Congress and was assigned responsibility for establishing uniform cost accounting standards to be followed by contractors and subcontractors performing certain defense contracts for the U.S. government. The board was composed of five members who held four-year terms and was supported by a full-time staff of research accountants. The CASB issued several Standards, compliance with which is mandatory for defense contractors and subcontractors. Verification of compliance is provided by the individual defense-contracting agencies such as the Defense Contract Audit Agency. The CASB was terminated in 1980 because Congress decided it had accomplished its mission.

THE NAA

The National Association of Accountants consists primarily of industrial accountants and educators whose interests are cost and managerial accounting. It supports research in various cost and managerial accounting areas and publishes a monthly publication, *Management Accounting*. In addition, it sponsors the Institute of Management Accounting, which offers a program leading to a *Certificate in Management Accounting* (CMA). To qualify for the certificate, the candidate must pass a series of rigorous professional examinations and meet specified educational and professional experience standards. To maintain their certification, CMAs must take continuing-education courses each year. Because of its activity in the development of quantitative methods and computer applications in accounting, the NAA is expected to play an increasingly important role in the development of accounting standards.

FORMS OF BUSINESS ORGANIZATION

Business organizations may be in the form of single proprietorships, partnerships, or corporations.

A **single proprietorship** is a business owned by one person. Many small service enterprises, retail stores, and professional practices are operated as single proprietorships. The owner of a single proprietorship is legally liable for its debts. From an accounting standpoint, however, the business is treated as an entity separate from its owner.

A **partnership** is a business owned by two or more people acting as partners. No special legal requirements need be met to form a partnership. All that is necessary is an agreement among the persons joining together as partners. Although the partnership agreement may be oral, a written agreement is preferred in order to avoid disagreements among the partners.

Partnerships are not separate legal entities. Consequently, the individual partners are personally liable for the debts of the partnership. From an accounting viewpoint, however, partnerships are treated as entities separate from their owners. Like single proprietorships, partnerships are widely used for small service enterprises, retail stores, and professional practices.

A **corporation** is a separate legal entity formed under the incorporation laws of individual states or the federal government. Its owners are called **stockholders** or **shareholders** because their ownership interests are represented by shares of the corporation's stock. Because a corporation is a separate legal entity, its stockholders are not liable for the corporation's debts. Separate legal entity status enables a corporation to conduct its business affairs in its own name as a legal person. Thus, a corporation can buy, own, and sell property; it can sue or be sued in its own name; and it can enter into contracts with others. In essence, a corporation is treated as a legal person with all the rights, duties, and responsibilities of a person.

Corporate stockholders are free to sell all or part of their shares at any time. This ease of transferability of ownership, coupled with the lack of personal liability for corporate debts, generally adds to the attractiveness of investing in corporate stock.

Although corporations conduct the majority of business activity in the United States, single proprietorships are more numerous. Because of the relatively simple nature of the single-proprietorship form, it will be used as the basis for the early discussion and illustrations in this book. Partnerships and corporations and their special accounting problems will be discussed in Chapters 14, 15, and 16.

FINANCIAL STATEMENTS

Accounting, as we have seen, is an information system designed to provide financial data to interested parties for decision-making purposes. The final result of the accounting process is the preparation of financial statements that serve as important communication devices. Some knowledge of the content of financial statements and the types of information they are designed to communicate will help you better understand the underlying concepts and measurement processes followed in accounting. The purpose of these statements is to communicate to users the effect of operating activities during a specified time period and the financial position at the end of the period for a specific business. Financial statements generally prepared are a balance sheet, an income statement, a capital statement, and a statement of changes in financial position.

The balance sheet, income statement, and capital statement will be discussed briefly here. The statement of changes in financial position, which is somewhat more complex, will be discussed in detail in Chapter 19.

THE BALANCE SHEET

The balance sheet reports the financial position of a business at a specific point in time. It is sometimes called a Statement of Financial Position. Financial position is reflected by the assets of the business, its liabilities or debts owed, and owner's equity. Figure 1-2 shows a balance sheet for Acme Repair Company as of December 31, 1984.

The heading of the balance sheet indicates the name of the business, the name of the statement, and the date. The assets (resources) of the business are listed on the left side and the liabilities and owner's equity are listed on the right side. Note that the two sides of the balance sheet are equal. This equality must exist because the left side lists the assets of the business and the right side shows the sources of the assets. Of the total assets of $169,480 owned by the business, $73,920 of them were provided by creditors and the remainder of $95,560 was provided by the owner, Mary Brady, by direct investment or by retaining part of the earnings of the business.

The basic accounting model (accounting equation) for the balance sheet is:

$$\text{Assets} = \text{Liabilities} + \text{Owner's Equity}$$

All transactions of a business could be analyzed using this basic model, although we will see later that better analyses can be made by expanding the

Figure 1-2
Balance Sheet

ACME REPAIR COMPANY			
Balance Sheet			
December 31, 1984			
Assets		**Liabilities**	
Cash	$ 16,780	Accounts payable	$ 6,920
Accounts		Mortgage payable	67,000
receivable	5,930	Total liabilities	73,920
Repair supplies	4,870		
Repair equipment	36,900	**Owner's Equity**	
Land	20,000	Mary Brady, capital	
Building	85,000		95,560
		Total liabilities and	
Total assets	$169,480	owner's equity	$169,480

equation to include the effect of the income statement. The balance sheet is divided into three main sections: assets, liabilities, and owner's equity.

Assets

Assets are the resources owned by a business, cash as well as noncash resources. They may be tangible (having physical characteristics, such as land, buildings, and equipment) or intangible (assets without physical existence such as legal claims or such rights as accounts receivable from customers, patent rights, or rights to use leased assets). Assets have economic value because they contain service benefits that can be used in future operations.

Liabilities

Liabilities are the debts owed by a business to outside parties called creditors and include such things as amounts owed to suppliers for goods or services purchased on credit (accounts payable), amounts borrowed from banks or other lenders (*notes payable* and *mortgages payable*), and amounts owed to employees for wages and salaries that have not yet been paid. Liabilities require the release of assets, generally cash, or the performance of future services to cancel them. Liabilities may also be thought of as claims of creditors against the assets of the business.

Owner's Equity

Owner's equity is the interest of the owner or owners in the assets of the business and may be thought of as the owner's claims against the assets of the business. The basic accounting model introduced earlier (Assets = Liabilities + Owner's Equity) indicates that the total assets of the business equal the total claims against those assets by creditors and owners. Creditors' claims take legal precedence over owner's claims; if the assets are sold, creditors must be paid before the claims of the owners are recognized. Thus, owner's equity is considered a residual claim, and the basic accounting model is sometimes expressed as

$$\text{Assets} - \text{Liabilities} = \text{Owner's Equity}$$

Other terms often used for owner's equity are *proprietorship,* and *capital.*

In summary, the two sides of the balance sheet are always equal because they simply reflect two views of the same thing. The list of assets shows the resources owned by the business. The lists of liabilities and owner's equity show the amounts of the resources provided to the business by the creditors and the owners. Thus, all of the firm's assets are provided to it by its creditors or its owners. Because creditors' claims take legal precedence, a business with a relatively large ratio of liabilities to owner's equity is considered financially weaker than a business with a relatively large ratio of owner's equity to liabilities.

THE INCOME STATEMENT

The income statement reports the results of earning activities for a specific time period such as a month, quarter, or year. Net income for the period is the excess of revenues over expenses for that time. If expenses for the period exceed revenues, a net loss is incurred. Figure 1-3 shows an income statement for Acme Repair Company.

The heading identifies the business being reported upon—Acme Repair Company—the name of the statement, and the time period covered by the statement. Identification of the time period covered is particularly important because it indicates the length of time (here, one year) it took to earn the reported net income. The data in the income statement would have little if any meaning to a user of the statement without a clear indication of the period covered.

Revenues

Revenues are increases in owner's equity from the sale of goods or the performance of services. They are measured by the amount of cash or other assets received. Although revenue often consists of cash, it may consist of any asset received, such as a promise by a customer to pay in the future (an account

Figure 1-3
Income Statement

ACME REPAIR COMPANY		
Income Statement		
For the Year Ended December 31, 1984		
Revenues		
Repair revenue		$147,500
Expenses		
Advertising	$ 6,750	
Repair supplies used	30,570	
Salaries and wages	42,600	
Rent expense	13,420	
Telephone expense	6,730	
Utilities expense	15,980	
Total expenses		116,050
Net income		$ 31,450

receivable) or the receipt of property from a customer. Regardless of the type of asset, to represent revenue it must reflect payment for the sale of goods or the performance of services. Other types of revenues are interest, dividends received on stock owned, and rent.

Expenses

Expenses are decreases in owner's equity resulting from the costs incurred to earn revenue. They are measured by the amount of assets consumed or the amount of liabilities incurred. They may be immediate cash payments, as for current wages and salaries, or promises to pay cash in the future for services received, such as advertising, that have not yet been paid for. In some cases, cash may be paid out before the expense is incurred, as in payment for next month's or next year's rent. These prepayments represent assets in the balance sheet until they are used. The total of all expenses incurred during 1984 by Acme Repair Company was $116,050. Subtracting these expenses from revenues produces net income of $31,450. It is important to understand that the net income earned represents an increase in owner's equity. Because revenues result in an increase in owner's equity and expenses result in a decrease in owner's equity, the difference between the two—**net income**—must represent a net increase in owner's equity. Similarly, a **net loss** represents a decrease in owner's equity.

THE CAPITAL STATEMENT

The capital statement (Figure 1-4) serves as a connecting link between the balance sheet and the income statement and explains the changes that took place in owner's equity during the period. For example, assuming that Mary Brady's capital balance on December 31, 1983, was $79,110 and that she withdrew $15,000 from the business for personal use during 1984, the capital statement for 1984 would be:

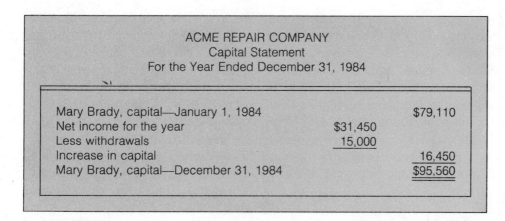

ACME REPAIR COMPANY
Capital Statement
For the Year Ended December 31, 1984

Mary Brady, capital—January 1, 1984		$79,110
Net income for the year	$31,450	
Less withdrawals	15,000	
Increase in capital		16,450
Mary Brady, capital—December 31, 1984		$95,560

Figure 1-4
Capital Statement

SOME UNDERLYING ACCOUNTING CONCEPTS, PRINCIPLES, AND ASSUMPTIONS

We have described accounting as a service activity designed to accumulate, classify, and summarize financial data of a business for use in making economic decisions. As accounting evolved, questions arose concerning the nature of the unit to be accounted for, the measurement principles to be used, and the general guidelines to be followed in order to make the financial data useful in decision-making. Accountants gradually produced responses to these questions and developed underlying accounting concepts, principles, and assumptions that are followed in present-day accounting.

THE BUSINESS ENTITY CONCEPT

If the transactions of a business are to be recorded, classified, and summarized into financial statements, the accountant must be able to identify clearly the boundaries of the unit being accounted for. Under the **business entity concept,** the business (Acme Repair Company, for example) is considered a separate entity distinguishable from its owner and from all other entities. It is assumed that each entity owns its assets and incurs its liabilities. The assets, liabilities, and business activities of the business are kept completely separate from those of the owner of the business as well as from those of other businesses. For example, the personal assets, debts, and activities of Mary Brady are not included in the records of Acme Repair Company because they do not constitute part of the business. A separate set of accounting records is maintained for each business, and the financial statements prepared represent the financial position and results of operations of that business only. If the personal activities of the owner were included, both the financial position and the results of operations would be distorted.

THE COST PRINCIPLE

Resources of a business are recorded initially at their cost under the **cost principle.** Cost is determined by the exchange price agreed upon by the parties to the exchange and is measured by the amount of cash to be given in exchange for the resource received. If the consideration given is something other than cash, cost is measured by the fair value of what is given or the fair value of the asset or service received, whichever is more clearly evident. For example, the land reported on the balance sheet of Acme Repair Company reflects the $20,000 consideration given to acquire the land on the date it was acquired. Even though Mary Brady may have considered the land to be worth more than $20,000 when she purchased it, thereby obtaining a bargain purchase, the cost principle in accounting limits the recorded value of the land to the $20,000 paid to acquire it. And although the land may have a current sales value of $40,000, it will continue to be reported at its cost of $20,000 under the cost principle. Thus, in reading a balance sheet, *it is important to remember that the dollar amounts reported do not show the amounts that would be received if the assets were sold, but the cost of the assets on the date they were acquired.*

THE OBJECTIVITY PRINCIPLE

It is appropriate to ask why accountants do not record changes in the values of assets to reflect their current market values. One explanation is the **objectivity principle** in accounting, which holds that accounting data must be reported on an objective or factual basis. Cost of the resource acquired is determined objectively on the basis of the exchange price negotiated by the independent parties to the exchange. The recording of current market values requires use of estimates, appraisals, or opinions, all of which are much more subjective. Users of accounting information should be given the most objective, factual data available.

THE GOING CONCERN ASSUMPTION

Another reason for the use of historical cost rather than current market value is that many assets are acquired for use rather than for resale. In fact, some assets, like land, buildings, and equipment, cannot be sold without disrupting ongoing business operations. Financial statements are prepared on the assumption that the existing business will continue to operate in the future—the **going concern assumption.** It is assumed that the business will not be sold in the near future but will continue to use its resources in operating activities. The current market values of the assets are, therefore, of little importance to decision-makers.

In the event that management is planning the sale or liquidation of the business, the going concern assumption and cost principle are set aside and the financial statements are prepared on the basis of estimated sales or liquidation values. When this is the case, the statements should identify clearly the basis upon which values are determined.

THE STABLE-DOLLAR ASSUMPTION

Another underlying assumption of accounting is the **stable-dollar assumption,** under which changes in the purchasing power of money are ignored. In our country, accounting transactions are recorded and reported in terms of dollars that are assumed to have a constant value. As a result, 1984 dollars are intermingled with 1980 and 1970 dollars as though they all represented the same purchasing power. Unfortunately, this is not realistic. When the general purchasing power of the dollar changes, the value of money also changes. As inflation occurs, the purchasing power of money declines. Although accountants recognize this fact, changes in the value of the measuring unit are ignored. As a result, gains are often reported on the disposal of assets when there has, in fact, been little or no gain in purchasing power. Assume that a business acquired a piece of land for $50,000 when the general price level (the average of prices in our economy) was 100 and sold it for $100,000 when the general price level had increased to 200. The doubling of the general price level reflects a decrease in the purchasing power of the dollar from 100 cents to 50 cents. Current accounting practice reports a $50,000 gain on the sale of the land even though the company is no better off from a purchasing-power standpoint because it would take $100,000 on the date of sale to buy the same amount of goods and services that could have been purchased for $50,000 on the date the land was acquired.

Recent high inflation rates have raised serious doubts about the wisdom of following the stable-dollar assumption. Methods have been devised to convert the dollar amounts in financial statements into dollars of current purchasing power. These restated financial statements are called *constant-dollar financial statements*. Accounting standards require that large companies disclose the effects of inflation on certain assets and net income. These disclosures, however, are supplemental disclosures only; the primary financial statements are still prepared following the stable-dollar assumption. If inflation rates continue to be high, we might reasonably expect a shift away from the stable-dollar assumption—and possibly the cost principle—to some other valuation basis for financial statements. A detailed discussion of this topic will be found in Chapter 13.

THE EFFECT OF TRANSACTIONS ON THE ACCOUNTING EQUATION

The basic accounting model or **accounting equation** was expressed earlier as

Assets = Liabilities + Owner's Equity

The sum of the assets of a business will always be equal to the total sources from which those assets came—liabilities plus owner's equity. Business transactions result in changes in assets, liabilities, and owner's equity. Even though the elements of the accounting equation change as a result of transactions, its basic equality remains unchanged, as may be demonstrated by illustrating some transactions undertaken by Sam's Cleaners.

Transaction 1   Assume that Sam Drew decided to open Sam's Cleaners on January 2 by taking $30,000 from his personal savings account and depositing it in a checking account he opened for Sam's Cleaners. This investment by Sam Drew represents the first transaction of Sam's Cleaners (1). After this initial investment, the new business has one asset (cash) and no liabilities. Thus, the equation for Sam's Cleaners would be

Assets	=	Liabilities	+	Owner's Equity
Cash				Sam Drew, Capital
(1) $30,000	=			$30,000

The effect of this transaction was to increase assets by $30,000, with an equal increase in owner's equity on the other side of the equation. (Remember that the equation relates only to the business entity.) Following the business entity concept, Sam Drew's personal assets and debts are not part of the business endeavor and are therefore excluded from the equation.

Transaction 2   After making the initial investment, Sam Drew, who manages the business himself, engaged in his next transaction by purchasing some cleaning equipment. The list price of the equipment was $16,000, but after some hard negotiation, the supplier agreed to sell the equipment to Sam's Cleaners for $14,000 cash. The equation before this transaction (2), the effect of the transaction on the equation, and the equation after the transaction are:

Assets			=	Liabilities	+	Owner's Equity
Cash	+	Cleaning Equipment				Sam Drew, Capital
(1) $30,000			=			30,000
(2) −14,000		+14,000				
16,000 +		14,000	=			30,000

This transaction resulted in an exchange of one asset (cash) for another asset (cleaning equipment). No liabilities were incurred and Sam Drew's equity remained unchanged. Note that, following the *cost principle*, the cleaning equipment was recorded at its cost of $14,000; the list price of the equipment is irrelevant.

Transaction 3   Sam Drew then purchased $4,500 worth of cleaning supplies from Adam Supply Company on account, with an agreement to pay for the supplies later. The effect of this transaction (3) is an increase in assets of $4,500 and an increase in liabilities, accounts payable, of $4,500:

		Assets			=	Liabilities	+	Owner's Equity
	Cash	+	Cleaning Equipment	+ Cleaning Supplies	=	Accounts Payable	+	Sam Drew Capital
(1)	$30,000				=			30,000
(2)	− 14,000	+	14,000					
	16,000	+	14,000		=			30,000
(3)				+4,500		+4,500		
	16,000	+	14,000	+ 4,500	=	4,500	+	30,000
			34,500				34,500	

Sam Drew's equity in the business did not change because assets and liabilities increased by equal amounts. The accounting equation is still in balance, with $34,500 in total assets and $34,500 of liabilities and owner's equity.

One of the prime objectives of a business is to engage in operating activities that will result in net income to its owners. As explained earlier, net income is the excess of revenues over expenses for a specific time period. Revenues for Sam's Cleaners are earned by charging a fee for the performance of cleaning and laundry services for its customers. Because the assets received as revenues belong to the owner, revenues increase owner's equity. Expenses for Sam's Cleaners consist of such things as wages and salaries paid to employees, newspaper advertising, and cleaning supplies used. Just as revenues increase owner's equity, expenses decrease owner's equity. The excess of revenues over expenses therefore results in an increase in the net assets of the business and a net increase in owner's equity. Of course, an excess of expenses over revenues (net loss) has the opposite effect.

Transactions 4 and 5 To illustrate the effect of revenues on the accounting equation, assume that Sam's Cleaners performed cleaning and laundry services for customers in the amount of $1,200, which was received in cash. In addition, Sam's Cleaners completed the cleaning of draperies for a local hotel and sent the customer a bill for $550. The effects of these transactions on the accounting equation are indicated in (4) and (5):

		Assets				=	Liabilities	+	Owner's Equity	
	Cash	+ Cleaning Equipment	+ Cleaning Supplies	+ Accounts Receivable		=	Accounts Payable	+	Sam Drew, Capital	
(1)	$30,000					=			30,000	
(2)	− 14,000	+14,000								
	16,000 +	14,000				=			30,000	
(3)			+4,500				+4,500			
	16,000 +	14,000 +	4,500			=	4,500	+	30,000	
(4)	+1,200								+ 1,200	(Revenue)
	17,200 +	14,000 +	4,500			=	4,500	+	31,200	
(5)				+550					+550	(Revenue)
	17,200 +	14,000 +	4,500 +	550		=	4,500	+	31,750	
		36,250						36,250		

Observe that the effect of transaction (4) is to increase the asset cash and, because it represents a receipt for the performance of services (revenue), to increase owner's equity by an equal amount. Transaction (5) introduces another important principle in accounting, the **revenue recognition principle** (sometimes called the *realization principle*), which requires the recognition of revenue when the earning process is completed rather than when cash is received. The revenue is represented by the receipt of an asset, in this case an **account receivable,** which represents the right to collect cash in the future.

Transactions 6 and 7 To see the effect of expenses on the accounting equation, assume that Sam's Cleaners paid cash in the amount of $300 for employee wages and $150 for advertising. In addition, a count of the cleaning supplies showed that cleaning supplies on hand amounted to $3,700. The other $800 ($4,500 − $3,700) of cleaning supplies had been used. The effects of these transactions on the accounting equation are shown in (6) and (7):

	Cash	+	Cleaning Equipment	+	Cleaning Supplies	+	Accounts Receivable	=	Accounts Payable	+	Sam Drew, Capital	
					Assets			**=**	**Liabilities**	**+**	**Owner's Equity**	
(1)	$30,000							=.			30,000	
(2)	−14,000		+14,000									
	16,000	+	14,000					=			30,000	
(3)					+4,500				+4,500			
	16,000	+	14,000	+	4,500			=	4,500	+	30,000	
(4)	+1,200										+1,200	(Revenue)
	17,200	+	14,000	+	4,500			=	4,500	+	31,200	
(5)							+550				+550	(Revenue)
	17,200	+	14,000	+	4,500	+	550	=	4,500	+	31,750	
(6)	−450										−450	(Expense)
	16,750	+	14,000	+	4,500	+	550	=	4,500	+	31,300	
(7)					−800						−800	(Expense)
	16,750	+	14,000	+	3,700	+	550	=	4,500	+	30,500	

35,000   35,000

Note that expenses have an effect opposite the recognition of revenue, with a decrease in assets and a decrease in owner's equity. The basic **expense recognition principle** in accounting requires that, in general, expenses should be recognized in the period in which the asset or benefit is used in the process of earning revenue. In transaction (6), the benefits received from employees and newspaper advertising had been used at the time payment was made. Thus the payment represents expenses that reduced the asset cash as well as owner's equity by equal amounts of $450. The initial purchase of cleaning supplies in transaction (3) resulted in the acquisition of an asset that will benefit several accounting periods. The counting of cleaning supplies at the end of the period indicated that $800 of the supplies had been used during the period and are therefore treated as an expense by decreasing cleaning supplies and decreasing owner's equity.

The combination of the principle of recognizing revenue when it is earned rather than when it is collected and the principle of recognizing expenses when assets or benefits are used rather than when they are paid for is referred to as *accrual accounting*. We will have more to say about this important concept later.

Transactions 8, 9, and 10   As one last illustration of the effect of transactions on the accounting equation, assume that Sam's Cleaners collected the account receivable recognized in transaction (5) and paid the amount due Adam Supply Company for the purchase of cleaning supplies in transaction (3). In addition, Sam Drew withdrew $200 from the business for his personal use. The effects of these transactions on the accounting equation are demonstrated in (8), (9), and (10):

	Cash	+	Cleaning Equipment	+	Cleaning Supplies	+	Accounts Receivable	=	Accounts Payable	+	Sam Drew, Capital	
					Assets			=	*Liabilities*	=	*Owner's Equity*	
(1)	$30,000							=			30,000	
(2)	−14,000		+14,000									
	16,000	+	14,000					=			30,000	
(3)					+4,500				+4,500			
	16,000	+	14,000	+	4,500			=	4,500	+	30,000	
(4)	+1,200										+1,200	(Revenue)
	17,200	+	14,000	+	4,500			=	4,500	+	31,200	
(5)							+550				+550	(Revenue)
	17,200	+	14,000	+	4,500	+	550	=	4,500	+	31,750	
(6)	−450										−450	(Expense)
	16,750	+	14,000	+	4,500	+	550	=	4,500	+	31,300	
(7)					−800						−800	(Expense)
	16,750	+	14,000	+	3,700	+	550	=	4,500	+	30,500	
(8)	+550						−550					
	17,300	+	14,000	+	3,700			=	4,500	+	30,500	
(9)	−4,500								−4,500			
	12,800	+	14,000	+	3,700			=			30,500	
(10)	−200										−200	(Withdrawal)
	12,600	+	14,000	+	3,700			=			30,300	

30,300   30,300

The effect of the collection of the account receivable in transaction (8) is to increase one asset (cash) and decrease another asset (accounts receivable). There is no effect on total assets and none on liabilities or owner's equity. The payment of the account payable in transaction (9) results in a decrease in cash and an equal decrease in liabilities, with no effect on owner's equity. The withdrawal by Sam Drew in transaction (10) decreases cash and owner's equity by equal amounts.

A review of this illustration brings out two important facts. First, every transaction recorded affected at least two items in the equation. This dual recording process, known as **double-entry accounting,** is the method followed in the vast majority of accounting systems. Second, after the effects of each transaction were recorded, the equation remained in balance, with the sum of the assets equal to the sum of the liabilities plus owner's equity.

Observe that, after all transactions have been recorded, Sam Drew's equity (or capital) is $30,300, composed of the $30,000 he invested at the inception of the business plus $500 net income, representing the excess of revenues ($1,750) over expenses ($1,250) for the period minus the $200 withdrawal. In addition, total assets of Sam's Cleaners are $30,300, and the business owes no liabilities. Assets have therefore increased by $300 during the period.

After taking the effects of the above transactions into account, we would arrive at the financial statements for Sam's Cleaners shown in Figure 1-5 on page 28.

GLOSSARY

ACCOUNTING.   The process of recording, classifying, and summarizing the financial data of a business that will be useful to decision-makers (p. 5).

ACCOUNTING EQUATION.   An algebraic expression of the equality of assets to liabilities and owner's equity: Assets = Liabilities + Owner's Equity (p. 22).

ACCOUNTING PRINCIPLE.   A rule adopted by the accounting profession as a guide to measuring and reporting business transactions (p. 12).

ACCOUNT PAYABLE.   An amount owed to a creditor for the purchase of goods or services (p. 17).

ACCOUNT RECEIVABLE.   An amount due from a customer for the sale of goods or services (p. 25).

ASSET.   A resource or thing owned by a business (p. 17).

AUDIT.   An examination by an independent CPA of the financial statements and supporting documents of a business (p. 9).

BALANCE SHEET.   A report listing the assets, liabilities, and owner's equity of a business as of a specific date (p. 16).

BUDGET.   A plan for the operating activities of a business (p. 10).

BUSINESS ENTITY CONCEPT.   The assumption that a business entity is separate and distinct from its owners and from other business entities (p. 20).

CERTIFIED PUBLIC ACCOUNTANT.   An accountant who has met the qualifications and received a license to practice public accounting (p. 8).

Financial Statements

SAM'S CLEANERS
Balance Sheet
January 31, 1984

Assets		Owner's Equity	
Cash	$12,600	Sam Drew, capital	$30,300
Cleaning supplies	3,700		
Cleaning equipment	14,000		
Total assets	$30,300	Total owner's equity	$30,300

Income Statement
For the Month Ended January 31, 1984

Cleaning revenue		$1,750
Operating expenses:		
Advertising	$150	
Cleaning supplies used	800	
Employee wages	300	
Total operating expenses		1,250
Net income		$ 500

Capital Statement
For the Month Ended January 31, 1984

Sam Drew, capital—January 2, 1984		$30,000
Net income for the month	$500	
Less withdrawals	200	
Increase in capital		300
Sam Drew, capital—January 31, 1984		$30,300

CONTROLLER. The chief accounting officer of a business (p. 10).

CORPORATION. A form of business organization licensed to operate as a business by state or federal laws (p. 15).

COST ACCOUNTING. The phase of accounting that deals with the collection, allocation, and control of the cost of producing a product or service (p. 10).

COST PRINCIPLE. The accounting practice that resources and services acquired by a business are recorded initially at cost (p. 20).

CREDITOR. A person or business to whom a debt is owed (p. 17).

DOUBLE-ENTRY. The concept that every transaction affects two or more items in the accounting equation (p. 27).

EXPENSE. Resources consumed in the process of earning revenues (p. 19).

EXPENSE RECOGNITION PRINCIPLE. The rule that expenses should be recognized when an asset is used to produce revenue rather than when it is paid for (p. 25).

FINANCIAL ACCOUNTING STANDARDS BOARD. The current rule-making body of the accounting profession (p. 13).

GOING CONCERN ASSUMPTION. The assumption that a business will continue in the future and use its assets in operations rather than sell them (p. 21).

INCOME STATEMENT. A financial report listing the revenues, expenses, and net income or net loss of a business for some time period (p. 18).

INTERNAL AUDITING. The ongoing investigation of compliance with established procedures and policies of a business by its internal audit staff (p. 11).

LIABILITIES. Debts owed by a business (p. 17).

NET INCOME. The excess of revenues over expenses (p. 19).

NET LOSS. The excess of expenses over revenues (p. 19).

OBJECTIVITY PRINCIPLE. The rule that accounting data should be reported on a factual basis (p. 21).

OWNER'S EQUITY. The owner's interest in the assets of a business (p. 17).

PARTNERSHIP. A form of business organization under which the business is owned by two or more people as partners (p. 14).

REVENUE. The inflow of assets into a business from the sale of goods or the performance of services (p. 18).

REVENUE RECOGNITION PRINCIPLE. The rule that revenues should be recognized or recorded when the revenue is earned rather than when the asset is received (p. 25). (Also called the REALIZATION PRINCIPLE.)

SHAREHOLDER. A person or entity owning shares of stock in a corporation (p. 15).

SINGLE PROPRIETORSHIP. A form of business organization in which the business is owned by an individual (p. 14).

STABLE-DOLLAR ASSUMPTION. The assumption in accounting that the purchasing power of the dollar does not change (p. 21).

TRANSACTIONS. The events that make up the economic activity of a business (p. 5).

DISCUSSION QUESTIONS

1. What is the purpose of accounting?
2. Who are the primary users of accounting information?
3. Explain and give an example of each of the two types of business transactions: external transactions and internal transactions.

4. What is the purpose of classifying and summarizing accounting data?
5. Accounting data is useful in decision-making. List six examples of business decisions requiring the use of accounting information.
6. Distinguish between recording and reporting accounting information.
7. What are the main services offered by public accountants?
8. What is the purpose of an audit?
9. Private accounting includes a number of phases. List four of them.
10. What is the Financial Accounting Standards Board? What is its function?
11. What is the Securities and Exchange Commission? What is its function?
12. A business may take one of three forms. What are they?
13. What is the general purpose of a balance sheet?
14. Define assets and give five examples.
15. Define liabilities and give three examples.
16. State two forms of the accounting equation.
17. Define revenue; expense.
18. Explain what is meant by the business entity concept.
19. If an asset is appraised at $12,000 but a company pays $10,000 for it with full knowledge of its appraised value, at what amount should the asset be recorded? Why?
20. Explain what is meant by the stable-dollar assumption.
21. If a company has assets of $30,000 and owner's equity of $17,000, how much are its liabilities?
22. What is meant by double-entry accounting?
23. Why are the two sides of a balance sheet always equal?
24. Give an example of a transaction that will:
    (a) Increase an asset and decrease another asset.
    (b) Increase an asset and increase a liability.
    (c) Increase an asset and increase owner's equity.
    (d) Decrease an asset and decrease a liability.
    (e) Decrease an asset and decrease owner's equity.
25. What are the two sources of owner's equity?
26. The term *accrual accounting* encompasses two fundamental accounting principles. What are they?

EXERCISES

Exercise 1-1 (Preparing a Balance Sheet)

Balance sheet items for Sally's Stenographers on May 31, 1984, are presented below in alphabetical order. Use these items to prepare a balance sheet similar to the one in Figure 1-2.

L	Accounts payable	$ 2,300	A	Land	$ 8,000
A	Accounts receivable	2,800	L	Mortgage payable	34,000
A	Building	56,500	O	Sally Strand, Capital	44,800
A	Cash	2,930	A	Supplies	1,420
A	Equipment	9,450			

(handwritten) A 81,100   L 36,300   OE 44,800
(handwritten) 81,100

Exercise 1-2 (Effects of Transactions on Total Assets)

The following transactions were completed by Franz Company. Indicate the effect of each transaction on total assets of Franz Company. Use the terms: increase total assets, decrease total assets, and no effect on total assets.

1. Invested cash in the business. +
2. Purchased office equipment for cash. ✔
3. Sold land for an amount equal to its cost. ✔
4. Paid a liability. —
5. Collected an account receivable. +
6. Sold land for an amount in excess of its cost. +
7. Borrowed money from a bank. +
8. Sold land for an amount less than its cost. —
9. Purchased equipment at a total cost of $3,000; paid $1,000 cash with the balance due in 90 days. +

Exercise 1-3 (Effect of Transactions on Accounting Equations)

Set up headings across a piece of paper as follows:

Transaction	Assets = Liabilities + Owner's Equity

For each of the following transactions, indicate its effect on the accounting equation by placing a + (increase), — (decrease), or 0 (no effect) below the elements of the accounting equation. Transaction (a) is given as an example.

Transaction	Assets	=	Liabilities	+	Owner's Equity
(a)	+	=	0	+	+

The owner:

(a) Invested cash in the business. + 0 +
(b) Purchased supplies on account. + — 0
(c) Purchased equipment for cash. 0 0 0
(d) Sent a bill to a customer for services performed. + 0 +
(e) Paid rent expense for a month. — — 0
(f) Collected the amount billed in (d). + — 0
(g) Purchased equipment, paying half of the purchase price in cash and agreeing to pay the remainder in three months. + + 0
(h) Paid for the supplies purchased in (b). — — 0

Exercise 1-4 (Explaining Accounting Transactions)

The following schedule shows the effect of several transactions on the accounting equation of Valley Company and the balance of each item in the equation after each transaction. Write a sentence to explain the nature of each transaction.

		Assets				=	Liabilities	+	Owner's Equity
		Cash	+ Accounts Receivable	+ Equipment	+ Supplies	=	Accounts Payable	+	Lee Jones, Capital
Inv. In Co.	(1)	+10,000							+10,000
Buy equ. for cash	(2)	− 4,000		+4,000					
		6,000		+ 4,000		=			10,000
Bill Payed in cash	(3)	+ 2,000							+ 2,000
		8,000		+ 4,000		=			12,000
Sent Bill out	(4)		+5,000						+ 5,000
		8,000 +	5,000	+ 4,000		=			17,000
Got Sup. on acct.	(5)				+3,000		+3,000		
		8,000 +	5,000	+ 4,000	+ 3,000	=	3,000	+	17,000
Bill Paided	(6)	+ 3,000	−3,000						
		11,000 +	2,000	+ 4,000	+ 3,000	=	3,000	+	17,000
withdrawal	(7)	− 4,500							− 4,500
		6,500 +	2,000	+ 4,000	; 3,000	=	3,000	+	12,500
Sup. used up ?	(8)				− 1,000				− 1,000
		6,500 +	2,000	+ 4,000	; 2,000	=	3,000	+	11,500
Paid for Sup.	(9)	− 3,000					−3,000		
		3,500 +	2,000	+ 4,000	+ 2,000	=	−0−	+	11,500

Exercise 1-5 (Preparation of a Balance Sheet)

Month-end balance sheet amounts for the legal practice of Dave Krasner, a local attorney, for three consecutive months are presented below. The information is complete except for the balance in the capital account.

	October 31	November 30	December 31
Cash	$ 9,100	$ 3,900	$ 3,000
Accounts receivable	16,100	15,000	8,050
Prepaid insurance	700	1,800	1,600
Office equipment	29,800	29,700	39,300
Building	41,000	40,800	40,600
Land	3,000	3,000	3,000
Accounts payable	10,100	3,100	3,000
Wages payable	5,100	4,100	4,800
Mortgage note payable	34,700	34,300	33,900
Dave Krasner, Capital	?	?	?

Required:
A. Determine the balance in Dave Krasner's capital account at the end of each month.
B. Assuming that Mr. Krasner made no additional investments and did not withdraw any money from the business during the three months, determine net income for November and for December.
C. Prepare a balance sheet for the business at the end of December. (The heading should read: Dave Krasner, Attorney.)

Exercise 1-6 (Examples of Business Transactions)

For each of the following, describe a transaction that would have the stated effect on the accounting equation.

1. Increase an asset and increase a liability.
2. Increase one asset and decrease another asset.
3. Decrease an asset and decrease owners' equity.
4. Increase an asset and increase owners' equity.
5. Decrease a liability and decrease an asset.

Exercise 1-7 (Recording Transactions)

Don's Shoe Repair began operations on August 1 and completed the following transactions during the first month.

1. Don Murphy deposited $12,000 of his personal funds in a checking account opened in the name of the business.
2. Shoe repair equipment was purchased at a cost of $8,000, of which $5,000 was paid in cash. A note payable was given for the remainder of $3,000.
3. Don collected $1,500 from customers for repair services performed.
4. Rent was paid for the month of August, $600.
5. Supplies amounting to $850 were purchased on account.
6. Wages of $250 were paid as well as a utility bill for electricity and water, $125.
7. Don paid for the supplies purchased in (5) above.
8. Supplies used during August amounted to $140.

Required:

A. Prepare a schedule similar to that on page 26. List the following assets, liabilities, and owner's equity as column headings: Cash, Supplies, Equipment, Notes Payable, Accounts Payable, D. Murphy, Capital.
B. Show the effects of each of the transactions on the accounts listed. Indicate totals after each transaction and complete the schedule as shown on page 26.
C. Prepare an income statement, balance sheet, and capital statement.

18,900

PROBLEMS

Problem 1-1 (Preparation of Income Statement and Balance Sheet)

Asset, liability, owner's equity, revenue, and expense amounts for Alicia's Interior Design at December 31, 1984, are presented below:

Cash	$ 4,100
Accounts receivable	19,600
Supplies	4,400
Equipment	19,200
Accounts payable	3,800
Alicia Jones, Capital	?

Design revenue	59,000
Advertising expense	5,000
Insurance expense	1,000
Rent expense	5,400
Supplies expense	2,100
Telephone expense	1,600
Utilities expense	3,000
Wage expense	17,600

Required:

A. Prepare an income statement for the business for the year ended December 31, 1984.

B. Prepare a balance sheet at December 31, 1984.

Problem 1-2 (Determining Missing Elements in Accounting Equation)

Compute the two missing amounts for each independent case below.

Case	Total Assets	Total Liabilities	Owner's Equity	Total Revenue	Total Expenses	Net Income (Loss)
A	$40,000	$15,000	$?	$39,000	$?	$ 9,000
B	?	49,000	52,000	85,000	?	(15,000)
C	70,000	?	42,000	60,000	44,000	?
D	?	26,000	44,000	?	22,000	15,000
E	51,000	?	31,000	?	33,000	(14,000)

Problem 1-3 (Preparation of Income Statement and Balance Sheet)

Data for Day Company as of December 31, 1984, follow:

handwritten: C- Beg Cap 38,000   C- withdrawals 2,000

A – Accounts receivable	$12,000	E – Wage expense	$14,000
R – Revenue	34,000	E – Advertising expense	6,000
L – Accounts payable	8,000	A – Land	15,000
C – Joe Crain, Capital	?	A – Equipment	11,000
A – Cash	9,000	L – Notes payable	10,000
L – Mortgage payable	26,000	E – Utilities expense	4,000
A – Building	42,000	E – Telephone expense	1,000

Required:

Prepare an income statement and balance sheet for Day Company.

Problem 1-4 (Recording Transactions and Preparing Financial Statements)

Balance sheet item balances for Drey Company on April 30 are given below in accounting equation form similar to the chapter illustrations.

Assets				=	Liabilities		+	Owner's Equity
Cash	+ Receivable	+ Supplies	+ Equipment =		Accounts Payable	+ Notes Payable +		Janice Drey, Capital
Bal. $6,340	$10,600	$800	$15,900		$1,940	$7,000		$24,700

During May, Drey Company entered into the following transactions:

1. Collected $6,000 of the accounts receivable.
2. Paid $1,200 on accounts payable.
3. Billed customers for services performed, $4,200.
4. Purchased equipment for $3,400. Paid $1,400 in cash and signed a note payable for $2,000.
5. Paid expenses in cash $1,950. (Employee wages, $1,100; utilities, $550; advertising, $300)
6. Purchased supplies on account, $250.
7. Used $400 of supplies during the period.
8. Janice Drey withdrew $650 for personal use.

Required:

A. List the April 30 balances for assets, liabilities, and owner's equity in table form as shown above.
B. Record the effects of each transaction. Show the total of each column after recording each transaction.
C. Prepare an income statement, capital statement, and balance sheet for Drey Company.

Problem 1-5 (Identifying Transactions from Balance Sheet Changes)

During the month of June 1984, Aaron Haynes was in the process of organizing a new business, Aaron's Cafe. After each transaction he entered into, Aaron prepared a balance sheet. During June, the following balance sheets were prepared:

(1)
AARON'S CAFE
Balance Sheet
June 4, 1984

Assets		Owner's Equity	
Cash	$ 75,000	Aaron Haynes, capital	$ 75,000

(2)
AARON'S CAFE
Balance Sheet
June 13, 1984

Assets		Owner's Equity	
Cash	$ 46,000	Aaron Haynes, capital	$ 75,000
Equipment	29,000		
Total	$ 75,000	Total	$ 75,000

(3)
AARON'S CAFE
Balance Sheet
June 18, 1984

Assets		Liabilities and Owner's Equity	
Cash	$ 26,000	Note payable	$ 40,000
Equipment	29,000	Aaron Haynes, capital	75,000
Land	10,000		
Building	50,000		
Total	$115,000	Total	$115,000

(4)
AARON'S CAFE
Balance Sheet
June 26, 1984

Assets		Liabilities and Owner's Equity	
Cash	$ 26,000	Accounts payable	$ 18,000
Food supplies	18,000	Note payable	40,000
Equipment	29,000	Total liabilities	58,000
Land	10,000	Aaron Haynes, capital	75,000
Building	50,000		
Total	$133,000	Total	$133,000

Required:
Describe the nature of each of the four transactions that took place during June.

ALTERNATE PROBLEMS

Problem 1-1A (Preparation of Financial Statements)
Dawson Industries began operations early in January 1983. On December 31, 1983, the Company's records showed the following asset, liability, owner's equity, revenue, and expense amounts:

Accounts receivable	$ 25,600
Rent expense	13,500
Cash	10,250
Supplies expense	5,250
Accounts payable	9,500
Service revenue	147,500
Supplies	11,000
Equipment	48,000
Lee Dawson, Capital	?

Utilities expense	7,200
Telephone expense	4,900
Advertising	12,500
Insurance	2,500
Wages	44,000
Withdrawals	23,400

Required:

A. Prepare an income statement for Dawson Industries for the year ended December 31, 1983.

B. Prepare a balance sheet as of December 31, 1983.

C. Prepare a capital statement for 1983.

Problem 1-2A (Determining Missing Elements in Accounting Equation)

Compute the two missing elements for each independent case below.

Case	Total Assets	Total Liabilities	Owner's Equity	Total Revenue	Total Expenses	Net Income (Loss)
1	$110,000	$ 30,000	$?	$136,000	$?	$13,200
2	?	25,000	30,000	79,000	?	4,250
3	70,000	?	50,000	83,000	73,000	?
4	?	104,000	172,000	?	260,000	31,000
5	121,000	?	69,000	?	62,000	(14,000)

Problem 1-3A (Preparation of Income Statement and Balance Sheet)

Data for East Company as of December 31, 1985, follows:

Accounts receivable	$102,000	Wages	$116,000
Revenue	289,000	Advertising	56,000
Accounts payable	68,000	Land	127,500
Gary Toliver, Capital	?	Equipment	93,500
Cash	76,500	Notes payable	83,000
Mortgage payable	221,000	Utilities expense	32,000
Building	335,000	Telephone expense	7,000

Required:

Prepare an income statement and balance sheet for East Company.

Problem 1-4A (Recording Transactions and Preparing Financial Statements)

Balance-sheet item balances for Easley Company on June 30 are given below in accounting equation form similar to the chapter illustrations.

	Assets				=	Liabilities		+	Owner's Equity
	Cash	+ Accounts Receivable	+ Supplies	+ Equipment	=	Accounts Payable	+ Notes Payable	+	Tom Easley, Capital
Bal.	$15,850	$26,500	$2,000	$39,750		$4,850	$17,500		$61,750

During the early part of July, Easley Company entered into the following transactions:

1. Collected $14,800 of the accounts receivable.
2. Paid $4,300 on accounts payable.
3. Billed customers for services performed, $10,900.
4. Purchased equipment for $8,400. Paid $3,000 in cash and signed a note payable for $5,400.
5. Paid expenses in cash $8,500 (advertising, $1,200; rent, $4,000; employees' wages, $3,300).
6. Purchased supplies on account, $680.
7. Used $1,000 of supplies during the period.
8. Collected $13,500 of accounts receivable.
9. Tom Easley withdrew $1,200 for his personal use.

Required:

A. List the June 30 balances for assets, liabilities, and owner's equity in table form as shown above.
B. Record the effects of each transaction. Show the total of each column after recording each transaction.
C. Prepare an income statement, capital statement, and balance sheet for Easley Company.

Problem 1-5A (Identifying Transactions from Balance Sheet Changes)

After obtaining her real estate broker's license, Melissa Davis spent the month of May organizing her own business, Melissa's Realty. Melissa prepared a new balance sheet after each transaction she entered into. During May, the following balance sheets were prepared:

(1)

MELISSA'S REALTY
Balance Sheet
May 5, 1984

	Assets		Owner's Equity	
Cash		$ 90,000	Melissa Davis, capital	$ 90,000

(2)

MELISSA'S REALTY
Balance Sheet
May 11, 1984

	Assets		Liabilities and Owner's Equity	
Cash		$ 65,000	Note payable	$ 57,000
Land		22,000	Melissa Davis, capital	90,000
Building		60,000		
Total		$147,000	Total	$147,000

(3)
MELISSA'S REALTY
Balance Sheet
May 22, 1984

Assets		Liabilities and Owner's Equity	
Cash	$ 65,000	Accounts payable	$ 2,500
Office supplies	2,500	Note payable	57,000
Land	22,000	Total liabilities	59,500
Building	60,000	Melissa Davis, capital	90,000
Total	$149,500	Total	$149,500

(4)
MELISSA'S REALTY
Balance Sheet
May 25, 1984

Assets		Liabilities and Owner's Equity	
Cash	$ 61,000	Accounts payable	$ 2,500
Office supplies	2,500	Note payable	53,000
Land	22,000	Total liabilities	55,500
Building	60,000	Melissa Davis, capital	90,000
Total	$145,500	Total	$145,500

(5)
MELISSA'S REALTY
Balance Sheet
May 30, 1984

Assets		Liabilities and Owner's Equity	
Cash	$ 56,000	Accounts payable	$ 2,500
Office supplies	2,500	Note payable	53,000
Land	22,000	Total liabilities	55,500
Building	60,000	Melissa Davis, capital	85,000
Total	$140,500	Total	$140,500

Required:
Describe the nature of each of the five transactions that took place during May.

CASE FOR CHAPTER 1

(Discussion—Preparation of Financial Statements)

Alice Miller was raised on a farm in the midwest. While in high school, she was an active member of the local 4H club and raised several prize animals that she sold at auction at state and local fairs. She saved her earnings and by the time she graduated from high school, Alice had nearly $7,000 in a savings account. She was undecided on whether to go to college to continue her education or use her savings in a business venture. Because of her love for animals, she believed she could successfully operate a pet grooming shop and decided to use the summer months as a trial.

During the month of April, Alice located a small building that she could rent for $200 per month. After transferring $5,000 from her savings account to a business checking account in the name of Alice's Pet Grooming Service, she wrote checks for rent and the purchase of grooming equipment and grooming supplies. Although she would not keep a full set of accounting records, she decided to deposit all receipts from services performed into the checking account and to make all payments by check. In this way she would have a relatively complete record of her business activities. Alice also kept a daily work book in which she recorded all services performed for customers.

On May 1, Alice opened her shop to the public. During the first three months, she was unusually busy. Early in August she needed to make a decision on continuing the operation of her business or to enroll for the fall semester of college. To aid her in making this important decision, Alice reviewed her checking account and daily work book to determine how well she had done. The review disclosed the following:

1. Total cash deposited in the checking account (including the initial $5,000 deposit) was $8,920.
2. The daily work book showed that on July 31 customers owed her $800 for services performed, which she expected to collect during August.
3. Checks were written for:
   a. Rent payments, $800 for the months of May through August.
   b. The purchase of grooming equipment, $1,500. The equipment cost $2,000 and Alice still owed the supplier $500 on the purchase.
   c. Grooming supplies, $960. Alice estimated that the cost of grooming supplies on hand on July 31 was $260.
   d. The payment of electric and water bills for the months of May and June, $522. She had just received her bill for the month of July in the amount of $279, but had not yet paid it.
   e. Advertising, $216.
   f. Withdrawals made by Alice to pay for personal expenses, $1,300.

Required:
A. Prepare an income statement for Alice's Pet Grooming Service for the three month period from May 1 to July 31.
B. Prepare a balance sheet on July 31 and a capital statement for the three month period.
C. What other information would you need to determine how well Alice had done during the three month period?

CHAPTER 2
RECORDING BUSINESS TRANSACTIONS

OVERVIEW AND OBJECTIVES

This chapter describes the basic procedures used to record the effects of transactions on a firm's financial position. When you have completed the chapter, you should understand:

- The nature of accounting transactions (pp. 42–43).
- A basic accounting model used to record, classify, and summarize transactions (pp. 43–57).
- The purpose and basic formats of accounts (pp. 45–46).
- The rules of debit and credit and how to apply these rules in analyzing transactions (pp. 52–54).
- The purpose and format of the general journal (pp. 54–57).
- The purpose and format of the general ledger (pp. 45, 51–52, 57).
- How to record transactions in the journal and how to transfer the information to the ledger (pp. 55–57).
- How to determine account balances and prepare a trial balance (pp. 45–46, 70).
- How to correct errors made in the journal or ledger (pp. 71–73).

In this chapter, we will examine the basic procedures used in a manual accounting system to record and summarize the effects of transactions. The recording and summarizing functions are performed by machines in many firms today, as we shall see in Chapter 6, but the data gathered and stored in an automated system are based on an analysis quite similar to the one in this chapter. To be an effective user of financial reports, you must have an understanding of the underlying accounting framework. Knowledge of the accounting system is most easily acquired by studying the procedures used in a manually operated system.

The focus in this chapter is on a business that performs a service for its customers. Accounting for businesses that manufacture a product or engage in a merchandising operation will be examined later.

TRANSACTIONS

TYPES OF TRANSACTIONS

A firm may enter into transactions with outside parties that affect the firm's financial statements. Examples include the purchase of office supplies, the performance of a service for others, the performance by others of a service for the firm, borrowing cash from a bank, and the purchase of equipment. These transactions are recorded by the accountant and (as we saw in Chapter 1) are called **external transactions** because there is an exchange of economic resources and/or obligations between the firm and one or more outside parties. In other words, in an external transaction the firm gives up something and receives something in return.

Other business activities that do not involve a transaction with outside parties are recorded because they affect the relationship between the firm's assets, liabilities, and owner's equity. Use of office supplies by an employee and use of equipment to perform a service are examples of **internal transactions.** Other events, such as the destruction of an office building by fire, are also given accounting recognition because assets and owner's equity are decreased. As noted in Chapter 1, the term *transaction* is often used to refer to all events that are given accounting recognition.

Some events of importance to the firm are not recorded because there has not been an exchange of goods or services. Examples include receiving an order from a customer, entering into a commitment to purchase an asset in the future, the hiring or retiring of an employee, and changing interest rates. These examples are not recorded because a transaction has not taken place at this point. In other words, initially such events do not affect the firm's recorded assets, liabilities, or owner's equity. The events will be given accounting recognition in the future if an exchange takes place.

Financial accounting is based on a framework of rules for determining which events constitute accounting transactions. Two of the difficulties you will encounter in the study of accounting are determining which events to record and deciding at what stage an event should be given accounting recognition. Unfortunately, there are no simple rules.

TYPICAL TRANSACTIONS OF A BUSINESS ENTITY

Assets were defined in Chapter 1 as resources owned by the business. The initial source of assets is an investment by the owners. Although the investment may take various forms (such as cash, land, or equipment), the initial investment is frequently cash. Individuals invest in a business in anticipation of eventually being able to withdraw assets in excess of those invested. They expect that the firm will operate at a profit and that they will receive a return on their investment. The mere holding of cash invested by the owners will not provide a return, however. Cash is useful as a medium of exchange or as a measure of value but it is essentially a nonproductive asset. In order to generate revenues, the firm acquires productive assets such as machinery, equipment, and buildings. The noncash assets are used to provide goods or services for customers in exchange for revenue in the form of cash or the customer's promise to pay cash in the future. Cash received from customers is then used to pay the operating expenses and obligations of the business. Any remaining cash may be retained in the business to pay future obligations, to finance future expansion, or to distribute to owners as a return on their investment.

THE ACCOUNTING CYCLE

Most businesses engage in a continuous series of transactions for an indefinite period of time that may span many years. The most complete and accurate measure of a firm's success is achieved when the firm discontinues its operations and goes out of existence. At that time, the firm's life cycle is complete and all facts concerning its performance are known. However, statement users must make current decisions regarding the firm and cannot wait an indefinite period for information. Thus statement users must be provided more timely information. In order to report on the periodic progress of the firm, its life is divided into artificial time periods of equal length called **accounting periods.** The division of the operating life of a firm into equal time intervals is called the **time period assumption.**

Accounting periods of equal length are established to enable the statement user to make meaningful comparisons of operating results of the current period with those of prior periods. A complete set of financial statements (often called an **annual report**) is issued to interested parties once a year.[1] A firm may select any 12 consecutive months for reporting—the **fiscal year.** Many firms select a natural business year as a reporting period. A **natural business year**

[1]Examples of annual reports for three companies are presented in an appendix to the text.

is a 12-month period that ends when business activities are at their lowest level. If a firm's annual period ends on December 31, it is referred to as a **calendar year** firm.

Annual reports are used by creditors, investors, and other interested parties to assess the firm's progress from year to year. Although the basic accounting period for which financial statements are presented is one year, quarterly statements are also commonly issued to external parties to provide timely information on the operation of the firm. Many firms also prepare monthly or weekly statements for internal use by management. Statements prepared before the end of the annual period are called **interim statements.**

During each fiscal period, a sequence of accounting procedures called the **accounting cycle** is completed. The occurrence of a business transaction is the initial step in the accounting cycle, the end product of which is the firm's year-end financial statements. The first four steps of the accounting cycle, listed below, are carried out during the period as transactions occur. These four steps of the cycle are described in detail in this chapter in the following order:

The First Four Steps in the Accounting Cycle

Step 1. Transactions are identified and business documents are prepared.

Step 2. Transactions are analyzed on the basis of the business document and are recorded in a journal.

Step 3. Information is transferred (posted) from the journal to ledger accounts.

Step 4. A trial balance is prepared from the account balances in the ledger to prove the equality of debits and credits.

The remaining part of the accounting cycle, completed at the end of the accounting period, is discussed in Chapters 3 and 4.

BUSINESS DOCUMENTS

Some type of **business document** such as a sales invoice, purchase order, or check is prepared for every transaction entered into by a business and serves two basic purposes. First, it provides written evidence of a transaction and is used by the accounting department as support for entries in the accounting records. Second, it serves as an important element in the control of the firm's resources. The arrival of a business document in the accounting department generally initiates the recording process.

RECORDING BUSINESS TRANSACTIONS— THE USE OF ACCOUNTS

Each transaction recorded results in an increase or decrease in one or more asset, liability, owner's equity, revenue, or expense items. A part of the accounting function is to classify the effects of transactions into meaningful categories and to summarize the results in the firm's financial statements. To facilitate accumulating financial statement data, transactions are recorded in accounts. An **account** is a device used to provide a record of increases and decreases in each item that appears in a firm's financial statements. Thus, as a part of its accounting system, a firm will typically maintain an account for each kind of asset, liability, owner's equity, revenue, and expense item. For example, a firm will maintain a separate account to record increases and decreases in cash, a separate account to record increases and decreases in accounts receivable, a separate account for accounts payable, and another account for capital investment. The **general ledger** is a collection of the complete set of accounts established by a specific firm.

Each account has three basic parts: (1) a title, which should be descriptive of the nature of the items being recorded in the account; (2) a place for recording increases; and (3) a place for recording decreases. Also, accounts typically provide space for recording an account number, the date of the transaction, an explanation of the transaction, and a posting reference column. One simplified format, called a **T account** because of its similarity to the letter T, is shown below. Two other formats are illustrated later in this chapter.

Account Title

Left side or debit side (Abbreviation—Dr.)	Right side or credit side (Abbreviation—Cr.)

A T account has a left side and a right side, called respectively the **debit** side and **credit** side. An account is debited when an amount is entered on the left side and credited when an amount is entered on the right side. A debit is also called a **charge** to the account.

After the transactions are entered, the **account balance** (the difference between the sum of its debits and the sum of its credits) can be computed. If the sum of the debits exceeds the sum of the credits, the account has a debit balance. A credit balance results when the sum of the credits is greater than the sum of the debits. An account will have a zero balance if the sum of the debits equals the sum of the credits.

To illustrate the mechanics involved, assume that a general ledger contained the following cash account after certain transactions had been recorded.

Cash

Debit (Dr.)	Credit (Cr.)
10,000	6,200
7,200	4,000
3,000	10,200
20,200	
Balance 10,000	

Cash receipts are recorded on the debit side of the account and cash payments are entered on the credit side. Recording the receipts and payments separately facilitates the determination of the account balance. Cash receipts of $20,200 exceeded the payments of $10,200, resulting in a debit balance of $10,000.

In a T account format the totals (called **footings**) are sometimes written smaller or in a different color than the postings so the totals will not be interpreted as additional debits and credits. The debit balance of $10,000 in the cash account is inserted on the debit side of the account. A balance sheet prepared at this time would report $10,000 in cash as an asset.

STANDARD ACCOUNT FORMS

The T account format described above is a convenient way to show the effects of transactions on individual accounts and is used primarily in accounting textbooks and in classroom illustrations. In practice, however, ledger accounts generally take one of the formats shown in Figure 2-1.

INDIVIDUAL ACCOUNTS COMMONLY USED

As mentioned previously, the accountant establishes an account for each type of asset, liability, owner's equity, revenue, and expense reported in the financial statements. The number of accounts and specific account titles will vary, depending on the nature and complexity of the business operation. For example, the accounts used to record transactions of a real estate sales office will differ significantly from those of a manufacturing firm. You will also find that the same type of account will be given different titles by different firms. In addition, the number of accounts can reflect the amount of information desired by the statement users. For example, although one account could be used for recording all expenses, it would generally not provide sufficient detail to monitor and control the firm's operations.

The title or name given to a specific account should be descriptive of the items recorded in the account. Because some account titles consist of terms new to you or with special technical meaning in accounting, it will be helpful to look first at the nature of the accounts normally used by a service organization before discussing the recording of transactions. Additional accounts are introduced in later chapters.

Figure 2-1
Examples of Two
Account Formats

Balance-column account

ACCOUNT **Cash**   Account No. **100**

Date		Explanation	Post* Ref.	Debit	Credit	Balance
1985						
Nov.	6		1	10,000		10,000
			1	7,200		17,200
			1		6,200	11,000
	7		2	3,000		14,000
			2		4,000	10,000

Four-column account

ACCOUNT **Cash**   Account No. **100**

Date		Explanation	Post Ref.	Debit	Credit	Balance	
						Debit	Credit
1985							
Nov.	6		1	10,000		10,000	
			1	7,200		17,200	
			1		6,200	11,000	
	7		2	3,000		14,000	
			2		4,000	10,000	

*The purpose of the Post Ref. column is discussed later in this chapter.

BALANCE SHEET ACCOUNTS

Asset Accounts

Cash. The cash account is used to record receipts and payments of cash. The cash balance includes cash on hand and the balance on deposit in a bank.

Notes Receivable. This account is used to record claims against another party that are evidenced by signed legal documents called promissory notes. A note is signed by the maker and contains, among other things, a promise to pay a definite sum of money at a specified time. Typically a note receivable is requested by the firm when an account receivable from a customer is to be extended beyond the normal due date. Notes receivable are usually interest-bearing.

Accounts Receivable. Accounts receivable are amounts owed to a firm by customers who have purchased goods or received services on credit. An account receivable, less formal than a note, is generally based on an oral agreement to pay. Parties outside the firm that owe the firm are called **debtors.**

Other Receivables. At the end of the period, the firm may have receivables resulting from a variety of other transactions. For example, cash advances may have been made to employees, deposits may have been made with another firm for goods or services to be received in the future, utilities frequently require a deposit before service is provided, interest revenue may have accumulated on an outstanding note receivable, and a tenant may owe the firm rent. (The latter two items are sometimes called *accrued revenue* or *accrued assets* and are discussed in more detail in Chapter 3.) A firm will normally establish an individual account for each type of receivable.

Prepaid Expenses. Prepaid expenses are goods or services that have been paid for but not yet received or used. At the time of payment, an asset is recorded and subsequently expensed as the asset is used to produce revenue. Included in this category are advance payments of rent and insurance premiums. Each type of prepaid expense may be recorded in a separate account.

Land. The land account is used to record land owned by the firm. Land is recorded in an account separate from the building.

Buildings. The buildings account, sometimes called the plant account, is used to record purchases of buildings to be used by a firm to carry out its normal operations.

Equipment. Physical items used in the business for a relatively long period of time are recorded in the equipment account. In general, this account includes any item not permanently attached to the land or building. The account is used to record acquisitions of delivery equipment, office furniture and machines, factory equipment, store and office fixtures, and store furniture. Greater detail may be obtained by establishing a separate account for each major type of equipment owned.

Land, buildings, and equipment accounts are used for items to be used in the operations of the firm. Assets held for resale are reported in separate accounts.

Liability Accounts

Accounts Payable. An account payable is an obligation to pay an amount to an outside party—a **creditor**—for the purchase of goods, supplies, or services on account.

Notes Payable. A note payable is a written promise to pay a specified amount to a creditor at a specified time. A note may be issued to a lending institution in exchange for cash, or the purchase of other assets may be made on credit by issuing a note payable. Notes payable are normally interest-bearing.

Unearned Revenue. Advances received from customers for goods to be delivered or services to be performed are not reported as revenue. The firm has a liability to the customer until the goods are delivered or the services performed. In other words, in accordance with the revenue recognition principle and accrual accounting, revenue is not recognized upon receipt of the cash but is reported as a liability because it represents an obligation to perform a service or deliver goods in the future. When the revenue is earned by delivering the goods or performing the required services, the amount earned is transferred from the unearned revenue account, a liability, to a revenue account. Examples are rent collected in advance from a tenant and a magazine subscription for two years received by a publisher.

Other Short-Term Liabilities. At any given time, the firm may owe money to employees, taxing authorities, or other parties for services received by the firm. (Obligations for unpaid expenses are called *accrued expenses* or *accrued liabilities* and are discussed in more detail in Chapter 3.) For example, most firms are required to collect a sales tax on goods sold; a company may owe state and federal income taxes; telephone service may have been received for the month but not yet paid; interest may be due on a note payable. It is not possible to list here all of the potential liabilities a firm may incur. The important fact at the moment is that an individual account can be used for each type of liability.

Mortgage Notes Payable. This account is used to record a particular kind of note for which the creditor has what is called a secured claim against one or more of the firm's assets. A secured claim means that if the firm is unable to pay the obligation when due, the creditor may force the sale of the assets pledged as security to recover the debt.

Owner's Equity Accounts

Four main types of transactions affect the owner's interest in the firm: (1) investment of assets in the firm by the owner, (2) withdrawal of assets by the owner, (3) earning of revenue, and (4) incurring of expenses to produce revenue. Thus the owner's equity part of the accounting equation may be expanded as follows:

Assets = Liabilities + Owner's equity
Owner's equity = Investment by the owner − Withdrawal by the owner
+ Revenue earned − Expenses incurred

In Chapter 1, transactions affecting the owner's equity in the business were recorded in a single column under the owner's name. However, separate accounts are maintained for each of these four categories as a convenient means for preparing a report of the changes in owner's equity that occurred during the period.

Capital.   Assets invested in the firm by the owner are recorded as an increase in assets and an increase in the capital account established in the name of the owner.

Withdrawals or Drawing.   The withdrawal account (sometimes called the drawing account) is used to record the withdrawal of assets, usually cash, from the business by the owner. Thus, withdrawals are recorded as a reduction in both assets and owner's equity. An owner of a single proprietorship will often establish a fixed amount to be withdrawn at specific intervals for personal living expenses. Although the owner may think of these withdrawals as a salary, neither law nor tax codes recognize a single proprietor as an employee of the firm because the owner cannot hire himself. Consequently, recurring withdrawals made in anticipation of earning income are not considered a salary nor an expense of the business.

Occasionally, personal expenses of the owner may be paid directly from the cash of the firm. Such payments are withdrawals and not expenses of doing business since they are not associated with producing revenue.

Income Statement Accounts

Revenue and expense accounts are subclassifications of owner's equity. Because of the variety and volume of revenue and expense transactions, it is helpful in the preparation of the income statement to maintain accounts separate from other owner's equity accounts. In addition, a separate account is maintained for each major type of revenue and expense item involved so that statement users will know the amount and source of revenue and the expenses used to produce revenue. Relatively insignificant amounts are normally recorded in a Miscellaneous Revenue or a Miscellaneous Expense account.

Revenues.   Revenues are increases in owner's equity from the performance of services or the sale of goods. They are measured by the fair value of assets received. The asset received as payment for the goods or services is normally cash or a receivable. In a double-entry accounting system, revenue is recorded as both an increase in an asset and an increase in owner's equity. Revenue is reported in a separate owner's equity account in order to disclose a particular source of assets.

Expenses. The costs of services acquired and assets consumed to produce revenue are called expenses. Expenses are recorded by decreasing an asset account and increasing the appropriate expense account (a decrease in the owner's equity in the firm). If an expense has not yet been paid for, a liability is recorded rather than decreasing an asset. A number of expense accounts are normally needed to report the wide variety of expense items.

When revenues exceed expenses, the difference is called **net income, earnings,** or **profit.** When expenses exceed revenue, the firm is said to be operating at a **net loss.** The earning of net income is obviously a major objective of a business, and one important function of accounting is to provide a measurement of the firm's profitability.

GENERAL LEDGER

In a manual system, each account is usually maintained on a separate card or on a separate sheet in a loose-leaf binder. As previously defined, the collection of all the individual accounts for a particular business is referred to as a *general ledger*.

SEQUENCE AND NUMBERING OF ACCOUNTS

Accounts are normally contained in the ledger in the order they appear in the balance sheet and the income statement, making it easier to find them and prepare financial statements. Each account has an identification number that is useful for reference and as a means for cross-referencing the transactions entered in a specific account. A **chart of accounts** is a listing of the complete account titles and their related numbers.

When analyzing transactions, one refers to the chart of accounts to identify specific accounts to be increased or decreased. A flexible numbering system permits the addition of accounts as necessary. For example, all assets could be assigned a three-digit number from 100 to 199, liabilities could be 200 to 299, owner's equity 300 to 399, revenues 400 to 499, and expenses 500 to 599. Some numbers would not be assigned within each classification of accounts to permit the insertion of new accounts as they are needed.

A chart of accounts used in this and later chapters to illustrate the accounting for the Starbuck Real Estate Office is as follows:

Balance Sheet Accounts		Income Statement Accounts	
Account Title	Acct. No.	Account Title	Acct. No.
Assets		*Revenue*	
Cash	100	Commission Revenue	400
Accounts Receivable	104	Appraisal Fee Revenue	401
Prepaid Insurance	110	Service Fee Revenue	402
Office Supplies Inventory	111	*Expenses*	
Land	150	Salary Expense	500
Building	160	Commission Expense	505
Accumulated Depreciation—		Utilities Expense	510
Building	161	Advertising Expense	520
Office Equipment	170	Insurance Expense	521
Accumulated Depreciation—		Office Supplies	
Office Equipment	171	Expense	530
Liabilities		Depreciation Expense	540
Accounts Payable	200	Interest Expense	560
Salaries Payable	210		
Commissions Payable	211		
Interest Payable	215		
Utilities Payable	216		
Unearned Appraisal Fees	220		
Mortgage Notes Payable	230		
Owner's Equity			
Mike Starbuck, Capital	300		
Mike Starbuck, Drawing	310		
Income Summary	350		

TRANSACTION ANALYSIS

In Chapter 1, transactions were analyzed in columnar form in terms of the accounting equation. In performing this analysis, it was necessary to determine which item was affected and the amount each item was increased or decreased. We emphasized that after every transaction the accounting equation had to be in balance. We also noted that each transaction affected at least two financial statement items, a system called double-entry accounting. When accounts are used in the accounting process, each transaction must also be analyzed to determine what type of accounts are affected, and whether each account is increased or decreased so as to determine whether they are to be debited or credited.

DEBIT AND CREDIT RULES

Balance Sheet Accounts

As noted earlier, the *left side* of a T account is called the *debit side* and the *right side* is called the *credit side*. When accounts are maintained in the formats shown on page 47 and in the general journal, which is discussed later in this chapter, "debit" simply means the left column and "credit" means the right column. Whether a debit or a credit is an increase or a decrease to the account balance depends on whether the account is an asset, a liability, or an owner's equity account. Increases and decreases are recorded in the three categories of balance sheet accounts as shown in T account format below:

Assets		=	Liabilities		+	Owner's Equity	
Debit to increase	Credit to decrease		Debit to decrease	Credit to increase		Debit to decrease	Credit to increase

An increase to an asset account is recorded as a debit; an increase in a liability or owner's equity account is recorded as a credit. Note the relationship of the debit/credit rules to the accounting equation. In other words, assets are on the left side of the equation and are increased on the left side of the T account, the debit side, whereas liabilities and owner's equity accounts are on the right side of the equation and are increased on the right side of the T account, the credit side. A decrease in an asset is recorded as a credit; a decrease in a liability or an owner's equity account is recorded as a debit.

The recording of increases to liability and owner's equity accounts on the credit side and decreases on the debit side, a procedure that is opposite that of assets, permits an additional check for accuracy. Thus, not only must the accounting equation be in balance, but the sum of the accounts with debit balances must equal the sum of the accounts with credit balances.

Income Statement Accounts

The debit/credit rules for revenues and expenses can be developed by examining the relationship of revenue and expense accounts to the owner's equity account. As explained earlier, revenues increase and expenses decrease owner's equity. Thus increases in revenues are recorded as credits consistent with the recording of increases in owner's equity. Increases in expenses are recorded as debits, because they decrease owner's equity. Although a debit to an expense account is a reduction in owner's equity, it is also an increase in an expense account.

Debit and credit rules for income statement accounts are shown below in T account format:

Revenues		Expenses	
Debit to decrease	Credit to increase	Debit to increase	Credit to decrease
		Note: A debit increases the account balance but is a decrease in owner's equity.	

Understanding the rules of debit and credit is fundamental to understanding the material in the rest of this book. Because of the importance of understanding these rules, you should master them now. Remember that to debit (credit) an account simply means to enter the amount on the left (or right) side of the account. A debit may increase or decrease the account balance, depending on whether the account is on the left or right side of the accounting equation. The same is true for a credit. Don't think of a debit or credit as an increase or decrease but simply as an entry on the left or right side.

NORMAL ACCOUNT BALANCES

It is helpful in finding ledger errors to know the normal account balance for an account. In particular, if the balance-column account format illustrated on page 47 is used, the balance does not indicate whether it is a debit or credit. The **normal balance** of an account is the side on which increases to the account are recorded:

Account	Side Increases Recorded on	Normal Balance
Assets	Debit	Debit
Liabilities	Credit	Credit
Owner's Equity		
Investment	Credit	Credit
Withdrawals	Debit	Debit
Revenues	Credit	Credit
Expenses	Debit	Debit

If an account has a balance different from its normal balance, it is likely that an error has been made. We would not expect to find a credit balance in the land account or a debit balance in a revenue account. However, a credit balance in the cash account could result for a limited time if the bank account had been overdrawn.

GENERAL JOURNAL

In the typical manual accounting system, a transaction is analyzed and recorded first in a book called a **journal** before the effects of the transaction are entered in the individual accounts in the ledger. Since this is the initial recording of a transaction, journals are referred to as **books of original entry.** Although transactions could be entered directly to the accounts in the ledger, it is more convenient in a manual system to record them first in a journal; then when convenient, the debit and credit amounts can be transferred to the proper ledger accounts.

The journal provides in one place a complete record of all transactions as they occur in chronological order—by date. That is, in the journal the title and dollar amounts of each account or accounts to be debited or credited are listed for each transaction. Thus, in a journal it is possible to review the full effect of a particular transaction on the business. Since an individual transaction is recorded in two or more accounts in the ledger, no single account will contain a complete record of each transaction.

In addition to providing a complete record of every transaction, the journal is a useful device for reducing and locating errors. If a transaction is recorded directly to ledger accounts, the effect of the transaction may inadvertently be recorded initially as two debits or two credits, or one side of a transaction may be omitted entirely, and such errors would be difficult to locate. However, in the journal the debit and credit information for each transaction is shown together in one place. The omission of a debit or a credit or the inclusion of two debits without an offsetting credit, for instance, would be evident (although errors may still be made when transferring the effects of the transaction from the journal to the ledger). With a complete record of each transaction in the journal, some errors can be isolated by retracing the debits and credits to ledger accounts to ensure that the correct amounts were transferred (or posted) to the proper accounts.

RECORDING TRANSACTIONS IN A JOURNAL

The number of journals and the design of each varies from firm to firm, depending on the nature of the firm's operations and the frequency of a particular type of transaction. In this chapter, we are concerned with using the **general journal,** or the **two-column** journal, so called because it contains two columns for entering dollar amounts. Special journals are discussed in Chapter 6.

The standard form of a general journal and the steps followed in recording a journal entry are shown in Figure 2-2. Recording transactions in a journal is called **journalizing,** and each transaction recorded is a separate **journal entry.** Two transactions are illustrated in Figure 2-2. The first journal entry records the receipt of cash for services performed for a customer. The second entry records the purchase of equipment with a partial payment in cash and the issuance of a note payable for the balance. An entry similar to the one on July 10 involving three or more accounts is called a **compound journal entry.**

Before a journal entry is prepared, it is necessary to analyze the transaction for its effect on the various ledger accounts. Note that the rules of double-entry accounting are observed for each transaction. First, two or more accounts

Figure 2-2
Example of a General Journal

				GENERAL JOURNAL		Page 64
Date			Description	Post Ref.	Debit	Credit
1984			②			
①July	5		Cash	⑧	③14,000	
			④Service Fee Revenue			⑤14,000
			⑥To record services performed in exchange for cash.			
			⑦			
	10		Office Equipment		62,000	
			Cash			22,000
			Notes Payable			40,000
			Purchased equipment for cash and issued a short-term note.			

are affected by each transaction; second, the sum of the debit amount(s) for every transaction equals the sum of the credit amount(s); and third, the equality of the accounting equation is maintained.

Every page in the journal is numbered for future reference. Before an entry is made in the journal, the year and month are written at the top of the first column. The year and month are not repeated until the start of a new page or a new month. The process for journalizing transactions is described below, and the steps in the process are keyed to the first entry in Figure 2-2.

1. The date each transaction occurred is entered in the second column.
2. The name of the account to be debited is entered against the left margin of the description column.
3. The amount to be debited to each account is entered in the debit-amount column on the same line as the account name.
4. The name of the account to be credited is entered on the line immediately below the account to be debited and is indented to set the account apart from the account to be debited.
5. The amount to be credited to each account is entered in the credit-amount column on the same line as the account name.
6. A brief explanation of the transaction may be entered on the line immediately below the journal entry. Unless a transaction is unusual, this step is often omitted because the nature of the transaction is obvious from the accounts debited and credited.
7. A single line is sometimes skipped between each journal entry.

8. At the time the journal entry is made, the posting reference column (discussed in the next section) is left blank.

In the analysis of a transaction, the chart of accounts should be referred to in order to ensure that proper account titles are being used. If an appropriate account title is not listed in the chart of accounts, an additional account may be added.

TRANSFERRING INFORMATION FROM THE JOURNAL TO THE LEDGER ACCOUNTS

The process of transferring amounts entered in the journal to the proper ledger accounts is called **posting**. The objective is to classify the effects of transactions on each individual asset, liability, owner's equity, revenue, and expense account.

The posting of one journal entry from Figure 2-2 with one debit and one credit is shown in Figure 2-3. The debit is posted in the top half of the figure and the credit is posted in the bottom half.

The steps involved in the posting process are:

1. Locate in the ledger the account to be debited.
2. Enter the date that the transaction occurred as shown in the journal.
3. Enter the debit amount in the debit column of the ledger account.
4. Enter in the posting reference column of the ledger account the page number of the journal from which the entry is being posted.
5. Enter in the posting reference column of the journal the account number to which the debit amount was posted.
6–10. Repeat steps 1 through 5 for the credit part of the entry.

Steps 4 and 5 provide a cross-reference between the accounts in the ledger and the original journal entry, a convenient means for locating additional information related to an amount recorded in an individual account in the ledger.

ILLUSTRATIVE PROBLEM

The June transactions for the Starbuck Real Estate Office are used to illustrate the analysis of transactions and the sequence of steps to be followed in recording and summarizing the transactions. Each transaction is stated below followed by an analysis of the transaction and a journal entry. In practice, the journal entries would appear sequentially in the general journal and would be

Figure 2-3
Posting from the
General Journal to
the General Ledger

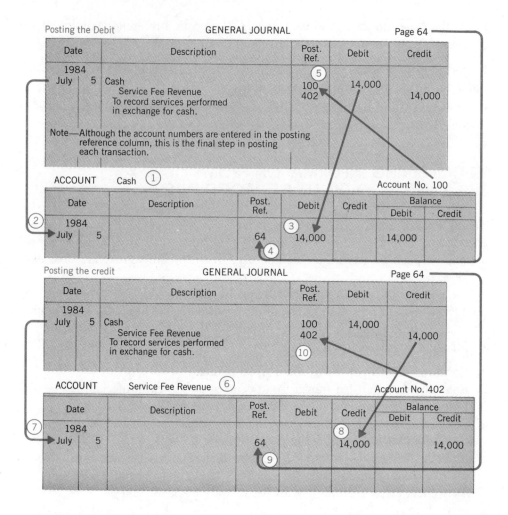

Posting the Debit — GENERAL JOURNAL — Page 64

Date	Description	Post. Ref.	Debit	Credit
1984 July 5	Cash	⑤ 100	14,000	
	Service Fee Revenue	402		14,000
	To record services performed in exchange for cash.			
	Note—Although the account numbers are entered in the posting reference column, this is the final step in posting each transaction.			

ACCOUNT   Cash ①   Account No. 100

Date	Description	Post. Ref.	Debit	Credit	Balance Debit	Balance Credit
1984 July 5		64	③ 14,000		14,000	

② ④

Posting the credit — GENERAL JOURNAL — Page 64

Date	Description	Post. Ref.	Debit	Credit
1984 July 5	Cash	100	14,000	
	Service Fee Revenue	402		14,000
	To record services performed in exchange for cash.	⑩		

ACCOUNT   Service Fee Revenue ⑥   Account No. 402

Date	Description	Post. Ref.	Debit	Credit	Balance Debit	Balance Credit
1984 July 5		64		⑧ 14,000		14,000

⑦ ⑨

uninterrupted by the analysis. Recall that in transaction analysis each transaction is analyzed to determine which accounts are affected (chart of accounts is on page 52) and whether an account is increased or decreased. The rules of debit and credit are then applied. Note that each transaction affects two or more accounts with equal debits and credits recorded and that after each entry is posted to the accounts the accounting equation is still in balance. Because the analysis explains the nature of the transaction, explanations that may appear in the general journal after each journal entry are omitted. For illustrative purposes, accounts affected by a transaction are shown after each journal entry using the T-account format for simplicity.

After the transactions are journalized, the information is posted to the firm's general ledger, presented in Figure 2-4 on pages 67–70. The information accumulated in the accounts is then used as in Chapter 3 to adjust the accounts and prepare financial statements for the month of June. A time period of one month is used for illustrative purposes. However, as noted earlier, financial statements may be prepared at other intervals desired by management, such as every quarter, but must be prepared at least annually.

June 1 Mike Starbuck deposited $60,000 cash in a checking account opened for the real estate business.

Analysis The asset cash is increased by a debit. At the same time the investment by the owner increases his equity in the firm and is recorded by a credit to his capital account.

GENERAL JOURNAL					Page 1
Date		Description	Post Ref.	Debit	Credit
1984					
June	1	Cash	100	60,000	
		Mike Starbuck, Capital	300		60,000

Cash	**100**	**Mike Starbuck, Capital**	**300**
6/1 60,000		6/1	60,000

June 1 Signed an agreement for the firm to manage an apartment complex for a monthly fee of $400 to be paid on the fifth day of the following month.

Analysis Initially, signing the agreement does not create a recordable asset or revenue and therefore is not given accounting recognition. That is, the signing of the agreement does not constitute an accounting transaction. In the future, as the service is performed, the fee is earned by the firm and becomes recordable.

June 2 Purchased land and office building for $72,000. The terms of the agreement provided for a cash payment of $12,000, the remainder to be financed with a 20-year mortgage bearing interest at 12% per year. The purchase price is allocated $10,000 to land and $62,000 to the building.

Analysis The land and building are both assets that are increased by a debit. The decrease in cash is recorded by a credit. The unpaid portion of the purchase price is a claim against the firm. A liability is increased by a credit. Although this transaction involves more than two accounts (a compound entry), the sum of the dollar amounts of the accounts debited equals the sum of the dollar amounts of the accounts credited.

June	2	Land	150	10,000	
		Building	160	62,000	
		Cash	100		12,000
		Mortgage Notes Payable	230		60,000

Cash		**100**		**Land**		**150**
6/1 60,000	6/2	12,000	6/2	10,000		

Building		**160**		**Mortgage Notes Payable**		**230**
6/2 62,000					6/2	60,000

June　3　Cash payment of $960 was made for a 24-month fire and business liability insurance policy.

Analysis The advance cash payment is recorded as a debit to an asset account, Prepaid Insurance. The asset acquired is insurance protection for 24-months, which will subsequently be expensed at some regular interval as insurance protection benefits are received and as a portion of the premium expires. Entries needed to adjust asset and liability accounts are covered in Chapter 3. A payment of cash decreases the Cash account and is recorded as a credit.

June	3	Prepaid Insurance	110	960	
		Cash	100		960

Cash		**100**		**Prepaid Insurance**	**110**
6/1 60,000	6/2	12,000	6/3	960	
	6/3	960			

June   5   Purchased office supplies in the amount of $620 on credit.

Analysis This transaction increases both an asset and a liability by the same amount. Increases in assets are recorded by debits and increases in liabilities are recorded by credits. As the supplies are consumed, an expense account will be increased by a debit and the Office Supplies Inventory account will be decreased by a credit.

June	5	Office Supplies Inventory	111	620	
		Accounts Payable	200		620

Office Supplies Inventory	**111**	**Accounts Payable**	**200**
6/5	620	6/5	620

June   5   Purchased office furniture and equipment for a total price of $9,600. Paid $5,000 in cash with the balance due in 60 days.

Analysis The account Office Equipment is debited for $9,600 to record the purchase of the asset. At the same time, cash is decreased by a credit of $5,000 and Accounts Payable, a liability, is increased by a credit of $4,600 to recognize a claim against the firm.

June	5	Office Equipment	170	9,600	
		Cash	100		5,000
		Accounts Payable	200		4,600

Cash		**100**	**Office Equipment**	**170**	**Accounts Payable**	**200**
6/1 60,000	6/2	12,000	6/5 9,600		6/5	620
	6/3	960			6/5	4,600
	6/5	5,000				

June   5   Hired two sales agents and an office secretary.

Analysis The hiring of employees is an important event to the firm but is not given accounting recognition since there are no effects at this time on the firm's accounting equation.

June 6 Paid $120 for radio commercials aired on June 3 and 4.

Analysis Advertising is an operating expense. The benefits were considered to be received when the commercial announcements were made. The Advertising Expense account is increased by a debit. Expenses decrease owner's equity (a debit), but a separate account, Advertising Expense, is established to facilitate preparation of the income statement. The cash account is decreased by a credit.

| June | 6 | Advertising Expense | 520 | 120 | |
| | | Cash | 100 | | 120 |

Cash			100		Advertising Expense	520
6/1	60,000	6/2	12,000	6/6	120	
		6/3	960			
		6/5	5,000			
		6/6	120			

June 15 Sold a residence that had been listed with the firm. A commission of $4,200 was earned on the sale, to be received when the agreement is closed.

Analysis Under accrual accounting, this is a revenue transaction even though no cash was received. The asset Accounts Receivable is therefore increased (a debit) to recognize the right to receive cash in the future. When the cash is received, Cash will be debited and Accounts Receivable credited. Revenues increase owners' equity (a credit), but a separate account, Commission Revenue, is established to facilitate preparation of the income statement.

| June | 15 | Accounts Receivable | 104 | 4,200 | |
| | | Commission Revenue | 400 | | 4,200 |

Accounts Receivable		104		Commission Revenue	400
6/15	4,200			6/15	4,200

June 19 Sold a residence that had been listed with the firm. A commission of $5,400 was earned on the sale, to be received when the loan is closed.

Analysis Same as the revenue transaction on June 15.

	GENERAL JOURNAL			Page 2
Date	Description	Post Ref.	Debit	Credit
1984				
June 19	Accounts Receivable	104	5,400	
	Commission Revenue	400		5,400

Accounts Receivable		**104**		**Commission Revenue**		**400**
6/15	4,200			6/15	4,200	
6/19	5,400			6/19	5,400	

June 22 Paid salaries of $1,800 to the secretary, part-time employees, and sales staff for services rendered during last two weeks.[2] Withholdings from the employees' salaries for taxes are ignored for now.

Analysis Analysis is similar to the transaction on June 6. However, the transactions differ as to the kind of expense involved. A separate expense account is established for each significant expense category.

June 22	Salary Expense	500	1,800	
	Cash	100		1,800

[2]The term *salary* is usually used to refer to fixed compensation paid on a regular basis for services received from employees. The term *wage* is commonly used to refer to compensation stated in terms of an hourly rate or a similar basis. Here, for convenience, the term *salary* applies to both.

	Cash		**100**		**Salary Expense**		**500**
6/1	60,000	6/2	12,000	6/22	1,800		
		6/3	960				
		6/5	5,000				
		6/6	120				
		6/22	1,800				

June   23 Conducted a real estate appraisal for a customer and received a fee of $250 in cash.

Analysis   The performance of the service is a revenue transaction and the receipt of cash increases both assets (debited) and owner's equity (credited). A separate revenue account is established to recognize the kind of revenue earned.

June	23	Cash	100	250	
		Appraisal Fee Revenue	401		250

	Cash		**100**		**Appraisal Fee Revenue**	**401**
6/1	60,000	6/2	12,000		6/23	250
6/23	250	6/3	960			
		6/5	5,000			
		6/6	120			
		6/22	1,800			

June   23 Starbuck withdrew $600 cash from the business for his personal use.

Analysis   This transaction is a withdrawal of assets or a negative investment by the owner and is not an expense related to the production of revenue. A debit is made to the Drawing account to reflect the decrease in capital, and the decrease in the Cash account is recorded by a credit.

June	23	Mike Starbuck, Drawing	310	600	
		Cash	100		600

	Cash		**100**		**Mike Starbuck, Drawing**		**310**
6/1	60,000	6/2	12,000	6/23	600		
6/23	250	6/3	960				
		6/5	5,000				
		6/6	120				
		6/22	1,800				
		6/23	600				

June   27 Paid $620 to creditors for office supplies purchased on credit.

Analysis   The payment reduced a creditor's claim against the assets of the firm. A decrease in liabilities is recorded by a debit and the asset Cash is decreased by a credit.

June	27	Accounts Payable	200	620	
		Cash	100		620

	Cash		**100**		**Accounts Payable**		**200**
6/1	60,000	6/2	12,000	6/27	620	6/5	620
6/23	250	6/3	960			6/5	4,600
		6/5	5,000				
		6/6	120				
		6/22	1,800				
		6/23	600				
		6/27	620				

June   29 Received a check for $280 for appraisals to be performed in July.

Analysis   Cash is increased by a debit. Since the service has not yet been performed, the revenue has not been earned. A liability, Unearned Appraisal Fees, is therefore recorded to reflect the obligation of the firm to perform the appraisal at some future date.

June	29	Cash	100	280	
		Unearned Appraisal Fees	220		280

	Cash		100		Unearned Appraisal Fees		220
6/1	60,000	6/2	12,000			6/29	280
6/23	250	6/3	960				
6/29	280	6/5	5,000				
		6/6	120				
		6/22	1,800				
		6/23	600				
		6/27	620				

June   30   Paid telephone bill in the amount of $72.

Analysis   Analysis is similar to transaction on June 6.

June	30	Utilities Expense	510	72	
		Cash	100		72

	Cash		100		Utilities Expense		510
6/1	60,000	6/2	12,000	6/30	72		
6/23	250	6/3	960				
6/29	280	6/5	5,000				
		6/6	120				
		6/22	1,800				
		6/23	600				
		6/27	620				
		6/30	72				

June   30   A check for $4,200 was received for commissions earned on the
              residence sold on June 15.

Analysis   The increase in cash is recorded by a debit. The receipt also reduced
the firm's claims against a debtor. A decrease in the asset Accounts Receivable
is recorded by a credit. Note that this transaction increases one asset and
decreases another. Recall that revenue was recorded on June 15 when it was
earned. That is, the revenue was earned when the residence was sold for the
client rather than when the cash was collected.

June	30	Cash	100	4,200	
		Accounts Receivable	104		4,200

Cash			100	Accounts Receivable			104
6/1	60,000	6/2	12,000	6/15	4,200	6/30	4,200
6/23	250	6/3	960	6/19	5,400		
6/29	280	6/5	5,000				
6/30	4,200	6/6	120				
		6/22	1,800				
		6/23	600				
		6/27	620				
		6/30	72				

The general ledger for the Starbuck Real Estate Office showing the effects of the above transactions on the accounts maintained by the firm is presented in Figure 2-4. In an actual accounting system, each account would be a separate page in the ledger. The four-column account format is used to replace the simpler T account form that was used above to illustrate the effects of the transactions on the accounts.

Figure 2-4
General Ledger

STARBUCK REAL ESTATE OFFICE

Account   **Cash**   Account No. **100**

Date	Item	Post Ref.	Debit	Credit	Balance Debit	Balance Credit
1984						
June 1		1	60,000		60,000	
2		1		12,000	48,000	
3		1		960	47,040	
5		1		5,000	42,040	
6		1		120	41,920	
22		2		1,800	40,120	
23		2	250		40,370	
23		2		600	39,770	
27		2		620	39,150	
29		2	280		39,430	
30		2		72	39,358	
30		2	4,200		43,558	

Account   **Accounts Receivable**   Account No. **104**

Date	Item	Post Ref.	Debit	Credit	Balance Debit	Balance Credit
1984						
June 15		1	4,200		4,200	
19		2	5,400		9,600	
30		2		4,200	5,400	

Figure 2-4
Continued

Account	Prepaid Insurance						Account No. **110**
			Post			Balance	
Date		Item	Ref.	Debit	Credit	Debit	Credit
1984							
June	3		1	960		960	

Account	Office Supplies Inventory						Account No. **111**
			Post			Balance	
Date		Item	Ref.	Debit	Credit	Debit	Credit
1984							
June	5		1	620		620	

Account	Land						Account No. **150**
			Post			Balance	
Date		Item	Ref.	Debit	Credit	Debit	Credit
1984							
June	2		1	10,000		10,000	

Account	Building						Account No. **160**
			Post			Balance	
Date		Item	Ref.	Debit	Credit	Debit	Credit
1984							
June	2		1	62,000		62,000	

Account	Office Equipment						Account No. **170**
			Post			Balance	
Date		Item	Ref.	Debit	Credit	Debit	Credit
1984							
June	5		1	9,600		9,600	

Account	Accounts Payable						Account No. **200**
			Post			Balance	
Date		Item	Ref.	Debit	Credit	Debit	Credit
1984							
June	5		1		620		620
	5		1		4,600		5,220
	27		2	620			4,600

Account   Unearned Appraisal Fees   Account No. **220**

Date		Item	Post Ref.	Debit	Credit	Balance	
						Debit	Credit
1984 June	29		2		280		280

Account   Mortgage Notes Payable   Account No. **230**

Date		Item	Post Ref.	Debit	Credit	Balance	
						Debit	Credit
1984 June	2		1		60,000		60,000

Account   Mike Starbuck, Capital   Account No. **300**

Date		Item	Post Ref.	Debit	Credit	Balance	
						Debit	Credit
1984 June	1		1		60,000		60,000

Account   Mike Starbuck, Drawing   Account No. **310**

Date		Item	Post Ref.	Debit	Credit	Balance	
						Debit	Credit
1984 June	23		2	600		600	

Account   Commission Revenue   Account No. **400**

Date		Item	Post Ref.	Debit	Credit	Balance	
						Debit	Credit
1984 June	15		1		4,200		4,200
	19		2		5,400		9,600

Account   Appraisal Fee Revenue   Account No. **401**

Date		Item	Post Ref.	Debit	Credit	Balance	
						Debit	Credit
1984 June	23		2		250		250

Figure 2-4
Continued

Figure 2-4
Continued

Account Salary Expense						Account No. 500
		Post			Balance	
Date	Item	Ref.	Debit	Credit	Debit	Credit
1984						
June 22		2	1,800		1,800	

Account Utilities Expense						Account No. 510
		Post			Balance	
Date	Item	Ref.	Debit	Credit	Debit	Credit
1984						
June 30		2	72		72	

Account Advertising Expense						Account No. 520
		Post			Balance	
Date	Item	Ref.	Debit	Credit	Debit	Credit
1984						
June 6		1	120		120	

TRIAL BALANCE

One aspect of a double-entry accounting system is that for every transaction there must be equal dollar amounts of debits and credits recorded in the accounts. The equality of debits and credits posted to the ledger accounts is verified by preparing a **trial balance**—a list of all of the accounts in the order in which they appear in the ledger with their current balances. The dollar amounts of accounts with debit balances are listed in one column, and the dollar amounts of accounts with credit balances are listed in a second column. The sum of the two columns should be equal. When this occurs, the ledger is said to be ''in balance.'' Figure 2-5 is a trial balance taken from the ledger of Starbuck Real Estate Office (see Figure 2-4).

A trial balance may be prepared at any time to test the equality of debits and credits in the ledger.

Figure 2-5
Trial Balance

STARBUCK REAL ESTATE OFFICE
Trial Balance
June 30, 1984

Account Title	Debit	Credit
Cash	$ 43,558	
Accounts Receivable	5,400	
Prepaid Insurance	960	
Office Supplies Inventory	620	
Land	10,000	
Building	62,000	
Office Equipment	9,600	
Accounts Payable		$ 4,600
Unearned Appraisal Fees		280
Mortgage Notes Payable		60,000
Mike Starbuck, Capital		60,000
Mike Starbuck, Drawing	600	
Commission Revenue		9,600
Appraisal Fee Revenue		250
Salary Expense	1,800	
Utilities Expense	72	
Advertising Expense	120	
Totals	$134,730	$134,730

DISCOVERY AND CORRECTION OF ERRORS

The fact that the sum of the debit column equals the sum of the credit column in the trial balance does not guarantee that errors have not been made. The trial balance is simply a verification that equal debits and credits have been recorded in the accounts. It also verifies that the account balances were computed correctly, based on the recorded data. However, errors could be made that do not affect the equality of debits and credits. For example, a correct amount could have been posted to the wrong account, a journal entry might have been omitted, or an incorrect amount could have been posted to both of the correct accounts. The possibility of making such errors should serve to emphasize the need to exercise due care in journalizing and posting transactions.

Some errors discussed in the preceding paragraph are discovered by chance or during normal operations. For example, if an account receivable is overstated, the customer usually will inform the firm when the monthly billings are made. Other errors may be identified through procedures established by the firm to check on the accuracy of its records. For example, as will be discussed in Chapter 7, a firm performs a bank reconciliation each month to verify the balance in the cash account.

A trial balance that does not balance is a clear indication of one or more errors in the accounts, or an error in preparing the trial balance. Although there is no one correct procedure for locating all types of errors, this systematic approach will be helpful.

1. Check the accuracy of the trial balance totals by adding the columns again.
2. Compute the difference between the totals. Certain types of error may be identified by performing a couple of simple mathematical exercises. For example, the amount of the difference may be equal to a debit or credit that was omitted; or if a debit or credit was recorded twice, the amount of the difference will be twice the erroneous posting. This is also true if a debit account balance is listed accidentally in the trial balance as a credit or vice versa. The trial balance and journal should first be reviewed for each of these amounts.

   If the difference between the two trial balance totals is divisible evenly by 9, it may be an indication of two common errors called **transpositions** and **slides.** To illustrate, assume that an expense account should have been debited for $4,613. If the error is a transposition, the order of the digits in a number is altered, as in posting the amount as $4,163. In a slide, the decimal point is shifted to the left or right, as by writing $461.30. In both types of error, the difference between the correct number and the incorrect number can be divided evenly by 9.
3. Compare the balances listed in the trial balance with the ledger accounts to verify that all account balances were included and copied correctly.
4. Recompute the account balances.
5. Verify that the debits equal the credits for each entry in the journal.
6. Trace the entries as recorded in the journal to the ledger accounts, and place a small check mark by each account in the journal and ledger as each posting is verified. Be alert for the posting of wrong amounts and debits posted as credits or vice versa. If the error is not found before this process is completed, review the journal and ledger, looking for amounts without a check mark.

CORRECTING ERRORS

Once an error is located, it must be corrected. An error in a journal entry discovered before the amount is posted is corrected by crossing out the wrong amount with a single line and inserting the correct amount immediately above. An error in a ledger amount is corrected in the same way. Errors should not be erased because erasures may give the impression that something is being concealed.

Journal entries that have been posted in the wrong accounts should be corrected by a journal entry. For example, assume that the following journal entry to record the receipt of cash for the performance of a service for a customer was made in the journal and posted in the ledger:

Feb.	14	Accounts Receivable	862.00	
		Service Revenue		862.00
		To record the performance of service		
		on account.		

A correcting entry is needed to cancel the incorrect debit to Accounts Receivable and to record a correct debit to the Cash account.

March	10	Cash	862.00	
		Accounts Receivable		862.00
		To correct an entry recorded on Feb.		
		14 in which a cash receipt was		
		debited to Accounts Receivable.		

USE OF DOLLAR AMOUNTS, COMMAS, AND PERIODS

Note that in the figures in this chapter dollar signs are not used in the journal or the ledger. Dollar signs are used, however, in the financial statements and other financial reports. A common practice in formal reports is to place a dollar sign before the first amount in a column of figures and also before the total amount.

When dollar amounts are entered in the journal or ledger and the columns are ruled, commas and periods are not necessary. The ruled columns serve to separate thousands of dollars and cents from dollars. For the convenience of the statement reader, commas and periods should be used if the paper is unruled.

DEMONSTRATION PROBLEM

At the ends of Chapters 2, 3, and 4, a demonstration problem and suggested solution are presented for you to use as a tool to test your comprehension of the chapter material. To make the best use of this material, you should attempt to solve the problem before studying the suggested solution.

Mary Johnson established an interior decorating service to be operated out of her home, called the Johnson Decorating Service. During the first month of operation, she completed the following transactions:

1984
July

1 Deposited $4,000 in the business checking account.
1 Purchased office equipment on credit for $1,200.
2 Purchased a used automobile for $4,200, paying $1,200 cash and signing a 12% note for the balance.
2 Paid $180 cash for a one-year insurance policy on the automobile.
8 Purchased office supplies on account, $140.
15 Completed a decorating assignment for a client and received $280 cash.
17 Received a deposit from a customer for services to be performed in August, $80.
28 Billed a client for services completed in July, $240.

Required:
A. Set up a general ledger in T account format using the following account titles and numbers:

Cash	100	Accounts Payable	200
Accounts Receivable	105	Unearned Service Fees	220
Office Supplies Inventory	120	Notes Payable	250
Prepaid Insurance	131	Mary Johnson, Capital	300
Automobile	160	Service Fee Revenue	400
Office Equipment	180		

B. 1. Journalize the above transactions.
   2. Post the entries to the T accounts.
   3. Prepare a trial balance as of July 31.

ANSWER TO DEMONSTRATION PROBLEM

B. 1. Recording transactions in the general journal. The posting reference column of the journal would be completed as the entries are posted in part B.2.

GENERAL JOURNAL					Page 1
Date		Description	Post Ref.	Debit	Credit
1984					
July	1	Cash	100	4,000	
		Mary Johnson, Capital	300		4,000
		The owner invested cash in the business.			

		Description	Ref.	Debit	Credit
	1	Office Equipment	180	1,200	
		Accounts Payable	200		1,200
		Purchased office equipment on account.			
	2	Automobile	160	4,200	
		Cash	100		1,200
		Notes Payable	250		3,000
		Purchased an automobile for $1,200 cash and signed a $3,000 note.			
	2	Prepaid Insurance	131	180	
		Cash	100		180
		Purchased a one-year insurance policy on the automobile.			
	8	Office Supplies Inventory	120	140	
		Accounts Payable	200		140
		Purchased office supplies on account.			
	15	Cash	100	280	
		Service Fee Revenue	400		280
		Earned revenue by completing assignment.			
	17	Cash	100	80	
		Unearned Service Fees	220		80
		Received an advance payment for services			
	28	Accounts Receivable	105	240	
		Service Fee Revenue	400		240
		Billed customers for services performed.			

A. and B. 2.

Cash   **100**

7/1	4,000	7/2	1,200
7/15	280	7/2	180
7/17	80		
Bal.	2,980		

Prepaid Insurance   **131**

7/2	180		

Accounts Receivable   **105**

7/28	240		

Automobile   **160**

7/2	4,200		

Office Supplies Inventory   **120**

7/8	140		

Office Equipment   **180**

7/1	1,200		

Accounts Payable		200
	7/1	1,200
	7/8	140
	Bal.	1,340

Mary Johnson, Capital		300
	7/1	4,000

Unearned Service Fees		220
	7/17	80

Service Fee Revenue		400
	7/15	280
	7/28	240
	Bal.	520

Notes Payable		250
	7/2	3,000

B. 3. Preparation of trial balance on July 31.

JOHNSON DECORATING SERVICE
Trial Balance
July 31, 1984

Account Title	Debit	Credit
Cash	$2,980	
Accounts Receivable	240	
Office Supplies Inventory	140	
Prepaid Insurance	180	
Automobile	4,200	
Office Equipment	1,200	
Accounts Payable		$1,340
Unearned Service Fees		80
Notes Payable		3,000
Mary Johnson, Capital		4,000
Service Fee Revenue		520
Totals	$8,940	$8,940

GLOSSARY

ACCOUNT. A device used to record increases and decreases for each item that appears in a financial statement (p. 45).

ACCOUNT BALANCE. The difference between the dollar amounts of debits and credits recorded in a particular account (p. 45).

ACCOUNTING CYCLE. The sequence of accounting procedures that take place during each accounting period (p. 44).

ACCOUNTING PERIOD. A period of time covered by a set of financial statements (p. 43).

ANNUAL REPORT. A set of financial statements issued at the end of a firm's fiscal period (p. 43).

BOOK OF ORIGINAL ENTRY (JOURNAL). A book in which transactions are first recorded (p. 54).

BUSINESS DOCUMENT. A paper or form that provides evidence that a transaction has occurred (p. 44).

CALENDAR YEAR FIRM. A firm whose annual period begins on January 1 and ends on December 31 (p. 44).

CHARGE. A debit to an account (p. 45).

CHART OF ACCOUNTS. A schedule listing the titles of all accounts contained in the ledger (p. 51).

COMPOUND JOURNAL ENTRY. A journal entry involving three or more accounts (p. 55).

CREDIT. An amount entered on the right side of an account (p. 45).

CREDITORS. Parties to whom the firm has an obligation (p. 49).

DEBIT. An amount entered on the left side of an account (p. 45).

DEBTORS. Parties that have an obligation to the firm (p. 48).

EXTERNAL TRANSACTIONS. Transactions involving parties outside the business (p. 42).

FISCAL YEAR. An accounting or reporting period of any 12 consecutive months (p. 43).

FOOTING. Computing the total of a column of figures (p. 46).

GENERAL JOURNAL (TWO-COLUMN JOURNAL). A book containing a chronological listing of transactions (p. 55).

GENERAL LEDGER. A collection of a group of accounts, with each account appearing on a separate page (p. 45).

INTERIM STATEMENTS. Financial statements prepared between the annual reports (p. 44).

INTERNAL TRANSACTIONS. Business activities in which only the single business entity participates, such as the use of supplies by an employee (p. 42).

JOURNAL ENTRY. The format in which a transaction is entered in the general journal (p. 55).

JOURNALIZING. The process of recording a transaction in the journal (p. 55).

NATURAL BUSINESS YEAR. A 12-month period that ends when business activities are at their lowest (p. 43).

NET INCOME (EARNINGS OR PROFIT). Excess of revenues over expenses (p. 51).

NET LOSS. Excess of expenses over revenues (p. 54).

NORMAL ACCOUNT BALANCE. The side of the account on which increases are recorded (p. 54).

POSTING. The process of transferring information recorded in the journal to the individual accounts in the ledger (p. 57).

SLIDE. An error in which the decimal point is shifted to the left or right (p. 72).

T ACCOUNT. An account format shaped like the letter T, in which the left side of the account is the debit side and the right side is the credit side (p. 45).

TIME PERIOD ASSUMPTION. The assumption that the operating life of a firm can be divided into specific time periods of equal length (p. 43).

TRANSPOSITION. An error in which the order of the digits of a number is altered (p. 72).

TRIAL BALANCE. A statement listing all of the accounts in the general ledger and their debit or credit balances. A trial balance is prepared to verify the equality of debits and credits made to the accounts (p. 70).

DISCUSSION QUESTIONS

1. Tell whether each of the following events is an internal transaction, an external transaction, or not a recordable business transaction:
   (a) Purchase of land.
   (b) Received payment from a customer on account.
   (c) Equipment is used to provide a service for a customer.
   (d) Land owned by the firm increased in value.
   (e) Money is borrowed from the First National Bank.
   (f) Supplies are used by an employee.
   (g) A prospective employee is interviewed.
2. What is the accounting cycle?
3. List the following steps in their proper sequence:
   (a) The journal entry is posted to the ledger.
   (b) A business document is prepared.
   (c) Analysis of the transaction is performed.
   (d) A business transaction occurs.
   (e) A trial balance is prepared.
   (f) An entry is made in the general journal.
4. Explain the purpose of an account. Explain the purpose of a ledger.
5. Explain the following terms as they pertain to a T account.
   (a) Debit side.
   (b) Credit side.
   (c) To debit.
   (d) To credit.
6. What are the four types of transactions that affect the owner's equity in the firm?
7. Define the term *revenues* and indicate how they affect owner's equity.

8. What is net income? What is net loss?
9. One sometimes hears the statement; "Debits are bad and credits are good for the business." Do you agree with this statement? Why or why not?
10. How are the accounts usually ordered in the ledger?
11. On what side of the account are increases recorded for (a) assets, (b) liabilities, (c) owner's equity, (d) revenue, and (e) expenses?
12. What is the normal balance of the following accounts:
    (a) Equipment
    (b) Rental Revenue
    (c) Accounts Payable
    (d) H. R. Wicks, Drawing
    (e) Salaries Expense
13. What is the purpose of the journal?
14. What is the purpose of posting references?
15. Give an example of a transaction that results in
    (a) An increase in one asset and an increase in a liability.
    (b) A decrease in one asset but no change in the total assets.
    (c) An increase in one asset and an increase in owner's equity.
    (d) A decrease in one asset and a decrease in a liability.
    (e) A decrease in one asset and a decrease in owner's equity.
    (f) One asset is increased, one asset is decreased, and one liability is increased.
16. What is the purpose of taking a trial balance?
17. Explain the fact that errors can exist even though the sum of the debit account balances may equal the sum of the credit account balances in the trial balance.
18. When the trial balance totals are not equal, what indicates that the error may be a transposition or a slide?
19. Identify the transposition and the slide in the following two examples:
    (a) An account that should have been debited for $9,840 is debited for $9,480.
    (b) A credit of $570 is listed as $57.

EXERCISES

Exercise 2-1 (Identification of Type of Account)
For each of the accounts listed, indicate whether it is an asset, a liability, an owner's equity, a revenue, or an expense.

1. Unearned Revenue
2. Accounts Receivable
3. Prepaid Insurance
4. Rent Expense
5. Service Fees Revenue
6. Cash
7. Kay Adams, Capital
8. Taxes Payable

9. Wages Expense
10. Interest Revenue
11. Kay Adams, Drawing
12. Land
13. Building
14. Note Payable

Exercise 2-2 (Debits and Credits and Normal Balance)

For each of the accounts listed in Exercise 2-1, (1) indicate whether increases are recorded as debits or credits and (2) indicate whether the normal balance is a debit or a credit.

Exercise 2-3 (Transaction Analysis)

Analyze each of the following transactions. Indicate whether each of the accounts affected is an asset, a liability, an owner's equity, a revenue, or an expense. Also indicate whether the account is being increased or decreased and whether the increase or decrease is a debit or credit.

> Example: Paid the rent
> Increase an expense (debit), decrease an asset (credit)

1. Purchased supplies on account.
2. Owner contributed cash.
3. Sold equipment for cash.
4. Billed customer for a service performed.
5. Purchased land for cash and a note payable.
6. Paid cash to a creditor.
7. Owner withdrew cash.
8. Cash payment made for a 36-month insurance policy.
9. Paid for an advertisement that appeared in last week's newspaper.
10. Received payment on an account receivable.

Exercise 2-4 (Normal Balance and Classification in Financial Statements)

For each of the following accounts, indicate whether the normal balance is a debit or a credit and whether the account would appear in the balance sheet or in the income statement.

1. Mortgage Notes Payable
2. Office Supplies Inventory
3. Service Revenue
4. Repair Expense
5. Accounts Receivable
6. Cash
7. Unearned Service Fees
8. Interest Revenue
9. John Heller, Capital

10. Accounts Payable

11. Telephone Expense

12. Equipment

13. John Heller, Drawing

14. Prepaid Advertising

3,900 CR

Cash 975 DR

Acc. Rec. 2925 CR

Exercise 2-5 (Recording Transactions in General Journal)

The following accounts appear in the ledger of the Green Valley Spa: Cash, Accounts Receivable, Exercise Equipment, Accounts Payable, Drawing—B. Buchanan, Membership Fees, Salaries Expense, and Advertising Expense.

Required:

Prepare the general journal entries to record the following transactions that occurred during May.

May   1 Purchased exercise equipment for $2,100. Paid $300 in cash and agreed to pay the balance in 60 days.

3 Paid salaries of $790.

8 B. Buchanan withdrew $1,050 from the business for his personal use.

14 Paid $490 for radio commercials.

19 Paid $370 to creditors for supplies that had been purchased on credit.

23 Received $185 from customers to reduce the balance in their accounts.

30 Earned $3,900 in membership fees during the month. Twenty-five percent of the fees were collected in cash and 75% will be paid within two months.

Exercise 2-6 (Recording Transactions in General Journal)

Record the following transaction in general journal format. Include a brief explanation of the transaction after each entry.

Feb.   1 Increase Rent Expense and decrease Cash by $750.

4 Increase Cash and decrease Accounts Receivable by $310.

6 Increase Capital and Cash by $1,300.

13 Increase Equipment by $4,700. Increase Note Payable by $4,200. Decrease Cash by $500.

20 Increase Cash and Unearned Revenue by $580.

24 Decrease Cash and Accounts Payable by $150.

Exercise 2-7 (Recording Transactions in General Journal)

Prepare the general journal entries that are needed to record the following transactions of the Collins Print Shop.

1. P. Collins, owner, transferred $1,700 in cash to the business.
2. Collins hired a new employee at an annual salary of $13,400.
3. The shop completed an order and billed the customer $125.
4. Collins purchased a piece of equipment for $9,400. The shop paid $1,200 in cash and signed a one-year, 13% note payable for the remainder.
5. Collins Print Shop signed an agreement with the high school to print 4,900 programs for $1,290.
6. Collins paid $700 to a creditor for paper purchased on account.
7. The shop paid $600 for property taxes.
8. P. Collins withdrew $480 from the business for personal use.
9. The shop will no longer be open on Sunday. The business will lose approximately $270 in revenue per week because of this decision.

Exercise 2-8 (Recording Transactions in General Journal)

Prepare the general journal entries needed to record the following transactions of Mack's Auto Repairs.

1. Paid the telephone bill of $58.
2. Purchased supplies for $130 on credit.
3. Mack Garson, the owner, invested an additional $3,400 in the business.
4. Received $205 in cash from a customer as advance payment for repair work to be done.
5. Paid $130 for supplies purchased on credit.
6. Billed a customer $480 for services performed.
7. Mack Garson withdrew $600 from the business for living expenses.

Exercise 2-9 (Preparation of Corrected Trial Balance)

The trial balance of the Douglas Company presented on page 83 does not balance. In examining the general journal and the general ledger you discover the following information.

1. A purchase of supplies for $210 in cash was erroneously recorded as a purchase on account.
2. The debits and credits to Accounts Receivable totaled $9,400 and $6,900 respectively.
3. The balance in the Taxes Payable account is $2,300.
4. A $790 payment for salaries was not posted to the cash account.
5. The debit to record the withdrawal of $500 in cash by the owner was not posted.

Prepare a corrected trial balance.

Exercise 2-10 (Effect of Errors on Trial Balance)

A. For each of the following errors: (1) indicate if the error would cause the trial balance to have unequal totals; (2) determine the amount by which the trial balance totals would differ, and (3) determine if the error would cause the debit total or the credit total to be larger.

Trial Balance
March 31, 1984

Account Title	Debit	Credit
Cash	$ 2,400	
Accounts Receivable	2,500	$ 2,480
Supplies Inventory	390	
Equipment	6,700	
Accounts Payable		2,610
Salaries Payable	310	
Taxes Payable		2,300 3,200
E. Douglas, Capital		7,200
E. Douglas, Drawing	3,920	
Service Revenues		13,800
Salary Expense	5,100	
Rent Expense	3,200	
Tax Expense	2,300	
Totals	$24,320	$29,290

1. A $21 debit to Cash was posted as a credit.
2. Receipt of a payment on account from a customer was recorded as a debit to Cash for $85 and a credit to Accounts Payable for $85.
3. A purchase of supplies for $78 was recorded as a debit to Supplies for $78 and a credit to Accounts Payable for $87.
4. A $117 credit to Sales Revenue was not posted.
5. A $315 debit to the Drawing account was debited to the Capital account.
6. A $450 debit to Rent Expense was posted as a $45 debit.

B. How would each error be corrected? Give the correcting journal entry where appropriate.

PROBLEMS

Problem 2-1 (Identification of Type of Account, Debit/Credit Analysis, and Normal Balance)

Listed below are the ledger accounts of Green Acres Memorial Park:

1. Cash
2. Land
3. Salary Expense
4. Interest Revenue

5. Miscellaneous Revenue
6. Building
7. Mortgage Notes Payable
8. Hank Green, Drawing

9. Accounts Receivable
10. Sales Tax Payable
11. Supplies Inventory
12. Insurance Expense
13. Notes Payable to Bank
14. Deposits with Utility Company
15. Service Fee Revenue
16. Accrued Interest Receivable
17. Salaries Payable

18. Prepaid Insurance
19. Accounts Payable
20. Maintenance Equipment
21. Unearned Revenue
22. Hank Green, Capital
23. Interest Expense
24. Property Taxes Payable
25. Notes Receivable
26. Rent Revenue

Required:

For each account listed above, complete the solution form shown below by placing a check mark in the proper columns to indicate the type of account, the side of a T account the item increases on, and the normal balance of the account.

Suggested solution form:

Account	Type of Account			Increases		Normal Balance	
	Asset	Liability	Owner's Equity (includes revenues and expenses)	Debit	Credit	Debit	Credit
1. Cash (List remaining 25 accounts.)	✓			✓		✓	

Problem 2-2 (Journal Entries, Posting to Four-Column Ledger, and Trial Balance)

Bruce Richards opened a barber shop in July. The following transactions occurred during the first month of the business.

July		
	2	Richards invested $2,300 in cash in the business.
	2	Paid rent of $410 for the first month.
	3	Purchased equipment for $1,500 cash and a $2,900 note.
	3	Purchased supplies for $240 cash.
	5	Paid advertising expense of $75.
	15	Recorded revenue for the first half of the month of $410 in cash and $25 on account.
	20	Paid insurance expense for July of $290.
	24	Received a $21 payment from customers on account.
	27	Withdrew $105 for personal living expenses.
	31	Recorded revenue for the second half of the month of $435 in cash and $18 on account.
	31	Paid utilities expense of $95.

Use the following account titles and numbers: Cash, 100; Accounts Receivable, 101; Supplies Inventory, 102; Equipment, 103; Note Payable, 200; Bruce Richards— Capital, 300; Bruce Richards—Drawing, 301; Revenue, 400; Rent Expense, 500; Advertising Expense, 501; Insurance Expense, 502; Utilities Expense, 503.

Required:
A. Prepare the general journal entries to record each transaction.
B. Post the entries from the general journal to the general ledger (four-column format) and enter the posting references in the general journal.
C. Prepare a trial balance as of July 31.

Problem 2-3 (Journal Entries, Entering Beginning Account Balances, Posting to T Accounts, and Trial Balance)

The January 31 trial balance of Margaret Hoffman, M.D. is shown below:

MARGARET HOFFMAN, M.D.
Trial Balance
January 31

Account Title	Debit	Credit
Cash	$ 240	
Accounts Receivable	1,205	
Supplies Inventory	310	
Prepaid Insurance	205	
Furniture and Equipment	6,580	
Accounts Payable		$ 245
Utilities Payable		240
Unearned Revenue		74
M. Hoffman, Capital		7,950
M. Hoffman, Drawing	4,070	
Revenue		9,231
Salary Expense	4,300	
Utilities Expense	240	
Rent Expense	590	
Totals	$17,740	$17,740

The following transactions were completed during February.

Feb. 1 Purchased supplies on account for $115.
4 Received $319 from patients as payment on account.
5 Paid the January utility expense of $240, previously recorded.
11 Performed services to earn revenue of $60 that was recorded previously as unearned revenue.
14 Recorded revenue earned of $4,300 in cash and $310 on account.

Feb. ~~15~~ Paid salaries of $1,900.
      ~~21~~ Purchased furniture for $178 in cash.
      ~~23~~ Paid creditors $160.
      ~~24~~ Withdrew $2,100 from the business for personal use.
      ~~26~~ Purchased 36-month insurance policy for $203.
      ~~27~~ Received $396 from patients as payment on account.
      ~~28~~ Recorded revenue earned of $3,850 in cash and $460 on account.
       28 Paid rent of $590.

Required:
A. Prepare journal entries to record each transaction.
B. 1. Open T accounts for the accounts shown in the trial balance.
     2. Enter the January 31 balance in each account.
     3. Post the February journal entries to the T accounts.
C. Prepare a trial balance at February 28.

Problem 2-4 (Journal Entries, Posting to Four-Column Ledger, and Trial Balance for Two Consecutive Months)

Lenny Plotkin opened Strike Bowling Alley in April and completed the following transactions during the month.

April 1 Invested $13,000 in the business.
       2 Paid the April rent of $504.
       4 Purchased bowling equipment for $10,000 in cash and a $15,000 mortgage.
       5 Paid $190 for a 12-month insurance policy.
       6 Purchased supplies for $230 on account.
      15 Paid salaries expense of $429.
      30 Recorded cash revenue earned for April of $1,400.
      30 Paid advertising expense of $163.

Chart of Accounts:

Account Title	Account number	Account Title	Account Number
Cash	10	L. Plotkin, Capital	30
Supplies Inventory	11	L. Plotkin, Drawing	31
Prepaid Insurance	12	Revenue	40
Bowling Equipment	13	Rent Expense	50
Accounts Payable	20	Salaries Expense	51
Mortgage Payable	21	Advertising Expense	52

Required:

A. Prepare general journal entries to record the April transactions.

B. Post the entries from the journal to the four-column ledger and enter the posting references in the journal.

C. Prepare a trial balance as of April 30.

The following transactions were completed during May.

May	1	Paid salaries expense of $495.
	1	Paid $75 on account for supplies purchased in April.
	9	Withdrew $260 from the business for personal use.
	16	Paid salaries expense of $507.
	16	Recorded cash revenue earned for the first half of May of $985.
	19	Paid $107 for radio advertisements.
	23	Purchased supplies for $96 on account.
	31	Recorded cash revenue earned for the second half of May of $1,173.

Required:

D. Prepare general journal entries to record the May transactions.

E. Post the entries from the general journal to the general ledger.

F. Prepare a trial balance as of May 31.

Problem 2-5 (Preparation of Trial Balance)

The ledger account balances for the Perry Public Golf Course as of December 31, 1984, are shown below. Each of the accounts contained a normal balance. The Cash account balance has been intentionally omitted.

Accounts Payable	$ 7,000	Equipment	$ 25,000
Accounts Receivable	2,000	Golf Lessons Revenue	22,000
Bill Perry, Capital	144,000	Green Fees Revenue	185,000
Bill Perry, Drawing	40,000	Insurance Expense	620
Building	145,000	Land	240,000
Cash	X	Mortgage Note Payable	250,000
Unearned Green Fees	3,100	Prepaid Insurance	480
Utilities Expense	58,000	Salary Expense	90,000

Required:

Prepare a trial balance inserting the correct Cash account balance. The accounts should be listed in the sequence in which they would normally appear in the ledger.

Problem 2-6 (Correction of Errors)

Your first assignment on your new job was to determine why the December 31, 1984, trial balance did not balance. In your review of the records you uncovered a number of errors described below:

1. A $1,298 debit to Cash was posted as $1,928.

2. A $280 credit to be made to the Sales account was credited to the Accounts Receivable account instead.
3. A cash collection of $1,200 from customers in partial settlement of their accounts was posted twice to the Cash account and the Accounts Receivable account.
4. The Accounts Payable account balance of $42,900 was listed in the trial balance as $49,200.
5. A $1,450 credit to Sales was posted as a $145 credit. The debit to Cash was for the correct amount.
6. A purchase of office supplies for $200 on account was not recorded.
7. A purchase of a delivery truck for $6,200 cash was posted as a debit to the Cash account and a debit to the Equipment acount.
8. The Drawing account balance of $28,000 was listed as a credit balance in the trial balance.
9. A $400 payment to employees for their weekly salaries was posted twice to the expense account. The credit to cash was made only once.
10. The Miscellaneous Expense account with a balance of $780 was omitted from the trial balance.
11. A payment of $550 on a Notes Payable was posted correctly to the Cash account, but was not posted to the Notes Payable account.

Required:

A. Indicate in the solution format shown below how each error would affect the trial balance totals. If the error does not cause the trial balance to be out of balance and you check "no" in the third column, write "equal" in the Difference Between Trial Balance Totals column. Each error is to be considered independent of the others.

	Would the error cause the trial balance to be out of balance?		Difference Between Trial Balance	Column having largest total	
Error	Yes	No	Totals	Debit	Credit
1.			$		
2.					
etc.					
through					
11.					

B. Prepare the journal entries necessary to correct errors number 2, 3, and 6.

ALTERNATE PROBLEMS

Problem 2-1A (Journal Entries, Posting to Four-Column Ledger, and Trial Balance)

Chris Rutgers opened a Beauty Salon in May. The following transactions occurred during the first month of the business.

May 1 Rutgers invested $3,300 in cash in the business.

2 Paid $390 for the first month's rent.

3 Purchased equipment costing $5,800 for $2,750 cash and a $3,050 note.

3 Purchased supplies costing $179 on account.

15 Recorded revenue for the first half of the month of $620 in cash and $84 on account.

17 Paid $179 to a creditor on account.

19 Paid insurance expense for May of $140.

23 Received payment from customers on account of $32.

27 Purchased supplies costing $40 on account.

31 Recorded revenue for the second half of the month of $648 in cash and $79 on account.

31 Paid telephone expense of $42.

Use the following account titles and numbers:

Cash, 101
Accounts Receivable, 102
Supplies Inventory, 103
Equipment, 104
Accounts Payable, 201
Note Payable, 202

Capital, 301
Revenue, 401
Rent Expense, 501
Insurance Expense, 502
Telephone Expense, 503

Required:

A. Prepare the general journal entries to record each transaction.

B. Post the entries from the general journal to a four-column general ledger and enter the posting references in the general journal.

C. Prepare a trial balance as of May 31.

Problem 2-2A (Journal Entries, Entering Beginning Account Balances, Posting to T Account, and Trial Balance)

Gary Birker, CPA, recently started his own practice. The trial balance at February 28 is shown at the top of the following page:

The following transactions were completed during March.

Mar. 2 Paid the rent for March of $370.

3 Received $704 from clients as payment on account.

6 Purchased supplies on account for $114.

8 Billed clients $1,684.

13 Withdrew $395 from the business for personal use.

15 Paid wages of $490.

17 Received $1,030 from clients as payment on account.

20 Paid maintenance service $64 for cleaning the office.

23 Paid creditors $103.

GARY BIRKER, CPA
Trial Balance
February 28

Account Title	Debit	Credit
Cash	$ 710	
Accounts Receivable	1,070	
Supplies Inventory	210	
Prepaid Insurance	156	
Equipment	4,475	
Accounts Payable		$ 305.
Notes Payable		1,500
G. Birker, Capital		4,600
G. Birker, Drawing	3,540	
Revenue		6,801
Wages Expense	2,100	
Rent Expense	740	
Interest Expense	48	
Cleaning Expense	157	
Totals	$13,206	13,206

Mar. 25 Paid $250 on the note plus interest of $21.
29 Purchased a typewriter for $240 on account.
30 Paid $45 for a three-month insurance policy.

Required:
A. Prepare general journal entries to record the transactions.
B. 1. Open T accounts for the accounts shown in the trial balance.
2. Enter the March 1 balance in each account.
3. Post the March journal entries to the T accounts.
C. Prepare a trial balance at March 31.

Problem 2-3A (Journal Entries, Posting to Four-Column Ledger, and Trial Balance for Two Consecutive Months)

Butch Slab opened Slab's Pool Hall during August and completed the following transactions during the month.

Aug. 1 Invested $10,500 of his own money into the business.
1 Paid rent for August of $437.
2 Purchased pool tables and other equipment for $9,500 in cash and a $18,000 note.
4 Paid $106 for advertising.

Aug. 6 Purchased supplies on account for $196.

15 Recorded cash revenue for the first half of the month of $570.

24 Withdrew $340 from the business for personal use.

31 Recorded cash revenue for the second half of the month of $790.

31 Paid wages of $214.

Use the following account titles and numbers:

Cash, 110   Butch Slab, Capital, 310
Supplies Inventory, 111   Butch Slab, Drawing, 311
Equipment, 112   Revenue, 410
Accounts Payable, 210   Rent Expense, 510
Notes Payable, 211   Advertising Expense, 511
                                   Wages Expense, 512

Required:
A. Prepare general journal entries to record the August transactions.
B. Post the entries from the general journal to a four-column general ledger and enter the posting references in the journal.
C. Prepare a trial balance as of August 31.

The following transactions took place in September.

Sept. 1 Paid rent for September of $437.

3 Paid $125 of the amount owed for supplies.

8 Paid $63 for newspaper advertisements.

13 Withdrew $415 from the business.

15 Recorded cash revenue for the first half of September of $820.

15 Paid wages of $305.

19 Purchased supplies on account for $107.

30 Recorded cash revenue for the second half of September of $816.

Required:
D. Prepare journal entries to record the September transactions.
E. Post the entries to the ledger.
F. Prepare a trial balance as of September 30.

Problem 2-4A (Journal Entries, Posting to T Accounts, and Trial Balance)

Raymond Oster decided to start his own lawn mowing service. He completed the following transactions during June.

June 1 Invested $5,250 cash and a lawnmower valued at $185 in the business.

2 Purchased a truck for $4,500 cash and a $3,000 note.

June   2   Purchased a lawnmower for $210 cash.

          7   Paid $115 for insurance on the truck.

       12   Recorded service fees earned of $120 cash and $106 on account.

       13   Paid assistant $85 for 20 hours of work.

       13   Paid $25 to have fliers printed advertising the lawn service.

       14   Paid $24 for gas for the truck.

       15   Paid $26 for insurance on the two lawnmowers.

       18   Received $84 from customers previously billed.

       27   Paid assistant $68 for 16 hours of work.

       28   Recorded service fees earned of $137 cash and $114 on account.

       30   Paid $200 on the note signed for the truck consisting of $170 principal and $30 interest.

       30   Paid $21 for gas for the truck.

Required:

A. Open the following T accounts: Cash, 1; Accounts Receivable, 2; Prepaid Insurance, 3; Equipment, 4; Truck, 5; Notes Payable, 10; R. Oster, Capital, 20; Service Fees, 30; Wages Expense, 40; Advertising Expense, 41; Truck Expense, 42; Interest Expense, 43.

B. Enter the transactions in the general journal.

C. Post the entries from the general journal to the general ledger.

D. Prepare a trial balance at June 30.

Problem 2-5A (Preparation of Trial Balance)

The ledger of the Alta Vista Laundry contains the following account titles and balances at June 30, 1984. Each account has a normal balance. The balance in the cash account has been intentionally omitted.

Accounts Payable	$ 600	Laundry Revenue	$49,300
Accounts Receivable	400	M. Webster, Capital	17,210
Alterations Revenue	8,100	M. Webster, Drawing	9,200
Cash	X	Note Payable	10,000
Dryers	8,000	Prepaid Rent	550
Interest Expense	300	Rent Expense	12,850
Interest Payable	300	Salary Expense	25,600
Utilities Expense	2,400	Supplies Inventory	210
Washing Machines	18,300	Supplies Expense	1,500

Required:

Prepare a trial balance at June 30, 1984. Include the correct balance in the cash account. List the accounts in the proper order.

CHAPTER 3
ADJUSTING THE ACCOUNTS AND PREPARING FINANCIAL STATEMENTS

OVERVIEW AND OBJECTIVES

This chapter describes the effect of year-end adjustments on financial statements. When you have completed the chapter, you should understand:

- The nature of business income (pp. 94–97).
- The need for adjusting entries and how to prepare them (p. 97–109).
- How to prepare financial statements from the adjusted trial balance (pp. 109–116).
- The meaning of the operating cycle (pp. 117–118).
- The major categories commonly used to classify accounts in the balance sheet (pp. 115–121).

A major objective of a business is to earn a profit or net income. To accomplish this, most businesses engage in a continuous series of transactions. As discussed in Chapter 2, in order to provide timely information to statement users, the operating life of a business is divided into relatively short intervals of equal length called accounting periods. One important function of accounting is to measure the net income earned or loss incurred during an accounting period. The amount of net income or loss is the difference between revenues and expenses. In the measurement of revenues and expenses, accountants apply generally accepted accounting principles. In this chapter we shall look more closely at how accountants define and determine net income. To comprehend the income statement, you must understand the term *net income* as it is used by accountants.

MEASUREMENT OF NET INCOME

CASH BASIS

Revenues and expenses may be measured on either a cash basis or an accrual basis. Under the cash basis of accounting, revenues are recorded in the period in which cash is received and expenses are recorded in the period in which cash is paid. In this system, net income is the excess of cash inflow from revenues over cash outflow for expenses. This method does not recognize revenue from the sale of goods or the performance of a service on credit. In addition, the costs of goods and services used during the current period to produce revenue, but not paid for, are recognized as expenses in a subsequent period when cash is paid. Thus, a cash basis system does not properly match the efforts of the firm to produce revenue with revenues earned.

Although the cash basis approach is used by small businesses and professional people who conduct most of their activities in cash, it is not satisfactory for most businesses that conduct a significant portion of their business on credit. The cash basis system can be justified only because it is simple to operate and, in some cases, will produce results essentially the same as those produced by accrual accounting.

ACCRUAL BASIS

Under the accrual basis of accounting, revenue is considered earned in the period in which a business sells goods or performs services. Expenses are recognized when incurred, that is, when goods are used or services are received. Accrual basis net income for an accounting period is determined by subtracting expenses incurred during the period from revenues reported as earned in accordance with the revenue realization principle. The process of associating expenses with revenues generated during the period is called **matching.** To develop a more thorough understanding of accrual accounting, the important concepts of revenue and expense will be discussed in more detail.

Revenues

Revenues are increases in owner's equity from the sale of goods or performance of services. They are measured by the fair value of assets received. Normally, the asset received is cash or the right to receive cash from customers in the future (an account receivable). Occasionally a firm may receive property or services may be performed for the firm in payment for goods sold or services performed, in which case the amount of revenue recorded is the fair value of the asset or service received. Thus, for a given accounting period, revenue earned is the sum of cash, accounts receivable, and the fair value of other assets received from customers for the sale of goods or performance of services during that period.

To illustrate the accrual concept of revenue, assume that a firm was organized in 1984 and received $100,000 in cash for services performed before the fiscal year-end. Assume also that its clients were billed $20,000 for services completed in 1984 for which the cash is to be received in 1985. Revenue earned in 1984 is $120,000, which is the sum of cash received ($100,000) and accounts receivable ($20,000) from customers for services performed in 1984. Recall from Chapter 2 that when services are performed for customers on credit, both accounts receivable and revenue are increased. In 1985, the cash collection of $20,000 is not revenue but is recorded as an increase in cash and a decrease in accounts receivable. Thus, revenue is recorded when earned regardless of the period in which the resulting cash is collected.

Some businesses perform services for their clients and charge a fee or commission for the services rendered. Examples are a real estate office, a barber or beauty salon, a law office, an accounting firm, or an investment advisory service. Various account titles are used to describe the major sources of revenue, and the account titles should be descriptive of the nature of the revenue. For example, Management Services Fees Earned and Tax Services Fees Earned may be used by an accounting firm to account for major categories of revenue. Other firms, called merchandising firms, earn revenue by selling a finished product. An account entitled Sales is commonly used by merchandising firms to record revenue from the sale of merchandise.

Expenses (Expired Costs)

Costs are incurred as a necessary part of the revenue-generating process. The portion of the cost that is expected to be used in the production of revenue in the future is reported as an asset and is called an unexpired cost. The costs of assets that can be identified with the revenue earned during the current period is reported in the income statement as an expense (sometimes called an expired cost) and is deducted from revenue in the determination of net income. In other words, as mentioned previously, expenses are the costs of services acquired and assets consumed to produce revenue.

Under the accrual basis of accounting, expenses are recognized in the period in which they are incurred rather than in the period in which the cash is paid. For example, salaries earned by employees this period are reported as a current expense even though payment may not be made until the next period. In other cases, such as the prepayment of rent for the next period and the purchase of office equipment for cash, cash is paid before an expense is incurred. These prepayments are accounted for as assets (unexpired costs) until the benefits are received, at which time they are transferred to expense accounts. In many cases, however, the expense and cash payment occur in the same period. Whatever the situation, it is important to realize that an expense incurred and the cash payment for it often do not occur in the same accounting period.

As noted in the preceding paragraph, the cost of assets must be allocated to the current and future period in order to provide proper matching of expenses incurred with revenue earned. Allocating the cost of long-term assets such as a building must be based on estimates because of the accountant's inability to predict the future and know the length of time an asset will be used. The need for timely information (the *time period assumption*), however, takes precedence over the lack of precision involved in preparing accrual basis financial statements. Although the estimates should be made as accurately as possible, the financial statements are only tentative and the actual results can be determined only at the time the firm ends operations. Despite the allocation problems, financial statements are prepared on the assumption that the firm will continue to operate in the future (the *going concern concept*) unless there is evidence to the contrary. The going concern concept and the time period assumption are the underlying bases for accrual accounting. If there were no need for periodic reports or if the firm were to liquidate in the near future, the cash basis would be satisfactory.

Although expenses decrease owner's equity, not all decreases in owner's equity are expenses. For example, a withdrawal of an asset by the owner decreases owner's equity but is not an expense of the business. Remember also that not all cash payments are expenses. Examples are the repayment of a loan, the cash purchase of office equipment (the cost will be expensed in future periods as the asset is used), and cash withdrawals by the owners.

Temporary (Nominal) and Permanent (Real) Accounts.   Although revenues increase and expenses decrease owner's equity, separate accounts are maintained for each major type of revenue and expense to provide detailed information about the dollar amount and sources of revenues as well as the dollar amount and type of expenses. This information is reported to interested parties via the income statement. Income statements are prepared for periods of equal length to enable the statement users to make meaningful comparisons of current period results with those of prior periods. To facilitate the preparation of the next period's income statement, all revenue and expense accounts are reduced to a zero balance at the end of the fiscal year—a process called *closing the accounts*—by transferring account balances to an owner's equity account. (This step in the accounting cycle is described in the next chapter.) Because the revenue and expense accounts are reduced to a zero balance at the end of the fiscal period, they are called **temporary** or **nominal accounts.** Balance sheet accounts are not closed; their ending balances of one period are carried forward and become the beginning balances of the next period. Balance sheet accounts are called **permanent** or **real accounts.**

WHY ARE ADJUSTING ENTRIES NEEDED?

In many cases, the payment or receipt of cash coincides with the accounting period in which the expense is incurred or the revenue is earned. However, some transactions will affect the firm's operating results and financial position for two or more accounting periods. In these cases, the period in which the cash is paid or received will not coincide with the period in which the expense is incurred or the revenue is earned. As a result, some of the accounts must be adjusted as of the last day of the accounting period to provide for the proper recognition of revenues earned and expenses incurred during the period. In addition, adjusting entries are necessary to achieve an accurate reporting of asset and liability balances on the last day of the accounting period.

The adjusting process involves an analysis of the accounts and supporting documents to determine if entries are needed to adjust account balances to their proper amounts for financial statement purposes. Once this analysis is completed, **adjusting entries** are recorded in the journal and posted to the accounts.

ADJUSTING ENTRIES

Adjusting entries normally are classified into two major categories with two types of items within each category. The categories are:

1. Deferrals (prepaid or precollected items)
   (a) *Prepaid expenses* are costs that have been paid for before they are used. They must be allocated to the periods in which they are used. Examples are rent expense paid by a firm in advance of occupancy and

insurance premiums paid for protection to be received in the future.

(b) *Unearned revenue* is revenue that is received from customers before it is earned. Examples are the receipt of cash for a two-year magazine subscription and rent revenue received from a tenant before occupancy occurs.

2. Accruals (unrecorded items)

(a) *Accrued expenses* are expenses that have been incurred but not yet entered in the records. Examples are unpaid wages earned by the firm's employees and interest expense that has accumulated on an outstanding note payable.

(b) *Accrued revenue* is revenue earned for services that have been performed or for goods that have been delivered but that have not yet been recorded. Examples are sales commissions earned but not yet received and interest revenue accumulated on a note receivable.

The two major categories of adjusting entries are usually referred to as deferrals and accruals. A **deferral** is a prepayment of an expense or revenue received in advance. An **accrual** is the recognition of an expense for benefits received but not yet paid for or the recognition of revenue that has been earned but for which cash has not yet been received.

To demonstrate each of these four types of adjusting entries, the illustration of Starbuck Real Estate Office will be continued. A trial balance on June 30 was prepared in Chapter 2 and is shown again in Figure 3-1. For illustrative purposes it is assumed that monthly financial statements are to be prepared and that monthly adjusting entries are made in the general journal. However, it is common practice to prepare formal adjusting journal entries at the end of the fiscal period only. If more frequent reports are prepared, the adjusting entries are entered on a worksheet only, as illustrated in Chapter 4.

PREPAID EXPENSES

A business often pays for some expense items (such as rent, insurance, and supplies) in advance of their use. Under the accrual basis of accounting, the payment of cash does not necessarily result in the recognition of an expense. Although the cost of goods and services paid for in advance is considered an asset, it is common accounting practice to charge the payment directly to an expense account if it will benefit the current period only. For example, the payment of one month's rent in advance on the first of the month is debited to Rent Expense. Other goods and services that are paid for in advance and are expected to benefit several periods are *normally* recorded as assets at the time of payment. At the end of the accounting period, the portion of the cost associated with the goods that have been used or with services that have been

STARBUCK REAL ESTATE OFFICE
Unadjusted Trial Balance
June 30, 1984

Account Title	Account Balance	
	Debit	Credit
Cash	$ 43,558	
Accounts Receivable	5,400	
Prepaid Insurance	960	
Office Supplies Inventory	620	
Land	10,000	
Building	62,000	
Office Equipment	9,600	
Accounts Payable		$ 4,600
Unearned Appraisal Fees		280
Mortgage Notes Payable		60,000
Mike Starbuck, Capital		60,000
Mike Starbuck, Drawing	600	
Commission Revenue		9,600
Appraisal Fee Revenue		250
Salary Expense	1,800	
Utilities Expense	72	
Advertising Expense	120	
Total	$134,730	$134,730

Figure 3-1
Unadjusted Trial Balance

received is transferred to an expense account. The remaining unexpired or unused portion of the cost is reported as an asset in the balance sheet. Thus, before the financial statements are prepared, the balance in the asset account is analyzed and is apportioned between an asset and an expense.

Prepaid Insurance

On June 3 a 24-month fire and insurance policy was purchased by the Starbuck Real Estate Office for $960. Insurance coverage began on June 1.
The transaction was recorded as follows:

June	3	Prepaid Insurance	960	
		Cash		960

The balance in the Prepaid Insurance account remains the same until the end of the month, at which time the cost of the insurance protection for the month of June is computed. The cost of the insurance protection per month is $40 ($960/24 months). The following adjusting entry is made on June 30 to record insurance expense and to reduce the Prepaid Insurance account:

(a) June	30	Insurance Expense	40	
		Prepaid Insurance		40
		(The adjusting entries are identified by		
		letters in this illustration for reference		
		purposes only.)		

After the adjusting entry is posted, the account balances are:

Prepaid Insurance				Insurance Expense	
6/3	960	6/30	40	6/30	40
6/30 Bal.	920				

The entry reduced the Prepaid Insurance account balance to $920, which is the unexpired portion of the cost applicable to future periods and is reported as an asset. The portion of the cost that expired in this period ($40) is properly matched as an expense with the revenue reported in June. If the adjusting entry were not made, net income, assets, and owner's equity would all be overstated.

In future periods, the $920 balance is reduced by $40 each month as insurance protection is received by the firm. The costs of additional policies purchased are debited to the Prepaid Insurance account and allocated to expense by following similar procedures.

Prepaid Expense Recorded Initially in an Expense Account.

In the above discussion, the insurance premium paid in advance was originally debited to an asset account. It is possible, however, to record prepaid items in more than one way. Some businesses find it more convenient to record all payments for goods or services initially in expense accounts, whether a particular cost will benefit the current period only or is expected to benefit several accounting periods. Whichever method is used, the accounts must be adjusted at the end of the period to properly match the expense of the current period with revenue and recognize an asset for the prepaid portion of the payment.

To illustrate, assume that Starbuck recorded the payment for the insurance policy as follows:

June	3	Insurance Expense	960	
		Cash		960

At the end of the period an adjusting entry is needed to remove the unexpired portion of the insurance coverage from the expense account.

| (a) June | 30 | Prepaid Insurance (23 months × $40 per month) | 920 | |
| | | Insurance Expense | | 920 |

After these entries are posted, the two accounts appear as follows:

Prepaid Insurance			Insurance Expense			
6/30	920		6/3	960	6/30	920
			6/30 Bal.	40		

Note that the June 30 balances are the same (Prepaid Insurance, $920; Insurance Expense, $40) as when the insurance premium payment was made initially to the Prepaid Insurance account.

When this method is used to record prepayments, a journal entry is normally made on July 1 to restore the prepaid portion of the premium of $920 to the Insurance Expense account. The entry is as follows:

| July | 1 | Insurance Expense | 920 | |
| | | Prepaid Insurance | | 920 |

Additional payments for insurance premiums are then added to the balance in the Insurance Expense account. At the end of the next reporting period, the account is analyzed and the prepaid portion is removed, as was done in entry (a) above.

Office Supplies

Starbuck Real Estate Office made the following journal entry on June 5 to record the purchase of office supplies:

| June | 5 | Office Supplies Inventory | 620 | |
| | | Accounts Payable | | 620 |

The cost of unused office supplies is reported as an asset in the balance sheet. As the office supplies are used, their cost is transferred to an expense account. Normally the recognition of the expense is deferred until the end of the accounting period. In other words, no journal entry is made during the period to record the cost of supplies consumed because this information is not needed on a day-to-day basis. Before financial statements are prepared, an adjusting entry is made to remove the cost of the supplies used from the asset account.

For control purposes the supplies are normally kept in a central location and employees may be required to requisition them as needed. The requisitions are then totaled to determine the cost of the supplies used during the period. If a requisition system is not used, the cost of the supplies on hand is determined by counting and pricing them.

In the case of Starbuck, assume that the cost of the supplies on hand at the end of June was determined to be $540. The cost of supplies used this period must be $80, since a total of $620 was available for use during the period. The following adjusting entry is made to record the supplies used:

(b) June	30	Office Supplies Expense	80	
		Office Supplies Inventory		80

After this entry is posted, the accounts will appear as follows:

Office Supplies Inventory				Office Supplies Expense	
6/5	620	6/30	80	6/30	80
6/30 Bal.	540				

The $540 balance left in the Office Supplies Inventory account is the cost of supplies available for use in future periods (an asset). The $80 balance in the Office Supplies Expense account is the cost of supplies used during June, which is matched with revenue earned this period in the income statement.

In future periods, the cost of additional purchases of supplies is debited to the Office Supplies account. The same analysis and process described above is performed at the end of each subsequent accounting period.

Depreciation of Equipment and Building

Included in the June transactions entered into by the Starbuck Real Estate Office were the purchases of a building for $62,000 and office equipment for $9,600. These assets were acquired and held by the firm for use in performing the operating activities of the firm. To provide proper matching, the cost of each asset less its estimated sales value at the end of its useful life is allocated to expense in the current and future periods as the assets are used to produce revenue. The amount of time that the asset is expected to be used is called its **estimated useful life.** The portion of the asset's cost assigned to expense is referred to as **depreciation.**

The adjusting entry to record depreciation is similar in concept to the entries made to allocate the cost of the insurance policy and office supplies described above. That is, an expense account is debited for the portion of the cost allocated to the current period and an asset is decreased. However, unlike the insurance policy and office supplies, which generally are used for one or two periods, items of equipment and buildings are frequently used for extended periods of time, sometimes up to 30 years or longer. It is often impossible for the accountant to know exactly the useful life of such assets or the sales values at the end of their useful lives. Consequently, amounts computed for depreciation are by necessity based on estimates of the asset's useful life and expected sales value. Depreciation must then be recognized as only an estimate.

In making the adjusting entry for depreciation, a separate account entitled Accumulated Depreciation is credited for the cost associated with the period rather than making a direct credit to the asset account. The balance in the **Accumulated Depreciation** account reflects the portion of the cost that has been assigned to expense since the item was purchased. The Accumulated Depreciation account is called a **contra account.** A contra account is reported as an offset to or a deduction from a related account. Thus in the balance sheet, the Accumulated Depreciation account is reported as a deduction from the original cost reported in the related asset account. Reporting both the original cost of the asset and the accumulated depreciation provides useful information about the age of the asset to statement users.

To illustrate, assume the building has an estimated useful life of 25 years, at which time it is expected to have a sales value of $2,000. The machinery has an eight-year useful life and a zero expected sales value at the end of eight years. The monthly depreciation expense for each asset is computed as follows:

Office Equipment	Building
$\dfrac{\$9{,}600}{96 \text{ months}} = \$100 \text{ per month}$	$\dfrac{\$62{,}000 - \$2{,}000}{300 \text{ months}} = \$200 \text{ per month}$

The adjusting entries to record depreciation for the month of June are:

(c) June	30	Depreciation Expense		100	
		Accumulated Depreciation—Office Equipment			100
(d) June	30	Depreciation Expense		200	
		Accumulated Depreciation—Building			200

(Rather than preparing two entries, the adjustments could be accomplished by one combined entry.)

The depreciation expense is reported as an expense in the income statement. The Building and Office Equipment accounts will be shown in the balance sheet as follows:

Building	$62,000	
Less: Accumulated Depreciation	200	$61,800
Office Equipment	$ 9,600	
Less: Accumulated Depreciation	100	9,500

book values

The difference between the original cost of the asset and its accumulated depreciation is called the **book value** of the asset and represents the unexpired cost of the asset.

As long as the assets are used, the same adjusting entries are made until the cost less expected sales value is fully assigned to expense. Thus, in successive balance sheets the Accumulated Depreciation—Office Equipment account increases $100 each month and the Accumulated Depreciation—Building account will increase $200 each month. The original cost of the two assets remains in the Office Equipment and Building accounts and does not change. A more complete discussion of depreciation is included in Chapter 10.

UNEARNED REVENUE (PRECOLLECTED REVENUE)

A firm may receive payment in advance for services that are to be performed in the future. Until the service is performed, a liability equal to the amount of the advance payment is reported in the balance sheet to reflect the obligation of the firm to perform future services. That is, recognition of the revenue is postponed until the earnings process is completed by performing the services.

For example, Starbuck Real Estate Office received a $280 advance payment on June 29 for an appraisal to be completed in July. The following entry was made to record the receipt of cash:

| June | 29 | Cash | 280 | |
| | | Unearned Appraisal Fees | | 280 |

Since the appraisal would not be performed by June 30, the credit was made to an *unearned revenue* account (a liability) at the time the cash was received. The revenue will be earned in July when the appraisal is performed for the client. Assuming that the appraisal was completed in July, an entry is made either at the time the revenue is earned or at the end of the period when the accounts are reviewed to transfer the earned portion of the advance payment to revenue as follows:

| July | 16 | Unearned Appraisal Fees | 280 | |
| | | Appraisal Fee Revenue | | 280 |

Note that the revenue is recognized in July, when the service is performed, rather than in June, when the cash was received.

The receipt of cash for services to be performed in the future could be recorded originally in a revenue account rather than a liability account. If so, an adjusting entry is needed at the end of the period to reduce the balance in the revenue account and record a liability for the unearned portion of the prepayment.

Another Unearned Revenue Illustration

The Starbuck Real Estate Office illustration contained one example of adjusting an unearned revenue account. In practice, some other common unearned revenue items are rent received in advance, magazine subscriptions and advertising fees received in advance by a publisher, and deposits received from customers before merchandise is delivered.

To further illustrate the accounting for unearned revenue, another example *unrelated to Starbuck's operations* will be used. Assume that on September 8, People of the World, publishers of a monthly magazine, received $24 for a one-year subscription beginning with the October issue. The company made the following entry upon receipt of the cash:

Sept.	8	Cash	24	
		Unearned Subscription Revenue		24

On December 31, the fiscal year-end, the balance in the Unearned Subscription Revenue account includes three months (3/12) of the revenue that was earned this period and nine months (9/12) of the revenue that will be earned and reported as revenue in the next period. Therefore, the following entry must be made to remove $6 (3/12 $\times$ $24) from the liability account and record the revenue earned in the current period.

Dec.	31	Unearned Subscription Revenue	6	
		Earned Subscription Revenue		6

After the two journal entries are posted the accounts will appear as follows:

Unearned Subscription Revenue				Earned Subscription Revenue	
12/31	6	9/8	24	12/31	6
		12/31 Bal.	18		

The adjusting entry leaves a balance of $18 in the Unearned Subscription Revenue account, which is reported as a liability in the balance sheet; the subscription revenue earned of $6 will appear as revenue in the income statement. In the next period, an adjusting entry for $18 will be made to transfer the liability balance to a revenue account.

UNRECORDED EXPENSES

During the period, most operating expenses are recorded when they are paid. At the end of the accounting period, there are usually some expenses that have been incurred but have not been recorded because payment has not been made.

An adjusting entry is needed to recognize the expense in the period in which it is incurred rather than in the period of payment. An offsetting credit is made to a liability account to record the firm's obligation to pay for the goods or services that have been received. These items are called accrued expenses or accrued liabilities.

Accrued Salary Expense (Liability)

Starbuck follows the practice of paying employees every two weeks. On Friday, June 22, the employees of Starbuck Real Estate Office were paid $1,800 for the preceding two weeks of service. A diagram of the salaries earned between this payment and June 29 is presented in Figure 3-2. No particular problem was encountered on June 22 when salaries were paid for the period of June 8 through June 22 because both the payment and the expense occurred in the same period. The following entry was made to record the payment:

June	22	Salary Expense	1,800	
		Cash		1,800
		(Withholdings from the employees		
		salaries for taxes are ignored for now.)		

When the end of the period (June 30) occurs before the next salary payment date (July 6), however, an adjusting entry is required to provide a proper matching of expenses incurred in June with revenues earned in June and to provide a record of the firm's liabilities at the end of June. Even though the employees are not paid until July 6, a portion of the $1,700 payment is for employees' services that were received in June. The entry to accrue the unpaid wages up to June 30 is:

(e) June	30	Salary Expense	990	
		Salaries Payable		990

The accounts after the adjusting entry is posted are as follows:

Salaries Payable			Salary Expense	
	6/30 990	6/22	1,800	
		6/30	990	
		6/30 Bal.	2,790	

The adjusting entry records an expense ($990) for the services received in June and reported in the June income statement along with the salaries previously paid for ($1,800). The credit of $990 in the Salaries Payable account reflects *the amount owed* to the employees for services performed up to June

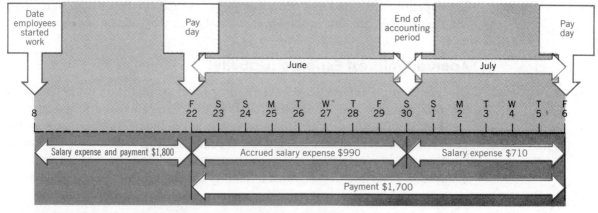

The total salaries vary each pay period because some employees work part-time.

Figure 3-2
Diagram of Salaries
Paid and Accrued

30 and is reported as a liability in the balance sheet. Failure to make the June 30 adjusting entry will result in an understatement of expenses and an overstatement of net income for June. In the balance sheet, liabilities would be understated and owner's equity would be overstated.

The liability of $990 is eliminated on July 6, when the payment of $1,700 is made to the employees. The $710 earned by the employees in July is recorded as an expense, as shown in the following entry:

July	6	Salaries Payable	990	
		Salary Expense	710	
		Cash		1,700

The effect of the above entries is to recognize the expense and liability in the period that an expense was incurred rather than in the period that payment is made to the employees.

Accrued Commission Expense (Liability)

Employees on the sales staff of Starbuck Real Estate Office are paid commissions on the tenth day of the month following the month in which a sale is made. At the end of June, $4,800 in sales commission was owed on the two residences that had been sold. Since this is an expense directly associated with the revenue earned in June, the following adjusting entry is needed to provide proper matching:

| (f) June | 30 | Commission Expense | 4,800 | |
| | | Commissions Payable | | 4,800 |

The expense is reported as a deduction from revenues in the income statement, and the payable amount is shown as a liability in the balance sheet.

Accrued Interest Expense (Liability)

On June 2, the Starbuck Real Estate Office financed a portion of the land and building purchase with a 20-year, $60,000, 12% mortgage. An annual payment of $3,000 plus accrued interest is made on June 2 of each subsequent year. As with accrued salaries, interest accumulates daily. Therefore, Starbuck must prepare an adjusting entry on June 30 to record the interest expense incurred in June and to recognize a liability for the unpaid interest. The entry is:

(g) June	30	Interest Expense[1]	600	
		Interest Payable		600

Note that only the $600 additional liability for the accrued interest is recorded on June 30. The Mortgage Notes Payable is already on the books as a result of making the June 2 entry to record the asset purchase. Interest expense is shown as an expense in the income statement for June, and interest payable is reported as a liability on the June 30 balance sheet.

Accrued Utilities Expense (Liability)

A utility company bills its customers after the service has been provided. Assume that on July 5 Starbuck Real Estate Office received a bill in the amount of $210 for electricity used in June. The adjusting entry to record the expense in June is:

(h) June	30	Utilities Expense	210	
		Utilities Payable		210

This entry increases expenses and liabilities by equal amounts. Note that even though the bill was not received until July 5, the journal entry is dated June 30 so that the expense and liability are properly reflected in the June financial statements. However, in practice when the amounts are immaterial, service companies often follow the cash basis for utility expenses and recognize the expense in the period in which the cash is paid.

[1]The formula for computing interest is as follows:

$$\text{Principal} \times \text{Rate} \times \text{Time} = \text{Interest}$$

For this entry the interest is $600, computed as follows:

$$\$60,000 \times 12\% \times \tfrac{1}{12} = 600$$

UNRECORDED REVENUE

In most cases when a service is performed by the firm, an entry is made to recognize the transaction. Even if cash is not received immediately, an account receivable is established in order to maintain a record of amounts owed to the firm and to recognize revenue earned. No entry is required at the end of a period since the receivable and revenue have been recorded. There are occasions in most firms, however, when revenue has been earned but not recorded. Earned revenue that is unrecorded at the end of the period must be included in the accounting records by debiting a receivable and crediting a revenue account. Such items are often called accrued revenues or accrued receivables.

To illustrate, Starbuck Real Estate Office signed an agreement on June 1 to manage an apartment complex for a monthly fee of $400. Although the service fee is earned by the firm in one month, the agreement provides for payment to be made on the fifth day of the following month. No entry was made on June 1, when the agreement was made, because there was not an exchange of goods or services and none of the fee was earned at that time. However, as services are performed, a portion of the fee is earned from day-to-day. By June 30, the full fee of $400 is earned and is recorded by the following entry:

(i) June	30	Accounts Receivable	400	
		Service Fee Revenue		400

The accounts receivable are shown in the balance sheet as an asset and the revenue account is reported with the other sources of revenue in the income statement.

Now that the various types of adjusting entries have been illustrated, they are summarized in Figure 3-3 for you to review.

ADJUSTED TRIAL BALANCE

The ledger accounts after the adjusting entries were journalized and posted are shown in T account form in Figure 3-4. A trial balance called an **adjusted trial balance** is taken to verify the equality of debits and credits in the accounts. An adjusted trial balance taken from the ledger of Starbuck Real Estate Office on June 30 is presented in Figure 3-5 on page 113.

PREPARATION OF FINANCIAL STATEMENTS

After the adjusting process is completed, the adjusted trial balance is used to prepare the financial statements.

Figure 3-3
Summary of Adjusting Entries

Type of Adjustment	Original Entry	Adjusting Entry	Errors in Financial Statements if Adjusting Entry Is Not Made − = unaffected O = overstated U = understated					
			Income Statement			Balance Sheet		
			Rev.	Exp.	NI	Asset	Liab.	O.E.
DEFERRALS Prepaid Expense—expense paid in advance; e.g., rent paid in advance of occupancy.	Asset Cash	Expense (for the amount used) Asset	−	U	O	O	−	O
	OR Expense Cash	Asset (for the amount unused) Expense	−	O	U	U	−	U
Unearned Revenue—revenue received before earned; e.g., rent received from a tenant before occupancy occurs.	Cash Liability	Liability (for the amount earned) Revenue	U	−	U	−	O	U
	OR Cash Revenue	Revenue (for the amount unearned) Liability	O	−	O	−	U	O
ACCRUALS Accrued Expense—expense incurred but not paid for; e.g., salaries earned by employees but not paid for.	None	Expense (for the amount incurred) Liability	−	U	O	−	U	O
Accrued Revenue—revenue earned but not yet received; e.g., interest earned on notes receivable but not yet received.	None	Asset (for the amount earned) Revenue	U	−	U	U	−	U

Assets

Cash — 100

6/1	60,000	6/2	12,000
6/23	250	6/3	960
6/29	280	6/5	5,000
6/30	4,200	6/6	120
		6/22	1,800
		6/23	600
		6/27	620
		6/30	72
6/30 Bal.	43,558		

Accounts Receivable — 104

6/15	4,200	6/30	4,200
6/19	5,400		
6/30 (i)	400		
6/30 Bal.	5,800		

Prepaid Insurance — 110

| 6/3 | 960 | 6/30 (a) | 40 |
| 6/30 Bal. | 920 | | |

Office Supplies Inventory — 111

| 6/5 | 620 | 6/30 (b) | 80 |
| 6/30 Bal. | 540 | | |

Land — 150

| 6/2 | 10,000 | | |

Building — 160

| 6/2 | 62,000 | | |

Accumulated Depr.—Bldg. — 161

| | | 6/30 (d) | 200 |

Office Equipment — 170

| 6/5 | 9,600 | | |

Accumulated Depr.—Off. Equip. — 171

| | | 6/30 (c) | 100 |

Liabilities

Accounts Payable — 200

6/27	620	6/5	620
		6/5	4,600
		6/30 Bal.	4,600

Salaries Payable — 210

| | | 6/30 (e) | 990 |

Commissions Payable — 211

| | | 6/30 (f) | 4,800 |

Interest Payable — 215

| | | 6/30 (g) | 600 |

Utilities Payable — 216

| | | 6/30 (h) | 210 |

Unearned Appraisal Fees — 220

| | | 6/29 | 280 |

Mortgage Notes Payable — 230

| | | 6/2 | 60,000 |

Owner's Equity

Mike Starbuck, Capital — 300

| | | 6/1 | 60,000 |

Mike Starbuck, Drawing — 310

| 6/23 | 600 | | |

Figure 3-4
General Ledger After Adjusting Entries Were Posted

Figure 3-4
Continued.

Commission Revenue		400
	6/15	4,200
	6/19	5,400
	6/30 Bal.	9,600

Appraisal Fee Revenue		401
	6/23	250

Service Fee Revenue		402
	6/30 (i)	400

Salary Expense		500
6/22	1,800	
6/30 (e)	990	
6/30 Bal.	2,790	

Commission Expense		505
6/30 (f)	4,800	

Utilities Expense		510
6/30	72	
6/30 (h)	210	
6/30 Bal.	282	

Advertising Expense		520
6/6	120	

Insurance Expense		521
6/30 (a)	40	

Office Supplies Expense		530
6/30 (b)	80	

Depreciation Expense		540
6/30 (c)	100	
6/30 (d)	200	
6/30 Bal.	300	

Interest Expense		560
6/30 (g)	600	

INCOME STATEMENT

An income statement for Starbuck Real Estate Office may be prepared from the adjusted trial balance as shown in Figure 3-6 on page 114. Note that the heading contains the name of the company, the type of financial statement, and the length of time it took to earn the reported income. For a service firm, the accounts are commonly classified into two major categories, revenue and operating expenses. Such a format is called a *single-step* income statement. The difference between revenue and operating expenses is the net income or net loss for the period.

The income statement normally is prepared before the balance sheet because the net income or net loss is needed to complete the owner's equity section of the balance sheet. For example, in this illustration a net income of $1,238

Figure 3-5
Adjusted Trial
Balance

STARBUCK REAL ESTATE OFFICE
Adjusted Trial Balance
June 30, 1984

Account Title	Debit	Credit
	Account Balance	
Cash	$ 43,558	
Accounts Receivable	5,800	
Prepaid Insurance	920	
Office Supplies Inventory	540	
Land	10,000	
Building	62,000	
Accumulated Depreciation—Building		$ 200
Office Equipment	9,600	
Accumulated Depreciation—Office Equipment		100
Accounts Payable		4,600
Salaries Payable		990
Commissions Payable		4,800
Interest Payable		600
Utilities Payable		210
Unearned Appraisal Fees		280
Mortgage Notes Payable		60,000
Mike Starbuck, Capital		60,000
Mike Starbuck, Drawing	600	
Commission Revenue		9,600
Appraisal Fee Revenue		250
Service Fee Revenue		400
Salary Expense	2,790	
Commission Expense	4,800	
Utilities Expense	282	
Advertising Expense	120	
Insurance Expense	40	
Office Supplies Expense	80	
Depreciation Expense	300	
Interest Expense	600	
Totals	$142,030	$142,030

is derived. This means the sum of the credit balances in the revenue accounts ($10,250) exceeded the sum of the debit balances in the expense accounts ($9,012) by $1,238. The net income of $1,238 must be added to owner's equity to equalize the total liabilities and owner's equity with the total assets. In other words, during the period there was an increase in net assets from

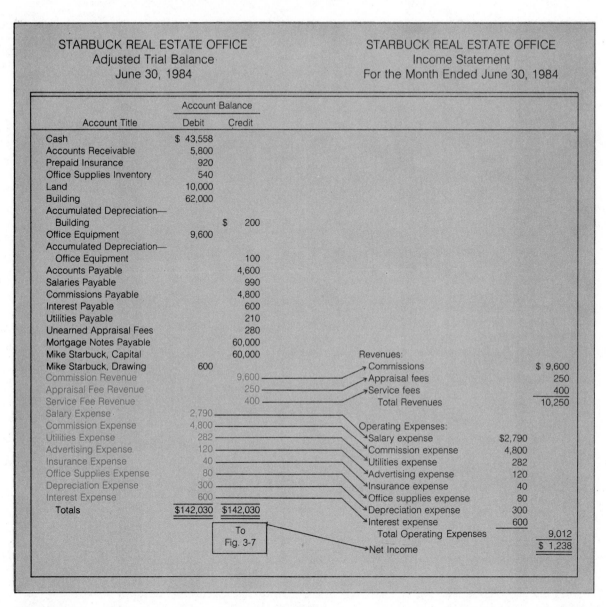

STARBUCK REAL ESTATE OFFICE
Adjusted Trial Balance
June 30, 1984

STARBUCK REAL ESTATE OFFICE
Income Statement
For the Month Ended June 30, 1984

Account Title	Account Balance Debit	Credit
Cash	$ 43,558	
Accounts Receivable	5,800	
Prepaid Insurance	920	
Office Supplies Inventory	540	
Land	10,000	
Building	62,000	
Accumulated Depreciation— Building		$ 200
Office Equipment	9,600	
Accumulated Depreciation— Office Equipment		100
Accounts Payable		4,600
Salaries Payable		990
Commissions Payable		4,800
Interest Payable		600
Utilities Payable		210
Unearned Appraisal Fees		280
Mortgage Notes Payable		60,000
Mike Starbuck, Capital		60,000
Mike Starbuck, Drawing	600	
Commission Revenue		9,600
Appraisal Fee Revenue		250
Service Fee Revenue		400
Salary Expense	2,790	
Commission Expense	4,800	
Utilities Expense	282	
Advertising Expense	120	
Insurance Expense	40	
Office Supplies Expense	80	
Depreciation Expense	300	
Interest Expense	600	
Totals	$142,030	$142,030

Revenues:
Commissions	$ 9,600
Appraisal fees	250
Service fees	400
Total Revenues	10,250

Operating Expenses:
Salary expense	$2,790
Commission expense	4,800
Utilities expense	282
Advertising expense	120
Insurance expense	40
Office supplies expense	80
Depreciation expense	300
Interest expense	600
Total Operating Expenses	9,012
Net Income	$ 1,238

To Fig. 3-7

Figure 3-6
Preparation of Income Statement from Adjusted Trial Balance

earning a net income. This increase in net assets (assets minus liabilities) belongs to the owner and should be added to the owner's capital account in the balance sheet.

BALANCE SHEET

A balance sheet for the Starbuck Real Estate Office is prepared from the adjusted trial balance in Figure 3-7. The heading indicates the name of the company, the title of the statement, and the statement date. Recall that the balance sheet reports the financial position on a specified date, June 30 in this illustration, whereas the income statement reports the flow of revenues and expenses during the month of June. The form of the balance sheet presented in Figure 3-7 is called the **report form.** In the report form, the accounts are listed in a single vertical column. This format is commonly used when the balance sheet is presented on one page. In contrast, the **account form** shows the assets on the left side of a page with the liabilities and owner's equity accounts listed on the right side of the page. In annual reports, the assets are frequently listed on one page and the liabilities and owner's equity accounts are placed on the facing page.

There are three major categories of accounts reported in the balance sheet: assets, liabilities, and owner's equity. When a number of accounts are reported, statement users have found the information contained in the balance sheet more useful if the assets and liabilities are further classified (called a **classified balance sheet**) into several important sub-categories:

Assets	Liabilities
Current assets	Current liabilities
Long-term investments	Long-term liabilities
Property, plant, and equipment	
Intangible assets	
Other assets	

These categories facilitate the evaluation of financial data and are arranged in the balance sheet so that important relationships between two sub-categories are shown. For example, the **liquidity** of a firm—its ability to satisfy short-term obligations as they become due—is of primary concern to most statement readers. To facilitate the evaluation of a firm's liquidity, assets and liabilities are classified as short-term (current) and long-term. The excess of current assets over current liabilities is called **working capital.** The use of the categories to perform analyses and interpretations is discussed in more detail in Chapter 20.

In Figure 3-7 only two of the asset categories are shown—current assets and property, plant, and equipment. Transactions involving accounts classified in the other categories were not experienced by the firm. A detailed discussion of these accounts is deferred to later chapters.

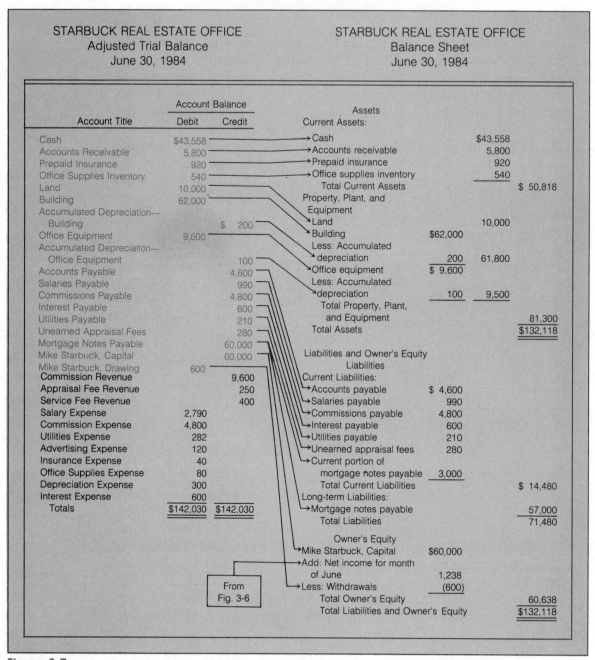

Figure 3-7
Preparation of Balance Sheet from Adjusted Trial Balance

Current Assets

Current assets are cash and other types of assets that are reasonably expected to be converted to cash, sold, or consumed either during the normal operating cycle of the firm or within one year after the balance sheet date, whichever is longer. For a merchandising firm, the **normal operating cycle** is the average length of time that it takes for a firm to acquire inventory, sell the inventory to its customers, and ultimately collect cash from the sale. The cycle is diagrammed:

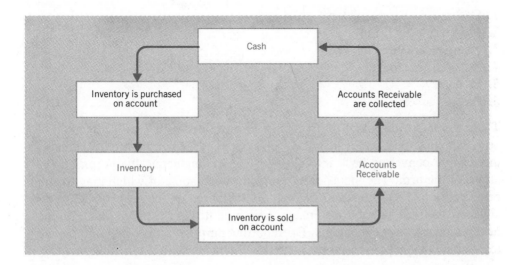

The cash collected from customers is used to pay for the inventory purchased and other operating activities of the firm, and then the cycle starts over again. Any resource, including cash, that has been committed to a specific long-term use is excluded from the current asset category.

The length of the operating cycle tends to vary for different businesses and is dependent on a number of factors. Obviously the length is affected by certain management policies such as the length of the credit period granted to customers. The type of inventory involved and the nature of the firm's operations will also affect the cycle. For example, a grocery store should have a shorter operating cycle than a jewelry store because it sells its inventory faster. Service organizations, of course, will not purchase and hold inventory. An operating cycle for a service organization involves using cash to acquire supplies and services, using the supplies and services acquired to perform a service for a customer, and then collecting cash from the customer. For many merchandising or service firms the operating cycle is less than one year. Thus, the one-year rule is applied in classifying current assets. However, many firms have an operating cycle that is longer than 12 months. Examples include firms involved with large construction projects, distilled products, and lumber operations. For these firms, the operating cycle rather than the one-year period is used to classify current assets. Unless indicated otherwise, it will be assumed in the remainder of this text that a one-year time period is to be used as the basis for classifying current assets.

Current assets are listed in the order of their liquidity. Here the term *liquidity* refers to the average length of time it takes to convert a non-cash asset into cash. The following major items, in their order of liquidity, are commonly found in a current asset section of a balance sheet:

1. Cash
2. Marketable securities
3. Notes receivable
4. Accounts receivable
5. Inventory
6. Prepaid assets

These items are discussed individually in more detail in later chapters. For now, note that marketable securities (discussed in Chapter 18) are investments that can be converted back into cash for use in conducting the normal operations of the firm. The inclusion of prepaid assets, some of which may expire or be consumed over a period of years, is supported on the grounds that if an advance payment had not been made, a cash outflow would be required in the next period to acquire the items. For reporting purposes, it is common practice to combine the prepaid assets into one account rather than list them separately.

Long-term Investments

Assets that are held for investment purposes rather than for use in normal operations are classified in the **long-term investment** section. Investments normally consist of stocks and bonds of other companies, land held for speculation, and cash or other assets set aside for specific long-term purposes such as a retirement fund for the firm's employees.

Property, Plant, and Equipment (Plant Assets)

The property, plant, and equipment category consists of assets of a physical nature (tangible) that are used in the normal operations of the firm to produce goods, sell goods, or perform services for customers. Several other terms are used for this classification; included are fixed assets, plant assets, and operational assets. **Plant assets** are expected to be used by the business for a number of years and are not held for resale. Examples include land, buildings, equipment, furniture, fixtures, patterns, dies, and tools used in operating the business.

Plant assets have limited useful lives, and their cost is depreciated over their estimated useful life. The depreciation recorded to date on an asset is shown in the *Accumulated Depreciation* account, which is deducted from the cost of the asset in the balance sheet to reflect the asset's book value. Because land has an unlimited life, it is not depreciated.

Intangible Assets

An **intangible asset** is one that does not have a physical substance but is expected to provide future benefits to the firm. Intangibles derive their value from the rights that possession and use confer to their owner. Like plant assets, intangibles are recorded initially at cost, which is allocated to future periods over the asset's estimated useful life. Examples are patents, trademarks, copyrights, franchise fees, secret processes, and trade names.

Other Assets

The other assets category is used to report those assets that do not readily fit into one of the categories described above. Some examples are plant and equipment no longer being used in operations but held for future disposal and costs incurred to rearrange equipment for a more efficient operation.

Current Liabilities

Current liabilities are obligations of the firm that are reasonably expected to be paid or settled in the next 12 months or the normal operating cycle, whichever is longer. Most current liabilities will require the payment of cash in the short term. Examples include short-term notes payable (notes that are *not* due within 12 months or the normal operating cycle are reported as long-term liabilities), accounts payable, interest payable, and other accrued liabilities. However, some current liabilities such as cash advances received from customers do not require the payment of cash, but are settled by the delivery of goods or the performance of a service. Also included as a current liability is the portion of long-term debt that is due within one year. To illustrate, recall that the Starbuck Real Estate Office issued $60,000 in mortgage notes payable to partially finance the purchase of certain assets. The contract provided for Starbuck to make a $3,000 payment plus accrued interest on June 2 for the next 20 years. In Figure 3-7, the $3,000 due within the next year is reported with the current liabilities of the firm. The remaining $57,000 due beyond 12 months of the balance sheet date is reported as a long-term liability.

Within the current liability section, in practice there is no agreed uniform order of presenting accounts. One approach is to list the accounts from the largest amount due to the smallest. Another approach commonly used is to list the notes payable first, followed by accounts payable, accrued liabilities, and the current portion of the long-term debt.

Long-term Liabilities

Long-term liabilities are those obligations of the firm that do not require payment within the next year or the normal operating cycle, whichever is longer. In other words, liabilities not classified as current are reported in this section of the balance sheet. Thus, if a firm's normal operating cycle is less than one year, obligations that mature more than one year beyond the balance sheet date are reported as long term. If the normal operating cycle is longer than 12 months, obligations due beyond the next operating cycle are reported as long-term liabilities.

In the case of the Starbuck Real Estate Office, the only long-term debt is that portion of the mortgage notes due after one year. Note in Figure 3-7 that only the interest that has accrued up to June 30 on the $60,000 outstanding debt is reported as interest payable. In other words, the total interest that will be paid over the life of the notes is not recognized as a liability at this time. Interest accrues with the passage of time and is not reported as a liability until it is accrued. The interest accrued on both the long-term and short-term portion of the debt is reported as a current liability because the interest payment is due on June 2, which is 11 months after the balance sheet date.

Owner's Equity

The owner's equity section of the balance sheet reports the equity of the owner in the assets of the firm. Owner's equity is increased by the contribution of assets and the earning of a net income. It is decreased by the withdrawal of assets and operating at a net loss for the period. Normally, the changes in owner's equity during the period are disclosed as follows in a schedule called a capital statement:

STARBUCK REAL ESTATE OFFICE
Capital Statement
For the Month Ended June 30, 1984

Mike Starbuck, Capital, June 1, 1984	$60,000
Add: Net income for the month of June	1,238
Total	61,238
Less: Withdrawals during June	600
Mike Starbuck, Capital, June 30, 1984	$60,638

The above statement is a supplemental schedule to the balance sheet. When the capital statement is prepared, the total owner's equity on June 30 of $60,638 is reported as a single amount in the balance sheet rather than showing the detailed information as presented in Figure 3-7.

DEMONSTRATION PROBLEM

The unadjusted trial balance prepared for the Johnson Decorating Service on July 31 is as follows:

JOHNSON DECORATING SERVICE
Unadjusted Trial Balance
July 31, 1984

Account Title	Debit	Credit
Cash	$2,980	
Accounts Receivable	240	
Office Supplies Inventory	140	
Prepaid Insurance	180	
Automobile	4,200	
Office Equipment	1,200	
Accounts Payable		$1,340
Unearned Service Fees		80
Notes Payable		3,000
Mary Johnson, Capital		4,000
Service Fee Revenue		520
Totals	$8,940	$8,940

Other information available at the end of July is as follows:

1. Depreciation on the automobile for one month is $100 and on the office equipment is $20.
2. Interest accrued on the notes payable is $30.
3. Received a $48 invoice from Jayhawk Oil Company for gasoline used in the business and charged on a credit card.
4. Office supplies of $85 were determined by a physical count.
5. The balance in the Prepaid Insurance account is the cost of a 12-month policy purchased on July 1.
6. Utilities used in July but not paid for; $165.

Required:
A. Journalize the required adjusting entries.

The following account titles are to be added to those listed in the trial balance:

Depreciation Expense
Automobile Expense
Insurance Expense
Office Supplies Expense
Utilities Expense
Interest Expense
Interest Payable
Accrued Expenses Payable
Accumulated Depreciation—Automobile
Accumulated Depreciation—Office Equipment

B. Prepare an adjusted trial balance.

ANSWER TO DEMONSTRATION PROBLEM

A.

Date		Description	Post. Ref.	Debit	Credit
July	31	Depreciation Expense		120	
		Accumulated Depreciation— Automobile			100
		Accumulated Depreciation— Office Equipment			20
		To record depreciation for the month of July.			
	31	Interest Expense		30	
		Interest Payable			30
		To record interest on notes payable.			
	31	Automobile Expense		48	
		Accrued Expenses Payable			48
		To record unpaid gasoline bills.			
	31	Office Supplies Expense		55	
		Office Supplies Inventory			55
		To record office supplies used in July			
	31	Insurance Expense		15	
		Prepaid Insurance			15
		To record expired insurance.			
	31	Utilities Expense		165	
		Accrued Expenses Payable			165
		To record accrued expense.			

B.

JOHNSON DECORATING SERVICE
Adjusted Trial Balance
July 31, 1984

Account Title	Account Balance	
	Debit	Credit
Cash	$2,980	
Accounts Receivable	240	
Office Supplies Inventory	85	
Prepaid Insurance	165	
Automobile	4,200	
Accumulated Depreciation—Automobile		$ 100
Office Equipment	1,200	
Accumulated Depreciation—Office Equipment		20
Accounts Payable		1,340
Unearned Service Fees		80
Notes Payable		3,000
Interest Payable		30
Accrued Expenses Payable		213
Mary Johnson, Capital		4,000
Service Fee Revenue		520
Depreciation Expense	120	
Automobile Expense	48	
Insurance Expense	15	
Office Supplies Expense	55	
Utilities Expense	165	
Interest Expense	30	
Totals	$9,303	$9,303

GLOSSARY

ACCOUNT FORM. A balance sheet format in which the assets are listed on the left side of the statement and the liabilities and owner's equity accounts are listed on the right side (p. 115).

ACCRUALS. Expenses that have been incurred but not recorded or revenues that have been earned but not recorded (p. 98).

ACCUMULATED DEPRECIATION. The amount of depreciation that has been recorded on an asset since it was acquired (p. 103).

ADJUSTING ENTRIES. Journal entries made at the end of an accounting period to update or correct the account balances (p. 97).

ADJUSTED TRIAL BALANCE. A trial balance taken from the ledger after the adjusting entries have been posted (p. 109).

BOOK VALUE. The original cost of an asset less its accumulated depreciation (p. 104).

CLASSIFIED BALANCE SHEET. A balance sheet with assets and liabilities arranged into significant groups that have some common basis (p. 115).

CONTRA ACCOUNT. An account that is deducted from a related account (p. 103).

CURRENT ASSETS. Cash and other forms of assets that are reasonably expected to be converted to cash, sold, or consumed either during the normal operating cycle of the firm or within one year of the balance sheet date, whichever is longer (p. 117).

CURRENT LIABILITIES. Obligations of the firm that are reasonably expected to be paid or satisfied within one year of the balance sheet date or the normal operating cycle, whichever is longer (p. 119).

DEFERRALS. The postponement of the recognition of expenses or revenues that have been paid for or received during the period (p. 98).

DEPRECIATION. That portion of the cost of a plant asset that is assigned to expense (p. 102).

ESTIMATED USEFUL LIFE. The period of time a plant asset is expected to be used (p. 102).

EXPIRED COST. The cost of an asset used to produce revenue; an expense (p. 95).

INTANGIBLE ASSETS. Assets that do not have a physical existence and derive value from the rights that possession confers to their owners (p. 119).

LIQUIDITY. The ability of a firm to satisfy its short-term obligations. Also refers to the average length of time it takes to convert a non-cash asset into cash (p. 115).

LONG-TERM INVESTMENTS. Investments that are restricted for use to other than current operations (p. 118).

LONG-TERM LIABILITIES. Obligations of the firm that do not require payment within one year of the balance sheet date or the normal operating cycle, whichever is longer (p. 120).

MATCHING PRINCIPLE. The process of associating expenses with revenues earned during the period (p. 94).

NORMAL OPERATING CYCLE. The average period of time it takes for a company to purchase inventory and then receive cash from its sale (p. 117).

PERMANENT (REAL) ACCOUNTS. Balance sheet accounts (p. 97).

PLANT ASSETS. Resources of the firm that are tangible in nature, have a relatively long useful life, and are used in the normal operations of the firm (p. 118).

REPORT FORM. A balance-sheet format in which the accounts are listed in a single vertical column (p. 115).

TEMPORARY (NOMINAL) ACCOUNTS. The revenue, expense, and drawing accounts are called temporary accounts because they are reduced to a zero balance at the end of an accounting period (p. 97).

UNEXPIRED COST. A cost that has not been used to produce revenue and has future economic benefit to the firm. Unexpired costs are reported as assets (p. 95).

WORKING CAPITAL. The excess of current assets over current liabilities (p. 115).

DISCUSSION QUESTIONS

1. How is net income determined under (a) the cash basis of accounting and (b) the accrual basis of accounting?
2. A company receives a machine as payment in full for services rendered. The machine has a book value of $1,250 on the books of the customer and a fair value of $1,400. How much revenue should the company record?
3. What generally accepted accounting principles are the bases for accrual accounting?
4. Differentiate between temporary and permanent accounts.
5. The withdrawal of cash by the owner is not an expense. Explain.
6. The owner of a business reviews the income statement you prepared and asks, "Why do you show a net income of only $30,000 when cash collections of $100,000 were received and cash payments of $50,000 were made for expenses during the year?" How would you respond to this question?
7. What are the objectives of making adjusting entries?
8. Define the following terms: (a) prepaid expense, (b) unearned revenue, (c) accrued expense, and (d) accrued revenue. What is generally the balance-sheet classification of each item?
9. Explain the difference between prepaid expenses and expenses incurred.
10. Explain why the purchase of supplies is usually recorded in an asset account rather than an expense account.
11. If supplies were expensed when purchased, which accounts should be debited and which credited at the end of the period to reflect the amount of supplies on hand?
12. What is a contra account? Give an example of one contra account used in the adjusting process.
13. During the year, *Aerobics for Women*, a monthly magazine, received cash for a three-year magazine subscription. A credit was made to the Unearned Subscription Revenue account.
    (a) Is the required adjusting entry made at the end of the period an example of an accrual or a deferral?
    (b) What types of accounts will be affected by the required adjusting entry?
    (c) What effect will omission of the adjusting entry have on net income and the balance sheet?

14. What would be the effect on the financial statements if an adjusting entry was not made to record revenue earned but not yet received?
15. Which financial statement is usually prepared first? Why?
16. What is a classified balance sheet?
17. What is the normal operating cycle?
18. Define current assets. In what order are current assets listed in the balance sheet?
19. Define current liabilities. Define long-term liabilities.
20. In what section of the balance sheet should the following items appear, if shown at all?
    (a) Cash
    (b) Notes payable due in six months
    (c) Bond investment to be disposed of in the near future to finance operations
    (d) Land held for speculation
    (e) Patent
    (f) Prepaid insurance
    (g) Equipment
    (h) Merchandise inventory
    (i) Land on which the office is located
    (j) Trademark
    (k) Mortgage note due in five years
    (l) Salary expense
    (m) Current portion due on long-term debt
    (n) Accumulated depreciation on office building

EXERCISES

Exercise 3-1 (Cash Versus Accrual Basis of Accounting)

At the end of the first year of operations, Linda Martin, owner of the Fifth Avenue Modeling, contracted with you to prepare 1984 financial statements on both the cash basis and the accrual basis. The firm's fiscal year-end is December 31. The following data are a summary of selected transactions that occurred during the year.

1. Fees of $72,000 were collected for services rendered during the year.
2. There were $5,000 in receivables at the end of 1984 for services performed on credit.
3. Cash payments of $45,000 were made for salaries, utilities, rent, insurance, and other operating expenses *incurred* during the year.
4. On December 15, 1984, a client paid $2,000 in advance for services to be rendered in 1985.
5. Expenses of $4,000 were prepaid (not included in the $45,000) at December 31.

Required:

A. Prepare condensed income statements for both the cash basis and the accrual basis.

B. Indicate how the following items would be reported in the firm's balance sheet under the accrual basis.
1. The $5,000 receivable.
2. The unpaid expenses of $6,000.
3. The $2,000 advance received on December 15.
4. The prepaid expense of $4,000.

Exercise 3-2 (Accrual Basis Income Statement)

After graduating from medical school in 1982, Dr. Art Taylor established his family medical practice in Akron. An income statement for the current period is presented below:

Dr. Art Taylor, Family Medical Practice
Income Statement
For the Year Ended December 31, 1984

Office fees revenue	$190,000
Less: Operating expenses	115,000
Net income	$ 75,000

Additional data:

1. Services performed in 1983 in the amount of $6,000 were collected in 1984 and are included in the 1984 revenue figure.
2. Services performed in 1984 in the amount of $8,000 are expected to be collected in 1985 and were not included in 1984 revenues.
3. Depreciation expense of $16,000 is not included in the operating expenses.
4. Accrued salaries at the end of 1983 and 1984 were $4,000 and $5,000, respectively. Expenses were recognized when cash payment was made.

Required:
A. Using the above information, prepare a condensed income statement on the accrual basis. Show all computations in good form.
B. Briefly explain why the statement you prepared is considered a better measure of net income.
C. Dr. Taylor withdrew $1,000 per week as a salary to cover his personal living expenses. The withdrawals were not included with the operating expenses. Is this a correct accounting procedure? Explain.

Exercise 3-3 (Adjusting Entry for Accrued Salaries)

Adams Company pays its employees every Friday for a five-day work week that begins on Monday and ends on Friday. The weekly payroll amounts to $1,500.

Required:
A. Assuming that December 31 falls on Wednesday, give the year-end adjusting entry.
B. If no adjusting entry were made on December 31, by how much would net income be overstated or understated? What would be the errors in the balance sheet?

C. Assuming that January 1 is a paid holiday, give the entry to pay the employees on January 2.

Exercise 3-4 (Adjusting Entry for Unearned Rent)

A law firm owns the building it occupies. The firm rents one office to a tenant who paid six months' rent in advance on November 1. The firm credited Unearned Rental Income to record the $2,100 received.

Required:
A. Prepare the adjusting entry for December 31.
B. What are the effects on the firm's financial statements from omitting the adjusting entry?
C. Prepare the entry to be made in the next period to recognize the remaining portion of the rent earned.

Exercise 3-5 (Adjusting Entry for Prepaid Insurance)

Hunter Company purchased a three-year insurance policy on March 1. The entire premium of $5,220 was recorded by debiting Prepaid Insurance.

Required:
A. Give the December 31 adjusting entry.
B. What amount should be reported in the December 31 balance sheet for Prepaid Insurance?
C. If no adjusting entry was made on December 31, by how much would net income be overstated or understated? Would assets be overstated or understated?
D. Give the adjusting entry for December 31 of the following year.
E. What would your adjusting entry in requirement A be if the premium of $5,220 was recorded by debiting Insurance Expense?

Exercise 3-6 (Adjusting Entries)

The annual accounting period for Russell Realty ends on June 30. Prepare adjusting entries for each of the following:

1. Russell Realty earned commissions of $4,300 during June that will not be received until July.
2. The telephone expense for June amounted to $115. This amount has not been recorded because it will not be paid until July.
3. The office supplies account had a $135 debit balance on July 1 of the preceding year. Supplies in the amount of $750 were purchased during the year and $90 worth of supplies are on hand on June 30.
4. The secretary's salary of $170 for the five-day work period ending July 2 will be paid on July 2.

Exercise 3-7 (Adjusting Entry for Accrued Revenue)

Dell Company sells service contracts on office machines. Its clients are billed a fixed fee per machine at the end of each month, payable by the fifteenth of the next month. On December 31, the end of the current fiscal year, billings for services performed in December in the amount of $8,200 were prepared and mailed to clients, but no entry was made to reflect the revenue earned.

Required:

A. Prepare the adjusting entry needed at December 31.

B. Indicate the financial statement classification of each account affected by the adjusting entry.

C. Give the journal entry on January 15, assuming that the full $8,200 was collected.

Exercise 3-8 (Adjusting Entries and Effect on Financial Statements)

The following information pertains to the R. J. Weber Company at the end of the current fiscal year.

1. Interest income of $430 has been earned but has not been received or recorded.
2. Property taxes of $590 have accrued but have not been recorded.
3. The balance of $1,430 in the Prepaid Insurance account includes $1,050 paid for insurance for the next year.

Required:

A. Prepare the necessary adjusting entries.

B. If no adjusting entries are made, will net income be overstated or understated, and by how much?

C. If no adjusting entries are made, what will be the effect on the asset section of the balance sheet? The liability section? The equity section?

Exercise 3-9 (Adjusting Entries—Missing Data)

Selected T accounts for the Warner Company are shown below. Adjusting entries for the period have been posted.

Prepaid Insurance		Insurance Expense	
12/31 Bal. 725		12/31 Adjusting entry 495	

Supplies Inventory		Supplies Expense	
12/31 Bal. 290		12/31 Adjusting entry 260	

Rental Revenue Receivable		Unearned Rental Revenue		Earned Rental Revenue	
1/1 Bal. -0-			12/31 Bal. 700		12/31 Bal. 9,000
12/31 Bal. -0-					

Required:

A. The balance in the Prepaid Insurance account on January 1 was $650. Compute the total cash payment made during the year for insurance premiums.

B. Supplies in the amount of $280 were purchased during the year. Compute the January 1 balance in the Supplies Inventory account.

C. No balance existed in the Unearned Rental Revenue account on January 1. Compute the total amount of rental fees that were received in cash during the period.

Exercise 3-10 (Adjusting Entries and Effect on Financial Statements)

Condensed financial statements for Ace Auto Rental before adjusting entries were made are shown in the first column of the schedule presented on page 131. The following items were not reflected in the statements:

1. Wages earned by employees but not paid at year-end, $620.
2. Depreciation on automobiles not recorded, $8,000.
3. Rental revenue earned but not collected or recorded, $720.
4. The company requires the first day rental in advance as a deposit for making a reservation. The deposit is either deducted from the total rental charges or is forfeited. During the last week of December, deposits earned were not recorded as revenue, $480.

Required:
A. Prepare the necessary adjusting entries in general journal form.
B. Determine the effects of the adjustments on the firm's financial statements by completing the schedule presented on page 131.
C. 1. Did net income increase or decrease? By how much?
   2. What was the effect of the adjusting entries on the total assets of the firm? Total liabilities? Total owner's equity?

Exercise 3-11 (Classified Balance Sheet)

Presented below are the captions of a balance sheet:

A. Current assets
B. Long-term investments
C. Property, plant, and equipment
D. Intangible assets
E. Other assets
F. Current liabilities
G. Long-term liabilities
H. Owner's equity
I. Not reported on the balance sheet

Required:
Indicate by letter where each of the following items would be classified:

_____ 1. Land held for speculation
_____ 2. Cash held for operations
_____ 3. Accounts receivable
_____ 4. Copyright
_____ 5. Accrued wages payable
_____ 6. Earned revenue
_____ 7. Unearned revenue
_____ 8. Stock in other companies held in employees' retirement fund
_____ 9. Furniture and fixtures
_____ 10. Notes payable due in two months.
_____ 11. Mortgage note payable due in 20 years
_____ 12. Interest receivable
_____ 13. Depreciation expense
_____ 14. Merchandise inventory
_____ 15. Ron Heck, Capital
_____ 16. Land and building held for sale

ACE AUTO RENTAL
Financial Statements

	Unadjusted Balances	Adjustments	Adjusted Balances
Income Statement			
Rental revenue	$142,000	————	————
Operating expenses:		————	————
Depreciation expense	—	————	————
Insurance expense	26,000	————	————
Wages expense	78,000	————	————
Miscellaneous			
expense	12,000	————	————
Net income	$ 26,000	————	————
Capital Statement			
Beginning capital	$ 50,000	————	————
Add: Net income	26,000	————	————
Less: Withdrawals	(40,000)	————	————
Ending capital	$ 36,000	————	————
Balance Sheet			
Cash	$ 26,000	————	————
Accounts receivable	—	————	————
Other receivables	6,000	————	————
Automobiles	68,000	————	————
Less: Accumulated		————	————
depr.	(32,000)	————	————
Totals	$ 68,000	————	————
Wages payable	$ —	————	————
Unearned deposits	4,000	————	————
Notes payable	28,000	————	————
Jim Dalton, Capital	36,000	————	————
Totals	$ 68,000	————	————

PROBLEMS

Problem 3-1 (Correction of Income Statement)

Navajo Airlines completed its third year of operations. The income statement prepared by the firm's bookkeeper is shown below:

NAVAJO AIRLINES
Income Statement
For the Year Ended December 31, 1984

Revenues—Airline tickets	$320,000	
Miscellaneous revenues	4,000	
Total revenues		$324,000
Operating Expenses:		
Salaries and wages expense	$ 78,000	
Depreciation expense	62,000	
Airport rental fees expense	46,000	
Gas and oil expense	31,000	
Maintenance expense	18,000	
Insurance expense	14,000	
Miscellaneous expense	6,000	
Total operating expenses		255,000
Net Income		$ 69,000

This is the first year the company has shown a profit. Concerned that the new and inexperienced bookkeeper may have made some errors, the owner of the firm asked your firm to review the records and financial statements. In conducting your review, you uncover the following:

1. Depreciation of $10,000 on a new airplane purchased during the year had not been recorded.
2. Advance ticket sales of $12,780 were included in the $320,000 revenue figure. This revenue will be earned next year.
3. Employees had not been paid $5,000 for salaries and wages earned during the last week of December.
4. An airport rental fee of $5,400 paid on December 1 for a three-month period was debited to Prepaid Rent. An entry had not been made to adjust the account at year-end.
5. Navajo Airlines has a contract to fly employees of Western Valley Electric to a remote coal-fired generating plant. Western is billed at the end of each quarter and makes payment by the fifteenth of the following month. Revenues of $7,200 earned for the quarter ending December 31 had not been collected or recorded.

Required:

A. Prepare the entries necessary to correct the accounts of Navajo Airlines.

B. Prepare a revised income statement incorporating the corrections made in requirement A.

C. The owner of the company could not understand why you excluded the advance ticket sales of $12,780 from revenues since the cash was received during the year. How would you respond to the concern of the owner?

Problem 3-2 (Adjusting Entries)

The following transactions pertaining to the business of Wayne Martin, CPA, occurred during December.

1. December 1. Purchased office furniture for $2,100. The furniture will be depreciated over a useful life of three years at which time it is expected to have a zero sales value.

2. December 1. Purchased a 24-month fire insurance policy for $1,056.

3. December 2. Borrowed $6,000 from State Bank by signing a promissory note. The principal, plus 15% annual interest, will be repaid in three months. Interest of $75 accrued on the note during December.

4. December 11. Purchased supplies for $115. On December 31, supplies worth $70 remained in inventory.

5. December 15. Paid $420 for one month's rent for the period December 15 to January 15.

6. December 18. Received a check from a client for $750 as an advance payment for services to be performed. Only 10% of the work was completed by December 31.

7. December 28. Received a bill for $245 for accrued property taxes.

Required:

Prepare the journal entries to record each transaction and prepare the adjusting entries for December 31, the end of the fiscal year.

Problem 3-3 (Adjusting Entries and Effect on Financial Statements)

A. The fiscal year for Daisy Dry Cleaning Company ends on December 31. Using the following information, make the necessary adjusting entries at year-end.

1. On October 15, Daisy Company borrowed $4,500 from Northern Bank at 12% interest. The principal and interest are payable on April 15. Interest of $113 had accrued on the loan by December 31.

2. Property taxes of $750 for the six-month period ending January 31 are due in February.

3. The annual depreciation on equipment is estimated to be $6,200. The January 1 balance in the Accumulated Depreciation account was $18,600.

4. Daisy Company purchased a one-year insurance policy on October 1 of the previous year for $228. A three-year policy was purchased on May 1 of the current year for $540. Both purchases were recorded by debiting Prepaid Insurance.

5. Daisy Company has two employees who each earn $30 a day. They both worked the last four days in December for which they have not yet been paid.
6. On November 1, the Restful Resort paid Daisy Company $450 in advance for doing their dry cleaning for the next three months. This was recorded by a credit to Unearned Dry Cleaning Revenue.
7. Utilities for December of $300 are unpaid and unrecorded.
8. The supplies account had a $135 debit balance on January 1. Supplies in the amount of $545 were purchased during the year and $120 of supplies are in the inventory as of December 31.

B. As you know, all adjusting entries affect one balance sheet account and one income statement account. Based on your adjusting entries prepared above:
   1. Complete the schedule given below.
   2. Compute the increase or decrease in net income.
   3. Compute the increase or decrease in total assets, total liabilities, and total owner's equity.

Entry	Account	Balance in the Account Before Adjustment	Dollar Effect of Adjusting Entries	Balance Reported in 12/31 Balance Sheet	Balance Sheet Classification*
1.	Interest Payable	_____	$ _____	_____	_____
2.	Property Tax Payable	_____	_____	_____	_____
3.	Accumulated Depreciation	_____	_____	_____	_____
4.	Prepaid Insurance	_____	_____	_____	_____
5.	Wages Payable	_____	_____	_____	_____
6.	Unearned Dry Cleaning Revenue	_____	_____	_____	_____
7.	Utilities Payable	_____	_____	_____	_____
8.	Supplies Inventory	_____	_____	_____	_____

*For each account, indicate whether it is an asset, liability, or owner's equity, and whether it is classified as a current asset or liability.

Problem 3-4 (Adjusting Entries, Posting to T Accounts, and Effect on Net Income)

At the end of the fiscal year, the trial balance of Fred Burkhart's Law Firm appeared as follows:

BURKHART'S LAW FIRM
Unadjusted Trial Balance
December 31, 1984

Account Title	Debit	Credit
Cash	$ 1,945	
Accounts Receivable	3,300	
Notes Receivable	4,000	
Prepaid Rent	1,050	
Prepaid Insurance	1,300	
Office Supplies Inventory	1,560	
Office Equipment	4,700	
Accumulated Depreciation—Off. Equip.		$ 950
Accounts Payable		105
Unearned Legal Fees		410
Notes Payable—Due 1987		3,500
F. Burkhart, Capital		8,000
F. Burkhart, Withdrawals	20,000	
Legal Fees Earned		53,090
Salaries Expense	22,000	
Utilities Expense	2,350	
Rent Expense	3,850	
Totals	$66,055	$66,055

Required:

A. Using the following information, prepare adjusting entries. Use the accounts shown in the trial balance and these additional accounts: Interest Expense, Depreciation Expense, Office Supplies Expense, Insurance Expense, Interest Payable, Utilities Payable, Salaries Payable.

1. A physical inventory of office supplies on December 31 showed $125 of unused supplies on hand.
2. One-half of the amount in the Unearned Legal Fees account had been earned by the end of the year.
3. Interest expense of $175 has accrued on the note payable.
4. The utility expense for December of $215 has not been recorded or paid.
5. Salaries expense accrued for the last four days in December amounts to $460.
6. Sixty percent of the prepaid insurance expired this period.
7. The amount in the prepaid rent account consists of rent for this December plus January and February of the following year.
8. Depreciation on the office equipment this year is estimated to be $400.

B. Open T accounts for the accounts shown in the trial balance and enter the December 31 balance in each account. Post the adjusting entries to the T accounts.

C. Prepare an adjusted trial balance, an income statement, and a classified balance sheet.

D. Compute the amount of net income that would be reported, assuming the adjusting entries were not made. Compare this amount to the net income derived in requirement C. What is the difference between the two figures?

Problem 3-5 (Determination of Adjusting Entries from Changes in Two Trial Balances)

The following accounts are taken from the ledger of the S. Reed Company. Account balances appear both before and after the year-end adjustments were made.

	Before Adjustments	After Adjustments
Interest Receivable	$ —	$ 220
Supplies Inventory	720	180
Prepaid Advertising	1,250	370
Prepaid Insurance	—	510
Accumulated Depreciation	330	530
Wages Payable	—	790
Property Taxes Payable	—	225
Unearned Service Fees	1,000	450
Interest Revenue	1,200	1,420
Service Fees Revenue	35,900	36,450
Supplies Expense	—	540
Advertising Expense	—	880
Insurance Expense	1,605	1,095
Depreciation Expense	—	200
Wages Expense	23,530	24,320
Property Tax Expense	1,940	2,165

Required:
Give the adjusting entries that resulted in the balances found in the After Adjustments column.

Problem 3-6 (Determination of Adjusting Entries from Changes in Two Balance Sheets)

Brian Carson, owner of the On Time Watch and Clock Repair Shop, prepared the first of the following balance sheets. He then realized that he had not made the adjusting entries, so he prepared the second, correct balance sheet.

Required:
A. Give the adjusting entries that caused the differences between the two balance sheets.

You may find the following format helpful in solving these types of problems:

	Original Balances		Adjustments		Revised Balance	
Account	Debit	Credit	Debit	Credit	Debit	Credit

B. Compute the amount of increase or decrease in net income resulting from the adjusting entries.

ON TIME WATCH AND CLOCK REPAIR SHOP
Balance Sheet
at December 31, 1984

	Before Adjustments		After Adjustments
Assets			
Cash		$ 1,745	$1,745
Accounts Receivable		820	820
Supplies Inventory		940	90
Prepaid Rent		1,050	700
Prepaid Insurance		930	430
Spare Parts Inventory		675	675
Shop Fixtures	$5,670		$5,670
Accumulated Depreciation	1,890	3,780	2,835 2,835
Total Assets		$ 9,940	$7,295
Liabilities and Owner's Equity			
Accounts Payable		$ 1,635	$1,635
Salaries Payable		—	110
Utilities Payable		—	75
Unearned Service Fees		430	200
B. Carson, Capital		10,050	7,450
B. Carson, Withdrawals		(2,175)	(2,175)
Total Liabilities and Owner's Equity		$9,940	$7,295

Problem 3-7 (Adjusting Entries for Prepaid Insurance, Unearned Revenue, and Prepaid Rent)

The ledger of the Duane Publishing Company includes these accounts: Prepaid Insurance, Insurance Expense, Subscription Revenue, Unearned Subscription Revenue, Prepaid Rent, and Rent Expense.

Required:

For each of the situations listed below, enter the beginning balance in the proper T account and post the transactions directly to the ledger accounts listed above. Then record the necessary adjusting entry at June 30, 1984, the end of the fiscal year.

Insurance:

July 1, 1983. The Prepaid Insurance account contained a debit balance of $1,755, which is allocable to the period July 1 through March 31.

October 15, 1983. Duane Publishing Company paid $2,880 for a 12-month policy beginning coverage on October 15.

Subscriptions:

July 1, 1983. The Unearned Subscriptions Revenue account contained a credit balance of $11,850. Of this balance, $3,100 is for subscriptions expiring at the end of September and $8,750 is for subscriptions expiring at the end of April.

October 1, 1983. Duane received $1,990 for subscriptions lasting six months.

February 1, 1984. Duane received $4,560 for subscriptions lasting 24 months.

May 1, 1984. Duane received $2,760 for subscriptions lasting six months.

Rent:

July 1, 1983. The Prepaid Rent account contained a debit balance of $1,975, which is allocable to July through November.

December 1, 1983. Duane paid $3,609 for nine months' rent.

Problem 3-8 (Opening T Accounts, Adjusting Entries, and Preparation of Financial Statements)

The unadjusted trial balance of the Ace Answering Service is shown below:

ACE ANSWERING SERVICE
Unadjusted Trial Balance
December 31, 1984

Account Title	Debit	Credit
Cash	$ 5,480	
Accounts Receivable	1,940	
Office Supplies Inventory	260	
Furniture and Equipment	6,060	
Accumulated Depreciation—Furniture and Equipment		$ 1,100
Accounts Payable		700
Unearned Fees		930
Note Payable		2,500
Martha Whitby, Capital		6,150
Martha Whitby, Drawing	5,400	
Service Fees Revenue		33,000
Rent Expense	3,440	
Salaries Expense	21,300	
Miscellaneous Expenses	500	
Totals	$44,380	$44,380

The following adjustment information is given:

1. Depreciation expense is $950.
2. The company paid $540 on December 1 for two months' rent in advance.
3. Office supplies on hand at December 31 total $70.
4. Accrued interest on the note payable is $180.
5. Salaries earned but not paid amount to $310.
6. The balance in the Unearned Fees account includes $70 received for services rendered during December.
7. A $120 payment for salaries was inadvertently recorded as a Miscellaneous Expense.

Required:

A. Set up T accounts for the accounts listed in the trial balance and these additional accounts: Depreciation Expense, Interest Expense, Interest Payable, Office Supplies Expense, Prepaid Rent, Salaries Payable.
   1. Post the balances shown in the trial balance to the T accounts.
   2. Post the adjustments directly to the T accounts.
B. Prepare an adjusted trial balance.
C. Prepare an income statement for the year ended December 31, 1984.
D. Prepare a classified balance sheet at December 31, 1984.

ALTERNATE PROBLEMS

Problem 3-1A (Conversion from Cash to Accrual Basis of Accounting)

Joan Robinson established the Robinson Accounting Service in 1981. The accounting records were maintained on a cash basis. During 1983, Joan decided to switch to the accrual basis and has asked you to assist in converting the 1981 and 1982 financial statements to an accrual basis. Your analysis of the accounting records revealed the following data:

	1981	1982
Accounting Fees Revenue		
Cash collected for services performed during the year	$28,000	$29,000
Charged customers for services performed during the year, but cash was not received until the following year	8,000	10,000
Prepaid (Unearned) Revenue collected in 1981 for services performed in 1982	1,500	
Operating Expenses		
Cash paid for services received	16,000	17,000
Accrued expenses at end of the year paid for in the following year	7,000	7,600
Prepaid expenses		
Cash paid during the year	4,000	6,000
Amount prepaid at the end of the year	3,000	7,000

Required:

A. Using the above data, you are to complete abbreviated income statements in the form shown below for the years 1981 and 1982 for both the cash basis and accrual basis of accounting.

	Cash Basis		Accrual Basis	
	1981	1982	1981	1982
Accounting Fees Revenue				
Operating expenses	___	___	___	___
Net income	═══	═══	═══	═══

Show supporting computations in good form.

B. Show the differences that would result in the December 31, 1982, balance sheet accounts from using the accrual basis as compared to the cash basis.

Problem 3-2A (Adjusting Entries)

The following transactions of the World-Wide Travel Agency occurred during June.

1. June 1. Purchased a 36-month insurance policy for $2,016.
2. June 1. Borrowed $5,500 from American Bank. The principal, plus 13% annual interest, is due in six months. A note was signed as evidence of the loan. Accrued interest on the note amounted to $60 on June 30.
3. June 3. Purchased three typewriters for $1,650. The typewriters will be depreciated over their estimated useful life of four years at which time they are expected to have a zero sales value.
4. June 6. Purchased supplies for $95. On June 30, supplies costing $10 remained in inventory.
5. June 15. Prepaid $780 rent for the period ending August 15.
6. June 29. Earned a commission of $780, which will be received in July.

Required:

Give the journal entries to record each transaction and give the adjusting entries for June 30, the end of the fiscal year.

Problem 3-3A (Adjusting Entries and Effect on Financial Statements)

Suburban Realty ends its fiscal year on June 30.

Required:

A. Using the following information, make the necessary adjusting entries.
1. Property taxes of $435 for the three-month period ending July 31 are due in August.
2. The June telephone expense of $105 is unpaid and unrecorded.
3. The supplies account had a $205 debit balance on July 1 of the preceding year. Supplies costing $980 were purchased during the year, and $180 of supplies are in inventory as of June 30.

4. Suburban Realty borrowed $9,500 from Town Bank on March 15. The principal, plus 17% interest, is payable on September 15. Accrued interest on June 30 was $471.
5. The annual depreciation on equipment is estimated to be $4,700. The balance in the Accumulated Depreciation account at the beginning of the fiscal year was $7,050.
6. The secretary earns $32 a day. She will be paid in July for the five-day period ending July 3.
7. On June 1, Suburban received two-months' rental income in advance, totaling $640. This was recorded by a credit to Unearned Rental Revenue.
8. Suburban Realty purchased a six-month insurance policy for $405 on November 1. A 24-month policy was purchased on April 30 for $1,272. Both purchases were recorded by debiting Prepaid Insurance.

B. As you know, all adjusting entries affect one balance sheet account and one income statement account. Based on your adjusting entries prepared in requirement A:
1. Complete the schedule given below.
2. Compute the increase or decrease in net income.
3. Compute the increase or decrease in total assets, total liabilities, and total owner's equity.

Entry	Account	Balance in the Account Before Adjustment	Dollar Effect of Adjusting Entries	Balance Reported in 6/30 Balance Sheet	Balance Sheet Classification*
1.	Property Tax Payable	_____	$ _____	_____	_____
2.	Telephone Expense Payable	_____	_____	_____	_____
3.	Supplies Inventory	_____	_____	_____	_____
4.	Interest Payable	_____	_____	_____	_____
5.	Accumulated Depreciation	_____	_____	_____	_____
6.	Salaries Payable	_____	_____	_____	_____
7.	Unearned Rental Revenue	_____	_____	_____	_____
8.	Prepaid Insurance	_____	_____	_____	_____

*For each account, indicate whether it is an asset, liability, or owner's equity account, and whether it is classified as a current asset or liability.

Problem 3-4A (Adjusting Entries, Posting to T Accounts, and Preparation of Financial Statements)

The trial balance of Speedy Print Shop at the end of the fiscal year appeared as follows:

SPEEDY PRINT SHOP
Unadjusted Trial Balance
December 31, 1984

Account Title	Debit	Credit
Cash	$ 1,640	
Accounts Receivable	295	
Supplies Inventory	1,780	
Prepaid Insurance	1,790	
Equipment	13,770	
Accumulated Depreciation		$ 2,015
Accounts Payable		205
Marilyn Ross, Capital		12,080
Marilyn Ross, Withdrawals	10,200	
Printing Revenues		29,030
Wages Expense	9,640	
Rent Expense	3,020	
Utilities Expense	1,195	
Totals	$43,330	$43,330

Required:

A. Using the following information, prepare adjusting entries. Use the accounts shown in the trial balance and these additional accounts: Supplies Expense, Wages Payable, Insurance Expense, Unearned Printing Revenues, Utilities Payable, Depreciation Expense.
 1. Insurance expense is $137 per month.
 2. Depreciation on the equipment this year is estimated to be $1,350.
 3. Supplies costing $220 remained in inventory on December 31.
 4. The December utility expense of $107 has not been paid or recorded.
 5. Wages accrued but not paid amounted to $95.
 6. The balance in the Printing Revenues account includes $130 received as payment in advance for an order to be started in January.
B. Open T accounts for the accounts shown in the trial balance and enter the December 31 balance in each account. Post the adjusting entries to the T accounts.
C. Prepare an adjusted trial balance, an income statement, and a classified balance sheet.
D. Compute the difference between the net income that would be reported assuming the adjusting entries were not made and the net income derived in requirement C.

Problem 3-5A (Determination of Adjusting Entries from Changes in Two Trial Balances)

The following accounts are taken from the ledger of the Boyce Company. Account balances are shown both before and after the year-end adjustments were made.

	Before Adjustments	After Adjustments
Service Fees Receivable	$ —	$ 385
Supplies Inventory	320	215
Unexpired Insurance	1,450	590
Prepaid Rent	740	370
Accumulated Depreciation	795	1,180
Salaries Payable	—	215
Utilities Expense Payable	—	195
Service Fees Revenue	21,600	21,985
Interest Income	2,460	2,460
Supplies Expense	930	1,035
Insurance Expense	—	860
Rent Expense	4,070	4,440
Depreciation Expense	—	385
Salaries Expense	9,745	9,960
Utilities Expense	2,060	2,255

Required:

Give the adjusting entries that resulted in the balances found in the column labeled After Adjustments.

Problem 3-6A (Determination of Adjusting Entries from Changes in Two Balance Sheets)

The first of the following balance sheets (see page 144) of the D. M. Cooper Company was inadvertently prepared before the year-end adjusting entries had been made. The second balance sheet is correct.

Required:

Give the adjusting entries that were made. You may find the following format helpful in developing your solution.

Account	Unadjusted Balances		Adjustments		Adjusted Balances	
	Debit	Credit	Debit	Credit	Debit	Credit

D. M. COOPER COMPANY
Balance Sheet
at December 31, 1984

		Before Adjustments		After Adjustments
Assets				
Cash		$ 2,490		$ 2,490
Accounts Receivable		1,650		1,650
Interest Receivable		—		425
Note Receivable		3,000		3,000
Supplies Inventory		1,510		120
Prepaid Insurance		680		425
Machinery and Equipment	$14,900		$14,900	
Accumulated Depreciation	5,960	8,940	7,940	6,960
Total Assets		$18,270		$15,070
Liabilities and Owner's Equity				
Accounts Payable		$ 4,570		$ 4,570
Telephone Expense Payable		—		65
Wages Payable		—		270
Unearned Revenue		2,165		325
D. M. Cooper, Capital		23,160		21,465
D. M. Cooper, Withdrawals		(11,625)		(11,625)
Total Liabilities and Owner's Equity		$18,270		$15,070

Problem 3-7A (Adjusting Entries for Supplies Inventory, Unearned Rent, and Prepaid Interest)

The ledger of the R. H. Klein Company includes these accounts: Supplies Inventory, Unearned Rent, and Prepaid Interest. The accounts are adjusted only at December 31, the end of the fiscal year.

Required:

For each situation, enter the information directly in the accounts listed above. Also record and post the adjusting entries at December 31 directly to the accounts. The chart of accounts also includes these accounts: Supplies Expense, Rent Revenue, and Interest Expense.

Supplies:

January 1. The supplies account contained a $0 balance.
January 3. Supplies costing $290 were purchased.
August 22. Supplies costing $395 were purchased.
December 31. A physical inventory count shows $105 of supplies on hand.

Rent:

January 1. The Unearned Rent account contained a credit balance of $4,150. The balance represents $1,250 for the period January–April and $2,900 for the period January–August.

September 1. Rent of $1,800 is received for the six-month period ending February 28.

November 15. Rent of $580 is received for a two-month period ending January 15. *break into ½ months*

Interest:

January 1. The Prepaid Interest account contained a debit balance of $150, which is allocable to the period January–March.

May 7. Interest of $185 was paid in advance on a three-month loan.

October 15. Interest of $300 was paid in advance on a six-month loan.

Problem 3-8A (Opening T Accounts, Adjusting Entries, and Preparation of Financial Statements)

United Rentals rents appliances and furniture. The unadjusted trial balance of the company appears below.

UNITED RENTALS
Unadjusted Trial Balance
December 31, 1985

Account Title	Debit	Credit
Cash	$ 3,500	
Accounts Receivable	2,400	
Prepaid Insurance	1,200	
Appliances	31,400	
Accumulated Depreciation—Appliances		$ 17,600
Furniture	47,300	
Accumulated Depreciation—Furniture		23,000
Accounts Payable		6,800
Brian Shakey, Capital		18,710
Brian Shakey, Drawing	18,310	
Rental Fees Earned		74,700
Salaries Expense	26,500	
Rent Expense	5,700	
Maintenance Expense	3,100	
Utilities Expense	1,400	
Totals	$140,810	$140,810

The following information pertains to adjustments.

1. Expired insurance amounts to $790.
2. The December utility bill for $120 has not been paid or recorded.
3. Depreciation on the appliances is $5,870. Depreciation on the furniture is $9,200.
4. Rental fees of $1,030 were received in advance and have not yet been earned.
5. The Rent Expense account contains $440 paid for January 1986 rent.
6. A rental fee of $110 paid in cash was recorded by debiting Accounts Receivable.
7. Salaries earned amounting to $180 will be paid in January and have not been recorded.

Required:
A. Set up T accounts for the accounts listed in the trial balance and the following accounts: Depreciation Expense, Insurance Expense, Prepaid Rent, Salaries Payable, Unearned Rental Fees, Utilities Payable.
    1. Post the account balances from the trial balance to the T accounts.
    2. Post the adjusting information directly to the T accounts.
B. Prepare an adjusted trial balance.
C. Prepare an income statement for the year ending December 31, 1985.
D. Prepare a classified balance sheet.

CASE FOR CHAPTER 3

(Discussion—Accrual Basis of Accounting)

A friend of yours, Fred Frost, started a business with a $20,000 investment. Business had been better than Fred had expected and on June 1 he hired an assistant so that he could spend more time soliciting new business. Anxious to determine whether his business had been profitable during the first year of operation, Fred prepared the financial statements shown below from the account balances contained in the general ledger. The ledger had been maintained by a bookkeeping service he had contracted with to keep the firm's records.

FROST SURVEYING
Income Statement
For the Year Ended December 31, 1983

Surveying fees revenue (includes $4,000 received in advance)		$46,600
Operating expenses:		
Salary expense	$ 8,400	
Fred Frost, withdrawals	36,000	44,400
Net income		$ 2,200

FROST SURVEYING
Balance Sheet
December 31, 1983

Cash	$11,200	Notes payable	$15,000
Office supplies	1,200	Fred Frost, Capital	20,000
Prepaid rent	4,800	Net income	2,200
Furniture and equipment	20,000		
Total	$37,200	Total	$37,200

Fred was quite disturbed with the level of income and was unable to reconcile a declining cash position with a net income for the year. Knowing that you were enrolled in an accounting course, he showed the results to you and asked you to review them and confirm his computations.

In discussing the results of operations, Fred states, ''The furniture and equipment was purchased on January 2 for $20,000. I paid cash of $5,000 and signed an 18% note for the balance. Due to my meticulous care, the items are just as useful today as when I bought them. I expect to use these items five years after which they will probably be obsolete and will be worth approximately $2,000. The interest on the note along with a $500 principal payment are not due until January 2, 1984.'' He adds that if he is successful, he plans to buy a building after he uses the office space he had rented for two years. Rent for the two years in the amount of $4,800 was prepaid on January 2, 1983.

Confidently he tells you that hiring the assistant had permitted him to obtain new clients and that he received $4,000 in advance for services to be performed in 1984. He adds that at the end of the year, clients owed him $2,200, but that because of his persistent efforts these accounts had all been collected by January 10, 1984. Asking about the employee, you are told that her monthly salary of $1,400 is paid on the fifth of the following month. Fred then asks, ''I know that the office supplies account shows a balance of $1,200, but when I counted them on December 31 to see if I needed to place an order, there was only $420 in the supply closet. What happened to the difference?''

Required:
A. Following the accrual basis of accounting, prepare a revised income statement and an unclassified balance sheet for the fiscal year.
B. Explain to Fred how a company with profits could have a reduction in cash during the year.

CHAPTER 4
THE PREPARATION OF A WORKSHEET AND COMPLETION OF THE ACCOUNTING CYCLE

OVERVIEW AND OBJECTIVES

This chapter completes the accounting cycle and introduces a worksheet used to accumulate the needed information. When you have completed the chapter, you should understand:

- How to prepare a worksheet (pp. 150–156).
- How to prepare financial statements from the worksheet (pp. 156–157).
- Journalizing adjusting entries using information from the worksheet (pp. 157–160).
- The closing process and how to prepare closing entries using information from the worksheet (pp. 160–169).
- How to prepare a post-closing trial balance (pp. 174–175).
- The accounting for accrued items in subsequent periods (pp. 176–177).
- The difference in the owners' equity section of a balance sheet prepared for a partnership or a corporation (pp. 177–180).
- The purpose of reversing entries (pp. 180–183).

In Chapter 3, adjusting entries were made directly in the journal and then posted to the ledger, after which an adjusted trial balance, a balance sheet, and an income statement were prepared. Before performing these steps, many firms prepare a worksheet to assemble in one place all the information needed to adjust the accounts and prepare the financial statements. In addition, the worksheet contains the information needed to close the income statement accounts at the end of the accounting period.

COMPLETION OF THE ACCOUNTING CYCLE

The accounting cycle is completed at least once each fiscal period; the sequence of steps is diagrammed in Figure 4-1. As noted in Chapter 2, the first three steps in the cycle are carried out during the year as transactions occur.

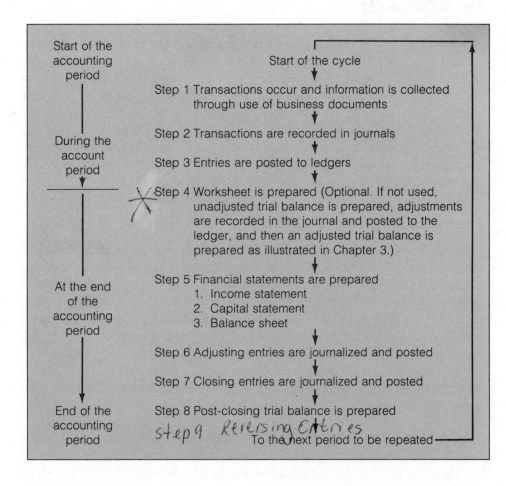

Figure 4-1
Diagram of the Accounting Cycle

The steps in the accounting cycle performed at the end of an accounting period include the preparation of a worksheet (Step 4), the preparation of the financial statements (Step 5), journalizing and posting adjusting entries (Step 6), journalizing and posting closing entries (Step 7), and preparation of a post-closing trial balance (Step 8). A trial balance is prepared as part of the worksheet in Step 4, but may be prepared at any time during the period to prove the equality of debits and credits.

As noted in Step 4 and as shown in Chapter 3, the cycle can be completed without using a worksheet. Nevertheless, because of the volume of work and the amount of detail involved in completing the accounting cycle for most firms, accountants often prepare a worksheet to help organize their work and minimize errors. We will use the worksheet as a tool to assist in completing the accounting cycle.

THE WORKSHEET

A **worksheet** is a form designed to bring together in one place the information needed to prepare formal financial statements and to record the adjusting and closing entries. It replaces neither the financial statements nor the necessity to journalize and post the adjusting and closing entries; it is simply a tool used to gather and organize the information needed to complete these steps of the accounting cycle. The worksheet is not a part of the permanent accounting records and is not prepared for use by the owners or management of the firm. For these reasons it is generally prepared in pencil so that errors can be erased and corrected before the entries are recorded in the journal.

PREPARATION OF THE WORKSHEET

The basic format of a worksheet is shown in Figure 4-2. The heading contains the usual three parts: the name of the firm, the title of the form, and the period it covers. The first column is used for the account titles. This column is followed by five sets of money columns provided for the (1) unadjusted trial balance, (2) adjusting entries, (3) adjusted trial balance, (4) income statement, and (5) balance sheet. Each set consists of a debit column and a credit column making a total of 10 columns for entering dollar amounts.

The steps followed in preparing a worksheet will be illustrated and described by using the information developed in Chapters 2 and 3 for the Starbuck Real Estate Office.

Step 1. Enter the ledger account titles and balances in the Account Title and Unadjusted Trial Balance columns. After all of the transactions that occurred during the period have been posted, a trial

STARBUCK REAL ESTATE OFFICE
Worksheet
For the Month Ended June 30, 1984

Account Title	Unadjusted Trial Balance		Adjustments		Adjusted Trial Balance		Income Statement		Balance Sheet	
	Debit	Credit	Debit	Credit	Debit	Credit	Debit	Credit	Debit	Credit
Cash	43,558									
Accounts Receivable	5,400									
Prepaid Insurance	960									
Office Supplies Inventory	620									
Land	10,000									
Building	62,000									
Accumulated Depreciation— Building										
Office Equipment	9,600									
Accumulated Depreciation— Office Equipment										
Accounts Payable		4,600								
Unearned Appraisal Fees		280								
Mortgage Notes Payable		60,000								
Mike Starbuck, Capital		60,000								
Mike Starbuck, Drawing	600									
Commission Revenue		9,600								
Appraisal Fee Revenue		250								
Salary Expense	1,800									
Utilities Expense	72									
Advertising Expense	120									
Totals	134,730	134,730								

Figure 4-2
Worksheet Format with Unadjusted Trial Balance Entered (Step 1 in the preparation of a worksheet.)

balance is prepared to verify the equality of debit and credit account balances, as shown in Figure 4-2. The trial balance is taken directly from the general ledger. This is an unadjusted trial balance because it is taken before any adjusting entries have been posted to the ledger.

Step 2. Enter the necessary adjusting entries in the Adjustments columns. The adjusting entries are entered first in the worksheet in the Adjustments columns. After the worksheet is completed, the adjusting entries are recorded in the journal. To aid in journalizing the entries and locating errors, each adjusting entry is identified by a separate letter so that the debit part of the entry can be cross-referenced to the credit part of the entry. The adjustments made in Figure 4-3 are the same as those explained in detail in Chapter 3. Adjustments were required for the following items:

STARBUCK REAL ESTATE OFFICE
Worksheet
For the Month Ended June 30, 1984

Account Title	Unadjusted Trial Balance		Adjustments		Adjusted Trial Balance		Income Statement		Balance Sheet	
	Debit	Credit	Debit	Credit	Debit	Credit	Debit	Credit	Debit	Credit
Cash	43,558				43,558					
Accounts Receivable	5,400		(i) 400		5,800					
Prepaid Insurance	960			(a) 40	920					
Office Supplies Inventory	620			(b) 80	540					
Land	10,000				10,000					
Building	62,000				62,000					
Accumulated Depreciation— Building				(d) 200		200				
Office Equipment	9,600				9,600					
Accumulated Depreciation— Office Equipment				(c) 100		100				
Accounts Payable		4,600				4,600				
Unearned Appraisal Fees		280				280				
Mortgage Notes Payable		60,000				60,000				
Mike Starbuck, Capital		60,000				60,000				
Mike Starbuck, Drawing	600				600					
Commission Revenue		9,600				9,600				
Appraisal Fee Revenue		250				250				
Salary Expense	1,800		(e) 990		2,790					
Utilities Expense	72		(h) 210		282					
Advertising Expense	120				120					
Totals	134,730	134,730								
Insurance Expense			(a) 40		40					
Office Supplies Expense			(b) 80		80					
Depreciation Expense			(c) 100							
			(d) 200		300					
Salaries Payable				(e) 990		990				
Commission Expense			(f) 4,800		4,800					
Commissions Payable				(f) 4,800		4,800				
Interest Expense			(g) 600		600					
Interest Payable				(g) 600		600				
Utilities Payable				(h) 210		210				
Service Fee Revenue				(i) 400		400				
Totals			7,420	7,420	142,030	142,030				

Figure 4-3
Adjusting Entries are Entered in Adjustments Columns and Account Balances Extended to the Adjusted Trial Balance Columns (Steps 2 and 3 in the preparation of a worksheet.)

Entry (a) Prepaid insurance expired, $40.

Entry (b) Office supplies used, $80.

Entry (c) Depreciation on office equipment, $100.

Entry (d) Depreciation on the building, $200.

Entry (e) Salaries earned but not paid, $990.

Entry (f) Commissions earned by employees but not paid, $4,800.

Entry (g) Accrued interest on mortgage notes payable, $600.

Entry (h) Utilities used but not paid for, $210.

Entry (i) Revenue earned from management of apartment complex but not received, $400.

When entering the adjustments, if an account already has a balance in the Unadjusted Trial Balance columns, the adjusting amount is entered on the same line. The account titles required by adjusting entries that were not listed in the Unadjusted Trial Balance columns are added on lines immediately below the trial balance.

For example, in adjusting entry (a) the Insurance Expense account is debited and the Prepaid Insurance account is credited for $40. To enter the debit amount of this entry, it is necessary to add an Insurance Expense account on the line below the trial balance because the account had a zero balance before the adjusting entry and consequently was not included in the unadjusted trial balance. The $40 credit is entered in the Adjustments credit column on the same line as the Prepaid Insurance account balance of $960. Thus, in this entry it is necessary to add only one new account. However, in adjusting entry (f), observe that both accounts affected by the entry must be entered below the unadjusted trial balance. The appropriate account titles were selected from the chart of accounts presented in Chapter 2 on page 52.

After all of the adjustments are entered, the two Adjustments columns are totaled to prove that the total debit adjustments equal the total credit adjustments. Adding the amount entered in a vertical column is called **footing** the column.

Step 3. Prepare an adjusted trial balance.

In this step, each account balance in the Unadjusted Trial Balance columns is combined with the corresponding adjustments, if any, in the Adjustments columns and the resulting balance is extended on the same line to the proper Adjusted Trial Balance column, as shown in Figure 4-3. The combined amounts entered in these two columns will be the same as the ledger account balances after the adjusting entries are recorded in the journal and posted to the ledger. Combining the amounts entered on each line—that is, adding or subtracting across the worksheet horizontally—is called **crossfooting.** The crossfooting must be done very carefully because it is easy to make an error.

For those accounts unaffected by the adjustments, such as Cash, Accounts Payable, and Commission Revenue, the balance is simply extended directly to the appropriate debit or credit column in the Adjusted Trial Balance columns. If an account has a debit balance in the Unadjusted Trial Balance column, a debit adjustment will increase the balance (see the Salary Expense account), whereas a credit adjustment will decrease the balance (see the Prepaid Insurance account). An account with a credit balance is increased by a credit adjustment and decreased by a debit adjustment. In some cases, an account may not have a balance in the Unadjusted Trial Balance columns, but an adjustment is made to the account. In such cases, the amount of the adjustment is extended directly to the Adjusted Trial Balance column. Examples are those accounts added below the unadjusted trial balance. After all adjusted account balances have been determined, the equality of debits and credits is verified by footing the two columns.

Step 4. Extend every account balance listed in the Adjusted Trial Balance columns to its proper financial statement column.
Every account balance listed in the Adjusted Trial Balance columns is extended to either the Balance Sheet columns or the Income Statement columns, as shown in Figure 4-4. Asset, liability, and owner's equity accounts are extended to the proper Balance Sheet debit or credit column. Revenue accounts are extended to the Income Statement credit column, and expense accounts are extended to the Income Statement debit column. In other words, accounts are sorted on the basis of their financial statement classification in this part of the process. Note that the drawing account is extended to the Balance Sheet debit column rather than to the Income Statement debit column. To avoid leaving out an account, the process should start by extending the first account listed, which is usually cash, and then proceeding vertically down the worksheet line by line. As a word of caution, the accounts listed in the Unadjusted Trial Balance are in Balance Sheet and Income Statement order. However, the accounts added below the unadjusted trial balance must be analyzed to determine whether the balance is extended to the Balance Sheet or Income Statement columns.

Step 5. Total the two Income Statement and the two Balance Sheet columns. Compute the difference between the totals of the two Income Statement columns and enter this as a balancing amount in both the Income Statement and Balance Sheet columns. Compute the four column totals again with the balancing amount included.
After all the amounts have been extended to either the Income Statement or the Balance Sheet columns, the four columns are totaled and their amount entered at the bottom of each column. The net income or net loss for the period is determined by computing the difference between the totals of the two Income Statement columns as shown in Figure 4-4. The computation in our illustration is:

Total of the credit column	$10,250
Total of the debit column	9,012
Difference	$ 1,238

In this illustration, the revenues earned ($10,250) exceeded the expenses incurred ($9,012), resulting in a net income of $1,238. This difference is entered in the Income Statement debit column to balance the two columns and is also entered on the same line in the Balance Sheet credit column because net income for the period is an increase in owner's equity. Stated another way,

Figure 4-4
Account Balances Extended to Financial Statement Columns and Totals Computed (Steps 4 and 5 in the preparation of a worksheet.)

STARBUCK REAL ESTATE OFFICE
Worksheet
For the Month Ended June 30, 1984

Account Title	Unadjusted Trial Balance Debit	Unadjusted Trial Balance Credit	Adjustments Debit	Adjustments Credit	Adjusted Trial Balance Debit	Adjusted Trial Balance Credit	Income Statement Debit	Income Statement Credit	Balance Sheet Debit	Balance Sheet Credit
Cash	43,558				43,558				43,558	
Accounts Receivable	5,400		(i) 400		5,800				5,800	
Prepaid Insurance	960			(a) 40	920				920	
Office Supplies Inventory	620			(b) 80	540				540	
Land	10,000				10,000				10,000	
Building	62,000				62,000				62,000	
Accumulated Depreciation— Building				(d) 200		200				200
Office Equipment	9,600				9,600				9,600	
Accumulated Depreciation— Office Equipment				(c) 100		100				100
Accounts Payable		4,600				4,600				4,600
Unearned Appraisal Fees		280				280				280
Mortgage Notes Payable		60,000				60,000				60,000
Mike Starbuck, Capital		60,000				60,000				60,000
Mike Starbuck, Drawing	600				600				600	
Commission Revenue		9,600				9,600		9,600		
Appraisal Fee Revenue		250				250		250		
Salary Expense	1,800		(e) 990		2,790		2,790			
Utilities Expense	72		(h) 210		282		282			
Advertising Expense	120				120		120			
Totals	134,730	134,730								
Insurance Expense			(a) 40		40		40			
Office Supplies Expense			(b) 80		80		80			
Depreciation Expense			(c) 100							
			(d) 200		300		300			
Salaries Payable				(e) 990		990				990
Commission Expense			(f) 4,800		4,800		4,800			
Commissions Payable				(f) 4,800		4,800				4,800
Interest Expense			(g) 600		600		600			
Interest Payable				(g) 600		600				600
Utilities Payable				(h) 210		210				210
Service Fee Revenue				(i) 400		400		400		
Totals			7,420	7,420	142,030	142,030	9,012	10,250	133,018	131,780
Net Income for the Period							1,238			1,238
							10,250	10,250	133,018	133,018

the amounts extended to the Balance Sheet columns from the Adjusted Trial Balance columns are end-of-period balances except for the owner's capital account of $60,000. The excess of revenues over expenses for the period represents an increase in owner's equity. Extending the net income of $1,238 to the Balance Sheet credit column, therefore, updates the owner's equity in the business to the end of the period. On the same line in the Account Title column, a caption "Net Income for the Period" is entered to identify the nature of the item being entered in the two sets of columns.

The four columns are totaled again with the net income of $1,238 included as a balancing amount in the columns. If the debit and credit columns under Balance Sheet are not equal, there is an error in extending the amounts from the Adjusted Trial Balance columns.

If the Income Statement debit column had exceeded the Income Statement credit column, a net loss for the period would be indicated. In this case, the difference between the two columns would be captioned "Net Loss for the Period" and that difference entered in the Income Statement credit column and the Balance Sheet debit column.

Totaling the debit and credit columns as work proceeds across the worksheet does not ensure that an error has not been made. For example (as discussed in Chapter 2), not all errors in the accounts are uncovered by the trial balance. Needed adjustments may have been omitted entirely or the wrong adjusting amounts may have been entered in the worksheet. In Step 4, an amount may be extended to the wrong column—as in extending the credit balance in the Unearned Appraisal Fees account, a liability, to the Income Statement credit column. This will not destroy the equality of debits and credits, but it will result in an overstatement in revenues in the income statement, an understatement in liabilities, and an overstatement in owner's equity in the balance sheet.

USING THE WORKSHEET TO COMPLETE THE ACCOUNTING CYCLE

Once the worksheet is completed, it is used to prepare the financial statements and to journalize adjusting and closing entries.

PREPARATION OF FINANCIAL STATEMENTS

Because account balances are already sorted between the income statement and the balance sheet in the worksheet, preparation of the formal financial statements is a relatively easy step. The income statement (Figure 4-5) is prepared from account balances listed in the two Income Statement columns in Figure 4-4. The Capital Statement (Figure 4-6) and the Balance Sheet

Figure 4-5
Income Statement

STARBUCK REAL ESTATE OFFICE
Income Statement
For the Month Ended June 30, 1984

Revenues:		
Commissions		$ 9,600
Appraisal fees		250
Service fees		400
Total Revenues		$10,250
Operating Expenses:		
Salary expense	$2,790	
Commission expense	4,800	
Interest expense	600	
Depreciation expense	300	
Utilities expense	282	
Advertising expense	120	
Office supplies expense	80	
Insurance expense	40	
Total Operating Expenses		9,012
Net income		$ 1,238

Figure 4-6
Capital Statement

STARBUCK REAL ESTATE OFFICE
Capital Statement
For the Month Ended June 30, 1984

Mike Starbuck, Original investment, June 1, 1984	$60,000
Add: Net income for the month of June	1,238
Total	61,238
Less: Withdrawals during the month of June	600
Mike Starbuck, Capital, June 30, 1984	$60,638

_-103,250_

(Figure 4-7) are prepared from items contained in the Balance Sheet columns of Figure 4-4.

RECORDING ADJUSTING ENTRIES

After the financial statements have been prepared, the adjusting entries are entered in the general journal as shown in Figure 4-8. The necessary information is available directly from the Adjustments columns of the worksheet. Note that the entries are dated on the last day of the accounting period and generally the caption "Adjusting Entries" is written in the general journal to separate these entries from other transactions. After the adjusting entries are

Figure 4-7
Balance Sheet

STARBUCK REAL ESTATE OFFICE
Balance Sheet
June 30, 1984

Assets
Current Assets:
Cash $43,558
Accounts receivable 5,800
Prepaid insurance 920
Office supplies inventory 540
   Total Current Assets .... $ 50,818
Property, Plant, and Equipment:
Land $10,000
Building $62,000
Less: Accumulated depreciation ... 200 ... 61,800
Office equipment .... $ 9,600
Less: Accumulated depreciation ... 100 ... 9,500
   Total Property, Plant, and Equipment 81,300
Total Assets $132,118

Liabilities and Owner's Equity
Liabilities
Current Liabilities:
Accounts payable $4,600
Commissions payable 4,800
Salaries payable 990
Interest payable 600
Unearned appraisal fees 280
Utilities payable 210
Current portion of mortgage notes
  payable 3,000
   Total Current Liabilities .... $ 14,480
Long-term Liabilities
Mortgage notes payable 57,000
   Total Liabilities 71,480

Owner's Equity
Mike Starbuck, Capital, June 30, 1984 60,638
Total Liabilities and Owner's Equity $132,118

		GENERAL JOURNAL			Page 3

Date		Description	Post Ref.	Debit	Credit
		Adjusting Entries			
June	30	Insurance Expense	521	40	
		Prepaid Insurance	110		40
		To record insurance expense for June.			
	30	Office Supplies Expense	530	80	
		Office Supplies Inventory	111		80
		To record office supplies used in June.			
	30	Depreciation Expense	540	100	
		Accumulated Depreciation—Off. Equip.	171		100
		To record depreciation for June on office equipment.			
	30	Depreciation Expense	540	200	
		Accumulated Depreciation—Building	161		200
		To record depreciation for June on building.			
	30	Salary Expense	500	990	
		Salaries Payable	210		990
		To record unpaid salaries at the end of June.			
	30	Commission Expense	505	4,800	
		Commissions Payable	211		4,800
		To record unpaid commissions at the end of June.			
	30	Interest Expense	560	600	
		Interest Payable	215		600
		To record accrued interest on mortgage notes payable at the end of June.			
	30	Utilities Expense	510	210	
		Utilities Payable	216		210
		To record unpaid utilities at the end of June.			
	30	Accounts Receivable	104	400	
		Service Fee Revenue	402		400
		To record revenue earned from management of apartment complex during June.			

Figure 4-8
Recording Adjusting Entries

4-3
4-4
4-5

P. 42

posted, the ledger account balances should agree with the balances reported in the worksheet.

CLOSING THE ACCOUNTS

The income statement reports revenues earned and expenses incurred during a single accounting period. Data needed to prepare the income statement are accumulated in the individual revenue and expense accounts. Once the income statement has been prepared for the current period, the revenue and expense accounts have served their intended purpose. To facilitate the preparation of the income statement for the next accounting period, all revenue and expense account balances are closed or cleared (reduced to a zero balance) by transferring their balances to another account. This step in the accounting cycle is referred to as the closing process, and journal entries made to close the temporary accounts are called **closing entries.**

The closing process results in each revenue and expense account beginning the next period with a zero balance, which prepares them for accumulating information for the next period's income statement. (Recall from Chapter 3 that because revenue and expense accounts are closed each period, they are called *temporary* or *nominal* accounts.) In addition, revenues increase and expenses decrease owner's equity. Because they are recorded in separate temporary accounts rather than directly to the owner's capital account, journal entries are needed to transfer the net change in owner's equity from operations during the period to the owner's capital account.

In the closing process, a new temporary account called the Income Summary account is established to summarize the balances in the revenue and expense accounts. This is the only time in the accounting process that this account is used. Closing entries are generally made in the following sequence:

1. The balance in each revenue account is transferred to the Income Summary account.
2. The balance in each expense account is transferred to the Income Summary account.
3. The balance in the Income Summary account is transferred to the owner's capital account.
4. The owner's Drawing account is transferred to the owner's Capital account.

The information needed to prepare the closing entries is conveniently available from the Income Statement columns of the worksheet. The process is diagrammed in Figure 4-9 in T account format, using the totals from the Income Statement columns in the worksheet presented in Figure 4-4. When the closing entries are entered in the journal, the individual revenue and expense accounts are debited or credited.

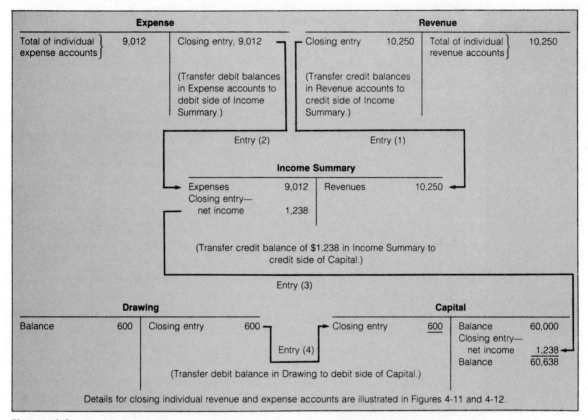

Figure 4-9
Diagram of the Closing Process

Closing Entries Illustrated

The owner's equity and income statement account balances after the adjusting entries were posted are shown in Figure 4-10 for the Starbuck Real Estate Office.

Figure 4-10

The Capital and Nominal Accounts of
STARBUCK REAL ESTATE OFFICE
After Adjusting Entries and Before Closing Entries Are Posted

Account   **Mike Starbuck, Capital**   Account No. **300**

Date		Item	Post Ref.	Debit	Credit	Balance Debit	Balance Credit
1984 June	1		1		60,000		60,000

Figure 4-10
Continued

Account   Mike Starbuck, Drawing   Account No. 310

Date		Item	Post Ref.	Debit	Credit	Balance Debit	Balance Credit
1984							
June	23		2	600		600	

Account   Income Summary   Account No. 350

Date		Item	Post Ref.	Debit	Credit	Balance Debit	Balance Credit

Account   Commission Revenue   Account No. 400

Date		Item	Post Ref.	Debit	Credit	Balance Debit	Balance Credit
1984							
June	15		1		4,200		4,200
	19		2		5,400		9,600

Account   Appraisal Fee Revenue   Account No. 401

Date		Item	Post Ref.	Debit	Credit	Balance Debit	Balance Credit
1984							
June	23		2		250		250

Account   Service Fee Revenue   Account No. 402

Date		Item	Post Ref.	Debit	Credit	Balance Debit	Balance Credit
1984							
June	30	Adj. ent. (i)	3		400		400

Account   Salary Expense   Account No. 500

Date		Item	Post Ref.	Debit	Credit	Balance Debit	Balance Credit
1984							
June	22		2	1,800		1,800	
	30	Adj. ent. (e)	3	990		2,790	

Account   Commission Expense   Account No. 505

Date		Item	Post Ref.	Debit	Credit	Balance Debit	Balance Credit
1984							
June	30	Adj. ent. (f)	3	4,800		4,800	

Account Utilities Expense Account No. **510**

Date		Item	Post Ref.	Debit	Credit	Balance Debit	Balance Credit
1984							
June	30		2	72		72	
	30	Adj. ent. (h)	3	210		282	

Account Advertising Expense Account No. **520**

Date		Item	Post Ref.	Debit	Credit	Balance Debit	Balance Credit
1984							
June	6		1	120		120	

Account Insurance Expense Account No. **521**

Date		Item	Post Ref.	Debit	Credit	Balance Debit	Balance Credit
1984							
June	30	Adj. ent. (a)	3	40		40	

Account Office Supplies Expense Account No. **530**

Date		Item	Post Ref.	Debit	Credit	Balance Debit	Balance Credit
1984							
June	30	Adj. ent. (b)	3	80		80	

Account Depreciation Expense Account No. **540**

Date		Item	Post Ref.	Debit	Credit	Balance Debit	Balance Credit
1984							
June	30	Adj. ent. (c)	3	100		100	
	30	Adj. ent. (d)	3	200		300	

Account Interest Expense Account No. **560**

Date		Item	Post Ref.	Debit	Credit	Balance Debit	Balance Credit
1984							
June	30	Adj. ent. (g)	3	600		600	

Figure 4-10
Continued

Closing the Revenue Accounts. A revenue account normally contains a credit balance. As a result, to close the account, a revenue account must be debited for an amount equal to its credit balance. The offsetting credit is made to the Income Summary account. The compound journal entry needed to close the revenue accounts is:

Date		Description	Post Ref.	Debit	Credit
		GENERAL JOURNAL			Page 4
		Closing Entries			
June	30	Commission Revenue	400	9,600	
		Appraisal Fee Revenue	401	250	
		Service Fee Revenue	402	400	
		Income Summary	350		10,250
		To close the revenue accounts.			

In the journal, the adjusting entries are separated from the closing entries by the caption "Closing Entries." For posting purposes, it is assumed that the closing entries are entered on page 4 of the general journal. Also, account numbers are entered in the posting reference column to indicate that the amounts have been posted.

The effect of this entry is to reduce the revenue accounts to a zero balance for the start of the next period and transfer the sum of their credit balances to the credit side of the Income Summary account, as shown in Figure 4-11.

Closing the Expense Accounts. Expense accounts normally have debit balances. Each expense account is therefore credited for an amount equal to its balance, and the Income Summary account is debited for the sum of the individual balances. The compound journal entry is:

Date		Description	Post Ref.	Debit	Credit
June	30	Income Summary	350	9,012	
		Salary Expense	500		2,790
		Commission Expense	505		4,800
		Utilities Expense	510		282
		Advertising Expense	520		120
		Insurance Expense	521		40
		Office Supplies Expense	530		80
		Depreciation Expense	540		300
		Interest Expense	560		600
		To close the expense accounts.			

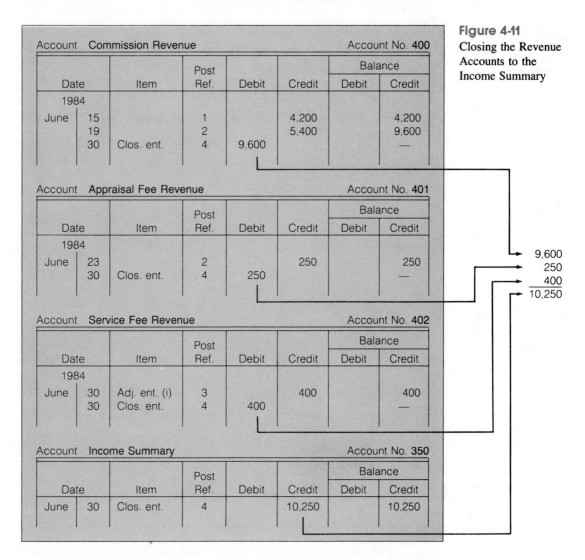

Figure 4-11

Closing the Revenue Accounts to the Income Summary

As shown in Figure 4-12, the entry reduces the expense accounts to a zero balance and transfers the total of $9,012 as a debit to the Income Summary account.

Closing the Income Summary Account.

After the first two closing entries are posted, the balances formerly reported in the individual revenue and expense accounts are summarized in the Income Summary account. If revenues exceed expenses, a net income is earned and the Income Summary account will contain a credit balance. If expenses exceed revenues, a net loss is indicated and the account will have a debit balance. In either case, the balance is transferred to the owner's Capital account.

Figure 4-12
Closing the Expense Accounts to the Income Summary

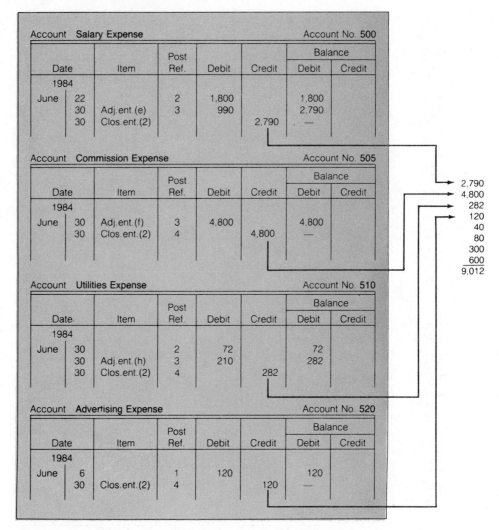

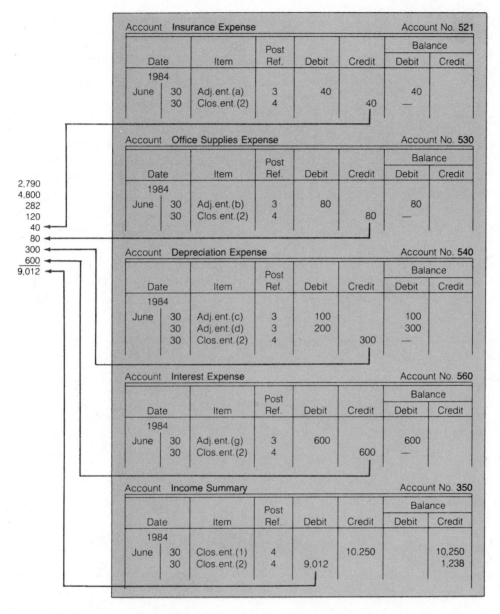

Figure 4-12
Continued

Account   Insurance Expense   Account No. **521**

Date		Item	Post Ref.	Debit	Credit	Balance Debit	Balance Credit
1984							
June	30	Adj.ent.(a)	3	40		40	
	30	Clos.ent.(2)	4		40	—	

Account   Office Supplies Expense   Account No. **530**

Date		Item	Post Ref.	Debit	Credit	Balance Debit	Balance Credit
1984							
June	30	Adj.ent.(b)	3	80		80	
	30	Clos.ent.(2)	4		80	—	

Account   Depreciation Expense   Account No. **540**

Date		Item	Post Ref.	Debit	Credit	Balance Debit	Balance Credit
1984							
June	30	Adj.ent.(c)	3	100		100	
	30	Adj.ent.(d)	3	200		300	
	30	Clos.ent.(2)	4		300	—	

Account   Interest Expense   Account No. **560**

Date		Item	Post Ref.	Debit	Credit	Balance Debit	Balance Credit
1984							
June	30	Adj.ent.(g)	3	600		600	
	30	Clos.ent.(2)	4		600	—	

Account   Income Summary   Account No. **350**

Date		Item	Post Ref.	Debit	Credit	Balance Debit	Balance Credit
1984							
June	30	Clos.ent.(1)	4		10,250		10,250
	30	Clos.ent.(2)	4	9,012			1,238

2,790
4,800
282
120
40
80
300
600
9,012

The Starbuck Real Estate Office earned a net income during June. The credit balance of $1,238 in the Income Summary account is closed as follows:

June	30	Income Summary	350	1,238	
		Mike Starbuck, Capital	300		1,238
		To close the Income			
		Summary account.			

This entry is posted to the accounts as shown in Figure 4-13. The effect of this entry is to recognize that the net assets (assets minus liabilities) increased this period due to profitable operations, and this increase in net assets adds to the owner's interest in the firm. If a net loss is reported, the Income Summary account is credited to reduce the account to a zero balance and the Capital account is debited to reflect a decrease in owner's equity from operations.

Closing the Drawing Account. The debit balance in the Drawing account reflects the decrease in the owner's interest during the period from the withdrawal of cash and/or other assets for personal use. The balance in the

Figure 4-13
Closing the Income Summary and Drawing Account

Income Summary — Account No. 350

Date		Item	Post Ref.	Debit	Credit	Balance Debit	Balance Credit
1984							
June	30	Clos. ent.	4		10,250		10,250
	30	Clos. ent.	4	9,012			1,238
	30	Clos. ent.	4	1,238			—

Mike Starbuck, Drawing — Account No. 310

Date		Item	Post Ref.	Debit	Credit	Balance Debit	Balance Credit
1984							
June	23		2	600		600	
	30	Clos. ent.	4		600	—	

Mike Starbuck, Capital — Account No. 300

Date		Item	Post Ref.	Debit	Credit	Balance Debit	Balance Credit
1984							
June	1		1		60,000		60,000
	30	Clos. ent.	4		1,238		61,238
	30	Clos. ent.	4	600			60,638

account is transferred directly to the owner's Capital account by the following entry:

June	30	Mike Starbuck, Capital	300	600	
		Mike Starbuck, Drawing	310		600
		To close the Drawing			
		account.			

After the entry is posted, the Drawing account will have a zero balance, as shown in Figure 4-13. Note that the Drawing account is not closed to the Income Summary account because the withdrawal of assets by the owner is not an expense of doing business.

ACCOUNT BALANCES AFTER COMPLETION OF THE CLOSING PROCESS

The accounts for the Starbuck Real Estate Office, after both the adjusting and closing entries have been posted, are presented in Figure 4-14. Note that the

STARBUCK REAL ESTATE OFFICE

Account **Cash**   Account No. **100**

Date		Item	Post Ref.	Debit	Credit	Balance Debit	Balance Credit
1984							
June	1		1	60.000		60.000	
	2		1		12.000	48.000	
	3		1		960	47.040	
	5		1		5.000	42.040	
	6		1		120	41.920	
	22		2		1.800	40.120	
	23		2	250		40.370	
	23		2		600	39.770	
	27		2		620	39.150	
	29		2	280		39.430	
	30		2		72	39.358	
	30		2	4.200		43.558	

Account **Accounts Receivable**   Account No. **104**

Date		Item	Post Ref.	Debit	Credit	Balance Debit	Balance Credit
1984							
June	15		1	4.200		4.200	
	19		2	5.400		9.600	
	30		2		4.200	5.400	
	30	Adj. ent. (i)	3	400		5.800	

Figure 4-14
General Ledger After Completion of the Closing Process

Figure 4-14
Continued

Account   Prepaid Insurance   Account No. 110

		Item	Post Ref.	Debit	Credit	Balance Debit	Balance Credit
1984							
June	3		1	960		960	
	30	Adj. ent. (a)	3		40	920	

Account   Office Supplies Inventory   Account No. 111

		Item	Post Ref.	Debit	Credit	Balance Debit	Balance Credit
1984							
June	5		1	620		620	
	30	Adj. ent. (b)	3		80	540	

Account   Land   Account No. 150

		Item	Post Ref.	Debit	Credit	Balance Debit	Balance Credit
1984							
June	2		1	10.000		10.000	

Account   Building   Account No. 160

		Item	Post Ref.	Debit	Credit	Balance Debit	Balance Credit
1984							
June	2		1	62.000		62.000	

Account   Accumulated Depreciation—Building   Account No. 161

		Item	Post Ref.	Debit	Credit	Balance Debit	Balance Credit
1984							
June	30	Adj. ent. (d)	3		200		200

Account   Office Equipment   Account No. 170

		Item	Post Ref.	Debit	Credit	Balance Debit	Balance Credit
1984							
June	5		1	9.600		9.600	

Account   Accumulated Depreciation—Office Equipment   Account No. 171

		Item	Post Ref.	Debit	Credit	Balance Debit	Balance Credit
1984							
June	30	Adj. ent. (c)	3		100		100

Figure 4-14
Continued

Account Accounts Payable   Account No. 200

Date		Item	Post Ref.	Debit	Credit	Balance Debit	Balance Credit
1984							
June	5		1		620		620
	5		1		4.600		5.220
	27		2	620			4.600

Account Salaries Payable   Account No. 210

Date		Item	Post Ref.	Debit	Credit	Balance Debit	Balance Credit
1984							
June	30	Adj. ent. (e)	3		990		990

Account Commissions Payable   Account No. 211

Date		Item	Post Ref.	Debit	Credit	Balance Debit	Balance Credit
1984							
June	30	Adj. ent. (f)	3		4.800		4.800

Account Interest Payable   Account No. 215

Date		Item	Post Ref.	Debit	Credit	Balance Debit	Balance Credit
1984							
June	30	Adj. ent. (g)	3		600		600

Account Utilities Payable   Account No. 216

Date		Item	Post Ref.	Debit	Credit	Balance Debit	Balance Credit
1984							
June	30	Adj. ent. (h)	3		210		210

Account Unearned Appraisal Fees   Account No. 220

Date		Item	Post Ref.	Debit	Credit	Balance Debit	Balance Credit
1984							
June	29		2		280		280

Account Mortgage Notes Payable   Account No. 230

Date		Item	Post Ref.	Debit	Credit	Balance Debit	Balance Credit
1984							
June	2		1		60.000		60.000

Figure 4-14
Continued

Account   Mike Starbuck, Capital — Account No. **300**

Date		Item	Post Ref	Debit	Credit	Balance Debit	Balance Credit
1984							
June	1		1		60.000		60.000
	30	Clos ent (3)	4		1.238		61.238
	30	Clos ent (4)	4	600			60.638

Account   Mike Starbuck, Drawing — Account No. **350**

Date		Item	Post Ref	Debit	Credit	Balance Debit	Balance Credit
1984							
June	23		2	600		600	
	30	Clos ent (4)	4		600	—	

Account   Income Summary — Account No. **350**

Date		Item	Post Ref	Debit	Credit	Balance Debit	Balance Credit
1984							
June	30	Clos ent (1)	4		10.250		10.250
	30	Clos ent (2)	4	9.012			1.238
	30	Clos ent (3)	4	1.238			—

Account   Commission Revenue — Account No. **400**

Date		Item	Post Ref	Debit	Credit	Balance Debit	Balance Credit
1984							
June	15		1		4.200		4.200
	19		2		5.400		9.600
	30	Clos ent (1)	4	9.600			—

Account   Appraisal Fee Revenue — Account No. **401**

Date		Item	Post Ref	Debit	Credit	Balance Debit	Balance Credit
1984							
June	23		2		250		250
	30	Clos ent (1)	4	250			—

Figure 4-14
Continued

Account   Service Fee Revenue   Account No. **402**

Date		Item	Post Ref.	Debit	Credit	Balance Debit	Balance Credit
1984							
June	30	Adj. ent. (i)	3		400		400
	30	Clos. ent. (1)	4	400			—

Account   Salary Expense   Account No. **500**

Date		Item	Post Ref.	Debit	Credit	Balance Debit	Balance Credit
1984							
June	22		2	1,800		1,800	
	30	Adj. ent. (e)	3	990		2,790	
	30	Clos. ent. (2)	4		2,790	—	

Account   Commission Expense   Account No. **505**

Date		Item	Post Ref.	Debit	Credit	Balance Debit	Balance Credit
1984							
June	30	Adj. ent. (f)	3	4,800		4,800	
	30	Clos. ent. (2)	4		4,800	—	

Account   Utilities Expense   Account No. **510**

Date		Item	Post Ref.	Debit	Credit	Balance Debit	Balance Credit
1984							
June	30		2	72		72	
	30	Adj. ent. (h)	3	210		282	
	30	Clos. ent. (2)	4		282		

Account   Advertising Expense   Account No. **520**

Date		Item	Post Ref.	Debit	Credit	Balance Debit	Balance Credit
1984							
June	6		1	120		120	
	30	Clos. ent. (2)	4		120	—	

Figure 4-14
Continued

Account	Insurance Expense						Account No. 521

			Post			Balance	
Date		Item	Ref.	Debit	Credit	Debit	Credit
1984							
June	30	Adj.ent.(a)	3	40		40	
	30	Clos.ent.(2)	4		40	—	

Account	Office Supplies Expense						Account No. 530

			Post			Balance	
Date		Item	Ref.	Debit	Credit	Debit	Credit
1984							
June	30	Adj.ent.(b)	3	80		80	
	30	Clos.ent.(2)	4		80	—	

Account	Depreciation Expense						Account No. 540

			Post			Balance	
Date		Item	Ref.	Debit	Credit	Debit	Credit
1984							
June	30	Adj.ent.(c)	3	100		100	
	30	Adj.ent.(d)	3	200		300	
	30	Clos.ent.(2)	4		300	—	

Account	Interest Expense						Account No. 560

			Post			Balance	
Date		Item	Ref.	Debit	Credit	Debit	Credit
1984							
June	30	Adj.ent.(g)	3	600		600	
	30	Clos.ent.(2)	4		600	—	

revenue, expense, and drawing accounts all have zero balances and are ready for recording transactions of the next period. The balances in the balance sheet accounts are carried forward to the next period and are the only accounts that have a balance.

THE POST-CLOSING TRIAL BALANCE

After the closing entries have been posted, it is desirable to prepare a **post-closing trial balance** to verify the equality of debits and credits in the ledger.

At this point, only the balance sheet accounts (permanent accounts) should have balances. A post-closing trial balance for the Starbuck Real Estate Office is presented in Figure 4-15.

Figure 4-15
Post-closing Trial
Balance

STARBUCK REAL ESTATE OFFICE
Post-closing Trial Balance
June 30, 1984

Account Title	Account Balance	
	Debit	Credit
Cash	$ 43,558	
Accounts Receivable	5,800	
Prepaid Insurance	920	
Office Supplies Inventory	540	
Land	10,000	
Building	62,000	
Accumulated Depreciation—Building		$ 200
Office Equipment	9,600	
Accumulated Depreciation—Office Equipment		100
Accounts Payable		4,600
Salaries Payable		990
Commissions Payable		4,800
Interest Payable		600
Utilities Payable		210
Unearned Appraisal Fees		280
Mortgage Notes Payable		60,000
Mike Starbuck, Capital		60,638
Totals	$132,418	$132,418

PREPARING INTERIM STATEMENTS
WITHOUT CLOSING THE ACCOUNTS

It is common practice for a firm to prepare monthly financial statements for use by management, and most large firms issue quarterly statements to external statement users. Such statements are called **interim statements** because they are prepared between the annual reports issued at fiscal year-end. In the preceding illustration, it was assumed that monthly financial statements were to be prepared. It was also assumed that the accounting cycle, including journalizing and posting both adjusting and closing entries, was completed at the end of the month. However, most firms adjust and close their accounts at the end of the fiscal period only. Information needed to prepare interim financial statements is accumulated in the worksheet only. In other words, adjustments are made in the worksheet but are not entered in the accounting records except at the end of the fiscal period. At that time the accounts are also closed.

ENTRIES MADE IN SUBSEQUENT PERIODS RELATED TO ACCRUALS

As part of the adjusting process, entries must be made to recognize expenses that have been incurred but not yet paid for or recorded and also revenues that have been earned but not yet collected or recorded. Recall that such adjustments are collectively called accruals. Adjusting entries (e) through (i) in the worksheet illustrated in Figure 4-3 are all examples of accruals. In subsequent periods, cash received or paid for accruals must be analyzed to properly apportion the amount involved between two or more periods.

For example, during June, $1,800 in salaries was paid and $990 in unpaid salaries was accrued at the end of June [adjusting entry (e)] to be paid on July 6. The following entry is required on July 6, assuming a $1,700 payment is made for salaries earned from June 23 to July 6:

July	6	Salaries Payable	990	
		Salary Expense	710	
		Cash		1,700
		To record payment of salaries for the period June 23 to July 6.		

After posting this entry, the Salary Expense and Salaries Payable accounts appear as follows:

Account **Salaries Payable**						Account No. **210**	
			Post			Balance	
Date		Item	Ref.	Debit	Credit	Debit	Credit
1984							
June	30	Adj. ent. (e)	3		990		990
July	6			990			—

Account Salary Expense					Account No. 500	
		Post			Balance	
Date	Item	Ref.	Debit	Credit	Debit	Credit
1984						
June 22		2	1,800		1,800	
30	Adj.ent.(e)	3	990		2,790	
30	Clos.ent.(2)	4		2,790	—	
July 6		5	710		710	

On July 1 the Salaries Payable account has a credit balance of $990, and the Salary Expense account has a zero balance. The zero balance results from making an entry on June 30 to close all expense accounts. Because the $1,700 payment is for salaries earned during two different accounting periods, the payment must be divided into two elements. First, the $990 debit settles the liability for the salaries earned by employees in June that were reported as an expense in June. The second debit of $710 properly recognizes as an expense that portion of the payment made for salaries incurred in July.

A similar analysis would be required for the other accruals when a cash payment is made or cash is received after June 30. However, in some cases the total amount of cash paid or received in a subsequent period is a settlement of a liability or a receivable accrued at the end of June with none of the cash apportioned as a revenue earned or an expense incurred in July. For example, the payment to be made on July 10 for accrued commissions is:

July	10	Commissions Payable	4,800	
		Cash		4,800
		To record payment of commissions		
		earned in June.		

Thus none of the payment is allocated as an expense in July, and the full payment is a settlement of the liability established by adjusting entry (f). The full amount of $4,800 was reported as an expense in June.

ACCOUNTING PROCEDURES APPLICABLE TO A PARTNERSHIP OR A CORPORATION

In the preceding illustration, Starbuck Real Estate Office was owned by one person, who had elected to operate the firm as a single proprietorship. Although single proprietorships are the most numerous form of business organization in the United States, the majority of business activity is conducted by the corporate form of business organization. A *corporation* is a business entity incorporated under the laws of a particular state or the federal government. A third form of business organization is the *partnership,* which is a business owned by two or more persons acting as partners. Accounting and reporting for partnerships and corporations are similar in most respects to accounting and reporting for single proprietorships. The income statement and the balance sheet are essentially the same for all three forms of business organization except for transactions that directly affect the owners' equity accounts. These differences are discussed briefly below. Special accounting problems associated with partnerships and corporations are discussed in more detail in Chapters 14–16.

ACCOUNTING FOR A PARTNERSHIP

In accounting for a partnership, separate capital and withdrawal accounts are maintained for each partner. An investment by a partner is credited to his or her capital account, and a withdrawal of cash or other assets from the partnership is debited to his or her withdrawal account. At the end of the period, the Income Summary account is closed by making a compound journal entry that allocates the balance in the account to each partner's capital account in accordance with the partners' profit and loss sharing agreement.

ACCOUNTING FOR A CORPORATION

The owners of a corporation are called stockholders or shareholders because their ownership interests are represented by shares of the corporation's stock. In a corporate balance sheet, the total interest of the owners in the assets of the corporation is called stockholders' equity. The stockholders' equity section is separated into two categories or sources of capital: (1) **Contributed Capital** represents the amount of assets invested in the corporation by the stockholders, and (2) **Retained Earnings** reflect the accumulated income earned by the corporation and retained in the business.

The investment of assets in a corporation is recorded by debits to the asset accounts and a credit to a contributed capital account such as Common Stock. When an investment is made in the corporation, the investors are given shares of the corporation's stock as evidence of their ownership. For example, assume that Starbuck Real Estate Office was organized on January 1, 1984, as a corporation and initially issued 10,000 shares of its $10 par value common stock for $100,000. The entry to record the issue is as follows:

1984				
Jan.	1	Cash	100,000	
		Common Stock		100,000

Just as the owner of a single proprietorship may periodically withdraw cash from the business in anticipation of profits, cash distributions called **dividends** may be made to the owners of a corporation. However, before a dividend can be paid, it must be declared by the corporation's board of directors. Assume that on December 1 Starbuck's board of directors declared a cash dividend of $1.00 per share on the 10,000 shares issued and outstanding. The dividend is to be paid on December 20. Entries to record the declaration and payment are:

Dec.	1	Dividends Declared	10,000	
		Cash Dividends Payable		10,000
		Declared a cash dividend of $1 per share on the 10,000 common shares outstanding.		
Dec.	20	Cash Dividends Payable	10,000	
		Cash		10,000
		To record payment of the dividend declared.		

The Dividends Declared account is a temporary Retained Earnings account rather than an expense account because dividends are considered a distribution of profits and are not a cost incurred for the purpose of producing revenue. At the end of the period, the Dividends Declared account is closed to the Retained Earnings account.

If net income for the year is $25,000, the Income Summary account will have a credit balance and will be closed by the following entry:

Dec.	31	Income Summary	25,000	
		Retained Earnings		25,000

At the end of the period, a corporation will normally prepare a Statement of Retained Earnings similar to the following:

STARBUCK REAL ESTATE OFFICE
Statement of Retained Earnings
For Year Ended December 31, 1984

Retained earnings, January 1, 1984	–0–
Add: Net income for the year	$25,000
Total	25,000
Less: Cash dividends for the year	10,000
Retained earnings, December 31, 1984	$15,000

Based on the above entries, the stockholders' equity section of the balance sheet will appear as follows:

Stockholders' Equity	
Common Stock, $10 par value, 10,000 shares issued and outstanding	$100,000
Retained earnings, December 31, 1984	15,000
Total Stockholders' Equity	$115,000

One important difference between the three forms of business organization is the way income taxes are computed. Although all three forms are recognized as separate business entities for accounting purposes, single proprietorships and partnerships are nontaxpaying entities. Single proprietors or partners must include their share of business income or loss in their individual tax returns. Thus, income tax expense will not appear in the income statement of a single proprietorship or partnership. Except for the Subchapter S corporations described in Chapter 28, corporations are separate taxable entities that must file tax returns and pay a state and federal tax on their taxable income. Therefore, in its financial statements, a corporation must show the amount of income tax expense incurred for the period and any unpaid portion of the tax as a liability. The amount of income tax to be paid each period is computed in accordance with the Internal Revenue Code. Some provisions of the Code are discussed in more detail in Chapter 28. Until then, we will assume a simplified tax computation for illustrative purposes.

REVERSING ENTRIES

In the Starbuck Real Estate Office illustration, the closing process was the last step in the accounting cycle. After this step is completed, the records are ready for entering the transactions of the next period. However, some firms add another step to the cycle after the closing entries are posted to the ledger. This added step involves making reversing entries. **Reversing entries** are dated as of the first day of the next accounting period and are so called because they reverse the effects of certain adjusting entries that were made on the last day of the preceding accounting period. Reversing entries are a bookkeeping technique made to simplify the recording of regular transactions in the next period.

To illustrate reversing entries, we will continue with the accrued salaries adjustment. Recall that $1,800 in salaries was paid during June and that $990 was accrued on June 30. Salaries earned for the period June 23 to July 6 in the amount of $1,700 are to be paid on July 6. Throughout an accounting period, the normal entry to record the payment of salaries is to debit Salary Expense and credit Cash.

At the end of June, accrued salaries were recorded in the following *adjusting entry*:

June	30	Salary Expense	990	
		Salaries Payable		990
		To record unpaid salaries at the end of June.		

At the end of the period, the balance of $2,790 in the Salary Expense account is closed to the Income Summary account and the Salaries Payable balance of $990 is reported as a liability in the balance sheet.

If the adjusting entry is not reversed, the following entry is made on July 6 to record payment:

July	6	Salaries Payable	990	
		Salary Expense	710	
		Cash		1,700
		To record payment of salaries for the period June 23 to July 6.		

Note that this entry requires two debits, a variation from the normal entry of one debit to the Salary Expense account. Thus, a change from the normal procedures is necessary and requires that the adjusting entry or the Salary Expense account in the general ledger be referred to in order to divide the payment between the two accounts. To simplify the July 6 entry, a *reversing entry* may be made to reverse the effects of the adjusting entry as follows:

July	1	Salaries Payable	990	
		Salary Expense		990
		To reverse the adjusting entry to accrue unpaid salaries.		

Compare this reversing entry to the adjusting entry on June 30. Observe that the debit and credit amounts are the same in both entries, but the account debited (Salary Expense) in the adjusting entry is credited in the reversing entry, while the account credited (Salaries Payable) in the adjusting entry is debited in the reversing entry. In other words, the reversal is the opposite of the adjusting entry.

The debit in the reversing entry transfers the liability to the expense account. This produces a temporary credit balance (a liability) of $990 in the expense account since it had a zero balance before the reversing entry as a result of the closing process. This permits making the normal entry to record the payment on July 6 as follows:

July	6	Salary Expense	1,700	
		Cash		1,700
		To record payment of salaries for the period June 23 to July 6.		

The debit of $1,700 is partially offset by the credit of $990 made in the reversing entry. This leaves a balance of $710 in the Salary Expense account, which is the expense for July.

As shown in Figure 4-16, the two approaches produce identical results. Salary expenses for June and July are $2,790 and $710, respectively, and a liability for $990 is reported in the balance sheet.

Figure 4-16
Illustration of Reversing Entries

	Without Reversing Entry			With Reversing Entry		
1. Payment of Salaries						
	6/22 Salary Expense	1,800		Salary Expense	1,800	
	Cash		1,800	Cash		1,800
2. Adjusting entry to accrue salaries						
	6/30 Salary Expense	990		Salary Expense	990	
	Salaries Payable		990	Salaries Payable		990
3. Closing entry						
	6/30 Income Summary	2,790		Income Summary	2,790	
	Salary Expense		2,790	Salary Expense		2,790
4. Reversing entry						
	7/1 No entry is made			Salaries Payable	990	
				Salary Expense		990
5. Payment of salaries						
	7/6 Salaries Payable	990				
	Salary Expense	710		Salary Expense	1,700	
	Cash		1,700	Cash		1,700

Salaries Payable		Salary Expense		Salaries Payable		Salary Expense	
7/6 990	6/30 990	6/22 1,800		7/1 990	6/30 990	6/22 1,800	
		6/30 990	6/30 2,790			6/30 990	6/30 2,790
		2,790	2,790			2,790	2,790
		7/6 710				7/6 1,700	7/1 990
						Bal. 710	

Cash			Cash		
6/22	1,800		6/22	1,800	
7/6	1,700		7/6	1,700	

Reversing entries are also useful when many similar transactions involve the computation of accruals. For example, a bank may have thousands of outstanding notes receivable. At the end of the period, interest earned but not received must be accrued in order to properly report interest revenue and interest receivable in the financial statements. If a reversing entry is not made, each time an interest payment is received in the next period, an employee must refer back to the list of accruals in order to divide the amount of the payment between the reduction in the receivable balance and the interest earned in the current period. If the adjusting entry is reversed, the receipt of cash for interest is simply recorded as a debit to Cash and a credit to Interest Revenue. In this case, reversals will result in saving a great deal of time since an employee will not have to allocate each interest payment between two periods.

A detailed study of reversing entries is reserved for a more advanced Accounting course. A thorough knowledge of reversing entries is not essential to understanding accounting concepts and procedures. For this reason, they are not made in the remainder of this text. For now it should be emphasized that reversing entries are optional and are made to facilitate the recording of routine transactions in future periods. Furthermore, only certain adjusting entries should be reversed if it is beneficial to do so. A general rule is that adjusting entries for accruals can be reversed. The prepayment of expenses and the advance receipt of revenues (deferrals) normally are recorded initially in a permanent account and are not reversed.

DEMONSTRATION PROBLEM

The unadjusted trial balance for Meadows Law Office at the end of the current fiscal year is presented on page 184.

Additional information needed to adjust the accounts is:

(a) The office supplies inventory determined by physical count was $620.
(b) The balance in the Prepaid Rent account is for three months' rent paid on November 1.
(c) Unpaid salaries earned by employees amounted to $1,300.
(d) Insurance expired during the period, $600.
(e) The balance in the Unearned Fees account consists of advance payments of $700 for law services to be performed next year. The remaining advance payments were earned this period.
(f) Estimated depreciation on office equipment, $800.
(g) Accrued interest on notes payable due on January 15 is $210.
(h) Travel expenses incurred by employees but unpaid were $220.

Required:
A. Prepare a 10-column worksheet.
B. Prepare closing entries.

MEADOWS LAW OFFICE
Unadjusted Trial Balance
December 31, 1984

Account Title	Debit	Credit
Cash	$ 9,880	
Accounts Receivable	4,310	
Prepaid Rent	1,500	
Prepaid Insurance	1,320	
Office Supplies Inventory	1,280	
Office Equipment	4,000	
Accumulated Depreciation—Office Equipment		$ 2,400
Accounts Payable		630
Unearned Fees		1,800
Notes Payable		3,000
Jane Meadows, Capital		10,000
Jane Meadows, Drawing	36,000	
Fees Earned		79,320
Salary Expense	25,200	
Rent Expense	5,000	
Utility Expense	2,490	
Research Expense	4,310	
Travel Expense	1,860	
Totals	$97,150	$97,150

ANSWER TO DEMONSTRATION PROBLEM

A.

MEADOWS LAW OFFICE
Worksheet
For Year Ended December 31, 1984

Account Title	Unadjusted Trial Balance Debit	Credit	Adjustments Debit	Credit	Adjusted Trial Balance Debit	Credit	Income Statement Debit	Credit	Balance Sheet Debit	Credit
Cash	9,880				9,880				9,880	
Accounts Receivable	4,310				4,310				4,310	
Prepaid Rent	1,500			(b) 1,000	500				500	
Prepaid Insurance	1,320			(d) 600	720				720	
Office Supplies Inventory	1,280			(a) 660	620				620	
Office Equipment	4,000				4,000				4,000	
Accumulated Depreciation—Office Equipment		2,400		(f) 800		3,200				3,200
Accounts Payable		630				630				630
Unearned Fees		1,800	(e) 1,100			700				700
Notes Payable		3,000				3,000				3,000
Jane Meadows, Capital		10,000				10,000				10,000
Jane Meadows, Drawing	36,000				36,000				36,000	
Fees Earned		79,320		(e) 1,100		80,420		80,420		
Salary Expense	25,200		(c) 1,300		26,500		26,500			
Rent Expense	5,000		(b) 1,000		6,000		6,000			
Utility Expense	2,490				2,490		2,490			
Research Expense	4,310				4,310		4,310			
Travel Expense	1,860		(h) 220		2,080		2,080			
Totals	97,150	97,150								
Office Supplies Expense			(a) 660		660		660			
Salaries Payable				(c) 1,300		1,300				1,300
Insurance Expense			(d) 600		600		600			
Depreciation Expense			(f) 800		800		800			
Interest Expense			(g) 210		210		210			
Interest Payable				(g) 210		210				210
Travel Expense Payable				(h) 220		220				220
Totals			5,890	5,890	99,680	99,680	43,650	80,420	56,030	19,260
Net Income for the Period							36,770			36,770
Totals							80,420	80,420	56,030	56,030

B.

Dec.	31	Fees Earned	80,420	
		Income Summary		80,420
		To close the revenue account.		
	31	Income Summary	43,650	
		Salary Expense		26,500
		Rent Expense		6,000
		Utility Expense		2,490
		Research Expense		4,310
		Travel Expense		2,080
		Office Supplies Expense		660
		Insurance Expense		600
		Depreciation Expense		800
		Interest Expense		210
		To close the expense accounts.		
	31	Income Summary	36,770	
		Jane Meadows, Capital		36,770
		To close the Income Summary account.		
	31	Jane Meadows, Capital	36,000	
		Jane Meadows, Drawing		36,000
		To close the Drawing account.		

GLOSSARY

CLOSING ENTRIES. Journal entries made at the end of an accounting period to reduce revenue and expense accounts to a zero balance and transfer the net balance to the owner's capital account (p. 160).

CONTRIBUTED CAPITAL. The capital invested in the corporation by its stockholders (p. 178).

CROSSFOOTING. Adding or subtracting horizontally across a worksheet (p. 153).

DIVIDEND. A distribution of cash by a corporation to its stockholders (p. 179).

FOOTING. Adding the amounts entered in a vertical column (p. 153).

INTERIM STATEMENTS. Financial statements prepared between the annual reports (p. 175).

POST-CLOSING TRIAL BALANCE. A trial balance taken after the adjusting and closing entries have been posted to the accounts (p. 174).

RETAINED EARNINGS. Earnings of a corporation that have been retained in the business rather than distributed to stockholders (p. 178).

REVERSING ENTRIES. Entries made to reverse the effects of certain adjusting entries (p. 180).

WORKSHEET. A form used by accountants to gather and organize the information needed to complete the accounting cycle (p. 150).

DISCUSSION QUESTIONS

1. Why do accountants prepare a worksheet?
2. Which one of the following steps in the accounting cycle may be omitted: (a) posting the entries to the ledger, (b) preparing a worksheet, (c) journalizing the adjusting entries, or (d) posting the closing entries to the ledger?
3. Why are the entries in the Adjustments column of the worksheet identified by either letters or numbers?
4. Define the terms *footing* and *crossfooting*.
5. In which columns of the worksheet is the net income for the period entered?
6. Will the columns of the worksheet balance if an expense is accidentally entered in the debit column of the Balance Sheet rather than the Income Statement? What will be the effect on the reported net income?
7. In a sole proprietorship, which accounts are involved in closing entries? Why are these accounts closed?
8. What is the purpose of the Income Summary account?
9. List the four steps in closing the accounts of a sole proprietorship.
10. Why is a post-closing trial balance prepared?
11. Which accounts appear on the post-closing trial balance?
12. Which steps in the accounting cycle are performed in order to prepare interim financial statements?
13. Describe the owners' equity section of a corporation's balance sheet and compare it to the owners' equity of a partnership.

14. Explain the difference between the payment of cash dividends and the withdrawal of cash by a sole proprietor. What is the effect of each on assets? Owners' equity? Net income?
15. Why are reversing entries so named?
16. What is the purpose of reversing entries? Which adjusting entries may be reversed?
17. At the end of the preceding period, the company accrued salaries payable of $1,500. On January 2, the company debited Salary Expense and credited Cash for $2,000.
    (a) If a reversing entry had not been made on January 1, would the financial statements be in error for the month of January? Explain.
    (b) What entry should have been made on January 2 given that a reversing entry was not made?
    (c) If the company made reversing entries, what reversing entry should have been made on January 1?

EXERCISES

Exercise 4-1 (Extention of Account Balances to Proper Worksheet Columns)

Listed below are ledger accounts that appear in the Adjusted Trial Balance columns of a worksheet. You are to complete the tabulation shown below by entering a check mark in the proper worksheet column in which the amount in each account would be extended in completing the worksheet.

1. Cash
2. Building
3. Service Revenue
4. Wages Expense
5. Sam Holly, Capital
6. Accumulated Depreciation
7. Depreciation Expense
8. Accounts Receivable
9. Wages Payable
10. Sam Holly, Withdrawals
11. Prepaid Insurance
12. Equipment
13. Office Supplies Inventory
14. Office Supplies Expense
15. Interest Revenue
16. Interest Expense
17. Interest Receivable
18. Interest Payable

Solution Format

Account	Income Statement		Balance Sheet	
	Debit	Credit	Debit	Credit
1. Cash	_____	_____	✓	_____

Exercise 4-2 (Completion of Worksheet, Preparation of Financial Statements, and Closing Entries)

The following unadjusted trial balance was taken from the ledger of Matlock Company on December 31, 1984.

Account	Debit	Credit
	(000 omitted)	
Cash	$10	
Accounts Receivable	8	
Prepaid Insurance	2	
Equipment	20	
Accumulated Depreciation		$ 8
Accounts Payable		4
Charles Matlock, Capital		27
Charles Matlock, Drawing	5	
Service Revenue		32
Wages Expense	17	
Utility Expense	6	
Miscellaneous Expense	3	
Totals	$71	$71

Required:

A. Prepare a 10-column worksheet using the following additional information on December 31, 1984 (000 omitted). Add the following account titles to those listed in the trial balance: Insurance Expense, Accrued Wages Payable, Depreciation Expense.

    1. Expired insurance, $1.

    2. Accrued wages, $2.

    3. Depreciation on equipment, $4.

B. Prepare an income statement, a capital statement, and an unclassified balance sheet.

C. Record the adjusting and closing entries in the general journal.

Exercise 4-3 (Closing Entries)

The following accounts and account balances were taken from the adjusted trial balance columns of the worksheet of the Wolek Company for the year ending December 31, 1985.

Jay Wolek, Capital	$12,300
Jay Wolek, Drawing	9,450
Fees Earned	47,230
Interest Revenue	5,100
Salaries Expense	19,700
Rent Expense	6,100
Advertising Expense	3,970
Depreciation Expense	5,340
Utilities Expense	2,100

Required:

Prepare the closing entries.

Exercise 4-4 (Preparation of Capital Statement)

The adjusted trial balance of the J. M. Lewis Company is shown below:

J. M. LEWIS COMPANY
Trial Balance
December 31, 1984

	Debit	Credit
Cash	$ 2,430	
Accounts Receivable	1,710	
Supplies on Hand	240	
Accounts Payable		$ 1,790
J. M. Lewis, Capital		2,050
J. M. Lewis, Drawing	5,850	
Fees Earned		12,630
Wages Expense	4,210	
Supplies Expense	330	
Advertising Expense	1,700	
Totals	$16,470	$16,470

Required:

Prepare a capital statement for the year ending December 31, 1984. Assume that J. M. Lewis did not contribute any additional capital during 1984.

6240

Exercise 4-5 (Closing Entries)

The income statement of Allied Rental Cars is presented below:

ALLIED RENTAL CARS
Income Statement
For the Year Ended June 30, 1984

Revenue:		
Car rental fees		$34,610
Truck rental fees		29,740
Total Revenue		64,350
Operating Expenses:		
Salaries expense	$18,990	
Depreciation expense	21,730	
Insurance expense	1,970	
Maintenance expense	2,650	
Supplies expense	460	
Advertising expense	830	
Total Operating Expenses		46,630
Net Income		$17,720

6390

8440

Required:
Given that the owner, Ron Jones, withdrew $16,800 from the business during the year, prepare the closing entries.

Exercise 4-6 (Preparation of Capital Statement)
The following accounts are taken from the ledger of the Bixler Company on December 31, the end of the current fiscal year.

W. Bixler, Capital				W. Bixler, Drawing			
12/31	16,230	1/1	6,740	2/15	2,800	12/31	16,230
		12/31	15,980	4/29	4,130		
				5/17	3,950		
				9/4	5,350		

Income Summary			
12/31	24,390	12/31	40,370
12/31	15,980		

Required:
Prepare a capital statement.

Exercise 4-7 (Determination of Cash Paid—Missing Data)
Selected accounts of the Haskins Company contain the following balances at the beginning and the end of the year. The year-end adjusting entries have been made.

	Jan. 1	Dec. 31
Prepaid Insurance	$ 200	$780
Supplies Inventory	155	270
Salaries Payable	1,100	915

The following items appear on the income statement for the year ended December 31.

Insurance Expense	$ 650
Supplies Expense	525
Salaries Expense	32,180

Required:
Determine how much cash was used during the year:

A. To purchase insurance
B. To purchase supplies
C. For salaries

Exercise 4-8 (Recording Capital Transactions of a Corporation)
Prepare the general journal entries that are needed to record the transactions of Atlas Corporation.

1. Issued 1,000 shares of $10 par value stock for $10,000.
2. The board of directors declared a cash dividend of $1 per share.
3. The cash dividend declared in (2) above was paid.
4. Close a $7,800 credit balance in the Income Summary account.

Exercise 4-9 (Closing Accounts and Preparation of Capital Statement for a Corporation)

On January 1, 1984, the owners' equity of the Williams Corporation consisted of common stock of $420,000 and retained earnings of $205,000. During the period, the company declared and paid a cash dividend of $60,000. The general ledger contains only two income statement accounts—Revenues Earned and Operating Expenses. On December 31, the balance in the Revenues Earned account was $620,000 and the balance in the Operating Expenses account was $545,000.

Required:
A. Prepare closing entries.
B. Prepare a statement of retained earnings at the end of 1984.
C. Compute the total owners' equity in the assets of the firm at the end of 1984.

Exercise 4-10 (Reversing Entries—Accrued Expense)

On December 31, 1984, the accountant for Hoover Plumbing determined that one month's interest of $24 had accrued on a note payable. An interest payment of $96 was made on March 31, 1985.

Required:
A. Give the adjusting entry needed on December 31, 1984.
B. Give the closing entry.
C. Give the reversing entry that could be made and the subsequent entry to record the payment of March 31, 1985.
D. Assuming no reversing entry, give the entry to record the interest payment.

Exercise 4-11 (Reversing Entries—Accrued Revenue)

Paula Pany operates a telephone answering service. Her clients are charged $75 a month for the service and are billed four times a year on January 31, April 30, July 31, and October 31. Quarterly payments are due by the fifteenth of the month following the end of a quarter. The balance in the Answering Service Fees Revenue account was $27,000 on December 31, the end of the fiscal period. Service fees earned in November and December but not yet recorded were $4,350.

Required:
A. Prepare the adjusting entry in the general journal to record the earned fees.
B. Assuming that reversing entries are not made, record the receipt of a $225 quarterly payment from a client on February 12 and the receipt of $150 on February 13 from a new client who had contracted for the service to start on December 1.
C. Assuming that reversing entries are made to facilitate the bookkeeping process, prepare the appropriate reversing entry, if any, and the receipt of cash on February 12 and 13.

Exercise 4-12 (Reversing Entries—Unearned Revenue)

During the 1984 fiscal year, Classic Publishing Company received $76,600 for magazine subscriptions. The bookkeeper credits Unearned Subscriptions, a liability account, for the full amount when cash is received. At December 31, 1984, it is determined that $28,400 of the subscriptions relate to magazines that are to be published and delivered in future periods.

Required:

A. What amount should be reported in the 1984 income statement for earned subscriptions revenue?

B. What amount should be reported in the December 31, 1984, balance sheet for unearned subscriptions?

C. Prepare the adjusting entry needed at December 31, 1984.

D. What reversing entry, if any, would you make on January 1, 1985?

E. The bookkeeper could have recorded the receipt of cash initially in a revenue account. Prepare the adjusting entry assuming that the Earned Subscriptions Revenue account contains a credit balance of $76,600 at December 31.

F. Compare the balances in the Unearned Subscriptions account and the Earned Subscriptions Revenue account derived in requirement E with those computed in requirements A and B.

G. What reversing entry, if any, would you make on January 1, 1985, to reverse the adjusting entry made in requirement E?

PROBLEMS

Problem 4-1 (Preparation of Worksheet)

The unadjusted trial balance of Royal Limousine Service is shown below:

ROYAL LIMOUSINE SERVICE
Unadjusted Trial Balance
December 31, 1984

	Debit	Credit
Cash	$ 5,300	
Accounts Receivable	4,610	
Prepaid Insurance	3,790	
Limousines	81,000	
Accumulated Depreciation, Limousines		$ 32,000
Office Equipment	2,100	
Accumulated Depreciation, Office Equipment		890
Accounts Payable		5,930
Notes Payable		25,000
Unearned Limousine Fares		840
Charles Jenkins, Capital		33,160
Charles Jenkins, Drawing	8,300	
Limousine Fares Earned		36,270
Salaries Expense	15,200	
Rent Expense	2,630	
Limousine Maintenance and Repair Expense	2,960	
Gas and Oil Expense	6,800	
Telephone Expense	1,400	
Totals	$134,090	$134,090

The following additional information is available at the end of December:

1. Expired insurance amounted to $3,400.
2. Depreciation on the limousines for one year is $7,600. Depreciation on the office equipment is $390.
3. Accrued interest on the note payable is $2,240.
4. The balance in the Unearned Limousine Fares account includes $125 received for services rendered on December 27.
5. Chauffeurs' salaries earned but not paid amounted to $940.
6. Limousine repair work done in December for $470 has not been paid for or recorded.
7. The December telephone bill of $110 was received during January and has not been recorded.

Required:

A. Prepare a 10-column worksheet for the year ended December 31, 1984.
B. Add the following account titles to those listed in the trial balance: Depreciation Expense, Telephone Expense Payable, Interest Payable, Interest Expense, Insurance Expense, Salaries Payable.

Problem 4-2 (Preparation of Worksheet, Financial Statements, and Closing Entries)

The ledger of Rick Clayton, Veterinarian, contains the following accounts and account balances on December 31, 1984.

Account	Debit	Credit
Cash	$ 3,410	
Accounts Receivable	2,950	
Prepaid Insurance	420	
Land	17,300	
Building	49,000	
Accumulated Depreciation—Building		$ 28,220
Equipment	5,030	
Accumulated Depreciation—Equipment		2,200
Accounts Payable		4,010
Mortgage Note Payable		7,130
R. Clayton, Capital		25,960
R. Clayton, Drawing	31,840	
Fees Earned		56,980
Rent Revenue		3,600
Salaries Expense	15,900	
Utilities Expense	1,130	
Interest Expense	770	
Insurance Expense	350	
Totals	$128,100	$128,100

The following account titles are included in the Chart of Accounts:

Interest Payable	Unearned Fees
Property Tax Payable	Property Tax Expense
Salaries Payable	Depreciation Expense

Consider the following information for adjusting entries:

1. Property tax for 1984 is $530.
2. Depreciation on the equipment is $810. Depreciation on the building is $2,320.
3. An advance fee payment of $100 for surgery to be performed in January was credited to Fees Earned.
4. The mortgage contract provides for a monthly payment of $250 plus accrued interest. The December payment was not made. Interest of $70 is accrued on the mortgage note.
5. Prepaid insurance of $310 has expired.
6. Salaries earned but not paid amount to $590.

Required:

A. Prepare a 10-column worksheet for the year ended December 31, 1984.
B. Prepare an income statement, a capital statement, and a balance sheet.
C. Journalize the closing entries.

Problem 4-3 (Preparation of Worksheet, Financial Statements, and Closing Entries)

Marie Townley owns United Employment Agency. Her accountant prepared the following unadjusted trial balance on June 30, 1984, the end of the fiscal year.

UNITED EMPLOYMENT AGENCY
Unadjusted Trial Balance
June 30, 1984

	Debit	Credit
Cash	$ 2,035	
Accounts Receivable	6,540	
Prepaid Advertising	940	
Office Supplies Inventory	305	
Office Equipment	7,790	
Accumulated Depreciation, Office Equipment		$ 1,140
Accounts Payable		5,835
Unearned Fees		1,290
M. Townley, Capital		4,635
M. Townley, Drawing	11,830	
Placement Fees Earned		44,790
Rent Expense	5,440	
Salaries Expense	21,750	
Telephone Expense	1,060	
Totals	$57,690	$57,690

The following additional information is available at June 30:

1. Advertising costing $630 expired during the year.
2. Unused supplies on hand on June 30 totaled $85.
3. Estimated depreciation on the office equipment is $1,035.
4. The Unearned Fees account includes $155 received for fees earned during June.

Required:
A. Prepare a 10-column worksheet for the year ending June 30, 1984.
B. Prepare an income statement, a capital statement, and a balance sheet.
C. Journalize the closing entries.

Problem 4-4 (The Complete Accounting Cycle)

Mario Coselli owns Harmony Piano Tuning and Repairs. The post-closing trial balance at December 31, 1984, is shown below:

Account Title	Account Number	Debit	Credit
Cash	100	$ 1,640	
Accounts Receivable	101	1,940	
Prepaid Insurance	105	95	
Supplies Inventory	110	105	
Truck	116	10,700	
Accumulated Depreciation, Truck	117		$ 4,013
Accounts Payable	200		970
Interest Payable	204		220
Note Payable	210		3,500
M. Coselli, Capital	300		5,777
Totals		$14,480	$14,480

Transactions completed during 1985 are summarized below:

1. Piano tuning fees of $14,300 were earned during the year; $11,970 of this total was received in cash. The remainder consisted of transactions on account.
2. Revenue from piano repairs was $12,190. Cash received totaled $8,400, and accounts receivable increased by $3,790.
3. Supplies costing $170 were purchased during the year on account.
4. On June 29, the company paid $1,500 on the note payable plus interest of $430. The interest payment consisted of $220 accrued during 1984 and $210 accrued during the first half of 1985.
5. Gas and oil for the truck, paid for in cash, totaled $1,340.
6. Insurance on the truck, paid in advance, was $420.
7. Telephone expense of $1,120 was paid.
8. Accounts receivable of $6,950 were collected.
9. Mario Coselli withdrew $16,460 in cash from the business.

The following information relating to adjusting entries is available at the end of 1985:

10. A physical count of the supplies showed supplies costing $90 on hand at December 31, 1985.
11. Accrued interest on the note payable is $120.
12. Insurance costing $410 expired during the year.
13. Depreciation on the truck is $2,675.
14. The December telephone bill for $90 has not been paid or recorded.

Required:

A. Open T accounts for each of the accounts listed in the post-closing trial balance and the accounts listed below. Insert beginning balances in the accounts as shown in the post-closing trial balance.

Account Title	Account Number
Telephone Expense Payable	205
M. Coselli, Drawing	301
Income Summary	305
Piano Tuning Fees	400
Piano Repair Fees	401
Gas and Oil Expense	500
Telephone Expense	501
Supplies Expense	502
Insurance Expense	503
Depreciation Expense	504
Interest Expense	505

B. Prepare journal entries to record the transactions (numbers 1–9) completed in 1985.
C. Post the entries to the T accounts.
D. Prepare a 10-column worksheet.
E. Prepare an income statement, a capital statement, and a balance sheet.
F. Journalize and post the adjusting entries.
G. Journalize and post the closing entries.
H. Prepare a post-closing trial balance.

Problem 4-5 (Adjusting and Reversing Entries)

The records of the Thomas Company contain the following information at December 31, the end of the fiscal year.

1. Interest of $130 has accrued on a note payable.
2. Wages earned but not paid total $570.
3. Depreciation on the office equipment is $3,345.
4. On September 15, the company paid $1,080 for a six-month advertising campaign beginning on that date. This transaction was recorded by debiting Prepaid Advertising. At the end of the year, advertising costing $720 had expired.

Required:

A. Prepare an adjusting entry for each transaction.
B. Prepare reversing entries where appropriate.

Problem 4-6 (Adjusting Entries, Posting to T Accounts, Reversing Entries, and Entries in Subsequent Period)

Selected accounts taken from the general ledger of Booker Company showed the following balances at December 31, the fiscal year-end.

Prepaid Insurance

12/31 Bal.   1,720

Insurance Expense

12/31 Bal.   -0-

Accrued Interest Receivable

12/31 Bal.   -0-

Interest Revenue

12/31 Bal.   4,200

Accrued Wages Payable

12/31 Bal.   -0-

Wages Expense

12/31 Bal. 77,800

Required:

A. Prepare adjusting entries for the above accounts based on the following data that is not yet recorded:
1. Insurance expired during the year, $620.
2. Wages earned by employees but not paid at year-end, $1,360.
3. Interest accrued but not yet received on notes receivable, $290.

B. Open T accounts for each of the accounts listed above. Enter the December 31 balances and the adjusting entries.

C. Enter in the appropriate accounts the effects of the closing entries that would be made at year-end.

D. Complete the following tabulation:

Account	Balance Before Adjustment	Effects of Adjusting Entries	Balance After Adjustments	Effect of Closing Entries	Balance After Closing Entries
Prepaid Insurance	$1,720	−$620	$1,100	-0-	$1,100
Insurance Expense					
Accrued Interest Receivable					
Interest Revenue					
Accrued Wages Payable					
Wages Expense					

E. The Booker Company follows the practice of making reversing entries. Prepare the reversing entries that would be made on January 1 of the next period. In a balance sheet prepared on January 1, how would the balance in the Interest Revenue and Wages Expense accounts be reported?

F. Record the payment of $1,840 in weekly wages on January 3 and the collection of $350 in interest on January 18. What are the balances in the Wages Expense and Interest Revenue after these entries are posted?

G. Prepare the two entries given in requirement F assuming the company did not prepare reversing entries.

ALTERNATE PROBLEMS

Problem 4-1A (Preparation of Worksheet)

The unadjusted trial balance of the Starr Moving Company is presented below:

STARR MOVING COMPANY
Unadjusted Trial Balance
December 31, 1984

	Debit	Credit
Cash	$ 3,200	
Accounts Receivable	6,430	
Office Supplies Inventory	320	
Moving Vans	46,800	
Accumulated Depreciation, Moving Vans		$ 19,700
Office Equipment	3,100	
Accumulated Depreciation, Office Equipment		1,750
Accounts Payable		5,400
Unearned Transporting Fees		1,130
Paula Starr, Capital		38,300
Paula Starr, Drawing	10,300	
Transporting Fees Earned		46,350
Insurance Expense	4,090	
Wages Expense	27,310	
Advertising Expense	1,940	
Maintenance Expense	3,800	
Gas Expense	5,340	
Totals	$112,630	$112,630

The following additional information should be considered for adjusting entries:

1. A physical inventory showed office supplies totaling $130 on hand at December 31.

2. Depreciation for one year on the moving vans is $4,260. Depreciation on the office equipment is $760.
3. The balance in the Unearned Transporting Fees account includes $340 received in November for moving done in December.
4. Wages earned but not paid amounted to $530.
5. Gas purchased on account for $120 and used during the last week in December has not been paid for or recorded.
6. The December insurance premium of $370 is past due and has not been recorded.
7. The balance in the Advertising Expense account includes $300 prepayment for an advertising campaign beginning in January.

Required:

A. Prepare a 10-column worksheet for the year ended December 31, 1984.
Add the following account titles to those listed in the trial balance: Prepaid Advertising, Depreciation Expense, Office Supplies Expense, Wages Payable, Insurance Expense Payable.

Problem 4-2A (Preparation of Worksheet, Financial Statements, and Closing Entries)

The ledger of Rodney Sinclair, Dentist, contains the following accounts and account balances on December 31, 1984.

Account	Debit	Credit
Cash	$ 2,400	
Accounts Receivable	4,630	
Supplies Inventory	570	
Land	12,800	
Building	73,000	
Accumulated Depreciation—Bldg.		$ 21,900
Dental Equipment	6,750	
Accumulated Depreciation—Equip.		3,210
Accounts Payable		3,980
Unearned Dental Fees		780
Mortgage Notes Payable		44,300
R. Sinclair, Capital		21,035
R. Sinclair, Drawing	26,390	
Dental Fees Earned		78,430
Insurance Expense	830	
Salaries Expense	43,970	
Advertising Expense	380	
Interest Expense	1,045	
Telephone Expense	870	
Totals	$173,635	$173,635

The following account titles are included in the chart of accounts:

Interest Payable   Supplies Expense   Prepaid Insurance
Telephone Expense Payable   Depreciation Expense

The following additional information is also available:

1. According to a physical inventory count, supplies totaling $155 are on hand at December 31.
2. The balance in the Unearned Dental Fees account includes $80 earned for services rendered the last week of December.
3. Estimated depreciation on the dental equipment is $1,240. Depreciation on the building is $3,650.
4. A six-month insurance policy was purchased on September 1 for $450.
5. The December monthly mortgage payment of $450 has not been paid or recorded. In each payment, $95 is attributable to interest.
6. The December telephone bill for $68 is unrecorded.

Required:
A. Prepare a 10-column worksheet for the year ended December 31, 1984.
B. Prepare an income statement, a capital statement, and a balance sheet.
C. Journalize the closing entries.

Problem 4-3A (Preparation of Worksheet, Financial Statements, and Closing Entries)

Executive Travel had the following unadjusted trial balance prepared on September 30, 1984, the end of the fiscal year.

EXECUTIVE TRAVEL
Unadjusted Trial Balance
September 30, 1984

	Debit	Credit
Cash	$ 3,450	
Accounts Receivable	2,670	
Prepaid Rent	1,400	
Office Supplies Inventory	405	
Office Equipment	8,640	
Accumulated Depreciation, Office Equipment		$ 3,105
Accounts Payable		1,970
Note Payable		5,000
Jay Trayner, Capital		3,940
Jay Trayner, Drawing	13,155	
Fees Earned		30,240
Rent Expense	3,500	
Wages Expense	9,740	
Utilities Expense	1,295	
Totals	$44,255	$44,255

Consider the following information for making year-end adjustments.

1. Rent of $1,400 for the four-month period beginning August 1 was paid in advance.
2. A physical inventory count showed supplies totaling $145 on hand at September 30.
3. Depreciation on the office equipment is $1,160.
4. Interest accrued on the note payable amounts to $735.

Required:
A. Prepare a 10-column worksheet for the year ended September 30, 1984.
B. Prepare an income statement, a capital statement, and a balance sheet.
C. Journalize the closing entries.

Problem 4-4A (The Complete Accounting Cycle)

The post-closing trial balance of the Family Counseling Service is shown below:

FAMILY COUNSELING SERVICE
Post-closing Trial Balance
December 31, 1984

Account Title	Account Number	Debit	Credit
Cash	100	$ 3,720	
Accounts Receivable	101	2,950	
Prepaid Rent	102	380	
Office Supplies Inventory	106	410	
Furniture and Equipment	110	8,975	
Accumulated Depreciation, Furniture & Equip.	111		$ 3,040
Accounts Payable	200		1,700
Salaries Payable	201		130
Julie Long, Capital	300		11,565
Totals		$16,435	$16,435

Transactions completed during 1985 are summarized below:

1. Counseling fees of $27,860 were earned during the year. Clients are billed after their appointments and are given 30 days in which to pay.
2. Collections on accounts receivable totaled $25,910.
3. $4,560 was spent to pay the rent in advance.

4. Office supplies were purchased during the year for $55 in cash and $130 on account.
5. Salary payments amounted to $9,980, of which $130 was for salaries accrued in 1984.
6. Utilities expense of $1,035 was paid.
7. Advertising totaling $950 was purchased on account.
8. Accounts payable of $830 were paid.
9. Julie Long withdrew $6,980.

The following additional information should be considered for adjusting entries.

10. Depreciation on the furniture and equipment is $1,340.
11. Rent for six months of $2,280 was paid in advance on February 1 and August 1.
12. Unused office supplies on hand at the end of the year totaled $210.
13. Salaries earned but not paid amount to $270.

Required:
A. Prepare the company's ledger by opening T accounts for the accounts listed in the post-closing trial balance and for the accounts listed below. Post the December 31, 1984, balances.

Account Title	Account Number
Julie Long, Drawing	301
Income Summary	320
Counseling Fees Revenue	400
Salaries Expense	500
Utilities Expense	503
Advertising Expense	504
Depreciation Expense	505
Rent Expense	512
Office Supplies Expense	513

B. Prepare journal entries to record the transactions completed (numbers 1–9) during 1985.
C. Post the entries to the T accounts.
D. Prepare a 10-column worksheet for the year ended December 31, 1985.
E. Prepare an income statement, a capital statement, and a balance sheet.
F. Journalize and post the adjusting entries.
G. Journalize and post the closing entries.
H. Prepare a post-closing trial balance.

Problem 4-5A (Adjusting and Reversing Entries)
The following information concerning Kramer and Sons Company is available at June 30, the end of the fiscal year.

1. Kramer and Sons received $780 rental income on May 1 for the three-month period beginning on that date. The transaction was recorded by a credit to Unearned Rental Income.
2. The June utilities bill for $115 has not been paid or recorded.
3. Interest earned but not received totals $614.
4. Prepaid Insurance was debited for $420 on February 28 to record the cost of a six-month policy beginning March 1.

Required:
A. Prepare an adjusting entry for each item.
B. Prepare reversing entries where appropriate.

CHAPTER 5
ACCOUNTING FOR MERCHANDISING OPERATIONS

OVERVIEW AND OBJECTIVES

This chapter describes accounting procedures for businesses that buy and sell merchandise inventory. When you have completed the chapter, you should understand:

- The nature of merchandise inventory (p. 205).
- The basic format of an income statement prepared for a merchandising firm (pp. 225–227).
- The various credit terms related to the sale of inventory (pp. 207–209).
- How to identify the various accounts used to record the purchase and sale of inventory (pp. 206–217).
- The difference between perpetual and periodic inventory systems (pp. 218–220).
- How to record inventory transactions for both inventory systems (pp. 211–217).
- How to prepare a worksheet for both inventory systems (pp. 220–225).
- How to complete the closing process for both inventory systems (pp. 223–225).

In preceding chapters, a business organized to render personal services was used to illustrate the accounting cycle. Service firms, which make up a significant part of our economy and provide a wide range of important services, include law firms, accounting firms, motels, barber and beauty shops, airlines, advertising agencies, golf courses, theaters, and photography studios. The primary business activity of many other firms centers on goods rather than services. *Manufacturing firms* (accounting for which is covered in later chapters) purchase raw materials and component parts for conversion into finished products. *Merchandising* or *trading firms,* which often distribute at both the wholesale and retail levels, purchase goods that are in a form ready to be sold to their customers. In this chapter, we will consider the accounting problems associated with the operations of a merchandising firm. Although the accounting principles and methods described in earlier chapters apply to merchandising firms, a number of additional accounts and procedures are used to record inventory transactions.

MERCHANDISE INVENTORY

The term **merchandise inventory** or simply **inventory** is used in a merchandising operation to designate tangible assets held for sale in the normal course of the business. Other assets held for future disposition but not normally sold as part of the regular business activities, such as an item of used office equipment that is no longer needed, are not included in the inventory category.

MERCHANDISING FIRM OPERATIONS

As described in Chapter 3, the normal operating cycle for a merchandising firm is the average length of time it takes for the firm to acquire inventory, sell that inventory to its customers, and collect cash from the sale. At the time of purchase, inventory is recorded at cost—in accordance with the cost principle. The cost of inventory available for future sale is reported in the balance sheet as a current asset. When a sale is made, both an asset and a revenue are recorded in an amount equal to the sales price. In the income statement, the cost of inventory sold during the current period is matched with revenue received from selling it. Proper matching of costs and revenues is, in fact, a major objective of accounting for inventory. It involves determining the amount of the total inventory cost to be deducted from sales in the current period and the amount to be carried forward as an asset to be expensed in some future period.

Inventory is one of the most active assets in a merchandising firm. It is continually being acquired, sold, and replaced. Inventories also make up a significant part of a firm's total assets. The cost of goods sold for a given period is frequently the firm's largest expense, sometimes exceeding the sum of all operating expenses. For these reasons, the control and safeguarding of inventory is essential for efficient and profitable operations.

INCOME STATEMENT FOR A MERCHANDISING FIRM

A condensed income statement for Sunrise Hi-Fi Sales, a merchandising firm, is shown below:

SUNRISE HI-FI SALES
Income Statement
For Year Ended December 31, 1986

Net sales		$172,000
Less: Cost of goods sold		103,000
Gross profit on sales		$ 69,000
Less: Operating expenses		
Selling expenses	$26,000	
Administrative expenses	18,000	
Total operating expenses		44,000
Net income		$ 25,000

A comparison of this income statement with the one prepared for Starbuck Real Estate Office on page 114 reveals several differences. First, revenue earned is the first item reported in both cases, but for a merchandising firm revenue is called **sales.** Second, a major difference is the inclusion in the income statement of Sunrise Hi-Fi Sales of a **cost of goods sold** section that shows the total cost of the inventory that was sold during the period. The cost of goods sold is subtracted from sales to arrive at an intermediate income amount called **gross profit** or **gross margin on sales.** Third, operating expenses are subtracted from gross profit on sales to determine the net income (or net loss) for the period. Although many of the operating expenses incurred by a service firm are also incurred by a merchandising firm, additional expenses that relate to buying and selling inventory are incurred by a merchandising firm. Operating expenses are normally separated by function. **Selling expenses** result from efforts to sell the inventory and include storage costs, advertising, sales salaries and commissions, and the cost of delivering goods to customers. **Administrative expenses** are those associated with operating such subdivisions of the firm as the general office, accounting, personnel, and credit and collection departments.

ACCOUNTING FOR SALES TRANSACTIONS

A sales transaction is generally recorded by the seller when the inventory is transferred from the firm to the customer. To record the sale, an asset account is debited and the Sales account is credited. The asset recorded in exchange for the inventory is normally cash or accounts receivable. The entry to record a credit sale is:

Aug.	5	Accounts Receivable* Sales Sold merchandise to Ray Stevens on account.	180	180

*Cash account is debited if a cash sale.

At year's end, the balance in the Sales account shows the total amount of cash and credit sales made during the accounting period. When a sale is made on account, the cash may be received in a subsequent period. As a result, there may be a significant difference between cash collections from sales and the balance accumulated in the Sales account.

SALES RETURNS AND ALLOWANCES

In order to maintain good customer relations and honor warranty agreements, most businesses permit a customer to return unsatisfactory goods. Alternatively, the customer may agree to keep the goods in exchange for a reduction in the sales price. The return of goods or an adjustment to the sales price is a reduction in the amount of recorded sales, and either a cash refund is made to the customer or his or her account receivable is credited. Handling returned merchandise is time-consuming and results in increased costs. For these reasons management must look for the cause of excessive returns and correct the problem whenever possible. To provide information on the volume of returns and allowances, a contra sales account called **Sales Returns and Allowances** is debited as follows:

Aug.	8	Sales Returns and Allowances Accounts Receivable Ray Stevens returned unsatisfactory merchandise sold on Aug. 5 for credit. (Making only one entry at this time assumes use of the periodic inventory system, discussed in a later section of this chapter.)	30	30

As shown on page 209, sales returns and allowances are subtracted from sales in the income statement.

CASH DISCOUNTS

The parties involved in an inventory transaction may agree that payment is to be made immediately upon transfer of the goods as a cash sale, or payment may be delayed for some specific length of time called the **credit period.** The length of the credit period varies among firms.

When inventory is sold on credit, the terms of payment, called the **credit terms,** agreed to by the buyer and seller should be clear as to the amount due and the credit period. The terms of payment normally appear in the business document called the *sales invoice* by the seller and the *purchase invoice* by the buyer. The credit period is usually abbreviated in the following form: *"n/10 EOM" or "n/30."* In the first case, the invoice price is due 10 days after the end of the month. In the second case, the invoice price is due within 30 days after the invoice date.

To provide an incentive for the buyer to make payment before the end of the credit period, the seller may grant a **cash discount** called a **sales discount** by the seller and **purchase discount** by the buyer. A cash discount entitles the buyer to deduct a specified percentage of the net sales price if payment is received within a given time span, the **discount period.** The terms are normally quoted in a format such as: *"2/10, n/30"* (Read "two ten, net thirty"). This notation means that the buyer has two payment options. If payment is made within 10 days of the invoice date, the buyer may deduct 2% from the amount of the invoice. If payment is not made within the 10-day discount period, the full price is due 30 days from the invoice date.

To illustrate, assume that the credit terms were 2/10, n/30 on the $180 sale to Ray Stevens recorded above. The entry to record the collection within the discount period, net of the $30 return, is:

Aug.	15	Cash	147	
		Sales Discounts ($150 × 2%)	3	
		Accounts Receivable ($180 − $30)		150
		Received payment from Ray		
		Stevens within the discount		
		period.		

The above entries are based on the assumption that sales are recorded at the gross invoice price, called the **gross invoice method.** Under this method, sales discounts are not recorded unless the customer takes advantage of the cash discount. If the customer pays within the discount period, as above, a sales discount is recorded in a separate account in order to provide information to management on the amount of sales discount taken by customers. A sales discount is considered a reduction in the sales price of the goods and is reported as a subtraction from sales revenue in the income statement.

From the seller's point of view, the purpose for granting cash discounts is to have the cash available for use before the end of the credit period. The earlier payment may also tend to reduce losses from uncollectible accounts receivable. To the buyer, taking advantage of the discount results in a favorable return for the use of the money, which can be shown by converting the discount rate to an annual rate. For example, with terms of 2/10, n/30 on a $300 invoice, the added cost of waiting 20 days to make payment at the end of the credit period is $6 ($300 × 2%). This is equivalent to an effective annual interest rate of 36% (360/20 = 18 periods per year × 2% per period).

Sales returns and allowances and sales discounts are subtracted from sales to arrive at net sales in the income statement as illustrated below:

Revenue from sales:		
Gross sales		$177,600
Less: Sales returns & allowances	$3,400	
Sales discounts	2,200	5,600
Net sales		$172,000

TRADE DISCOUNTS

A **trade discount** is a percentage reduction granted to a customer from the suggested list price. In contrast to a cash discount, a trade discount is not related to early payment but is used in determining the actual invoice price to the customer. Trade discounts enable the firm to print one price list but still vary prices.

Trade discounts are not normally recorded in the accounts by either the buyer or the seller. For example, assume that a wholesaler quotes a list price of $200 per item but grants a trade discount of 30% to retailers if they purchased in quantities of 10 or more. If included in the terms of the sale, a cash discount is computed on the $1,400 sales price less any subsequent returns or allowances. The entry to record the sale of 10 units is:

July	10	Accounts Receivable	1,400	
		Sales ($200 × 10 units × 70%)		1,400
		To record the sale of inventory on credit subject to a 30% trade discount.		

The buyer will record a purchase of inventory in the amount of $1,400.

FREIGHT-OUT

The sales invoice will normally indicate which party to the transaction must pay the cost of shipping the goods. If the goods are sold **FOB (free on board) shipping point,** freight costs incurred from the point of shipment are paid by the buyer. The term **FOB destination** means that the seller is responsible for paying the freight cost.

When the terms of the sale are FOB destination, the seller will normally record the payment of freight costs as a debit to a **Freight-out** or **Delivery Expense** account. Freight-out is an expense and should be reported in the selling expense category of the income statement. Freight charges paid by the seller on goods sold should not be confused with freight charges incurred on goods purchased, which is discussed later in the chapter.

ACCOUNTING FOR INVENTORY AND COST OF GOODS SOLD

Two distinctly different inventory systems, perpetual and periodic, are used to determine the amounts reported for the ending inventory and the cost of goods sold. The system adopted by a firm is largely determined by the type of inventory held.

PERPETUAL INVENTORY SYSTEM

A **perpetual inventory system** involves keeping a current and continuous record of all inventory transactions on a separate inventory card for each type of inventory item held. Each inventory card shows the quantity, unit cost, and total cost for each purchase, each sale, and the inventory balance. When each item is different, as with automobiles that have different options and cost, a separate inventory card is maintained for each item. Figure 5-1 is an example of an inventory card for a certain type of refrigerator. The total dollar value of all inventory held by the firm on any given date is determined by adding the balances of the individual cards.

A perpetual inventory system is often used because it provides more timely information to management for use in controlling and planning for inventory. However, because the maintenance of individual records involves much cler-

Figure 5-1
Inventory Card

Item Code	Refrigerator GE1120				Location 1 unit showroom, Remainder—Warehouse				Minimum Stock 4 Maximum Stock 17		
		Purchases			Sales			Balance			
Date	Explanation	Units	Unit Cost	Total Cost	Units	Unit Cost	Total Cost	Units	Unit Cost	Total Cost
1/1	Beginning Balance							4	650	2,600
1/15	Purchase	10	650	6,500				14	650	9,100
1/21	Sales				3	650	1,950	11	650	7,150
1/23	Purchase returns	(1)	650	(650)				10	650	6,500
1/24	Sales returns				(1)	650	(650)	11	650	7,150

ical work, the system is usually used by firms that sell inventory of high unit value such as automobiles, heating and air-conditioning units, works of art, pianos, television sets, stereo equipment, and home appliances. In the past, many small firms and firms that sold a large number of items with a low cost found the cost of maintaining a perpetual inventory system prohibitive. In recent years, with the introduction of computers and other electronic business machines with various capabilities, more and more firms have found it feasible to use a perpetual inventory system in order to better plan and control their investment in inventory. In particular, the development of on-site computers has been a real breakthrough for the perpetual inventory system. For example, many grocery stores now use optical-scan cash registers that not only record the sales price of the item but also enter the item sold for inventory purposes. Firms adopt the perpetual system because they believe the benefits obtained from detailed inventory records outweigh the additional cost of maintaining the system.

ILLUSTRATION OF A PERPETUAL INVENTORY SYSTEM

In a merchandising firm, when the perpetual inventory method is used, a single account is maintained in the general ledger to record all inventory transactions. Supporting details are entered in individual inventory cards. One card is maintained for each type of item held in inventory. The balance in the general ledger account should equal the sum of the dollar amounts shown on the inventory cards. Entries to record inventory transactions are made to both the inventory account and the appropriate inventory cards. A purchase of inventory is recorded as an increase; the cost of goods sold is recorded as a decrease. To determine the dollar cost of each sale, the accountant refers to the individual inventory card of the item sold. An item sold must therefore be identified so that the unit and related cost may be removed from the proper inventory card and the cost removed from the inventory account in the general ledger.

To illustrate the entries required under a perpetual inventory system, assume that a firm sells high-cost home appliances. The entries that follow are based on the transactions recorded on the inventory card presented in Figure 5-1.

The Merchandise Inventory account in the general ledger at the beginning of the period in T account form is:

Merchandise Inventory	
1/1 Beg. Bal. 2,600	
(4 units @ $650)	

(In actuality, the balance in this account would be much larger and would show the total cost of all types of appliances held at the beginning of the period rather than the cost of these refrigerators only.)

Entries to record the transactions for January are presented below:

Transaction 1: Purchased 10 units @ $650 per unit.

Jan.	15	Merchandise Inventory	6,500	
		Accounts Payable		6,500
		Purchased 10 refrigerators at $650		
		per unit on account from Frig King		
		Incorporated. Terms 2/10, n/30.		
		Invoice Date: Jan. 15.		

The purchase is recorded as a debit to the Merchandise Inventory account and a credit to Accounts Payable in the amount of the gross invoice price. At the same time, the purchase is entered on the perpetual inventory card and a new balance is computed.

Transaction 2: Paid freight cost of $426 on inventory shipped FOB shipping point.

Conceptually, the cost of an asset, in this case inventory, includes the invoice price plus freight charges and other costs directly related to acquiring the merchandise. If the seller charges the list price and pays the freight, it is not separated on the invoice and becomes a part of the inventory cost when the entry is made to record the purchase transaction. If the seller pays the freight and charges the buyer, it will normally be listed separately on the invoice and is debited to an account called **Freight-in** or **Transportation-in.** This same account is used to record freight costs paid by the buyer when the terms of the sale are FOB shipping point. Freight costs that are listed separately are normally recorded in a Freight-in account because of the practical problem of allocating freight cost to individual units when several different inventory items are included in a single shipment. Furthermore, in most cases the allocation of freight cost would not significantly change the financial statements of the firm. To illustrate, assume that the terms of the January 15 transaction were FOB shipping point and costs of $426 were incurred. The entry to record payment of the freight is:

Jan.	17	Freight-in	426	
		Cash		426
		Paid freight cost on merchandise		
		purchased FOB shipping point.		

In the income statement, the freight-in for the period is generally added as a separate item to the cost of goods sold or is combined directly into the amount reported as the cost of goods sold.

Transaction 3: Sold 3 units for $1,050 per unit; cost $650 per unit.

Jan.	21	Accounts Receivable	3,150	
		Sales		3,150
		Sold three refrigerators on account		
		($1,050 × 3 units)		
Jan.	21	Cost of Goods Sold	1,950	
		Merchandise Inventory		1,950
		To remove the cost of refrigerators		
		sold from the Merchandise		
		Inventory account ($650 × 3		
		units).		

When a perpetual inventory system is used, each sale will require two entries. One entry records the sale. A second entry records the expense in the Cost of Goods Sold account and reduces the Merchandise Inventory account. Thus, reductions are made to the Merchandise Inventory account and to the individual inventory card at the time a sale occurs. Note carefully that the sales entry is based on the sales price, whereas the amount of the inventory entry is based on the cost of the units sold as shown in the inventory card.

Transaction 4: Returned to the manufacturer a defective unit, which cost $650.

Jan.	23	Accounts Payable	650	
		Merchandise Inventory		650
		Defective unit returned to Frig King		
		for credit on account.		

When the buyer and seller agree that an item is to be returned for credit, the Merchandise Inventory account and the inventory card are both reduced to show that the item is no longer being held.

Transaction 5: Paid for purchases made on January 15 within the discount period.

Accounting for cash discounts by the seller and the notation (2/10, n/30) used to describe the credit terms have already been discussed. Recall that a cash discount entitles the buyer to deduct a specified amount from the invoice price if payment is made within a specified time period.

The entry to record the payment within the discount period is:

Jan.	24	Accounts Payable ($6,500 − $650)	5,850	
		Cash		5,733
		Purchase Discounts ($5,850 × 2%)		117
		Paid for inventory purchased on		
		Jan. 15.		

If the payment were not made within the discount period, the credit to Cash in the entry would be for $5,850. Although the Purchase Discounts account has a credit balance, it is not revenue to the firm. A firm does not realize revenue by purchasing goods; it realizes revenue from selling them. When purchases are recorded at the gross invoice price, in a perpetual inventory system purchase discounts should be reported as a reduction in cost of goods sold.

Transaction 6: A unit that was sold for $1,050 is returned by a customer for credit. The unit cost $650.

Jan.	24	Sales Returns and Allowances	1,050	
		Accounts Receivable		1,050
		A refrigerator sold on 1/21 was		
		returned by customer.		
Jan.	24	Merchandise Inventory	650	
		Cost of Goods Sold		650
		Returned refrigerator was placed		
		back in stock.		

An item returned by a customer also requires two entries. The first entry records the sales return. Because it is assumed that the unit is still suitable for sale, a second entry is necessary to eliminate the cost of goods sold and restore the unit to the Merchandise Inventory account. The unit is also entered in the inventory card. Again note that the first entry is based on the original sales price of $1,050 whereas in the second entry the inventory is recorded at its cost, $650.

The Merchandise Inventory account in the general ledger after the above transactions are posted would appear as follows:

Merchandise Inventory

1/1 Beg. Bal.	2,600	1/21	1,950
1/15	6,500	1/23	650
1/24	650		
1/31 Balance	7,150		

Observe that the balance in the inventory account agrees with the balance in the inventory card (see Figure 5-1 on page 210). By maintaining a continuous inventory record, it is not necessary to take a physical count of the inventory on hand to determine the inventory balance. Firms using a perpetual inventory system nevertheless should take a physical inventory once a year to verify the accuracy of the inventory records. A **physical inventory** involves first counting all inventory units on hand. Next, the unit cost of each type of item in stock is determined from purchase invoices and multiplied by the appropriate number of units to determine the dollar cost of that particular item. The dollar cost of the entire inventory is the sum of the individual costs determined for each item. Differences between the physical count and the inventory records could result from clerical error, theft of goods, breakage, and obsolescence. Causes of large discrepancies should be identified and eliminated if at all possible. In some cases, the difference may result from natural causes such as evaporation or shrinkage. Taking a physical inventory is discussed in more detail in Chapter 9.

When the physical inventory and the inventory account balances differ, a journal entry is made to bring the account balance into agreement with the physical count. The entry to reduce the Merchandise Inventory account by $386 is:

Dec.	31	Inventory Loss	386	
		Merchandise Inventory		386
		To adjust the inventory account to the physical count.		

The Inventory Loss account is for management information only. Normally the account is included with the cost of goods sold in the income statement.

PERIODIC INVENTORY SYSTEM

Many firms that sell a large number of items with a low cost per unit find the maintenance of perpetual inventory records too costly and time-consuming to be practical unless they have access to a computer. Such firms include drugstores, variety stores, hardware stores, and grocery stores. A store operating with high volume may conveniently record the amount of each sale, but would find it difficult to trace each item sold back to detailed inventory cards. Firms that do not use a perpetual inventory system use a **periodic inventory system.**

ILLUSTRATION OF A PERIODIC INVENTORY SYSTEM

In a periodic inventory system, the beginning balance in the Merchandise Inventory account is not changed until the end of the accounting period. The costs of additional inventory purchases made during a period are recorded in a Purchases account rather than in the Merchandise Inventory account. When inventory is sold, only one entry is made and that is to record the sale. The additional entry made to record the cost of goods sold when a perpetual inventory system is used is not made under a periodic inventory system. Since no record of the goods sold is maintained during the period, it is necessary to count the units on hand and multiply the number of units times the cost per unit to determine the cost of goods on hand. Once this is completed, the cost of goods sold is computed as follows:

Cost of beginning inventory	$2,600
Add: Net cost of goods purchased during the current period	6,159
Cost of goods available for sale	8,759
Less: Cost of ending inventory (per physical count)	7,150
Cost of goods sold	$1,609

The ending inventory for the current period will become the beginning inventory for the following period. The process of adjusting the inventory account to its end of year balance is discussed later in this chapter.

A periodic inventory system is illustrated below. So that you may compare a periodic system with a perpetual system, the illustration is based on the same data used in the perpetual illustration. In practice, remember, the periodic system would be used when selling a volume of low-priced items. The inventory account at the beginning of the period is:

Merchandise Inventory

1/1 Beg. Bal. 2,600	
(4 units @ $650)	

The beginning inventory of $2,600 is the ending inventory determined by a physical inventory conducted on the last day of the preceding period.

Transaction 1: Purchased 10 units @ $650 per unit.

Jan.	15	Purchases	6,500	
		Accounts Payable		6,500
		Purchased 10 refrigerators at $650		
		per unit on account from Frig King		
		Incorporated. Terms 2/10, n/30.		
		Invoice Date: Jan 15.		

The **Purchases** account is a temporary account used to accumulate the cost of all merchandise acquired for resale during the period. This account is used to record inventory purchases only. Other acquisitions of assets are recorded in appropriate asset accounts. Because the balance is closed at the end of each accounting period, the accumulated account balance reflects the purchases for the current period.

Transaction 2: Paid freight cost of $426 on inventory purchased FOB shipping point.

Jan.	17	Freight-in	426	
		Cash		426
		Paid freight cost on merchandise		
		purchased FOB shipping point.		

Freight-in is reported as an addition to purchases.

Transaction 3: Sold 3 units for $1,050 per unit, which cost $650 per unit.

Jan.	21	Accounts Receivable	3,150	
		Sales		3,150
		Sold inventory on account.		

At the time of sale, only one entry is made to record the sale. A second entry is not made to record the cost of goods sold.

Transaction 4: Returned to the manufacturer a defective unit, which cost $650 per unit.

Jan.	23	Accounts Payable	650	
		Purchase Returns and Allowances		650
		Defective unit returned to Frig King for		
		credit on account.		

There is a cost to the firm to order merchandise, receive and inspect the merchandise, and to repack it for return to the seller. To provide relevant information to management concerning the total amount of goods returned, the return is recorded in a contra purchases account, **Purchase Returns and Allowances,** rather than directly as a credit to the Purchases account. The entry is the same if the goods are kept by the buyer and an adjustment is made to the invoice price.

Transaction 5: Paid for purchases made on January 15 within the discount period.

Jan.	24	Accounts Payable ($6,500 − $650)	5,850	
		Cash		5,733
		Purchase Discounts ($5,850 × 2%)		117
		Paid for inventory purchased on		
		Jan. 15.		

Note that this entry is the same as the one made under the perpetual inventory system. In a periodic system, purchase discounts are reported as a contra account to purchases.

Transaction 6: A unit that was sold for $1,050 is returned by a customer for credit.

Jan.	24	Sales Returns and Allowances	1,050	
		Accounts Receivable		1,050
		A refrigerator sold on 1/21 was		
		returned by customer.		

When a periodic inventory system is used, only one entry is needed to record the merchandise returned. A second entry, to reverse the cost of goods sold, is not needed here because the cost of goods sold was not recorded on the date of sale.

PERPETUAL AND PERIODIC INVENTORY SYSTEMS CONTRASTED

The two basic differences between the perpetual and periodic inventory systems are illustrated with the entries shown in Figure 5-2. First, under the perpetual inventory system the balance in the Merchandise Inventory account provides a continuous and current record of inventory on hand. Second, a perpetual system provides for an accumulation of the cost of goods sold during the period. In contrast, a physical inventory must be taken to determine the inventory on hand and the cost of goods sold when a periodic inventory system is used. A physical inventory is taken under the perpetual system only to verify the accuracy of the ending inventory. Also note that a Purchases account is maintained with a periodic system, whereas a Cost of Goods Sold account is maintained with a perpetual system.

Based on the six transactions recorded in Figure 5-2, income statements are prepared in Figure 5-3 for both systems. It is assumed that a physical inventory taken at the end of the period confirmed that 11 units were on hand. The dollar amount is computed to be $7,150 (11 units × $650). Note that the net sales, cost of goods sold, and gross profit on sales are the same in both income statements.

Some relationships shown in statement format for the periodic inventory system are summarized below:

1. Gross profit on sales = Net sales − Cost of goods sold

   or

   Net Sales = Cost of goods sold + Gross profit on sales
2. Cost of goods available for sale = Cost of beginning inventory + cost of net purchases
3. Cost of goods sold = Cost of goods available for sale − cost of ending inventory

   or

   Cost of goods sold = Cost of beginning inventory + cost of net purchases − cost of ending inventory

Familiarity with these relationships will aid you in understanding the characteristics of the periodic inventory system and make it easier for you to determine the effect of inventory errors.

Observe that under the periodic inventory system, the cost of goods sold is a residual amount that is left after deducting the ending inventory from the cost of goods available for sale. As a result, losses of inventory from causes such as theft, shrinkage, breakage, and clerical error are difficult to identify. Techniques used to determine any large inventory losses are examined in Chapter 9.

Figure 5-2
Comparison of Entries to Record Inventory Transactions Under Perpetual and. Periodic Inventory Systems

Data: Cost per unit $ 650
        Selling price per unit $1,050
        Beginning inventory   4 units

Perpetual Inventory System   Periodic Inventory System

Merchandise Inventory account—Beginning of the period.

Merchandise Inventory		**Merchandise Inventory**	
4 units 2,600		4 units 2,600	

1. Purchased 10 units of merchandise on credit. Terms 2/10, n/30; FOB shipping point.

Merchandise Inventory	6,500		Purchases	6,500	
(10 × $650)					
Accounts Payable		6,500	Accounts Payable		6,500

2. Paid freight cost.

Freight-in	426		Freight-in	426	
Cash		426	Cash		426

3. Sold 3 units to customers on account.

Accounts Receivable	3,150		Accounts Receivable	3,150	
Sales (3 × $1,050)		3,150	Sales		3,150
Cost of Goods Sold	1,950				
Merchandise					
Inventory (3 × $650)		1,950			

4. Returned 1 unit for credit on account.

Accounts Payable	650		Accounts Payable	650	
Merchandise			Purchase Returns		
Inventory (1 × $650)		650	and Allowances		650

5. Paid for purchases within discount period.

Accounts Payable	5,850		Accounts Payable	5,850	
Cash		5,733	Cash		5,733
Purchase Discounts		117	Purchase Discounts		117

6. Customer returned 1 unit for credit on account.

Sales Returns and			Sales Returns and		
Allowances	1,050		Allowances	1,050	
Accounts Receivable		1,050	Accounts Receivable		1,050
Merchandise Inventory					
(1 × $650)	650				
Cost of Goods Sold		650			

Figure 5-3
Partial Income Statements, Perpetual and Periodic Inventory Systems

Perpetual Inventory System

Sales	$3,150
Less: Sales returns and allowances (discounts)	1,050
Net sales	2,100
Cost of goods sold*	1,609
Gross profit on sales	491

*Freight-in and purchase discounts are combined with cost of goods sold.
1,609 = 1,300 + 426 − 117   inv loss +

Periodic Inventory System

Sales			$3,150
Less: Sales returns and allowances			1,050
Net sales			2,100
Cost of goods sold:			
Cost of beginning merchandise inventory		$2,600	
Add: Cost of purchases	$6,500		
Freight-in	426		
	6,926		
Less: Purchase returns and allowances	650		
Purchase discounts	117	767	
Cost of net purchases		6,159	
Cost of goods available for sale		8,759	
Less: Cost of ending merchandise inventory		7,150	
Cost of goods sold			1,609
Gross profit on sales			491

END OF PERIOD PROCESS

ILLUSTRATION OF WORKSHEETS FOR A MERCHANDISING FIRM

At the end of the accounting period, after all the year's transactions have been posted to the ledger, a worksheet can be used to organize the information needed to prepare financial statements and closing entries. Worksheets for a perpetual and a periodic inventory system are presented in Figures 5-4 and 5-5 for Sunrise Hi-Fi Sales, a corporation.

In both illustrations, the first two columns (Unadjusted Trial Balance) contain a listing of the account balances taken from the general ledger of the company. For simplicity, the various types of selling and administrative expense accounts have been combined into one account for each category. Usually, a trial balance would consist of a complete listing of all accounts. The next two columns are for the end of year adjustments based on the following information:

SUNRISE HI-FI SALES
Worksheet
For Year Ended December 31, 1985

	Unadjusted Trial Balance		Adjustments		Adjusted Trial Balance		Income Statement		Balance Sheet	
	Debit	Credit	Debit	Credit	Debit	Credit	Debit	Credit	Debit	Credit
Cash	41,170				41,170				41,170	
Accounts Receivable	98,710				98,710				98,710	
Inventory	53,260				53,260				53,260	
Prepaid Insurance	1,910			(d) 610	1,300				1,300	
Store Equipment	72,000				72,000				72,000	
Accumulated Depr.—Store Equipment		46,600		(b) 7,600		54,200				54,200
Office Equipment	26,400				26,400				26,400	
Accumulated Depr.—Office Equipment		13,300		(c) 3,200		16,500				16,500
Accounts Payable		107,610				107,610				107,610
Common Stock		50,000				50,000				50,000
Retained Earnings		36,000				36,000				36,000
Dividends Declared	10,000				10,000				10,000	
Sales		714,280				714,280		714,280		
Sales Returns & Allowances	21,390				21,390		21,390			
Sales Discount	3,260				3,260		3,260			
Cost of Goods Sold	464,280				464,280		464,280			
Freight-in	6,210				6,210		6,210			
Purchase Discounts		2,860				2,860		2,860		
Selling Expenses	90,470		(a) 2,200 (b) 7,600		100,270		100,270			
Administrative Expenses	73,990		(a) 1,050 (c) 3,200 (d) 610		78,850		78,850			
Income Tax Expense	9,000		(e) 1,470		10,470		10,470			
Interest Expense	1,000				1,000		1,000			
Rent Revenue		2,400				2,400		2,400		
	973,050	973,050								
Salaries Payable				(a) 3,250		3,250				3,250
Income Taxes Payable				(e) 1,470		1,470				1,470
			16,130	16,130	988,570	988,570	685,730	719,540	302,840	269,030
Net Income for the Period							33,810			33,810
							719,540	719,540	302,840	302,840

Figure 5-4
Perpetual Inventory System

1. Accrued salaries: Sales $2,200
                   Administrative   1,050
2. Depreciation: Store Equipment   7,600
                   Office Equipment   3,200
3. Prepaid insurance expired during the year   610
4. Unpaid income taxes at the end of the period   1,470

Based on a physical inventory taken December 31 of each year, the ending merchandise inventory was determined to be $53,260 at the end of the current period and was $58,400 at the end of the prior period.

Figure 5-5
Periodic Inventory System

SUNRISE HI-FI SALES
Worksheet
For Year Ended December 31, 1985

	Unadjusted Trial Balance		Adjustments		Adjusted Trial Balance		Income Statement		Balance Sheet	
	Debit	Credit	Debit	Credit	Debit	Credit	Debit	Credit	Debit	Credit
Cash	41,170				41,170				41,170	
Accounts Receivable	98,710				98,710				98,710	
Inventory—1/1	58,400				58,400		58,400	53,260	53,260	
Prepaid Insurance	1,910			(d) 610	1,300				1,300	
Store Equipment	72,000				72,000				72,000	
Accumulated Depr.—Store Equipment		46,600		(b) 7,600		54,200				54,200
Office Equipment	26,400				26,400				26,400	
Accumulated Depr.—Office Equipment		13,300		(c) 3,200		16,500				16,500
Accounts Payable		107,610				107,610				107,610
Common Stock		50,000				50,000				50,000
Retained Earnings		36,000				36,000				36,000
Dividends Declared	10,000				10,000				10,000	
Sales		714,280				714,280		714,280		
Sales Returns & Allowances	21,390				21,390		21,390			
Sales Discount	3,260				3,260		3,260			
Purchases	472,620				472,620		472,620			
Freight-in	6,210				6,210		6,210			
Purchase Returns & Allowances		13,480				13,480		13,480		
Purchase Discounts		2,860				2,860		2,860		
Selling Expenses	90,470		(a) 2,200 (b) 7,600		100,270		100,270			
Administrative Expenses	73,990		(a) 1,050 (c) 3,200 (d) 610		78,850		78,850			
Income Tax Expense	9,000		(e) 1,470		10,470		10,470			
Interest Expense	1,000				1,000		1,000			
Rent Revenue		2,400				2,400		2,400		
	986,530	986,530								
Salaries Payable				(a) 3,250		3,250				3,250
Income Taxes Payable				(e) 1,470		1,470				1,470
			16,130	16,130	1,002,050	1,002,050	752,470	786,280	302,840	269,030
Net Income for the Period							33,810			33,810
							786,280	786,280	302,840	302,840

A worksheet prepared for a business organized as a corporation is essentially the same as the one illustrated in Chapter 4 for a single proprietorship. In the trial balance columns there are new owners' equity accounts—Common Stock ($50,000 credit), Retained Earnings ($36,000 credit), and Dividends Declared ($10,000 debit)—that appear in place of the owner's capital and drawing accounts. These new accounts are extended to the appropriate Balance Sheet columns. In addition, an Income Tax Expense balance of $9,000 is included in the Unadjusted Trial Balance debit column. As noted in Chapter 4, the income of a corporation is subject to state and federal income taxes. Federal tax laws and some states require that a corporation estimate its tax liability at the beginning of the year and pay the tax in installments. Such advance payments are recorded as debits to Income Tax Expense. In this illustration, $9,000 in taxes had been prepaid during the year. At the end of the period, the income subject to tax and the resulting tax expense is computed on forms provided by the Internal Revenue Service. It is assumed that the total tax expense for Sunrise Hi-Fi Sales is $10,470. To recognize the unpaid portion of the taxes ($10,470 − $9,000), one additional adjusting entry [entry (e)] is made in the Adjustments column to debit Income Tax Expense and credit Income Taxes Payable. The Income Tax Expense account is extended to the Income Statement debit column, and the Income Taxes Payable is extended to the Balance Sheet credit column.

PERPETUAL INVENTORY SYSTEM

When a perpetual inventory system is used to account for the flow of goods, the balance in the Merchandise Inventory account is the ending inventory amount. This balance is extended to the balance sheet debit column. The cost of goods sold, freight-in, and purchases discounts are extended along with the other temporary accounts to the proper Income Statement columns. The rest of the worksheet is completed in the manner illustrated in Chapter 4.

Closing entries based on the Income Statement columns are presented in Figure 5-6. Except for the new accounts introduced in this chapter, the closing process for a merchandising business is similar to that illustrated for a service firm. For comparison purposes, the closing entries based on the periodic inventory system are also shown.

PERIODIC INVENTORY SYSTEM

Under a periodic inventory system (Figure 5-5), the merchandise inventory balance of $58,400 listed in the Unadjusted Trial Balance debit column is the beginning inventory amount. This amount is extended to the Income Statement debit column because it is added to the cost of net purchases to determine the

Figure 5-6
Closing Entries, Perpetual and Periodic Inventory Systems

	Perpetual		Periodic	
	Debit	Credit	Debit	Credit
Income Summary	685,730		752,470	
Merchandise Inventory		—		58,400
Sales Returns & Allowances		21,390		21,390
Sales Discounts		3,260		3,260
Cost of Goods Sold		464,280		—
Purchases		—		472,620
Freight-in		6,210		6,210
Selling Expenses		100,270		100,270
Administrative Expenses		78,850		78,850
Income Tax Expense		10,470		10,470
Interest Expense		1,000		1,000
Sales	714,280		714,280	
Purchase Returns &				
Allowances		—		13,480
Purchase Discounts	2,860		2,860	
Rent Revenue	2,400		2,400	
Merchandise Inventory		—		53,260
Income Summary		719,540		786,280
Income Summary	33,810		33,810	
Retained Earnings		33,810		33,810
Retained Earnings	10,000		10,000	
Dividends Declared		10,000		10,000

cost of goods available for sale. The accounts that enter into the cost of net purchases—Purchases, Purchase Returns and Allowances, Purchase Discounts and Freight-in—are also extended to the appropriate Income Statement columns. The ending merchandise inventory of $53,260 is entered directly in the Income Statement credit column since it is a deduction from the cost of goods available for sale when computing the cost of goods sold. The amount is also entered in the Balance Sheet debit column because the ending inventory is an asset to the firm, and because it is necessary to enter an equal debit to maintain the equality of debits and credits in the worksheet.

At the end of the period, it is necessary to remove the beginning inventory balance and record the ending inventory in the Merchandise Inventory account. There are several ways to accomplish this, and each method produces the same cost-of-goods-sold amount. One approach is to adjust the Merchandise Inventory account during the closing process at the same time the other income statement accounts are closed. This approach is illustrated in Figure 5-6 for Sunrise Hi-Fi Sales. The credit to the Merchandise Inventory account of $58,400 in the first closing entry removes the beginning inventory balance and transfers it to the Income Summary account. The ending inventory balance of $53,260 is recorded in the second closing entry. Before this second entry is made and posted, the ending inventory is not reported in any ledger accounts.

INCOME STATEMENT OF A MERCHANDISING FIRM

An income statement for Hi-Fi Sales is presented in Figure 5-7 to show how a merchandiser's income statement accounts are reported. The company uses a periodic inventory system and reports a detailed cost of goods sold section. In practice, there is considerable variation in income statement formats. As a general rule, only the net sales and cost-of-goods-sold amounts are reported in annual reports. The format shown in Figure 5-7 is called a **multiple-step** income statement. Note that in this format, items that do not result from regular operations of the firm are reported near the bottom of the statement in a section called Other Revenue and Expense. In other words, other revenue and expense results from transactions related to secondary or miscellaneous activities of the firm. Included in this category are items such as interest expense, dividend revenue, interest revenue, miscellaneous earnings from rentals, and gains and losses from the sale of assets. Also note that in this format, the expenses are classified by function, such as cost of goods sold, selling expenses, and administrative expenses.

In this illustration, operating expenses are separated into two categories: selling expenses and administrative expenses. In Figure 5-7, individual types of expenses and amounts are assumed within each category. A detailed listing of individual expenses was not included in the worksheet. In some cases, such as for rent expense, it may be necessary to allocate or divide certain expenses between selling expenses and administrative expenses. Several methods can be used to allocate an expense. The allocation should be based on a logical relationship between the expense to be allocated and the benefits from the expense. For example, rent could be allocated based on square feet occupied by each department. Allocation methods are covered in more detail in Chapter

Figure 5-7
Income Statement

SUNRISE HI-FI SALES
Income Statement
For Year Ended December 31, 1985

Gross Sales			$714,280
Less: Sales returns and			
allowances		$ 21,390	
Sales discount		3,260	24,650
Net Sales			689,630
Cost of Goods Sold			
Merchandise Inventory, 1/1		58,400	
Add: Purchases	$472,620		
Freight-in	6,210		
	478,830		
Less: Purchase returns and			
allowances	$13,480		
Purchase discount	2,860	16,340	
Net cost of purchases		462,490	
Cost of goods available for			
sale		520,890	
Less: Merchandise			
Inventory, 12/31		53,260	
Cost of Goods Sold			467,630
Gross Profit on Sales			222,000
Operating Expenses			
Selling Expenses:			
Sales salaries and			
commission expense	61,040		
Delivery expense	6,210		
Advertising expense	8,420		
Rent expense—store			
space	17,000		
Depreciation expense—			
store equipment	7,600		
Total Selling Expense		100,270	
Administrative Expenses			
Office salaries expense	48,840		
Rent expense—office space	12,000		
Depreciation expense—			
office equipment	3,200		
Bad debts expense	14,200		
Insurance expense	610		
Total Administrative			
Expenses		78,850	
Total Operating Expenses			179,120
Income from Operations			42,880
Other Revenue and Expense			
Other Revenue			
Rent revenue			2,400
			45,280
Other Expense			
Interest expense			1,000
Income before income taxes			44,280
Income taxes			10,470
Net income for the year			$33,810

[handwritten margin notes:] formula B.I + Purch. available − E.I COGS   23.6%

21. Although not illustrated here, a worksheet is used to facilitate preparation of the financial statements and completion of the accounting cycle.

NET INVOICE METHOD OF RECORDING PURCHASES AND SALES

Purchases and sales were recorded at the *gross invoice price* in the preceding illustrations. Under the gross invoice method, merchandise inventory is recorded at the gross, or full, invoice price and purchase discounts (a contra purchases account) are not recorded unless payment is made within the discount period. Discounts lost are not separately reported for use by management and become a part of the inventory cost. Conceptually, however, a purchase discount reduces the unit cost of the inventory purchased; if the payment is not made within the discount period, the discount lost should be reported as interest expense. Thus, use of the gross method overstates inventory costs and understates interest expense. On the books of the seller, when the gross invoice method is used, a sale is recorded for the full invoice price and a sales discount (a contra sales account) is recorded if the customer pays within the discount period. If a discount is not taken, it is not separately reported and the amount of the discount is included in the sales account. However, a discount not taken is an added charge to the customer for permitting the deferral of the payment and should be reported as a separate revenue item.

Another procedure used by some firms, called the **net invoice method,** is to debit purchases or inventory (credit sales in the case of the selling firm) for the *net invoice amount (invoice price less the cash discount),* when recording the initial transaction. To illustrate the net invoice method, assume the purchase of goods for $5,850 on terms of 2/10, n/30, and a settlement of the account balance within the discount period. The entries for both the buying and selling firm, assuming both use the periodic inventory system, are as follows:

Buying Firm			Selling Firm		
Jan. 15 Purchases	5,733		Accounts Receivable	5,733	
Accounts Payable		5,733	Sales		5,733
(Invoice price of $5,850 less 2% discount of $117 = $5,733.)					
Jan. 24 Accounts Payable	5,733		Cash	5,733	
Cash		5,733	Accounts Receivable		5,733

If payment is not made within the discount period, the full invoice price of $5,850 must be paid since the cash discount is lost. The entry is as follows:

Accounts Payable	5,733		Cash		5,850
Purchase Discounts Lost			Sales Discounts Earned		
(Interest Expense)	117		(Interest Revenue)		117
Cash		5,850	Accounts Receivable		5,733

Note that the Accounts Payable (Accounts Receivable) account must be reduced by $5,733 to offset the initial credit (debit) of $5,733 made to the account on January 15 even though cash of $5,850 was eventually paid (received). The difference of $117 is the discount. Purchase discounts lost is a financing expense that results from delaying payment and is reported along with interest expense in the other expense section of the income statement. Sales discounts earned is considered interest revenue and reported as other revenue.

The net method is conceptually preferable because the cost of the asset purchased (or sales revenue earned) is recorded in terms of the cash price. This method also results in reporting the amount of purchase discounts lost and sales discounts earned as a separate item for use by management in evaluating financial management practices since discounts should normally be taken. Nevertheless, the gross method is commonly used in practice because it avoids the practical problem of allocating the discount to individual units when a physical inventory is taken and when the amounts are entered on individual record cards with the perpetual inventory system. In addition, the discount amounts are often immaterial.

GLOSSARY

ADMINISTRATIVE EXPENSES. Expenses associated with the operations of the general, accounting, personnel, and credit offices (p. 206).

BEGINNING INVENTORY. Merchandise on hand at the beginning of an accounting period that is available for sale to customers in the normal course of business (p. 216).

CASH DISCOUNT. An incentive offered to the buyer to induce early payment of a credit sale. Cash discounts are a reduction in the invoice price (p. 208).

COST OF GOODS SOLD. An amount that is deducted from sales in the income statement and is a measure of the cost of the inventory sold during the accounting period (p. 206).

CREDIT PERIOD. The period of time granted for the payment of an account (p. 208).

CREDIT TERMS. The agreement made between buyer and seller concerning the sale of goods on credit (p. 208).

DISCOUNT PERIOD. The period of time in which a cash discount may be subtracted from the invoice price (p. 208).

ENDING INVENTORY. Merchandise on hand at the end of an accounting period that is available for sale to customers in the normal course of the business (p. 216).

FOB DESTINATION. Shipping terms in which freight is paid by the seller (p. 209).

FOB SHIPPING POINT. Shipping terms in which freight is paid by the buyer (p. 209).

FREIGHT-IN (TRANSPORTATION-IN). An account used to accumulate the expense incurred by the buyer in transporting inventory purchases (p. 212).

FREIGHT-OUT (DELIVERY EXPENSE). Transportation expense incurred by the seller to deliver goods to customers (p. 209).

GOODS AVAILABLE FOR SALE. The cost of beginning inventory plus the cost of net purchases (p. 216).

GROSS INVOICE METHOD. A procedure in which sales revenue and purchases of inventory are recorded at the gross or full invoice price (p. 208).

GROSS PROFIT OR GROSS MARGIN ON SALES. Net sales less cost of goods sold (p. 206)

MERCHANDISE INVENTORY (INVENTORY). Goods acquired by a merchandising firm for the purpose of resale in the normal course of business (p. 205).

MULTIPLE-STEP. An income statement format in which operating and nonoperating items are separated and expenses are classified by function (p. 225).

NET INVOICE METHOD. A procedure in which sales revenue and purchases of inventory are recorded at the net invoice amount, invoice price less the stated cash discount (p. 227).

PERIODIC INVENTORY SYSTEM. A system of accounting for inventory in which the goods on hand are determined by a physical count. Cost of goods sold is equal to the beginning inventory plus net purchases less ending inventory (p. 215).

PERPETUAL INVENTORY SYSTEM. A system of accounting for inventory that provides a continuous and detailed record of the goods on hand and the cost of goods sold (p. 210).

PHYSICAL INVENTORY. The process of counting and pricing the goods on hand (p. 214).

PURCHASES. An account used in a periodic inventory system to record the cost of goods acquired for resale to customers (p. 216).

PURCHASE DISCOUNTS. An account used to record cash discounts taken by a firm on goods purchased for resale (p. 208).

PURCHASE RETURNS AND ALLOWANCES. An account used to record the return by a firm of inventory or adjustments made to the purchase price (p. 217).

SALES. A revenue account used by a merchandising firm to record the sales price of goods sold (p. 206).

SALES DISCOUNT. An account used to record cash discounts taken by customers on the sale of inventory (p. 208).

SALES RETURNS AND ALLOWANCES. The selling price of inventory returned by customers or adjustments made to the sales price (p. 207).

SELLING EXPENSES. Expenses that result from efforts to store, sell, and deliver goods to customers (p. 206).

TRADE DISCOUNTS. A reduction in the suggested list price granted to certain customers. Trade discounts are not normally recorded in the accounts (p. 209).

DISCUSSION QUESTIONS

1. Define ''merchandise inventory'' as the term is used in a merchandising operation.
2. What is the normal operating cycle for a merchandising firm?
3. How is the gross profit on sales computed?
4. Differentiate between selling expenses and administrative expenses.
5. What is the purpose of recording sales returns and allowances in a contra sales account rather than debiting a return or allowance directly to the sales account?
6. What is a cash discount? What are the benefits to the seller of granting cash discounts?
7. For the credit terms, 1/15, n/45, what is the length of the discount period? What is the length of the credit period? Prepare the journal entry to record a $200 sale assuming that the firm uses the gross method to record sales. Also, record the collection within the discount period.
8. At what amount would a seller record merchandise sold for a list price of $140 and a 20% trade discount?
9. Five accounts are shown below in T-account format. Prepare in general journal form the entries to record the transactions reflected in the accounts. Include an explanation with each entry.

Cash			Accounts Receivable			
(3)	388		(1)	500	(2)	100
					(3)	400

Sales			Sales Returns and Allowances			Sales Discounts		
	(1)	500	(2)	100		(3)	12	

10. What does the term FOB shipping point mean when included in the terms of a sale? Why is freight-in considered a part of the cost of purchasing merchandise?
11. Why is there no Purchases account when a perpetual inventory system is used? How is the return of purchases to the supplier recorded under a perpetual inventory system?
12. Why do firms that use a perpetual inventory system take a physical count of the inventory at least once a year?

13. Why do high volume merchandisers, such as grocery stores, tend to use a periodic inventory system?
14. When a periodic inventory system is used, what does the balance in the Inventory account during the period represent?
15. Roach Hardware purchased $160,000 in merchandise during the year. Compute the cost of goods sold for each of the following independent situations.

	Beginning Inventory	Ending Inventory
(a)	–0–	–0–
(b)	$20,000	–0–
(c)	–0–	$30,000
(d)	$20,000	$30,000

16. Where on the income statement do losses from inventory theft, shrinkage, and breakage appear when a periodic inventory system is used?
17. Under the periodic inventory system, in which columns of the worksheet does the beginning inventory appear? In which columns does ending inventory appear?
18. Distinguish between the gross invoice method and the net invoice method of recording cash discounts.
19. Where do the following items appear on the income statement: sales discounts, purchase discounts, sales discounts earned, and purchase discounts lost? What is the normal balance of each account?

EXERCISES

Exercise 5-1 (Journal Entries for Both Buyer and Seller—Periodic Inventory System)

A. Prepare general journal entries to record the following transactions (1) for the Vern Company and (2) for the Dox Company. Both companies use a periodic inventory system and the gross invoice method of recording cash discounts.

April 2 Vern Company sold merchandise to the Dox Company for $780 with terms 2/10, n/30, FOB shipping point.
  6 Dox Company paid the transportation cost of $42.
  8 Dox Company returned merchandise worth $60.
  9 Dox Company paid Vern Company the amount due.

B. Indicate how each account balance should be reported in the financial statements of Vern Company and Dox Company.

Exercise 5-2 (Journal Entries—Perpetual Inventory System)

Using a perpetual inventory system, record the following transactions in the general journal:

1. Purchased 50 units for $70 each on account.
2. Returned 3 units to the manufacturer.

3. Sold 26 units for $105 each on credit.
4. Purchased office supplies for $121 cash.
5. Customer returned 4 of the units sold in (3).
6. Sold 10 units for $106 each on credit.
7. The physical inventory at the end of the period consisted of 3 fewer units than the inventory account balance.

Exercise 5-3 (Journal Entries—Periodic Inventory System)

Using a periodic inventory system, prepare general journal entries for the following transactions.

1. Purchased merchandise on account for $9,800.
2. Sold merchandise for $4,200 in cash and $3,240 on credit.
3. A customer returned merchandise he had bought on credit for $310.
4. Purchased a typewriter to be used in the business for $275 cash.
5. Returned merchandise for credit that was previously purchased for $179.
6. Purchased merchandise on account with $2,900 list price and a 20% trade discount.
7. Sold merchandise for $306 on credit.

Exercise 5-4 (Income Statement—Periodic Inventory System)

Use the following information from the books of Best Company to prepare a multiple-step income statement.

Purchases	$97,600
Merchandise Inventory, January 1	8,150
Merchandise Inventory, December 31	10,942
Selling Expenses	23,016
Sales	143,200
Purchase Returns and Allowances	2,630
Sales Returns and Allowances	3,100
Administrative Expenses	9,800
Sales Discounts	874
Freight-in	2,046
Purchase Discounts	1,090

Exercise 5-5 (Income Statement—Perpetual Inventory System)

Use the following account balances taken from the books of Best Company to prepare a multiple-step income statement.

Cost of Goods Sold	$92,178
Merchandise Inventory, December 31	10,942
Selling Expenses	23,016
Sales	143,200
Sales Returns and Allowances	3,100
Administrative Expenses	9,800
Sales Discounts	874
Freight-in	2,046
Purchase Discounts	1,090

If you have also worked Exercise 5-4, compare the two income statements you prepared.

Exercise 5-6 (Completion of Worksheet—Periodic Inventory System)

Select accounts and a partial section of a worksheet are shown below:

Account	Adjusted Trial Balance Debit	Adjusted Trial Balance Credit	Income Statement Debit	Income Statement Credit	Balance Sheet Debit	Balance Sheet Credit
Merchandise Inventory	?					
Sales		82,000				
Sales Returns and Allowances	2,000					
Sales Discounts	1,500					
Purchases	60,000					
Purchase Returns and Allowances		1,000				
Purchase Discounts		800				
Freight-in	600					
Income Tax Expense	4,200					
Income Taxes Payable		460				

Required:
The beginning and ending merchandise inventory were $14,000 and $16,000, respectively. You are to enter the beginning and ending inventory amounts in the proper columns and extend the other account balances listed to their proper columns.

Exercise 5-7 (Computing Missing Data in Income Statement)

For each of the following independent cases, compute the missing amounts.

	Cases 1	Cases 2	Cases 3
Sales	54,300	22,160	g
Beginning Inventory	a	3,700	6,500
Purchases	26,000	d	24,000
Ending Inventory	15,730	4,600	h
Cost of Goods Sold	b	14,700	25,300
Gross Profit on Sales	25,630	e	i
Operating Expenses	c – 40990	7,460	10,100
Net Income (loss)	13,310	f	(2,700)

Exercise 5-8 (Closing Entries—Periodic Inventory System)

The following information is taken from the trial balance of Hiram's Health Food Store:

	Debit	Credit
Merchandise Inventory, January 1	$ 29,600	
Hiram Boyd, Withdrawals	21,840	
Sales		$548,600
Sales Returns and Allowances	10,041	
Sales Discounts	1,780	
Purchases	361,035	
Purchase Returns and Allowances		4,400
Purchase Discounts		1,230
Freight-in	6,310	
Selling Expenses	87,500	
Administrative Expenses	53,740	

Given that the cost of the inventory on December 31 is $35,230, prepare the closing entries.

Exercise 5-9 (Closing Entries—Perpetual Inventory System)

The trial balance of the Hiram's Health Food Store contains the following account balances at December 31:

	Debit	Credit
Merchandise Inventory	$ 35,230	
Hiram Boyd, Withdrawals	21,840	
Sales		$548,600
Sales Returns and Allowances	10,041	
Sales Discounts	1,780	
Cost of Goods Sold	351,005	
Purchase Discounts		1,230
Freight-in	6,310	
Selling Expenses	87,500	
Administrative Expenses	53,740	

Prepare the closing entries.

Exercise 5-10 (Net Invoice Method to Record Sales)

A. A. G. Jaxs Company sold merchandise to a customer for $375 on February 11. The credit terms were 2/15, n/45. A. G. Jaxs Company uses a periodic inventory system and the net invoice method is used to record sales.

1. Give the general journal entry to record the sale.

2. Assume that the customer paid in full on February 23. Give the entry to record the receipt of cash.

3. Assume that the customer paid in full on March 21. Give the entry to record the payment.

B. Indicate how the sales discount earned would be reported in the firm's financial statements.

Exercise 5-11 (Net Invoice Method to Record Purchases)

A. Action Book Company purchased merchandise for $400 on February 11. The credit terms were 2/15, n/45 and the goods were shipped FOB destination. Action Book

Company uses a periodic inventory system and the net invoice method is used to record purchases.

1. Give the general journal entry to record the purchase.
2. Assume that Action paid for the goods in full on February 23. Give the entry to record the cash payment.
3. Assume that Action paid for the goods in full on March 21. Give the entry to record the cash payment.
4. Determine the effective annual interest rate of forgoing the cash discount.
B. Indicate how purchase discounts lost would be reported in the firm's financial statements.

PROBLEMS

Problem 5-1 (Journal Entries for Both Buyer and Seller—Periodic Inventory System)

Prepare general journal entries to record the following transactions for the Davis Company and for the Ford Company. Assume that both companies use a periodic inventory system and use the gross invoice method to record purchases and sales.

May   2   Davis Company sold merchandise to Ford Company for $1,800 with terms of 1/10, n/30.
           11   Ford Company paid for the merchandise.
           15   Davis Company sold merchandise to Ford Company for $300 with terms of 1/10, n/30.
           30   Ford Company paid for the merchandise.

Problem 5-2 (Journal Entries—Perpetual Inventory System)

The following transactions related to Product S-2 occurred in July. Prepare journal entries to record the transactions assuming that a perpetual inventory system is used. The beginning inventory on July 1 consisted of 150 units at $9 each.

July   1   Purchased 302 units for $9 each on credit.
         7   Returned 8 units, which were defective.
       12   Sold 190 units for $15 each on account.
       24   A customer returned 11 units.
       25   Sold 64 units for $15 each on account.
       31   A physical inventory count shows 201 units at a total cost of $1,809. Assuming that the company closes its books each month, prepare entries to close the income statement accounts based on the above data and assuming that operating expenses for July were $1,420.

Problem 5-3 (Journal Entries—Periodic Inventory System)

Using the data given in Problem 5-2, prepare the required journal entries assuming that a periodic inventory system is used by the company.

Problem 5-4 (Journal Entries Involving Purchases and Sales Discounts, Closing Entries, and Income Statements— Both Perpetual and Periodic Inventory Systems)

The Fallon Company buys lamps, model #k37, for $30 each and sells them for $50 each. The company uses the gross invoice method to record purchases and sales. On April 1, 24 lamps were in inventory. Fallon Company completed the following transactions during April.

April		
	3	Purchased 40 lamps on account. Terms: 2/10, n/30, FOB shipping point.
	4	Paid freight cost of $60 on April 3 purchase.
	5	Sold 22 lamps on account. Terms: 3/10, n/30, FOB destination. Paid freight cost of $27.
	9	Returned 10 of the lamps purchased on April 3 and paid the amount due on the lamps retained in stock.
	10	A customer returned 3 of the lamps sold on April 5. The lamps were not defective and were returned to stock.
	13	Purchased 20 lamps on account. Terms: 2/10, n/30, FOB shipping point.
	14	Received payment from customer for the amount due on April 5 sale.
	19	Sold 39 lamps for cash.
	20	Four of the lamps sold on April 19 were returned by the customer for a cash refund. The lamps were not defective.
	22	Paid the supplier the amount owed for the April 13 purchase.

A physical inventory taken on April 30 shows 20 lamps in stock.

Required:

A. In two columns, prepare general journal entries to record the transactions assuming that:
  1. A perpetual inventory system is used.
  2. A periodic inventory system is used.
B. Assuming Fallon Company closes its books every month, prepare entries to close the accounts that enter into the determination of net sales and cost of goods sold.
C. Prepare two separate income statements through gross profit on sales for April, assuming that:
  1. The perpetual inventory system was used.
  2. The periodic inventory system was used.

Problem 5-5 (Worksheet and Completion of Accounting Cycle— Perpetual Inventory System)

A trial balance for Heller's Sporting Goods Store is shown below:

HELLER'S SPORTING GOODS
Unadjusted Trial Balance
December 31, 1984

Account Title	Debit	Credit
Cash	$ 3,600	
Accounts Receivable	9,300	
Merchandise Inventory	24,850	
Prepaid Rent	2,700	
Store Equipment	41,400	
Accumulated Depreciation—Store Equipment		$ 6,200
Accounts Payable		8,750
Common Stock		54,670
Retained Earnings		20,000
Dividends Declared	26,160	
Sales		219,840
Sales Returns and Allowances	4,120	
Sales Discounts	980	
Cost of Goods Sold	127,650	
Purchase Discounts		1,030
Freight-in	2,310	
Rent Expense	19,000	
Income Tax Expense	10,000	
Other Operating Expenses	38,420	
Totals	$310,490	$310,490

Required:

A. Prepare a worksheet using the following information to make adjusting entries:
1. Depreciation on the store equipment, $2,800.
2. Expired prepaid rent, $1,600.
3. Accrued utilities expense, $205.
4. Unpaid income taxes at the end of the period, $3,460.

Add the following account titles to those listed in the trial balance: Utilities Payable and Income Taxes Payable.

B. Prepare an income statement, a statement of retained earnings, and a balance sheet for the year ended December 31, 1984.
C. Prepare adjusting and closing entries.
D. Prepare a post-closing trial balance.

Problem 5-6 (Worksheet and Completion of Accounting Cycle— Periodic Inventory System)

The unadjusted trial balance of Efficient Business Equipment is shown below:

EFFICIENT BUSINESS EQUIPMENT
Unadjusted Trial Balance
December 31, 1984

Account Title	Debit	Credit
Cash	$ 21,900	
Accounts Receivable	26,230	
Merchandise Inventory (January 1)	59,170	
Prepaid Insurance	2,400	
Store Equipment	39,060	
Accumulated Depreciation, Store Equipment		$ 11,560
Delivery Truck	9,800	
Accumulated Depreciation, Delivery Truck		4,100
Accounts Payable		12,780
Note Payable		15,000
Common Stock		66,120
Retained Earnings		21,500
Dividends Declared	21,780	
Sales		357,960
Sales Returns and Allowances	14,610	
Sales Discounts	1,800	
Purchases	199,570	
Purchase Returns and Allowances		12,800
Purchase Discounts		1,070
Freight-in	4,120	
Operating Expenses	91,320	
Income Tax Expense	9,000	
Interest Expense	2,130	
Totals	$502,890	$502,890

Required:

A. Prepare a worksheet for Efficient Business Equipment. Use the following information to make the year-end adjustments.

1. Prepaid insurance expired during the year, $1,700.
2. Depreciation on the store equipment, $4,100.
3. Depreciation on the delivery truck, $2,030.
4. Accrued interest on the note payable, $980.
5. Total income tax expense for the period, $11,500.

In making the adjustments, Interest Payable and Income Taxes Payable accounts are to be added to those listed in the trial balance. The ending merchandise inventory determined by physical count was $47,930.

B. Prepare an income statement, a statement of retained earnings, and a balance sheet for the year ended December 31, 1984.

C. Prepare adjusting and closing entries.

D. Prepare a post-closing trial balance.

Problem 5-7 (Net Invoice Method for Both Buyer and Seller)

A. Prepare general journal entries to record the following transactions for the Davis Company and for the Ford Company. Assume that both companies use a periodic inventory system and use the net invoice method to record purchases and sales.

May	2	Davis Company sold merchandise to Ford Company for $1,800 with terms of 1/10, n/30.
	11	Ford Company paid for the merchandise.
	15	Davis Company sold merchandise to Ford Company for $300 with terms of 1/10, n/30.
	30	Ford Company paid for the merchandise.

B. Indicate how the sales discounts earned and the purchase discounts lost would be reported in the financial statements of each firm.

ALTERNATE PROBLEMS

Problem 5-1A (Journal Entries for Both Buyer and Seller—Periodic Inventory System)

Prepare general journal entries to record the following transactions for the Hollins Company and for the Schrader Company. Both companies use a periodic inventory system and use the gross invoice method to record purchases and sales.

Sept.	14	Hollins Company sold merchandise to Schrader Company for $2,700. Terms were 2/15, n/30.
Sept.	26	Schrader Company paid Hollins Company the net amount due.
Sept.	29	Hollins Company sold merchandise to Schrader Company for $1,400. Terms were 2/15, n/30.
Oct.	18	Schrader Company paid for the merchandise.

Problem 5-2A (Journal Entries—Perpetual Inventory System)

The following transactions related to Product Item 3X-L occurred in March. Prepare journal entries to record the transactions assuming that a perpetual inventory system is used. The beginning inventory on March 1 consisted of 29 units at $16 each.

March	2	Purchased 85 units for $16 each on credit.
	11	Returned 3 units to the manufacturer for credit on account.
	13	Sold 41 units for $29 each on account.
	17	The customer returned 6 units.
	28	Sold 32 units for $29 each on account.
	31	According to a physical inventory count, 44 units are on hand at a total cost of $704. Assuming the company closes its books each month, prepare entries to close the income statement accounts based on the above data and operating expenses of $640.

Problem 5-3A (Journal Entries—Periodic Inventory System)

Using the data given in Problem 5-2A, prepare the required journal entries assuming that a periodic inventory system is used by the company.

Problem 5-4A (Journal Entries Involving Purchases and Sales Discounts, Closing Entries, and Income Statements— Both Perpetual and Periodic Inventory Systems)

The Hawthorne Company sells alarm clock model #NC004 for $20 each. It buys the clocks for $10 each. Hawthorne uses the gross invoice method to record purchases and sales. On November 1, 46 clocks are in inventory. Hawthorne Company completed the following transactions during November:

Nov.

3 Sold 6 clocks for cash.

4 Paid the supplier for 20 clocks purchased October 5. Terms: 2/10, n/30.

5 Purchased 27 clocks on account. Terms: 2/10, n/30, FOB shipping point.

6 A customer returned 2 of the clocks sold on November 3 and received cash. The clocks were not defective in any way.

9 Paid $32 in freight charges on November 5 purchase.

12 Returned 7 of the clocks purchased on November 5 for credit.

13 Sold 15 clocks on account. Credit terms: 2/10, n/30.

14 Paid the supplier the amount due on the November 5 purchase.

22 A customer returned 5 clocks sold on November 13 and included a check for the amount due on the other 10 clocks. The clocks were not defective and were returned to inventory.

23 Purchased 35 clocks on account. Terms: 2/10, n/30, FOB shipping point.

30 Paid the supplier for the November 23 purchase.

A physical inventory count taken on November 30 verified that 87 clocks were on hand.

Required:

A. In two columns prepare general journal entries to record the transactions assuming that:
   1. A perpetual inventory system is used.
   2. A periodic inventory system is used.
B. Assuming that Hawthorne Company completes the closing process each month, prepare entries to close the accounts that enter into the determination of net sales and cost of goods sold.
C. Prepare two separate income statements through gross profit on sales for November, assuming that:
   1. The perpetual inventory system was used.
   2. The periodic inventory system was used.

Problem 5-5A (Worksheet and Completion of Accounting Cycle— Perpetual Inventory System)

A trial balance for Fashionable Fabrics Store is shown below:

FASHIONABLE FABRICS STORE
Unadjusted Trial Balance
December 31, 1984

Account Title	Debit	Credit
Cash	$ 15,870	
Accounts Receivable	16,970	
Merchandise Inventory	22,300	
Supplies	310	
Store Equipment	35,550	
Accumulated Depreciation, Store Equipment		$ 7,940
Accounts Payable		3,600
Note Payable		10,000
Common Stock		38,270
Retained Earnings		28,270
Dividends Declared	19,750	
Sales		114,190
Sales Returns and Allowances	1,030	
Sales Discounts	450	
Cost of Goods Sold	66,220	
Purchase Discounts		975
Freight-in	1,095	
Income Tax Expense	5,000	
Operating Expenses	18,700	
Totals	$203,245	$203,245

Required:

A. Prepare a worksheet for Fashionable Fabrics Store. Use the following information to make adjusting entries.
  1. Supplies on hand at December 31, $120.
  2. Depreciation on the store equipment, $3,150.
  3. Interest accrued on the note payable, $1,370.
  4. Unpaid income taxes at the end of the year, $1,960.
  Add the following account titles to those listed in the trial balance: Interest Payable, Income Taxes Payable, Interest Expense.
B. Prepare an income statement, a statement of retained earnings, and a balance sheet for the year ended December 31, 1984.
C. Prepare closing entries.

Problem 5-6A (Worksheet and Completion of Accounting Cycle— Periodic Inventory System)

The unadjusted trial balance of the Plaza Hobby Shop appears below:

PLAZA HOBBY SHOP
Unadjusted Trial Balance
December 31, 1985

Account Title	Debit	Credit
Cash	$ 17,650	
Accounts Receivable	21,700	
Merchandise Inventory (January 1)	17,640	
Prepaid Rent	1,240	
Shop Equipment	15,700	
Accumulated Depreciation, Shop Equipment		$ 4,310
Accounts Payable		5,700
Common Stock		34,260
Retained Earnings		28,450
Dividends Declared	9,890	
Sales		107,980
Sales Returns and Allowances	3,200	
Sales Discounts	930	
Purchases	61,300	
Purchase Returns and Allowances		1,420
Purchase Discounts		560
Freight-in	2,100	
Rent Expense	6,820	
Salaries Expense	13,410	
Income Tax Expense	3,600	
Other Operating Expenses	7,500	
Totals	$182,680	$182,680

The following accounts listed in the chart of accounts contained a zero balance: Salaries Payable, Income Taxes Payable, Telephone Expense Payable, Depreciation Expense.

Required:

A. Prepare a worksheet. The ending inventory was determined to be $21,530. Use the following information to make the year-end adjustments.

1. Prepaid rent expired during the year, $620.
2. Depreciation on the shop equipment, $3,020.
3. Accrued salaries expense, $770.
4. Accrued telephone expense, $110.
5. Unpaid income taxes at the end of the period, $600.

B. Prepare an income statement, a statement of retained earnings, and a balance sheet for the year ended December 31, 1985.

C. Prepare closing entries.

Problem 5-7A (Net Invoice Method for Both Buyer and Seller)

A. Prepare general journal entries to record the following transactions for the Hollins Company and the Schrader Company. Assume both companies use a periodic inventory system and use the net invoice method to record purchases and sales.

Sept. 14 Hollins Company sold merchandise to Schrader Company for $2,700. Terms were 2/15, n/30.

26 Schrader Company paid Hollins Company the net amount due.

29 Hollins Company sold merchandise to Schrader Company for $1,400. Terms were 2/15, n/30.

Oct. 18 Schrader Company paid for the merchandise.

B. Indicate how the sales discounts earned and the purchase discounts lost would be reported in the financial statements of each firm.

CASE FOR CHAPTER 5

(Discussion—Perpetual versus the Periodic Inventory System)

The Grand Forks Discount Office Furniture is a retailer for office furniture and equipment. The firm stocks about 70 different items ranging in retail price from $60 to $1,200 per unit. Throughout the fiscal year, the inventory balance at cost is maintained at approximately $90,000. This requires that the company make 15–20 purchases a month from 20 manufacturers. Approximately 70% of the sales are on terms n/30, and 70 to 100 sales are made on a typical day. The dollar sales volume is not seasonal, but is sensitive to the general economic conditions of the area.

Required:

Management has been using the periodic inventory system, but is considering changing to the perpetual inventory system to ascertain the information needed to prepare monthly statements, and for placing orders with their suppliers. Management has asked you to explain the advantages and disadvantages of each system and to recommend one for them to use.

PART TWO
ACCOUNTING SYSTEMS AND CONTROLS

CHAPTER 6
ACCOUNTING SYSTEMS

OVERVIEW AND OBJECTIVES

This chapter describes accounting systems. When you have completed the chapter, you should understand:

- The basic structure of an accounting system (pp. 247–248).
- How data are transformed into information with an accounting system (p. 247).
- The development of an accounting system with systems analysis, systems design, and systems implementation (pp. 248–250).
- How control accounts and subsidiary ledgers are used in a manual accounting system (pp. 251–252).
- The advantages of special journals (pp. 252–253).
- The formats of and procedures used with a sales journal, purchases journal, cash receipts journal, and cash disbursements journal (pp. 253–265).
- The use of a general journal when special journals are utilized (pp. 265–266).
- The need for electronic data processing (p. 268).
- The basic components of a digital computer (pp. 269–270).
- How a computer can be used in an accounting system (pp. 271–272).

In earlier chapters, we have seen that the effects of various business transactions are *collected, processed, and reported* with a firm's accounting system. An **accounting system** is a collection of business forms (also called source documents), records, procedures, management policies, and data-processing methods used to transform economic data into useful information. Accounting systems can take many forms, ranging from simple manual systems to sophisticated computerized systems.

We have limited the consideration of an accounting system in earlier chapters to one that is both *simple* and *manually operated* in order to introduce basic accounting procedures. Such a system may be satisfactory for a small business with a limited number of transactions. In most cases, however, even relatively small businesses will require a more sophisticated accounting system for two reasons. First, the procedures described earlier may be too time-consuming for rapid data processing and timely reporting. The volume of transactions may be so great that the accounting staff cannot process the data manually at a reasonable cost and on a sufficiently prompt basis. Second, many of the transactions will be so repetitive that they can be handled more efficiently with more specialized treatment than the general procedures so far discussed. Special journals can be used for such repetitive transactions as sales, purchases, cash receipts, and cash disbursements instead of the less efficient general journal. This chapter describes accounting systems as they are designed and installed for efficient and dependable processing of financial data. We will begin by considering the fundamental concepts associated with any accounting system.

OPERATION OF AN ACCOUNTING SYSTEM

The operation of an accounting system consists of three basic phases: *input, processing,* and *output.* Transactions are recorded as they occur on numerous business forms such as sales invoices, purchase invoices, checks, bank deposit tickets, and payroll cards. The documents serve as input that is entered into some type of journal as a chronological record of the transactions. Periodically the debits and credits in the journal are posted to a general ledger that represents a permanent file classified as assets, liabilities, owners' equity, revenues, and expenses. Financial reports such as an income statement, a balance sheet, a statement of changes in financial position, and other special reports are prepared from the data in the general ledger as output from the system. The reports provide useful information concerning the operating results and financial position of the firm for a variety of interested parties. Some of the parties are outside the firm (such as creditors and taxing authorities) while others are insiders as members of the management team. Consequently, both financial and managerial accounting information is produced with the same system.

In the conversion of input to output, data are transformed into information. While the two terms *data* and *information* are often used synonymously, a useful distinction between them can be made. *Data* are recorded facts; *information* is data that have been processed in some prescribed manner so they are more useful to a potential user. For example, sales data are collected chronologically on invoices, processed through the accounting system, and reported as sales information (revenue) on the income statement. The development of information from data in an accounting system can be diagrammed as:

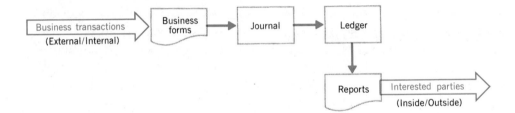

INTERNAL CONTROL

The procedures adopted by a business to control its operations are defined collectively as a system of internal control. Chapter 7 covers the basic elements of internal control, but at this point we must mention the relationship of internal control to an accounting system. One of the primary objectives of internal control is to ensure the reliability of accounting information. As we have seen, financial data are transformed into information with a number of accounting procedures such as preparing business forms, analyzing transactions, recording transactions in journals, posting journal entries to ledger accounts, and developing financial reports.

Users of financial information need assurance that these accounting procedures are performed correctly so that the resulting information is accurate and dependable. This assurance is provided to a large extent by a sound system of internal control that actually provides the foundation for a reliable accounting system. We will discuss the basic characteristics of internal control in Chapter 7.

DEVELOPMENT OF AN ACCOUNTING SYSTEM

When a new business is started, one of the first steps taken is the development of a dependable accounting system. In many instances, the system is designed and installed by a member or members of the firm's own accounting department, although the system may be developed by an outside source such as a CPA firm. With either approach, the development of an accounting system must be based on a thorough *understanding* of the business and the industry in which it operates.

As the business grows and engages in different activities, the accounting system must be *revised frequently* to accommodate a larger volume of transactions and changes in the nature of those transactions. The design of an accounting system, then, is not a one-time affair but requires continuous development to ensure that the capability of the system is compatible with the changing needs of a business. Many large firms have a systems department that has responsibility for reviewing the accounting system continuously to determine whether portions or all of it require revision. The installation or revision of an accounting system consists of three phases: systems analysis, systems design, and systems implementation.

SYSTEMS ANALYSIS

The objective of the systems analysis phase is to gather facts that provide a thorough understanding of a business's information requirements and the sources of information. Systems analysis is performed in the installation of a new system or the evaluation of an existing system. A study of the organization and how it functions is performed to determine the best combination of personnel, forms, records, procedures, and equipment. Such questions as these must be considered: How is the business organized? What is its history? What type of business is involved? What activities are performed? Who is responsible for the activities? What decisions must be made to properly manage the business? What needs to be reported, to whom, and for what purposes? How often is information required? How much money will be devoted to the development and operation of the system? What is the projected growth and direction of the firm? What are the strengths and weaknesses of the business? What are management's plans for future changes in operations? What business forms, records, procedures, reports, and equipment currently are being used?

In existing systems, much of the information required for systems analysis may be available in the form of an operating manual—a detailed description of how the system should function. A major consideration in such cases is an evaluation of how closely the instructions in the manual are followed in the actual operation of the accounting system. Any deficiencies in procedures and data-processing methods currently in use should be corrected with the analysis. In the installation of a new system, many of the facts gathered during the systems analysis phase are used later in the preparation of an operating manual.

SYSTEMS DESIGN

A new system is developed or improvements are made to an existing system in the systems-design phase based on the facts gathered through systems analysis. A team approach using accountants, managers, engineers, computer experts, and other specialists is often required in the design of an accounting system. The specific means to be used for input, processing, and output must be selected in terms of the information requirements of the business.

The design must include a consideration of the *personnel* required to operate the system, the *business forms* needed to document transactions, the *account-*

ing records and *procedures* to be used to process data, the *reports* to be prepared for interested parties, and *any automated features* of the system. The basic concern in the design phase is to develop an accounting system with the most *efficient flow of information,* given the funds committed to the system and the information requirements involved. A fundamental part of the design phase is the development of reliable internal control. The guiding principle in the choice of output in the form of reports is that the benefits from each must exceed the costs. Some reports, such as financial statements and tax returns, are mandatory but should still be produced at a reasonable cost. The value of other reports, such as those prepared for management, must be compared continuously with the preparation cost. The information in these reports must be accurate, timely, and relevant to be beneficial to users. In most cases, the ultimate measure of the benefits from the information is the quality of the decision-making based on it. Cost/benefit analysis of accounting information is particularly important when a large investment of funds in a computer and other electronic equipment is required.

SYSTEMS IMPLEMENTATION

Systems implementation is the final phase in the development or revision of an accounting system. This step involves the implementation of the decisions made during the design stage. The business forms, records, and equipment chosen must be purchased. The personnel needed to operate the system must be selected, trained, and supervised closely to assure that they understand how the system should function. An operating manual should be prepared as a formalized description of the procedures required to transform economic data into useful information. When an existing system is being revised, the old system often is operated parallel to the new one until management is certain that the new system is reliable. Major revisions are usually accomplished gradually rather than all at once to aid in ensuring reliable data flows. Any new accounting system should be tested thoroughly to be certain that its output is compatible with the desired results. Modifications should be made whenever necessary.

MANUAL ACCOUNTING SYSTEMS

As its name suggests, a manual accounting system is operated by human effort. Clerical personnel or bookkeepers prepare business forms, make journal entries, post to ledger accounts, and prepare financial reports. Many small businesses are able to satisfy their information requirements with a manual system, although the number has decreased significantly in recent years because of the increasing popularity and decreasing cost of the computer. In earlier chapters, we illustrated basic accounting procedures by recording each transaction with an entry in a general journal and later posting each debit and credit to an appropriate account in the general ledger. We now can extend this basic version of a manual accounting system to one that is more streamlined and efficient by introducing subsidiary ledgers and special journals. Similar subsidiary ledgers and special journals are used in a computer accounting system.

CONTROL ACCOUNTS AND SUBSIDIARY LEDGERS

The coverage so far of a ledger as an essential part of an accounting system has been limited to a general ledger. For more timely and efficient processing, we need to examine the use of control accounts and subsidiary ledgers. Before doing so, assume that a business sells merchandise on credit to 5,000 customers. If the firm used only one Accounts Receivable account—as we have done for illustrative purposes so far—it would not provide adequate detail concerning the amount of merchandise sold to individual customers, amount of money received from them, and amount still owed by them. Consequently, the firm will want to establish a separate Accounts Receivable account for each customer. If this were done in the general ledger, 5,000 accounts would have to be established and combined with the other assets, liabilities, owners' equity, revenues, and expenses. As a result, the general ledger would be unwieldy, and the likelihood of errors would be high. The trial balance prepared from such a large general ledger would also be very long and difficult to work with. This situation is complicated further by the fact that other general ledger accounts, such as Accounts Payable and Inventory, require the same detailed information.

When a large amount of detailed information about a certain general ledger account must be kept, a separate record called a **subsidiary ledger** is used. With this, the detailed information is recorded outside the general ledger. For example, one Accounts Receivable account can be used in the general ledger and an Accounts Receivable account can be established for each customer (5,000 in the case above) in the subsidiary ledger. The Accounts Receivable account in the general ledger is called a **control account,** a general ledger account supported by the detail of a subsidiary ledger. A subsidiary ledger consists of a group of individual accounts, the total of which should equal the balance of the related control account in the general ledger. Control accounts and subsidiary ledgers are used for a number of general ledger accounts such as Accounts Receivable, Accounts Payable, Inventory, Marketable Securities, and Plant Assets.

To illustrate the relationship between accounts receivable as a control account and its subsidiary ledger, consider the following simplified illustration, which summarizes the November sales and cash receipts activities of a firm with three customers, given their beginning-of-the-month account balances:

General Ledger Accounts Receivable					Subsidiary Ledger P. Able			
Date	Debit	Credit	Balance		Date	Debit	Credit	Balance
Nov. 1			6,500		Nov. 1			3,200
Nov. 30	5,100	6,900	4,700		Nov. 8	1,800		5,000
					Nov. 16		3,200	1,800

Proof of Agreement Between Control
Account and Subsidiary Ledger
Beginning balances:
$6,500 = $3,200 + $1,100 + $2,200
Ending balances:
$4,700 = $1,800 + $2,400 + $500

R. Baker			
Date	Debit	Credit	Balance
Nov. 1			1,100
Nov. 3		1,100	
Nov. 20	2,400		2,400

D. Cane			
Date	Debit	Credit	Balance
Nov. 1			2,200
Nov. 12	900		3,100
Nov. 28		2,600	500

The accounts receivable subsidiary ledger is an alphabetical file with a separate account for each customer. Note that at the beginning and end of November the totals of the subsidiary ledger accounts are in agreement with the Accounts Receivable control account in the general ledger. The use of a subsidiary ledger has three major advantages: it relieves the general ledger of a mass of detail; it allows a division of labor in maintaining the ledgers; and it provides effective internal control.

SPECIAL JOURNALS

The general journal described in earlier chapters can be used to record all types of transactions—sales, purchases, cash receipts, cash disbursements, sales returns and allowances, and purchase returns and allowances. The universal nature of the general journal imposes some limitations that will adversely affect the efficiency of processing data. Each debit and credit recorded in the general journal must be posted individually, requiring a large amount of posting time. As the number of transactions increases, this inefficiency can make it difficult to provide accounting information on a timely basis. Also, only one person at a time can record the effects of transactions and post debits and credits to the ledger accounts, since all of the entries are recorded in one journal.

To avoid the limitations of using only a general journal, transactions are grouped into like categories and a **special journal** is set up for each category. Most of a typical firm's transactions fall into four categories, which in turn require four special journals:

Category of Transaction	Special Journal
Sales of merchandise on credit	Sales journal
Purchases of merchandise on credit	Purchases journal
Receipts of cash	Cash receipts journal
Disbursements of cash	Cash disbursements journal

The general journal is retained for recording transactions other than those in the four categories above. For example, sales returns and allowances, purchase returns and allowances, adjusting entries, and closing entries are recorded in the general journal. If the sales returns and allowances or the purchase returns and allowances occur frequently, special journals may also be designed for them. The combination of the five journals represents a much more efficient way to process data than the use of a general journal alone. As we will see later, the time required to journalize entries will be less and totals rather than individual entries can be posted to ledger accounts in many cases, thus reducing the cost of accounting labor. Also, an efficient division of labor can be achieved by assigning different journals to different employees so work can be performed concurrently. Several selected transactions involving the Baldwin Video Equipment Store during the month of January illustrate the four special journals in the next section. The formats used for the four special journals are typical and not unique. The nature of a given business determines the exact formats required.

SALES JOURNAL

A **sales journal** such as the one shown in Figure 6-1 is used solely for recording sales of merchandise on credit. (Cash sales are recorded in the cash receipts journal, as we shall see later.) As each credit sale occurs, several copies of a sales invoice are prepared to document the transaction. The information shown on a sales invoice includes the customer's name, date of sale, invoice number (usually prenumbered), amount of sale, and the credit terms. One copy of the sales invoice is used by the seller to record the sale in the sales journal. In

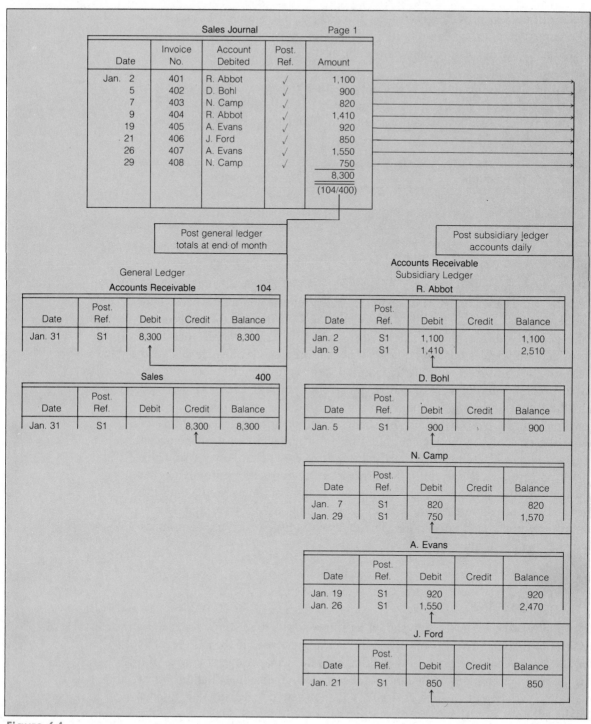

Figure 6-1
Relationship of Sales Journal and Ledger Accounts

Figure 6-1, eight sales to five different customers have been recorded. All credit sales are made on the basis of 2/10, n/30. Other columns can be added to the sales journal to satisfy the needs of a specific business. If credit terms vary among customers, an additional column can be added to the sales journal to identify the terms of each sale. In addition, a sales tax payable column can be used to record the amount of sales tax to be collected from customers when a business is required to do so for state or local taxing authorities.

ADVANTAGES OF A SALES JOURNAL

The sales journal shown in Figure 6-1 has these time-saving advantages:

1. Each sales transaction is recorded on a *single line*. All credit sales are alike in that they result in a debit to Accounts Receivable and a credit to Sales. Recordkeeping efficiency is achieved by simply identifying the customer who is the debtor instead of entering the account titles—Accounts Receivable and Sales—for each transaction.
2. The entries in the sales journal do not require an explanation for two reasons. First, all the transactions involved are the same, as discussed above. Second, the detailed information related to each sale is documented on a sales invoice that is referenced in the second column of the sales journal. If additional information concerning a particular sale is required, the interested party can simply identify the invoice number and refer to the details of the sales invoice.
3. Posting efficiency is achieved with the sales journal since only one amount, the total credit sales for the month, is posted to the general ledger. Note in Figure 6-1 that the total credit sales of $8,300 are posted twice—once to the Accounts Receivable control account and once to the Sales account. This procedure eliminates posting separate debits and credits during the month. In addition, the sales information needed for each customer in the accounts receivable subsidiary ledger is posted daily from the line items of the sales journal. A checkmark is recorded in the Post. Ref. (posting reference) column to indicate that each sale has been posted to the subsidiary ledger. The account numbers for Accounts Receivable (104) and Sales (400) are entered below the total credit sales for the month to show that the general ledger accounts have been posted. A posting reference column is also included in the ledger accounts to indicate the source of the entries posted for cross-referencing purposes. The S1 refers to the first page of the sales journal.

SUMMARY OF SALES JOURNAL PROCEDURES

The procedures used with the sales journal illustrated in Figure 6-1 can be summarized as follows:

1. From each sales invoice, enter the date of the sale, invoice number, customer's name, and amount of sale on a line of the sales journal.
2. *At the end of each day,* post each sale to the related customer's account in the subsidiary ledger. Place a checkmark in the posting reference column of the sales journal and S1 in the posting reference column of the customer's account.
3. *At the end of each month,* total the amount column of the sales journal and post the total amount as a debit and credit to the two general ledger accounts, Accounts Receivable and Sales, respectively. Place the general ledger account numbers (104/400) below the total credit sales and S1 in the posting reference columns of the two general ledger accounts.
4. Add the account balances of the Accounts Receivable subsidiary ledger to verify that the total is equal to the Accounts Receivable control account balance in the general ledger. In Figure 6-1, the amount involved is $8,300.

Purchases Journal

The **purchases journal** can be set up as either a single-column or a multi-column journal. In either case, the purchases of merchandise must be recorded separately from the acquisition of other assets because, as we have seen earlier, the total purchases of merchandise for a period are used to compute cost of goods sold. A single-column purchases journal such as that shown in Figure 6-2 is used solely for recording the purchases of merchandise on credit with a periodic inventory system. Cash purchases of merchandise are recorded in the cash disbursements journal, as discussed later. Other purchases such as the acquisition of an automobile or an office machine, will be recorded in some other journal, determined by the means of payment involved. If such assets are acquired for cash, the transactions are recorded in the cash disbursements journal; if purchased on credit, they are recorded in the general journal.

The advantages of and procedures required for a single-column purchases journal are similar to those described earlier for a sales journal. Recall from the discussion in Chapter 5 that the purchase of merchandise on credit with a periodic inventory system is recorded with a debit to Purchases and a credit to Accounts Payable. If a perpetual inventory system is used, the debit is to the Inventory account. The account credited on each line item of a purchases journal is an Account Payable with a particular creditor to whom the business has an obligation. A subsidiary ledger is maintained to provide the detailed information concerning each individual Account Payable. An Accounts Payable control account also is established in the general ledger. The procedures used with a single-column purchases journal, as illustrated in Figure 6-2, can be summarized as:

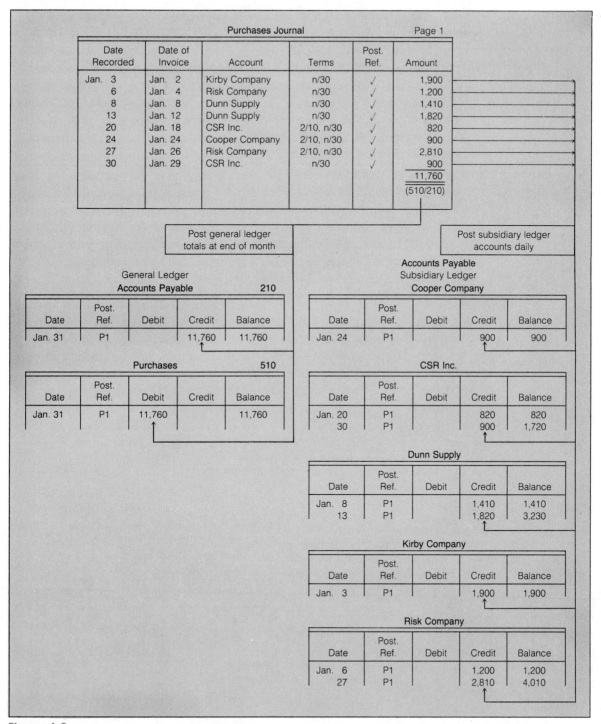

Figure 6-2
Relationship of Purchases Journal and Ledger Accounts

1. Enter the recording date, invoice date, supplier's name, credit terms if applicable, and the dollar amount of the purchase on a single line of the journal from each purchase invoice.
2. *At the end of each day,* post each purchase to the related supplier's account in the subsidiary ledger. Place a checkmark in the posting reference column of the purchases journal and P1 (indicating page one of the purchases journal) in the posting reference column of the creditor's account. These posting reference marks indicate that the journal entry has been posted and identify the source of the entry.
3. *At the end of each month,* total the amount column of the purchases journal and post the total amount as a debit and a credit to the two general ledger accounts, Purchases and Accounts Payable, respectively. Place the general ledger account numbers (510/210) below the total credit purchases and P1 in the posting reference columns of the two general ledger accounts.
4. Add the account balances of the Accounts Payable subsidiary ledger to verify that the total is equal to the Accounts Payable control account balance in the general ledger. In Figure 6-2, the total amount is $11,760.

A single-column purchases journal can be expanded to a multicolumn format such as the one shown in Figure 6-3. This journal has a single credit column for accounts payable and several debit columns for purchases of merchandise, purchases of store supplies, purchases of office supplies, and other debits. The other debits column can be used to record such transactions as the acquisition of equipment or the incurrence of freight-in charges. All of the transactions recorded in this journal will involve credit rather than cash because of the single accounts payable credit column. The recording and posting procedures with a multicolumn purchases journal are similar to those described next for the cash receipts journal.

Date	Account	Post. Ref.	Purchases Debit	Stores Supplies Debit	Office Supplies Debit	Other Debits Account	Post. Ref.	Amount	Accounts Payable Credit
Jan 3	Hull Co.	✓	1,900						1,900
10	Kirk, Inc.	✓	2,800						2,800
14	Deckers, Inc.	✓		810					810
19	Short Co.	✓			465				465
24	Zinn Co.	✓				Office Equipment	170	1,155	1,155

Figure 6-3
Multicolumn Purchases Journal

Cash Receipts Journal

The **cash receipts journal** is used to record all transactions involving the receipt of cash (a debit to cash). Typical sources of cash are the sale of merchandise for cash, the collection of accounts receivable from customers, investments by owners, and bank loans. A multicolumn cash receipts journal is necessary because of the numerous sources of cash possible. Two debit columns are required—one for the actual cash collected, the other for sales discounts. To keep the required number of columns manageable but at the same time achieve efficient processing, three credit columns often are used to separate the sources of cash in the journal. The headings on the three credit columns as shown in Figure 6-4 are Sales, Accounts Receivable, and Other Accounts. The first two credit columns are used to record collections from cash sales and accounts receivable. All other sources of cash are entered in the third credit column.

These cash receipts transactions for the Baldwin Video Equipment Store provide the basis for the entries in Figure 6-4:

1. The owner of the business, Betty Baldwin, invested $10,000 of her own cash on January 3.
2. Video equipment was sold for $285 cash on January 8.
3. Received payment from Robert Abbot for an eight-day-old account receivable of $1,100 less a 2% sales discount of $22 on January 10. Therefore, $1,078 cash was received. Credit terms are 2/10, n/30 and the cash was received within 10 days.
4. Received payment from Don Bohl for a 15-day-old account receivable of $900 on January 20. No discount was involved since the cash was not received within 10 days.
5. Video equipment was sold for $220 cash on January 21.
6. A bank loan of $2,500 was received on January 31.

The two debit columns and three credit columns of the cash receipts journal shown in Figure 6-4 are used as follows:

Debits

Cash. The cash column is used in *every* entry because *only* cash receipt transactions are recorded in the cash receipts journal.

Sales Discounts. This column is used to record all sales discounts allowed customers for prompt payment. Note that on January 10 a 2% discount (.02 × $1,100 = $22) was given to R. Abbot because the payment was made within 10 days in accordance with the credit terms. The total debits to Cash ($1,078) and Sales Discounts ($22) are equal to the $1,100 Accounts Receivable, all of which are recorded on one line.

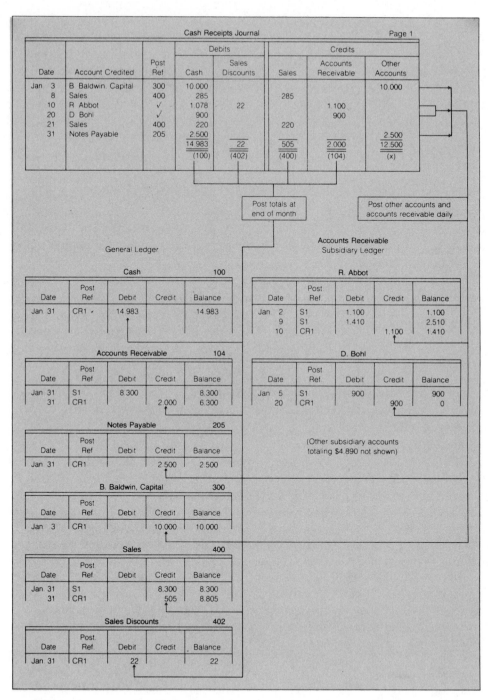

Figure 6-4
Relationship of Cash Receipts Journal and Ledger Accounts

Credits

Sales. All cash sales are recorded in the sales column. Most firms use cash registers to account for daily cash sales. At the end of a day, a sales tape showing the total cash sales is removed from the cash register and used to make the entry in the sales column.

Accounts Receivable. This column is used to record the collections on accounts from customers. The name of the customer is written in the account credited column to identify the proper account to be credited in the subsidiary ledger.

Other Accounts. This column is used for all cash collections other than from cash sales and accounts receivable. The title of the specific account to be credited is identified in the account credited column. For example, Betty Baldwin's Capital account is credited on January 3 for the $10,000 investment.

SUMMARY OF POSTING PROCEDURES FOR CASH RECEIPTS JOURNAL

The procedures required to post the entries in the cash receipts journal can be summarized as:

1. The entries in the accounts receivable column should be *posted daily* to the subsidiary ledger. A checkmark is placed in the posting reference column of the cash receipts journal, and CR1 (representing page one of the cash receipts journal) is entered in the posting reference columns of the subsidiary ledger accounts.
2. The credits in the other accounts column should be posted *daily or at other frequent intervals* during the month. The number of the account involved is recorded in the posting reference column as the entries are posted to show that the posting has been accomplished. In addition, CR1 is entered in the posting reference column of each account to indicate the source of each entry.
3. *At the end of the month,* the entries in each column should be totaled. The sum of the debit columns should be compared with the sum of the credit columns to verify that the debits and credits are equal. This procedure is called crossfooting, which gives the following results, using the totals of the journal columns:

Debit Columns		**Credit Columns**	
Cash	$14,983	Sales	$ 505
Sales discounts	22	Accounts receivable	2,000
		Other accounts	12,500
Total debits	$15,005		$15,005

Crossfooted

After the totals have been crossfooted, the following four column totals are posted:

Cash debit column. Posted as a debit to the Cash account. The account number (100) is entered below the total to indicate that the posting has been done, and CR1 is recorded in the posting reference column of the Cash account.

Sales discounts debit column. Posted as a debit to the Sales Discounts account. The account number (402) is placed below the total to show that the posting has been accomplished, and CR1 is entered in the Sales Discounts account.

Sales credit column. Posted as a credit to the Sales account. The account number (400) is entered below the total as an indication that the posting has taken place, and CR1 is recorded in the Sales account.

Accounts receivable credit column. Posted as a credit to the Accounts Receivable control account. The account number (104) is recorded below the total, and CR1 is entered in the control account.

The total of the other accounts column *is not posted at the end of the month* because each entry was posted individually during the month. Some accountants use a special symbol—such as (x)—at the bottom of the column to indicate that it is not posted as a total.

Cash Disbursements Journal

The **cash disbursements journal,** also called the cash payments journal, is used to record all transactions involving payments of cash—cash purchases of merchandise, payment of accounts payable to creditors, disbursements for operating expenses, and payment of bank loans. The multicolumn format of the cash disbursements journal is similar to the one described earlier for the cash receipts journal. Three debit columns (Purchases, Accounts Payable, and Other Accounts) are used along with two credit columns (Cash and Purchases Discounts), as illustrated in Figure 6-5. These transactions for Baldwin Video Equipment Store illustrate the cash disbursements journal:

1. Merchandise costing $680 was purchased for cash on January 4.
2. Store rent of $325 was paid on January 7.
3. Store equipment costing $410 was purchased for cash on January 14.
4. Merchandise costing $840 was purchased for cash on January 28.
5. A one-year premium for an insurance policy amounting to $510 was paid on January 29.
6. The $1,900 account payable to the Kirby Company was paid on January 30.

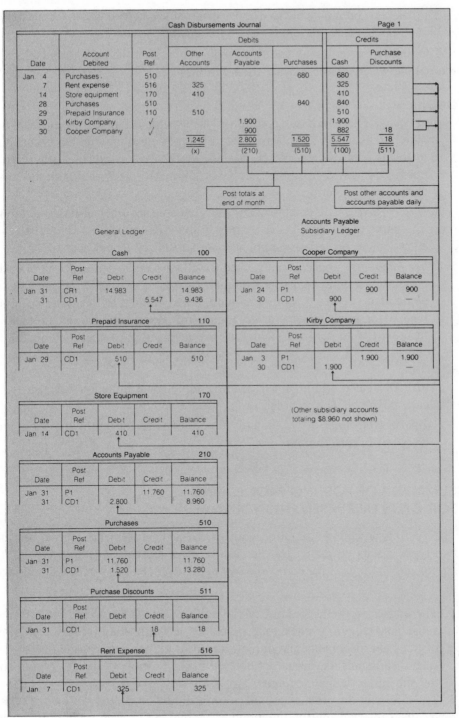

Figure 6-5
Relationship of Cash Disbursements Journal and Ledger Accounts

7. The $900 account payable to Cooper Company was paid less a 2% discount of $18 on January 30. Therefore, $882 cash was paid.

The three debit columns and two credit columns of the cash disbursements journal shown in Figure 6-5 are used as follows:

Debits

Purchases. The purchases column is used to record all cash purchases of merchandise. The total of this column is posted to the Purchases account in the general ledger. When posted, the amount is added to the credit purchases posted from the purchases journal to determine the total purchases for the period.

Accounts Payable. Payments of accounts payable are entered in this column. The name of the supplier is written in the account debited column so the entry can be posted to the appropriate subsidiary ledger account.

Other Accounts. This column is used for all cash disbursements *except* cash purchases and payments of accounts payable. The title of the account to be debited is entered in the account debited column to identify a specific type of cash disbursement. In Figure 6-5, rent expense and prepaid insurance were paid for along with the acquisition of store equipment.

Credits

Cash. The cash column must be used for *each* transaction because *only* cash payments are recorded in the journal.

Purchase Discounts. Any purchase discounts taken for prompt payment are recorded in this column.

SUMMARY OF POSTING PROCEDURES FOR CASH DISBURSEMENTS JOURNAL

The posting procedures required with the cash disbursements journal are the two types discussed earlier for the cash receipts journal—*postings during the month* and *postings at the end of the month*. The procedures can be summarized as:

1. The entries in the accounts payable column should be posted *daily* to the subsidiary ledger. A checkmark is placed in the posting reference column of the cash disbursements journal, and CD1 (representing page one of the cash disbursements journal) is entered in the posting reference columns of the subsidiary ledger accounts.

2. The debits in the other accounts column should be posted *daily or at other frequent intervals* during the month. The number of each account involved is recorded in the posting reference column as the entries are posted to

indicate that the posting has been done. CD1 is entered in the posting reference column of each account to show the source of each entry.

3. *At the end of the month,* the dollar amounts entered in each column should be totaled and crossfooted to verify that the debits and credits are equal as follows:

Debit Columns		Credit Columns	
Other accounts	$1,245	Cash	$5,547
Accounts payable	2,800	Purchase discounts	18
Purchases	1,520		
Total debits	$5,565	Total credits	$5,565
		Crossfooted	

4. The column totals for accounts payable, purchases, cash, and purchase discounts are posted *at the end of the month* to their respective accounts in the general ledger. The account numbers are entered below the column totals, and CD1 is recorded in the posting reference columns of the general ledger accounts. The total of the other accounts column is *not* posted at the end of the month because the individual entries were posted earlier. An (x) can be placed below the column total to indicate that it is not posted at the end of the month.

USE OF GENERAL JOURNAL

Despite the inefficiency of a general journal for repetitive transactions such as sales, purchases, cash receipts, and cash disbursements, it is an essential part of every accounting system. A *limited number* of transactions (such as sales returns and allowances, purchase returns and allowances, and the purchase or sale of equipment on credit) are recorded in the general journal *during* an accounting period. If a particular transaction cannot be recorded efficiently in one of the special journals, it should be entered in the general journal. The general journal is also used for all *adjusting* and *closing entries* at the end of the accounting period. The procedures used to record entries in the general journal and to post them to ledger accounts have already been described. As we have seen in the description of special journals, the ledger accounts should indicate the journal from which each debit and credit is posted. The symbol GJ typically is used in the ledger accounts for postings from the general journal; GJ1 would refer to page one of the general journal. The following symbols can be used to identify the sources of entries posted from the five journals discussed so far:

S1—page 1 of the sales journal
P2—page 2 of the purchases journal

CR3—page 3 of the cash receipts journal

CD4—page 4 of the cash disbursements journal

GJ5—page 5 of the general journal

To illustrate the use of the general journal, assume that Betty Baldwin agreed to give A. Evans a $72 allowance on his account because of a faulty component on video equipment sold on January 19. The sales allowance would be recorded in the general journal as shown in Figure 6-6. Both the Accounts Receivable control account and the customer's subsidiary ledger account must be credited; otherwise the control account would not be in balance with the subsidiary ledger. The number of the accounts receivable account (104) and a checkmark are recorded in the posting reference column to indicate that both postings are made.

REFINEMENTS OF AN ACCOUNTING SYSTEM

We have emphasized that a given business often refines the general accounting records discussed so far with a manual system to provide more efficient data processing and to satisfy its own information requirements. Two means of refinement are worthy of noting at this point because of their popularity: *direct posting from invoices* and a *one-write system.* Many businesses maintain a numerical file of sales invoices from which sales and accounts receivable information is posted to ledger accounts. The sales invoices are numbered serially and filed as they are prepared in a binder of some sort, so in effect the binder takes the place of the sales journal. Each sales invoice total is posted directly to the related customer's account in the accounts receivable subsidiary ledger on a daily basis. At the end of the month, all invoices for that month are totaled, and a general journal entry is made debiting the Accounts Receivable control account and crediting the Sales account for the total monthly sales. The same procedures can be used in recording purchase invoices in lieu of maintaining a purchases journal.

As the name suggests, a one-write system eliminates the need to enter the same data more than once. Several business forms for different recording functions can be held in alignment on some type of writing board so that a single entry on the top form produces the same entries on the forms beneath it. Since only the one entry is made, repetitive copying is avoided, reducing clerical costs. For example, a one-write approach can be used with a cash disbursements journal. When a check is written, the information also is recorded in the appropriate column of the cash disbursements journal and in the accounts payable subsidiary ledger whenever applicable. This is accomplished by using special paper that reproduces what is written on the check on the other records.

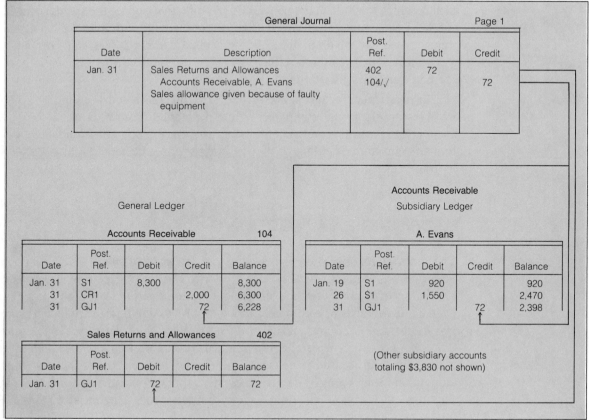

Figure 6-6
Relationship of General Journal and Ledger Accounts

DATA-PROCESSING EQUIPMENT

To process data accurately and rapidly, most businesses use some type of equipment. Even in the manual accounting applications discussed earlier, such equipment as calculators, typewriters, cash registers, and copy machines are used to reduce the workload and errors. A wide range of additional equipment is available and can be adopted to satisfy the information requirements and operating conditions of a firm. For example, a bookkeeping machine can be utilized for a number of accounting applications. **Bookkeeping machines** can perform relatively simple arithmetic operations and generate financial reports. They can be used to record such repetitive transactions as sales, purchases, cash receipts, cash disbursements, and payroll. In essence, the special journals and ledger accounts discussed earlier are maintained with a bookkeeping machine. However, the dramatic technological advances of electronic computers, particularly small computers, have significantly reduced the number of bookkeeping machines used today.

The most modern and sophisticated type of automated accounting system involves an electronic computer. While a detailed description of a computer accounting system is beyond the scope of this book, we should develop a fundamental understanding of how a computer operates and the importance of its role in the accounting function.

ELECTRONIC DATA PROCESSING

The terms **electronic data processing (EDP)** and *computer data processing* are often used interchangeably. They refer to the use of electronic equipment, consisting of a computer and its peripheral equipment, to process data. The primary advantages of a computer as a data-processing device are its *accuracy, speed, storage capacity,* and *versatility* for performing analytical operations. As a firm grows in size and complexity, the volume of paperwork from transactions to be processed increases significantly. At some point the cost, inaccuracy, and time delays of a manual system force a business to consider using a computer. For example, think about the data-processing requirements of a medium-sized commercial bank with assets of $150,000,000. The bank must have an accounting system to process data related to revenue and expense transactions as well as its balance sheet accounts. It also must maintain detailed records concerning such functions as credit card activity, installment loans, business loans, real estate loans, check processing, customer deposits, and savings accounts. Hundreds of thousands of transactions are involved, and a computerized operation of some sort will be required to cope with the volume of data. A similar situation confronts a variety of other operations such as an airline, a retail-store chain, a stockbrokerage firm, a hospital, a hotel chain, or a manufacturing company.

Today, the increasing popularity of minicomputers, microcomputers, and time-sharing services have made EDP affordable even for small businesses. As its name suggests, a *minicomputer* is a small, low-cost machine capable of performing many of the operations of a large computer, although on a more limited scale. A *microcomputer* is even smaller; it can have most of its essential components on a single silicon chip smaller than a key on a pocket calculator. A *time-sharing application* exists when one business shares a computer's time with other users, as happens when time is rented from a service bureau specializing in data processing.

WHAT IS A COMPUTER?

A computer is a high-speed electronic machine that receives data and instructions, processes the data into information, and reports the results in a form readable by a human being or another machine. The type of computer used in an accounting system is a **digital computer,** a machine that processes discrete numbers in accordance with a sequence of internally stored instructions. The other type of computer is an analog computer, which manipulates some physical quantity such as voltage or temperature change and is used in engineering applications. Today's large digital computers can execute an instruction in a nanosecond—one billionth of a second—and can process a large volume of data in a fraction of the time required with human effort. For example, a large company with thousands of employees can process its payroll in a *few hours* with a computer instead of the *several days* required with manual processing. Today, hundreds of thousands of digital computers are being used in the United States.

A digital computer has five basic components, illustrated in Figure 6-7:

Input. Receives data and instructions from the computer operator or an electronic device. Many different means can be used for the input process: *punched cards, diskettes, paper tape, magnetic cards, magnetic tape,* or a *keyboard*.

Memory unit. The primary storage of the computer, where data and instructions are stored and from which data are obtained when needed.

Arithmetic-logic unit. Performs arithmetical and logical operations such as addition, subtraction, multiplication, division, and comparison of two values. Data in the memory section are manipulated according to instructions from the control unit in the arithmetic-logic unit.

Control unit. Directs the sequencing of operations that process input data according to well-defined instructions fed into the memory unit.

Output. Translates the results of processed data into such usable form as *printed copy, punched cards, diskettes, paper tape, magnetic cards, magnetic tape,* or *lines on a display screen*.

The central processing unit (CPU) of a computer consists of its memory, arithmetic-logic, and control components. The CPU determines the operating capacity of the computer since it controls the flow of data into the system, performs calculations and other manipulations on the data, and regulates the flow of output. In addition to the primary storage of the memory component, a computer usually is supported with secondary storage external to the computer that allows the storage of a larger volume of data than permitted in the memory of the computer itself. The secondary-storage capacity is normally less expensive than the computer memory.

Figure 6-7
Components of a
Computer

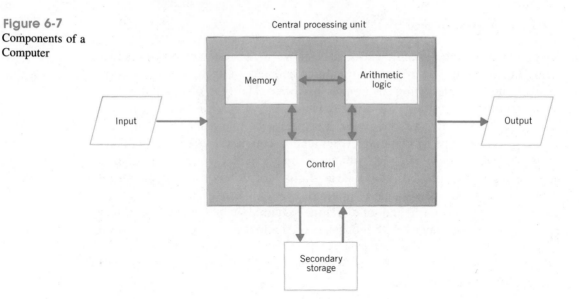

Central processing unit

HOW DOES A COMPUTER WORK?

A computer must be told exactly *where to find data input, how to process the data, and what to do with the output*. These instructions are given to the CPU in the form of **computer programs,** a series of precise instructions that tell the computer what it is to do step by step. Programs are read into the memory of the computer to provide these instructions. Whereas the term **hardware** is used to denote the components of the computer and its peripheral equipment, **software** refers to the programs that will make the equipment function along with documentation and instructions for using the programs.

A **computer programmer** is a person who writes computer programs. These programs usually are written in a language people can work with, such as BASIC, FORTRAN, or COBOL. They are translated later into a machine-readable form through the use of special programs called compilers. COBOL, an acronym for Common Business Oriented Language, is particularly useful for such accounting applications as updating ledgers, processing payrolls, preparing financial statements, and maintaining inventories. In a computerized accounting system, a computer program must be written to tell the computer how to proceed through each accounting application. To do so, the programmer must know whether the data processing will be performed with batch processing or online processing. In **batch processing,** transaction data are accumulated until a large volume is processed at one time. This method often is used for such routine procedures as payroll, customer billing, and general ledger accounting. For example, payroll data can be collected at the end of each pay period, batched, and processed by the computer. **Online processing** involves processing transactions as they occur so that a user can obtain current information at any time. An example of online processing is the system used for airline reservations. Each ticket counter has a terminal with which an agent can instantly communicate with a computer concerning flight information and available space. Online processing can be applied to such accounting activities as accounts receivable, accounts payable, and inventories.

COMPUTER ACCOUNTING SYSTEMS

It is important to note the similarities between a basic accounting system and a computer. Each involves three essential phases: *input, processing,* and *output.* The integration of a computer into an accounting system is, therefore, a relatively simple task. A significant amount of software available today supports such accounting applications as accounts receivable, accounts payable, payroll, inventory control, and general ledger accounting. Remember that a manual accounting system consists of business forms, journals, ledgers, and reports. In a computer accounting system, basically the same business forms can be used but must be converted into a machine-readable format to be accepted as input to the computer. Business transactions are recorded on coding forms similar to the special journals discussed earlier. The data are then put into the computer through some device such as a keyboard, which is similar to an ordinary typewriter.

The programs supporting a particular accounting application are moved into the primary storage area of the computer, the work area of the CPU. Input, programs, and output are moved in and out of the primary storage area as the computer processes data according to well-defined instructions. **Files,** which are ordered sets of accessible records, are used to process the accounting data. For example, the accounts receivable master file (consisting of a record for each customer) at the beginning of an accounting period can be updated by the computer to record credit sales billed to customers as follows:

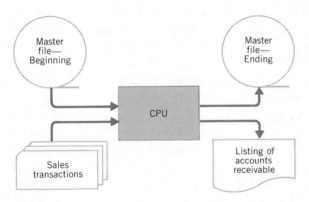

(Note the similarities between this updating of the accounts receivable file and the manual procedures discussed earlier with the sales journal.)

In this simple case, there are two sources of input and output. The input consists of the accounts receivable file at the beginning of the period and the sales transactions required to update the beginning balances. On the output side, an updated accounts receivable master file and a listing of accounts receivable billed are produced through the computer processing. A master file and a transaction file would be used for updating accounts receivable. In general, the transformation of data into information with a computer accounting system can be diagrammed as:

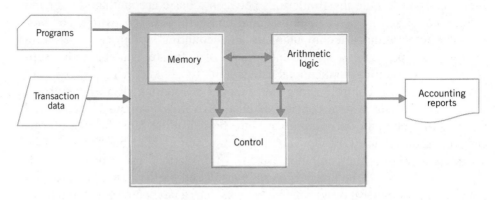

GLOSSARY

ACCOUNTING SYSTEM. A collection of business forms, records, procedures, management policies, and data-processing methods used to transform economic data into useful information (p. 246).

BATCH PROCESSING. Accumulating a volume of data and processing it at one time (p. 270).

BOOKKEEPING MACHINE. A mechanical or electronic machine that can perform relatively simple arithmetic computations and generate reports (p. 267).

CASH DISBURSEMENTS JOURNAL. A special journal used to record all cash payments (p. 262).

CASH RECEIPTS JOURNAL. A special journal used to record transactions involving the receipt of cash (p. 259).

COMPUTER PROGRAM. A sequence of instructions stored in the computer's memory that tell the computer what to do and when to do it (p. 270).

COMPUTER PROGRAMMER. A person who writes computer programs, usually in a language understandable by humans that is later converted into a machine-readable form by a compiler (p. 270).

CONTROL ACCOUNT. A general ledger account that is supported by the detail of a subsidiary ledger (p. 251).

DIGITAL COMPUTER. An electronic machine that processes discrete values and consists of input, a memory unit, an arithmetic-logic unit, a control unit, and output (p. 269).

ELECTRONIC DATA PROCESSING. The use of a digital computer and its peripheral equipment to process data (p. 268).

FILE. An ordered set of records used to process data (p. 271).

HARDWARE. The components of the computer and its peripheral equipment (p. 270).

ONLINE PROCESSING. A technique that involves immediate access to the computer whenever a user wants information (p. 270).

PURCHASES JOURNAL. A special journal used to record all purchases of merchandise on credit (p. 256).

SALES JOURNAL. A special journal used to record all sales of merchandise on credit (p. 253).

SOFTWARE. Programs that make the computer function along with documentation and instructions for using the programs (p. 270).

SPECIAL JOURNALS. Books of original entry used for such repetitive transactions as sales, purchases, cash receipts, and cash disbursements (p. 253).

SUBSIDIARY LEDGER. A group of individual accounts, the total of which should equal the balance of a related control account in the general ledger (p. 251).

SYSTEMS ANALYSIS. The initial stage in the development of an accounting system through which an understanding of a business's information requirements and sources of information is provided (p. 249).

SYSTEMS DESIGN. The second stage in the development of an accounting system through which the specific means to be used for input, processing, and output are determined (p. 249).

SYSTEMS IMPLEMENTATION. The final stage in the development of an accounting system through which the system is made operational (p. 250).

DISCUSSION QUESTIONS

1. What are the three phases of an accounting system? Explain each one.
2. Distinguish between data and information in the sense the two terms are used technically in an accounting system.
3. Why is internal control important in the operation of an accounting system?
4. What are the three phases of the installation of an accounting system? Explain each one.
5. What is the basic limitation of a manual accounting system?
6. How are control accounts and subsidiary ledgers used? What are their major advantages?

7. What are the advantages of using special journals? Why is the general journal needed even when special journals are used?
8. How often are sales transactions posted from the sales journal to the general ledger? To the subsidiary ledger?
9. What are the advantages of the sales journal?
10. How often are purchase transactions posted from the purchases journal to the general ledger? To the subsidiary ledger?
11. Why is it necessary to crossfoot both the cash receipts journal and the cash disbursements journal?
12. Why is a multicolumn journal used for cash receipts and cash disbursements?
13. Identify the major sources of cash receipts recorded in the cash receipts journal. Identify the major transactions involving cash payments recorded in the cash disbursements journal.
14. Explain how copies of sales invoices can be used as a sales journal.
15. What is meant by the term *one-write system* as it is applied to an accounting system?
16. What are the primary advantages of computer data processing?
17. What are the five basic components of a computer?
18. Distinguish between the terms *hardware* and *software* as they are used in electronic data processing.
19. What is a computer program and why is it important in data processing?
20. Differentiate batch processing from online processing.
21. What is a file in the application of electronic data processing?

EXERCISES

Exercise 6-1 (Matching Transactions with Journals)
The Genesee Company uses a purchases journal, a cash receipts journal, a cash disbursements journal, a sales journal, and a general journal. Indicate in which journal each of the following transactions would most likely be recorded.

1. Sales of merchandise on credit
2. Payment of monthly rent
3. Received payment on a customer's account
4. Purchased merchandise on account
5. Cash purchase of merchandise
6. Year-end closing entries
7. Sale of marketable securities for cash
8. Received credit memo for defective merchandise, which was purchased on account and returned to the supplier
9. Sale of capital stock for cash
10. Cash refund to a customer who returned merchandise

Exercise 6-2 (Matching Ledger Accounts with Journals)
The Strong Company has an accounting system that uses sales, purchases, cash receipts, cash disbursements, and general journals. Identify the most probable journal used for each posting to the following accounts.

Cash		Sales		Purchases		Accounts Payable	
(a) 11,900	(g) 8,740	(b) 21,000 (d) 2,000	(h) 900 (k) 12,000			(j) 8,000	(l) 12,000

Accounts Receivable		Sales Discounts		Purchase Discounts	Purchase Allowances
(c) 21,000	(e) 10,000	(f) 100		(i) 160	(m) 150

Exercise 6-3 (Relating Special Journals to Subsidiary Ledger)

The sales and cash receipts journals of the Victor Company for the month of July are presented below. The company maintains an accounts receivable subsidiary ledger, which is balanced with the general ledger account each month. On July 1, the subsidiary ledger was comprised of four accounts: B. Allen—$150; J. Kline—$200; M. Feldman—$300; B. Lang—$125.

	Sales Journal		P. 15			Cash Receipts		P. 11
Date	Invoice	Account	Amount		Date	Account	Cash	Accounts Receivable
7/2	503	R. Raman	130		7/5	B. Allen	75	75
7/6	504	B. Allen	60		7/10	J. Kline	200	200
7/7	505	J. Kline	125		7/23	M. Feldman	190	190
7/15	506	M. Feldman	100		7/27	B. Lang	125	125
7/25	507	K. Light	95					

Required:

A. Post the amounts to the accounts receivable subsidiary ledger and to the general ledger.

B. Prepare a trial balance of the subsidiary ledger and compare it to the balance in the control account.

Exercise 6-4 (Accounting with Several Journals)

The Thomas Company uses sales, purchases, cash receipts, cash disbursements, and general journals. The following column totals were taken from the company's journals at the end of September:

1. Sales journal	$1,500
2. Purchases journal	800
3. Cash receipts journal:	
(a) Cash	1,240
(b) Accounts receivable	1,040
(c) Sales	210
(d) Sales discounts	10

4. Cash disbursements journal:

(a) Cash	1,180
(b) Accounts payable	1,000
(c) Purchase discounts	20
(d) Purchases	200

The balance in the Accounts Receivable control account on September 1 was $600 and the Accounts Payable control account balance was $850.

Required:

A. At the end of September, the total of the sales journal should be posted to what account or accounts?

B. At the end of September, the total of the purchases journal should be posted to what account or accounts?

C. For each column total in the cash receipts and the cash disbursements journals, specify whether it would be posted to the general ledger as a debit or a credit.

D. After the journals have been posted to the general ledger for September, what would be the balances in the Accounts Receivable and the Accounts Payable control accounts?

Exercise 6-5 (Detecting Errors in an Accounting System)

The Gross Company has an accounting system that uses sales, purchases, cash receipts, cash disbursements, and general journals. At various times during the year, the following errors have occurred. Specify a procedure that would detect each error.

1. An error was made in totaling the cash column in the cash receipts journal.

2. A customer's check, net of the applicable sales discount, was correctly entered in the cash column at the net amount and in the accounts receivable column at the gross amount. No entry was made in the sales discounts column.

3. The amount column in the purchases journal was incorrectly totaled.

4. A subtraction error was made on a customer's account in the accounts receivable subsidiary ledger.

5. The amount of a bank loan entered in the Other column of the cash receipts journal was posted as a debit to notes payable.

6. A sales return, journalized in the general journal, was posted to the Accounts Receivable control account and to the Sales Return and Allowances account but was not posted to the accounts receivable subsidiary ledger.

7. A credit sale for $750 was posted as $75 in the accounts receivable subsidiary ledger.

8. A purchase discount was not entered in the cash disbursements journal. The gross amount of vendor's invoice was entered in the accounts payable column and the net amount of the check was entered in the cash column.

9. A purchase allowance for merchandise purchased on account was entered in the general journal. The entry was posted to only two accounts—the Accounts Payable subsidiary account and to Purchase Returns and Allowances.

10. The sales journal was incorrectly totaled.

PROBLEMS

Problem 6-1 (Relating Journals to Accounts Receivable Control Account)

The Holland Company uses sales, cash receipts, and general journals in its accounting system. The company also maintains an accounts receivable subsidiary ledger that contained the following five accounts on May 31.

B. Phillips

Date		Post Ref.	Debit	Credit	Balance
5/1	Balance				1,500
5/7		CR3		1,200	300

E. Dewey

Date	Post Ref.	Debit	Credit	Balance
5/5	S7	700		700
5/15	S7	600		1,300
5/21	CR3		500	800

E. Cook

Date	Post Ref.	Debit	Credit	Balance
5/10	S7	500		500
5/19	CR3		200	300

J. Scofield

Date		Post Ref.	Debit	Credit	Balance
5/1	Balance				900
5/11		CR3		400	500
5/21		S7	200		700

T. Morrow

Date		Post Ref.	Debit	Credit	Balance
5/1	Balance				1,250
5/19		GJ4		200	1,050
5/30		CR3		1,050	–0–

Required:

Establish an Accounts Receivable control account and post all entries for the month of May in chronological order with the necessary posting references.

Problem 6-2 (Accounting with Sales and Purchases Journals)

The Lilac Company uses sales and purchases journals in its accounting system. The following transactions occurred during February 1985.

Feb.
3 Purchased merchandise on account from the Scott Co., Invoice 307, $500, terms 2/10, n/30

7 Purchased merchandise on account from the Harris Co., Invoice 737, $350, terms 2/10, n/30.

10 Sold merchandise on account to the Brookman Co., Invoice 126, $950.

15 Sold merchandise on account to the Lyman Co., Invoice 127, $825.

17 Purchased merchandise on account from the Conn Co., Invoice 238, $425, terms 2/10, n/30.

25 Sold merchandise on account to the Miles Co., Invoice 128, $650.

27 Sold merchandise on account to the Lyman Co., Invoice 129, $500, terms 2/10, n/30.

Required:

A. Open all necessary general ledger accounts, accounts receivable subsidiary ledger accounts, and accounts payable subsidiary ledger accounts. Use the following account numbers: Accounts Receivable—105; Accounts Payable—200; Sales—400; Purchases—500.
B. Journalize the February transactions in the appropriate journals.
C. Post the data from the journals to the correct general ledger and subsidiary accounts.
D. Prepare a schedule of the accounts receivable subsidiary ledger and the accounts payable subsidiary ledger as of February 28 to prove the subsidiary ledger balance for the control accounts.

Problem 6-3 (Accounting with Sales, Cash Receipts, and General Journals)

The Dorchester Company maintains a sales journal, a cash receipts journal, a general journal, and an accounts receivable subsidiary ledger. The terms of all credit sales are 2/10, n/30 and all account receivable balances as of November 1, 1985, arose from transactions prior to October 20, 1985. The trial balance as of November 1 included the following accounts, among others:

Acct. No.	Acct. Title	Acct Balance	Acct. No.	Acct. Title	Acct Balance
100	Cash	$ 7,000	410	Sales Discounts	$ 800
120	Marketable Securities	12,000	420	Sales Returns and	
150	Accounts Receivable	5,000		Allowances	1,000
151	Notes Receivable	–0–	430	Dividend Revenue	400
200	Notes Payable	1,000	440	Interest Revenue	300
400	Sales	80,000	490	Gain on Sale of Stock	100

The accounts receivable subsidiary ledger balances were as follows:

L. Lamb	$ 750
M. Mulligan	1,250
N. Nettles	300
P. Peterson	1,500
S. Sweet	1,200
.V. Viceroy	–0–

The following transactions in November involved the sales, cash receipts, and general journals:

Nov.
1 Issued a credit memo to L. Lamb for defective merchandise sold on account during October, $75.

3 Sold merchandise on account to V. Viceroy, $800, Invoice 254.

6 Received a check from N. Nettles for payment of an October purchase, $300.

7 Sold merchandise on account to M. Mulligan, $100, Invoice 255.

8 Sold merchandise on account to P. Peterson, $180, Invoice 256.

10 Received payment from V. Viceroy for Invoice 254 less 2% discount.

11 Received payment in full from L. Lamb.

13 Borrowed $5,000 cash from the bank for three months at 18%.

14 Sold merchandise for cash, $125.

17 Sold common stock that had been held as a short-term investment for $6,500. The stock had been purchased for $5,000.

19 Received a 60-day note from M. Mulligan in settlement of his account receivable balance.

25 Received a check from P. Peterson, $1,500, for payment on his account.

27 Sold merchandise on account to N. Nettles, $300, Invoice 257.

30 Received payment from N. Nettles for Invoice 257 less 2% discount.

Required:

Record the November transactions in the appropriate journals. Make all postings to the proper general ledger accounts and to the accounts receivable subsidiary ledgers.

Problem 6-4 (Accounting for Transactions with Several Journals)

The Newcastle Company started operations March 1. Its accounting system includes a sales journal, a purchases journal, a cash receipts journal, a cash disbursements journal, and a general journal. During March, the following accounts were used:

100	Cash	405	Sales Discounts
110	Accounts Receivable	410	Sales Allowances
115	Prepaid Insurance	500	Purchases
150	Office Equipment	503	Purchase Returns
201	Accounts Payable	505	Purchase Discounts
210	Notes Payable	550	Rent Expense
300	Common Stock	560	Insurance Expense
400	Sales	570	Utilities Expense

During March, the transactions were as follows:

March 1 Sold common stock at par value, $10,000
       3 Borrowed $5,000 from a local bank for one year at 20%.
       3 Paid rent for March, $1,000.
       5 Purchased merchandise on account from the Gibson Co., $2,000, Invoice 433, terms 2/10, n/60.
       6 Purchased merchandise on account from the Murray Co., $750, Invoice 220, terms 1/10, n/30.
       7 Purchased office equipment for cash, $500.
       8 Sold merchandise on account to McHenry Co., $600, terms 2/10, n/30, Invoice 301.
      10 Paid for merchandise purchased from the Gibson Co., Invoice 433.
      11 Received a credit memo from the Murray Co. for merchandise returned, $50.
      12 Paid Murray Co. in full for balance of Invoice 220.
      13 Sold merchandise for cash, $210.
      17 Paid for a 12-month insurance policy, $600. The effective date of the policy was March 1.
      19 Purchased merchandise on account from the Abell Co., $1,200, Invoice 760, terms n/60.
      20 Purchased merchandise on account from the Croydon Co., $650, Invoice 406, terms 2/10, n/30.
      25 Sold merchandise on account to the Beresford Co., $525, Invoice 302, terms 2/10, n/30.
      26 Received payment from the McHenry Co. in full settlement of Invoice 301.
      27 Sold merchandise on account to the Palm Co., Invoice 303, $1,050, terms 2/10, n/30.
      28 Paid the Croydon Co. in full for merchandise purchased March 20.
      30 Paid the electric bill, $90.
      30 Issued a credit memo to the Palm Co. for defective merchandise sold March 27, $30.

Required:

Record the transactions in the proper journals. Indicate how the postings would be made from the journals by entering the appropriate posting references.

Problem 6-5 (Journalizing Transactions and Completing the Accounting)

The Ludington Company uses sales, purchases, cash receipts, cash disbursements, and general journals along with subsidiary ledgers for accounts receivable and accounts payable. The post-closing trial balance as of April 30, 1984, and the trial balances of the subsidiary ledgers are presented below on page 281.

LUDINGTON COMPANY
Post-Closing Trial Balance
April 30, 1984

100	Cash	$ 6,000	
110	Accounts Receivable	3,000	
150	Inventory	5,000	
170	Equipment	10,000	
175	Accumulated Depreciation		$ 1,000
200	Accounts Payable		4,000
300	Common Stock		10,000
350	Retained Earnings		9,000
400	Sales		–0–
405	Sales Returns	–0–	
410	Sales Discounts	–0–	
500	Purchases	–0–	
510	Purchase Discounts		–0–
515	Purchase Returns		–0–
530	Rent Expense	–0–	
540	Utilities Expense	–0–	
550	Commissions Expense	–0–	
		$24,000	$24,000

Accounts Receivable Subsidiary Ledger

Highland Co.	$ 700
Radcliffe Co.	1,400
Cedarwood Co.	900
Total	$3,000

Accounts Payable Subsidiary Ledger

Ramsey Co.	$1,000
Yarmouth Co.	1,600
Gramercy Co.	1,400
Total	$4,000

The following transactions occured in May 1984:

May   ① Received a check from Highland Co. for payment on account, $700.

          3 Sold merchandise to the Blossom Co. on account, Invoice 502, $900, terms 2/10, n/30.

          4 Paid rent for May, $750.

          5 Purchased merchandise on account from the East Co., $1,050, Invoice 123, terms 2/10, n/30.

6 Paid Ramsey Co. for merchandise purchased previously, $1,000.

8 Received payment from Blossom Co. for full settlement of Invoice 502.

9 Received a credit memo from the East Co. for merchandise returned, $50.

11 Paid the East Co. in full, Invoice 123.

12 Paid sales commissions, $2,050.

13 Received a check from the Radcliffe Co. in partial payment of the account, $700.

17 Paid $3,000 for new office equipment.

18 Cash sales, $560.

19 Sold merchandise on account to the Highland Co., $950, Invoice 503, terms 2/10, n/30.

21 Sold merchandise on account to the Garson Co., $450,. Invoice 504, terms 2/10, n/30.

23 Paid the Yarmouth Co. for merchandise purchased in April, $1,600.

25 Cash sales, $625.

27 Paid utility bills for May, $275.

30 Received a check from Cedarwood Co., $900, for payment on account.

30 Received a check from Garson Co. for payment on account.

Required:

A. Journalize the transactions in the appropriate journals.

B. Make all necessary postings for the month.

C. Prepare a trial balance of the general ledger and subsidiary ledgers on May 30.

ALTERNATE PROBLEMS

Problem 6-1A (Relating Journals to Accounts Receivable Control Account)

The Caso Company uses sales, cash receipts, and general journals in its accounting system. The company also maintains an accounts receivable subsidiary ledger that contained the following five accounts on June 30:

			D. Ford		
Date		Post Ref.	Debit	Credit	Balance
6/1	Balance				1,800
6/10		CR4		1,440	360

J. Jones

Date	Post Ref.	Debit	Credit	Balance
6/6	S9	840		840
6/16	S9	720		1,560
6/22	CR4		600	960

A. Robinson

Date	Post Ref.	Debit	Credit	Balance
6/9	S9	600		600
6/18	CR4		240	360

R. Cohn

Date		Post Ref.	Debit	Credit	Balance
6/1	Balance				1,080
6/11		CR4		480	600
6/22		S9	240		840

C. Plant

Date		Post Ref.	Debit	Credit	Balance
6/1	Balance				1,500
6/20		GJ5		240	1,260
6/29		CR3		1,260	–0–

Required:

Establish an Accounts Receivable control account. Then post all entries for the month of June in chronological order and show the necessary posting references.

Problem 6-2A (Accounting with Sales and Purchases Journals)

The Shirlee Company uses sales and purchases journals in its accounting system. The following transactions took place during March:

March 2 Purchased merchandise on account from the Dye Co., Invoice 408, $420, terms 2/10, n/30.

6 Purchased merchandise on account from the Rider Co., Invoice 606, $600, terms 2/10, n/30.

11 Sold merchandise on account to the Jett Co., Invoice 228, $1,140.

14 Sold merchandise on account to the Dynamics Co., Invoice 229, $990.

19 Purchased merchandise on account from the Donoley Co., Invoice 1614, $510, 2/10, n/30.

23 Sold merchandise on account to the Dockey Co., Invoice 230, $780.

28 Sold merchandise on account to the Peck Co., Invoice 231, $600, 2/10, n/30.

Required:

A. Establish all necessary general ledger accounts, accounts receivable subsidiary ledger accounts, and accounts payable subsidiary ledger accounts. Use the following account numbers: Accounts Receivable—104; Accounts Payable—201; Sales—400; Purchases—500.

B. Journalize the March transactions in the appropriate journals.

C. Post the data from the journals to the appropriate general ledger and subsidiary ledger accounts.

D. Develop a schedule of the accounts receivable subsidiary ledger and the accounts payable subsidiary ledger as of March 31 to prove the subsidiary ledger balances for the control accounts.

Problem 6-3A (Accounting with Sales, Cash Receipts, and General Journals)

The Plaza Company uses a sales journal, a cash receipts journal, a general journal, and an accounts receivable subsidiary ledger. The terms of all credit sales are 2/10, n/30 and all account receivable balances as of October 1, 1985, were the result of transactions prior to September 15, 1985. The trial balance as of October 1 included the following accounts, among others:

	Acct. Title	Acct. Balance
100	Cash	$ 8,400
120	Marketable Securities	14,400
150	Accounts Receivable	6,000
151	Notes Receivable	–0–
200	Notes Payable	1,200
400	Sales	96,000
410	Sales Discounts	960
420	Sales Returns	1,200
430	Dividend Revenue	480
440	Interest Revenue	360
490	Gain on Sale of Stock	120

The accounts receivable subsidiary ledger balances were:

P. Dickens	$ –0–
D. Fields	1,800
S. Lamb	360
R. Roberts	1,500
S. Sheets	1,440
J. Tinker	900
Total	$6,000

The following transactions during October were recorded in the sales, cash receipts, or general journals:

October 1 Issued a credit memo to J. Tinker for defective merchandise sold on account during September, $90.
4 Sold merchandise on account to P. Dickens, $960, Invoice 324.
8 Received a check from S. Lamb for payment of a September purchase, $360.
9 Sold merchandise on account to R. Roberts, $120, Invoice 325.
10 Sold merchandise on account to D. Fields, $216, Invoice 326.
13 Received payment from P. Dickens for Invoice 324 less 2% discount.
17 Received payment in full from J. Tinker.
20 Borrowed $6,000 cash from the bank for three months at 18%.
21 Sold merchandise for cash, $150.
24 Sold common stock that had been held as a short-term investment for $7,800. The stock was originally purchased for $6,000.
27 Received a 60-day note from R. Roberts in settlement of his account receivable balance.
27 Received a check from D. Fields, $1,800, for payment on his account.
27 Sold merchandise on account to S. Lamb, $360, Invoice 327.
30 Received payment from S. Lamb for Invoice 327 less 2% discount.

Required:
Record the October transactions in the appropriate journals. Make all postings to the proper general ledger accounts and to the accounts receivable subsidiary ledgers.

Problem 6-4A (Accounting for Transactions with Several Journals)

The Ping Company started operations on April 1 with an accounting system that includes a sales journal, a purchases journal, a cash receipts journal, a cash disbursement journal, and a general journal. During April, the following accounts were used:

100 Cash
110 Accounts Receivable
115 Prepaid Insurance
150 Office Equipment
201 Accounts Payable
210 Notes Payable
300 Common Stock
400 Sales

405 Sales Discounts
410 Sales Allowances
500 Purchases
503 Purchase Returns
505 Purchase Discounts
550 Rent Expense
560 Insurance Expense
570 Utilities Expense

The following transactions took place during April:

April 1 Sold common stock at par value, $12,000.
3 Borrowed $6,000 from a local bank for one year at 20%.
3 Paid rent for April, $1,200.
5 Purchased merchandise on account from the Rolley Co., $2,400, Invoice 483, terms 2/10, n/60.

6 Purchased merchandise on account from the Dickens Co., $900, Invoice 284, terms 1/10, n/30.

7 Purchased office equipment for cash, $600.

8 Sold merchandise on account to the Rogers Co., $720, terms 2/10, n/30, Invoice 101.

10 Paid for merchandise purchased from the Rolley Co., Invoice 483.

11 Received a credit memo from the Dickens Co. for merchandise returned, $60.

12 Paid Dickens Co. in full for balance of Invoice 284.

13 Sold merchandise for cash, $252.

17 Paid for a 12-month insurance policy, $720. The effective date of the policy was April 1.

19 Purchased merchandise on account from the Ace Co., $1,440, Invoice 980, terms, n/60.

20 Purchased merchandise on account from the Keri Co., $780, Invoice 1012, terms 2/10, n/30.

25 Sold merchandise on account to the Richards Co., $630, Invoice 102, terms 2/10, n/30.

26 Received payment from the Rogers Co. in full settlement of Invoice 101.

27 Sold merchandise on account to the River Co., Invoice 103, $1,260, terms 2/10, n/30.

28 Paid the Keri Co. in full for merchandise purchased April 20.

29 Paid the electric bill, $108.

30 Issued a credit memo to the River Co. for defective merchandise sold April 27, $36.

Required:

Record the transactions in the appropriate journals. Indicate how the postings would be made from the journals by entering the posting references involved.

Problem 6-5A (Journalizing Transactions and Completing the Accounting)

The Jackson Company uses sales, purchases, cash receipts, cash disbursements, and general journals along with subsidiary ledgers for accounts receivable and accounts payable. The post-closing trial balance as of May 31, 1984, and the trial balances of the subsidiary ledgers are presented below:

JACKSON COMPANY
Post-Closing Trial Balance
May 31, 1984

100	Cash	$ 7,200
110	Accounts Receivable	3,600
115	Inventory	6,000
170	Equipment	12,000

175 Accumulated Depreciation		$ 1,200
200 Accounts Payable		4,800
300 Common Stock		12,000
350 Retained Earnings		10,800
400 Sales		–0–
405 Sales Returns	–0–	
410 Sales Discounts	–0–	
500 Purchases	–0–	
510 Purchase Discounts		–0–
515 Purchase Returns		–0–
530 Rent Expense	–0–	
540 Utilities Expense	–0–	
550 Commissions Expense	–0–	
	$28,800	$28,800

Accounts Receivable Subsidiary Ledger

Schott Co.	$840
Naville Co.	1,680
Feller Co.	1,080
Total	$3,600

Accounts Payable Subsidiary Ledger

Bruce Co.	1,200
Rickard Co.	1,920
Flinger Co.	1,680
Total	$4,800

The following transactions took place during June 1984:

June
1   Received a check from the Schott Co. for payment on account, $840.

3   Sold merchandise to the Bloom Co. on account, Invoice 602, $1,080, terms 2/10, n/30.

4   Paid rent for June, $900.

5   Purchased merchandise on account from the West Co., $1,260, Invoice 383, terms 2/10, n/30.

6   Paid the Bruce Co. for merchandise purchased previously, $1,200.

8   Received payment from the Bloom Co. for full settlement of Invoice 602.

9   Received a credit memo from the West Co. for merchandise returned, $60.

11   Paid the West Co. the amount due on Invoice 383.

12   Paid sales commissions, $2,460.

13   Received a check from the Naville Co. in partial payment of the account, $840.

17   Paid $3,600 for new office equipment.

18   Cash sales, $672.

19 Sold merchandise on account to the Schott Co., $1,140, Invoice 603, terms 2/10, n/30.
21 Sold merchandise on account to the Garner Co., $540, Invoice 604, terms 2/10, n/30.
23 Paid the Rickard Co. for merchandise purchased in May, $1,920.
25 Cash sales, $750.
27 Paid utility bills, $330.
30 Received a check from Feller Co., $1,080, for payment on account.
30 Received a check from Garner Co. for payment on account.

Required:
A. Journalize the transactions in the appropriate journals.
B. Make all necessary postings for the month.
C. Prepare a trial balance of the general ledger and subsidiary ledgers on June 30.

CASE FOR CHAPTER 6

Financial Report Analysis (Accounting System Considerations)
Refer to the financial statements of General Motors Corporation in the appendix.

Required:
1. The management of General Motors Corporation must take the responsibility for preparing the financial statements. What are the ramifications of these responsibilities for the firm's accounting system?
2. What steps would be taken continuously to revise an accounting system as large as the one operated by General Motors Corporation?
3. What balance sheet accounts of the firm would be maintained as control accounts with subsidiary ledgers supporting them?

CHAPTER 7
CASH AND
CASH CONTROLS

OVERVIEW AND OBJECTIVES

This chapter discusses the nature of cash and internal control concepts. When you have finished the chapter, you should understand:

- What cash consists of (p. 289).
- The general internal control concepts (p. 290).
- The distinction between administrative controls and accounting controls (pp. 290–291).
- The procedures used to control cash receipts and cash disbursements (pp. 295–298).
- The purpose and operation of a petty cash fund (pp. 298–300).
- The purpose and preparation of a bank reconciliation (pp. 302–307).
- The purpose and operation of a voucher system in controlling cash disbursements (Appendix p. 308–316).

Cash is a term used in accounting to identify money and any other instrument, such as a check or money order, that a bank will normally accept as a deposit to the depositor's bank account. Cash does not include accounts or notes receivable, postdated checks, IOUs, or postage stamps (which represent prepaid postage expense). Cash is a medium of exchange as well as a measure of value in our economy. Although companies may have several bank accounts as well as cash on hand, the sum of all of the cash items is reported as a single item in the current asset section of the balance sheet. Users of financial statements are interested in the current cash position of a company because it aids them in evaluating the ability of the company to pay short-run cash expenses and to meet currently maturing obligations. Practically every business transaction will eventually result in an inflow or outflow of cash.

The control and proper use of cash is an important management function. Cash is an unproductive asset because it produces no revenue. Any cash accumulated in excess of that needed for current use should be invested, even temporarily, in some type of revenue-producing investment. Cash is a liquid asset, easily subject to misappropriation, and therefore must be adequately protected by controlling access to and use of it. Several techniques have been developed to aid in cash management, the most important of which is the establishment of an internal control system for cash. Other techniques are the preparation of cash forecasts and cash investment planning.

GENERAL INTERNAL CONTROL CONCEPTS

All assets have value to a business because they represent scarce resources that will be used by the business in future operations. The efficient use and protection of these resources is a primary management function. In a single proprietorship, the owner often controls the entire operation through direct involvement in all operating activities of the business. As the business grows, however, the owner or owners must place increasing reliance on others to help manage and control operations. The system designed to aid managers in controlling operations is called an **internal control system.** This system consists of all the measures employed by a business to safeguard its resources against waste, fraud, and inefficiency; promote the reliability of accounting data; and encourage compliance with company policies and governmental regulations.

ADMINISTRATIVE CONTROLS AND ACCOUNTING CONTROLS

Internal controls consist of two types: administrative controls and accounting controls. *Administrative controls* are those established to provide operational efficiency and adherence to prescribed company policies. An example of an administrative control is a written directive to the personnel department of a company identifying the standards to be followed in hiring new employees. Other examples are the manuals identifying purchasing and sales procedures and the various performance reports required from employees.

Accounting controls are the methods and procedures used to protect assets and ensure the reliability of accounting records. They include procedures for the authorization of transactions and the separation of recordkeeping duties from custodianship of the company's assets. Accounting controls are designed to provide reasonable assurance that:

1. Transactions are executed in accordance with management's general or specific authorization.
2. Transactions are recorded as necessary (a) to permit preparation of financial statements in conformity with generally accepted accounting principles or

any other criteria applicable to such statements and (b) to maintain accountability for assets.

3. Access to assets is permitted only in accordance with management's authorization.
4. The recorded accountability for assets is compared with the existing assets at reasonable intervals and appropriate action is taken with respect to any differences.[1]

THE FOREIGN CORRUPT PRACTICES ACT

During the 1970s, several large corporations admitted making payments to foreign officials to obtain or retain business. Although these payments were not necessarily illegal under the laws of the countries in which the payments were made, they were considered illegal, or at least unethical, in the United States. Payments were often made from secret funds that did not appear in the company's records, and top executives of some companies maintained that they were not even aware that the payments were being made.

In an effort to halt these practices, the U.S. Congress passed the Foreign Corrupt Practices Act in 1977. The act contains two types of provisions: antibribery provisions and accounting standards provisions. The *antibribery provisions* apply to all American businesses and individuals. The law prohibits the offer, payment, promise to pay, or authorization of a payment of anything of value to a foreign official or foreign political party for the purpose of obtaining or retaining business. The act also makes it illegal to make such a payment to any person while knowing or having reason to believe that the person will offer, give, or promise the item of value to a foreign official.

The *accounting standards provisions* require that all publicly held corporations keep reasonably detailed and accurate accounting records. They must also maintain internal controls sufficient to provide reasonable assurance that transactions are properly authorized, that transactions are recorded in accordance with generally accepted accounting principles, and that assets are used only in accordance with management's authorization. These accounting standards provisions apply to all companies that must file annual reports with the SEC, even if they do no business in a foreign country. Violators are subject to severe penalties, including prison terms and fines.

One of the main accomplishments of the act is to emphasize that responsibility for the maintenance of an adequate internal control system and for the accuracy of the financial statements rests with management. As a result, top corporate management has directed much more attention to strengthening in-

[1]Professional Standards No. 1, "Auditing, Management Advisory Services, Tax Practice, and Accounting and Review Services," (Chicago: Commerce Clearing House, Inc., June, 1980), Sec. AU 320.28.

ternal control systems. Corporate boards of directors regularly assure compliance with the act by obtaining written evidence about management's evaluation and review of the internal control system. In addition, annual reports generally contain a statement expressing management's primary responsibility for the content of the financial statements as well as the adequacy of internal controls. An example from an annual report of Smith International, Inc., is presented in Figure 7-1.

Although each business must design its own internal control system to meet its specific needs, several general elements of internal accounting control can be identified as discussed below.

CLEARLY ESTABLISHED LINES OF RESPONSIBILITY

Control ultimately involves people. Individuals initiate business transactions, record the transactions, and handle the assets resulting from those transactions. Thus the cornerstone of a good internal control system is the employment of competent personnel and assignment of responsibilities to them. Responsibility should be commensurate with ability and authority. If employees are to operate effectively, they must have a clear understanding of their responsibilities. In addition, responsibility must be assigned so that there are no overlapping or undefined areas. If two or more employees share responsibility and something goes wrong, it is very difficult to determine who is at fault and therefore difficult to take corrective action. If two or more employees use the same cash register, for example, each should be assigned a separate drawer and register key so that any errors or cash shortages can be identified with individuals on a daily basis. Or one employee might be assigned the responsibility of making change for all transactions recorded on a specific cash register.

Responsibilities and duties should be rotated among employees periodically so that they can become familiar with the entire system. Rotation of duties also tends to discourage deviation from prescribed procedures since employees know that other employees may soon be taking over their duties and reviewing their activities.

SEPARATION OF RECORD-KEEPING AND CUSTODIANSHIP

Whenever possible, responsibility for initiating business transactions and for custody of the business' assets should be separated from responsibility for maintaining the accounting records in order to help avoid the misappropriation or misuse of assets. The person with custody of an asset is unlikely to misappropriate or misuse it because a record of the asset is kept by another employee. The employee maintaining the records has no reason to falsify them because he or she has no access to the asset. A theft of the asset and falsification of records to cover up the theft would therefore require collusion between the two employees.

Report of Management

The accompanying consolidated financial statements have been prepared in conformity with generally accepted accounting principles and, as such, include amounts that are based on our best estimates and judgments, giving due consideration to materiality. Financial information included elsewhere in this Annual Report is consistent with that in the financial statements.

The integrity and objectivity of data in these financial statements are the responsibility of management. To this end management maintains a system of accounting and controls, which includes an internal audit function. The system of controls includes a careful selection of people, a division of responsibilities, and the application of formal policies and procedures that are consistent with high standards of accounting and administrative practices. Management is continually reviewing, modifying and improving its system of accounting and controls in response to changes in business conditions and operations. We believe our controls provide reasonable assurance that assets are safeguarded against loss from unauthorized use or disposition and that accounting records are reliable for preparing financial statements.

The independent public accountants, recommended by the Audit Committee of the Board of Directors and selected by the Board of Directors and the shareholders at the annual meeting, are engaged to express an opinion on our financial statements. Their opinion is based on procedures performed in accordance with generally accepted auditing standards, including tests of the accounting records and such other auditing procedures as they considered necessary in the circumstances.

The Board of Directors, acting through the Audit Committee composed solely of outside directors, is responsible for determining that management fulfills its responsibilities in the financial control of operations and preparation of financial statements. The Committee meets regularly with management, the internal auditors and the independent public accountants to discuss the Company's system of accounting and controls and financial reporting matters. The independent public accountants have full and free access to the Audit Committee.

Management has long recognized its responsibility for conducting the Company's affairs in a manner which is responsive to the ever increasing complexities of the business environment. The responsibility is reflected in key Company policies regarding, among other things, potential conflicting outside business interests of Company employees, proper conduct of domestic and international business activities and compliance with anti-trust laws.

JERRY W. NEELY
Chairman of the Board,
President and Chief Executive Officer

FRED J. BARNES
Group Vice President and
Chief Financial Officer

Figure 7-1

Management Report

DIVISION OF RESPONSIBILITY FOR RELATED TRANSACTIONS

To minimize the possibility of errors, fraud, and theft, responsibility for a series of related transactions should be divided among two or more employees or departments so that the work of one employee acts as a check on the work of another. For example, if one employee were permitted to order goods, receive the goods, and pay the supplier, that employee might be tempted to order goods for personal use, have the goods delivered to his or her home, and pay for them from business funds. Or an employee might be tempted to place orders with personal friends rather than seek the best quality at the lowest price. To avoid such potential abuses, authority for ordering goods should be placed with a purchasing department, the goods should be physically received by a receiving department, and payment for the order should be performed by a third department or employee. Documents (purchase orders, receiving reports, invoices) showing the work done by each department or employee are then sent to the accounting department for recording purposes. In this way, the work of each employee acts as a check on the work performed by others.

MECHANICAL AND ELECTRONIC DEVICES

Mechanical and electronic devices designed to protect assets and to improve the accuracy of the accounting process should be used wherever feasible. Cash registers are used to provide an accurate record of cash sales, produce a receipt for the customer, and protect the cash received. A safe or vault may be provided for the protection of cash on hand and important documents. Measuring devices such as those used to measure yards of cloth sold and check protectors that perforate the amount of the check on its face, thereby making alteration of the amount difficult, are other examples of devices used to strengthen internal control.

ADEQUATE INSURANCE AND BONDING OF EMPLOYEES

Another element of good internal control is the provision of adequate insurance on business assets to protect them against loss, theft, or casualty. In addition, employees having access to cash and negotiable instruments should be bonded by coverage with fidelity insurance to insure against losses by fraud on the part of those employees. Bonding companies generally investigate an employee's background before issuing a bond on the employee. Consequently, bonding also serves as a deterrent to misappropriation of funds because employees are aware that they are bonded and will have to deal with the bonding company if a shortage is discovered. Bonding companies generally will not cover a loss unless the employer is willing to prosecute employees who misappropriate funds.

INTERNAL AUDITING

As mentioned in Chapter 1, many companies have internal auditors who are responsible for a continuing review and study of the internal control system. Deviations from established procedures and suggestions for improving the system are reported to top management. Internal auditors also often aid the independent CPA who conducts the annual audit.

CONTROL OF CASH

Because cash is a liquid asset, easily transferable and not easily identified, it is the asset most subject to misappropriation. It is therefore important to provide a good internal control system for handling cash and cash transactions. Such a system must contain procedures for protecting cash on hand as well as for handling both cash receipts and cash disbursements. Three particularly important elements of the internal control system for cash are the separation of responsibility for handling and custodianship of cash from responsibility for maintaining cash records, the deposit of each day's cash receipts intact, and the policy of making all cash payments by check. The first element is necessary to prevent misappropriation of cash and falsification of accounting records without collusion among employees. The deposit of each day's cash receipts intact prevents the cash custodian from borrowing the funds for a few days and replacing them before they are deposited. By depositing each day's cash receipts intact and making all cash payments by check, internal control is strengthened since the bank record of all cash transactions may be used as a cross-check on the accuracy of the internal cash records of the business.

Because the details of a system of internal control for cash will vary with the size and type of business, we only will consider a general system that might be used. Procedures used to build a system of internal control for cash can be illustrated best by considering cash receipts and cash disbursements separately.

CONTROL OF CASH RECEIPTS

Cash receipts normally consist of two types, over-the-counter receipts from cash sales and cash received through the mail from customers making payments on charge accounts. Different control procedures are established for each type.

Receipts from Cash Sales

Cash received over the counter from cash sales should be rung up on a cash register located in a position that permits the customer to see the amount recorded. The register prints a receipt that is given to the customer. Each register has a locked-in tape on which each cash sale is recorded. The basis for internal control is the principle of separation of record-keeping from custodianship. The salesclerk who collects the cash should not have access to the tape in the register. At the end of each business day, the salesclerk counts the cash in the register and records the amount on a memorandum form that is sent to the accounting department. An employee other than the salesclerk removes the tape and cash from the register, counts the cash, and compares the count with that of the salesclerk, noting any discrepancies. The cash is then forwarded to the cashier for deposit, and the tape, along with any discrepancy noted, is sent to the accounting department, where it is used to prepare appropriate accounting entries. In this way, neither the salesclerk nor the cashier has access to the accounting records, and the accounting department personnel have no access to cash.

Prenumbered Sales Tickets. Additional internal control of cash receipts can be obtained by the use of prenumbered sales tickets, prepared in duplicate for each cash sale. The sale is recorded on the cash register, the original copy of the sales ticket is given to the customer, and the carbon copy of the sales ticket is retained. At the end of the day, an employee other than the salesclerk adds the total of the sales tickets and verifies that none are missing. The total of the sales tickets is then compared with the total sales recorded on the cash register tape.

Cash Received Through the Mail

Procedures for the control of mail receipts are also based on the separation of recordkeeping and custodianship. The employee who opens the mail prepares a list of the amounts received. One copy is sent to the cashier along with the receipts (usually checks or money orders). The receipts are combined with those from the cash registers in preparing the daily bank deposit. Another copy of the list is forwarded to the accounting department for use in preparing entries in the cash receipts journal and the customers' accounts. Again, neither the mail clerk nor the cashier has access to the accounting records, and accounting department personnel have no access to cash. Thus, fraud is generally avoided unless there is collusion.

Cash Short and Over

When numerous individual cash sales are recorded, it is inevitable that some errors will be made by salesclerks and customers will be given the wrong change. As a result, a cash shortage or overage will be detected when the actual cash in the cash register is compared with the register tape. For example, assume that the cash register tape shows that total sales recorded were $1,272, and the cash in the register amounted to $1,264. The cash shortage is recorded when the daily sales are recorded as follows:

April	4	Cash	1,264	
		Cash Short and Over	8	
		Sales		1,272
		To record the day's cash sales.		

If the cash count had exceeded the amount of sales recorded, the Cash Short and Over account would have been credited for the difference. The Cash Short and Over account is closed to the Income Summary account at year end as part of the normal closing process. If the account has a debit balance (shortages exceed overages), it will be reported as miscellaneous expense on the income statement. If the account has a credit balance (overages exceed shortages), it is normally reported as an item of other income on the income statement.

We have presented the above entry in general journal form for illustration purposes. If special journals are used, the entry would be recorded in the cash receipts journal. Throughout the remainder of this book, we will illustrate entries in general journal form but the reader should remember that the entry would be made in the appropriate special journal if such journals are used.

CONTROL OF CASH DISBURSEMENTS

Just as an adequate system of internal control must contain procedures for controlling cash receipts, it must also provide for the protection of cash balances and procedures for the control of cash disbursements. To accomplish these objectives, each day's cash receipts should be deposited intact in a bank account and all cash disbursements should be made by check. Checks should be prenumbered so that all checks can be accounted for. These procedures are supported by a division of responsibility for the approval and payment of invoices. The employee designated to approve invoices for payment should have no checkwriting or accounting responsibility. Before authorizing payment, the employee should verify that the goods or services represented by the invoice were properly ordered and actually received. Approval of the invoice for payment is generally indicated by placing an approval stamp on its face.

The employee responsible for signing checks should have no invoice-approval or accounting responsibilities. Checks presented for signature should be signed only upon receipt of a properly approved invoice indicating that payment is justified. At the time the check is signed, the related invoice should be canceled by perforating it or placing a *paid* stamp on it to prevent the possibility of having the invoice presented for payment a second time. The approved invoice and a copy of the check are forwarded to the accounting department, where the appropriate entry is made to record the payment. The combination of these procedures makes it difficult for a fraudulent disbursement to be made without collusion by two or more employees.

Internal control of cash disbursements can be strengthened by use of a voucher system. A detailed description of a voucher system and its use is presented in the appendix to this chapter.

THE PETTY CASH FUND

As emphasized earlier, a basic principle of internal control is that all disbursements should be made by check. An exception, however, is made to avoid the expense and inconvenience of writing many small checks for minor expenditures for items such as postage stamps and miscellaneous supplies. To permit such payments to be made in cash and still retain control of cash disbursements, most firms establish a **petty cash fund**—a specified amount of cash, placed under the control of a specific employee (the petty cash fund cashier)—for use in making small payments.

Establishing the Fund

The petty cash fund is established by writing a check to the petty cash fund cashier, who will cash the check and place the proceeds in a locked box to which only he or she has access. The fund is generally established in a round amount, such as $100 or $200, expected to be sufficient to handle petty cash payments for a relatively short period such as a month. The check is recorded by a debit to a Petty Cash account and a credit to the Cash account. For example, assuming a fund of $100 is established on January 2, the journal entry is:

Jan.	2	Petty Cash	100	
		Cash		100
		To establish a petty cash fund.		

Making Disbursements from the Fund

As cash payments are made from the fund, the recipient is required to sign a **petty cash receipt** that is prepared by the cashier of the fund. The receipt shows the amount paid, the purpose of the payment, and the date paid. A receipt is prepared for every payment made from the fund and is placed in the petty cash fund box. Thus, at all times the total of the receipts plus cash in the fund should be equal to the amount originally placed in the fund, $100 in our illustration. An example of a petty cash receipt follows:

PETTY CASH RECEIPT

No. ___2___ .   Date ___January 4, 1984___   Amount ___$12.35___
Purpose _____Miscellaneous Office Supplies_____

Debit to _____Office Supplies Expense_____
Approved by _____   _J. B. Small_____
                              Signature

Replenishing the Fund

Because payments from the fund will gradually decrease the cash available, the fund must be replenished periodically by writing a check in the amount of the sum of the receipts in the fund. Each receipt is stamped *paid* by the cashier and sent to the accounting department to serve as a basis for the entry needed to record the replenishment. The check is cashed by the cashier of the fund and the proceeds are placed in the petty cash box. Various expense accounts are debited as indicated by the petty cash receipts, and cash is credited for the amount needed to replenish the fund. For example, assume that the petty cash box contained the following receipts and cash at the end of the first month of operations:

Receipt No.	Purpose	Amount
1	Postage Stamps	$ 30.00
2	Office Supplies	12.35
3	Postage	26.47
4	Gasoline	15.22
	Cash in Box	15.96
		$100.00

Because the cash in the fund is low, the fund is replenished and the following journal entry is prepared:

Jan.	31	Auto Expense	15.22	
		Office Supplies Expense	12.35	
		Postage Expense	56.47	
		Cash		84.04
		To replenish the petty cash fund.		

Since the petty cash receipts are supplementary records, this entry is needed so that the expenses are properly recorded in the journal and general ledger accounts. Thus, expense accounts are debited when the fund is replenished. Note that the Petty Cash account is not affected by the replenishing entry. The Petty Cash account is debited only when the fund is initially established, and no other entries are made to the Petty Cash account unless a decision is made to increase or decrease the size of the fund. The petty cash fund is normally included with other cash amounts and reported as a single amount on the balance sheet.

The petty cash fund is also replenished at the end of an accounting period, even though the amount of cash in the fund is not running low, in order to have the expenses represented by the receipts in the fund recorded during the current accounting period. If the fund is not replenished, cash will be overstated on the balance sheet and expenses will be understated on the income statement for the period.

On occasion the custodian of the fund may forget to obtain a signed receipt for a payment from the fund, in which case the fund will be short. When this occurs, the Cash Short and Over account is debited for the shortage when the fund is replenished.

BANK CHECKING ACCOUNTS

As mentioned earlier, an important element of internal control of cash is the requirement that each day's cash receipts be deposited intact into a bank checking account and that all disbursements be made by check. Internal control is strengthened because the bank record of deposits received and checks paid provides a cross-check on the internal cash records of the business. Deposits of cash receipts are made by preparing a deposit ticket (Figure 7-2) that includes the amount of currency and coin and a list of the checks included with the deposit. Each check deposited is identified by the code number of the bank on which the check is drawn. The deposit ticket is prepared in duplicate; one copy is sent to the bank with the deposit and the other copy is retained by the depositor. Disbursements from the checking account are authorized by checks written by the depositor. Checks are legal instruments signed by the depositor, ordering the bank to pay a specified amount of money to the person or company identified on the check. Figure 7-3 shows a copy of a typical check.

THE BANK STATEMENT

Each month the bank sends the depositor a **bank statement** detailing the activity that has taken place in the account during the month. The statement shows the balance in the account at the beginning of the month, the individual deposits received and checks paid during the month, any other adjustments made during the month, and the account balance at month end. Along with the bank statement, the bank will include the depositor's canceled checks

Figure 7-2
A Deposit Ticket

DEPOSIT TICKET
United Bank
Akron, Ohio

Date Sept. 4, 1984

Depositor: Calhoun, Inc.
4214 Stemmer Avenue
Akron, Ohio

⑆122ı028З⑆:248ı‖05208Оı055‖

CASH	Currency	126	00
	Coin	7	80
CHECKS: 18-122		86	23
45-41		214	25
19-162		74	56
18-113		316	31
Total		825	15
Less Cash Received		–0–	
Net Deposit		825	15

Figure 7-3
A Check

No. 368
July 6, 1984   91-283/1221
PAY TO THE ORDER OF   Brandon Wholesale Company $ 422.56
Four hundred twenty-two and 56/100   Dollars

UNITED BANK

Akron, Ohio   Calhoun, Inc.
                     B. J. Jones
⑆122ı028З⑆:2454‖05208Оı055‖

(checks written by the depositor and paid by the bank) and debit and credit memoranda identifying miscellaneous charges and credits made to the account during the month by the bank. The depositor's cash balance in the account represents a liability on the part of the bank and is therefore reflected on the bank's books by a credit balance. Thus debit memos identify charges (debits or decreases) in the depositor's account during the month for such things as bank service and check-printing charges and nonsufficient funds (NSF) checks—checks that were included in a depositor's deposit but were not paid by the maker's bank because of the lack of sufficient funds to cover the check. NSF checks are charged back to the depositor's account and the depositor is notified by a debit memo. Credit memos identify credits (increases) made to the depositor's account by the bank. For example, the bank may have collected a note receivable for the depositor and placed the proceeds in the depositor's account. Debit and credit memos are also used by the bank to correct errors made by the bank in previous months. An example of a bank statement is shown in Figure 7-4.

Reconciling the Bank Account

The cash balance reported on the bank statement will seldom agree with the balance shown in the depositor's general ledger cash account. As a result, a bank reconciliation is prepared for each bank account to reconcile the cash balance reported on the bank statement with the balance per the depositor's records. The purpose is to prove the accuracy of both records. The bank statement balance may differ from the depositor's records for several reasons:

1. Amounts added to cash on the depositor's books have not yet been added to the bank account by the bank. These generally reflect what are called "deposits in transit," deposits recorded on the depositor's books and, because they were deposited late in the day on the last day of the month or were mailed to the bank, were not yet recorded by the bank at the time of the preparation of the bank statement.

2. Amounts deducted from cash on the depositor's books have not yet been deducted from the bank account balance by the bank. The most common example is outstanding checks—checks written by the depositor that have not yet cleared the bank.

3. Amounts added to the depositor's bank account by the bank and not yet recorded on the depositor's books. An example is a note or other receivable collected by the bank on behalf of the depositor and credited directly to the bank account.

4. Amounts deducted from the depositor's account by the bank but not yet

Figure 7-4
A Bank Statement

UNITED BANK
Tempe, Arizona

STATEMENT OF ACCOUNT WITH
DATA COMPANY
1842 Elm Street
Tempe, Arizona 85282

Account No.
052181059

Page
1

Period Covered
9/1/84 to 9/30/84

Date	Check No.	Amount	Deposits/Credits	Balance
	Checks/Debits			
8/31				4,260.82
9/2	1016	326.50		
	1017	219.18		
	1018	182.96	972.85	4,505.03
9/5	1019	494.22		
	1020	384.60	618.42	4,244.63
9/9	1021	66.43		
	1022	198.39		
	1023	764.80	866.34	4,081.35
9/15	1024	36.72		
	1025	117.81		
		89.78 DM	544.54	4,381.58
9/22	1026	127.94		4,253.64
9/27	1028	313.30		
	1030	123.65	614.88	4,431.57
9/29	1033	197.54		4,234.03
9/30		8.50 SC	1,200.00 CM	5,425.53

Beginning Balance	Debits		Credits		Current Balance
	No.	Amount	No.	Amount	
4,260.82	16	3,652.32	6	4,817.03	5,425.53

SYMBOLS: DM = Debit Memo   CM = Credit Memo
NSF = Nonsufficient Funds   SC = Service Charge

recorded on the depositor's books—service charges, check-printing charges, and NSF checks.

The form of bank reconciliation generally followed consists of the four parts shown below. The numbers in parentheses refer to the four reasons for differences between the bank statement balance and the cash balance per depositor's books discussed above.

Balance per Bank Statement	$2,000
Add: (1) Amounts added to the books that have not yet been	
added to the bank account, e.g., deposits in transit	500
	2,500
Deduct: (2) Amounts deducted from the books that have not	
yet been deducted from the bank account, e.g.,	
outstanding checks	900
Adjusted Bank Balance	$1,600
Balance per Books	$1,310
Add: (3) Amounts added to the bank account by the bank	
that have not yet been recorded on the depositor's	
books, e.g., note collected by the bank on behalf of	
the depositor	300
	1,610
Deduct: (4) Amounts deducted from the bank account by the	
bank that have not yet been recorded on the de-	
positor's books, e.g., bank service charges	10
Adjusted Book Balance	$1,600

The objective of the bank reconciliation is to reconcile both the cash balance on the depositor's records and the bank cash balance to the correct amount that would be included on a balance sheet prepared at the end of the period.

Procedures for Locating Reconciling Items. The following procedures are generally used to locate reconciling items in the determination of the correct cash balance:

1. The individual deposits listed on the bank statement are compared with those recorded on the depositor's books. Any errors are identified for correction. Any deposits unrecorded by the bank are added to the balance per bank statement on the reconciliation.
2. Canceled checks returned with the bank statement are placed in numerical order and their amounts are compared with the amounts listed on the depositor's records. Any errors are identified for correction. Checks issued that have not yet cleared the bank are listed to be deducted from the bank balance on the reconciliation as outstanding checks.
3. Any debit memos included with the bank statement are separated so they can be deducted from the book balance as reconciling items. They also serve as the basis for preparing adjusting entries on the depositor's books.
4. Any credit memos included with the bank statement are separated so they can be added to the book balance as reconciling items. Like debit memos, they also serve as the basis for the preparation of adjusting entries on the depositor's books.

5. Errors discovered in the preceding steps are listed separately as reconciling items. The bank is notified of errors in the bank's records so that bank employees can make appropriate adjustments to the bank account. Errors discovered in the depositor's records are corrected by preparing appropriate journal entries.

To illustrate the bank reconciliation process, assume that Data Company received the bank statement presented in Figure 7-4. The bank statement shows a bank balance of $5,425.53 on September 30. Assume the cash balance shown on Data Company's books is $4,215.51. The following differences between the bank statement and Data Company's cash records were identified in applying the procedures described above.

1. A deposit in the amount of $546.87 was placed in the night depository at the bank on the evening of September 30 by Data Company's cashier.
2. Checks issued and recorded by Data Company that were not returned with the bank statement were:

Check No.	Amount
1027	$ 94.67
1029	174.83
1031	102.62
1032	39.58
1034	216.47
Total	$628.17

3. Two debit memos were included with the bank statement:
   (a) One debit memo, in the amount of $89.78, represented a check received from a customer (Mary Jonas) and deposited by Data Company that was returned for lack of sufficient funds in Mary Jonas's account.
   (b) The second debit memo, amounting to $8.50, represented bank service charges for the month of September.
4. A credit memo included with the bank statement indicated that the bank had collected a noninterest-bearing note receivable for Data Company in the amount of $1,225. The bank charged a collection fee of $25 and credited the remaining $1,200 to Data Company's account.
5. Comparison of the canceled checks with the accounting records showed that check number 1024 in the amount of $36.72, in payment for the purchase of office supplies, had been incorrectly entered in the cash disbursements journal as $63.72, thereby producing an understatement of the cash account of $27.

The bank reconciliation for Data Company as of September 30 is shown in Figure 7-5.

Figure 7-5
Bank Reconciliation

DATA COMPANY		
Bank Reconciliation as of September 30, 1984		
Balance per Bank Statement		$5,425.53
Add: Deposit in transit		546.87
		5,972.40
Deduct: Outstanding checks		628.17
Adjusted Bank Balance		$5,344.23
Balance per Books		$4,215.51
Add: Proceeds from note collected, less collection		
fee ($1,225 − $25)	$1,200.00	
Error in recording check No. 1024	27.00	1,227.00
		5,442.51
Deduct: NSF Check—Mary Jonas	89.78	
Bank service charge	8.50	98.28
Adjusted Book Balance		$5,344.23

Notice that the correct cash balance of $5,344.23 is different from both the balance on the bank statement and the balance in Data Company's general ledger cash account. After the bank records the deposit in transit and the outstanding checks clear, the bank records will show the correct balance of $5,344.23. In order to adjust Data Company's cash balance to the correct amount, adjusting journal entries must be prepared on its books for those reconciling items made to the book balance on the bank reconciliation. Individual adjusting entries might be made as follows:

Sept.	30	Cash	1,200.00	
		Miscellaneous Expense	25.00	
		Notes Receivable		1,225.00
		To record the collection of a note receivable by the bank, less collection fee.		

The entry records the collection of the note receivable by increasing cash, recording the collection fee as miscellaneous expense, and reducing notes receivable.

Sept.	30	Cash	27.00	
		Office Supplies Inventory		27.00
		To record correction of Check No. 1024.		

The purchase of office supplies was recorded as a debit to Office Supplies

Inventory and a credit to Cash in the incorrect amount of $63.72. The actual amount of the purchase and check was $36.72. The entry above corrects the error by increasing the Cash account and decreasing the Office Supplies Inventory account by the amount of the error, $27.

Sept.	30	Accounts Receivable—Mary Jonas Cash To set up NSF check as a receivable from Mary Jonas.	89.78	89.78

This entry establishes an account receivable from Mary Jonas for the amount of the NSF check. As with other accounts receivable, an attempt will be made to collect from Ms. Jonas. In the event the attempt is unsuccessful, the account will be written off as a bad debt.

Sept.	30	Miscellaneous Expense Cash To record bank service charges for September.	8.50	8.50

This entry charges the bank service charge to miscellaneous expense so that it will be included on the income statement for the month of September, if one is prepared.

Rather than preparing individual entries, the adjustments to the accounting records normally would be accomplished by one combined entry such as the following:

Sept.	30	Cash
		Miscellaneous Expense
		Accounts Receivable—Mary Jonas
		  Notes Receivable
		  Office Supplies Inventory
		To record bank reconciliation items for
		September.
			1,128.72
			33.50
			89.78
				
				1,225.00
				27.00

After the adjusting entry above has been posted, the Cash account will have a balance of $5,344.23 as indicated below:

Cash

Balance before adjustment	4,215.51
Adjustment	1,128.72
9/30 Balance	5,344.23

The account balance now agrees with the adjusted book balance on the bank reconciliation and is also the amount of cash that should be included in the September 30, 1984, balance sheet if one is prepared on that date.

APPENDIX: CASH DISBURSEMENTS AND THE VOUCHER SYSTEM

A **voucher system** consists of the procedures followed to accumulate, verify, and record all cash disbursements made for the acquisition of goods or services. Four relatively distinct steps make up the cycle involved in the ordering, receipt, and payment for goods and services:

1. Orders are placed.
2. Goods or services are received.
3. The accuracy of invoices is verified and the invoices are approved for payment.
4. Checks are written in payment of approved invoices.

In a small business, the steps are often controlled and performed entirely by the owner or manager. In a large business, control is achieved by assigning the various steps to specific individuals or departments. One or more business documents are prepared at each step to provide verification that the step was completed properly. Although the same general procedures are followed for the acquisition of both goods and services, the following description concentrates on the acquisition of goods—merchandise and other physical assets.

PLACING ORDERS

Operating department managers are normally prohibited from placing orders directly with suppliers; to permit them to do so would prohibit effective centralization of the control of the total goods ordered and the resulting liabilities. Operating managers, who have responsibility for determining the goods needed by their departments, prepare a form called a **purchase requisition** (Figure 7-6) that lists the items needed by the department. The purchase requisition is sent to a central purchasing department that has responsibility for placing orders, and a copy is forwarded to the accounting department. Purchasing department personnel determine the appropriate source of supply, negotiate the terms of the purchase with the supplier, and place the order by preparing a **purchase order**—a business form that authorizes a supplier to ship specific goods (Figure 7-7). The original of the purchase order is sent to the supplier, a copy is sent to the requisitioning department to inform the manager that the order has been placed, and a copy is forwarded to the accounting department, which will eventually approve payment for the order.

RECEIPT OF GOODS

When goods are shipped, the supplier prepares a document called an **invoice** or bill (Figure 7-8) that itemizes the goods shipped, the price charged for each

Figure 7-6
A Purchase Requisition

PURCHASE REQUISITION

Data Company

No. _____ 269 _____

Date _____ August 6, 1984 _____

From: Assembly Department
To: Purchasing Department

Please place the following order:

Quantity	Number	Description
200	142 JX	J-type Gear Boxes
400	142 JY	Gear Box Brackets

For Purchasing Department Use:
Date Ordered _____ August 9, 1984 _____

Betty Wallace
Approved

Purchase Order No. _____ 348 _____

Figure 7-7
A Purchase Order

PURCHASE ORDER

No. _____ 348 _____

Data Company
1842 Elm Street
Tempe, Arizona 85282

To: Croyden Gear Supply
1478 Sundown Avenue
Los Angeles, California 94412

Date _____ August 9, 1984 _____
Ship Via _____ Acme Trucking _____
Terms _____ 2/10, n/30 _____

Please ship the following:

Quantity	Description	Price	Total
200	142 JX J-type Gear Boxes	$ 4.95	$990.00
400	142 JY Gear Box Brackets	.78	312.00

Data Company
By *P. Schneider*

Figure 7-8
An Invoice

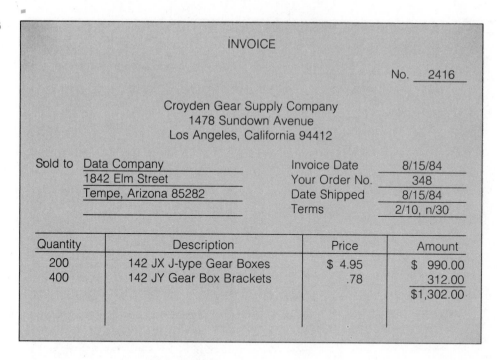

INVOICE

No. 2416

Croyden Gear Supply Company
1478 Sundown Avenue
Los Angeles, California 94412

Sold to Data Company   Invoice Date   8/15/84
         1842 Elm Street   Your Order No.   348
         Tempe, Arizona 85282   Date Shipped   8/15/84
                                          Terms   2/10, n/30

Quantity	Description	Price	Amount
200	142 JX J-type Gear Boxes	$ 4.95	$ 990.00
400	142 JY Gear Box Brackets	.78	312.00
			$1,302.00

item, and the total amount of the invoice. A copy of the invoice is mailed to
the purchaser. The invoice represents a sales invoice to the supplier and a
purchase invoice to the buyer. When the invoice is received, it is sent to the
accounting department, where it is held until the goods are received and in-
spected. Most large companies maintain a separate department responsible for
receiving and inspecting the goods as they are received. The receiving department prepares a **receiving report** (Figure 7-9), which lists the type and
quantity of goods received. Copies are sent to the requisitioning department
and the purchasing department to serve as notification that the goods have
been received, and a copy is sent to the accounting department for comparison
with the purchase requisition, purchase order, and purchase invoice.

The flow of documents in the acquisition of goods can be depicted as
follows:

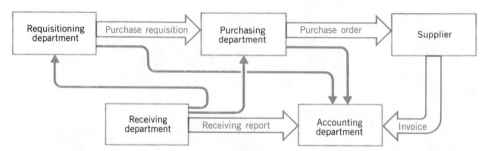

Figure 7-9
A Receiving Report

RECEIVING REPORT

No. ___694___

Data Company
Tempe, Arizona

To: Accounting Department
From: Receiving Department

Date Received	8/19/84
Purchase Order No.	348
Supplier	Croyden Gear Supply Co.

The following items have been received:

Description	Quantity	Condition
142 JX J-type Gear Boxes	200	Good
142 JY Gear Box Brackets	400	Good

SB.Frandin
Signed

VERIFICATION OF THE ACCURACY OF INVOICES AND APPROVAL OF PAYMENT

Upon receipt of the receiving report, the accounting department will possess copies of the purchase requisition, purchase order, purchase invoice, and receiving report, all of which relate to a specific purchase from a specific supplier. Accounting department personnel then perform several important verification procedures, after which the invoice is approved for entry into the accounting records and for payment. Verification procedures generally followed are:

1. Items on the purchase invoice are compared with those listed on the purchase requisition to verify that the goods shipped by the supplier were properly requisitioned.
2. Items on the purchase invoice are compared with those listed on the purchase order to verify that the goods shipped are the same as those ordered.
3. Items listed on the purchase invoice are compared with those listed on the receiving report to verify that the goods billed by the supplier were actually received.
4. Additional verification is performed on the purchase invoice to assure that prices charged and credit terms are those agreed upon and that computations and price extensions are accurate.

The Voucher

As each purchase invoice is received by the accounting department, a document called a **voucher** (Figure 7-10) is attached to the invoice. The other related documents (requisition, purchase order, and receiving report) will also be attached to the voucher as they are received so they can be used by the accounting department employee who will perform the verification process. The voucher typically contains the types of information shown in the sample voucher in Figure 7-10.

Figure 7-10
A Voucher

Voucher No. 341

DATA COMPANY
Tempe, Arizona

Pay to *Reardon Wholesale*
224 W. Oak
Phoenix, Az 85042

Date *Sept 1, 1984*

Due Date *Sept 10, 1984*

Date of Invoice *Sept 1, 1984*
Invoice Number *2163*
Payment Terms *2/10, N/30*

Invoice Amount *$2,147.80*
Cash Discount *42.97*
Net Amount *2,104.83*

Verification of:

	Approved by
Proper Purchase Requisition	*B.J.*
Quantities on Purchase Order with Invoice	*B.J.*
Quantities on Receiving Report with Invoice	*B.J.*
Prices on Purchase Order with Invoice	*B.J.*
Credit Terms in Agreement with Purchase Order	*B.J.*
Invoice Extensions and Footings	*B.J.*
Approved for Payment	*Don Allen*

Account Distribution / Amount

Purchases	*$2,147.80*
Freight In	
Office Supplies	
Advertising	
Office Salaries	
Sales Salaries	
Utilities	
Miscellaneous Expense	
Total Vouchers Payable Credit	*$2,147.80*

Payment Record:
Date Paid *9/10/84* Check No. *260* Amount *$2,104.83*

The voucher contains five sections, used to record various information:

1. The name of the creditor, the date the voucher is prepared, and the last date on which payment can be made to obtain cash discounts or the date on which payment is otherwise due.
2. General invoice data such as the date of the invoice, payment terms, the amount of the invoice, and the net amount due after allowing for cash discounts, if any.
3. The initials of the person performing the verification steps and of the employee authorized to approve payment of the invoice.
4. Amounts to be debited to identified general ledger accounts by the accounting department and the total amount to be credited to vouchers payable.
5. Payment data identifying the date paid, the check number, and the amount of the check.

Every cash payment, including reimbursement of the petty cash fund, requires a voucher regardless of whether the payment is for services, merchandise, equipment, or a mortgage payment. Even the receipt of a bill (such as a utility bill) that is to be paid immediately must first be vouchered. Probably the greatest benefit received from use of a voucher system is the assurance that every cash expenditure has been thoroughly reviewed and amounts verified before payment is made. If there is no collusion among employees, management is assured that all expenditures were made for valid business purposes.

The Voucher Register

After the voucher is prepared it is recorded in a **voucher register,** a book of original entry that, in combination with a check register under the voucher system, takes the place of the cash disbursements journal described in Chapter 6. The function of a check register is described in a later section of this appendix, and a voucher register is shown in Figure 7-11.

Under the voucher system, a Vouchers Payable account takes the place of the Accounts Payable account. Every voucher is entered in the voucher register with a debit to various asset, expense, or liability accounts and a credit to vouchers payable. All information in the voucher register is entered from the voucher at the time it is approved for recording with the exception of the payment information, which is entered as each voucher is paid.

The posting of the voucher register follows the same general procedures used to post the cash disbursements journal. Columns are totaled and crossfooted at month end to verify the equality of debits and credits. The total of all debit columns, including the "other debits" column, must equal the total of the vouchers payable column. The total of each column, with the exception of the "other debits" column, is posted as a debit or credit to the appropriate

Date 1984	Voucher No.	Payee	Payment Date	Chk. No.	Vouchers Payable Credit	Purchases Debit	Freight In Debit	Advertising Debit	Sales Salaries Debit	Office Salaries Debit	Account	P/R	Amt.
9/1	341	Reardon Wholesale	9/10	260	2,147 80	2,147 80							
9/1	342	Daly Freight Co.	9/3	251	122 50		122 50						
9/4	343	Haried Insurance Co.	9/5	253	347 80						Prepaid Insurance	136	347 80
9/6	344	Acme Office Supply	9/12	263	89 40						Office Supplies	124	89 40
9/6	345	The Leader	9/11	261	138 00			138 00					
9/7	346	Doug Johnson	9/7	256	236 50				236 50				
9/7	347	Rick Burdick	9/7	257	149 30					149 30			
9/7	348	Charles Myler	9/7	258	220 00				220 00				
9/8	349	Zylon Equipment Co.	9/20	284	370 00						Office Equipment	158	370 00
9/30	382	United Bank	9/30	349	2,060 00						Notes Payable / Interest Expense	210 / 535	2,000 00 / 60 00
9/30	383	Turner Supply Co.			896 22	896 22							
9/30	384	Adventure Travel	9/30	350	384 50						Travel Expense	574	384 50
9/30	385	The Leader			74 90			74 90					
					18,249 24	6,483 94	286 89	399 40	1,839 42	597 20			8,642 39
					(202)	(533)	(520)	(504)	(562)	(572)			(X)

Figure 7-11
A Voucher Register

account listed in the column heading. Evidence of the posting is indicated by placing the general ledger account number in parentheses just below the column total. Entries in the ''other debits'' column are posted individually as debits to the account listed and the account number is entered in the posting reference column.

Unpaid Vouchers File

Some vouchers—particularly those prepared for the payment of ongoing expenses such as sales salaries, office salaries, and utilities—are often paid on the date they are recorded in the voucher register. With other payments, however, there may be a time lag between the receipt of an invoice and its due date. In these cases, the voucher is prepared and filed in an **unpaid vouchers file.** To protect the company's credit rating and to assure the payment of invoices in time to obtain cash discounts, the vouchers are filed under the dates on which payment is due. The unpaid vouchers file constitutes a subsidiary ledger of vouchers payable and, under a voucher system, takes the place of the accounts payable subsidiary ledger described in Chapter 6. The elimination of the accounts payable subsidiary ledger often results in a considerable cost savings to the business. At the end of the month, after month-end posting has taken place, the total of all vouchers in the unpaid voucher file should be equal to the balance in the Vouchers Payable account in the general ledger. A reconciliation should be prepared at month-end to verify

Date 1984		Check No.	Payee	Voucher No.	Vouchers Payable Debit		Purchase Discounts Credit		Cash Credit	
Sept.	1	251	Daly Freight Co.	342	122	50			122	50
	3	252	Haried Insurance	343	347	80			347	80
	5	254	Reardon Wholesale	335	1,246	00	24	92	1,221	08
	6	255	Batho Company	334	1,322	80	26	46	1,296	34
	7	256	Doug Johnson	346	236	50			236	50
	7	257	Rick Burdick	347	149	30			149	30
	7	258	Charles Myler	348	220	00			220	00
	30	349	United Bank	382	2,060	00			2,060	00
	30	350	Adventure Travel	384	384	50			384	50
					18,629	90	193	48	18,436	42
					(202)		(534)		(101)	

Figure 7-12
A Check Register

that the total of unpaid vouchers in the voucher register agrees with the total of all vouchers in the unpaid vouchers file and the balance of the vouchers payable general ledger account.

The Check Register

On each business day, the vouchers in the unpaid vouchers file under that date are removed and sent to the employee authorized to approve vouchers for payment. The employee reviews the voucher to assure that all verification steps have been completed; initials the voucher to signify approval for payment; fills in the payment-record section of the voucher indicating the date paid, check number, and amount; prepares a check; and forwards the check and voucher to the person authorized to sign checks, usually the company's treasurer. The treasurer then reviews the voucher for proper authorization of payment, signs the check and mails it to the payee, and sends the voucher to the accounting department.

When the voucher is received by the accounting department, an entry is made in the "payment" column of the voucher register to indicate that the voucher has been paid. The check is then recorded in a check register (Figure 7-12), which serves as a record of all cash disbursements, and the paid voucher is filed in numerical order in a paid vouchers file.

Because checks are written only in payment of specific vouchers, every check drawn results in a debit to Vouchers Payable and a credit to Cash, with the exception of cases where a check is drawn in payment of a voucher on which a cash discount is involved. In those cases, the entry in the check register results in a debit to Vouchers Payable for the gross amount, a credit to Purchase Discounts, and a credit to Cash for the net amount paid. At the end of the month, the columns of the check register are footed and cross-footed, and the column totals are posted to the general ledger accounts specified in the column headings. As with the posting of other special journals, the general account ledger numbers are written in parentheses at the bottom of each column to indicate that the total has been posted.

Making Partial Payments

If an invoice is to be paid in installments, a separate voucher is prepared for each installment when the invoice is received. However, if installment payments are decided upon after the invoice has been vouchered, the original voucher is canceled and new vouchers prepared, one for each installment.

Recording Purchase Returns and Allowances

On occasion a defective item is returned to a supplier or an allowance is received from a supplier. If this occurs prior to the preparation of the voucher, the voucher is prepared for the amount of the corrected invoice. If returns are made or allowances received after the voucher has been prepared and entered in the voucher register, a general journal entry is prepared debiting Vouchers Payable and crediting Purchase Returns and Allowances for the appropriate amount. A reference to this general journal entry is then made on the appropriate line in the voucher register and the amount of the return or allowance is deducted on the voucher. A copy of the credit memorandum or other document verifying the return is attached to the voucher. The check drawn in payment of the voucher is then written for the corrected amount.

GLOSSARY

BANK RECONCILIATION.   A form prepared to reconcile the cash balance reported on the bank statement with the balance per the depositor's records (p. 302).
BANK STATEMENT.   A statement prepared by the bank that provides the detail of activity that has taken place in a checking account for a period (p. 300).
CANCELED CHECKS.   Checks written by the depositor and paid by the bank (p. 301).

CASH.   Money and any instrument such as a check or money order that a bank will accept for immediate deposit in a bank account (p. 289).

CHECK REGISTER.   A book in which all checks written are recorded in numerical order (p. 315).

INTERNAL CONTROL SYSTEM.   The overall procedures adopted by a business to safeguard its assets, promote the reliability of accounting data, and encourage compliance with company policies (p. 290).

INVOICE.   A business form prepared by a supplier that itemizes the goods shipped, prices charged, and total amount due. To the buyer it is a purchase invoice; to the seller it is a sales invoice (p. 308).

NSF CHECK.   A check that was included in a depositor's deposit, but was not paid by the maker's bank because of insufficient funds (p. 302).

OUTSTANDING CHECKS.   Checks written by a depositor that have not yet cleared the bank (p. 302).

PAID VOUCHERS FILE.   A file in which vouchers are placed in numerical order after they have been paid (p. 315).

PETTY CASH FUND.   A specified amount of cash placed under the control of an employee for use in making small cash payments (p. 298).

PETTY CASH RECEIPT.   A form used as a receipt for payments from a petty cash fund (p. 298).

PURCHASE ORDER.   A business form prepared by the buyer that authorizes a supplier to ship specific goods (p. 308).

PURCHASE REQUISITION.   A business form used by operating managers to request the purchasing department to place orders for goods and services (p. 308).

RECEIVING REPORT.   A business form prepared by the receiving department that lists the type and quantity of goods received (p. 310).

UNPAID VOUCHERS FILE.   A file in which unpaid vouchers are stored under the date on which they must be paid (p. 314).

VOUCHER.   A business form used to summarize a purchase transaction and approve the invoice for recording and payment (p. 312).

VOUCHER REGISTER.   A book of original entry in which all vouchers prepared are listed in numerical order (p. 313).

VOUCHER SYSTEM.   An accounting system used to control all cash disbursements (p. 308).

DISCUSSION QUESTIONS

1. What items are included as Cash on the balance sheet?
2. Distinguish between internal administrative controls and internal accounting controls. Give an example of each.
3. What is one of the main accomplishments of the Foreign Corrupt Practices Act?
4. Why are clearly established lines of responsibility an important element of internal accounting controls?

5. How does the policy of rotating duties among employees aid in strengthening internal control?
6. A company's cashier has the responsibility of determining the specific accounts receivable to be written off as uncollectible. What general element of internal control is lacking?
7. An employee is responsible for ordering goods, receiving the goods, and paying the supplier. What general element of accounting control is lacking?
8. Procedures for the control of receipts from cash sales and for the control of mail receipts are based on the same general principle of internal control. What is this principle? Why is the possibility of fraud decreased when this principle is followed?
9. Why is it important that the employee designated to approve invoices for payment not have checkwriting or accounting responsibilities?
10. What account(s) is debited when (a) establishing a petty cash fund and (b) replenishing a petty cash fund?
11. Why is the petty cash fund replenished at the end of an accounting period even though the amount of cash in the fund is not running low?
12. What document serves as the basis for the entry needed to record the replenishment of a petty cash fund? Who makes such an entry?
13. Why is internal control strengthened by requiring that each day's cash receipts be deposited intact and by further requiring that all disbursements be made by check?
14. Define the terms *debit memo* and *credit memo*. Give an example of each.
15. Identify each of the following bank reconciliation items as: (a) an addition to the bank statement balance, (b) a deduction from the bank statement balance, (c) an addition to the book balance, and (d) a deduction from the book balance.
    (1) Bank service charges.
    (2) Outstanding checks.
    (3) Deposit in transit.
    (4) Check of a customer returned by the bank because of insufficient funds.
    (5) A note collected for the depositor by the bank.
    (6) Depositor's check written for $200 but charged by the bank as $20.
16. In reconciling a bank statement, what reconciling items require a journal entry on the depositor's books?
17. What entry should be made when a customer's check is deposited and returned later by the bank marked "NSF"?
18. What documents are used in the verification procedures performed by the accounting department prior to approving an invoice for payment?
19. What account(s) is debited in the voucher register? What account is credited?
20. What accounts are debited and credited in the check register?

EXERCISES

Exercise 7-1 (Composition of Cash)
On June 30 the safe of Jud Company contained the following items:

1. Currency and coin, $1,826.42.
2. A $50 IOU from an employee representing a temporary loan that is to be deducted from the employee's next paycheck.
3. Checks dated June 30 in the total amount of $1,616.30 received from customers on June 30.
4. A check for $420 received from a customer on June 30, but dated July 3.

Required:
A. What dollar amount should be included in "cash" on the June 30 balance sheet?
B. Explain how any items not included in "cash" should be reported in the June 30 balance sheet.

Exercise 7-2 (Cash Internal Control Procedures)

Brian Doty, owner of Doty Equipment Sales, is troubled by the fact that his business consistently shows good earnings but is often short of cash. He explains to you that he has made a serious effort to establish good internal control procedures for cash transactions. He says "I have made one employee responsible for keeping the accounting records, making cash collections, and making bank deposits. I have assigned to another employee the responsibility for ordering merchandise, receiving and counting the goods when they arrive, and writing checks to pay for the merchandise. I want to be sure that we are actually getting what we're paying for."

Required:
Evaluate Brian's internal control procedures and explain the reasoning behind any criticism you have.

Exercise 7-3 (Petty Cash and Cash Receipts)

Prepare journal entries for the following transactions of Pete Company. If an entry is not required, indicate so and explain why.

1. A petty cash fund was established in the amount of $150.
2. Cash sales for Monday recorded on the cash register tape amounted to $846.22. A count of the cash in the register showed a total of $892.12. The cash register contained a $50.00 change fund at the beginning of the day.
3. An employee paid $5.29 postage to mail a package and was reimbursed from the petty cash fund.
4. Cash sales for Tuesday recorded on the cash register tape amounted to $796.44. A count of the cash in the register showed a total of $849.13. The register contained a $50.00 change fund at the beginning of the day.

Exercise 7-4 (Petty Cash Fund Transactions)

On July 1, Wilson Company established a $200 petty cash fund. On July 31, the petty cash box contained the following cash and expense receipts:

Cash $24.31

Expense Receipts

Receipt No.	Purpose	Amount
1	Postage	61.09
2	Office supplies	40.35
3	Taxi fares	21.50
4	Gasoline	34.75
5	Newspapers	18.00

Required:

A. Prepare the entry that was made to establish the petty cash fund.

B. Prepare the entry needed to replenish the petty cash fund. (Taxi and newspaper expenditures should be charged to Miscellaneous Expense.)

C. Assume that a decision was made to increase the petty cash fund to $300. Prepare the journal entry to do so.

Exercise 7-5 (Petty Cash)

Braden Company's petty cash box contained the following items on December 31, the end of the fiscal year:

Cash	$93.20
Expense Receipts	
Office supplies	22.96
Postage	35.87
Freight in	29.41
Taxi fares (miscellaneous expense)	18.56

Required:

A. Explain why the petty cash fund should be replenished on December 31 even though there is a substantial amount of cash in the fund.

B. Prepare the entry to replenish the petty cash fund.

Exercise 7-6 (Bank Reconciliation)

Johnson Company received its bank statement for the month of July, which showed a bank balance of $2,392.30. The cash balance on Johnson Company's books on July 31 was $2,185.55. The following reconciling items were identified:

1. Outstanding checks amounted to $410.

2. The bank statement included a $7.75 debit memorandum for bank service charges for the month and a $12.50 debit memorandum for printing checks.

3. Cash receipts of $700 for July 31 were placed in the bank's night depository and were unrecorded by the bank at the time the July bank statement was prepared.

4. A credit memorandum received with the bank statement indicated that a noninterest-bearing note receivable in the amount of $600 was collected for Johnson Company by the bank. The bank charged a collection fee of $20 and credited the remaining $580 to Johnson Company's account.

5. Johnson Company's bookkeeper discovered that check No. 301 in the amount of $92.40 in payment of office supplies purchased had been incorrectly recorded as $29.40.

Required:
Prepare a bank reconciliation for Johnson Company as of July 31.

Exercise 7-7 (Adjusting Entries from Bank Reconciliation)
Prepare the journal entries needed on Johnson Company's books as a result of the bank reconciliation in Exercise 7-6.

Exercise 7-8 (Recording Transactions Using a Voucher System)
(This exercise is based on information in the appendix to the chapter.)

Sampson Company uses a voucher system. Selected transactions during June are as follows:

June	2	Voucher No. 540 was prepared for the purchase of merchandise from Leesburg Wholesale Company, $1,240; terms, 2/10, n/30.
	5	Voucher No. 546 was prepared for an advertising bill received from Taylor Associates, $560; terms, n/20.
	7	Voucher No. 549 was prepared for the purchase of office equipment from Whipple Brothers, $900; terms, 2/10, n/30.
	11	Issued check No. 1242 to Leesburg Wholesale Company in payment of voucher No. 540.
	16	Issued check No. 1245 to Whipple Brothers in payment of voucher No. 549.
	25	Issued check No. 1248 to Taylor Associates in payment of voucher No. 546.

Required:
Record each of the transactions in general journal form.

PROBLEMS

Problem 7-1 (Petty Cash Transactions)
Transactions and events affecting the petty cash fund of Cochran Company are as follows:

1. Paid $14 for the repair of an office typewriter.
2. Paid $30 for postage.
3. Purchased office supplies, $19.50.
4. Paid $11.75 for newspapers and magazines.
5. Paid $21.50 C.O.D. charges on merchandise purchased.
6. The custodian of the fund exchanged the receipts in the petty cash box for a check to reimburse the fund and to increase the size of the fund from $100 to $200.
7. Paid National Express $36 for overnight delivery of some important machinery replacement parts.
8. Paid $6 to have the office windows washed.
9. Paid $7.50 for coffee and supplies for the employee lounge.
10. Reimbursed an employee $10 for taxi fares.

11. Paid $13 to a dry cleaner for office drapes cleaned.
12. Paid $22.50 to the driver of the company's delivery truck for gasoline purchased.

Required:
Prepare general journal entries to:
A. Establish the petty cash fund in the amount of $100.
B. Replenish the fund after transaction (5) and increase its size to $200. (C.O.D. charges and express payments may be debited to Freight-in. Expenses unrelated to autos, office supplies, and postage should be debited to Miscellaneous Expense.)
C. Replenish the fund after transaction (12).

Problem 7-2 (Bank Reconciliation)

Brown Company received its bank statement for the month of April, showing a bank balance of $3,321.16. The cash balance on Brown Company's books on April 30 was $3,086.47. The following reconciling items were identified:

1. Outstanding checks amounted to $435.24.
2. Debit memos were included with the bank statement as follows:
   (a) A $241.40 check received from a customer (Davis Company) and deposited by Brown Company was returned for lack of sufficient funds in Davis Company's account.
   (b) Service charges for the month were $12.35.
3. A credit memo received with the bank statement indicated that a note receivable in the amount of $700 plus interest of $80 had been collected by the bank. The bank charged a collection fee of $20 and credited the remaining $760 to Brown Company's account.
4. A deposit of $742.80 was in transit on April 30.
5. The bookkeeper discovered that check No. 462 in the amount of $159.20 in payment of insurance expense had been incorrectly recorded as $195.20.

Required:
A. Prepare a bank reconciliation as of April 30.
B. Prepare any adjusting general journal entries required.

Problem 7-3 (Bank Reconciliation)

The following information was taken from the bank statement of Westside Company dated June 30.

May 31 Balance			$3,955.25
	Checks/Debits		**Deposits/**
Date	**Check No.**	**Amount**	**Credits**
June 1	488	88.00	385.50
	480	135.75	
2	489	150.00	
4	490	248.60	345.50
6	491	301.80	490.70
	494	49.70	

7	493	175.75	
10	492	704.50	615.65
12	499	315.80	295.35
16	495	440.40	340.60
21	496	201.15	455.75
	497	195.45	
	498	180.10	
23	500	87.60	410.25
	501	138.70	
26			425.10
27	503	165.00	
28			385.30
29	504	114.10	
30		85.00 DM	
		5.75 SC	245.00 CM
Totals		3,783.15	4,394.70
June 30 Balance			$4,566.80

On June 30, the bank debited Westside's account for $85 for a check returned because of insufficient funds and for $5.75 for bank service charges. The NSF check was written by Larry King, a customer. On June 30, the bank also credited the company's account for $245 for the net proceeds ($250 less $5 collection fee) of a note receivable it had collected on behalf of the company.

The number and amount of each check written during the month was recorded in the cash disbursements journal as follows:

Check No.	Amount	Check No.	Amount	Check No.	Amount
489	$150.00	495	$440.40	501	$138.70
490	248.60	496	210.15	502	201.40
491	301.80	497	195.45	503	165.00
492	704.50	498	180.10	504	114.10
493	175.75	499	315.80	505	174.00
494	49.70	500	87.60		

The date and the amount of each deposit as recorded in Westside's books during June were as follows:

Date	Amount	Date	Amount
June 4	$345.50	June 21	$455.75
6	490.70	23	410.25
10	615.65	26	425.10
12	295.35	28	385.30
16	340.60	30	342.90

The bookkeeper discovered that check No. 496 (in payment for the purchase of office equipment) was correctly issued for $201.15 but incorrectly recorded in the cash disbursements journal as $210.15.

Outstanding checks at the last statement date, May 31, were: No. 480 for $135.75; No. 488 for $88.00; and No. 486 for $106.50.

The balance in the cash account on the company's books on June 30 was $4,264.55.

Required:

A. Prepare a bank reconciliation for Westside Company as of June 30.

B. Prepare general journal entries needed to reconcile the company's cash account with the correct balance.

Problem 7-4 (Bank Reconciliation)

Information about cash transactions and cash balances for Zepper Company for the month of September is:

1. The general ledger cash account had a balance of $6,329.15 on August 31.
2. The cash receipts journal showed total cash receipts of $22,458.98 for September.
3. The cash disbursements journal showed total cash payments of $23,622.40 for September.
4. The September bank statement reported a bank balance of $4,931.96 on September 30.
5. Cash receipts of $960.20 for September 30 were placed in the bank's night depository on September 30 and were not included in the September bank statement.
6. Outstanding checks at the end of September were: No. 764, $89.62; No. 766, $214.30; and No. 770, $119.89.
7. Included with the bank statement were:
   (a) A debit memo for service charges, $8.42.
   (b) A check written by Nance Company, a customer, for $286.46 marked NSF.
   (c) A credit memo for $642.50 indicating the collection of a note receivable of $600 plus interest that the bank had credited to Zepper Company's account.
8. Comparison of the canceled checks with the entries in the cash disbursements journal disclosed that check No. 742 for $872 written, in payment of rent expense, had been incorrectly recorded as $827.

Required:

A. Prepare a bank reconciliation for September.

B. Prepare general journal entries to adjust the accounts.

C. What is the amount of cash that should be reported on the September 30 balance sheet?

Problem 7-5 (Recording Transactions Using a Voucher System)

(This problem covers information contained in the chapter appendix.)

Lamber Company completed the following transactions affecting Vouchers Payable during May:

May	1	Prepared voucher No. 531 payable to Mint Company for merchandise purchased, $975.60; invoice dated April 29; terms, 2/10, n/30.
	7	Prepared voucher No. 532 payable to Ace Insurance for one year's insurance premiums, $375.51.
	8	Issued check No. 876 in payment of voucher No. 531.

10 Prepared voucher No. 533 for sales salaries, $822.60, and administrative salaries, $1,216.40.

10 Issued check No. 877 in payment of voucher No. 533. Cashed the check and distributed cash to employees.

11 Issued check No. 878 in payment of voucher No. 532.

18 Prepared voucher No. 534 payable to Brice Company for merchandise purchased, $1,426.82; invoice dated May 17; terms, 2/10, n/30.

20 Prepared voucher No. 535 payable to Acme Company for office furniture, $822.19; invoice dated May 18; terms, n/30.

22 Prepared voucher No. 536 payable to River Power Company, $266.87, for monthly utility bill.

23 Issued check No. 879 in payment of voucher No. 536.

24 Prepared voucher No. 537 for sales salaries, $892.80, and administrative salaries, $1,422.40.

24 Issued check No. 880 in payment of voucher No. 537. Cashed the check and distributed cash to employees.

26 Issued check No. 881 in payment of voucher No. 534.

28 Prepared voucher No. 538 payable to Bell Telephone Company for telephone bill, $89.22.

29 Prepared voucher No. 539 payable to Mint Company for merchandise purchased, $860.40; invoice dated May 27; terms, 2/10, n/30.

Required:

A. Prepare a Voucher Register and Check Register similar to those illustrated in this chapter and record the transactions in the registers. Set up separate debit columns for Purchases, Sales Salaries, Administrative Salaries, and Utilities Expense.

B. Post the appropriate amounts to a Vouchers Payable account (No. 516).

C. Prove the balance in the Vouchers Payable account by preparing a list of unpaid vouchers.

ALTERNATE PROBLEMS

Problem 7-1A (Petty Cash Transactions)

James Welch set up a petty cash fund for his business and appointed an office secretary custodian of the fund. The following transactions and events affecting the petty cash fund were then completed:

1. Wrote a $200 check payable to the petty cash fund custodian to establish the petty cash fund.
2. Paid $35 for postage (Postage Expense).
3. Paid $24 C.O.D. charges on merchandise purchased (Delivery Expense).
4. Paid for janitorial supplies purchased, $27.50 (Miscellaneous Expense).
5. Paid $29 for the repair of an office machine (Repairs Expense).
6. Paid $10.25 for newspapers and magazines (Miscellaneous Expense).
7. The custodian of the fund exchanged the receipts in the petty cash box for a check to reimburse the fund and to increase the size of the fund from $200 to $300.

8. Paid Speedy Delivery Service for the overnight delivery of an important contract, $42 (Delivery Expense).
9. Paid $22.50 for the installation of a new regulator in the company's automobile (Repairs Expense).
10. Paid $35.60 to have the office windows washed and carpet cleaned (Miscellaneous Expense).
11. Paid $22.25 for coffee and supplies for the employee lounge (Miscellaneous Expense).

Required:
Prepare general journal entries to:

A. Establish the petty cash fund.
B. Replenish the fund after transaction (6) and increase its size to $300.
C. Replenish the fund after transaction (11).

Problem 7-2A (Bank Reconciliation)
Porter Company received its bank statement for the month of September showing a bank balance of $4,188.30. The cash balance on Porter Company's books on September 30 was $4,029.30. The following reconciling items were identified:

1. Outstanding checks amounted to $501.25.
2. Debit memos were included with the bank statement as follows:
    (a) A $225.00 check received from a customer (Leonard Company) and deposited by Porter Company was returned marked "NSF."
    (b) Service charges for the month were $11.75.
    (c) Check printing charge, $12.00..
3. A credit memo received with the bank statement indicated that a note receivable in the amount of $630 plus interest of $71 had been collected by the bank. The bank charged a collection fee of $20 and credited the remaining $681 to Porter Company's account.
4. A deposit of $801.50 was in transit on September 30.
5. The bookkeeper discovered that check No. 103 in the amount of $225.00 in payment of insurance expense had been incorrectly recorded on the books as $252.00.

Required:
A. Prepare a bank reconciliation as of September 30.
B. Prepare any adjusting general journal entries required.

Problem 7-3A (Bank Reconciliation with Errors)
The March bank statement and general ledger cash accounts of Davison Company are given below:

Bank Statement

	Checks	Deposits	Balance
Balance, March 1			$ 6,200
Deposits recorded during March		$43,000	49,200
Checks paid during March	$39,900		9,300
NSF check—B. D. Foote	240		8,960
Bank service charges	26		8,934
Balance, March 31			8,934

Cash

| March 1 balance | 6,600 | March checks written | 42,100 |
| March deposits | 44,500 | | |

Petty Cash

| March 31 balance | 200 | |

Cash on hand for making change (included in the Cash account) on March 1 and March 31 was $400.

Required:

A. Prepare a bank reconciliation. (*Hint:* You might find an error made by either the bank or the company.)

B. Prepare any adjusting general journal entries necessary.

C. What total amount of cash should be reported on the March 31 balance sheet?

Problem 7-4A (Bank Reconciliation)

The accountant for Watson Company gathered the following information concerning cash transactions and cash balances for the month of August:

1. The general ledger cash account had a balance of $2,380.25 on August 1.

2. Total cash receipts and cash disbursements during August were: cash receipts, $16,283.45; cash disbursements, $14,908.90.

3. The August bank statement showed a cash balance of $3,860.85 on August 31.

4. Outstanding checks at the end of August were: No. 230, $28.35; No. 233, $101.20; and No. 248, $370.50.

5. Included with the bank statement were:

(**a**) A check written by Adams Company (a customer) for $350.75 marked NSF.

(**b**) A debit memo for service charges, $10.10.

(**c**) A credit memo for $670.00 indicating the collection of a note receivable of $600 plus interest that the bank had credited to Watson Company's account.

6. Cash receipts for the last day of August amounting to $748.15 were placed in the bank's night depository on August 31 and were not included in the August bank statement.

7. Comparison of the canceled checks with the entries in the cash disbursements journal disclosed that check No. 241 for $549 written in payment of utilities expense had been incorrectly recorded as $594.

Required:

A. Prepare a bank reconciliation as of August 31.

B. Prepare general journal entries to adjust the accounts.

C. What is the amount of cash that should be reported on the August 31 balance sheet?

Problem 7-5A (Recording Transactions Using a Voucher System)

(This problem covers information contained in the chapter appendix.)

Molson Company began operations on November 1 and decided to use a voucher system to aid control of cash disbursements. During November, Molson Company completed the following transactions affecting vouchers payable.

Nov. 4 Prepared voucher No. 1 payable to Thompson Company for merchandise purchased, $189.80; invoice dated November 2; terms, 3/10, n/60.

6 Prepared voucher No. 2 payable to Acme Realty for November rent, $401.50.

10 Prepared voucher No. 3 payable to Dixon Company for office equipment, $365.75; invoice dated November 9; terms, n/20.

10 Prepared voucher No. 4 for employee wages, $822.60.

11 Issued check No. 100 in payment of voucher No. 4. Cashed the check and distributed cash to employees.

14 Issued check No. 101 in payment of voucher No. 1.

15 Issued check No. 102 in payment of voucher No. 2.

17 Prepared voucher No. 5 payable to Ritchie Company for merchandise purchased, $1,580.88; invoice dated November 17; terms, 2/10, n/30.

20 Prepared voucher No. 6 payable to Aztec Press for advertising, $601.10; invoice dated November 18; terms, n/30.

21 Prepared voucher No. 7 payable to Western Power Company, $305.10 for monthly utility bill.

23 Issued check No. 103 in payment of voucher No. 7.

24 Prepared voucher No. 8 for employee wages, $1,010.40.

24 Issued check No. 104 in payment of voucher No. 8. Cashed the check and distributed cash to employees.

26 Issued check No. 105 in payment of voucher No. 5.

29 Prepared voucher No. 9 payable to Miller Company for merchandise purchased, $860.40; invoice dated November 27; terms, 2/10, n/30.

30 Issued check No. 106 in payment of voucher No. 3.

Required:
A. Prepare a Voucher Register and Check Register similar to those illustrated in this chapter and record the transactions in the registers. Set up separate debit columns for Purchases, Wages, and Utilities Expense.
B. Post the appropriate amounts to a Vouchers Payable account (No. 403).
C. Prove the November 30 balance in the Vouchers Payable account by preparing a list of unpaid vouchers.

CASE FOR CHAPTER 7

(Discussion—Internal Control Procedures)

Jerry Barnes took over the management of his family's successful retail business shortly after graduating from Westwood University with a degree in economics. Because Jerry had little knowledge of internal control procedures, he relied heavily upon the company's new bookkeeper, Ted Crawford. Ted, with the help of an assistant bookkeeper, had full responsibility for keeping the company's accounting records, preparing financial statements, making bank deposits, preparing checks for payment for purchases and expenses, maintaining the petty cash fund, and preparing the monthly bank reconciliation.

The monthly income statements received by Jerry Barnes from Ted Crawford reported a highly satisfactory net income. However, Jerry noticed that the amount of cash in the bank was steadily declining. After several months he was forced to apply for a bank loan in order to meet his current obligations. The bank loan officer reviewed the company's financial statements and, expressing his belief that "there must be something wrong," recommended that Jerry review his operating procedures for cash receipts and disbursements. Upon return to the company's premises, Jerry announced that he intended to begin a review of operating procedures the next morning. On the following morning Ted Crawford did not report for work and telephone calls to his home went unanswered. With the help of a friend with some experience in accounting, Jerry began his review of cash procedures and discovered the following:

1. At the close of business each day, Ted Crawford removed the cash and the tape from the two cash registers, prepared a cash deposit ticket, and made the bank deposit in the night depository at the company's bank. He also prepared the daily cash receipts summary that was given to the assistant bookkeeper for the preparation of accounting entries. A comparison of daily cash register tapes with daily bank deposits showed that deposits were often much smaller than cash receipts.
2. Ted Crawford was custodian of the petty cash fund. For each payment from the fund, Ted prepared a petty cash receipt that he signed to verify the disbursement. Investigation showed that the $500 fund had been replenished frequently during the past several months.
3. Ted Crawford relieved the salesclerks and recorded cash sales on their registers during the salesclerks' lunch hours.
4. Ted Crawford prepared all purchase orders. He also approved payment of all purchase invoices, wrote and properly signed the check in payment, and mailed the payment to the vendor. Investigation revealed that payment was made to one company for several large purchases of store equipment that could not be located on the premises.

Required:
For each of the numbered paragraphs above, describe the internal control procedures that should be established to help prevent the occurrence of fraudulent events.

PART THREE
ACCOUNTING FOR ASSETS AND LIABILITIES

CHAPTER 8
ACCOUNTING FOR RECEIVABLES AND PAYABLES

OVERVIEW AND OBJECTIVES

This chapter describes the accounting treatment of short-term receivables and payables—those classified as current assets and current liabilities. When you have completed the chapter, you should understand:

- The different types of short-term receivables and payables and how to account for them (pp. 333–351).
- The nature of uncollectible accounts (pp. 334–336).
- The difference between the income statement and balance sheet approaches to estimating bad debts expense (pp. 337–339).
- How to compute and account for interest (pp. 342–344).
- What is meant by discounting notes receivable and notes payable (pp. 345–347, 349–351).

Today's U.S. economy is essentially a credit economy. Manufacturers, wholesalers, and retailers regularly extend credit to buyers of their goods and services as a means of increasing sales. The willingness of businesses to extend credit is an important factor in the significant growth of our economy. Most businesses not only extend credit to customers, which results in receivables, but also receive credit from suppliers, resulting in payables.

RECEIVABLES

Receivables are amounts due from other persons or businesses. Although arising from various business transactions, receivables most often result from the sale of goods or services on credit. Credit is often extended to customers on open account, which means that the buyer has a specified length of time such as 30 or 60 days before payment is due. These open accounts are called **accounts receivable** by the business granting credit.

Sometimes credit is granted only upon receipt of a formal legal instrument such as a promissory note. A promissory note is a **negotiable instrument** that can be transferred by **endorsement**—a signature on the back that assigns the rights therein to another party. To the grantor of credit the note is a **note receivable.** Creditors favor promissory notes for three main reasons: First, if a lawsuit arises concerning the debt, the note represents a legal, written acknowledgment by the debtor of both the debt and its amount. Second, notes are generally interest-bearing and thereby produce interest revenue for the credit grantor. Third, notes receivable are more easily converted into cash than are accounts receivable before their maturity date by transferring them by endorsement to a bank or finance company. Promissory notes are generally used for transactions that have a long payment period, such as sales on an installment plan or sales of large items like machinery or equipment. A promissory note is often demanded by the creditor when a customer requests an extension of payment of an open account.

Other types of receivables include amounts receivable from officers and employees for loans or salary advances, amounts receivable from the sale of assets other than inventory, and amounts receivable from lending money to affiliated companies or outside parties.

CLASSIFICATION OF RECEIVABLES

Accounts and notes receivable that arise from the sale of merchandise or services in the normal course of business are called **trade receivables.** They are normally classified as current assets on the balance sheet because they are scheduled for collection in cash within the operating cycle. Other receivables, such as those from officers and employees and from the sale of non-merchandise assets, are called *nontrade receivables*. They are considered current assets if they are to be collected within one year or within the operating cycle; otherwise, they are classified as noncurrent assets under the caption "Other Receivables" or "Investments." To facilitate the proper classification of receivables, a general ledger account should be used for each type, and subsidiary ledgers provided where necessary.

ACCOUNTS RECEIVABLE

Accounts receivable arise from the sale of goods or services on open account as was already noted. Although businesses would prefer to collect the sales price at the time of sale, experience has shown that extending credit can increase revenue and net income significantly for many firms. To accomplish an increase in net income, however, the additional gross profit generated by credit sales must exceed the additional expenses incurred in extending credit. These expenses include investigation of the creditworthiness of prospective customers, additional recordkeeping, and provision for uncollectible accounts. The lack of adequate control of receivables is often a major cause of business failures.

No business wants to extend credit to a customer who is unlikely to pay the account when due. Most large companies therefore maintain a credit department, which has responsibility for investigating the credit history and determining the debt-paying ability of customers who apply for credit. If the customer is a business, the credit department normally requests a set of its audited financial statements for use in judging its ability to pay. If the customer is an individual, the credit department will ask for information about current earnings, current expenses, outstanding debts, and general financial position. In addition, the credit department normally obtains a credit report from a local or national credit-rating agency that accumulates data on the credit history of individuals and businesses.

Uncollectible Accounts

Regardless of the diligence and care exercised in extending credit, there are always some customers who do not pay their accounts. Credit department personnel may have misjudged a customer's ability to pay, or sudden financial reverses may have resulted in an inability to pay. A downturn in general economic conditions often results in an increase in business failures and personal bankruptcies, resulting in uncollectible accounts to those who have extended credit. At the time they make the decision to sell goods and services on credit, business managers know that some of the resulting accounts receivable will eventually prove to be uncollectible. These uncollectible accounts (sometimes called **bad debts**) are expected to occur and therefore are considered an expense of doing business on a credit basis.

The accounting principle of matching expenses against revenues requires that the expense of uncollectible accounts be deducted in the same accounting period in which the credit sales were recognized. There is no general rule for determining the time at which a receivable actually becomes uncollectible. The fact that the debtor fails to pay the receivable on its due date does not by itself establish uncollectibility. The debtor may simply have forgotten to pay or may be temporarily short of cash and cannot pay until later. The creditor normally will make a continued effort to collect past-due accounts through oral or written communication with the debtor, and may eventually turn the receivable over to a collection agency or begin legal action. This process may take several months or years to complete, with receivables arising in one accounting period being collected or written off in the following accounting period or later. Because the specific accounts that will eventually become uncollectible are unknown, bad debts expense is estimated at the end of the accounting period by the allowance method of accounting for uncollectible accounts.

Allowance Method of Accounting for Uncollectible Accounts

At the end of the accounting period, before the books are closed and the financial statements prepared, an estimate is made of the amount of accounts receivable expected to become uncollectible. An adjusting entry is prepared with a debit to Bad Debts Expense and a credit to an account called Allowance for Uncollectible Accounts. To illustrate, assume that Cardon Company began operations in January, 1984, made credit sales in the amount of $400,000 during 1984, and collected $300,000 of these accounts during the year. The balance in the accounts receivable account at the end of the year is therefore $100,000. After a careful review of the accounts receivable, the management of Cardon Company estimated that $6,000 of the accounts will be uncollectible. An adjusting entry is made on December 31, 1984, the end of the fiscal year for Cardon Company, as follows:

Dec.	31	Bad Debts Expense	6,000	
		Allowance for Uncollectible Accounts		6,000
		To record estimated bad debts expense.		

The entry serves two important purposes. First, it records the estimated bad debts of $6,000 as an expense of the period in which the revenue from credit sales was recognized, thereby properly matching expenses and revenues. Bad debts expense will be deducted on the income statement for 1984. Second, the entry establishes an allowance account that is deducted from accounts receivable on the balance sheet in order to report accounts receivable at their estimated realizable (collectible) value.

The Allowance for Uncollectible Accounts. Why credit an allowance account rather than crediting accounts receivable directly when recording the entry for estimated bad debts? You will recall that the general ledger Accounts Receivable account is a control account supported by a subsidiary ledger that identifies the amounts owed by individual customers. Any debit or credit to the accounts receivable control account requires a like debit or credit to one of the subsidiary-ledger accounts. But it is impossible to determine in advance which specific accounts will prove uncollectible. A direct credit to the Accounts Receivable control account would produce an imbalance between it and the accounts receivable subsidiary ledger, thereby destroying an important element of internal control. The alternative is to credit an allowance account (called a contra-asset account) that, when subtracted from accounts receivable on the balance sheet, results in the reporting of accounts receivable at the estimated amount expected to be collected (the expected realizable value of accounts receivable) as shown in Figure 8-1.

Figure 8-1
Allowance for Uncollectible Accounts

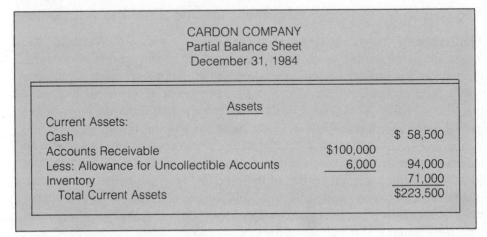

it and the accounts receivable subsidiary ledger, thereby destroying an important element of internal control.

CARDON COMPANY
Partial Balance Sheet
December 31, 1984

Assets

Current Assets:		
Cash		$ 58,500
Accounts Receivable	$100,000	
Less: Allowance for Uncollectible Accounts	6,000	94,000
Inventory		71,000
Total Current Assets		$223,500

Estimating the Amount of Bad Debts Expense

The estimate of the amount of bad debts is generally based on a combination of past experience and forecasts of future economic and business conditions, with considerable personal judgment involved. The goal is to produce a reasonable estimate of the amount of accounts receivable that will be eventually collected in cash. However, the practice of conservatism in accounting often comes into play and accountants may have a tendency to estimate the amount at the upper end of the "reasonable" range to produce a relatively low asset value for accounts receivable as well as a conservative net income figure.

Two methods are widely used to estimate bad debts expense. One method determines the amount as a percentage of net credit sales for the period. Because this method uses net credit sales (credit sales less credit sales returns and allowances, and discounts on credit sales) as a base, it is sometimes called the *income statement approach*. The method places emphasis on the relationship between credit sales and uncollectible accounts and is therefore more in accordance with the matching principle. The other method analyzes the age and probability of collection of the individual accounts receivable and is called aging the accounts receivable. Since this method bases bad debts expense on an analysis of accounts receivable, it is often called the *balance sheet approach*. Emphasis is placed on the realizable value of accounts receivable on the balance sheet. Most firms will use either of these two methods, but not both.

Estimate Based on Net Credit Sales. An analysis of past accounting data will usually show some predictable percentage relationship between the amount of bad debts and the amount of net credit sales. This percentage is then applied to net credit sales for the period to estimate the amount of bad debts expense. The logic of this method is that credit sales produce the accounts receivable that may become uncollectible in the future. As an example, assume that past experience shows that about 1% of net credit sales each year have been uncollectible and that net credit sales for the year amounted to $847,000. The year-end adjustment to recognize bad debts expense would be:

Dec.	31	Bad Debts Expense	8,470	
		Allowance for Uncollectible Accounts		8,470
		To record bad debts expense for the		
		year in the amount of 1% × $847,000.		

Under this method, any existing balance in the Allowance for Uncollectible Accounts is ignored in computing the amount of bad debts expense. Basically, this method addresses the question, "How much of this year's net credit sales is expected to be uncollectible?" and the Allowance for Uncollectible Accounts is adjusted by that amount.

Estimate Based on an Analysis of Accounts Receivable. If the estimate of bad debts expense is based on an analysis of accounts receivable, the estimate is derived from a schedule that analyzes and classifies accounts receivable by age. The preparation of the schedule is called *aging the accounts receivable,* and generally takes the following form:

Aging of Accounts Receivable
December 31, 1984

Customer	Balance	Not Yet Due	Number of Days Past Due				
			1–30	31–60	61–90	91–180	Over 180
Apex Co.	$ 680		$ 680				
B. D. Brent	335	$ 335					
Carr Company	590	240	350				
Darnett Co.	860			$ 420	$ 440		
J. C. Evans	470						$ 470
R. S. Fox	215					$ 215	
E. J. Zare	740	740					
B. K. Zuny	930	830		100			
Total	$83,400	$55,800	$10,600	$6,600	$4,200	$3,800	$2,400

The older an account receivable is, the greater the probability that it will be uncollectible. Past accounting records are therefore analyzed to determine the approximate percentage of each age group that will become uncollectible. For example, assume that an analysis of past accounting records shows the following percentages of accounts receivable that were written off as uncollectible:

Age Category	Percent
Not yet due	1%
1 to 30 days past due	5%
31 to 60 days past due	10%
61 to 90 days past due	20%
91 to 180 days past due	30%
Over 180 days past due	60%

With these data, the balance needed in the allowance for uncollectible accounts to reduce the accounts receivable to their estimated realizable value is computed as follows:

Age Category	Amount	Estimated Uncollectible Accounts	
		Percentage	Amount
Not yet due	$55,800	1	$ 558
1–30 days past due	10,600	5	530
31–60 days past due	6,600	10	660
61–90 days past due	4,200	20	840
91–180 days past due	3,800	30	1,140
Over 180 days past due	2,400	60	1,440
Total	$83,400		$5,168

The total determined, $5,168, is the balance needed in the allowance for uncollectible accounts. Consequently, any existing balance in the allowance account must be taken into consideration in determining the amount of the year-end adjustment. For example, if the Allowance for Uncollectible Accounts has a $1,540 credit balance before adjustment, bad debts expense must be charged for the difference of $3,628 ($5,168 − $1,540) and the following adjusting entry prepared:

Dec.	31	Bad Debts Expense	3,628	
		Allowance for Uncollectible Accounts		3,628
		To record bad debts expense for the year.		

After this entry is posted, the Accounts Receivable and Allowance for Uncollectible Accounts will appear as follows:

Accounts Receivable

12/31 balance	83,400	

Allowance for Uncollectible Accounts

	12/31 balance before adjusting	1,540
	12/31 adjustment	3,628
	12/31 balance	5,168

The allowance for uncollectible accounts may sometimes have a debit balance at year-end because more accounts than estimated actually became uncollectible. If the allowance for uncollectible accounts had a debit balance (for example $260) before adjustment, that balance would be added to the $5,168 and the total of $5,428 would be debited to Bad Debts Expense and credited to the Allowance for Uncollectible Accounts to produce the desired balance of $5,168 in the allowance account.

Rather than preparing an aging schedule, some companies simply analyze past data to determine a percentage relationship between uncollectible accounts and accounts receivable. This percentage is multiplied by the balance in accounts receivable at the end of the year to determine the balance needed in the Allowance for Uncollectible Accounts. The allowance account is then adjusted to that balance by an entry similar to the one above.

Writing Off an Uncollectible Account

When an account receivable is determined to be uncollectible, it is written off against the allowance for uncollectible accounts by debiting the allowance account and crediting Accounts Receivable. Of course, the related account in the accounts receivable subsidiary ledger is also credited. For example, assume that after an extended effort to collect, the $470 account of J. C. Evans is determined to be uncollectible. The following entry would be made:

Dec.	31	Allowance for Uncollectible Accounts	470	
		Accounts Receivable—J. C. Evans		470
		To write off the account receivable as uncollectible.		

Two important things should be noted concerning this entry. First, the write-off is debited to the Allowance for Uncollectible Accounts rather than to Bad Debts Expense. Expense was recognized on an estimated basis at the end of the year in which the sale was made. To charge an expense account again at the time the account is written off would result in a double recording of expense with a resulting understatement of net income. Second, the net amount of accounts receivable is unchanged by the entry to write off an uncollectible account. After the write-off entry is posted, the general ledger accounts would appear as follows:

Accounts Receivable

12/31 balance before write-off	83,400	12/31 write-off	470
balance	82,930		

Allowance for Uncollectible Accounts

12/31 write-off	470	12/31 balance before write-off	5,168
		balance	4,698

Note that the estimated realizable value of accounts receivable is the same after the write-off as it was before the write-off:

	Before Write-off	After Write-off
Accounts Receivable	$83,400	$82,930
Less: Allowance for Uncollectible Accounts	5,168	4,698
Estimated Realizable Value	$78,232	$78,232

The fact that the write-off did not change the net amount of accounts receivable demonstrates clearly the notion that no expense results from the write-off of an account receivable. The expense from uncollectible accounts is properly charged to the period in which the credit sale was made rather than to the period in which the account is written off.

The total amount of accounts receivable written off against the allowance account during a period will seldom agree with the amount in the allowance account at the beginning of the period. If write-offs during the period are less than the opening balance in the account, the account will have a credit balance at the end of the period before adjustment. If write-offs exceed the opening balance, the account will have a debit balance at the end of the period before adjustment. After the year-end adjustment to record bad debts expense, however, the allowance for uncollectible accounts will have a normal credit balance.

Recovery of an Account Written Off

In some cases, an account that has been written off will be collected in part or in full at a later date. If this occurs, the account receivable should be reestablished in the accounts in order to maintain a complete history of the customer's activity. Assume, for example, that J. C. Evans underwent bankruptcy proceedings and that a final settlement of his account was received on May 4 in the amount of $250. The entry to reinstate the account receivable is:

May	4	Accounts Receivable—J. C. Evans	250	
		Allowance for Uncollectible Accounts		250
		To reestablish part of the account		
		receivable written off as uncollectible.		
		on December 31.		

After the account is reestablished, the cash collection is recorded as usual by a debit to Cash and a credit to Accounts Receivable—J. C. Evans.

Direct Write-off Method

Although the allowance method is the one that properly matches expenses and revenues and is the method most widely used, some companies use the **direct write-off method.** With this method, uncollectible accounts are charged to expense at the time an account is determined to be uncollectible. This is done by debiting Bad Debts Expense and crediting Accounts Receivable. No attempt is made to match expense with related revenue. The direct write-off method is therefore not generally accepted and its use can be justified only on the basis of immateriality. Some companies sell goods and services primarily on a cash basis and make only occasional small sales on account. Any uncollectible accounts written off will be small and therefore immaterial in relation to total revenue and net income. In the event that an account previously written off is collected later, the collection is normally recorded by a debit to Cash and a credit to either Bad Debts Expense, if that account has a debit balance large enough to absorb it, or a credit to an appropriately titled miscellaneous revenue account such as Bad Debts Recovered.

NOTES RECEIVABLE

As specified earlier, credit is sometimes extended only upon receipt of a **promissory note,** often referred to simply as a *note*. A promissory note is an unconditional written promise to pay a sum certain in money on demand or at a future determinable date. The person making the promise to pay by signing the note is called the **maker** of the note, and the person to whom payment is to be made is called the **payee.** In the note illustrated on the following page, DMF Corporation is the maker and Baker Wholesale Company is the payee. To Baker Wholesale the note is a *note receivable,* and to DMF Corporation it is a *note payable*.

If the note bears interest, the interest rate must be stipulated and the note is called an *interest-bearing note*. If no interest rate is stipulated, the note is called a *noninterest-bearing note*. **Interest** is a charge made for the use of money. To the payee, interest is revenue; to the maker of the note it is an expense.

```
┌─────────────────────────────────────────────────────────────────────┐
│    $3,000                        Tempe, Arizona  February 12  19  84  │
│ ───────────                                                           │
│              90 days             after date            we             │
│ ─────────────────────────────                 ────────────────────── │
│ promise to pay to the order of          Baker Wholesale Company       │
│ ───────────────────────────────        ───────────────────────────   │
│     three thousand and 00/100---------------------------------- dollars│
│ ────────────────────────────                                          │
│ payable at       United Bank of Tempe                                 │
│ ─────────────   ───────────────────────────────────────────────────  │
│ for value received with interest at      10%    .                     │
│                                        ─────────                       │
│                                                                       │
│                                          DMF Corporation              │
│                                          Jake Smith                   │
│                                          ──────────────────────────── │
│                                          Treasurer                    │
└─────────────────────────────────────────────────────────────────────┘
```

The amount printed on the note is called its **face value,** or **principal,** and the amount due is called the **maturity value.** The maturity value of a short-term interest-bearing note is the sum of its face value plus interest. The maturity value of a noninterest-bearing note is its face value.

Computing Interest

The formula for computing interest is:

$$\text{Principal} \times \text{Rate} \times \text{Time} = \text{Interest}$$

Interest rates are normally stated in terms of a period of one year. Thus the interest rate of 10% on the note illustrated is an annual interest rate. If the term of the note is expressed in days, the exact number of days should be used to compute interest. For convenience, however, it is generally assumed that a year contains 360 days. Interest on the note illustrated therefore is computed as follows:

$$\text{Principal} \times \text{Rate} \times \frac{\text{days}}{360} = \text{Interest}$$

or

$$\$3,000 \times .10 \times \frac{90}{360} = \$75$$

On the maturity date of the note, DMF Corporation must pay the maturity value of $3,075 ($3,000 principal plus $75 interest).

Determining Due Date

The period of time from the issue date of a note to its due date is generally expressed in days or months, and the date on which the note is due is called the **maturity date.** If expressed in months, the note is due in the month of its maturity on the day of the month it was issued. Thus a four-month note issued on February 14 has a due date of June 14; a two-month note issued on December 30 is due on February 28 since February does not have 30 days. In computing interest, each month is considered to be 1/12 of a year so interest on the four-month note would be computed by taking 4/12 of the annual interest amount.

If a note is expressed in days, the maturity date is computed as follows, assuming a 90-day note dated February 14:

Term of the note in days		90
Number of days in February	28	
Date of Note	14	
Number of days outstanding in February		14
Number of days remaining		76
Number of days in March		31
Number of days remaining		45
Number of days in April		30
Due date in May		15

Accounting for Receipt and Collection of a Note

Some companies, particularly manufacturing and wholesale firms that sell in large quantities, often request a note from a buyer who asks for credit. Other companies, such as retail firms, may receive notes only occasionally, although some retailers sell high-priced items on an installment plan under which the buyer makes a down payment and gives a note (or a series of notes with different maturity dates) for the balance. Firms that regularly sell goods on open account are sometimes asked for an extension of credit beyond the normal due date. In these cases, the company generally insists that the customer give it an interest-bearing note to replace the account receivable.

A single notes receivable account is normally maintained in the general ledger. The notes receivable account is a control account, with a subsidiary ledger consisting of a file of the actual notes received arranged in order of due date. No other record is necessary because the notes themselves contain all the information needed—the name of the maker, maturity date, and interest rate.

To illustrate the accounting for a note receivable, assume that Cardon Company has an account receivable from Dennis Mead in the amount of $1,500 that is past due. Mead requested a 90-day extension of the payment date, and Cardon Company agreed by accepting a 90-day, 10% note in exchange for the account receivable. Upon receipt of the note, Cardon Company would make the following entry:

July	9	Notes Receivable	1,500	
		Accounts Receivable—Dennis Mead		1,500
		To record the receipt of a note in		
		settlement of an account receivable.		

This entry simply substitutes a note receivable for the account receivable. If a note had been received at the time of the original sale, the entry above would be the same except that the credit would be to Sales rather than to Accounts Receivable.

On October 7, when Mead pays the note, the entry in general journal form is:

Oct.	7	Cash	1,537.50	
		Notes Receivable		1,500.00
		Interest Revenue		37.50
		($1,500 $\times$ 10% $\times$ 90/360)		
		To record collection of a note receivable		
		from Dennis Mead.		

Dishonored Notes Receivable

If the maker of a note fails to pay on the maturity date, the note is said to have been **dishonored** and the maker is said to have *defaulted* on the note. Because the maturity date has passed, the note is no longer negotiable and cannot be sold or discounted at a bank. The maker, however, is not relieved from legal responsibility for the debt, and the payee will make the normal effort to collect. For these reasons, the payee generally transfers the claim, including any interest due, to an accounts receivable account.

To illustrate, assume that in the previous illustration Dennis Mead failed to pay the note on its maturity date. Cardon Company would make the following entry:

Oct.	8	Accounts Receivable—Dennis Mead	1,537.50	
		Notes Receivable		1,500.00
		Interest Revenue		37.50
		To record Dennis Mead's dishonored		
		note.		

This entry removes the note from the Notes Receivable account and reinstates an account receivable from Mead, thereby maintaining a complete history concerning his payment activities. The Notes Receivable account will then contain only those notes that have not yet matured and therefore represent collectible items.

Notice that the account receivable includes the interest on the note, which was credited to Interest Revenue even though it has not yet been collected.

Mr. Mead's legal obligation to Cardon Company is for the maturity value of the note—principal and interest—and his account should contain the full amount owed. In addition, since interest is earned over time, the accrued interest on the note is revenue of the current period.

Discounting Notes Receivable

One of the positive features of a note receivable is its relative ease of conversion to cash before its maturity date. The note may be endorsed by the holder and sold to a bank in exchange for cash. The bank then holds the note until its maturity date, when it expects to collect the maturity value from its maker. This process is called *discounting notes receivable* because the bank will deduct in advance an interest charge called a **discount.** The discount is based on the maturity value of the note for the period the bank will hold the note—the time between the date the note is transferred to the bank and its due date. The maturity value of the note less the discount deducted, called the **proceeds,** is then paid to the endorser by the bank.

To illustrate, assume that Cardon Company received a $2,000, 90-day, 10% note dated March 16 from Frank Morgan, a customer. Cardon Company held the note until April 15, when it discounted it at a bank at a discount rate of 12%. Since the maturity date of the note is June 14 (15 days in March, 30 days in April, 31 days in May, and 14 days in June total 90 days), the bank will hold the note for 60 days (15 days in April, 31 days in May, and 14 days in June—60 days). The period of time the bank holds the note before its collection is called the **discount period,** for which the bank will charge interest (discount) at 12%. The bank will deduct from the maturity value of the note 60 days' interest at 12% and give Cardon Company the proceeds as follows:

Face Value of the Note	$2,000
Interest at 10% for 90 days (2,000 × 10% × 90/360)	50
Maturity Value	2,050
Less: Discount at 12% for 60 days (2,050 × 12% × 60/360)	41
Proceeds	$2,009

The entry to record the discounting of the note by Cardon Company would be:

Apr.	15	Cash	2,009	
		Notes Receivable		2,000
		Interest Revenue		9
		Discounted Frank Morgan's note at the bank at 12%.		

The excess of the proceeds received over the face value of the note is recorded as interest revenue. It represents the amount of interest Cardon Company would have earned if it had held the note to maturity ($50) less the amount deducted as discount by the bank when it purchased the note ($41). In this case, the proceeds exceed the face value of the note, resulting in interest revenue. If the proceeds are less than the face value, the difference is debited to interest expense.

Contingent Liability.   A discounted note must be endorsed by the holder, who then becomes contingently liable for payment of the note. Contingent liability means that the endorser (Cardon Company in our illustration) must pay the note on its maturity date if the maker (Frank Morgan) fails to do so. The discounting of the note therefore creates a contingent liability for Cardon Company that continues until the due date of the note. If the maker pays the note on its due date, the contingent liability ceases. If the maker defaults, the contingent liability becomes an actual, that is, real liability.

The nature and amount of any contingent liability must be disclosed in the financial statements. Consequently, the contingent liability for notes receivable discounted must be disclosed if a balance sheet is prepared earlier than the maturity date of the notes. Disclosure is normally made by a footnote to the financial statements that explains the nature and amount of the contingent liability.

Dishonor of a Discounted Note

Normally the bank collects a discounted note directly from the maker so that no further obligation remains for the endorser. If the maker fails to pay on the maturity date, however, the note has been *dishonored* and the bank is required by law to notify the endorser promptly that it intends to collect from the endorser. To accomplish this, the bank normally protests the dishonored note by sending the endorser a notarized statement called a *notice of protest*. A fee called a protest fee is often assessed by the bank when a dishonored note is protested, and the endorser is legally obligated to pay the maturity value of the note plus the protest fee. When the endorser pays the bank, the amount paid is recorded as a receivable from the maker of the note.

As an example, assume in the previous illustration that instead of paying the $2,000 note on its maturity date, Frank Morgan dishonored it and the bank sent Cardon Company a notice of protest and assessed a protest fee of $20. Cardon Company will pay the bank and make the following entry:

June	15	Accounts Receivable—Frank Morgan	2,070	
		Cash		2,070
		To establish a receivable for a dishonored note.		

The amount of the receivable includes the maturity value of the note ($2,050) plus the protest fee ($20). Cardon Company will make the normal effort to collect the receivable from Frank Morgan. If this fails, the receivable will be written off against the allowance for uncollectible accounts.

End-of-period Adjustment for Interest Revenue

Interest is a function of time, that is, interest is earned as time passes. When an interest-bearing note receivable is held at the end of the accounting period, accrued interest should be computed and recorded to recognize the interest earned as well as interest receivable. For example, assume Cardon Company received a $4,000, 75-day, 12% note on November 1. On December 31, the end of the fiscal year for Cardon Company, the following adjusting entry will be made to accrue interest for 60 days on the note:

Dec.	31	Interest Receivable	80	
		Interest Revenue		80
		($4,000 × 12% × 60/360)		
		To accrue interest on a note receivable.		

This entry results in the recognition of interest revenue during the period it was earned and establishes a receivable for interest to be reported as a current asset on the December 31 balance sheet.

When the note is collected on January 15, the collection is recorded as follows:

Jan.	15	Cash	4,100	
		Notes Receivable		4,000
		Interest Receivable		80
		Interest Revenue		20
		To record collection of a note receivable.		

This entry eliminates the note and interest receivable, and recognizes $20 of interest revenue for the 15 days the note was held during the current accounting period.

PAYABLES

Payables are the opposite of receivables, representing amounts due to creditors of the business. They result from various transactions, such as the purchase of merchandise or other assets on credit and from borrowing money from banks or finance companies. The business also may owe amounts for accrued expenses, such as salaries and wages due to employees, interest accrued on loans, and taxes due to governmental agencies. Payables are also called liabilities.

CLASSIFICATION OF PAYABLES

Payables are classified into two broad groups, current liabilities and long-term liabilities, based on the time they are due. *Current liabilities* are those obligations that must be settled within one year or the operating cycle, whichever is longer. They require the use of current assets (or the incurring of other current liabilities) to eliminate them. Among the common current liabilities are accounts payable, short-term notes payable, and accrued expenses. *Long-term liabilities* are those whose settlement date is beyond one year or the operating cycle and generally include mortgage notes payable, bonds payable, and obligations for employee pensions. Accounting for current liabilities is discussed here. Payroll liabilities are discussed in Chapter 12, and long-term liabilities in Chapter 17.

Accounts Payable

Accounts payable designates amounts owed to creditors for the purchase of merchandise, supplies, and services in the normal course of business. Because they are not evidenced by a formal debt instrument such as a note, they often are referred to as *open accounts* or *payables*. Each time merchandise, supplies, or services are acquired on open account, the appropriate asset or expense account is debited and Accounts Payable is credited.

Short-term Notes Payable

Notes payable differ from accounts payable in that the liability is evidenced by a promissory note. They are often issued when a business borrows money from a bank. In some industries it is normal practice for the purchaser of merchandise to give a note payable to the seller at the time of purchase, as we have seen. Other transactions that result in notes payable are purchases of relatively high-cost items of machinery or equipment, and the substitution of a note payable for a past-due open account payable.

Note Issued for a Bank Loan.   When money is borrowed from a bank, the borrower may issue an interest-bearing note payable to the bank under which the borrower agrees to repay the amount of the note plus interest on its maturity date. For example, assume that Cardon Company borrowed $20,000 from a bank on June 1, and signed a six-month note for $20,000 at an interest rate of 12%. The journal entry on Cardon Company's books to record the note would be:

June	1	Cash	20,000	
		Notes Payable		20,000
		Borrowed $20,000 for 6 months at 12%.		

No interest is recorded on the note until it is paid on December 1, when the entry would be:

Dec.	1	Notes Payable	20,000	
		Interest Expense ($20,000 × 12% × 6/12)	1,200	
		Cash		21,200
		Paid a note payable.		

In this illustration, the note provided for the payment of its face value plus interest at a stipulated rate. The borrower received the face amount of the note at the time it was given to the bank and repaid that amount plus interest on the maturity date. As an alternative, banks sometimes have the borrower sign a noninterest-bearing note for the amount to be repaid at maturity. Interest is deducted in advance, and the borrower receives the difference between the face value of the note and the amount of interest deducted, the proceeds. This practice is called discounting a note payable. By this practice, the note in the preceding illustration would be recorded by Cardon Company as follows:

June	1	Cash	18,800	
		Discount on Notes Payable	1,200	
		Notes Payable		20,000
		Discounted a 6-month, $20,000 note at 12%.		

The discount on notes payable is deducted as a contra-liability in the current liability section of the balance sheet as shown below:

Current Liabilities		
Accounts Payable		$46,500
Notes Payable	$20,000	
Less: Discount on Notes Payable	1,200	18,800
Accrued Expenses		6,700
Total Current Liabilities		$72,000

Because the discount on notes payable represents interest deducted in advance, it will be transferred to interest expense over the term of the note. In our illustration, the maturity date of the note falls within the same year as the issue date. Thus the discount will be charged to interest expense when the note is paid on December 1 as follows:

Dec.	1	Notes Payable	20,000	
		Interest Expense	1,200	
		Discount on Notes Payable		1,200
		Cash		20,000
		Paid a $20,000 note payable.		

Discounting a noninterest-bearing note increases the effective annual interest rate on the loan as compared to borrowing on an interest-bearing note. This results because the same amount of interest is paid under either method, but the borrower has the use of less money under the discounting method. If the effective interest rate on a $20,000, one-year, 12% interest-bearing note is compared with the effective interest rate on a $20,000, one-year note discounted at 12%, we obtain the following results:

	Annual Interest Amount	Amount Borrowed	Effective Interest Rate
Interest-bearing Note	$2,400	$20,000	12.00%
Discounted Note	2,400	17,600	13.64%*

*$2,400/$17,600

End-of-period Adjustments for Interest

When a note payable is issued in one accounting period and matures in another, an adjusting entry must be made at the end of the first period to allocate interest expense properly. For example, assume that the $20,000, six-month, 12% note of Cardon Company in the previous illustration was issued on November 1 rather than on June 1. If the note is an interest-bearing note, an adjusting entry is needed on December 31 to accrue interest expense for two months as follows:

Dec.	31	Interest Expense	400	
		Interest Payable		400
		($20,000 × 12% × 2/12)		
		To accrue interest at 12% for two months		
		on a $20,000 note.		

When the note is paid on May 1, the following entry is prepared:

May	1	Notes Payable	20,000	
		Interest Payable	400	
		Interest Expense	800	
		Cash		21,200
		To record payment of a note plus		
		interest.		

The adjustment process is slightly different if the note had been discounted at 12% on November 1. The year-end adjustment is:

Dec.	31	Interest Expense	400	
		Discount on Notes Payable		400
		To record interest for two months on		
		discounted note.		

The entry to record payment of the note on May 1 is:

May	1	Notes Payable	20,000	
		Interest Expense	800	
		Discount on Notes Payable		800
		Cash		20,000
		Paid a $20,000 discounted note.		

In either case, the amount of interest expense allocated to each accounting period is the same, $400 to the period in which the note was issued and $800 to the following period.

Other Current Liabilities

In addition to accounts payable and short-term notes payable, other payables are reported as current liabilities because they will require the use of current assets or the incurring of other current liabilities to settle the obligation. Expenses incurred but unpaid at the end of the period are accrued for such items as interest on notes payable, rent, and wages due employees in order to include them in the accounting period in which they were incurred. Any portion of long-term debt that matures within one year is also reported as a current liability. In addition, cash received before it is earned, such as rent received in advance and magazine subscriptions received by a publishing company, is classified as a current liability. These cash advances are often called **deferred revenue** or *unearned revenue* such as Unearned Subscription Revenue. They are classified as current liabilities because they will normally be earned within the operating cycle or a period of one year, whichever is longer.

GLOSSARY

ACCOUNTS PAYABLE.   Amounts owed to creditors for the purchase of merchandise, supplies, and services in the normal course of business (p. 348).

ACCOUNTS RECEIVABLE.   Amounts due from customers for sales or services performed on credit (p. 333).

AGING OF ACCOUNTS RECEIVABLE.   The process of classifying accounts receivable on the basis of the length of time they have been outstanding (p. 336).

ALLOWANCE FOR UNCOLLECTIBLE ACCOUNTS. The estimated amount of accounts receivable expected to be uncollectible (p. 335).

BAD DEBTS EXPENSE. The expense resulting when a customer fails to pay an account receivable (p. 334).

CONTINGENT LIABILITY. A possible liability that may become actual if certain future events occur (p. 346).

DEFERRED REVENUE. Cash advances that will be earned in future accounting periods (p. 351).

DIRECT WRITE-OFF METHOD. The recognition of uncollectible accounts expense at the time an account receivable is deemed to be uncollectible (p. 341).

DISCOUNT. Interest deducted in advance (p. 345).

DISCOUNT PERIOD. The period of time for which a bank will charge interest on a discounted note (p. 345).

DISHONORED NOTE. A note the maker has failed to pay on its maturity date (p. 344).

ENDORSEMENT. A signature on the back of a negotiable instrument that assigns the rights therein to another party (p. 333).

INTEREST. A charge made for the use of money, computed as Principal × Rate × Time (p. 341).

MAKER. The person who promises to pay a note on its maturity date (p. 341).

MATURITY DATE. The date on which the maturity value of a note is due (p. 342).

MATURITY VALUE. The amount of a note due on its maturity date; it includes principal as well as interest (p. 342).

NEGOTIABLE INSTRUMENT. A legal document that can be transferred to another party by an endorsement (p. 333).

NOTE PAYABLE. An obligation evidenced by a formal written promise to pay (p. 348).

NOTE RECEIVABLE. A receivable evidenced by a formal written promise to pay (p. 333).

PAYEE. The person to whom a promissory note is made payable (p. 341).

PRINCIPAL. The face amount of a note. Also called FACE VALUE (p. 342).

PROCEEDS. The maturity value of a note less discount (p. 345).

PROMISSORY NOTE. An unconditional written promise to pay a sum certain in money on demand or at a future determinable date (p. 341).

PROTEST FEE. A fee assessed by a bank when a note is dishonored (p. 346).

TRADE RECEIVABLES. Accounts and notes receivable that arise from the sale of merchandise or services in the normal course of business (p. 333).

DISCUSSION QUESTIONS

1. What is a note receivable? Why do creditors favor promissory notes over accounts receivable?

2. Where are accounts and notes receivable reported on the balance sheet?
3. Explain briefly how the allowance method of accounting for uncollectible accounts works.
4. Two methods are widely used to estimate bad debts expense. Name them and explain how each works.
5. What is the direct write-off method of accounting for uncollectible accounts? What is its main shortcoming?
6. What type of account is the Allowance for Uncollectible Accounts?
7. Explain how the Allowance for Uncollectible Accounts might have a debit balance before the end-of-period adjustment is made.
8. After the accounts are adjusted at the end of the fiscal year, Accounts Receivable has a balance of $135,000 and Allowance for Uncollectible Accounts has a balance of $7,000.
   (a) What is the net realizable value of accounts receivable?
   (b) If a $1,000 account receivable is written off as uncollectible, what effect will the write-off have on the net realizable value of accounts receivable?
9. A $700 account receivable is considered to be uncollectible and is to be written off. Give the journal entry to record the write-off assuming that (a) the allowance method is used and (b) the direct write-off method is used.
10. What entry is made when an account receivable that has been written off is collected in part or in full at a later date? Why?

For questions 11 through 17, assume a fiscal year-end of December 31.

11. A note dated June 8 provides for payment after 90 days of $1,000 plus interest at 10%. What is the face value, maturity value, and maturity date of the note?
12. On March 6, a company accepts a 90-day, 10% note with a face amount of $5,000. Give the journal entry to record collection of the note at its maturity date.
13. Assume that the maker of the note in question 12 defaulted on the note. Give the entry to record the default.
14. X Company received a $5,000, 90-day, 10% note dated July 9 from a customer and discounted it at a bank at 11% after holding the note for 30 days. How much will X Company receive from the bank? Give the journal entry to record the discounting of the note.
15. Brad Company issued a 120-day, 15% note payable dated February 16 to replace an account payable to Cleve Company in the amount of $10,000. Give the journal entries to record the issuance of the note payable and the payment of the note on its maturity date.
16. A company borrowed $5,000 from a bank and signed a six-month note payable dated May 1 for $5,000 at an interest rate of 15%. Give the entry to record payment of the note on its maturity date.
17. Assume the note in question 16 was issued on October 1 rather than May 1. What entry should be made on December 31 concerning the note?
18. What would the effective interest rate on the note in question 16 be if the company had discounted the $5,000 note at a discount rate of 15%?

EXERCISES

Exercise 8-1 (Accounting for Bad Debts)

Prepare journal entries to record the following transactions:

Dec. 31 Based on past experience, Lynch Company estimates that 1% of the year's credit sales of $205,000 will be uncollectible.

Feb 27 After a concerted effort to collect, an account receivable of $355 from Gessler Company was written off as uncollectible.

April 28 Gessler Company unexpectedly paid the amount written off on Feb. 27.

Exercise 8-2 (Accounting for Bad Debts)

At the end of its fiscal year, December 31, Henderson Company aged its accounts receivable and determined that an allowance for uncollectible accounts of $4,236 was needed to report accounts receivable at their net realizable value.

Required:

A. Prepare the entry to record bad debts expense assuming that the allowance for uncollectible accounts currently has a $740 credit balance.

B. Prepare the entry to record bad debts expense assuming that the allowance for uncollectible accounts currently has a $310 debit balance.

C. Prepare the entry to write off as uncollectible a $275 account receivable from R. D. Minton.

D. Assume that before the entry recorded in C above, the net amount of accounts receivable on Henderson Company's books was $33,850. What is the net amount of accounts receivable after recording the write-off of the Minton account? Why?

Exercise 8-3 (Note Received in Exchange for Account Receivable)

Flynn Company has an account receivable from Dave Roberts in the amount of $2,200 that is past-due. On March 3, Mr. Roberts requested a 90-day extension of the payment date, and Flynn Company agreed to accept a 90-day, 12% note in exchange for the account receivable.

Required:

A. Prepare a journal entry to record the receipt of the note.

B. Prepare a journal entry to record the receipt of payment of the note on its maturity date, assuming the fiscal year ends on December 31.

C. Assume that Mr. Roberts defaulted on the note on its maturity date. Prepare the journal entry Flynn Company would make to record the default.

Exercise 8-4 (Note Received in Exchange for Account Receivable)

On December 1, Brooks Company accepted a $6,000, 90-day, 10% note from Jill Morgan in exchange for a $6,000 account receivable that was past due.

Required:

Prepare all entries that should be made for this note from the time of its receipt to the time of its collection. (Brooks Company's fiscal year ends on December 31.)

Exercise 8-5 (Discounting a Note Receivable)

Jorgen Company sold merchandise to Bailor Company and accepted a $5,400, 90-day, 12% note dated July 24 in payment. On September 22, Jorgen Company discounted the note at its bank at a discount rate of 14%. Bailor Company dishonored the note on its maturity date and the bank sent Jorgen Company a notice of protest including a protest fee of $15. Jorgen Company paid the bank for the maturity value of the note plus the protest fee. Jorgen Company's fiscal year ends on December 31.

Required:

A. Prepare the journal entry to record the receipt of the note.
B. Prepare the journal entry to record the discounting of the note by Jorgen Company.
C. Prepare the journal entry to record Jorgen Company's payment to the bank when the note was dishonored.

Exercise 8-6 (Accounting for a Note Payable)

Campo Company borrowed $12,000 from its bank on March 1 and signed a six-month, 14% note payable for $12,000.

Required:

A. Prepare journal entries to record the issue of the note and its payment on its maturity date. Campo Company's fiscal year ends on December 31.
B. Assume that the note was issued on October 1 rather than March 1. Prepare journal entries to record the issue of the note, the accrual of interest on December 31, and the payment of the note.

Exercise 8-7 (Borrowing by Discounting a Note Payable)

On November 1, Dorsey Company borrowed money by issuing a $12,000, six-month note payable to a local bank. The bank deducted interest at 14% and gave Dorsey Company the proceeds.

Required:

A. Prepare all entries needed to record the issue of the note, the adjustment for interest expense at year-end, and the payment of the note on its maturity date. (Dorsey Company's fiscal year ends on December 31.)
B. Compute the effective interest rate Dorsey Company paid for the use of the borrowed money.

PROBLEMS

Problem 8-1 (Accounting for Bad Debts)

On January 1, Dram Company had accounts receivable of $214,320 and an allowance for uncollectible accounts with a credit balance of $12,240. During January of the current year, the following transactions occurred:

1. Sales on account	$162,000
2. Sales returns and allowances on credit sales	6,480

3. Accounts receivable collected	147,600
4. Accounts written off as uncollectible	4,960

Based on an aging of accounts receivable on January 31, the company determined that the allowance for uncollectible accounts should have a credit balance of $13,690 on the January 31 balance sheet.

Required:

A. Prepare journal entries to record the summary data in the four items above and to adjust the allowance for uncollectible accounts.

B. Show how accounts receivable and the allowance for uncollectible accounts would appear on the January 31 balance sheet.

C. On March 23, Brad Company, whose $1,680 account had been written off as uncollectible in January, paid its account in full. Prepare the journal entries to record the collection.

D. Assume that Dram Company bases its estimate of uncollectible accounts on net credit sales and that 1% of net credit sales is expected to become uncollectible. Prepare the entry to recognize bad debts expense and determine the balance in the Allowance for Uncollectible Accounts.

Problem 8-2 (Accounting for Bad Debts)

All transactions related to a company's uncollectible accounts for the fiscal year ended December 31 are presented below:

Jan.	19	Wrote off the $480 account of Rocky Company as uncollectible.
April	9	Reestablished the account of James Fulbright and recorded the collection of $1,100 in full payment of his account, which was written off earlier.
July	31	Received 40% of the $340 balance owed by Carl Wilson and wrote off the remainder as uncollectible.
Aug.	15	Wrote off as uncollectible the accounts of Welch Company, $2,800, and D. Fleetman, $725.
Sept.	26	Received 25% of the $4,200 owed by Western Company and wrote off the remainder as uncollectible.
Oct.	16	Received $790 from D. Jackson in full payment of his account, which had been written off earlier as uncollectible.
Nov.	20	Recorded an account receivable for a $2,000, 11%, 90-day note of N. Vassar that was dishonored at maturity date.
Dec.	31	Estimated bad debts expense for the year to be 1½% of net credit sales of $399,000.

The accounts receivable account had a balance at December 31 of $110,850, and the beginning (January 1) balance in the allowance for uncollectible accounts was $5,300.

Required:

A. Prepare journal entries for each of the transactions.

B. Determine the balance in the allowance account after the December 31 adjustment and the expected realizable value of the accounts receivable at December 31.

C. Assume that, instead of basing the allowance for uncollectibles on net credit sales, the estimate of uncollectible accounts is based on an aging of accounts receivable and that $7,050 of the accounts receivable at December 31 were estimated to be uncollectible. Determine:
   1. The adjustment necessary to bring the allowance account to the desired balance.
   2. The expected realizable value of the accounts receivable at December 31.

Problem 8-3 (Comparison of Direct Write-off and Allowance Methods)

Ventura Company has used the direct write-off method of recording uncollectible accounts since it began operations four years ago. Recently the company has liberalized its credit policy, which has resulted in a significant increase in credit sales and therefore the amount of uncollectible accounts. In light of these facts, the company is considering a change to the allowance method of accounting for uncollectible accounts.

The following information was extracted from the accounting records.

	Net Credit Sales	Total of Accounts Written Off	Year of Origin of Accounts Receivable Written off as Uncollectible			
Year			1	2	3	4
1	$ 20,000	$ 200	$200			
2	35,000	350	100	$250		
3	50,000	500	50	100	$350	
4	160,000	1,200		125	400	$675
			$350	$475	$750	$675

Management intends to estimate uncollectible accounts based on net credit sales, and they are curious as to the effect that an annual provision of 1½% of net credit sales would have had on the amount of bad debts expense reported during each of the last four years.

Required:
A. Determine for each year:
   1. The amount of bad debts expense based on 1½% of net credit sales.
   2. The increase over the expense that was actually reported that such an estimate would cause.
   3. The balance in the allowance for uncollectible accounts at year-end.
B. Do you think the 1½% figure is a good estimate, or would some other figure be more appropriate? Base your determination on the amount of uncollectible accounts originating during the first two years. (AICPA Adapted)

Problem 8-4 (Comprehensive Problem on Receivables and Payables)

Selected transactions of Landers Company for the year 1984 are presented below:

Feb. 13 Wrote off the $537 account receivable from Snider Company as uncollectible.

28 Accepted a 60-day, 10% note in exchange for a $2,000 past-due account receivable of Morton Company.

March 20 Sold merchandise to Silone Company and accepted a 90-day, 11% note in the amount of $6,500.

30 Issued to Andrews Wholesale an $8,000, 10%, 90-day note for merchandise purchased.

30 Discounted at First Bancorp the note received from Morton Company on February 28. The bank discount rate was 10%.

May 31 Borrowed $6,000 from Eastern Bank, issuing a $6,000, 11%, 9-month note.

June 2 Received from Betty Jolsen a 30-day, 10% note for $2,000 in settlement of her account receivable.

18 Received from Silone Company the amount due on the note dated March 20.

28 Paid the Andrews Wholesale note issued on March 30.

July 2 Betty Jolsen dishonored her note of June 2.

Dec. 31 Recorded accrued interest on the note payable to Eastern Bank.

Required:

A. Prepare journal entries to record the above transactions, assuming that Landers Company uses the allowance method of accounting for uncollectible accounts.

B. Prepare a journal entry to record the payment of the note payable to Eastern Bank on February 28, 1985.

Problem 8-5 (Accounting for Notes Receivable, Including Discounting)

During the last three months of the fiscal year, a company received the following notes:

	Date of Note	Face Amount	Term of Note	Interest Rate	Date of Discount	Discount Rate
1.	Oct. 10	$ 7,000	60 days	10%	Nov. 9	11%
2.	Nov. 2	8,000	90 days	9%	Dec. 10	10%
3.	Nov. 12	2,000	60 days	11%		
4.	Dec. 1	4,000	90 days	13%		
5.	Dec. 8	6,000	90 days	12%	Dec. 23	14%
6.	Dec. 16	10,000	60 days	10%		

Required:

A. Determine the due date and maturity value for each note, and for notes 1, 2, and 5, determine the discount period, the amount of discount, and the proceeds.

B. Prepare journal entries to record the discounting of notes 1, 2, and 5 at the bank.

C. Prepare a journal entry to accrue interest on notes 3, 4, and 6 on December 31.

D. Prepare journal entries to record the collection of notes 3, 4, and 6 in the next fiscal period.

Problem 8-6 (Comprehensive Problem on Accounts and Notes Receivable)

The following transactions occurred during fiscal year 1984 (July 1, 1983, through June 30, 1984) at Chiles Company:

July	9	The company accepted an 8%, 90-day, $4,000 note in exchange for the past-due account receivable of Joe Lane.
Aug.	1	Wrote off the $520 account receivable of H. Roberts as uncollectible.
Sept.	7	The note receivable from Joe Lane was discounted at the bank at a discount rate of 9%.
Oct.	7	Joe Lane defaulted on his note and the bank assessed a protest fee of $10. Chiles Company paid the maturity value of the note plus the $10 protest fee.
Nov.	6	Joe Lane unexpectedly paid the maturity value of his dishonored note plus the protest fee and interest at 8% on both for 30 days beyond the note's maturity date.
Dec.	2	Chiles Company received $500 cash and a $5,500, 60-day, 10% note from P. Putnam in granting an extension on his past-due account receivable.
Jan.	31	Received payment from P. Putnam on his note of Dec. 2.
May	1	The company accepted a $7,000, 90-day, 11% note from C. Carr in settlement of an account receivable.
May	1	The company discounted a 6-month, 10%, $15,000 note payable at a local bank.
June	30	Interest was accrued on the note receivable from C. Carr and on the note payable to the bank.
June	30	Bad debts expense is to be recorded at 1% times net credit sales of $301,000.

Required:

A. Prepare journal entries to record the transactions on Chiles Company's books assuming the use of the allowance method of accounting for uncollectible accounts.

B. Prepare journal entries to record the collection of the C. Carr note and the payment of the note payable to the bank during fiscal year 1985.

ALTERNATE PROBLEMS

Problem 8-1A (Accounting for Accounts Receivable)

On October 1, Dawson Company had accounts receivable and an allowance for uncollectible accounts as follows:

Accounts Receivable

Oct. 1 balance	482,220

Allowance for Uncollectible Accounts

Oct. 1 balance	8,920

During October, the following transactions occurred:

1.	Sales on account	$364,500
2.	Sales returns and allowances on credit sales	14,580
3.	Accounts receivable collected	332,100
4.	Accounts written off as uncollectible	11,160

Based on an aging of accounts receivable on October 31, the company determined that the allowance for uncollectible accounts should have a credit balance of $22,500 on the October 31 balance sheet.

Required:

A. Prepare journal entries to record the summary data for the four items above and to adjust the allowance for uncollectible accounts.

B. Show how accounts receivable and the allowance for uncollectible accounts would appear on the October 31 balance sheet.

C. On November 29, Travis Company, whose $2,100 account had been written off as uncollectible in October, paid its account in full. Prepare journal entries to record the collection.

Problem 8-2A (Accounts and Notes Receivable)

Transactions affecting Bradford Company's accounts receivable for the fiscal year ended December 31 are presented below:

Feb.	3	Wrote off the $700 account of Elm Company as uncollectible.
March	6	Received 50% of the $650 balance owed by Jack Wiley and wrote off the remainder as uncollectible.
April	16	Recorded the collection of $475 from Glenn Rhodes in full payment of his account, which had been written off earlier.
July	15	Wrote off as uncollectible the accounts of Pauley Company, $1,100, and Rob Donley, $360.
Sept.	9	Received $500 from E. Dawkins in full payment of his account, which had been written off earlier as uncollectible.
Oct.	8	Received 25% of the $2,800 owed by North Company and wrote off the remainder as uncollectible.
Dec.	4	Recorded an account receivable for a $5,000, 10%, 90-day note of D. Martin that was dishonored at maturity date.
Dec.	31	Estimated bad debts expense for the year to be 1% of net credit sales of $503,500.

Required:

A. Prepare journal entries for each of the transactions.

B. Determine the balance in Allowance for Uncollectible Accounts after the December 31 adjustment. (Assume the allowance account had a $1,960 credit balance on January 1.)

C. Assume that, instead of basing the allowance for uncollectibles on net credit sales, the estimate of uncollectible accounts is based on an aging of accounts receivable and that $8,110 of the accounts receivable at December 31 were estimated to be uncollectible. Determine the adjustment necessary to bring the allowance account to the desired balance. (Assume the allowance account had a $1,960 credit balance on January 1.)

Problem 8-3A (Default on a Note Receivable)

Portland Company sells much of its merchandise on credit with terms of n/30. Customers sometimes ask for an extension of credit beyond 30 days, in which case Portland Company requires that the customer give an interest-bearing note. A sequence of transactions with a customer, Nance Company, follows:

Mar. 10 Sold merchandise to Nance Company for $4,500; received $1,000 cash and the balance was debited to accounts receivable.

Apr. 9 Received a 12%, 90-day note from Nance Company in settlement of its account receivable. The note was dated April 9.

July 8 On the due date of the note, Nance Company defaulted.

Sept. 6 Nance Company paid the defaulted note plus interest at 12% on the defaulted amount from July 8 to September 6.

Required:
Prepare journal entries for the above events. Show interest computations and round to the nearest dollar. Portland Company's fiscal year ends on December 31.

Problem 8-4A (Discounting and Default of a Note Receivable)

Simmons Company entered into the following transactions during 1984:

Jan. 6 Accepted a 10%, 90-day, $1,500 note in exchange for the past-due account receivable of Jim Davies.

March 7 The note received from Jim Davies was discounted at the bank at a discount rate of 12%.

April 6 Jim Davies defaulted on his note and the bank assessed a protest fee of $15. Simmons Company paid the maturity value of the note plus the protest fee.

May 6 Jim Davies paid the maturity value of his dishonored note plus the protest fee and interest at 10% on both for 30 days beyond the note's maturity date.

Nov. 16 Accepted an $11,000, 90-day, 12% note from Tim Williams in settlement of his account receivable.

Nov. 30 Discounted a 6-month, 10%, $9,000 note payable at Central Bank.

Dec. 31 Interest was accrued on the note receivable from Tim Williams.

31 Interest expense was accrued on the note payable to Central Bank.

Required:
A. Prepare journal entries to record the transactions on Simmons Company's books.
B. Prepare journal entries to record the collection of the Tim Williams note and the payment of the note payable to Central Bank during 1985.

Problem 8-5A (Accounting for Notes Payable)

On February 1, Prince Company purchased office equipment at a cost of $55,000. A cash down payment of $15,000 was made and a 15%, six-month note payable was given for the balance. The note requires two payments of $20,000 each plus interest on the amount of the payment. Payments are due on May 1 and August 1.

Required:

A. Prepare journal entries on February 1, May 1, and June 30, the end of the fiscal year for Prince Company.

B. Prepare the journal entry for the final payment on August 1.

CASE FOR CHAPTER 8

(Annual Report Analysis)

Refer to the financial statements of Mary Moppet's Day Care Schools, Inc. for the years ended September 30, 1981 and 1980 in the appendix, and answer the following questions.

1. What types and classes of receivables did Mary Moppet's hold on September 30, 1981?

2. Does Mary Moppet's use the allowance method or direct-write-off method of accounting for uncollectible accounts?

3. What types and classes of payables did Mary Moppet's owe on September 30, 1981?

4. What was the average interest rate paid on notes payable during the year ended September 30, 1981?

5. What was the balance in the allowance for doubtful accounts at the end of 1980? 1981? Can you explain the reason for the significant change in the account balance?

CHAPTER 9
ACCOUNTING FOR INVENTORIES

OVERVIEW AND OBJECTIVES

This chapter describes various methods used to assign cost to ending inventory and cost of goods sold. When you have completed the chapter, you should understand:

- How to determine when the title to inventory transfers (pp. 364–366).
- How to allocate the total inventory cost between ending inventory and cost of goods sold using four different costing methods (pp. 366–371, 380–383).
- How to determine inventory values by applying the lower of cost or market rule (pp. 376–380).
- The effects of inventory errors on the balance sheet and income statement (pp. 386–388).
- How to estimate a value for the ending inventory using the retail inventory and gross profit methods (pp. 388–391).

In Chapter 5, the term *merchandise inventory* was used to designate all goods owned by a merchandising firm and held for future sale to the firm's customers in the normal course of the business. Two inventory systems, perpetual and periodic, were described and illustrated assuming that the cost per unit was the same for the beginning inventory and purchases made during the year. However, in today's markets the prices of most goods change frequently during the period. When prices change, the firm is confronted with the problem of determining what portion of the total cost of goods available for sale should be assigned to ending inventory and what portion to cost of goods sold. In this chapter, we will consider four alternative methods used to assign the total cost of goods to ending inventory and cost of goods sold when prices are changing. We will also address some additional issues related to accounting for inventory.

DETERMINING THE INVENTORY ON HAND

When a periodic inventory system is maintained, the cost of inventory purchased during the period is recorded in the Purchases account, as we saw in Chapter 5. The balance in the Merchandise Inventory account is the cost of the inventory on hand at the beginning of the period. To determine the cost of the ending inventory, the units on hand must be counted and priced. The ending inventory is then reported as a current asset in the balance sheet and is also deducted from the cost of goods available for sale in the income statement to determine the cost of goods sold. Although the inventory on hand and the cost of goods sold balances are available in the accounts when a perpetual inventory system is used, a physical inventory is also taken at least once a year to verify the balances reported.

Before conducting the actual physical count of units on hand (commonly referred to as *taking an inventory*) and pricing the units, the entire process must be carefully planned. During the process, the procedures established must be supervised to ensure that all units owned by the firm are properly counted. Although the specific details vary, this is a typical approach employed:

1. An inventory ticket for each type of item in stock is prenumbered and issued to each department. A space is provided on the ticket to record a description or code number of the item, the number of units counted, the initials of the person making the count, and the initials of the person verifying the count.
2. An employee counts the units and enters on the inventory ticket the type of item counted and the number of units on hand, and initials to identify the person performing the count. The inventory ticket is then attached to the units counted. Because conducting the physical count is often difficult, this step is frequently performed when the firm is closed to business.
3. A supervisor recounts a sufficient number of items to ensure the accuracy of the recorded count and initials the inventory ticket.
4. A supervisor examines the inventory in each department to be sure that an inventory ticket has been attached to all items. Any group of like items without a ticket attached has obviously not been counted.
5. The inventory tickets are collected and forwarded to the accounting department, where the prenumbered tickets are all accounted for. The information on the inventory tickets is summarized on an inventory summary sheet.
6. The unit cost of each individual item in stock is determined from purchase invoices or other supplementary records.
7. The number of units of each individual item is multiplied by their cost and added together to compute the total ending inventory value.

TRANSFER OF OWNERSHIP

During an inventory count, care must be exercised to assure that all goods legally owned by the firm on the inventory date are included in the ending inventory, regardless of where the inventory is located. Transfer of ownership normally depends on the terms of the shipment. Recall from Chapter 5 that when goods are sold **FOB (free on board) shipping point,** freight is paid by the buyer and title ordinarily transfers when the goods are delivered to the transportation company by the seller. If the terms are **FOB destination,** the seller is responsible for paying the freight and title usually does not transfer until delivery is made to the buyer.

From an accounting point of view, at the time title to the goods transfers, the seller may record a sales transaction and the buyer a purchase of inventory. In practice, however, sales are normally recorded when shipment is made and purchases are recorded when the inventory is received irrespective of the shipping terms. To increase the accuracy of the financial statements at year-end, purchase and sales invoices for the last week or two of the current accounting period and for the first week or two of the next period should be reviewed to determine whether there were units in transit on the date of the inventory that should be included with the units counted. For example, goods purchased FOB shipping point and in transit at year-end should be recorded as a purchase and included in the physical count even though they were not on hand when the actual count was made. Although exclusion of this inventory will have no effect on net income (purchases, goods available for sale, and ending inventory are all understated by an equal amount), total assets and total liabilities are understated if the purchase is not recorded. Similarly, goods sold FOB destination should be included in the seller's ending inventory if in transit at year-end since title to the goods has not transferred. The sale and related cost of goods sold are transactions to be recorded in the succeeding period.

In some cases, the seller may have received orders for goods but shipment may not have been made. In such situations, a sale is not recorded because the revenue has not been earned. However, an exception is made when an order for goods has been received and the goods have been readied for shipment, but the buyer requests that the goods be held for later delivery. Such items should be excluded from the inventory of the seller and included in the inventory of the buyer. In still other cases, it may not be clear that title has transferred. The accountant must then use judgment and attempt to assess when the parties to the transaction intended the title to transfer.

GOODS ON CONSIGNMENT

Another problem sometimes encountered in taking an inventory is the treatment of goods held on **consignment.** A consignment is a marketing arrangement whereby a business (the **consignor**) ships goods to a dealer (the **consignee**) who agrees to sell the goods for a commission. Although a transfer of goods has taken place, title to the goods in this case remains with the consignor. Since title to the goods has not transferred, the shipment of consigned goods is not considered a sales/purchase transaction. Goods out on consignment are therefore part of the consignor's inventory even though physical possession of the goods is with the consignee. The goods are excluded from the inventory of the consignee since they remain the property of the consignor.

DETERMINING THE COST OF INVENTORY

As with the accounting for other assets, cost is the primary basis of accounting for inventory. Applied to inventory, cost means the sum of all direct and indirect costs incurred to bring the merchandise to a salable condition and to its existing location. Conceptually, the invoice price, freight charges, insurance on the goods while in transit, special handling costs, adjustments and assembly costs incurred in preparing the goods for sale, costs incurred to operate a purchasing department, costs associated with receiving and inspecting the goods, and storage costs incurred before the goods are sold are among the costs that may be properly identified and allocated to inventory. However, when several types of inventory are acquired in one shipment, it may be difficult to allocate the incidental costs, such as freight and insurance, to individual items so that a unit cost can be computed. In addition, the allocation of storage costs and costs related to operating a purchasing and a receiving department requires an arbitrary allocation method and does not produce enough benefits to justify the additional cost of making the allocation. Many inventory costs are thus expensed in the period incurred rather than added to the cost of inventory. As a result, only the invoice price is often used in computing a unit cost of goods purchased.

ASSIGNMENT OF COST TO ENDING INVENTORY AND COST OF GOODS SOLD

In Chapter 5, it was assumed that the unit cost of the beginning merchandise inventory and the unit cost of additional units acquired during the period were the same. As is more often the case, however, units purchased at different dates have different unit costs. When this happens, the accountant is confronted with a problem of selecting the unit cost to be matched against sales. To adhere to the matching principle, the allocation of total inventory cost between merchandise inventory and cost of goods sold is based on some cost flow assumption. This is true whether a periodic or perpetual inventory system is being used. Four methods are commonly used to assign cost: (1) specific identification, (2) first-in, first-out (FIFO), (3) last-in, first-out (LIFO), and (4) average cost. The terminology for the average cost method will vary with the inventory system in use. The method is called the *weighted average* method when using a periodic system and is called the *moving average* method when using a perpetual system. All four methods are considered acceptable for accounting purposes, but when prices are changing each will produce different ending inventory and cost of goods sold amounts. FIFO, LIFO, and average cost are the most commonly used methods, as shown by three surveys of 600 companies reported in Figure 9-1.

The cost flow assumption does not have to conform to the actual physical movement of goods. A firm may rotate its stock so that the oldest units are sold first. However, in determining the cost of units sold, the cost of the most recent purchases may be assigned to cost of goods sold.

To illustrate the effects of the four inventory costing methods on the allocation of the total cost of goods available for sale ($412) to ending inventory and cost of goods sold, the following inventory record of a single item will be assumed for the fiscal period:

Date	Number of Units	Unit Cost	Total Cost
Jan. 1 Beginning merchandise inventory	10	$10	$100.00
Purchases made during the current period:			
April 15 Purchase	12	11	$132.00
July 7 Purchase	15	12	180.00
Total purchases	27		312.00
Goods available for sale	37		$412.00
Sales made during the current period:			
April 20 Sales	8	?	
Aug. 12 Sales	10	?	
Total cost of sales	18		?
Dec. 31 Ending merchandise inventory	19		?

If a perpetual inventory system were in operation, the units purchased, sold, and on hand would be available from the inventory card. In a periodic inventory system, the 19 units on hand at December 31 would have been determined by taking a physical inventory.

Figure 9-1
Inventory Cost
Methods Used by
600 Companies

Costing Method	1964		1971		1979	
	No.	%	No.	%	No.	%
FIFO	199	31	333	40	390	37
LIFO	190	29	144	18	374	35
Average Cost	163	25	220	27	241	23
Other	96	15	125	15	56	5
Totals	648	100	822	100	1,061	100

(The total exceeds 600 companies because a company may adopt a different method for different types of inventory held.)
Source: Accounting Trends and Techniques, 1980, 1975, and 1965 editions (New York: AICPA, 1980, 1975, 1965).

PERIODIC INVENTORY SYSTEM

With a periodic inventory system, the number of units on hand at the end of the period must be counted and priced before the cost of goods available for sale of $412 can be allocated between the ending inventory and cost of goods sold. That portion of the total inventory cost assigned to the ending inventory depends on the cost flow assumption the firm adopts. Once the cost of the ending inventory is determined, the cost of goods sold is computed by deducting the ending inventory cost from the cost of goods available for sale. The determination of the cost to be matched against revenues is considered to be the most important objective of inventory measurement.

Specific Identification Method

The **specific identification** method requires that each unit sold and each unit on hand be identified with a specific purchase invoice. To do this, the firm must use some form of identification such as serial numbers. For illustration, assume that the 19 units in the ending inventory can be separately identified as 10 units from the July 7 purchase and 9 units from the beginning inventory. Costs are assigned as follows:

Cost of goods available for sale—37 units			$412.00

Less: Cost of 19 units in the ending merchandise inventory

Date	Units	Unit Cost	Total Cost
1/1	9	$10	$ 90.00
7/7	10	12	120.00

Cost of ending merchandise inventory—19 units	210.00
Cost of goods sold—18 units	$202.00

As can be seen, the cost of goods sold is a residual amount, but the $202 figure can be verified as follows:

Cost of goods sold—18 units	
1 unit from the beginning inventory at $10 per unit	$ 10.00
12 units from the April 15 purchase at $11 per unit	132.00
5 units from the July 7 purchase at $12 per unit	60.00
Total cost of goods sold	$202.00

Using the amounts computed for the specific identification method, the cost allocation procedure is diagrammed below:

*Allocation of the cost of goods available for sale to cost of ending inventory and cost of goods sold will vary depending on the cost flow method used.

Under a periodic inventory system, the ending inventory of $210 is reported as a current asset in the balance sheet and as a deduction from cost of goods available for sale in the income statement. As shown in Chapter 5, these amounts may be entered in the ledger accounts as part of the closing process. Recall that in one closing entry, merchandise inventory is credited for $100 to remove the beginning inventory balance from the account and transfer it to the Income Summary account. In a second closing entry, merchandise inventory is debited for $210 to record the ending inventory. These procedures are the same for the other three costing methods that follow, but the amounts will vary with the costing method used.

First-in, First-out (FIFO) Method

The **FIFO** method of determining the cost of goods sold is based on the assumption that the first units acquired are the first units sold. Therefore, the cost of the units on hand is that of the most recent purchases. Once again, this is a cost flow assumption and need not represent the actual physical movement of goods. It should be emphasized that the name of the inventory method, in this case FIFO and in the next section LIFO, refers to the flow of cost and the determination of cost of goods sold and not the ending inventory. That is, under FIFO, the cost of goods sold is made up of the *first units* purchased, while the ending inventory is made up of the *last units* purchased.

In the periodic inventory system, the ending inventory is generally computed first and is subtracted from the cost of goods available for sale to compute the cost of goods sold as follows:

Cost of goods available for sale—37 units $412.00
Less: Cost of 19 units in ending inventory

Date	Units	Unit Cost	Total Cost
7/7	15	$12	$180.00
4/15	4	11	44.00

Cost of ending merchandise inventory—19 units   224.00
Cost of goods sold—18 units $188.00

Note that the 19 units in the ending inventory are associated with the last two purchases. In a periodic inventory system, the cost of goods sold is a residual amount, but in this simplified example it can be verified as follows:

Cost of goods sold—18 units
10 units from the beginning inventory at $10 per unit $100.00
8 units from the April 15 purchase at $11 per unit   88.00
   Total cost of goods sold $188.00

The cost of the 18 units sold in this period consists of the beginning inventory and a portion of the cost of the first purchase made on April 15. The other four units from the April 15 purchase were assumed to be on hand.

Last-in, First-out (LIFO) Method

Under the **LIFO** method, the *last units* purchased are assumed to be the first units sold. Consequently, the costs of the most recent purchases are matched with sales revenues in the income statement. The cost of the ending inventory consists of the cost of the *earliest* acquisitions. The cost allocation is:

Cost of goods available for sale—37 units $412.00
Less: Cost of 19 units in the ending inventory

Date	Units	Unit Cost	Total Cost
1/1	10	$10	$100.00
4/15	9	11	99.00

Cost of ending merchandise inventory—19 units   199.00
Cost of goods sold—18 units $213.00

The cost of goods sold can be verified as follows:

Cost of goods sold—18 units
15 units from the July 7 purchase at $12 per unit $180.00
3 units from the April 15 purchase at $11 per unit   33.00
   Total cost of goods sold $213.00

Notice that when the LIFO method is used with a periodic inventory system, no attempt is made to compare the dates of sales with those of purchases. Units sold during the period are identified with the most recent purchases. In other words, it is possible to expense the cost of units sold even though they were not on hand at the time of sale. For example, if a purchase had been made after August 12, the date of the last sale, those units would be considered sold first in applying the LIFO method.

Weighted Average Method

Under the **weighted average** method, an **average cost** per unit is computed by dividing the total cost of goods available for sale, including the cost of the beginning inventory and all purchases, by the total number of units available for sale. This weighted average is then multiplied by the number of units on hand to determine the cost of the ending inventory as follows:

$$\frac{\text{Cost of goods available for sale}}{\text{Number of units available for sale}} = \frac{\$412.00}{37 \text{ units}} = \$11.14 \text{ per unit}$$

Ending inventory $-$ 19 units $\times$ \$11.14 per unit = \$211.66

The cost of goods sold is:

Cost of goods available for sale—37 units	\$412.00
Less: Cost of ending merchandise inventory—19 units	211.66
Cost of goods sold—18 units	\$200.34

The cost assigned to cost of goods sold is confirmed as follows:

18 units $\times$ \$11.14 per unit = \$200.52
(Difference is due to rounding the unit cost.)

The use of this method results in all units sold and on hand being priced at the average of \$11.14 per unit.

COMPARISON OF COSTING METHODS

In the preceding sections, the procedural aspects of each costing method were illustrated. Let us now examine the justifications, features, and disadvantages of each method. In doing so, it is helpful to compare the effects of the four methods on the firm's financial statements. The results obtained in applying the four methods in the previous examples are summarized in Figure 9-2. It is assumed that the 18 units were sold for \$360, operating expenses were \$120, and the average income tax rate was 30%. The sales and operating expenses are the same in all cases because the inventory method used does

Figure 9-2
Comparison of Four
Costing Methods

Periodic Inventory System				
	Specific Identifi- cation	FIFO	LIFO	Weighted Average
Sales—18 units	$360	$360	$360	$360
Beginning inventory	$100	$100	$100	$100
Add: Purchases	312	312	312	312
Goods available for sale	412	412	412	412
Less: Ending inventory	210	224	199	212
Cost of goods sold	202	188	213	200
Gross profit on sales	158	172	147	160
Less: Operating expenses	120	120	120	120
Net income before taxes	38	52	27	40
Less: Income taxes— 30%*	11	16	8	12
Net income	$ 27	$ 36	$ 19	$ 28
Ending inventory also reported in the balance sheet	$210	$224	$199	$212

*Income taxes are rounded to the nearest dollar.

not affect these income statement items. The beginning inventory in each case was assumed to be 10 units costing $100. In the next period, the beginning inventory value will vary depending on the costing method selected and will be equal to the ending inventory computed in the current period.

Note that the computations in Figure 9-2 are based on the assumption that the unit cost increased steadily from $10 to $12 during the period. If the unit cost had not changed during the period, cost of goods sold, net income, and ending inventory values would be the same for all four methods. When costs change during a period, the costing method selected can have a significant effect on the firm's reported assets and net income figures. Even in our simple example of increasing prices and only one inventory item held for sale, FIFO net income was almost twice as much as LIFO net income. The absolute difference between the methods would be even greater if the volume of purchases and sales and the variety of individual items held for sale were increased. However, keep in mind that all four methods are based on the cost concept. Although cost of goods sold and net income may vary between accounting periods, the total cost of goods sold and total net income reported over the life of the firm will be the same for all four methods since only the actual cost incurred for inventory can be expensed.

SPECIFIC IDENTIFICATION

Under the specific identification method, when a sale is made, the item sold is identified and the cost of that item is matched against revenues. Thus, the method is based on the actual physical flow of goods. For most firms, this method is not practical and is too costly to apply. Its use is limited primarily to businesses that sell easily identified items with a high unit cost (automobile dealerships and jewelry stores, for example). Another disadvantage of the method is that if the inventory units are identical and have different costs, it is possible for management to manipulate income by choosing to sell a unit with a low or high cost.

FIRST-IN, FIRST-OUT

The FIFO method is widely used because it is easy to apply. When stock is rotated so that the oldest units are sold first, the method's cost flow assumption will approximate the actual physical flow of goods. The method does not permit manipulation of income, since management is not free to pick the cost of a certain item to be matched with revenue, but must expense the oldest unit cost available for sale. As can be seen in Figure 9-2, during periods of consistently rising unit cost, this method results in reporting a lower cost of goods sold and higher net income than the LIFO and weighted average methods. In the balance sheet, the ending inventory will reflect the higher cost of the most recent purchases, which is a more realistic measure of the current value of the inventory than is provided by the other methods. On the other hand, during a period of declining unit cost, FIFO will produce the highest cost of goods sold, the lowest net income, and the lowest ending inventory values.

Many accountants agree that using FIFO during periods of consistently rising prices results in an overstatement in real net income. To illustrate this point, consider the data used in our previous illustration.

January 1	Beginning inventory	10 units @ $10
April 15	Purchases	12 units @ $11
April 20	Sales	8 units @ $20
July 7	Purchases	15 units @ $12
August 12	Sales	10 units @ $20

On April 20, the firm sold 8 units for $20 per unit. Under FIFO, the company charged $10 per unit to cost of goods sold, which resulted in a gross profit of $10 per unit. However, these units were replaced on July 7 with units costing $12. Therefore, $2 of the gross profit was used to replace the units sold and only $8 represents the real gross profit to the firm. Inclusion of the $2 in gross profit is considered misleading because it cannot be distributed to the owners or reinvested in other aspects of the business without reducing the firm's ability to replace units sold. For this reason, it is sometimes called ''phantom profit'' or ''illusory profit.'' The same line of reasoning applies to the units sold on August 12, which, if prices continue to rise, must be replaced with higher cost units.

LAST-IN, FIRST-OUT

The basic assumption of the LIFO method is that the firm must maintain a certain level of inventory to operate. When inventory is sold, it must be replaced at its current replacement cost. Income is not considered earned unless the sales price exceeds the cost to replace the units sold. It is frequently argued that LIFO provides a better measure of net income by matching the more recent costs with current revenues. Since prices have generally moved upward, the effect of this method is to produce a higher cost of goods sold and a lower net income than the other methods (see Figure 9-2). However, balance sheet values soon become outdated because the oldest unit costs remain in the inventory. This creates some problems in evaluating the working capital position of a firm. In addition, if there is a reduction in the inventory below its normal quantity, there is a matching of old costs with current revenues, which distorts income in the year of the inventory liquidation. Another disadvantage of LIFO is that the possibility exists for management to manipulate net income by buying, or not buying, goods at the end of the year.

Note in Figure 9-2 that the income tax expense under LIFO is $8, the lowest of the four methods. This reduction in tax liability is one of the major reasons this method is adopted. As can be seen from the survey on page 368, a number of companies changed their inventory costing method to LIFO during the 1970s. One reason for the change is the high inflation rates of those years. Although all four methods are acceptable for computing taxable income, using LIFO during periods of rising prices produces a tax benefit. LIFO matches the most recently acquired, more expensive units against the revenues recorded during the period, resulting in reduced taxable income and lower income taxes. The reduced cash outflow for taxes makes more cash available for use in the firm's operations. However, as noted earlier, only the actual cost incurred is deductible as an expense. Thus, if the beginning inventory is eventually sold or prices decline, the total cost of goods sold will be lower and taxable income will be greater under LIFO. Of course, over the life of the firm these items will be the same for all four methods. Why then, have we seen the switch to LIFO in recent years? The reason is that a tax reduction in the current period is preferred to one in a later period.

Despite the tax benefit, some firms have been reluctant to switch to LIFO because current tax laws require that if LIFO is used for tax purposes, it must also be used for financial reporting purposes. As a result, the firms will report lower earnings which may have an unfavorable effect on investors.

WEIGHTED AVERAGE

The average cost method is usually justified because the method is simple to apply and is not subject to income manipulation as are some of the other methods. In applying this method, the average unit cost is affected by the units and cost in the beginning inventory and all purchases made during the year. As a result, the cost of goods sold, net income, and ending inventory amounts reported under the average cost method will be between the extremes produced by FIFO and LIFO when prices are rising or falling. Thus, the use of the average cost method tends to smooth out net income and inventory values with neither the cost of goods sold nor the ending inventory reported at current values. Although the average method is not used as frequently as FIFO and LIFO, it is sometimes used when the inventory units involved are homogeneous in nature and when it is difficult to establish a flow assumption. Examples are grain in a grain elevator or gasoline in a storage tank.

WHICH METHOD TO SELECT?

The selection of the cost method to use for a particular type of inventory depends on many factors such as the effect that each method will have upon the firm's financial statements, income tax considerations, information needs of management and statement users, and clerical cost of applying a costing method. In practice, more than one of the methods may be considered appropriate in accounting for the same type of inventory. That is, generally accepted accounting standards do not prescribe the use of a specific costing method as being ''best'' for a particular set of inventory conditions. It is up to management and the firm's accountant to decide which method provides the most useful information to its statement users.

CONSISTENCY IN USING A COSTING METHOD

Clearly, the inventory costing method selected can have a significant impact on the firm's reported net income and asset figures. For this reason, *the method* used to assign cost to inventory and cost of goods sold *should be disclosed in the financial statements*.

Once a costing method has been selected, management cannot indiscriminately switch to another. When alternative accounting methods or procedures are considered acceptable in a given situation, the principle of **consistency** requires that a firm apply the same method from one accounting period to the next. If a company were permitted to switch from one accounting method to another, the accounting data produced in different accounting periods would not be comparable.

Consistency does not completely rule out switching to an alternative acceptable method if the new method results in improved financial reporting. For tax purposes, a change in inventory costing methods must, however, first be approved by the Internal Revenue Service. When a change is approved and made, the nature of the change, the effect of the change on the financial statements, and the reasons the newly adopted method is preferred must be fully disclosed in notes accompanying the financial statements. Such disclosure is illustrated in Figure 9-3 for Merck & Co., Inc. Without such disclosure, the statement reader may assume that no material changes in accounting methods were made during the period.

THE LOWER OF COST OR MARKET RULE

Cost is the primary basis for recording and reporting most assets. The four inventory costing methods we have been discussing are alternatives for arriving at the cost of inventory when the unit cost fluctuates during the period. When there has been a decrease in the value of inventory or in the cost to replace the units in inventory, however, it is considered appropriate in certain circumstances to report inventory at an amount below its cost. The decline in value could result from obsolescence, damage, deterioration, or a decline in the unit cost caused by supply and demand factors. At the end of the period, the cost of the inventory is compared with the cost to replace it. If the cost of replacing the inventory is less than its historical cost, the inventory is written down to the lower replacement cost and a loss is reported. This valuation approach is referred to as the **lower of cost or market (LCM)** rule. *Market,* as the term is used here, is *the cost to replace* the inventory in the quantities typically purchased through the usual source of supply.

Using a valuation figure that is lower than cost is justified by the principle of **conservatism.** Under this principle, probable losses are recorded in the accounts in the period in which the loss occurs. Thus, application of the LCM rule results in a loss in inventory value being recorded (matched against revenue) in the period in which the decline in value occurs rather than in a

Report of Independent Public Accountants

ARTHUR ANDERSEN & CO.
1345 Avenue of the Americas
New York, New York

January 26, 1982

To the Board of Directors
of Merck & Co., Inc.:

We have examined the consolidated balance sheets of Merck & Co., Inc. (a New Jersey corporation) and Subsidiaries as of December 31, 1981 and 1980, and the related statements of consolidated income, retained earnings, and changes in financial position for each of the three years in the period ended December 31, 1981. Our examinations were made in accordance with generally accepted auditing standards and, accordingly, included such tests of the accounting records and such other auditing procedures as we considered necessary in the circumstances.

As more fully explained in Note 2 to the accompanying financial statements, the company changed from the first-in, first-out (FIFO) method to the last-in, first-out (LIFO) method of determining the cost of substantially all its domestic inventories as of January 1, 1980.

In our opinion, the financial statements referred to above present fairly the financial position of Merck & Co., Inc. and Subsidiaries as of December 31, 1981 and 1980 and the results of their operations and the changes in their financial position for each of the three years in the period ended December 31, 1981, in conformity with generally accepted accounting principles, which, except for the change (with which we concur) in the method of accounting for inventories referred to in the preceding paragraph, have been applied on a consistent basis.

Arthur Andersen & Co.

Footnote accompanying financial statements.

2. Inventories

Inventories at December 31 consisted of:

	($ in Millions)	
	1981	1980
Finished goods	$310.7	$268.4
Raw materials and work in process	369.5	347.5
Supplies	43.7	41.8
Total (approximates current cost)	723.9	657.7
Less reduction to LIFO cost	76.3	35.7
	$647.6	$622.0

As of January 1, 1980, the Company adopted LIFO for substantially all domestic inventories in order to provide an appropriate matching of current costs with revenues under inflationary conditions. Inventories valued at LIFO comprised approximately 44% and 46% of inventories in 1981 and 1980, respectively. The change to LIFO had the effect of reducing 1981 net income by $21,108,000 ($.28 per share) and 1980 net income by $18,588,000 ($.25 per share), with a positive increase to cash flow of $19,500,000 in 1981 and $17,100,000 in 1980 as a result of decreased U.S. taxes.

Figure 9-3
Illustration of Reporting Change in Inventory Costing Methods

subsequent period when the inventory is sold. Increases in the cost to replace inventory are not recorded.

To illustrate the application of the LCM rule, assume that 10 units of an item costing $180 per unit were priced to sell for $300 per unit and 5 units were sold during the period. The expected gross profit is $120 per unit or 40% ($120 ÷ $300) of sales price. At the end of the period, the cost of replacing the units declined to $135, a 25% decrease in cost. Assume also that the decline in cost resulted in the firm reducing the sales price per unit to $225 on the remaining inventory. Gross profit on sales based on cost and LCM is computed below in the year of the price decline.

| | Ending inventory valued at | | Differ- |
	Cost	LCM	ence
Sales (5 units × $300)	$1,500	$1,500	–0–
Cost of goods available for sale	$1,800	$1,800	–0–
Less: Ending inventory			
5 units × $180*	900		
5 units × $135		675	– $225
Cost of goods sold	900	1,125	+ $225
Gross profit on sales	$ 600	$ 375	– $225

*When the unit cost fluctuates, cost would be determined by using any of the four cost flow assumptions:

Applying the LCM rule in this example results in the ending inventory being $225 [5 units × ($180 − $135)] less than the historical cost ending inventory figure. The reduction in the ending inventory value becomes a part of the cost of goods sold, reducing the gross profit by $225. In the next period, when the goods are sold, gross profit on sales based on cost and LCM is $225 and $450 respectively:

	Cost	LCM	Difference
Sales (5 units × $225)	$1,125	$1,125	–0–
Less: Beginning inventory	900	675	– $225
Gross profit on units sold	$225	$450	+ $225

As shown in the cost column, if the write-down is not made in the preceding period, gross profit is expected to be $225 in the year the units are sold. When the write-down of the inventory to LCM in the preceding period is made, the gross profit is expected to be $450. Thus, applying the LCM rule results in the $225 decline in the replacement cost being recognized in the period in which it occurs rather than in the period in which the goods are sold.

In the above example, it was assumed that a 25% decrease in the replacement cost resulted in the sales price being decreased 25% [($300 − $225) ÷ $300]. In practice, however, the cost of an item and its selling price do not always change proportionately. In some cases, the sales price may not be reduced, and as a result the asset has not lost its revenue-producing power. If so, then a write-down to replacement cost is not justified. In still other cases, the anticipated sales price may be decreased, but not in the same proportion as the decrease in replacement cost. In these cases, the write-down of the inventory to replacement cost may result in a misstatement in the asset and the reported income amounts. Because of this potential for misstatement, several modifications to the LCM rule as illustrated above are used in practice to determine the market value to be compared to historical cost. These modifications and other issues related to applying the LCM rule are discussed in Intermediate Accounting.

NET REALIZABLE VALUE

The inventory of a retail or wholesale business often contains units that have been used or are obsolete, shopworn, or damaged. Such inventory items are generally reported at **net realizable value**—the anticipated sales price in the normal course of the business less the estimated cost of selling and disposal. To illustrate, assume a company is holding a tape deck that cost $380 and normally sells for $460. Because the unit was used as a demonstrator, however, it is estimated that it could be sold for $345 after the unit is reconditioned for a cost of $50. A sales commission on the unit is expected to be $20. The value of the unit for inventory purposes is computed as follows:

Estimated sales value	$345
Estimated selling and disposal cost	70
Estimated net realizable value	$275

Since the estimated net realizable value is below the historical cost of $380, the unit should be carried in the ending inventory at $275. This will result in a loss of $105 ($380 − $275) being reported in the period in which it occurs rather than in the period in which the unit is sold. Under a periodic inventory system, the loss becomes a part of the cost of goods sold. If a perpetual inventory system is used, the inventory card is adjusted to reflect the lower value, and an entry is made to reduce the Merchandise Inventory account and recognize a loss.

If the net realizable value is greater than historical cost, the inventory is not written up to reflect the higher value. Again, the historical cost of the unit is the upper value to be used in valuation. In addition, if inventory is written down to net realizable value or replacement cost, the new value substitutes for the original cost figure for computations in future periods.

PERPETUAL INVENTORY SYSTEMS

Recall that in Chapter 5 two inventory systems—periodic and perpetual—were discussed and illustrated. Earlier in this chapter, the specific identification, FIFO, LIFO, and weighted average cost flow assumptions were discussed and illustrated assuming that the firm had adopted a periodic inventory system. One or more of these same four methods may also be adopted if the firm uses a perpetual inventory system. Because under the perpetual system the cost of goods sold is determined at the time of sale rather than at the end of the period, the two systems will in some cases produce different net income and ending inventory figures. In this part of the chapter, application of the four cost flow methods with a perpetual inventory system is illustrated. As we have noted before, with the availability of more versatile and less costly computers, the trend is for more companies to adopt the perpetual inventory system in order to achieve better inventory control.

PERPETUAL INVENTORY SYSTEM ILLUSTRATED

In a perpetual inventory system, an inventory card is maintained for each item in stock and an inventory control account is kept in the general ledger. To provide a continuous and current record of inventory transactions, the appropriate inventory card and the Merchandise Inventory account are adjusted as purchases and sales transactions occur. Inventory purchases are recorded at cost in the Merchandise Inventory account and in the individual inventory cards. We saw in Chapter 5 that the following two entries are made at the time of sale:

(1)	Accounts Receivable (or Cash)	20	
	Sales		20
	Sold one unit of inventory for $20.		
(2)	Cost of Goods Sold	10	
	Merchandise Inventory		10
	Transferred cost of unit sold.		

The dollar amount of the first entry is based on the sales price. If the per-unit cost varies, the dollar amount recorded in the second entry will depend on the cost flow method used.

A perpetual inventory card using the same data presented earlier for the periodic inventory system is shown in Figure 9-4 for three cost flow assumptions: FIFO, LIFO, and moving average. Note that the perpetual inventory record shows the unit and dollar amounts on a continuous basis for goods on hand, goods purchased, and goods sold. The computations for the specific identification method would be the same as those described earlier under a periodic inventory system and will not be repeated here. The only difference is that an entry is made at the time of sale to record the transfer of cost from the Inventory account to the Cost of Goods Sold account.

Justifications and disadvantages of using each method are the same as those discussed earlier for the periodic inventory system and will not be repeated here. Furthermore, the relative dollar amounts of cost of goods sold, net income, and ending inventory produced by the four methods will also be the same. That is, in periods of rising prices, LIFO will produce a higher cost of goods sold, a lower net income, and a lower ending inventory than the FIFO or average cost methods.

First-in, First-out Method

Under the FIFO method (Part A of Figure 9-4), the cost of units removed from inventory is assumed to be from the *first units available for sale* at the time of each sale. The cost of the units on hand is composed of the most recent purchases. Thus in Figure 9-4, the cost of the 8 units sold ($80) on April 20 is computed from the unit cost of the earliest units available, which are those in the beginning inventory. The 14 remaining unsold units are assumed to be from the beginning inventory (2 units) and from the April 15 purchase (12 units). The identification of units from separate purchases results in what are frequently called "inventory cost layers." For the next sale, the cost of 2 units from the beginning inventory ($20) and 8 units from the first purchase ($88) are transferred to cost of goods sold. This leaves an ending inventory of 19 units, valued at $224. The Cost of Goods Sold account will show a balance of $188 ($80 + $108) at the end of the period.

Last-in, First-out Method

When the LIFO method (Part B of Figure 9-4) is used in conjunction with a perpetual inventory system, the cost of goods sold is determined at the point of each sale based on the assumption that the *last units acquired* are sold first. Thus the cost of the units sold on April 20 consists of the cost of the most recent units purchased on April 15. The inventory balance of 14 units consists of two inventory cost layers—10 units from the beginning inventory and

4 from the April 15 purchase. Similarly, the units sold on August 12 are identified with the most recent units acquired on July 7. The cost of goods

Figure 9-4
Inventory Card Perpetual Inventory System

Item:	Pencil Sharpener								Minimum Stock:	10	
Code:	1800			Location:	Store Display				Maximum Stock:	30	

		Purchases			Cost of Goods Sold			Balance			
Date	Explanation	Units	Unit Cost	Total Cost	Units	Unit Cost	Total Cost	Units	Unit Cost	Total Cost	
A. FIFO Method											
1/1	Beginning balance							10	10.00	100.00	
4/15	Purchases	12	11.00	132.00				10	10.00	100.00	
								12	11.00	132.00	
4/20	Sales				8	10.00	80.00	2	10.00	20.00	
								12	11.00	132.00	
7/7	Purchases	15	12.00	180.00				2	10.00	20.00	
								12	11.00	132.00	
								15	12.00	180.00	
8/12	Sales				2	10.00	20.00	4	11.00	44.00	
					8	11.00	88.00	15	12.00	180.00	
B. LIFO Method											
1/1	Beginning balance							10	10.00	100.00	
4/15	Purchases	12	11.00	132.00				10	10.00	100.00	
								12	11.00	132.00	
4/20	Sales				8	11.00	88.00	10	10.00	100.00	
								4	11.00	44.00	
7/7	Purchases	15	12.00	180.00				10	10.00	100.00	
								4	11.00	44.00	
								15	12.00	180.00	
8/12	Sales				10	12.00	120.00	10	10.00	100.00	
								4	11.00	44.00	
								5	12.00	60.00	
C. Moving Average Method											
1/1	Beginning balance							10	10.00	100.00	
4/15	Purchases	12	11.00	132.00				22	10.55	232.00	
4/20	Sales				8	10.55	84.40	14	10.55	147.60	
7/7	Purchases	15	12.00	180.00				29	11.30	327.60	
8/12	Sales				10	11.30	113.00	19	11.30	214.60	

Computations
4/15 ($100.00 + $132.00)/(10 units + 12 units) = $10.55 per unit
7/7 ($147.60 + $180.00)/(14 units + 15 units) = $11.30 per unit

sold for the period is $208 ($88 + $120) and the ending inventory is $204 ($100 + $44 + $60.)

Moving Average Method

Under the **moving average** method (Part C of Figure 9-4), a new average cost per unit is computed after each purchase. The average is called a moving average because a new weighted average cost is computed after each purchase rather than simply computing a weighted average at year-end. The moving average cost, computed after a purchase, is used to compute the cost of goods sold and inventory on hand until additional units are acquired at a different unit price. The moving average cost is computed as follows:

$$\frac{\text{Cost of goods available for sale currently}}{\text{Total number of units available for sale currently}} = \text{moving average cost}$$

In our illustration the average cost per unit after the April 15 purchase is:

$$(\$100 + \$132)/(10 \text{ units} + 12 \text{ units}) = \$10.55 \text{ per unit}$$

Since there were no additional purchases made before the sale of 8 units on April 20, the cost of these units sold is $84.40 (8 units × $10.55 per unit). The 14 units on hand are valued at $147.60 ($232.00 − $84.40). As a result of rounding, the ending inventory is approximately equal to the 14 units times the $10.55 per unit. This average cost of $10.55 would be used to cost additional units sold until another purchase is made, at which time a new moving average cost is computed, as shown in Part C of Figure 9-4.

COMPARISON OF INVENTORY SYSTEMS

Application of the four alternative cost flow assumptions have now been illustrated using the same data for both the periodic and perpetual inventory systems. For comparison, the results obtained for both methods are presented in Figure 9-5 assuming that the 18 units were sold for $360, operating expenses were $120, and the average income tax rate was 30%. A comparison of the specific identification and the FIFO methods in Figure 9-5 reveals that each method assigns the same amount of cost to the ending inventory and to cost of goods sold under both the perpetual and the periodic inventory systems. Using FIFO, the same amounts are obtained because in computing the cost of goods sold it is always the oldest units available for sale that are assumed to be the units sold. (Another way to say this is that the ending inventory cost under both systems is made up of the most recent purchases.) The values obtained with the specific identification method are the same because the units identified as sold

Figure 9-5
Comparison of Inventory Systems and Four Costing Methods

Perpetual Inventory System

	Specification Identification	FIFO	LIFO	Moving Average
Sales—18 units	$360	$360	$360	$360
Less: Cost of goods sold	202	188	208	197
Gross profit on sales	158	172	152	163
Less: Operating expenses	120	120	120	120
Net income before taxes	38	52	32	43
Less: Income taxes—30%*	11	16	10	13
Net income	$ 27	$ 36	$ 22	$ 30
Ending inventory	$210	$224	$204	$215

Periodic Inventory System
(From Figure 9-2)

	Specific Identification		FIFO		LIFO		Weighted Average
Sales—18 Units		$360		$360		$360	$360
Beginning inventory	100		100		100		100
Add: Purchases	312		312		312		312
Goods Available for sale	412		412		412		412
Less: Ending inventory	210		224		199		212
Cost of goods sold		202		188		213	200
Gross profit on sales		158		172		147	160
Less: Operating expenses		120		120		120	120
Net income before taxes		38		52		27	40
Less: Income taxes—30%*		11		16		8	12
Net income		$ 27		$ 36		$ 19	$ 28
Ending inventory		$210		$224		$199	$212

*Income taxes are rounded to the nearest dollar.

were the same under both inventory systems.

When the LIFO method is used, both the ending inventory and cost of goods sold dollar amounts may vary between the perpetual and periodic systems. The periodic system with LIFO produced a cost of goods sold of $213 and an ending inventory of $199. The amounts for a perpetual inventory system were $208 and $204, respectively. The two methods produce different results because of the timing of the computation of cost of goods sold. Under the periodic system, cost of goods sold is computed at the end of the period and the dates of sale are ignored. With the perpetual system, cost of goods sold is computed at the time of each sale. The cost of goods sold and ending inventory computations for both inventory systems are:

Periodic Inventory System (See page 370)				Perpetual Inventory System (See Figure 9-4)			
			Cost of Goods Sold				
Date Acquired	**Units**	**Unit Cost**	**Total**	**Date Acquired**	**Units**	**Unit Cost**	**Total**
4/15	3	$11	$ 33	4/15	8	$11	88
7/7	15	12	180	7/7	10	12	120
Cost of goods sold			$213	Cost of goods sold			$208
			Ending Inventory				
1/1	10	$10	$100	1/1	10	$10	$100
4/15	9	11	99	4/15	4	11	44
—	—	—	—	7/7	5	12	60
Ending inventory			$199	Ending inventory			$204
Total cost of goods available for sale			$412				$412

When the perpetual system is used and prices are rising, units with a lower cost (the more recent purchases at the time of sale) are charged to cost of goods sold, which in this example results in some units of the last purchase, on July 7, being considered still on hand. Under a periodic system, these more expensive units are included in the cost of goods sold computation; the lower cost units in the beginning inventory and first purchase are considered to still be on hand in the ending inventory.

Although the computation of average cost is essentially the same under both systems, the two systems produce different results when prices change during the reporting period. The results differ because the cost transferred to cost of goods sold each time a sale is made is based on a moving average that changes whenever new goods are purchased under the perpetual system. Under the periodic system, one weighted average cost for the entire period is used to cost all goods sold during the period. When prices increase during a period, a moving average will yield a lower cost of goods sold and a higher ending inventory than a periodic weighted average. This happens because the periodic weighted average is computed at the end of the period and is affected by the higher unit cost of purchases made late in the period.

In summary, when prices are changing, the periodic and perpetual systems will produce different net income figures under the LIFO and average costing methods. The extent of the variation is determined primarily by the rate of change in prices during the period and the frequency with which the inventory is purchased and sold.

INVENTORY ERRORS

Cost of goods sold is the largest expense for many firms. The inventory balance of unsold goods is often the largest current asset reported in the balance sheet. The determination of correct dollar amounts to be reported for these two financial statement items is therefore very important. Because of the large volume of inventory transactions and the necessity of making numerous computations, errors can occur at various stages in accounting for inventory.

If a perpetual inventory system is maintained, a physical inventory is taken at the end of the period to verify the balances shown in the individual inventory cards. Even if the inventory records and the physical count are in agreement, there may still be errors in the accounts. A common error is the failure to record goods in transit owned by the firm at the end of the period. As discussed earlier, such errors have no effect on net income, but inventory and accounts payable are both understated by the same amount. Another common error is the failure to observe a proper cut-off for recording sales and the related cost of goods sold. For example, a sale made after the year-end may have been recorded before year-end. If this error occurs, sales, cost of goods sold, gross profit, and net income are overstated. In the balance sheet, accounts receivable are overstated and inventory is understated—resulting in a net overstatement in total assets and owners' equity equal to the amount of the gross profit on the sale.

Under a periodic inventory system, errors may occur in counting and pricing the inventory and in the failure to use the proper cut-off dates for recording purchases and sales. To illustrate the effects of errors in a periodic inventory system, it is helpful to consider the calculation of cost of goods sold. In Figure 9-6, it is assumed that a $10,000 understatement in the ending inventory occurred while taking the physical inventory at the end of 1985. As can be seen when compared with the "correct" column, this error resulted in an overstatement in the cost of goods sold and an understatement in both gross profit and net income. Since the ending inventory is also reported as a current asset, this error will cause current assets, total assets, and owners' equity all to be understated by $10,000. The opposite happens if the ending inventory is overstated rather than understated.

The failure to discover the error in the ending inventory will also cause the

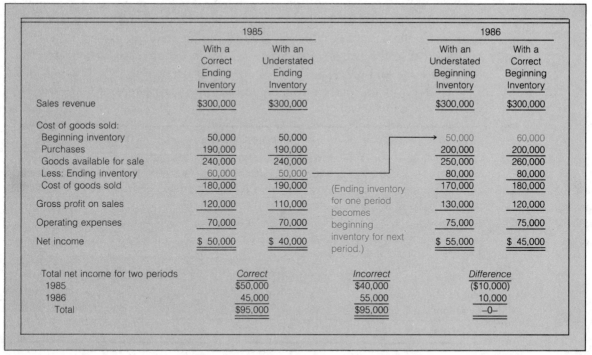

	1985			1986	
	With a Correct Ending Inventory	With an Understated Ending Inventory		With an Understated Beginning Inventory	With a Correct Beginning Inventory
Sales revenue	$300,000	$300,000		$300,000	$300,000
Cost of goods sold:					
Beginning inventory	50,000	50,000		50,000	60,000
Purchases	190,000	190,000		200,000	200,000
Goods available for sale	240,000	240,000		250,000	260,000
Less: Ending inventory	60,000	50,000		80,000	80,000
Cost of goods sold	180,000	190,000	(Ending inventory for one period becomes beginning inventory for next period.)	170,000	180,000
Gross profit on sales	120,000	110,000		130,000	120,000
Operating expenses	70,000	70,000		75,000	75,000
Net income	$ 50,000	$ 40,000		$ 55,000	$ 45,000

Total net income for two periods	Correct	Incorrect	Difference
1985	$50,000	$40,000	($10,000)
1986	45,000	55,000	10,000
Total	$95,000	$95,000	–0–

Figure 9-6
Comparative Income Statements Showing Effects of Inventory Errors in Two Operating Periods (all amounts are assumed)

income statement for the next period to be incorrect, since the ending inventory for one period becomes the beginning inventory for the next period. In the next year, cost of goods sold is understated by $10,000, and both gross profit and net income are overstated by $10,000. Again, the opposite is true if the beginning inventory had been overstated.

In the absence of any other errors, the balance sheet amounts are correct at the end of 1986. This results because inventory errors offset one another over two consecutive periods. That is, the net income in 1985 is understated by $10,000, but the net income in 1986 is overstated by $10,000. Thus, although each year is in error, the total net income for the two periods of $95,000 is correct and the owners' equity accounts at the end of 1986 will also be correct.

If the errors are discovered after 1986 and comparative financial statements are prepared, the appropriate amounts reported in the financial statements should be corrected even though the errors are offsetting. Failure to do so will distort the trend of the firm's earnings. For example, in Figure 9-6 the correct inventory amounts yielded a declining earnings trend, whereas the incorrect amounts show increasing net income amounts. Finally, if the error is discovered before the close of the 1986 year end, a correcting entry should be made to increase the inventory account. The offsetting credit is made to owners' equity because the net income closed to owners' equity was understated by $10,000 at the end of 1985.

The effects of inventory errors on various financial statement items can be summarized as follows:

	Income Statement			Balance Sheet	
	Cost of Goods Sold	Gross Profit	Net Income	Inventory Balance	Owners' Equity
Year 1—Ending inventory is understated	+	−	−	−	−
Year 2—Beginning inventory is understated	−	+	+	0	0
Year 1—Ending inventory is overstated	−	+	+	+	+
Year 2—Beginning inventory is overstated	+	−	−	0	0

+ Overstated   − Understated   0 Correct Balance

ESTIMATING INVENTORIES

When a perpetual inventory accounting system is used, the cost of goods sold and the dollar amount of the inventory on hand is readily determinable throughout the period from the accounting records. However, many businesses such as department stores frequently use a periodic inventory system. As we know, a periodic system requires that a physical inventory be taken to determine the ending inventory balance. Taking a physical inventory is so time-consuming and expensive that it is usually performed only at the end of the fiscal period. However, management and other statement users desire interim financial statements at regular intervals during the accounting period in order to assess the performance of the firm. If a periodic inventory system is used, the preparation of the income statement requires that the inventory on hand be determined for the computation of the cost of goods sold. The *retail inventory method* and the *gross profit method* are two approaches commonly used to *estimate* the dollar amount of unsold goods without taking a physical count.

In addition, the two methods are also useful to test the reasonableness of a physical inventory taken by the firm's employees, to provide some insights into the dollar amount of inventory shortages from such causes as theft and damage, and to compute an estimate of the goods on hand when a physical inventory cannot be taken, such as when the inventory has been destroyed by fire or flood. The retail method is also used by a retail business to convert a physical inventory taken at retail prices to an estimated cost amount.

RETAIL INVENTORY METHOD

To use the **retail inventory** method, the firm must maintain records of the beginning inventory and purchases made during the period at both cost and retail (selling price). The goods available for sale at cost are divided by the goods available for sale at retail to calculate a relationship between cost and selling price called the *ratio of cost to retail* or simply the *cost ratio*. An estimate of the inventory at retail is then determined by subtracting the sales recorded during the period from the goods available for sale at retail. The ending inventory at retail is multiplied by the cost ratio to arrive at an estimate of the ending inventory at cost.

To illustrate, assume that the following information was accumulated in the accounts and supplementary records:

	Cost	Retail
Beginning inventory	$24,500	$ 40,000
Net purchases to date	35,500	60,000
Net sales	—	80,000

The ending inventory at cost is estimated as follows:

	Cost	Retail
Beginning inventory	$24,500	$ 40,000
Net purchases	35,500	60,000
Goods available for sale	$60,000	$100,000

Ratio of cost to retail:

$$\frac{\$60,000}{\$100,000} = 60\%$$

Less: Net sales	80,000
Estimate of ending inventory at retail	$ 20,000
Cost ratio	× 60%
Estimate of ending inventory at cost	$ 12,000

The cost of goods sold can now be determined as $48,000 ($60,000 cost of goods available for sale minus $12,000 ending inventory at cost). The ending inventory, as computed above, is an estimate acceptable for interim statements. The firm should still conduct a physical inventory at least once a year for control purposes and to assure a proper measurement of the cost of goods sold.

The retail inventory method is also a convenient means to convert a physical inventory taken at retail to a cost amount. In other words, in a retail store each item for sale is generally marked to indicate the sales price. Consequently, during a physical inventory the units are listed at current retail prices as they are counted. This procedure eliminates the need to look up purchase invoices to determine the unit cost of each item. The retail dollar value of the ending inventory is converted to cost by applying the cost ratio calculated as shown above. Remember that the cost ratio is applied to the inventory value determined by a physical count. An estimate of the ending inventory at retail is still calculated as a control measure because significant differences between the actual retail value and the estimate may indicate problems in the accounting system or excessive losses from theft or other causes.

The accuracy of the ending inventory determined by the retail inventory method depends on the mix or composition of goods in the ending inventory in relation to the mix of goods used to compute the cost ratio. The method assumes that the ending inventory consists of the same mix of goods at various cost percentages as was contained in the goods available for sale.

In practice, the originally established sales price of many items does not remain constant during the period, but in fact changes frequently during the year as prices are reduced for special sales or are increased as the market value of the item increases. Frequent changes in the original selling price make the calculation of a cost ratio actually more complicated than illustrated here. Modifications needed to adjust the retail inventory method for price changes are a refinement covered in Intermediate Accounting.

GROSS PROFIT METHOD

Some businesses do not maintain a record of the retail price of beginning inventory and purchases. If this information is not available, the retail inventory method cannot be used. However, the goods on hand may be estimated without taking a physical count by applying the **gross profit method.** This method is based on the assumption that the gross profit percentage remains approximately the same from period to period.

To illustrate, assume that the inventory of a business was totally destroyed by fire. A review of the last two years' operations revealed that the gross profit percentage was 40%. On the date of the fire, the ledger had been posted up to date and as part of the company's internal control system was locked in a fireproof safe every night after closing. Selected account balances were:

	Dr. (Cr.) Balance
Sales	($140,000)
Sales returns and allowance	8,000
Purchases	83,100
Inventory—Beginning balance	16,300
Purchases returns and allowances	(2,500)
Freight-in	700

The inventory on hand on the date of the fire can be estimated for insurance purposes by preparing a partial section of the income statement, using the available information:

Sales		$140,000	
Less: Sales returns and allowances		8,000	
Net sales		132,000	100%
Cost of goods sold:			
Beginning inventory		$16,300	
Purchases	$83,100		
Less: Purchases returns & allowances	(2,500)		
Add: Freight-in	700		
Net purchases		81,300	
Goods available for sale		97,600	
Less: Estimated ending inventory		?	
Estimated cost of goods sold ($132,000 × .60)		79,200	60%
Estimated gross profit on sales ($132,000 × .40)		$ 52,800	40%

It can be determined from the records that the company had $97,600 of goods available for sale up to the date of the fire. The cost of goods sold is estimated to be $79,200 by applying the cost percentage of 60% to the net sales. The goods that were available for sale but had not been sold must have been on hand; their cost is the difference between the estimated cost of goods sold ($79,200) and the cost of goods available for sale ($97,600), which is $18,400.

PRESENTATION IN FINANCIAL STATEMENTS

The method used to account for inventory can affect significantly a firm's financial position and results of operations. Because of the importance of inventory, additional information is provided in footnotes to the financial statements. The disclosure commonly contains the composition of the inventory (raw materials, work in process, and finished goods), the cost flow method that is used and whether it is applied to all of the inventory, the method of valuing the inventory (cost or lower of cost or market), and whether the cost flow method was used consistently from one period to another. Figure 9-7 shows examples of the disclosure provided by two companies. Other examples are contained in the Appendix to the text.

GLOSSARY

AVERAGE COST.   An inventory costing method in which an average unit cost is computed by dividing the total cost of goods available for sale by the total number of units available for sale. Moving average and weighted average are variations of the average cost method (p. 371).

Figure 9-7
Illustrations of Disclosure of Inventories in Financial Statements

JOHNSON & JOHNSON
Footnote accompanying financial statements

Inventories
While cost is determined principally by the first-in, first-out (FIFO) method, the majority of domestic inventories are valued using the last-in, first-out (LIFO) method. Inventories are valued at the lower of cost or market.
Note 5. Inventories

(Dollars in Millions)	1981	1980
Raw materials and supplies	$304.1	300.9
Goods in process	204.7	184.9
Finished goods	391.3	363.0
	$900.1	848.8

If all inventories were valued on the FIFO basis, total inventories would have been $1,023.8 million and $954.5 million at January 3, 1982 and December 28, 1980, respectively.

J.C. PENNEY COMPANY, INC.
Footnote accompanying financial statements

Merchandise inventories at year end 1981 were $1,578 million, a slight increase from $1,571 million at year end 1980.
Substantially all inventories are valued at the lower of cost, last-in, first-out (LIFO), or market, determined by the retail method. If the first-in, first-out (FIFO) method of inventory valuation had been used by the Company, inventories at year end would have been approximately $345 million higher for 1981 and 1980 and $233 million higher for 1979.

CONSERVATISM. An accounting concept that specifies that when equally acceptable accounting procedures or estimates are available, an accountant should select the one that produces the lowest asset or net income amount. An example is the lower of cost or market approach to inventory valuation (p. 376).

CONSIGNEE. A firm or individual holding goods on consignment. The consignee does not own the goods held on consignment (p. 366).

CONSIGNMENT. A marketing arrangement whereby physical control of merchandise, but not title, is transferred from one business (the consignor) to another (the consignee) (p. 365).

CONSIGNOR. A firm or individual that ships goods on consignment. Title to the goods is retained by the consignor until the goods are sold by the consignee (p. 366).

CONSISTENCY. An accounting principle that calls for the use of the same acceptable accounting procedure from period to period (p. 376).

FIRST-IN, FIRST-OUT (FIFO). An inventory costing method that assumes the first units purchased were the first units sold. The ending inventory consists of the cost of the most recently purchased units (p. 369).

FOB DESTINATION. Shipping terms in which freight is paid by the seller. Title to goods normally transfers when delivered to the location specified by the buyer (p. 365).

FOB SHIPPING POINT. Shipping terms in which freight is paid by the buyer. Title to goods normally transfers when goods are delivered to the transportion company (p. 365). ·

GROSS PROFIT METHOD. A method used to estimate ending inventory value based on the assumption that the gross profit percentage is approximately the same from period to period (p. 390).

LAST-IN, FIRST-OUT (LIFO). An inventory costing method that assumes the most recent units purchased were the first units sold. Ending inventory consists of the cost of the earliest units purchased (p. 370).

LOWER OF COST OR MARKET. An inventory valuation method by which inventory is valued at lower of original cost or market on the financial statement date (p. 376).

MOVING AVERAGE. An inventory costing method by which an average unit cost is computed after each purchase (p. 383).

NET REALIZABLE VALUE. The anticipated sales price of an item less the estimated cost of selling and disposal (p. 379).

RETAIL INVENTORY METHOD. A method used to estimate the ending inventory value based on the relationship of cost to retail prices (p. 389).

SPECIFIC IDENTIFICATION. An inventory costing method by which the cost of a specific item sold can be separately identified from the cost of other units held in the inventory (p. 368).

WEIGHTED AVERAGE. An inventory costing method by which an average cost per unit is computed by dividing the total cost of the units available for sale by the total number of units available for sale (p. 371).

DISCUSSION QUESTIONS

1. Explain the terms *FOB shipping point* and *FOB destination*. If goods are shipped FOB shipping point at a cost of $600, which party to the transaction must pay the freight bill?
2. There are two parties to a consignment transaction. Which party should include goods being held on consignment in his or her inventory?
3. What costs should be included in the cost of an item of inventory?
4. Why are inventory costing methods needed?

5. Must a company use the inventory costing method that best conforms to the actual physical movement of the goods? Explain.
6. Explain the assumptions behind the FIFO method and the LIFO method.
7. Compare the effects of LIFO and FIFO on net income and ending inventory values during a period of increasing prices.
8. Explain the income tax benefits from using LIFO during periods of inflation.
9. What effect does the principle of consistency have on the selection of an inventory costing method? Why is it important that an accounting method be applied consistently from period to period?
10. Define the term *market* as used in the phrase ''lower of cost or market.''
11. What accounting principle justifies the use of the lower of cost or market valuation approach? Explain the principle.
12. Define net realizable value.
13. Differentiate between the weighted average cost method and the moving average cost method.
14. Will the cost of goods sold necessarily be the same under both a perpetual and a periodic inventory system when the following cost methods are used: (a) specific identification, (b) FIFO, (c) LIFO, and (d) average cost?
15. Explain why the LIFO method used with a periodic inventory system will generally produce different results than when it is used with a perpetual inventory system.
16. Why do inventory errors affect two periods?
17. If the ending inventory is mistakenly understated, what is the effect on net income in that period and the next period? What is the effect on the year-end balance sheet values reported for each year?
18. What uses can be made of the retail inventory method and the gross profit method of estimating the cost of inventory?
19. What records must be maintained to use the retail inventory method?
20. Explain the gross profit method as it is used to estimate the ending inventory.

EXERCISES

Exercise 9-1 (Inventory Cost Flow Methods—Periodic Inventory System)

The beginning inventory and the purchases of a product during June are shown.

June 1	Inventory	600 units at $3.00
June 8	Purchase	350 units at $2.50
June 19	Purchase	400 units at $2.80
June 23	Purchase	200 units at $3.10
June 29	Purchase	510 units at $3.50

On June 30, 450 units remain in inventory. The company uses a periodic inventory system. Determine the cost of the ending inventory and the cost of goods sold using three methods.

1. Weighted average
2. FIFO
3. LIFO

Exercise 9-2 (Lower of Cost or Market)

The inventory of the Jordan Company contains the following items at December 31.

Item	Quantity	Cost	Market
		Unit price	
#33	57	$ 3	$ 3.50
#24	30	7	6.00
#6	12	24	22.00
#45	65	4	4.00
#27	50	6	5.50

Required:

A. Determine the ending inventory value at December 31, applying the lower of cost or market rule to the individual items.
B. What effect did application of the LCM rule have on the financial statements of the firm?

Exercise 9-3 (Net Realizable Value)

Grand Rapids Auto is an automobile dealership. One of its models was used as a demonstrator during the year. Presented below is the information related to the demonstrator as of December 31, the end of the current fiscal year.

Normal sales price	$9,280
Original cost	8,300
Estimated sales value in existing condition	7,900
Estimated selling and disposal cost	670

Required:

From the information above, determine the value at which the demonstrator should be reported in the December 31 financial statements. Is there an affect on net income reported for the current period?

Exercise 9-4 (Inventory Cost Methods—Perpetual Inventory System)

The following information relates to the inventory of the Peterson Company during March.

March 1	Beginning Inventory	100 units at $8
3	Purchased	55 units at $9
10	Sold	70 units
12	Purchased	60 units at $10
17	Sold	35 units
25	Sold	40 units

Assume the ending inventory on March 31 consisted of 8 units from the beginning inventory, 43 units from the March 3 purchase, and 19 units from the March 12 purchase. The Peterson Company uses a perpetual system. Determine the cost of the ending inventory and the cost of goods sold using four methods.

1. The moving average
2. Specific identification
3. LIFO
4. FIFO

Exercise 9-5 (LIFO Cost Flow Method— Periodic and Perpetual Inventory Systems)

The beginning inventory, purchases, and sales of Product X for the month of November are shown.

Nov. 1	Inventory	3 2	11 units at $31
5	Sold	2 1	8 units
16	Purchased 11	3 4 1	9 units at $29
21	Purchased	2 6 1	12 units at $33
23	Sold	3 9 6	7 units
29	Sold	9 9 8	6 units

Required:

A. Determine the cost of the inventory on November 30 using a perpetual inventory system and the LIFO method.

B. Determine the cost of the inventory on November 30 using a periodic inventory system and the LIFO method.

Exercise 9-6 (LIFO and FIFO Cost Flow Methods— Periodic and Perpetual Inventory Systems)

The following transactions relate to the inventory of Item C-7.

Jan. 1	Beginning Inventory		6 at $103 = $618	
Feb. 14	Purchased		7 at $110 = $770	
March 25	Sold		9	
July 8	Purchased	2 6	5 at $114 = $570	
Sept. 3	Purchased	-2 1	8 at $115 = $920	
Oct. 13	Sold	5	9	2 8 7 8
Dec. 10	Sold		3	

Required:

A. Using a periodic system and the LIFO method, determine the cost of the 5 items in inventory on December 31 and the cost of sales for the year.

B. Using a perpetual system and the LIFO method, determine the cost of the year-end inventory and the cost of sales.

C. Using a periodic system and the FIFO method, determine the cost of the 5 items in inventory on December 31 and the cost of sales for the year.

D. Using a perpetual system and the FIFO method, determine the cost of the year-end inventory and the cost of sales.

Exercise 9-7 (Effects of Inventory Errors)

The Gardiner Company's income statements for the past three years are as shown.

	1984	1985	1986
Net Sales	$34,000	$39,000	$35,000
Beginning Inventory	8,000	9000 ~~7,000~~	9000 ~~10,000~~
Net Purchases	15,000	2700 ~~18,000~~	11,000
Goods Available for Sale	23,000	25,000	20,000
Ending Inventory	9000 ~~7,000~~	9000 ~~10,000~~	6,000
Cost of Goods Sold	14000 ~~16,000~~	18000 ~~15,000~~	14000 ~~15,000~~
Gross Margin	20000 ~~18,000~~	24,000	21000 ~~20,000~~
Operating Expenses	8,000	7,000	9,500
Net Income	12000 ~~$10,000~~	14000 ~~$17,000~~	11500 ~~$10,500~~

Because of errors, the 1984 ending inventory is understated by $2,000 and the 1985 ending inventory is overstated by $1,000. The 1986 ending inventory is correct.

Required:
A. Determine the correct amount of net income for each of the three years.
B. Determine the total income for the three-year period as shown and as corrected.

Exercise 9-8 (Effects of Inventory Errors)

ME Corporation was formed in 1983. Partial income statements for its first two years of operations are shown below

	1983		1984	
Sales		$60,000		$68,000
Cost of Goods Sold:				
Beginning Inventory	$15,000		$10,000	
Purchases (net)	35,000		43,000	
Cost of Goods Available for Sale	50,000		53,000	
Less: Ending Inventory	10,000		16,000	
Cost of Goods Sold		40,000		37,000
Gross Profit on sales		$20,000		$31,000

After the 1984 income statement was prepared, the firm's accountant noted that the gross profit percentage varied significantly between the two years and that the 1984 gross profit increased $11,000 with only a $8,000 increase in sales. After an extensive review of the records, he found that inventory in the amount of $4,000 was correctly recorded as a purchase in 1983 but was not included in the physical count taken on December 31, 1983. The 1984 ending inventory was determined to be correct.

Required:

A. Prepare corrected partial income statements for the two years.

B. What effect did this error have on the gross profit of each year? What effect did the error have on the combined gross profit for the two years? Explain your answer.

C. What effect did this error have on the balance sheet accounts for each year?

Exercise 9-9 (Retail Inventory Method)

Using the following information, determine the cost of the April 30 inventory by the retail inventory method.

	Cost	Retail
Beginning Inventory, April	$21,000	$30,000
Purchases During April	14,000	20,000
Sales During April		38,000

Exercise 9-10 (Gross Profit Method)

The following information relates to the inventory of the C. B. Owens Company during September.

Inventory, September 1	$26,000
Purchases	34,000
Purchase returns	2,500
Sales	69,000
Average gross profit on sales	34%

Use the gross profit method to estimate the cost of the inventory at September 30.

PROBLEMS

Problem 9-1 (Inventory Cost Flow Methods— Periodic Inventory System)

During the year, the Hopkins Company sold 9,300 units of its product at $7 each. Operating expenses of $1.25 per unit were incurred. Purchases of the product are shown below.

Jan. 1	Inventory	1,206 at $3.50
Feb. 4	Purchases	2,600 at $3.80
April 29	Purchases	2,200 at $4.00
July 23	Purchases	2,350 at $4.05
Sept. 6	Purchases	1,300 at $4.10
Dec. 11	Purchases	1,850 at $4.25

Hopkins Company uses a periodic inventory system.

Required:

A. Prepare a schedule to compute the number of units and cost of goods available for sale during the year.

B. Determine the cost of the inventory at December 31 using the following inventory costing methods:
1. FIFO
2. LIFO
3. Weighted average

C. Prepare three income statements in adjacent columns using each of the above inventory costing methods.

Problem 9-2 (Lower of Cost or Market)
The following information relates to barrels of oil held in the inventory of Robertson Oil Company during 1984.

		Barrels	Unit Cost
January 1	Beginning inventory	40,000	$35
April 15	Purchases	30,000	35
May 13	Sales ($45 per barrel)	(50,000)	
August 9	Purchases	30,000	35
October 28	Sales ($45 per barrel)	(40,000)	

Due to an oil glut, the replacement cost for a barrel of the same grade of oil was $28 per barrel on December 31. In 1985, the company disposed of the 10,000 barrels of oil in the ending inventory for $360,000. No additional purchases were made in 1985. Robertson Company uses a periodic inventory system and the average cost flow method.

Required:
Complete the following partial income statements for 1984 and 1985 under the average cost flow method and under the lower of cost or market rule.

	Average Cost		LCM	
	1984	1985	1984	1985
Sales	___	___	___	___
Cost of goods sold				
Beginning inventory	___	___	___	___
Purchases	___	___	___	___
Cost of goods available for sale	___	___	___	___
Less: Ending inventory	___	___	___	___
Cost of goods sold	___	___	___	___
Gross profit on sales	___	___	___	___

Problem 9-3 (Inventory Cost Flow Methods— Periodic Inventory System)
The following information relates to the inventory of the Washburn Company during the month of December

3.96

	Units	Unit Cost	Total Cost
12/1 Beginning Inventory	400	$5.00	$2,000
12/10 Purchases	400	5.30	2,120
12/23 Purchases	500	5.60	2,800
Totals	1,300		$6,920

Washburn uses the periodic inventory system. During the month, 700 units were sold for $6,300. A physical count on December 31 verified that 600 units were on hand.

Required:

A. Prepare an income statement through gross profit on sales for December using each of the following costing methods.
   1. Specific identification, assuming that 300 units were sold from the beginning inventory and 400 units were sold from the first purchase.
   2. FIFO.
   3. LIFO.
   4. Weighted average.
B. Which cost flow method resulted in the highest gross profit on sales? The highest ending inventory? Explain why your results differ.
C. Prepare an income statement through gross profit on sales for December using the FIFO and LIFO costing methods and assuming the December 23 purchase had not been made.
D. Management of Washburn Company is expecting the unit cost to increase to $6.00 early in the next period. In anticipation of the price increase, assume that a purchase of 600 additional units was made on December 29 at a unit cost of $5.80. Prepare an income statement through gross profit on sales for December using the FIFO and LIFO costing methods.
E. Compare your results obtained in requirements A, C, and D. Explain why your results are or are not the same.

Problem 9-4 (Inventory Cost Flow Methods— Perpetual Inventory System)

The Robinson Company buys and sells home computers. The inventory on October 1 consisted of 7 units at $2,100 each. Transactions during October are shown below.

Oct. 5	Purchased	3 units at $2,180 per unit
11	Sold	4 units
20	Purchased	6 units at $2,300 per unit
23	Sold	3 units
28	Sold	5 units

Required:

A. Record the information on perpetual inventory cards using each of the following methods:
   1. LIFO.
   2. FIFO.
   3. Moving average.

B. Robinson Company sold its product for $3,750 each throughout October. Operating expenses for the month totaled $4,200. Prepare an income statement based on each of the following inventory costing methods:
1. LIFO.
2. FIFO.
3. Moving average.
4. Specific identification.(Assume the first sale was out of the beginning inventory, the second sale was out of the October 5 purchase, and the third sale was out of the October 20 purchase.)

Problem 9-5 (LIFO Cost Flow Method—Perpetual Inventory System)

The beginning inventory, purchases, and sales of Product FM19 during August are shown below:

Aug. 1	Inventory	7 units at $31
2	Purchased	9 units at $30
5	Sold	10 units
8	Purchased	6 units at $31.50
14	Sold	4 units
15	Purchased	5 units at $33
20	Sold	6 units
23	Sold	3 units
27	Purchased	8 units at $32

Required:

A. Record the beginning inventory, the purchases, the cost of goods sold, and the running balance on a perpetual inventory card using the LIFO method.
B. The 10 units sold on August 5 were sold on credit for $50 each. Give the general journal entries to record the sale and the cost of goods sold using LIFO and assuming that a perpetual inventory system is used.

Problem 9-6 (FIFO and LIFO Cost Flow Methods— Perpetual Inventory System)

Fiesta Electronic Games adopted a perpetual inventory system to account for its inventory in video games. The inventory on June 1 contained three units of Cosmo Invaders, a model that cost $350 per unit. The following data related to this model was accumulated during the month of June. All transactions were for cash.

	Purchases		Sales	
Date	Number of Units	Cost per Unit	Number of Units	Unit Sales Price
6/6	2	$400		
6/10			1	$700
6/16	3	420		
6/23			2	730
6/28			2	750

Operating expenses were $600 for the month.

Required:

A. Prepare a perpetual inventory card for this model for the month of June assuming (1) FIFO and (2) LIFO cost flow methods.

B. Record the sale of two units on June 23 for both the FIFO and LIFO cost flow methods.

C. Prepare income statements for both cost flow methods assuming a 30% income tax rate.

D. Which cost flow method resulted in the highest gross profit from sales? Under what conditions would you expect the other method to result in the highest net income?

E. What amount is reported for the inventory in the June 30 balance sheet under each cost flow method? Explain why there is a difference in inventory values when the number of units in the ending inventory is the same for both methods.

F. How much did income taxes differ between the two methods?

G. Assume that there were no additional units purchased and all of the units in the ending inventory were sold in the next period for $750 per unit. Which method will show the highest net income in the next period? The income tax rate for the next year is expected to be 30%.

Problem 9-7 (Effects of Inventory Errors)

The income statements for Arnold Company for two years are shown below:

	1983	1984
Sales Revenue	$350,000	$375,000
Cost of Goods Sold		
Beginning Inventory	70,000	100,000
Purchases	190,000	145,000
Goods Available for Sale	260,000	245,000
Ending Inventory	100,000	65,000
Cost of Goods Sold	160,000	180,000
Gross Profit on Sales	190,000	195,000
Operating Expenses	90,000	100,000
Net Income	$100,000	$ 95,000

The following information concerning 1983 has been discovered.

1. Arnold Company recorded on December 23 goods purchased at a cost of $200. The terms were FOB shipping point. The goods were delivered by the seller to the transportation company on December 27. The goods were not included in the ending inventory since they had not arrived.

2. Arnold sells goods that it does not own on a consignment basis. Consigned goods on hand at year-end were included in inventory at a cost of $1,100.

3. A purchase of goods worth $950 was made in December but not recorded until January. The goods were received on December 28 and included in the physical inventory.

4. A sale of goods costing $1,400 was made and recorded in December. Since the buyer requested that the goods be held for later delivery, the items were on hand and included in inventory at year end.   ↑ inv ↓ 1400
5. Arnold sold goods costing $700 for $1,300 on December 26. The terms were FOB destination. The goods arrived at the destination in January. The sale was recorded in 1983 and the goods were excluded from the ending inventory.

↑ inv
↓ sale

Required:

A. Determine the correct ending inventory figure for 1983.
B. Prepare revised income statements for 1983 and 1984.
C. Determine the total net income for the two-year period both before and after the revisions. Why are these figures similar or different?

Problem 9-8 (Retail Inventory Method)

Fifi's Boutique uses the retail inventory method to estimate the ending inventory for the purpose of preparing interim financial statements. The following information is available for the first three months of the year.

	Cost	Retail
Jan. 1 Beginning Inventory	$15,500	$26,750
Net Purchases	24,500	37,250
Net Sales		51,460
Operating Expenses	8,560	

Required:

A. Determine the cost of the March 31 inventory.
B. Prepare an income statement for the first quarter of the year.

Problem 9-9 (Retail Inventory Method)

Skeeter's Sporting Goods takes the year-end physical inventory at retail and converts it to cost by the retail inventory method. Since Skeeter suspects that one of his employees has been stealing merchandise, he also wants to use the retail inventory method to estimate the cost of the ending inventory. The following information is available at December 31.

	Cost	Retail
January 1 Beginning Inventory	$28,100	$46,400
Purchases	46,576	74,500
Purchase Returns	3,500	6,100
Net Sales		87,000
December 31, Physical Inventory		21,600

Required:

A. Convert the retail dollar value of the December 31 physical inventory to cost.
B. Estimate the cost of the December 31 inventory.
C. Calculate the loss due to theft at cost and at retail.

Problem 9-10 (Gross Profit Method)

The inventory of the Dakotan Shop was totally destroyed by fire on March 15. The accounting records were not destroyed, and they contained the following information for the period January 1 to March 15.

Inventory balance, January 1	$24,200
Sales	61,800
Sales returns and allowances	3,500
Purchases	29,900
Purchases returns and allowances	1,800
Freight-in	1,400

The gross profit on sales over the last four years has averaged 42%. Estimate the inventory on hand at the date of the fire.

ALTERNATE PROBLEMS

Problem 9-1A (Inventory Cost Flow Methods— Periodic Inventory System)

The C.D. Underwood Company sells only one product, which had a price of $20 throughout the past year. Total sales for the year amounted to $96,000. Selling and administrative expenses of $19,200 were incurred. The product was purchased as follows:

January 1 inventory	805 at $10.00
Purchases:	
March 3	990 at $10.25
May 14	895 at $10.40
Aug. 2	1030 at $10.75
Sept. 23	1200 at $10.80
Nov. 5	790 at $11.00

The company uses a periodic inventory system.

Required:

A. Prepare a schedule to compute the number of units and cost of goods available for sale during the year.

B. Determine the cost of the year-end inventory using each of the following methods:
1. FIFO.
2. LIFO.
3. Weighted average.

C. Prepare three income statements in adjacent columns using each of the above methods to determine the cost of goods sold.

Problem 9-2A (Lower of Cost or Market)

The following information applies to the inventory of the Morenci Camera Shop at December 31.

Camera Model	Quantity	Unit Price	
		Actual Cost	Replacement Cost
A-4	21	$24	$21
C-7	17	19	19
G-1	8	87	85
Z-8	19	33	36

Required:

A. Compute the ending inventory value at December 31, applying the lower of cost or market rule to each item in stock.
B. What effect did application of the LCM rule have on the financial statements of the firm?
C. Assume that at the end of the next fiscal period, 18 units of Model A-4 are still on hand and the replacement cost is $23 per unit. How would this increase in replacement cost affect the inventory value of the 18 units?

Problem 9-3A (Inventory Cost Flow Methods— Perpetual Inventory System)

The F. E. McDonnell Company sells one type of phone answering machine. The November 1 inventory consisted of 15 units at $105 each. During November, the selling price was $200 and total operating expenses were $850. Transactions for the month were as follows:

Nov. 3	Purchased	8 units at $107 per unit
10	Sold	9 units
16	Purchased	10 units at $115 per unit
21	Sold	6 units
25	Sold	8 units

Required:

A. Record the information on perpetual inventory cards using each of the following methods:
  1. Moving average.
  2. LIFO.
  3. FIFO.
B. Prepare an income statement based on the perpetual inventory system for each of the following methods:
  1. Moving average.
  2. LIFO.
  3. FIFO.
  4. Specific identification.

For specific identification, assume that the first sale was out of the beginning inventory, the second sale was out of the November 16 inventory, and the third sale was out of the November 3 inventory.

Problem 9-4A (LIFO Cost Flow Method—Perpetual Inventory System)

The beginning inventory of Article LW4 and information about purchases and sales made during February are shown below:

Feb.	1	Inventory	1,000 units @ $4.00
	4	Purchase	2,500 units @ $3.50
	9	Sale	2,000 units
	12	Purchase	3,000 units @ $4.25
	21	Sale	1,000 units
	24	Sale	1,500 units
	26	Purchase	2,000 units @ $4.00
	27	Sale	1,000 units

Required:

A. Using the LIFO method, record the beginning inventory, the purchases, the cost of goods sold, and the running balance on a perpetual inventory card.

B. All the units sold on February 21 were sold for cash at $8 each. Prepare the general journal entry to record the sale and the entry to record the cost of goods sold. Use LIFO and assume that a perpetual inventory system was adopted by the firm.

Problem 9-5A (Effects of Inventory Errors)

Two consecutive annual income statements of the Alpha Company are shown below:

	1983	1984
Sales Revenue	$286,000	$279,000
Cost of Goods Sold		
Beginning Inventory	55,000	68,000
Purchases	160,750	149,300
Goods Available for Sale	215,750	217,300
Ending Inventory	68,000	74,000
Cost of Goods Sold	147,750	143,300
Gross Profit on Sales	138,250	135,700
Operating Expenses	65,400	71,700
Net Income	$ 72,850	$ 64,000

The following information concerning 1983 has been discovered.

1. Alpha Company sells goods of the Omega Corporation on consignment. Consigned goods on hand at December 31 were included in the inventory at a cost of $1,100.
2. On December 27, Alpha sold goods costing $450 for $940. The terms were FOB destination, and the goods reached the buyer on January 6. Alpha recorded the sale in 1983 and the goods were excluded from the ending inventory.
3. On December 19, Alpha made and recorded a purchase of goods worth $1,500. The terms were FOB shipping point, and Alpha received notice that the goods were delivered to the transportation company on December 23. Since the goods had not arrived by the end of the year, they were not included in inventory.
4. On December 31, a customer had goods costing $205 out on trial. These goods were excluded from ending inventory.

5. On December 26, Alpha purchased goods for $870. The terms were FOB destination. Since the goods arrived in January, they were excluded from the ending inventory. The purchase was recorded in December.

Required:
A. Determine the correct ending inventory figure for 1983.
B. Prepare revised income statements for 1983 and 1984.
C. Determine the total net income for the two-year period both before and after the revisions. Explain why the figures are similar or different.

Problem 9-6A (Retail Inventory Method)
Main Street Gift Shop takes the year-end inventory at retail and converts it to cost by the retail inventory method. For control purposes, the Gift Shop also estimates the cost of the ending inventory using the retail inventory method. The accounting records contain the following information on December 31.

	Cost	Retail
Inventory, January 1	$52,300	$ 88,000
Purchases	79,000	119,500
Purchase Returns	3,300	7,500
Net Sales		136,800
Physical Inventory, December 31		54,350

Required:
A. Convert the retail dollar value of the December 31 physical inventory to cost.
B. Estimate the cost of the December 31 inventory.
C. Calculate the amount of the inventory shortage at cost and at retail.

Problem 9-7A (Gross Profit Method)
An explosion occurred at the Paducah Paint Store on the night of April 11 and destroyed the entire inventory. The accounting records, which survived the explosion, contained the following information about the period January 1 to April 11.

Sales	$45,200
Sales returns and allowances	6,700
Purchases	23,100
Purchases returns and allowances	2,000
Freight-in	400
Inventory balance, January 1	16,000

The gross profit on sales has averaged 39% over the last three years. Estimate the cost of the inventory that was destroyed.

CASE FOR CHAPTER 9

(Annual Report Analysis)
For this case refer to the General Motors 1981 annual report presented in the Appendix to the text.

Required:

Answer the following questions and perform the necessary computations.

1. What were the inventory balances reported in the 1981 and 1980 comparative balance sheets? Compute inventory as a percentage of current assets for both years. Discuss the primary reason for the change in the percentage.

2. What were the company's policies with respect to accounting for domestic inventories and inventories held outside the United States? Discuss the major advantages of using the LIFO method. With respect to balance sheet valuation, what is a major disadvantage of the LIFO method?

3. What would the inventory balances have been if the FIFO method had been used? Ignoring income taxes, what effect would a change from LIFO to FIFO have on stockholders' equity? On operating income (loss)? Assuming an effective income tax rate of 46%, compute how much income taxes were reduced or increased in 1981 by using the LIFO method.

4. Sometimes a company using LIFO faced with a strike or material shortages will find it necessary to reduce its normal inventory levels to satisfy current sales. In Note 1, General Motors states that a portion of its inventory was liquidated at a lower cost than current purchases. Did this liquidation result in an increase or decrease in cost of sales and net income? Why is this data disclosed to statement users? Compute the cost of sales in 1981 if the LIFO inventory had not been liquidated.

5. Compute the cost of sales and other operating charges, exclusive of the other expenses listed separately, as a percentage of net sales for 1979–1981. Briefly discuss any important changes revealed by the computations.

6. How much did the inventories balance increase or decrease in 1979, 1980, and 1981?

CHAPTER 10
PLANT AND EQUIPMENT: ACQUISITION AND ALLOCATION

OVERVIEW AND OBJECTIVES

This chapter explores the nature of plant and equipment assets, the components of their cost, and the methods used to allocate their cost to expense. When you have completed the chapter, you should understand:

- How the cost of different plant assets is determined (pp. 410–411).
- How to apportion the cost of a lump-sum purchase of assets (p. 412).
- The nature of depreciation (p. 414).
- The factors that should be considered in determining a plant asset's useful life (p. 415).
- How to calculate depreciation expense under each of the commonly used depreciation methods (pp. 416–420).
- The difference between capital expenditures and revenue expenditures (pp. 424–426).

The terms *plant and equipment, property, plant, and equipment,* and *plant assets* are commonly used in accounting to describe those long-lived assets acquired by a business for use in operations rather than for resale to customers. Examples include land, buildings, equipment, machinery, storage facilities, and vehicles. The term **fixed assets,** although seldom used today in the formal financial statements of large companies, often has been used in the past to describe this general category of assets and is still used frequently in conversation and in some of the general accounting literature.

Management's intention to use these assets for the future production of goods or services over several accounting periods is the primary factor that distinguishes them from other assets. Since they have value in use, they are said to contain future service benefits for the business. Buildings contain future housing services, automobiles contain future transportation services, and computers contain future data processing services. All of these assets are expected to be used in the future to produce goods or services for sale to customers. Assets that have physical characteristics similar to plant and equipment but are not intended for future use to produce goods or services should not be included in the plant and equipment category. For example, construction equipment held by an equipment dealer is inventory but the same type of equipment held by a construction company represents plant and equipment. Similarly, land held for future expansion or as an investment should be excluded from plant and equipment and classified as a long-term investment.

Because the service benefits contained in plant assets will be used over two or more accounting periods, the cost of the assets is allocated in a systematic manner to the accounting periods that benefit from their use. As the assets are used to produce goods or services, their cost is transferred to depreciation expense to match it with the revenue produced by the sale of the goods or services (matching principle).

DETERMINING THE COST OF PLANT ASSETS

The cost of a plant asset includes all of the expenditures necessary to obtain the asset and to get it ready for the use intended by the purchaser. An **expenditure** is a cash payment or the incurring of a liability to acquire a good or service. For example, the cost of acquiring a machine includes its invoice price (minus any cash discounts), sales taxes, freight, insurance in transit, and installation expenditures such as power hook-up and any initial adjustments needed to make the machine function properly. Assume, for example, the purchase of a machine at a list price of $25,000 with terms of 3/20, n/60. In addition, a sales tax of 4% must be paid, freight charges amount to $820, and installation expenditures amount to $675. The cost of the machine to be debited to the machinery account is computed as follows:

List price of the machine	$25,000
Less: cash discount (3% × $25,000)	750
Net cash price	24,250
Sales tax (4% × $24,250)	970
Freight	820
Installation	675
Total	$26,715

The cost of an asset should not exceed the amount for which it could be acquired in a cash transaction plus the other expenditures necessary to get the asset ready for use. Therefore, if payment is not made in time to take the cash discount, the $750 should be charged to interest expense rather than as a part of the cost of the machine. In effect, an extra $750 was paid for the privilege of waiting an extra 40 days to make payment. The cost of a used or *secondhand* asset should include its purchase price plus initial expenditures made for repairs, new parts, paint, and any other conditioning necessary to get the asset ready for use.

Care should be taken that only *reasonable* and *necessary* expenditures are included. Expenditures that could be avoided or that do not increase the usefulness of the asset should be excluded from its cost. For example, expenditures required to repair damage to an asset caused by carelessness during installation should be charged to an expense account rather than to the asset account.

When a company *constructs an asset for its own use,* cost includes all expenditures made directly for construction, such as labor, materials, and insurance premiums paid during construction. The cost of buildings also includes architectural fees, engineering fees, and building permits. In addition, a reasonable amount of general overhead for such things as power, management supervision during construction, and depreciation on machinery used for construction should be included. Interest incurred on borrowed money during the construction period is also included as part of the cost of a self-constructed asset.[1]

The cost of *land* includes the price paid to the seller plus the broker's commission and other necessary expenditures such as title-search and survey fees. If the buyer pays delinquent taxes on the property, they should also be included in the cost of the land. If the land contains a building that is to be demolished in order to construct a new building, the total purchase price plus the cost of removing the old building (less amounts received from the sale of salvaged materials) is included in the cost of the land. The cost of removing the old building is considered part of the land cost because it was incurred to get the land into condition for its intended use—the construction of a new building. In addition, expenditures made for leveling and landscaping are properly included as part of the cost of the land.

Although land is not depreciable because it has an unlimited life, some expenditures related to its acquisition and use, such as driveways, fences, and parking lots, do have limited lives and are properly depreciated. Consequently, these items are normally charged to a separate *land improvements* account and depreciated over their estimated useful lives.

---

[1]*Statement of Financial Accounting Standards No. 34,* ''Capitalization of Interest Cost'' (Stamford: Financial Accounting Standards Board, 1979), par. 6.

APPORTIONING THE COST OF A LUMP-SUM ACQUISITION

Several plant assets may be acquired for a **lump-sum payment** without an identification of the cost of each asset. In these cases, the total cost must be allocated in some systematic way to the assets purchased because they may have different depreciable lives or they may not be depreciable at all. The most common method is to allocate total cost on the basis of the fair values of the assets acquired. Fair values may be either estimates of current selling prices or appraised values. For example, assume that a building, land, and office equipment were acquired for a lump-sum payment of $800,000. Fair values of the assets were determined by an independent appraisal as follows:

	Fair Value
Building	$595,000
Land	170,000
Office Equipment	85,000
Total Fair Value	$850,000

The total cost of $800,000 is allocated to each asset on the basis of these fair values by use of the following formula:

$$\frac{\text{Fair value of specific asset}}{\text{Total fair value}} \times \text{Cost} = \frac{\text{Cost allocated to the}}{\text{specific asset}}$$

The allocation would be as follows:

$$\text{Building} = \frac{595,000}{850,000} \times \$800,000 = \$560,000$$

$$\text{Land} = \frac{170,000}{850,000} \times \$800,000 = 160,000$$

$$\text{Equipment} = \frac{85,000}{850,000} \times \$800,000 = \underline{80,000}$$

$$\text{Total} \qquad\qquad \underline{\underline{\$800,000}}$$

The acquisition would be recorded with the following entry:

Jan.	2	Buildings	560,000	
		Land	160,000	
		Office Equipment	80,000	
		Cash		800,000
		To record the purchase of plant assets.		

EXCHANGING A NOTE FOR PLANT ASSETS

When a plant asset is purchased on credit, a note is often given in exchange. The note may contain a specific interest rate, in which case the face value of the note will be equal to the cash price of the asset. For example, if a $20,000, 10%, 18-month note is exchanged for a machine, the transaction is recorded as follows:

Jan.	2	Machinery	20,000	
		Notes Payable		20,000
		Exchanged a $20,000, 10%, 18-month		
		note for machinery.		

Interest expense on the note will be accrued at the end of the year with the following entry:

Dec.	31	Interest Expense	2,000	
		Interest Payable		2,000
		To accrue interest on a note payable for		
		one year ($20,000 × 10%).		

When the note is paid on its maturity date, the entry is:

July	2	Notes Payable	20,000	
		Interest Payable	2,000	
		Interest Expense	1,000	
		Cash		23,000
		Paid a note payable plus interest.		

Notice that the machinery account is debited only for the cash price of the asset. Interest on the note is not a part of the asset's cost and is therefore debited to interest expense when accrued or paid.

If no interest rate is specified on the note, or if the specified rate is unreasonable, a portion of the face value must be assumed to represent interest. The asset acquired with the note is recorded at its cash value or the market value of the note, whichever is more clearly determinable. This process is called **imputing interest** on a note.[2] To illustrate, assume that an 18-month, $23,000 noninterest-bearing note was exchanged for a machine with a cash price of $20,000. The transaction would be recorded as follows:

Jan.	2	Machinery	20,000	
		Discount on Notes Payable	3,000	
		Notes Payable		23,000
		Exchanged a noninterest-bearing note		
		for machinery.		

[2]Accounting Principles Board, ''Interest on Receivables and Payables,'' *APB Opinion No. 21* (New York: AICPA, August 1971), par. 12.

Notice that the machine is recorded at its cash value of $20,000 rather than at the face value of the note. This is the machine's cost and is the amount that is depreciated over the machine's useful life. The remaining $3,000 represents discount or interest on the note that will be recognized as interest expense over the term of the note.

An adjusting entry is made on December 31 to recognize interest expense for the first year as follows:

Dec.	31	Interest Expense	2,000	
		Discount on Notes Payable		2,000
		To record interest expense on a note		
		payable.		

When the note is paid on its maturity date, the entry is:

July	2	Notes Payable	23,000	
		Interest Expense	1,000	
		Discount on Notes Payable		1,000
		Cash		23,000
		To record payment of a note payable.		

THE NATURE OF DEPRECIATION

As described earlier, plant assets contain service benefits a business intends to use over the life of the assets in the production of goods or services. All plant assets except land have limited useful lives and their service benefits will be consumed by the end of their useful lives. The cost of the service benefits is therefore assigned to depreciation expense as the benefits are used. This process is called **depreciation** in accounting. Depreciation is nothing more than the allocation of the cost of an asset to the accounting periods benefiting from its use. The meaning of depreciation is often misunderstood because the term is generally used by nonaccountants to refer to the decline in the market value of assets. Although plant assets are subject to changes in market values, accountants are not concerned with recognizing these changes because plant assets are acquired for use, not for sale. Depreciation is therefore an allocation process, not a valuation process.

DETERMINING THE AMOUNT OF DEPRECIATION

Factors needed to determine the amount of periodic depreciation for a plant asset are its cost, its estimated useful life, and its estimated residual value. Determination of the initial cost of plant assets was discussed earlier. A discussion of estimated useful life and estimated residual value follows.

Estimated Useful Life

In order to allocate the cost of a plant asset to the periods benefiting from its use, an estimate must be made of the asset's **useful life**—the time period during which it is expected to be used by the purchaser in the production of goods or services. This period is generally much shorter than the asset's physical life. For example, the physical life of an automobile may be 8 to 10 years. Because it will require more maintenance and will operate less efficiently as it becomes older, however, the purchaser may decide that it is economical to trade in the automobile for a new one after three years. The cost of the automobile, less estimated residual value, therefore should be charged to depreciation expense over the three-year period.

Three major factors generally are considered in estimating the useful life of an asset—physical wear and tear, obsolescence, and inadequacy. *Physical wear and tear* is affected by such things as frequency of use, climatic conditions under which the asset is used, and the frequency of expected maintenance. For some assets like construction equipment, these physical factors are the most important ones affecting useful life. **Obsolescence** results when technological advances produce new assets that can provide the same service more efficiently than the existing assets, thereby causing them to become out of date. Obsolescence is the most important factor affecting the useful life of assets such as computers. The rapid improvements made in the design and performance of computers generally make them obsolete long before they wear out physically.

Inadequacy refers to the inability of an asset to meet the increasing needs of the user caused by growth of the firm. When a company acquires plant assets, it generally attempts to acquire those that will provide adequate capacity to meet foreseeable operating needs. When demand for the company's product increases more rapidly than anticipated, the plant assets may not have the capacity to meet that demand and the assets are said to have become inadequate. Because obsolescence and inadequacy cannot be easily predicted, accountants often are conservative in estimating the useful lives of plant assets that are most affected by these factors. Estimates of useful lives are made on the basis of past experience. If the company has no past experience, estimated useful lives of various assets can be obtained from industry publications.

Estimated Residual Value

The **residual value** of a plant asset is its estimated value at the end of its useful life. It is the amount expected to be received from the sale or other disposition of the asset at the end of its useful life. Assets such as automobiles and trucks may have significant resale values; other assets like specifically designed machinery and equipment may have value only as scrap metal at the end of their useful lives. The cost of an asset less its residual value is the amount that should be charged to depreciation expense over the asset's useful life. When residual value is expected to be an insignificant amount in relation to the asset's cost, it is often ignored in computing depreciation. Residual value is sometimes also called *salvage value* or *trade-in value*.

Depreciation Methods

Several methods can be used to allocate the cost of an asset over its useful life. The four most frequently used are the straight-line, units-of-production, sum-of-years'-digits, and double declining-balance methods. All are generally accepted in accounting because they result in a systematic and rational allocation of the cost of an asset to the periods that benefit from its use. It is not necessary that a company use a single depreciation method for all of its depreciable assets. The methods chosen will vary with management's expectations about the way the service benefits incorporated in the assets are to be used. In addition, the methods adopted by management for use in the accounts and financial statements may differ from those used in the preparation of income tax returns.

Straight-line Method. The **straight-line depreciation method** allocates an equal amount of depreciation to each full accounting period in the asset's useful life. The amount of depreciation for each period is determined by dividing the cost of the asset minus its residual value by the number of periods in the asset's useful life. For example, assume a machine has a cost of $33,000, a residual value of $3,000, and a useful life of five years. Depreciation for each year is computed as follows:

$$\frac{\text{Cost} - \text{Residual value}}{\text{Useful life}} = \frac{\$33,000 - \$3,000}{5 \text{ years}} = \$6,000 \text{ annual depreciation}$$

The entry to record the depreciation is:

Dec.	31	Depreciation Expense	6,000	
		Accumulated Depreciation—Machinery		6,000
		To record depreciation for the year.		

Annual depreciation expense is $6,000. If the asset is acquired during a fiscal period, the annual depreciation amount should be prorated for the first and last partial years of its use. For example, if the machine were purchased on April 1, depreciation for the first year would be 9/12 × $6,000, or $4,500. Although depreciation could be computed to the exact day when an asset is acquired during a month, computation to the nearest month is generally sufficient. A full month's depreciation is taken on an asset acquired during the first half of a month, and no depreciation is taken for the month if the asset is acquired during the last half of the month. In fact, because depreciation is an estimate, many companies compute depreciation only to the nearest full year.

Units-of-production Method.
The **units-of-production method** relates depreciation to use rather than to time. This method is particularly appropriate for assets whose use varies significantly from one period to another because it results in a better matching of expenses with revenues. Accounting periods with greater production from the asset will be charged with a greater amount of depreciation expense. A disadvantage of the method is that it requires additional recordkeeping to determine the units produced during each period by each asset.

Under the units-of-production method, the cost of the asset minus residual value is divided by the estimated number of production units expected from the asset during its estimated life. Production units might be expressed in several ways—miles, operating hours, units of product. The result of the division is a depreciation rate per production unit. The amount of depreciation for a period is then determined by multiplying the depreciation rate per production unit times the number of production units used or produced during the period.

To illustrate, assume that a machine with a cost of $33,000 and an estimated residual value of $3,000 is estimated to have a useful life of 15,000 operating hours. The depreciation rate per operating hour is:

$$\frac{\text{Cost} - \text{Residual value}}{\text{Operating hours}} = \text{Depreciation per operating hour}$$

or

$$\frac{\$33,000 - \$3,000}{15,000 \text{ hours}} = \$2.00 \text{ per operating hour}$$

If the machine was operated for 2,500 hours during an accounting period, that period would be charged with depreciation of $5,000 (2,500 hours × $2.00), and the following depreciation entry is prepared:

Dec.	31	Depreciation Expense	5,000	
		Accumulated Depreciation—Machinery		5,000
		To record depreciation expense for the year.		

Sum-of-years'-digits Method.
The **sum-of-years'-digits method** results in a decreasing depreciation charge over the useful life of the asset. Depreciation for each period is determined by multiplying the cost less residual

value by successively smaller fractions. The denominator of the fractions, which is constant, is determined by adding the years in the asset's useful life. The numerators of the fractions, which change each year, are the years remaining in the asset's life at the beginning of the period.

To illustrate, assume that the sum-of-years'-digits method is used to allocate depreciation on a machine with a cost of $33,000, a residual value of $3,000, and an estimated life of five years. The sum of the years' digits (the denominator) is computed as:

$$1 + 2 + 3 + 4 + 5 = 15$$

The depreciation charge for each year is then calculated as shown in the following tabulation:

Year	Cost Less Residual Value	Fraction	Depreciation for the Year	Total Accumulated Depreciation	Book Value
1	$30,000 ×	5/15 =	$10,000	$10,000	$23,000
2	30,000 ×	4/15 =	8,000	18,000	15,000
3	30,000 ×	3/15 =	6,000	24,000	9,000
4	30,000 ×	2/15 =	4,000	28,000	5,000
5	30,000 ×	1/15 =	2,000	30,000	3,000

Notice that the method results in a book value equal to the asset's residual value at the end of its useful life.

When the asset has a long life, the sum of the years' digits can be calculated by using the formula: $S = n\left(\dfrac{n + 1}{2}\right)$, where S equals the sum of the years' digits and n equals the number of years in the asset's life. The sum of the years' digits for an asset with a 10-year life is therefore $10\left(\dfrac{10 + 1}{2}\right) = 55$.

When an asset is acquired during a fiscal year, it is necessary to allocate each full year's amount to the fiscal years benefiting from the asset's use. Consequently, if the asset was acquired on April 1, the depreciation recorded in the first year would be 9/12 × $10,000, or $7,500. Depreciation for the second year would be:

3/12 × $10,000 (from year 1 above)	$2,500
9/12 × $8,000 (from year 2 above)	6,000
Depreciation for second year	$8,500

Depreciation for each of the remaining years would be computed in a similar manner.

Double Declining-balance Method.

Like the sum-of-years'-digits method, the **double declining-balance method** results in a decreasing depreciation charge over the useful life of the asset. Depreciation expense for each period is determined by multiplying a fixed depreciation rate equal to twice the straight-line rate times the declining *undepreciated cost* of the asset, called its **book value.**

To illustrate, assume the same asset used in the previous illustrations. The asset has a cost of $33,000, an estimated residual value of $3,000, and a useful life of five years. The straight-line rate is determined by dividing 100% by the useful life (5 years) of the asset. This rate (20%) is then doubled to determine the declining-balance rate (40%). The declining-balance rate is then applied to the book value of the asset at the beginning of the year to compute depreciation expense for each period, as indicated in the following tabulation:

Year	Book Value at Beginning of Year		Rate		Annual Depreciation Expense	Book Value at End of Year
1	$33,000	×	.40	=	$13,200	$19,800
2	19,800	×	.40	=	7,920	11,880
3	11,880	×	.40	=	4,752	7,128
4	7,128	×	.40	=	2,851	4,277
5	4,277				1,277	3,000

Three things should be specifically noted in this tabulation. First, the 40% depreciation rate is applied to the *book value* of the asset. Estimated residual value is *not* deducted under the double declining-balance method. Second, the amount of depreciation declined each year. Third, depreciation for the last year was *not* determined by multiplying $4,277 by 40% (which would result in a book value less than the asset's residual value). Depreciation expense of $1,277 was computed for the last year by simply subtracting the residual value of $3,000 from the book value at the beginning of the year, $4,277.

It was assumed in the above illustration that the asset was acquired at the beginning of the fiscal period, which seldom actually occurs. When an asset is acquired during a fiscal period, the amount of depreciation for the first year should be prorated. For example, if the asset was purchased on April 1, the first year's depreciation would be 9/12 × $13,200, or $9,900. The method of computing depreciation for subsequent years is unaffected, although the amounts will differ:

Year	Book Value at Beginning of Year	Rate				Annual Depreciation Expense	Book Value at End of Year
1	$33,000	× .40	= $13,200 × 9/12	=		$9,900	$23,100
2	23,100	× .40			=	9,240	13,860
3	13,860	× .40			=	5,544	8,316
4	8,316	× .40			=	3,326	4,990
5	4,990		(4,990 − 3,000)		=	1,990	3,000

COMPARISON OF DEPRECIATION METHODS

The straight-line depreciation method is the one most widely used, as shown in the following table from the 1980 edition of *Accounting Trends & Techniques,* an annual survey of 600 companies conducted by the American Institute of Certified Public Accountants:

Depreciation Method	No. of Companies
Straight-line	556
Double declining-balance	63
Sum-of-years'-digits	34
Units-of-production	46

(The number of companies exceeds 600 because some companies use more than one method.)

The different methods allocate different amounts to depreciation expense over the life of an asset even though the cost, residual value, and useful life are the same. The straight-line method produces uniform charges to depreciation over the life of the asset. Depreciation, under the straight-line method, is considered a function of time. The benefits received from the use of the asset are assumed to be received evenly throughout the asset's life. The units-of-production method produces depreciation charges that may vary significantly from one accounting period to another as the use of the asset varies. Thus, depreciation is considered a function of asset use.

Both the sum-of-years'-digits and the double declining-balance methods charge greater amounts of depreciation to the first year of an asset's life and gradually decreasing charges thereafter. For that reason, these methods are called accelerated depreciation methods. Although depreciation is considered a function of time, the benefits received from the use of the asset are assumed to be greater in the early years of use. As the asset ages, it becomes less efficient and requires increasing expenditures for repairs and maintenance. The combination of decreasing depreciation expense and increasing repair and maintenance expense tends to equalize the total periodic expense of the asset

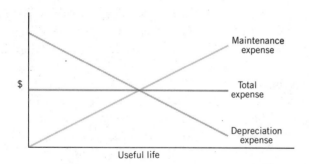

Figure 10-1
Depreciation and
Maintenance Expense

(as illustrated in Figure 10-1), thereby achieving a better matching of expense with revenue.

A comparison of the periodic depreciation charges under the straight-line and accelerated methods for the machine used in previous illustrations is presented in the table below, based as before on a machine cost of $33,000, a residual value of $3,000, and a useful life of five years.

Year	Straight-line	Sum-of-years'-digits	Double Declining-balance
1	$ 6,000	$10,000	$13,200
2	6,000	8,000	7,920
3	6,000	6,000	4,752
4	6,000	4,000	2,851
5	6,000	2,000	1,277
Total	$30,000	$30,000	$30,000

DEPRECIATION FOR INCOME TAX PURPOSES

Accelerated depreciation methods (for example, double declining-balance and sum-of-years' digits) were widely used for income tax purposes for property acquired prior to 1981. *The Economic Recovery Act of 1981* established new depreciation rules for income tax purposes under an *accelerated cost recovery system (ACRS)*. ACRS generally permits more rapid depreciation than was allowed under previous tax laws. This is accomplished by a significant reduction in the number of years over which property is depreciated. For example, buildings that were previously depreciated over 30 or 40 years are now depreciated over 15 years. The new rules apply to property placed in service after 1980. For property placed in service prior to 1981, depreciation must continue to be computed under the old methods.

Acceleration of depreciation for tax purposes results in larger depreciation expense, lower taxable income, and lower income tax payments during the early years of the asset's life. Tax payments are thereby deferred until later years when the lower depreciation charges will result in higher taxable income and higher income taxes. Even though larger tax payments must be made in later years, the company has the interest-free use of the deferred tax dollars until the later years of the asset's life. Accounting for the differences between depreciation expense taken for financial reporting purposes and depreciation expense taken for income tax purposes is discussed in Chapter 28.

REVISION OF DEPRECIATION RATES

Two of the factors used to determine periodic depreciation, residual value and useful life, are based on estimates, which are rarely precise. Small errors in estimates occur frequently and are generally ignored because their effect is not material. Large errors, however, should be corrected when discovered. The generally accepted procedure is to spread the remaining undepreciated cost of the asset over its remaining useful life.[3] Annual depreciation is increased or decreased enough in the current and future periods to offset the effect of the error in prior periods. For example, assume the following case:

Asset cost	$38,000
Estimated useful life	6 years
Estimated residual value	$ 8,000
Accumulated depreciation at the end of four years	$20,000

Early in the fifth year, it is decided that the asset will last for four more years, at which time its residual value is estimated to be $4,000. The amount of depreciation to be recognized in the fifth year and each of the remaining years is $3,500, as computed below:

Undepreciated Cost at the End of the 4th Year ($38,000 − $20,000)	$18,000
Less: Estimated Residual Value	4,000
Remaining Cost to Be Depreciated	$14,000
Useful Life Remaining	4 years
Revised Annual Depreciation ($14,000 ÷ 4 years)	$ 3,500

Sometimes a company changes depreciation methods during a plant asset's useful life. A change in depreciation method—from straight-line to double declining-balance, for example—is called a *change in accounting principle*. The treatment of a change in accounting principle is presented in Chapter 16.

[3]Accounting Principles Board, "Accounting Changes," *APB Opinion No. 20* (New York: AICPA, July 1971), par. 31.

REPORTING DEPRECIATION IN THE FINANCIAL STATEMENTS

For financial reporting purposes, the Accounting Principles Board has ruled that depreciation expense must be disclosed, that both the cost of plant assets and their accumulated depreciation must be shown in the statements by major classes, and that a general description of the depreciation method or methods used must be presented in the financial statements or in statement footnotes.[4] To comply with these requirements, companies generally report depreciation expense as a separate item in the income statement or in a footnote. Plant assets may be reported on the face of the balance sheet or in an accompanying schedule as follows:

Property, Plant, and Equipment:		
Land (at cost)	$164,000	
Buildings at cost ($849,000) less		
Accumulated Depreciation ($231,500)	617,500	
Machinery and Equipment at cost		
($236,400) less Accumulated Depreciation		
($172,600)	63,800	
Total Property, Plant, and Equipment		$845,300

With information presented in this manner and with knowledge of the depreciation methods used, the reader of the balance sheet can determine the approximate age of the plant assets. If the plant assets are old, they are likely to be less efficient in producing future goods and services. In addition, knowledge of the age of the assets is useful in judging the approximate time at which expenditures will be needed to replace them. For example, assuming the use of straight-line depreciation, the machinery and equipment presented above have been used for about 75% of their useful lives. Financing the replacement of these assets will probably be required in the relatively near future.

ACCUMULATED DEPRECIATION DOES NOT REPRESENT CASH

A common misunderstanding of those who have not studied accounting is that accumulated depreciation represents cash that can be used to replace the assets when they wear out. The informed user knows that accumulated depreciation represents nothing more than the portion of an asset's cost that has been transferred to depreciation expense since the asset was acquired. The cash account is not affected by the periodic entries made to transfer the asset's cost to depreciation expense. The accumulated depreciation account is a contra-asset account with a credit balance and, as we have learned, cash is an asset having a debit balance.

---

[4]Accounting Principles Board, "Omnibus Opinion—1967," *APB Opinion No. 12* (New York: AICPA, December 1967), par. 5.

This misunderstanding probably occurs because depreciation expense, unlike most other expenses, does not require a cash outlay in the same period in which the expense is deducted from revenue. As a result, most companies have a net cash inflow from operations (cash receipts from revenues less cash payments for expenses) in excess of reported net income. To illustrate, assume that Beta Company sells services only in exchange for cash and pays cash for all expenses with the exception of depreciation in the same period in which the expense is incurred. During 1984, Beta Company made cash sales of $230,000, paid cash expenses of $170,000, and recognized depreciation expense of $10,000 on equipment purchased with cash in 1982. A comparison of cash flow from operations with net income reported for 1984 is:

	1984 Cash Flow		1984 Net Income	
Cash receipts from sales		$230,000		$230,000
Cash expenses	$170,000		$170,000	
Depreciation expense	–0–	170,000	10,000	180,000
Net cash flow		$ 60,000		
Net income				$ 50,000

Beta Company had a $10,000 greater net cash flow from operations than the amount of net income reported. This results because the depreciation expense deducted in arriving at net income did not require a cash payment in 1984. You might ask, "Isn't the $10,000 cash in the bank account, and couldn't it be used to replace the equipment when it wears out?" The answer is that the $10,000 may or may not be in the bank. It may have been used already, or will be used before the equipment needs replacement, for any of the purposes for which a company normally uses cash. It may be used to pay cash expenses or to pay off long-term debt, for example, or it may be withdrawn by the owners for their personal use.

CAPITAL AND REVENUE EXPENDITURES

Expenditures made to acquire, improve, and maintain plant assets are of two types: capital expenditures and revenue expenditures. **Capital expenditures** are those that add to the utility or usefulness of a plant asset for more than one accounting period either by lengthening the asset's useful life or by increasing its capacity. Examples are expenditures made for building additions, extraordinary repairs, asset replacements, and the installation of escalators to replace stairwells. Capital expenditures are debited to asset accounts and allocated to the current and future periods through depreciation. **Revenue ex-**

penditures are those that benefit the current accounting period only and are debited to expense accounts when incurred. They are called revenue expenditures because they are matched against revenues in the period in which they are made. Ordinary repairs and maintenance are examples.

It is important to distinguish carefully between capital and revenue expenditures because improper treatment affects both the determination of periodic income and balance sheet values. For example, if the cost of equipment (a capital expenditure) is charged to expense when purchased, the net income of the current period is understated and the net income of future periods will be overstated because of the absence of depreciation expense on the asset. In addition, plant and equipment, as well as owners' equity, will be understated on the balance sheet until the asset is disposed of or reaches the end of its useful life.

ORDINARY REPAIRS AND MAINTENANCE

Ordinary repairs and maintenance are those relatively small recurring outlays necessary to keep a plant asset in good operating condition. Buildings need painting and minor repairs to their electrical and plumbing systems. Machines must be lubricated, cleaned, and reconditioned on a regular schedule. Engines require tune-ups and the replacement of small parts. Expenditures for these purposes do not materially add to the economic value or useful life of the asset. Rather, they are made to assure the obtaining of benefits from the asset over its original estimated useful life. Ordinary repairs and maintenance expenditures are therefore matched against revenue of the current period. For example, if a company spent $675 for new tires, a new battery, and an engine tune-up for its delivery truck, the entry would be:

June	6	Repairs and Maintenance Expense	675	
		Cash		675
		To record ordinary repairs on delivery truck.		

EXTRAORDINARY REPAIRS

Extraordinary repairs are major reconditioning and overhaul expenditures made to extend a plant asset's useful life beyond the original estimate. For example, assume a delivery truck was purchased for $14,000 and was estimated to have a useful life of five years with a residual value of $2,000. At the end of the truck's fourth year, its book value is $4,400, as shown below:

Cost	$14,000
Accumulated depreciation (4 × $2,400)	9,600
Book value	$ 4,400

At the beginning of the fifth year, it is decided to replace the truck's engine at a cost of $4,200, after which the truck will last for three more years and have a residual value of $2,000. The entry to record this capital expenditure is:

Jan.	4	Delivery Truck	4,200	
		Cash		4,200
		To record the installation of a new engine.		

Depreciation expense for each of the remaining three years of the truck's life is computed as follows:

Total Cost ($14,000 + $4,200)	$18,200
Accumulated Depreciation	9,600
Book Value	8,600
Less : Estimated Residual Value	2,000
New Depreciable Amount	$6,600
Annual Depreciation Expense ($6,600 ÷ 3 years)	$2,200

Sometimes an extraordinary repair is debited to the accumulated depreciation account rather than to the asset account with the reasoning that the expenditure cancels out some of the depreciation recorded in past periods. The effect of the debit to accumulated depreciation is to increase the book value of the asset, and depreciation expense for each of the remaining years would be computed as illustrated.

PLANT AND EQUIPMENT RECORDS

Plant assets are normally divided into functional groups with a separate general ledger account and accumulated depreciation account provided for each group. For example, a retail furniture company would have separate asset and accumulated depreciation accounts for delivery equipment, office equipment, and store equipment. The company might have several delivery trucks and numerous items of office equipment and store equipment. For example, the Office Equipment account may contain the cost of calculators, chairs, desks, typewriters, and filing cabinets. These items may have been acquired on different dates and will have different useful lives and residual values. In addition, the composition of the group of assets will change over time as individual assets are disposed of and new ones acquired. Because it is impossible to keep all of the detailed information needed for each asset in the general ledger accounts, each plant asset account and its related accumulated depreciation account become control accounts, with the detail about each item maintained in a subsidiary ledger.

Although there are many variations in the form of subsidiary ledgers, one commonly used method consists of a card file with a separate card for each item included in the control account. Each card contains a number that is also placed on the asset itself as a means of identification and to aid in control over the items. To illustrate, assume a simplified case of a company that has two delivery trucks, both purchased on April 1, 1982. The general ledger Delivery Equipment and Accumulated Depreciation control accounts and subsidiary records for these assets are presented in Figure 10-2.

Delivery Equipment   Account No. 216

Date	Explanation	P/R	Debit	Credit	Balance
4/1/82		CD 18	18,400		18,400

Accumulated Depreciation—Delivery Equipment   Account No. 217

Date	Explanation	P/R	Debit	Credit	Balance
12/31/82		GJ 12		2,025	2,025
12/31/83		GJ 29		2,700	4,725
12/31/84		GJ 41		2,700	7,425

PLANT ASSET RECORD

Account No. 216

Item 3/4 Ton Truck   General Ledger Account Delivery Equipment
Serial No. 3AG64243321
Purchased from Bextell Motors
Useful Life 5 years   Estimated Residual Value $1,600
Depreciation per Year $1,200   Depreciation Method straight-line

Date	Explanation	P/R	Asset Dr.	Asset Cr.	Asset Bal.	Dep. Dr.	Dep. Cr.	Dep. Bal.
4/1/82		CD 18	7,600		7,600			
12/31/82		GJ 12					900	900
12/31/83		GJ 29					1,200	2,100
12/31/84		GJ 41					1,200	3,300

Figure 10-2
Plant Asset Records

Figure 10-2
Continued.

PLANT ASSET RECORD

Account No. _____216_____

Item _One-ton Truck_   General Ledger Account _Delivery Equipment_
Serial No. ___4SG7215B4312___
Purchased from _____Bextell Motors_____
Useful Life ___6 years___   Estimated Residual Value ___$1,800___
Depreciation per Year ___$1,500___   Depreciation Method _straight-line_

			Asset			Depreciation		
Date	Explanation	P/R	Dr.	Cr.	Bal.	Dr.	Cr.	Bal.
4/1/82		CD 18	10,800		10,800			
12/31/82		GJ 12					1,125	1,125
12/31/83		GJ 29					1,500	2,625
12/31/84		GJ 41					1,500	4,125

Notice that the account number on the subsidiary ledger cards is the same as the general ledger account number for Delivery Equipment. Notice also that the balance in the general ledger account, Delivery Equipment, is equal to the total of the balances of the asset section of the subsidiary ledger cards. Likewise, the balance in the general ledger account, Accumulated Depreciation—Delivery Equipment, is equal to the sum of the balances of the depreciation section of the subsidiary ledger cards. An inventory of plant assets is taken periodically to maintain control over the assets and to prove the equality of the general ledger accounts and subsidiary records.

The subsidiary ledger cards provide information for the preparation of income tax returns and for supporting insurance claims in the event of loss from theft and casualty. The cards also contain information for preparing year-end adjustments for depreciation and space for entries to record the disposal of the asset. When the asset is disposed of, the asset section of the subsidiary card is credited and the depreciation section is debited, thereby reducing both sections to zero. The card is then removed from the subsidiary ledger and filed in a permanent file for possible future reference.

GLOSSARY

ACCELERATED DEPRECIATION METHOD. Any depreciation method that results in greater depreciation expense in the early years of a plant asset's life than in later years (p. 420).

BOOK VALUE.   The cost of a plant asset minus accumulated depreciation (p. 419).

CAPITAL EXPENDITURE.   An expenditure that adds to the utility or usefulness of a plant asset for more than one accounting period (p. 424).

DOUBLE DECLINING-BALANCE DEPRECIATION.   A depreciation method under which double the straight-line rate is applied to the book value of a plant asset to arrive at annual depreciation expense (p. 419).

DEPRECIATION.   The allocation of a plant asset's cost to the periods benefiting from its use (p. 414).

EXPENDITURE.   A cash outlay or the incurring of a liability to acquire a good or service (p. 410).

FIXED ASSETS.   A term sometimes used to refer to plant assets (p. 409).

IMPUTING INTEREST.   Assigning a portion of the face value of a note to interest when no interest rate is specified or when the interest rate specified is clearly unreasonable (p. 413).

INADEQUACY.   The inability of a plant asset to meet current demand for its product (p. 415).

LUMP-SUM ACQUISITION.   The purchase of a group of plant assets for one total payment (p. 412).

OBSOLESCENCE.   A condition under which a plant asset is out of date and can no longer produce on a competitive basis (p. 415).

RESIDUAL VALUE.   The estimated value of a plant asset at the end of its useful life (p. 415).

REVENUE EXPENDITURE.   An expenditure that benefits the current accounting period only (p. 425).

STRAIGHT-LINE DEPRECIATION.   A depreciation method that allocates an equal amount of a plant asset's cost to each period in its useful life (p. 416).

SUM-OF-YEARS'-DIGITS DEPRECIATION.   A depreciation method under which the cost of a plant asset is allocated to depreciation on a fractional basis. The denominator of the fraction is the sum of the digits in the asset's useful life. The numerators of the fractions are the years remaining in the asset's useful life at the beginning of the period (p. 417).

UNITS-OF-PRODUCTION DEPRECIATION.   A depreciation method under which the cost of a plant asset is allocated to depreciation expense based on the number of production units produced during the period (p. 417).

USEFUL LIFE.   The time period a plant asset is expected to be used to produce goods or services (p. 415).

DISCUSSION QUESTIONS

1. What are plant assets? What is the primary characteristic that distinguishes them from other assets?
2. Why is the cost of a plant asset allocated to accounting periods?
3. In a general sense, what should be included in the cost of a plant asset? Explain which of the following should be included in the cost of equipment: (a) sales tax,

(b) installation charges, (c) freight charges, (d) cost of a permanent foundation, (e) new parts needed to replace those damaged while unloading.

4. Strum Company purchased a piece of open land for speculation purposes. It is expected that the value of the land will increase so that it can be sold in the future at a gain. Where should this land be reported in the balance sheet?

5. Jones Company acquired land, a building, and office equipment for a lump-sum payment of $280,000. Fair values of each asset as determined by an independent appraiser are: land, $84,000; building, $186,000; office equipment, $50,000. How much of the total payment of $280,000 should be allocated to each asset?

6. A $10,000, 12%, 12-month note was exchanged for a machine with a fair value of $10,000 on June 30. What entry should be made on December 31 to accrue interest expense on the note? How would this entry differ if a 12-month, noninterest-bearing note in the amount of $11,200 had been given?

7. Explain what is meant by the term *depreciation* as it is used in accounting.

8. Should depreciation be recorded on a building for a year in which the market value of the building has increased? Explain.

9. What is the difference between obsolescence and inadequacy as it relates to plant assets?

10. What are accelerated depreciation methods? Why are they sometimes used?

11. Explain why accelerated depreciation methods are often used for income tax purposes.

12. What are the main advantage and the main disadvantage of using a units-of-production depreciation method?

13. An asset with a cost of $11,000, a residual value of $1,000, and an estimated life of four years was purchased at the beginning of Year 1. What is the amount of depreciation expense for Years 1 and 2 if the sum-of-years'-digits method is used?

14. What would be the amount of depreciation for Years 1 and 2 for the asset purchased in question 13 if the double declining-balance method were used?

15. What is the sum-of-the-years'-digits of a plant asset with an estimated useful life of 25 years?

16. Explain what the balance in the Accumulated Depreciation—Machinery account represents. How is the account treated in the financial statements?

17. What is meant by the term *book value?* Does a credit to Accumulated Depreciation increase or decrease book value?

18. If a company changes its estimate of the useful life of a plant asset, how should the change be accounted for?

19. What is the distinction between capital expenditures and revenue expenditures? Give an example of each and explain how the accounting treatment is different.

EXERCISES

Exercise 10-1 (Lump-sum Purchase)

Valley Manufacturing Company purchased a building, land, and equipment on July 21 for a cash payment of $1,200,000. Appraised values of the assets on the date of purchase were:

Building	$ 750,000
Land	375,000
Equipment	125,000
Total	$1,250,000

Required:
Compute the amount of cost that should be assigned to each of the assets and prepare a journal entry to record the purchase.

Exercise 10-2 (Determining Cost and Annual Depreciation)
On January 2, 1984, Dexter Company purchased a machine with a list price of $22,500 and credit terms of 2/10, n/30. Payment was made within the discount period and included sales tax of 4% on the net price. Freight costs of $540 and installation costs of $528 were also paid. The machine has an estimated useful life of four years and a residual value at the end of its useful life of $2,400.

Required:
A. Determine the amount that should be debited to the machinery account and prepare a journal entry to record the purchase.
B. Determine the amount of depreciation expense for each of the four years assuming use of:
   1. The straight-line depreciation method.
   2. The double declining-balance method of depreciation.
C. Prepare a journal entry to record depreciation expense for 1985 under the double declining-balance method.

Exercise 10-3 (Acquisition by Issuing a Note Payable)
On February 28, 1984, Trexon Company purchased a machine on credit, giving a $34,000, 12%, 15-month note payable.

Required:
Prepare journal entries to:

A. Record the purchase of the machine.
B. Accrue interest on the note on December 31, 1984.
C. Record payment of the note in 1985.

Exercise 10-4 (Depreciation Methods)
Matthews Company purchased a new machine on January 2, 1984, for $49,000. The machine has an estimated useful life of four years and a residual value of $4,000.

Required:
A. Compute depreciation expense for each year (1984 through 1988) under the double declining-balance method and under the sum-of-years'-digits method.
B. Assume that Matthews Company decided to use the units-of-production depreciation method and that the useful life of the machine is estimated to be 25,000 operating hours. Prepare the journal entry to record depreciation expense on December 31, 1985, if the machine was operated for 7,000 hours during 1985.

Exercise 10-5 (Depreciation Methods)

Canyon Company purchased office equipment on April 1, 1984, for $36,000. The equipment has an estimated useful life of five years and an estimated residual value of $6,000.

Required:

Determine the amount of depreciation expense to be recorded for each of the first two years under the straight-line, double declining-balance, and sum-of-years'-digits depreciation methods assuming that Canyon Company records depreciation expense to the nearest month.

Exercise 10-6 (Revision of Depreciation Rates)

Clayton Company purchased a machine on January 1, 1984, for $34,000. The machine had an estimated useful life of four years and an estimated residual value of $4,000. Clayton Company uses the straight-line depreciation method.

During 1986, following a review of the adequacy of depreciation rates, Clayton Company's controller determined that the machine would have a useful life of four more years (including 1986) and an estimated residual value of $2,000.

Required:

A. Compute the amount of depreciation expense that should be recognized for each of 1984 and 1985.
B. Compute the amount of revised depreciation expense to be recorded for 1986 and each year thereafter.

Exercise 10-7 (Extraordinary Repairs and Revision of Depreciation)

On January 2, 1983, Rader Company purchased for $18,000 a machine with an estimated useful life of five years and an estimated residual value of $3,000. In order to keep the machine running properly, the company has performed regular maintenance and repairs each year since its acquisition. In year 4 (1986), ordinary repairs amounted to $450.

At the beginning of 1987, Rader Company decided to completely overhaul the machine's major operating parts at a cost of $4,800, after which the machine is expected to have an estimated useful life and residual value of four more years and $2,000, respectively. Rader Company uses the straight-line depreciation method.

Required:

Prepare journal entries to record:

A. The purchase of the machine on January 2, 1983.
B. The ordinary repairs on the machine in 1986.
C. The major overhaul of the machine on January 3, 1987.
D. Depreciation expense on the machine on December 31, 1987.

PROBLEMS

Problem 10-1 (Depreciation Methods)

Nu-tech Company recently paid $170,000 for manufacturing equipment, which is expected to have a useful life of five years and a residual value of $20,000. The manager of Nu-tech desires information about the effect that various depreciation methods will have on net income and asks you to prepare a schedule comparing the straight-line, double declining-balance, and sum-of-years'-digits methods of depreciation.

Required:

Prepare a schedule like the following and compute the annual depreciation charge and end-of-year book value for the expected life of the equipment.

	Straight-line		Declining-balance		Sum-of-years'-digits	
Year	Depre-ciation	Book Value	Depre-ciation	Book Value	Depre-ciation	Book Value
Acquisition		$170,000		$170,000		$170,000
1						
2						
3						
4						
5						

Problem 10-2 (Determining Cost of Various Assets)

Weedout Company began operations during 1984. The company had a building constructed and acquired manufacturing equipment during the first six months of the year; manufacturing operations began early in July, 1984. The company's bookkeeper, who was unsure how to treat plant asset transactions, opened a Plant Assets account and debited (credited) that account for all of the expenditures and receipts involving plant assets as presented below:

1. Cost of real estate purchased: Land	$ 86,000
Old Building	41,000
2. Paid for the demolition of the old building to prepare the site for a new building	15,000
3. Paid for delinquent taxes on the property in (1)	8,200
4. Paid fee for title search on property in (1)	1,500
5. Received for sale of salvaged materials from old building	(2,500)
6. Paid architect for designing new building	24,000
7. Paid for a temporary fence around the construction site	3,100
8. Paid excavation costs for new building	12,500
9. Partial payment to building contractor	196,000

10. Paid for construction of parking lot and installation of parking lot lights — 15,900
11. Paid interest on building loan during construction — 18,400
12. Made final payment to building contractor — 260,000
13. Paid for manufacturing equipment — 118,000
14. Paid freight bill on manufacturing equipment — 1,900
15. Paid installation costs of manufacturing equipment — 2,600
16. Paid for removal of temporary fencing around construction site — 1,200
17. Received for temporary fencing materials salvaged — (400)
18. Paid for repair of manufacturing equipment that was damaged during installation — 1,800

Plant Assets account balance — $804,200

Required:

A. Prepare a schedule like the one presented below, analyze each transaction, and enter the payment (receipt) in the appropriate column. Total the columns.

Item	Land	Land Improvements	Building	Manufacturing Equipment	Other

B. Prepare a journal entry to close the $804,200 balance in the Plant Assets account and allocate the transactions to their appropriate accounts.

C. Prepare an entry to record depreciation expense for one-half year on land improvements, building, and manufacturing equipment using straight-line depreciation. Useful lives and residual values are:

	Useful Life	Residual Value
Land improvements	10 years	$ –0–
Building	25 years	40,000
Manufacturing equipment	8 years	20,000

(AICPA adapted)

Problem 10-3 (Comprehensive Problem)

On January 2, 1984, Porter Industries purchased, by exchanging $300,000 cash and a $180,000, 12%, 18-month note payable, assets with the following independently determined appraised values:

	Appraised Value
Building	$320,000
Land	80,000
Machinery and equipment	100,000
Total	$500,000

The estimated useful life of the building is 30 years and its residual value is $20,000.

The $100,000 machinery and equipment amount consists of three machines independently appraised at $30,000 each, and some office equipment appraised at $10,000.

The estimated useful lives and residual values for these assets are:

	Useful Life	Residual Value
Machine 1	6 years	$3,000
Machine 2	9 years	3,000
Machine 3	4 years	4,000
Office equipment	5 years	500

Porter Industries uses the straight-line depreciation method.

Required:

A. Prepare journal entries to record:
  1. The purchase of the assets.
  2. The accrual of interest expense on the note payable on December 31, 1984.
  3. Depreciation expense for the year 1984.
  4. The payment of the note on July 2, 1985.
B. Show how the plant assets would be reported on the December 31, 1984, balance sheet.

Problem 10-4 (Comprehensive Problem)

Over a five-year period, Trent Company completed the following transactions affecting plant assets. The company uses straight-line depreciation on all depreciable assets and records depreciation to the nearest month.

1982

Jan. 3 Purchased a new machine having a cash price of $26,000. A $30,500, 15-month, noninterest-bearing note payable was given in exchange. Freight charges of $340 and installation expenditures of $1,660 were paid in cash. The machine has an estimated useful life of 5 years and a residual value of $3,000.

June 20 Purchased a used delivery truck for $3,600 cash. The truck was repainted at a cost of $250, and a new battery (cost: $50) and tires (cost: $200) were installed. The truck has an estimated useful life of 3 years and an expected residual value of $500.

Dec. 31 Recorded depreciation expense on the assets.

Dec. 31 Amortized discount on the note payable issued on January 3.

1983

Apr. 2 Paid the note payable issued on January 3, 1982.

July 30 Paid for ordinary repairs and maintenance on the machine and truck at a cost of $187.

Dec. 31 Recorded depreciation expense on the assets.

1984

April 9 Installed a fence around the company property at a cost of $4,800. The fence has an estimated useful life of 12 years with no residual value. (Debit the cost to a Land Improvements account.)

Dec. 31 Recorded depreciation expense on the assets.

1985

June   30 Recorded the final depreciation on the delivery truck.

June   30 The company completed construction of a new warehouse. Construction costs incurred (all paid in cash) were: labor, $14,000; materials, $19,000; building permits, $1,400; architectural fees, $1,800; and overhead, $2,300. The warehouse is expected to have a residual value of $3,500 and a useful life of 35 years. (Debit the cost to a Buildings account.)

Dec.   27 Completely overhauled the machine purchased on January 3, 1982, at a cost of $5,000, after which the useful life was estimated to be four additional years. The new residual value was estimated to be $1,000.

Dec.   31 Recorded depreciation expense on the assets.

1986

Dec.   31 Recorded depreciation expense on the assets.

Required:

A. Prepare journal entries to record the transactions of Trent Company.

B. Prepare a schedule showing the cost and accumulated depreciation of each plant asset after recording depreciation on December 31, 1986.

Problem 10-5 (Comprehensive Problem)

Valano Company completed the following transactions during 1984. The company uses sum-of-years'-digits depreciation and records depreciation to the nearest month.

1984

Jan.   6 Purchased a used machine (No. 1) for $7,000 cash. The machine was painted and reconditioned at a cost of $800. During installation, one of the major operating parts was dropped and had to be repaired at a cost of $250, paid in cash. The machine is expected to have a useful life of three years and a residual value of $600.

Mar.   7 Purchased land and a building with the intention of tearing down the building and constructing a new office complex. Valano Company paid $110,000 for the property plus a broker's commission of $15,000 and title search fees of $4,000.

Mar.   20 Paid Tex Demolition Company $9,000 to demolish the building acquired on March 7.

Apr.   10 The company's parking lot was paved at a cost of $16,500. The lot has an estimated useful life of 10 years with no residual value.

June   23 Purchased for cash a machine (No. 2) with a list price of $18,000. The seller granted a 2% cash discount. A sales tax of 5% on the net purchase price and freight charges of $478 were also paid. The machine's useful life is estimated to be 10 years and its residual value $2,500.

Nov.   1 Purchased for $27,000 cash a machine (No. 3) with an estimated useful life of 4 years and a residual value of $3,000.

Required:

A. Prepare journal entries to record the transactions of Valano Company.

B. Prepare an entry to record depreciation expense on December 31, 1984.

Problem 10-6 (Plant Asset Records)

Selected transactions of Dawson Company are given below. The company uses straight-line depreciation and computes depreciation expense to the nearest month.

1984

Jan.   12 Purchased from Fairchild Sales Company a bottle washer (Serial No. 78135A) for $24,000 cash. The estimated life of the machine is 5 years and its residual value is expected to be $4,000.

Apr.   10 Purchased from Goodrich Distributors a dryer (Serial No. YA1341) for $13,000 cash. The machine has a useful life of 6 years and a residual value of $1,000.

Required:

A. Prepare journal entries to record the purchase of the assets and to record depreciation expense on December 31, 1984 and 1985.

B. Open a Machinery account (No. 230) and an Accumulated Depreciation—Machinery account (No. 231), and prepare subsidiary plant asset records for the two assets. Post the journal entries to the general ledger accounts and to the subsidiary plant asset records.

ALTERNATE PROBLEMS

Problem 10-1A (Determining Cost of Various Assets)

Zing Company was organized early in 1984. During the first nine months, the company acquired real estate for the construction of a building and other facilities. Operating equipment was purchased and installed and the company began operating activities in October, 1984. The company's accountant, who was not sure how to record some of the transactions, opened a Plant Property account and recorded debits and (credits) to the account as follows:

1. Cost of real estate purchased as a building site	$189,000
2. Paid architect's fee for the design of a new building	18,500
3. Paid for the demolition of an old building on the building site purchased in (1)	21,000
4. Paid delinquent property taxes on the real estate purchased as a plant site in (1)	3,000
5. Paid excavation costs for the new building	22,000
6. Made the first payment to the building contractor	243,000
7. Paid for equipment to be installed in the new building	137,500
8. Received from the sale of salvaged materials from the demolition of the old building	(6,700)

9. Made final payment to the building contractor	262,000
10. Paid interest on building loan during construction	14,800
11. Paid freight bill on equipment purchased	2,600
12. Paid installation costs of equipment	4,900
13. Paid for repair of equipment damaged during installation	2,800
Plant property account balance	$914,400

Required:

A. Prepare a schedule like the one below, analyze each transaction, and enter the payment (receipt) in the appropriate column. Total the columns.

Item	Land	Building	Equipment	Other

B. Prepare a journal entry to close the $914,400 balance in the Plant Property account and allocate the transactions to the appropriate accounts.

C. Prepare an entry to record depreciation expense from October 1 to December 31, 1984. Useful lives and residual values are:

Building	30 years and $20,300
Equipment	5 years and $5,000

Zing Company uses the straight-line depreciation method.

Problem 10-2A (Depreciation Methods)

Prince Company purchased new equipment on July 1, 1984, at a cost of $280,000. The equipment has a useful life of four years and an estimated residual value of $20,000.

Required:

Assuming a fiscal year ending December 31, compute the amount of depreciation expense for each year (1984 through 1988) with each of the following methods:

A. Straight-line.
B. Sum-of-years'-digits.
C. Double declining-balance.

Problem 10-3A (Extraordinary Repairs and Revision of Depreciation)

Rebo Company purchased machinery on January 2, 1983, at a cost of $184,220. The machinery is depreciated by the straight-line method over a useful life of four years with a residual value of $24,220.

On January 3, 1986, extraordinary repairs were made to the machinery at a cost of $38,500. Because of these extensive repairs, the useful life was reestimated at three years from January 3, 1986, and the residual value was reestimated at $12,720.

Required:

Prepare journal entries to record:

A. The purchase of the machinery on January 2, 1983.
B. Depreciation expense for 1983, 1984, and 1985.

C. The expenditure for repairs on January 3, 1986.

D. Depreciation expense for 1986.

Problem 10-4A (Comprehensive Problem)

Over a four-year period, Samson Company completed the following transactions affecting plant assets. The company uses straight-line depreciation and records depreciation to the nearest month.

1982

Jan.   3   Purchased a new machine having a cash price of $30,000. A $34,500 18-month, noninterest-bearing note payable was given in exchange. Freight charges of $290 and installation expenditures of $1,250 were paid in cash. The machine has an estimated useful life of 4 years and a residual value of $1,540.

July   2   Purchased a used delivery truck for $4,500. Cash expenditures were made to repaint the truck at a cost of $400 and for new tires costing $300. The truck has an estimated useful life of 4 years and an expected residual value of $1,000.

Dec. 31 Recorded depreciation expense on plant assets.

       31 Amortized discount on the note payable issued on January 3.

1983

July   3   Paid the note payable issued on January 3, 1982.

     30 Paid for ordinary repairs and maintenance on the machine and truck at a cost of $230.

Dec. 31 Recorded depreciation expense on plant assets.

1984

June 26 Installed a fence around the company property at a cost of $7,800. The fence has an estimated useful life of 15 years with no residual value. (Debit the cost to a Land Improvements account.)

Dec. 31 Recorded depreciation expense on plant assets.

1985

Jan.   5   Completely overhauled the machine purchased on January 3, 1982, at a cost of $7,000, after which the useful life was estimated to be 3 more years. The new residual value was estimated to be $500.

Dec. 31 Recorded depreciation expense on plant assets.

Required:

A. Prepare journal entries to record the transactions of Samson Company.

B. Prepare a schedule showing the cost, accumulated depreciation, and book value of each plant asset after recording depreciation on December 31, 1985.

Problem 10-5A (Correcting Errors)

At the end of Beacon Company's fiscal year, December 31, 1983, the following items must be resolved before financial statements can be prepared:

1. On January 1, 1983, Beacon Company purchased a used machine for $46,000 cash. The cost was debited to the Machinery account. Prior to use, additional cash

expenditures were made for (a) painting and repairing the machine, $3,800, and (b) installing and testing the machine, $4,200. These additional expenditures were debited to Repairs and Maintenance Expense. The repairs and installation were completed on April 1, 1983, and the machine was placed into use. The machine has an estimated useful life of five years with a residual value of $4,000. Beacon Company uses straight-line depreciation and records depreciation to the nearest month.

2. A small building and land were purchased on January 2, 1983, for $110,000 cash, which was debited to the Land account. The appraised values of the building and land were $90,000 and $30,000, respectively. The building has an estimated useful life of 20 years with a residual value of $2,500. Beacon Company uses straight-line depreciation for buildings.

3. A new truck was purchased on September 1, 1983, Beacon Company giving cash of $2,000 and a 12-month noninterest-bearing note payable in the amount of $8,200. The Trucks account was debited for $10,200. The truck had a cash value of $9,000 on September 1. The truck has an estimated life of five years with a residual value of $1,000 and is depreciated by the double declining-balance method.

Required:

A. Prepare journal entries on December 31, 1983, to correct the accounts.

B. Prepare journal entries to record depreciation expense after the corrections in requirement A have been made.

Problem 10-6A (Plant Asset Records)

Selected transactions affecting the Machinery account of Rocktown Company are given below. The company uses double declining-balance depreciation and computes depreciation expense to the nearest month.

1984
Jan.   12 Purchased from Beech Company a dye machine (Serial No. 6913A1) for $36,000 cash. The estimated life of the machine is 5 years and its residual value is expected to be $6,000.

June   30 Purchased from Park & Sons a drill press (Serial No. X12344) for $41,000 cash. The machine has a useful life of 4 years and a residual value of $3,000.

Required:

A. Prepare journal entries to record the purchase of the assets and to record depreciation expense on December 31, 1984 and 1985.

B. Open a Machinery account (No. 202) and an Accumulated Depreciation—Machinery account (No. 203), and prepare subsidiary plant asset records for the two assets. Post the journal entries to the general ledger accounts and to the subsidiary plant asset records.

CASE FOR CHAPTER 10

(Annual Report Analysis)

Refer to the financial statements of General Motors and Modern Merchandising, Inc. in the appendix and answer the following questions:

1. How much was total depreciation expense reported by General Motors for 1981? By Modern Merchandising, Inc.?
2. What depreciation method is used by General Motors? By Modern Merchandising, Inc.?
3. What was the book value of General Motor's Land improvements and Furniture and Office equipment on December 31, 1981?
4. What was the book value of Owned property and equipment of Modern Merchandising, Inc. on February 2, 1980?
5. Can you determine the approximate useful lives of General Motor's plant and equipment assets? How about Modern Merchandising, Inc.?
6. Can you determine the book value of Modern Merchandising, Inc.'s buildings on January 31, 1981?

CHAPTER 11
PLANT AND EQUIPMENT DISPOSALS: NATURAL RESOURCES AND INTANGIBLES

OVERVIEW AND OBJECTIVES

This chapter covers the accounting procedures followed when disposing of plant assets and those followed for the acquisition and allocation of natural resources and intangible assets. When you have completed the chapter, you should understand:

- How to record the discarding, sale, or exchange of plant assets (pp. 442–449).
- The nature of composite-rate depreciation (pp. 449–451).
- How to account for natural resources (pp. 451–453).
- How to account for the various kinds of intangible assets (pp. 453–460).

When a plant asset is no longer useful, it is discarded, sold, or traded in on a new asset. The entry to record the disposal varies with the nature of the disposal. In all cases, however, it is necessary to remove the book value of the asset from the accounts. This is accomplished by debiting the appropriate accumulated depreciation account for the amount of depreciation accumulated on the asset to the date of its disposal and crediting the asset account for its cost.

A plant asset should not be removed from the accounts merely because it has become fully depreciated. If the asset is still used, its cost and accumulated depreciation should remain on the books until it is sold, discarded, or traded in. If the asset is removed from the accounts, there will be no evidence of its continued use and the control provided by the subsidiary ledger will be eliminated. Of course, no additional depreciation can be recorded on the asset because its cost has been fully allocated to expense.

DISCARDING PLANT ASSETS

When a plant asset is no longer useful to the business and has no sales value, it is discarded or scrapped. If the asset is fully depreciated, there is no loss on disposal. For example, if a machine with a fully depreciated cost of $7,000 is discarded because it is worthless, the entry is:

Jan.	2	Accumulated Depreciation—Machinery	7,000	
		Machinery		7,000
		Discarded a fully depreciated machine.		

Sometimes a plant asset is discarded as worthless before it is fully depreciated, in which case the undepreciated cost of the asset represents a loss on disposal. If the machine above was discarded when it had an accumulated depreciation balance of $6,500, a $500 loss would be recorded when the asset is removed from the accounts:

Jan.	2	Accumulated Depreciation—Machinery	6,500	
		Loss on Disposal of Plant Assets	500	
		Machinery		7,000
		Discarded a partially depreciated machine.		

If expenditures are incurred for the removal of the asset, they increase the loss on disposal. Assuming the company had to pay $400 to have the machine dismantled and hauled away, the discarding entry would be:

Jan.	2	Accumulated Depreciation—Machinery	6,500	
		Loss on Disposal of Plant Assets	900	
		Machinery		7,000
		Cash		400
		Discarded a partially depreciated machine and paid disposal costs of $400.		

In the illustrations above, the asset was disposed of at the beginning of the year. When plant assets are disposed of during the year, an entry should be made to record depreciation expense for the fractional portion of the year prior to disposal, regardless of the method of disposal. If the monthly depreciation on the machine above was $100, for example, and the machine was discarded on March 1, the entry to record depreciation for the two months prior to disposal would be:

Mar.	1	Depreciation Expense	200	
		Accumulated Depreciation—Machinery		200
		To record depreciation on discarded machine.		

The entry to record the discarding of the machine would then be:

Mar.	1	Accumulated Depreciation—Machinery	6,700	
		Loss on Disposal of Plant Assets	300	
		Machinery		7,000
		Discarded a partially depreciated machine.		

SALE OF PLANT ASSETS

A second means of disposing of a plant asset is to sell it. If the selling price exceeds the book value of the asset, there is a gain on disposal. If the selling price is less than book value, there is a loss. When material in amount, these gains and losses should be reported separately on the income statement as a part of income from operations. Immaterial gains and losses are generally offset and the net gain or loss is included on the income statement with other income or other expense.

To illustrate the various possibilities for reporting a gain or loss, assume that a machine with a cost of $22,000, an estimated residual value of $2,800, and a useful life of eight years was acquired on January 3, 1979. After the adjusting entry for depreciation was made on December 31, 1983, the accounts showed the following balances:

Machinery $22,000
Accumulated Depreciation—Machinery 12,000*
*($22,000 − $2,800) ÷ 8 = $2,400
$2,400 × 5 years = $12,000

The machine was sold on August 1, 1984.

Before recording the sale, seven months' depreciation should be recorded for the period of January through July 1984:

Aug.	1	Depreciation Expense	1,400	
		Accumulated Depreciation—Machinery		1,400
		($2,400 × 7/12)		
		To record depreciation to the date of		
		sale.		

After recording depreciation to the date of sale, the book value of the machine is $8,600 ($22,000 − $13,400). Entries to record the sale of the machine under three different assumptions as to selling price are presented below:

1. *The machine is sold for $8,600.*

Aug.	1	Cash	8,600	
		Accumulated Depreciation—Machinery	13,400	
		Machinery		22,000
		Sold a machine for its book value.		

Because the machine was sold for its book value, no gain or loss is recognized. The cash received is recorded and the cost of the machine and its related accumulated depreciation are removed from the accounts.

2. *The machine is sold for $9,300.*

Aug.	1	Cash	9,300	
		Accumulated Depreciation—Machinery	13,400	
		Machinery		22,000
		Gain on Disposal of Plant Assets		700
		Sold a machine for more than its book		
		value.		

Since the machine was sold for more than its book value, a gain is recognized equal to the difference between the selling price ($9,300) and the book value ($8,600) of the machine.

3. *The machine is sold for $8,200.*

Aug.	1	Cash	8,200	
		Accumulated Depreciation—Machinery	13,400	
		Loss on Disposal of Plant Assets	400	
		Machinery		22,000
		Sold a machine for less than its book		
		value.		

Because the machine was sold for less than its book value, a loss is recognized equal to the difference between the selling price ($8,200) and the book value ($8,600) of the machine.

EXCHANGING PLANT ASSETS

Another means of disposing of a plant asset is to trade it for another asset. Such exchanges occur frequently with machinery, automobiles, and equipment. A trade-in allowance for the old asset is deducted from the price of the new asset, and the balance is paid in accordance with the normal credit terms. Accounting procedures used for the exchange of assets depend upon whether the assets exchanged are similar or dissimilar.

EXCHANGING SIMILAR ASSETS

Similar assets are those that are of the same general type and that perform the same function in a business. The exchange of a truck for another truck or a typewriter for another typewriter are examples. The entry to record an exchange of similar assets will vary according to whether there is a book gain or a book loss on the exchange. When the trade-in allowance exceeds the book value of the asset traded in, a book gain results. If the trade-in allowance is less than the book value of the asset traded in, a book loss results. Book losses on an exchange of similar assets are recognized immediately. Book gains are not recognized, and the recorded value of the new asset is decreased by the amount of the unrecognized gain.[1]

Recognition of a Book Loss

To illustrate the recognition of a book loss on an exchange, assume that a machine with a cost of $22,000 and accumulated depreciation to date of exchange of $15,000 is traded for a new machine with a cash price of $30,000. A trade-in allowance of $4,000 is received and the remaining $26,000 is paid in cash. The excess of the book value of the old machine ($7,000) over the trade-in allowance received ($4,000) results in a book loss of $3,000 and the exchange is recorded as follows:

Jan.	3	Machinery	30,000	
		Accumulated Depreciation—Machinery	15,000	
		Loss on Disposal of Plant Assets	3,000	
		Machinery		22,000
		Cash		26,000
		Exchanged an old machine plus cash for a new machine.		

---

[1]Accounting Principles Board, "Accounting for Nonmonetary Transactions," *APB Opinion No. 29* (AICPA: New York, May 1973), par. 22.

This entry records the new machine at its cash price of $30,000, the amount that would have been paid in a straight cash transaction and therefore the maximum amount that should be debited to the asset account. The entry also removes the old machine and its related accumulated depreciation from the accounts and recognizes a loss on the exchange. The immediate recognition of book losses on exchanges of similar assets is justified under the accounting principle of conservatism.

Nonrecognition of a Book Gain

When there is a book gain on the exchange of similar assets, accounting rules require that the gain *not* be recognized at the time of the exchange. The amount of the gain serves to reduce the recorded value of the asset received, and the new asset is recorded at its cash price less the nonrecognized gain. Another way of viewing this is that the new asset is recorded at the book value of the old asset plus cash paid in acquiring the new asset. To illustrate, assume that a trade-in allowance of $9,500 rather than $4,000 was received for the old machine in the preceding illustration and the balance of $20,500 was paid in cash. Although the exchange results in a book gain of $2,500 ($9,500 trade-in allowance minus $7,000 book value), the gain is not recognized and the exchange is recorded as follows:

Jan.	3	Machinery	27,500	
		Accumulated Depreciation—Machinery	15,000	
		Machinery		22,000
		Cash		20,500
		Exchanged an old machine plus cash for a new machine.		

The recorded amount of the new machine is its cash price of $30,000 less the unrecognized gain of $2,500. Or, looked at another way, the recorded amount is equal to the book value of the old machine ($7,000) plus the amount of cash paid in the exchange ($20,500). The recorded amount of $27,500 is the machine's "cost" and is the amount that will be used in recording depreciation over its useful life. The nonrecognition of the gain at the time of exchange is actually a *postponement* of the gain. Total depreciation expense over the life of the new machine will be $2,500 less and net income $2,500 greater than if depreciation were based on the $30,000 cash price of the machine. Thus the gain is recognized gradually over the life of the new machine in the form of lower annual depreciation expense.

Two important facts support the nonrecognition of book gain. First, the amount of the gain is difficult to measure objectively because the price of the new asset may have been set higher than the amount of cash the seller would realistically expect to receive in a cash sale (the cash price) in order to offer an inflated trade-in allowance. Anyone who has traded in an automobile on a new one is fully aware of this practice. Second, as expressed by the Accounting Principles Board, "revenue should not be recognized merely because one productive asset is substituted for a similar productive asset but rather should be considered to flow from the production and sale of the goods or services to which the substituted productive asset is committed."[2] Thus the exchange is considered a continuation of a past transaction rather than the creation of a new one.

EXCHANGING DISSIMILAR ASSETS

When assets that perform different functions in a business are exchanged, both gains and losses are recognized immediately. Examples are the exchange of machinery for land or the exchange of a building for equipment. These exchanges are considered new transactions. The asset and related accumulated depreciation accounts for the old asset are removed from the books, the asset received is recorded at its fair market value, and gain or loss is recognized for the difference between the book value of the old asset and the fair market value of the new asset. To illustrate, assume that Dell Company exchanged a building with a cost of $125,000, accumulated depreciation of $60,000, and a fair market value of $90,000 for construction equipment with a fair market value of $90,000. The exchange would be recorded as follows:

Jan.	5	Construction Equipment	90,000	
		Accumulated Depreciation—Buildings	60,000	
		Buildings		125,000
		Gain on Disposal of Plant Assets		25,000
		Exchanged a building for construction equipment.		

Note that the construction equipment received is recorded at its fair market value ($90,000); the cost of the building ($125,000) and its related accumulated depreciation ($60,000) are removed from the accounts; and a gain is recognized in the amount of $25,000, which is the difference between the fair market value of the equipment received ($90,000) and the book value of the building given in exchange ($65,000).

If the fair market value of the construction equipment received were $50,000 rather than $90,000, a loss would be recognized and the entry would be:

[2]*Ibid.*, par. 16.

Jan.	5	Construction Equipment	50,000	
		Accumulated Depreciation—Buildings	60,000	
		Loss on Disposal of Plant Assets	15,000	
		Buildings		125,000
		Exchanged a building for construction		
		equipment.		

Notice in this case that a loss of $15,000 results because the fair market value of the equipment received ($50,000) is less than the book value ($65,000) of the building given.

FEDERAL INCOME TAX RULES FOR EXCHANGES OF PLANT ASSETS

Federal income tax laws provide that neither gain nor loss is recognized for income tax purposes when an asset is traded for another similar asset. The cost basis of the new asset is the sum of the book value of the old asset plus additional consideration given in the exchange. Thus the treatment of a non-recognized gain is consistent with the acceptable method for financial reporting purposes. Rules differ in the case of a trade-in involving a loss, however. Financial accounting rules require the immediate recognition of the loss, whereas income tax regulations do not permit a loss recognition.

To illustrate, assume that a machine with a cost of $22,000 and accumulated depreciation of $15,000 was traded for a new machine with a cash price of $30,000. A trade-in allowance of $4,000 was received and the remaining $26,000 was paid in cash. For income tax purposes, the new machine has a depreciation basis of $33,000, which is equal to the book value of the old machine ($7,000) plus the $26,000 cash paid. The $3,000 difference between the book value of $7,000 and the trade-in allowance of $4,000 is not recognized immediately for tax purposes but is deferred and recognized over the useful life of the new machine. Depreciation expense for tax purposes will be based on $33,000 rather than on the cash price of $30,000. Thus the $3,000 loss will be recognized over the life of the new machine through higher depreciation charges.

COMPOSITE-RATE DEPRECIATION

In previous illustrations, depreciation was computed on each individual asset. An alternative approach, called composite-rate depreciation, is often used in practice by companies with many similar assets. Under this approach, a single average depreciation rate is applied to the cost of a functional group of assets such as office equipment or store equipment. The average depreciation rate is computed by dividing the sum of the annual depreciation charges for each asset in the group by the total cost of the assets. For example, the computation of the composite rate for office equipment might be made as follows:

Asset	Cost	Salvage Value	Depreciable Cost	Useful Life	Annual Depreciation
Chair	$ 150	$ 22	$128	8	$ 16
Desk	470	70	400	10	40
Typewriter	850	150	700	5	140
Typewriter	780	100	680	5	136
Calculator	560	60	500	4	125
File Cabinet	390	70	320	10	32
Total	$9,750				$731

$$\frac{\$731 \text{ annual depreciation}}{\$9,750 \text{ cost}} = 7.5\% \text{ composite rate}$$

Although the total cost of office equipment will change as new assets are added and old assets retired, the general mix is assumed to remain relatively the same. Additions and retirements are assumed to occur uniformly throughout the year; the composite rate is therefore applied to the average of the beginning and ending balances in the account for the year. If the office equipment account had a $9,750 balance at the beginning of the year and a $12,500 balance at the end of the year, the year-end adjustment for depreciation would be $834 ($9,750 + $12,500 = $22,250 ÷ 2 = $11,125 × .075), and the following depreciation entry would be prepared:

Dec.	31	Depreciation Expense	834	
		Accumulated Depreciation—Office Equipment		834
		To record depreciation on office equipment.		

When assets within the composite group are disposed of, no gain or loss is recognized. The cost of the asset is credited to the asset account and accumulated depreciation is debited for the difference between the asset's cost and the amount realized from the sale. For example, assume a typewriter with a cost of $850 is sold for $300. The following entry would be made to record the disposal:

Jan.	10	Cash	300	
		Accumulated Depreciation—Office Equipment	550	
		Office Equipment		850
		To record the sale of a typewriter.		

When an asset in the group is traded in on a new one, the transaction is recorded in a similar manner. If the typewriter above was traded for a new one with a fair value of $1,000, a trade-in allowance of $400, and $600 paid in cash, the entry would be:

Jan.	10	Office Equipment	1,000	
		Accumulated Depreciation—Office Equipment	450	
		Office Equipment		850
		Cash		600
		Traded in an old typewriter for a new one.		

NATURAL RESOURCES

Natural resources are often called *wasting assets*. Examples are mineral deposits, oil and gas reserves, and standing timber. In their natural state they represent inventories that will be consumed in the future by mining, pumping, or cutting to convert them into various products. For example, a copper mine is a deposit of unmined copper ore, an oil field is a pool of unpumped oil, and standing timber is an inventory of uncut lumber. When mined, pumped, or cut they are converted into products for sale to customers. Until converted they are noncurrent assets shown on the balance sheet under such descriptive titles as Mineral Deposits, Oil and Gas Reserves, and Timber Lands.

Natural resources are recorded in the accounts at their cost, which may include costs of exploration and development in addition to the purchase price. As the resource is converted by mining, pumping, or cutting, the asset account must be reduced proportionately. The carrying value of a copper mine, for example, is reduced for each ton of copper ore mined. As a result, the original cost is gradually transferred from the asset account to a depletion account to be matched against the revenue produced from the copper produced and sold.

DEPLETION

The periodic allocation of the cost of natural resources to the units removed is called depletion. Depletion is computed in the same way depreciation is under the units-of-production method. The cost of the natural resource (minus residual value) is divided by the estimated number of units available, such as tons of copper ore, to arrive at a depletion rate per unit. This depletion rate is then multiplied by the number of units removed during the period to determine the total depletion charge for the period. If a copper mine is purchased for $10,000,000, has an estimated residual value of $1,000,000, and contains an estimated 4,500,000 tons of copper ore, the depletion rate per ton is $2 ($10,000,000 − $1,000,000 = $9,000,000/4,500,000 tons). If 400,000 tons of ore are mined during the first year, the depletion charge for the year is $800,000, and is recorded as follows:

Dec.	31	Depletion of Copper Mine	800,000	
		Accumulated Depletion—Copper Mine		800,000
		To record depletion for the year.		

On the balance sheet at the end of the first year, the copper mine would be reported as follows:

Mineral Deposits	$10,000,000	
Less: Accumulated Depletion	800,000	$9,200,000

Depletion represents a part of the cost of the resource extracted or product produced. It is possible that a natural resource extracted in one year may not be sold until a later year. In that case, the unsold portion represents inventory and should be reported as a current asset on the balance sheet. For example, if only 300,000 tons of the copper ore in the illustration were actually processed and sold during the year, $600,000 would be reported on the income statement as depletion (included in cost of goods sold) and the remaining $200,000 would be shown as Inventory of Copper Ore on the balance sheet. In other words, depletion is recorded in the year in which the copper ore is mined and is then allocated to cost of goods sold and inventory based on the number of units sold and the number of units retained in inventory by the following entry:

Dec.	31	Cost of Goods Sold	600,000	
		Inventory of Copper Ore	200,000	
		Depletion of Copper Mine		800,000
		To allocate depletion of copper mine.		

Of course, the cost of the inventory on hand at year-end also would include labor costs and other extraction costs.

DEPRECIATION OF RELATED PLANT ASSETS

The extraction of natural resources often requires the construction of on-site buildings and the installation of equipment that may be useful only at that particular location. These plant assets should be depreciated over their useful lives or over the life of the natural resource, whichever is shorter. Most often, depreciation is computed on the same basis as depletion by use of the units-of-production depreciation method.

To illustrate, assume that mining equipment with a cost of $450,000 and a normal useful life of 15 years is installed at the copper mine in the preceding illustration. The copper ore is being mined at a rate that will exhaust the mine in approximately 10 years. At the end of that time, the equipment will be abandoned. Thus the useful life of the equipment is only 10 years. In this case, depreciation on the equipment should be based on the life of the mine and computed in the same way as depletion by use of the units-of-production method. The depreciation rate per ton would be $.10 ($450,000 ÷ 4,500,000 tons), and the depreciation charge for mining equipment in the first year would be $40,000 ($.10 × 400,000 tons). The depreciation entry would be:

Dec.	31	Depreciation of Equipment	40,000	
		Accumulated Depreciation—Equip.		40,000
		To record depreciation for the year.		

Like depletion, depreciation is allocated to expense and inventory based on the number of units sold and the number of units retained in inventory.

INTANGIBLE ASSETS

Long-lived assets that are useful to a business but have no physical substance are called **intangible assets.** Their value is derived from the long-term legal and economic rights obtained from ownership. The primary types are patents, copyrights, leaseholds, and goodwill. Some assets that lack physical substance, such as accounts receivable and prepaid expenses, are not classified as intangible assets because they are short-term. Consequently, intangible assets are those that are used in the operation of a business but have no physical substance and are long-term in nature.

The principles followed in accounting for intangible assets are similar to those used to account for plant assets. Accounting for intangibles is somewhat more difficult, however, because the lack of physical substance makes the identification, valuation, and estimation of useful lives more difficult. Intangible assets are recorded initially at their acquisition cost. Some intangibles like trademarks and trade names may have been acquired without incurring any cost. Although they may be extremely valuable to the business—even essential to profitable operations—they should not be included in the balance sheet unless they have an acquisition cost. Intangible assets are normally shown in a separate section of the balance sheet immediately after the plant and equipment section and are reported at cost or the portion of their cost that has not yet been amortized.

AMORTIZATION

The allocation of the cost of intangible assets to the periods benefiting from their use is called amortization. Amortization is therefore similar to depreciation of plant assets. Unlike depreciation, however, an accumulated amortization account normally is not used and the amortization entry consists of a debit to amortization expense and a credit directly to the intangible asset account.

For many years accountants supported the view that some intangible assets had unlimited lives and therefore should not be amortized. At the same time, many businesses elected to write their intangible assets down to the nominal figure of $1 on the basis of conservatism and the inability to determine a reasonable useful life. Accounting rules today require that all intangible assets be amortized over their useful lives, with a maximum amortization period of 40 years.[3] The arbitrary write-down of intangible assets is not permitted. Significant changes in estimated useful life are accounted for by spreading the unamortized cost of the intangible assets over their remaining useful lives. The straight-line method of amortization is generally used to account for intangible assets.

PATENTS

A patent is an exclusive right, granted by the federal government, to produce and sell a particular product or to use a specific process for a period of 17 years. The reason for issuing patents is to encourage the invention of new machines, processes, and mechanical devices.

American businesses spend billions of dollars yearly on research and development for new products and new processes. These expenditures are vital in contributing to economic growth and increasing productivity. Before 1975, some companies charged research and development expenditures to expense when incurred. Other companies capitalized such expenditures and amortized them over future periods. Because of this lack of uniformity, accounting rules were established requiring that all research and development expenditures not reimbursable from governmental agencies or other parties must be charged to expense in the period incurred.[4]

[3]Accounting Principles Board, "Intangible Assets," *APB Opinion No. 17* (AICPA: New York, August 1970), par. 27, 29.
[4]Financial Accounting Standards Board, "Accounting for Research and Development Costs," *Statement of Financial Accounting Standards No. 2* (FASB: Stamford, Conn., October 1974), par. 12.

Since research and development expenditures are charged to expense as incurred, often the only additional costs involved in a patent developed internally are the legal and filing fees paid to obtain the patent. Because these fees are usually relatively small, they are generally also charged to expense as incurred. When a patent is purchased from its inventor or holder, rather than developed internally, the purchase price should be debited to the Patents account. In addition, any legal costs of a successful defense of the patent (which occurs quite frequently) should also be debited to the Patents account.

For example, if a patent was purchased for $80,000 on January 4, the entry would be:

Jan.	4	Patents	80,000	
		Cash		80,000
		To record the purchase of a patent.		

Although a patent grants exclusive rights to the holder for 17 years, new inventions often make the patent obsolete sooner. The cost of a patent should therefore be amortized over its estimated useful life with a maximum of 17 years. If the patent recorded above is expected to have a useful life of eight years, the following adjusting entry is made each year to record amortization:

Dec.	31	Amortization Expense	10,000	
		Patents		10,000
		To record amortization of patents.		

Amortization expense is reported on the income statement as an expense.

COPYRIGHTS

A copyright is an exclusive right, granted by the federal government, to reproduce and sell an artistic or published work. The exclusive right exists for the life of the creator plus 50 years. If a copyright is purchased, the purchase price is debited to a copyrights account and amortized over its useful life, not to exceed 40 years. As with a patent, the cost of a successful legal defense of a copyright should be debited to the Copyrights account. Because it is difficult to determine how long benefits will be received, most copyrights are amortized over a relatively short period. Often the only additional cost to the creator of an artistic work is the fee paid for the copyright because research and development costs have been expensed. Since the fee is nominal, it is often charged to expense immediately.

TRADEMARKS AND TRADE NAMES

The exclusive right to trademarks and trade names can be obtained by registering them with the federal government. The main cost of developing trademarks and trade names lies in advertising, which should be charged to expense in the period incurred. Other costs such as registration fees and design costs should be capitalized and amortized if their amount is material. Because these costs are often small, they are generally charged to expense when incurred. If a trademark or trade name is purchased, however, the purchase price may be significant and its cost should be debited to the appropriate intangible asset account and amortized over its useful life, not to exceed 40 years.

LEASEHOLDS

Many companies rent property under a contract called a lease. The owner of the property is the lessor and the person or company obtaining the rights to possession and use of the property is the lessee. The rights of possession and use granted to the lessee by the contract are called a leasehold.

Some leases provide for regular monthly rent payments and the lease can be canceled at any time by either the lessor or lessee. In these cases, a leasehold account is not used and the monthly rent payments are debited to rent expense. Sometimes a lease agreement provides that the rent for the entire period of the lease must be paid in advance or a lump-sum payment is made in advance in addition to periodic rental payments. In these cases, it is necessary to allocate the payments to the proper accounting periods. If the lease covers a short time period, the prepayments are debited to a current asset account, Prepaid Rent, and transferred to rent expense as illustrated in earlier chapters. If the lease covers a long time period, the prepayment is debited to a Leasehold account and is generally classified on the balance sheet as an intangible asset or as a deferred charge. In either case, the prepayment is allocated to rent expense as the lease benefits are received.

For example, assume an agreement was made to lease a portion of a building from Baxter Realty for four years beginning on January 1, 1984. The lease agreement requires a prepayment of $40,000 plus an annual payment of $20,000 on December 31 of each year. The prepayment would be recorded as follows:

Jan.	1	Leasehold	40,000	
		Cash		40,000
		To record a four-year building lease prepayment.		

On December 31 of each year the additional payment would be recorded and the Leasehold (prepayment) amortized as follows:

Dec.	31	Rent Expense	30,000	
		Leasehold		10,000
		Cash		20,000
		To record rent payment and the amortization of a leasehold.		

At times, the life of the lease covers essentially the full useful life of the leased property. In these cases, the lease is treated as the equivalent of an installment purchase of property and the lessee records both the leased asset (such as Leased Machinery) and an equal lease liability. Both the asset and the liability are recorded at the discounted present value of the future lease payments required under the lease contract. Accounting for this type of lease is discussed further in Chapter 17.

LEASEHOLD IMPROVEMENTS

Long-term leases often require that special improvements to the leased property must be paid for by the lessee. Examples are partitions and permanent store fixtures installed in a leased building. These **improvements** become a permanent part of the property and cannot be removed by the lessee at the end of the lease. As a result, the cost of these improvements is debited to a Leasehold Improvements account and amortized to expense over the life of the improvements or the life of the lease, whichever is shorter. The amortization entry consists of a debit to Rent Expense and a credit to Leasehold Improvements.

To illustrate, if $10,000 was paid to install partitions and permanent fixtures in a building leased for five years, the payment would be recorded as:

Jan.	10	Leasehold Improvements	10,000	
		Cash		10,000
		To record payment for improvements to		
		leased building.		

The Leasehold Improvements would then be amortized each year as follows:

Dec.	31	Rent Expense	2,000	
		Leasehold Improvements		2,000
		To record amortization of leasehold		
		improvements.		

FRANCHISES

A **franchise** is a right granted by a company or governmental body to conduct business at a specified location or in a specific geographical area. Examples are the right to operate a fast-food operation such as McDonald's or Kentucky Fried Chicken and the right to operate a municipal bus line or private water company. The initial cost of a franchise may be substantial and should be capitalized and amortized over the term of the franchise. If the franchise is perpetual, it should be amortized over a period not to exceed 40 years. If initial franchise costs are small, they may be expensed when incurred. Periodic annual payments under a franchise agreement should be expensed.

GOODWILL

The term goodwill is used by accountants and the public to mean various things. It is often thought of as the favorable reputation of a business among its customers. From an accounting standpoint, however, goodwill has a special meaning not limited to good customer relations. Goodwill is the potential of a business to earn a rate of return on its net assets (assets minus liabilities) in excess of the normal rate of return in the industry in which the business operates. It arises from many factors, including customer confidence, superior management, favorable location, manufacturing efficiency, good employee relations, and competitive advantages. A successful business continually builds goodwill as it develops these factors, but the expenditures made in doing so generally cannot be specifically identified with the development of goodwill. Thus, goodwill is often called the ''unidentifiable'' intangible represented by the overall ability of a business to earn above normal returns on its net identifiable assets (net assets other than goodwill).

To illustrate the meaning of above-normal earnings, assume that two businesses in the same industry are offered for sale and that the normal return on the fair value of net assets in the industry is 15%. Data for the two companies follow:

	Able Company	Bay Company
Fair market value of net assets	$5,000,000	$5,000,000
Normal rate of return for the industry	× 15%	× 15%
Normal earnings	750,000	750,000
Actual average earnings for the past five years	900,000	750,000
Average earnings in excess of normal	$ 150,000	$ –0–

A potential buyer would be willing to pay $5,000,000 for Bay Company because it is earning a normal return on the fair value of its net assets. Thus, assuming the same level of earnings in the future, the buyer would receive a 15% return on the purchase price of $5,000,000. Although Able Company has the same fair value of net assets, a potential buyer would be willing to pay more for Able Company than for Bay Company because Able Company has been obtaining above-normal earnings that should continue for some time into the future.

Although a potential buyer would be willing to pay more for Able Company than for Bay Company, the data above do not tell us how much more the buyer would be willing to pay. The actual amount paid for goodwill will be the amount the buyer is willing to pay and the seller is willing to accept. Several approaches to estimating the amount of goodwill are available to the buyer and seller as a basis for negotiation.

1. The buyer and seller may agree on an arbitrary amount for goodwill. For example, if the buyer offers $5,400,000 for Able Company and the seller accepts the offer, the payment for goodwill is $400,000, the excess of the purchase price over the fair market value of the net assets. Thus the buyer and the seller are placing an arbitrary value of $400,000 on goodwill.
2. Goodwill may be valued arbitrarily at some multiple of excess earnings. For example, if excess earnings are expected to continue for about four years into the future, goodwill may be valued at four times the average above-normal earnings, or $600,000 (4 × $150,000) in our illustration. If agreed upon by the buyer and seller, the purchase price for Able Company would be $5,600,000, of which $600,000 represents payment for goodwill.
3. Goodwill may be valued by capitalizing the average above-normal earnings at the average rate of return for the industry. Capitalizing above-normal earnings means dividing those earnings by the normal rate of return. For example, if Able Company is expected to continue to have $150,000 of excess earnings each year, these excess earnings may be capitalized at 15% and a $1,000,000 value may be placed on goodwill ($150,000 ÷ 15% = $1,000,000). This approach values the goodwill at the amount that would have to be invested at the normal rate of return in order to earn the extra $150,000 each year ($1,000,000 × 15% = $150,000). This is the most theoretically correct approach if excess earnings are expected to continue indefinitely. However, because this will seldom occur, the excess earnings are often capitalized at a higher capitalization rate to reflect the limited life of the goodwill. For example, if the excess earnings of Able Company are capitalized at 30%, goodwill is valued at $500,000 ($150,000 ÷ 30%).

Regardless of the approach used to value goodwill, its recorded value will always be determined in the final analysis by the amount the buyer is willing to pay and the seller is willing to accept. *Goodwill is recorded in the accounts only when it has been purchased.* Because goodwill generally cannot be purchased or sold separately, this usually occurs only when a business is purchased in its entirety. The purchase price of the business is assigned first to the fair values of the identifiable assets acquired and any remainder of the purchase price is recorded as goodwill.

Many businesses have goodwill that has been developed internally by establishing good customer relations, acquiring or training superior management, and obtaining the other factors that contribute to above-normal earnings. This internally developed goodwill is not recorded in the accounts, however, because the expenditures made to develop it have been charged to expense in the periods incurred.

As with other intangible assets, goodwill is considered by accountants to have a limited life. Goodwill must therefore be amortized to expense over its useful life, not to exceed a maximum period of 40 years.

GLOSSARY

AMORTIZATION. The allocation of the cost of intangible assets to the periods benefiting from their use (p. 454).

COMPOSITE-RATE DEPRECIATION. A depreciation method under which a single average depreciation rate is applied to the cost of a functional group of assets (p. 449).

COPYRIGHT. An exclusive right granted by the federal government to reproduce and sell an artistic or published work (p. 455).

DEPLETION. The periodic allocation of the cost of natural resources to the units removed (p. 451).

FRANCHISE. A right granted by a company or governmental body to conduct business at a specified location or in a specific geographical area (p. 457).

GOODWILL. The ability of a business to earn a rate of return in excess of the normal rate of return in an industry (p. 458).

INTANGIBLE ASSETS. Long-lived assets that are useful to a business but have no physical substance (p. 453).

LEASE. A contract for the rental of property (p. 456).

LEASEHOLD. The rights of possession and use of property granted under a lease contract (p. 456).

LEASEHOLD IMPROVEMENTS. Permanent improvements to leased property made by the lessee (p. 457).

LESSEE. The person or company obtaining the rights to possession and use of leased property (p. 456).

LESSOR. The owner of property leased to others (p. 456).

PATENT. An exclusive right granted by the federal government to produce and sell a particular product or process for a period of 17 years (p. 454).

DISCUSSION QUESTIONS

1. Accounting for the disposal of a plant asset varies with the nature of the disposal. However, it is necessary to do one thing in all cases. What is this? How is it accomplished?
2. When a plant asset is sold for cash, how is the gain or loss measured? How is the gain or loss reported in the financial statements?
3. What entry should be made prior to the disposal of a plant asset in the middle of the year?

4. A factory machine and $8,000 cash are exchanged for a delivery truck. How should the cost of the delivery truck be determined for financial accounting purposes?

5. A duplicating machine with a cost of $12,000 and accumulated depreciation of $8,000 is traded for a new improved duplicating machine with a cash price of $17,000. Cash of $11,000 is also given. What is the cost of the new machine for financial accounting purposes? For federal income tax purposes?

6. What logic supports the nonrecognition of book gains on the exchange of similar assets?

7. What is composite-rate depreciation?

8. At what amount are natural resources recorded in the accounts? What is the expense from the extraction of natural resources called? How is it computed?

9. Connor Coal Company recognizes $2 of depletion for each ton of coal mined. If 400,000 tons of coal are mined but only 300,000 tons are sold during the current year, how much should be charged for depletion expense for the year?

10. What are intangible assets? What are the most common types?

11. A building with an estimated life of 30 years is constructed on the site of a silver mine. The silver ore is expected to be entirely extracted over a period of 20 years. Assuming the building will be abandoned after all the silver ore is extracted, over what time period should the building be depreciated? What depreciation method should probably be used?

12. What is amortization? In general, what should be the length of the amortization period? What amortization method is generally used?

13. Several years ago Baxter Company purchased for $170,000 a patent for the manufacture of special "seal tight" plastic containers. After five years, the manufacture of these containers was discontinued because of the development of a new, improved container by a competitor. Baxter Company is continuing to deduct amortization expense of $10,000 per year based on a patent life of 17 years, which the president of Baxter Company says is required by generally accepted accounting standards. Do you agree?

14. What are leasehold improvements? Over what time period should they be amortized? Why?

15. What is goodwill from an accounting standpoint? When and in what amount is it recorded in the accounts? Is it necessary to amortize goodwill?

EXERCISES

Exercise 11-1 (Discarding Plant Assets)
Clark Company discarded the following machines as worthless.

Machine	Cost	Accumulated Depreciation Jan. 2, 1984	Removal Expense Paid	Date of Purchase	Date of Disposal
1	$4,800	$4,800	–0–	1/2/80	1/2/84
2	5,000	4,500	$300	6/30/79	1/2/84
3	8,000	7,000	–0–	6/30/80	4/1/84

Depreciation expense was recorded last on December 31, 1983.

Required:
Prepare separate entries to record the disposal of the machines.

Exercise 11-2 (Sale of Plant Assets)

On January 3, 1979, Joslen Company paid $16,500 for a machine with an estimated useful life of 10 years and a residual value of $1,500. On December 31, 1983, accumulated depreciation on the machine was $7,500. The machine was sold on May 31, 1984.

Required:
A. Prepare an entry to record depreciation expense on the machine for the five months in 1984. Use the straight-line depreciation method.
B. Prepare an entry to record the sale of the machine on May 31, 1984 assuming a selling price of:
1. $8,000.
2. $8,900.

Exercise 11-3 (Exchange of Similar Assets)

On January 3, 1984, a company exchanged a machine with a cost of $18,000 and accumulated depreciation of $13,000 for a new similar machine with a cash price of $24,000.

Required:
A. Prepare an entry to record the exchange of the machines for financial accounting purposes assuming a trade-in allowance of $4,000 was received for the old machine and the balance of $20,000 was paid in cash.
B. Prepare an entry to record the exchange of machines for financial accounting purposes assuming a trade-in allowance of $7,000 was received for the old machine and the balance of $17,000 was paid in cash.

Exercise 11-4 (Exchange of Dissimilar Assets)

A company exchanged machinery with a cost of $100,000 and accumulated depreciation of $60,000 for a parcel of land.

Required:
Prepare an entry to record the exchange assuming:

A. The fair value of the land was $50,000.
B. The fair value of the land was $32,000.

Exercise 11-5 (Depletion of Natural Resources)

Western Zinc Mine was purchased for $29,000,000, has an estimated residual value of $2,000,000, and contains an estimated 10,000,000 tons of zinc ore. Mining equipment with an estimated useful life of 15 years was installed at a cost of $1,200,000. The ore is being extracted at a pace that will exhaust the mine in about 12 years, after which the equipment will be abandoned.

Required:

A. Prepare entries to record depletion of the mine and depreciation of the mining equipment for the first year assuming that 820,000 tons of ore were mined and sold.

B. Prepare a partial balance sheet showing how the zinc mine and the mining equipment would be reported at the end of the first year.

Exercise 11-6 (Composite-rate Depreciation)

Woodward Company uses the composite-rate method to record depreciation of its store equipment. On January 1, the company owned the following store equipment:

Item	Cost	Residual Value	Useful Life
Display cases	$26,000	$3,000	10 years
Cash registers	19,000	5,000	5 years
Shopping carts	14,000	2,000	6 years
Shelving	22,000	1,200	8 years
Display racks	9,000	1,000	4 years
Total	$90,000		

Required:

A. Compute the composite rate for depreciating the store equipment.

B. Prepare the entry to record depreciation expense on December 31 assuming the store equipment account had a balance of $104,000 at year-end.

C. Prepare an entry to record the sale of a display case for $1,200. The case had an original cost of $1,900.

D. Prepare an entry to record the exchange of a cash register with an original cost of $4,000 for a new cash register with a cash price of $6,000. The company received a trade-in allowance of $1,500 for the old register and paid the balance of $4,500 in cash.

Exercise 11-7 (Goodwill)

LaRue Company is considering the purchase of Retsin Company, which produces a product that LaRue uses in its manufacturing process. Relevant data for Retsin Company is:

Fair market value of net assets	$1,000,000
Normal rate of return in the industry in which Retsin Company operates	15%
Actual average annual earnings for the past five years	$ 180,000

Required:

Determine the total price LaRue Company would pay for Retsin Company under each of the following assumptions:

A. LaRue will pay an amount equal to five years' above-normal earnings for Retsin Company's goodwill.

B. Above-normal annual earnings are to be capitalized at 30% to determine the amount to be paid for goodwill.

C. Actual average annual earnings are to be capitalized at 15% to determine the total purchase price.

PROBLEMS

Problem 11-1 (Exchanges and Disposals of Plant Assets)

Brent Company entered into the following transactions during 1984:

Jan.	4	Discarded a machine that cost $5,000 and had accumulated depreciation of $4,600. Disposal costs of $100 were incurred.
March	29	Sold for $10,000 a machine that had cost $23,000 on January 2, 1980. The machine's estimated useful life and residual value were five years and $3,000, respectively. Accumulated depreciation on the machine through December 31, 1983 was $16,000.
April	1	Exchanged a machine with a cost of $30,000 and accumulated depreciation to the date of exchange of $21,000 for a new similar machine with a cash price of $40,000. A trade-in allowance of $10,000 was received for the old machine and the remainder of the purchase price was paid in cash.
July	1	Exchanged a parcel of land that had cost $30,000 for machinery with a fair market value of $55,000.
Sept.	30	Exchanged a building with a cost of $100,000 and accumulated depreciation to the date of exchange of $70,000 for a machine with a fair market value of $25,000.
Oct.	31	Sold for $18,000 cash a machine that cost $60,000 on November 1, 1979. The machine had an estimated useful life of six years and a residual value of $6,000 when purchased. On December 31, 1983, straight-line depreciation of $9,000 was recorded. No depreciation has yet been recorded for 1984.
Dec.	31	Recorded depletion of the company's mine. The mine was purchased on January 1, 1984, for $30,000,000. On the date of purchase, the mine was estimated to contain 10,000,000 tons of ore and to have a residual value of $2,000,000. One million tons of ore were mined during 1984.

Required:

Prepare journal entries to record the above transactions.

Problem 11-2 (Intangible Assets)

The following transactions and events of Baxter Industries occurred during the current year.

1. The company's copper mine produced 800,000 tons of ore this year. The mine, which was purchased last year for $16,000,000, has an estimated residual value of $800,000 and is estimated to contain about 7,600,000 tons of ore. Production is expected to continue at about the same level as the current year.

2. A patent with an estimated useful life of 12 years was purchased from its inventor for $120,000 in November of last year.

3. Mining equipment with a cost of $760,000 was installed at the copper mine [discussed in (1) above] shortly after the mine was purchased. The equipment has a normal useful life of 12 years with no salvage value.

4. Timber rights were purchased for $500,000. The stand of timber is estimated to contain about 1,000,000 board feet. One hundred thousand board feet of timber was cut this year.

5. A four-year lease agreement was signed by the company at the end of last year, requiring that rent for the entire period in the amount of $100,000 be paid in advance.

6. In early July of this year, the company made some improvements to the property leased in (5) above in the amount of $17,500. The improvements are estimated to have a useful life of five years.

7. In late June of this year, the company purchased a franchise from a regional restaurant chain for $120,000. The franchise is to be amortized over 15 years.

8. On October 2 of the current year the company purchased a highly profitable local engineering firm for $1,900,000. The fair value of the net identifiable assets of the firm was $1,500,000. Goodwill is to be amortized over its expected life of 10 years.

Required:

Prepare separate journal entries to record amortization, depletion, and depreciation for the current year ending December 31.

Problem 11-3 (Exchanges of Similar Assets)

The beginning balance in the Machinery account and credits to the account for various machinery disposals during the year are presented in the Machinery account below:

Machinery

1/1/84 balance	430,500	1/5/84 Sold machine No. 102	11,000
1/11/84	?	1/8/84 Sold machine No. 94	8,000
1/14/84	?	1/11/84	10,000
4/2/84	?	1/14/84	24,000
8/30/84	?	2/26/84 Sold machine No. 98	19,000
		4/2/84	54,000
		6/30/84 Sold machine No. 104	9,500
		8/30/84	5,500

Four exchange transactions took place during 1984 as indicated below:

Jan. 11 Exchanged an old machine and $13,000 cash for a similar machine with a cash price of $18,000. The old machine had a cost of $10,000 and accumulated depreciation of $7,000.

Jan. 14 A machine with a cost of $24,000 and accumulated depreciation of $20,000 was traded for a similar machine having a cash price of $36,000. A trade-in allowance of $3,000 was received, with the balance paid in cash.

April 2 A machine with a cost of $54,000 and accumulated depreciation of $40,000 on December 31, 1983, was exchanged for a new similar machine with a cash price of $75,000. A trade-in allowance of $10,000 was received and the balance was paid in cash. Monthly depreciation on the old machine was $300.

Aug. 30 A machine with a cost of $5,500 and a book value at the date of exchange of $1,600 was traded in for a new similar machine with a cash price of $7,000. Received a trade-in allowance of $2,000 and paid the remaining $5,000 in cash.

Required:

A. Determine the amount that should be debited to the machinery account for each of the exchanges and reproduce the Machinery account showing its ending balance.

B. Assuming that the composite-rate depreciation method is used with a composite rate of 8%, prepare the journal entry to record depreciation expense for 1984.

C. Determine the cost for income tax purposes of the four machines acquired during 1984.

Problem 11-4 (Goodwill)

Harry Bensen, who recently received an inheritance from his grandmother's estate, quit his high school coaching job and began a search for a business that he would purchase and operate. He found what he believed was an ideal business for his background, Sunrise Sporting Goods, which had been earning an average of $65,000 per year over the last four years.

Harry has a copy of Sunrise's current balance sheet as shown below:

Current Assets:			
Cash		$ 28,000	
Inventory		76,000	
Total Current Assets			$104,000
Long-term Assets:			
Land		32,000	
Building	$149,000		
Less: Accumulated Depreciation	37,000	112,000	
Equipment	124,000		
Less: Accumulated Depreciation	38,000	86,000	
Total Long-term Assets			230,000
Total Assets			$334,000
Liabilities:			
Accounts Payable			$ 16,000
Mortgage Payable			85,000
Total Liabilities			101,000
Melvin Akers, Capital			233,000
Total Liabilities and Owner's Equity			$334,000

Harry Bensen and Melvin Akers agree that the book values of assets and liabilities are equal to their fair market values with the exception of land, which has a fair market value of $80,000, and inventory, which has a fair market value of $68,000. Harry proposes to purchase the assets (except for cash) and assume the liabilities of Sunrise.

Required:
A. Determine the fair value of the net assets of Sunrise.
B. What is the average rate of return Sunrise has earned on its net assets as determined in (A)?
C. Determine the amount Harry will pay for Sunrise assuming he is willing to pay for goodwill:
   1. Four times average earnings in excess of an 18% return on the net assets acquired.
   2. Average earnings in excess of an 18% return on net assets acquired capitalized at 30%.

Problem 11-5 (Correcting Errors)
The following errors were made and discovered during the current year:

1. Depreciation of machinery, $2,140, was incorrectly credited to Accumulated Depreciation—Buildings.
2. A machine with a cost of $22,500 and accumulated depreciation to the date of sale of $16,000 was sold for $8,000. The sale was recorded by a debit to cash and a credit to machinery for $8,000.
3. Property taxes of $6,420 were paid and debited to Property Tax Expense. Of this amount, $3,600 represented delinquent taxes from previous years on land purchased during the current year.
4. Delivery equipment, purchased on July 1 for $7,900, was debited to the Purchases account. The equipment has a useful life of four years and an estimated residual value of $900. The straight-line depreciation method is used for delivery equipment.
5. The cost of installing lighting in the company parking lot, $12,000, was charged to Maintenance Expense on January 4. The lights have a useful life of eight years and no residual value. Assume straight-line depreciation.
6. A machine with a cost of $26,000 and accumulated depreciation to the date of exchange of $19,000 was exchanged on December 23 for a new similar machine with a cash price of $35,000. A trade-in allowance of $9,000 was allowed on the old machine. The bookkeeper made the following entry:

Machinery	35,000	
Accumulated Depreciation—Machinery	19,000	
Machinery		26,000
Cash		26,000
Gain on Exchange		2,000

Required:
Prepare journal entries to correct the errors assuming the books have not been closed for the current year ending December 31.

Problem 11-6 (Comprehensive Review Problem)

Feron Company completed the following transactions over a period of several years:

1983

Jan.   2   Purchased land and a building for $350,000 cash. The land and building had appraised values at that time of $100,000 and $300,000, respectively.

March.   20   Paid $32,500 to Re-Nu Company for renovation costs on the building acquired on January 2. Feron Company opened for business on March 25. The building has an estimated life of 25 years and an expected residual value of $20,000. Assume straight-line depreciation.

Dec.   31   Recorded depreciation expense on the building.

1984

May   21   Paid $2,642 to repair damage to the building caused by a windstorm.

Dec.   31   Recorded depreciation expense on the building.

1985

Jan.   6   Paid $54,250 for an addition to the building. The addition is expected to increase the useful life to 30 years from the date of the addition and to increase the building's residual value to $30,000.

Dec.   31   Recorded depreciation expense on the building.

1986

Oct.   4   The land and building were sold for $432,000 cash.

Required:

A. Prepare journal entries to record the transactions.

B. Open general ledger accounts for Land, Buildings, and Accumulated Depreciation—Buildings, and post the relevant portion of the entries to these accounts.

ALTERNATE PROBLEMS

Problem 11-1A (Plant Asset Disposals)

During 1984, Jax Company disposed of four different plant assets. On January 1, 1984, the accounts showed the following:

Asset	Cost	Residual Value	Estimated Life	Accumulated Depreciation
Truck No. 4	$18,000	$3,000	5 years	$12,000
Truck No. 6	24,000	4,000	4 years	15,000
Machine A	42,000	8,000	10 years	23,800
Machine B	36,000	6,000	15 years	21,000

Jax Company depreciates its trucks and machines by the straight-line method and records depreciation to the nearest month. Assets were disposed of as follows:

Truck No. 6, which was not insured, was completely destroyed by fire on January 6, 1984. A towing company was paid $600 to remove the truck and to clean up any debris.

Truck No. 4 was traded for a new truck on July 3, 1984. The new truck had a cash price of $26,000. The old truck plus cash of $19,500 were given in exchange.

Machine A was sold for $17,000 cash on October 1, 1984.

Machine B was traded for a new similar machine with a cash price of $41,000 on December 22, 1984. The old machine plus cash of $30,500 were given in exchange.

Required:
Prepare all journal entries needed to account for the above transactions.

Problem 11-2A (Various Methods of Disposing of a Plant Asset)
On January 2, 1981, Mason Company purchased a truck for $19,000. The truck had an estimated life of five years and a residual value of $4,000. Straight-line depreciation is used.

Required:
Assuming the truck is to be disposed of on July 1, 1984:

A. What entry should be made to record depreciation prior to the disposal?
B. Prepare journal entries to record the disposal of the truck under each of the following assumptions:
 1. The truck is sold for $9,000 cash.
 2. The truck is sold for $7,500 cash.
 3. The truck and cash of $12,000 are exchanged for a new truck with a cash price of $22,400.
 4. The truck was completely destroyed by fire and cash of $7,000 was received from the insurance company.
 5. The truck and cash of $10,000 are exchanged for a new truck with a cash price of $16,300.

Problem 11-3A (Intangibles)
The following transactions and events affect the accounts of Dawn Company for the current year:

1. A patent with an estimated useful life of 10 years was purchased for cash of $375,000 on January 3 of last year.
2. On January 8 of the current year Dawn Company paid $54,000 in legal fees for the successful defense of a patent infringement suit against the patent purchased in (1) above.
3. On January 10 of the current year, Dawn Company signed a contract to lease a small warehouse from Ajax Company. The lease is for five years and required an

advance payment of $100,000 plus a $40,000 cash payment at the end of each year.

4. On February 6 of the current year, Dawn Company purchased a coal mine for $6,400,000. Of the total purchase price, $5,200,000 was assigned to the coal mine and the remaining $1,200,000 was assigned to mining machinery. The mine has a residual value of $500,000 and contains an estimated 10,000,000 tons of coal. The mining machinery is expected to be useful for the entire life of the mine and will be abandoned when the coal deposits are depleted. During the current year, 1,500,000 tons of coal were mined.

5. Improvements were made to the leased warehouse [(3) above] on June 30 of the current year at a cost of $27,000. The estimated life of the improvements is eight years.

Required:

A. Prepare journal entries to record the expenditures made during the current year.

B. Prepare journal entries to record amortization, depletion, and depreciation for the current year. Record to the nearest month.

Problem 11-4A (Intangibles)

Morley Company has four different intangible assets at the end of 1984. Facts concerning each are:

1. *Copyright.* On January 3, 1984, the company purchased a copyright for $87,000. The remaining legal life of the copyright was 22 years, and it is expected to have a useful life of 15 years to Morley Company with no residual value.

2. *Franchise.* On April 2, 1984, Morley Company purchased a franchise to distribute a new product for a 10-year period with no right of renewal. Cost of the franchise was $60,000.

3. *Patent.* Morley Company purchased a patent on July 1, 1984, from Bay Company for $128,100. The patent had been registered initially on January 1, 1978, and is expected to be useful to Morley Company until the end of its legal life.

4. *Goodwill.* Morley Company began operations on January 2, 1980, by purchasing another company for a total cash payment of $389,000. Included in the purchase price was a payment of $80,000 for goodwill. The president of Morley Company believes that ''the goodwill is such an important long-term asset of the company that it should last for 100 years.''

Required:

A. Prepare journal entries to record the acquisition of intangible assets during 1984.

B. Prepare journal entries for each intangible asset that are necessary at the end of the annual accounting period on December 31, 1984.

Problem 11-5A (Correcting Errors)

During an audit of Lever Company at the end of 1984, the following errors made in 1984 were discovered:

1. Store fixtures with a cost of $12,000 and accumulated depreciation to the date of sale of $8,500 were sold for $1,200 cash. The sale was recorded by a debit to Cash and a credit to Store Fixtures for $1,200.

2. The $9,000 cost of installing a fence around the office building was charged to Maintenance Expense on July 1. The fence has a useful life of 10 years and no residual value. Assume straight-line depreciation.
3. The $16,700 cost of a truck purchased on January 4 was inadvertently debited to the Purchases account. The truck has a useful life of five years and is to be depreciated by the double declining-balance method with a residual value of $2,200.
4. On July 1, land with a cost of $26,000 was exchanged for a machine having a cash value of $48,000. The machine has a useful life of eight years and an estimated residual value of $4,000. The exchange was recorded by a debit to Machinery and a credit to Land for $26,000. Machinery is depreciated using the straight-line method.

Required:

A. Prepare journal entries that should be made to correct the accounts at December 31, 1984 before the adjusting entries are made. Assume closing entries have not yet been made.
B. Prepare adjusting entries on December 31, 1984, after the corrections in (A) have been made.

CASE FOR CHAPTER 11

(Annual Report Analysis)

Refer to the financial statements in the appendix and answer the following questions:

1. With reference to Modern Merchandising, Inc.
   a. What is the nature of the intangible assets reported?
   b. Are intangible assets being amortized?
   c. Can you determine the amortization period?
2. With reference to General Motors
   a. General Motors reports only one type of intangible asset. What is it?
   b. Can you determine the amount of amortization expense for 1981?
   c. Can you determine the amortization period?
   d. What do you think is the most logical amortization period?
3. With reference to Mary Moppet's Day Care Schools, Inc.
   a. What is the nature of the intangible assets reported?
   b. Are the intangibles being amortized?
   c. If intangibles are being amortized, over what time period?
   d. What amortization method is used?

CHAPTER 12
PAYROLL SYSTEMS

OVERVIEW AND OBJECTIVES

This chapter describes the essential features of a payroll system. When you have completed the chapter, you should understand:

- The importance of accounting for labor costs and related payroll taxes (pp. 472–473).
- How internal control is applied to payroll accounting (pp. 473–474).
- The determination of an employee's gross earnings (pp. 475–476).
- The different deductions from gross earnings (pp. 476–479).
- The computation of an employee's net earnings (pp. 479–480).
- Which payroll taxes are withheld from employees' earnings and which are paid by the employer (pp. 476–478, 480–481).
- The basic records and procedures used in a payroll system (pp. 481–486).
- How to prepare journal entries for payroll accounting (pp. 483, 488).

The combined cost of labor and related payroll taxes represents a major expense of operating every business. Norfolk and Western Railway Company reported in 1980 that it employed 23,051 employees with payroll expenses amounting to approximately $615 million, or 39 percent of sales. Ford Motor Company had 426,700 employees worldwide in 1980 with total labor costs of over $12 billion. In addition to the dollar amounts involved, accounting for payroll expenses is complicated by the impact of many federal and state laws. These laws require employers to maintain certain payroll records, collect and pay taxes on a timely basis, and comply with specific minimum standards for the amount of compensation paid and hours worked.

Another important consideration of payroll accounting is the increasing popularity of such fringe benefits as insurance premiums and retirement plans. The substantial dollar amounts involved have added to the need for detailed payroll records. Large and small businesses alike must operate a sound payroll system that will ensure that each payroll is paid on time, federal and state laws are complied with, and sound internal control is maintained to prevent errors or fraudulent activities. A payroll system is an integral part of the accounting system discussed in Chapter 6. Like the accounting system itself, a good payroll system must be capable of receiving input data (such as employees' names, social security numbers, pay rates, and hours worked), processing the data, and generating output (such as payroll checks, payroll records, and reports to taxing authorities). This chapter describes the essential features of an effective payroll system.

IMPORTANCE OF INTERNAL CONTROL

Sound internal control, as discussed in Chapter 7, is a fundamental part of an effective payroll system. This is particularly important because payroll fraud has been experienced by many businesses in the past. Common payroll frauds, often substantial in amount, have been overpaying employees' compensation, continuing former employees on the payroll after termination, making payments to fictitious employees, overstating payroll deductions, and issuing duplicate checks. In a small business with only a few employees, the owner may be able to handle all the payroll procedures personally. As a business grows, various payroll duties are delegated to several people, thereby introducing the possibility of fraud. The likelihood of error also increases with the separation of responsibilities for payroll functions.

To achieve sound internal control over payroll procedures, a business should separate these duties: hiring employees, timekeeping, preparing checks and maintaining payroll records, and distributing checks to employees. In small businesses, two or more of these functions may have to be combined because of the lack of personnel. However, some separation of duties is essential even in small businesses to satisfy the basic characteristics of sound internal control. Internal control over payroll should begin when a new employee is hired and continue until the employment is terminated. Written notice of employment, job description, amount of earnings, and deduction authorizations originate in the personnel department at the time of employment. Each new employee must complete an **Employee's Withholding Allowance Certificate, Form W-4,** such as the one shown on page 479, to indicate the appropriate number of withholding allowances. Payroll deductions for such items as union dues, insurance, retirement plan, or uniforms must be authorized by each employee. Subsequent changes in pay rate, job assignment, or payroll deductions are recorded by the personnel department. The employee information maintained by the personnel department will be sent to the payroll department to place a new employee on the payroll and assure that he or she is paid properly.

Some type of document must be utilized to record the amount of time for which the employee will be paid. Most businesses use a time clock to record the number of hours worked by each employee paid on an hourly basis. Employees clock in when work begins and clock out at the end of the work day. The manager responsible for the related work activity is in charge of the time cards used for timekeeping purposes. In large businesses, a timekeeping department may supervise the time-recording process. A weekly or monthly time report is usually maintained for salaried personnel. At the end of each payroll period, the documents used to record employees' time are reviewed by the responsible managers to verify their accuracy and then are sent to the payroll department.

Ideally, employees in the payroll department should have no payroll responsibilities other than checking the accuracy of the timekeeping documents, preparing payroll checks, and maintaining payroll records. Timekeeping forms are combined with information from the personnel department to process the payroll. In many cases, the payroll is processed with a computer, using the procedures discussed in Chapter 6. Payroll checks are prepared, and individual employee records of earnings and deductions are updated. The payroll checks are signed by the treasurer of the company or some other specified officer. A separate bank account should be used to control payroll expenditures in most cases, as will be discussed later. The final step in the payroll process is the distribution of paychecks. This should be accomplished by someone who is independent of the payroll function and is not responsible for supervising employees. In large businesses, this person often is called the paymaster. By separating the various duties involved in the payroll function for internal control purposes, collusion on the part of two or more people is necessary for fraudulent activity.

EMPLOYER–EMPLOYEE RELATIONSHIP

Businesses obtain services from their own employees and from outsiders who are independent contractors. In the operation of a payroll system, a firm is concerned only with payments made as compensation to employees and not with disbursements to independent contractors. We thus need to be able to recognize the essential features of an employer–employee relationship. In general, such a relationship exists when the business or person for whom the service is performed (the employer) has the right to direct and control not only the results to be accomplished but also how the results are to be accomplished by another person (the employee). In contrast, an independent contractor chooses the specific means used to perform services and is at liberty to work for other businesses or persons at the same time.

A bookkeeper and the controller of a business are employees; a CPA performing an audit for the firm is an independent contractor. As such, the CPA is not an employee because he or she will determine the scope of the audit work and will not be subject to the control of the client. The fees paid to independent contractors are kept separate from compensation to employees and, to repeat, are not part of the payroll system.

GROSS EARNINGS

The first step in computing the amount paid to a particular employee during a given payroll period is determining his or her **gross earnings** (also called gross compensation) in the form of wages or salary. The term **wages** is used for compensation paid to an employee on the basis of an hourly rate or piecework (this means that a worker is paid on the basis of some measure of productivity such as the number of units produced). **Salary** refers to compensation paid on a weekly, biweekly, or monthly basis. Usually salaries are paid to management, sales, and administrative personnel. Both wages and a salary may be supplemented by bonuses, profit sharing, commissions, and cost-of-living escalators.

Gross earnings are also increased by overtime pay, which may be determined by agreement between an employer and the employees (often in the form of a union contract) or by law. The **Federal Fair Labor Standards Act** (also called the Wages and Hours Law) regulates overtime pay for any employer who engages in interstate commerce. The act also establishes certain minimum-wage and equal-pay standards. For example, an employee covered by the act had to be paid a minimum wage of $3.35 in 1981. In most cases, the actual hourly wage agreed on by an employer and the employee will be higher than the minimum wage.

The law also provides that a covered employee must be paid overtime at a rate that is at least 1½ times the regular rate for every hour worked in excess of 40 hours a week. Exemptions from the overtime requirements are provided in the law for executive, administrative, and certain supervisory personnel. Employees in certain industries such as restaurants, motels, and farms also are exempt from overtime. Many employment agreements provide an overtime pay rate in excess of 1½ times the regular rate for weekends or holidays. Some employment agreements recognize overtime rates for hours worked in excess of 8 during any given day. The act also requires that females and males be paid equally for performing jobs involving equal skills, effort, responsibility, and working conditions.

To illustrate the calculation of gross earnings with overtime pay, assume that Leonard Smith, a construction worker for the Five Star Remodeling Company, earns a regular hourly wage of $8. In addition, he is paid an overtime rate of 1½ times the regular rate for all hours over 8 in any weekday and twice the regular rate for work performed on a weekend or a holiday. During the week ending February 11, 1984, Smith worked the following hours:

	Total Hours	Regular Hours	Overtime Hours
Monday	8	8	0
Tuesday	8	8	0
Wednesday	10	8	2
Thursday	9	8	1
Friday	10	8	2
Saturday	3	0	3
Total hours	48	40	8

Smith's gross earnings for the week are computed as:

Regular pay	40 hours × $8	=	$320
Overtime pay, weekdays	5 hours × $8 × 1.5	=	60
Overtime pay, weekend	3 hours × $8 × 2	=	48
Gross earnings			$428

DEDUCTIONS FROM GROSS EARNINGS

The **net earnings** paid an employee will be less than gross earnings because of certain deductions that must be made. Many of these deductions are required because of federal, state, or local laws, while others are authorized by agreement between an employer and the employees. In the example above, Leonard Smith will not receive $428, because his employer will deduct certain amounts for such items as FICA taxes, federal income taxes, state income taxes, and union dues.

FICA TAXES

The Social Security System was created by the **Federal Insurance Contributions Act of 1935 (FICA).** The purpose of the system is to provide qualified workers with a continuing source of income during their retirement years. In addition, certain medical, disability, and survivorship benefits are provided by the system. The principal source of financing for the Social Security System is a tax on wages or salaries and self-employment income. Most sources of compensation are subject to FICA taxes. Special rules apply to certain types of employment such as agricultural labor, casual labor, domestic workers, and government employees.

   FICA taxes are levied on both the employee and the employer according to a schedule established by Congress. The schedule includes a tax rate on wages and salaries up to a maximum or ceiling amount of earnings. While the schedule is subject to change by congressional action, the following indicates the FICA taxes schedule as of mid-1982:

Year	Maximum Compensation Limitation	Tax on Employee	Tax on Employer
1982	$31,800	6.70%	6.70%
1983	33,900	6.70	6.70
1984	36,000	6.70	6.70
1985	38,100	7.05	7.05
1986	40,200	7.15	7.15
1987	42,600	7.15	7.15

outdated table

Since FICA taxes are paid by both employee and employer, the total rate scheduled to be paid in 1984 is 13.4% (6.7 × 2). An employer must withhold from wages or salary the FICA taxes owed by each employee and pay a payroll tax equal to the amount withheld. For example, assume that construction worker Leonard Smith earns $23,500 in 1984. His employer, Five Star Remodeling Company, would withhold FICA taxes amounting to $1,574.50 ($23,500 × 6.70%) during the year and would owe a like amount as the employer's share of FICA taxes. Consequently, the total tax contributed to the Social Security System on Smith's behalf in 1984 is $3,149. If Smith's annual wages were $38,000, only $36,000 would be subject to FICA taxes and the total amount withheld would be $2,412. FICA taxes would not have to be paid on the $2,000 ($38,000 less $36,000) balance, because it exceeds the maximum compensation taxable.

FEDERAL INCOME TAXES

The federal income tax system of the United States is on a "pay-as-you-go" basis. This means that an employer must withhold certain amounts of federal income tax from each employee's wages or salary based on the amount of gross earnings and the number of **withholding allowances** claimed by the employee. Employers use **withholding tables** such as the one illustrated in Figure 12-1 to determine the amount of federal income tax to be withheld except for unusual cases. Each employee is required by law to complete a Form W-4 like the one in Figure 12-2 at the time he or she is hired. At that time, the employee indicates the number of income tax withholding allowances claimed, and the marital status of the employee is recorded. At the time of this writing, each allowance causes $1,000 of gross earnings to be exempted from federal income tax. One allowance can be claimed for the employee, one for the employee's spouse, and one for each of the employee's dependents. Additional allowances are taken if the employee or spouse is blind or at least

And the wages are—		And the number of withholding allowances claimed is—										
		0	1	2	3	4	5	6	7	8	9	10
At least	But less than	The amount of income tax to be withheld shall be—										
$310	$320	$46.20	$41.40	$37.50	$33.70	$29.80	$26.00	$22.50	$19.50	$16.40	$13.40	$10.70
320	330	48.70	43.80	39.50	35.70	31.80	28.00	24.10	21.10	18.00	14.90	12.10
330	340	51.20	46.30	41.50	37.70	33.80	30.00	26.10	22.70	19.60	16.50	13.50
340	350	53.70	48.80	44.00	39.70	35.80	32.00	28.10	24.30	21.20	18.10	15.00
350	360	56.20	51.30	46.50	41.70	37.80	34.00	30.10	26.30	22.80	19.70	16.60
360	370	58.70	53.80	49.00	44.20	39.80	36.00	32.10	28.30	24.40	21.30	18.20
370	380	61.20	56.30	51.50	46.70	41.90	38.00	34.10	30.30	26.40	22.90	19.80
380	390	63.70	58.80	54.00	49.20	44.40	40.00	36.10	32.30	28.40	24.60	21.40
390	400	66.20	61.30	56.50	51.70	46.90	42.10	38.10	34.30	30.40	26.60	23.00
400	410	68.70	63.80	59.00	54.20	49.40	44.60	40.10	36.30	32.40	28.60	24.80
410	420	71.20	66.30	61.50	56.70	51.90	47.10	42.30	38.30	34.40	30.60	26.80
420	430	73.70	68.80	64.00	59.20	54.40	49.60	44.80	40.30	36.40	32.60	28.80
430	440	76.20	71.30	66.50	61.70	56.90	52.10	47.30	42.50	38.40	34.60	30.80
440	450	78.70	73.80	69.00	64.20	59.40	54.60	49.80	45.00	40.40	36.60	32.80
450	460	81.60	76.30	71.50	66.70	61.90	57.10	52.30	47.50	42.70	38.60	34.80
460	470	84.70	78.80	74.00	69.20	64.40	59.60	54.80	50.00	45.20	40.60	36.80
470	480	87.80	81.90	76.50	71.70	66.90	62.10	57.30	52.50	47.70	42.90	38.80
480	490	90.90	85.00	79.00	74.20	69.40	64.60	59.80	55.00	50.20	45.40	40.80
490	500	94.00	88.10	82.10	76.70	71.90	67.10	62.30	57.50	52.70	47.90	43.10
500	510	97.10	91.20	85.20	79.20	74.40	69.60	64.80	60.00	55.20	50.40	45.60

MARRIED Persons—WEEKLY Payroll Period

Figure 12-1
Income Tax Withholding Table

65 years old. Consequently, a married couple (neither of whom is blind nor 65 years old or older) with three dependent children would claim five allowances for a total dollar amount of $5,000. Whenever the number of allowances or marital status changes, the employee must file a new Form W-4. The employer will match the gross earnings and number of allowances with the proper withholding table to determine the amount to be withheld from each paycheck. (It should be noted that an employee can, with certain limitations, claim a different number of allowances than he or she actually has because of the expected income tax liability for a given year.)

OTHER INCOME TAXES

Most states and some local authorities (city or county) levy income taxes that must be withheld by an employer. The procedures used for such taxes are similar to those discussed above for withholding federal income taxes.

Form **W-4** (Rev. January 1982)	Department of the Treasury—Internal Revenue Service **Employee's Withholding Allowance Certificate**	OMB No. 1545-0010 Expires 4-30-83

1 Type or print your full name
   Leonard E. Smith

2 Your social security number
   306-39-6193

3 Marital Status
   ☐ Single   ☒ Married
   ☐ Married, but withhold at higher Single rate
   Note: If married, but legally separated, or spouse is a nonresident alien, check the Single box.

Home address (number and street or rural route)
   1056 Rush Street

City or town, State, and ZIP code
   Indianapolis, Indiana   46206

4 Total number of allowances you are claiming (from line F of the worksheet on page 2) 5

5 Additional amount, if any, you want deducted from each pay . . . . $

6 I claim exemption from withholding because (see instructions and check boxes below that apply):
   a ☐ Last year I did not owe any Federal income tax and had a right to a full refund of **ALL** income tax withheld, **AND**
   b ☐ This year I do not expect to owe any Federal income tax and expect to have a right to a full refund of **ALL** income tax withheld. If both a and b apply, enter "EXEMPT" here . . . . ▶
   c If you entered "EXEMPT" on line 6b, are you a full-time student? . . . . ☐ Yes ☐ No

Under the penalties of perjury, I certify that I am entitled to the number of withholding allowances claimed on this certificate, or if claiming exemption from withholding, that I am entitled to claim the exempt status.

Employee's signature ▶ *Leonard E. Smith*   Date ▶ January 8   19 80

7 Employer's name and address (including ZIP code) (FOR EMPLOYER'S USE ONLY)
   Five Star Remodeling Company
   Indianapolis, Indiana   46222

8 Office code

9 Employer identification number
   35-1299693

Figure 12-2
Employee's Withholding Allowance Certificate

OTHER DEDUCTIONS

In addition to the mandatory deductions for taxes, several other deductions must be accounted for. Examples are union dues, insurance premiums, retirement-plan contributions, parking charges, savings bond purchases, uniform allowances, and charitable contributions. These deductions are taken out of the employee's paycheck by the employer and later remitted to the appropriate organization.

COMPUTATION OF NET EARNINGS

Gross earnings less the deductions described above equals the **net earnings** or take-home pay received by an employee. To illustrate how net earnings are computed, we assume that construction worker Leonard Smith is paid weekly. Recall that his regular and overtime pay combined for the period ending February 11, 1984, was $428. All of his earnings are subject to FICA taxes, and he has union dues of $4 per week. In addition, he has medical insurance premiums of $17.80 and contributes $5 per week to United Way—a charitable organization. His federal and state income tax withholdings have been determined by his employer to be $53.30 and $8.56, respectively.[1] His net earnings are computed as:

[1]Since the withholding table presented in Figure 12-1 was applicable in 1982, it was not used to compute the $53.30 withheld for Leonard Smith. If it had been used, the amount withheld would have been $49.60.

Gross earnings		$428.00
Deductions:		
FICA taxes (at 6.70%)	$28.68	
Federal income taxes	53.30	
State income taxes	8.56	
Union dues	4.00	
Medical insurance	17.80	
United Way contribution	5.00	
Total deductions		117.34
Net earnings		$310.66

EMPLOYER'S LIABILITY FOR WITHHOLDING

The amounts withheld from an employee's paycheck are liabilities of the employer, who performs the duties of a collection agent. In the case of Leonard Smith, his employer owes a total of $117.34 to the different parties involved with the withholdings. The various deductions must be paid when due to the federal government, state government, union, insurance company, and United Way. After the deductions are withheld but before they are remitted to the appropriate organization, the amounts are *liabilities* of the employer. In turn, the employer is responsible for maintaining adequate records that will provide the basis for filing any reports concerning the withholdings and for making payments on time. The withholdings are classified as current liabilities on the employer's balance sheet until they are paid.

EMPLOYER PAYROLL TAXES

Payroll taxes are paid by both employers and employees. As indicated earlier, employers are required to *match* the amount of the employee's contribution to the Social Security System. In the case of Leonard Smith, his employer would pay FICA taxes amounting to $28.68, based on his weekly earnings. Employers also must make payments for federal and state unemployment compensation tax. The **Federal Unemployment Tax Act (FUTA)** provides certain benefits for a limited period to employees who lose their jobs through no fault of their own. FUTA is a part of the Social Security System and is a joint federal and state unemployment program. The act establishes certain minimum standards that must be complied with by each state. The major portion of the tax is levied by the states and a minor portion by the federal government. Actual unemployment benefits are paid by the state involved, while administrative expenses are paid from the amount of the tax remitted to the federal government. The amount of the total tax can change, but recently for most states the federal and state portions combined amounted to 3.4 percent of the first $6,000 earned by each employee. By law, the federal portion of the unemployment tax itself is 3.4% but a credit against that amount is granted for the state portion up to a maximum of 2.7%. In turn, the actual amount paid to a state may be less than 2.7% if a particular employer has had a sufficiently low unemployment record in the past. Nevertheless, the credit for federal purposes will still be 2.7%, so the federal liability is .7% (3.4% less 2.7%). A few states also require employees to pay state unemployment taxes. Indiana, the state in which Leonard Smith works, does not require a contribution from employees, but his employer has to pay the state the full 2.7% of the first $6,000 earned by each employee. The employer's share of the state unemployment taxes in a given year will be $162 and the federal unemployment taxes $42, a total of $204.

PAYROLL RECORDS AND PROCEDURES

The payroll system selected by a particular firm will depend on the number of employees and amount of automation, but several records and procedures are common to most payroll systems. Many small companies process their payrolls manually, although the number has decreased significantly in recent years because of the increasingly detailed recordkeeping involved and the availability of in-house computers or timesharing services that process payrolls for a fee. One of the oldest and most popular computer applications in business is preparing a payroll, because of its repetitive nature. A computer enables a business to process its payroll accurately, economically, and rapidly. In this section, we describe the basic records and procedures common to most payroll systems.

INPUT DATA

Two types of input data, *permanent* and *current*, are used to process a payroll. A permanent file, maintained at all times for each employee, includes such items as the employee's name, address, Social Security number, rate of pay, Form W-4 information, other deductions from gross earnings, and year-to-date payroll figures. A current file is developed each time a payroll is processed to record such items as regular hours worked, overtime hours worked, bonuses, commissions, vacation pay, tips, and sick pay. The permanent and current data are combined to determine net earnings, prepare a payroll check, and update year-to-date payroll figures such as gross earnings, various types of deductions, and net earnings. Many businesses maintain the related payroll records on a departmentalized basis so the source of the expenditure can be readily identified for control purposes. For example, a medical clinic can departmentalize its payroll for medical services performed, such as pediatrics, surgery, laboratory, radiology, and internal medicine.

PAYROLL REGISTER

A **payroll register** is a detailed listing of a firm's complete payroll for a particular pay period. Each employee's earnings and deductions for the period are reported in this register. The specific form chosen by a business for a payroll register will vary depending on the number of employees, payroll classifications required, and the use of automation. The Five Star Remodeling Company's payroll register, shown in Figure 12-3, is typical of one used by a business and itemizes the gross-to-net earnings for each employee. The firm's payroll is divided into categories for office salaries and construction wages. Note that the beginning point of the accounting by employee is the gross earnings for a current payroll period. A column is presented for each type of deduction from gross earnings. Also, the net earnings (take-home pay) are reported, computed as gross earnings less the total deductions. The cumulative gross earnings column keeps the employer informed about the total compensation paid to date. By totaling each of the columns, the business has the

Figure 12-3
Payroll Register

		Gross Earnings			Deductions							
												Payroll Register 2/11/84 Page 1
Employee	Hours	Regular	Over-time	Total	FICA Tax	Fed. Tax	State Tax	Union Dues	Insur-ance	United Way	Net Earnings	Cumula-tive Gross
Office Salaries												
M. Andrews	40	200.00		200.00	13.40	15.80	4.00		17.80	2.00	147.00	1,200.00
J. Miller	40	220.00		220.00	14.74	15.90	4.40		17.80	4.00	163.16	1,540.00
Subtotal		420.00		420.00	28.14	31.70	8.40		35.60	6.00	310.16	2,740.00
Construction Wages												
A. Baker	40	240.00		240.00	16.08	26.40	4.80	4.00	17.80	4.00	166.92	1,720.00
D. Cohn	40	240.00		240.00	16.08	26.40	4.80	4.00	17.80	4.00	166.92	1,700.00
R. King	44	280.00	42.00	322.00	21.58	35.10	6.44	4.00	17.80	6.00	231.08	2,260.00
B. Maier	50	320.00	136.00	456.00	30.55	55.80	9.12	4.00	17.80	6.00	332.73	3,260.00
L. Smith	48	320.00	108.00	428.00	28.68	53.30	8.56	4.00	17.80	5.00	310.66	2,100.00
C. Thomas	40	400.00		400.00	26.80	53.10	8.00	4.00	17.80	5.00	285.30	2,700.00
Subtotal		1800.00	286.00	2086.00	139.77	250.10	41.72	24.00	106.80	30.00	1493.61	13,740.00
Total		2220.00	286.00	2506.00	167.91	281.80	50.12	24.00	142.40	36.00	1803.77	16,480.00

information required to record the payroll expense classified as office salaries and construction wages as well as the related liabilities in the accounting system. This is accomplished with a general journal entry:

Feb.	11	Office Salaries Expense	420.00	
		Construction Wages Expense	2,086.00	
		FICA Taxes Payable		167.91
		Federal Income Taxes Payable		281.80
		State Income Taxes Payable		50.12
		Union Dues Payable		24.00
		Medical Insurance Payable		142.40
		United Way Contribution Payable		36.00
		Salaries and Wages Payable		1,803.77
		To record the payroll for the week ended February 11.		

At the same time, the employer payroll taxes can be recorded—although some firms do so with an end-of-the month adjusting entry. Remember that the employer is required to pay an amount equal to the employee's share of FICA taxes as well as the unemployment taxes based on a maximum amount of compensation ($6,000 in 1981). Consequently, the employer would compute the federal and state unemployment tax liability, match the employees' FICA tax liability of $167.91, and make the following entry:

Feb.	11	Payroll Taxes Expense	253.11	
		FICA Taxes Payable		167.91
		State Unemployment Taxes Payable		67.66
		($2,506 × 2.7%)		
		Federal Unemployment Taxes Payable		17.54
		($2,506 × .7%)		
		To record payroll taxes expense for the week ended February 11.		

As a result, the total payroll expense for the week ended February 11 is $2,759.11 ($2,506.00 + $253.11). After the two payroll entries above are recorded, the Five Star Remodeling Company also has liabilities amounting to $2,759.11 that must be paid on a timely basis to the employees, governmental agencies, and various other organizations. This will be done by debiting the liabilities and crediting cash for the amounts accrued in the two entries above, as will be discussed later.

EMPLOYEE EARNINGS RECORD

An **employee earnings record,** such as the one shown in Figure 12-4, provides a detailed description of an employee's hours worked, gross earnings, deductions, and net earnings for the year to date. The information is posted

		Earnings			Deductions						Net	Cumulative
Period Ending	Total Hours	Reg.	O.T.	Gross	FICA	Fed.	State	Union	Insur.	United Way	Earnings	Gross
Jan. 7	42	320.00	24.00	344.00	23.05	35.20	6.88	4.00	17.80	5.00	252.07	344.00
14	44	320.00	48.00	368.00	24.66	39.40	7.36	4.00	17.80	5.00	269.68	712.00
21	40	320.00		320.00	21.44	31.00	6.40	4.00	17.80	5.00	234.36	1,032.00
28	40	320.00		320.00	21.44	31.00	6.40	4.00	17.80	5.00	234.36	1,352.00
Feb. 4	40	320.00		320.00	21.44	31.00	6.40	4.00	17.80	5.00	234.36	1,672.00
11	48	320.00	108.00	428.00	28.68	53.30	8.56	4.00	17.80	5.00	310.66	2,100.00

Employee Earnings Record — Name: Leonard E. Smith, Address: 1056 Rush St. Indianapolis, IN 46206, Soc. Sec. No. 306-39-6193, Date of Birth July 19, 1948, Marital Status M, Exemptions 5, Pay Rate $8.00, Position Carpenter, 1984

Figure 12-4
Employee Earnings Record

from the related line of the payroll register at the end of each pay period. The employee earnings record must be kept current because it serves four important purposes: (1) It provides the information needed for certain payroll tax returns; (2) it indicates when an employee's gross earnings have reached the maximum limitations for FICA and unemployment taxes; (3) it furnishes the information required to prepare a Wage and Tax Statement, Form W-2 (discussed later), at the end of the year; and (4) it keeps the employer informed about the amount of earnings for each employee. Note in Figure 12-4 that the last column shows the cumulative gross earnings for the year to date.

PAYMENT OF EMPLOYEES

We noted earlier that for internal control reasons the preferred treatment is to pay employees with checks written on a separate **payroll bank account.** At the end of each pay period, a check is written for the total of the net earnings of all employees. It is drawn on the regular bank account and is deposited in the payroll bank account. Paychecks such as the one illustrated in Figure 12-5 are later drawn on the payroll bank account, which should be reduced to zero after all the paychecks have cleared the bank. The use of only one check drawn on the regular bank account for the payroll simplifies the reconciliation of that account at the end of the month. The separation of paychecks drawn on a special account facilitates the preparation, control, and reconciliation of what often is a large number of checks. In the case of Five Star Remodeling Company, a check in the amount of $1,803.77 would be drawn on the regular bank account. Salaries and Wages Payable would be debited and Cash would be credited for $1,803.77 in the cash disbursements journal. The payroll register provides detailed information concerning specific amounts paid to individual employees.

A business with only a few employees may not need the control feature of a special payroll bank account. In such cases, paychecks are drawn from the regular bank account, and entries are made in the cash disbursements journal debiting Salaries and Wages Payable and crediting Cash. Although it is not required by law, most employers provide each employee an earnings statement for each pay period. As can be seen in Figure 12-5, the earnings statement is usually attached to the paycheck and shows hours worked, gross earnings, deductions, and net earnings for the current period and year to date.

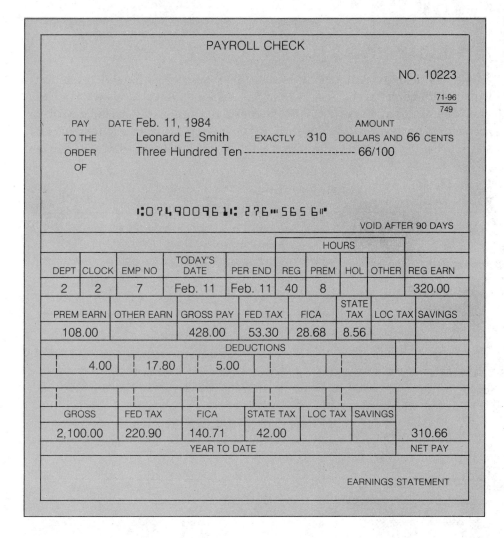

Figure 12-5
Paycheck/Earnings
Statement

WAGE AND TAX STATEMENT

By January 31 of every year, an employer must provide each employee several copies of a **Wage and Tax Statement, Form W-2,** for the preceding calendar year. The form shows the total earnings paid to the employee, the federal income taxes withheld, the state income taxes withheld, the earnings subject to FICA taxes, the FICA taxes withheld, and certain other information. The employer also must send a copy of each employee's Form W-2 to the Social Security Administration, which processes the information and then sends the Internal Revenue Service the income tax information it requires from the form. The Form W-2 furnishes information needed by the employee to file his or her income tax returns, and a copy of the form must be attached to each return filed. An example of a Form W-2, prepared for Leonard Smith, is shown in Figure 12-6.

PAYROLL TAX RETURNS

Employers also are required by law to file a number of payroll tax returns with governmental agencies. An example is the **Employer's Quarterly Federal Tax Return, Form 941.** Every business must use a calendar year in accounting for payroll taxes even if it has chosen a fiscal year for financial and income tax reporting. Form 941 must be prepared quarterly and filed no

Figure 12-6
Wage and Tax Statement

Copy B To be filed with employee's FEDERAL tax return

Five Star Remodeling Company
P.O. Box 682
Indianapolis, IN. 46222

2 Employer's name, address, and ZIP code

3 Employer's identification number: 35-1299693	4 Employer's State number
5 Stat. employee ☐ Deceased ☐ Pension plan ☐ Legal rep. ☐	942 emp. ☐ Correction ☐
6	7 Advance EIC payment
8 Employee's social security number: 306-39-6193	9 Federal income tax withheld: 2603.00
10 Wages, tips, other compensation: 18,200.00	11 FICA tax withheld: 1,219.00
13 FICA wages: 18,200.00	14 FICA tips
16 Employer's use	

12 Employee's name, address, and ZIP code

Leonard E. Smith
1056 Rush Street
Indianapolis, IN. 46206

17 State income tax	18 State Wages, tips, etc.	19 Name of State
364.00		Indiana
20 Local income tax	21 Local wages, tips, etc.	22 Name of locality

Form **W-2 Wage and Tax Statement 1981** This information is being furnished to the Internal Revenue Service. Department of the Treasury Internal Revenue Service 13-2678063 IRS APP. 3/19/81 later than the end of the month following a given quarter. Information concerning FICA taxes and federal income tax withholdings are combined on Form 941. It shows the total gross earnings paid by an employer, the earnings subject to FICA taxes, the amount of FICA taxes, and the amount of federal income taxes withheld. Similar payroll tax returns are required for state income taxes, local income taxes, and unemployment taxes.

PAYROLL TAX PAYMENTS

The employer acts as a collection agent and is liable to remit the amount of tax withheld to the appropriate governmental agency. Whenever the amounts withheld are large, they must be paid frequently by the employer. The exact timing of the payments depends on the nature of the tax and the amounts involved. For federal purposes, the FICA taxes (both employees' and employer's portions) and the federal taxes withheld must be combined to determine when the total must be paid. In 1981, the total taxes due were paid quarterly if they did not exceed $500 during the quarter. Whenever the total was more than $500 during a quarter, the employer had to pay the amount due on a timely basis through deposits made to the credit of the Internal Revenue Service at a *federal depository bank*. Large businesses are required to make such deposits because of the size of their payroll. The deposits later are reconciled with the tax liability shown on Form 941. Similar procedures must be followed with the federal portion of unemployment taxes. State and local governments also have specific schedules that must be complied with for timely payment of tax liabilities. When the amounts previously withheld are paid, an entry is made in the cash disbursements journal debiting the liability accounts and crediting cash.

PAYMENT OF OTHER WITHHOLDING

The employer remits the amounts withheld for such items as union dues, insurance premiums, and charitable contributions at various times according to agreements with the external organizations involved. Five Star Remodeling Company owes the union $24, an insurance company $142.40, and United Way $36. When the amounts accumulated in the three liability accounts are paid by the company, entries will be made in the cash disbursements journal debiting the liability accounts and crediting cash.

SUMMARY OF JOURNAL ENTRIES FOR PAYROLL ACCOUNTING

The journal entries required to record the payroll of Five Star Remodeling Company and the ultimate payment by the firm to the various parties can be summarized as follows (these entries are shown for illustration only; the actual entries may take different forms because of the timing of the cash payments involved):

Payroll Transaction	Journal Entry			Journal Used
Accrue Payroll	Office Salaries Expense	420.00		General
	Construction Wages Expense	2,086.00		
	FICA Taxes Payable		167.91	
	Federal Income Taxes Payable		281.80	
	State Income Taxes Payable		50.12	
	Union Dues Payable		24.00	
	Medical Insurance Payable		142.40	
	United Way Contribution Payable		36.00	
	Salaries and Wages Payable		1,803.77	
Accrue Payroll Taxes	Payroll Taxes Expense	253.11		General
	FICA Taxes Payable		167.91	
	State Unemployment Taxes Payable		67.66	
	Federal Unemployment Taxes Payable		17.54	
Pay Employees	Salaries and Wages Payable	1,803.77		Cash
	Cash		1,803.77	Disbursements
Pay Taxes	FICA Taxes Payable	335.82		Cash
	Federal Income Taxes Payable	281.80		Disbursements
	State Income Taxes Payable	50.12		
	State Unemployment Taxes Payable	67.66		
	Federal Unemployment Taxes Payable	17.54		
	Cash		752.94	
Pay Other Withholdings	Union Dues Payable	24.00		Cash
	Medical Insurance Payable	142.40		Disbursements
	United Way Contribution Payable	36.00		
	Cash		202.40	

GLOSSARY

EMPLOYEE EARNINGS RECORD. A record maintained for each employee showing hours worked, gross earnings, deductions, and net earnings for the year to date (p. 483).

EMPLOYEE'S WITHHOLDING ALLOWANCE CERTIFICATE (FORM W-4). A form completed by each employee stating the number of withholding allowances claimed and marital status (p. 473).

EMPLOYER'S QUARTERLY FEDERAL TAX RETURN (FORM 941). A report prepared each quarter by the employer to provide the federal government with information concerning gross earnings, FICA taxes, and income taxes withheld (p. 486).

FEDERAL FAIR LABOR STANDARDS ACT.   A law that regulates overtime, minimum wages, and equal pay standards (p. 475).

FEDERAL INSURANCE CONTRIBUTIONS ACT (FICA).   The law governing the Social Security System (p. 476).

FEDERAL UNEMPLOYMENT TAX ACT (FUTA).   A law providing certain benefits for a limited period to employees who lose their jobs through no fault of their own (p. 480).

FEDERAL UNEMPLOYMENT TAXES.   The federal portion of FUTA taxes paid by an employer (p. 481).

FICA TAXES.   Taxes paid by both an employer and the employee to finance the Social Security System (p. 476).

GROSS EARNINGS.   The total amount of an employee's salary or wages before any payroll deductions (p. 475).

NET EARNINGS.   Gross earnings of an employee less the payroll deductions (p. 479).

PAYROLL BANK ACCOUNT.   A special bank account used for payroll purposes only (p. 484).

PAYROLL REGISTER.   A detailed listing of a firm's complete payroll for a given period (p. 482).

PAYROLL TAXES.   Taxes withheld from an employee's gross earnings or paid by an employer (p. 480).

SALARY.   Compensation on a weekly, biweekly, or monthly basis paid to an employee (p. 475).

STATE UNEMPLOYMENT TAXES.   The state's portion of FUTA taxes paid by an employer or in a limited number of states by an employee (p. 481).

WAGE AND TAX STATEMENT (FORM W-2).   A form furnished by an employer to every employee showing gross earnings and certain tax information for a particular year (p. 486).

WAGES.   Compensation computed on an hourly rate or piecework basis paid to an employee (p. 475).

WITHHOLDING ALLOWANCE.   The amount of an employee's gross earnings not subject to income tax (p. 477).

WITHHOLDING TABLES.   Tables showing amounts of tax to be withheld for different levels of gross earnings (p. 477).

DISCUSSION QUESTIONS

1. Why is sound internal control essential for an effective payroll system? What duties should be separated to achieve good internal control in a payroll system?

2. What is the difference between an employee and an independent contractor? Why is this difference important for payroll accounting?

3. What are the two major types of gross earnings? Why is the Federal Fair Labor Standards Act important in the determination of gross earnings?

4. Identify the federal taxes that most employers are required to withhold from employees' gross earnings.

5. Explain which of the following taxes related to an employee's gross earnings are paid by the employee, by the employer, or by both:
   (a) FICA taxes
   (b) Federal income taxes
   (c) Federal unemployment taxes
   (d) State unemployment taxes
   (e) State income taxes

6. Why are deductions from gross earnings liabilities of the employer?

7. Is the total compensation expense for a given period equal to gross earnings or net earnings? Why?

8. What is meant by the statement, "An employer acts as a collection agent in the operation of a payroll system"?

9. What was the basic purpose of the Federal Insurance Contributions Act (FICA)?

10. What was the basic purpose of the Federal Unemployment Tax Act (FUTA)?

11. What is meant by the statement, "The federal income tax system of the United States is on a pay-as-you-go basis"? Why is this important in the operation of an accounting system?

12. When is an Employee's Withholding Allowance Certificate (Form W-4) prepared? What is its purpose?

13. What are the two basic types of input data in a payroll system?

14. Why is a payroll register an essential part of a payroll system?

15. What is an employee earnings record? Distinguish between it and a payroll register.

16. Why is a separate bank account usually used except with a small payroll?

17. What is the basic purpose of a Wage and Tax Statement (Form W-2)?

18. When is an Employer's Quarterly Federal Tax Return (Form 941) filed? Are all payments for the employees' share of FICA taxes and their taxes withheld always paid when Form 941 is filed?

19. Robert Davis earns $400 per week; he is married and has two children. State income tax withholding is 2 percent of gross earnings. Insurance premiums amounting to $20 per week are deducted and all of his compensation is subject to FICA taxes (6.7 percent). Use the withholding table on page 478 to compute his net earnings. Assuming he is the only employee, what journal entry is required to accrue his compensation as an expense?

EXERCISES

Exercise 12-1 (Determining Gross and Net Earnings)

Bill Powers is a factory worker who is paid at the rate of $8 per hour. During the past week, he worked 46 hours. He is paid overtime at 1 1/2 times his regular hourly rate. His gross earnings prior to this past week were $4,000. Powers is married and claims 5 withholding allowances on his Form W-4. His union dues are $3 per week, and he has authorized a contribution to United Way of $2 each week. Assume a FICA tax rate of 6.7%. Use the withholding table on page 478 for federal taxes and assume the state rate is 2%.

Required:
Compute the following for Powers' weekly wages:

1. Gross earnings   **4.** Deductions from gross earnings
2. Regular earnings   **5.** Net earnings
3. Overtime earnings

Exercise 12-2 (Journal Entries for Payroll Accounting)

On January 21, the weekly payroll register showed gross wages and salaries of $150,000. The entire payroll was subject to FICA and unemployment taxes. The company withheld $19,500 of federal income taxes, $3,000 of state income taxes, $2,300 of medical insurance premiums, and $970 of union dues from the employees' payroll checks. The applicable FICA rate is 7.05%, the state unemployment tax rate is 2.7%, and the federal unemployment tax rate is .7%.

Required:
A. Prepare a journal entry to record the payroll and payroll deductions.
B. Prepare a journal entry to record the employer's payroll tax expense.

Exercise 12-3 (Computing Employer Payroll Tax Expenses)

The Douglas Company is estimating its payroll taxes for the upcoming year. The company estimates that the amount of gross wages will be $790,000, of which $180,000 will be employee earnings not subject to FICA taxes. It also anticipates that $270,000 of the wages paid will not be subject to unemployment taxes. The FICA rate will be 7.15%, the state unemployment tax rate 1.6%, and the federal unemployment tax rate .7%.

Required:
Calculate the amounts the company estimates it will pay for payroll tax expenses for the year, showing separately the amount of each of the three taxes.

Exercise 12-4 (Journal Entries for Payroll and Related Tax Expenses)

The Beltline Company has four employees; the payroll data for the week ending October 12 are presented below.

Employee	Gross Pay	Cumulative Earnings to End of Prior Week	Federal Income Tax	State Income Tax
A. Altier	$ 500	$ 5,700	$ 35	$10
C. Ralph	350	6,500	47	7
E. Lubberts	950	30,050	108	19
D. Lindner	1,050	31,200	250	21

The FICA tax rate is 6.7% on the first $31,800 paid each employee. The state unemployment tax rate is 2.7% and the federal unemployment tax rate is .7% on each employee's first $6,000 of wages.

Required:
Prepare journal entries to record the payroll and to record the employer's payroll tax expenses.

Exercise 12-5 (Calculating and Recording a Payroll)
The Tanya Company is calculating the net pay of a married employee who claims four income tax withholding allowances. The employee worked 48 hours during the past week and his hourly rate is $7.50. The company pays an overtime rate of 1½ times the regular hourly rate, and the FICA rate is 6.7% on each employee's first $31,800 of wages. The employee's year-to-date pay to the end of the prior week was $31,600.

Required:
Prepare a journal entry to record the employee's payroll. Use Figure 12-1 on page 478 to calculate the income tax withholding. Assume a state income tax rate of 2.0% of gross wages.

PROBLEMS

Problem 12-1 (Determining and Recording Gross and Net Earnings)
Tina Walker is a department supervisor at a local retail store who earns $6 per hour. She receives 1½ times her regular pay rate for any hours worked over 8 hours on a weekday, twice her regular pay rate for any hours worked on the weekend, and three times her regular rate for holidays. Tina's hours for the past week were:

M	T	W	T	F	S	S
7	9	8	8	6	3	0

Monday was a legal holiday. The FICA rate is 6.7%, and the state income tax rate is 2% of gross pay. Tina is married and claims one withholding allowance. She has authorized her employer to withhold $10 a week for health insurance premiums and $2 a week as a contribution to United Way. Her year-to-date gross earnings prior to this past week were $7,500.

Required:
A. Compute Tina's gross and net earnings. Use the withholding table on page 478 for federal taxes.
B. Prepare a journal entry to accrue Tina's compensation.

Problem 12-2 (Calculations and Journal Entries for a Payroll)
The following payroll data for the week ending September 20 were taken from the company's payroll records. The FICA tax rate is 7.05% on the first $38,100 paid each

employee. The state and federal unemployment tax rates are 1.5% and .7%, respectively, on each employee's first $6,000 of wages.

Employee	Gross Pay	Federal Income Taxes	State Income Taxes	United Way Deductions	Health Insurance Deduction	Compensation to September 13
A. Frasier	$ 300	$ 35	$ 6	$ 5	$ 8	$ 4,500
R. Birdwell	600	85	9	5	10	6,100
H. Dailey	950	200	19	15	12	37,900
D. Ralph	1,200	300	25	15	8	38,200

Required:
A. Calculate the FICA tax withheld and the net pay for each employee.
B. Prepare a journal entry to accrue the payroll.
C. Prepare a journal entry to accrue the employer's payroll tax expense.

Problem 12-3 (Preparing a Payroll Register and Recording a Payroll)
The Windmill Company has provided the following information for the weekly payroll ending November 27.

Employee	Daily Time M T W T F S S	Pay Rate	Federal Income Taxes	State Income Taxes	Medical Insurance	Earnings to End of Prior Week
R. Allen	8 9 9 9 8 0 0	$7.50	$33.00	$ 7.00	$15.00	$31,800
A. Bult	8 8 8 8 8 5 0	6.00	30.00	6.00	10.00	31,700
P. Greaves	12 8 10 8 8 2 0	9.00	55.00	10.00	15.00	4,200
W. May	8 8 10 8 8 0 0	5.00	20.00	5.00	15.00	5,800

The FICA tax rate is 6.7% of the first $31,800 paid each employee. All employees receive 1½ times their hourly rate for all hours over 8 in any weekday and twice their regular rate for work performed on a weekend. The state unemployment tax rate is 2.7% and the federal unemployment tax rate is .7% of an employee's first $6,000 of wages.

Required:
A. Prepare a payroll register for the week ending November 27.
B. Prepare a journal entry to record the payroll and an entry to record the employer's payroll tax expense.

Problem 12-4 (Preparing a Payroll Register and Recording a Payroll)
The Brooks Company has provided the following information for the weekly payroll ending September 15.

	Daily Hours									**Earnings to End of**
						Pay	**Fed. Tax**	**State**	**United**	**Prior**
Employee	**M**	**T**	**W**	**T**	**F**	**Rate**	**Exemptions**	**Tax**	**Way**	**Week**
J. Clifford	8	9	8	8	10	$7.00	1	$9.30	$ 5.00	$ 3,000
M. Lyell	9	8	12	8	8	7.00	4	9.95	10.00	29,800
G. Goodman	9	9	12	8	8	9.00	2	8.82	5.00	4,300
P. Oliver	8	8	8	8	9	9.00	3	7.47	5.00	5,800

The FICA tax rate is 7.05% of the first $38,100 paid each employee. Each employee's first $6,000 of wages are subject to unemployment taxes; the state rate is 2.7%, and the federal rate is .7%. All employees are married and receive 1½ times their regular rate for all hours over 8 in any weekday.

Required:

A. Prepare a payroll register for the week ending September 15. Refer to Figure 12-1 on page 478 to calculate the federal income tax withholdings.

B. Prepare journal entries to record the payroll and the employer's payroll tax expense.

Problem 12-5 (Journalizing Payroll Transactions)

The following accounts and balances appeared in the ledger of the Brunsting Company on August 30.

FICA Taxes Payable	$750
Federal Income Taxes Payable	490
State Income Taxes Payable	125
Federal Unemployment Taxes Payable	70
State Unemployment Taxes Payable	270
Medical Insurance Payable	190
United Way Contributions Payable	80

The following transactions occurred during September and October:

Sept. 1 Issued check payable to First National Bank (a federal depository bank) in payment of employee's federal income tax and FICA tax due.

Sept. 30 Prepared a journal entry to record the monthly payroll.

Gross wages	$3,500
Federal income taxes withheld	300
FICA taxes withheld	247
State income taxes withheld	70
Medical insurance premiums withheld	85
United Way deductions	40

Sept. 30 Issued check payable to the payroll bank account for the net amount of the monthly payroll.

Sept.	30	Prepared a journal entry to record the employer's payroll tax expense. The federal unemployment tax rate is .7%, and the state unemployment tax rate is 2.7%. Gross wages earned by employees in excess of the unemployment tax limit amounted to $500.
Oct.	1	Issued a check payable to First National Bank in payment of the employees' federal income tax and FICA tax due.
Oct.	15	Issued a check in payment of the company's federal unemployment taxes for the third quarter.
Oct.	20	Issued a check payable to the United Way in payment of employee deductions to date.
Oct.	25	Paid the ABC Insurance Co. the medical insurance premiums withheld from employees' paychecks during the quarter.
Oct.	30	Remitted to the State Department of Revenue state income taxes payable for the quarter.
Oct.	30	Issued a check to the State Unemployment Division for the quarter's state unemployment taxes.

Required:
Prepare journal entries to record the September and October transactions.

ALTERNATE PROBLEMS

Problem 12-1A (Determining and Recording Gross and Net Earnings)

Larry Roman is a manager of a local store who earns $8 an hour. He receives overtime pay at a rate of 1½ times his regular pay rate for hours worked in excess of 40 from Monday through Friday and twice his regular pay rate for any hours worked on the weekend. The FICA rate is 7.05%, and he lives in a state which imposes an income tax of 3% on gross wages. Larry's employer withholds $15 from his weekly paycheck for health insurance and $5 for a United Way contribution. He is married and has year-to-date wages of $16,500 prior to this week. His hours for the week were as follows:

M	T	W	T	F	S	S
8	9	10	8	8	4	0

Required:
A. Calculate Larry's gross and net earnings for the week. Use the withholding table on page 478 for federal taxes.
B. Prepare a journal entry to record Larry's paycheck.

Problem 12-2A (Calculations and Journal Entries for a Payroll)

The Abbott Company is preparing the payroll for November 14 and has compiled the following data. The FICA rate is 6.7% on the first $33,900 paid each employee. The state unemployment rate is 2.7% and the federal unemployment tax rate is .7% on each employee's first $6,000 of wages.

Employee	Gross Pay	Federal Income Taxes	State Income Taxes	Union Dues	Health Insurance Deduction	Compensation through November 7
S. Wilson	$500	$195	$15	$10	$12	$ 5,700
K. May	450	110	12	10	12	16,000
S. Burns	800	250	18	15	18	33,800
C. White	600	205	16	15	20	33,600

Required:
A. Calculate the FICA withheld for each employee.
B. Prepare a journal entry to record the payroll.
C. Prepare a journal entry to record the employer's payroll tax expense.

Problem 12-3A (Preparing a Payroll Register and Recording a Payroll)

The Brighton Company has provided the following data for the week ending November 27.

Employee	M	T	W	T	F	S	S	Hourly Pay Rate	Federal Income Taxes	State Income Taxes	United Way Deduction	Earnings to End of Prior Week
M. McConnell	8	8	8	8	8	2	0	$5.00	$20.00	$3.00	$ 5.00	$ 5,900
C. Breeze	8	8	9	9	8	1	0	6.00	30.00	3.50	10.00	13,200
H. Fairport	8	8	8	8	8	0	0	4.00	15.00	2.00	10.00	8,500
M. Penfield	8	10	10	8	8	0	0	9.00	55.00	8.00	25.00	37,900

The state and federal unemployment tax rates are 2.7% and .7%, respectively, on the first $6,000 paid each employee. The FICA rate is 7.05% of each employee's first $38,100 of wages. The company pays each employee 1½ times the hourly rate for all hours over 8 on a weekday and for all weekend hours worked.

Required:
A. Prepare a payroll register for the week ending November 27.
B. Prepare journal entries to record the payroll and to record the employer's payroll tax expense.

Problem 12-4A (Preparing a Payroll Register and Recording a Payroll)

The Phipps Company has asked you to record the payroll for the week ending October 12 and has provided the following data:

Employee	Daily Hours					Fed. Tax Exemptions	Pay Rate	Earnings to End of Prior Week
	M	T	W	T	F			
A. Devon	8	8	8	8	10	0	$ 8.00	$ 5,800
B. Essex	8	9	9	9	7	1	8.50	25,500
C. Ferry	5	4	8	6	8	2	10.00	12,100
D. Salem	9	9	8	8	8	1	8.35	33,600
F. Union	8	8	8	8	8	3	8.00	7,500

Each employee receives 1½ times the regular pay rate for all hours over 8 in any day. The FICA rate is 6.7% of each employee's $33,900 of wages. Each employee's first $6,000 of wages are subject to federal and state unemployment taxes of .7% and 2.7%, respectively. The state income tax is 2% of gross wages.

Required:

A. Refer to Figure 12-1 on page 478 to calculate each employee's federal income tax withholding and prepare a payroll register for the week ending October 12.

B. Prepare a journal entry to record the payroll and an entry to record the employer's payroll tax expense.

Problem 12-5A (Journalizing Payroll Transactions)

The Lenox Company has provided the following general ledger balances as of May 31:

Federal Income Taxes Payable	$4,400
FICA Taxes Payable	2,680
Federal Unemployment Taxes Payable	280
Medical Insurance Payable	470
State Income Taxes Payable	760
State Unemployment Taxes Payable	580
United Way Contributions Payable	200

The following transactions occurred in June and July:

June 1   Made a deposit at the Federal Trust Bank (a federal depository bank) for payment of employee's federal income taxes and FICA tax payable.

30   Prepared a journal entry to record the monthly payroll as follows:

Gross wages	$21,000
Federal income taxes withheld	3,900
FICA taxes withheld	1,050
State income taxes withheld	390
United Way deductions	100
Medical insurance premiums withheld	235

	30	Issued a check payable to the payroll bank account for the net amount of the monthly payroll.
	30	Gross wages earned by employees in excess of the $6,000 unemployment tax limit were $18,000. The federal and state unemployment tax rate is .7% and 2.7%, respectively.
July	1	Issued a check for payment of the employee's federal income tax and FICA tax due from the June 30 payroll.
	10	Paid the company's federal unemployment taxes for the second quarter.
	18	Issued a check to the United Way for payment of unremitted employee deductions to date.
	27	Issued a check to Safety Insurance Co. for medical insurance premiums withheld from employee's paychecks during the second quarter.
	30	Issued a check to the State Department of Revenue for state income taxes payable in the quarter.
	30	Remitted unemployment taxes to the state for the second quarter.

Required:
Prepare journal entries to record the June and July transactions.

CASE FOR CHAPTER 12

Decision Problem (Determining the Real Cost of Labor)

The Pilgrim Moving and Storage Company is located in a Midwestern university community. Last year's sales revenue totaled $500,000 and produced a net income of $40,000. Bill Shuman, president of the company, is concerned about profit margins that have been declining recently because of increasing labor costs and stable sales revenue. The moving and storage business in a campus town is seasonal, with 70% of sales typically occurring from May through September.

Mr. Shuman is looking for ways to reduce labor costs. During the busy season, 10 employees are needed to pack household goods for intrastate or interstate shipments. These people do not have chauffeur's licenses, so they cannot drive the trucks used to haul furniture and household goods. Each packer works approximately 860 hours from May through September. During the rest of the year, only five people are needed for a full 40 hours each week. However, the firm has found it necessary to guarantee the other five workers a minimum of 20 hours per week from October through April to retain their services during the busy season. Mr. Shuman estimates that the five people will be paid for a total of 3,000 hours during the period October through April, but only 1,500 of the hours will be spent productively. The rest will be idle time because the employees will have nothing to do.

Mary Blair, a marketing representative of Temporary Help, Inc., recently has made a proposal to Mr. Shuman that is an alternative way for him to hire the extra five packers. Mrs. Blair's firm provides temporary services with all types of skilled and unskilled workers. The workers supplied would be billed to Pilgrim on an hourly basis and would be on Temporary Help, Inc.'s payroll. Mrs. Blair has offered to provide workers who are capable of packing household goods to replace the five employees for the entire year at a fixed hourly rate of $6 each. Pilgrim would pay only for the hours worked by the temporary help during the year. At first glance, Mr. Shuman is tempted to reject the offer because his company can hire packers at an hourly rate of $5. However, he realizes that the "true" cost of using his own employees must be greater than $5 per hour and has asked for your assistance in evaluating Mrs. Blair's proposal. You have determined that in addition to the $5 per hour labor rate, the firm pays 6.7% on total wages for FICA taxes and 3.4% on wages of $6,000 or less for FUTA taxes. The firm also pays $60 per month for each employee's health insurance.

Required:
A. Based strictly on the economics involved, should Pilgrim continue to hire the five additional packers or accept Mrs. Blair's offer?
B. What other factors, if any, should Mr. Shuman consider in the decision-making process?

CHAPTER 13
ACCOUNTING CONCEPTS: EFFECTS OF INFLATION

OVERVIEW AND OBJECTIVES

This chapter examines the nature of basic accounting concepts and principles as well as the effect of changing prices on financial reporting. When you have completed the chapter, you should understand:

- Why accounting standards are needed (p. 501).
- The nature of generally accepted accounting principles (pp. 501–502).
- The basic rules governing revenue recognition (pp. 505–506).
- How to apply the percentage-of-completion method of recognizing revenue on long-term construction contracts (pp. 506–507).
- The matching principle and the basic rules governing the timing of expenses (pp. 509–510).
- The nature of inflation (p. 513).
- The difference between general price-level changes and specific price changes (pp. 513–514).
- The distinction between constant dollar accounting and current value accounting (pp. 515–521).
- FASB requirements for reporting the effects of inflation (pp. 521–523).

Chapter 1 contains a brief description of some basic accounting concepts as well as the sources of accounting principles and practices. The theory underlying accounting concepts and standards has also been discussed throughout the preceding chapters as it related to the focus of those chapters. Thus, many important accounting concepts have been discussed in a relatively piecemeal fashion. In learning a new discipline, however, it is worthwhile to pause occasionally to consider what has been learned and to attempt to relate that learning to a general framework. That is one of the purposes of this chapter (Part A). An additional purpose is to study the effects of inflation on financial reporting (Part B).

PART A: ACCOUNTING CONCEPTS
THE NEED FOR ACCOUNTING STANDARDS

We have described the objective of financial reporting as that of providing financial information for use in making economic decisions. Business managers, investors, creditors, governmental agencies, and other outside parties use accounting information in making decisions concerning the allocation of scarce resources. These decisions have a significant effect on all of society since they have impact on the form and direction of our economy. The effectiveness of decision-makers is enhanced if they have information that is both reliable and understandable. In addition, decision-making requires information about a business that is comparable with prior periods as well as with other businesses. In other words, accountants need standards to guide them in preparing financial reports that contain information that is reliable, understandable, and comparable over time and between businesses when used by decision-makers.

GENERALLY ACCEPTED ACCOUNTING PRINCIPLES

The rules, conventions, and practices developed over time by the accounting profession are called **generally accepted accounting principles.** Sometimes also called *standards,* they include the assumptions, concepts, and practices that serve as general guidelines in the preparation of financial reports to make accounting information reliable, understandable, and comparable.

Principles or standards become ''generally accepted'' by obtaining the ''substantial authoritative support'' of the accounting profession. As noted in Chapter 1, the most active authoritative bodies are the American Institute of Certified Public Accountants, the Financial Accounting Standards Board, and the Securities and Exchange Commission. These groups, with the help of extensive research staffs, study reporting alternatives for various transactions and select the one that results in the most useful presentation of financial information. Other groups such as the American Accounting Association, the National Association of Accountants, and the Financial Executives Institute also influence the development of accounting principles by conducting research and recommending reporting alternatives to those responsible for setting accounting standards, chiefly the FASB and the SEC. Selection of the best alternatives has come about gradually and in some areas has not yet been completed. Accounting standards are continually reviewed and revised to keep abreast with the increasing complexity of business operations. Accounting principles are not fundamental natural laws like those of the physical sciences; they are man-made guidelines that attain their status when they are accepted by the accounting profession.

Since accounting principles evolve in accordance with changes in the business environment, it is not possible to present a complete list of generally accepted accounting principles. There are, however, several broad principles that serve as basic guides in the selection of specific rules and practices. Knowledge of these broad principles will help us to better understand the general framework within which accounting standards are developed.

THE ENTITY CONCEPT

A basic principle of accounting is that information is accumulated for a specific area or unit of accountability called an entity. An **accounting entity** is an economic unit that controls resources and engages in economic activity. To accumulate financial information, the accountant must be able to clearly identify the boundaries of the unit being accounted for. Business activities of the entity are separated from both the personal activities of its owners and those of other entities. An entity may be an individual, a governmental agency, a nonprofit organization, a business enterprise, or an organizational subunit. For example, we may want to prepare a report for a single division of a company, in which case the division is considered a separate unit of accountability.

Attention in accounting is normally focused on the economic activities of individual businesses, but the boundaries of the accounting entity may not be the same as those of the legal entity. For example, a parent company and its subsidiaries (other companies a parent company controls) are considered an economic unit of accountability for which consolidated financial statements are prepared as discussed in Chapter 18. However, each of the individual companies is a legal entity and therefore also an accounting entity. When financial reports are prepared, they must identify clearly the entity being reported on.

THE GOING CONCERN ASSUMPTION

Accounting reports are prepared under the assumption that the business will continue to operate in the future, unless there is evidence to the contrary. Because it is not possible to predict how long a business will exist, an assumption must be made. Past experience indicates that the continuation of operations in the future is highly probable for most companies. Thus, it is assumed that the business will continue to operate at least long enough to carry out its existing commitments. This assumption is called the **going concern assumption** or sometimes the *continuity assumption*.

Adoption of the going concern assumption has important implications in accounting. For example, it provides justification for the use of historical costs in accounting for plant assets and for the systematic allocation of their cost to depreciation over their useful lives. Because it is assumed that the assets will not be sold in the near future but will continue to be used in operating activities, current market values of the assets are of little importance. If the business continues to use the assets, fluctuations in their market values cause no gain or loss, nor do they increase or decrease the usefulness of the assets. The going concern assumption also supports the inclusion of some assets, such as prepaid expenses and purchased goodwill, in the balance sheet even though they may have little if any sales value.

Although the going concern assumption is followed in most cases, it should not be applied when there is conclusive evidence that the business will not continue. If management intends to liquidate the business, the going concern and historical cost principles are set aside and financial statements are prepared on the basis of expected liquidation values. Thus, assets are reported at their expected sales values and liabilities at the amount needed to settle them immediately.

THE TIME PERIOD ASSUMPTION

A completely accurate report of the degree of success achieved by a business cannot be obtained until the business is liquidated. Only then can net income be determined precisely. Users of financial information, however, need timely information for decision-making purposes. Accountants must thus prepare periodic reports on the results of operations, financial position, and changes in financial position. To do so, accountants have adopted the **time-period assumption**—that is, they assume that economic activity can be associated realistically with relatively short time intervals.

Because of the many estimates, professional judgments, and assumptions required, dividing the continuous economic activity of a business into time periods such as months, quarters, and years creates many problems for accountants. The shorter the time period, the more inaccurate are the cost allocations needed to determine net income. As a result, monthly net income is generally a less reliable figure than quarterly net income, which in turn is less reliable than net income determined on a yearly basis. Since cost allocations affect asset and liability amounts, the shorter the reporting period, the more inaccurate the balance-sheet amounts. Periodic measurements of net income and financial position are estimates and therefore tentative. Users of financial statements should be fully aware of the tentative nature of the statement amounts when making decisions. There is a trade-off between the reliability of accounting information and its timely reporting—the more timely the information, the more subject it is to error.

THE MONETARY UNIT PRINCIPLE

Money is used in accounting as the common denominator by which economic activity is measured and reported. Accountants assume that data expressed in terms of money are useful in making economic decisions and that the monetary unit (the dollar) represents a realistic unit of value that can be used to measure net income, financial position, and changes in financial position.

Inherent in the use of money as a unit of measure is the assumption that the value of money remains constant over time. As a result, 1983 dollars are combined with 1980 and 1975 dollars as though they all represented the same purchasing power. For example, land purchased in 1975 for $50,000 is added to land purchased in 1983 for $100,000 and reported as a dollar investment of $150,000. Although accountants recognize that when the general purchasing power of the dollar changes, the value of money also changes and that money therefore is not a stable unit of measure, these changes in the value of the measuring unit are ignored. Recent high inflation rates have raised serious doubts about the wisdom of ignoring changes in the purchasing power of money, and current accounting standards require the supplementary disclosure of the effects of inflation. Methods of disclosure, as well as the problems and benefits involved, are discussed later in this chapter.

THE OBJECTIVITY PRINCIPLE

The **objectivity principle** holds that, if possible, accounting information should be factual (free from bias) and verifiable. **Verifiability** means that the data are supported by adequate evidence that supports the validity of the data. If information is objective and verifiable, essentially similar measures and results would be produced if two or more qualified persons examined the same data. For example, the price agreed upon in an arms-length exchange transaction is objective because it is based upon negotiation between independent parties. The price is also verifiable if it is supported by an invoice, contract, paid check, or other document. Accountants rely on various types of evidence to support the figures presented in accounting reports. Business documents such as contracts, purchase orders, invoices, paid checks, and physical counts of inventory and other assets provide objective, verifiable evidence in accounting.

Although accountants seek the most objective evidence available, we must recognize that accounting data are not completely objective because there are many cases in which estimates must be made on the basis of personal judgments and observations. For example, the cost of a plant asset may be highly objective, but the amount of depreciation charged to each accounting period is affected by estimates of useful life and residual value as well as by the selection of an appropriate depreciation method. However, as long as estimates are based on data and methods that can be verified by outside parties, the information is considered basically objective and verifiable.

THE COST PRINCIPLE

The need for objective, verifiable data is the basic reason for the use of historical cost in accounting. Resources acquired are recorded at their cost as measured by the amount of cash or cash equivalent given to acquire them. Changes in the market value of the resources are generally ignored and the cost of the resources is allocated to the periods that benefit from their use. Thus, the income statement reflects the cost of resources used as expenses and the balance sheet reports the unallocated cost of the resources.

Some accountants believe that current market value (rather than cost) should be used as the basis for measuring resources and expenses. They argue that current values are more relevant to users of accounting data. Current values, however, are less objective than historical costs, which raises the question of which concept is more important—reliability or relevancy. As discussed in a later section of this chapter, many accountants support the presentation of both historical cost and current value data as at least a partial solution of the problem.

THE REVENUE REALIZATION PRINCIPLE

An important accounting function is the determination of periodic net income—the process of identifying and measuring revenues and expenses for a specified time period. Revenue for a period is determined by applying the **revenue realization principle,** which provides guidance as to when revenue should be recognized. Essentially, the realization principle provides that revenue should be recognized under accrual accounting when it is earned.

Some revenue, like interest revenue and rent revenue, is earned with the passage of time and is therefore not difficult to associate with specific time periods. On the other hand, sales revenue is earned in a continuous process as the activities that give rise to revenue take place. For example, the earning process for a manufacturing firm involves acquisition of goods and services, production of a product, sale of the finished product, and collection from customers. Although all of these activities contribute to the earning process, it is difficult to determine objectively how much revenue is earned at each step. To provide a practical guide, accountants have adopted the realization principle, which provides that revenue should be recognized when (1) the earning process is complete or essentially complete and (2) an exchange has taken place. Following this principle, most revenue is recognized when goods are sold (which normally means when they are delivered) or services are rendered and become billable. At this point the earning process is essentially completed and the exchange price provides objective evidence of the amount of revenue to recognize. The only part of the earning process remaining is the collection of the sales price, which is considered relatively assured in our credit-oriented society.

Although most revenue is recognized at the time of sale, two major exceptions are the percentage-of-completion method and the installment sales method.

Percentage-of-completion Method

Construction companies often undertake projects that may take two or more years to complete. For example, assume a company signed a contract to construct a major section of interstate highway that is expected to take four years to complete. If the basic realization principle were followed, net income on the project would not be recognized until the end of construction. Annual income statements would clearly be of little use to investors and other users who must make timely decisions. As a result, departure from the realization principle is recommended for long-term construction projects when estimates of costs to complete and the extent of progress toward completion are reasonably dependable.[1] Estimates are made of the percentage of the project completed each year and gross profit is recognized in proportion to the work completed. This approach is called the **percentage-of-completion method** of accounting for long-term construction projects. The method works as follows:

1. An estimate is made of the total cost expected to be incurred on the project. The difference between the contract price and total estimated cost is the estimated gross profit.
2. At the end of each year, the percentage of the project completed during the year is estimated. This may be done by comparing the actual project costs incurred during the year to the most recent estimate of the total cost of the project, or an estimate may be made by engineers or other qualified personnel.
3. The percentage determined above is multiplied by the estimated gross profit on the project, as computed in Step 1, to determine the amount of gross profit for the year.

[1] "Long-term Construction-type Contracts," *Accounting Research Bulletin No. 45* (New York: AICPA, 1955), par. 15.

4. In the final year of the project, no estimate is needed because total actual costs are known. The difference between the actual gross profit and the cumulative amount of gross profit recognized in prior years constitutes the gross profit for the final year.

To illustrate, assume that Bates Construction Company signed a contract to construct a section of interstate highway at a price of $10,000,000. The project is expected to take three years to complete at an estimated cost of $7,000,000. Estimated gross profit on the project is therefore $3,000,000. The actual costs incurred and the amount of gross profit recognized each year are:

Year	Actual Costs Incurred	÷	Estimated Total Costs	=	Percent	×	Estimated Gross Profit	=	Gross Profit for the Year
1	$2,450,000	÷	$7,000,000	=	35%	×	$3,000,000	=	$1,050,000
2	2,800,000	÷	7,000,000	=	40%	×	3,000,000	=	1,200,000
3	1,850,000				a				650,000
Total	$7,100,000								$2,900,000

aBalance to complete the contract:

Contract price	$10,000,000
Actual cost	7,100,000
Actual gross profit	2,900,000
Gross profit recognized in the first two years (1,050,000 + 1,200,000)	2,250,000
Remaining gross profit	$ 650,000

In Year 1, the actual costs incurred represented 35% of the estimated total cost of the project. The percentage-of-completion method assumes that incurring costs represents a valid reflection of progress toward completion of the project. Thus, 35% of the estimated gross profit is recognized in Year 1. Similarly, 40% of the total estimated cost was incurred in Year 2 and 40% of the estimated gross profit is therefore recognized. In Year 3, gross profit is recognized in an amount equal to the actual total gross profit on the contract minus the cumulative amount of gross profit recognized in Years 1 and 2.

The percentage-of-completion method is based on estimates and therefore introduces an element of subjectivity into the determination of net income. In spite of this, the financial statements are considered more useful than they would be if none of the profit were recognized until the end of the project.

Although the percentage-of-completion method is appropriate in accounting for long-term contracts expected to produce a profit, it is not an appropriate method if a loss is expected. When it becomes apparent that a loss is expected, the estimated loss must be recognized immediately.

The Installment Method

It is common practice in some businesses to make sales on an installment basis. The purchaser normally makes a down payment and agrees to pay the remainder of the purchase price in equal installments at specified times. The seller often retains title to the property until final payment is received or makes other arrangements to permit the repossession of the property in the event the purchaser defaults. In spite of these provisions, installment sales ordinarily should be accounted for in the same manner as regular sales on account, and revenue should be recognized at the time of sale.[2] Of course, appropriate provision should be made for estimated uncollectible accounts. In the relatively rare situations in which collection of the sales price is not reasonably assured, the installment method of accounting may be used.[3]

Under the **installment method,** each cash receipt is considered to consist of a partial recovery of the cost of the property sold and partially gross profit. For example, if the gross profit rate on the installment sale is 40%, each cash receipt is considered to consist of 40% gross profit and 60% recovery of cost of goods sold. To illustrate, assume that on July 1, 1984, Croy Company sold land that cost $18,000 for $30,000. The gross profit rate is 40% ($30,000 − $18,000)/$30,000. The purchaser made a down payment of $6,000 and agreed to pay the remaining $24,000 at the rate of $1,000 per month for 24 months beginning on August 1.[4] The amount of gross profit from installment sales recognized in each period, assuming all payments are received when due, is:

Year	Amount Collected	×	Gross Profit Rate	=	Gross Profit
1984	$11,000	×	40%	=	$ 4,400
1985	12,000	×	40%	=	4,800
1986	7,000	×	40%	=	2,800
Total	$30,000				$12,000

The $11,000 collected in 1984 consists of the down payment of $6,000 plus five monthly payments of $1,000 each. Under the installment method, gross profit is deferred and recognized when payment is received.

---

[2]Accounting Principles Board, "Omnibus Opinion—1966," *APB Opinion No. 10* (New York: AICPA, 1966), par. 12.

[3]The Internal Revenue Code permits the use of the installment method; it is often used for income tax purposes because it permits the deferral of income tax payments until the cash is received.

[4]Installment sales contracts generally provide for interest on the unpaid balance. Although ignored in our illustration, the amount of each payment representing interest is recognized as interest revenue when received.

EXPENSE RECOGNITION—THE MATCHING PRINCIPLE

Revenue is an inflow of assets from the sale of goods or performance of services. Expenses are the assets used up in the process of producing revenue. In general terms, under accrual accounting, revenues are recognized when they are earned and expenses recognized (or matched against revenue) as assets are used. Just as the realization principle has been developed by accountants to serve as a guide in the timing of revenue, the **matching principle** has been developed to guide the timing of expense recognition. Three basic rules specify the bases for recognizing expenses. They are associating cause and effect, systematic and rational allocation, and immediate recognition.

Associating Cause and Effect

Some expenses are recognized on the basis of a relatively direct association with revenues earned and are therefore recorded in the same period the revenue is recognized. Examples are the cost of goods sold during the period and sales commissions. The sale of goods produced the sales revenue; sales commissions relate directly to the revenue generated by the salespeople.

Systematic and Rational Allocation

Many expenses cannot be associated directly with revenue-producing transactions but can be associated with specific accounting periods and are allocated to those accounting periods in a systematic and rational way. Examples are depreciation of plant assets, amortization of intangible assets, and allocation of rent and insurance. The depreciation, amortization, and allocation methods described in earlier chapters provide a systematic and rational allocation of asset costs to the periods that benefit from their use.

Immediate Recognition

Some expenses are associated with the current accounting period because (1) they cannot be associated directly with revenue transactions, (2) they have no discernible benefits for future accounting periods, or (3) their allocation among several accounting periods serves no useful purpose. Application of this rule results in a charge to expense in the period in which payment is made or a liability incurred. Examples are officers' salaries, selling expenses such as advertising, and research and development expenditures. In addition, items carried as assets that are determined to have no discernible benefit for future periods are charged to expense. One example is equipment that has suddenly become obsolete before the end of its original useful life.

In applying these expense-recognition rules, costs are first analyzed to see whether they can be associated with revenue on the basis of cause and effect. If not, an attempt is made to apply systematic and rational allocation procedures. If neither cause and effect nor systematic and rational allocation is appropriate, costs are recognized as expenses in the period incurred.

THE PRINCIPLE OF CONSISTENCY

Several generally accepted alternative accounting methods have been described in preceding chapters. For example, inventory methods include FIFO, LIFO, and average, and depreciation methods include straight-line, sum-of-years'-digits, declining balance, and units-of-production. The methods adopted have a significant effect on the amount of net income reported for a period as well as on financial position at the end of the period. Although accounting statements for any given period may be useful in themselves, they are more useful if they can be compared with similar statements of prior periods. To improve the comparability of accounting data, accountants follow the **consistency principle,** which requires that once a particular accounting method is adopted, it will not be changed from period to period. Without this principle, large changes in net income and financial position may result from an arbitrary change in the accounting methods used rather than from changes in business conditions or general managerial effectiveness.

The principle of consistency does not mean that a company can never change an accounting method. In fact, a change to a new method should be made if the new method provides more useful information than the previous method. If a company changes an accounting method, however, the nature of and justification for the change and its effect on net income must be disclosed in the financial statements of the period in which the change is made.[5] The justification should explain clearly why the new method is preferable. For example, a change in method may be disclosed in a footnote such as this one:

During the year, the company changed from the first-in, first-out to the last-in, first-out method of accounting for inventory because the last-in, first-out method more clearly reflects net income. The effect of the change was to decrease net income by $460,000 for the period.

We should also note that the consistency principle does not require that a given accounting method be applied throughout the company. A company may very well use different inventory methods for different types of inventory and different depreciation methods for different kinds of plant assets.

---

[5]Accounting Principles Board, ''Accounting Changes,'' *APB Opinion No. 20* (New York: AICPA, 1971), par. 17.

THE FULL DISCLOSURE PRINCIPLE

The **full disclosure principle** requires that all relevant information affecting net income and financial position must be reported in the financial statements or in footnotes to the financial statements—although this does not mean that information must be reported in great detail. Too much detailed information, in fact, may impede rather than improve the usefulness of information. A list of the customers who owe money to a company and the amount owed by each would be of little use to statement users. On the other hand, if a single customer owes a large portion, say 60%, of the total accounts receivable, that fact may be significant and usually should be disclosed. In general, the goal is to disclose information in sufficient detail to permit the knowledgeable reader to make an informed decision.

Because many alternative accounting methods exist and because the methods adopted can affect significantly the financial position and results of operations of a company, knowledge of the methods used is essential for statement users. A summary of the accounting methods used must therefore be presented as an integral part of the financial statements.[6] This summary is generally included as the first footnote to the financial statements (for example, see footnote 1 of the General Motors financial statements in the Appendix). In addition to the disclosure of accounting methods, other items typically disclosed include:

1. The components of inventory such as raw materials, work in process, and finished goods.
2. The components of the income tax provision.
3. The terms of major debt agreements.
4. The nature of any contingent liabilities such as lawsuits.
5. Identification of assets pledged as security for loans.
6. The nature of contractual agreements for leases, pension plans, and stock-option plans.
7. Major transactions affecting stockholders' equity.
8. The effect of changes in accounting methods and estimates.

MATERIALITY

Materiality is used in accounting to refer to the relative size or importance of an item or event. Accounting is a practical art rather than an exact science. Although accountants generally apply the most theoretically sound treatment to transactions and events, they sometimes deviate from that practice because

---

[6]Accounting Principles Board, "Disclosure of Accounting Policies," *APB Opinion No. 22* (New York: AICPA, 1972), par. 8.

the effect of a transaction or event is not significant enough to affect decisions: the effect is not relevant. For example, small expenditures for plant assets are often expensed immediately rather than depreciated over their useful lives to save clerical costs of recording depreciation and because the effects on the income statements and balance sheets over their useful lives are not large enough to affect decisions. Another example of the application of materiality is the common practice by large companies of rounding amounts to the nearest thousand dollars in their financial statements.

Materiality is a relative matter: what is material for one company may be immaterial for another. A $10,000 error in the financial statements of a multi-million-dollar company may not be important, but it may be critical to a small company. The materiality of an item may depend not only upon its relative size but also on its nature. For example, the discovery of a $10,000 bribe is a material event even for a large company. Judgments as to the materiality of an item or event are often difficult. Accountants make them based on their knowledge of the company and on past experience, and users of financial statements must generally rely on the accountants' judgment. In summary, an item is material if there is a reasonable expectation that knowledge of it would influence the decisions of financial statement users.

CONSERVATISM

Accountants must make many difficult judgments and estimates when determining the proper treatment of business transactions. In reaching a decision, they must rely on the principles described earlier in an effort to make a fair presentation of the factual effects of the transactions. When this approach fails and doubt exists, accountants apply the convention of **conservatism,** which says in essence: *When in doubt, choose the solution that is least likely to overstate assets and income for the current period.*

Conservatism is apparent in the tendency to defer the recognition of gains until the earning process is essentially completed but to recognize losses as soon as they become known. For example, in the application of the lower of cost or market rule to inventory valuation, a loss is recognized if the market value of the inventory is less than its cost. If the market value exceeds cost, however, the gain is not recognized until the inventory is sold.

Conservatism is a useful approach in accounting but should be applied only when uncertainty prevents the reporting of factual results. Nothing in the convention of conservatism suggests that accountants should understate income or assets. An overapplication of conservatism produces incorrect results in both the current accounting period and future periods.

PART B: EFFECTS OF INFLATION

In our economy, money (the dollar) is used as both a medium of exchange and as a measure of "real" value as determined by the amount of goods and services for which it can be exchanged. The amount of goods or services for which a dollar can be exchanged is called the **purchasing power of the dollar.** Although the price of some goods (such as calculators, digital watches, and computers) has decreased in recent years, the economy of the United States and of most other countries has been characterized by significantly increasing prices of most goods and services. The general increase in prices results in **inflation,** which can be defined as a decrease in the purchasing power of the dollar or as an increase in the general price level. The **general price level** is the weighted average price of all goods and services in our economy.

Price changes are of two types: specific price changes and general price level changes. It is important to distinguish these two types because they reflect quite different things. **Specific price changes** are changes in the prices of specific goods or services such as bread, computers, and medical services. These specific prices may increase or decrease from one period to another. As indicated earlier, the prices of calculators and digital watches, for example, have been decreasing, whereas the prices of real estate and medical services have increased steadily.

General price level changes are changes in the weighted average of all goods and services in the economy. A general price level change therefore represents a change in the value of money in all its uses. Specific price changes affect the general price level because the prices of specific goods and services constitute the items used to determine the general price level. Although the general price level may decrease (deflation), that has occurred only once in the United States during the last 35 years—in 1949. Thus, the more common occurrence is an increase in the general price level (inflation).

When the general price level increases, it takes more dollars to acquire a given amount of goods or services. Stated another way, a dollar will buy a smaller amount of goods or services. The general price level is expressed in the form of an index number with a specific base year set equal to 100. Although agencies of the United States government publish several general price indexes, the most widely recognized is the Consumer Price Index (CPI), which is published monthly by the Bureau of Labor Statistics. The Financial Accounting Standards Board requires this index to restate financial statements for general price level changes because it is readily available, timely, and produces results that are comparable to other general price indexes. A partial listing of the CPI and the yearly inflation rate is shown in Figure 13-1.

As can be seen in Figure 13-1, the general price level almost doubled from 1967 to 1978; that is, the 1978 dollar purchased only about half as much goods

Figure 13-1
Consumer Price In-
dex

Year	Average Index* (1967 = 100)	Year-end Index	Inflation Rate
1967	100.0	101.6	
1968	104.2	106.4	4.2%
1969	109.8	112.9	5.4
1970	116.3	119.1	5.9
1971	121.3	123.1	4.3
1972	125.3	127.3	3.3
1973	133.1	138.5	6.2
1974	147.7	155.4	11.0
1975	161.2	166.3	9.1
1976	170.5	174.3	5.8
1977	181.5	186.1	6.5
1978	195.4	202.9	7.7
1979	217.4	229.9	11.3
1980	246.8	258.4	13.5

*Source: U.S. Department of Labor, Bureau of Labor Statistics

and services as the 1967 dollar. Stated another way, it would take $195.40 in 1978 to purchase the same goods and services that could have been purchased in 1967 for $100. The inflation rate was determined on the basis of the change in the average index for the year. Thus, for example, the inflation rate for 1975 was computed as $(161.2 - 147.7)/147.7 = 9.1\%$.

REPORTING THE EFFECTS OF INFLATION

As discussed earlier, accountants prepare financial statements based on historical cost under the stable-dollar assumption. These historical cost financial statements consist of aggregated amounts of dollars from different years, which represent different purchasing powers. The impact of inflation is difficult to assess by statement users. Because of the persistent nature of inflation and relatively high inflation rates, many accountants and users of financial information question the usefulness of the dollar measurements in the traditional historical-cost financial statements. They disagree, however, on what should be done to make the financial statements more useful. Although several approaches have been suggested, two primary methods of reporting the effects of inflation have received relatively wide support. One is to restate the historical-cost financial statements for changes in the general price level: **constant dollar accounting.** The other is to prepare the financial statements on the basis of current prices: **current value accounting.**

CONSTANT DOLLAR ACCOUNTING

Under constant dollar accounting, historical cost figures in the financial statements are converted to the number of current dollars representing an equivalent amount of purchasing power through the use of a general price level index such as the CPI. This is accomplished by multiplying the historical cost amounts by a fraction. The numerator of the fraction is the current index number. The denominator is the index number at the date the historical cost figure originated. The objective is to state all amounts in dollars of current purchasing power. For example, assume that land was purchased on December 31, 1972 for $100,000. The land would be restated to an equivalent number of 1980 dollars as follows:

$$\frac{\text{Current price index}}{\text{Historical cost price index}} \times \text{Historical cost} = \text{Restated cost}$$

$$\frac{258.4}{127.3} \times \$100,000 = \$202,985$$

If additional land was purchased on December 31, 1975 for $50,000, it would be converted to 1980 dollar purchasing power as:

$$\frac{258.4}{166.3} \times \$50,000 = \$77,691$$

Land would be reported on the 1980 constant dollar balance sheet at $280,676 ($202,985 + $77,691).

Restatement for general price-level changes is not considered a departure from the historical-cost principle because historical costs are merely adjusted to a constant 1980 measuring unit. Thus the restated amount for land of $280,676 does not represent the current market value of the land. The restatement does, however, represent a departure from the stable-dollar assumption.

Monetary and Nonmonetary Items

When preparing constant-dollar financial statements, one must distinguish monetary items from nonmonetary items because their treatment is different. Monetary items are those assets and liabilities that represent claims to a fixed number of dollars. Cash, accounts receivable, and notes receivable therefore are monetary assets. Most liabilities are monetary because they represent obligations to pay fixed amounts of dollars. Since monetary items represent claims to fixed amounts of dollars, they are already stated in terms of current purchasing power and therefore do not need to be restated.

Purchasing power gains and losses result from holding monetary items over time. Holding monetary assets during a period of rising prices results in a loss in purchasing power since the value of money is falling. On the other hand, owing money (holding monetary liabilities) during a period of rising prices results in a purchasing-power gain since the debts can be paid in the future with dollars of smaller purchasing power.

To illustrate a purchasing-power loss, assume that Bray Company held $20,000 in cash throughout 1980. The loss in purchasing power would be:

Number of dollars needed to maintain purchasing power

$$\left(\$20,000 \times \frac{258.4}{229.9}\right)$$
$22,479

Actual number of dollars held at year end   20,000

Purchasing power loss $ 2,479

If Bray Company also held a $30,000 note payable throughout 1980, the gain in purchasing power would be:

Number of year-end dollars representing the same purchasing power
  as the amount owed at the beginning of the year

$$\left(\$30,000 \times \frac{258.4}{229.9}\right)$$
$33,719

Number of dollars actually owed   30,000

Purchasing power gain $ 3,719

Nonmonetary items are those items that are not monetary in nature. Examples are inventory, plant assets, intangibles, and stockholders' equity. Since these items do not represent claims to fixed amounts of cash, no purchasing-power gain or loss results and the nonmonetary items must be restated in terms of constant dollars. By restating them, recognition is given to the effect of changes in the general price level from the time the items were originally acquired.

Constant-dollar Balance Sheet

To illustrate the preparation of a constant-dollar balance sheet, the historical-cost balance sheet, restatement computations, and constant-dollar balance sheet for Troy Company adjusted to year-end dollars are shown in Figure 13-2. Assumptions are that:

1. Restatement is based on the CPI (Figure 13-1).
2. Troy Company was formed on December 31, 1974. Capital stock was issued and all plant assets and land were acquired at that time.
3. Inventory was acquired evenly throughout 1980; the average CPI for 1980 was 246.8 (Figure 13-1).

Notice that the monetary assets and liabilities are not restated. Nonmonetary assets and capital stock are restated on the basis of the current (1980) index

Figure 13-2
Constant Dollar Balance Sheet

TROY COMPANY
Constant-dollar Balance Sheet
December 31, 1980

	Historical Cost	Computation	Constant Dollar
Assets			
Cash	$ 48,000	Monetary—not restated	$ 48,000
Accounts receivable	76,000	Monetary—not restated	76,000
Inventory	80,000	(258.4/246.8) × $ 80,000	83,760
Plant and equipment	148,000	(258.4/155.4) × $148,000	246,095
Accumulated depreciation	(42,000)	(258.4/155.4) × $ 42,000	(69,838)
Land	60,000	(258.4/155.4) × $ 60,000	99,768
Total	$370,000		$483,785
Liabilities			
Accounts payable	$ 53,000	Monetary—not restated	$ 53,000
Notes payable, 1985	40,000	Monetary—not restated	40,000
Stockholders' Equity			
Capital stock	180,000	(258.4/155.4) × $180,000	299,305
Retained earnings	97,000	Balancing amount	91,480
Total	$370,000		$483,785

over the index at the time the nonmonetary assets were acquired and capital stock issued. The restated retained earnings figure is an amount that is entered to bring the constant-dollar balance sheet into balance.

Constant-dollar Income Statement

A historical-cost and constant-dollar income statement for Troy Company is given in Figure 13-3. Assumptions are that:

1. Sales were made and expenses (other than depreciation) incurred evenly throughout the year.
2. The purchasing power loss of $2,640, which resulted because Troy Company carried an excess of monetary assets over monetary liabilities through the year, is an assumed amount. The computation of the purchasing power gain or loss in an actual situation is quite complex and is therefore covered in detail in more advanced accounting courses.

Figure 13-3
Constant Dollar Income Statement

TROY COMPANY
Constant-dollar Income Statement
For Year Ended December 31, 1980

	Historical Cost	Computations	Constant Dollar
Sales	$394,000	(258.4/246.8) × $394,000	$412,519
Expenses:			
Cost of goods sold	241,000	(258.4/246.8) × $241,000	252,327
Depreciation	20,000	(258.4/155.4) × $ 20,000	33,256
Other expenses	73,000	(258.4/246.8) × $ 73,000	76,431
Total expenses	334,000		362,014
Net income	$ 60,000		
Net income before purchasing power loss			50,505
Purchasing power loss			(2,640)
Constant dollar net income			$ 47,865

Notice that sales, cost of goods sold, and other expenses were converted on the basis of the current CPI over the average CPI for the year. Depreciation expense is converted on the basis of the CPI that existed when the related depreciable assets were acquired in 1974.

The need for constant dollar financial statements is an unsettled issue. Those who support their preparation argue that the stable-dollar assumption does not reflect reality, particularly when inflation rates are high. They believe that the aggregation of dollars with different purchasing power may mislead users of financial information and thereby cause poor decisions. In addition, they argue that the financial data in constant-dollar statements are just as reliable and verifiable as historical-cost data. Critics of constant-dollar accounting argue that both historical-cost and constant-dollar financial statements are inadequate because they ignore real value changes. Most critics consequently support the preparation of current-value financial statements.

CURRENT-VALUE ACCOUNTING

As explained earlier, constant-dollar accounting does not depart from the historical-cost concept, but merely restates historical costs in terms of the current purchasing power of money—that is, historical costs are adjusted only for general price level changes. Current-value accounting, however, is a departure from historical cost because it gives effect to specific price changes. Two basic concepts of current value exist: net realizable value and current replacement cost (current cost). **Net realizable value** is an exit value, an estimate of the amount an asset could be sold for in its present condition minus disposal costs. **Current replacement cost** is an entry value, an estimate of the amount that would have to be paid currently to acquire an asset in its present condition, and is generally referred to simply as *current cost*.

Proponents of current-value accounting tend to support the use of current cost rather than net realizable value for two reasons. First, current costs are believed to be more objectively determinable by the use of current price lists of suppliers, prices in established markets for used assets, and specific price indexes. Second, most assets are held for use rather than for direct sale. In addition, the Financial Accounting Standards Board requires the disclosure of selected current cost information as discussed later in this chapter. Our discussion, although limited, will thus concentrate on current-cost accounting.

To illustrate the preparation of current-cost financial statements, assume that the replacement cost of Troy Company's nonmonetary assets on December 31, 1980, and the replacement cost of goods sold at the time they were sold were as follows:

Inventory	$ 92,000
Plant and equipment (net of depreciation)	300,000
Land	110,000
Cost of goods sold	275,000

Plant and equipment items are depreciated by the straight-line method and have a 10 year remaining life.

The current cost balance sheet would be:

TROY COMPANY
Current-cost Balance Sheet
December 31, 1980

Cash	$ 48,000
Accounts receivable	76,000
Inventory	92,000
Plant and equipment (net)	300,000
Land	110,000
Total Assets	$626,000
Accounts payable	$ 53,000
Notes payable	40,000
Common stock (258.4/155.4 × $180,000)	299,305
Retained earnings (balancing amount)	233,695
Total Equities	$626,000

In the current-cost balance sheet, monetary assets (cash and accounts receivable) and monetary liabilities (accounts and notes payable) are not changed from their historical amounts because they already reflect current values. Nonmonetary assets are reported at the current cost to replace them in their present condition. Contributed capital accounts are normally restated for general price-level changes and retained earnings is computed as a balancing amount.

The current-cost income statement for Troy Company would be:

TROY COMPANY
Current-cost Income Statement
For Year Ended December 31, 1980

Sales		$394,000
Expenses:		
Cost of goods sold	$275,000	
Depreciation	30,000	
Other expenses	73,000	378,000
Net Income		$ 16,000

In the current-cost income statement, sales and those expenses resulting from current cash payments or current accruals are reported at their historical cost amounts. Historical costs are used because sales resulted in an increase in monetary assets (cash or accounts receivable) and expenses resulted in a decrease in monetary assets (cash) or an increase in monetary liabilities (accrued expenses). Expenses that will differ from historical costs (primarily cost of goods sold and depreciation) are reported at their current cost. Cost of goods sold is computed by multiplying the number of units sold by the replacement cost of the units at the time of sale. Depreciation expense is determined by applying the depreciation methods used to the plant assets' replacement costs. By reporting current costs, each company recognizes the effect of the specific price changes that affect the resources used by that company.

Proponents of current-cost accounting argue that current-cost information is much more realistic than historical-cost or constant-dollar information—and therefore more useful. They also believe that a company has net earnings only if it has recovered the replacement cost of resources used, thereby permitting it to maintain its productive capacity. Critics of current-cost accounting maintain that replacement costs are too subjective and difficult to verify and may therefore mislead decision-makers. In addition, they believe that the use of LIFO to determine cost of goods sold and the use of rapid depreciation methods are objective and verifiable and will result in reported earnings that approach those that would be reported under current cost accounting. Consequently, they argue, essentially the same earnings results could be obtained without departing from the historical-cost basis.

FASB REQUIREMENTS

The Financial Accounting Standards Board has been concerned with the reporting problems created by inflation but has had difficulty reaching an agreement as to the proper solution. Each reporting basis—historical cost, constant dollar, and current cost—has its advantages and disadvantages. Because decision-makers use financial information daily, a major change in the reporting basis has the potential of disrupting the decision-making process and, therefore, the allocation of resources within our economy. In order to obtain experience in the preparation and use of different reporting bases, the FASB requires that some companies must present selected data on a constant-dollar and current-cost basis in supplementary schedules to the historical-cost-based financial statements. Specific reporting requirements are contained in *Statement of Financial Accounting Standards No. 33,* "Financial Reporting and Changing Prices."

Statement No. 33 applies only to large publicly held companies—those with inventories and property, plant, and equipment (before deducting accumulated depreciation) of more than $125 million, or with total assets of more than $1 billion (after deducting accumulated depreciation). The main disclosures required, supplementary to the regular historical-cost-based financial statements, are:

1. Income from continuing operations for the current fiscal year on a constant-dollar basis.
2. The purchasing power gain or loss on net monetary items for the current fiscal year.
3. Income from continuing operations for the current fiscal year on a current-cost basis.
4. The current-cost amounts of inventory and property, plant, and equipment at the end of the current fiscal year.[7]

An example of these disclosures by Zenith Radio Corporation is reproduced in Figure 13-4.

---

[7]Financial Accounting Standards Board, "Financial Reporting and Changing Prices," *Statement of Financial Accounting Standards No. 33* (Stamford: FASB, 1979), par. 29, 30.

Figure 13-4
Zenith Radio
Effects of Price
Changes

Income and Net Assets as Reported and as Adjusted for Changing Prices
for the Year ended December 31, 1980 (in millions)

	As Reported	General Inflation (Constant dollar)	Changes in Specific Prices (Current cost)
Net sales	$1,186	$1,186	$1,186
Cost of sales	955	976	957
Depreciation	19	27	31
Other costs, expenses and income, net	165	165	165
Provision for income taxes	21	21	21
Net income (loss)	$ 26	$ (3)	$ 12
Effective tax rate	44%	117%	64%
Inflationary impact on purchasing power of:			
Monetary assets for time held		$ (22)	$ (22)
Monetary liabilities for time outstanding		36	36
		14	14
Net income and purchasing power gain		$ 11	$ 26
At December 31, 1980:			
Inventory	$ 236	$ 326	$ 263
Property, plant and equipment, net	151	221	265

For 1979, current cost values (in average 1979 dollars) of cost of sales, depreciation, and net income were $904 million, $25 million, and $9 million, respectively. Inventory and property, plant and equipment, net at December 31, 1979, in average 1979 dollars, were $267 million and $223 million, respectively.

The 1980 cost of sales under the constant dollar method included an $8 million reduction of inventory to net realizable value.

In addition to the above disclosures, *Statement No. 33* requires the disclosure of other selected information for each of the five most recent fiscal years.[8] An example of these disclosures by Zenith Radio Corporation is given in Figure 13-5.

[8]*Ibid.*, par. 35.

Selected Inflation-adjusted Data in Average 1980 Dollars
Prepared in Accordance with Financial Accounting Standards Board (FASB)
Statement No. 33 Requirements

	1980	1979	1978	1977	1976
Net sales	$1,185.9	$1,220.6	$1,237.8	$1,310.0	$1,371.4
Constant dollar information:					
Net income (loss)	(3)	12			
Per share	(.16)	.66			
Stockholders' equity at year-end	456	417			
Current cost information:					
Net income	12	10			
Per share	.64	.54			
Stockholders' equity at year-end	437	428			
Inventory and fixed assets based on current cost method over					
(under) those based on constant dollar method	(19)	9			
Other information:					
Gain from decline in purchasing power of net amounts owed	14	5			
Cash dividends per share—As reported	.60	.90	1.00	1.00	1.00
—Adjusted for general inflation	.60	1.02	1.26	1.36	1.45
Market price at year-end—As reported	19.50	9.75	12.88	13.50	27.38
—Adjusted for general inflation	$18.62	$10.47	$15.66	$19.23	$38.76
Average consumer price index	247	217	195	182	171

Figure 13-5
Zenith Radio Inflation-adjusted data

GLOSSARY

ACCOUNTING ENTITY.   An economic unit that controls resources and engages in economic activity (p. 502).

CONSERVATISM.   An accounting convention which provides that when in doubt, choose the solution least likely to overstate assets and income for the current period (p. 512).

CONSISTENCY PRINCIPLE.   The concept that once a particular accounting method is adopted it should not be changed from period to period unless a different method provides more useful information (p. 510).

CONSTANT DOLLAR ACCOUNTING.   The restatement of historical-cost financial statements for changes in the general price level (p. 514).

COST PRINCIPLE.   A basis on which resources and the allocation of resources are accounted for at their cost. Changes in the market value of resources are not recognized (p. 505).

CURRENT-VALUE ACCOUNTING (CURRENT-COST ACCOUNTING).   The preparation of financial statements on the basis of current costs (p. 514).

CURRENT REPLACEMENT COST (CURRENT COST).   The amount that would have to be paid currently to acquire an asset in its present condition (p. 519).

FULL-DISCLOSURE PRINCIPLE.   The accounting principle that financial statements should disclose all relevant information affecting net income and financial position of a company (p. 511).

GENERAL PRICE LEVEL.   The weighted average of the prices of all goods and services in an economy (p. 513).

GENERAL PRICE LEVEL CHANGE.   A change in the weighted average of the prices of all goods and services in an economy (p. 513).

GENERALLY ACCEPTED ACCOUNTING PRINCIPLES.   The body of rules, conventions, and practices followed by accountants (p. 501).

GOING CONCERN ASSUMPTION (CONTINUITY).   The assumption that a business will continue to operate in the future unless there is evidence to the contrary (p. 503).

INFLATION.   A decrease in purchasing power of money; also defined as an increase in the general price level (p. 513).

INSTALLMENT METHOD.   A method of accounting for installment sales under which gross profit is recognized in proportion to the amount of cash collected. Its use is permitted for financial reporting purposes only when collection of the sales price is not reasonably assured (p. 508).

MATCHING PRINCIPLE.   The guide followed in accounting to determine the time period in which expenses will be deducted from revenues (p. 509).

MATERIALITY.   The relative size or importance of an item or event. An item or event is considered material if knowledge of it would affect a user's decision (p. 511).

MONETARY ITEMS.   Assets and liabilities that represent claims to fixed amounts of dollars (p. 515).

MONETARY UNIT PRINCIPLE.   The use of money in accounting as the common denominator by which economic activity is measured and reported (p. 504).

NET REALIZABLE VALUE.   The amount an asset could be sold for, less disposal costs (p. 519).

NONMONETARY ITEMS.   All financial statement amounts that are not monetary in nature—that is, do not represent claims to fixed amounts of cash (p. 516).

OBJECTIVITY PRINCIPLE (VERIFIABILITY).   The concept that accounting data should be free from bias and supported by evidence that establishes its validity (p. 504).

PERCENTAGE-OF-COMPLETION METHOD.   A method of accounting for long-term construction projects under which gross profit is recognized in proportion to the work completed during the period (p. 506).

PURCHASING POWER.   The amount of goods or services for which a dollar can be exchanged (p. 513).

PURCHASING POWER GAIN (LOSS).   The gain (loss) from holding monetary liabilities (assets) during a period of rising prices (p. 515).

REVENUE REALIZATION PRINCIPLE.   The rule in accounting that revenue should be recognized when the earning process is substantially completed and an exchange has taken place (p. 505).

SPECIFIC PRICE CHANGE.   A change in the price of a specific good or service (p. 513).

TIME PERIOD ASSUMPTION.   Accountants' assumption that economic activity can be associated realistically with relatively short time intervals (p. 503).

DISCUSSION QUESTIONS

1. Why have accountants developed accounting standards of "generally accepted accounting principles"?
2. How do accounting principles become "generally accepted"?
3. Why is it so important that the business activities of an accounting entity be separated from the personal activities of its owners and the activities of other entities?
4. What is meant by the going concern assumption? What accounting practices receive their justification from this assumption?
5. How is the time period assumption related to the trade-off between the reliability of accounting information and its timely reporting?
6. What is the basic problem created by the monetary unit principle when inflation rates are high?
7. Explain what is meant by the cost principle. Why is it used instead of current market values?
8. What is the objectivity principle?
9. Explain what is meant by the revenue realization principle.
10. What is the matching principle? Briefly explain each of the three bases for recognizing expenses and give an example of each.
11. What is required by the consistency principle? Why?
12. What is meant by the full disclosure principle?
13. How is the concept of materiality used in accounting?
14. Explain what is incorporated in the convention of conservatism and when it is applied. Given an example of its application.
15. Distinguish between general price level changes and specific price changes.
16. What is constant-dollar accounting?
17. What is meant by the term *monetary items?* Give some examples.
18. What is current-value accounting?
19. What are the main disclosures required as a supplement to the regular historical-cost-based financial statements under FASB Statement No. 33?

EXERCISES

Exercise 13-1 (Matching Accounting Concepts)
Match the items in Column I with the appropriate descriptions in Column II.

Column I	Column II
_9_ a. Going concern (continuity)	1. The measurement basis used to record and report economic activity.
_11_ b. Consistency	2. The normal basis used to account for assets.
_10_ c. Materiality	3. Business activity is separated from the owner's personal activity.
_8_ d. Conservatism	4. Measurement of net income and financial position necessarily requires estimates.
_3_ e. Entity concept	5. Data can be corroborated by reference to business documents, physical counts, and measurements by several qualified persons.
_4_ f. Time period assumption	6. The basis for determining when expenses should be recognized.
_1_ g. Monetary unit assumption	7. The earning process must be completed and an exchange taken place.
_2_ h. Cost principle	8. Used to discourage overoptimism in recording assets and net income.
_12_ i. Full disclosure	9. An inappropriate assumption for a firm undergoing bankruptcy.
_5_ j. Verifiability (objectivity)	10. Relates to the relative size or importance of an item or event.
_7_ k. Revenue realization	11. The same accounting methods should be used by a firm from one period to another.
_6_ l. Matching principle	12. Financial reports should include all relevant and significant information affecting net income and financial position.

Exercise 13-2 (Violation of Accounting Principles)
Several independent situations are described below:

1. Depreciation expense was not recorded because to do so would result in a net loss for the period.
2. The LIFO inventory method was used in Year 1, FIFO in Year 2, and weighted average in Year 3.
3. The cost of three small files (cost $8.27 each) was charged to expense when purchased even though they had a useful life of several years.

4. The owner of a company included his personal medical expenses on the company's income statement.
5. Land was reported at its estimated selling price, which is substantially higher than its cost. The increase in value was included on the income statement.
6. No mention was made of a major lawsuit filed against the company even though the company's attorney believes there is a high probability of losing the suit.

Required:
Indicate for each situation the accounting principle(s) (if any) that is violated.

Exercise 13-3 (Percentage-of-completion Method)
Simmons Construction Company signed a contract to construct a dam on the Verde River for $16,000,000. The project is expected to take four years to complete at an estimated cost of $12,000,000. Actual costs incurred each year were:

Year	Costs Incurred
1	$ 2,400,000
2	3,360,000
3	3,600,000
4	2,760,000
Total	$12,120,000

Assume that the estimated total cost of the project remained at $12,000,000 through the end of the third year.

Required:
Determine the amount of gross profit that should be recognized each year under the percentage-of-completion method.

Exercise 13-4 (Installment Sale and Constant-dollar Accounting)
On March 1, 1984, Harding Company sold land held as an investment at a selling price of $800,000. The land had been acquired for $540,000 on January 1, 1977. The purchaser made a down payment of $400,000 and agreed to pay the remaining $400,000 at the rate of $10,000 per month for 40 months beginning on April 1, 1984.

Required:
A. Assuming all payments were received when due, determine the amount of gross profit that should be recognized each year under the installment basis. Harding's fiscal year-end is December 31.
B. Assume that the entire purchase price was received on the date of sale and that the Price Index was 224 on March 1, 1984, and 165 on January 1, 1977. Compute the gain or loss on the sale of land on a constant-dollar basis.
C. Assuming an income tax rate of 30%, and the situation described in (B) above, compute the after-tax gain or loss on a constant-dollar basis.

Exercise 13-5 (Constant-dollar Accounting)
Carol Company has landholdings that were purchased for a total of $210,000. The year of purchase and the purchase price for each of the three parcels owned are:

Parcel	Year Purchased	Purchase Price
1	1975	$120,000
2	1977	35,000
3	1978	55,000

Required:

A. Determine the amount at which land should be reported on a 1980 constant-dollar balance sheet. Base your computation on the CPI presented in Figure 13-1 on page 514. All purchases were made at year-end, December 31.

B. Assuming the land was sold early in 1981 for $285,000, compute the gain or loss from the sale based on:

  1. Historical-cost measurement.

  2. Constant-dollar measurement.

Exercise 13-6 (Purchasing Power Gain or Loss)

Bailey Company held $35,000 cash and a $10,000 note receivable throughout the year 1984. The company also held a note payable for $25,000 throughout the year. Assume the Price Index was 196 on January 1, 1984, and 217 on December 31, 1984.

Required:

Determine the purchasing power gain or loss on the monetary items.

Exercise 13-7 (Purchasing Power Gain or Loss)

Mrs. Drew had $30,000 cash in a safety deposit box at her bank during the entire year of 1984. On July 1, 1984, Mrs. Drew borrowed $10,000 from a friend and promised to repay the loan one year later. No interest was charged. Assume the Price Index was 155 on January 1, 1984; 160 on July 1, 1984; and 170 on December 31, 1984.

Required:

What purchasing power gain or loss did Mrs. Drew have for 1984? (Round computations to the nearest dollar.)

Exercise 13-8 (Comparing Historical Cost, Constant Dollar, and Current Cost)

Blair Company purchased equipment for $100,000 on January 1, 1978, when the Price Index was 120. The equipment has a 10-year life and a residual value of $10,000. Replacement cost of the equipment on December 31, 1984, was $162,000 and its residual value was still estimated to be $10,000. The average Price Index for 1984 was 180.

Required:

Compute the amount of straight-line depreciation expense that would be deducted in the 1984 income statement, assuming the income statement is prepared on the basis of:

A. Historical cost.

B. Constant dollar.

C. Current Cost.

PROBLEMS

Problem 13-1 (Violation of Accounting Principles)

During an audit of Bryne Company, you discover that the following transactions and events were recorded during the current year.

1. A patent with a cost of $120,000 was being amortized over its useful life of 10 years. The amortization entry made at the end of the current year was:

[handwritten: matching]

~~Retained Earnings~~ *Amortization Exp*	12,000	
Patents		12,000

2. Inventory was acquired at $30 per unit throughout the current year until the last purchase was made in November. At that time the company was able to negotiate a special price and acquired 10,000 units at $25 per unit. The purchase was recorded as follows:

[handwritten: cost revenue]

Inventory	~~300,000~~ *250,000*	
Cash		250,000
~~Revenue~~		~~50,000~~

3. An accelerator control device was installed on each of the company's 10 delivery trucks at a cost of $12.40 each. The transaction was recorded as follows:

[handwritten: o.k. materiality]

Maintenance Expense	124	
Cash		124

4. On January 2 of the current year, a new truck was purchased for $18,000. The truck had an estimated useful life of four years and a residual value of $2,000. Depreciation expense for the year was recorded as follows in order to avoid reporting a net operating loss.

[handwritten: conservatism matching objectivity]

Depreciation Expense	4,000	
Accumulated Depreciation—Trucks		4,000

5. The company borrowed $500,000 from a bank at an interest rate of 10% to construct a new warehouse. At the completion of construction, the loan was repaid and the following entry was made:

[handwritten: o.k.]

Note Payable	500,000	
Warehouse *pg 411*	30,000	
Cash		530,000

6. Ending inventory for the current year was overstated by ignoring the fact that the replacement cost of the inventory was $18,000 lower than its cost.

[handwritten: conserv. exp. recogn.]

Required:

For each item above, determine which generally accepted accounting principle(s) (if any) is violated, and explain why. For each violation, indicate the correct treatment.

Problem 13-2 (Revenue Realization Principle)

This problem focuses on the revenue principle and consists of three parts.

Part I. Required:

Critique each of the following statements.

A. Revenue is earned when goods are shipped or delivered to the buyer.

B. Revenue should be recognized when the cash is received.

Part II. Required:

Indicate the amount of revenue that should be recognized in 1983 in each of the following cases and explain why.

A. Net credit sales for 1983 amounted to $200,000, three-fourths of which were collected in 1983. Past experience indicates that about 98% of all credit sales are eventually collected.

B. Cash of $50,000 is received from a customer during 1983 in payment for special purpose machinery, which is to be manufactured and shipped to the customer early in 1984.

Part III. Required:

Determine the amount of gross profit that should be recognized in each of 1983, 1984, and 1985 for each of the following cases.

A. Construction equipment with a cost of $100,000 was sold for $160,000. A $40,000 down payment was received in 1983 and the purchaser agreed to pay the balance in eight equal quarterly installments during 1984 and 1985. Collection of the full sales price is not reasonably assured.

B. Bryant Construction Company signed a contract to construct an office complex at a contract price of $8,000,000. The project is expected to take three years to complete at an estimated total cost of $5,600,000. Actual costs incurred on the project were: 1983, $1,680,000; 1984, $2,520,000; 1985, $1,500,000. Estimates of cost to complete and the extent of progress toward completion are reasonably dependable. Estimated total costs remained $5,600,000 until early in 1985.

Problem 13-3 (Constant-dollar Accounting)

WPC Inc. purchased land and machinery early in 1975 for $500,000, of which $150,000 was allocated to land. The machinery had an estimated useful life of eight years and a salvage value of $30,000. Machinery is depreciated on the straight-line basis. Additional land was purchased by WPC Inc. on January 1, 1977 for $50,000 and on December 31, 1979 for $70,000. The machinery purchased in 1975 was sold on January 1, 1981, for $190,000.

Required: Using the CPI data in Figure 13-1 on page 514,

A. Determine the net amount at which machinery should be reported on a constant-dollar balance sheet on December 31, 1980.

B. Determine the amount at which land should be reported on a constant dollar balance sheet on December 31, 1980.

C. Determine the amount of depreciation expense on machinery that should be reported on a constant dollar income statement for 1979 and 1980.

D. How much gain would be reported on the sale of machinery in the historical-cost income statement for the year ended December 31, 1981?

E. In terms of constant dollars, how much gain (loss) was realized on the sale of the machinery?

Problem 13-4 (Constant-dollar Financial Statements)

The December 31, 1980, balance sheet and 1980 income statement for Leeman Company are presented below:

LEEMAN COMPANY
Balance Sheet
December 31, 1980

Assets

Cash	$ 40,000
Accounts receivable	57,000
Inventory	64,000
Plant and equipment	120,000
Accumulated depreciation	(25,000)
Land	35,000
Investment in bonds of Dart Company	10,000
Total Assets	$301,000

Liabilities

Accounts payable	$ 70,000
Notes payable, 1985	65,000
Total Liabilities	135,000

Stockholders' Equity

Capital stock	$80,000	
Retained earnings	86,000	$166,000
Total Liabilities and Stockholders' Equity		$301,000

Income Statement
Year Ended December 31, 1980

Sales		$400,000
Cost of goods sold		230,000
Gross profit		170,000
Expenses:		
Depreciation	$ 10,000	
Other expenses	115,000	125,000
Net Income		$ 45,000

Other Information:

1. Inventory was acquired evenly throughout 1980.
2. The company was formed on January 1, 1974, at which time the capital stock was issued and the plant and equipment were acquired.
3. The investment in bonds of Dart Company was made on December 31, 1978.
4. Sales were made and expenses (except for depreciation) were incurred evenly throughout the year.
5. A purchasing power gain of $3,600 was computed for the year.
6. The land was acquired in two purchases. The first parcel was purchased with the plant and equipment in 1974 for $20,000; the second portion was acquired on January 1, 1977 for $15,000.

Required:
Using the CPI data in Figure 13-1 on page 514,

A. Prepare a constant-dollar balance sheet at December 31, 1980.
B. Prepare a constant-dollar income statement for the year ended December 31, 1980.

Problem 13-5 (Constant-dollar and Current-cost Financial Statements)

An income statement for the year ended December 31, 1983, and a balance sheet on December 31, 1983, for Dressler Company are presented below:

Income Statement

Net sales		$1,694,000
Cost of goods sold		1,205,000
Gross profit		489,000
Expenses:		
Depreciation	$ 38,000	
Other expenses	353,000	391,000
Net Income		$ 98,000

Balance Sheet

Assets		Liabilities and Owners' Equity	
Cash	$125,000	Accounts payable	$165,000
Accounts receivable	189,000	Notes payable	200,000
Inventory	240,000	Capital stock	300,000
Plant and equipment (net)	416,000	Retained earnings	305,000
Total	$970,000	Total	$970,000

Dressler Company was formed in 1976, at which time the capital stock was issued and the plant and equipment were purchased. Inventory was purchased evenly throughout 1983, and sales were made and cost of goods sold and expenses (other than depreciation) were incurred evenly throughout the year.

Other information:
1. Depreciation expense computed on the basis of plant asset replacement costs is $75,000.
2. The replacement cost of goods sold during 1983 was $1,265,000.
3. A purchasing power gain of $15,500 was computed for 1983.
4. The replacement cost of the December 31, 1983, inventory was $276,000.
5. The replacement cost of plant and equipment on December 31, 1983, was $686,000.
6. Assumed Price Indexes:

When the company was formed	145
December 31, 1983	200
Average for 1983	190

Required:
A. Prepare a constant-dollar and a current-cost income statement for Dressler Company for the year ended December 31, 1983.
B. Prepare a constant-dollar and a current-cost balance sheet at December 31, 1983.

ALTERNATE PROBLEMS

Problem 13-1A (Violation of Accounting Principles)
While reviewing the business activities of Basley Company, you discover that the following transactions and events were recorded:

1. A new machine was purchased at a warehouse auction sale for cash of $16,000. Since the cash price of the machine would have been $19,000 if purchased from Basley Company's normal supplier, the machinery account was debited for $19,000 and the following entry made:

Machinery	19,000	
Cash		16,000
Gain from bargain purchase		3,000

2. Leasehold improvements with an estimated useful life of eight years were completed early in the current year at a cost of $88,000. Basley Company had a five-year nonrenewable lease on the property to which the improvements were made. To record amortization for the current year, the accountant made the following entry:

Amortization Expense	11,000	
Leasehold Improvements		11,000

3. On December 28 of the current year, Basley Company signed a contract with a customer under which Basley Company agreed to manufacture equipment for the

customer during January of the following year at a price of $26,000. Basley Company received a check for $5,000 from the customer on December 28 and made the following entry:

Accounts Receivable	21,000	
Cash	5,000	
Sales		26,000

4. Steering wheel covers were installed in each of Basley Company's five delivery trucks at a cost of $20 each. The trucks had an average remaining useful life of four years. The transaction was recorded as:

Repairs Expense	100	
Cash		100

5. Ending inventory for the current year had a cost of $96,000 and a replacement cost of $85,000. The inventory was not reduced to its replacement cost because the company's accountant believed that "the purchase price of similar inventory items will probably increase again during the next year."

6. Basley Company borrowed $200,000 from a bank at an interest rate of 15% to finance the construction of a new building. At the completion of construction the loan was repaid and the following entry was made:

Note Payable	200,000	
Buildings	22,000	
Cash		222,000

Required:
For each item above, determine which generally accepted accounting principle(s), if any, is violated, and explain why. For each violation, indicate the correct treatment.

Problem 13-2A (Constant-dollar Accounting)

Wallach Company purchased a building and land on January 4, 1978, for $300,000, of which $60,000 was assigned to land. The building had an estimated useful life of 15 years and a residual value of $30,000. Buildings are depreciated by the straight-line method. Additional land was purchased for $70,000 on January 2, 1980, and for $90,000 on July 1, 1981. The land purchased in 1980 was sold on January 2, 1984, for $110,000. The assumed Price Index at relevant dates was:

January 1, 1978	140
January 1, 1980	170
July 1, 1981	185
January 1, 1984	190
December 31, 1984	200

Required:
A. Determine the net amount at which the building should be reported on a constant-dollar balance sheet on December 31, 1984.
B. Determine the amount at which land should be reported on a constant-dollar balance sheet on December 31, 1984.

C. Determine the amount of depreciation expense on the building that should be reported on a constant-dollar income statement for 1983 and 1984.

D. How much gain or loss would be reported on the sale of land in the historical-cost income statement for the year ended December 31, 1984?

E. In terms of constant dollars, how much gain or loss was realized on the sale of the land?

Problem 13-3A (Revenue Realization Principle)

This problem concerns the correct application of the revenue principle and consists of three parts.

Part I. Required:

Critique each of the following statements.

A. The revenue principle provides that revenue should be recognized under accrual accounting at the time of sale.

B. Revenue is earned with the passage of time.

Part II. Required:

Indicate the amount of revenue that should be recognized in 1984 in each of the following cases and explain why.

A. Cash of $35,000 is received from a customer during 1984 in payment for equipment that is to be manufactured and shipped to the customer during 1985.

B. Net credit sales for 1984 amounted to $150,000, three-fourths of which were collected in 1984. Past experience indicates that about 98% of all credit sales are eventually collected.

Part III. Required:

Determine the amount of gross profit that should be recognized in each of 1983, 1984, and 1985 for each of the following cases.

A. Kenny Construction Company signed a contract to construct a dam on the Lulu River at a contract price of $5,000,000. The project is expected to take three years to complete at an estimated cost of $3,600,000. Actual costs incurred on the project were: 1983, $1,080,000; 1984, $1,620,000; 1985, $960,000. Estimates of costs to complete and the extent of progress toward completion are reasonably dependable. Estimated total costs remained $3,600,000 until early in 1985.

B. Office equipment with a cost of $60,000 was sold for $100,000. A $20,000 down payment was received in 1983 and the purchaser agreed to pay the balance in eight equal quarterly installments during 1984 and 1985. Collection of the full sales price is not reasonably assured.

Problem 13-4A (Constant-dollar Financial Statements)

An income statement for the year ending December 31, 1983, and a December 31, 1983, balance sheet for Darby Company follow:

Sales		$139,600
Expenses:		
Cost of goods sold	$71,300	
Depreciation expense	·6,600	
Other expenses	22,200	100,100
Net Income		$ 39,500

Assets		Liabilities	
Cash	$ 19,000	Accounts payable	$ 21,100
Accounts receivable	31,000	Notes payable	17,200
Inventory	32,500	Total Liabilities	38,300
Plant and equipment	58,600	Owners' Equity	
Accumulated depreciation	(18,300)	Capital stock	74,500
Land	26,900	Retained earnings	36,900
Total	$149,700	Total	$149,700

Darby Company began operations in January, 1976, at which time the capital stock was issued and plant and equipment and land were purchased. Sales were made and expenses (except for depreciation) were incurred evenly throughout 1983. Inventory was acquired evenly throughout 1983. In addition, a purchasing power loss of $1,140 was computed for 1983.

Assume the Price Index was:

146 on January 1, 1976
208 on December 31, 1983
204 average for 1983

Required:

A. Prepare a constant-dollar income statement for 1983.

B. Prepare a constant-dollar balance sheet at December 31, 1983. (Round to the nearest dollar.)

Problem 13-5A (Constant-dollar Financial Statements)

An income statement for 1984 and a balance sheet on December 31, 1984, for Knox Company are presented below:

Income Statement
For Year Ended December 31, 1984

Sales		$620,000
Cost of goods sold		356,500
Gross profit		263,500
Expenses:		
Depreciation	$ 15,400	
Other expenses	178,000	193,400
Net Income		$ 70,100

Balance Sheet
December 31, 1984

Cash		$ 56,000
Accounts receivable		79,800
Inventory		89,000
Plant and equipment		172,000
Accumulated depreciation		(35,000)
Land		49,000
Investment in bonds of Stacy Company		15,000
Total Assets		$425,800
Accounts payable		$ 98,000
Notes payable, due in 1990		91,000
Total Liabilities		189,000
Capital stock	$115,000	
Retained earnings	121,800	236,800
Total Liabilities and Stockholders' Equity		$425,800

Additional information:

1. Inventory was acquired evenly throughout 1984.
2. The company was formed in 1977, at which time the capital stock was issued and the plant and equipment purchased.
3. The investment in bonds of Stacy Company was made in 1980.
4. Sales were made and expenses (except for depreciation) were incurred evenly throughout the year.
5. A purchasing power gain of $4,650 was computed for the year.
6. The land was acquired in two purchases. The first parcel was purchased with the plant and equipment in 1977 for $30,000; the second portion was purchased in 1980 for $19,000.
7. The assumed Price Index on various dates was:

In 1977 when the company was formed	150
In 1980 when the bond investment and land were purchased	180
On December 31, 1984	220
Average for the year 1984	210

Required:
A. Prepare a constant-dollar income statement for the year ended December 31, 1984.
B. Prepare a constant-dollar balance sheet at December 31, 1984.

Problem 13-6A (Constant-dollar and Current-cost Financial Statements)

An income statement for the year ended December 31, 1984, and a balance sheet on December 31, 1984, for Lewis Company are presented below:

Income Statement

Net sales		$1,355,200
Cost of goods sold		939,900
Gross profit		415,300
Expenses:		
Depreciation	$ 30,000	
Other expenses	282,900	312,900
Net Income		$ 102,400

Balance Sheet

Assets		Liabilities and Owners' Equity	
Cash	$100,000	Accounts payable	$130,000
Accounts receivable	151,000	Notes payable	120,000
Inventory	192,000	Capital stock	280,000
Plant and equipment (net)	332,800	Retained earnings	245,800
Total	$775,800	Total	$775,800

Lewis Company was formed in 1979, at which time the capital stock was issued and the plant and equipment acquired. Inventory was purchased evenly throughout 1984 and sales were made and cost of sales and expenses (other than depreciation) were incurred evenly throughout the year.

Additional information:
1. Depreciation expense computed on the basis of plant asset replacement costs is $52,000 for 1984.
2. The replacement cost of goods sold during 1984 was $959,500.
3. A purchasing power loss of $2,400 was incurred during 1984.
4. The replacement cost of the December 31, 1984, inventory was $205,000.
5. The replacement cost of plant and equipment on December 31, 1984, was $568,000.
6. Assumed Price Indexes were:

When the company was formed in 1979	130
December 31, 1984	190
Average for 1984	185

Required:
A. Prepare a constant-dollar and a current-cost income statement for Lewis Company for the year ended December 31, 1984.
B. Prepare a constant-dollar and a current-cost balance sheet at December 31, 1984.

CASE FOR CHAPTER 13

(Annual Report Analysis)

Refer to the financial statements and the supplementary financial data on the effects of changing prices for Modern Merchandising, Inc. in the appendix and answer the following questions:

1. What was the net income (loss) reported for the year ended January 31, 1981 on an historical cost basis?
2. How much net income (loss) would have been reported for the year ended January 31, 1981 if the company had used:
   a. Constant-dollar accounting?
   b. Current cost accounting?
3. What was the total amount of monetary assets held on January 31, 1981?
4. How much purchasing power gain or loss would have been reported on a constant-dollar income statement for the year ended January 31, 1981? Explain, in general terms, why the amount was a gain or loss.
5. What was the amount of Modern Merchandising Inc.'s net assets on January 31, 1981:
   a. On an historical cost basis?
   b. On a constant-dollar basis?
   c. On a current cost basis?
6. What was the amount of Modern Merchandising Inc.'s inventory on January 31, 1981:
   a. On an historical cost basis?
   b. On a current cost basis?

PART FOUR
PARTNERSHIPS AND CORPORATIONS

CHAPTER 14
ACCOUNTING FOR PARTNERSHIPS

OVERVIEW AND OBJECTIVES

This chapter discusses the partnership form of business organization and the accounting procedures used for it. When you have completed the chapter, you should understand:

- The advantages of partnerships (p. 543).
- The major characteristics of partnerships (pp. 543–545).
- How to account for the formation of a partnership (pp. 546–548).
- Methods of sharing profits and losses (pp. 548–552).
- How to record the admission of a new partner (pp. 553–556).
- How to record the withdrawal of a partner (pp. 556–559).
- How to record the liquidation of a partnership (pp. 559–562).

Many of the accounting principles and practices discussed so far are also appropriate when accounting for a partnership. Nevertheless, some aspects of partnership accounting are different. These unique aspects mainly involve accounting for owners' equity transactions, allocation of net income or loss, the admission or withdrawal of a partner from the partnership, and partnership liquidation. We will examine briefly some of the characteristics of a partnership before these areas are discussed. Partnership law also has a significant influence on accounting practice. Most states have adopted the **Uniform Partnership Act (UPA)** or some modification of it to govern the formation, operation, and liquidation of partnerships; provisions of the UPA will be discussed briefly throughout this chapter when appropriate. More extensive study of the legal aspects of a partnership is part of most business law courses.

PARTNERSHIP DEFINED

A **partnership,** as defined by the UPA, is "an association of two or more persons to carry on as co-owners a business for profit." Because a written agreement is not necessary to form a partnership, it is sometimes difficult to determine if a partnership does in fact exist. Three attributes are necessary for a business partnership: (1) There must be an agreement between two or more legally competent persons; (2) the business must be operated for the purpose of earning a profit; and (3) members of the firm must be co-owners of the business. Co-ownership (often the most difficult attribute to determine) involves the right of each partner to share in the profits of the firm, to participate with the other partners in the management of the firm, and to own jointly with the other partners the property of the partnership. The right to participate in management may be limited by an express agreement among the partners.

REASONS FOR FORMING A PARTNERSHIP

We have already noted that a business can be a sole proprietorship, a partnership, or a corporation. Each of these forms has certain advantages and disadvantages. One of the major advantages of a partnership over a sole proprietorship is that it permits the pooling of both capital resources and the multiple skills of the individual partners. A partnership is easier and less costly to establish than a corporation and is generally not subject to as much governmental regulation. Furthermore, the partners may be able to operate with more flexibility because they are not subject to the control of a board of directors. There also may be certain tax advantages to a partnership, primarily because a partnership is not taxed as a separate entity.[1] Instead, the partnership's net income or net loss is allocated to the individual partners to be reported on their individual tax returns, whether or not the income is distributed to the partners. Except for Subchapter S corporations described in Chapter 28, a corporation is considered a separate taxable entity, so its income is taxed to the corporation and again to the stockholders when distributed by the corporation.

CHARACTERISTICS OF A PARTNERSHIP

A prospective owner of a business should consider the tax and legal aspects of the various forms of business organizations carefully before selecting the

---

[1]The tax advantages of the various forms of business organizations are covered in Chapter 28.

one that meets his or her organizational objectives and personal goals. The partnership form may turn out to be unattractive because of one or more of the following characteristics:

UNLIMITED LIABILITY

In a **general partnership,** the most common form, each partner is personally liable for the obligations of the partnership. This means that if the creditors of the partnership are not paid from assets of the partnership, they can look to an individual partner's personal assets for recovery of any unpaid claims. In contrast, a **limited partnership** exists when one or more of the partners have limited their liability for partnership debts to the amount of assets they have contributed to the partnership. However, a limited partner may not participate in the management of the business. In a limited partnership, one or more of the partners must be a general partner.

LIMITED LIFE

A partnership is dissolved for a number of reasons, including the death of a partner, the bankruptcy of the partnership or an individual partner, the withdrawal of a partner from the partnership, the expiration of the period specified in a contract, or a judgment by a court that a partner is unsound of mind and incapable of performing his or her partnership duties. In some of these cases, the partnership activities are terminated and the partnership ceases to exist. In other cases, the continuing partners may form a new partnership and continue to operate without any visible interruption of business activities.

MUTUAL AGENCY

Normally, every partner acts as an agent for the partnership and for every other partner. Thus, a partner can represent the other partners and bind them to a contract if he or she is acting within the apparent scope of the business. For example, in the case of a merchandising firm, a partner can enter into contracts to buy and sell merchandise, hire employees, and acquire office equipment. Activities outside the normal course of the business, such as selling land owned by the partnership, must be authorized by all partners.

TRANSFER OF PARTNERSHIP INTEREST

A capital interest in a partnership is a personal asset of the individual partner that can be sold or disposed of in any legal way. However, partnership law recognizes the highly personal relationship of partners and provides that the purchaser of a partner's interest does not have the right to participate in management of the firm unless he or she is accepted by all the other partners. The new partner is entitled to the profit allocation acquired and, in the event of liquidation, to receive whatever assets the selling partner would have received had he or she continued in the partnership. Obtaining approval to participate in management from the other partners may make it difficult to transfer a partnership interest.

The above discussion underlines the importance of careful selection of the individuals to be associated with in a partnership. In particular, the mutual-agency and unlimited liability characteristics could result in extensive personal liability resulting from the acts of other partners.

Because of these characteristics, it may be more difficult for a partnership to raise capital than it is for a corporation. Partnerships are thus most common in comparatively small businesses, professional organizations such as a medical clinic or an accounting practice, and some limited projects undertaken to accomplish a single goal such as an oil and gas exploration project or a real estate development project.

PARTNERSHIP AGREEMENT

A partnership is a voluntary association based on the contractual agreement between or among legally competent persons. The contract between the parties is called the **partnership agreement, partnership contract,** or **articles of partnership.** Although the partnership agreement may be oral, sound business practice dictates that the agreement be in writing for the protection of the individual partners. The partners should clearly express their intentions and the document should cover all aspects of operating the partnership. If there are subsequent disputes and the partners are unable to reach a satisfactory agreement, it may be necessary to resort to litigation. During litigation, the court will attempt to interpret the partnership agreement and the intentions of the partners. For example, in the absence of a specific agreement, courts have held that the intent of the individual partners must have been to share equally in profits of the firm. To avoid as many conflicts as possible, the partners should seek professional guidance from an attorney in drafting the agreement.

The partnership agreement should be as explicit as possible and should include these important points:

1. Partnership name and identity of the partners.
2. Nature, purpose, and scope of the business.
3. Location of the place of business.
4. Provision for the allocation of profit and loss.

5. Provision for the withdrawal of assets by a partner.
6. Fiscal period of the partnership.
7. Whether or not an audit is to be performed.
8. Authority of each partner in contract situations.
9. Identification and valuation of initial asset contributions and specification of capital interest each respective partner is to receive.
10. Accounting practices to be followed, such as depreciation methods to be used.
11. Procedures to be followed in the event of disputes among the partners.
12. Provisions covering how operations are to be conducted and how the various partners' interests are to be satisfied upon the death or withdrawal of a partner.

ACCOUNTING FOR A PARTNERSHIP

For accounting purposes, a partnership is a separate business entity. The transactions and events that affect the assets, liabilities, and capital accounts of the partnership are accounted for separately from the personal activities of the individual partners. For reporting purposes, however, a creditor may require information concerning the personal assets and debts of individual partners as well as financial statements of the firm because a general partner has unlimited liability for the partnership debts.

Accounting for a partnership involves essentially the same procedures and generally accepted accounting principles examined in preceding chapters. A major difference, however, is accounting for owners' equity. In a partnership, ownership interests generally are not equal because the capital investments and withdrawals of each partner vary. Furthermore, as we shall see, the profit or loss reported each fiscal period is allocated to the partners in accordance with the partnership agreement. Because the capital interest of each partner can vary, a separate capital account and separate withdrawal account is maintained for each partner.

The capital account of each partner is credited when assets are invested in the partnership by that person. Each partner's withdrawal account is debited to record the withdrawal of assets or the payment of personal expenses by an individual partner from partnership assets. At the end of the period, the withdrawal account of each partner is typically closed to his or her capital account and the balance in the Income Summary account is allocated to the partners and closed to their respective capital accounts. Except for the additional accounts and the need to divide the profit or loss, these are the same procedures followed in accounting for the capital transactions of a sole proprietorship.

RECORDING THE FORMATION OF A PARTNERSHIP

Assets contributed to a partnership, liabilities assumed by a partnership, monetary amounts to be assigned to specific assets and liabilities, and the capital interest each partner is to receive should be agreed upon and specified in the partnership agreement. Once the agreement is made, the entry to record the initial investment can be made.

To illustrate, assume that Art Becker and Robin Cook, operators of competing businesses, agree to form the BC Partnership. The book value and fair value of the assets being contributed and the liabilities assumed by the partnership were agreed upon as follows:

	Book Value		Fair Value	
	Becker	**Cook**	**Becker**	**Cook**
Cash	$ 60,000	$ 20,000	$ 60,000	$ 20,000
Inventory	43,000	9,000	40,000	10,000
Equipment	80,000	42,000	50,000	20,000
Accumulated Depreciation	(35,000)	(18,000)	—	—
Land	—	15,000	—	40,000
Building	—	110,000	—	50,000
Accumulated Depreciation	—	(70,000)	—	—
Total Assets Contributed	148,000	108,000	150,000	140,000
Mortgage Assumed	—	40,000	—	40,000
Net Assets Contributed	$148,000	$ 68,000	$150,000	$100,000

Assuming that Becker and Cook agree that each partner is to receive a capital credit equal to the amount of net assets contributed, journal entries to record the initial investment are:

Jan.	1	Cash	60,000	
		Inventory	40,000	
		Equipment	50,000	
		Becker, Capital		150,000
	1	Cash	20,000	
		Inventory	10,000	
		Equipment	20,000	
		Land	40,000	
		Building	50,000	
		Mortgage Payable		40,000
		Cook, Capital		100,000

Note that the noncash assets and liabilities are recorded at their fair value and each partner receives a capital credit equal to the fair value of the net assets contributed as agreed to by the two partners. The recorded amounts in the books of the partnership may differ from the book-value amounts recorded in the books of the separate businesses. For example, the equipment recorded at $50,000 in the entry above had a book value of $45,000 ($80,000 − $35,000). The use of fair value provides a more equitable measure of the amount invested by each partner and is a better measure of the acquisition cost to the partnership. Entries to record additional investments after the partnership is formed are based on the same concepts.

ALLOCATION OF PARTNERSHIP NET INCOME OR NET LOSS

The partners may agree to any allocation of profit or loss that they consider appropriate, and the allocation method should be included in the partnership agreement. In the absence of an agreement or if the partners are unable to reach an agreement, the law provides that profits are to be divided equally, regardless of the amount invested by the individual partners. Also, if a profit agreement is made but a loss agreement is not, a loss is allocated in the same way as a profit.

In establishing an equitable way to allocate partnership profit and loss, the partners should consider the three distinct elements that make up partnership income: (1) a return for the personal services performed by the partners, (2) a return on the capital provided by the partners, and (3) a return for the business risks assumed by the partners. If profits are to be allocated equitably, the allocation method should take into consideration any difference in the amount of resources and services contributed. For example, if one partner is more actively involved in the management of the firm or if his or her services are more valuable to the firm, this fact should be recognized in the profit and loss agreement. Likewise, if the partners' capital investments are not equal, a provision to recognize these differences should be included in the agreement.

As noted, the objective of the profit and loss agreement is to reward each partner for resources and services contributed to the firm. Some of the more common agreements are:

1. A fixed ratio.
2. A ratio based on capital balances.
3. Interest on capital contributions, salaries to partners for services rendered for the partnership, and the remainder in a fixed ratio established by the partners.

In the following illustrations, it is assumed that Art Becker and Robin Cook formed the BC Partnership with capital investments of $150,000 and $100,000, respectively. At the end of the first year of operations, the Income Summary account had a credit balance of $60,000 (net income). To complete the closing process, the Income Summary account is closed to the individual partners' capital accounts. The amount credited to each capital account is dependent on the income allocation method agreed to by the partners.

FIXED RATIO

One of the simplest profit and loss agreements is for each partner to be allocated profits or losses based on some specified ratio. This method may be appropriate if the partners' contribution can be stated in terms of a fixed percentage. For example, assume that Becker and Cook agree to a 70:30 sharing of profits and losses, respectively. The entry to close the Income Summary account is:

Dec.	31	Income Summary	60,000	
		Becker, Capital		42,000
		Cook, Capital		18,000

Losses would be allocated using the same 70:30 ratio unless a separate loss agreement is stated in the partnership contract.

RATIO BASED ON CAPITAL BALANCES

The allocation of profits based on the ratio of capital balances may result in an equitable allocation when invested capital is considered the most important factor and/or the partnership operations require little of the partners' time. Since the capital balances normally change during the period, the agreement should specify whether the ratio is to be computed from the original investment, the beginning-of-year balances, end-of-year balances, or an average of the balances.

The $60,000 net income is allocated as follows, assuming that the ratio is to be computed from the beginning-of-year balances:

	Capital Investment	Net Income Allocation	
Becker	$150,000	($150,000/$250,000) × $60,000 =	$36,000
Cook	100,000	($100,000/$250,000) × $60,000 =	24,000
Totals	$250,000		$60,000

The entry to close the Income Summary account is:

Dec.	31	Income Summary	60,000	
		Becker, Capital		36,000
		Cook, Capital		24,000

INTEREST, SALARIES, AND THE REMAINDER IN A FIXED RATIO

Frequently, the individual partners make unequal capital contributions, and the amount of time as well as the nature of services performed in the management function are not the same. Unless provided for in the partnership agreement, however, a partner is not legally entitled to receive compensation for services performed for the partnership or interest on capital investments. Thus, if an equitable allocation of net income is to be made to compensate the partners for unequal contributions, a profit allocation method that contains a provision for interest and/or salaries must be included in the partnership agreement. To illustrate, assume the partnership agreement of BC Partnership contains this profit agreement:

1. Each partner is to be allowed interest of 10% on their initial capital investment.
2. Art Becker and Robin Cook are to receive salary allowances per year of $18,000 and $10,000, respectively.
3. Any remaining net income or loss is to be shared equally. (Equal percentages are used here under the assumption that business risk is assumed equally by each partner.)

The allocation of $60,000 net income would be:

	Becker	Cook	Total
Interest on capital contribution			
$150,000 × 10%	$15,000		
$100,000 × 10%		$10,000	$25,000
Salaries to partners	18,000	10,000	28,000
Total interest and salary allocation	33,000	20,000	53,000
Remainder to be divided equally	3,500	3,500	7,000*
Totals	$36,500	$23,500	$60,000

*The remainder is the difference between the net income of $60,000 and the salary and interest allocation of $53,000. It is allocated equally to each partner as provided for in Step 3 of the partnership agreement.

The entry to allocate the balance in the Income Summary account to the partners is:

Dec.	31	Income Summary	60,000	
		Becker, Capital		36,500
		Cook, Capital		23,500

Note that the salary and interest provisions are not accounted for as an increase in expenses of the partnership but are considered determinants in the allocation of net income.

A salary agreement is sometimes confused with an agreement that permits withdrawals of assets. Since the term *salary* is commonly understood to mean a cash payment for services rendered, it is important that the partners specify clearly their intentions as to whether the salary is part of the profit agreement or an agreement to permit withdrawals during the period. That is, the partners may agree that each is permitted to withdraw a certain amount of cash from the business at regular intervals for personal living expenses. The partners may further agree that the withdrawals are salaries in anticipation of profitable operations and are to be considered part of the profit allocation to be made at the end of the period. Or the partners may provide for a profit agreement that is independent of the withdrawal agreement. In the remainder of this chapter and in the end-of-chapter materials, a salary agreement is considered an allocation of profit or loss only.

In the preceding example, the net income of $60,000 was greater than the interest and salary allocations of $53,000. The same method is used to allocate net income that is less than the interest and salary allocation or to allocate a net loss if the partners fail to provide alternative allocations for these two possibilities in the partnership agreement. For example, assume that the net income for the period had been $41,000 rather than $60,000. The allocation would then be:

	Allocation of $41,000 Net Income		
	Becker	Cook	Total
Interest on capital contributions	$15,000	$10,000	$25,000
Salaries to partners	18,000	10,000	28,000
Total interest and salary allocation	33,000	20,000	53,000
Deficiency allocated equally	(6,000)	(6,000)	(12,000)*
Totals	$27,000	$14,000	$41,000

*Net income minus interest and salary allocation: $41,000 − 53,000 = ($12,000)

If there had been a loss of $12,000, the allocation of $53,000 still follows the procedures shown above, and the deficiency allocation of $65,000 ($53,000 + $12,000) would be allocated equally to the partners. Thus, the capital account of Becker would be credited for $500 and Cook's capital account would be debited for $12,500:

	Allocation of $12,000 Net Loss		
	Becker	Cook	Total
Total interest and salary allocation	$33,000	$20,000	$53,000
Deficiency allocated equally	(32,500)	(32,500)	(65,000)*
Totals	$ 500	($12,500)	($12,000)

*Net loss plus interest and salary allocation, $12,000 + $53,000 = $65,000

To avoid the above allocations when the net income is insufficient to cover the interest and salary allocations, the partnership agreement may contain an alternative allocation.

FINANCIAL STATEMENTS FOR A PARTNERSHIP

The income statement, balance sheet, and statement of changes in financial position for a partnership are prepared in much the same manner as for other forms of business organizations. The following items that are specifically related to partnership reporting should be noted:

1. Each individual partner's equity in the business is reported separately on the balance sheet or in a separate schedule.
2. Salaries authorized for each partner and interest on capital investments are not reported as expenses but recognized as an allocation of net income.
3. There is no income tax expense since a partnership is required to file an information return only.
4. The profit or loss allocation for the period is normally disclosed in the financial statements either on the face of the income statement or in a supplementary schedule.
5. A statement is prepared to report the changes in partners' capital that occurred during the period.

The latter schedule may appear as shown in Figure 14-1 for the BC Partnership.

Figure 14-1
Statement of Partners' Capital

BC PARTNERSHIP
Statement of Partners' Capital
For the Year Ended December 31, 1984

	Becker	Cook	Total
Capital balances, 1/1	$150,000	$100,000	$250,000
Add: Additional investment	10,000	–0–	10,000
Net income allocation	36,000	24,000	60,000
	196,000	124,000	320,000
Less: Withdrawals*	14,000	14,000	28,000
Capital balances, 12/31	$182,000	$110,000	$292,000

*Withdrawal amounts are assumed.

CHANGES IN THE MEMBERS OF A PARTNERSHIP

A new partner may be admitted to an existing partnership by purchasing all or part of an interest directly from one or more existing partners or by making an investment in the partnership itself. In the first instance, a current member of the firm is selling all or part of an interest in the partnership. The net assets of the firm are not changed since this is a personal transaction between individuals. If an investment is made in the partnership, the net assets and total capital of the firm are increased by the amount of the investment. Similarly, a partner may retire from a partnership by withdrawing partnership assets in settlement of his or her capital interest.

ADMISSION OF A NEW PARTNER

A partner cannot be prevented from selling his or her interest in a partnership, but the remaining partners must agree to the transfer of interest before the buyer can participate in management. The UPA provides that the buyer of a partnership interest acquires the same right to share in profits and assets upon liquidation for which the selling partner would otherwise be entitled.

Admission of a New Partner by Purchasing an Existing Interest

When an individual buys an interest in a partnership by making payment directly to a current partner or partners, the only entry required in the partnership books is transfer of the capital interest acquired from the selling partner to the buying partner. To illustrate, assume that Lori Monk and Frank Jordan are partners with current capital balances of $30,000 and $50,000, respectively. Their profit and loss sharing ratio is 60:40. Monk and Jordan negotiate with Mary Dart to sell one-half of their capital interests for $60,000. The entry to record the transfer of capital interests is:

May	6	Monk, Capital ($30,000 × 50%)	15,000	
		Jordan, Capital ($50,000 × 50%)	25,000	
		Dart, Capital		40,000

Note that the capital transferred to Dart is equal to the selling partners' recorded capital interest times the percentage interest acquired by Dart. This entry is the same, regardless of the amount of cash paid by Dart. Note also that the net assets and total capital of the partnership are the same ($80,000) after the transfer is recorded because the cash transfer is between the partners as individuals and is not recorded in the partnership books.

Admission of a New Partner by Contributing Assets

An individual may also gain admission to an existing partnership by investing assets in the business. Because assets are contributed to the partnership, total assets and owners' equity of the partnership are increased by the same amount. To illustrate, assume again that Monk and Jordan are partners with current capital account balances of $30,000 and $50,000, respectively. Their profit and loss sharing ratio is 60:40. Dart is to invest $40,000 for a one-third interest in the firm. The entry to record Dart's investment is:

May	6	Cash	40,000	
		Dart, Capital		40,000
		[($30,000 + $50,000 + $40,000) × ⅓ = $40,000]		

After the entry is posted, the total capital and net assets are $120,000, of which Dart has a one-third capital interest of $40,000. If Dart had contributed noncash assets, the assets contributed should be recorded at their fair value.

Although Dart has a one-third interest in the net assets of the firm, her right to share in profits of the new partnership may be less than, equal to, or greater than one-third. As already pointed out, the profit-sharing ratio is a separate agreement and is not necessarily related to the capital interest. Thus, for the protection of the partners, a new profit and loss agreement should be determined and included in the partnership agreement.

A Bonus to the Old Partners.

In the preceding illustration, Dart contributed $40,000 in assets and received a $40,000 capital interest in the partnership. In some situations, an incoming partner may invest assets that have a fair value greater than the capital interest received. The difference between the two is called a **bonus** to the old partners and is credited to their capital accounts in the profit-sharing ratio that existed prior to the admittance of the new partner. The incoming partner may be willing to give such a bonus to the old partners because the partnership has been earning above-normal profits and he or she wants to acquire the right to share in them; or the new partner may perceive other advantages in the partnership operations.[2]

Assume that Monk and Jordan share profits in the ratio of 60:40 and currently report capital balances of $30,000 and $50,000, respectively. An agreement is made with Dart that she invest $40,000 cash in the partnership for a one-fourth interest in capital. Dart's capital interest may then be computed:

[2]Another method, called the goodwill method, is sometimes used to record the admission of a new partner or the withdrawal of an existing partner. This method is covered in more advanced accounting courses.

Capital interest of old partners ($30,000 + $50,000)	$ 80,000
Investment by new partner	40,000
Total capital interest in new partnership	120,000
Dart's capital interest ($120,000 × 25%)	30,000
Old partners' capital interest ($120,000 × 75%)	$ 90,000

Note that the old partners' capital interest has increased by $10,000.

The entry to record the investment by Dart is:

May	6	Cash	40,000	
		Monk, Capital ($10,000 × 60%)		6,000
		Jordan, Capital ($10,000 × 40%)		4,000
		Dart, Capital		30,000

Note that the $10,000 bonus is allocated to Monk and Jordan in their profit and loss sharing ratio. After the investment entry is posted, Dart has a capital interest equal to one-fourth of the net assets of $120,000 and the old partners have the remaining three-fourths interest of $90,000.

A Bonus to the New Partner. Sometimes a partnership may need an additional investment of working capital or the new partner may possess some skills or business contacts required by the firm. In such conditions, the old partners may be willing to grant the incoming partner a capital interest greater than the value of the assets invested.

To illustrate, assume the same facts as stated above except that Dart is to invest $40,000 for a one-half capital interest in the firm. The capital interests are computed as:

Capital interest of old partners	$ 80,000
Investment by the new partner	40,000
Total capital interest of the new partnership	120,000
Dart's capital interest ($120,000 × 50%)	60,000
Old partners' capital interest ($120,000 × 50%)	$ 60,000

Note that the old partners' capital interest has decreased by $20,000.

The entry to record the admission of the new partner is:

May	6	Cash	40,000	
		Monk, Capital ($20,000 × 60%)	12,000	
		Jordan, Capital ($20,000 × 40%)	8,000	
		Dart, Capital		60,000

Note once again that the bonus of $20,000 to the new partner is contributed by the old partners according to their old profit and loss ratio. After the debits are posted to the capital accounts, the old partners' total equity in the new partnership is $60,000, or half of $120,000. Dart has the remaining half interest of $60,000.

WITHDRAWAL OF A PARTNER

A partner wishing to withdraw from a partnership may sell his or her interest to an outside party or to one or more of the existing partners. In such cases, the payment is made from personal funds of the buying party and goes directly to the withdrawing partner. The only entry required in the partnership books is to transfer the amount in the capital account of the withdrawing partner to the capital account of the new partner or existing partners as appropriate. The transaction does not affect the assets of the partnership. In other cases, the equity interest of the withdrawing partner may be settled by withdrawing partnership assets.

The legal issues related to the withdrawal of a partner are rather complex and should be reviewed carefully by the parties involved. For example, the retiring partner may still have some responsibility for the liabilities existing at the time of withdrawal. Furthermore, to avoid as much potential conflict as possible, the partnership agreement should set out the procedures to be followed and the method for determining settlement.

Withdrawal of Assets from the Partnership

A partnership agreement may require an audit of the accounting records and a revaluation of assets and liabilities before a partner withdraws. Normally, any increase or decrease in values is allocated to the partners in their profit and loss ratio. The withdrawing partner is often permitted to withdraw assets or accept a note payable from the new partnership equal to his or her existing capital interest.

Assume that Art Becker, Robin Cook, and Mary Dart are partners in the BCD Partnership, sharing profits 40:30:30, respectively. The partners agree that Cook is to retire from the partnership. The partnership agreement requires the revaluation of assets and liabilities on retirement of a partner and provides for the retiring partner to withdraw from the firm cash equal to his or her revalued capital account balance. Furthermore, if the cash balance is insufficient to settle the capital interest and leave enough cash to operate the business, the withdrawing partner is to receive promissory notes for the balance with a stated rate of interest equal to the current prime rate. A balance sheet for the BCD Partnership before the accounts are revalued is:

Cash	$ 25,000	Liabilities	$ 35,000
Accounts Receivable	20,000	Becker, Capital	30,000
Inventories	40,000	Cook, Capital	40,000
Plant Assets (net)	70,000	Dart, Capital	50,000
Total	$155,000	Total	$155,000

Appraisals indicate the inventories are understated by $3,000 due to the use of the LIFO inventory method, plant assets are understated by $20,000, and the liabilities are understated by $8,000. The entries to record the revaluations and the withdrawal, assuming Cook agrees to take cash of $12,000 ($13,000 is needed to operate the business) and the balance in a promissory note, are:

Nov.	5	Inventories	3,000	
		Plant Assets	20,000	
		Liabilities		8,000
		Becker, Capital ($15,000 × 40%)		6,000
		Cook, Capital ($15,000 × 30%)		4,500
		Dart, Capital ($15,000 × 30%)		4,500
		To record the revaluation of assets and liabilities prior to withdrawal of a partner.		
	5	Cook, Capital ($40,000 + $4,500)	44,500	
		Cash		12,000
		Notes Payable		32,500
		To record the withdrawal of Cook from the partnership.		

Note that the net gain resulting from the revaluation of the firm's assets and liabilities is allocated in the profit and loss sharing ratio.

A balance sheet after these entries are posted would be:

Cash	$ 13,000	Liabilities	$ 43,000
Accounts Receivable	20,000	Notes Payable	32,500
Inventories	43,000	Becker, Capital	36,000
Plant Assets (net)	90,000	Dart, Capital	54,500
Total	$166,000	Total	$166,000

Since a new partnership is now formed, Becker and Dart should draft a new partnership agreement.

In this example, the book value of the assets and note received by Cook were equal to the book value of her revalued capital interest. Sometimes, however, a withdrawing partner may receive assets that have a value greater than the book value of his or her capital interest. This could happen because a profitable firm may be worth more than the fair value of its net assets, or the continuing partners may be anxious to rid themselves of a specific partner. On the other hand, a partner may be anxious to withdraw from a partnership and therefore be willing to receive assets that have a value less than the book value of his or her interest. When the book value of the net assets withdrawn does not equal the book value of the capital interest, the difference may be accounted for as a bonus to the remaining or withdrawing partner that is assigned to the remaining partners in their relative profit and loss ratio.

To illustrate the withdrawal of assets with greater value than the book value interest, assume that Cook is to withdraw from the BCD Partnership and is to receive $12,000 in cash and a promissory note for $39,500 for her $44,500 capital interest. The entry to record the withdrawal is:

Nov.	5	Cook, Capital	44,500	
		Becker, Capital ($7,000 × 4/7)	4,000	
		Dart, Capital ($7,000 × 3/7)	3,000	
		Cash		12,000
		Notes Payable		39,500
		To record the withdrawal of Cook from		
		the partnership.		

Note that the excess payment of $7,000 (the bonus) is charged against the capital accounts of Becker and Dart in their profit and loss sharing ratio of 4:3.

Instead, assume that Cook is anxious to withdraw and agrees to take a payment of $12,000 in cash and a $25,500 promissory note in settlement of her $44,500 capital interest. The entry to record the withdrawal is:

Nov.	5	Cook, Capital	44,500	
		Becker, Capital ($7,000 × 4/7)		4,000
		Dart, Capital ($7,000 × 3/7)		3,000
		Cash		12,000
		Notes Payable		25,500
		To record the withdrawal of Cook from		
		the partnership.		

In this case, Cook is receiving a settlement less than the book value of her equity interest. The bonus is credited to the capital accounts of the remaining partners in their profit and loss sharing ratio of 4:3.

DEATH OF A PARTNER

A partnership is dissolved upon the death of a partner and the deceased partner's estate is entitled to receive his or her current equity interest in the partnership assets. Determining a partner's equity interest in the firm can result in a number of controversies. To avoid litigation, the partnership agreement should contain procedures for determining a deceased partner's equity interest and the method of settlement. In the absence of specific provisions, the surviving partners and the executor of the estate must negotiate a settlement.

To determine a partner's equity interest at the time of death, the assets and liabilities are normally adjusted to their fair values and the accounts are closed to determine the net income or loss earned since the end of the last fiscal period. Although the old partnership is dissolved, the agreement usually provides that operations do not terminate but are continued by the surviving partners. If so, the method of settlement should be specified in the partnership agreement. Entries to record the settlement either by the distribution of partnership assets to the estate or by the direct payment to the estate by those who purchase the interest are similar to those of earlier illustrations.

PARTNERSHIP LIQUIDATION

When a partnership is liquidated, the operations of the firm are discontinued and the business ceases to exist. The **liquidation** process involves the sale of noncash assets, payment of creditors' claims, and distribution of the remaining assets to the partners according to their capital interests.

To illustrate the accounting for a partnership liquidation, assume that ABC Partnership reported this trial balance immediately after the closing process had been completed:

ABC PARTNERSHIP
Trial Balance

Account Title	Debit	Credit
Cash	$ 30,000	
Accounts Receivable	60,000	
Inventory	80,000	
Plant Assets (net)	130,000	
Liabilities		$ 80,000
Able, Capital (50%)		120,000
Baker, Capital (30%)		70,000
Carter, Capital (20%)		30,000
Totals	$300,000	$300,000

Each partner's share of profit or loss is shown in parentheses.

DISPOSAL OF NONCASH ASSETS—EACH PARTNER'S CAPITAL BALANCE SUFFICIENT TO ABSORB SHARE OF LOSSES

The first step in the liquidation process is to convert the noncash assets into cash, referred to as realization. If the sales price is greater than or less than book value, there is a gain or loss from the sale. The gain or loss is shared by the partners in their profit and loss sharing ratio.

The following entries are made to record the liquidation of ABC Partnership, assuming that the noncash assets are sold for $190,000:

Jan.	2	Cash	190,000	
		Loss on Sale of Assets	80,000*	
		Accounts Receivable		60,000
		Inventory		80,000
		Plant Assets		130,000
		To record the sale of all noncash assets.		

*(60,000 + 80,000 + 130,000) − 190,000 = 80,000 loss

	2	Able, Capital ($80,000 × 50%)	40,000	
		Baker, Capital ($80,000 × 30%)	24,000	
		Carter, Capital ($80,000 × 20%)	16,000	
		Loss on sale of assets		80,000
		To allocate the loss on the sale of noncash assets.		

If the assets had been sold at a gain, a Gain on Sale of Assets account would be credited in the first entry and the gain would be allocated to the partners in their profit ratio.

After these entries are posted to recognize a loss, a balance sheet would appear as follows:

ABC PARTNERSHIP Balance Sheet			
Cash	$220,000	Liabilities	$ 80,000
		Able, Capital	80,000
		Baker, Capital	46,000
		Carter, Capital	14,000
Totals	$220,000	Totals	$220,000

The available cash must now be distributed first to satisfy the claims of the creditors in full; then the remaining cash is distributed to the partners. The entries are:

Jan.	2	Liabilities	80,000	
		Cash		80,000
		To pay creditors in full.		
	2	Able, Capital	80,000	
		Baker, Capital	46,000	
		Carter, Capital	14,000	
		Cash		140,000
		To record the distribution of cash to partners.		

Observe that the amount of cash distributed to the partners is equal to the balances remaining in their respective capital accounts rather than in the profit and loss ratio. The distribution represents a final settlement with the partners for their capital interest, rather than an allocation of profit or loss. After the entries shown above are posted, all accounts in the partnership books will have a zero balance.

A PARTNER WITH A DEBIT CAPITAL BALANCE

In the preceding illustration, each partner's capital balance was sufficient to absorb his or her share of the $80,000 loss. In some cases, however, the allocation of the loss may result in a debit balance in one or more capital accounts. A debit capital balance is referred to as a **deficit** or **deficiency.** If a partner has a debit capital balance, the partnership has a claim against the partner for the amount of the debit balance. Accordingly, the debit balance is reported as a receivable in a balance sheet of the partnership.

To illustrate, assume that the noncash assets of ABC Partnership were sold for $80,000. Allocation of the $190,000 loss ($270,000 book value − $80,000 sales price) results in an $8,000 debit balance in the capital account of Carter:

	Capital Balances Before Allocation of the Loss	Allocation of the Loss	Capital Balances After Allocation of the Loss
Able (50%)	$120,000	$ 95,000	$25,000
Baker (30%)	70,000	57,000	13,000
Carter (20%)	30,000	38,000	(8,000)
Totals	$220,000	$190,000	$30,000

After the creditors are paid in full ($80,000), a balance sheet would appear as follows:

ABC PARTNERSHIP
Balance Sheet

Cash	$30,000	Able, Capital	$25,000
Carter, Capital		Baker, Capital	13,000
(Receivable)	8,000		
Totals	$38,000	Totals	$38,000

If Carter is able to eliminate the deficit by paying $8,000 to the partnership, the liquidation is completed as follows:

Jan.	2	Cash	8,000	
		Carter, Capital		8,000
		To record additional investment by Carter.		
	2	Able, Capital	25,000	
		Baker, Capital	13,000	
		Cash		38,000
		To record the distribution of the remaining cash to partners.		

If Carter is unable to contribute the $8,000 to the firm, the deficit is written off to the other partners' capital accounts in their profit and loss sharing ratio, 5:3 in this case. The entry to record the allocation of Carter's deficit is:

Jan.	2	Able, Capital	5,000	
		Baker, Capital	3,000	
		Carter, Capital		8,000
		To allocate deficit in Carter's capital account.		

After this entry, the capital accounts of Able and Baker ($20,000 and $10,000, respectively) will be equal to the remaining cash balance of $30,000. The cash is distributed and an entry prepared as follows:

Jan.	2	Able, Capital	20,000	
		Baker, Capital	10,000	
		Cash		30,000
		To distribute cash to partners.		

Note again that the amount distributed to each partner is determined by the balance in their respective capital accounts.

GLOSSARY

BONUS.   The transfer of a portion of the capital interest of one or more partners to another partner. The bonus method is used to record the admission or withdrawal of a partner (p. 554).

DEFICIT (DEFICIENCY).   A debit balance in a partner's capital account (p. 561).

GENERAL PARTNERSHIP.   A partnership in which each partner is individually liable for the partnership liabilities (p. 544).

LIMITED PARTNERSHIP.   A partnership in which one or more of the partners have limited their liability for partnership liabilities to the amount of their investment (p. 544).

LIQUIDATION.   The termination of a business by the sale of noncash assets, payment of creditors, and distribution of the remaining cash to the owners (p. 559).

MUTUAL AGENCY.   A characteristic of a partnership whereby each partner is an agent for the partnership and can bind the partnership to a contract if acting within the normal scope of the business (p. 544).

PARTNERSHIP.   An association of two or more persons to carry on as co-owners a business for profit (p. 543).

PARTNERSHIP AGREEMENT (PARTNERSHIP CONTRACT, ARTICLES OF PARTNERSHIP).   The contract or agreement made among the partners to form and operate a partnership (p. 545).

STATEMENT OF PARTNERS' CAPITAL.   A financial statement that shows the changes in each partners' capital interest during the period (p. 552).

UNIFORM PARTNERSHIP ACT (UPA).   Statutes of substantially uniform substance, adopted by most states, that govern the formation, operation, and liquidation of a partnership (p. 542).

UNLIMITED LIABILITY.   A characteristic of a partnership whereby each general partner is responsible for all debts of the partnership (p. 544).

DISCUSSION QUESTIONS

1. Define a partnership and list some of the advantages of the partnership form of business organization.
2. A partner withdrew $18,000 from the partnership during the year. His share of partnership net income is $14,000. How much income from the partnership must he report on his individual income tax return?
3. Define the terms *unlimited liability* and *mutual agency* as they apply to a partnership.
4. Ray sells his partnership interest to Henry even though the other partners do not agree to admit Henry as a partner. Does Henry have the right to take over Ray's position as manager of the business? Is Henry entitled to a share of the profits, and if so, how large a share?

5. Mark contributes land with a book value of $80,000 and a fair value of $100,000 to a new partnership being formed. The partnership assumes a $30,000 mortgage on the land. What is Mark's capital interest in the partnership, assuming that he is to receive a capital credit equal to his asset contribution?

6. The partnership agreement provides that Tom and Sue are to share profits in a 70:30 ratio but does not mention losses. How would a $10,000 net loss be allocated?

7. Jan and Don receive salaries of $12,000 and $10,000, respectively. They allocate the remainder of the partnership income in the ratio of 40:60. How would they share a net income of $18,000?

8. Keith has a $15,000 capital balance when he sells his partnership interest to Scott for $21,000. What is Scott's capital balance?

9. Mary and Kay have partnership capital balances of $40,000 and $60,000, respectively, when they agree to give Larry a one-fourth capital interest in the partnership upon his investment of $30,000. How much is the bonus, and is it credited to Larry's account or to the accounts of Mary and Kay?

10. What is the purpose of revaluing assets and liabilities before a partner withdraws from the partnership?

11. In the liquidation process, how is a gain or loss on the sale of the assets shared by the partners?

12. Jerry and Ken share profits and losses in the ratio of 40:60. They have capital balances of $30,000 and $45,000 when they decide to liquidate. After they sell all noncash assets and pay the creditors, there is a cash balance of $100,000. How should the cash be distributed between the partners?

13. Explain how liquidation procedures can cause a partner to have a debit capital balance. What obligations does a partner with a debit balance have to the partnership?

EXERCISES

Exercise 14-1 (Partnership Formation)

Mary Logan and Kate Branson agree to combine their businesses and form a partnership. The fair value and the book value of the assets contributed by each partner and the liabilities assumed by the partnership are shown below:

	Mary Logan		Kate Branson	
	Book Value	Fair Value	Book Value	Fair Value
Cash	$ 5,000	$ 5,000	$ 3,600	$ 3,600
Accounts Receivable	8,000	7,800	4,100	4,000
Inventory	14,900	13,500	13,700	15,000
Equipment	47,000	34,000	48,000	37,000
Accumulated Depreciation— Equipment	(20,000)		(25,000)	
Accounts Payable	12,000	12,000	9,100	9,100

Required:
Prepare separate journal entries to record the initial investment of each partner, assuming assets are accepted by the firm at fair market value.

Exercise 14-2 (Allocation of Net Income)

90,000

Washington and Horne form a partnership by investing $50,000 and $40,000, respectively. The partnership has a net income of $24,000 for the first year.

Required:

A. Prepare the journal entry to record the allocation of net income under each of the following assumptions:
  1. Washington and Horne agree to a 55:45 sharing of profits.
  2. The partners agree to share profits in the ratio of their original capital investments.
  3. The partners agree to recognize a $10,000 per year salary allowance to Washington and a $4,000 per year salary allowance to Horne. Each partner is entitled to 8% interest on his original investment, and any remaining income is to be shared equally.

B. Repeat requirement (3) assuming the partnership has a net income *loss* of $15,000 for the first year.

Exercise 14-3 (Admission of a New Partner)

Robins and High are partners having capital balances of $80,000 and $40,000, respectively. They share profits in the ratio of 70:30. They agree to admit Wilson to the partnership for an investment of machinery worth $30,000.

Required:
Prepare the journal entry to record Wilson's investment under each of the following conditions:

A. Wilson receives a one-fourth capital interest.
B. Wilson receives a one-fifth capital interest.
C. Wilson receives a one-sixth capital interest.

Exercise 14-4 (Admission of a New Partner)

Ray Baron and Linda Morris are partners. Their respective capital balances are $100,000 and $125,000, and they share profits and losses equally.

Required:
Prepare the journal entry to record the admission of Carol Green into the partnership under each of the following conditions:

A. Carol acquires one-fourth of Ray's capital interest by paying $30,000 directly to him.
B. Carol acquires one-fifth of both Ray's and Linda's capital interests. Ray receives $20,000 and Linda receives $23,000 directly from Carol.
C. Carol acquires a one-third interest for a $150,000 cash investment in the partnership.

Exercise 14-5 (Withdrawal of a Partner)

Greg Jax, Ed Marx, and Frank Sax are partners who share profits and losses in a 5:3:2 ratio. They have respective capital balances of $80,000, $60,000, and $50,000 at the time of Jax's withdrawal from the partnership.

Required:

Prepare the journal entry to record the withdrawal of Jax under each of the following assumptions:

A. Jax receives $80,000 in cash.
B. Jax receives $100,000 in cash.
C. Jax receives $75,000 in cash.

Exercise 14-6 (Partnership Liquidation)

Batt, Carroll, and Martin are partners with capital accounts of $28,000, $20,000, and $40,000, respectively. They share profits and losses in the ratio of 30:30:40. When the partners decide to liquidate, the business has $15,000 in cash, noncash assets totaling $105,000, and $32,000 in liabilities. The noncash assets are sold for $130,000, and the creditors are paid.

Required:

Prepare journal entries to record each of the following transactions:

A. The sale of the noncash assets and the allocation of the gain or loss from the sale of the assets.
B. The payment to the creditors.
C. The distribution of cash to the partners.

Exercise 14-7 (Partnership Liquidation—Partner With a Deficit Balance)

The partnership of Crane, Darling, and Hare is being liquidated. After the noncash assets are sold and the creditors are paid, the business has $70,000 cash. Crane has a $40,000 credit capital balance, Darling's account has a $50,000 credit balance, and Hare's capital account has a debit balance of $20,000. The partners share profits and losses in the ratio of 40:40:20.

Required:

A. Assuming that Hare pays the money he owes to the partnership, prepare the journal entries to record Hare's payment and the distribution of the cash to the partners.
B. Assuming that Hare does not pay any of the money he owes, prepare the journal entries to record the allocation of Hare's debit balance and the distribution of the cash.

Exercise 14-8 (Recording Partnership Transactions)

Warner and Fannin had capital balances of $70,000 and $50,000, respectively, on January 1, 1983. They completed the following transactions during the year:

March 8	Warner withdrew $30,000 in cash from the partnership. Fannin withdrew $4,000 of inventory.

July 27	Warner contributed equipment valued at $12,000. Fannin contributed $6,000 cash.
December 31	The net income of $22,000 was allocated in the ratio of 60% to Warner and 40% to Fannin.
December 31	The partners' Withdrawal accounts were closed.

Required:
A. Prepare journal entries to record each of the above transactions.
B. Prepare a statement of partners' capital for the year ended December 31, 1983.

PROBLEMS

Problem 14-1 (Partnership Formation)

Dana Bethany and Bryan Taylor formed a partnership on September 1, 1983. They agreed to share profits and losses in the ratio of 80:20. Bethany contributed $50,000 in cash and land worth $150,000. Assets contributed to the partnership and liabilities assumed by the partnership from Taylor's business are shown below at both book value and fair value.

	Book Value	Fair Value
Cash	$ 3,000	$ 3,000
Accounts Receivable	5,000	4,700
Inventory	10,000	13,000
Equipment	35,000	38,000
Accounts Payable	7,500	7,500
Note Payable	5,000	5,000

During the first year, Bethany contributed an additional $6,000 in cash. The partnership's net income was $16,000. Bethany withdrew $4,000, and Taylor withdrew $7,000.

Required:
A. Prepare the journal entries to record each partner's initial investment.
B. Prepare the partnership's balance sheet at September 1, 1983.
C. Prepare a statement of partners' capital for the year ended August 31, 1984.

Problem 14-2 (Allocation of Net Income and Net Loss)

Julie Young and Steve Armstrong have agreed to form a partnership. Julie is contributing $90,000, and Steve is contributing $60,000. They are considering each of the following methods of allocating profits and losses:

1. Allocate in the ratio of 55:45.
2. Allocate in the ratio of their original investments.
3. Allocate interest of 10% of their original investments, a $12,000 salary to Julie, a $15,000 salary to Steve, and the remainder in the ratio of 60:40.
4. Allocate a $5,000 salary to Steve, interest of 6% on their original investments, and the remainder equally.

Required:
For each allocation method, determine each partner's share of the net income or loss assuming:

A. A net income of $80,000.
B. A net income of $20,000.
C. A net loss of $15,000.

Problem 14-3 (Allocation of Net Income)
Tom Ranier, Sally Shigela, and Edward Coli are forming a partnership. Tom is investing $20,000, Sally is investing $40,000, and Edward is investing $30,000. Tom will work full-time, Sally will work half-time, and Edward will work one-fourth of the time. Profits and losses will be allocated according to one of the following plans.

1. Allocate interest of 10% on their original investments and the remainder in proportion to the time devoted to the business.
2. Allocate a $30,000 salary to Tom, a $16,000 salary to Sally, a $7,000 salary to Edward, and the remainder in the ratio of their original investments.
3. Allocate a $6,000 salary to Tom and the remainder in the ratio of 25:45:30.
4. Allocate in the ratio of 20:40:40.

Required:
Determine each partner's share of the profits under each plan for a net income of

A. $100,000
B. $30,000

Present the data in a table similar to the one below.

Plan	$100,000 Net Income			$30,000 Net Income		
	Tom	Sally	Edward	Tom	Sally	Edward

Problem 14-4 (Admission of a New Partner)
Nancy, Lois, and Mary Beth are partners. They share profits and losses in the ratio of 50:30:20. On May 15, 1983, when they have capital balances of $100,000, $50,000, and $60,000, respectively, they agree to admit Bill to the partnership.

Required:
Prepare the journal entry to record Bill's admission to the partnership for each of the following situations:

A. Bill invests $90,000 cash in the partnership for a 30% interest in the partnership.
B. Bill invests $40,000 cash in the partnership for a 20% interest.
C. Bill invests $40,000 cash in the partnership for a 10% interest.
D. Bill pays Lois $30,000 for 50% of her interest.
E. Bill pays Nancy $20,000 and Mary Beth $15,000 for 25% of each of their partnership interests.

Problem 14-5 (Withdrawal of a Partner)

The November 16, 1984, balance sheet of the Ace Partnership is shown.

ACE PARTNERSHIP
Balance Sheet
November 16, 1984

Assets	
Cash	$ 45,000
Accounts Receivable	25,000
Inventory	56,000
Equipment	220,000
Total Assets	$346,000
Liabilities and Partners' Equity	
Accounts Payable	$ 35,000
Andrews, Capital	155,000
Charles, Capital	60,000
Edwards, Capital	96,000
Total Liabilities and Partners' Equity	$346,000

Andrews, Charles, and Edwards share profits and losses in the ratio of 45:20:35. Charles withdraws from the partnership on November 16, 1984.

Required:
Prepare the journal entry or entries to record the withdrawal of Charles under each of the following situations:

A. Charles receives $40,000 cash and a $20,000 note from the partnership for his interest.
B. Edwards purchases Charles' interest for $74,000.
C. The partnership gives Charles $25,000 cash and equipment with a book value of $45,000 for his interest.
D. The partnership gives Charles $40,000 cash for his interest.
E. Charles sells one-third of his interest to Andrews for $25,000 and two-thirds to Edwards for $38,000.

F. Appraisals reveal that accounts receivable are overstated by $4,000, inventory is understated by $5,000, and equipment is understated by $10,000. These assets are revalued, and Charles is given a promissory note equal to his revalued capital account.

Problem 14-6 (Partnership Liquidation)

Ann, Lisa, and Harry are partners who share profits and losses in the ratio of 30:20:50. On July 18, 1985, they decide to liquidate the business. The balance sheet on that date is presented below.

ANN, LISA, AND HARRY
Balance Sheet
July 18, 1985

Assets		
Cash		$ 20,000
Accounts Receivable	$ 30,000	
Less: Allowance for Doubtful Accounts	5,000	25,000
Inventory		60,000
Equipment	160,000	
Less: Accumulated Depreciation	30,000	130,000
Building	800,000	
Less: Accumulated Depreciation	100,000	700,000
Land		200,000
Total Assets		$1,135,000
Liabilities and Partners' Equity		
Accounts Payable		$ 50,000
Mortgage Payable		600,000
Ann, Capital		175,000
Lisa, Capital		60,000
Harry, Capital		250,000
Total Liabilities and Partners' Equity		$1,135,000

Required:

A. Prepare one journal entry to summarize the following transactions:
  1. Collected $10,000 on accounts receivable and wrote off the remaining accounts.
  2. Sold the inventory for $20,000.
  3. Sold the equipment for $80,000.
  4. Sold the building and the land for $600,000. The buyer assumed the mortgage.
B. Prepare the journal entry to allocate the loss to the partners' capital accounts.
C. Prepare a balance sheet just after the entries for (A) and (B) are posted.
D. Prepare journal entries to record the payment of accounts payable, the receipt of

cash from the partner(s) with a deficit balance for the amount of the deficit, and the distribution of the remaining cash to the partners.

Problem 14-7 (Partnership Liquidation)

West, Gordon, and Carter are partners who share profits and losses in the ratio of 60:30:10. They have decided to liquidate the business. The latest balance sheet appears below.

WEST, GORDON, AND CARTER
Balance Sheet
October 10, 1984

Assets	
Cash	$10,000
Other Assets	82,000
Total Assets	$92,000
Liabilities and Partners' Equity	
Accounts Payable	$35,000
West, Capital	38,000
Gordon, Capital	12,000
Carter, Capital	7,000
Total Liabilities and Partners' Equity	$92,000

Required:

Prepare all the journal entries needed to record the sale of the noncash assets, the allocation of any gain or loss on liquidation, the payment to creditors, and the distribution of cash to the partners, assuming:

A. The noncash assets are sold for $60,000.
B. The noncash assets are sold for $38,000, and the partner with a deficit is unable to contribute to the partnership.
C. The noncash assets are sold for $33,000, and the partner with a deficit is able to contribute only one-half the amount of the deficit.
D. The noncash assets are sold for $90,000.

ALTERNATE PROBLEMS

Problem 14-1A (Partnership Formation)

On October 1, 1984, Rick Sorg and Roger Jackson formed a partnership. Sorg contributed some business assets and the liabilities assumed by the partnership, which are listed below at both book value and fair value.

	Book Value	Fair Value
Cash	$ 40,000	$ 40,000
Marketable Securities	28,000	36,000
Accounts Receivable	43,000	39,000
Inventory	100,000	103,000
Machinery and Equipment	250,000	260,000
Accounts Payable	80,000	80,000

Jackson contributed a building worth $300,000, land worth $100,000, and a $250,000 mortgage was assumed by the partnership. They agreed to share profits and losses in the ratio of 70:30. During the first year of the partnership, Sorg invested $50,000 in the business and withdrew $35,000. Jackson invested $75,000 and withdrew $10,000. The partnership had a net income of $60,000.

Required:
A. Prepare the journal entries to record the initial investments of both partners.
B. Prepare a balance sheet as of October 1, 1984.
C. Prepare a statement of partners' capital for the year ended September 30, 1985.

Problem 14-2A (Allocation of Net Income and Net Loss)
Tad Goode and Len Gomer have decided to form a partnership by investing $30,000 and $20,000, respectively. The following plans for dividing profits and losses are under consideration:

1. In the ratio of 50:50.
2. A $10,000 salary to Tad, a $20,000 salary to Len, and the remainder in the ratio of 70:30.
3. A $15,000 salary to Len, 12% interest on their original investments, and the remainder equally.
4. In the ratio of their original investments.

Required:
For each plan, determine the division of the net income or loss assuming:

A. A net income of $90,000.
B. A net loss of $2,000.
C. A net income of $25,000.

Problem 14-3A (Allocation of Net Income)
Kevin, Tony, and Gary form a partnership by contributing $90,000, $80,000, and $30,000, respectively. Kevin will work 15 hours a week for the business, Tony will work 25 hours a week, and Gary will work 40 hours a week. The partners are considering the following plans for the division of profits and losses:

1. Divide according to the amount of time worked in the business.

2. Allocate an $8,000 salary to Kevin, a $14,000 salary to Tony, a $20,000 salary to Gary, interest of 8% on their original investments, and the remainder in the ratio of 50:40:10.
3. Divide in the ratio of their original investments.
4. Allocate a $3,000 salary to Tony, a $7,000 salary to Gary, 12% interest on their original investments, and the remainder in the ratio of 40:40:20.

Required:
For each plan, determine each partner's share of the profits assuming a net income of:

A. $80,000
B. $36,000

Present the data in the following format.

Plan	$80,000 Net Income			$36,000 Net Income		
	Kevin	Tony	Gary	Kevin	Tony	Gary

Problem 14-4A (Admission of a New Partner)
Adams, Davis, and Johnson are partners in the DAW Company. They share profits and losses in the ratio of 70:20:10. Their current capital balances are $250,000, $90,000, and $40,000. The partners have agreed to admit Robinson to the partnership.

Required:
Prepare the journal entry to record Robinson's admission to the partnership under each of the following conditions:

A. Robinson pays directly to Adams $210,000 for 50% of his partnership interest.
B. Robinson contributes to the partnership $100,000 for a 25% interest.
C. Robinson contributes to the partnership $20,000 for a 5% interest.
D. Robinson contributes to the partnership $300,000 for a 40% interest.
E. Robinson pays Adams $150,000, Davis $60,000, and Johnson $10,000 for 50% of each of their interests.

Problem 14-5A (Withdrawal of a Partner)
The balance sheet of the HRB partnership at March 10, 1984, is shown on page 574.

```
                        HRB PARTNERSHIP
                          Balance Sheet
                         March 10, 1984

        Assets
        Cash                                            $ 30,000
        Accounts Receivable                               14,000
        Inventory                                         28,000
        Plant and Equipment                              103,000
          Total Assets                                  $175,000


        Liabilities and Partners' Equity
        Accounts Payable                                $ 50,000
        Hoover, Capital                                   25,000
        Romley, Capital                                   70,000
        Boyle, Capital                                    30,000
          Total Liabilities and Partners' Equity        $175,000
```

Hoover, Romley, and Boyle divide profits and losses in a 20:50:30 ratio. On March 10, 1984, Hoover retires from the partnership.

Required:

Prepare journal entries to record Hoover's retirement from the partnership under each of the following assumptions:

A. Boyle pays directly to Hoover $20,000 for his partnership interest.
B. Hoover receives $30,000 of partnership cash for his interest.
C. Hoover receives inventory from the partnership with a book value of $19,000 and a $25,000 fair market value. The inventory is not to be revalued on the partnership books.
D. An analysis of the assets reveals that inventory is overstated by $8,000 and plant and equipment are understated by $20,000. The assets are revalued, and Hoover is given $28,000 of partnership cash for his interest.
E. Hoover sells one-half of his interest to his friend Jones for $12,000. Romley buys the other half for $15,000.
F. The partners agree that accounts receivable are overstated $4,000. The account balance is adjusted, and Hoover is given partnership cash equal to his adjusted capital balance for his interest.

Problem 14-6A (Partnership Liquidation)

On May 4, 1983, Jerry, Mark, and Scott decide to liquidate their partnership. The balance sheet on that date appears on page 575.

```
                    JERRY, MARK, AND SCOTT
                         Balance Sheet
                          May 4, 1983


Assets
Cash                                                   $ 10,000
Marketable Securities                                    15,000
Accounts Receivable                       $ 20,000
Less: Allowance for Doubtful Accounts        3,000      17,000
Inventory                                               46,000
Plant and Equipment                        190,000
Less: Accumulated Depreciation              32,000     158,000
     Total Assets                                     $246,000


Liabilities and Partners' Equity
Accounts Payable                                      $ 42,000
Notes Payable                                           15,000
Jerry, Capital                                          94,000
Mark, Capital                                           73,000
Scott, Capital                                          22,000
     Total Liabilities and Partners' Equity          $246,000
```

Jerry, Mark, and Scott share profits and losses in a 40:40:20 ratio.

Required:

A. Prepare one journal entry summarizing the transactions listed below:
1. The inventory is sold for $21,000.
2. Collections on accounts receivable total $6,000. The remaining accounts receivable are written off.
3. The plant and equipment are sold for $75,000. The buyer assumed the $15,000 notes payable and paid the balance in cash.
4. The marketable securities are sold for $16,000.

B. Prepare the entry to allocate the gain or loss on liquidation to the partners' capital accounts.

C. Prepare a balance sheet for the partnership just after the entries in (A) and (B) are posted.

D. Prepare journal entries to record the payment in full to creditors, the receipt of cash in the amount of his deficit from one of the partners, and the distribution of the remaining cash to the partners.

Problem 14-7A (Partnership Liquidation)

The Mercury Company is being liquidated. The current balance sheet is shown below:

```
                        MERCURY COMPANY
                         Balance Sheet
                        January 14, 1984

        Assets
        Cash                                          $ 6,000
        Other Assets                                    50,000
           Total Assets                                $56,000

        Liabilities and Partners' Equity
        Accounts Payable                              $15,000
        Firth, Capital                                  22,000
        Jones, Capital                                  14,000
        Malcolm, Capital                                 5,000
           Total Liabilities and Partners' Equity     $56,000
```

Firth, Jones, and Malcolm share profits and losses in a 40:30:30 ratio.

Required:

Prepare all the necessary journal entries to record the sale of the other assets, the allocation of any gain or loss on the sale, the payment to creditors, and the distribution of cash to the partners, assuming:

A. The other assets are sold for $25,000, and the partner with a deficit is unable to eliminate any of the deficit.
B. The other assets are sold for $60,000.
C. The other assets are sold for $20,000, and the partner with a deficit is able to contribute only $1,000 to the partnership.
D. The other assets are sold for $42,000.

CASE FOR CHAPTER 14

The AB Partnership was formed by Art Abbott and Bill Bradley in 1980. The partners agreed to share profits and losses equally. Abbott manages the business and spends 45 to 60 hours per week. Bradley is a salesperson with extensive experience in marketing. The balance sheet for AB Partnership as of December 31, 1983, is as follows:

Assets		Liabilities and Capital	
Cash	$10,000	Accounts payable	$90,000
Accounts receivable	60,000	Other current liabilities	60,000
Inventory (LIFO cost)	90,000	Long-term note (22% due in 1987)	50,000
Land	40,000	Abbott, Capital	55,000
Building (net)	60,000	Bradley, Capital	40,000
Equipment (net)	35,000		
	$295,000		$295,000

Since its formation, the partnership has not produced a profit and has had cash flow problems. Unable to meet their short-term obligations, the partners borrowed $50,000 from Carl Cline giving a long-term note. Abbott and Bradley feel that the major problems confronting the partnership have been eliminated and that the firm is an attractive investment. They recognize that management of their liquid assets will be required and they are also concerned about the high level of interest costs. Together they approached Cline and convinced him to become a partner in a new partnership called the ABC Partnership. The long-term note is to be converted to a partnership interest of the same amount plus Cline is to invest cash in the firm so that he will have a ⅓ capital interest. Cline insisted, however, that the accounts be adjusted to reflect any errors and omissions. Abbott and Bradley agree to this and counter by insisting that assets and liabilities should be adjusted to reflect current values. They argue that Cline should not be permitted to benefit from price appreciations that have already occurred. After a review of the assets and the liabilities of the firm, the partners and Cline agree that the following adjustments are needed:

1. The business had not followed a strict accrual basis of accounting. As a result the following items were omitted from the December 31 balance sheet:

Accrued expenses	$1,200
Prepaid expenses	600
Unearned revenues	400
2. No provisions had been made for a loss on uncollectible accounts. It is estimated that 10% of the accounts receivable are uncollectible.
3. Current cost to replace the inventory is $98,000.
4. The fair value of the land is $60,000. The book value of the other fixed assets is equal to their current fair value.

Required:

A. Prepare the necessary journal entries on the books of the old partnership to adjust the accounts. Assume that the adjustments are made to an account called the "Valuation Adjustment" account. This account is then closed to the partners' capital accounts in accordance with their agreed profit and loss sharing ratio.
B. Record the admission of Cline by recognizing the conversion of the long-term debt to capital and the additional cash investment.
C. Prepare a balance sheet on December 31, 1983 as it would appear after the adjustments and the admission of Cline.
D. Discuss why it is equitable to restate the accounts of the old partnership before the admission of Cline.

CHAPTER 15
CORPORATIONS: ORGANIZATION AND OPERATION

OVERVIEW AND OBJECTIVES

This chapter discusses the way corporations are organized, the types of stock they issue, and accounting procedures for stockholders' equity. When you have completed the chapter, you should understand:

- The advantages and disadvantages of the corporate form of business organization (pp. 579–582).
- How a corporation is formed (pp. 582–583).
- The management structure of a corporation (pp. 583–585).
- The rights attached to stock ownership (pp. 583–584).
- Why a distinction is made between contributed capital and retained earnings (pp. 586–587).
- The difference between authorized, issued, and outstanding stock (pp. 587–588).
- How to record the issue of corporate stock (pp. 588–591).
- The effect of dividends on assets and stockholders' equity (pp. 591–592).
- The differences between common and preferred stock (pp. 593–596).
- How to record stock subscriptions (pp. 596–597).
- The meaning of book value per common share and how to compute it (pp. 597–598).

Although there are fewer corporations than single proprietorships and partnerships in the United States, corporations transact about six times more business than the other two combined and control vast amounts of resources. Most large businesses as well as many small ones are organized as corporations. Because of the dominant role they play in our economy and because many of you will at some time either work for or own shares in a corporation, it is important to have an understanding of corporations and their accounting practices.

The domination of our economy by corporations has led to increasing demands for information about them. Almost everyone is affected by the activities of corporations. We all buy goods and services produced by them. Many people work for corporations, receive interest and dividends from them, or sell goods and services to them. All segments of society—including investors and prospective investors, creditors, labor unions, governmental agencies, and consumers—are necessarily interested in the financial strength and profitability of corporations as a means of assessing the efficiency with which they have used their resources.

THE CORPORATION

Probably the most widely quoted definition of a corporation is that given by Chief Justice John Marshall in the Dartmouth College Case in 1819, in which he described a corporation as "an artificial being, invisible, intangible, and existing only in contemplation of the law." A corporation is a legal entity or artificial person separate and distinct from its owners. As a separate entity, it has many of the rights and responsibilities of a person. As a legal entity, it can, through its agents, buy, own, and sell property in its own name and engage in business activity by entering into contracts with others. It has legal status in a court and can sue and be sued, is legally responsible for its liabilities, and must pay income taxes just as a person does.

Corporations may be classified in several ways. They may be organized for profit or for nonprofit purposes. A **profit corporation** is one that engages in business activity with the goal of earning a profit for its owners. Its continued existence is dependent upon profitable operations. **Nonprofit corporations** are organized to engage in educational, charitable, health research, and other society-benefiting activities and generally depend upon public contributions for their continued existence.

Corporations are also often classified as public corporations and nonpublic corporations. **Public corporations** are those whose shares of stock are widely held and traded through national stock exchanges. Corporations whose shares of stock are held by a small group, often by the members of a single family, and are not publicly traded are called **nonpublic** (or **closely held**) **corporations.**

ADVANTAGES OF THE CORPORATE FORM

The corporate form of business has several advantages over the single proprietorship and partnership forms. The main ones are discussed on page 580.

Limited Liability

As a separate legal entity, a corporation is responsible for its actions and liabilities. Creditors have claims only against the assets of the corporation, not against the personal assets of the stockholders. Because owners of a corporation are not personally liable for corporate debts, the maximum amount they can lose is the amount they invest. To investors, this is one of the most important advantages of the corporate form, since under the alternative forms of business organization, owners may be personally liable for business debts.

Broad Source of Capital

Ownership rights in corporations are represented by transferable shares of stock. By dividing ownership of the business into many shares with a relatively small value per share, both large and small investors are able to participate in the ownership of the business. Most large corporations can therefore draw upon the savings of many people to obtain the capital they need.

Continuity of Existence

A corporation has an indefinite life and continues in existence even if its ownership changes. The transfer of shares from one owner to another has no effect on a corporation. In contrast, the death, incapacity, or withdrawal of an owner terminates a single proprietorship or a partnership.

Ready Transferability of Shares

Corporate shares may be transferred easily without disrupting the activities of the corporation. Shares in public corporations can be bought and sold on practically every weekday through one of the national stock exchanges. Consequently, a stockholder can readily convert his/her investment into cash if the need arises.

Use of Professional Management

Although the stockholders own the corporation, they do not manage its daily activities. Stockholders elect a board of directors, which has overall responsibility for administrative decisions. The board then hires a president and other officers to manage the business. In contrast to a partnership, no mutual agency exists in a corporation. An individual stockholder does not have the right to bind the corporation to a contract unless he or she has been hired as a corporate officer. This separation of management and ownership permits the corporation to hire the best managerial talent available.

DISADVANTAGES OF THE CORPORATE FORM

The corporate form also has some disadvantages when compared to the single proprietorship and partnership forms. The main disadvantages are described below.

Heavier Tax Burden

Single proprietorships and partnerships are not subject to income tax as separate business units. Instead, the income they earn is taxed only as personal income to the owners. In contrast, a corporation's income is taxed twice. Because the corporation is a separate legal entity, its income is subject to federal and state income taxes, the total of which often exceeds 40% of corporate income. When the corporation's after-tax income is distributed to its stockholders as dividends, the income is taxed again as personal income to the stockholders receiving the dividends. This double taxation is the primary disadvantage of the corporate form of business.[1]

Greater Governmental Regulation

Corporations come into existence under specific state laws. Consequently, they are said to be creatures of the state and are subject to a much greater degree of control and supervision by the state than are single proprietorships or partnerships. In addition, public corporations must file periodic reports with the Securities and Exchange Commission and the stock exchanges on which their shares are traded. Meeting these additional reporting requirements often can be very costly.

Separation of Ownership and Management

The use of professional managers was cited earlier as an advantage of the corporate form. In some cases, however, this separation of ownership from management may prove to be a disadvantage because managers have sometimes operated corporations for their own benefit rather than for the benefit of the stockholders. Considerable harm may be done before stockholders become aware of the condition and take action to change mangagement. A summary comparison of the corporate form of business with the single proprietorship or partnership form is given in Figure 15-1.

---

[1] When specific conditions of the Internal Revenue Code are met, the stockholders of some corporations may avoid the double taxation of income by electing to be taxed as partnerships.

Figure 15-1
Summary Comparison of Forms of Business Organization

Characteristic	Form of Business Organization	
	Proprietorship/ Partnership	Corporation
Limited liability of owners	Disadvantage	Advantage
Ease of raising capital	Disadvantage	Advantage
Continuity of existence	Disadvantage	Advantage
Ease with which ownership may be transferred	Disadvantage	Advantage
Tax burden	Advantage	Disadvantage
Extent of government regulation	Advantage	Disadvantage

FORMING A CORPORATION

Some corporations, such as national banks and savings and loan associations, are formed under federal laws. The majority of corporations, however, are created by obtaining a charter from one of the 50 states. To form a corporation, states require that individuals called **incorporators** must sign an application for a corporate charter and file it with the appropriate state official. Although state laws vary, the application generally must include:

1. The name and address of the proposed corporation.
2. The purpose of the proposed corporation.
3. A description of the different classes of stock and their par or stated value per share, if any.
4. The number of shares of each class of stock authorized.
5. A description of the rights, preferences, and restrictions of each class of stock.
6. The names and addresses of the original subscribers to shares of stock and the amount of each subscription.

If the application is approved, a legal contract between the state and the incorporators, called a **corporate charter,** is entered into and the corporation is authorized to conduct business. The incorporators hold an initial meeting to adopt the bylaws to be followed in conducting corporate affairs and to elect a board of directors. The board of directors then meets to appoint the president and other officers who will manage the company. After capital is raised through the issue of shares of stock, the corporation is ready to begin operating activities.

Organization Costs

The costs incurred in forming a corporation are called **organization costs** and include the incorporation fee paid to the state, attorneys' fees, promotors' fees, the cost of printing stock certificates and corporate records, and various other expenditures needed to form the corporation. These costs represent an intangible asset that will benefit the corporation throughout its life and are therefore debited to an asset account called Organization Costs. Since the life of a corporation is indeterminate, the number of years that the corporation will benefit from organization costs is also indeterminate. Current accounting practice requires that organization costs, like other intangible assets, be amortized over their estimated useful life with a maximum of 40 years.

Current income tax rules permit a corporation to amortize organization costs over a period of not less than five years. Many companies therefore amortize their organization costs over five years for both income tax and accounting purposes. Although not conceptually correct, the practice is accepted by accountants because organization costs are generally not material in amount (materiality principle).

MANAGING THE CORPORATION

Although control of a corporation rests ultimately with its stockholders, that control is exercised only indirectly. Stockholders elect a board of directors, which sets overall corporate policies. The board, in turn, appoints a president and other officers to manage the corporation's day-to-day affairs and carry out the policies established by the board.

The Stockholders

An individual stockholder is not directly involved in the daily management of the company unless he or she has been elected to serve on the board of directors or has been appointed an officer or manager. Stockholders are generally involved only in electing the board of directors and voting on certain important corporate actions specified in the corporate bylaws. For example, many corporate bylaws provide that stockholders must approve such actions as the merger with or acquisition of another company and changes in the capital structure of the corporation.

Ownership of stock usually carries certain rights and privileges that can be modified only by specific contract at the time the shares are issued. These basic rights are:

1. The right to vote for directors and on other matters described in the corporate bylaws. (We will see later that this right is generally eliminated for preferred stockholders.)
2. The right to share in profits by receiving dividends declared by the board of directors.
3. The right to share in the distribution of the corporation's assets if it is liquidated. When a corporation is liquidated, creditors must be paid in full,

and any remaining assets are distributed to the stockholders in proportion to the number of shares held.

4. The right to purchase a portion of any additional stock issued by the corporation. This right, called the preemptive right, permits stockholders to maintain their percentage interests in a corporation by purchasing new shares in proportion to their current holdings. For example, if Maria Martinez owns 4,000 of the 40,000 outstanding shares of a corporation, she has a 10% interest. If the corporation issues 10,000 additional shares, Maria has the right to purchase 10% of them, or 1,000 shares, so that she will maintain her 10% interest in the corporation after the issue of the additional shares. Because this right is burdensome and may unduly restrict the actions of management of widely held corporations, it is frequently waived by stockholders in the bylaws.

Stockholders generally meet once a year to elect directors and to conduct other business as provided by the corporate bylaws. Each share of stock is entitled to one vote. A stockholder who owns more than 50% of a corporation's stock can thus elect the board of directors and control the corporation. Because many of the stockholders of a widely held company do not attend the annual meeting, however, a corporation can often be controlled through the ownership of a much smaller percentage of stock. Stockholders who do not attend the annual meeting may delegate their voting right to an agent by signing a legal document called a proxy statement. Often the voting right is delegated to the current management in order to permit them to continue in control.

The Board of Directors

Although the board of directors has final responsibility for managing the corporation, it normally restricts its role to formulating the major business policies of the company and to appointing the officers who will have responsibility for carrying out these policies. Duties of the board are normally identified in the corporate bylaws and generally include such things as (1) taking responsibility for protecting the rights of stockholders and creditors, (2) setting officers' salaries, (3) declaring dividends, (4) authorizing long-term borrowing, additional stock issues, and major expansion projects, and (5) reviewing the system of internal control. The board of directors is normally composed of corporate executives and holders of large blocks of corporate stock. In addition, the board normally includes several outside directors to ensure a more objective evaluation of management performance.

Official actions of the board are recorded in the minutes of their meetings. The *minutes book* is important to the accountant because it contains board decisions that serve as the basis for the authorization of certain transactions and the preparation of many accounting entries.

The Corporate Officers

A corporation's administrative officers usually include a president, who is the chief executive with responsibility to the board of directors for managing and controlling business activities. The president is normally supported by one or more vice-presidents, who are responsible to the president for managing specific functional areas. For example, a corporation may have a vice-president of finance, a vice-president of production, and a vice-president of marketing. Other officers are the controller, the treasurer, and the secretary.

The *controller* is the chief accountant and is generally responsible for maintaining the accounting records and an adequate internal control system, preparing financial statements, tax returns, and other reports, and developing the budget. The controller also often advises the board of directors about the accounting and tax consequences of proposed corporate actions. The *treasurer* is the main manager of cash. He or she normally has custody of the company's funds and is responsible for planning and controlling the company's cash position. The *secretary* maintains the minutes of meetings of the directors and stockholders, and represents the corporation in many legal and contractual matters. In a small corporation, the secretary normally also maintains the records of stockholders and the amount of their stock interests. Large corporations use outside registrars and transfer agents to perform this stockholder-record function. Some corporations, particularly smaller ones, combine the positions of secretary and treasurer.

The following diagram illustrates a typical corporate organization chart. Lines of authority extend from the stockholders to the board of directors to the president to other officers.

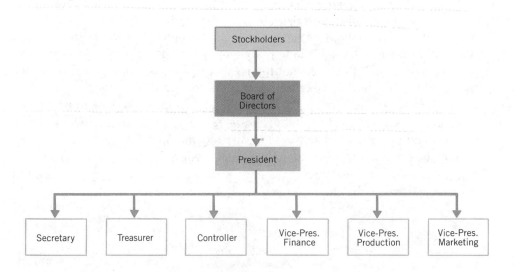

CORPORATE CAPITAL

Accounting for a corporation is similar in most respects to accounting for a single proprietorship or a partnership. The income statement and the asset and liability sections of the balance sheet are esentially the same for all forms of business organization. There is a major difference, however, in accounting for owners' equity. In a corporation, the term *stockholders' equity*—sometimes called *shareholders' equity* or simply *capital*—is used instead of *owners' equity*. The stockholders' equity section of a typical corporate balance sheet might appear as follows:

Stockholders' Equity	
Contributed Capital:	
Preferred stock, $100 par value, 10,000 shares authorized, 5,000 shares issued and outstanding	$ 500,000
Common stock, $10 par value, 500,000 shares authorized, 200,000 shares issued and outstanding	2,000,000
Contributed capital in excess of par—Preferred	50,000
Contributed capital in excess of par—Common	1,450,000
Total contributed capital	4,000,000
Retained Earnings	870,000
Total Stockholders' Equity	$4,870,000

State incorporation laws generally require that stockholders' equity must be separated into two broad categories, contributed capital and retained earnings. Contributed capital represents the amount of assets invested in the corporation by its stockholders. When stockholders invest cash or other assets in a corporation, they are given shares of the corporation's stock as evidence of their investment. The contributed capital section includes information about the types of stock, their par value, and the number of shares authorized and outstanding. We will discuss these concepts later in this chapter.

Retained earnings reflect the amount of income (assets) earned by the corporation and retained in the business. When a corporation's income statement accounts are closed at year-end, the Income Summary account is closed to Retained Earnings. For example, if net income for the year is $120,000, the Income Summary account will have a credit balance and will be closed to Retained Earnings by the following entry:

Dec.	31	Income Summary	120,000	
		Retained Earnings		120,000
		To close the income summary account.		

If the corporation incurred a net loss for the year, the Income Summary account would have a debit balance and the closing entry would consist of a debit to Retained Earnings and a credit to the Income Summary account. A debit balance in the Retained Earnings account is called a **deficit** and is deducted in arriving at total stockholders' equity.

AUTHORIZED CAPITAL STOCK

When a corporation is formed, its charter indicates the maximum number of shares of stock it is permitted to issue and the par or stated value per share, if any. This maximum number of shares is called **authorized stock.** A corporation may be authorized to issue only one type of stock, called **common stock** (or *capital stock*), or it may be authorized to issue both common stock and preferred stock. (Preferred stock is discussed later in this chapter.) A corporation normally obtains permission to issue more stock than it plans to sell immediately, which permits the corporation to raise additional capital in the future without asking the state to authorize more stock each time the corporation wishes to issue additional shares. For example, a corporation may be authorized to issue 500,000 shares of common stock even though it intends to issue only 200,000 shares initially to raise the capital needed to begin operations. The remaining 300,000 shares may then be issued in the future if additional capital is needed.

Par Value

The par value of stock is an arbitrary amount per share placed on the stock by the incorporators at the time they apply for the corporate charter. They may select any value they wish, and par values of $1, $5, and $10 are common. For example, Alpha Portland Company's common stock has a par value of $10, Idaho Power Company's is $5, and J. C. Penney, Inc.'s is 50¢. Most corporations set a par value substantially below the value at which the stock is initially issued because most states prohibit the issue of stock for less than its par value. If the market price of the stock drops below its par value, the corporation is unable to issue additional stock. Establishing a relatively large spread between the initial issue price of the stock and its par value minimizes the possibility of its market price dropping below par value.

If a corporation issues par value stock, the par value is printed on each stock certificate and is the amount recorded in the capital stock accounts. The only significance of par value is that it establishes a minimum amount of capital, called *legal capital,* which provides an element of protection for creditors. Legal capital cannot be reduced except by operating losses or legal action by a majority vote of the stockholders. Because a corporation's creditors have claims only against the assets of the corporation, additional protection is provided them by maintaining a minimum amount of assets equal to legal capital. This minimum amount of assets cannot be returned to the stockholders until all creditors' claims have been paid. Total legal capital of a corporation issuing par value stock is equal to the number of shares outstanding times par value per share.

The par value of stock has no relationship to its worth or market value. Par value is a fixed amount per share; market value generally fluctuates daily. For example, the market value of Color Tile, Inc.'s common stock ranged from $12.32 to $25.25 per share during 1980; its par value remained at $1 per share.

OUTSTANDING STOCK

The outstanding stock of a corporation consists of the shares held by stockholders at any given time. As authorized stock is issued, it becomes outstanding stock. If 500,000 shares are authorized and 200,000 shares have been issued, the remaining 300,000 shares are called unissued stock and contain no rights until they are issued. The holders of the 200,000 shares own 100% of the corporation. At times, a corporation's issued stock may exceed the number of shares outstanding because some of the shares may have been repurchased by the corporation. These repurchased shares are called "treasury stock" (discussed in Chapter 16.)

THE ISSUE OF COMMON STOCK

When common stock is issued for cash, the Cash account is debited, the Common Stock account is credited for the par value of the shares issued (legal capital), and a separate account called Contributed Capital in Excess of Par is credited for the excess of the selling price over par value. For example, if 10,000 shares of $1 par value common stock are issued at $20 per share, the entry is:

Jan.	5	Cash	200,000	
		Common Stock		10,000
		Contributed Capital in Excess of Par		190,000
		Issued 10,000 shares of common stock at $20 per share.		

Contributed capital in excess of par is sometimes called *premium on common stock*. It is important to recognize that this premium on common stock does not constitute income to the corporation. It is a part of total contributed capital that, because it is not legal capital, is reported on the balance sheet as a separate element of contributed capital as follows:

Stockholders' Equity:
Common Stock, $1 par value, 60,000 shares authorized, 10,000

shares issued and outstanding	$ 10,000
Contributed Capital in Excess of Par	190,000
Total Contributed Capital	200,000
Retained Earnings (assumed amount)	50,000
Total Stockholders' Equity	$250,000

A few states permit the issue of stock for less than its par value, in which case a Discount on Common Stock account is debited for the difference between the issue price and the par value of the stock. If stock is issued at a discount, the purchasers of the stock are contingently liable to the corporation's creditors for the amount of the discount. Consequently, the issue of stock at a discount is rare.

Issuing Stock for Assets Other than Cash

Corporations normally issue their stock for cash and use the cash to acquire the goods and services needed. At times, however, a corporation may issue stock directly for assets such as land, buildings, or equipment. When this occurs, the assets received are recorded at the fair value of the stock issued or the fair value of the assets received, whichever is more objectively determinable. If the stock is publicly traded, the market value of the shares given is often a better measure of value than is the appraised value of the assets received. If 3,000 shares of common stock are exchanged for a piece of land and the stock has a current market value of $15 per share, it is reasonable to record the cost of the land at $45,000 (3,000 × $15) since the stock could have been sold for $45,000 and the cash used to acquire the land. For a new corporation or a closely held one, the market value of the stock is unknown and the fair value of the assets received must be determined. For example, assume a new corporation issued 10,000 shares of $10 par value common stock to one of the incorporators in exchange for land with an appraised value of $60,000 and a building appraised at $350,000. The issue of the stock would be recorded as follows:

Jan.	5	Land	60,000	
		Buildings	350,000	
		Common Stock		100,000
		Contributed Capital in Excess of Par		310,000
		Exchanged 10,000 shares of common stock for land and a building.		

Because the fair value of the stock is unknown, the land and buildings are recorded at their appraised values. Common Stock is credited for the par value of the shares issued and the difference between the fair value of the assets and the par value of the stock is credited to Contributed Capital in Excess of Par.

Sometimes a new corporation issues stock to its promoters in exchange for their services in organizing and promoting the corporation. If the fair value of the services received is $20,000 and 500 shares of $10 par value common stock is given, the entry is:

Jan.	5	Organization Costs	20,000	
		Common Stock		5,000
		Contributed Capital in Excess of Par		15,000
		Exchanged 500 shares of stock for		
		organizational services.		

DONATED CAPITAL

Sometimes a corporation may receive a donation of assets from a stockholder or other party. In order to increase their tax base and provide employment to residents, for example, cities often donate land to a corporation to encourage construction of facilities in their localities. When this occurs, the asset received is recorded at its fair value and a separate Contributed Capital–Donations account is credited. For example, if a corporation received a donation of land with a fair value of $140,000, the entry would be:

Jan.	4	Land	140,000	
		Contributed Capital—Donations		140,000
		To record the fair value of land donated by		
		Tuba City.		

If major restrictions are placed on the use of donated assets, a footnote explaining the restrictions should be included with the financial statements.

NO-PAR STOCK

In the early history of the American corporation, all stock was required to have a par value. Today, however, all states permit the issue of **no-par stock.** Some states require that the entire proceeds from the sale of no-par stock must be credited to the capital stock account as legal capital. This type is referred to as *straight no-par stock.* In other states, the board of directors may assign a stated value per share to their no-par stock. From an accounting standpoint, stated value and par value are the same thing in that they both identify the amount that must be recorded as legal capital in the capital stock account.

To illustrate the accounting for no-par stock, we assume that a corporation issues 10,000 shares of no-par common stock at $25 per share. If the stock does not have a stated value, the entire proceeds are recorded in the no-par common stock account as follows:

Jan.	5	Cash	250,000	
		Common Stock—No-par		250,000
		Issued 10,000 shares of no-par stock at $25 per share.		

If the board of directors has assigned a stated value of $5 to the no-par stock, the difference between the issue price and the stated value is credited to Contributed Capital in Excess of Stated Value as follows:

Jan.	5	Cash	250,000	
		Common Stock—No-par		50,000
		Contributed Capital in Excess of Stated Value		200,000
		Issued 10,000 shares of no-par stock with a stated value of $5 per share for $25 per share.		

CASH DIVIDENDS

A **dividend** is a distribution of cash, other assets, or a corporation's own stock to its stockholders. Cash dividends are the most common and will be discussed here. Distributions of other assets or corporate stock are discussed and illustrated in Chapter 16.

Many corporations distribute part of their earnings periodically to their stockholders by declaring a dividend. The authority to declare dividends rests solely with the board of directors, which is responsible for determining both the legality of the dividend and the corporation's ability to pay it. Most states prohibit the payment of dividends in excess of retained earnings, but some states do permit the payment of dividends from any capital other than legal capital. When a dividend is declared from capital other than retained earnings, the corporation is returning to its stockholders a portion of their contributed capital. These dividends are called **liquidating dividends** because they do not represent income to the stockholders. That is, liquidating dividends represent a return of stockholders' investments rather than a return on their investments.

In addition to retained earnings, the corporation must have sufficient cash or other assets to distribute to stockholders without putting an undue strain on the ability of the corporation to continue to operate efficiently. The board of directors must therefore determine the wisdom of distributing assets to stockholders rather than retaining them for operating activities or for financing growth. Once the board has declared a dividend, the obligation to pay it becomes a current liability and cannot be rescinded.

Cash dividends are stated in terms of so many dollars or cents per share of stock. For example, a corporation may declare a dividend of $2 per share on outstanding stock and a stockholder owning 100 shares will receive a dividend check for $200.

A corporation's stockholders change as shares are traded on the market. To assure that dividends are paid to the rightful owner of the shares, dividends are declared on one date, payable on some future date to the stockholders of record on some date between the declaration date and the payment date. For example, the board may declare a dividend on May 25 (the declaration date) to be paid on June 20 (the payment date) to the stockholders of record on June 10 (the date of record). Investors buying stock between May 25 and June 10 will therefore have time to get the ownership of their shares recorded before payment of the dividend.

To illustrate, assume that on May 25 the board of directors declared a $2-per-share dividend on 40,000 outstanding shares of common stock to be paid on June 20 to stockholders of record on June 10. Because a dividend liability is created on the declaration date that will not be settled until the payment date, two journal entries are required. The entry on the declaration date is:

May	25	Retained Earnings	80,000	
		Dividends Payable		80,000
		Declared a cash dividend of $2 per share		
		on the 40,000 common shares		
		outstanding.		

This entry recognizes the dividend liability, which is reported as a current liability on the May 31 balance sheet.

The entry to record payment of the dividend is:

June	20	Dividends Payable	80,000	
		Cash		80,000
		To record payment of the dividend		
		declared on May 25.		

No entry is required on the date of record since that date is used only to determine the owners of the stock who are to receive the dividends.

Companies that normally declare several dividends within a fiscal year—such as quarterly dividends—often debit a separate account called *Dividends Declared* rather than Retained Earnings when the dividend is declared. The Dividends Declared account is then closed to Retained Earnings at the end of the year. If a company declares dividends on both common and preferred stock, it may use a separate Dividends Declared and Dividends Payable account for each type of stock. Regardless of the procedures followed, the net effect of a cash dividend is to reduce both retained earnings and cash by the amount of the dividend.

PREFERRED STOCK

In addition to common stock, many corporations issue one or more types of preferred stock. Preferred stock receives its name from the fact that preferred stockholders receive preferential treatment over common stockholders in one or more respects. Common stock is the residual equity in a corporation, which means that common stockholders are the last to receive asset distributions if the corporation is liquidated. Common stockholders take the greatest risk of loss if the corporation is unsuccessful, but also have the greatest potential for gain if the company is profitable. As a result, the market value of common stock is closely related to profitability and will increase or decrease as stockholders' expectations about future profits rise and fall.

Preferred stock is normally given several preferences over common stock. The most common are preferences as to dividend distributions as well as asset distributions if the corporation is liquidated. In addition, preferred stock is generally callable at the option of the corporation and sometimes is convertible into common stock at the option of the preferred stockholders. In exchange for these preferences, preferred stockholders normally relinquish the right to vote. Preferences and other special features of preferred stock vary widely. Consequently, the preferred stock contract must be read carefully to determine its specific provisions.

Dividend Preference

If stock is preferred as to dividends, its holders are entitled to some specified dividend before any dividend is paid to common stockholders. The annual dividend is usually stated as a dollar amount per share or as a percentage of the stock's par value. For example, Armstrong Cork Company's balance sheet includes no-par preferred stock with a $3.75 annual dividend per share, and Tenneco Inc.'s balance sheet shows 8.52%, $100 par preferred stock, which means that $8.52 must be paid yearly on each share of preferred stock before a dividend can be paid to common stockholders.

Because the obligation to pay a dividend arises only if the board of directors declares one, preferred stockholders are not assured of receiving a dividend each year. Although dividends must be paid on preferred stock before any are paid on common stock, the board of directors may decide not to declare a dividend on either preferred or common stock because of a lack of retained earnings, a shortage of cash, or both. The dividend preference on most preferred stock is cumulative, which means that undeclared dividends accumulate and the accumulated amount plus the current year's preferred dividend must be paid before any dividend can be paid to common stockholders. Dividends that are not declared in the year they are due are called dividends in arrears. Current accounting standards require that dividends in arrears must be disclosed. Disclosure is generally made in a footnote to the financial statements.

To illustrate cumulative dividends, assume that a corporation has 50,000 shares of $5 cumulative preferred stock outstanding and that no dividends were declared in the preceding year. In addition, there are 100,000 shares of common stock outstanding. If the board of directors declares a $700,000 dividend, it will be distributed to preferred and common stockholders as follows:

	Preferred	Common
Dividends in Arrears (50,000 × $5)	$250,000	–0–
Current Year's Dividend	250,000	$200,000
Total	$500,000	$200,000

If the board declared a $400,000 dividend, it would all be distributed to preferred stockholders; common stockholders would receive no dividends, and dividends in arrears on preferred stock would still exist in the amount of $100,000.

If preferred stock is **noncumulative,** any undeclared dividends at the end of the year are lost. Because investors would be hesitant to purchase such stock, very few noncumulative preferred stocks are issued.

Asset Preference

In addition to a dividend preference, most preferred stocks include a preference as to assets if the corporation is liquidated. If the corporation is terminated, the preferred stockholders are entitled to receive payment (after creditors have been paid) equal to the par value of their stock—or a higher liquidation value if one is included—before common stockholders receive any portion of the corporation's assets. This preference also includes any dividends in arrears on cumulative preferred stock.

Callable Preferred Stock

Preferred stock contracts generally include a **call provision,** which gives the corporation the right to repurchase the stock from the stockholders at a predetermined call price. The call price—sometimes called *redemption price*—is usually slightly higher than par value. For example, Johns-Manville's $65 stated value preferred stock has a call price of $67.70 per share. When preferred stock is called, the stockholder is paid the call price plus any dividends in arrears and a pro rata portion of the current year's dividend. A call provision gives the corporation some flexibility in structuring its equity. A preferred stock may be called and retired, for example, in order to distribute greater dividends to common stockholders. Or a preferred stock may be retired and replaced with another preferred stock with a lower dividend rate.

Convertible Preferred Stock

Some preferred stock is convertible, which permits the preferred stockholder to convert the stock into common stock at a predetermined exchange ratio. For example, each share of Borg-Warner Corporation's preferred stock is convertible into 2.5 shares of common stock at the option of the holder. The conversion privilege is an attractive feature to investors. If the corporation is successful and the market price of its common stock rises, the market price of the preferred stock will also increase proportionately since it is convertible into common stock. If the market price of the common stock does not increase, the preferred stock still has its preference as to regular fixed dividends.

To illustrate, assume that a corporation issued 20,000 shares of 7%, $100 par convertible preferred stock on January 2, 1981, at a price of $100 per share. Each preferred share is convertible into three shares of the corporation's $5 par value common stock at any time. The market price of the common stock was $30 per share on January 2, 1981, and an annual dividend of $1.50 per share was being paid. During the next several years earnings increased significantly, and by January 1, 1984, the market price of the common stock had risen to $50 per share and annual dividends were increased to $3.50 per share. The preferred stock would have a market price of approximately $150 per share since it could be converted into three shares of common stock with a total market price of $150.

When the market price and annual dividends on common stock increase, some preferred stockholders may convert their preferred stock into common stock. For example, if the holders of 5,000 of the preferred shares converted their stock, the entry would be:

Jan.	2	Preferred Stock	500,000	
		Common Stock		75,000
		Contributed Capital in Excess of Par		425,000
		Converted 5,000 shares of $100 par value preferred stock into 15,000 shares of $5 par value common stock.		

This entry transfers the stockholders' equity associated with the preferred shares converted to appropriate common stockholders' equity accounts. The preferred stock account is reduced by $500,000 (5,000 shares × $100 par value per share) and the common stock account is credited for the par value of the common stock issued (15,000 shares × $5 = $75,000). The difference between the par value of the preferred stock retired and the par value of the common stock issued is credited to Contributed Capital in Excess of Par. Note that the market price of the common stock issued has no effect on the transaction.

Capital Stock Subscriptions

Corporations sometimes issue stock on a subscription basis under which the purchaser (subscriber) agrees to pay for the shares at a future time or in a series of installments. In these cases, a receivable from the subscriber is recorded for the total purchase price. Legal capital is credited to a separate account called Common (or Preferred) Stock Subscribed. A separate Stock Subscribed account is used to show that the stock has not been fully paid for and, therefore, the stock certificate has not yet been issued. The difference between legal capital and the issue price is credited to Contributed Capital in Excess of Par. To illustrate, assume that on January 2 a corporation sold 5,000 shares of $5 par value common stock on a subscription basis for $30 per share. Payment terms provide for a down payment of one-third of the purchase price, with the remainder due in two equal installments on March 1 and June 1. The entries to record the sale and collection of the down payment are:

Jan.	2	Subscriptions Receivable—Common	150,000	
		Common Stock Subscribed		25,000
		Contributed Capital in Excess of Par		125,000
		To record subscriptions for 5,000 shares of $5 par value common stock at $30 per share.		
Jan.	2	Cash	50,000	
		Subscriptions Receivable—Common		50,000
		To record collection of stock subscriptions receivable.		

When installment payments are received on March 1 and June 1, Cash is debited and Subscriptions Receivable—Common is credited as follows:

March and June	1 1	Cash	50,000	
		Subscriptions Receivable—Common		50,000
		To record collections of stock subscriptions receivable.		

After full payment is received, the stock certificate will be issued to the investor and the following entry prepared:

June	1	Common Stock Subscribed	25,000	
		Common Stock		25,000
		To record the issue of a stock certificate for 5,000 shares of $5 par value common stock.		

Subscriptions receivable are generally reported as current assets on the balance sheet and the Common Stock Subscribed account is reported as an item of stockholders' equity.

BOOK VALUE PER SHARE OF COMMON STOCK

Common stockholders' equity is often reported in statistical summaries in annual reports and in the financial press as an amount per share, generally called **book value per share of common stock.** It is computed by dividing total common stockholders' equity by the number of common shares outstanding. If a corporation has only one type of stock, book value per share is determined by dividing total stockholders' equity by the number of shares outstanding. For example, assume a corporation has the following stockholders' equity:

Common Stock, $5 par, 100,000 shares authorized, 50,000 shares issued and outstanding	$ 250,000
Contributed Capital in Excess of Par	600,000
Retained Earnings	430,000
Total Stockholders' Equity	$1,280,000

Book value per share is $1,280,000 ÷ 50,000 shares = $25.60.

When a corporation has both preferred and common stock outstanding, total stockholders' equity must be allocated to the two classes of stock. Because book value per share is generally reported for common stock only, the approach is to subtract from total stockholders' equity the amount that would be distributed to preferred stockholders if the corporation were terminated. Thus, the equity allocated to preferred stock is its call price plus any dividends in arrears. To illustrate, assume a corporation has the following stockholders' equity:

7% Cumulative Preferred Stock, $100 par, 5,000 shares issued and outstanding, callable at $105	$ 500,000
Common Stock, $5 par, 100,000 shares authorized, 50,000 shares issued and outstanding	250,000
Contributed Capital in Excess of Par	600,000
Retained Earnings	430,000
Total Stockholders' Equity	$1,780,000

Assume further that there are no dividends in arrears for prior years, but that the current year's preferred dividend has not yet been declared. Book value per common share is computed as follows:

Total Stockholders' Equity		$1,780,000
Allocated to Preferred Stock:		
Call Price (5,000 × $105)	$525,000	
Preferred Dividends	35,000	560,000
Common Stockholders' Equity		1,220,000
Divided by Common Shares Outstanding		÷ 50,000
Book Value per Common Share		$24.40

The main purpose of including the book value per share of common stock in statistical summaries is to give some indication to readers of financial statements of the effect of the retention of earnings on growth of the corporation. For example, the book value per common share of Marathon Oil Company increased from $16.85 to $27.88 during a recent five-year period. Since the number of common shares outstanding remained relatively constant during this period, the effect of retaining earnings, rather than distributing them as dividends, was to increase book value per share by $11.03.

Book value should not be confused with liquidation value. If the corporation were liquidated, its assets would probably be sold at prices quite different from their book values. In addition, book value normally has little relationship to a stock's market value. The level of current earnings, earning capacity, and dividend policy are more important factors affecting the market value of common stock.

Several types of stockholders' equity accounts have been introduced in this chapter. An example of the stockholders' equity section of a balance sheet that includes these accounts is shown in Figure 15-2.

GLOSSARY

AUTHORIZED STOCK. The maximum amount of stock a corporation is permitted to issue under the terms of its charter (p. 587).

BOOK VALUE PER COMMON SHARE. The amount of common stockholders' equity related to each share of common stock (p. 597).

CALL PROVISION. The right of a corporation to repurchase preferred stock from its stockholders at a predetermined price (p. 594).

COMMON STOCK. Stock of a corporation having only one class of stock; if there is more than one class, the class that has no preferences relative to the other classes of stock (p. 587).

CONTRIBUTED CAPITAL. The capital invested in the corporation by its stockholders (p. 586).

Stockholders' Equity Accounts

Contributed Capital:	
Cumulative, 10%, preferred stock, $100 par value, 100,000 shares authorized, 20,000 shares issued and outstanding	$2,000,000
Common stock, $10 par value, 1,000,000 shares authorized, 300,000 shares issued and outstanding	3,000,000
Common stock subscribed, 10,000 shares	100,000
Contributed capital in excess of par—preferred	160,000
Contributed capital in excess of par—common	2,400,000
Contributed capital—donations	300,000
Total Contributed Capital	7,960,000
Retained Earnings	310,000
Total Stockholders' Equity	$8,270,000

Figure 15-2
Stockholders' Equity Accounts

CORPORATE CHARTER.   The legal contract between the state and the incorporators (p. 582).

CUMULATIVE PREFERRED STOCK.   Preferred stock on which undeclared dividends accumulate and must be paid before any dividend can be paid to common stockholders (p. 593).

DEFICIT.   A negative (debit) balance in retained earnings (p. 587).

DIVIDEND.   A distribution of cash, other assets, or a corporation's own stock to its stockholders (p. 591).

DIVIDENDS IN ARREARS.   Dividends on cumulative preferred stock that are not declared in the year in which they are due (p. 593).

INCORPORATORS.   Individuals who form a corporation and sign the application for a corporate charter (p. 582).

LIQUIDATING DIVIDEND.   A dividend declared from capital other than retained earnings. It is a return of capital rather than a return on capital. (p. 591).

NONCUMULATIVE PREFERRED STOCK.   Preferred stock on which the right to receive dividends is lost in any year in which dividends are not declared (p. 594).

NONPROFIT CORPORATION.   A corporation organized for nonprofit purposes; it generally depends upon public contributions for its continued existence (p. 579).

NONPUBLIC (CLOSELY HELD) CORPORATION.   A corporation whose shares are not publicly traded (p. 579).

NO-PAR STOCK.   A type of capital stock that is not assigned a par value (p. 590).

ORGANIZATION COSTS.   The expenditures made to form a corporation. They include incorporation fees, attorneys' fees, and promoters' fees (p. 582).

PREEMPTIVE RIGHT.   The right that permits stockholders to maintain their percentage interests in a corporation by purchasing new shares in proportion to their current holdings (p. 584).

PREFERRED STOCK. A type of stock that has certain preferences, such as a preference in dividend distributions or a preference in asset distributions if the corporation is liquidated (p. 593).

PROFIT CORPORATION. A corporation organized with the goal of earning a profit for its shareholders (p. 579).

PROXY STATEMENT. A legal document under which a stockholder assigns his or her vote to an agent (p. 584).

PUBLIC CORPORATION. A corporation whose shares are widely held and traded through national stock exchanges (p. 579).

RETAINED EARNINGS. Earnings of a corporation that have been retained in the business rather than distributed to stockholders (p. 586).

DISCUSSION QUESTIONS

1. What is the difference between public corporations and nonpublic corporations?
2. What are the main advantages of the corporate form of business organization? The main disadvantages?
3. What are organization costs? How should they be accounted for?
4. What is a proxy statement?
5. List the general rights of common stockholders.
6. Explain what is meant by the preemptive right.
7. Distinguish between contributed capital and retained earnings.
8. When stock is issued for assets other than cash, accountants must determine the amount at which to record the transaction. What is the rule generally followed?
9. X Corporation has retained earnings at the beginning of the year of $200,000. The only entry affecting this account during the year was the entry to close the $220,000 debit balance in the income summary account. What is the balance in the retained earnings account at year-end? What is this balance called?
10. Why is an investment in noncumulative preferred stock generally not a desirable investment?
11. What is legal capital? What does it consist of?
12. What entry would be made to record the issuance of 10,000 shares of $2 par value common stock for $20 per share? How much (if any) of the amount received represents income to the corporation?
13. What accounts are involved when recording the declaration of a cash dividend? The payment of the cash dividend?
14. Define each of the following terms in the context of their application to preferred stock: (a) cumulative; (b) dividends in arrears; (c) call provision; (e) convertible.
15. Classify (asset, liability, stockholders' equity, revenue, expense) each of the following accounts:
   (a) Common Stock Subscribed
   (b) Organization Costs

    (c) Subscriptions Receivable

    (d) Dividends Payable

    (e) Contributed Capital in Excess of Par

    (f) Retained Earnings

16. How is book value per share of common stock determined when a corporation has both common stock and preferred stock outstanding?

17. What relationship is there between book value per share of common stock and the market price of the common stock?

EXERCISES

Exercise 15-1 (Recording the Issue of Stock)

Bolton Company's charter contains authorization to issue 100,000 shares of common stock.

Required:

Prepare a journal entry to record the issue of 20,000 shares of stock at $40 per share assuming:

A. The stock has a par value of $5 per share.

B. The stock is no-par stock.

C. The stock is no-par stock with a stated value of $10 per share.

Exercise 15-2 (Preparing Stockholders' Equity Section of Balance Sheet)

Croydon Corporation was organized on January 2, 1984, and was authorized to issue 50,000 shares of $100 par value, 9%, cumulative preferred stock and 100,000 shares of $1 par value common stock. One-half of the preferred stock was issued at par value and 40,000 shares of common stock were issued at $30 per share.

Required:

Prepare the stockholders' equity section immediately after the issue of the shares.

Exercise 15-3 (Dividend Distributions)

Dux Corporation has 10,000 shares of $100 par value, 7%, cumulative preferred stock outstanding in addition to its common stock. The company began operations and issued both classes of stock on January 2, 1982. Dividends declared in each of the first four years were:

1982	$100,000
1983	20,000
1984	90,000
1985	140,000

Required:

Determine how the dividends will be distributed to each class of stock and the amount of dividends in arrears (if any) at the end of each year.

Exercise 15-4 (Exchange of Stock for Noncash Assets)

Harlen Corporation completed the following transactions during its first year of operations:

1. Accepted land with a fair value of $100,000 as a donation from the city of Midtown.
2. Exchanged 1,000 shares of $10 par value common stock for organizational services having a fair value of $25,000.
3. Issued 20,000 shares of $10 par value common stock in exchange for a building appraised at $420,000 and machinery with a fair value of $80,000.

Required:
Record the transactions in general journal form.

Exercise 15-5 (Effects of Transactions on Retained Earnings)

Dawson Corporation completed the following transactions over a six-month period:

Dec.	31	Closed the $75,000 credit balance in the Income Summary account to Retained Earnings.
April	30	Declared a cash dividend of $2 per share on the 25,000 common shares outstanding.
June	6	Paid the dividends declared on April 30.

Required:
Prepare journal entries to record the transactions.

Exercise 15-6 (Stock Subscriptions)

On April 30, a corporation sold 20,000 shares of $2 par value common stock on a subscription basis for $50 per share. Payment terms required a down payment of 25% of the purchase price with the remainder due in two equal installments on June 30 and August 30.

Required:
Prepare journal entries to record the stock subscription, cash collection, and the issue of the stock certificates.

Exercise 15-7 (Conversion of Preferred Stock to Common Stock)

Sampson Corporation has 10,000 shares of 10%, $75 par value convertible preferred stock outstanding, in addition to its 100,000 shares of $1 par value common stock. The preferred stock was originally issued at par value. Each preferred share is convertible into three shares of common stock. On May 10 of the current year, 5,000 of the preferred shares were converted into common stock.

Required:
A. Prepare the journal entry to record the conversion.
B. Assume that the common stock is no-par with a stated value of $5 per share. Prepare the journal entry to record the conversion.

Exercise 15-8 (Book Value per Share of Common Stock)

Box Corporation has the following stockholders' equity:

Preferred Stock, $100 par, 8%, cumulative, 30,000 shares authorized, issued, and outstanding	$ 3,000,000
Common Stock, $10 par, 200,000 shares authorized, 100,000 shares issued and outstanding	1,000,000
Contributed Capital in Excess of Par	4,250,000
Retained Earnings	4,875,000
Total Stockholders' Equity	$13,125,000

There are no dividends in arrears on the preferred stock, but the current year's dividend has not yet been declared. The preferred stock is callable at $104.

Required:

A. Determine the book value per share of common stock.

B. Assume that the preferred stock is callable at $106 and that no dividends have been declared in the current or prior year. Determine the book value per share of common stock.

PROBLEMS

Problem 15-1 (Issuing Stock and Preparing Stockholders' Equity Section)

Preston Corporation was organized early in 1983. The corporate charter authorizes the issue of 50,000 shares of $100 par value, 9%, cumulative preferred stock and 100,000 shares of $5 par value common stock. The following transactions affecting stockholders' equity were completed during the first year:

1. Issued 100 shares of preferred stock at par value for organizational services.
2. Issued 5,000 shares of common stock at $30 per share and 1,000 shares of preferred stock at par.
3. Exchanged 10,000 shares of common stock for land with an appraised value of $70,000 and a building with an appraised value of $230,000.
4. Declared the required preferred stock dividend and a $2 per share dividend on common stock.
5. Closed the $87,500 credit balance in the Income Summary account.

Required:

A. Prepare journal entries to record the above transactions.

B. Prepare the stockholders' equity section of the balance sheet.

Problem 15-2 (Comprehensive Problem)

Monroe Corporation received its charter authorizing the issue of 20,000 shares of $50 par value, 10%, cumulative preferred stock and 100,000 shares of no-par common stock. The board of directors elected to assign a stated value of $10 per share to the common stock. The preferred stock is callable at $55 per share. The following transactions affecting stockholders' equity were completed during the first year:

Jan.	8	Issued 20,000 shares of common stock at $15 per share and 2,000 shares of preferred stock at $55 per share.
	15	Received subscriptions to 10,000 shares of common stock at $18 per share along with one-third of the subscription price. The remainder of the subscription price is payable in two equal installments due on June 30 and September 30.
Apr.	26	Issued 4,000 shares of preferred stock in exchange for land with a fair value of $212,000.
June	30	Collected the first installment on the subscribed stock of Jan. 15.
Sept.	30	Collected the last installment on the subscribed stock of Jan. 15 and issued the stock certificates.
Dec.	9	Declared the required dividend on preferred stock and a $1.50 per share dividend on common stock.
	18	Received subscriptions to 5,000 shares of common stock at $20 per share. The subscription price is payable in two equal installments on January 31 and May 31 of the following year.
Dec.	31	Closed the $118,000 credit balance in the Income Summary account.

Required:

A. Prepare journal entries for the above transactions.

B. Prepare the stockholders' equity section of the balance sheet on December 31.

C. Compute book value per share of common stock. (The common shares subscribed should be included with common stock outstanding.)

extra step added

Problem 15-3 (Determining Number of Shares Outstanding)

Stockholders' equity data of several corporations on December 31, 1983, are presented below:

1. Preferred Stock, 8%, $100 par, __?__ shares issued and
outstanding, callable at 104% of par $1,000,000
Common Stock, $2 par, 80,000 shares authorized, __?__ shares
issued and outstanding 80,000
Contributed Capital in Excess of Par 1,720,000
Retained Earnings 580,000
    Total Stockholders' Equity $3,380,000

2. Cumulative Preferred Stock, 7%, $75 par, __?__ shares issued
and oustanding, callable at $80 .... $ 375,000
Common Stock, $5 par, 200,000 shares authorized, __?__ shares
issued and outstanding 375,000
Contributed Capital in Excess of Par 2,200,000
Retained Earnings 20,000
    Total Stockholders' Equity $2,970,000

how long Alive
Years - 20
Days - 7300
hours - 175,200
min - 10,512,000
sec. - 630,720,000

Preferred dividends are in arrears for 1981 and 1982.

3. Cumulative Preferred Stock, 8%, $100 par, ___?___ shares issued
   and outstanding, callable at $106 ... $2,500,000
   Contributed Capital in Excess of Par—Preferred ... 50,000
   Common Stock, $10 par, 500,000 shares authorized, ___?___ shares
   issued and outstanding ... 4,500,000
   Contributed Capital in Excess of Par—Common ... 3,000,000
   Retained Earnings ... 1,400,000
   Total Stockholders' Equity ... $11,450,000

Dividends are in arrears on preferred stock for 1982.

4. Cumulative Preferred Stock, $6 preferred dividend, $70 par, ___?___
   shares issued and outstanding, callable at $75 ... $ 350,000
   Common Stock, no-par, 250,000 shares authorized, 150,000
   shares issued and outstanding ... 2,800,000
   Retained Earnings (Deficit) ... (70,000)
   Total Stockholders' Equity ... $3,080,000

Dividends are in arrears on preferred stock for 1981 and 1982.

Required:

A. Determine the number of preferred and common shares outstanding for each corporation.

B. Assuming that none of the corporations has yet declared dividends for 1983, determine book value per share of common stock.

Problem 15-4 (Comprehensive Problem)

The stockholders' equity section of Zee Corporation's balance sheet on December 31 of last year is presented below:

Stockholders' Equity		
Contributed Capital:		
Convertible Preferred Stock, $100 par, 7%, cumulative, 50,000 shares authorized, 10,000 shares issued and outstanding	$1,000,000	
Contributed Capital in Excess of Par—Preferred	110,000	$1,110,000
Common Stock, $10 par, 500,000 shares authorized, 200,000 shares issued and outstanding	2,000,000	
Contributed Capital in Excess of Par—Common	480,000	2,480,000
Retained Earnings		440,000
Total Stockholders' Equity		$4,030,000

Each share of preferred stock is convertible into two shares of common stock. There are no preferred dividends in arrears.

Required:

A. Assume that each class of stock was issued in a single transaction. Prepare the entries that were made for the issue of each class of stock.

B. Assume that Zee Corporation paid total cash dividends last year in the amount of $160,000 on November 20 to stockholders of record on November 1. The dividends were declared on September 28. Prepare separate entries for each class of stock for each date if required. A Dividends Declared account is not used.

C. Prepare the entry that was made to close last year's net income of $400,000 from the Income Summary account to Retained Earnings.

D. Prepare an entry to record the conversion of 5,000 preferred shares into common shares.

Problem 15-5 (Correcting Errors)

McNulty, Inc. completed its first year of operations as of December 31, 1984. The stockholders' equity section of the corporation's balance sheet as prepared by McNulty's bookkeeper is presented below:

Stockholders' Equity	
Preferred Stock	$ 30,000
Common Stock, no-par	220,000
Retained Earnings	70,100
Total Stockholders' Equity	$320,100

You have been asked to review the accounts and make any corrections necessary. During your review, you learn the following:

1. Preferred Stock: $50 par, $3 cumulative, 10,000 shares authorized, 600 shares issued and outstanding. The issue price was $54 per share and the difference between par value and the issue price was credited to Retained Earnings.

2. Common Stock: No-par, stated value of $5 per share, 50,000 shares authorized, 25,000 shares issued and outstanding, 11,875 of which were issued for cash at $8 per share and credited in full to the Common Stock account. The other 13,125 shares were issued in exchange for a building with a fair value of $105,000. The Common Stock account was credited for the full $105,000.

3. Land with a fair value of $40,000 was donated to the corporation by the city of Yorktown. The bookkeeper debited Land and credited Retained Earnings for $40,000.

4. Common stock subscriptions were received for 2,500 shares of stock at $8 per share. The Common Stock account was credited for the full subscription price of

$20,000. One-half of the subscription price was received as a down payment; the remainder is due early in 1985 and is included on the balance sheet as an account receivable. The stock certificates will not be issued until full payment is received.

Required:
A. Prepare individual entries to correct any errors in recording the transactions above.
B. Prepare a corrected stockholders' equity section for McNulty on December 31, 1984.

Problem 15-6 (Comprehensive Problem)

Touhey Corporation began operations five years ago by issuing 5,000 shares of $7 cumulative, $100 par value preferred stock at $102 and 30,000 shares of $10 par value common stock at $50 per share. The amount of stock outstanding has remained unchanged since the first day of operations (with the exception of the conversion of preferred stock into common stock). Dividends distributed each year are listed below. (Dividends in Year 5 were distributed before the preferred stock was converted.)

Year 1	$ –0–
Year 2	65,000
Year 3	76,000
Year 4	25,000
Year 5	127,500

The preferred stock is convertible into three shares of common stock and is callable at $105. At the end of the fifth year, the corporation had a credit retained earnings balance of $340,000.

Required:
A. Determine for each year the total and per-share dividends on each class of stock and the amount of dividends in arrears on preferred stock, if any.
B. Assume that in Year 5 dividends were declared on August 10 to be paid on September 30 to stockholders of record on September 18. Prepare entries for each class of stock for each date if required. A Dividends Declared account is used, one for each class of stock.
C. Assume that 2,500 shares of preferred stock were converted into common stock on December 30, Year 5. Prepare the journal entry to record the conversion.
D. Assume that 15,000 shares of preferred stock and 50,000 shares of common stock are authorized. Prepare the stockholders' equity section of the balance sheet at the end of Year 5. (Remember that preferred stock was converted into common stock prior to year-end.)
E. Determine the book value per share of common stock at the end of Year 5.

ALTERNATE PROBLEMS

Problem 15-1A (Recording Stock Issues)

Morton Corporation received a corporate charter authorizing it to issue 20,000 shares of $100 par value, 8%, cumulative preferred stock and 200,000 shares of no-par common stock with a stated value of $2 per share. The following transactions affecting stockholders' equity were completed during the first year.

1. Issued 200 shares of preferred stock at par value for organizational services.
2. Issued, for cash, 20,000 shares of common stock at $40 per share and 1,000 shares of preferred stock at par.
3. Exchanged 12,750 shares of common stock for land with an appraised value of $300,000 and machinery with an appraised value of $210,000.
4. Declared the required preferred stock dividend and a $1 per share dividend on common stock.
5. Closed the Income Summary account. A $92,500 net income was earned.

Required:
A. Prepare journal entries to record the above transactions.
B. Prepare the stockholders' equity section of the balance sheet.

Problem 15-2A (Comprehensive Problem)

Press Corporation received a corporate charter in 1984 authorizing it to issue 100,000 shares of $10 par value common stock. It then completed the following transactions:

1984		
March	8	Issued 5,000 shares of common stock for cash at $18 per share.
	10	Issued 500 shares of common stock to the corporation's attorney for services performed in organizing the corporation. The board of directors placed a value of $9,000 on the services.
June	16	Issued 12,000 shares of common stock in exchange for the following assets at their fair values: building, $110,000; land, $60,000; equipment, $52,000.
Dec.	5	Received subscriptions to 10,000 shares of common stock at $18 per share. Twenty-five percent down payments were received with the subscriptions.
	31	Closed the $12,800 debit balance in the Income Summary account.
1985		
March	18	Received the balance due on the stock subscriptions of December 5 and issued the stock.
Dec.	31	Closed the $87,500 credit balance in the Income Summary account.
1986		
Feb.	6	The board of directors declared a $1 per share dividend on the common stock. The dividend was payable on March 1 to stockholders of record on February 22.
March	1	Paid the dividends declared on February 6.

Required:
A. Prepare journal entries for the transactions.
B. Prepare the stockholders' equity section of the balance sheet on December 31, 1984.

Problem 15-3A (Issuing Stock for Assets and Preparing Balance Sheet)

Robert Drum has operated a successful business for several years as a single proprietorship. In June, 1984, Robert decided to incorporate the business in order to raise additional capital for expansion. On June 15, a corporate charter was received for Drum Corporation authorizing the corporation to issue 5,000 shares of $100 par, 10% cumulative preferred stock and 50,000 shares of $2 par value common stock.

During June, Drum Corporation completed the following transactions:

June 16   Robert Drum transferred assets with fair values indicated below from the single proprietorship to the corporation in exchange for 18,000 shares of common stock:

Inventory	$54,000
Equipment	60,000
Building	120,000
Land	40,000

18   Issued 500 shares of preferred stock for cash at $105 per share.

29   Subscriptions to 1,000 shares of preferred stock were received at $105 per share. A down payment of 10% of the subscription price accompanied the subscription.

Required:

A. Prepare journal entries to record the transactions.

B. Prepare a balance sheet for Drum Corporation as of June 30, 1984.

Problem 15-4A (Comprehensive Problem)

The stockholders' equity section of the balance sheet of Monroe Corporation on December 31, 1984, is presented below:

MONROE CORPORATION
Stockholders' Equity
December 31, 1984

Cumulative preferred stock, 10%, $50 par,		
20,000 shares authorized:		
Issued	$350,000	
Subscribed	200,000	$550,000
Common stock, $5 par, 500,000 shares		
authorized:		
Issued	520,000	
Subscribed	240,000	760,000
Contributed Capital in Excess of Par:		
Preferred stock	33,000	
Common stock	420,000	453,000
Retained Earnings (deficit)		(120,000)
Total Stockholders' Equity		$1,643,000

Listed as part of the assets on the balance sheet are: Preferred Stock Subscriptions Receivable, $145,750; Common Stock Subscriptions Receivable, $168,000.

Required:

Answer the following questions and show your computations:

A. How many shares of preferred and common stock have been issued?
B. How many shares of preferred and common stock have been subscribed to?
C. What is the total contributed capital of Monroe Corporation?
D. What is the total legal capital of Monroe Corporation?
E. What was the average issue price of the preferred stock, including preferred stock subscribed?
F. What was the average issue price of the common stock, including common stock subscribed?
G. What is the average amount per share still owed by subscribers of common stock?
H. What is the book value per share of common stock, assuming that preferred stock dividends have all been paid and that preferred stock is callable at $54 per share?

Problem 15-5A (Preparing a Classified Balance Sheet)

The following data were taken from the general ledger of Brackett Company on December 31 of the current year:

Cash	$ 22,400
Accounts receivable	36,300
Common stock	42,000
Accounts payable	18,300
Preferred stock	30,000
Inventory	41,200
Preferred stock subscriptions receivable	56,000
Retained earnings	82,500
Plant assets	368,000
Accumulated depreciation—plant assets	97,500
Mortgage note payable	49,000
Allowance for uncollectible accounts	2,100
Organization costs	8,100
Preferred stock subscribed	100,000
Employee wages payable	3,600
Contributed capital in excess of par—common	89,000
Contributed capital in excess of par—preferred	18,000

The company is authorized to issue 10,000 shares of $50 par value, 10%, cumulative preferred stock and 50,000 shares of $5 par value common stock.

Required:

Prepare a classified balance sheet for Brackett Company.

CASE FOR CHAPTER 15

(Annual Report Analysis)

Refer to the financial statements and supporting schedules in the appendix and answer the following questions:

1. What is the par value or stated value per share of
   a. General Motor's common stock?
   b. General Motor's preferred stock?
   c. Modern Merchandising's common stock?
   d. Mary Moppet's common stock?
2. With reference to Mary Moppet's, how many shares of common stock on September 30, 1981 were
   a. Authorized?
   b. Issued?
   c. Outstanding?
3. With reference to General Motors
   a. What is the annual dividend per share on preferred stock?
   b. How many shares of preferred stock are
      1. Authorized?
      2. Issued?
      3. Outstanding?
   c. What redemption feature applies to the preferred stock?
   d. What is the trend in dividend payments on common stock?
   e. What was the market price per common share on December 31, 1981? On December 31, 1977?
4. With reference to Modern Merchandising Inc. for the year ended January 31, 1981
   a. What was the total amount of dividends declared during the year?
   b. What was the total amount of dividends paid during the year?
   c. How many shares of common stock were issued during the year?

CHAPTER 16
CORPORATIONS: OTHER TRANSACTIONS, INCOME, AND RETAINED EARNINGS

OVERVIEW AND OBJECTIVES

This chapter continues the discussion of transactions that affect stockholders' equity. When you have completed the chapter, you should understand:

- The meaning of treasury stock and how to account for it (pp. 612–615).
- How to record the retirement of stock (pp. 615–616).
- The nature of stock dividends and stock splits and how to account for them (pp. 617–620).
- The meaning of retained earnings restrictions (pp. 620–621).
- How to report the effect of discontinued operations, extraordinary items, and changes in accounting principles (pp. 621–628).
- How to compute and report earnings per share (pp. 628–630).
- The nature of prior period adjustments and how to report them (pp. 630–632).

TREASURY STOCK

Treasury stock is a corporation's own stock that has been issued and reacquired but not retired or reissued. Treasury stock may be either preferred or common stock, but when preferred stock is reacquired, it is normally retired and will not be reissued. Most treasury stock is therefore common stock.

Among the most common reasons a corporation reacquires its own common stock are: (1) to support the current market price of the stock since stockholders often judge management performance on the basis of the market value of the stock, (2) to have stock available for issue to employees and officers under stock purchase or stock option plans, and (3) to have stock available for use in acquiring other companies. For these reasons, many large corporations reacquire and reissue their own shares on a fairly regular basis.

Most treasury stock is acquired by cash purchase on the open market and results therefore in a decrease in the corporation's assets and a decrease in stockholders' equity by an equal amount. The treasury shares may be held for an indefinite period, reissued at any time, or retired. While held by the corporation, treasury stock is similar to unissued stock in that it contains none of the stockholder rights. Thus, treasury stock is not entitled to vote, receive dividends, receive assets if the corporation is liquidated, or exercise the preemptive right. Treasury stock is different from unissued stock, however, in one important respect. If stock was originally issued at an amount in excess of its par value and later purchased as treasury stock, it can be reissued (sold) for less than its par value without incurring a discount liability. When par value stock is originally issued at a price below its par value, the purchasers of the stock are contingently liable to the corporation's creditors for the amount of the discount.

PURCHASE OF TREASURY STOCK

Purchases of treasury stock are normally recorded at cost by debiting a Treasury Stock account and crediting Cash. For example, assume Brett Corporation purchased 2,000 shares of its own $10 par value common stock at $35 per share. The entry to record the purchase is:

July	6	Treasury Stock	70,000	
		Cash		70,000
		Purchased 2,000 shares of treasury stock at $35 per share.		

The Treasury Stock account is debited for the total cost of the shares acquired. The par or stated value and the original issue price of the stock have no effect on the entry.

When treasury stock is purchased, the corporation essentially pays off some of its stockholders, thereby reducing both stockholders' equity and corporate assets. Because the stock may be reissued later, it is recorded in a Treasury Stock account, which is a contra-stockholders' equity account that is subtracted from the total of contributed capital and retained earnings in the stockholders' equity section of the balance sheet:

Stockholders' Equity	
Contributed capital:	
Common stock, $10 par value, 50,000 shares authorized, 30,000 shares issued, 28,000 shares outstanding	$300,000
Contributed capital in excess of par	185,000
Total contributed capital	485,000
Retained earnings	162,000
Total contributed capital and retained earnings	647,000
Less: Treasury stock, 2,000 shares, at cost	70,000
Total stockholders' equity	$577,000

The stockholders' equity section of the balance sheet shows that 30,000 shares of common stock were issued, of which 2,000 are held as treasury stock. The number of shares outstanding is therefore 28,000, which constitutes the total ownership of the corporation.

Restriction of Retained Earnings for Treasury Stock Purchased

We saw earlier that when a corporation purchases treasury stock, some corporate assets are distributed to the stockholders from whom the shares were purchased. If assets are distributed to stockholders, the amount of assets left to pay creditors, of course, is reduced. To protect creditors, most states limit the distribution of assets to stockholders to the amount of retained earnings. Our discussion in Chapter 15 indicated that dividend distributions reduce retained earnings and corporate assets. If a corporation were to declare dividends in the amount of its total retained earnings and also acquire treasury stock, it would obviously distribute assets in excess of retained earnings. Therefore, to limit total distributions of assets to the amount of retained earnings, most states restrict the availability of retained earnings for dividends to the extent of the cost of treasury stock purchased. For the corporation whose stockholders' equity is presented above, dividend declarations would be limited to $92,000 ($162,000 − $70,000) until the corporation either obtains additional earnings or reissues part or all of the treasury stock. The restriction on the amount of retained earnings available for dividends is normally disclosed in a footnote to the financial statements.

Reissue of Treasury Stock

When treasury stock is reissued, Cash (or other assets received) is debited, the Treasury Stock account is credited for the cost of the shares reissued, and any difference between cost and the reissue price is credited or debited to Contributed Capital from Treasury Stock Transactions. To illustrate, assume that Brett Corporation reissues 1,000 of the 2,000 treasury shares acquired on

July 6 for $35 per share at a reissue price of $50 per share. The reissue entry would be:

Oct.	9	Cash	50,000	
		Treasury Stock		35,000
		Contributed Capital from Treasury Stock		
		Transactions		15,000
		Reissued at $50 per share 1,000 shares of treasury stock with a cost of $35 per share.		

If treasury stock is reissued at a price below its cost, Contributed Capital from Treasury Stock Transactions is debited. For example, if Brett Corporation reissued 500 of its remaining 1,000 treasury shares at $30 per share, the entry would be:

Dec.	4	Cash	15,000	
		Contributed Capital from Treasury Stock		
		Transactions	2,500	
		Treasury Stock		17,500
		Reissued at $30 per share, 500 shares of treasury stock with a cost of $35 per share.		

If there is no contributed capital from previous treasury stock transactions, or if the balance in that account is insufficient to cover the excess of cost over the reissue price, the debit is made to Retained Earnings.

The difference between the reissue price and cost of the treasury stock is credited or debited to Contributed Capital rather than to a gain or loss account. Corporations earn profits or incur losses from the sale of goods or services to customers, not from the retirement or reissue of capital stock. Although not exactly the same, the purchase of treasury stock is similar to a withdrawal, and the reissue of the treasury stock is similar to a new investment by a single proprietor or a partner. That is, these transactions are disinvestment and investment transactions that do not affect gain or loss.

RETIREMENT OF STOCK

A corporation may reacquire shares of its own stock with the intention of formally retiring them. When shares are retired, the stockholders' equity amounts related to the retired shares are removed from the capital accounts. If the shares are reacquired at a price less than their average issue price, the excess of the average issue price over cost is credited to Contributed Capital—Stock Retirement. For example, assume a corporation issued its $5 par value common stock at an average of $15 per share. If 10,000 shares are later reacquired at $13 per share and formally retired, the entry would be:

May	6	Common Stock (10,000 × $5)	50,000	
		Contributed Capital in Excess of Par*	100,000	
		Cash		130,000
		Contributed Capital—Stock Retirement		20,000
		Purchased and retired 10,000 shares of		
		common stock at $13 per share.		
		*(10,000 × $10)		

If the shares are reacquired at a price in excess of their average issue price, the excess of cost over average issue price is debited to retained earnings. For example, if the 10,000 shares above were acquired at $18 per share, the entry would be:

May	6	Common Stock	50,000	
		Contributed Capital in Excess of Par	100,000	
		Retained Earnings	30,000	
		Cash		180,000
		Purchased and retired 10,000 shares of		
		stock at $18 per share.		

Note that the retirement does not result in gain or loss to the corporation. Like treasury stock transactions, stock retirement transactions are disinvestments affecting balance sheet stockholders' equity accounts only. Revenues and expenses are unaffected.

If the stock being retired is held as treasury stock, the entries are similar to those presented above except that the Treasury Stock account (rather than Cash) is credited. For example, if the stock had been purchased at $13 per share and held as treasury stock, the acquisition entry would have been:

Apr.	4	Treasury Stock	130,000	
		Cash		130,000
		Purchased 10,000 shares of treasury stock		
		at $13 per share.		

If the stock is retired formally later, the entry is:

May	6	Common Stock	50,000	
		Contributed Capital in Excess of Par	100,000	
		Treasury Stock		130,000
		Contributed Capital—Stock Retirement		20,000
		Formally retired 10,000 shares of stock held		
		as treasury stock.		

STOCK DIVIDENDS

A **stock dividend** is a pro-rata distribution of additional shares of a corporation's stock to its stockholders, normally consisting of the distribution of additional shares of common stock to common stockholders. Stock dividends should be clearly distinguished from cash dividends. Unlike cash dividends, which reduce corporate assets and stockholders' equity, stock dividends have no effect on corporate assets or on total stockholders' equity. The only effect of a stock dividend is a transfer of retained earnings to contributed capital.

Stock dividends often are declared by successful companies that have used their earnings to expand operations. These companies use their cash earnings to acquire additional plant and equipment in order to grow and therefore generally declare only minimal cash dividends. The declaration of a stock dividend gives stockholders some additional shares as evidence of the increase in their equity in the corporation without distributing cash or other assets to them. Another reason for stock dividends is to reduce the market price of the common stock by increasing the number of shares outstanding. When a corporation grows, the market price of its common stock tends to increase. By reducing the market price of its shares, the corporation can encourage a broader ownership by both small and large investors. To accomplish this objective, the stock dividend must be a relatively large one. As an alternative, the corporation may undertake a stock split, which is described later in this chapter.

When stock dividends are declared, retained earnings are transferred to contributed capital. As discussed in Chapter 15, state incorporation laws generally require the maintenance of legal capital at an amount equal to the number of shares outstanding times par or stated value per share. Consequently, a minimum amount equal to the par or stated value of the additional shares issued must be transferred from Retained Earnings to the Common Stock account. Accounting rules, however, distinguish between small and large stock dividends. *Small stock dividends* (defined as about 20% or less of outstanding shares) tend to have little immediate effect on the market price of the stock; some investors therefore consider them to be distributions of earnings. Accounting rules provide that retained earnings should be transferred to contributed capital in an amount equal to the number of additional shares issued times the market price per share.

Large stock dividends (those in excess of about 20% of shares outstanding) generally have the effect of an immediate and proportionate reduction in the market price of the stock. For example, if the market price of the stock was $50 before a stock dividend, the declaration of a 100% stock dividend would reduce the market price immediately to about $25 per share, since there would be twice as many shares outstanding. Because stockholders observe that the total market value of their shares remains unchanged after a large stock dividend, they do not tend to view it as a distribution of earnings. As a result, accounting rules require the transfer of retained earnings in an amount sufficient only to comply with state laws, which is the par or stated value of the additional shares issued.

To illustrate a small stock dividend, assume that Brett Corporation has the following stockholders' equity:

Stockholders' Equity

Contributed capital:	
Common stock, $5 par value, 100,000 shares authorized, 50,000	
shares issued and outstanding	$250,000
Contributed capital in excess of par	300,000
Total contributed capital	550,000
Retained earnings	400,000
Total stockholders' equity	$950,000

Assume further that the board of directors declares a 5% stock dividend on December 20, distributable on January 10 to stockholders of record on December 31. The market price of the stock was $22 per share on December 20. The entry to record the declaration of the stock dividend is:

Dec.	20	Retained Earnings	55,000	
		Stock Dividend Distributable (2,500 × $5)		12,500
		Contributed Capital in Excess of Par*		42,500
		To record the declaration of a 5% stock dividend on 50,000 shares of outstanding common stock.		
		*(2,500 × $17)		

Note that, like cash dividends, stock dividends are declared on outstanding shares only. Because this is a small stock dividend, the Retained Earnings account is debited for the market value of the shares to be distributed, computed as follows:

$$50,000 \text{ shares} \times .05 = 2,500 \text{ shares} \times \$22 = \$55,000$$

The Stock Dividend Distributable account is credited for the par value of the shares to be issued, and the excess of the total market value over par value is credited to Contributed Capital in Excess of Par. The Stock Dividend Distributable account would be reported as a separate item of contributed capital on the December 31 balance sheet as illustrated in Figure 16-1 on page 622. Note that it is not a liability because there is no obligation to distribute corporate assets.

When the shares are distributed on January 10, the entry is:

Jan.	10	Stock Dividend Distributable	12,500	
		Common Stock		12,500
		To record the distribution of a 2,500-share		
		stock dividend.		

The net effect of the entries on December 20 and January 10 is to decrease retained earnings by $55,000 and to increase contributed capital by the same amount, of which $12,500 is an increase in legal capital and $42,500 increases Contributed Capital in Excess of Par. Thus total stockholders' equity remained unchanged by the stock dividend as demonstrated below:

	Before Stock Dividend	After Stock Dividend
Common stock	$250,000	$262,500
Contributed capital in excess of par	300,000	342,500
Retained earnings	400,000	345,000
Total stockholders' equity	$950,000	$950,000

Because total stockholders' equity remained unchanged, each stockholder's interest in total stockholders' equity also would remain unchanged. For example, assume that Paula Dean owned 5,000 shares (10%) of Brett Corporation before the distribution of the stock dividend. Her share of the stockholders' equity before and after the dividend would be:

$$\text{Before} \quad \frac{5,000 \text{ shares}}{50,000 \text{ shares}} = 10\% \times \$950,000 = \$95,000$$

$$\text{After} \quad \frac{5,250 \text{ shares}}{52,500 \text{ shares}} = 10\% \times \$950,000 = \$95,000$$

STOCK SPLITS

Many investors prefer to spread their investment risk by purchasing stock in several corporations. Since stock is normally traded in 100-share lots, the purchase of 100 shares of a stock with a market price of $100 per share requires a $10,000 investment, which may prohibit small investors from diversifying their holdings. Consequently, as mentioned earlier, a company may want to reduce the market price of its stock in order to make it available to a wider range of investors. One method of accomplishing this objective is to declare a large stock dividend. An alternative is to *split the stock* by decreasing the par or stated value of the stock and increasing the number of shares proportionally.

To illustrate, assume that Brett Corporation's stockholders' equity is as follows:

Stockholders' Equity

Contributed capital:	
Common stock, $5 par value, 100,000 shares authorized, 50,000 shares issued and outstanding	$250,000
Contributed capital in excess of par	300,000
Retained earnings	400,000
Total stockholders' equity	$950,000

Assume further that the common stock has a current market price of $100 per share. In order to reduce the market price, the board of directors votes to split the stock 4 for 1, which should reduce the market price per share to about $25. When the stock is split, the par value per share is decreased to $1.25 ($5 ÷ 4) and the number of authorized shares is increased to 400,000. Outstanding stock is recalled and new stock certificates are issued, four new shares given for each share recalled.

A stock split does not change the balance of any of the stockholders' equity accounts. Legal capital remains the same—at $250,000—since 200,000 shares are outstanding with a par value of $1.25 each. Thus, all that is necessary is a memo entry in the journal and Common Stock account indicating that the par value has been reduced and the number of shares increased.

Comparison of Large Stock Dividends and Stock Splits

Large stock dividends are sometimes mistakenly called stock splits. Although both have the same effect on the market price of the stock, so that a 2-for-1 stock split and a 100% stock dividend both result in a doubling of the number of shares outstanding and a market price of about one-half of the previous market price, they are legally different. All stock dividends result in an increase in the amount of legal capital and a decrease in retained earnings; stock splits do not.

RETAINED EARNINGS RESTRICTIONS

Restrictions are often placed on retained earnings so that the retained earnings reported in the balance sheet are not entirely available for dividend declarations. Some restrictions are legal ones. As discussed earlier, many states restrict the payment of dividends to the extent of the cost of treasury stock held by the corporation. Some restrictions are contractual. For example, bond indentures and other borrowing agreements often include a restriction on the amount of dividends that can be paid until the debt is repaid. The purpose of such a restriction is to provide an additional element of protection to creditors—since corporate assets that are not distributed as dividends are more likely to be available for interest payments and debt retirement. Other restrictions may be made voluntarily by the board of directors. For example, many corporations have contingent liabilities such as lawsuits in process. Regardless of the nature of the restriction—legal, contractual, or voluntary—its purpose is to retain assets in the business rather than distribute them as dividends.

Restrictions on the payment of dividends are normally disclosed in footnotes to the financial statements. For example, recent financial statements of St. Regis Paper Company included the following footnote:

> *Agreements covering the long-term debt of St. Regis contain certain restrictions on the payment of cash dividends. The most restrictive of such agreements relates to the 8-7/8% promissory notes. At December 31, 1980, the retained earnings that were free of such restrictions amounted to approximately $411,000,000.*

The December 31, 1980, balance sheet reported total retained earnings of $956,103,000. Thus, less than one-half of St. Regis' retained earnings were available for dividends at that time.

COMPREHENSIVE ILLUSTRATION OF STOCKHOLDERS' EQUITY

In this and the preceding chapter, several illustrations of the treatment of stockholders' equity items were presented. Although the terminology used and the amount of detail provided vary considerably in practice, Figure 16-1 shows one possible presentation of stockholders' equity.

SPECIAL INCOME STATEMENT ITEMS

Determining periodic net income is one of the primary functions of accounting. The amount of net income earned as well as the trend of earnings over time are important to users of accounting information because they serve as a measure of management efficiency, a measure of creditworthiness, and a factor in the prediction of future earnings. Stock market prices and dividends are both affected by net income earned. Earnings from normal, recurring operating activities are presumed to be more useful in predicting future earnings. Consequently, they are separated on the income statement from those earnings

Figure 16-1
Stockholders' Equity

Stockholders' Equity

Contributed capital:	
8% Cumulative preferred stock, $100 par, 50,000 shares authorized, 25,000 shares issued and outstanding	$2,500,000
Common stock, stated value $5 per share, 500,000 shares authorized, 200,000 shares issued, 195,000 shares outstanding	1,000,000
Common stock subscribed, 30,000 shares	150,000
Common stock dividend distributable, 20,000 shares	100,000
*Contributed capital in excess of par—preferred	200,000
*Contributed capital in excess of stated value—common	1,870,000
*Contributed capital from retirement of preferred stock	75,000
*Contributed capital from treasury stock transactions	160,000
Total contributed capital	6,055,000
Retained earnings (of which $580,000 is restricted under debt agreements and for treasury stock purchased)	1,690,000
Total contributed capital and retained earnings	7,745,000
Less: Treasury stock, 5,000 common shares at cost	125,000
Total stockholders' equity	$7,620,000

*These items are often combined into one figure called Other Contributed Capital. The items making up other contributed capital are then presented in a footnote to the financial statements.

resulting from unusual transactions that are not expected to recur on a regular basis. Three categories of unusual transactions are identified by current accounting practice: discontinued operations, extraordinary gains and losses, and changes in accounting principle.

DISCONTINUED OPERATIONS—DISPOSAL OF A BUSINESS SEGMENT

Most large corporations have many segments. For the purpose of reporting discontinued operations, a segment is defined as "a component of an entity whose activities represent a separate major line of business or class of customer."[1] For example, assume that Pratt Communications, Inc. has four segments—newspaper publishing, magazine publishing, radio, and television. If one of these segments is sold, the income statement for the year will not be comparable with those of other years. Current accounting standards require

[1]"Reporting the Results of Operations," *APB Opinion No. 30* (AICPA: New York, June 1973), par. 13.

that the gain or loss on sale and the operating net income or loss of the current year to the date of sale must be presented in a separate section of the income statement after Income from Continuing Operations.

To illustrate, assume that Pratt Communications, Inc. sold its radio stations on August 1, 1984, at an after-tax gain of $800,000. Prior to August 1, the radio stations had earned $60,000 net income after tax. The sale would be reported in a separate Discontinued Operations section of the income statement as shown in Figure 16-2.

PRATT COMMUNICATIONS, INC.
Income Statement
For the Year Ended December 31, 1984

Revenue:		
Advertising revenue		$4,600,000
Subscription revenue		3,280,000
Total revenue		7,880,000
Operating expenses:		
Selling expenses	$4,800,000	
General and administrative expenses	1,640,000	
Interest expense	390,000	6,830,000
Income from continuing operations before tax		1,050,000
Income tax expense		420,000
Income from continuing operations		630,000
Discontinued operations:		
Operating income of discontinued segment (Net of $39,000 income tax)	$ 60,000	
Gain on sale of discontinued segment (Net of $267,000 income tax)	800,000	860,000
Net income		$1,490,000

Figure 16-2
Income Statement—
Special Items

Revenues and expenses reported in the income statement include those of the newspaper, magazine, and television segments only. The revenues and expenses of the radio segment between January 1 and August 1 are reported at their net amount in determining the operating income of the discontinued segment, which is added to the gain on sale of the radio division in the Discontinued Operations section. By reporting in this way, income from continuing operations can be used to estimate the earning power of those segments that will continue to operate in the future.

Income Tax Allocation

When a segment of the business is disposed of, total income tax expense for the year of $726,000 ($420,000 + $39,000 + $267,000) must be allocated to show the amount that relates to income from continuing operations ($420,000) and the amount identified with discontinued operations ($39,000 + $267,000). The income tax effects on discontinued operations are generally shown parenthetically, as illustrated in Figure 16-2. We will see later that this approach is also used in reporting extraordinary items and changes in accounting principle.

If a loss is incurred on operations of the discontinued segment to the date of sale, or if a loss is incurred on the sale of the segment, income tax savings result and serve to reduce the amount of the loss incurred. For example, if Pratt Communication, Inc. had incurred an operating loss of $99,000 before tax on the radio segment to the date of sale, the income statement presentation would be:

Income from continuing operations before tax		$1,050,000
Income tax expense		420,000
Income from continuing operations		630,000
Discontinued operations:		
Operating loss of discontinued segment (Net of $39,000 tax savings)	$ (60,000)	
Gain on sale of discontinued segment (Net of $267,000 income tax)	800,000	740,000
Net income		$1,370,000

Note that income from continuing operations remains the same, $630,000. The results of discontinued operations have no effect on the amount of income from continuing operations.

EXTRAORDINARY ITEMS

Some gains and losses result from events so unusual that they are reported separately on the income statement in order to distinguish them from the results of normal operating activities. These events, called **extraordinary items,** are relatively rare because they must be both unusual in nature and occur infrequently. Unusual and infrequent events are described in APB Opinion No. 30 as:

Unusual Nature—the underlying events or transaction should possess a high degree of abnormality and be of a type clearly unrelated to, or only incidentally related to, the ordinary and typical activities of the entity, taking into account the environment in which the entity operates.

Infrequency of Occurrence—the underlying event or transaction should be of a type that would not reasonably be expected to recur in the foreseeable future, taking into account the environment in which the entity operates.[2]

The environment includes such factors as the characteristics of the industry in which the firm operates, the geographical location of its operations, and the nature and extent of governmental regulations. A given event may be unusual in nature for one firm but not for another because of differences in their environments. Past experience of a company may be used to determine the probability of recurrence of an event, but is not sufficient by itself to satisfy the criterion of infrequency of occurrence. If the event is a type that occurs frequently in the environment in which the firm operates, it is not extraordinary.

Because the criteria for extraordinary items are somewhat subjective, judgment is required to distinguish extraordinary events from normal operating activities. APB Opinion No. 30 offers some guidance by including examples of events that might be considered extraordinary as well as examples of events that generally are not extraordinary as follows:

Extraordinary	Not Extraordinary
1. Major casualties such as an earthquake, if infrequent in the area.	1. Write-down or write-off of receivables, inventories, equipment leased to others, deferred research and development costs, or other intangible assets.
2. Expropriation of assets by a foreign government.	2. Gains or losses from exchange or translation of foreign currencies, including those relating to major devaluations and revaluations.
3. Loss from a prohibition under a newly enacted law or regulation.	3. Gains or losses on disposal of a segment of a business.
	4. Other gains or losses from sale or abandonment of property, plant, or equipment used in the business.
	5. Effects of a strike, including those against competitors and major suppliers.
	6. Adjustments of accruals on long-term contracts.[3]

[2]*Ibid.*, par. 20.
[3]*Ibid.*, par. 23

In addition, any material gain or loss on the early extinguishment of debt must be reported as an extraordinary item net of related income tax effect.[4] When an event qualifies as an extraordinary item, it is reported on the income statement after discontinued operations (if any) under the caption of *Extraordinary Items*. To illustrate, assume that Pratt Communications, Inc. had a television station damaged by an earthquake in an area where no quake had ever occurred before. The loss would be reported on the income statement as follows:

Income from continuing operations		$ 630,000
Discontinued operations:		
Operating income of discontinued segment (Net of $39,000 income tax)	$ 60,000	
Gain on sale of discontinued segment (Net of $267,000 income tax)	800,000	860,000
Income before extraordinary item		1,490,000
Extraordinary item: Loss from earthquake (Net of $200,000 tax savings)		600,000
Net income		$ 890,000

Note that, as with the disposal of a segment of a business, the extraordinary loss is reported net of its related tax effect. That is, we have assumed an $800,000 pre-tax earthquake loss, of which $200,000 reduces income tax expense, thereby producing a tax savings.

Sometimes events occur that meet only one of the criteria for extraordinary items. In those cases, any gain or loss resulting should be reported as a separate item in the determination of income from continuing operations. For example, assume that Pratt Communications, Inc. had a gain of $400,000 on the sale of land held as an investment. The gain is not extraordinary because the sale of investments is not unusual. The gain is so large that it should be brought to the attention of users of the financial statements. Thus, it is reported separately in determining income from continuing operations as illustrated in Figure 16-3 on page 631.

CHANGE IN ACCOUNTING PRINCIPLE

As discussed in earlier chapters, alternative methods may be used to account for some types of transactions. For example, several methods are acceptable in accounting for depreciation and for inventory. Different methods may result in material differences in income statement and balance sheet amounts. The accounting **principle of consistency** generally requires that once an accounting

---

[4]*Statement of Financial Accounting Standards No. 4,* "Reporting Gains and Losses from Extinguishment of Debt" (FASB: Stamford, Conn., March 1975), par. 8

method is adopted, it must be used consistently in order to provide comparable data from one accounting period to another. An exception to the consistency principle is permitted and an accounting method may be changed, however, if a new method is clearly preferable to the old one. A company may change from the straight-line method to an accelerated depreciation method, for example, because the service benefits are actually being used on an accelerated basis.

When an accounting principle is changed, a description of the change and its effect on net income for the period must be disclosed in a footnote to the financial statements. In addition, the change in principle is assumed to have been made at the beginning of the year of change, and the cumulative effect of the change to the beginning of the year generally must be reported on the income statement immediately after extraordinary items, if any. The *cumulative effect* is the total effect the new method would have had on retained earnings if it, instead of the old method, had been applied in past periods.[5]

To illustrate, assume that Pratt Communications, Inc. adopted the sum-of-years'-digits depreciation method for printing equipment purchased at the beginning of 1982. The equipment cost $630,000 and had an estimated useful life of six years with a zero residual value. In 1984, management decided to change to the straight-line method because it more closely reflected the pattern of asset use. The cumulative effect of the change to the beginning of 1984 is computed as follows:

Depreciation taken under SYD method for 1982 and 1983:

$$\frac{6}{21} + \frac{5}{21} = \frac{11}{21} \times \$630,000 = \qquad \$330,000$$

Depreciation that would have been taken under the straight-line method for 1982 and 1983:

$$\$630,000 \div 6 \text{ years} = \$105,000 \times 2 \text{ years} = \qquad \underline{210,000}$$

Cumulative effect of the change $\qquad \underline{\underline{\$120,000}}$

A journal entry would be prepared to adjust the accumulated depreciation account and to recognize the cumulative effect of the change as follows:

Dec.	31	Accumulated Depreciation—Equipment	120,000	
		Cumulative Effect of Accounting Change		120,000
		To record the cumulative effect of a change		
		from SYD to straight-line depreciation.		

---

[5]Some changes in accounting principle are disclosed by restating the financial statements of prior years rather than by recognition of the cumulative effect of the change in the current year. For a complete discussion of accounting changes, see *APB Opinion No. 20*, ''Accounting Changes,'' AICPA (New York: 1972).

The cumulative effect of the change, assuming an income tax rate of 40%, would be reported on the income statement as follows:

Income from continuing operations		$ 630,000
Discontinued operations:		
Operating income of discontinued segment (Net of $39,000 income tax)	$ 60,000	
Gain on sale of discontinued segment (Net of $267,000 income tax)	800,000	860,000
Income before extraordinary item		1,490,000
Extraordinary item: Loss from earthquake (Net of $200,000 tax savings)		600,000
Income before the effect of an accounting change		890,000
Cumulative effect on prior years' income from change in depreciation method (Net of $48,000 income tax)		72,000
Net income		$ 962,000

Again, note that the cumulative effect of the accounting change is reported net of its related income tax effect. Because it is an income statement account, the Cumulative Effect of Accounting Change account is closed to the Income Summary account at year-end.

EARNINGS PER SHARE

One of the most widely publicized accounting statistics is **earnings per share of common stock** (EPS). Earnings-per-share data are used to evaluate the past performance of a business, to form an opinion as to its potential future performance, and to compare the operating performance of different companies. If a company has only common stock outstanding, earnings per share is computed by dividing net income by the average number of shares outstanding.

The average number of shares is computed on a weighted-average basis. For example, if Merk Company had 100,000 shares of common stock outstanding at the beginning of the year and issued 20,000 additional shares on April 1, the weighted average is based on the number of months that the shares were outstanding during the year ended December 31, and the computation would be:

100,000 shares × 3/12 =	25,000
120,000 shares × 9/12 =	90,000
Weighted Average Shares Outstanding	115,000

or

100,000 shares × 12/12 =	100,000
20,000 shares × 9/12 =	15,000
Weighted Average Shares Outstanding	115,000

Basing the computation of EPS on the weighted average number of shares recognizes the fact that the assets received from the issue of shares on April 1 were available for earning revenue during three-fourths of the year only.

If Merk Company reported net income of $287,500 for the year, earnings per share would be:

$$\frac{\text{Net income}}{\text{Average shares outstanding}} = \frac{\$287,500}{115,000} = \$2.50$$

Note that earnings per share pertain to common stock only. If a company has both cumulative preferred stock and common stock outstanding, the preferred dividend requirement for the year must be subtracted from net income and the remaining net income divided by the average number of common shares outstanding. For example, assume that Merk Company has $400,000 of $100 par value, 6% cumulative preferred stock outstanding. The computation of earnings per share of common stock would be:

$$\frac{\text{Net income} - \text{preferred dividends}}{\text{Average common shares outstanding}} = \frac{\$287,500 - \$24,000}{115,000} = \$2.29$$

PRIMARY AND FULLY DILUTED EARNINGS PER SHARE

When a company has a simple capital structure like the one illustrated above, the computation of earnings per share is relatively straightforward. Many companies, however, have a **complex capital structure** that includes convertible securities or stock purchase rights, the conversion or exercise of which have the potential of decreasing or *diluting* earnings per share of common stock. In other words, the conversion of preferred stock or the exercise of stock purchase rights will increase the number of common shares outstanding and might therefore reduce earnings per share.

To indicate the potential dilution, two earnings-per-share figures are generally presented, primary earnings per share and fully diluted earnings per share. **Primary earnings per share** is computed as illustrated above.[6] **Fully diluted earnings per share** is computed under the assumption that all potentially dilutive securities were converted or exercised at the beginning of the year. Thus, users are notified as to the potential dilution that might occur.

To illustrate, assume that each of the 4,000 shares of Merk Company's $100 par, 6%, cumulative preferred stock is convertible into 4 shares of common stock. The computation of primary and fully diluted earnings per share,

---

[6]Convertible securities and stock purchase rights that have a high probability of being converted or exercised are called common stock equivalents and are sometimes included in the computation of primary earnings per share. The rules for determining when and how to include them are beyond the scope of this book. They are described and illustrated in *APB Opinion No. 15*, "Earnings Per Share" (AICPA: New York, 1969).

assuming the convertible preferred stock affects only the computation of fully diluted earnings per share, would be:

$$\text{Primary} = \frac{\$287{,}500 - \$24{,}000}{115{,}000} = \$2.29$$

$$\text{Fully diluted} = \frac{\$287{,}500}{115{,}000 + 16{,}000} = \$2.19$$

In the numerator of the fully diluted computation, the preferred stock is assumed to have been converted at the beginning of the year. Consequently, there would have been no dividends on the preferred stock. However, there would have been 16,000 additional shares of common stock outstanding during the year, which are added to the outstanding common shares in the denominator.

EARNINGS PER SHARE ON THE INCOME STATEMENT

Because of the significance attached by investors and others to earnings-per-share data, publicly held corporations are required to present earnings-per-share data on the face of the income statement. If a company has discontinued operations, extraordinary items, or the cumulative effect of a change in accounting principle reported on the income statement, earnings per share data must be presented for each of these components as well as for final net income. The presentation of earnings per share is illustrated in Figure 16-3.

COMPREHENSIVE INCOME STATEMENT ILLUSTRATED

A comprehensive income statement for Pratt Communications, Inc., is shown in Figure 16-3. Although a company would seldom have all of these transactions and events in a single year, they are included to illustrate their treatment.

PRIOR PERIOD ADJUSTMENTS

Generally, all items of profit and loss recognized during a period must be included in the determination of net income of that period. A major exception to this general policy is the correction of a material error in the financial statements of a prior period.[7]

---

[7]"Prior Period Adjustments," *Statement of Financial Accounting Standards No. 16* (Stamford, Conn., FASB, 1977), par. 11.

Errors result from mathematical mistakes, mistakes in the application of accounting principles, or oversight or misuse of facts that existed at the time

262,500 (handwritten)

Figure 16-3
Comprehensive Income Statement

PRATT COMMUNICATIONS, INC.
Income Statement
For the Year Ended December 31, 1984

Revenue:		
Advertising revenue		$4,600,000
Subscription revenue		3,280,000
Total revenue		7,880,000
Operating expenses:		
Selling expenses	$4,800,000	
General and administrative expenses	1,640,000	
Interest expense	390,000	6,830,000
Income from operations		1,050,000
Gain on sale of land		400,000
Income from continuing operations—before tax		1,450,000
Income tax expense		580,000
Income from continuing operations		870,000
Discontinued operations		
Operating income of discontinued segment (Net of $39,000 income tax)	$ 60,000	
Gain on sale of discontinued segment (Net of $267,000 income tax)	800,000	860,000
Income before extraordinary item		1,730,000
Extraordinary item: Loss from earthquake (Net of $200,000 tax savings)		600,000
Income before the effect of an accounting change		1,130,000
Cumulative effect on prior years' income of a change in depreciation method (Net of $48,000 income tax)		72,000
Net income		$1,202,000

Earnings (loss) per common share for:	Primary	Fully Diluted
Continuing operations	$1.74	$1.45
Discontinued operations	1.72	1.43
Extraordinary loss	(1.20)	(1.00)
Cumulative effect of accounting change	.14	.12
Net income	2.40	2.00

The earnings per share data assume 500,000 common shares outstanding for primary earnings per share and 600,000 for fully diluted earnings per share.

(handwritten annotations: 580000/1450000 = 40% rate; adjust for cumm. affect; equals)

the financial statements were prepared. Errors discovered in the same period in which they occurred are corrected in the current period's financial statements. Errors in net income not discovered until a later accounting period are excluded from the current year's income statement to avoid distorting net income of the current period. Because net income is closed to retained earnings, the correction of an error in a prior year's net income is adjusted to the beginning balance of retained earnings in the year in which the error is discovered. These adjustments, which are made net of income tax effects, are called **prior period adjustments.**

To illustrate, assume that in the process of preparing closing entries at the end of 1984 the accountant discovered that the company had failed to record depreciation of $65,000 on machinery acquired at the beginning of 1983. Assuming no income tax effect, the entry to correct the error would be made as follows:

Dec.	31	Retained Earnings	65,000	
		Accumulated Depreciation—Machinery		65,000
		To correct the failure to record depreciation for 1983.		

The net income credited to retained earnings in closing the books at the end of 1983 was overstated by $65,000. In addition, accumulated depreciation on machinery was understated on the 1983 balance sheet. The debit to retained earnings in the entry above corrects the balance in the Retained Earnings account, and the credit to Accumulated Depreciation—Machinery corrects the balance in that account. The correction of the beginning balance of retained earnings for 1984 is reported as shown on the retained earnings statement presented in Figure 16-4.

Figure 16-4
Retained Earnings
Statement

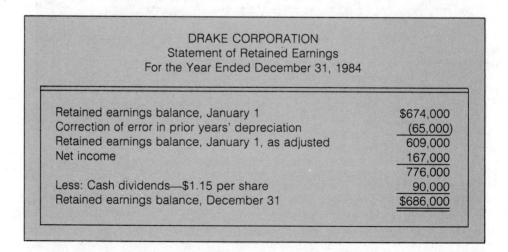

DRAKE CORPORATION
Statement of Retained Earnings
For the Year Ended December 31, 1984

Retained earnings balance, January 1	$674,000
Correction of error in prior years' depreciation	(65,000)
Retained earnings balance, January 1, as adjusted	609,000
Net income	167,000
	776,000
Less: Cash dividends—$1.15 per share	90,000
Retained earnings balance, December 31	$686,000

RETAINED EARNINGS STATEMENT

In addition to a balance sheet, an income statement, and a statement of changes in financial position, a retained earnings statement is prepared either as a separate statement or as part of a combined statement of income and retained earnings. The retained earnings statement summarizes the changes that have taken place in the retained earnings account during the year:

GLOSSARY

CHANGE IN ACCOUNTING PRINCIPLE.   A change from one acceptable method of accounting to another acceptable method (p. 626).

COMPLEX CAPITAL STRUCTURE.   A capital structure that contains potentially dilutive securities (p. 629).

CONSISTENCY PRINCIPLE.   The requirement that, once adopted, an accounting method must be used consistently from one accounting period to another (p. 626).

EARNINGS PER SHARE.   The amount of net income identified with each share of common stock (p. 628).

EXTRAORDINARY ITEM.   An event that is unusual in nature and occurs infrequently considering the environment in which a firm operates (p. 624).

FULLY DILUTED EARNINGS PER SHARE.   An earnings-per-share figure computed under the assumption that all potentially dilutive securities were converted or exercised at the beginning of the year (p. 629).

PRIMARY EARNINGS PER SHARE.   Net income identified with common stock divided by the weighted average number of common shares outstanding during the year (p. 629).

PRIOR PERIOD ADJUSTMENT.   A direct adjustment to retained earnings to correct an error in the net income of a prior period (p. 632).

SEGMENT OF A BUSINESS.   A component of an entity whose activities represent a separate major line of business or class of customer (p. 622).

STOCK DIVIDEND.   A pro-rata distribution of additional shares of a corporation's own stock to its stockholders (p. 617).

STOCK SPLIT.   A decrease in the par or stated value of stock with a proportionate increase in the number of shares (p. 619).

TREASURY STOCK.   A corporation's own stock that has been issued and reacquired but not retired or reissued (p. 612).

QUESTIONS

1. What is treasury stock? For what purposes might a corporation reacquire its own shares?
2. How is treasury stock similar to unissued stock? How is it different?

3. A corporation purchased 1,000 shares of its own $1 par value common stock at a price of $20 per share. What is the entry to record the purchase? What kind of account is the Treasury Stock account? How is this account reported on the balance sheet?

4. XYZ Corporation has retained earnings of $480,000 and holds treasury stock purchased at a cost of $180,000. In most states, what is the maximum amount of retained earnings that could be declared as a dividend? Why? Where is information regarding restrictions on retained earnings disclosed?

5. What accounts are involved when recording the purchase for cash of a corporation's own par value stock at a price less than its average issue price, if the shares are to be formally retired? How is this entry different if the shares are purchased at a price in excess of their average issue price?

6. What is a stock dividend? What effect do stock dividends have on corporate assets and on total stockholders' equity? How does a stock dividend affect book value per share of stock?

7. ABC Corporation has 50,000 shares of $1 par value common stock issued and outstanding. What entry would be made to record the declaration of a 5% stock dividend at a time when the market price of the shares is $25?

8. What is a stock split? What effect does a stock split have on total stockholders' equity?

9. A corporation with 20,000 shares of common stock outstanding splits its stock 3 for 1. How many shares are outstanding after the split?

10. Indicate where each of the following items should be reported in the income statement:
   (a) Gain on sale of all refining operations by an oil company.
   (b) Loss on the disposal of obsolete manufacturing equipment.
   (c) An uninsured loss from the total destruction of a company's office building caused by a tornado. Tornados are rare in the area in which the company operates.
   (d) A change from the straight-line method of depreciation to the double declining-balance method.
   (e) Gain on the sale of one of several investments in the common stock of other companies.
   (f) Correction of an error in recording depreciation expense in a prior period.

11. Which of the following items would generally be considered extraordinary?
   (a) Bonus payments to management personnel.
   (b) Uninsured flood loss.
   (c) Bad debts expense.
   (d) Loss on the sale of a plant asset.
   (e) Loss from the passing of a new federal law prohibiting the sale of a certain product.
   (f) Loss from the expropriation of corporate assets by a Latin American country.

12. What is the general accounting practice followed when reporting the income tax effects of "special" income statement items?

13. A corporation decides in 1984 to change its method of depreciating plant machinery from the straight-line method to the double declining-balance method.

The machinery was purchased for $100,000 at the beginning of 1982 and had an estimated useful life of four years with no residual value. What journal entry is necessary to adjust the accumulated depreciation account and to recognize the cumulative effect of the change?

14. Prepare a partial income statement showing how the effect of the accounting change in question 13 would be reported. Assume an income tax rate of 40%. Income before the effect of the accounting change amounted to $964,000.

15. Lockhart Company had 60,000 shares of common stock outstanding at the beginning of the year and issued 30,000 additional shares on May 1. What is the weighted average number of shares outstanding during the year? How much is earnings per share, assuming a net income for the year of $680,000?

16. Assume the company in question 15 has $800,000 of $100 par value, 8%, cumulative preferred stock outstanding. What is earnings per share now? Assume further that each of the 8,000 preferred shares is convertible into three shares of common stock. What is fully diluted earnings per share under this assumption?

17. Is it necessary to present earnings-per-share data for such "special" income statement items as gains (losses) from discontinued operations?

18. An accountant discovered during 1984 that her company failed to record 1983 depreciation expense of $25,000 on equipment. What entry would be made to correct the error? What is this entry called?

19. What is the purpose of the retained earnings statement?

EXERCISES

Exercise 16-1 (Preparing Journal Entries and Stockholders' Equity Section)

Kennington Corporation had the following stockholders' equity on January 1:

Common Stock, $5 par, 100,000 shares authorized, 50,000 shares issued and outstanding	$ 250,000
Contributed Capital in Excess of Par	480,000
Retained Earnings	275,000
Total Stockholders' Equity	$1,005,000

During the year, the company entered into the following treasury stock transactions:

May	1	Purchased 3,000 of its own shares at $25 per share.
Aug.	6	Sold 1,200 of the treasury shares purchased on May 1 for $30 per share.
Dec.	3	Sold 800 of the treasury shares purchased on May 1 for $20 per share.

Required:
A. Prepare journal entries to record the transactions.
B. Prepare the stockholders' equity section of the balance sheet on December 31.

Exercise 16-2 (Retirement of Stock)

A corporation reacquired at $40 per share, 25,000 shares of its own $10 par value common stock that were issued at an average price of $46 per share. All 25,000 shares were then retired.

Required:

A. Prepare the journal entry to record the stock retirement.

B. Assume the shares were reacquired at $50 per share rather than $40. Prepare the entry to record the stock retirement.

C. Assume that the shares purchased above at $50 per share were initially intended to be held as treasury stock. Prepare the entries to record the purchase of the shares and retirement of the shares at a later date.

Exercise 16-3 (Retained Earnings Statement)

In the process of preparing closing entries at the end of 1984, the accountant for New West Corporation discovered that depreciation on one of the machines, in the amount of $10,000, had not been recorded at the end of 1982. The January 1, 1984, balance in retained earnings was $810,000. Net income for 1984 is $81,000 and a cash dividend of $1.80 was declared on the 30,000 common shares outstanding. The company has no preferred stock.

Required:

A. Prepare the journal entry needed to correct for the failure to record depreciation. Assume there is no income tax effect.

B. Prepare a statement of retained earnings for the year ended December 31, 1984.

Exercise 16-4 (Stock Dividends and Stock Splits)

A corporation with 100,000 shares of $2 par value common stock issued and outstanding declared a 10% stock dividend on July 18, distributable on August 15 to stockholders of record on July 31. The market price of the stock on July 18 was $32 per share. The corporation has contributed capital in excess of par of $425,000 and retained earnings of $360,000.

Required:

A. Prepare the journal entries to record the declaration and distribution of the stock dividend.

B. Assume that the corporation declared a 100% stock dividend instead of a 10% one. Prepare the entries to record the declaration and distribution of the stock dividend and prepare a schedule detailing the components of stockholders' equity before and after the stock dividend.

C. Assume that the board of directors choose to split the stock 2 for 1 instead of declaring a stock dividend. Prepare the memo entry to record the stock split.

D. Prepare the stockholders' equity section of the balance sheet as it would appear assuming:

1. (B) above had occurred.
2. (C) above had occurred.

Exercise 16-5 (Preparation of Income Statement)

Clarion Company had sales revenue of $4,450,000 and service revenue of $805,000 for the year ended December 31, 1984. Cost of goods sold amounted to $2,725,000, selling and administrative expenses were $1,500,000, and income tax expense on continuing operations was $135,000.

During 1984, the company sold one of its operating divisions at a gain of $280,000 net of income tax of $80,000. Operating income of the division to the date of sale (which is excluded from the data given above) was $80,000 net of income tax of $30,500.

Required:
Prepare an income statement for Clarion Company for the year ended December 31, 1984.

Exercise 16-6 (Income Statement Classification)

Selected transactions and events of International Corporation are given below:

1. An earthquake in Midtown, where the company's largest plant is located, resulted in an uninsured loss of $1.8 million. Earthquakes have never occurred before in the Midtown area.
2. Long-term investments were sold at a loss of $350,000.
3. A strike at the Danville plant by the machinists union resulted in a loss to the corporation of $2.3 million.
4. Excess machinery was sold at a gain of $240,000.
5. The company disposed of its unprofitable meat packing operations incurring a loss of $1.1 million.
6. The meat packing operations had incurred a loss of $105,000 up to the date of sale.
7. The company sold one of its shoe manufacturing factories at a gain of $589,000.

Required:
Indicate in which section of the income statement each of the transactions or events should be reported. Your choices are: (1) income from continuing operations; (2) disposal of a segment of the business; (3) extraordinary item.

Exercise 16-7 (Cumulative Effect of Accounting Change)

Murin Company had revenues and operating expenses for the year 1984 as follows:

Sales	$1,636,000
Cost of goods sold	780,000
Administrative expenses	190,000
Selling expenses	220,000
Depreciation expense	200,000

During 1984, the depreciation method used on two machines was changed from the straight-line method to the double declining-balance method. (The $200,000 depreciation expense shown above was computed under the new method.) Relevant data for the two machines is presented below:

	Cost	Date of Purchase	Estimated Useful Life	Estimated Salvage Value
Machine A	$180,000	1/1/82	5 years	$12,000
Machine B	72,000	1/1/81	8 years	5,000

Assume an income tax rate of 40%.

Required:

A. Prepare the journal entry needed to record the effect of the change in depreciation method.

B. Prepare an income statement for 1984 for Murin Company.

Exercise 16-8 (Earnings per Share)

A partial income statement for Johnson, Inc., is given below:

Income from Continuing Operations		$540,000
Discontinued Operations:		
Operating Income of Discontinued Segment (Net of $28,000 Income Tax)	$ 70,000	
Gain on Sale of Segment (Net of $100,000 Income Tax)	280,000	350,000
Net Income		$890,000

The corporation had 200,000 common shares outstanding throughout the year along with 10,000 shares of $100 par, 7% preferred stock. Each preferred share is convertible into three shares of common stock, which affects the computation of fully diluted earnings per share.

Required:

Determine primary and fully diluted earnings per common share for continuing operations, discontinued operations, and net income.

PROBLEMS

Problem 16-1 (Journal Entries for Stockholders' Equity Items)

Selected transactions and events affecting the stockholders' equity of Rizke Company during 1984 are given below:

1. Purchased 4,000 shares of treasury stock at $28 per share.
2. Reissued at $36 per share 1,500 of the treasury shares purchased in (1).
3. Reissued at $22 per share the 2,500 remaining treasury shares purchased in (1).
4. Declared a 10% common stock dividend on the 200,000 shares of outstanding $10 par value common stock. The market price of the common stock on the declaration date was $34 per share.
5. Distributed the stock dividend declared in (4).
6. Changed from the straight-line to the sum-of-years'-digits depreciation method for machinery purchased at the beginning of 1982. The machinery cost $160,000 and

had an estimated useful life of five years with a salvage value of $10,000. Rizke's fiscal year ends on December 31.

7. The $10 par value common stock was split on a 2 for 1 basis.

8. Discovered that the bookkeeper failed to record depreciation expense of $18,000 on machinery for the prior year.

Required:

Prepare journal entries to record the above items.

Problem 16-2 (Income Statement with Special Items)

SRW Inc. had revenues and operating expenses for the year ended December 31, 1984 as follows:

Sales revenues	$10,580,000
Cost of goods sold	7,370,000
Administrative expenses	940,000
Selling expenses	760,000
Interest expense	320,000

Other events affecting 1984 net income were:

1. SRW sold its food processing division on May 31, 1984, at a pretax gain of $480,000. Operating income before tax for the division to the date of sale was $54,000, which is not included in the data above.

2. A mining venture in Central America, partially owned by SRW in a joint venture with other firms, was expropriated by the foreign government. SRW's share of the loss amounted to $750,000 before tax effects.

Required:

Prepare an income statement for SRW Inc. for the year ended December 31, 1984. Assume a uniform income tax rate of 40%. Include earnings per share data under the assumption that SRW had 250,000 shares of common stock outstanding throughout the year.

Problem 16-3 (Preparing Journal Entries and Stockholders' Equity Section)

Carson Corporation had stockholders' equity at the beginning of 1984 as follows:

Common Stock, $10 par value, 400,000 shares authorized, 150,000 shares issued and outstanding	$1,500,000
Contributed Capital in Excess of Par	975,000
Retained Earnings	1,096,000
Total Stockholders' Equity	$3,571,000

During 1984, the corporation completed the following transactions:

Jan.   6 Issued at par value 5,000 shares of $100 par, 9%, cumulative preferred stock.
Jan.   15 Purchased 10,000 shares of common stock at $25 per share to be held as treasury stock.
Mar.   30 Reissued at $33 per share 2,500 of the treasury shares.
Dec.   15 Declared a 5% stock dividend on common stock, distributable on January 20, to stockholders of record on December 29. The market price of the stock was $24 per share.

Required:
A. Prepare journal entries to record the transactions.
B. Prepare the stockholders' equity section of the balance sheet on December 31, assuming that net income for 1984 was $356,000.

Problem 16-4 (Dividends and Preparation of Stockholders' Equity Section)

Clark Company had the following stockholders' equity at the beginning of 1984:

Common Stock, $2 par value, 1,000,000 shares authorized, 400,000 shares issued and outstanding	$ 800,000
Contributed Capital in Excess of Par	1,025,000
Retained Earnings	2,384,000
Total Stockholders' Equity	$4,209,000

During 1984, the following transactions and events occurred:

1. On September 2 the company declared a $.50 per share cash dividend and a 5% stock dividend on its outstanding common stock. The dividends were payable or distributable on October 10 to stockholders of record on September 20. The market price of the stock on September 2 was $20 per share.
2. Net income for 1984 was $671,000.
3. While preparing closing entries at the end of 1984, the accountant discovered that two errors were made in recording depreciation for 1983:
   (a) Depreciation of $30,000 on machinery was overlooked and, therefore, not recorded.
   (b) Depreciation on office equipment was recorded in the amount of $100,000. The correct amount should have been $10,000.

Required:
A. Prepare journal entries for the declaration and payment (distribution) of dividends and to correct the accounts for the depreciation errors.

B. Prepare the stockholders' equity section of the balance sheet on December 31, 1984.

C. Prepare a retained earnings statement for the year ended December 31, 1984.

Problem 16-5 (Earnings per Share)

Largent Company had 142,000 shares of common stock and 50,000 shares of $50 par value, 10%, cumulative preferred stock outstanding on January 1. During the year, the company entered into the following transactions:

April	1	Issued 20,000 shares of common stock.
June	1	Purchased 6,000 common shares as treasury stock.
August	1	Reissued 3,000 shares of treasury stock.
October	1	Issued 10,000 shares of common stock.

Required:

A. Compute the weighted average number of common shares outstanding during the year.

B. Net income for the year was $632,500. Compute earnings per share assuming:
  1. The preferred stock is nonconvertible.
  2. Each share of preferred stock is convertible into four shares of common stock, which affects the computation of fully diluted earnings per share.

ALTERNATE PROBLEMS

Problem 16-1A (Comprehensive Problem)

Bretz Corporation has been in existence for several years. On January 1, 1984, its stockholders' equity consisted of the following:

Common Stock, $5 par value, 500,000 shares authorized, 300,000 shares issued and outstanding	$1,500,000
Contributed Capital in Excess of Par	400,000
Retained Earnings	386,000
Total Stockholders' Equity	$2,286,000

During 1984 Bretz Corporation completed the following transactions:

Jan.	9	Purchased 20,000 shares of treasury stock at $12 per share.
Feb.	16	Reissued at $16 per share 10,000 of the treasury shares purchased on January 9.
Mar.	10	Declared a 5% common stock dividend on the outstanding common stock. The market value of the common stock was $15 per share. (Reminder: Don't forget that some of the shares are held as treasury stock and are not, therefore, outstanding.)
Apr.	2	Reissued at $15 per share 5,000 of the treasury shares purchased on January 9.

Apr.	5	Distributed the stock dividend declared on March 10.
June	12	Changed from the straight-line to the double declining-balance depreciation method for equipment purchased on January 2, 1982. The equipment cost $140,000 and had an estimated useful life of five years with a salvage value of $20,000.
Sept.	8	Discovered that the accounting department failed to record depreciation expense of $12,500 on machinery for 1983.
Dec.	31	Closed the $86,400 credit balance in the Income Summary account.

Required:

A. Prepare journal entries to record the transactions.

B. What is the balance in the Treasury Stock account on December 31? How should the balance be reported in the December 31, 1984, financial statements?

C. How is the effect of changing from the straight-line to the double declining-balance method of depreciation reported in the financial statements?

D. What type of entry is the September 8 entry?

E. Determine the amount of total stockholders' equity on December 31, 1984.

F. Prepare a retained earnings statement for 1984.

Problem 16-2A (Effects of Transactions and Earnings per Share)

At the beginning of 1984, Ambro Company had 35,000 shares of common stock outstanding and total stockholders' equity was $752,500. During 1984, Ambro Company completed the following transactions:

Jan.	31	Purchased 4,000 shares of its outstanding stock as treasury stock at a price of $30 per share.
Apr.	1	Declared and distributed a 10% stock dividend on its outstanding common stock. The market price of the stock was $32 per share.
July	1	Reissued for $35 per share 2,000 of the treasury shares purchased on January 31.
Dec.	10	Declared a cash dividend of $1 per share payable on January 8, 1985.
Dec.	31	Closed the $76,300 credit balance in the Income Summary account.

Required:

A. Set up a schedule with headings for (1) Total Stockholders' Equity, (2) Number of Shares Outstanding, and (3) Book Value per Share, and enter the amount of each of these three items on January 1, 1984, and after each of the above transactions.

B. Compute earnings per share for 1984.

Problem 16-3A (Income Statement with Special Items)

Carlin-Ross Company earned revenues and incurred operating expenses for the year ended December 31, 1983, as follows:

Sales revenue	$2,380,000
Cost of goods sold	1,358,000
Administrative expenses	212,000
Selling expenses	371,000
Interest expense	72,000

Other events affecting 1983 income were:

1. An extraordinary loss of $245,000 before tax was incurred when a tornado severely damaged one of Carlin-Ross Company's warehouses.
2. Carlin-Ross sold its quick-food division on July 31, 1983, at a pretax gain of $160,000. An operating loss of $72,000 before tax was incurred by the division to the date of sale.
3. Carlin-Ross changed from the double declining-balance to the straight-line method of depreciation. The cumulative effect of the change to the beginning of 1983 was $96,000 (credit) before tax.

Required:
Prepare an income statement for Carlin-Ross Company for the year ended December 31, 1983. Assume a uniform income tax rate of 30%. Include earnings-per-share data under the assumption that Carlin-Ross had 122,000 shares of common stock outstanding throughout the year.

Problem 16-4A (Earnings per Share)

Spraling Company had 210,000 shares of common stock and 30,000 shares of $100 par value, 9%, cumulative preferred stock outstanding on January 1. During the year, the company entered into the following transactions:

March	30	Issued 80,000 additional shares of common stock.
July	31	Purchased 20,000 common shares as treasury stock.
Nov.	1	Reissued 10,000 shares of treasury stock.

Required:
A. Compute the weighted average number of common shares outstanding during the year.
B. Net income for the year was $825,000. Compute earnings per share assuming:
   1. The preferred stock is nonconvertible.
   2. Each share of preferred stock is convertible into five shares of common stock, which affects the computation of fully diluted earnings per share.

Problem 16-5A (Correction of Errors)

Early in 1984, the head bookkeeper for Lowrey Company, Sue McKinley, became seriously ill and had to be hospitalized. During her absence, her relatively inexperienced assistant made the following journal entries to record the transactions described in the explanations.

1. Cost of Goods Sold   20,000
      Inventory   20,000
To correct for the overstatement of inventory at the end of 1983.

2. Retained Earnings   90,000
      Dividends Payable   90,000
To record the declaration of a $1.50 per share dividend on 60,000 shares of outstanding common stock.

3. Treasury Stock   15,000
      Cash   15,000
To record the purchase of 1,000 shares of $5 par value common stock for $15 per share to be held as treasury stock.

4. Land   100,000
      Common Stock   100,000
To record the issue of 20,000 shares of $5 par value common stock in exchange for land with a fair value of $290,000.

5. Dividend Payable   90,000
      Cash   90,000
To record payment of the dividend declared in (2).

6. Cash   10,000
      Treasury Stock   10,000
To record the reissue of 500 shares of treasury stock at $20 per share.

7. Contributed Capital in Excess of Par   40,000
      Common Stock Dividend Distributable   10,000
      Contributed Capital in Excess of Par   30,000
To record a small stock dividend of 2,000 shares of $5 par value common stock with a market value of $20 per share.

8. Common Stock Dividend Distributable   10,000
      Common Stock   10,000
To record the distribution of the stock dividend declared in (7).

9. Accumulated Depreciation—Equipment   8,000
      Depreciation Expense   8,000
To correct for the overstatement of depreciation expense on equipment at the end of 1983.

Required:

Analyze each transaction and state whether the entry made was correct or incorrect. If the entry is incorrect, make the entry that should have been made to record the transaction.

CASE FOR CHAPTER 16

(Annual Report Analysis)

Refer to the financial statements and supporting schedules in the appendix, and answer the following questions:

1. With reference to Mary Moppet's,
   a. How many shares of common stock were held as treasury stock on September 30, 1981?
   b. What was the total cost of the treasury shares on September 30, 1981?

2. With reference to Modern Merchandising, Inc.,
   a. What was the amount of retained earnings on January 31, 1981?
   b. How much of the January 31, 1981 retained earnings were available for dividend distribution?
   c. Note I to the financial statements refers to a prior period adjustment. Describe the nature of the prior period adjustment. How was its effect treated in the financial statements?
   d. Note G explains the effect of a fire that destroyed the Company's Minnnetonka, Minnesota showroom. How much was the pretax gain from insurance recovery? Was the gain treated as an extraordinary item? Why or why not?
3. With reference to General Motors,
   a. How much were earnings (loss) per share in 1981? in 1980?
   b. Why doesn't the company report a fully diluted earnings (loss) per share figure for 1981?
   c. How were dividends on preferred stock treated in computing earnings per share?

PART FIVE
ADDITIONAL FINANCIAL REPORTING ISSUES

CHAPTER 17
ACCOUNTING FOR LONG-TERM LIABILITIES

OVERVIEW AND OBJECTIVES

This chapter describes accounting for bonds payable and other long-term liabilities. When you have completed the chapter, you should understand:

- Why a firm obtains funds by long-term borrowing (pp. 650–652).
- The features commonly included in a bond issue (pp. 653–654).
- How to record the issuance of bonds at par value, at a discount, and at a premium (pp. 654–664).
- How bond prices are determined (pp. 656–659).
- How to amortize a bond discount or premium by the straight-line method of amortization (pp. 659–664).
- How to account for bonds issued between interest payment dates (pp. 664–665).
- Why an adjusting entry is needed to accrue bond interest expense and how to prepare the entry (pp. 665–666).
- How to record the retirement of bonds before maturity (p. 667).
- How to record the conversion of bonds into common stock (pp. 667–668).
- The purpose of a bond sinking fund and how to account for one (pp. 668–669).
- How to amortize a bond discount or premium by the effective interest method of amortization (pp. 669–672).
- How to account for a mortgage note payable (p. 673).
- The difference between an operating lease and a capital lease (pp. 673–675).
- The nature of a pension plan and when a pension liability results (p. 675).

The acquisition of assets through investment by owners and the retention of working capital generated from operations has been discussed in earlier chapters. Firms also obtain the funds needed to operate a business from a variety of lending sources. The method of financing depends on several factors, one of which is the length of time required to convert the assets acquired with the borrowed funds back into cash. Inventories that will be sold in the near future, for example, are usually financed through short-term credit. Cash needed to finance seasonal activities is generally borrowed on short-term notes because current operations are expected to produce sufficient cash to repay the loan. On the other hand, when a firm finds it necessary to obtain funds for long-term purposes such as the acquisition of plant assets, the funds are often obtained by long-term borrowing. Deferring the payment for an extended period will allow time for the acquired assets to generate sufficient cash to cover interest payments and accumulate the funds needed to repay the loan.

The repayment of long-term debt is often deferred for a period of 30 years or longer. The agreement between the lender and the borrower usually provides for periodic interest payments on specified dates as well as the repayment of the amount borrowed. The borrower is receiving current dollars in exchange for a promise to make payments to the lender at different times in the future. Dollars received and paid at different times are made comparable by considering the time value of money. To thoroughly understand the accounting for long-term liabilities, one should have some knowledge of present value concepts. If you have not been exposed to the concepts before, turn to the Appendix to this chapter and study the concepts and computations presented there.

THE NATURE OF LONG-TERM LIABILITIES

A liability is considered long-term if it is due beyond one year from the balance sheet date or the operating cycle, whichever is longer. In other words, when the operating cycle is less than one year, a one-year period is used to classify liabilities as current or long-term. When the operating cycle is longer than one year, the length of the operating cycle is used to classify the obligations of the firm. The portion of long-term debt that will mature within one year or the operating cycle, whichever is longer, and is to be retired with current assets is reported as a current liability.

The principal long-term liabilities are:

1. **Unsecured note payable.** A promissory note that is backed by a legal claim against the general assets of the borrower.

2. Mortgage note payable. A form of a promissory note in which specific property of the borrower serves as collateral (security) for the loan. Collateral is something of value acceptable to the lender that can be converted into cash to satisfy the debt if the borrower defaults.
3. Bond payable. A form of a promissory note generally issued when a large amount is borrowed from many investors.

Long-term notes and mortgages are normally issued when money is borrowed from one or a few lending institutions such as banks or insurance companies. Frequently, however, a few lenders may not be able or willing to lend the total amount of money needed. In such situations, long-term funds may be obtained by issuing bonds to many investors.

Other types of long-term liabilities are lease contracts, pension liabilities, and deferred income tax credits. The fundamentals of lease and pension liabilities are considered in later sections of this chapter. Deferred income taxes are discussed briefly in Chapter 28. Accounting for these items is complex and is therefore covered more thoroughly in more advanced accounting courses.

WHY FINANCE THROUGH LONG-TERM DEBT?

One function of management is to select the types of financing that are most advantageous to the firm. The major advantages and disadvantages of issuing long-term debt rather than common stock result from the legal distinction between creditors and owners. A creditor does not have a voting right and therefore cannot participate in the management of the firm. As a result, the issuance of bonds does not dilute the control of the existing owners. If the firm is liquidated, however, creditors must be paid in full before any asset distribution is made to stockholders. In addition, interest payments to creditors must be made each period as specified in the debt instrument regardless of whether the firm is profitable. Default on an interest commitment could result in forced bankruptcy of the firm. On the other hand, if funds are raised through the issue of stock, dividends do not have to be paid. Consequently, the risk of losing the investment and return earned on the investment each period is less for creditors. As a result, long-term notes and bonds are attractive investments for investors who prefer not to assume the risks of ownership.

Even though a firm may be able to raise funds by selling stock, long-term debt is often issued because of the leverage provided and the income tax treatment of interest payments. Leverage is the use of borrowed funds to earn a return greater than the interest paid on the debt. The use of debt has the additional advantage of interest expense being deductible in computing taxable income, whereas dividends on preferred and common stock are not tax deductible.

To illustrate the effect of debt financing versus equity financing (raising capital by selling stock), assume that a firm with $2,000,000 in $10 par value common stock is currently earning $400,000 a year before income taxes. The firm needs to raise $1,000,000 in additional funds to finance a planned expansion of the plant. Management estimates that after the expansion the firm will earn $700,000 annually before interest and income taxes. The $1,000,000 can be obtained from one of the three plans that are proposed for consideration: Plan 1—issue 100,000 shares of $10 par value common stock; Plan 2—issue 10%, cumulative, nonparticipating preferred stock; Plan 3—issue 12% bonds. It is assumed that each security is issued at its total par value of $1,000,000. Income taxes are assumed to be 40% of income. The effect of these three plans on the net income available to common stockholders is shown in Figure 17-1.

	Existing Operations	Plan 1 Common Stock	Plan 2 Preferred Stock	Plan 3 Bonds
Shares of Common Stock Outstanding				
Common Shares Currently Outstanding	200,000	200,000	200,000	200,000
Additional Common Shares Issued	—	100,000	—	—
Total	200,000	300,000	200,000	200,000
Net Income Before Bond Interest and Income Taxes	$400,000	$700,000	$700,000	$700,000
Less: Bond Interest Expense	—	—	—	120,000
Net Income Before Income Taxes	400,000	700,000	700,000	580,000
Less: Income Taxes (40%)	160,000	280,000	280,000	232,000
Net Income	240,000	420,000	420,000	348,000
Less: Preferred Stock Dividend	—	—	100,000	—
Net Income Available to Common Stockholders	$240,000	$420,000	$320,000	$348,000
Number of Common Shares Outstanding	200,000	300,000	200,000	200,000
Net Income (Earnings) per Share on Common Stock	$1.20	$1.40	$1.60	$1.74

Figure 17-1
Illustration of Three Plans to Finance Expansion

Using earnings per share as the sole criterion for making the decision, Plan 3 is clearly the most attractive to the existing common stockholders despite the payment of $120,000 in interest each period. This results from a combination of two factors. First, the firm is predicting that after-tax net income will increase $180,000 [$300,000 − (40% × $300,000)] before bond interest expense is deducted. Second, because interest is a tax-deductible expense, the cost of borrowing is considerably less than the $120,000 paid to the bondholders. In other words, the after-tax cost of borrowing is $72,000, which is the $120,000 expense minus the $48,000 (40% × $120,000) reduction in income tax expense. The net increase in earnings of $108,000 ($180,000 − $72,000) accrues to the existing stockholders. Although Plan 1 shows an increase in net income of $180,000, the increase is divided over 50 percent more shares. Plan 3 has an advantage over Plan 2 because the dividends on preferred stock are not deductible in computing taxable income.

This analysis was based on the effect of the alternative plans on earnings per share of common stock and on a favorable leverage assumption. In financial planning, however, management cannot ignore the fact that the bonds will eventually mature and that the fixed interest cost must be paid each period. At lower levels of net income, Plan 1 becomes more attractive. For example, if the company were to earn $120,000 before interest and taxes, the entire amount would be offset by the interest cost. At lower earnings levels, the firm may be unable to generate sufficient cash to satisfy the interest payments and could be forced into bankruptcy.

BONDS PAYABLE

A **bond** is a written promise to pay a principal amount at a specified time as well as interest on the principal at a specified rate per period. Once issued (sold), the bond becomes a long-term obligation to the issuer and an investment to the buyer. When a bond is issued, a bond certificate is given to the buyer as evidence of the firm's indebtedness. The terms of the agreement constitute a contract called the bond **indenture.** The bond indenture indicates the interest rate to be paid, the dates interest is to be paid, the maturity date, the principal amount, and other features included in this particular issue such as the bondholders' right to convert the bonds into common stock.

Bonds are generally issued in denominations of $1,000, which is called the **par value, face value, principal,** or **maturity value.** On the **maturity date** the borrower must pay the par value to the bondholder. Maturity dates vary, but terms of 20 to 30 years are common for corporate bonds. A total bond issue of $4,000,000 would generally consist of 4,000 individual bonds of $1,000 par value each. The division of the total issue into relatively small units permits more investors to participate in the issue.

When a company issues bonds, it normally sells the entire bond issue to an investment firm called an **underwriter.** The underwriter then sells the bonds to investors at a higher price, thereby earning a profit. Because the bonds may be held by numerous individual investors, a third party called a **trustee** is appointed by the issuing company to represent the bondholders. In most cases, the trustee is a large bank or trust company whose primary duty is to ensure that the issuing company fulfills the terms of the bond indenture.

A specified rate of interest is paid on the par value throughout the life of the bonds. The rate, called the **coupon rate, nominal rate,** or **stated rate,** is expressed as a percentage of par value. Interest payments are normally made semiannually, although the stated rate of interest is expressed as an annual rate.

Bond prices are quoted as a percentage of par value. For example, the price of a $1,000 par value bond quoted at 104 is $1,040 ($1,000 × 104%). Like stock quotations, the minimum variation in a bond price is 1/8 of a dollar. Thus a $1,000 bond quoted at 83 5/8 would sell for $836.25 ($1,000 × 83.625%). Bonds may be sold at par, which means that the bond price was 100. If the bond price is below 100, the bonds sell at a **discount;** if the bond price is above 100, the bonds sell at a **premium.** The amount of the discount or premium is the difference between the issue price and the par value of the bond. For example, a bond quoted at 104 is selling at a $40 ($1,040 − $1,000) premium. Alternatively, if the firm received $920 for a bond, there is an $80 discount.

CLASSIFICATION OF BONDS

A bond indenture is written to satisfy the financial needs of the borrower, but the agreement also must be attractive to a sufficient number of investors. Consequently, individual bond issues with a variety of features have been created. Some of the more common features are:

1. Bond Features Related to the Underlying Security
   (a) **Secured or Mortgage Bonds.** A secured bond is one in which specific assets of the firm serve as collateral for the bond. If the firm fails to satisfy its obligations as specified in the bond indenture, the specific assets may be sold and the proceeds used to satisfy the indebtedness.
   (b) **Debenture Bonds or Unsecured Bonds.** Holders of debenture bonds rely for their security on the general credit standing of the issuing firm.
2. Bond Features Related to Evidence of Ownership and Payment of Interest
   (a) **Registered Bonds.** The name and address of the holder of a registered bond must be on file, called the bond register, with the issuing company or the trustee. Interest payments are made by check to the currently registered owners. If ownership of the bond is transferred, the issuing

company must be notified so that the new owner can be entered in the bond register.

(b) **Coupon (Bearer) Bonds.** These bonds have a printed coupon attached to the bond for each interest payment. The amount of interest due and interest payment date is specified on each coupon. When interest is due, the bondholder detaches the proper coupon from the bond, endorses it, indicates his or her address, and then normally presents it to a bank for collection. When coupon bonds are issued, the issuing company normally does not maintain a record of the bondholders. The title to the bond is assumed to be with the holder or bearer.

3. Bond Features Related to the Maturity Date
  (a) **Term Bonds.** The principal of a term bond issue is paid in full on a single specified date. That is, the entire issue matures on the same date.
  (b) **Serial Bonds.** Serial bonds mature in installments on a series of specified dates. For example, $100,000 of a $1,000,000 bond issue may mature at the end of each year for a period of 10 years.

4. Bond Features Related to Potential Early Retirement
  (a) **Callable Bonds.** Some bonds can be called in by the issuing company before they mature. The price the issuer must pay, called the *call price,* is stipulated in the indenture and is usually slightly higher than the par value of the bonds. Most bonds issued today are callable bonds.
  (b) **Convertible Bonds.** These are bonds that can be exchanged for common stock at the option of the bondholder.

A bond issue may contain other special features. The agreement may permit a corporation to pay dividends to stockholders only if a stipulated level of working capital is maintained. It may also require that the issuing company make periodic deposits to a bond retirement fund (called a bond sinking fund) to accumulate the cash needed to retire the bonds when they mature.

Although bond issues may contain different features, accounting for the various issues is similar. Because the features of a long-term debt are important to potential investors, they are disclosed in a footnote to the financial statements. The disclosure usually contains the interest rate, interest payment dates, maturity date, effective rate of interest, and any assets pledged as security. An example of such disclosures is presented in Figure 17-2.

ACCOUNTING FOR BONDS ISSUED AT PAR VALUE

A formal journal entry is not required when bonds are authorized for sale, but a memorandum entry describing the issue may be entered in the Bonds Payable account. To illustrate, assume that on May 15, 1984, Jordan Corporation's board of directors authorized the issue of $100,000 of 11%, five-year bonds

Footnote accompanying financial statements:

Note 9—Long-term debt
The components of long-term debt were:

In millions	December 31 1981	1980
9.95% promissory note due 1999	$110.0	$110.0
8.375% convertible subordinated debentures due 2005	50.0	50.0
Capitalized lease obligations	2.5	3.0
Total	$162.5	$163.0

The terms of the 9.95% promissory note include annual sinking fund requirements of $6.875 million, beginning December 1984. The note agreement contains certain restrictive covenants which, among other things, require a minimum level of working capital and place restrictions concerning additional borrowing and retained earnings available for stock repurchases and payment of dividends. At December 31, 1981, $44 million of retained earnings were free of limitations set forth in the agreement.

The debentures are unsecured general obligations subordinated in right of payment to certain other debt obligations and are convertible into common stock at $20.375 per share. Terms of the debenture agreement include annual sinking fund requirements of $2.5 million, beginning in 1991.

Source: Zenith 1981 annual report.
(A subordinated debenture is an obligation that ranks behind previously issued debt.)

Figure 17-2
Illustration of Long-term Debt Disclosures

dated June 30, 1984.[1] Interest is payable semiannually on June 30 and December 31. There are no other special features contained in the bond indenture. The memorandum may take the following form:

Bonds Payable

1984 May 15	Received authorization to issue $100,000 of 11%, 5-year debenture bonds dated June 30, 1984. Interest is payable semiannually on June 30 and December 31.	

Assuming that the entire bond issue is sold at par value on June 30, the entry to record the issue is:

June	30	Cash	100,000	
		Bonds Payable		100,000
		Issued 11%, 5-year bonds at par value.		

In this case, interest of $5,500 ($100,000 × 11% × 6/12) is due each June 30 and December 31 until the bonds mature. The entry to record the first semiannual interest payment is:

[1]For illustrative purposes, the bonds are issued for an unusually small amount and are assumed to be outstanding for a relatively short period of time.

Dec.	31	Bond Interest Expense		5,500	
		Cash			5,500
		Paid semiannual interest on 11% bonds.			

During the five-year period that the bonds are outstanding, total interest expense of $55,000 is reported.

When the bonds mature five years later, the entry to record the payment of the principal is:

1989					
June	30	Bonds Payable		100,000	
		Cash			100,000
		Paid the par value of 11% bonds at			
		maturity.			

Once the bonds are issued, they may be traded on the open market. Depending on a number of factors, such as current interest rates and the financial position of the borrower, the price of the bonds will fluctuate above or below their par value. Changes in the market price of the bonds are not entered in the firm's books because such changes do not alter the firm's commitment to make the stated semiannual interest payments and to pay the par value when the bonds mature.

THE EFFECT OF MARKET INTEREST RATES ON BOND PRICES

In the above example, Jordan Corporation agreed to pay $100,000 when the bonds mature on June 30, 1989, and 11 percent of the par value annually in two semiannual payments of $5,500 each on June 30 and December 31. Thus the stated rate of interest, interest payment dates, the maturity value, and the maturity date are specified in the bond indenture and usually remain fixed during the life of the bonds. Although the stated rate of interest of 11 percent establishes the amount of interest to be paid annually, the actual interest rate incurred by the firm will be equal to the market rate of interest at the time the bonds are issued. The **market rate** of interest on a bond, sometimes called the **effective rate** or **yield rate,** is the actual rate of interest an investor will earn if bonds purchased at a certain price are held to maturity. The market rate tends to fluctuate daily as investors' perceived risk of an investment changes. The greater the risk associated with an investment, the greater will be the rate of return required by investors. Because securities vary in risk, there is no single market rate of interest. Instead, there is a schedule of rates corresponding to the risk associated with a particular security.

In the case of Jordan Corporation, the firm will receive the $100,000 par value for the bonds only if the market rate of interest for comparable alternative investments is equal to the stated rate of 11 percent on the bonds. If the market rate of interest is higher on other investments of similar risk, investors will offer less than the par value so that they can earn the prevailing market rate of interest. That is, investors will not pay $1,000 for a Jordan Corporation bond and get $110 interest per year if they could receive 12 percent, or $120, annually from an alternative investment considered to have the same risk. In contrast, if other investments of similar risk are selling to yield 10 percent, investors will bid up the price of the Jordan Corporation bonds until a price is reached that will yield the market rate of 10 percent. Thus, the market price of a bond is determined by the prevailing market rate of interest for comparable alternative investments. Because the stated rate is fixed, an adjustment to the price of the bond is necessary to bring the yield on the bonds in line with the prevailing market rate of interest.

The issuer generally establishes a stated rate of interest approximately equal to the market rate on the date the bonds are to be issued. However, to allow sufficient time for printing the certificates, drafting a security agreement, and obtaining the necessary approvals, the stated rate must be determined in advance of the issue date. Because the market rate fluctuates daily, sometimes widely over a short period of time, the issue price is often not equal to par value and the bonds will be issued at a discount or a premium.

HOW IS THE ISSUE PRICE OF A BOND DETERMINED?

(The illustrations in this section are dependent on your understanding of present value concepts presented in the Appendix to this chapter.)

To illustrate how the issue price of a bond is determined, assume that the Jordan Corporation 11%, five-year bonds were issued when the market rate of interest was 12% (6% per semiannual period). Jordan Corporation will pay $1,000 per bond five years later when the bonds mature, and an interest payment of $55 every six months for the next five years. To determine an issue price that will yield a return of 12% to an investor, the two separate cash flows—principal and interest payments—are discounted using the market rate of interest as shown below:

Present value of $1,000 due after 10 semiannual periods at 6%:
$1,000 × .5584 (Table 3, page 698)   = $558.40
Present value of $55 payable semiannually for 10 periods at 6%:
$55 × 7.3601 (Table 4, page 700)   =   404.80
Present value of future cash flows discounted at 6% $963.20

Because the market rate of interest is higher than the fixed stated rate, the bond issue will sell at a discount. An investor paying $963.20 for a bond and holding it until maturity will earn a return of 12% on the bonds.

After the bonds are issued, the market price of the bonds will fluctuate with changes in the market rate of interest. Given a market rate of interest, the desired market price of the bonds can be determined by using essentially the same procedures shown above.

To illustrate the computation of the bond price when the bonds are issued at a premium, assume that the market rate of interest was 10% when the bonds were issued. The issue price per bond is computed as follows:

Present value of $1,000 due after 10 semiannual periods at 5%:
  $1,000 × .6139 (Table 3, page 698)   = $ 613.90
Present value of $55 payable semiannually for 10 periods at 5%:
  $55 × 7.7217 (Table 4, page 700)   =   424.70
Present value of the future cash flows discounted at 5%   = $1,038.60

The bonds will be issued for a premium because the market rate of interest is lower than the stated rate.

Note that bond prices move in an opposite direction to the market rate of interest. If the market rate of interest increases, the price of a bond will decline. Conversely, if the market rate of interest decreases, the price of a bond will increase. These relationships are summarized in the following schedule.

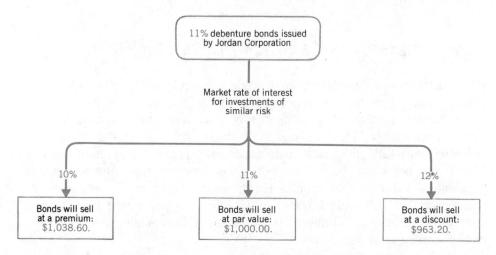

ACCOUNTING FOR BONDS ISSUED AT A DISCOUNT

To illustrate accounting for bonds issued at a discount, assume that Jordan Corporation issued its $100,000, 11%, five-year bonds on June 30 for $96,320 to yield the prevailing market rate of interest of 12%. The issuance of the bonds is recorded as follows:

June	30	Cash	96,320	
		Discount on Bonds Payable	3,680	
		Bonds Payable		100,000
		Issued 11%, 5-year bonds at a discount.		

In a balance sheet prepared immediately after the bonds were issued, the bonds would be reported in this manner:

Long-term Liabilities:
    11% Bonds Payable, due 6/30/1989 $100,000
  Less: Unamortized Discount on Bonds Payable   3,680 $96,320

The discount is deducted from the Bonds Payable account to show the **carrying value** of the debt. On the date of issuance, the carrying value is equal to the amount borrowed. In subsequent periods, the debit balance in the discount account is amortized (allocated to interest expense) over the life of the bonds, which results in a gradual increase in the carrying value from period to period. When the bonds mature, the discount will be fully amortized and the carrying value of the bonds will equal their par value.

AMORTIZING THE BOND DISCOUNT

Because the par value, rather than the amount received, must be paid to the bondholders at the maturity date, the discount is an increased cost to the firm. The total cost for using the borrowed funds is computed as follows:

Cash to be paid to the bondholders:
  Principal at maturity $100,000
  Interest payments ($100,000 × 11% × 5 years)   55,000
Total cash paid $155,000
Cash received when the bonds were issued   96,320
Total interest cost $ 58,680

As can be seen, the total interest cost is the difference between the amount borrowed ($96,320) from the bondholders and the amount paid back to them ($155,000). The total interest cost consists of the discount of $3,680 paid when the bonds mature plus the $55,000 total cash interest payments. In other words, the amount of cash received when the bonds were issued ($96,320) is less than the cash to be paid back at maturity ($100,000) by the amount of the discount ($3,680). Therefore, the company must pay back $3,680 more than was borrowed in addition to the 10 semiannual interest payments that total $55,000. Although the discount is not paid until the bonds mature, it is allocated (called *amortization*) over the life of the bonds because each period benefits from the use of the money. Thus the amount of the discount increases the cost of borrowing, and as shown later, amortization of the discount results in an interest expense each period that is greater than the semiannual cash payment. The effect of the discount is to increase the stated rate of interest of 11% to the effective rate of 12% desired by the investors.

Two methods may be used to amortize a discount or premium, the *straight-line method* and the *effective-interest method*. The straight-line method of amortization is easier to apply and is often used in practice. However, as will be discussed in the next section, the method is conceptually deficient. Although the effective-interest method (described in a later section of the chapter) is theoretically preferred, a discount or premium may be amortized using the straight-line method if the results obtained from using the method are not materially different from those that would be obtained if the effective-interest method were used.

Straight-line Method of Amortization

The straight-line method allocates an equal amount of the discount to bond interest expense in each interest period. In our illustration, the discount of $3,680 is amortized over 10 six-month periods, which is $368 per period. The entry to record the first semiannual interest payment is:[2]

Dec.	31	Bond Interest Expense	5,868[3]	
		Discount on Bonds Payable		368
		Cash ($100,000 × 11% × 6/12)		5,500
		Paid semiannual interest and amortized		
		discount on 11%, 5-year bonds.		

[2]In this chapter, one compound journal entry is made to amortize any discount or premium on bonds payable. However, it is sometimes easier to see the effects of amortization on the accounts if two entries are made: (1) to record the payment of interest and (2) to record the amortization of the discount or premium. For this illustration, these entries are as follows:

Dec.	31	Bond Interest Expense	5,500	
		Cash		5,500
		To record the payment of semiannual interest.		
Dec.	31	Bond Interest Expense	368	
		Discount on Bonds Payable		368
		To record the amortization of discount.		

Both the compound journal entry and the two entries above are considered acceptable alternatives.

[3]When the straight-line method of amortization is used, the bond interest expense can be verified by dividing the total interest cost of $58,680 by the 10 semiannual interest periods.

Notice that interest expense of $5,868 is reported although cash of only $5,500 is paid. The added expense of $368 does not involve cash until the par value is paid when the bonds mature. The bonds payable and discount accounts will appear as follows after the December 31 entry is posted:

Bonds Payable			Discount on Bonds Payable			
	6/30	100,000	6/30	3,680	12/31	368
			12/31 Bal.	3,312		

The credit of $368 to the contra-liability account, Discount on Bonds Payable, results in an increase of $368 in the carrying value of the bonds. The bonds would be reported as follows in the December 31 balance sheet:

Long-term Liabilities:

11% Bonds Payable, due 6/30/1989	$100,000	
Less: Unamortized Discount on Bonds Payable		
($3,680 − $368)	3,312	$96,688

In each subsequent interest period, the carrying value will increase $368 as the discount is amortized. When the bonds mature, the carrying value will be equal to the par value of $100,000.

When the straight-line method is used, total interest cost is allocated equally to each period over the life of the bonds. Because the carrying value is increasing each period, interest expense as a percentage of the carrying value of the debt will decrease over time. Conversely, the straight-line amortization of a bond premium will result in a decreasing carrying value for the bonds, and interest as a percentage of carrying value will increase. Since the effective rate of interest is a fixed rate, use of the straight-line method distorts the actual cost of borrowing. For this reason, the APB and its successor the FASB support the use of the effective interest method of amortization. Although the effective interest method is required, the straight-line method of amortization is permitted "if the results obtained are not materially different from those which would result from the 'interest method.' "[4]

ACCOUNTING FOR BONDS ISSUED AT A PREMIUM

Bonds will sell at a premium if the stated rate of interest on the bonds is greater than the prevailing market rate of interest at the time of issue. For example, as shown earlier, the 11%, five-year bonds of the Jordan Corporation

---

[4]"Interest on Receivables and Payables," *Opinion of the Accounting Principles Board No. 21* (New York: AICPA, 1971), par. 15.

will sell for $103,860 if the market rate of interest is 10% at the time of issue. The entry to record the sale on June 30 is:

June	30	Cash	103,860	
		Premium on Bonds Payable		3,860
		Bonds Payable		100,000
		Issued 11%, 5-year bonds at a premium.		

The bonds would be shown in a balance sheet prepared immediately after their issue as:

Long-term Liabilities:
11% Bonds Payable, due 6/30/1989	$100,000	
Add: Unamortized Premium on Bonds Payable	3,860	$103,860

Both the unamortized bond premium and bonds payable accounts have a credit balance, so they are added together to derive the carrying value of the debt. In subsequent periods, the premium is allocated over the life of the bonds as a reduction in interest expense to reflect the fact that the actual rate of borrowing is less than the stated rate. By the time the bonds mature, the premium account will be reduced to a zero balance, leaving a carrying value of $100,000— the amount due the bondholders.

AMORTIZING THE BOND PREMIUM

Because the bonds were issued at a premium, the cost of borrowing is $51,140, as computed below:

Cash to be paid the bondholders:		
Principal at maturity	$100,000	
Interest payments ($100,000 × 11% × 5 years)	55,000	
Total cash paid to bondholders		$155,000
Cash received when the bonds were issued		103,860
Total interest cost		$ 51,140

The total interest cost is equal to the sum of the periodic interest payments less the amount of the premium. That is to say, the amount of cash received when the bonds were issued ($103,860) is greater than the amount to be paid back at maturity ($100,000) by the amount of the premium ($3,860). The premium received over the cash to be paid back reduces the total cost of borrowing and is amortized over the life of the bonds because each period benefits from the lower interest cost. Amortization of the premium results in an interest expense each period that is less than the semiannual cash payment.

The bond premium may be amortized using the straight-line method of amortization or the effective interest method of amortization, although the latter is preferred conceptually, as mentioned earlier with bond discount amortization.

Straight-line Method of Amortization

If the straight-line method is used to amortize a premium, an equal amount is amortized as a reduction in interest expense each period. Thus amortization per period is $386 ($3,860 ÷ 10 interest periods). The entry to record the first interest payment on December 31 is:[5]

Dec.	31	Bond Interest Expense	5,114	
		Premium on Bonds Payable	386	
		Cash		5,500
		Paid semiannual interest and amortized the premium on 11%, 5-year bonds.		

This entry is the same in each interest period. Note that the interest expense is less than the cash payment by the amount of the premium amortization. The interest expense is lower because the actual cost of borrowing (10%) is less than the 11% stated rate. However, interest expense reported each period as a percentage of the bond carrying value does not portray the actual effective rate of interest incurred by the firm.

After the December 31 entry is posted, the Bonds Payable and Premium on Bonds Payable accounts will appear as follows:

Bonds Payable		Premium on Bonds Payable			
6/30	100,000	12/31	386	6/30	3,860
				12/31 Bal.	3,474

These accounts will be reported in the December 31 balance sheet as shown below:

Long-term Liabilities:
11% bonds payable, due 6/30/1989 $100,000
Add: Unamortized premium on bonds payable   3,474 $103,474

[5]The payment and amortization may be recorded by making two entries as follows:

Dec.	31	Bond Interest Expense	5,500	
		Cash		5,500
		To record the payment of semiannual interest.		
Dec.	31	Premium on Bonds Payable	386	
		Bond Interest Expense		386
		To record the amortization of premium.		

Note that the carrying value of $103,474 is $386 less than the carrying value of $103,860 on June 30, the date of issue. In each subsequent interest period, the carrying value will decrease $386 until the bonds mature, at which time the carrying value will be equal to the par value of the bonds.

ADDITIONAL PROBLEMS RELATED TO ACCOUNTING FOR BONDS PAYABLE

Accounting for bonds is a complex topic. In order to focus on the basic issues of accounting for bonds payable, it was assumed in the previous section of this chapter that bonds were sold on their issue date, an interest-payment date coincided with the fiscal year-end, the straight-line method of amortization was used, and the bonds were held to maturity. Accounting for a bond issue when these assumptions do not hold is discussed and illustrated in this section of the chapter, along with several other related issues. These topics are:

1. Accounting for bonds issued between interest-payment dates.
2. Year-end adjusting entry for bond interest expense.
3. Retirement of bonds before maturity.
4. Conversion of bonds into common stock.
5. Accounting for a bond sinking fund.
6. The interest-rate method of amortization.

BONDS ISSUED BETWEEN INTEREST-PAYMENT DATES

In the above example, the bonds were issued on an interest-payment date and were outstanding a full six months before the first semiannual interest payment was made. However, bonds are frequently issued between interest-payment dates. In such cases, the buyer must pay the issuing company the interest accrued from the interest payment date to the date of issue plus the issue price of the bonds. On the first interest-payment date, a full six months' interest is paid on the bonds outstanding regardless of when the bonds were issued. Thus in the first payment, the accrued interest collected from the buyer is returned along with the payment for the interest accrued after the date of issue. If the firm did not collect accrued interest at the time of issue, it would be necessary to maintain a record of each bondholder and the date the bonds were issued. At the first interest payment date, interest due each bondholder would have to be computed separately—resulting in increased recordkeeping costs.

If a bond is later sold by an investor, the buyer must pay the seller accrued interest from the last payment date to the sales date. The holder of the bond then receives a full six months' interest on the next interest-payment date.

To illustrate, assume that the Jordan Corporation bonds dated June 30 were issued on September 30 at par value plus three months' accrued interest. The entry to record the issue is:

Sept.	30	Cash	102,750	
		Bonds Payable		100,000
		Bond Interest Expense		2,750
		Issued 11%, 5-year bonds at par value plus accrued interest for 3 months ($100,000 × 11% × 3/12).		

Note that the credit of $2,750 for the accrued interest is made to the Bond Interest Expense account. Although the credit balance represents a liability at this time, a credit to an expense account avoids the need to split the first interest payment between a liability and the expense portion that accrues after the date of issue.

On December 31, the first semiannual interest payment date, a full six months' interest is paid to the bondholders even though the bonds were not issued until September 30. The entry is:

Dec.	31	Bond Interest Expense	5,500	
		Cash		5,500
		Paid semiannual interest on 11% bonds.		

After these two entries are posted, the Bond Interest Expense account in T account format would appear as follows:

Bond Interest Expense

12/31 (Interest Payment)	5,500	9/30 (Accrued Interest)	2,750
Balance	2,750		

The balance in the account is the proper amount of interest expense for the three-month period the bonds were outstanding ($100,000 × 11% × 3/12 = $2,750).

YEAR-END ADJUSTING ENTRY FOR BOND INTEREST EXPENSE

A company's fiscal year-end often does not correspond with an interest-payment date. In such cases, an adjusting entry must be made at year-end to record the interest accrued on the bonds and to amortize any discount or premium from the last interest-payment date to the fiscal year-end. For example, Jordan Corporation's 11%, five-year bonds were issued for $103,860 on June 30, 1984, in a preceding illustration. Interest is paid on June 30 and December 31. The entry to record the first interest payment on December 31, 1984, is:

Dec.	31	Bond Interest Expense	5,114	
		Premium on Bonds Payable	386	
		Cash		5,500
		Paid semiannual interest and amortize the		
		premium on 11%, 5-year bonds.		

If Jordan has a January 31 fiscal year-end, the following adjusting entry must be made on January 31, 1985, to accrue one month's interest and to amortize one month's bond premium.

1985				
Jan.	31	Bond Interest Expense	853	
		Premium on Bonds Payable	64	
		Accrued Bond Interest Payable		917
		To accrue interest and amortize premium		
		for one month on 11% bonds. ($100,000		
		× 11% × 1/12 = $917; premium		
		amortization for 6 months of $386 ÷ 6 =		
		$64)		

On January 31, 1985, the Bond Interest Expense account would appear as follows:

Bond Interest Expense

1984			
12/31	5,114		
1985			
1/31	853		
1/31 Bal.	5,967		

When interest is paid on June 30, the following entry is made:

June	30	Bond Interest Expense	4,261	
		Premium on Bonds Payable ($386 − $64)	322	
		Accrued Bond Interest Payable	917	
		Cash		5,500
		Paid semiannual interest, a portion of which		
		was accrued at fiscal year-end, and		
		amortized premium for 5 months on 11%		
		bonds.		

In this entry, the interest expense and premium amortization for the remaining five months is recorded and the accrued liability recorded at January 31 is satisfied. If bonds are issued at a discount, the accrual of interest and amortization of the discount is recorded in a similar manner.

RETIREMENT OF BONDS BEFORE MATURITY

As mentioned earlier, most bond issues are callable by the issuing company if it pays a specified price to the bondholders. Bonds are made callable to enable the company to retire the bonds and issue new ones at a lower effective interest rate. Bonds may also be retired by purchasing them on the open market.

In accounting for the early retirement of bonds, a material difference between the price paid and the bond's carrying value is reported separately in the income statement as an extraordinary gain or loss.[6] An extraordinary gain results if the purchase price of the bonds is less than their carrying value, and an extraordinary loss is incurred if the purchase price is greater than carrying value. To illustrate, assume that the $100,000 Jordan Corporation bonds issued for $103,860 contained a provision that the bonds could be called at 104 on any interest date after June 30, 1986. The company exercised its call option on July 1, 1987, when the unamortized bond premium was $1,544. The entry is:

1987					
July	1	Bonds Payable		100,000	
		Premium on Bond Payable		1,544	
		Extraordinary Loss on Retirement of Bonds		2,456	
		Cash ($100,000 × 104%)			104,000

A gain would result if the company were able to purchase the bonds for a price less than the carrying value of $101,544.

CONVERSION OF BONDS INTO COMMON STOCK

A bond may be convertible into common stock of the issuing company at the option of the bondholder if provided for in the bond indenture. The terms of conversion, such as the conversion ratio (the number of shares received for each bond converted) and the conversion period or dates, are specified in the bond agreement. Convertible bonds are popular because they offer advantages to both issuer and investor. From the point of view of the investor, a convertible bond provides a fixed rate of return and the security of being a creditor of the firm, but at the same time the investor retains the option of converting the bonds into common stock should conversion become attractive. The conversion option also gives the investor the opportunity to benefit from the price appreciation of the common stock because the price of a convertible bond will

[6]"Reporting Gains and Losses from Extinguishment of Debt," *Statement of Financial Accounting Standards No. 4* (Stamford, Conn.: FASB, 1975), par. 8.

increase with increases in the market price of the underlying common stock. An advantage to the issuing company is that the effective rate of interest is generally lower for convertible bonds than for nonconvertible bonds.

Up to the date of conversion, convertible bonds are accounted for in the same way as debenture bonds. If the bonds are converted, the carrying value of the debt is transferred to contributed capital accounts. For example, assume that each of the $1,000 Jordan Corporation bonds is convertible into 30 shares of $10 par value common stock. One-half of the bondholders elect to convert their bonds after the interest payment has been made on June 30, 1987. The entry for the conversion is:

1987					
June	30	Bonds Payable ($100,000 × 50%)		50,000	
		Premium on Bonds Payable		772	
		($1,544 × 50%)			
		Common Stock—$10 par value			15,000*
		Contributed Capital in Excess of Par			35,772
		*30 shares × 50 bonds = 1,500 shares ×			
		$10 = $15,000			

Note that there is no gain or loss recognized on the transaction. The essence of this entry is to recognize the carrying value of the debt as the payment for the stock. Accordingly, the excess of the carrying value of the bonds ($50,772) over the par value of the common stock ($15,000) is credited to Contributed Capital in Excess of Par.

BOND SINKING FUND

When bonds mature, the issuing company must have sufficient cash available to pay their maturity value. Bond indentures often provide that periodic deposits must be made to a **bond sinking fund** during the life of the bonds. In other cases, management may decide to make voluntary deposits to accumulate the cash needed at the maturity date. Sinking fund deposits are usually made to a trustee, who invests the cash in income-earning securities. The periodic deposits, plus the earnings on the investments, accumulate until the bonds mature, at which time the trustee sells the investments and uses the proceeds to retire the bonds. Any deficiency in the fund is made up by an additional deposit by the issuing company. If there is an excess of cash in the fund, it is returned to the issuing company.

The amount of each periodic deposit will depend on the rate of return earned from the investments. For example, assume that on January 1, 1984, Grant Corporation issued $1,000,000 of five-year bonds and agreed to deposit with a trustee at the end of each year for the next five years $200,000 less the earnings made on the fund investments during the year. The initial deposit is recorded as follows:

1984 Dec.	31	Bond Sinking Fund	200,000	
		Cash		200,000
		Made annual deposit to sinking fund.		

Although the assets in the sinking fund are physically held by the trustee, they are still the property of Grant Corporation. The Bond Sinking Fund account is reported in Grant Corporation's balance sheet as a long-term investment because the funds are not available for use in current operations.

The trustee will report the earnings on the investments each period to Grant Corporation. The entries at the end of 1985, assuming that earnings of $18,000 were reported by the trustee, are:

1985 Dec.	31	Bond Sinking Fund	18,000	
		Sinking Fund Revenue		18,000
		To record revenue earned from sinking fund investments.		
	31	Bond Sinking Fund	182,000	
		Cash		182,000
		Made annual deposit to sinking fund.		

Revenue earned from sinking fund investments is reported in the income statement in the Other Revenue section.

Similar entries are made at the end of each year for the remainder of the accumulation period. As the maturity date approaches, the trustee will sell the investments and will inform the company of any final deposit required to bring the accumulated balance up to the $1,000,000 needed to retire the debt. The entry to record the bond retirement is:

1989 Jan.	1	Bonds Payable	1,000,000	
		Bond Sinking Fund		1,000,000
		To record the payment of bonds at maturity.		

EFFECTIVE-INTEREST METHOD OF AMORTIZATION

As noted earlier, the effective-interest method is the preferred method for computing interest expense. However, the straight-line method is considered an acceptable alternative when the difference between the amortization amounts computed with both methods is not material. In order to contrast the two methods, the same data used earlier to illustrate the straight-line method of amortizing a discount or premium will now be used to illustrate the effective-interest method.

Amortization of a Discount: Effective-Interest Method

The following facts are assumed for the bond issue of Jordan Corporation.

Date of issue	June 30, 1984
Par value	$100,000
Stated rate of interest	11%
Interest payment dates	June 30, December 31
Term to maturity	5 years
Market rate of interest	12%
Issue price to yield 12%	$96,320

The journal entry to record the bond issue is:

1984					
June	30	Cash		96,320	
		Discount on Bonds Payable		3,680	
		Bonds Payable			100,000

Under the effective-interest method, interest expense for each period is computed by multiplying the carrying value of the bonds at the beginning of the period by the effective interest rate per period. The amount of the discount amortized each period is the difference between interest expense and the semi-annual interest payment. A discount amortization table for the Jordan Corporation bonds is presented in Figure 17-3. Amounts have been rounded to the nearest dollar.

Since the bonds were sold to yield 12% annually, the semiannual effective interest rate is 6%. The interest expense to be recorded each period is computed by multiplying the beginning carrying value (Column A) by 6%. During the first period, interest expense is $5,779 but only $5,500 was paid to the bond-holders. The difference of $279 is the amount of the discount amortization for the period. The entry to record the payment and discount amortization is:

Dec.	31	Bond Interest Expense		5,779	
		Discount on Bonds Payable			279
		Cash			5,500

In period two, interest expense is 6% times the net liability of $96,599, or $5,796. Because the liability increased during the first period, the interest cost

	(A)	(B)	(C)	(D)	(E)	(F)	(G)
Semiannual Interest Periods	Carrying Value Beginning of Period (Col. G for previous period)	Effective Semiannual Interest Expense (Col. A × 6%)	Semiannual Cash Payment ($100,000 × 5½%)	Discount Amortization (Col. B – Col. C)	Par Value	Bond Discount Balance (Col. F for previous period – Col. D)	Carrying Value—End of Period (Col. E – Col. F)
6/30/84					$100,000	$3,680	$ 96,320
12/31/84	$96,320	$ 5,779	$ 5,500	$ 279	100,000	3,401	96,599
6/30/85	96,599	5,796	5,500	296	100,000	3,105	96,895
12/31/85	96,895	5,814	5,500	314	100,000	2,791	97,209
6/30/86	97,209	5,832	5,500	332	100,000	2,459	97,541
12/31/86	97,541	5,852	5,500	352	100,000	2,107	97,893
6/30/87	97,893	5,874	5,500	374	100,000	1,733	98,267
12/31/87	98,267	5,896	5,500	396	100,000	1,337	98,663
6/30/88	98,663	5,920	5,500	420	100,000	917	99,083
12/31/88	99,083	5,945	5,500	445	100,000	472	99,528
6/30/89	99,528	5,972*	5,500	472	100,000	—	100,000
Totals		$58,680	$55,000	$3,680			

*In the last period, interest expense is equal to the semiannual interest paid plus the remaining balance in the bond discount column ($5,500 + $472 = $5,972). The carrying value at the beginning of the tenth interest period times 6% may not exactly equal this amount due to the accumulated effects of rounding errors.

Figure 17-3
Amortization Table for Bonds Issued at a Discount—Effective-Interest Amortization

is greater in the second period. In subsequent periods, the interest expense increases as the carrying value increases.

Note that interest expense (Column B) as a percentage of the beginning carrying value (Column A) is a constant 6% each period. Although the bond indenture requires a semiannual interest payment of $5,500, the interest expense reported each period reflects the effective interest rate incurred by the firm.

Amortization of a Premium: Effective-interest Method

To illustrate the amortization of a bond premium, we assume that the Jordan Corporation bonds were issued for $103,860 to yield an effective annual interest rate of 10%, 5% per semiannual period. A premium amortization table for the Jordan Corporation bonds under the effective-interest method is presented in Figure 17-4. The computations are based on the same concepts discussed earlier for the amortization of a discount. Observe, however, that the amount of premium amortized each period decreases interest expense. Interest expense reported each period is the effective semiannual rate of 5% times the carrying value at the beginning of the period.

Semiannual Interest Period	(A) Carrying Value Beginning of Period (Col. G for previous period)	(B) Effective Semiannual Interest Expense (Col. A × 5%)	(C) Semiannual Cash Payment ($100,000 × 5½%)	(D) Premium Amortization (Col. B − Col. C)	(E) Par Value	(F) Bond Premium Balance (Col. F for previous period − Col. D)	(G) Carrying Value—End of period (Col. E + Col. F.)
6/30/84					$100,000	$3,860	$103,860
12/31/84	$103,860	$ 5,193	$ 5,500	$ 307	100,000	3,553	103,553
6/30/85	103,553	5,178	5,500	322	100,000	3,231	103,231
12/31/85	103,231	5,162	5,500	338	100,000	2,893	102,893
6/30/86	102,893	5,145	5,500	355	100,000	2,538	102,538
12/31/86	102,538	5,127	5,500	373	100,000	2,165	102,165
6/30/87	102,165	5,108	5,500	392	100,000	1,773	101,773
12/31/87	101,773	5,089	5,500	411	100,000	1,362	101,362
6/30/88	101,362	5,068	5,500	432	100,000	930	100,930
12/31/88	100,930	5,047	5,500	453	100,000	477	100,477
6/30/89	100,477	5,023*	5,500	477	100,000	—	100,000
Totals		$51,140	$55,000	$3,860			

*In the last period, interest expense is equal to the semiannual interest paid less the remaining balance in the bond premium account ($5,500 − $477). The carrying value at the beginning of the tenth period times 5% may not exactly equal this amount due to the accumulated effects of rounding errors.

Figure 17-4
Amortization Table for Bonds Issued at a Premium—Effective-Interest Amortization

The first interest payment is recorded as follows:

Dec.	31	Bond Interest Expense	5,193	
		Premium on Bonds Payable	307	
		Cash		5,500
		Paid semiannual interest and amortized premium on 11%, 5-year bonds.		

Over the life of the bonds, the interest expense debit decreases with a corresponding increase in the debit to the premium account. This results because the carrying value of the bonds is decreasing each period as the premium is reduced through amortization.

OTHER LONG-TERM LIABILITIES

Usually a balance sheet will contain a number of different kinds of long-term liabilities other than bonds payable. In this section of the chapter, other common types of long-term liabilities are discussed. These are mortgage notes payable, lease obligations, and liabilities related to an employee pension plan.

MORTGAGE NOTES PAYABLE

A company may borrow money or finance the purchase of plant assets on credit by giving the lender or seller a promissory note secured by a legal document called a mortgage. The promissory note given is called a *mortgage note payable*. A **mortgage** is a lien on specific property of the borrower. If the debt is not paid, the mortgage holder may have the specific property sold and the proceeds applied to the debt.

Mortgage contracts generally require the borrower to make equal periodic payments that include both accrued interest and a reduction in principal. Each payment is applied first to the accrued interest; the remainder of the payment reduces the principal. As the principal balance declines over time, the portion of each payment assigned to interest decreases and the portion assigned to a reduction of principal increases.

To illustrate, assume that Midwest Airlines purchased a passenger airplane for $2,500,000 on September 1, 1984. Midwest gave the seller a 12% mortgage note that provided for a $252,250 down payment and 60 monthly payments of $50,000 each to begin on October 1, 1984. The division of the first five and last two monthly payments between interest and principal is shown in Figure 17-5. The entry to record the October 1 payment is:

Oct.	1	Interest Expense	22,478	
		Mortgage Note Payable	27,522	
		Cash		50,000
		Made the monthly mortgage payment.		

For reporting purposes, the part of the unpaid principal balance to be paid during the next year should be classified as a current liability, with the balance of the principal classified as a long-term liability.

LEASE OBLIGATIONS

A **lease** is a rental agreement in which the lessor (the owner) conveys to the lessee the right to use property for a specified period of time in return for periodic rental payments. Many companies lease much of their equipment rather than purchasing it, for one or more of the following reasons:

1. Leasing permits 100% financing rather than making a substantial down payment as required in most credit purchases.
2. The full lease payment, even for land, is deductible for tax purposes.
3. Lease contracts may be more flexible and contain fewer restrictions than most debt agreements.
4. The risk of obsolescence is shifted to the lessor.

Because of these advantages, the use of leasing has grown rapidly in recent years. As a result, the accounting profession has devoted a great deal of effort

Monthly Payment Number	(A) Payment Date	(B) Unpaid Balance at Beginning of Month	(C) Cash Payment	(D) Interest for One Month (Col. B × 1%)	(E) Reduction in Principal (Col. C − Col. D)	(F) Principal Balance at End of Month
	1984					
	Sept. 1	$2,500,000	$252,250	$ —	$252,250	$2,247,750
1	Oct. 1	2,247,750	50,000	22,478	27,522	2,220,228
2	Nov. 1	2,220,228	50,000	22,202	27,798	2,192,430
3	Dec. 1	2,192,430	50,000	21,924	28,076	2,164,354
	1985					
4	Jan. 1	2,164,354	50,000	21,644	28,356	2,135,998
5	Feb. 1	2,135,998	50,000	21,360	28,640	2,107,358
	1990					
59	Aug. 1	98,520	50,000	985	49,015	49,505
60	Sept. 1	49,505	50,000	495	49,505	–0–

Figure 17-5
Monthly Payment Schedule

to the establishment of accounting standards for lease reporting.

For accounting purposes, leases are of two types: capital leases and operating leases. Leases that transfer substantially all the benefits and risks of ownership to the lessee are installment purchases in substance and are called capital leases. Because the provisions contained in lease contracts vary widely, the FASB established four criteria to be applied in assessing whether a particular lease contract is in substance an installment purchase of property. A lease is classified as a capital lease if it is noncancelable and meets one or more of these four criteria:

1. The lease transfers ownership of the property to the lessee by the end of the lease term.
2. The lease permits the lessee to acquire the property at the end of the lease for a bargain price.
3. The length of the lease (lease term) is equal to 75% or more of the estimated economic life of the leased property.
4. The present value of the lease payments at the beginning of the lease term equals or exceeds 90% of the fair value of the leased property.[7]

To illustrate, assume that a major airline entered into an equipment lease to acquire its airplanes. The lease has a fixed noncancelable term of eight years and transfers ownership of the airplanes to the airline at the end of the lease

[7]"Accounting for Leases," *Statement of Financial Accounting Standards No. 13* (Stamford, Conn.: FASB, 1976), par. 7.

term. The estimated economic life of the airplanes is 10 years. Because the lease satisfies criteria one and three, the airline would account for the lease as a capital lease.

Capital leases are accounted for as if they were installment purchases. Accounting by the lessee is similar to that described earlier for a mortgage note payable. The lessee records the leased property as a plant asset and credits a long-term liability for the future lease payments. The asset and liability are recorded at an amount equal to the present value of the future lease payments. Part of each lease payment is recorded as interest expense, and the remainder is a reduction in the principal balance. In addition, the leased asset is depreciated over the period that it is expected to be used.

Leases that do not meet at least one of the four criteria for a capital lease are classified as operating leases. Operating leases are generally short-term or cancelable, and the lessor retains the usual risks and rewards of ownership. For example, a company that leases delivery trucks on a weekly basis during its peak demand periods, would account for the truck lease as an operating lease. The periodic lease payments are accounted for by the lessee as an expense. The leased property is not recorded as an asset, and the related obligation to make the lease payments is not recognized in the accounts. However, if the amounts involved are significant, the minimum future rental payments for each of the next five years and the total rental expense included in each income statement presented must be disclosed in a footnote.

PENSION PLANS

Most firms have pension plans to provide payments to eligible employees when they retire. The company normally appoints a trustee such as an insurance company to administer the plan and satisfies its pension obligation by making regular payments to the trustee. The trustee then invests the funds and uses the fund earnings and contributions to pay benefits to retired employees. This type of plan is called a funded plan.

The amount to be paid into the fund is determined jointly by the policies of the company, the trustee, and the provisions of the Pension Reform Act of 1974. Measurement of the pension expense is complex and beyond the scope of our coverage here. However, the amount reported as expense in the income statement is determined independently of the cash contribution. Payments to the pension funds are recorded by a debit to Pension Expense and a credit to Cash. If payments to the pension fund are equal to the pension expense computed each period, a liability will not appear in the balance sheet. A liability will arise, however, if payments to the fund are less than the pension expense recognized. Therefore, the liability that often appears in the balance sheet represents the accumulated excess of pension expense over the cash paid into the pension fund.

GLOSSARY

BOND (BOND PAYABLE). A certificate containing a written promise to pay the principal amount at a specified time plus interest on the principal at a specified rate per period (p. 650, 652).

BOND SINKING FUND. An investment fund established to provide for the retirement of bonds (p. 668).

CALLABLE BOND. A bond that may be purchased at the option of the issuing company for a specified price before the bond matures (p. 654).

CAPITAL LEASE. A lease that is in substance an installment purchase of property (p. 674).

CARRYING VALUE OF BONDS. The par value of a bond issue less any unamortized discount or plus any unamortized premium (p. 659).

COLLATERAL. Something of value that is acceptable to a lender as security for a loan (p. 650).

CONVERTIBLE BOND. A bond that may be converted into some other security of the issuing company (p. 654).

COUPON RATE (NOMINAL OR STATED RATE). The interest rate stated as a percentage of par value and used to determine the amount paid periodically to the bondholder (p. 653).

COUPON (BEARER) BOND. A bond that has a printed interest coupon attached for each interest-payment date. Title is assumed to be with the holder of the bond (p. 654).

DEBENTURE BOND (UNSECURED BOND). A bond backed only by the general credit rating of the company (p. 653).

DISCOUNT. The excess of the par value of a bond over its issue price (p. 653).

FUNDED PLAN. A pension plan in which deposits are made to an outside agency appointed to manage the fund (p. 675).

INDENTURE. The terms of a bond agreement (p. 652).

LEASE. A rental agreement in which the lessor conveys to the lessee the right to use property for a specified period of time in return for periodic rental payments (p. 673).

LEVERAGE. The use of borrowed funds that have a fixed cost to earn a higher rate of return for the purpose of increasing the earnings of the owners (p. 650).

MARKET RATE (EFFECTIVE RATE, YIELD RATE). Actual rate of interest an investor will earn if bonds are purchased at a certain price and held to maturity (p. 656).

MATURITY DATE. The date on which the borrower must pay the par value of a note (p. 652).

MORTGAGE. A legal document setting forth the specific assets serving as collateral for a loan (p. 673).

MORTGAGE NOTE PAYABLE. A form of a promissory note in which specific property of the borrower serves as collateral for a loan (p. 650).

OPERATING LEASE.   A lease that is not a capital lease. In an operating lease, the lessor retains the risks and rewards of ownership (p. 675).

PAR VALUE (FACE VALUE, PRINCIPAL, MATURITY VALUE).   The amount due to a lender when a debt matures (p. 652).

PENSION PLAN.   A plan established to provide payments to eligible employees when they retire (p. 675).

PREMIUM.   The excess of the issue price of a bond over its par value (p. 653).

REGISTERED BOND.   A bond whose owner's name is on file with the issuing firm (p. 653).

SECURED (MORTGAGE) BOND.   A bond secured by a prior claim against specific property of the issuing company (p. 653).

SERIAL BONDS.   A bond issue that matures in installments (p. 654).

TERM BONDS (ORDINARY BONDS).   A bond issue in which all of the bonds mature on one date (p. 654).

TRUSTEE.   A third party appointed to represent the bondholders (p. 653).

UNDERWRITER.   An investment firm that markets a bond issue (p. 653).

UNSECURED NOTE PAYABLE.   A promissory note backed by a legal claim against the general assets of the borrower (p. 649).

DISCUSSION QUESTIONS

1. What are the advantages and disadvantages of debt financing rather than equity financing?
2. ABC Company issued $1,000,000 of bonds on an interest-payment date. What amount of cash was received from the sale, assuming the bonds sold at (a) 100, (b) 97¼, and (c) 102?
3. Differentiate between the following bond terms: (a) secured and debenture, (b) registered and coupon, and (c) term and serial.
4. A corporation issued $500,000 of 7½% bonds at 96 ⅝ to yield 8%.
   (a) Were the bonds issued at a premium or at a discount?
   (b) What is the maturity value of the bonds?
   (c) What is the nominal (stated) rate of interest?
   (d) What is the effective rate of interest?
5. How do the market rate of interest and the stated rate of interest compare when a bond is sold at a discount?
6. The unamortized premium on a $1,000,000 bond issue is $340,500. What is the carrying value of the bonds?
7. Why must the buyer of a bond sold between interest-payment dates pay the seller accrued interest?
8. A company calls $500,000 of bonds at 101 when the discount account has a $21,000 balance.
   (a) What is the amount of the company's gain or loss?
   (b) What type of gain or loss is it?

9. What is the advantage to the issuing company of issuing convertible bonds?

10. (a) Where is the Bond Sinking Fund account classified on the balance sheet?
    (b) Where is the Bond Sinking Fund Revenue listed on the income statement?

11. Why does interest expense change each period when the effective-interest method of amortization is used?

12. What accounts are debited in an entry to record a payment on a mortgage note payable?

13. Differentiate between the journal entries to record a lease payment with a capital lease and with an operating lease.

14. When would a company have a credit balance in the Pension Fund Liability account?

EXERCISES

(For the exercises and problems in this chapter, round all computations to the nearest dollar.)

Exercise 17-1 (Alternative Financing Methods)

HIP Corporation has been very profitable in recent years and because of the increasing demand for its product is planning an expansion program. The program will require an investment of $2,000,000 and is expected to increase income before interest and taxes by $700,000. An income statement for the last fiscal period is presented below:

Revenues	$20,000,000
Costs and expenses	18,000,000
Interest expense	100,000
Income before income taxes	1,900,000
Income taxes (40%)	760,000
Net income	$ 1,140,000
Earnings per share	$1.14

Management is considering whether to finance the expansion by selling 200,000 shares at $10 per share or by issuing 14%, 20-year bonds at par value.

Required:

A. Assuming that the company maintains its current level of income and achieves the expected increase in income from the expansion, what will the earnings per share be for each of the alternative methods of financing?

B. Discuss the disadvantage(s) of the method that produces the highest earnings per share.

Exercise 17-2 (Computing Issue Price of Bonds and Recording the Issue)

On June 11, the Kona Corporation received authorization from its board of directors to issue $1,000,000 of 10%, 10-year bonds dated July 1. Interest is payable semi-annually on December 31 and June 30.

Required:

A. Compute the issue price of the bonds on July 1 for each of the following three cases:

1. The bonds are sold to yield 10%.
2. The bonds are sold to yield 12%.
3. The bonds are sold to yield 8%.

B. Record the issuance of the bonds for each case.

Exercise 17-3 (Straight-line Method of Amortization)

On July 1, 1984, Winfield Corporation issued $200,000, 9%, 10-year bonds. The bonds were dated July 1, 1984, and interest is payable each June 30 and December 31. Winfield Corporation's annual year-end is December 31, and because the difference between the two methods of amortization is not material, the company uses the straight-line method of amortization.

Required:

A. Prepare journal entries to record the issuance of the bonds and the payments of interest and the amortization of discount or premium on December 31, 1984, and June 30, 1985, assuming:

1. The bonds were issued at par.
2. The bonds were issued for $187,540.
3. The bonds were issued for $212,460.

B. Complete the following schedule as of December 31, 1984 after the December 31 interest payment had been recorded.

	Issue Price		
	$200,000	$187,540	$212,460
Bonds payable			
Unamortized discount			
Unamortized premium			
Carrying value of the bonds			
Change in carrying value from July 1			
Bond interest expense for 1984			
Cash payment for interest during 1984			
Discount or premium amortization during 1984			

Exercise 17-4 (Bonds Issued Between Interest Payment Dates)

The Banner Corporation issued $100,000 of 20-year, 10% bonds on May 1 at par value plus accrued interest. Interest is payable on February 1 and August 1. The corporation is a calendar-year firm.

Required:

Prepare general journal entries to record the following transactions:

A. Issuance of the bonds on May 1.
B. First interest payment on August 1.
C. Accrued interest on December 31.
D. The interest payment on February 1.

Exercise 17-5 (Accrual of Bond Interest)

On August 31, 1985, Hurst Company issued $500,000 of 8%, 15-year bonds for $480,000. Interest is payable on August 31 and February 28. The fiscal year of the company is the calendar year, and the company uses the straight-line method of amortization.

Required:

Prepare journal entries to record the following transactions:

A. Issue of the bonds on August 31, 1985.

B. Accrual of interest and amortization of the discount on December 31, 1985.

C. Payment of interest and amortization of discount on February 28, 1986.

Exercise 17-6 (Retirement of Bonds Before Maturity)

The Helms Company issued $1,000,000 of 12%, 10-year callable bonds on January 1, 1980, at 102. Interest is payable on June 30 and December 31, and the company uses the straight-line method of amortization.

Required:

A. Prepare the journal entry to record the interest payment and the amortization of the premium on June 30, 1984.

B. Prepare the entry to record the retirement of the bonds on July 1, 1984, at 103.

$900 \times 20 = 18,000$

Exercise 17-7 (Bond Conversion)

The Tracey Corporation has $900,000 of 11% convertible bonds outstanding. Each $1,000 bond is convertible into 20 shares of $20 par value common stock. On March 1, 1985, an interest-payment date, unamortized discount amounted to $9,000 after recording the current interest payment. On March 1, 1985, $400,000 of the bonds were converted.

Required:

Prepare the journal entry to record the conversion of the bonds.

Exercise 17-8 (Bond Sinking Fund)

On February 1, 1984, A & B Industrial Corporation issued $700,000 of 10-year bonds. The bond indenture requires that A & B deposit every January 29 for the next 10 years $70,000 less any earnings made on the fund investment during the year.

Required:

Prepare journal entries to record each of the following transactions:

A. The first deposit is made in the sinking fund on January 29, 1985.

B. On December 31, 1986, it is determined that the sinking fund investments earned $8,630 during the year.

C. The $700,000 accumulated in the sinking fund is used to retire the bonds on February 1, 1994.

Exercise 17-9 (Effective-interest Method of Amortization)

The Winfield Corporation issued $200,000 of 10-year, 9% bonds on July 1, 1984, for $187,540. Interest is payable on June 30 and December 31. The market rate of interest is 10%.

Required:

A. Prepare the journal entry to record the issue of the bonds on July 1, 1984.

B. Using the effective-interest method of amortization, prepare the general journal entries to record the payments of interest and the amortization of the discount or premium on the following dates: (1) December 31, 1984, (2) June 30, 1985, and (3) December 31, 1985.

C. Show how the bonds payable would be reported in the December 31, 1985, balance sheet.

D. How much bond interest expense is reported in the 1985 income statement?

E. How much cash was paid to the bondholders during 1985?

F. Explain why your answers to requirements (D) and (E) are different.

G. Prepare the journal entry to retire the bonds at the maturity date.

Exercise 17-10 (Effective-interest Method of Amortization)

Use the same information as given in Exercise 17-9 except that the bonds were issued for $213,590 to yield 8%.

Required:

Complete requirements (A) through (G) as given in Exercise 17-9.

Exercise 17-11 (Mortgage Notes Payable)

The Otter Corporation purchased a warehouse on May 1, 1985, for $350,000. Otter gave a down payment of $70,000 and signed a 9% mortgage note with monthly payments of $2,500.

Required:

A. Give the journal entry to record the first monthly payment on June 1, 1985.

B. Give the entry to record the payment on August 1, 1985.

PROBLEMS

Problem 17-1 (Computing Issue Price and Straight-line Method of Amortization)

On July 1, 1984, Wilcox Corporation issued $900,000 of 10-year bonds with a stated interest rate of 16%. The market rate of interest was 20% on that date. Semiannual interest is payable on June 30 and December 31. The company's fiscal year ends December 31.

Required:

A. Determine the issue price of the bonds.

B. Prepare a journal entry to record the issuance of the bonds.

C. Using the straight-line method, prepare journal entries to record bond interest expense and amortization on the first three interest payment dates.
D. Compute the carrying value of the bonds on January 1, 1986. Show how the bonds would be reported in the balance sheet.
E. Compute the total bond interest expense that would be reported in the 1985 income statement. How is the interest reported?
F. Prepare the journal entry to retire the bonds on their maturity date.

Problem 17-2 (Accrual of Interest and Bond Retirement Before Maturity)

The following transactions of the Eberhardt Corporation relate to its issuance of $2,000,000 of 14%, 20-year, callable bonds. Interest-payment dates are September 1 and March 1. The company's fiscal year is the calendar year, and it uses the straight-line method of amortization.

1. September 1, 1984. The bonds are issued for $2,300,000.
2. December 31, 1984. An adjusting entry is made to record accrued interest and to amortize a portion of the premium.
3. March 1, 1985. Interest is paid and a portion of the premium is amortized.
4. September 1, 1986. Interest is paid and a portion of the premium is amortized.
5. September 1, 1986. The company retires one-fourth of the bonds by calling them at 110.

Required:
Prepare general journal entries to record each of the transactions.

Problem 17-3 (Bond Transactions and Sinking Fund)

Blaine Corporation decided to issue $1,000,000 of 13%, five-year bonds. Interest is payable on June 30 and December 31. The fiscal year of the corporation ends June 30. The bond indenture requires Blaine Corporation to deposit $157,450 in a bond sinking fund at the end of every fiscal year during the life of the bonds. The sinking fund investments are expected to earn a 12% annual return each period. Some of the transactions relating to the bond issue and the sinking fund are listed below.

1. July 1, 1984. Sold the bond issue at 92¼.
2. December 31, 1984. Paid the semiannual interest and amortized the discount using the straight-line method.
3. June 30, 1985. Paid the interest on the bonds and amortized the discount.
4. June 30, 1985. Made the first sinking fund deposit.
5. June 30, 1986. Paid the interest on the bonds and amortized the discount.
6. June 30, 1987. Recorded the interest earned by the sinking fund investments during the fiscal year. The investments earned 12% as expected.
7. June 30, 1988. Made the fourth sinking fund deposit.
8. June 30, 1989. Retired the bonds and transferred the excess in the sinking fund to the cash account.

Required:
A. Prepare a table showing the interest earned by the sinking fund during the fiscal

year and the fund balance at June 30 for each of the five years during the life of the bonds.

B. Prepare journal entries to record the transactions shown above.

Problem 17-4 (Bonds Issued Between Interest-Payment Dates, Accrual of Interest, Bond Conversion, and Bond Retirement Before Maturity)

Raskin Company decided to issue $1,500,000 of 12%, 15-year, convertible bonds dated April 30, 1986. Each $5,000 bond is convertible into 200 shares of $10 par value common stock. Semiannual interest is due on April 30 and October 31. The fiscal year of the company is the calendar year and it uses the straight-line method to amortize bond discount and premium. Raskin Company completed the following transactions:

1. August 31, 1986. Issued the entire bond issue at a price of 100 plus accrued interest.
2. October 31, 1986. Paid the semiannual interest.
3. December 31, 1986. Recorded the accrued interest.
4. April 30, 1987. Paid the semiannual interest.
5. May 1, 1987. Bondholders converted $500,000 of the bonds.
6. October 31, 1987. Paid the semiannual interest on the bonds outstanding.

   Raskin Company then decided to issue $600,000 of 11%, 20-year, callable bonds dated December 31, 1986. Interest is payable on June 30 and December 31. The following transactions were completed:

7. December 31, 1986. Issued the entire issue at 98.
8. June 30, 1987. Paid the semiannual interest and amortized the discount.
9. December 31, 1987. Paid the semiannual interest and amortized the discount.
10. July 1, 1990. Called the bonds at 99½.

Required:
Prepare journal entries to record each of the transactions.

Problem 17-5 (Effective-interest Method of Amortization)
The Grovemont Corporation issued $600,000 of three-year bonds on February 1, 1985. Semiannual interest payments are due on January 31 and July 31. The fiscal year of the company ends July 31. The accountant prepared the following interest expense and amortization schedule.

Interest-Payment Date	Cash Paid	Interest Expense	Amount Amortized
July 31, 1985	$24,000	$26,304	$2,304
January 31, 1986	24,000	26,407	2,407
July 31, 1986	24,000	26,516	2,516
January 31, 1987	24,000	26,629	2,629
July 31, 1987	24,000	26,747	2,747
January 31, 1988	24,000	26,870	2,870

Required:
A. Determine the stated rate of interest.
B. Were the bonds sold at a discount or at a premium?
C. What method of amortization was used?
D. Determine the effective rate of interest.
E. Prepare the entry to record the sale of the bonds.
F. Prepare journal entries to record the interest payment and amortization on July 31, 1985, and on January 31, 1987.

Problem 17-6 (Effective-interest Method of Amortization)

On January 1, 1984, the GTX Corporation issued five-year, 10% bonds with a par value of $100,000. Interest is payable June 30 and December 31. The bonds were issued at a price to yield 8%.

Required:
A. Compute the issue price of the bonds.
B. Prepare journal entries to record the following transactions:
  1. January 1, 1984. All of the bonds were issued for cash.
  2. June 30, 1984. Paid the semiannual interest and amortized the premium or discount. (Use the effective-interest method to amortize the discount or premium.)
  3. December 31, 1984 (end of annual period). Paid the semiannual interest and amortized the premium or discount.
  4. June 30, 1985. Paid the semiannual interest and amortized the premium or discount.
  5. January 1, 1989. Paid the bonds at maturity.
C. Show how the bonds payable will be reported in the December 31, 1984 balance sheet.
D. Answer the following questions:
  1. What amount of bond interest expense is reported in 1984?
  2. Will the bond interest expense reported in 1985 be the same as, greater than, or less than the amount reported in 1984?
  3. Assuming the bonds are outstanding the full five-year period, what is the total bond interest expense to be recognized during the life of the bonds?
  4. Would the straight-line method of amortization result in the same amount, more than, or less than the bond interest expense reported in 1984 under the effective-interest method?
  5. If the straight-line method had been used, would the carrying value of the bonds be less than or greater than the carrying value computed in requirement (C) above?
  6. Would the total bond interest expense recognized over the life of the bonds using the straight-line method be the same as, greater than, or less than the amount computed in question (3)? Explain.

Problem 17-7 (Mortgage Notes Payable)

Yonkers, Incorporated, has decided to open another department store. It purchased a building and land for $3,300,000 on May 1, 1985, by giving a down payment of

$310,576 and signing a 16% mortgage note. The note provides for 80 quarterly payments of $125,000. The first quarterly payment was made on August 1, 1985. The company's fiscal year-end is December 31.

Required:
A. Prepare a quarterly payment schedule for payments made in 1985 and 1986. Head the columns with the following titles: Payment Date, Unpaid Balance at Beginning of Quarter, Cash Payment, Interest for One Quarter, Reduction in Principal, Principal Balance at End of Quarter.
B. Prepare journal entries to record the purchase of the land and building and the first three quarterly payments (80% of the purchase price is attributed to the building).
C. Show how the unpaid mortgage note principal would be classified on the balance sheet at December 31, 1985.

ALTERNATE PROBLEMS

Problem 17-1A (Computing Issue Price and Straight-line Method of Amortization)
R. D. Skelly Company issued $3,000,000 of 13%, 15-year bonds on October 1, 1985, when the market rate is 12%. Interest payments are due on March 31 and September 30. The fiscal year of the company ends September 30.

Required:
A. Determine the issue price of the bonds.
B. Prepare a journal entry to record the issuance of the bonds.
C. Prepare journal entries to record bond interest expense and amortization for the first three interest payments. Use the straight-line method of amortization.
D. Compute the carrying value of the bonds on October 1, 1986. Show how the bonds would be reported in the balance sheet.
E. Compute the total bond interest expense that would be reported in the income statement for the year ended September 30, 1986.
F. Prepare the journal entry to retire the bonds on their maturity date.

Problem 17-2A (Accrual of Interest and Bond Retirement Before Maturity)
The J. R. Marin Company issued $900,000 of 11%, 15-year, callable bonds. Interest-payment dates are May 31 and November 30. The company's fiscal year ends December 31 and it uses the straight-line method of amortization. The following transactions relate to the bond issue:

1. November 30, 1984. The bonds are issued for $968,625.
2. December 31, 1984. An entry is made to record interest accrued and to amortize a portion of the premium.
3. May 31, 1985. The first interest payment is made and a portion of the premium is amortized.

4. November 30, 1986. The fourth interest payment is made and a portion of the premium is amortized.
5. November 30, 1986. One-third of the bonds are called at 108 and retired.

Required:
Prepare general journal entries to record each of the transactions.

Problem 17-3A (Bond Transactions and Sinking Fund)

Geno Corporation decided to issue $750,000 of 12%, four-year bonds. Semiannual interest payments are due on June 30 and December 31. The company has agreed to deposit $161,700 in a bond sinking fund at the end of each year in the life of the bond issue. The sinking fund investments will earn an annual return of 10%. Geno Corporation uses the straight-line method of amortization. Some of the company's transactions are listed:

1. January 2, 1985. Sold the entire issue for 98 ⅜.
2. June 30, 1985. Paid the first interest payment and amortized a portion of the discount.
3. December 31, 1985. Deposited cash into the sinking fund.
4. June 30, 1986. Paid the third interest payment and amortized a portion of the discount.
5. December 31, 1986. Recorded the income earned during the year by the sinking fund investments.
6. December 31, 1987. Deposited cash into the sinking fund.
7. December 31, 1988. Recorded the sinking fund earnings for the year.
8. December 31, 1988. Paid the bondholders with proceeds from the sinking fund and received cash for the excess amount in the fund.

Required:
A. Prepare a table showing the interest earned by the sinking fund during the year and the year-end fund balance for each year during the life of the bonds.
B. Prepare journal entries to record the transactions listed.

Problem 17-4A (Bond Issued Between Interest-Payment Dates, Accrual of Interest, Bond Conversion, and Bond Retirement Before Maturity)

The DuBois Corporation decided to issue $2,000,000 of 9%, 10-year, convertible bonds. The bonds are dated October 1, 1984, and interest is payable on March 31 and September 30. Each $1,000 bond can be converted into 40 shares of $15 par value common stock. The company's fiscal year ends December 31. Because the difference between the two amortization methods is immaterial, the company uses the straight-line method of amortization. The following transactions relating to the bond issue were completed:

1. December 1, 1984. Issued the entire bond issue at par plus accrued interest.
2. December 31, 1984. Recorded the accrued interest.
3. March 31, 1985. Paid the semiannual interest.
4. September 30, 1985. Paid the semiannual interest.

5. September 30, 1985. $800,000 of the bonds were converted.
6. December 31, 1985. Recorded the accrued interest on the outstanding bonds.

DuBois Corporation then decided to issue $1,300,000 of 10%, 20-year, callable bonds. The bonds are dated January 1, 1986, and interest-payment dates are June 30 and December 31. DuBois completed these transactions:

7. January 1, 1986. Issued all the bonds for $1,313,000.
8. June 30, 1986. Paid the semiannual interest and amortized the premium.
9. June 30, 1990. Paid the semiannual interest and amortized the premium.
10. June 30, 1990. The entire bond issue was called at 102 and retired.

Required:
Prepare the general journal entries to record each transaction.

Problem 17-5A (Effective-interest Method of Amortization)

On June 30, 1984, Catamaran Corporation issued $500,000 of three-year bonds. Interest-payment dates are June 30 and December 31. The corporation's fiscal year is the calendar year. The following amortization table was prepared.

Interest-Payment Date	Cash Paid	Interest Expense	Amount Amortized
December 31, 1984	$28,750	$29,631	$ 881
June 30, 1985	28,750	29,684	934
December 31, 1985	28,750	29,740	990
June 30, 1986	28,750	29,799	1,049
December 31, 1986	28,750	29,862	1,112
June 30, 1987	28,750	29,931	1,181

Required:
A. What is the stated rate of interest on the bonds?
B. Were the bonds issued at a premium or at a discount?
C. Which method of amortization was used?
D. What was the market rate of interest when the bonds were sold?
E. Prepare the entry to record the sale of the bonds.
F. Prepare journal entries to record interest expense and amortization on June 30, 1985, and on June 30, 1986.

Problem 17-6A (Effective-interest Method of Amortization)

On January 1, 1984, the GTX Corporation issued five-year, 10% bonds with a par value of $100,000. Interest is payable June 30 and December 31. The bonds were issued at a price to yield 12%.

Required:
A. Compute the issue price of the bonds.
B. Prepare journal entries to record the following transactions:
   1. January 1, 1984. All of the bonds were issued for cash.
   2. June 30, 1984. Paid the semiannual interest and amortized the premium or

discount. (Use the effective-interest method to amortize the discount or premium.)

3. December 31, 1984 (end of annual period). Paid the semiannual interest and amortized the premium or discount.
4. June 30, 1985: Paid the semiannual interest and amortized the premium or discount.
5. January 1, 1989. Paid the bonds at maturity.

C. Show how the bonds payable will be reported in the December 31, 1984 balance sheet.

D. Answer the following questions:

1. What amount of bond interest expense is reported in 1984?
2. Will the bond interest expense reported in 1985 be the same as, greater than, or less than the amount reported in 1984?
3. Assuming the bonds are outstanding the full five-year period, what is the total bond interest expense to be recognized during the life of the bonds?
4. Would the straight-line method of amortization result in the same amount, more than, or less than the bond interest expense reported in 1984 under the effective-interest method?
5. If the straight-line method had been used, would the carrying value of the bonds be less than or greater than the carrying value computed in requirement (C) above?
6. Would the total bond interest expense recognized over the life of the bonds using the straight-line method be the same as, greater than, or less than the amount computed in question (3)? Explain.

Problem 17-7A (Mortgage Notes Payable)

Waverly Corporation purchased a building and the land it is on for $1,250,000. It gave the seller a down payment of $254,400 and a 14% mortgage note requiring 100 quarterly payments of $36,000 due the fifteenth of March, June, September, and December. Waverly Corporation purchased the building and land and made the down payment on June 16, 1984. It made the first quarterly payment on September 15, 1984. The company's fiscal year-end is December 31.

Required:

A. Prepare a quarterly payment schedule for 1984 and 1985. Use the following headings: Payment Date, Unpaid Balance at Beginning of Quarter, Cash Payment, Interest for One Quarter, Reduction in Principal, Principal Balance at End of Quarter.
B. Prepare journal entries to record the purchase and the first three quarterly payments (85% of the purchase price is attributed to the building).
C. Show how the mortgage note payable would be classified in the balance sheet at December 31, 1984.

CASES FOR CHAPTER 17

Case 17-1 (Annual Report Analysis)

For this case you are to refer to the Modern Merchandising, Inc. annual report presented in the Appendix to the text.

Required:

A. Compute the net increase or decrease in the firm's total long-term debt during the fiscal year ended January 31, 1981.

B. Determine the amount of long-term debt reported in the January 31, 1981 balance sheet that matures within the next fiscal year.

C. Prepare a list of the firm's notes and contracts payable that require a sinking fund payment, the amount of the payment required, and the date the first payment is to be made.

D. Are there restrictions on the payment of cash dividends to the common stockholders? How can the lender benefit from a restriction on dividends?

E. As of January 31, 1981, what is the amount of property and equipment pledged as collateral for notes and contracts payable? How can the lender benefit by this provision in the debt agreement?

F. When are the 10% subordinated debentures due? Which liabilities are they subordinate to? Are the debentures callable and, if so, at what call price?

G. How much interest expense on long-term debt did the company recognize for fiscal year ended January 31, 1981?

H. What would the interest expense on long-term debt have been for the fiscal year ended January 31, 1981 if there had not been an amortization of debt discount?

I. Does the amortization of debt discount indicate whether the debt was issued for an amount less than or greater than the face value of the debt?

Case 17-2 (Annual Report Analysis—Lease Obligations)

For this case you are to refer to the Modern Merchandising, Inc. annual report presented in the Appendix to the text.

Required:

A. How did the company record the signing of leases for substantially all of its showrooms?

B. The company shows total minimum obligations for capital leases of $226,369,612. However, only $97,894,244, including current maturities, is reported as a liability in the balance sheet. What does the difference between these two amounts represent? Explain how this difference is accounted for.

C. The company discloses the minimum lease payments for both capital leases and operating leases. What criteria must the company use to classify its leases as capital or operating?

APPENDIX: TIME VALUE OF MONEY

We have seen earlier that interest is the payment made for the use of money. As such, interest is the measure of the time value of money. A dollar expected sometime in the future is not equivalent to a dollar held today because of the time value of money. The dollar available today can be invested to earn interest so it will increase in value to more than one dollar in the future. We would consequently rather receive a dollar now than the same amount in the future even if we are certain of receiving it at the later date. Businesses often invest and borrow large sums of money, so the time value of money is an important topic. The dramatic increase in interest rates in recent years has had a corresponding impact on the time value of money. For example, the average interest rates on short-term bank loans between 1965 and 1970 ranged from 5% to 9%. By the middle part of the 1970s, the rate averaged as high as 14%. In the early 1980s, the interest on short-term bank loans exceeded 20% at times. We begin the examination of the time value of money with a discussion of simple and compound interest.

SIMPLE AND COMPOUND INTEREST

Simple interest is interest earned on an original amount invested (the *principal*). The amount of principal and the interest payments remain the same from period to period since interest is computed on the amount of principal only as:

Interest (in dollars) = Principal (in dollars) × Rate (% per year) × Time (in years)

To illustrate the computation of simple interest, assume that the Brown Supply Company sells merchandise in exchange for a $2,000 two-year note receivable bearing simple interest of 12% per year. The amount of interest due Brown Supply Company at the end of two years is:

$$\text{Interest} = \text{Principal} \times \text{Rate} \times \text{Time}$$
$$= \$2,000 \times .12 \times 2$$
$$= \$480$$

Compound interest is interest earned on the original amount invested (principal) plus previously earned interest. As interest is earned during any period, it is added to the principal; interest is computed on the new balance (often called the compound amount) during the next period. Interest can be compounded in a number of ways such as daily, monthly, quarterly, semiannually, or annually. As an illustration of compound interest, assume the note receivable held by the Brown Supply Company is the same as that described earlier except the interest is compounded annually. The total interest for the two-year period can be computed:

(1) Year	(2) Beginning Balance	(3) Compound Interest [Column (2) × .12]	(4) Ending Balance
1	$2,000.00	$240.00	$2,240.00
2	2,240.00	268.80	$2,508.80

In the second case, the total interest is $508.80, compared with the $480.00 computed earlier. The difference of $28.80 represents interest earned in the second year on the first year's interest ($240 × .12) and is the product of using compound rather than simple interest. In most cases involving the time value of money, compound interest is applicable, so we will consider only compound interest in the discussion that follows.

The time value of money is used in a wide variety of accounting applications, including the valuation of bonds, valuation of notes receivable/payable, determination of amounts to contribute to a pension plan, accounting for installment contracts, valuation of leases, and capital budgeting. Four cases must be considered in developing an understanding of the time value of money:

Case I   —Future value of a single amount
Case II   —Future value of an ordinary annuity
Case III   —Present value of a single amount
Case IV   —Present value of an ordinary annuity

CASE I (FUTURE VALUE OF A SINGLE AMOUNT)

As we have seen earlier, an amount of money invested today will have a higher future value than the original principal because of interest earned. The *future value of a single amount* invested today can be computed as follows:

$$FV = PV (1 + i)^n$$

where:

FV = Future value
PV = Present value of single amount invested (principal)
i = Interest rate per period
n = Number of periods

Schematically, the future-value computation can be shown as:

Present value (principal invested) $\longrightarrow$ Compounded at i interest rate for n periods $\longrightarrow$ Future value (accumulated amount)

The interest rate normally is expressed as an annual rate. However, interest often is compounded more frequently—daily, monthly, quarterly, or semi-annually. In such cases, the interest rate and number of periods must coincide with the compounding schedule. For example, if 12% per year interest is earned over a two-year period with quarterly compounding, the interest rate and number of periods used in the future-value formula are 3% and 8, respectively. This means that the annual interest rate (12%) is divided by the number of times compounding takes place (4) within a year, giving 3%, and the number of years (2) is multiplied by the number of compounding periods (4), giving 8 periods.

To illustrate the use of the future value formula with annual compounding, consider again the Brown Supply Company case with compound interest. The future value of the note receivable is found as follows:

$$FV = \$2,000 \ (1 + .12)^2$$

$$= \$2,508.80$$

As we see, the total amount due Brown Supply Company at maturity ($2,508.80) is the same as we computed earlier by adding the compound interest to the principal. If the note receivable involves quarterly compounding, we must revise the formula by dividing the 12% interest rate by 4 and multiplying 2 years by 4 as:

$$FV = \$2,000 \ (1 + .03)^8$$

$$= \$2,533.60$$

The amount of interest earned with quarterly compounding will be $24.80 more than it was with annual compounding. Note that the mathematics involved with the future-value formula becomes more tedious as we increase the number of periods involved. Fortunately, tables have been developed for various combinations of interest rates and periods to avoid the necessity of using the formula each time a future value of a single amount of money must be computed. Table 17.1 shows the future value of $1 for various interest rates and various periods.

Suppose we want to know how much a dollar invested today at 12% interest compounded annually will be worth 10 years from now. We simply find the amount (called a *factor*) in the 12% column and 10-periods row of Table 17.1—3.1058. Thus, the dollar invested now will become approximately $3.11 in 10 years because of the compound interest earned. Note that the left-hand column of Table 17.1 (and the other tables discussed later) refers to periods instead of years. This enables us to use the table even if interest is compounded more frequently than once a year. As we noted earlier for such cases, the number of years is multiplied by the number of times compounding occurs to determine the number of periods that must be considered. In addition, an

Periods	2%	3%	4%	5%	6%	8%	10%	12%	16%	20%
1	1.0200	1.0300	1.0400	1.0500	1.0600	1.0800	1.1000	1.1200	1.1600	1.2000
2	1.0404	1.0609	1.0816	1.1025	1.1236	1.1664	1.2100	1.2544	1.3456	1.4400
3	1.0612	1.0927	1.1249	1.1576	1.1910	1.2597	1.3310	1.4049	1.5609	1.7280
4	1.0824	1.1255	1.1699	1.2155	1.2625	1.3605	1.4641	1.5735	1.8106	2.0736
5	1.1041	1.1593	1.2167	1.2763	1.3382	1.4693	1.6105	1.7623	2.1003	2.4883
6	1.1262	1.1941	1.2653	1.3401	1.4185	1.5869	1.7716	1.9738	2.4364	2.9860
7	1.1487	1.2299	1.3159	1.4071	1.5036	1.7138	1.9487	2.2107	2.8262	3.5832
8	1.1717	1.2668	1.3686	1.4775	1.5938	1.8509	2.1436	2.4760	3.2784	4.2998
9	1.1951	1.3048	1.4233	1.5513	1.6895	1.9990	2.3579	2.7731	3.8030	5.1598
10	1.2190	1.3439	1.4802	1.6289	1.7908	2.1589	2.5937	3.1058	4.4114	6.1917
11	1.2434	1.3842	1.5395	1.7103	1.8983	2.3316	2.8531	3.4785	5.1173	7.4301
12	1.2682	1.4258	1.6010	1.7959	2.0122	2.5182	3.1384	3.8960	5.9360	8.9161
13	1.2936	1.4685	1.6651	1.8856	2.1329	2.7196	3.4523	4.3635	6.8858	10.6993
14	1.3195	1.5126	1.7317	1.9799	2.2609	2.9372	3.7975	4.8871	7.9875	12.8392
15	1.3459	1.5580	1.8009	2.0789	2.3966	3.1722	4.1772	5.4736	9.2655	15.4070
16	1.3728	1.6047	1.8730	2.1829	2.5404	3.4259	4.5950	6.1304	10.7480	18.4884
17	1.4002	1.6528	1.9479	2.2920	2.6928	3.7000	5.0545	6.8660	12.4677	22.1861
18	1.4282	1.7024	2.0258	2.4066	2.8543	3.9960	5.5599	7.6900	14.4625	26.6233
19	1.4568	1.7535	2.1068	2.5270	3.0256	4.3157	6.1159	8.6128	16.7765	31.9480
20	1.4859	1.8061	2.1911	2.6533	3.2071	4.6610	6.7275	9.6463	19.4608	38.3376
25	1.6406	2.0938	2.6658	3.3864	4.2919	6.8485	10.8347	17.0001	40.8742	95.3962
30	1.8114	2.4273	3.2434	4.3219	5.7435	10.0627	17.4494	29.9599	85.8499	237.3763

Table 17.1

Future Value of $1

annual interest rate is divided by the number of compounding periods to convert it to the appropriate interest rate. For example, assume the dollar invested earlier will earn 12% interest compounded semiannually instead of annually. We need to multiply 10 years by 2 (20-periods) and divide 12% by 2 (6 percent) to determine the appropriate factor in Table 17.1. The factor is 3.2071—located in the 6% interest rate column and 20-periods row. Therefore the dollar will grow to approximately $3.21 over the 10-year period. This same adjustment is required with the later tables whenever interest is compounded more frequently than once a year.

The factors in Table 17.1 were determined by using the future-value formula with a principal of $1. By multiplying a specific factor found in the table for the appropriate combination of interest rate and number of periods by the single amount of money involved, the future value of that amount can be calculated. To illustrate the use of Table 17.1 when the amount involved is more than $1, assume again that the two-year note receivable of Brown Supply Company has a 12% interest rate compounded annually. The factor in Table

17.1 for 12% interest and two years is 1.2544, so the note's future value is:

$$FV = \$2,000 \ (1.2544)$$

$$= \$2,508.80$$

This is the same result we obtained earlier with the future-value formula. If interest is compounded quarterly, the factor from the table is 1.2668 (3% and 8 periods) so the future value is:

$$FV = \$2,000 \ (1.2668)$$

$$= \$2,533.60$$

Again, the future value is the same as the one computed earlier with the formula approach.

CASE II (FUTURE VALUE OF AN ORDINARY ANNUITY)

In contrast to the single amount of money considered in Case I, an *annuity* consists of a series of payments over a specified number of periods, with compound interest on the payments. An *ordinary annuity* is a series of equal payments that occur at the end of each time period involved. We will consider here ordinary annuities only and defer the subject of annuities due (in which the payments occur at the beginning of the time periods) to more advanced accounting courses.

The future value of an ordinary annuity is the sum of all payments plus the compound interest accumulated on each. For example, if a business makes a deposit of $5,000 to a savings program at the end of three consecutive years with each payment earning 12% interest compounded annually, the total amount accumulated over the three-year period is the future value of an ordinary annuity. One way to calculate the future value of the series of payments would be to treat each payment separately and determine the amount of interest earned:

(1) Year	(2) Beginning Balance	(3) Annual Interest [Column (2) × .12]	(4) Payment	(5) Ending Balance
1			$5,000	$ 5,000
2	$ 5,000	$ 600	5,000	10,600
3	10,600	1,272	5,000	16,872

It can be seen from these calculations that interest is earned for only two periods even though three payments were made. As the number of payments increase, this approach obviously becomes more time-consuming.

A formula can be used also to calculate the future value of an ordinary annuity. The formula is more complicated than the one used for the future value of a single amount, however, so it is not normally utilized. Instead, a

Periods	2%	3%	4%	5%	6%	8%	10%	12%	16%	20%
1	1.0000	1.000	1.0000	1.0000	1.0000	1.0000	1.0000	1.0000	1.0000	1.0000
2	2.0200	2.0300	2.0400	2.0500	2.0600	2.0800	2.1000	2.1200	2.1600	2.2000
3	3.0604	3.0909	3.1216	3.1525	3.1836	3.2464	3.3100	3.3744	3.5056	3.6400
4	4.1216	4.1836	4.2465	4.3101	4.3746	4.5061	4.6410	4.7793	5.0665	5.3680
5	5.2040	5.3091	5.4163	5.5256	5.6371	5.8666	6.1051	6.3528	6.8771	7.4416
6	6.3081	6.4684	6.6330	6.8019	6.9753	7.3359	7.7156	8.1152	8.9775	9.9299
7	7.4343	7.6625	7.8983	8.1420	8.3938	8.9228	9.4872	10.0890	11.4139	12.9159
8	8.5830	8.8923	9.2142	9.5491	9.8975	10.6366	11.4359	12.2997	14.2401	16.4991
9	9.7546	10.1591	10.5828	11.0266	11.4913	12.4876	13.5795	14.7757	17.5185	20.7989
10	10.9497	11.4639	12.0061	12.5779	13.1808	14.4866	15.9374	17.5487	21.3215	25.9587
11	12.1687	12.8078	13.4864	14.2068	14.9716	16.6455	18.5312	20.6546	25.7329	32.1504
12	13.4121	14.1920	15.0258	15.9171	16.8699	18.9771	21.3843	24.1331	30.8502	39.5805
13	14.6803	15.6178	16.6268	17.7130	18.8821	21.4953	24.5227	28.0291	36.7862	48.4966
14	15.9739	17.0863	18.2919	19.5986	21.0151	24.2149	27.9750	32.3926	43.6720	59.1959
15	17.2934	18.5989	20.0236	21.5786	23.2760	27.1521	31.7725	37.2797	51.6595	72.0351
16	18.6393	20.1569	21.8245	23.6575	25.6725	30.3243	35.9497	42.7533	60.9250	87.4421
17	20.0121	21.7616	23.6975	25.8404	28.2129	33.7502	40.5447	48.8837	71.6730	105.9306
18	21.4123	23.4144	25.6454	28.1324	30.9057	37.4502	45.5992	55.7497	84.1407	128.1167
19	22.8406	25.1169	27.6712	30.5390	33.7600	41.4463	51.1591	63.4397	98.6032	154.7400
20	24.2974	26.8704	29.7781	33.0660	36.7856	45.7620	57.2750	72.0524	115.3797	186.6880
25	32.0303	36.4593	41.6459	47.7271	54.8645	73.1059	98.3471	133.3339	249.2140	471.9811
30	40.5681	47.5754	56.0849	66.4388	79.0582	113.2832	164.4940	241.3327	530.3117	1181.8816

Table 17.2
Future Value of an Ordinary Annuity of $1

table such as Table 17.2 is used because it contains factors for various combinations of interest rates and number of periods as computed with a *future value of an ordinary annuity* formula when payments of $1 are involved.

To illustrate the use of Table 17.2, consider again that the company makes 3 annual payments of $5,000 at the end of each year and earns 12% interest, compounded annually. The factor for 12% interest and 3 periods in Table 17.2 is 3.3744. Since the factor represents the future value of 3 payments of $1 at 12% interest, it is used to determine the future value of the actual payments made as:

$$FV = \$5,000 \ (3.3744)$$

$$= \$16,872$$

This is the same answer we found earlier by treating each payment separately. The three payments of $5,000 (total of $15,000) will increase in value to $16,872 over the three-year period. The difference between the $16,872 future value and the payments totaling $15,000 is interest amounting to $1,872. If semiannual payments of $2,500 had been involved during the three-year period, the appropriate factors from Table 17.2 would be for 6 periods and 6%. Again, this adjustment is required because of semiannual compounding. The factor for 6 periods and 6% from Table 17.2 is 6.9753, so the future value of the ordinary annuity is:

$$FV = \$2,500 \ (6.9753)$$

$$= \$17,438.25$$

As we see, the future value of $17,438.25 with semiannual compounding is higher than the $16,872.00 computed with annual compounding because additional interest is earned.

CASE III (PRESENT VALUE OF A SINGLE AMOUNT)

In Case I, we were concerned with the determination of the future value of a single amount of money. Many accounting applications of the time value of money involve the reverse of the future value consideration: the concern with computing the present value of some future amount of money. As noted earlier, money held today is worth more than the same amount of money received in the future because of the time value of money. Consequently, the present value of a given amount to be received in the future will be less than the future value. To determine the present value of a specific future amount, the future value must be discounted with an appropriate interest rate to the present. The interest rate involved often is called a *discount rate*. Future value and present value have a reciprocal relationship—as can be seen by comparing the formulas for the future value and present value of a single amount of money. Recall that the future value is computed as:

$$FV = PV \ (1 + i)^n$$

In contrast, the *present value of a single amount* of money is calculated as:

$$PV = \frac{FV}{(1 + i)^n}$$

where:

PV = Present value
FV = Future value of amount to be accumulated
i = Interest rate per period
n = Number of periods

Schematically, the present value computation can be shown as:

| Present value (amount to be invested now) | Discounted at i interest rate for n periods | Future value (amount to be accumulated) |

To illustrate the use of the present value of a single amount of money formula, consider again the note receivable held by Brown Supply Company. We determined earlier that the future value of the note was $2,508.80 when interest was compounded annually. By discounting the $2,508.80 for two years at 12%, we can determine its present value, which should be $2,000, as:

$$PV = \frac{\$2,508.80}{(1 + .12)^2}$$

$$= \$2,000.00$$

If the interest is compounded quarterly, we learned earlier that the future value of the note is $2,533.60. However, the present value of the note should remain at $2,000 when it is discounted for 8 periods at 3% interest per period, or:

$$PV = \frac{\$2,533.60}{(1 + .03)^8}$$

$$= \$2,000.00$$

As another example of calculating the present value of a single amount of money, assume that the Holmes Company has a liability of $23,958 that must be paid in three years. The company wants to know how much it must invest today to have $23,958 in three years if the amount earns 10% interest, compounded annually. The amount to be invested would be determined as:

$$PV = \frac{\$23,958}{(1 + .10)^3}$$

$$= \$18,000$$

Consequently, the $18,000 (present value) will increase in value to $23,958 (future value) by the end of the third year because interest amounting to $5,958 will be earned. Like the future-value formulas, the math involved with the computation of present value with a formula can be tedious, so a table is normally used. Table 17.3 shows factors for various combinations of interest rates and number of periods when the present value of $1 is computed. By multiplying an appropriate factor from the table by the single amount of money involved, its present value can be determined. For example, in the Brown Supply Company case with annual compounding, a value of .7972 is found in Table 17.3 for 12% interest and 2 periods. The present value of the note receivable is thus:

$$PV = \$2,508.80 \ (.7972)$$

$$= \$2,000.02[1]$$

---

[1]A small rounding difference may occur in the use of the factors from the tables.

Periods	2%	3%	4%	5%	6%	8%	10%	12%	16%	20%
1	0.9804	0.9709	0.9615	0.9524	0.9434	0.9259	0.9091	0.8929	0.8621	0.8333
2	0.9612	0.9426	0.9246	0.9070	0.8900	0.8573	0.8264	0.7972	0.7432	0.6944
3	0.9423	0.9151	0.8890	0.8638	0.8396	0.7938	0.7513	0.7118	0.6407	0.5787
4	0.9238	0.8885	0.8548	0.8227	0.7921	0.7350	0.6830	0.6355	0.5523	0.4823
5	0.9057	0.8626	0.8219	0.7835	0.7473	0.6806	0.6209	0.5674	0.4761	0.4019
6	0.8880	0.8375	0.7903	0.7462	0.7050	0.6302	0.5645	0.5066	0.4104	0.3349
7	0.8706	0.8131	0.7599	0.7107	0.6651	0.5835	0.5132	0.4523	0.3538	0.2791
8	0.8535	0.7894	0.7307	0.6768	0.6274	0.5403	0.4665	0.4039	0.3050	0.2326
9	0.8368	0.7664	0.7026	0.6446	0.5919	0.5002	0.4241	0.3606	0.2630	0.1938
10	0.8203	0.7441	0.6756	0.6139	0.5584	0.4632	0.3855	0.3220	0.2267	0.1615
11	0.8043	0.7224	0.6496	0.5847	0.5268	0.4289	0.3505	0.2875	0.1954	0.1346
12	0.7885	0.7014	0.6246	0.5568	0.4970	0.3971	0.3186	0.2567	0.1685	0.1122
13	0.7730	0.6810	0.6006	0.5303	0.4688	0.3677	0.2897	0.2292	0.1452	0.0935
14	0.7579	0.6611	0.5775	0.5051	0.4423	0.3405	0.2633	0.2046	0.1252	0.0779
15	0.7430	0.6419	0.5553	0.4810	0.4173	0.3152	0.2394	0.1827	0.1079	0.0649
16	0.7284	0.6232	0.5339	0.4581	0.3936	0.2919	0.2176	0.1631	0.0930	0.0541
17	0.7142	0.6050	0.5134	0.4363	0.3714	0.2703	0.1978	0.1456	0.0802	0.0451
18	0.7002	0.5874	0.4936	0.4155	0.3503	0.2502	0.1799	0.1300	0.0691	0.0376
19	0.6864	0.5703	0.4746	0.3957	0.3305	0.2317	0.1635	0.1161	0.0596	0.0313
20	0.6730	0.5537	0.4564	0.3769	0.3118	0.2145	0.1486	0.1037	0.0514	0.0261
25	0.6095	0.4776	0.3751	0.2953	0.2330	0.1460	0.0923	0.0588	0.0245	0.0105
30	0.5521	0.4120	0.3083	0.2314	0.1741	0.0994	0.0573	0.0334	0.0116	0.0042

Table 17.3
Present Value of $1

With quarterly compounding, the value in Table 17.3 is found for 3% interest and 8 periods (.7894) and used as follows:

$$PV = \$2{,}533.60 \,(.7894)$$

$$= \$2{,}000.02$$

Table 17.3 also can be used to determine the amount the Holmes Company must invest today to have $23,958 three years later with the same factors discussed earlier. The factor in Table 12.3 for 10% interest and 3 periods is .7513, so the present value of $23,958 is:

$$PV = \$23{,}958 \,(.7513)$$

$$= \$17{,}999.65$$

Note that each of the factors shown in Table 17.3 for a particular combination of interest rates and number of periods is one (1) divided by the corresponding factor found in Table 17.1. This must be true because of the reciprocal relationship between the formulas for future value and present value of a single amount. For example, the factor in Table 17.3 for 12% interest and 2 periods is .7972, which is the same as one (1) divided by 1.2544 (Table 17.1). Consequently, you can always determine the appropriate Table 17.3 factor from Table 17.1 and vice-versa if both tables are not available.

CASE IV (PRESENT VALUE OF AN ORDINARY ANNUITY)

In Case II, we considered how to determine the future value of an ordinary annuity—a series of equal payments made at the end of each time period involved. Our final concern with the time value of money is the reverse of Case II—that is, the present value of a series of equal future payments representing an ordinary annuity. The present value of an ordinary annuity is the amount that would have to be invested today at a certain compound interest rate to enable the investor to receive the series of future payments over a specified period of time. Assume that the Briden Corporation has obligations of $6,000 that must be repaid at the end of each of the next three years, including the current one. The firm wants to know how much it would have to invest today to repay each of the obligations if the amount invested earns 10%, compounded annually. One way to determine the amount of the required investment would be to treat each $6,000 payment as a single amount. Each payment would be discounted to its present value (using Table 17.3), and the results would be added to determine the total amount needed to be invested. If this approach is taken, the following calculations are necessary:

(1)	(2)	(3)	(4) Present
Year	Payment	Factor	Value
		(Table 17.3—10%)	[Column (2) × Column (3)]
1	$6,000	.9091	$ 5,454.60
2	6,000	.8264	4,958.40
3	6,000	.7513	4,507.80
Total present value			$14,920.80

The firm would have to invest $14,920.80 today to have the money available to make payments of $6,000 at the end of each of the next three years. If numerous payments are involved, this approach obviously will be quite time-consuming. Since the $6,000 payments can be viewed as an annuity, an easier way to discount them to their present value is to use Table 17.4. The factors in Table 17.4 have been derived from a formula representing the *present value of an annuity of $1*. In the table, factors for various combinations of interest rates and number of periods are presented for the determination of the present value of an annuity of $1. Again, a given factor must be multiplied by the actual amount of each payment involved. The factor is 2.4869 for 10% and 3 periods. Therefore, the present value of the $6,000 payments can be calculated as:

Periods	2%	3%	4%	5%	6%	8%	10%	12%	16%	20%
1	0.9804	0.9709	0.9615	0.9524	0.9434	0.9259	0.9091	0.8929	0.8621	0.8333
2	1.9416	1.9135	1.8861	1.8594	1.8334	1.7833	1.7355	1.6901	1.6052	1.5278
3	2.8839	2.8286	2.7751	2.7232	2.6730	2.5771	2.4869	2.4018	2.2459	2.1065
4	3.8077	3.7171	3.6299	3.5460	3.4651	3.3121	3.1699	3.0373	2.7982	2.5887
5	4.7135	4.5797	4.4518	4.3295	4.2124	3.9927	3.7908	3.6048	3.2743	2.9906
6	5.6014	5.4172	5.2421	5.0757	4.9173	4.6229	4.3553	4.1114	3.6847	3.3255
7	6.4720	6.2303	6.0021	5.7864	5.5824	5.2064	4.8684	4.5638	4.0386	3.6016
8	7.3255	7.0197	6.7327	6.4632	6.2098	5.7466	5.3349	4.9676	4.3436	3.8372
9	8.1622	7.7861	7.4353	7.1078	6.8017	6.2469	5.7590	5.3282	4.6065	4.0310
10	8.9826	8.5302	8.1109	7.7217	7.3601	6.7101	6.1446	5.6502	4.8332	4.1925
11	9.7868	9.2526	8.7605	8.3064	7.8869	7.1390	6.4951	5.9377	5.0286	4.3271
12	10.5753	9.9540	9.3851	8.8633	8.3838	7.5361	6.8137	6.1944	5.1971	4.4392
13	11.3484	10.6350	9.9856	9.3936	8.8527	7.9038	7.1034	6.4235	5.3423	4.5327
14	12.1062	11.2961	10.5631	9.8986	9.2950	8.2442	7.3667	6.6282	5.4675	4.6106
15	12.8493	11.9379	11.1184	10.3797	9.7122	8.5595	7.6061	6.8109	5.5755	4.6755
16	13.5777	12.5611	11.6523	10.8378	10.1059	8.8514	7.8237	6.9740	5.6685	4.7296
17	14.2919	13.1661	12.1657	11.2741	10.4773	9.1216	8.0216	7.1196	5.7487	4.7746
18	14.9920	13.7535	12.6593	11.6896	10.8276	9.3719	8.2014	7.2497	5.8178	4.8122
19	15.6785	14.3238	13.1339	12.0853	11.1581	9.6036	8.3649	7.3658	5.8775	4.8435
20	16.3514	14.8775	13.5903	12.4622	11.4699	9.8181	8.5136	7.4694	5.9288	4.8696
25	19.5235	17.4131	15.6221	14.0939	12.7834	10.6748	9.0770	7.8431	6.0971	4.9476
30	22.3965	19.6004	17.2920	15.3725	13.7648	11.2578	9.4269	8.0552	6.1772	4.9789

Table 17.4

Present Value of an Ordinary Annuity of $1

$$PV = \$6,000\ (2.4869)$$
$$= \$14,921.40$$

As we see, the results are essentially the same as those obtained by discounting each payment and adding the individual present values. If semiannual payments of $3,000 were made to satisfy the firm's obligations, the present-value calculation would require an adjustment of the number of periods and the annual interest rate. Six periods (3 years × 2) and an interest rate of 5% (10% ÷ 2) would be used to determine the factor of 5.0757 from Table 17.4, and the present value of the annuity would be:

$$PV = \$3,000\ (5.0757)$$
$$= \$15,227.10$$

Note that the present value with semiannual payments is more than it was with annual payments. The reason for this is that the amount invested will not have as much time to earn interest because payments are made every six months rather than at the end of the year.

EXERCISES TO THE APPENDIX

Exercise 17A-1 (Compute Simple Interest)

The Hinkle Company has agreed to take a note receivable in exchange for an overdue account receivable from the Pay-Late Company. Simple interest at 15% is payable beginning March 1 (the date of the exchange) and the note receivable is for a three-year term. The amount of the note receivable is $4,000 and interest will be paid at the maturity of the note.

Required:
Calculate the amount of interest due at the end of three years.

Exercise 17A-2 (Compute Compound Interest)

Refer to Exercise 17A-1. How much interest would be due if compound interest were involved?

Exercise 17A-3 (Compute the Future Value of a Single Amount)

Using Table 17.1 on page 693, compute the following future values:

1. $10,000 invested at 12% for 5 years, compounded annually.
2. $10,000 invested at 12% for 5 years, compounded semiannually.
3. $10,000 invested at 12% for 5 years, compounded quarterly.

Exercise 17A-4 (Compute the Future Value of a Single Amount)

An investor wants to know how much a $5,000 investment made today will amount to in 15 years if it earns 12% interest, compounded annually.

Exercise 17A-5 (Compute the Future Value of an Annuity)

Using Table 17.2 on page 695, determine the following future values:

1. $10,000 invested at the end of each year for 5 years at 12%, compounded annually.
2. $5,000 invested at the end of each 6 months for 5 years at 12% per year, compounded semiannually.
3. $2,500 invested at the end of each 3 months for 5 years at 12% per year, compounded quarterly.

Exercise 17A-6 (Compute the Future Value of an Annuity)

An investor wants to know how much she will have if she makes annual payments of $5,000 at the end of the year for 10 years assuming the money will earn 12%.

Exercise 17A-7 (Compute the Present Value of a Single Annuity)

Using Table 17.3 on page 698, determine the present values of the following situations:

1. $10,000 in 5 years at 12%, compounded annually.
2. $10,000 in 5 years at 12%, compounded semiannually.
3. $10,000 in 5 years at 12%, compounded quarterly.

Exercise 17A-8 (Compute the Present Value of a Single Amount)

Don Clarkson wants to establish a college fund for his only daughter, who currently is eight years old. He wants to know how much he must invest today for it to accumulate to be $50,000 in 10 years at 12%. Ignore income taxes.

Exercise 17A-9 (Compute the Present Value of an Annuity)

Using Table 17.4 on page 700, compute the present values of the following situations:

1. $10,000 to be paid at the end of each year for 5 years, assuming 12% interest and annual compounding.
2. $5,000 to be paid at the end of each 6 months for 5 years, assuming 12% annual interest and semiannual compounding.
3. $2,500 to be paid at the end of each 3 months for 5 years, assuming 12% annual interest and quarterly compounding.

Exercise 17A-10 (Compute the Present Value of an Annuity)

An investor wants to receive $5,000 at the end of each year for the next 5 years (including the current year). How much must he invest today to achieve his objective assuming the money earns 12%?

CHAPTER 18
INTERCORPORATE INVESTMENTS AND CONSOLIDATED FINANCIAL STATEMENTS

OVERVIEW AND OBJECTIVES

This chapter discusses accounting for intercorporate investments in securities and the nature of consolidated financial statements. When you have completed the chapter, you should understand:

- The difference between temporary and long-term investments (pp. 704).
- How to account for temporary investments (pp. 704–706).
- The purpose of holding long-term investments in securities (pp. 706–707).
- The difference between the cost and equity methods of accounting for long-term investments in voting stock (pp. 707–712).
- How to account for long-term investments in bonds (pp. 712–716).
- The purpose of consolidated financial statements (pp. 716–717).
- The conditions that must be met before a subsidiary is included in the consolidated financial statements (pp. 729–730).
- Limitations in the use of information contained in consolidated financial statements (pp. 730–731).

In the three preceding chapters, we discussed accounting for the issue of securities and the payment of dividends and interest from the viewpoint of the issuing corporation. We now turn our attention to the accounting procedures followed by the investors who purchase these securities. Investors may be individuals, mutual funds, pension funds, or other corporations.

Although corporate securities may be purchased directly from the issuing corporation, most are purchased from other investors through brokers, who charge a commission for their services. Brokers act as agents since they buy and sell stocks and bonds for their clients through securities exchanges such as the New York Stock Exchange and the American Stock Exchange. Securities of some companies are not listed on a national exchange but are traded through brokers on the "over-the-counter" market. Millions of securities are traded each weekday and a record of the transactions is reported daily in the financial pages of many newspapers. As we noted earlier, stock prices are quoted in terms of dollars and fractions of dollars, with $\frac{1}{8}$ of a dollar normally being the minimum fraction. Thus, a quote of $42\frac{3}{8}$ means $42.375 per share and a stock quoted at $107\frac{1}{2}$ means it has a price of $107.50. Bond prices are quoted as a percentage of their par value, so a quote of $97\frac{1}{2}$ means that a $1,000 par value bond has a market value of $975 ($1,000 $\times$ 97.5%).

CLASSIFICATION OF INVESTMENTS

Investments are classified as temporary or long-term, depending upon the objective of the investment. Securities that management intends to hold for a short time are classified as **temporary investments,** while securities that management intends to hold for a longer period are classified as **long-term investments.**

TEMPORARY INVESTMENTS

Companies often have cash that is not needed immediately but will be needed later for operating purposes. To obtain revenue from interest, dividends, and market appreciation, this excess cash may be invested temporarily in U.S. government securities or in stocks and bonds of corporations with the intention of converting these securities back into cash when needed for operations. Because they are readily marketable, they can be converted to cash on short notice and are generally considered to be as liquid as cash itself. Consequently, they are reported on the balance sheet as current assets immediately after cash. For example, an annual report for Zenith Radio Corporation reported marketable securities as a part of current assets as follows:

Current Assets:	
Cash	$11,700,000
Marketable securities at cost approximating market	51,600,000

Temporary investments may be debt securities (bonds and notes payable of other companies or governmental bodies) or equity securities (preferred and common stock). When an investor holds debt securities or shares of stock in several companies, the group of debt securities or stocks is called a **portfolio.**

Temporary Investments in Debt Securities

A temporary investment in a portfolio of debt securities is normally accounted for at cost. However, if the market value of the portfolio is substantially less than its cost and the decline in market value is not due to a temporary condition, the investment should be reported at its market value.[1] The write-down to market value is recorded by a debit to a Loss on Temporary Investments account and a credit to the Temporary Investments account. Later recoveries in market value are not recognized. Interest revenue is accrued as earned. Discounts or premiums on the investments are not amortized because of the temporary nature of the investments.

Temporary Investments in Stock

A temporary stock portfolio is accounted for at the lower of its aggregate cost or aggregate market value at the date of the balance sheet.[2] For example, assume that Flank Corporation had the following temporary stock portfolio on December 31, 1984:

Investment	Cost	Market
Brad Company—Preferred Stock	$ 22,000	$ 18,000
Crance Company—Common Stock	46,000	49,000
Ever Company—Common Stock	35,000	35,000
Hulto Company—Common Stock	81,000	70,000
Total	$184,000	$172,000

Because the market value of the portfolio is $12,000 less than its cost, a $12,000 unrealized loss has been incurred and the portfolio should be reported in the balance sheet at its lower market value of $172,000. To record the loss and reduce the marketable securities to their market value, an entry is made as follows:

Dec.	31	Unrealized Loss on Marketable Securities	12,000	
		Allowance to Reduce Marketable		
		Securities to Market Value		12,000
		To reduce marketable securities to the		
		lower of cost or market.		

[1]*Accounting Research Bulletin No. 43,* "Restatement and Revision of Accounting Research Bulletins" (New York: AICPA, 1953), Ch. 3A, par. 9.

[2]*Statement of Financial Accounting Standards No. 12,* "Accounting for Certain Marketable Securities" (Stamford, Conn.: FASB, 1975), par. 8.

Although the loss is unrealized because the securities have not been sold, it must be deducted on the income statement. Large losses are reported as a separate item in determining income from continuing operations; small losses are normally included in the "other expense" category on the income statement. The Allowance to Reduce Marketable Securities to Market Value is a contra-asset account and is deducted from the cost of the marketable securities on the balance sheet as follows:

Current Assets:		
Cash		$ 78,000
Marketable equity securities	$184,000	
Less: Allowance to reduce marketable securities to		
market value	12,000	172,000

Reporting in this way discloses to statement users both the cost of the marketable securities and their current market value.

If the market value of the portfolio·is greater than its cost, the unrealized gain is not recorded and the marketable securities are reported at their cost. This treatment is consistent with the accounting convention of *conservatism,* under which gains are not recognized until realized by a sale but losses are recognized when they are incurred. If the portfolio's market value increases in subsequent periods, the unrealized loss is reversed up to its original amount and included in net income. Thus, when the temporary equity securities portfolio has been written down to its market value, it may be written back up to its original cost only. Dividends are recognized as revenue when they are declared or received.

LONG-TERM INVESTMENTS

Long-term investments are those that are not intended to be converted into cash for normal operating activities; they may be defined simply as all investments that are not temporary. Just like temporary investments, they may consist of equity securities or debt securities. Long-term investments also include funds set aside for special purposes, such as a bond sinking fund, and land or other assets owned by the company but not used in normal operations. Long-term investments are normally reported in a separate section of the balance sheet immediately after current assets under the caption "Long-term Investments" or simply "Investments."

Although there are several reasons a company makes long-term investments in the securities of other companies, the primary objective is to increase net income. Net income is increased, of course, by the receipt of interest or dividends and through market appreciation of the securities, which is recognized when the securities are sold. Another important means of increasing net income is through growth. When a company wants to expand, it has two main alternatives. It can expand by enlarging existing facilities or by purchasing or building new factories or other facilities in various locations. This process requires large amounts of capital and produces results rather slowly.

As an alternative, a company may expand its operations by acquiring sufficient voting stock of another company to influence or control its operations by electing members of its board of directors. The company acquiring the stock is called the **investor company** and the company whose stock is acquired is called the **investee company.** Many companies expand in this way for several reasons. One is that expansion is accomplished rapidly since the investee company already has operating facilities, customers, and suppliers, and may own natural resources needed in the investor company's operations. Another reason is that expansion can be obtained with a smaller capital commitment. By acquiring more than 50% of the voting stock of another company, the investor can control the investee with a much smaller investment than would be required to build or buy new equivalent facilities.

ACCOUNTING FOR LONG-TERM INVESTMENTS IN COMMON STOCK

Long-term investments in common stock are recorded initially at their cost. Accounting for the investment subsequent to acquisition, however, depends upon whether the investor owns enough stock to exercise significant influence over the investee's operating and financing policies. If the investor can exercise significant influence over the investee, the investment is accounted for by the **equity method;** otherwise it is accounted for by the **cost method,** applying normal lower of cost or market procedures. In order to provide a reasonable degree of uniformity in practice, current accounting rules state that—unless there is evidence to the contrary—the ownership of 20% or more of the voting stock of a corporation provides presumptive evidence of the ability to exercise significant influence.[3] Thus, common stock investments of 20% or more are normally accounted for by the equity method, whereas those of less than 20% are accounted for by the cost method.

---

[3]*APB Opinion No. 18,* "The Equity Method of Accounting for Investments in Common Stock" (New York: AICPA, 1971), par. 17.

PART FIVE   ADDITIONAL FINANCIAL REPORTING ISSUES

THE COST METHOD

When less than 20% of a corporation's common stock is purchased and held as a long-term investment, the investment is recorded at its cost, including any broker's commission. For example, assume that Apex Company purchased 10,000 (10%) of Lux Corporation's 100,000 outstanding common shares as a long-term investment at 18¾ plus a broker's commission of $1,000. The investment is recorded as follows:

Jan.	8	Investment in Lux Corp. Stock	188,500	
		Cash		188,500
		To record the purchase of 10,000 shares of Lux Corporation common stock at $18.75 per share plus $1,000 commission.		

Because less than 20% of Lux Corporation's outstanding stock was acquired, the investment is accounted for by the cost method. Dividends received are recognized as dividend revenue. For example, if Lux Corporation paid a $1 per share dividend, the entry would be:

Aug.	6	Cash	10,000	
		Dividend Revenue		10,000
		To record dividends received.		

A group of long-term stock investments, each less than 20% of the outstanding stock of the respective investee company, constitutes the investor's long-term stock portfolio. The lower of cost or market procedures also must be applied to a long-term stock investment portfolio accounted for by the cost method. Thus, the aggregate cost of the portfolio is compared with aggregate market value at the end of each accounting period. If aggregate market value is less than aggregate cost, an Unrealized Loss on Long-term Investments account is debited and an Allowance to Reduce Long-term Investments to Market is credited. Accounting procedures are the same as those used for the temporary stock portfolio *with one major exception*—the Unrealized Loss on Long-term Investments account is reported as a contra-stockholders' equity item rather than as a deduction in the income statement. Thus, the Unrealized Loss account is not closed at the end of the period. In subsequent periods, both the Unrealized Loss account and the Allowance account are adjusted by an amount sufficient to report the Long-Term Stock Investment at the lower of its cost or market. Any balance in the Unrealized Loss account is deducted directly from stockholders' equity and the Allowance account is deducted as a contra to Long-term Investments.

For example, assume a long-term stock investment portfolio had an aggregate cost of $490,000 and an aggregate market value of $420,000 on December

31, 1984. The unrealized loss and allowance accounts would be reported on the December 31, 1984, balance sheet as follows:

Assets

Current assets		$169,000
Plant and equipment (net of depreciation)		281,000
Long-term investments in stock	$490,000	
Less: Allowance to reduce long-term investments		
to market value	70,000	420,000
Total assets		$870,000
Liabilities		$100,000

Stockholders' Equity

Common stock, $10 par	$500,000	
Retained earnings	340,000	
Total	840,000	
Less: Unrealized loss on long-term investments	70,000	770,000
Total Liabilities and Stockholders' Equity		$870,000

The unrealized loss is subtracted directly from stockholders' equity rather than being deducted in the income statement as is done with the unrealized loss on temporary stock investments. The loss in value of temporary investments is more likely to be realized because management intends to sell the investment in the near future. Because management intends to hold the long-term stock investments for several years, during which time the market value of the stock may rise again, the FASB decided that these fluctuations in stock values should not be reflected in net income.

THE EQUITY METHOD

As mentioned earlier, when a company acquires 20% or more of the voting stock of a corporation, the investment is normally accounted for by the equity method. When the stock is acquired, the investment is recorded at its cost just as it is with the cost method. However, two main features distinguish the equity method from the cost method. Under the equity method:

1. The investor company recognizes its proportional share of the investee's income as an increase in the investment account and as revenue for the period. If the investee reports a loss for the period, the investor decreases the investment account for its proportional share and recognizes a loss.
2. Dividends received from the investee are credited to the investment account.

To illustrate, assume that on January 2, 1984, Apex Company purchased 25,000 (25%) of the 100,000 outstanding common shares of Lux Corporation at 18¾ plus a broker's commission of $2,000. On September 1, Lux Corporation paid a dividend of $1 per share and on December 31 reported net income of $200,000. To record the effects of these events, Apex Company would make the following entries:

Jan.	2	Investment in Lux Corporation	470,750	
		Cash		470,750
		To record the purchase of 25,000 common shares of Lux Corporation at $18.75 per share plus $2,000 commission.		
Sept.	1	Cash	25,000	
		Investment in Lux Corporation		25,000
		To record dividends received.		
Dec.	31	Investment in Lux Corporation	50,000	
		Investment Revenue		50,000
		To record 25% of Lux Corporation's reported net income of $200,000		

The investment is recorded at its initial cost. The distribution of the dividend on September 1 reduced Lux Corporation's stockholders' equity by $100,000 and reduced Apex Company's share of Lux Corporations stockholders' equity by $25,000 (25% × $100,000). Consequently, the receipt of the dividend is credited to the investment account to reflect the decrease in equity. Because Apex Company can influence significantly the operating policies of Lux Corporation, Apex Company recognized its share of Lux Corporation's net income for the period. Lux Corporation's stockholders' equity increased by the amount of income earned during the year ($200,000), and Apex Company's share of $50,000 (25% × $200,000) is added to the investment account. The investor's share of the increases and decreases in the investee's stockholders' equity are thus recorded as increases and decreases in the investment account. After recording these transactions, the investment account will appear as follows:

Investment in Lux Corporation

Jan. 2 purchase	470,750	Sept. 1 dividends	25,000
Dec. 31 net income	50,000		
Dec. 31 balance	495,750		

RECORDING THE SALE OF STOCK INVESTMENTS

When stock investments are sold, the appropriate investment account is credited for the carrying value of the shares sold, and the difference between the selling price (less broker's fees) and the carrying value is credited to Gain on

Sale of Investments or debited to Loss on Sale of Investments. For example, assume that Apex Company sold 2,500 shares of Lux Corporation stock on January 2, 1985, for $22 per share and paid a broker's fee of $1,000. The entry to record the sale of 10% of the shares (2,500/25,000) would be:

Jan.	2	Cash [(2,500 × $22) − $1,000]	54,000	
		Investment in Lux Corp.*		49,575
		Gain on Sale of Investments		4,425
		To record the sale of 2,500 shares of Lux		
		Corporation stock at $22 per share less		
		$1,000 broker's fees.		
		*(10% × $495,750)		

A comparison of accounting for long-term and temporary stock investments under the lower-of-cost-or-market method is presented in Figure 18-1. A comparison of accounting for long-term stock investments under the cost method versus the equity method is shown in Figure 18-2.

Item	Temporary	Long-term
Balance sheet location	Current assets	Investments
Allowance to reduce to lower of aggregate cost or market	Deducted from the cost of investment	Same as temporary
Unrealized loss	Unrealized loss in income statement	Unrealized loss subtracted from stockholders' equity
Recovery of market value	Adjusted through Recovery account in income statement	Adjusted through Unrealized Loss account in stockholders' equity
Sale of investment	Results in realized gain or loss in income statement	Same as temporary
Dividends declared	Reported as revenue in the income statement	Depends on use of cost or equity method as shown in Figure 18-2

Figure 18-1
Accounting for Long-term and Temporary Investments under the Lower of Cost or Market Method

Figure 18-2
Comparison of Cost
and Equity Methods

Item	Cost Method	Equity Method
Acquisition of investment	Recorded at acquisition cost (remains unchanged).	Same as Cost but balance changes each year.
Revenue from investment	Recorded only when dividends are declared.	Investment account increased by investor's share of earnings.
Dividends declared	Revenue recognized.	No revenue recognized. Credit Investment account.
Use of lower of cost or market method	Compare total cost and total market value of all equity securities classified as long-term. Write down in a contra account if market is lower than cost.	Investment account not written down unless market decline is material and permanent.

ACCOUNTING FOR LONG-TERM INVESTMENTS IN BONDS

Accounting for an investment in long-term bonds by the investor is essentially the reverse of accounting for the issue of the bonds by the issuing company. The bond investment is recorded at its cost, including broker's fees. Since interest on bonds accrues over time, the purchaser must also pay interest accrued between the date of the last interest payment and the purchase date. The amount paid for accrued interest is normally debited to Interest Revenue so that it will be offset against the credit to Interest Revenue when the first interest payment is received.

The amount paid for bonds often will be more or less than par value; that is, the bonds are purchased at a premium or a discount. As explained in Chapter 17, if the market rate of interest is less than the stated rate on the bonds, the bonds will sell at a premium. If the market interest rate is more than the stated rate, the bonds will sell at a discount. Premium or discount represents an adjustment to interest revenue and therefore must be amortized over the remaining life of the bonds.

BONDS PURCHASED AT A PREMIUM

To illustrate bonds purchased at a premium, assume that on May 1, 1984, Bay Company purchased 300, $1,000 par value, 10% bonds of Croy Corporation on the open market at 105 plus accrued interest of $7,500 and broker's fees of $3,000. The bonds pay interest semiannually on July 31 and January 31. They mature on January 31, 1988, and thus have 45 months remaining to maturity date. The entry to record the purchase is:

May	1	Investment in Croy Corp. Bonds	318,000	
		Interest Revenue	7,500	
		Cash		325,500
		To record the purchase of Croy Corp. bonds.		

The Investment account is debited for the total cost of the bonds [(300 × $1,000 × 105%) + $3,000 broker's fee] and interest revenue is debited for the three months accrued interest of $7,500 ($300,000 × .10 × 3/12). Note that, unlike the accounting for bonds by the issuing company, when accounting for bonds purchased a separate premium account for the investment is not used.

The receipt of the first semiannual interest payment and amortization of premium for three months are recorded as follows:

July	31	Cash	15,000	
		Investment in Croy Corp. Bonds		1,200
		Interest Revenue		13,800
		To record the receipt of interest and the amortization of premium.		

Because there were 45 months between the purchase of the bonds and their maturity date, amortization per month under the straight-line method is computed as follows:

Cost of the investment	$318,000
Par value of the bonds	300,000
Amount to be amortized	18,000
Amortization period (45 months)	÷ 45
Amortization per month	$ 400[4]

[4]As mentioned in Chapter 17, the interest method of amortization should be used if the difference between it and the straight-line method is material in amount. The straight-line method is generally used by companies that make only incidental investments in long-term bonds because interest revenue constitutes only a small part of their total income.

The debit to cash represents the amount received for the semiannual period ($300,000 × .10 × %12). The credit to the investment account reflects the amortization of premium for the months of May, June, and July (3 × $400).

The amount of interest earned each month can be computed as follows:

Amount to be received by the investor:	
Maturity value	$300,000
Interest for 45 months ($300,000 × .10 × 45/12)	112,500
Total	412,500
Cost of investment	318,000
Total interest revenue	94,500
Number of months to maturity	÷ 45
Interest revenue per month	$ 2,100

After the interest entry above is posted, the Interest Revenue account will appear as:

Interest Revenue

May 1	7,500	July 31	13,800

The credit balance in the account ($6,300) reflects the correct amount of interest earned for the three months from May 1 to July 31 ($2,100 × 3 months).

On December 31, the end of the fiscal year, interest is accrued and amortization is recorded as follows:

Dec.	31	Interest Receivable (1)	12,500	
		Investment in Croy Corp. Bonds (2)		2,000
		Interest Revenue (3)		10,500
		To accrue interest for 5 months and amortize premium.		
		(1) $300,000 × .10 × 5/12		
		(2) $400 × 5 months		
		(3) $2,100 × 5 months		

Notice that amortization is credited directly to the Investment in Croy Corporation Bonds account. This process will reduce the investment account to the par value of the bonds ($300,000) by their maturity date, at which time Bay Company will receive the maturity value and make the following entry:

1988 Jan.	31	Cash	300,000	
		Investment in Croy Corp. Bonds		300,000
		To record receipt of maturity value.		

BONDS PURCHASED AT A DISCOUNT

If the bonds are purchased at a discount rather than at a premium, the amount of periodic amortization is debited (rather than credited) to the investment account. In this way the investment account is gradually increased over time and will be equal to the maturity value of the bonds on their maturity date.

For example, assume that the Croy Corporation bonds in the previous illustration were purchased for $295,500 (including the broker's fee) plus accrued interest. Thus, the bonds were purchased at a $4,500 discount ($300,000 − $295,500). During the first year, the investment in bonds would be accounted for as follows:

May	1	Investment in Croy Corp. Bonds	295,500	
		Interest Revenue	7,500	
		Cash		303,000
		To record the purchase of Croy Corp. bonds.		
July	1	Cash	15,000	
		Investment in Croy Corp. Bonds[1]	300	
		Interest Revenue		15,300
		To record the receipt of interest and amortization of discount.		
		[1]$4,500 discount divided by 45 months = $100 per month. $100 × 3 months = $300		
Dec.	31	Interest Receivable	12,500	
		Investment in Croy Corp. Bonds ($100 × 5)	500	
		Interest revenue		13,000
		To accrue interest for 5 months and amortize discount.		

RECORDING THE SALE OF BOND INVESTMENTS

When bond investments are sold, the procedure is similar to that for the sale of stock investments. However, in addition to the selling price of the bonds, the seller will receive interest accrued since the last interest-payment date. Also, amortization of premium or discount on the investment to the date of sale should be recorded.

To illustrate, assume that Bay Company sold one-half of its Croy Corporation bonds on April 1, 1986, for $160,000 (net of broker's fees) plus accrued interest of $2,500. Assume also that the bonds were purchased at a premium as illustrated previously. Before recording the sale, amortization should be recorded from the last interest-payment date to the date of sale as follows:

Apr.	1	Interest Revenue	800	
		Investment in Croy Corp. Bonds		800
		To record amortization for February and March at $400 per month.		

After this entry is posted, the Investment in Croy Corporation Bonds account will appear as presented below:

Investment in Croy Corporation Bonds

5/1/84	318,000	7/31/84 amortization	1,200
		12/31/84 amortization	2,000
		1/31/85 amortization	400
		7/31/85 amortization	2,400
		12/31/85 amortization	2,000
		1/31/86 amortization	400
		4/1/86 amortization	800
4/1/86 Balance	308,800		9,200

The sale of the bonds can now be recorded by the following entry:

Apr.	1	Cash	162,500	
		Interest Revenue		2,500
		Investment in Croy Corporation Bonds		154,400
		Gain on Sale of Investment		5,600
		To record the sale of one-half of the Croy Corporation bonds.		

Cash is debited for the proceeds from the sale of $160,000 plus $2,500 accrued interest ($150,000 × .10 × 2/12), the Investment in Croy Corporation Bonds account is credited for half its carrying value (½ × $308,800) since only half the bonds were sold, and a gain on the sale of $5,600 is recorded. The gain can be verified as follows:

Selling price	$160,000
Carrying value of bonds sold (½ × $308,800)	154,400
Gain on sale of investment	$ 5,600

Since half the bonds were sold, interest received on each following July 31 and January 31 will be $7,500 ($150,000 × .10 × 6/12), and amortization of premium will be $200 per month rather than $400.

CONSOLIDATED FINANCIAL STATEMENTS

Corporations often own all or a majority (more than 50%) of the voting stock of other corporations. The company owning the stock is called the **parent company,** and the company whose stock is more than 50% owned is called a **subsidiary.** Thus, if Pratt Company owns more than 50% of the voting stock of Sweet Company, Pratt Company is the parent company and Sweet Company is a subsidiary. By owning more than 50% of the voting stock, Pratt Company can elect the board of directors of Sweet Company and thereby effectively control its activities and resources.

Each company is a separate legal entity, so each maintains its own accounting records and prepares separate financial statements. In the separate financial statements of Pratt Company, the Investment in Sweet Company will appear in the balance sheet as an investment accounted for by the equity method and the income statement will include Pratt Company's share of Sweet Company's net income or net loss. However, the equity method does not show the individual asset and liability amounts of Sweet Company represented by the investment account or the individual revenues and expenses of Sweet Company that produced Pratt Company's share of Sweet Company's net income. Because the parent company controls the activities and resources of the subsidiary, the two companies effectively function as a *single economic entity*. Investors in the parent company want financial information about the entire resources and operations under control of the parent company. Consequently, the separate financial statements of the parent company and its subsidiary (or subsidiaries) are combined into a single set of statements called **consolidated financial statements.**

The preparation of consolidated financial statements is quite difficult and is normally the subject of an advanced accounting course. However, because most publicly held corporations consist of a parent company owning one or more subsidiary companies, it is important to understand the basic principles followed in the preparation of consolidated financial statements.

PRINCIPLES OF CONSOLIDATION

Consolidated financial statements are prepared by combining the individual account balances of the parent company with those of the subsidiary in order to report them as single accounts. For example, the cash balance of the parent company is combined with the cash balance of the subsidiary; the parent company's accounts payable are combined with the subsidiary's accounts payable; and the parent company's sales are combined with those of the subsidiary. Before combining account balances, however, certain duplicate items must be eliminated so that the combined amounts are not overstated from a single-entity standpoint. Three basic types of elimination must be made: *elimination of the investment account and subsidiary stockholders' equity; elimination of intercompany receivables and payables;* and *elimination of intercompany revenues and expenses*. (The first two types are discussed in the following section on the preparation of the consolidated balance sheet. Elimination of intercompany revenues and expenses will be discussed in the later section on the preparation of a consolidated income statement.)

CONSOLIDATED BALANCE SHEET

The consolidated balance sheet shows the total assets under control of the parent company's board of directors, the total debts owed by the consolidated entity to outsiders, and owners' equity in the assets. To illustrate the preparation of a consolidated balance sheet, assume that Pratt Company and Sweet Company had the following balance sheets on January 1, 1984:

	Pratt Company	Sweet Company
Assets		
Cash	$320,000	$ 49,000
Note receivable from Sweet Company	30,000	–0–
Accounts receivable (net)	80,000	52,000
Inventory	125,000	71,000
Plant and equipment (net)	396,000	76,000
Total Assets	$951,000	$248,000
Liabilities and Stockholders' Equity		
Accounts payable	$ 86,000	$ 48,000
Note payable to Pratt Company	–0–	30,000
Common stock, $10 par	500,000	100,000
Retained earnings	365,000	70,000
Total Liabilities and Stockholders' Equity	$951,000	$248,000

On January 2, 1984, Pratt Company purchased for $170,000 on the open market all of the outstanding common stock of Sweet Company. Late in 1983 Pratt Company loaned Sweet Company $30,000, obtaining a note receivable as evidence of the loan.

To record the purchase of Sweet Company's stock, Pratt Company made the following entry:

Jan.	2	Investment in Sweet Company	170,000	
		Cash		170,000
		To record the purchase of 100% of Sweet Company's outstanding stock.		

Notice that the purchase price of the stock was equal to the book value of Sweet Company's net assets (stockholders' equity). The total purchase price of the stock is often greater (or less) than the book value of the net assets purchased. Accounting for these situations is discussed later in this chapter.

Data for the preparation of consolidated statements are normally accumulated on a worksheet similar to that in Figure 18-3. Because no operating
activity has yet taken place, the only consolidated financial statement prepared
on the date of stock acquisition is a consolidated balance sheet. Notice that Pratt
Company's balance sheet on the worksheet includes cash of $150,000, since
$170,000 was used to buy Sweet Company's stock, and also includes its invest-
ment in Sweet Company. The $170,000 cash was paid to Sweet Company's
stockholders and, therefore, is not incuded in Sweet Company's balance sheet.

The theory of consolidated statements is that the parent company and its
subsidiary are viewed as a single economic entity. Thus, before the accounts
of Pratt Company and Sweet Company are combined, it is necessary to prepare
the two types of eliminating entries mentioned earlier. *The eliminating entries*

Figure 18-3
Worksheet for Consolidated Balance Sheet—100% Ownership

PRATT COMPANY AND SUBSIDIARY
Worksheet for a Consolidated Balance Sheet
January 2, 1984

	Pratt Company	Sweet Company	Eliminations Dr.	Eliminations Cr.	Consolidated Balances
Cash	150,000	49,000			199,000
Note receivable from Sweet Company	30,000			(2) 30,000	
Accounts receivable	80,000	52,000			132,000
Inventory	125,000	71,000			196,000
Investment in Sweet Company	170,000			(1) 170,000	
Plant and equipment	396,000	76,000			472,000
Total	951,000	248,000			999,000
Accounts payable	86,000	48,000			134,000
Note payable to Pratt Company		30,000	(2) 30,000		
Common stock:					
Pratt Company	500,000				500,000
Sweet Company		100,000	(1) 100,000		
Retained earnings:					
Pratt Company	365,000				365,000
Sweet Company		70,000	(1) 70,000		
Total	951,000	248,000	200,000	200,000	999,000

(1) To eliminate the investment in Sweet Company.
(2) To eliminate intercompany note receivable and note payable.

are worksheet entries only—they are not made on either the parent company's or subsidiary company's books.

Eliminating entry (1) (Figure 18-3) is made to eliminate the Investment in Sweet Company and Sweet Company's stockholders' equity. When Pratt Company purchased the stock of Sweet Company, it effectively acquired Sweet Company's net assets, which were recorded in the Investment in Sweet Company account. Because Sweet Company's assets and liabilities will be combined with those of Pratt Company, failure to eliminate the interest in the net assets reported in the investment account would result in a double counting. In addition, since Sweet Company's stockholders' equity represents the source of the net assets, it also must be eliminated. In other words, one part of the consolidated entity (Pratt Company) owns the stock of another part of the consolidated entity (Sweet Company). An entity's ownership of its own stock does not constitute either an asset or stockholders' equity. Consequently, both the investment account and the subsidiary's stockholders' equity are eliminated to report the parent company and subsidiary company as a single economic entity.

Eliminating entry (2) is made to eliminate the intercompany note receivable and note payable. Failure to eliminate them would result in an overstatement of both assets and liabilities since the receivable and payable result from the transfer of funds within the consolidated entity—that is, no outside party is involved. Since a company cannot owe money to itself, the intercompany note receivable and note payable are eliminated.

After the eliminating entries have been made on the worksheet, the remaining balance sheet accounts are combined and carried into the consolidated balances column as assets, liabilities, and stockholders' equity of the consolidated entity. The consolidated balances column is then used to prepare the consolidated balance sheet as shown on page 721. Notice that the stockholders' equity of the consolidated entity is the same as Pratt Company's since Sweet Company's stockholders' equity was eliminated.

PURCHASE OF LESS THAN 100% OF SUBSIDIARY STOCK

In the preceding case, we assumed that Pratt Company purchased all (100%) of Sweet Company's outstanding stock. As mentioned earlier, however, control can be achieved by acquiring a majority—but less than 100%—of the subsidiary's outstanding shares. When this occurs, the subsidiary has stockholders other than the parent company. These other stockholders are called minority stockholders and their interest in the net assets of the subsidiary is called a **minority interest.** All of the subsidiary's assets and liabilities are included in the consolidated balance sheet in order to show the total resources and obligations under control of the parent company's board of directors. The

PRATT COMPANY AND SUBSIDIARY
Consolidated Balance Sheet
January 2, 1984

Current Assets:	
Cash	$199,000
Accounts receivable (net)	132,000
Inventory	196,000
Total Current Assets	527,000
Plant and equipment (net)	472,000
Total Assets	$999,000
Current Liabilities:	
Accounts payable	$134,000
Stockholders' Equity:	
Common stock, $10 par	500,000
Retained earnings	365,000
Total Liabilities and Stockholders' Equity	$999,000

minority interest in the net assets of the subsidiary is set out on the worksheet when the investment account and subsidiary's stockholders' equity is eliminated, as shown in Figure 18-4.

For example, assume that Pratt Company purchased only 70% of Sweet Company's stock on January 2, 1984, at a cost of $119,000. A worksheet for a consolidated balance sheet on the date of acquisition is shown in Figure 18-4.

Again, notice that the purchase price of the stock ($119,000) was equal to the book value of Sweet Company's net assets acquired (.70 × $170,000 = $119,000). Also, since Pratt Company used only $119,000 in cash to acquire Sweet Company stock, the cash balance is $201,000 ($320,000 − $119,000). Eliminating entry (1) is made to eliminate the investment account and Sweet Company's stockholders' equity. However, since only 70% of the stock was purchased, a minority interest in the net assets of Sweet Company exists in the amount of $51,000 (.30 × $170,000). This minority interest is set up on the last line of the worksheet as part of eliminating entry (1) and is reported as a separate item on the consolidated balance sheet. Most companies report minority interest as a separate item between liabilities and stockholders' equity. Thus, the liability and stockholders' equity section of the consolidated balance sheet may appear as shown on page 722.

PRATT COMPANY AND SUBSIDIARY
Worksheet for a Consolidated Balance Sheet
January 2, 1984

	Pratt Com- pany	Sweet Com- . pany	Eliminations Dr.	Eliminations Cr.	Consoli- dated Balances
Cash	201,000	49,000			250,000
Notes receivable from Sweet Company	30,000			(2) 30,000	
Accounts receivable	80,000	52,000			132,000
Inventory	125,000	71,000			196,000
Investment in Sweet Company	119,000			(1) 119,000	
Plant and equipment	396,000	76,000			472,000
Total	951,000	248,000			1,050,000
Accounts payable	86,000	48,000			134,000
Notes payable to Pratt Company		30,000	(2) 30,000		
Common stock:					
Pratt Company	500,000				500,000
Sweet Company		100,000	(1) 100,000		
Retained earnings:					
Pratt Company	365,000				365,000
Sweet Company		70,000	(1) 70,000		
Minority interest				(1) 51,000	51,000
Total	951,000	248,000	200,000	200,000	1,050,000

(1) To eliminate the investment in Sweet Company
(2) To eliminate intercompany note receivable and note payable.

Figure 18-4
Worksheet for Consolidated Balance Sheet—Minority Interest

Liabilities and Stockholders' Equity

Current liabilities:	
Accounts payable	$ 134,000
Minority interest	51,000
Stockholders' equity:	
Common stock, $10 par	500,000
Retained earnings	365,000
Total liabilities and stockholders' equity	$1,050,000

Eliminating entry (2) is made to eliminate intercompany notes receivable and notes payable, as explained in the preceding illustration.

PURCHASE OF STOCK FOR MORE (OR LESS) THAN BOOK VALUE

In the preceding examples we assumed that the parent company purchased its shares in the subsidiary company at a price equal to their book value. That assumption was made to simplify the examples and concentrate attention on the fundamentals followed in the preparation of a consolidated balance sheet. When a corporation purchases stock in another corporation, it must pay the market price of the shares—which will normally be more or less than their book value. In the preparation of consolidated statements, this difference between the cost of the investment and the book value of the subsidiary's equity acquired must be reported properly.

If the parent company pays more than book value for the shares, an excess of cost over book value will remain when the investment account is eliminated against the subsidiary's stockholders' equity. Among the main reasons a company may pay more than book value for the shares are:

1. The fair values of the subsidiary's assets may be greater than their book values. The application of conservative accounting procedures such as the use of accelerated depreciation and the LIFO inventory method often produces book values for plant and equipment and for inventory that are less than their fair values. Or some subsidiary assets such as land may have appreciated in value.
2. Long-term subsidiary liabilities may be overvalued as a result of an increase in general market interest rates.
3. The subsidiary may have unrecorded goodwill as evidenced by its above-normal earnings.
4. The parent company may be willing to pay a premium for the right to acquire a controlling interest in the subsidiary and the economic advantages it expects to obtain from integrated operations.

The Accounting Principles Board has identified the standards to be followed in assigning the cost of shares in a subsidiary company as follows: First, all identifiable assets acquired—and liabilities assumed—whether or not shown in the financial statements of the acquired company, should be assigned a portion of the cost of the acquired company, normally equal to their fair values at date of acquisition. Second, the excess of cost over the sum of the amounts assigned to identifiable assets acquired less liabilities assumed should be recorded as goodwill.[5]

To illustrate, assume that Pratt Company and Sweet Company had balance sheets on January 1, 1984, as shown on page 718. On January 2, 1984, Pratt

---

[5]Accounting Principles Board, "Business Combinations," *APB Opinion No. 16* (New York: AICPA, August 1970), par. 87.

Company purchased all of Sweet Company's stock for $220,000. Since the book value of Sweet Company's net assets (stockholders' equity) is $170,000, there is an excess of cost over book value of $50,000 ($220,000 − $170,000). Assume further that $30,000 of this excess relates to an undervaluation of Sweet Company's plant and equipment and the remaining $20,000 represents consolidated goodwill. A worksheet for the preparation of a consolidated balance sheet on the date of acquisition is shown in Figure 18-5.

Pratt Company's cash balance on January 2 is $100,000 because $220,000 was used to acquire Sweet Company's stock. Note that when the investment account is eliminated against Sweet Company's stockholders' equity, a $50,000 excess of cost over equity acquired remains, $30,000 of which is added to plant and equipment and $20,000 of which represents consolidated goodwill.

Figure 18-5
Worksheet for Consolidated Balance Sheet—Excess Cost

PRATT COMPANY AND SUBSIDIARY
Worksheet for a Consolidated Balance Sheet
January 2, 1984

	Pratt Company	Sweet Company	Eliminations Dr.	Eliminations Cr.	Consolidated Balances
Cash	100,000	49,000			149,000
Note receivable from Sweet Company	30,000			(2) 30,000	
Accounts receivable	80,000	52,000			132,000
Inventory	125,000	71,000			196,000
Investment in Sweet Company	220,000			(1) 220,000	
Plant and equipment	396,000	76,000	(1) 30,000		502,000
Goodwill			(1) 20,000		20,000
Total	951,000	248,000			999,000
Accounts payable	86,000	48,000			134,000
Note payable to Pratt Company		30,000	(2) 30,000		
Common stock:					
Pratt Company	500,000				500,000
Sweet Company		100,000	(1) 100,000		
Retained earnings:					
Pratt Company	365,000				365,000
Sweet Company		70,000	(1) 70,000		
Total	951,000	248,000	250,000	250,000	999,000

(1) To eliminate the investment in Sweet Company.
(2) To eliminate intercompany note receivable and note payable.

The $30,000 must be charged to depreciation expense on the worksheet over the remaining life of the plant assets in determining consolidated net income. Likewise, consolidated goodwill is amortized to expense on the worksheet over its estimated life, not to exceed 40 years.

Sometimes the parent company pays less than book value for the subsidiary company's shares because the fair values of the subsidiary's assets are less than their book values, its liabilities are understated, or it has incurred operating losses that have decreased the market value of its shares. If this occurs, the APB provides that the excess of book value over cost should be allocated to reduce the values assigned to noncurrent assets in determining their fair values.[6]

CONSOLIDATED INCOME STATEMENT

The consolidated income statement is prepared by combining the individual revenue and expense accounts of the parent company and its subsidiaries. Before combining the accounts, however, any intercompany revenues and expenses must be eliminated so that the consolidated income will reflect the results of operations from transactions with parties outside the affiliated group. Examples of intercompany items that must be eliminated are intercompany sales and purchases, intercompany rent revenue and rent expense, and intercompany interest revenue and interest expense.

To illustrate, assume that Pratt Company and Sweet Company had revenues and expenses during 1984 as shown in Figure 18-6. Assume also that Pratt Company sold $80,000 worth of merchandise to Sweet Company during the year, and that Sweet Company paid $2,400 interest to Pratt Company on the note payable to Pratt Company. Sweet Company sold all of the merchandise purchased from Pratt Company during the year. A worksheet for the preparation of a consolidated income statement is shown in Figure 18-6.

Eliminating entry (1) eliminates intercompany sales and purchases (included here in the cost of goods sold) so that the total sales and cost of goods sold reported on the consolidated income statement will include only those resulting from transactions with parties outside the affiliated group. Eliminating entry (2) eliminates intercompany interest revenue and interest expense since the intercompany note receivable and note payable were eliminated on the consolidated balance sheet. In addition, the interest payment resulted in a cash transfer within the consolidated entity since no outside party was involved.

The preparation of a consolidated income statement is normally much more complex than illustrated here. The consolidated financial statements would

[6]*Ibid.*, par. 91.

PRATT COMPANY AND SUBSIDIARY
Worksheet for a Consolidated Income Statement
Year Ended December 31, 1984

	Pratt Company	Sweet Company	Eliminations Dr.		Eliminations Cr.		Consolidated Balances
Sales	642,000	374,000	(1)	80,000			936,000
Interest revenue	2,400		(2)	2,400			
Total revenue	644,400	374,000					936,000
Cost of goods sold	376,000	208,000			(1)	80,000	504,000
Operating expenses	169,000	122,000					291,000
Interest expense		2,400			(2)	2,400	
Total expenses	545,000	332,400					795,000
Net Income	99,400	41,600		82,400		82,400	141,000

(1) To eliminate intercompany sales and purchases.
(2) To eliminate intercompany interest revenue and interest expense.

Figure 18-6
Worksheet for Consolidated Income Statement

also include a consolidated retained earnings statement and a consolidated statement of changes in financial position. Because their preparation is complex, they are appropriate topics of an advanced accounting course.

PURCHASE VERSUS POOLING OF INTERESTS

When a corporation and one or more other companies are brought together (become affiliated) into one economic unit, the transaction is called a **business combination.** Two methods of accounting for business combinations—the purchase method and the pooling-of-interests method—are acceptable, but not as alternatives for the same business combination.

In preceding examples we have assumed that Pratt Company acquired its controlling interest in Sweet Company by purchasing the subsidiary's shares for cash. This type of acquisition is called a **purchase** and the consolidated financial statements are prepared under the purchase method of accounting. Rather than using cash, the parent company could acquire the shares purchased with other assets, debt securities, equity securities, or a combination of these. As mentioned earlier, under the purchase method the investment in the subsidiary is recorded at its cost, which is assigned to the assets acquired and liabilities assumed in an amount equal to their fair values. Any excess of cost over the fair value of the net assets acquired is recorded as consolidated goodwill. Under the purchase method, it is assumed that the former stockholders of the subsidiary sell their shares to the parent company in exchange for the cash, other assets, or securities received.

If the parent company exchanges its voting stock for essentially all (defined as 90% or more) of the voting stock of a subsidiary and certain other specific conditions are met, the business combination must be accounted for as a **pooling of interests.**[7] Because the former stockholders of the subsidiary become stockholders in the combined or consolidated entity, and because no resources are distributed, the business combination is viewed as a transaction under which the stockholders of the combining companies pool their resources and stockholder interests to form the new company. In other words, no purchase and sale of the subsidiary's stock occurs. Based on this reasoning, the market price of the shares given and the fair values of the subsidiary's assets and liabilities are ignored. The net assets of the subsidiary are not revalued in the consolidated balance sheet. The *book values* of the subsidiary's assets and liabilities are combined with those of the parent company in the consolidated balance sheet and no excess of cost over book value (or excess of book value over cost) exists. As a consequence, no consolidated goodwill exists in a pooling of interests.

Under the pooling-of-interests method, the investment in a subsidiary is normally recorded at an amount equal to the par or stated value of the parent company shares issued. The investment account is then eliminated on the consolidated worksheet in a manner similar to that under the purchase method. To illustrate, assume that on January 2, 1984, Pratt Company exchanged 10,000 shares of its unissued common stock with a market value of $22 per share for all of the outstanding common stock of Sweet Company and that all other conditions for a pooling of interests were met. The exchange of stock would be recorded by Pratt Company as follows:[8]

Jan.	2	Investment in Sweet Company	100,000	
		Common Stock		100,000
		Issued 10,000 shares of $10 par stock for all of the outstanding shares of Sweet Company.		

Note that the market value of Pratt Company's shares is ignored. Note also, for comparison purposes later, that if the purchase method had been used, the

---

[7]*Ibid.*, par. 45–48.

[8]If the total par or stated value of the shares issued differs from the total par or stated value of the shares acquired, some reclassification of stockholders' equity is needed. Accounting for that situation is covered in more advanced accounting courses.

investment would have been recorded at its cost of $220,000 (10,000 shares × $22 per share), the same amount illustrated for the purchase method in Figure 18-5. A worksheet for the preparation of a consolidated balance sheet on the date of acquisition under the pooling-of-interests method is shown in Figure 18-7.

Note that Pratt Company's cash balance is $320,000 on the worksheet since none was used to acquire Sweet Company's stock. Notice also that Pratt Company's common stock is $600,000, which reflects the $100,000 increase resulting from the exchange of its shares for those of Sweet Company.

Eliminating entry (1) is made to eliminate the investment account and Sweet Company's common stock since Pratt Company's common stock has been substituted for Sweet Company's. Sweet Company's retained earnings of $70,000 become a part of consolidated retained earnings. Eliminating entry (2) is made to eliminate the intercompany note receivable and note payable.

Figure 18-7

Worksheet for Consolidated Balance Sheet—Pooling of Interests

PRATT COMPANY AND SUBSIDIARY
Worksheet for a Consolidated Balance Sheet
Pooling of Interests Method
January 2, 1984

	Pratt Company	Sweet Company	Eliminations Dr.	Eliminations Cr.	Consolidated Balances
Cash	320,000	49,000			369,000
Note receivable from Sweet Company	30,000			(2) 30,000	
Accounts receivable	80,000	52,000			132,000
Inventory	125,000	71,000			196,000
Investment in Sweet Company	100,000			(1) 100,000	
Plant and equipment	396,000	76,000			472,000
Total	1,051,000	248,000			1,169,000
Accounts payable	86,000	48,000			134,000
Note payable to Pratt Company		30,000	(2) 30,000		
Common stock:					
Pratt Company	600,000				600,000
Sweet Company		100,000	(1) 100,000		
Retained earnings	365,000	70,000			435,000
Total	1,051,000	248,000	130,000	130,000	1,169,000

(1) To eliminate the investment in Sweet Company.
(2) To eliminate intercompany note receivable and note payable.

Observe that total consolidated stockholders' equity ($1,035,000) is equal to the combined preacquisition stockholders' equity of the two companies ($865,000 + $170,000 = $1,035,000), and total consolidated assets ($1,169,000) and liabilities ($134,000) are equal to the combined preacquisition assets and liabilities of the two companies with the exception of the $30,000 intercompany note receivable and note payable that are eliminated.

Comparison of Figure 18-7 with Figure 18-5 demonstrates clearly that the pooling method ignores the revaluation of plant and equipment to its fair value and that no consolidated goodwill exists. Thus, consolidated net income in the future will be greater under the pooling method than under the purchase method because there will be no depreciation of the $30,000 increment in plant and equipment and no amortization expense for the goodwill.

Another important difference between the purchase and pooling of interests methods is the treatment of the subsidiary's earnings in the year of combination. If the business combination occurs during the subsidiary's fiscal year, under the purchase method only that portion of the net income earned by the subsidiary after the date of combination is included in consolidated net income. Under the pooling of interests method, the subsidiary's net income for the full year is included in consolidated net income even though the business combination may occur late in the year.

In summary, a business combination that meets the specific conditions for pooling must be accounted for by the pooling-of-interests method. All other business combinations must be accounted for by the purchase method. A comparison of the primary differences between the purchase and pooling of interest methods is given in Figure 18-8.

CONDITIONS FOR THE PREPARATION OF CONSOLIDATED FINANCIAL STATEMENTS

Certain conditions must be met before a given subsidiary is included in the consolidated financial statements. The most important condition is that the parent company must actually control the subsidiary by owning more than 50% of its voting stock. In addition, management of the parent company should actively exercise control and should expect to continue to control in the future. A parent company should not consolidate a subsidiary that it expects to sell in the near future.

Even though control conditions are met, there may be some situations, such as the following, in which the subsidiary should be excluded from the consolidated statements.

1. The activities of the subsidiary may be so unrelated to those of other subsidiaries or the parent company that it would be more informative to

Figure 18-8
Comparison of Purchase and Pooling of Interests

Purchase	Pooling of Interests
1. The investment is recorded at its cost. Subsidiary assets and liabilities are adjusted to their fair values and any excess of cost over the fair value of the subsidiary's net assets is consolidated goodwill.	The investment is recorded at the par or stated value of the parent company's shares issued. Subsidiary assets and liabilities are included in the consolidated balance sheet at their book values. No excess of cost over book value exists.
2. Subsidiary retained earnings do not become a part of consolidated retained earnings.	Subsidiary retained earnings are included in consolidated retained earnings.
3. The excess of cost over book value assigned to depreciable assets and goodwill is amortized to reduce consolidated net income.	No excess of cost over book value exists; thus, there is no amortization expense.
4. Subsidiary earnings are included in consolidated net income only from the date of combination.	Subsidiary earnings for the full year of combination are included in consolidated net income.

exclude the subsidiary from consolidation and disclose its activities separately. For example, General Motors Corporation does not consolidate its finance subsidiary, General Motors Acceptance Corporation.

2. The resources of the subsidiary, such as a bank or insurance company, are so restricted by statute that they are not generally available for use throughout the affiliated group. For example, Sears, Roebuck and Company does not consolidate its insurance subsidiary, Allstate Insurance Company.

3. The subsidiary is in a foreign country that has imposed currency restrictions such that the income and assets of the subsidiary cannot be withdrawn by the parent company.

When a subsidiary is excluded from consolidation, it is generally reported in the financial statements as an investment accounted for by the equity method.

LIMITATIONS OF CONSOLIDATED FINANCIAL STATEMENTS

Consolidated financial statements are prepared primarily for use by management, stockholders, and creditors of the parent company. They are of limited use to minority stockholders and creditors of the subsidiary companies because they contain no detailed information about the individual subsidiaries. Creditors and minority stockholders of a subsidiary have legal claims only against the resources of that subsidiary and, thus, must rely on the individual financial statements of the subsidiary to assess the safety and earning potential of their investments.

Information in consolidated financial statements of highly diversified companies that operate in several industries is often of limited use to investors and prospective investors of the parent company. Financial position and the results of operations of these companies cannot be compared with industry standards or with other companies since they may operate in different industries. To partially counter this deficiency, accounting standards require that diversified companies must report certain information by segments of the business. Specific requirements of segment reporting are contained in *Financial Accounting Standards No. 14*, "Financial Reporting for Segments of a Business Enterprise," and are explored in more advanced accounting courses.

GLOSSARY

BUSINESS COMBINATION. A transaction under which a corporation and one or more other companies are brought together into one economic unit (p. 726).

CONSOLIDATED FINANCIAL STATEMENTS. The financial statements of a parent company and its subsidiaries in which the assets and liabilities of the affiliates are combined into a consolidated balance sheet and their revenues and expenses are combined into a consolidated income statement (p. 717).

COST METHOD OF ACCOUNTING FOR STOCK INVESTMENTS. An accounting method under which the investment is recorded at its cost. Income is recognized on the investment as dividends are received (p. 707).

EQUITY METHOD OF ACCOUNTING FOR STOCK INVESTMENTS. An accounting method under which the investor company recognizes its share of the investee company's earnings or losses as they are reported by the investee. The investor increases or decreases the investment account for its share of the investee's earnings or losses and decreases the investment account for dividends received (p. 707).

INVESTEE COMPANY. A corporation whose stock is owned by another company (p. 707).

INVESTOR COMPANY. A company that owns stock in another company (p. 707).

LONG-TERM INVESTMENTS. Investments that are not intended to be converted into cash for normal operating needs (p. 706).

MINORITY INTEREST. The minority stockholders' interest in the net assets of a subsidiary company (p. 720).

PARENT COMPANY. A company that owns more than 50% of the voting stock of a corporation (p. 716).

POOLING-OF-INTERESTS. A method of accounting for a business combination in which the parent company exchanges its voting stock for essentially all of the voting stock of a subsidiary and certain other specific conditions are met. The assets and liabilities of the separate companies are combined at their book values (p. 727).

PORTFOLIO. A group of equity securities or debt securities held by an investor (p. 705).

PURCHASE METHOD. A method of accounting for a business combination in which the stockholders of the subsidiary company sell their shares to the parent company. Assets and liabilities of the subsidiary are reported at their fair values as measured by the total cost of the shares (p. 726).

SUBSIDIARY COMPANY. A corporation whose shares are more than 50% owned by another company (p. 717).

TEMPORARY INVESTMENTS. Investment securities that management intends to convert into cash when needed for current operating activities (p. 704).

DISCUSSION QUESTIONS

1. What is the distinction between temporary investments and long-term investments?
2. Contrast the accounting for a temporary debt security portfolio with accounting for a temporary stock investment portfolio.
3. Are unrealized gains on a temporary stock investment portfolio ever reported on the income statement? If so, when and how?
4. Long-term investments in voting stock are initially recorded at their cost. Subsequent to acquisition they are accounted for by one of two methods. Name each method and explain when the use of each is appropriate.
5. Explain briefly how the use of the cost method of accounting for long-term investments in voting stock differs from the accounting procedures used for temporary investments in voting stock.
6. Dade Company purchased 10,000 of the 40,000 outstanding common shares of Easy Company on January 3, 1984, paying $20 per share. During 1984, Easy Company declared a dividend of $90,000 and reported earnings for the year of $200,000. The market value of the stock was $18 per share on December 31, 1984. What should be the balance in the Investment in Dade Company Stock account on December 31, 1984?
7. Assume that the stock in (6) above was purchased on July 1, 1984, instead of January 3 and that the dividends were declared on April 1, 1984. Earnings of Easy Company for the year were $200,000. What would be the balance in the Investment account to be reported on the December 31, 1984, balance sheet of Dade Company?
8. Under what circumstances will a company's bonds sell on the market at (a) par, (b) a premium, and (c) a discount?
9. Why is it necessary to amortize a discount or a premium that arises from the purchase of a long-term investment in bonds at an amount below or above par value? Over what period should the discount or the premium be amortized?
10. Space Company purchased a $1,000 par value, 15% bond of Crafe Company on July 1, 1984, for $1,132. The bond matures on December 31, 1989. How much interest revenue should be reported by Space Company for the year ended December 31, 1984?
11. Describe how the sale of a stock investment is recorded.

12. What are consolidated financial statements? What is their purpose?
13. What are the three basic types of eliminations that must be made in the preparation of consolidated financial statements?
14. Why are the investment account and the subsidiary's stockholders' equity accounts eliminated on a worksheet for a consolidated balance sheet?
15. What is meant by the term *minority interest?* Where is this item generally reported on a consolidated balance sheet?
16. Briefly, explain when a business combination must be accounted for as a pooling of interests. Why does no consolidated goodwill ever result in such a combination?
17. Why might consolidated net income be greater under the pooling-of-interests method than under the purchase method?

EXERCISES

Exercise 18-1 (Temporary Stock Portfolio)

A corporation had the following temporary stock portfolio on December 31, 1984:

Stock	Cost	Market Value
Rodan Corporation—Preferred	$ 61,000	$ 65,000
Tellman Company—Common	135,000	120,000
B. J. Crane Company—Common	42,000	50,000
Total	$238,000	$235,000

Required:

A. Prepare the journal entry to reduce the marketable securities to the lower of cost or market.
B. Explain how the accounts in (A) should be reported in the financial statements for 1984.

Exercise 18-2 (Long-term Stock Investment—Cost and Equity Methods)

On January 2, 1984, Union Company purchased 10% of Klein Company's 50,000 outstanding common shares as a long-term investment at 31¼ plus a broker's commission of $1,200. On July 6, Klein Company paid a dividend of $2 per share on all outstanding common shares, and reported net income of $120,000 for the year.

Required:

A. Prepare the entries to record the purchase of the stock and the receipt of the cash dividend.
B. Assuming the market value of the Klein Stock investment was $149,000 at the end of 1984, explain how the difference between cost and market value should be reported in the financial statements.
C. Assume that Union Company purchased 25% of Klein Company's outstanding common stock instead of 10%. Prepare the journal entries Union Company would

make to account for its investment during 1984. [Broker's fees, net income, and dividends paid remain the same as in (A).]

Exercise 18-3 (Stock Investment—Equity Method)

On January 3, 1984, Baker Company purchased as a long-term investment 3,000 of the 10,000 outstanding common shares of Crater Company, paying $30 per share. On August 6, 1984, Crater Company paid a dividend of $.75 per share, and on December 31, Crater Company reported earnings for the year of $50,000. The market value of Crater Company's stock on December 31, 1984, was $28.50 per share.

Required:

A. Prepare all journal entries on the books of Baker Company to account for its investment in Carter Company for 1984.
B. Compute the balance in the investment account after all entries for 1984 have been posted.
C. Assume Baker Company sold 600 of its shares in Crater Company on January 5, 1985, for $29 per share less a broker's commission of $300. Prepare the journal entry to record the sale.

Exercise 18-4 (Long-term Bond Investment)

On May 1, 1984, Western Company purchased as a long-term investment 100, $1,000 par value, 10% bonds of Texor Company on the open market at 101 plus accrued interest of $2,500 and broker's fees of $2,000. The bonds pay interest semiannually on July 31 and January 31 and mature on July 31, 1990. Western Company's fiscal year ends on December 31.

Required:

A. Prepare all journal entries that would be made by Western Company to account for the bond investment during 1984.
B. Assuming that Western Company held the bonds until their maturity date, prepare the journal entry on Western's books on July 31, 1990.

Exercise 18-5 (Sale of Bond Investment)

Refer to Exercise 18-4. Assume that Western Company sold one-half of its Texor Company bonds on April 31, 1986, for $53,000 (net of broker's fees) plus accrued interest of $1,250.

Required:

Prepare the journal entries that Western Company should prepare on the date of sale.

Exercise 18-6 (Long-term Bond Investment)

On March 1, 1984, Quinn Company purchased as a long-term investment 50, $1,000 par value, 12% bonds of Rex Company on the open market for $48,260 plus accrued interest. The bonds pay interest semiannually on June 30 and December 31 and mature on December 31, 1988.

Required:

A. Prepare all journal entries that would be made by Quinn Company to account for this investment during 1984, assuming its fiscal year ends on December 31.

B. How much interest revenue was earned during 1984?

C. Assume that Quinn Company sold all of the bonds on July 1, 1986, for $49,300 and prepare the entry to record the sale.

Exercise 18-7 (Consolidated Worksheet Entries—100% Ownership)

Power Company and Sugar Company had balance sheets on January 1, 1984, as follows:

	Power	Sugar
Cash	$270,000	$ 50,000
Note receivable from Sugar Company	50,000	–0–
Accounts receivable	90,000	24,000
Inventory	100,000	30,000
Plant and equipment (net)	305,000	105,000
Total Assets	$815,000	$209,000
Accounts payable	$ 72,000	$ 20,000
Note payable to Power Company	–0–	50,000
Common stock, $2 par	400,000	70,000
Retained earnings	343,000	69,000
Total Liabilities and Stockholders' Equity	$815,000	$209,000

On January 2, 1984, Power Company purchased on the open market all of the outstanding common stock of Sugar Company for $139,000.

Required:

A. Prepare the entry Power Company would make to record the purchase of Sugar Company's stock.

B. Prepare, in general journal form, the eliminating entries that would be needed to prepare a consolidated balance sheet worksheet at the date of acquisition, January 2, 1984.

Exercise 18-8 (Consolidated Worksheet Entries—70% Ownership)

Refer to the data in Exercise 18-7 and assume that Power Company had purchased only 70% of Sugar Company's common stock (instead of 100%) at a purchase price of $97,300.

Required:

A. Prepare, in general journal form, the eliminating entries that would be needed in the preparation of a consolidated balance sheet worksheet on January 2, 1984.

B. Assume that Power Company purchased 100% of Sugar Company's stock for $175,000 and that $21,000 of the excess of cost over book value acquired relates to the undervaluation of Sugar Company's plant and equipment. The remainder of cost over book value acquired represents goodwill. Prepare, in general journal form, the eliminating entries that would be needed in the preparation of a consolidated balance sheet worksheet on January 2, 1984.

Exercise 18-9 (Journal and Worksheet Entries for Pooling of Interests)

On March 1, 1984, Porter Company exchanged 25,000 shares of its unissued $5 par value common stock with a market value of $21 per share for all of the outstanding common stock of Sanders Company in a transaction properly accounted for as a pooling of interests. On the date of exchange, Sanders Company had stockholders' equity as follows:

Common stock, $10 par	$125,000
Retained earnings	310,000
Total Stockholders' Equity	$435,000

At the time of the stock exchange, Sanders Company had a note payable outstanding that was payable to Porter Company in the amount of $20,000.

Required:

Prepare the journal entry needed to record the exchange of stock and prepare, in general journal form, the eliminating entries that would be made in the preparation of a consolidated balance sheet worksheet on March 1, 1984.

Exercise 18-10 (Consolidated Income Statement)

Palmer Company and Stone Company had revenues and expenses for the year 1984 as follows:

	Palmer	Stone
Sales	$910,000	$298,000
Interest revenue	5,000	–0–
Total revenue	915,000	298,000
Cost of goods sold	510,000	179,000
Operating expenses	265,000	82,000
Interest expense		5,000
Total expenses	775,000	266,000
Net Income	$140,000	$ 32,000

Stone Company is a wholly owned subsidiary of Palmer Company. During 1984, Palmer Company sold $60,000 of merchandise to Stone Company. The $5,000 interest expense of Stone Company was paid to Palmer Company on a note payable.

Required:

A. Prepare, in general journal form, the eliminating entries needed to prepare a consolidated income statement worksheet for 1984.

B. Prepare a consolidated income statement for the year ended December 31, 1984.

PROBLEMS

Problem 18-1 (Temporary Stock Investment Portfolio)

On January 1, 1984, Hod Company purchased the following securities as temporary investments:

Investment	Cost
Frame Company common stock	$ 26,000
Lake Company common stock	41,000
Monroe Company preferred stock	38,000
Total	$105,000

During 1984 Hod Company received $10,500 in dividends from these investments. On December 31, 1984, the market values of the investments were:

Investment	Market Value
Frame Company common stock	$29,000
Lake Company common stock	36,000
Monroe Company preferred stock	32,000
Total	$97,000

Required:

A. Prepare journal entries to:
  1. Record the receipt of dividends.
  2. Adjust the temporary stock investment portfolio at December 31, 1984.
B. Explain where the accounts used in (A.2.) above should be reported in the financial statements on December 31, 1984.
C. Assume that the Frame Company stock was sold on February 8, 1985, for $32,000 less a broker's fee of $1,000. Prepare the entry to record the sale.
D. If the total market value of the investment portfolio had been $110,000 on December 31, 1984, what entry would have been made? Explain.

Problem 18-2 (Cost vs. Equity Method for Long-term Stock Investment)

Drake Company purchased as a long-term investment some of the 20,000 shares of the outstanding common stock of Folk Company. The annual accounting period for each company ends on December 31. The following transactions took place during 1984:

Jan.	5	Purchased shares of common stock of Folk Company at $15 per share as follows: Case A 2,000 shares purchased Case B 5,000 shares purchased
Dec.	31	Received financial statements of Folk Company for the year ended December 31, 1984. Reported net income was $60,000.
	31	Received a cash dividend of $.75 per share from Folk Company.
	31	The market value of Folk Company common stock was $13 per share.

Required:

A. For each case, what accounting method should be used by Drake Company? Explain.

B. Prepare the journal entries that Drake Company should make for each case for the transactions above.

C. Give the amounts for each case that would be reported on the financial statements of Drake Company on December 31, 1984. Use the following format:

	Case A	Case B
Balance Sheet:		
Long-term investment		
Less: Allowance to reduce investment to market		
value		
Net investment		
Stockholders' equity:		
Unrealized loss		
Income Statement:		
Investment (dividend) revenue		

Problem 18-3 (Long-term Stock Investment)

On January 3, 1983, Lane Company purchased as a long-term investment 30,000 of the 100,000 outstanding common shares of Prince Company for $12.50 per share plus a broker's commission of $3,000. Prince Company declared and paid a cash dividend of $.50 per share on August 8, 1983, and reported net income for the year of $80,000 on December 31, 1983. The market value of Prince Company's stock on December 31, 1983, was $14 per share.

Required:

A. What method should Lane Company use to account for the investment in Prince Company? Why?

B. Prepare the entries Lane Company would make during 1983 to account for its investment in Prince Company.

C. Assume that Lane Company sold 3,000 of its shares of Prince Company on January 2, 1984, for $14 per share less a broker's commission of $800. Prepare the entry to record the sale.

Problem 18-4 (Long-term Bond Investment)

On June 1, 1984, Butler Company purchased as a long-term investment 200, $1,000 par value, 9% bonds of Daley Company at 101 plus accrued interest of $3,000 and a broker's commission of $3,700. The bonds pay interest semiannually on March 31 and September 30 and mature on September 30, 1990. On November 30, 1985, Butler Company sold one-half of the bonds for $104,400 (net of broker fees) plus accrued interest of $1,500, to finance plant expansion.

Required:

A. Prepare all journal entries concerning the bond investment during the years of 1984 and 1985. (Butler Company's fiscal year ends on December 31.)

B. What is the net amount of interest revenue earned during 1984?

C. Prepare the entry that would be made on September 30, 1990, when the remaining unsold bonds mature.

Problem 18-5 (Long-term Bond Investment)

Assume the same information given in Problem 18-4, except that the bonds were purchased at 96 instead of 101 and that the broker's commission was $3,440 instead of $3,700.

Required:

A. Prepare all journal entries concerning the bond investment during the years 1984 and 1985. (Butler Company's fiscal year ends on December 31.)

B. What is the net amount of interest revenue earned during 1984?

C. Prepare the entry that would be made on September 30, 1990, when the remaining unsold bonds mature.

Problem 18-6 (Worksheet for Consolidated Balance Sheet— 80% Ownership)

Balance sheets of Powell Company and Sands Company on January 3, 1984, are as follows:

	Powell Company	Sands Company
Cash	$ 420,000	$ 60,000
Note receivable from Sands Company	40,000	–0–
Accounts receivable (net)	102,000	59,000
Inventory	168,000	89,000
Plant and equipment (net)	510,000	170,000
Total assets	$1,240,000	$378,000
Accounts payable	$ 190,000	$115,000
Note payable to Powell Company	–0–	40,000
Common stock, $10 par	700,000	150,000
Retained earnings	350,000	73,000
Total Liabilities and Stockholders' Equity	$1,240,000	$378,000

On January 4, 1984, Powell Company purchased 80% of the outstanding common stock of Sands Company on the open market for $178,400.

Required:

A. Prepare the entry to record the purchase of Sands' stock.

B. Prepare a worksheet for a consolidated balance sheet on January 4, 1984.

C. Prepare a consolidated balance sheet.

Problem 18-7 (Worksheet for Consolidated Balance Sheet— 100% Ownership)

Refer to the data in Problem 18-6 and assume that Powell Company purchased all of the stock of Sands Company for $275,000. Assume also that $35,000 of the excess of cost over book value relates to an undervaluation of Sands Company's plant and equipment and the remainder represents goodwill.

Required:

A. Prepare the entry to record the purchase of Sands Company's stock.

B. Prepare a worksheet for a consolidated balance sheet on the date of acquisition.

Problem 18-8 (Consolidated Balance Sheet—Pooling of Interests)

On January 3, 1984, Peters Company exchanged 20,000 shares of its unissued $10 par value common stock with a market value of $20 per share for all of the outstanding common stock of Strand Company. The transaction is properly accounted for as a pooling of interests. Balance sheets for the two companies on January 2, 1984, are presented below:

	Peters	Strand
Cash	$ 310,000	$ 70,000
Note receivable from Strand Company	60,000	
Accounts receivable (net)	170,000	86,000
Inventory	465,000	125,000
Plant and equipment (net)	780,000	180,000
Total Assets	$1,785,000	$461,000
Accounts payable	$ 370,000	$ 91,000
Note payable to Peters Company		60,000
Common stock, $10 par	800,000	200,000
Retained earnings	615,000	110,000
Total Liabilities and Stockholders' Equity	$1,785,000	$461,000

Required:

A. Prepare the entry Peters Company would make to record the exchange of stock.

B. Prepare a worksheet for the preparation of a consolidated balance sheet on the date of acquisition.

ALTERNATE PROBLEMS

Problem 18-1A (Temporary Stock Investment Portfolio)

Early in 1984, Paro Company purchased the following equity securities as temporary investments:

Investment	No. of Shares	Percent of Investees' Stock	Cost per Share
Able Company—Preferred	400	5%	$112.00
Baker Company—Common	3,000	1%	16.50
Carter Company—Common	5,000	12%	18.00

During 1984, Paro Company received $17,200 in cash dividends from these investments. On December 31, 1984, the market values of the shares were:

Investment	Market Value per Share
Able Company—Preferred	$108.00
Baker Company—Common	13.00
Carter Company—Common	18.25

Required:
A. Prepare journal entries to:
   1. Record receipt of the cash dividends.
   2. Adjust the temporary stock investment portfolio at December 31, 1984.
B. Explain where the accounts used in (A.2.) above should be reported in the financial statements on December 31, 1984.
C. Assume that the Able Company stock was sold on February 15, 1985, for $107 per share less total broker fees of $300. Prepare the entry to record the sale.
D. Assume that the investments were purchased as long-term investments rather than temporary investments. Prepare the entry to adjust the stock investment portfolio on December 31, 1984.
E. Explain where the accounts used in (D) above should be reported in the financial statements on December 31, 1984.

Problem 18-2A (Cost vs. Equity Method of Accounting)

Barrow Company had 50,000 shares of $10 par value common stock outstanding. On January 2, 1984, Reed Company purchased as a long-term investment some of Barrow Company's common stock at $22 per share. On December 31, 1984, Barrow Company reported a net operating loss of $40,000 and declared and paid a cash dividend of $.60 per share. The market value of Barrow Company's stock on December 31, 1984, was $19 per share.

Required:
A. For each case given below, indicate the method of accounting that should be used by Reed Company. Explain why.
   Case A—Reed Company purchased 5,000 shares of Barrow Company stock.
   Case B—Reed Company purchased 20,000 shares of Barrow Company stock.
B. For each case, give the journal entries that Reed Company should make for each of the events below. (If no entry is required, explain why.)
   1. To record the purchase of the shares.
   2. To recognize the net loss reported by Barrow Company for 1984.
   3. To record the receipt of cash dividends.
   4. To recognize the effect of the market value on December 31, 1984.
C. Indicate the amounts that would be reported in the financial statements of Reed Company on December 31, 1984, relative to these cases. Follow the format presented below:

	Case A	Case B
Balance Sheet:		
Long-term investment in Barrow Stock	_____	_____
Less: Allowance to reduce to market	_____	_____
Net investment	_____	_____
Stockholders' equity:		
Unrealized loss	_____	_____
Income Statement:		
Investment or dividend revenue (loss)	_____	_____

Problem 18-3A (Long-term Stock Investment)

At the beginning of 1983, Trump Company purchased as a long-term investment 15,000 of the 50,000 outstanding common shares of Velure Company for $16 per share plus a broker's commission of $5,000. Velure Company declared and paid a cash dividend of $.80 per share on September 9, 1983, and reported a net loss of $60,000 for the year ended December 31, 1983.

Required:

A. What method should Trump Company use to account for the investment in Velure Company? Why?
B. Prepare the entries Trump Company would make during 1983 to account for its investment in Velure Company.
C. Assume that Trump Company sold 3,000 of its shares of Velure Company on January 5, 1984, for $13 per share less a broker's commission of $700. Prepare the entry to record the sale.

Problem 18-4A (Long-term Bond Investment)

On October 1, 1984, Mead Company purchased as a long-term investment 50, $1,000 par value, 12% bonds of Clark Company for $47,760 plus accrued interest of $2,000. The bonds pay interest semiannually on May 31 and November 30 and mature on May 31, 1989. On August 1, 1985, Mead Company sold one-half of the bonds for $23,800 (net of broker's fees) plus accrued interest of $500, to finance plant expansion.

Required:

A. Prepare all journal entries concerning the bond investment during the years 1984 and 1985. (Mead Company's fiscal year ends on December 31.)
B. What is the net amount of interest revenue earned during 1984?
C. Prepare the entry that would be made on May 31, 1989, when the remaining bonds mature.

Problem 18-5A (Long-term Bond Investment)

Assume the same information given in Problem 18-4A, except that the bonds were purchased for a total cost of $52,800 plus accrued interest of $2,000.

Required:

A. Prepare all journal entries concerning the bond investment during the years 1984 and 1985. (Mead Company's fiscal year ends on December 31.)

B. What is the net amount of interest revenue earned during 1984?

C. Prepare the entry that would be made on May 31, 1989, when the bonds mature.

Problem 18-6A (Worksheet for Consolidated Balance Sheet— 90% Ownership)

Peters Company and Sherril Company had balance sheets on January 2, 1984, as follows:

	Peters Company	Sherril Company
Cash	$1,470,000	$ 210,000
Note receivable from Sherril Company	140,000	–0–
Accounts receivable (net)	355,000	206,000
Inventory	590,000	312,500
Plant and equipment (net)	1,785,600	595,600
Total Assets	$4,340,600	$1,324,100
Accounts payable	$ 970,400	$ 398,100
Note payable to Peters Company	–0–	140,000
Common stock, $5 par	2,450,000	520,000
Retained earnings	920,200	266,000
Total Liabilities and Stockholders' Equity	$4,340,600	$1,324,100

On January 3, 1984, Peters Company purchased 90% of the outstanding common stock of Sherril Company on the open market for $707,400.

Required:

A. Prepare the entry to record the purchase of Sherril Company stock.

B. Prepare a worksheet for a consolidated balance sheet on January 3, 1984.

C. Prepare a consolidated balance sheet.

Problem 18-7A (Worksheet for Consolidated Balance Sheet— 100% Ownership)

Using the data in Problem 18-6A, assume that Peters Company purchased all of the stock of Sherril Company for $955,000. Any excess of cost over book value relates to an undervaluation of Sherril Company's land, which is included in the plant and equipment account.

Income statements for the two companies for the year ended December 31, 1984, are given below:

	Peters	Sherril
Sales	$6,050,000	$2,508,000
Interest revenue	10,000	–0–
Total Revenue	$6,060,000	$2,508,000
Cost of goods sold	3,921,000	1,580,700
Operating expenses	1,654,600	707,000
Interest expense	–0–	19,600
Total Expenses	5,575,600	2,307,300
Net Income	$ 484,400	$ 200,700

During 1984, Sherril Company made sales to Peters Company of $800,000. Sherril Company paid $10,000 in interest to Peters Company on the note payable.

Required:

A. Prepare the entry to record the purchase of Sherril Company's stock.

B. Prepare a worksheet for a consolidated balance sheet on the date of acquisition.

C. Prepare a worksheet for a consolidated income statement for 1984.

Problem 18-8A (Consolidated Worksheet—Pooling of Interests)

At the beginning of 1984, Prentice Company exchanged 44,000 shares of its unissued $10 par value common stock with a market value of $17.50 per share for all of the outstanding common stock of Shields Company. The transaction met all of the criteria for a pooling of interests. Balance sheets for the two companies immediately before the exchange of stock were:

	Prentice	Shields
Cash	$ 680,000	$ 155,400
Note receivable from Shields Company	132,000	–0–
Accounts receivable (net)	374,000	189,200
Inventory	1,025,000	275,000
Plant and equipment (net)	1,716,000	400,000
Total Assets	$3,927,000	$1,019,600
Accounts payable	$ 814,000	$ 200,200
Note payable to Prentice Company	–0–	132,000
Common stock, $10 par	1,765,000	440,000
Retained earnings	1,348,000	247,400
Total Equities	$3,927,000	$1,019,600

Required:

A. Prepare the entry Prentice Company would make to record the exchange of stock.

B. Prepare a worksheet for the preparation of a consolidated balance sheet on the date of acquisition.

CASE FOR CHAPTER 18

(Annual Report Analysis)

Refer to the financial statements of General Motors Corporation in the appendix and answer the following questions:

1. What method is used to account for temporary investments?
2. Why aren't temporary investments carried at the lower market figures?
3. What method is used to account for nonconsolidated subsidiaries and associated conpanies?
4. How much income was earned from investments in nonconsolidate subsidiaries and associated companies during 1981?
5. What is the general principle followed by General Motors in determining which subsidiaries should be included in the consolidated financial statements?
6. Why isn't General Motors Acceptance Corporation consolidated with other subsidiaries in the consolidated finanial statements?
7. How muh did General Motors Acceptance Corporation owe to General Motors Corporation and affiliated companies on Debember 31, 1981?

CHAPTER 19
STATEMENT OF CHANGES IN FINANCIAL POSITION

OVERVIEW AND OBJECTIVES

This chapter discusses the preparation and uses of a statement of changes in financial position. When you have completed the chapter, you should understand:

- The different concepts of funds (pp. 747–748).
- The kinds of transactions that produce changes in working capital (pp. 749–750).
- The normal sources and uses of working capital (pp. 750–753).
- How to report the effects of exchanges of noncurrent items (pp. 753–754).
- How to prepare a statement of changes in financial position worksheet (pp. 760–764).
- How to prepare a formal statement of changes in financial position (pp. 764–765).
- How to prepare cash flow statements (pp. 764–770).

As discussed earlier, a complete set of financial statements includes a balance sheet, an income statement, a retained earnings statement, and a statement of changes in financial position. The first three have been presented in preceding chapters. The fact that the statement of changes in financial position is discussed last does not imply that it is any less important than the others, however. It is a very useful statement for both investors and creditors because it identifies the sources and uses of resources as well as the changes that have taken place in the financial position of a business from one period to another. An analysis of comparative balance sheets for successive periods will identify the total changes that have taken place in asset, liability, and owners' equity accounts, but will not provide a ready explanation of what caused those changes. The income statement and retained earnings statement do give a partial explanation by indicating the sources and uses of funds from operating activities, the amount of earnings paid as dividends, and the amount of earnings retained for other uses. Neither statement, however, gives a full report of the sources of resources during the period and the uses to which they were committed.

The statement specifically designed to summarize all of the financing (sources of funds) and investing (uses of funds) activities of a business, including those involving operating activities, is the statement of changes in financial position. This statement aids users by providing answers to questions like: How were the funds obtained to pay off long-term debt and to acquire new plant assets during the period? How was the firm able to pay regular dividends even though it incurred a significant operating loss for the period? How were the funds from a new stock issue utilized? Why is the company in a worse working capital position when it had profitable operations for the period? The statement of changes in financial position provides answers to these and similar questions because it shows the individual sources and uses of funds during the period. In fact, in the past many firms called it a Statement of Sources and Applications of Funds, or simply a Funds Statement, but today the great majority of firms use the title Statement of Changes in Financial Position.

CONCEPTS OF FUNDS

The term **funds** has different meanings to different people. Many think of funds as cash; some view funds as cash and readily marketable securities; still others think of funds as **working capital**—the excess of current assets over current liabilities.[1] Although any of these concepts of funds may be used in the preparation of the statement of changes in financial position, the most widely used concept is that of working capital as indicated by the results of a survey of 600 companies reported in the 1980 edition of *Accounting Trends & Techniques* (p. 354):

Number of Companies Reporting:

Changes in working capital	549
Changes in cash	51
Total Companies	600

The working-capital concept of funds is most often used because business and financial executives recognize that short-term credit is often used as a substitute for cash. Over the operating cycle, current liabilities are incurred to

---

[1]Terminology used in the accounting and finance literature varies somewhat. Some authors refer to current assets as working capital and call the excess of current assets over current liabilities net working capital.

acquire inventory and services, the inventory is exchanged for an account receivable in a sales transaction, the account receivable is collected, and the cash is used in part to pay current liabilities. In other words, current liabilities are continually being incurred, current assets are constantly being converted into cash, and cash is continuously being used to pay current liabilities. At any given time, the excess of current assets over current liabilities (working capital) represents a fund of relatively liquid resources. For example, assume that Clark Corporation had the following current assets and current liabilities on January 1:

Cash	$ 60,000	Notes payable	$ 35,000
Accounts receivable	80,000	Accounts payable	90,000
Inventory	120,000	Accrued expenses	10,000
Total Current Assets	$260,000	Total Current Liabilities	$135,000

Clark Corporation's working capital is $125,000 ($260,000 − $135,000). As the inventory is sold and accounts receivable are collected, cash becomes available to pay off the current liabilities. In addition, there will be cash left over that management can use to replace inventory, pay current expenses, invest in plant assets, pay off long-term debt, or distribute as dividends. Thus, business executives generally think of working capital as a fund of net liquid assets that can be used for various operating and investing activities.

It is important to recognize that activity involving current assets and current liabilities only does not normally change the amount of working capital. For example, if Clark Corporation collects $40,000 of accounts receivable, total current assets and current liabilities remain unchanged; thus, working capital also remains unchanged. Likewise, if $35,000 cash is used to pay off the notes payable, current assets will be reduced to $225,000, current liabilities will be reduced to $100,000, and working capital will remain unchanged at $125,000.

SOURCES AND USES OF WORKING CAPITAL

When the statement of changes in financial position is prepared to report the sources and uses of working capital, any transaction that increases working capital is a **source of funds** and any transaction that decreases working capital is a **use of funds.** It is therefore important to recognize the effect of various transactions on working capital. As an aid in analyzing the effect of different transactions on working capital, it is helpful to view the balance sheet in account form as shown below:

a. Current Assets	b. Current Liabilities
c. Noncurrent Assets	d. Noncurrent Liabilities and Owners' Equity

To affect working capital, a transaction must involve both a current account and a noncurrent account. In other words, to affect working capital a transaction must involve accounts on both sides of the solid line (which might be called the working-capital line) in the balance sheet above. Transactions that affect accounts within one of the four parts only, as well as transactions that affect accounts on both sides of the broken line only, have no effect on working capital. Applying these rules, we can identify 10 general types of transactions, six of which do not affect working capital and four that do affect it.

Transactions That Do Not Affect Working Capital

Type of Transaction	Parts of Balance Sheet Affected	Examples
1.	Part a only	Purchased a temporary investment for cash; collected an account receivable.
2.	Part b only	Exchanged a short-term note payable for an account payable.
3.	Part c only	Exchanged land for equipment.
4.	Part d only	Exchanged common stock for bonds payable.
5.	Parts a and b	Paid an account payable; purchased inventory on account.
6.	Parts c and d	Issued common stock for land.

Notice that none of these six types of transactions involve accounts on both sides of the solid line. Types 1, 2, 3, and 4 affect accounts within each part only. An exchange of one current asset for another of equal value or the exchange of one current liability for another of equal value does not change total working capital. Likewise, an exchange of one noncurrent asset for another or an exchange of a noncurrent liability for another noncurrent liability or for stock has no effect on working capital. Type 5 transactions reduce or increase current assets and current liabilities by equal amounts and therefore do not affect total working capital. Type 6 transactions do not involve working capital because no current asset or current liability is affected.

Transactions That Affect Working Capital

Type of Transaction	Parts of Balance Sheet Affected	Examples
7.	Parts a and c	Purchased plant assets for cash; sold plant assets for a short-term receivable.
8.	Parts b and c	Purchased plant assets on short-term credit.
9.	Parts a and d	Issued bonds payable for cash; retired preferred stock for cash.
10.	Parts b and d	Exchanged a short-term note payable for a long-term note payable.

Each of these four types of transactions involves a current asset or current liability and a noncurrent asset, noncurrent liability, or element of owners' equity. Each type affects accounts on both sides of the solid line, thereby resulting in a source or use of working capital.

SOURCES OF WORKING CAPITAL

Firms obtain working capital primarily from four basic sources: current operating activities, the sale of noncurrent assets, the issue of long-term debt, and the issue of capital stock.

Current Operations

The main source of working capital for many companies is current operating activities. Sales result in an increase in current assets (cash or receivables) and an increase in owners' equity (revenue). The increase in current assets increases working capital. Cost of goods sold and most operating expenses decrease current assets or increase current liabilities and decrease owners' equity. Most expenses therefore reduce working capital. If the increase of funds from revenues exceeds the decrease of funds for cost of goods sold and operating expenses, there is a net increase of funds and therefore a net increase in working capital. Of course, if the decrease of funds for cost of goods sold and operating expenses exceeds the increase of funds from revenues, a net decrease in working capital results.

If all expenses represented decrease of current assets or the incurring of current liabilities, net income would represent a net increase in working capital for the period. This is seldom the case, however, because some expenses deducted on the income statement (such as depreciation, depletion, and amortization) do not reduce current assets or increase current liabilities during the current period. Depreciation, for example, is recorded by a debit to depreciation expense and a credit to accumulated depreciation (a contra asset account). Current assets and current liabilities are unaffected. The same is true for depletion of natural resources and amortization of intangible assets. Some items increase net income but do not involve working capital. One of them, gain on the sale of an asset, is discussed later in this chapter. Other items are covered in more advanced accounting courses.

In the preparation of the statement of changes in financial position, total revenues and those expenses that decrease working capital could be reported separately. However, since this detail is already provided in the income statement, the normal approach is to show net income as the first item on the statement of changes in financial position. Expenses that did not decrease working capital during the period are then added as illustrated below.

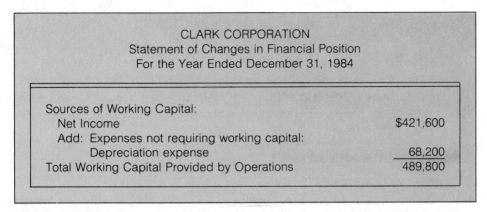

Other sources and uses of working capital are then listed separately to complete the statement, as will be shown later.

Unfortunately, the addition of depreciation expense to net income has led some people to view depreciation as a source of working capital. It is important that users of financial statements avoid this misconception. As explained earlier, the depreciation entry does not involve a current asset or current liability. Thus, no working capital flows into the company from the depreciation entry. The source of the $489,800 working capital from operations for Clark Corporation was the excess of sales revenues over those expenses that required the use of working capital. Depreciation and similar items are deducted from revenue in arriving at net income, but do not require the use of working capital. Thus they are added back to net income as a convenient short-cut for determining working capital provided by operations.

It is possible for a company to report a net operating loss for the period and still show working capital provided by operations. This will result when the total of depreciation, depletion, and amortization added back is greater than the operating loss. For example, refer to the statement of changes in financial position for General Motors on page A4. Although General Motors reported a net loss of approximately $750 million for 1980, operations provided about $3.5 billion of working capital.

Another type of adjustment to net income in determining working capital provided by operations is that needed for nonoperating gains and losses. Current accounting standards require that these gains and losses must be reported on the income statement. For example, if land with a cost of $40,000 is sold for $100,000, the sale would be recorded as follows:

June	5	Cash	100,000	
		Land		40,000
		Gain on Sale of Land		60,000

The entire proceeds from the sale ($100,000) is reported on the statement of changes in financial position as working capital provided from the sale of land. Since the $60,000 gain is reported in the income statement and included in net income, it must be deducted from net income on the statement of changes in financial position in order to reflect properly the working capital provided by operations. If the gain is not deducted, working capital provided by the transaction would be incorrectly reported as $160,000. In a similar manner, if the land were sold for $30,000 and a $10,000 loss reported, the loss must be added to net income in arriving at working capital provided by operations.

Sale of Noncurrent Assets

A company may obtain working capital by selling a plant asset, long-term investment, or other noncurrent asset in exchange for a current asset. Working capital will increase by the amount of current assets received regardless of whether the noncurrent asset is sold at a gain or a loss. For example, if long-term investments with a cost of $50,000 are sold for $70,000 cash, working capital increases by the $70,000 increase in current assets. If the cost of the long-term investments had been $80,000, resulting in a loss of $10,000, the increase in working capital would still be $70,000—since that is the amount by which current assets increased. As discussed earlier, any gain (loss) is deducted from (added to) net income in determining working capital provided by operations.

Issue of Long-term Debt

The issue of long-term debt, such as bonds payable, for cash increases current assets and noncurrent liabilities and is a major source of working capital for many companies. Short-term borrowing, however, increases both current assets and current liabilities by an equal amount and is therefore not a source of working capital.

Issue of Capital Stock

An additional issue of capital stock or the reissue of treasury stock for cash or other current assets is another source of working capital because current assets increase with an offsetting increase in stockholders' equity. In a similar manner, an additional investment of current assets by an individual owner or partner is a source of working capital to a single proprietorship or partnership. Capital stock issued in a stock dividend or stock split does not provide working capital, however, because only stockholders' equity accounts are affected.

USES OF WORKING CAPITAL

Most uses of working capital come about from transactions that are opposite of those that provide working capital. For example, a business may incur an operating loss in excess of depreciation and other items added back, thereby reducing working capital. More common uses of working capital are the purchase of noncurrent assets, the retirement of long-term debt, the retirement or reacquisition of capital stock, and the declaration of cash dividends.

Purchase of Noncurrent Assets

The purchase of plant assets, long-term investments, or other noncurrent assets in exchange for current assets or current liabilities is a major use of working capital for many companies. Noncurrent assets are increased and the decrease in current assets or increase in current liabilities reduces working capital.

Retirement of Long-term Debt

If current assets are used to pay long-term liabilities, working capital is reduced. In addition, when a portion of long-term debt becomes due within the next accounting period, it must be reclassified as a current liability. Since current liabilities increase with an offsetting decrease in noncurrent liabilities, the reclassification results in a decrease in working capital. Subsequent payment of the portion classified as a current liability will not affect working capital because both current assets and current liabilities will be reduced.

Retirement or Reacquisition of Capital Stock

When current assets are used to reacquire capital stock that is to be retired or held as treasury stock, working capital is decreased by the amount of the current assets given up. Likewise, the withdrawal of current assets by an individual owner or partner is a use of working capital to a single proprietorship or partnership.

Declaration of Cash Dividends

The declaration of a cash dividend results in a debit to retained earnings and a credit to a current liability, dividends payable. Since current liabilities are increased, the declaration of the dividend is a use of working capital. The later payment of the dividend reduces a current asset and a current liability by equal amounts and therefore does not affect working capital. In other words, it is the declaration of cash dividends rather than their payment that represents a use of working capital.

THE SPECIAL CASE OF EXCHANGE TRANSACTIONS

Companies sometimes give a long-term note payable or issue their capital stock in direct exchange for a noncurrent asset. For example, assume that common stock was issued in exchange for a building and the following entry made:

June	4	Buildings	600,000	
		Common Stock		600,000
		Exchanged common stock for a building.		

Since the transaction does not involve current assets or current liabilities, it has no effect on working capital. However, because the transaction does represent a significant investment and financing event, accounting standards require that the effects of the transaction be disclosed by reporting it as both a source and a use of working capital.[2] The acquisition of the building is reported therefore as a $600,000 use of working capital, and the issue of common stock is reported as a $600,000 source of working capital. In this way, significant investing and financing transactions are disclosed even though the net effect on working capital is zero. This approach to reporting exchange transactions is sometimes referred to as the **all financial resources approach** in the preparation of the statement of changes in financial position.

Other types of exchange transactions that are reported as both a source and use of working capital are the conversion of bonds payable or preferred stock into common stock and the exchange of long-term debt for plant assets. Most transactions that affect noncurrent accounts only are exchange transactions. A major exception is the issue of a stock dividend. Stock dividends are not exchange transactions and do not affect the company's resources, but merely result in a transfer of retained earnings to other stockholders' equity accounts. Thus, stock dividends are not reported in the statement of changes in financial position.

PREPARING THE STATEMENT OF CHANGES IN FINANCIAL POSITION—WORKING CAPITAL BASIS

The statement of changes in financial position consists of two main sections, one for reporting the sources of working capital and the other for reporting the uses of working capital. The difference between the totals of the two sections represents the increase or decrease in working capital for the period. The statement is supported by a schedule showing the changes in current assets and current liabilities for the period.

Much of the information needed to prepare the statement is contained in the comparative balance sheets, income statement, and retained earnings statement. Additional information is obtained by analyzing the changes that have taken place in the noncurrent general ledger accounts during the period. Since

---

[2]Accounting Principles Board, "Reporting Changes in Financial Position," *APB Opinion No. 19* (New York: AICPA, 1971), par. 8.

transactions that increase or decrease working capital must involve both current and noncurrent accounts, an examination of the changes in the noncurrent accounts helps identify the individual sources and uses of working capital.

WORKING CAPITAL FLOW: A SIMPLE ILLUSTRATION

Ace Company is a small corporation engaged in the retail sale of men's clothing. The company rents its store building but owns its store equipment. An income statement for 1984 and comparative balance sheets on December 31, 1983 and 1984, are shown in Figure 19-1.

Figure 19-1
Ace Company Financial Statements

ACE COMPANY
Income Statement
For the Year Ended December 31, 1984

Sales		$380,000
Cost of goods sold		196,000
Gross profit		184,000
Operating expenses:		
Administrative expense	$76,000	
Selling expense	56,000	
Depreciation expense	8,000	140,000
Net income		$ 44,000

Comparative Balance Sheets

	December 31 1984	December 31 1983
Assets		
Cash	$ 47,000	$ 36,000
Accounts receivable	26,000	18,000
Inventory	54,000	49,000
Store equipment	88,000	88,000
Less: accumulated depreciation	(43,000)	(35,000)
Land	55,000	–0–
Total assets	$227,000	$156,000
Liabilities and Owners' Equity		
Accounts payable	$ 13,000	$ 21,000
Short-term notes payable	15,000	10,000
Capital stock	150,000	100,000
Retained earnings	49,000	25,000
Total liabilities and owners' equity	$227,000	$156,000

In addition to normal operating activities, the following events occurred during 1984:

1. Land costing $55,000 was purchased for cash for the future construction of a store building.
2. Capital stock was issued at par value for cash of $50,000.
3. Dividends of $20,000 were declared and paid.

The first step in the preparation of a statement of changes in financial position is the computation of the change in working capital for the year. This can be done by preparing a schedule of changes in the components of working capital (Figure 19-2).

The statement of changes in financial position can now be prepared as shown in Figure 19-3.

Working capital provided by operations can be determined by analyzing the income statement. Net income of $44,000 is adjusted for expenses not requiring the use of working capital during the period, in this case depreciation expense of $8,000. Note that the $8,000 also represents the increase in accumulated depreciation (a noncurrent account) on the comparative balance sheets.

Remember that sources and uses of working capital must involve both current and noncurrent accounts. Thus, the other sources and uses of working capital can be determined by analyzing the changes in noncurrent accounts on the comparative balance sheets. The land account increased by $55,000, reflecting the purchase of land, which is a use of working capital. The capital stock account increased by $50,000, which represents a source of working capital from the issue of stock. In addition, the change in retained earnings for the year can be verified as follows:

Retained earnings balance, 1/1/84	$25,000
Add net income for 1984	44,000
Total	69,000
Less dividends declared in 1984	20,000
Retained earnings balance, 12/31/84	$49,000

A MORE COMPLEX ILLUSTRATION

The preparation of a more complex statement of changes in financial position involves four basic steps:

1. The change in working capital for the period is calculated.
2. A worksheet is prepared to analyze the changes in noncurrent accounts.

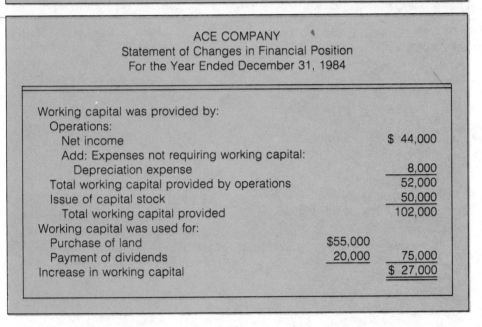

Figure 19-2
Change in Components of Working Capital

Changes in Components of Working Capital

| | December 31 | | Increase or (Decrease) in Working Capital |
	1984	1983	
Current assets:			
Cash	$ 47,000	$ 36,000	$11,000
Accounts receivable	26,000	18,000	8,000
Inventory	54,000	49,000	5,000
Total current assets	127,000	103,000	
Current liabilities:			
Accounts payable	$ 13,000	$ 21,000	8,000
Short-term notes payable	15,000	10,000	(5,000)
Total current liabilities	28,000	31,000	
Working capital	$ 99,000	$ 72,000	
Increase in working capital			$27,000

Figure 19-3
Statement of Changes in Financial Position

ACE COMPANY
Statement of Changes in Financial Position
For the Year Ended December 31, 1984

Working capital was provided by:		
Operations:		
Net income		$ 44,000
Add: Expenses not requiring working capital:		
Depreciation expense		8,000
Total working capital provided by operations		52,000
Issue of capital stock		50,000
Total working capital provided		102,000
Working capital was used for:		
Purchase of land	$55,000	
Payment of dividends	20,000	75,000
Increase in working capital		$ 27,000

3. Changes in noncurrent accounts are analyzed to determine whether they have resulted in a source or use of working capital.
4. The statement of changes in financial position is prepared from the information gathered on the worksheet.

The comparative balance sheets and statement of income and retained earnings of Clark Corporation presented in Figure 19-4 are used to illustrate the preparation of the statement of changes in financial position.

Figure 19-4
Clark Corporation
Financial Statements

CLARK CORPORATION
Comparative Balance Sheets

	December 31	
Assets	1984	1983
Current assets:		
Cash	$ 188,000	$ 162,000
Accounts receivable (net)	231,000	176,000
Inventory	314,000	322,000
Prepaid expenses	36,000	14,000
Total current assets	769,000	674,000
Property, plant, and equipment:		
Buildings	1,200,000	800,000
Accumulated depreciation—buildings	(348,000)	(315,000)
Equipment	674,000	516,000
Accumulated depreciation—equipment	(267,000)	(232,000)
Land	300,000	300,000
Total property, plant, and equipment	1,559,000	1,069,000
Long-term stock investment (at cost which is less than market)	100,000	200,000
Total assets	$2,428,000	$1,943,000
Liabilities and Stockholders' Equity		
Current liabilities:		
Notes payable	$ 62,000	$ 50,000
Accounts payable	238,000	269,000
Accrued expenses	21,000	16,000
Total current liabilities	321,000	335,000
Long-term liabilities:		
Notes payable, due January 1, 1987	100,000	–0–
Bonds payable, due July 1, 1998	600,000	500,000
Total long-term liabilities	700,000	500,000
Stockholders' equity:		
Common stock, $5 par	650,000	550,000
Contributed capital in excess of par	299,000	226,000
Retained earnings	458,000	332,000
Total stockholders' equity	1,407,000	1,108,000
Total liabilities & stockholders' equity	$2,428,000	$1,943,000

Figure 19.4
continued

Statement of Income and Retained Earnings
For the Year Ended December 31, 1984

Net sales		$4,620,000
Cost of goods sold		2,440,000
Gross profit on sales		2,180,000
Operating expenses other than depreciation	$1,770,000	
Depreciation expense	68,000	
Total operating expenses		1,838,000
Operating income		342,000
Gain on sale of investments		60,000
Net income before income tax		402,000
Income tax expense		160,000
Net income		242,000
Retained earnings, January 1		332,000
		574,000
Less: Cash dividends declared		116,000
Retained earnings, December 31		$ 458,000

During 1984, Clark Corporation entered into these transactions that affected noncurrent accounts:

1. A new wing was added to the building at a cost of $400,000 cash.
2. New equipment was purchased at a cost of $158,000; cash of $58,000 and a note payable for $100,000 due January 1, 1987, were given in exchange.
3. Long-term stock investments were sold for $160,000.
4. Bonds payable of $100,000 were issued for cash at par.
5. An additional 20,000 shares of $5 par value common stock were issued for $173,000.
6. Depreciation expense for the year was $33,000 on buildings and $35,000 on equipment.
7. Cash dividends of $116,000 were declared and paid.

COMPUTATION OF THE CHANGE IN WORKING CAPITAL FOR THE YEAR

The first step in the preparation of a statement of changes in financial position for Clark Corporation is to compute the increase or decrease in working capital during 1984 as follows:

	December 31		Increase (Decrease)
	1984	1983	
Current assets	$769,000	$674,000	$ 95,000
Current liabilities	321,000	335,000	14,000
Working capital	$448,000	$339,000	$109,000

Current assets increased by $95,000 from the end of 1983 to the end of 1984, resulting in an increase in working capital. In addition, current liabilities decreased by $14,000, which also represents an increase in working capital. Since working capital increased by a total of $109,000 during the year, the sources of working capital reported in the statement of changes in financial position must exceed the uses of working capital by $109,000.

PREPARATION OF THE WORKSHEET

After determining the net change in working capital, noncurrent accounts are analyzed to identify the individual sources and uses of working capital. To aid in this analysis and to gather the information needed to prepare the statement of changes in financial position, many companies prepare a worksheet. Although the statement could be prepared directly from an analysis of the changes in noncurrent accounts, the worksheet is particularly helpful when there have been numerous transactions affecting noncurrent accounts during the period. The worksheet for Clark Corporation, presented in Figure 19-5, consists of two main sections. The top section is used to reconcile beginning-of-year with end-of-year noncurrent account balances and to identify the individual sources and uses of working capital, which are listed in the bottom section. The basic steps in the preparation of the worksheet are:

1. Columns are used in the top section to record noncurrent account balances at the beginning of the year, analyze transactions for the year, and record noncurrent account balances at the end of the year.
2. Noncurrent accounts with debit balances are separated from those with credit balances. Working capital balances at the beginning of the year and the end of the year are listed as the first "debit" item, and the increase (decrease) in working capital is entered as a debit (credit) in the Analysis of Transactions column. The beginning-of-year and end-of-year debit balances are then listed, followed by the beginning-of-year and end-of-year credit balances.[3]

---

[3] If the company has negative working capital at the beginning or end of the year (if current liabilities exceed current assets), this is entered as the first item in the Credit part of the top section.

Figure 19-5
Worksheet for Statement of Changes in Financial Position

CLARK CORPORATION
Worksheet for Statement of Changes in Financial Position
Year Ended December 31, 1984

	Account Balance 1/1/84	Analysis of Transactions for 1984		Account Balance 12/31/84
		Debit	Credit	
Debits				
Working capital	339,000	109,000		448,000
Buildings	800,000	(3) 400,000		1,200,000
Equipment	516,000	(4) 158,000		674,000
Land	300,000			300,000
Long-term investments	200,000		(5) 100,000	100,000
Total Debits	2,155,000			2,722,000
Credits				
Accumulated depr.— buildings	315,000		(2) 33,000	348,000
Accumulated depr.— equipment	232,000		(2) 35,000	267,000
Notes payable	–0–		(4) 100,000	100,000
Bonds payable	500,000		(6) 100,000	600,000
Common stock	550,000		(7) 100,000	650,000
Contributed capital in excess of par	226,000		(7) 73,000	299,000
Retained earnings	332,000	(8) 116,000	(1) 242,000	458,000
Total Credits	2,155,000	783,000	783,000	2,722,000
Sources of Working Capital		Sources	Uses	
Operations				
Net income		(1) 242,000		
Add: Depreciation		(2) 68,000		
Less: Gain on sale of investment			(5) 60,000	
Issue of note payable for equipment		(4) 100,000		
Sale of long-term investments		(5) 160,000		
Issue of bonds payable		(6) 100,000		
Issue of common stock		(7) 173,000		
Uses of Working Capital				
Building addition			(3) 400,000	
Purchase of equipment			(4) 158,000	
Cash dividends declared			(8) 116,000	
		843,000	734,000	
Increase in working capital			109,000	
		843,000	843,000	

3. After beginning-of-year and end-of-year debit and credit balances are entered, the debits and credits are added to prove their equality.

4. After debits and credits are added, the heading Sources of Working Capital is entered in the bottom section of the worksheet. Several lines are skipped and then Uses of Working Capital is entered.

5. Changes in each noncurrent account are analyzed and explained. Entries are then made in the Analysis of Transactions columns to reconcile the beginning-of-year and end-of-year balances and to list the individual sources and uses of working capital in the bottom section of the worksheet. (Because the analysis of transactions is critical in the preparation of the statement of changes in financial position, an analysis of each transaction is presented in the next section.)

6. Each debit and credit item is totaled horizontally to prove the reconciliation of the beginning-of-year and end-of-year balances. Any item that does not reconcile is an indication that a transaction has been omitted.

7. The Sources and Uses columns in the bottom section are totaled and the increase (decrease) in working capital is entered as a balancing use (source) of working capital.

8. The debits and credits in the Analysis of Transactions columns are added to prove their equality.

After the worksheet is completed, all of the information needed to complete the statement of changes in financial position is contained in the bottom section and is then used to prepare the formal statement.

ANALYSIS OF TRANSACTIONS

The most important step in the preparation of the statement of changes in financial position is the analysis of the transactions that affected noncurrent accounts during the year. An analysis of each transaction is presented here, and the explanations are keyed to the numbers in Figure 19-5 and Figure 19-6.

1. Clark Corporation reported net income of $242,000 for 1984. Net income represents an increase in retained earnings (a noncurrent account) and, as discussed earlier, is an increase in working capital. On the worksheet, net income is therefore debited to a source of working capital from operations and is credited to the beginning balance of retained earnings as one reconciling item between the beginning and ending retained earnings balances. Recall, however, that the net income figure must be adjusted for items that affected net income but did not affect current assets or current liabilities during the period in order to report the net working capital provided by operations.

2. As explained earlier, depreciation expense reduces net income but does not decrease a current asset or increase a current liability during the period. Depreciation therefore has no effect on working capital. Depreciation expense was $33,000 on the building and $35,000 on equipment. Depreciation expense of $68,000 is shown on the worksheet as an addition to net income and as an addition to accumulated depreciation on buildings ($33,000) and equipment ($35,000). The worksheet entry adjusts working capital provided by operations and reconciles the beginning and ending balances in the accumulated depreciation accounts.

3. Cash of $400,000 was paid for a building addition during the year. This decrease in current assets represents a use of working capital. The worksheet entry is a debit to buildings and a credit to uses of working capital of $400,000. The entry reconciles the beginning and ending balances in the buildings account and reports the separate use of working capital.

4. Equipment was purchased during the year at a cost of $158,000, of which $58,000 was paid in cash and a $100,000 long-term note payable was given for the balance. The worksheet entry for this transaction is:

Source of Working Capital—Issue of Note Payable	100,000	
Equipment	158,000	
Notes Payable		100,000
Use of Working Capital—Purchase of Equipment		158,000

Notice that the purchase of equipment was financed in part by the use of working capital and in part by the issue of a long-term note payable. The net effect of the transaction is a $58,000 use of working capital. Under the all financial resources concept, however, the issue of the long-term note payable is shown as a source of working capital and the entire cost of the equipment ($158,000) is shown as a use of working capital. The debit to equipment and credit to notes payable serve to reconcile the beginning and ending balances of the Equipment and Notes Payable accounts.

5. Long-term investments with a cost of $100,000 were sold during the year for $160,000. The book entry to record the sale was:

Cash	160,000	
Long-term Investments		100,000
Gain on Sale of Investments		60,000

The $160,000 cash received increased current assets and therefore increased working capital. The $60,000 gain on sale of investments was included in net income on the income statement. Notice that the worksheet entry for this transaction shows the $160,000 source of working capital and the $100,000 credit to long-term investments reconciles the beginning and ending balances in the Long-term Investments account. In addition, the $60,000 gain is subtracted from net income to show working capital provided by operations. Since the full $160,000 cash received is shown as a source of working capital, failure to subtract the $60,000 gain would result in a double reporting of sources of working capital.

6. The issue of bonds payable provided $100,000 of working capital during the year. The worksheet entry shows the source of working capital and reconciles the beginning and ending balances in the Bonds Payable account.

7. The issue of common stock provided $173,000 of working capital. The worksheet entry shows the source of working capital and reconciles the beginning and ending balances in the Common Stock and Contributed Capital in Excess of Par accounts.

8. Cash dividends declared decreased working capital by $116,000. The worksheet entry shows the use of working capital and completes the reconciliation of the beginning and ending balances in the Retained Earnings account.

PREPARATION OF THE STATEMENT OF CHANGES IN FINANCIAL POSITION

When the worksheet is completed, all sources and uses of working capital have been identified. The formal statement is then prepared from the bottom section of the worksheet as shown in Figure 19-6. Notice that the net working capital provided by operations is $250,000, the other individual sources and uses of working capital are identified, and the increase in working capital for the year of $109,000 is shown as the final item.

In addition to the statement of changes in financial position, the net changes in each element of working capital must be disclosed either in the statement or in a separate schedule. (A schedule of changes in working capital for Clark Corporation is included in Figure 19-6.)

CASH FLOW STATEMENTS

As indicated earlier, the cash concept of funds is sometimes used as the basis for the preparation of the statement of changes in financial position, in which case the statement reports the sources and uses of cash rather than the sources and uses of working capital. Even when the working-capital basis is used for external reporting purposes, some type of cash flow statement is normally prepared for internal use in planning and controlling cash flows.

A cash flow statement may be prepared in any of various formats. If prepared for internal use only, it is often a simple listing of cash receipts (sources) and cash disbursements (uses) during the period. If prepared for external reporting purposes, it takes the same format as the statement of changes in financial position prepared on a working-capital basis. *Cash provided by operations* is reported first, followed by *other sources* and *other uses* of cash. The

Figure 19-6
Statement of
Changes in
Financial Position

CLARK CORPORATION
Statement of Changes in Financial Position
Year Ended December 31, 1984

Sources of Working Capital
Operations

Net income (1)	$242,000	
Add: Depreciation (2)	68,000	
Less: Gain on sale of investments (5)	(60,000)	
Net working capital provided by operations		250,000
Issue of long-term notes payable (4)		100,000
Sale of long-term investments (5)		160,000
Issue of bonds payable (6)		100,000
Issue of common stock (7)		173,000
Total sources of working capital		783,000

Uses of Working Capital

Building addition (3)	$400,000	
Purchase of equipment (4)	158,000	
Cash dividends (8)	116,000	
Total uses of working capital		674,000
Increase in working capital		$109,000

Changes in Elements of Working Capital

	December 31 1984	1983	Working Capital Increase (Decrease)
Current assets:			
Cash	$188,000	$162,000	$ 26,000
Accounts receivable	231,000	176,000	55,000
Inventory	314,000	322,000	(8,000)
Prepaid expenses	36,000	14,000	22,000
Total current assets	769,000	674,000	
Current liabilities:			
Notes payable	62,000	50,000	(12,000)
Accounts payable	238,000	269,000	31,000
Accrued expenses	21,000	16,000	(5,000)
Total current liabilities	321,000	335,000	
Working capital	$448,000	$339,000	
Increase in working capital			$109,000

difference between total sources and uses of cash represents the net increase or decrease in cash during the period. Following the all financial resources approach, exchange transactions are reported as both sources and uses of cash. An exchange of a long-term note payable for equipment, for example, is reported as though the note were issued for cash and the cash was then used to purchase equipment.

CASH PROVIDED BY OPERATIONS

The first step in the preparation of a cash flow statement is to determine the amount of cash provided by operations. Cash sales and the collection of accounts receivable result in a cash inflow to the company from current operations. The payment of current operating expenses and current liabilities that were incurred to obtain goods and services results in a cash outflow for operations. The difference between the cash inflow and the cash outflow from operating activities represents a net increase or decrease in cash from operations.

One approach to determining net cash flow from operations would be to list separately the cash received from cash sales and collections of accounts receivable and the cash paid out for operating expenses and payment of current liabilities. Another approach is similar to that used to determine working capital provided by operations, where items that affected net income but that did not provide or use working capital were added to or subtracted from net income. In determining cash flow, changes in current assets (other than cash) and current liabilities constitute sources and uses of cash. The normal approach in computing cash flow from operations is to convert the accrual basis income to a cash basis income. Each current asset (except cash) and current liability is adjusted to reflect its effect on revenues and expenses as if a cash basis rather than an accrual basis of determining income were used.

To convert the accrual basis income to cash basis income, we must consider the relationship between the effect of operating transactions on accrual income and cash movements within the company. Thus, accrual basis revenue is adjusted to show cash received from customers and accrual basis expenses are adjusted to show cash expenses. The difference between cash received from customers and cash paid for expenses represents the net cash flow from operating activities. The conversion process is presented below.

Cash Receipts from Customers

Under accrual accounting, sales on account are recognized by a debit to accounts receivable and a credit to sales at the time each sale is made. Under the cash basis, revenue is not recognized until cash is received. The conversion

of accrual basis sales revenue to cash basis sales revenue may be done as
follows:

$$\text{Net sales} \left\{ \begin{array}{c} + \text{ decrease in accounts receivable} \\ \text{or} \\ - \text{ increase in accounts receivable} \end{array} \right\} = \begin{array}{l} \text{Cash received} \\ \text{from customers} \end{array}$$

Clark Corporation's comparative balance sheets (Figure 19-4, page 758) show
that accounts receivable increased from $176,000 to $231,000 during 1984,
an increase of $55,000. Thus, cash receipts from customers may be computed
as:

Net sales (Figure 19-4)	$4,620,000
Less: Increase in accounts receivable	(55,000)
Cash received from customers	$4,565,000

Because accounts receivable increased by $55,000 during 1984, sales recorded
must have exceeded collections from customers by that amount. Sales recorded
on an accrual basis are therefore $55,000 higher than if the cash basis had
been used. The increase in accounts receivable is thus deducted from the
accrual basis net sales. If accounts receivable had decreased during the year,
cash collected would have exceeded sales recorded on an accrual basis. Consequently, the decrease in accounts receivable would be added to net accrual
sales to arrive at cash received from customers.

Cash Payments for Purchases

Under accrual accounting, purchases of merchandise on account are recognized when made by a debit to purchases (in a periodic system) and a credit
to short-term notes payable or accounts payable. Under the cash basis, purchases are not recognized until cash is paid. To convert from the accrual basis
to the cash basis, adjustments must be made for the changes during the year
in inventory, short-term notes payable, and accounts payable. (We assume
here that short-term notes payable were issued for the purchase of merchandise. If issued for other purposes, they would be reported as a separate source
of cash rather than as an adjustment to net income.) The conversion may be
made as follows:

$$\text{Cost of goods sold} \left\{ \begin{array}{c} + \text{ increase in inventory} \\ \text{or} \\ - \text{ decrease in inventory} \end{array} \right\} = \text{Purchases}$$

$$\text{Purchases} \left\{ \begin{array}{c} + \text{ decrease in accounts and notes payable} \\ \text{or} \\ - \text{ increase in accounts and notes payable} \end{array} \right\} = \begin{array}{l} \text{Cash paid for} \\ \text{purchases} \end{array}$$

Clark Corporation's comparative balance sheets show that inventory decreased by $8,000, notes payable increased by $12,000, and accounts payable decreased by $31,000. Giving effect to these adjustments, cash paid for purchases during 1984 may be computed as follows:

Cost of goods sold (Figure 19-4)	$2,440,000
Less: Decrease in inventory	(8,000)
Purchases made during the period	2,432,000
Add: Decrease in accounts payable	31,000
Less: Increase in notes payable	(12,000)
Cash paid for purchases	$2,451,000

Inventory decreased by $8,000 during the year, which means that the company sold more merchandise than it purchased. Thus, cost of goods sold is $8,000 higher under accrual accounting than it would have been on a cash basis. The net decrease of $19,000 in the combined amount of short-term notes payable and accounts payable means that the company paid for more purchases than it made during the year. As a result, cash paid for purchases is $19,000 higher than purchases recorded on an accrual basis.

Cash Payments for Expenses

Under accrual accounting, expenses are recognized when resources are used to earn revenues. Some expenses are prepaid, some are paid during the current period as incurred, and some are accrued at the end of the period. Under the cash basis, expenses are recognized when they are paid for. The relationship between expenses and cash payments depends on the changes in prepaid expenses and accrued liabilities. Thus, the conversion of accrual basis expenses to cash basis expenses may be made as follows:

paid more

Accrual expenses
operation
+ income
tax
{ + increase in prepayments
or
− decrease in prepayments }

and/or

{ + decrease in accrued liabilities
or
− increase in accrued liabilities
and
− depreciation expense } = Cash payments for expenses

Clark Corporation's comparative balance sheets show that prepaid expenses increased by $22,000 and that accrued expenses (liabilities) increased by $5,000. Consequently, cash paid for operating expenses, including income tax expense, during the year was:

Operating expenses plus income tax expense (Figure 19-4)	$1,998,000
Add: Increase in prepaid expenses	22,000
Less: Increase in accrued expenses (liabilities)	(5,000)
Depreciation expense	(68,000)
Cash paid for operating expenses	$1,947,000

The increase of $22,000 in prepaid expenses means that the company paid more cash than there are expenses recorded. Therefore, the increase is added to accrual basis operating expenses. The increase in accrued expenses means that more expenses were recorded than were paid for during the period. The increase is thus deducted from accrual basis operating expenses to arrive at cash basis operating expenses. In addition to the adjustments for prepaid and accrued expenses, depreciation expense must be subtracted because it did not require a cash outlay during the current period.

Using the cash basis information determined in the preceding paragraphs, we can compute the amount of cash provided by operations as shown in Figure 19-7.

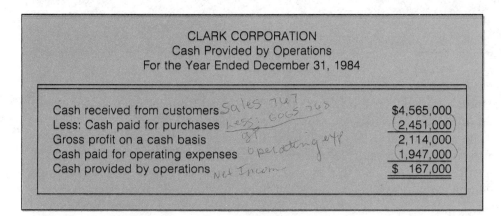

CLARK CORPORATION
Cash Provided by Operations
For the Year Ended December 31, 1984

Cash received from customers	$4,565,000
Less: Cash paid for purchases	(2,451,000)
Gross profit on a cash basis	2,114,000
Cash paid for operating expenses	(1,947,000)
Cash provided by operations	$ 167,000

Figure 19-7
Cash Provided by
Operations

PREPARING THE CASH FLOW STATEMENT

The cash provided by operations computed in Figure 19-7 does not explain the full story of cash flows during the year. Sources (uses) of cash from the nonoperating financing and investing activities of the company must be added (deducted) to explain fully the $26,000 increase in cash during the year, as shown in Figure 19-8.

Notice that the other (nonoperating) sources and uses of cash are the same as those shown in the statement of changes in financial position prepared on a working capital basis in Figure 19-6. Note also that the gain on sale of investments reported in the income statement (Figure 19-4) is not separately

Figure 19-8
Cash Flow Statement

CLARK CORPORATION
Cash Flow Statement
For the Year Ended December 31, 1984

Sources of Cash		
Cash provided by operations (Figure 19-7)		$167,000
Other sources:		
Issue of long-term notes payable	$100,000	
Sale of long-term investment	160,000	
Issue of bonds payable	100,000	
Issue of common stock	173,000	533,000
Total sources of cash		700,000
Uses of Cash		
Building addition	$400,000	
Purchase of equipment	158,000	
Cash dividends	116,000	
Total uses of cash		674,000
Increase in cash		26,000
Cash balance, January 1		162,000
Cash balance, December 31		$188,000

reported. Rather, the full $160,000 cash received from the sale of long-term investments is included as a separate, other source of cash.

The sources and uses of cash other than those provided by operations are relatively self-explanatory. Cash was obtained from the issue of bonds payable and from the issue of common stock. Cash was used to acquire a building addition, to purchase equipment, and to pay dividends. In addition, as mentioned earlier, the exchange of the long-term note for equipment is reported both as a source of cash from the issue of long-term notes payable and as a use of cash for the purchase of equipment.

GLOSSARY

ALL FINANCIAL RESOURCES APPROACH.   A reporting format for the statement of changes in financial position that includes exchanges of noncurrent items as both a source and use of working capital or cash (p. 754).

CASH FLOW STATEMENT.   A statement that reports the sources and uses of cash for a period (p. 764).

FUNDS.   When used in the statement of changes in financial position, funds are defined as working capital, cash, or cash and readily marketable securities (p. 747).

SOURCE OF FUNDS. A transaction that increases working capital or cash (p. 748).

USE OF FUNDS. A transaction that decreases working capital or cash (p. 748).

WORKING CAPITAL. The excess of current assets over current liabilities (p. 747).

DISCUSSION QUESTIONS

1. What are the primary concepts of "funds" that may be used in the preparation of a statement of changes in financial position?
2. What are the primary sources and uses of working capital?
3. Why are expenses such as depreciation and depletion added back to net income in determining working capital provided by operations? List some other items that would require adjustments to net income.
4. What is the effect on working capital of each of the following transactions? (Consider each item individually.)
   (a) The collection of a $6,000 account receivable.
   (b) The issue of a $1,000 par value bond payable at a premium of $20.
   (c) The purchase of equipment in exchange for a 90-day note payable amounting to $15,000.
   (d) The purchase of $5,000 of merchandise inventory on open account.
   (e) The exchange of a 120-day, $1,000, 10% note payable in settlement of an open account payable.
   (f) The exchange of 2,000 shares of common stock with a market value of $20 per share for machinery.
   (g) The sale for $16,000 of temporary marketable securities with a cost of $12,000.
5. If long-term investments with a cost of $25,000 are sold for $35,000, what will be the effect on working capital? On cash?
6. Is depreciation a source of working capital? Why or why not?
7. What effect would the issue of a stock dividend have on working capital? How would the issue affect cash flow?
8. A company reported a net loss of $40,000 on its income statement and a $20,000 source of working capital from operations on its statement of changes in financial position. Explain how this could happen.
9. What effect would the amortization of $500 of discount on bonds payable have on working capital? How should the $500 be treated on a statement of changes in financial position?
10. During the year, the holders of $100,000 of convertible bonds payable converted their bonds into 30,000 shares of $5 par value common stock. What effect would the conversion have on working capital? Do you think the conversion should be reported on the statement of changes in financial position? If so, how?
11. Explain how accrual basis net sales can be adjusted to show the amount of cash received from customers.
12. Total cost of goods sold for a company during the year under accrual accounting amounted to $80,000. If inventory decreased by $6,000 and accounts payable decreased by $12,000 during the year, how much cash was paid for purchases?

13. Accrual basis operating expenses other than depreciation for a company amounted to $62,000 for the year. If prepaid expenses increased by $8,000 and accrued expenses decreased by $6,000 during the year, how much cash was paid for operating expenses during the year?

14. Zee Company's fiscal year ends on June 30. The board of directors declared a cash dividend on June 20 of the current year, payable on July 15 to stockholders of record on June 30. What effect would this declaration have on a statement of changes in financial position prepared on a working-capital basis for the current year? What would be the effect on a cash flow statement for the current year? What would be the effect on working capital and cash flow in the following year, when the dividend was paid?

EXERCISES

Exercise 19-1 (Effects of Transactions on Working Capital)

Below is a list of transactions of Core Company during 1984. For each transaction, indicate whether it resulted in a source or use of working capital and the amount, if any. Use the letters S for source, U for use, and N for neither a source nor a use.

Transaction	Effect on Working Capital	Amount
1. Collected $94,000 of accounts receivable.		
2. Sold a machine with a book value of $4,000 for $5,500 cash.		
3. Borrowed $10,000 from a bank, giving a note payable on July 5, 1986.		
4. Paid $19,000 in settlement of accounts payable.		
5. Issued 1,000 shares of $10 par value common stock at $20 per share.		
6. Purchased a machine for $9,000, giving $2,000 cash and promising to pay the balance in 60 days.		
7. Recorded depreciation expense on equipment, $5,000.		
8. Issued a long-term note payable, $15,000, in settlement of a short-term note payable, $15,000.		
9. Issued 100 $1,000 par value bonds payable at 90.		
10. Purchased treasury stock, $67,000.		
11. Purchased land, giving a $40,000 note payable in 1987 in exchange.		
12. Declared a cash dividend of $17,000.		
13. Settled an account payable of $12,000 by giving the creditor 500 shares of unissued common stock.		
14. Sold a temporary investment with a cost of $6,000 for $8,000 cash		

15. Declared and distributed a 5% stock dividend on 100,000 shares of outstanding common stock when the market price of the stock was $8 per share. _____ _____
16. Issued 1,000 shares of $10 par value common stock with a market price of $20 per share in exchange for land. _____ _____
17. Wrote off a $900 uncollectible account receivable against the allowance for uncollectible accounts. _____ _____
18. Reissued one-half of the treasury stock acquired in (10) above for $40,000. _____ _____

Exercise 19-2 (Effects of Transactions on Cash)

For each of the transactions in Exercise 19-1, indicate whether it resulted in a source or use of cash and the amount, if any. Use the letters *S* for source, *U* for use, and *N* for neither a source nor a use.

Exercise 19-3 (Determining Working Capital Provided by Operations)

The following income statement was prepared for Kingman Company at the end of 1984.

KINGMAN COMPANY
Income Statement
For Year Ended December 31, 1984

Sales		$6,930,000
Cost of goods sold		3,600,000
Gross margin		3,330,000
Operating expenses:		
Distribution expense	$ 900,000	
Salaries and wages expense	1,300,000	
Depreciation expense	290,000	
Rent expense	90,000	
Patent amortization expense	26,500	
Uncollectible accounts expense	10,200	2,616,700
Operating income		713,300
Gain on sale of investments		10,000
Net income before income tax		723,300
Income tax expense		275,000
Net income		$ 448,300

Required:

Determine the amount of working capital provided by current operating activities for the year.

Exercise 19-4 (Changes in Elements of Working Capital)

The current sections of Lavelle Company's balance sheets at December 31, 1983 and 1984, were as follows:

	1984	1983
Current assets:		
Cash	$ 62,000	$ 31,500
Accounts receivable (net)	84,000	105,000
Inventory	231,000	190,000
Prepaid expenses	21,000	25,200
Total current assets	$398,000	$351,700
Current liabilities:		
Notes payable	$ 50,000	$ 40,000
Accounts payable	42,000	63,000
Accrued expenses payable	54,000	40,000
Total current liabilities	$146,000	$143,000

Required:

Prepare a schedule showing the net change in each element of working capital during 1984.

Exercise 19-5 (Working Capital and Cash Provided by Operations)

The following information was taken from the comparative financial statements of Cycle Company prepared on an accrual basis:

	1984	1983
Net sales	$196,000	$180,000
Cost of goods sold	82,000	71,000
Operating expenses (including depreciation expense of $14,000 each year)	74,000	70,000
Net income	40,000	39,000
Year-end accounts receivable (net)	37,000	34,000
Year-end inventory	26,000	30,000
Year-end accounts payable	17,000	16,000
Year-end wages payable	5,000	8,000

Required:

A. Prepare a schedule to show the amount of working capital provided by operations during 1984.

B. Prepare a schedule to show the amount of cash provided by operations during 1984..

Exercise 19-6 (Conversion from Accrual Basis to Cash Basis)

The following information was taken from the general ledger accounts of Layton Company, which uses the accrual basis of accounting.

	Year-end	
	1984	1983
Accounts receivable	$36,700	$21,800
Inventory	29,000	32,100
Prepaid insurance	800	1,200
Accounts payable for merchandise purchased	18,600	20,400
Wages payable	1,600	2,800
Sales	95,600	
Cost of goods sold	48,900	
Operating expenses (including $9,000 depreciation expense)	25,400	

Required:

Compute:

A. The amount of cash collected from customers during 1984.
B. The amount of cash paid for merchandise purchased during 1984.
C. The amount of cash paid for operating expenses during 1984.

Exercise 19-7 (Preparing Statement Without a Worksheet)

Comparative balance sheets for 1984 and 1983 and an income statement for 1984 for Zeeber Company are presented below:

	1984	1983
Cash	$ 8,600	$12,400
Accounts receivable	16,900	15,200
Inventory	22,700	24,800
Plant assets	58,000	40,000
Accumulated depreciation—plant assets	(20,000)	(17,000)
Total Assets	$86,200	$75,400
Accounts payable	$13,400	$12,100
Accrued expenses	2,900	3,900
Long-term note payable	5,000	–0–
Capital stock	10,000	10,000
Retained earnings	54,900	49,400
Total Liabilities and Owners' Equity	$86,200	$75,400

Sales	$88,700
Cost of goods sold	56,600
Gross profit on sales	32,100
Operating expenses including depreciation	24,600
Net income	$ 7,500

Plant assets were purchased during the year, but none was sold. Dividends were declared and paid during November 1984.

Required:

A. Compute the increase or decrease in working capital during 1984.
B. Prepare a statement of changes in working capital. (Because this is a relatively easy exercise, a worksheet should not be necessary.)

PROBLEMS

Problem 19-1 (Preparing a Statement Without a Worksheet)

The following data were taken from the financial statements of Boxer Company:

	December 31	
	1984	1983
Current assets	$169,000	$134,000
Building	230,000	230,000
Less: Accumulated depreciation	(90,000)	(80,000)
Equipment	88,000	76,000
Less: Accumulated depreciation	(28,000)	(22,000)
Long-term investments	20,000	40,000
Current liabilities	89,000	76,000
Capital stock	175,000	150,000
Retained earnings	125,000	152,000

No equipment was sold during the year; cash dividends declared and paid during the year amounted to $67,000; net income for 1984 was $40,000; long-term investments were sold at a gain of $4,000.

Required:

Prepare a statement of changes in financial position for 1984 on a working-capital basis. A worksheet should not be necessary.

Problem 19-2 (Worksheet for Statement of Changes in Financial Position)

Rhodes Company had balance sheets at the end of December, 1983 and 1984 as follows:

Assets	1984	1983
Cash	$113,500	$ 50,400
Accounts receivable (net)	89,000	99,750
Inventory	390,000	335,000
Prepaid expenses	40,000	12,500
Equipment	445,000	290,000
Accumulated depreciation—equipment	(84,000)	(50,400)
Total Assets	$993,500	$737,250
Liabilities and Owners' Equity		
Notes payable	$ 26,500	$ 16,000
Accounts payable	146,400	137,500
Accrued expenses	13,000	16,000
Long-term notes payable	70,000	100,000
Common stock, $5 par value	350,000	275,000
Contributed capital in excess of par	175,000	25,000
Retained earnings	212,600	167,750
Total Liabilities and Owners' Equity	$993,500	$737,250

An inspection of the firm's 1984 income statement and general ledger accounts revealed the following:

1. Net income for the year was $114,850.
2. Depreciation expense was recorded in the amount of $38,600, and a fully depreciated machine with a cost of $5,000 was discarded and its cost and accumulated depreciation removed from the accounts.
3. New equipment was purchased during the year at a cost of $160,000.
4. A long-term note payable of $30,000 was paid off.
5. Fifteen thousand shares of common stock were issued during the year at an issue price of $15 per share.
6. Cash dividends of $1 per share were declared and paid on outstanding shares, including those issued during the year.

Required:

A. Prepare a worksheet for a statement of changes in financial position on a working, capital basis.
B. Prepare a formal statement of changes in financial position including a schedule of changes in the elements of working capital.

Problem 19-3 (Cash Flow Statement)

Using the data presented in Problem 19-2 plus the additional income statement detail given below, prepare a cash flow statement for Rhodes Company for the year ended December 31, 1984.

Income Statement Detail	
Net sales	$1,046,000
Cost of goods sold	679,000
Operating expenses other than depreciation	213,550

Problem 19-4 (Preparing a Statement Without a Worksheet)

Brill Company had the following condensed balance sheet at the end of 1983:

BRILL COMPANY
Balance Sheet
December 31, 1983

Current assets	$ 56,250	Current liabilities	$ 22,500
Long-term investments	30,000	Long-term notes	
Plant and equipment (net)	101,250	payable	38,250
Land	60,000	Bonds payable	37,500
	60,000	Capital stock	112,500
		Retained earnings	36,750
	$247,500		$247,500

During 1984, the following events occurred:

1. Net income for 1984 was $31,500 after deducting depreciation of $13,500.
2. Bonds payable in the amount of $7,500 were retired at par.
3. Dividends totaling $11,250 were declared and paid.
4. Land was purchased at a cost of $9,000 cash.
5. Additional capital stock of $15,000 was issued at par.
6. Land was purchased by exchanging $27,000 in bonds payable.
7. Long-term investments that cost $15,000 were sold for $15,450.

Required:

A. Prepare a statement of changes in financial position for 1984.
B. Prepare a condensed balance sheet for Brill Company as it would appear on December 31, 1984. Assume that current liabilities remained at $22,500.

Problem 19-5 (Worksheet for Statement of Changes in Financial Position)

Comparative balance sheets for Fulkerson Company on June 30, 1983 and 1984, are presented below:

	June 30	
	1984	1983
Current Assets:		
Cash	$ 105,000	$ 122,600
Accounts receivable (net)	130,700	111,300
Inventory	275,000	221,200
Prepaid expenses	22,800	23,000
Total current assets	533,500	478,100
Plant and Equipment:		
Buildings	639,000	339,000
Accumulated depreciation—buildings	(111,400)	(97,600)
Equipment	361,200	331,200
Accumulated depreciation—equipment	(89,900)	(67,000)
Land	168,000	39,000
Total plant and equipment	966,900	544,600
Long-term investments	70,000	160,000
Total Assets	$1,570,400	$1,182,700
Current Liabilities:		
Notes payable	$ 45,000	$ 50,000
Accounts payable	170,000	168,000
Accrued expenses	10,500	14,000
Total current liabilities	225,500	232,000
Long-term Liabilities:		
Notes payable, due 3/30/87	200,000	150,000
Bonds payable, due 9/1/93	300,000	200,000
Total long-term liabilities	500,000	350,000
Stockholders' Equity:		
Common stock, $10 par	230,000	200,000
Contributed capital in excess of par	272,100	188,100
Retained earnings	342,800	212,600
Total stockholders' equity	844,900	600,700
Total Liabilities and Stockholders' Equity	$1,570,400	$1,182,700

Examination of the company's income statement and general ledger accounts disclosed the following:

1. Net income for the year was $199,200.
2. Depreciation expense was recorded during the year on buildings, $13,800, and on equipment, $22,900.
3. A new wing was added to the building at a cost of $300,000 cash.
4. Long-term investments with a cost of $90,000 were sold for $125,000.
5. A vacant lot next to the company's plant was purchased for $129,000 with payment consisting of $79,000 cash and a note payable for $50,000 due on June 30, 1987.

6. Bonds payable of $100,000 were issued for cash at par.
7. Three thousand shares of common stock were issued at $38 per share.
8. Equipment was purchased for $30,000 cash.
9. Cash dividends of $69,000 were declared and paid.

Required:

A. Prepare a worksheet for a statement of changes in financial position (working-capital basis).

B. Prepare a formal statement of changes in financial position. A schedule of changes in the elements of working capital is not necessary.

Problem 19-6 (Cash Flow Statement)

Using the data provided in Problem 19-5 and the income statement detail given below, prepare a cash flow statement for Fulkerson Company for the year ended June 30, 1984.

Income Statement Detail	
Net sales	$875,600
Cost of goods sold	525,300
Operating expenses other than depreciation	149,400

ALTERNATE PROBLEMS

Problem 19-1A (Effects of Transactions on Working Capital and Cash)

A list of business transactions and adjustments is given below. For each item in the list, indicate the effect (increase, decrease, or no effect) on both working capital and cash. Use the following format:

Item	Working Capital	Cash

A. Declared a cash dividend.
B. Recorded depreciation expense for the period. back out effect
C. Paid an account payable.
D. Sold a plant asset at a loss.
E. Paid a cash dividend previously declared.
F. Paid the income tax liability that was accrued at the end of last year.
G. Purchased equipment, giving a 90-day note payable.
H. Sold a temporary investment at a gain.
I. Wrote off an account receivable against the allowance for uncollectible accounts.
J. Issued common stock in exchange for convertible bonds, which were converted by the bondholders.
K. Recorded amortization expense on patents.
L. Exchanged 30,000 shares of authorized common stock for a building.
M. Paid in advance for a one-year insurance policy.

Problem 19-2A (Preparing Statement Without a Worksheet)

Hawes Company's financial statements contained the following information:

	September 30	
	1984	**1983**
Current assets	$148,000	$167,000
Building	271,000	271,000
Less: Accumulated depreciation	(129,000)	(118,000)
Machinery	200,000	98,000
Less: Accumulated depreciation	(41,000)	(32,000)
Long-term investments	23,000	47,000
Current liabilities	115,000	102,000
Capital stock	240,000	200,000
Retained earnings	117,000	131,000

No machinery was sold during the year; cash dividends declared and paid during the year amounted to $12,000; a net operating loss of $2,000 was incurred during the year; long-term investments were sold at a loss of $6,000.

Required:

Prepare a statement of changes in financial position for the year ending September 30, 1984, using a working capital basis. A worksheet is not necessary.

Problem 19-3A (Worksheet for Statement of Changes in Financial Position)

Comparative balance sheets for Blair Company at June 30, 1984 and 1983 were:

	1984	1983
Cash	$ 89,200	$112,600
Accounts receivable (net)	116,400	121,900
Inventory	73,300	58,400
Prepaid expenses	18,600	17,100
Long-term investments in stock	45,000	76,500
Plant assets	399,400	281,300
Less: Accumulated depreciation	(112,200)	(96,700)
Total Assets	$629,700	$571,100
Accounts payable	$ 98,400	$ 72,700
Accrued expenses	18,900	21,600
Long-term notes payable	40,000	60,000
Common stock, $10 par value	300,000	250,000
Contributed capital in excess of par	100,000	90,000
Retained earnings	72,400	76,800
Total Liabilities and Stockholders' Equity	$629,700	$571,100

Reference to Blair Company's income statement and general ledger accounts showed the following:

1. The income statement reported net income of $13,600.
2. Plant assets were purchased for cash during the year. No plant assets were sold.
3. Part of the long-term investment in stock was sold at a $7,500 loss.
4. Five thousand shares of common stock were issued during the year for $12 per share.
5. Cash dividends of $.60 per share were declared and paid on outstanding shares including those issued during the year.
6. Long-term notes payable became due and were paid during the year.

Required:

A. Prepare a worksheet for a statement of changes in financial position on a working capital basis.
B. Prepare a formal statement of changes in financial position including a schedule of changes in the elements of working capital.

Problem 19-4A (Cash Flow Statement)

Using the data provided in Problem 19-3A plus the additional income statement detail below, prepare a cash flow statement for Blair Company for the year ended June 30, 1984.

Income Statement Detail	
Net sales	$832,600
Cost of goods sold	529,400
Operating expenses including depreciation expense	282,100

Problem 19-5A (Preparing Statement Without a Worksheet)

Zorro Company had the following condensed balance sheet at the end of 1983.

ZORRO COMPANY
Balance Sheet
December 31, 1983

Current assets	$ 79,600	Current liabilities	$ 42,900
Long-term investment	47,500	Long-term notes payable	50,000
Plant assets (net)	163,900	Bonds payable	100,000
Land	75,000	Capital stock	150,000
Patents	44,600	Retained earnings	67,700
	$410,600		$410,600

The following events occurred during 1984:

1. Net income of $18,400 was reported in 1984 after deducting depreciation expense of $28,000 and amortization expense on patents of $4,000.
2. Bonds payable in the amount of $20,000 were issued at par.
3. Land valued at $25,000 was purchased by exchanging 1,000 shares of $25 par value capital stock.
4. Dividends totaling $16,000 were declared and paid.
5. Long-term investments that cost $26,000 were sold for $29,000.
6. Plant assets were purchased for cash, $36,000.

~Required:

A. Prepare a statement of changes in financial position—working capital basis—for 1984.
B. Prepare a condensed balance sheet for Zorro Company as it would appear on December 31, 1984. Assume current liabilities remained at $42,900.

Problem 19-6A (Worksheet for Statement of Changes in Financial Position)

Balance sheets for Benno Company on December 31, 1984 and 1983, contained the following items:

	1984	1983
Assets		
Cash	$ 38,200	$ 44,600
Accounts receivable, net	32,400	31,200
Inventory	100,400	102,800
Prepaid expenses	2,600	2,200
Long-term investments	–0–	30,000
Equipment	60,800	57,000
Accumulated depreciation—equipment	(13,200)	(9,800)
Building	200,000	–0–
Accumulated depreciation—building	(2,400)	–0–
Land	40,000	–0–
Total Assets	$458,800	$258,000
Liabilities and Stockholders' Equity		
Accounts payable	$ 40,600	$ 43,400
Income taxes payable	2,800	2,200
Mortgage payable	130,000	–0–
Common stock, $5 par	200,000	160,000
Other contributed capital	10,000	2,000
Retained earnings	75,400	50,400
Total Liabilities and Stockholders' Equity	$458,800	$258,000

Benno Company's 1984 income statement and general ledger accounts showed:

1. Net income earned during the year, $39,000.
2. Equipment was purchased during the year at a cost of $5,000.
3. Equipment with a cost of $1,000 and accumulated depreciation of $600 was traded for new equipment with a list price of $1,600. A trade-in allowance of $600 was received.
4. Fully depreciated equipment that cost $1,600 was discarded during the year and written off in the accounts.
5. Long-term investments were sold during the year for an amount equal to their cost.
6. Benno Company purchased the building and land it had been previously renting for a total of $240,000; $110,000 was paid in cash and a mortgage was given for the balance.
7. Depreciation expense for the year was: equipment, $5,600 and building, $2,400.
8. Eight thousand shares of common stock were issued during the year for cash of $6 per share.
9. Cash dividends of $14,000 were declared and paid during the year.

Required:

A. Prepare a worksheet for a statement of changes in financial position on a working capital basis.
B. Prepare a formal statement of changes in financial position including a schedule of changes in the elements of working capital.

Problem 19-7A (Cash Flow Statement)

Using the data provided in Problem 19-6A plus the additional income statement detail provided below, prepare a cash flow statement for Benno Company for the year ended December 31, 1984.

Income Statement Detail

Net sales	$542,600
Cost of goods sold	361,200
Operating expenses including depreciation expense	142,400

CASE FOR CHAPTER 19

(Annual Report Analysis)

Refer to the financial statements of General Motors Corporation in the appendix and answer the following questions:

1. What concept of funds is used in the Statement of Changes in Financial Position?
2. How much working capital did General Motors have on December 31, 1981? December 31, 1980?
3. What was the amount of funds provided by operations during 1981?
4. What was the increase (decrease) in funds during 1981?
5. How much did General Motors pay in dividends during 1981?
6. Reconcile the change in Long-term Debt during 1981.
7. Reconcile the change in the Special Tools account during 1981.
8. Assess General Motors working capital position at the end of 1981 versus the end of 1979.

CHAPTER 20
ANALYSIS OF FINANCIAL STATEMENTS

OVERVIEW AND OBJECTIVES

This chapter describes some of the techniques used to analyze a firm's financial statements. When you have completed the chapter, you should understand:

- The objectives of financial statement analysis (pp. 786–787).
- How to perform horizontal analysis, trend analysis, and vertical analysis (pp. 787–791).
- How to compute the ratios commonly used to analyze a firm's profitability, liquidity, and solvency (pp. 791–801).
- How to use ratios for analyzing a firm's profitability, liquidity, and solvency (pp. 791–801).
- The limitations of financial statement analysis (pp. 801–802).

The financial statements issued by a firm are used by various parties to evaluate the firm's financial performance. In the preceding chapter, we demonstrated how the statement of changes in financial position could be used to supplement the balance sheet and income statement in analyzing the financing and investing activities of a firm. In this chapter we will focus on the basic techniques commonly employed to analyze a firm's balance sheet and income statement. These statements are emphasized because they are the primary source of financial data for most outside parties.

SOURCES OF FINANCIAL INFORMATION

The financial statements of a firm are the end products of the accounting process. These statements, with their accompanying schedules and explanatory notes, are the primary means by which management communicates information about the firm to interested outside parties.

In addition to financial data published by a firm, a wealth of information is also available from other sources. Probably the most detailed information available on publicly held companies is contained in the reports that must be filed with the SEC. Financial advisory services such as Moody's Investors Service and Standard and Poor's Corporation also publish financial data for most companies. These are normally not as detailed as the SEC and company reports, but the advisory-service reports are more accessible; they are generally available in most public and university libraries. It is also useful to compare data of the company under study with that of competing firms. Industry data are available from Dun & Bradstreet, Inc. and Robert Morris and Associates. Individual company and industry analyses are also available from stockbrokerage firms. An abundance of useful information is also available in various economic and financial newspapers and magazines.

THE NEED FOR ANALYTICAL TECHNIQUES

Information contained in the various sources of financial data is expressed primarily in monetary terms. Although dollar amounts are necessary for many purposes, most individual items reported in financial statements are generally of limited usefulness when considered by themselves. Significant relationships may not be revealed in a review of absolute dollar amounts because they provide no indication of whether a particular item is good or bad for a given firm. For example, knowing that a company reported earnings of $100,000 for the current year is of limited use unless the amount is compared to other information such as last year's earnings, the current year's sales, the earnings of other companies in the same business, or some predetermined standard established by the statement user. To simplify the identification of significant changes and relationships, the dollar amounts reported in financial statements are frequently converted into percentages of some base item, referred to as horizontal analysis and vertical percentage analysis. In other cases, the relationship between two items is expressed as a ratio.

OBJECTIVES OF FINANCIAL STATEMENT ANALYSIS

Percentage analysis and ratio analysis have been developed to provide an efficient means by which a decision-maker can identify important relationships between items in the same statements and trends in financial data. Percentages and ratios are calculated in order to reduce the financial data to a more understandable basis for the evaluation of the financial condition and past operating performance of the firm. The information is used primarily to forecast a firm's ability to pay its debts when due and to operate at a satisfactory profit level. Because the special interests and objectives of users differ and because the analytical techniques are almost limitless, the choice of proper tools must vary.

Some users of financial data are concerned with evaluating the firm's ability to produce enough cash to pay its short-term debts when they mature and still have sufficient cash left to carry out its other activities. The ability of a firm to pay its short-term debts is referred to as liquidity, and the focus of the investigation is generally on the firm's current assets and liabilities. Other users, such as long-term creditors and stockholders, are also concerned with the firm's liquidity but, in addition, are interested in a firm's ability to pay its long-term obligations. This aspect of the analysis is concerned with the solvency of the firm. In a solvency analysis, the statement user assesses the financial structure of the firm and its prospects for operating at an earnings level adequate to provide sufficient cash for the payment of interest, dividends, and debt principal.

To serve as a basis for the discussion of percentage and ratio analysis, balance sheets and income statements for the Gordon Corporation during a two-year period are presented in the first two columns of Figures 20-1 and 20-2. In order to show the computations of ratios for two periods, a December 31, 1984, balance sheet is also included in Figure 20-1. It cannot be emphasized too strongly that, for the statement analysis of an individual company to be useful, the relationships must be compared to other data or standards. (In the following discussion, rather than stating the need for comparison every time a particular analysis is performed, it will be assumed that this additional step is taken by the statement user.)

PERCENTAGE ANALYSIS

HORIZONTAL ANALYSIS

An analysis of the preceding year's financial statements is generally performed as a starting point for forecasting future performance. Most firms include in their annual report financial statements for the two most recent years (comparative statements), and selected summary data for five to 10 years. An analysis of the change from year to year in individual statement items is called horizontal analysis.

In horizontal analysis, the individual items or groups of items on comparative financial statements are generally first placed side by side as in the first columns of Figures 20-1 and 20-2. Because it is difficult to compare absolute

GORDON CORPORATION
Comparative Balance Sheets
December 31, 1986, 1985, and 1984
(000's omitted)

Assets	Year Ended December 31			Change During the Year 1985–1986		Common Size* Statements	
	1986	1985	1984	Dollar Amount	Percent	1986	1985
Current Assets							
Cash	390	300	290	90	30.0	5.2	4.7
Marketable Securities	380	440	460	(60)	(13.7)	5.1	7.0
Accounts Receivable (net)	1,460	1,290	1,320	170	13.2	19.6	20.5
Inventory	2,010	1,770	1,860	240	13.6	27.1	28.1
Prepaid Expenses	100	100	100	–0–	–0–	1.3	1.6
Total Current Assets	4,340	3,900	4,030	440	11.3	58.3	61.9
Long-term Investments	400	500	500	(100)	(20.0)	5.4	7.9
Plant and Equipment	2,600	1,800	1,770	800	44.4	35.0	28.6
Other Assets	100	100	100	–0–	–0–	1.3	1.6
Total Assets	7,440	6,300	6,400	1,140	18.1	100.0	100.0
Liabilities							
Current Liabilities							
Accounts Payable	1,040	900	1,050	140	15.6	14.0	14.3
Notes Payable	620	600	750	20	3.3	8.4	9.5
Accrued Expenses	100	100	100	–0–	–0–	1.3	1.6
Total Current Liabilities	1,760	1,600	1,900	160	10.0	23.7	25.4
Long-term Liabilities—11%	1,900	1,700	1,800	200	11.8	25.5	27.0
Total Liabilities	3,660	3,300	3,700	360	10.9	49.2	52.4
Stockholders' Equity							
Preferred Stock	300	300	300	–0–	–0–	4.0	4.8
Common Stock ($10 par value)	1,500	1,200	1,200	300	25.0	20.2	19.0
Additional Paid-in Capital	502	400	400	102	25.5	6.7	6.3
Retained Earnings	1,478	1,100	800	378	34.4	19.9	17.5
Total Stockholders' Equity	3,780	3,000	2,700	780	26.0	50.8	47.6
Total Liabilities and Stockholders' Equity	7,440	6,300	6,400	1,140	18.1	100.0	100.0

*Computations are explained on page 791

Figure 20-1
Comparative Balance Sheets, Change During the Year, and Common Size Statements

dollar amounts, the difference between the figures of one year and the next is computed in dollar amounts and percentage change. In computing the increase or decrease in dollar amounts, the earlier statement is used as the base year. The percentage change is computed by dividing the increase or decrease from the base year in dollars by the base-year amount. For example, from 1985 to 1986 the Cash account of Gordon Corporation increased $90,000, from $300,000 to $390,000 (Figure 20-1). The percentage change is 30%, computed as follows:

$$\text{Percentage increase} = (100)\frac{90,000}{300,000} = 30\%$$

GORDON CORPORATION
Comparative Income Statement
For Year Ended December 31, 1986 and 1985
(000 omitted)

	Year Ended December 31		Change During Year		Percent of Net Sales	
	1986	1985	Dollar Amount	Percent	1986	1985
Sales	10,320	9,582	738	7.7	100.0	100.0
Less: Cost of Goods Sold	7,719	6,975	744	10.7	74.8	72.8
Gross Profit on Sales	2,601	2,607	(6)	(0.2)	25.2	27.2
Selling Expense	1,080	830	250	30.1	10.5	8.6
Administrative Expense	567	620	(53)	(8.5)	5.5	6.5
Interest Expense	252	230	22	9.6	2.4	2.4
Income Tax Expense	144	237	(93)	(39.2)	1.4	2.5
Total Expenses	2,043	1,917	126	6.6	19.8	20.0
Net Income	558	690	(132)	(19.1)	5.4	7.2
Preferred Stock Dividends	30	30	–0–		0.3	0.3
Net Income Available to Common Stockholders	528	660	(132)	(20.0)	5.1	6.9

Figure 20-2
Comparative Income Statements, Change During the Year, and Common Size Statements

A percentage change can be computed only when a positive amount is reported in the base year; the amount of change cannot be stated as a percentage if the item in the base year was reported as a negative or a zero amount.

A review of the percentage increases or decreases will reveal prominently those items that showed the most significant change between the periods under study, and important and unusual changes will be investigated further by the analyst. The objectives of the investigation are to determine the cause of the change, to determine whether the change was favorable or unfavorable, and to attempt to assess whether any trends are expected to continue. In so doing, the analyst must consider changes in other related items. For example, when reviewing the percentage changes in the balance sheet accounts included in Figure 20-1, attention is directed to the change in the Plant and Equipment account because of the size of the change ($800,000 or 44%). It appears that the firm is expanding its operations. An analyst would seek further answers to such questions as: How is the added investment being financed? Is expansion going to cause severe cash-flow problems? Are sales markets adequate to support the additional output? Sales in Figure 20-2 increased 7.7%, by itself a favorable trend. However, the rate of increase in cost of goods sold was 10.7%, and selling expenses increased by 30%. Thus, during the period the firm was unable to maintain its profit margin percentage [(sales − cost of goods sold)/sales], and it appears that the increase in sales is at least partially the result of an increased sales effort. These items would warrant further investigation by an analyst who was concerned with the profitability and long-term future of the firm.

TREND ANALYSIS

When financial data are presented for three or more years, trend analysis is a technique commonly employed by financial analysts. In this analysis, the earliest period is the base period, with all subsequent periods compared to the base. For example, assume that sales and net income were reported for the last five years as:

| | Base Year | | | | |
	1982	**1983**	**1984**	**1985**	**1986**
Sales	1,000,000	1,050,000	1,120,000	1,150,000	1,220,000
Net income	200,000	206,000	218,000	222,000	232,000

It is clear that the dollar amount of both sales and net income are increasing. However, the relationship between the change in sales and net income can be more easily interpreted if the changes are expressed in percentages by dividing the amount reported for each subsequent year by the base-year amount, thus producing:

	1982	**1983**	**1984**	**1985**	**1986**
Sales	100	105	112	115	122
Net income	100	103	109	111	116

Now it can be seen that net income is increasing more slowly than sales. Obviously, the trend in other accounts should also be investigated. The level of net income is affected not only by sales, but also by the expenses of the firm. In this case, it is possible that the firm's inventory costs are increasing faster than selling prices. Or the increase in sales may be the result of granting more liberal credit terms that are resulting in larger bad-debt expenses. The point is that other related operating data must also be reviewed before drawing conclusions about the significance of one particular item. The overall objective is to evaluate various related trends and attempt to assess whether the trend can be expected to continue.

VERTICAL ANALYSIS

Horizontal analysis compares the proportional changes in a specific item from one period to the next; **vertical analysis** involves restating the dollar amount of each item reported on an individual financial statement as a percentage of a specific item on the same statement, referred to as the base amount. For example, on the balance sheet, individual components are stated as a percentage of total assets or total liabilities and stockholders' equity. On the income statement, net sales or total revenue are usually set equal to a base of 100%, with each income-statement item expressed as a percentage of the base amount. Such statements are often called **common size statements** since all items are presented as a percentage of some common base amount.

Vertical analysis for Gordon Corporation is presented in the last two columns of Figures 20-1 and 20-2, pages 788 and 789. The analysis may be performed on condensed statements or on more detailed statements if available. Vertical analysis is useful for identifying the relative importance of items to the base used. It can be readily observed, for example, that the cost of goods sold as a percentage of sales increased from 72.8% to 74.8%. Vertical analysis is also an important tool for comparing data to other standards such as the past performance of the firm, the current performance of competing firms, and averages developed for the industry in which the firm operates.

RATIO ANALYSIS

A financial statement **ratio** is computed by dividing the dollar amount of one item reported in the financial statements by the dollar amount of another item reported. The purpose is to express a relationship between two relevant items that is easy to interpret and compare with other information. For example, the relationship of current assets to current liabilities is of interest to most statement users. For a firm reporting current assets of $210,000 and current liabilities of $120,000, the relationship between the two items is called the current ratio. It amounts to 1.75 (210,000/120,000), which means that current assets are 1.75 times greater than current liabilities. The relationship could also be converted to a percentage (175%) by multiplying the ratio by 100. In ratio form, however, the relationship between the two items can be more easily compared to such other standards as the current ratio of other companies or industrywide ratios.

Relevant relationships can exist between items in the same financial statement or between items reported in two different financial statements, so there are a number of ratios that could be computed. The analyst must therefore give careful thought initially to the selection of those ratios that express relationships relevant to the area of immediate concern. The user must keep in mind that a ratio is computed to show a significant relationship that, when used alone, may have little significance. Consequently, to evaluate the adequacy of a certain relationship the ratio should be compared to other standards.

Ratios are classified and presented in several different ways. In the remainder of this chapter, three general groups of ratios are discussed, those commonly used to evaluate a firm's *profitability, liquidity,* and *solvency.* Unless otherwise noted, computations are based on the financial statements presented for Gordon Corporation in Figures 20-1 and 20-2.

RATIOS TO ANALYZE PROFITABILITY

Profitability analysis consists of tests used to evaluate a firm's earning performance during the year. The results are combined with other data to forecast the firm's potential earning power. Potential earning power is important to long-term creditors and stockholders because, in the long run, the firm must operate at a satisfactory profit to survive. Earning power is also important to statement users such as suppliers and labor unions, who are interested in maintaining a continuing relationship with a financially sound company. A firm's financial soundness is obviously dependent on its future earning power.

Adequacy of earnings is measured in terms of the relationship between earnings and either total assets or stockholders' equity, the relationship between earnings and sales, and the availability of earnings to common stockholders. If earnings are not adequate, the next step is to determine why they are not. Is the sales volume too low? Are the cost of goods sold and/or other expenses too high? Is the investment in assets excessive in relation to the firm's sales?

Rate of Return on Total Assets

Rate of return on total assets is determined by dividing the sum of net income plus interest expense by average total assets for the year:

$$\text{Return on total assets[1]} = \frac{\text{Net income + Interest expense}}{\text{Average total assets}}$$

---

[1]There are variations in the way analysts compute the same ratios. For example, some analysts prefer to compute the return on total assets using one of the following alternatives as a substitute for the numerator shown above:

1. Net income + Interest expense (net of tax)

$$\frac{\text{Interest expense}}{\text{(net of tax)}} = \text{Pretax interest expense} - (1.0 - \text{the effective income tax rate})$$

2. Net income before interest expense and income taxes
3. Net income

The various approaches to computing the same ratio points out the need for an analyst to exercise care when comparing ratios computed by different individuals.

Interest is added back to net income in the numerator to reflect the fact that the efficient use of the resources is not affected by the method of financing acquisition of the assets. In other words, the interest expense is considered a return to the creditors for the assets they have provided. Average total assets is used in the denominator because the earnings were produced by employing resources throughout the period.

The management of Gordon Corporation produced a return on average total assets of 11.8% in 1986 and 14.5% in 1985 as computed below:

$$\underset{\text{1986}}{\frac{558 + 252}{(6,300 + 7,440)/2}} = 11.8\% \qquad \underset{\text{1985}}{\frac{690 + 230}{(6,400 + 6,300)/2}} = 14.5\%$$

During 1986, management produced approximately 12 cents in profit for every dollar invested in resources, compared with 14.5 cents in 1985. The decrease in rates between the two years is significant and results from decreased net income combined with an increased investment base. Such a decrease highlights the need for further investigation by the analyst.

Rate of Return on Common Stockholders' Equity

The return on total assets does not measure the return earned by management on the assets contributed by the common stockholders. The return to the common stockholders may be greater or less than the return on total assets because of the firm's use of leverage. As we saw in Chapter 17, leverage is the use of borrowed funds or other fixed-return securities, such as preferred stock, to earn a return greater than the interest or dividends paid to the creditors or preferred stockholders. Thus, if a firm is able to earn more on the borrowed funds than the fixed amount that must be paid to the creditors or preferred stockholders, the return to the common stockholders will be greater than the return on total assets. If the amount earned is less than the fixed interest and preferred dividend, the return to the common stockholders will be less than the return on total assets. The return may be computed as:

$$\text{Return on common stockholders' equity} = \frac{\text{Net income} - \text{Preferred dividend requirement}}{\text{Average common stockholders' equity}}$$

The preferred dividend requirement is subtracted from net income to yield the portion of net income allocated to the common stockholders' equity.

The computations for Gordon Corporation are:

---

[2]In the denominator, the sum of the beginning and ending total assets is divided by 2 to determine the average of these two amounts. If sufficient information were available, a monthly or quarterly average would be preferred to minimize the effects of seasonal fluctuations.

$$\frac{1986}{558 - 30}{(2,700 + 3,480)/2} = 17.1\% \qquad \frac{1985}{690 - 30}{(2,400 + 2,700)/2} = 25.9\%$$

Note that both of these rates are higher than the corresponding returns computed on total assets because the company earned a return on the assets financed by the creditors and preferred stockholders greater than the interest or dividends paid them. However, the percentage decreased from 25.9% to 17.1%, a decrease worthy of further investigation.

Return on Sales

Return on sales (also called profit margin) is calculated during a vertical analysis of the income statement. It reflects the portion of each dollar of sales that represents income and is computed by dividing net income by net sales:

$$\text{Return on sales} = \frac{\text{Net income}}{\text{Net sales}}$$

For Gordon Corporation the rates are:

$$\frac{1986}{558}{10,320} = 5.4\% \qquad \frac{1985}{690}{9,582} = 7.2\%$$

For 1986, each dollar of sales produced 5.4 cents in income. Consistent with the other rates computed, this ratio indicates a declining profitability trend for the firm. The rates should of course be compared to other standards to be more useful. If the return on sales for competing firms is 5%, the 5.4% appears favorable, but the declining trend between the two years should be investigated further.

Earnings Per Share

Earnings per share (EPS) of common stock is one of the most commonly quoted and most widely publicized ratios computed from a firm's financial statements. As the term implies, this ratio is the conversion of the absolute dollar amount of net income to a per-share basis and is computed:

$$\text{EPS} = \frac{\text{Net income} - \text{Preferred dividend requirements}}{\text{Weighted average number of shares outstanding}}$$

The computation of EPS is much more complex than it appears above if a company has issued securities that are convertible into common stock, complexities that are discussed in detail in more advanced accounting courses. In our illustration the calculations are:

$$\frac{\overset{1986}{558 - 30}}{150} = \$3.52 \qquad \frac{\overset{1985}{690 - 30}}{120} = \$5.50$$

The weighted average number of shares in 1986 is computed on an assumption that 30,000 additional shares were issued at the beginning of the year.[3] This ratio can be interpreted to mean that for 1986 the firm earned $3.52 per share of common stock outstanding. Because of the importance attached to the EPS figure, firms are required to disclose it on the face of the income statement.

Price-Earnings Ratio

The price-earnings ratio (P/E ratio) is computed by dividing the market price of a share of common stock by the earnings per share:

$$\text{P/E ratios} = \frac{\text{Market price per share of common stock}}{\text{Earnings per share}}$$

This ratio indicates how much an investor would have to pay for each dollar of earnings. It enhances a statement user's ability to compare the market value of one common stock relative to earnings to that of other companies.

Assuming a market price of $40 per share for Gordon Corporation common stock in 1986, the P/E ratio is:

$$\frac{40.00}{3.52} = 11.4 \text{ times}$$

The common stock of Gordon Corporation is said to be selling for 11.4 times its earnings.

P/E ratios vary widely between industries since they represent investors' expectations for a company. High P/E stocks are associated with growth companies, whereas more stable firms have low P/E stocks. Also, financially strong companies that have been successful and are expected to be so in the future will generally have higher P/E ratios.

Dividend Yield and Payout Ratio

Dividend yield is computed as:

$$\text{Dividend yield} = \frac{\text{Annual dividend per share of common stock}}{\text{Market price per share of common stock}}$$

[3]Computing EPS and the weighted average number of shares outstanding is covered in more detail in Chapter 16 (pages 628–630).

Cash dividends of $150,000 ($1 per share) were paid during 1986 to the common stockholders of Gordon Corporation. Assuming a market price of $40 per share, the dividend yield is computed as follows:

$$\frac{1.00}{40.00} = 2.5\%$$

This ratio is normally computed by an investor who is investing in common stock primarily for dividends rather than appreciation in the market price of the stock. The percentage yield indicates a rate of return on the dollars invested and permits easier comparison to returns from alternative investment opportunities.

Investors interested in dividend yields may also compute the percentage of common stock earnings distributed as dividends to the common stockholders each period. This ratio is referred to as the dividend payout ratio:

$$\text{Dividend payout} = \frac{\text{Total dividends to common stockholders}}{\text{Net income} - \text{Preferred dividend requirements}}$$

For the Gordon Corporation the 1986 ratio is:

$$\frac{150}{558 - 30} = 28.4\%$$

This ratio provides an investor some insights into management's policy of distributing dividends as a percentage of net income available to the common stockholders. A low payout ratio would indicate that management is reinvesting earnings internally. Such a company would be desirable for someone interested in investing for growth in the market price of the shares.

RATIOS TO ANALYZE LIQUIDITY

Liquidity is an important factor in financial statement analysis since a firm that cannot meet its short-term obligations may be forced into bankruptcy and will therefore not have the opportunity to operate in the long run. The focus of this aspect of analysis is on working capital or some component of working capital.

Current Ratio

Perhaps the most commonly used measure of a firm's liquidity is the current ratio, which is computed as:

$$\text{Current ratio} = \frac{\text{Current assets}}{\text{Current liabilities}}$$

Current ratio, a measure of the firm's ability to satisfy its obligations in the short term, measures a margin of safety to the creditors. It indicates how much current assets exceed current liabilities on a dollar-per-dollar basis. A low ratio may indicate that the firm would be unable to meet its short-term debt in an emergency. A high ratio is considered favorable to creditors, but may indicate excessive investment in working-capital items that may not be producing income for the firm. Analysts often contend that the current ratio should be at least 2:1; in other words, a firm should maintain $2 of current assets for every dollar of current liabilities. Although such rules may be one standard of comparison, they are arbitrary and subject to exceptions and numerous qualifications in the modern approach to statement analysis. Deviations from the rule nevertheless highlight an area that deserves further investigation.

The current ratios for Gordon Corporation for 1985 and 1986 are:

$$\underset{1986}{\frac{4{,}340}{1{,}760}} = 2.5 \qquad \underset{1985}{\frac{3{,}900}{1{,}600}} = 2.4$$

Gordon Corporation shows a slight improvement in the relationship between current assets and current liabilities and, in the absence of other information, would be considered liquid, at least in the short run. However, a ratio of 2.4 or higher may signify excessive investments in current assets.

Quick Ratio or Acid Test Ratio

One of the limitations of the current ratio is that it includes inventory and prepaid assets in the numerator. However, these items are not as liquid as cash, marketable securities, notes receivable, and accounts receivable. In the normal course of business, inventories must first be sold, and then the cash collected, before cash is available. Also, most prepaid assets are to be consumed and cannot be readily converted into cash. A ratio used to supplement the current ratio that provides a more rigorous measure of liquidity is the quick ratio or acid test ratio, as it is sometimes called. The quick ratio is computed as follows:

$$\text{Quick ratio} = \frac{\text{Cash} + \text{Marketable securities} + \text{Net receivables}}{\text{Current liabilities}}$$

The higher the ratio, the more liquid the firm is considered. A rule of thumb used by some analysts is that a 1:1 ratio is adequate. A lower ratio may indicate that in an emergency the company would be unable to meet its immediate obligations.

The quick ratio for Gordon Corporation is computed:

$$\underset{1986}{\frac{390 + 380 + 1{,}460}{1{,}760}} = 1.3 \qquad \underset{1985}{\frac{300 + 440 + 1{,}290}{1{,}600}} = 1.3$$

A ratio of 1.3:1 in both years indicates that the firm is highly liquid. However, this observation is dependent somewhat on the collectibility of the receivables included in the numerator.

The current ratio and quick ratio are used to measure the adequacy of the firm's current assets to satisfy its current obligations at one point in time, the balance sheet date. These ratios do not consider the movement of items making up the current assets. An important aspect of the firm's operations affecting liquidity is how long it takes for a firm to convert receivables and inventories into cash. Since receivables and inventories normally make up a large percentage of a firm's current assets, a quick ratio and a current ratio may be misleading if there is an extended interval between purchasing inventory, selling it, and collecting cash from the sale. The receivable-turnover and inventory-turnover ratios are two other measures of liquidity that can yield additional information.

Receivable Turnover

The receivable-turnover ratio is a measure of how many times the average receivable balance was converted into cash during the year. It is also considered a measure of the efficiency of the credit-granting and collection policies that have been established by the firm and is computed as follows:

$$\text{Receivable turnover} = \frac{\text{Net sales}}{\text{Average receivable balance}}$$

The higher the receivable-turnover ratio, the shorter the period of time between recording a sale and collecting the cash. To be competitive, the credit policies established by the firm are influenced by industry practices. Comparison of this ratio to industry norms can reveal deviations from competitors' operating results.

In computing this ratio, credit sales should be used in the numerator whenever the amount is available. However, such information is normally not available in financial statements, so net sales is then used as a substitute. Also, an average of monthly receivable balances should be used in the denominator. In the absence of monthly information, the year-end balance, or an average of the beginning of the year and end of the year balances, or averages of quarterly balances are used in the calculation. The computations for Gordon Corporation are:

$$\frac{1986}{10,320} \quad\quad\quad \frac{1985}{9,582}$$
$$\frac{10,320}{(1,290 + 1,460)/2} = 7.5 \quad\quad \frac{9,582}{(1,320 + 1,290)/2} = 7.3$$

Frequently, the receivable turnover is divided into 365 days to derive the average number of days it takes to collect receivables from sales on account.

1986	1985
$\dfrac{365 \text{ days}}{7.5} = 48.7$ days	$\dfrac{365 \text{ days}}{7.3} = 50.0$ days

During 1986, the corporation collected the average account receivable balance 7.5 times; or, expressed another way, it took 48.7 days to collect sales on account—an improvement over 1985. These measures are particularly useful if one knows the credit terms granted by the firm. Assuming credit terms of 60 days, the average collection period of 49 days provides some indication that the firm's credit policy is effective and that the firm probably is not burdened by excessive amounts of uncollectible accounts that have not been written off. A collection period significantly in excess of 60 days indicates a problem with either the granting of credit, collection policies, or both.

Inventory Turnover

The control of the amount invested in inventory is an important aspect of managing a business. The size of the investment in inventory and inventory turnover are dependent on such factors as type of business and time of year. A grocery store will have a higher turnover than an automobile dealership, and the inventory level of a seasonal business will be higher at certain times in the operating cycle than at others. The inventory turnover ratio is a measure of the adequacy of inventory and how efficiently it is being managed. The ratio is an expression of the number of times the average inventory balance was sold and then replaced during the year. The ratio is computed as follows:

$$\text{Inventory turnover} = \frac{\text{Cost of goods sold}}{\text{Average inventory balance}}$$

Cost of goods sold rather than sales is used in the numerator because it is a measure of the cost of inventory sold during the year, and the cost measure is consistent with the cost basis of the denominator. Ideally, an average of monthly inventory balances should be computed, but this information is generally not readily available. A quarterly average can be computed if quarterly reports are published by the firm.

The inventory turnover for Gordon Corporation is:

1986	1985
$\dfrac{7,719}{(1,770 + 2,010)/2} = 4.1$	$\dfrac{6,975}{(1,860 + 1,770)/2} = 3.8$

The average days per turnover can be computed by dividing 365 days by the turnover ratio:

$\dfrac{365 \text{ days}}{4.1} = 89.0$ days	$\dfrac{365 \text{ days}}{3.8} = 96.1$ days

The 1986 turnover ratio indicates that the average inventory was sold 4.1 times during the year as compared to 3.8 times in 1985. In terms of days, the firm held its inventory approximately 89 days in 1986 before it was sold.

The increased turnover in 1986 would generally be considered a favorable trend. Inventory with a high turnover is less likely to become obsolete and decline in price before it is sold. A higher turnover would also indicate greater liquidity since the inventory would be converted into cash in a shorter period of time. A very high turnover, however, may indicate that the company is carrying insufficient inventory and is losing a significant amount of sales.

RATIOS TO ANALYZE SOLVENCY

We will now focus on several tests used to analyze the firm's ability to satisfy its long-term commitments and still have sufficient working capital left over to operate successfully.

Debt to Total Assets

The proportion of total assets financed by creditors is important to long-term investors in a firm since the creditors have a prior claim to assets in the event of liquidation—the creditors must be paid before assets are distributed to stockholders. The greater the percentage of assets contributed by stockholders, the greater the protection to the creditors. The debt ratio is a measure of the relationship between total liabilities and total assets and is computed:

$$\text{Debt to total assets (Debt ratio)} = \frac{\text{Total liabilities}}{\text{Total assets}}$$

Since this ratio is a measure of the margin of safety to the creditors of the firm in the event of liquidation, the lower the ratio, the greater the asset protection to the creditors.

For Gordon Corporation the ratio is:

1986	1985
$\frac{3,660}{7,440} = .492$ or 49.2%	$\frac{3,300}{6,300} = .524$ or 52.4%

Thus, for both years, approximately 50% of the assets were provided by the firm's creditors. The fair value of the assets would have to decline to 50% below book value before the creditors would not be protected in liquidation. (Note that this ratio is already available if vertical percentage analysis has been performed.)

Times Interest Earned

Current interest charges are normally paid from funds provided by current operations. In recognition of this, analysts frequently compute the relationship between earnings and interest:

$$\text{Times interest earned} = \frac{\text{Net income} + \text{Interest expense} + \text{Income tax expense}}{\text{Interest expense}}$$

This ratio is an indication of the firm's ability to satisfy periodic interest payments from current earnings. Interest expense and income taxes are added back to net income in the numerator because the ratio is a measure of income available to pay the interest charges.

For our illustration the ratio is:

1986	1985
$\dfrac{558 + 252 + 144}{252} = 3.8$	$\dfrac{690 + 230 + 237}{230} = 5.0$

In 1985, earnings before interest and income taxes were 5 times greater than interest expense. This ratio declined to 3.8 in 1986, which is marginal but still an adequate coverage by most standards. A rough rule of thumb is that the company should earn 3 to 4 times its interest requirement. Again, the 3.8 should be considered in relation to other trends in the company's financial status and comparison with other standards.

LIMITATIONS OF FINANCIAL ANALYSIS

The analytical techniques introduced in this chapter are useful for providing insights into the financial position and results of operations for a particular firm. There are nevertheless certain limitations that should be kept in mind:

1. Financial analysis is performed on historical data primarily for the purpose of forecasting future performance. The historical relationships may not continue because of changes in the general state of the economy, the business environment in which the firm must operate, or internal factors such as change in management or changes in the policies established by management.

2. The measurement base used in computing the analytical measures is historical cost. Failure to adjust for inflation or changes in fair values may result in some computations providing misleading information on a trend basis and in any comparison between companies. For example, the return on total assets includes net income in the numerator, which is affected by the current year's sales and current operating expenses measured in current dollars. Fixed assets and other nonmonetary items, however, are measured in historical dollars—which are not adjusted to reflect current price levels. Thus the ratio divides items primarily measured in current dollar amounts by a total measured primarily in terms of historical dollars. This limitation is partially overcome by the recently enacted requirement that firms must report inflation-adjusted data as supplementary information to the historical cost statements (see Chapter 13).

3. Year-end data may not be typical of the firm's position during the year. Knowing that certain ratios are computed at year-end, management may attempt to improve a ratio by entering into certain types of transaction near the end of the year. For example, the current ratio can be improved by using cash to pay off short-term debt. Also, a firm usually establishes a fiscal year-end that coincides with the low point of activity in its operating cycle. Therefore, account balances such as receivables, accounts payable, and inventory may not be representative of the balances carried in these accounts during the year.

4. Companies may not be comparable. Throughout this chapter it has been emphasized that one important comparison is between competing companies. However, because of factors such as the use of different accounting methods, the size of the companies, and the diversification of product lines, data among companies may not provide meaningful comparisons.

Although there are other limitations of the techniques illustrated, those above should provide sufficient evidence that a statement user must be most careful in interpreting trends and ratios computed from reported financial statements.

A summary of the ratios discussed in this chapter is presented in Figure 20-3 on page 803.

GLOSSARY

COMMON SIZE STATEMENT. A financial statement in which the amount of each item reported in the statement is stated as a percentage of some specific base amount also reported in the same statement (p. 791).

COMPARATIVE STATEMENTS. Financial statements for the current year and prior years presented together to facilitate the analysis of changes in account balances (p. 787).

HORIZONTAL ANALYSIS. That part of an analysis based on the comparison of amounts reported for the same item in two or more comparative statements with an emphasis on the change from year to year (p. 787).

LIQUIDITY. A firm's ability to satisfy its short-term obligations (p. 787).

RATIO. Division of the amount reported for one financial statement item by the amount reported for another. Ratio analysis is the evaluation of the relationship indicated by this division (p. 791).

SOLVENCY. A firm's ability to satisfy its long-term obligations (p. 787).

VERTICAL ANALYSIS. That part of an analysis in which the focus of the study is on the proportion of individual items expressed as a percentage of some specific item reported in the same statement (p. 791). (See also *Common Size Statement*.)

Ratio	Method of Calculation	Significance of Each Ratio
Profitability Ratios		
Return on total assets	$\dfrac{\text{Net income} + \text{Interest expense}}{\text{Average total assets}}$	Measures rate of return earned on total assets provided by both creditors and owners.
Return on common stockholders' equity	$\dfrac{\text{Net income} - \text{Preferred dividend requirements}}{\text{Average common stockholders' equity}}$	Measures rate of return earned on assets provided by owners.
Return on sales	$\dfrac{\text{Net income}}{\text{Net sales}}$	Measures net profitability of each dollar of sales.
Earnings per share	$\dfrac{\text{Net income} - \text{Preferred dividend requirements}}{\text{Weighted average number of shares outstanding}}$	Measures net income earned on each share of common stock.
Price-earnings ratio	$\dfrac{\text{Market price per share of common stock}}{\text{Earnings per share}}$	Measures the amount investors are paying for a dollar of earnings.
Dividend yield	$\dfrac{\text{Annual dividend per share of common stock}}{\text{Market price per share of common stock}}$	Measures rate of return to stockholders based on current market price.
Dividend payout	$\dfrac{\text{Total dividends to common stockholders}}{\text{Net income} - \text{Preferred dividend requirements}}$	Measures the percentage of income paid out to common stockholders.
Liquidity Ratios		
Current ratio	$\dfrac{\text{Current assets}}{\text{Current liabilities}}$	A measure of short-term liquidity. Indicates the ability of a firm to meet its short-term debts from its current assets.
Quick ratio	$\dfrac{\text{Cash} + \text{Marketable securities} + \text{Net receivables}}{\text{Current liabilities}}$	A more rigorous measure of short-term liquidity. Indicates the ability of the firm to meet unexpected demands from liquid current assets.
Receivable turnover	$\dfrac{\text{Net sales}}{\text{Average receivable balance}}$	Measures effectiveness of collections; used to evaluate whether receivable balance is excessive.
Inventory turnover	$\dfrac{\text{Cost of goods sold}}{\text{Average inventory balance}}$	Indicates the liquidity of inventory. Measures the number of times inventory was sold on the average during the period.
Solvency Ratios		
Debt to total assets	$\dfrac{\text{Total liabilities}}{\text{Total assets}}$	Measures percentage of assets provided by creditors and extent of using leverage.
Times interest earned	$\dfrac{\text{Net income} + \text{Interest expense} + \text{Income tax expense}}{\text{Interest expense}}$	Measures the ability of the firm to meet its interest payments out of current earnings.

Figure 20-3
Summary of Ratios

DISCUSSION QUESTIONS

1. The dollar amounts of one year's financial statements have limited significance when presented alone. To what could the dollar amounts be compared to provide a more meaningful analysis?
2. Differentiate between horizontal analysis, trend analysis, and vertical analysis.
3. What is the purpose of computing ratios?

4. Name and define each of the three financial aspects of a firm that are commonly analyzed.
5. Identify the people who would have a primary interest in each of the three financial aspects of a firm.
6. Explain how the price-earnings ratios, dividend yield ratios, and dividend payout ratios of growth firms and more stable firms tend to differ.
7. What ratio will help to answer each of the following questions:
   (a) How effective are the credit policies of the firm?
   (b) How much confidence do investors have in the firm?
   (c) Are the assets being used efficiently?
   (d) How is the firm being financed?
8. How are the current ratio and the quick ratio similar? How do they differ?
9. Why is it preferable to use only credit sales as the numerator in computing the receivable turnover? Comment on a firm's credit policies if the receivable turnover is 8.1 and its credit terms are 30 days.
10. What risk does a company assume as the inventory turnover increases?
11. How could earnings per share decrease even though net income has increased from the previous year?
12. How can ratios be used to determine whether common stockholders benefit from the assets contributed by creditors and preferred stockholders?
13. A firm has a current ratio of 2.0 and a quick ratio of 1.5. If the current liabilities total $100,000, what is the sum of the inventory and prepaid assets?
14. Explain why financial statement analysis should be merely the beginning of a thorough investigation of a firm.
15. Why is the usefulness of financial analysis particularly limited during periods of high inflation?

EXERCISES

Exercise 20-1 (Common Size Statements)
Comparative income statements of the Hadley Company are shown below:

	1985	1984
Sales	$300,000	$280,000
Cost of goods sold	187,200	179,200
Gross profit on sales	112,800	100,800
Operating expenses	93,000	80,360
Net income	$ 19,800	$ 20,440

Required:
Prepare common size statements for both years.

Exercise 20-2 (Trend Analysis)
A company reported the following financial data over a five-year period.

	1983	1984	1985	1986	1987
Sales	$750,000	$795,600	$825,000	$807,300	$868,000
Gross profit on sales	315,000	337,000	343,350	347,130	368,550
Operating expenses	202,500	210,600	212,600	216,700	233,000

Required:
A. Prepare a trend analysis of the data.
B. Do the trends signify a favorable or unfavorable situation? Explain.

Exercise 20-3 (Trend Analysis)
The asset section of the balance sheet of the Safford Company is shown below:

	1985	1984
Cash	$ 15,000	$ 14,500
Accounts receivable	33,400	36,200
Inventory	110,600	108,000
Prepaid insurance	1,000	1,700
Furniture and fixtures	59,000	55,000
Machinery and equipment	105,000	94,000

Required:
Compute the changes in dollar amounts and percentages.

Exercise 20-4 (Liquidity Analysis)
The following information is taken from the financial statements of the Jasmine Company.

	1986	1985
Cash	$ 20,000	$ 22,000
Marketable securities	50,000	44,000
Accounts receivable	54,000	51,000
Inventory	130,000	129,000
Prepaid expenses	6,000	10,000
Plant and equipment	230,000	221,000
Current liabilities	127,000	125,000
Sales	560,000	554,000
Cost of goods sold	340,000	336,000

Required:
Compute the following items for 1986:

A. Current ratio
B. Quick ratio
C. Receivable-turnover ratio

D. Average collection period of accounts receivable
E. Inventory-turnover ratio
F. Average period for inventory turnover

Exercise 20-5 (Profitability and Solvency Analysis)

The following information is available for the Yag Company.

	1986	1985
Sales	$1,600,000	$1,470,000
Interest expense	69,000	71,000
Income tax expense	124,400	137,900
Net income	146,000	144,000
Preferred dividends	9,000	9,000
Total assets	1,300,000	1,230,000
Total liabilities	730,000	810,000
Preferred stock	150,000	150,000
Common stock	263,000	249,000
Retained earnings	157,000	21,000

Required:
A. Compute the following ratios for 1986:
  1. Return on total assets
  2. Return on common stockholders' equity
B. Compute the following ratios for 1985 and 1986:
  1. Return on sales
  2. Debt to total assets
  3. Times interest earned

Exercise 20-6 (Profitability Analysis)

The Burns Corporation had a net income of $760,000. The company distributed preferred dividends of $40,000, and dividends to common stockholders of $450,000. Throughout the year, 300,000 shares of common stock were outstanding. Common stock is currently selling for $35 per share.

Required:
Compute the following ratios:

A. Earnings per share
B. Price-earnings ratio
C. Dividend yield
D. Dividend payout

✓Exercise 20-7 (Effect of Transactions on Current Ratio)

Presented below is information related to ETG Company on December 29, 1983:

```
                        ETG COMPANY
                     Partial Balance Sheet
                      December 29, 1983


   Cash                 $  300,000  Short-term notes payable  $100,000
   Accounts receivable     210,000  Accounts payable           300,000
   Inventories             450,000  Accrued liabilities         90,000
   Prepaid expenses         40,000
        Total           $1,000,000      Total                 $490,000
```

Required:
A. Compute the current and quick ratio based on the data as of December 29, 1983.
B. A long-term debt agreement entered into by the company two years ago requires the company to maintain a minimum working capital ratio of 2:1. Management is concerned that this requirement will not be met and is considering entering into one or more of the following transactions before the close of the fiscal year-end, December 31. Compute the current ratio after each of the following transactions and indicate whether the ratio would be increased, decreased, or unaffected by the transaction.
  1. Borrow $100,000 on a long-term note.
  2. Pay $100,000 on accounts payable.
  3. Give existing creditors a $100,000 short-term note in settlement of accounts payable.
  4. Give existing creditors a $100,000 long-term note in settlement of accounts payable.

Exercise 20-8 (Limitations of Ratio Analysis)
A Company and B Company began operations on January 1, 1983. For illustrative purposes, we will assume that at that date their financial positions were identical and that their operations during 1983 were also identical. The only difference between the two companies is that they elected to use different accounting methods as shown below:

	A Company	B Company
Inventory	FIFO	LIFO
Plant and equipment	Straight-line depreciation	Accelerated depreciation

Financial statements for the two companies prepared at the end of 1983 are presented below:

Income Statement

	A Company	B Company
Revenues	$130,000	$130,000
Cost of goods sold	78,000	86,000
Gross profit on sales	52,000	44,000
Operating expenses*	28,000	38,000
Net income	$ 24,000	$ 6,000

*Includes interest expense of $5,000. Depreciation expense was $10,000 for A Company and $20,000 for B Company.

Balance Sheet

	A Company	B Company
Cash	$ 16,000	$ 16,000
Accounts receivable	40,000	40,000
Inventories	28,000	20,000
Property, plant, and equipment (net)	40,000	30,000
	$124,000	$106,000
Current liabilities	$ 20,000	$ 20,000
Long-term liabilities	30,000	30,000
Stockholders' equity	74,000	56,000
	$124,000	$106,000

Required:
Compute the following ratios for each company:

A. Return on total assets
B. Return on common stockholders' equity
C. Return on sales
D. Current ratio
E. Receivable turnover
F. Inventory turnover
G. Debt to total assets

PROBLEMS

Problem 20-1 (Horizontal and Vertical Analysis)
The comparative financial statements of McDonnell Company are shown.

McDONNELL COMPANY
Comparative Income Statements
For the Years Ended December 31, 1986 and 1985
(000 omitted)

	1986	1985
Sales	$4,000	$3,800
Less: Cost of goods sold	2,360	2,394
Gross profit on sales	1,640	1,406
Selling expenses	580	520
Administrative expenses	720	680
Income tax expense	150	103
Total Expenses	1,450	1,303
Net Income	$ 190	$ 103

McDONNELL COMPANY
Comparative Balance Sheets
December 31, 1986 and 1985
(000 omitted)

	1986	1985
Assets		
Cash	$ 50	$ 60
Accounts Receivable	110	90
Inventory	230	210
Long-term Investments	75	100
Plant and Equipment	1,100	840
Total Assets	$1,565	$1,300
Liabilities and Stockholders' Equity		
Accounts Payable	$ 130	$ 118
Notes Payable	25	35
Long-term Liabilities	580	580
Common Stock	600	440
Retained Earnings	230	127
Total Liabilities and Stockholders' Equity	$1,565	$1,300

Required:
A. Compute the changes in the financial statements from 1985 to 1986 in both dollar amounts and percentages.
B. Prepare a common size income statement and balance sheet for 1986 and 1985.
C. Comment on the significant relationships revealed by the horizontal and vertical analyses.

Problem 20-2 (Trend Analysis)

The comparative income statements and balance sheets of the M. L. Washington Company are shown below:

M. L. WASHINGTON COMPANY
Comparative Income Statements
For the Years Ended December 31, 1983–1988
(000 omitted)

	1983	1984	1985	1986	1987	1988
Sales	$300	$310	$308	$321	$400	$430
Less: Cost of goods sold	184	186	178	190	237	282
Gross profit on sales	116	124	130	131	163	148
Operating expenses	98	100	103	115	120	124
Net Income	$ 18	$ 24	$ 27	$ 16	$ 43	$ 24

M. L. WASHINGTON COMPANY
Comparative Balance Sheets
December 31, 1983–1988
(000 omitted)

	1983	1984	1985	1986	1987	1988
Assets						
Cash	$ 12	$ 10	$ 9	$ 14	$ 11	$ 8
Accounts Receivable	25	30	28	31	52	68
Inventory	74	78	85	120	160	157
Plant and Equipment	180	185	189	350	347	354
Total Assets	$291	$303	$311	$515	$570	$587
Liabilities and Stockholders' Equity						
Accounts Payable	$ 46	$ 44	$ 49	$ 47	$107	$120
Long-term Liabilities	60	57	53	143	118	118
Common Stock	155	155	155	255	255	255
Retained Earnings	30	47	54	70	90	94
Total Liabilities and Stockholders' Equity	$291	$303	$311	$515	$570	$587

Required:

A. Prepare a trend analysis of the data.

B. Comment on any significant situations revealed by the trends.

Problem 20-3 (Ratio Analysis)

The comparative financial statements of the Marvin Corporation are shown below and on page 812.

MARVIN CORPORATION
Comparative Balance Sheets
December 31, 1985 and 1984

	1985	1984
Assets		
Current Assets:		
Cash	$ 20,000	$ 18,000
Marketable Securities	21,000	25,000
Accounts Receivable	79,000	74,000
Inventory	210,000	203,000
Prepaid Expenses	4,000	5,000
Total Current Assets	334,000	325,000
Plant and Equipment	160,000	141,000
Total Assets	$494,000	$466,000
Liabilities		
Current Liabilities:		
Accounts Payable	$ 77,000	$ 64,000
Notes Payable	40,000	30,000
Total Current Liabilities	117,000	94,000
Bonds Payable	140,000	140,000
Total Liabilities	257,000	234,000
Stockholders' Equity		
Preferred Stock	40,000	40,000
Common Stock ($5 par value)	50,000	50,000
Additional Paid-in Capital	115,000	115,000
Retained Earnings	32,000	27,000
Total Stockholders' Equity	237,000	232,000
Total Liabilities and Stockholders' Equity	$494,000	$466,000

During 1985, Marvin Corporation declared and paid preferred dividends of $2,800 and common dividends of $23,200. On December 31, 1985, the market price of the common stock was $27 a share.

Required:

Compute the following ratios for 1985:

A. Return on total assets
B. Return on common stockholders' equity
C. Return on sales
D. Earnings per share
E. Price-earnings ratio

MARVIN CORPORATION
Comparative Income Statements
For the Years Ended December 31, 1985 and 1984

	1985	1984
Sales	$790,000	$773,000
Less: Cost of goods sold	494,000	456,000
Gross profit on sales	296,000	317,000
Operating expenses	220,000	241,000
Interest expense	15,000	14,000
Income tax expense	30,000	32,000
Total Expenses	265,000	287,000
Net Income	$ 31,000	$ 30,000

F. Dividend yield
G. Dividend payout
H. Current ratio
I. Quick ratio
J. Receivable turnover
K. Inventory turnover
L. Debt to total assets
M. Times interest earned

Problem 20-4 (Effect of Transactions on Ratios)

The Zenger Corporation completed the transactions listed below in the left-hand column.

Transaction	Ratio
1. Retired bonds payable by issuing common stock	Return on common stockholders' equity
2. Purchased inventory on account	Quick ratio
3. Sold inventory for cash	Current ratio
4. Issued additional shares of common stock for cash	Debt to total assets
5. Declared a cash dividend on common stock	Dividend payout
6. Paid the cash dividend	Dividend yield
7. Wrote off an uncollectible account receivable to Allowance for Doubtful Accounts	Current ratio
8. Collected on accounts receivable	Receivable turnover
9. Paid on accounts payable	Return on total assets
10. Sold obsolete inventory at cost	Return on sales
11. Issued a stock dividend on common stock	Earnings per share
12. Sold inventory on account	Inventory turnover

Required:

State whether each transaction would cause the ratio listed opposite to it to increase, decrease, or remain unchanged.

Problem 20-5 (Using Ratios to Compute Data Missing in Financial Statements)

The incomplete financial statements of the Euclid Corporation are shown below:

EUCLID CORPORATION
Income Statement
For the Year Ended December 31, 1985

Sales	$?
Less: Cost of goods sold	?
Gross profit on sales	?
Operating expenses	22,000
Interest expense	?
Total Expenses	?
Income before taxes	?
Less: Income tax (40%)	6,720
Net Income	$?

EUCLID CORPORATION
Balance Sheet
December 31, 1985

Assets	
Current Assets:	
Cash	$?
Accounts Receivable	?
Inventory	?
Total Current Assets	?
Plant and Equipment	?
Total Assets	$?
Liabilities and Stockholders' Equity	
Current Liabilities	$?
Long-term Liabilities, 12% interest	10,000
Common Stock, $20 par value	?
Retained Earnings	?
Total Liabilities and Stockholders' Equity	$94,000

The following additional information is available.

1. The current ratio is 2.5.
2. The quick ratio is 1.0.
3. The receivable turnover is 12.5 and the balance in Accounts Receivable on January 1, 1985 was $8,200.
4. The inventory turnover is 2.75. The January 1, 1985 inventory was $19,750.
5. The debt to total assets ratio is 25.0%.
6. Earnings per share are $4.032. No additional common stock was issued during the year.
7. All the interest expense is attributable to the long-term liabilities.

Required:
Complete the income statement and the balance sheet. Show all computations. (Hint: The debt to total asset ratio is the key to this problem.)

ALTERNATE PROBLEMS

Problem 20-1A (Horizontal and Vertical Analysis)
Comparative income statements and balance sheets of the Corona Corporation appear below:

CORONA CORPORATION
Comparative Income Statements
For the Years Ended December 31, 1985 and 1984

	1985	1984
Sales	$870,000	$730,000
Less: Cost of goods sold	504,600	467,200
Gross profit on sales	365,400	262,800
Operating expenses	257,000	154,000
Interest expense	22,000	14,000
Income tax expense	37,000	40,600
Total Expenses	316,000	208,600
Net Income	$ 49,400	$ 54,200

CORONA CORPORATION
Comparative Balance Sheets
December 31, 1985 and 1984

	1985	1984
Assets		
Cash	$ 43,500	$ 68,000
Accounts Receivable	98,500	85,000
Inventory	130,000	103,000
Plant and Equipment	490,000	380,000
Total Assets	$762,000	$636,000
Liabilities and Stockholders' Equity		
Accounts Payable	$130,000	$109,000
Bonds Payable	210,000	110,000
Common Stock	385,000	385,000
Retained Earnings	37,000	32,000
Total Liabilities and Stockholders' Equity	$762,000	$636,000

Required:

A. Compute the changes in the income statements and balance sheets from 1984 to 1985 in dollar amounts and in percentages.
B. Prepare common-size financial statements for both years.
C. Comment briefly on the relationships revealed by the horizontal and vertical analyses.

Problem 20-2A (Trend Analysis)

Comparative financial statements for the Gibbons Corporation appear below.

GIBBONS CORPORATION
Comparative Income Statements
For the Years Ended December 31, 1984–1988
(000 omitted)

	1984	1985	1986	1987	1988
Sales	$930	$965	$1,100	$1,650	$1,865
Less: Cost of goods sold	560	580	640	941	1,083
Gross profit on sales	370	385	460	709	782
Selling expenses	120	131	135	150	210
Administrative expenses	80	78	87	96	100
Interest expense	17	17	17	26	27
Income tax expense	60	62	85	172	178
Total Expenses	277	288	324	444	515
Net Income	$ 93	$ 97	$ 136	$ 265	$ 267

GIBBONS CORPORATION
Comparative Balance Sheets
December 31, 1984–1988
(000 omitted)

	1984	1985	1986	1987	1988
Assets					
Current Assets	$310	$347	$344	$ 390	$ 397
Plant and Equipment	530	550	585	745	816
Total Assets	$840	$897	$929	$1,135	$1,213
Liabilities and Stockholders' Equity					
Current Liabilities	$140	$162	$198	$ 174	$ 190
Bonds Payable	175	177	179	281	284
Common Stock	450	450	450	450	450
Retained Earnings	75	108	102	230	289
Total Liabilities and Stockholders' Equity	$840	$897	$929	$1,135	$1,213

Required:

A. Perform a trend analysis on the financial statements.

B. Comment on any significant relationships revealed by the trend analysis.

Problem 20-3A (Ratio Analysis)

The 1984 annual report of the Igloo Company contains the following information.

Preferred dividends declared and paid during 1984: $18,000
Common dividends declared and paid during 1984: $380,000
Market price per share of preferred stock on December 31, 1984: $23.00
Market price per share of common stock on December 31, 1984: $59.50

IGLOO COMPANY
Income Statement
For the Year Ended December 31, 1984
(000 omitted)

Sales	$9,000
Less: Cost of goods sold	5,540
Gross profit on sales	3,460
Selling expenses	1,200
Administrative expenses	920
Interest expense	270
Income tax expense	420
Total Expenses	2,810
Net Income	$ 650

IGLOO COMPANY
Comparative Balance Sheets
December 31, 1984 and 1983
(000 omitted)

	1984	1983
Assets		
Current Assets:		
Cash	$ 300	$ 280
Marketable Securities	80	70
Accounts Receivable	900	1,000
Inventory	1,100	1,140
Total Current Assets	2,380	2,490
Plant and Equipment	4,200	3,900
Total Assets	$6,580	$6,390
Liabilities		
Current Liabilities:		
Accounts Payable	$1,280	$1,320
Accrued Expenses	20	47
Total Current Liabilities	1,300	1,367
Notes Payable	50	45
Bonds Payable	1,750	1,750
Total Liabilities	3,100	3,162
Stockholders' Equity		
Preferred Stock (9%, $20 par value)	200	200
Common Stock ($10 par value)	1,000	1,000
Paid-in Capital in Excess of Par	1,810	1,810
Retained Earnings	470	218
Total Stockholders' Equity	3,480	3,228
Total Liabilities and Stockholders' Equity	$6,580	$6,390

Required:

Compute the following ratios at December 31, 1984:

A. Return on total assets
B. Return on common stockholders' equity
C. Return on sales
D. Earnings per share
E. Price-earnings ratio
F. Dividend yield
G. Dividend payout
H. Current ratio
I. Quick ratio
J. Receivable turnover
K. Inventory turnover
L. Debt to total assets
M. Times interest earned

Problem 20-4A (Effect of Transactions on Ratios)

Selected transactions of the Plymouth Company are listed below in the left-hand column.

Transaction	Ratio
1. Buy machinery on account	Debt to total assets
2. Write off an uncollectible account receivable to Allowance for Doubtful Accounts	Quick ratio
3. Retire bonds payable with cash	Return on total assets
4. Issue common stock in exchange for land	Return on common stockholders' equity
5. Pay on accounts payable	Debt to total assets
6. Declare a cash dividend on common stock	Current ratio
7. Sell inventory on account	Quick ratio
8. Collect on accounts receivable	Current ratio
9. Sell inventory for cash	Receivable turnover
10. Pay a cash dividend previously declared	Dividend payout
11. Record accrued interest on notes payable	Return on sales
12. Issue bonds payable	Return on total assets

Required:

Indicate whether each transaction will increase, decrease, or have no effect on the ratio listed across from it.

Problem 20-5A (Using Ratios to Compute Data Missing in Financial Statements)

The financial statements of the Finley Corporation appear below with most of the dollar amounts missing.

FINLEY CORPORATION
Income Statement
For the Year Ended June 30, 1984

Sales	$760,000
Less: Cost of goods sold	?
Gross profit on sales	?
Operating expenses	?
Interest expense	?
Total Expenses	?
Income before taxes	?
Less: Income tax (40%)	?
Net Income	$?

FINLEY CORPORATION
Balance Sheet
June 30, 1984

Assets	
Current Assets:	
Cash	$?
Accounts Receivable	?
Inventory	?
Total Current Assets	?
Plant and Equipment	?
Total Assets	$?
Liabilities and Stockholders' Equity	
Current Liabilities	$ 71,000
Long-term Liabilities, 12.5% interest	174,800
Common Stock, $10 par value	?
Retained Earnings	?
Total Liabilities and Stockholders' Equity	$?

The following additional information is available.

1. The current ratio is 2.0.
2. The quick ratio is 1.1.
3. The receivable turnover is 16.0, and the Accounts Receivable balance on July 1, 1983, was $49,000.
4. The inventory turnover is 6.4, and the balance in the Inventory account on July 1, 1983 was $76,725.
5. Return on sales is 6.9%.
6. Debt to total assets is 50.0%.
7. Earnings per share are $2.50. The number of shares of common stock outstanding remained constant during the year.
8. Times interest earned is 5.0.

Required:
Fill in all the missing dollar amounts. Show all computations. (Hint: The current ratio is the key to solving this problem.)

CASE FOR CHAPTER 20

(Ratio Analysis and Review of Financial Statements)
For this case you must use the financial statements for Modern Merchandising, Inc. presented in an Appendix to the text. Your company is planning to acquire an interest

in Modern Merchandising, Inc. As financial vice-president, the president of your company requested that you review the annual report and respond to certain questions, and that you prepare certain financial statistics for fiscal years ended January 31, 1981 and February 2, 1980. You elect to compute the following ratios for both years:

1. Current ratio
2. Quick ratio
3. Inventory turnover
4. Debt to total assets
5. Return on total assets
6. Return on common stockholders' equity
7. Return on sales

Required:

A. Respond briefly to the following questions asked by the president:
   Significant Accounting Policies
   1. What was the company's policy with respect to accounting for inventories?
   2. Which depreciation method does the company use?
   Accountants' Report
   3. In the opinion of the company's auditors, were the statements fairly presented in accordance with generally accepted accounting principles?
   4. Were accounting principles applied on a consistent basis from year to year?
   Income Statement
   5. Did the earnings per share increase or decrease between the two years?
   6. Were there any unusual or extraordinary items included in the determination of net income in either year?
   7. What was the percentage change in revenues and net earnings? Discuss the major reasons why these two percentage changes were significantly different.

B. Compute the ratios listed in the problem information above. Considering the ratios independently of any other data, discuss any significant trends that should be pointed out to management. In computing the ratios use year-end balances rather than computing averages in the denominators.

PART SIX
MANAGERIAL ACCOUNTING FUNDAMENTALS

CHAPTER 21
MANAGERIAL ACCOUNTING AND BUSINESS SEGMENTS

OVERVIEW AND OBJECTIVES

This chapter presents a transition from *financial accounting* to *managerial accounting*. When you have completed the chapter, you should understand:

- The way organizational structure affects the information needs of management (p. 823).
- The importance of efficiency and effectiveness performance measures (pp. 824).
- The role of management in an organization (pp. 823–826).
- The concept of different costs for different purposes (p. 826).
- The basic nature of business segmentation (pp. 826–827).
- The importance of responsibility accounting in a business firm (pp. 828–830).
- The use of departmental accounting (pp. 830–831).
- The difference between departmental gross profit, departmental contribution to indirect expenses, and departmental net income as profitability measures (pp. 831–843).
- The basic nature and limitations of indirect operating expense allocations (pp. 834–840).
- The analysis required to identify an unprofitable department (pp. 840–843).
- The basic procedures required for branch accounting (pp. 843–846).

As we mentioned at the outset, modern accounting serves a wide variety of users who have economic interests in business firms. The preceding chapters have examined the fundamentals of financial accounting with primary attention directed toward external parties such as creditors and investors. We now turn to the subject of **managerial accounting,** which is concerned with internal reporting to managers, who use the information at all levels of an organization for planning, controlling, and decision-making. The information needs of management are quite different from those of parties external to the firm. Managerial accounting is *not* restricted to the generally accepted accounting principles required for financial accounting, so management can establish its own guidelines for the type of accounting information it uses. However, both managerial and financial accounting information should be developed within the same general accounting system. The cost of maintaining two separate systems would be excessive, if not prohibitive, because of the duplication of such items as chart of accounts, journals, ledgers, bookkeeping costs, and computer time. Since it is management-oriented, our coverage of managerial accounting should be preceded by an understanding of what managers do and the organizational structure within which they operate.

ORGANIZATIONAL CONSIDERATIONS

The most basic form of economic enterprise is a one-person business. Its management and information needs obviously are simple because all decision-making responsibilities for such functions as purchasing, selling, production, accounting, and financing rest with the individual. This simple situation seldom exists, and if it does, it normally will be found only during the initial stage of a business firm's life cycle. As soon as the first employee is hired, a division of labor occurs and an organization is born. An **organization** can be defined as a group of people who share common goals with a well-defined division of labor. The management of an organization needs relevant information to integrate the activities of the various segments of the organization and insure that they are directed toward common goals. As an organization develops in size and complexity, authority and responsibility for performance are delegated to a number of people. Consequently, the role of management becomes increasingly important. This is true for a manufacturing corporation, a bank, an accounting firm, a medical clinic, or a retail store.

ROLE OF MANAGEMENT

A major goal of every firm is to achieve satisfactory financial results. The management of a business firm is accountable to its owners for adequate profits as indicators of a successful operation. Even not-for-profit entities such as charitable organizations must be certain that their expenses do not excee . revenues for an extended period. Every firm must accept the fact that its resources will be in limited supply and must be conserved if a satisfactory financial performance is to be achieved. Such factors as inflation, technological change, competition, government regulation, high interest rates, increased energy costs, and declining productivity have an adverse effect on most firms' financial performance.

If a business is to be financially successful, management must be both efficient and effective. **Efficiency** means maintaining a satisfactory relationship between a firm's resource inputs and its outputs of products or services (for example, the number of labor hours required to produce a product). **Effectiveness** refers to how well a firm attains its goals (for example, the number of products sold compared with the number planned). The efficiency and effectiveness performance of the management process diagrammed in Figure 21-1 is essential to the overall success of any business. It is important to note that these **management functions** are not always as sequentially dependent as Figure 21-1 may suggest, since they often are performed concurrently and are constantly interacting with each other.

PLANNING

A successful business plans for the future by carefully setting goals. Management must decide what action the firm should take in the future and how it should be accomplished. Alternative courses of action are identified, their probable results are evaluated, and the course of action that appears best for the achievement of the firm's goals is selected. Planning is required so that management can anticipate future events rather than react to actual circum-

Figure 21-1
Management Process

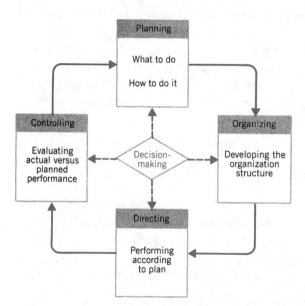

stances once they are known. Much of managerial planning will be concerned with the efficiency and effectiveness of future operations.

ORGANIZING

Plans are only words and numbers on paper until they are implemented. The organizing function provides the structure or capacity within which management will work to achieve its plans. The firm is divided into segments (such as departments, branches, divisions, plants, and offices) to take advantage of the specialization of skills and abilities. The right people are hired, trained, and assigned to specific jobs. Well-defined lines of authority and responsibility are established. Sources of operating resources (such as materials, utilities, and advertising) are selected, physical facilities (land, buildings, machinery, and equipment) are obtained, and financing commitments are arranged to fund the operations.

DIRECTING

This function deals with the day-to-day management of the firm. Actions, decision-making, communication, and leadership are combined to carry out the planned activities within the organizational structure. Problems are solved, questions are answered, disagreements are resolved, and coordination of the various operating segments is achieved.

CONTROLLING

Management must be sure that the actual performance of the firm and its segments compares favorably with the goals established during the planning function. If managers are to be held accountable for their performance, they should know where and why actual results differ from those planned. Control is based upon the concept of **management by exception,** which recognizes that since management time is a scarce resource, the primary concern should be for any performance that deviates significantly from the related plan. Performance reports are issued periodically to inform management of any significant variations from the expected results, so corrective action can be taken to improve the efficiency or effectiveness of future operations, whenever possible.

DECISION-MAKING

Competent decision-making is at the core of each of the functions performed by management. A wide range of decisions must be made. Top management will be concerned with strategic decisions relating primarily to the firm's environment (such as economic conditions, social problems, and market considerations). At lower levels of management, operating decisions are made regularly for such activities as product pricing, choice of inventory levels, production scheduling, and advertising media selection. All management decisions are concerned with the selection between alternatives and have one thing in common—*the need for reliable information*. Some of the information will be historical, while much of it will reflect management's expectations about the future. Most of the information will be objective, but some will be subjective. Much of the information will be available from internal sources, although some will be externally oriented. As we shall see, a significant amount of the information will come from managerial accounting.

DIFFERENT COST CLASSIFICATIONS

Two of the most frequently used terms in the accountant's vocabulary are *cost* and *expense*. Both the distinction between the two terms and the many ways costs are classified are of extreme importance in accounting. While the terms *cost* and *expense* are often used synonymously for convenience, there is a technical difference between the two. A cost is an economic sacrifice of resources made in exchange for a product or service, whereas an expense is an expired cost. In general, as long as a cost has future benefit, it is an asset reported on the balance sheet. The cost expires when it is consumed in the production of revenue or when it no longer has future benefit. Then the cost becomes an expense presented on the income statement.

Managerial accountants use a number of modifiers to identify specific meanings of cost since they are concerned with how one conception of cost is suitable for a given purpose while another is meaningless. Examples are direct cost, indirect cost, controllable cost, uncontrollable cost, variable cost, and fixed cost. Since most costs ultimately become expenses, the same modifiers can be associated with expenses. The important issue is that *different costs will be applicable for different purposes*. Once the purpose of the cost information is known, the managerial accountant will choose from the many cost classifications available to select the most pertinent meaning. We will explain each of the major cost classifications in our discussion of managerial accounting topics.

BUSINESS SEGMENTATION

We noted earlier that a key aspect of the organizing function is the structuring of a business firm's segments. **Business segmentation,** the division of work into specialized units, enables a firm to accomplish more than it otherwise could. Decision-making usually is better since managers of the segments are closest to the day-to-day activities and can control them more effectively. Departments, divisions, and branches are typical business segments within the same entity. Some corporations use subsidiaries organized as separate entities with common ownership of stock and top management. The choice of business segments depends upon such factors as the size of the organization, nature of the business activity, management philosophy, and geographical dispersion. For example, a franchised automobile dealership might be segmented into six departments: new car sales, used car sales, leasing, repair shop, body shop, and parts, as shown in Figure 21-2. Even service firms divide their activities into well-defined segments. An accounting firm typically is structured into departments for auditing, management services, and tax work.

Once the choice of specific business segments is made, a manager is assigned to each of them. He or she is given a certain amount of authority to make decisions and take whatever action is necessary to accomplish the goals of the segment. In turn, the manager is held responsible for the segment's performance. Ideally, both efficiency and effectiveness measures will be used to evaluate the performance of the segments. This means that resource inputs, outputs in the form of products or services, and the goals of the segment will be considered in the evaluation process whenever possible.

To evaluate the performance of a segment, the accounting system must be designed so that detailed financial information for each segment will be available. This detailed information usually is not made public since it would be valuable to competitors. Instead, it is for the use of management to plan activities for each segment, allocate scarce resources, evaluate actual performance, and take corrective action whenever necessary to improve the efficiency and effectiveness of future operations.

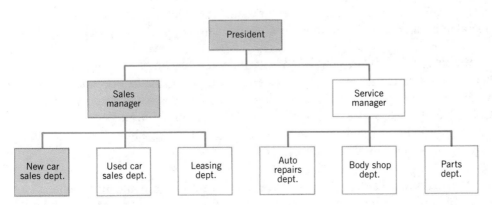

Figure 21-2
Automobile Dealership Organization Chart

RESPONSIBILITY ACCOUNTING

Responsibility accounting is an important managerial accounting topic that provides much of the personalized information needed to manage the segments of a business. In essence, responsibility accounting requires each manager to participate in the development of financial plans for his or her segment and provides timely performance reports that compare actual results with those planned. When responsibility accounting is used along with budgeting (which we will discuss in Chapter 24), the combination provides management with an effective means of planning and controlling a firm's financial performance.

FUNDAMENTALS OF RESPONSIBILITY ACCOUNTING

The most essential features of responsibility accounting can be summarized as follows:

Choice of Responsibility Centers. A **responsibility center** is a business segment such as a department that can be established as a cost center, a profit center, or an investment center. The choice between the three depends on the answer to the question "What aspect of the financial performance is to be controlled?" If management is concerned only with the costs incurred in a particular department, it will be defined as a *cost center*. Cost centers are the most popular form of responsibility center since many departments do not produce revenue. For example, a retailing firm's accounting department could be established as a cost center. A *profit center* exists when revenues as well as costs can be traced to a department. A sales department of a retail store can be organized as a profit center since earnings from the segment's activity can be measured. The most complete form of responsibility center, however, is an *investment center,* in which management is held responsible for the return on the resources used by the segment. As such, the manager of an investment center will be accountable for costs, revenues, and operating assets with the goal of generating a satisfactory return on investment. A department store operated by a chain-store organization is an example of an investment center.

Matching Accounting System and Organization. Once the choice between the different responsibility centers has been made, the accounting system must be designed to collect financial data for each responsibility center. Consequently, the accounting system itself is segmented to provide information for individual managers, as well as the firm as a whole, through the numbering system used to code the general ledger accounts.

Controllability Focus. In the evaluation of their responsibility centers' financial performances, managers should be accountable only for the financial items over which they have control. At their level of management, they must be able to regulate or at least influence all costs, revenues, or invested resources classified as being controllable during a given accounting period. The two key dimensions of controllability in responsibility accounting are therefore the *specific level of management* and the *given time period*. For example, a **controllable cost** is one that can be authorized by a particular manager during a specified time period. The manager of a sales department in a retail store usually is able to control the labor costs of the department but cannot influence the real estate taxes paid on the building occupied by the store. He or she would be held accountable for the labor cost but not the property taxes.

Participative Management.   The managers accountable for the performance of the responsibility centers should participate actively in the development of the planned financial performance, which usually is expressed in terms of a budget. When managers prepare their own estimates, the goals become *self-imposed* rather than ones established by higher management. This approach should motivate the managers to achieve the planned performance.

Performance Reporting.   The manager of a responsibility center is evaluated with performance reports that show the financial items for which he or she is responsible. The reporting phase of responsibility accounting is based upon the premise that the assignment of responsibility and authority flows from top to bottom in an organization while accountability flows from bottom to top. Consequently, the performance reports start at the lowest level of management and build upward, with the managers receiving information concerning their own performance as well as that of any other manager in their span of authority. Figure 21-3 is a partial version of a responsibility reporting system used to control the operating expenses of the automobile dealership shown in Figure 21-2. Cost centers have been established at three levels of management—departmental, sales or service manager, and the president of the firm. For illustrative purposes, we have restricted our attention to the shaded area of Figure 21-2, although all segments would be included in a real-life situation.

As the performance information flows from bottom to top, it is cumulative and less detailed. At the top of the organization, the president is accountable for one large responsibility center representing the entire business. The expected operating expenses are shown in the Budget column and the actual operating expenses incurred are presented in the Actual column. The **variances** shown in the right-hand column are the differences between the expected and actual results. The *U* indicates an unfavorable variance whenever the actual results are greater than those expected. A favorable variance, *F,* occurs when the actual expenses are less than those planned.

Figure 21-3
Automobile Dealership Partial Responsibility Reporting System Month of January, 1984

	Budget	Actual	Variance
President's Report:			
President's office	$ 12,800	$ 13,900	$ 1,100 U
Sales departments	102,900	112,370	9,470 U
Service departments	92,500	98,600	6,100 U
Total	208,200	224,870	16,670 U
Sales Manager's Report:			
Sales manager's office	9,500	9,900	400 U
New car sales department	56,600	61,970	5,370 U
Used car sales department	28,200	32,100	3,900 U
Leasing department	8,600	8,400	200 F
Total	102,900	112,370	9,470 U
New Car Sales Manager's Report:			
Sales salaries	18,200	19,800	1,600 U
Advertising	20,000	23,200	3,200 U
Utilities	4,400	4,850	450 U
Insurance	3,200	3,200	—
Rent	10,000	10,000	—
Other	800	920	120 U
Total	$ 56,600	$ 61,970	$5,370 U

Management by Exception. Significant variances between the planned and actual performance of each responsibility center should be emphasized in the performance reports so their causes can be determined and corrective action taken whenever necessary. For example, in the automobile dealership illustration, the unfavorable variances would be investigated to explain why the actual expenses reported are $16,670 higher than expected. The president can request the detailed copies of the performance reports from all levels of responsibility and can trace the variances downward through the performance reports to identify their sources so that corrective action can be taken to improve future operations. In turn, each accountable manager can do the same thing for his or her span of authority.

DEPARTMENTAL ACCOUNTING

Many firms are divided into departments to take advantage of the benefits of business segmentation and to differentiate between the products or services offered. More detailed accounting procedures are required to evaluate the financial performance of each department within an organization than are needed for the firm as a whole. Departmental accounting is used most frequently by large businesses, which are more likely to have control problems and will want to constantly evaluate the profitability of their different activities. However, even small firms can utilize departmental accounting to determine where their resources can be used best. For example, a small accounting firm may account separately for its accounting and tax services so that management can decide where the professional time of employees should be devoted to achieve desired financial results. Many of the procedures used for departmental accounting are actually extensions of responsibility accounting.

The income statement is typically the only accounting report used for departmental accounting, since the balance sheet is common to the entire firm. In developing departmental accounting information, the accountant must decide how complete the income statement should be for each of the departments. Some small firms segregate only revenue by departments. Many merchandising firms restrict their attention to the gross profit on sales, which is calculated by subtracting cost of goods sold from net sales. Other businesses consider certain direct operating expenses of the departments, and some prepare a complete income statement for each department by allocating indirect expenses among the departments. Each of these approaches has certain advantages, but keep in mind that the managers of the various departments should be held accountable for only those financial items they can control.

DEPARTMENTAL GROSS PROFIT: MERCHANDISING FIRM

Departmental gross profit (also called gross margin) on sales is a key indicator of profitability that is watched closely by the management of a merchandising firm. As we noted in Chapter 9, the gross profit percentage can even be used to estimate ending inventories. If a merchandising business is to achieve its profit goals, the gross profit must be sufficient to cover the operating expenses and produce the desired net income. The factors influencing department gross profit are the number of units sold, selling prices, mix of merchandise sold, and the cost of goods sold. In most cases, all four factors are controllable by the department managers so the gross profit receives a significant amount of attention. Faster inventory turnover, higher prices, a more profitable sales mix, and effective cost control are among the most important objectives of the department managers. This does not mean that the management ignores the operating expenses, since the ultimate measure of financial performance is net income. As we shall see, however, many of the operating expenses are beyond the control of the department managers.

A merchandising firm must select between two basic approaches for the development of departmental gross profit information. The first and most often used approach is to establish a complete set of general ledger accounts for the items that contribute to the gross profit in each department. Such accounts as sales, purchases, inventory, sales returns and allowances, freight in, and purchase returns and allowances are used in each department to record transactions as they occur. An alternative that is less accurate but may save time and expense is to use a single set of general ledger accounts for the firm as a whole and distribute the total amounts recorded to the various departments at the end of the accounting period. Analysis sheets that are not actually part of the general ledger provide the detail required in the alternative treatment. A separate analysis sheet would be used for sales, purchases, sales returns, freight in, and purchase returns. Figure 21-4 illustrates an analysis sheet used to account for the monthly sales of a hardware store. By combining the data in the analysis sheets with the amount of actual or estimated ending inventory for each department at the end of an accounting period, the departmental gross profit can be computed.

ELECTRONIC DATA PROCESSING

More complete and reliable departmental accounting information has been made available in recent years by electronic data processing applications. Data terminals located at customer checkout stations can capture sales and inventory information while they function as cash registers at the point of sale. In some cases, the data are collected through the terminal and transmitted directly or indirectly to a computer. In more modern applications, the data terminals are freestanding devices, which in essence means they have their own electronic capability to collect, process, and report information.

Data terminals used at the point of sale have become popular in drugstores, supermarkets, hardware stores, discount stores, and department stores. Even small stores often find a data terminal to be the most effective and economical means of performing departmental accounting. Inventory tags or labels are encoded with such information as department, type of merchandise, price, vendor, style, color, and original purchase cost. A coding system can be used to prevent customers from identifying anything except the price of the item. The checkout clerk punches the information into the terminal, where it is captured for subsequent processing into valuable management reports concerning the sales and inventory performance. For automatic data capture, an optical wand reader can be used at the point of sale to read the coded information and enter it into the terminal. Human key entry of the inventory information is eliminated, which saves time and can increase the accuracy of the data collection. The person operating the terminal simply passes the wand reader over the inventory tag and the information is automatically entered into the terminal. Alternatively, the reader may be contained in the checkout counter and the inventory items passed over it.

	Department			
	Tools	Hardware	Paint	Combined
1 (Store closed)	—	—	—	—
2	$ 905	$ 1,245	$ 310	$ 2,460
3	682	982	245	1,909
4	962	1,168	412	3,504
31	750	890	280	1,920
Totals—month	$24,440	$36,110	$16,405	$76,955

Figure 21-4
Sales Analysis Sheet
Month of January
1984

The electronic data processing capability provides management with timely and reliable information concerning each department's performance. Inventory turnover, gross profit calculations, the percentage of total inventory invested in each item, sales results by salesperson, and pricing structure information are among the many statistics made available to management.

INCOME STATEMENT WITH DEPARTMENTAL GROSS PROFITS

Figure 21-5 shows an income statement prepared for the Andrews Hardware Store, which operates three departments. The statement reveals departmental gross profits and their combined total. The operating expenses are not assigned to the departments when this format is used but instead are subtracted from the total gross profit. The gross profit is presented as a dollar amount and as a percentage of sales. The income statement provides management with useful information by which the departmental performance can be evaluated and the sources of profit can be identified. The combination of the volume of inventory sold and the gross profit rate for each sales dollar must be considered because the same total gross profit can be achieved with a large volume of sales at a low gross profit rate or with a smaller volume of sales at a higher gross profit rate. However, it should be noted that the analysis is not complete since some of the operating expenses will be related to specific departments, and the ultimate objective is to earn a satisfactory amount of net income. Because the focus of the income statement in Figure 21-5 is on departmental gross profit, an itemized listing of the selling and administrative expenses is omitted.

DEPARTMENTAL NET INCOME

Departmental profitability reporting can be extended beyond the gross profit calculation to show the net income of each department through the use of

ANDREWS HARDWARE STORE
Income Statement
(Departmental Gross Profit Format)
Year Ended December 31, 1984

	Tools Department		Hardware Department		Paint Department		Combined Departments
Sales	$352,000		$448,000		$224,000		$1,024,000
Less returns	8,000		4,800		3,200		16,000
Net sales	344,000		443,200		220,800		1,008,000
Cost of goods sold:							
Beginning inventory	68,800		88,640		36,800		194,240
Purchases	262,480		278,968		129,680		671,128
Freight in	4,800		5,600		3,200		13,600
Goods available for sale	336,080		373,208		169,680		878,968
Ending inventory	71,200		89,560		37,200		197,960
Cost of goods sold	264,880		283,648		132,480		681,008
Gross profit (%)	79,120	(23.0)	159,552	(36.0)	88,320	(40.0)	326,992 (32.4)
Operating expenses:							
Selling expenses							146,400
Administrative expenses							132,800
Total operating expenses							279,200
Net income							$ 47,792

(handwritten note: GP / Sales)

Figure 21-5
Departmental Income Statement

operating expense allocation. The reasoning used for such an extension is that a department is merely a part of the entire firm and could not function without the benefits provided by such operating expenses as advertising, rent, utilities, property taxes, insurance, and salaries. Since the firm's revenues are generated by the sales departments, a fair share of all expenses should be matched with them. Unfortunately, difficult expense allocation problems are inevitable in the determination of departmental net income and usually will have an adverse effect on the accuracy of the results. When **departmental net income** is computed, the reports must be interpreted and used carefully. They should not be utilized for responsibility accounting purposes if they contain expenses over which the departmental managers have no control. Instead, complete departmental income statements should be used by top management to assess the approximate profitability of the departments as separate businesses providing their own goods and services, given the methods used to allocate the operating expenses.

DIRECT AND INDIRECT OPERATING EXPENSES

To determine departmental net income, a distinction must be made between the direct and indirect operating expenses. Managerial accountants often use the terms *direct* and *indirect* in relation to some **cost objective,** which is defined as any activity for which separate cost measurement is performed. In general, a **direct cost** can be traced to a specific cost objective, whereas an **indirect cost,** also called a common cost, is incurred for multiple cost objectives. In this chapter, the cost objective is a department in a merchandising firm. However, managerial accounting uses a wide range of other cost objectives such as a product produced by a manufacturing firm, a service performed by a bank, or a branch office operated by an insurance company.

A direct operating expense can be traced to a particular department as a cost objective since it is incurred solely for the benefit of that department. Examples are the sales salaries and commissions paid to salespeople who work exclusively in one department. The direct operating expenses can be charged to separate departmental expense accounts when they are incurred. Alternatively, some accountants prefer to assign the direct expenses to the departments with a worksheet at the end of an accounting period. This approach reduces the number of departmental accounts needed without any loss of accuracy.

In contrast, an indirect operating expense is incurred for the benefit of the firm as a whole, so it cannot be traced to a particular department as a cost objective. An indirect operating expense is a common expense since it is incurred for the benefit of more than one cost objective. Rent, utilities, insurance, property taxes, and top management salaries are examples of indirect operating expenses. Another type of indirect operating expense would be one incurred by a service department. A **service department** supports the sales departments in some specific way that enables the sales departments to function. A personnel department, an advertising department, a general office department, an accounting department, and a maintenance department are service departments. Although certain expenses such as salaries and supplies are directly related to the service departments, they are indirect operating expenses for the selling departments.

Since none of the indirect operating expenses can be traced to the merchandising departments, they can be assigned to them only on some allocation basis. This means the indirect expenses are apportioned among the various departments that jointly benefit from them. A number of bases have been developed by accountants as potentially equitable ways to allocate indirect expenses. Since the guiding principle for proper allocation should be to match the expenses with the revenues they help produce, the merchandising departments ideally will be charged for indirect expenses on the basis of the benefits they receive. However, these benefits often are difficult to measure and sound judgment rather than absolute rules may be the only approach possible. Unfortunately, even accountants of equal capability often will disagree on the choice of the best allocation basis for a specific indirect expense. As a result, extreme caution must be exercised in interpreting income statements in which indirect expenses have been allocated.

BASES FOR ALLOCATING EXPENSES

To illustrate the allocation of indirect expenses to departments, we will continue to use the Andrews Hardware Store example. We assume that the direct operating expenses are assigned to the departments at the end of the accounting period instead of being recorded regularly in departmental accounts. The indirect operating expenses are allocated at the end of the period on bases that the firm's accountant believes best represent the benefits received from the expenses. A departmental expense allocation worksheet is used to allocate the operating expenses to the three departments—tools, hardware, and paint. The methods used for the distribution of the operating expenses are discussed next, and the results are shown on the allocation worksheet in Figure 21-6.

Sales Salaries. Each salesperson employed by Andrews Hardware Store works exclusively in one department, so all sales salaries are *direct expenses*. The payroll register is departmentalized and shows that the sales salaries are $36,960, $34,240, and $21,200 for the Tools Department, Hardware Department, and Paint Department, respectively.

Figure 21-6
Expense Allocation Worksheet

ANDREWS HARDWARE STORE
Departmental Expense Allocation Worksheet
Year Ended December 31, 1984

Operating Expenses	Amount	Allocation Base	Tools	Hardware	Paint
Selling expenses:					
Sales salaries	$ 92,400	Direct—payroll register	$36,960	$34,240	$21,200
Advertising	12,600	Direct—invoices	5,200	2,400	5,000
Advertising	17,640	Indirect—net sales	6,015	7,762	3,863
Inventory insurance	5,760	Direct—insurance policy	2,056	2,615	1,089
Bad debts	4,200	Direct—accounts written off	1,432	1,848	920
Sales supplies	3,800	Direct—requisitions	1,200	1,100	1,500
Depreciation—equipment	5,200	Direct—property records	1,900	1,500	1,800
Miscellaneous	4,800	Indirect—net sales	1,637	2,112	1,051
Total	146,400		56,400	53,577	36,423
Administrative expenses:					
Management salaries	48,000	Indirect—time	16,000	16,000	16,000
Building expenses	46,800	Indirect—space	11,700	23,400	11,700
Purchasing department	16,000	Indirect—purchases	6,240	6,656	3,104
General office department	16,200	Indirect—employees	6,480	5,670	4,050
Miscellaneous	5,800	Indirect—net sales	1,978	2,552	1,270
Total	$132,800		$42,398	$54,278	$36,124

Advertising Expense. Andrews Hardware Store relies primarily on newspaper and radio media for its advertising. The department managers have the authority to authorize a limited amount of advertising for their departments only. Invoices indicate that the direct departmental advertising amounted to $5,200, $2,400, and $5,000 for the three departments, or a total of $12,600. The remaining $17,640 was spent on store advertising that featured all three departments and is allocated on the basis of sales as the most realistic distribution of the related benefits. The indirect advertising expense of Andrews Hardware Store would be allocated according to the following schedule:

Department	Tools	Hardware	Paint	Combined
1984 net sales	$344,000	$443,200	$220,800	$1,008,000
Percentage of combined sales	34.1	44.0	21.9	100.0
Allocation of $17,640	$ 6,015	$ 7,762	$ 3,863	$ 17,640

Alternative treatments would be to distribute the indirect advertising on the basis of the direct advertising expense or the relative number of departmental products presented in the indirect advertising.

Inventory Insurance. The insurance premium paid to insure the store's merchandise inventory is treated as a direct expense since it is calculated on the basis of the average dollar amount of inventory maintained during the year. Consequently, the total insurance expense is divided among the departments proportionate to their average inventory balances. The computation of the average departmental inventories as percentages of the average inventory of the store is as follows:

Department	Tools	Hardware	Paint	Combined
Beginning inventory	$68,800	$88,640	$36,800	$194,240
Ending inventory	71,200	89,560	37,200	197,960
Average inventory	70,000	89,100	37,000	196,100
Percentage of combined	35.7	45.4	18.9	100.0
Allocation of $5,760	$ 2,056	$ 2,615	$ 1,089	$ 5,760

Bad Debts. Bad debt expense is charged directly to the departments on the basis of the accounts receivable written off during the period. When this approach is not feasible, bad debts are usually apportioned on the basis of departmental credit sales. The bad debt expenses are $1,432, $1,848, and $920 for the three departments.

Sales Supplies. The sales supplies are treated as direct expenses for each of the departments. The dollar amounts per department are determined from the requisition forms used to order the supplies. The amounts recorded are $1,200, $1,100, and $1,500 for the three departments.

Depreciation Expense.   Depreciation on the equipment used in each department is calculated from the property records, which are maintained on a departmental basis. Consequently, the depreciation expense is directly related to the departments and amounts to $1,900, $1,500, and $1,800 for the three departments.

Miscellaneous Expenses.   Since the expenses listed in this category originated from a variety of sources, it is assumed that allocating them on the basis of sales provides the best overall measure of the benefits received by each department. Therefore, the same percentages used in the distribution of indirect advertising expense would be applied to the miscellaneous sales expenses, which total $4,800.

Management Salaries.   These expenses are allocated on the basis of the approximate time devoted by the top management of the store to each department. Considerations such as sales volume, personnel requirements, promotional effort, and operating problems will affect the time spent by management on departmental activities. In the case of Andrews Hardware Store, management estimates that it devotes about the same amount of time to each department, so the total of $48,000 is divided equally among the departments.

Building Expenses.   All of the building occupancy expenses including rent, cleaning, real estate taxes, utilities, maintenance, and insurance are charged to one account—building expenses—and allocated to the sales departments on the basis of square feet occupied. If the building were owned, its depreciation would be allocated on the same basis. The Tools, Hardware, and Paint departments occupy one-quarter, one-half, and one-quarter of the total space, respectively, so their charges are $11,700, $23,400, and $11,700. All of the space is of approximately the same value. If significant differences in value exist because of a department's location in a store, they should be taken into consideration in the allocation of any building expenses affected. For example, if management believes the space near the store entrance is worth twice as much as the same area on the second floor because of higher sales, the building rent allocated should be twice as much for the more valuable space.

Purchasing Department Expenses.   The Purchasing Department is one of two service departments used by Andrews Hardware Store. The department has the responsibility of finding the best suppliers for purchases required by the selling departments and for placing specific orders. A variety of service departments may provide support to the selling departments of merchandising firms. Commonly used bases for allocating service department expenses to the selling departments are shown in Figure 21-7. Andrews Hardware Store uses the purchases of a given year to allocate the Purchasing Department's expenses since this is considered the best approximation of the services rendered to the selling departments. The resulting distribution is as follows:

Department	Tools	Hardware	Paint	Combined
1984 purchases	$267,280	$284,568	$132,880	$684,728
Percentage of combined purchases	39.0	41.6	19.4	100.0
Allocation of $16,000	$ 6,240	$ 6,656	$ 3,104	$ 16,000

General Office Department Expenses. The other service department of Andrews Hardware Store provides personnel, accounting, and payroll services to the three selling departments. The number of employees per department is the basis used to allocate the General Office Department expenses to the selling departments since it is considered the best approximation of the benefits provided. An evaluation of the personnel employed in each department indicates that the following schedule is appropriate:

indirect by no. of workers in dept.

Department	Tools	Hardware	Paint	Combined
Percentage of total employees	40	35	25	100
Allocation of $16,200	$6,480	$5,670	$4,050	$16,200

Service Department	Expense Allocation Bases
Advertising	Sales or number of ads placed in each selling department.
General office	Number of employees or sales in each selling department.
Janitorial	Square feet of floor space in each selling department.
Maintenance	Service rendered to each selling department.
Personnel	Number of employees in each selling department.
Purchasing	Dollar amounts of purchases by each selling department.
Storeroom	Dollar amounts of purchases or merchandise handled for each selling department.

Figure 21-7
Service Department Expense Allocation Bases

Miscellaneous Administrative Expenses. The miscellaneous administrative expenses are allocated to the departments on the basis of sales for the same reason discussed earlier for the miscellaneous selling expenses. Consequently, the distribution of the total amount of $5,800 is $1,978, $2,552, and $1,270 to the Tools Department, Hardware Department, and Paint Department respectively.

DEPARTMENTAL INCOME STATEMENT

Once the assignment of operating expenses is completed, an income statement showing the net income from operations by department, such as the one presented in Figure 21-8, can be prepared. The results indicate that two of the departments, Hardware and Paint, were profitable with net incomes of $51,697 and $15,773, respectively, while the Tools Department incurred à loss of $19,678. However, remember that these results should be evaluated cautiously. They do represent estimates of the "bottom line" net income performances of the departments when they are assigned "their share" of the indirect operating expenses. In turn, they represent approximations of the operating results of the departments as independent businesses. As suggested earlier, however, "their share" is subject to a great deal of judgment and depends upon the choice of the bases used to allocate the indirect operating expenses. Different accountants may choose different allocation bases and obviously will achieve different results. Also, the statements can be criticized on the basis that the departments are not really separate businesses but instead segments of the same firm. Therefore, their "bottom line" evaluation should be concerned only with the expenses for which they are directly accountable and the indirect expenses should be a common pool that benefits the entire firm rather than individual departments. Such a presentation would avoid arbitrary allocations and represent the contribution of each department to the united efforts of the firm as a whole.

DEPARTMENTAL CONTRIBUTION TO INDIRECT EXPENSES

An analysis of the net income results shown in Figure 21-8 may lead to the conclusion that the Tools Department is so unprofitable that management should consider eliminating it. The net loss of $19,678 may suggest to management that profits would have been $67,470 instead of $47,792 without the Tools Department. *But is this an accurate conclusion?* While it is true that the Tools Department does not have a sufficient amount of gross profit to cover its direct operating expenses plus its allocated indirect expenses, it nevertheless is making a contribution to the firm's profit results. The **departmental contribution to indirect expenses** is considered by many accountants and managers to be a more realistic assessment of a department's profitability performance than net income, which involves the allocation process described earlier. The advantage of departmental contribution to indirect expenses is that it usually consists of the revenue and expenses that would disappear if the department did not exist. Its use avoids the somewhat arbitrary allocation of indirect expenses required when an attempt is made to measure departmental net income.

The departmental contribution to indirect expenses is found by subtracting the direct operating expenses of a department from the departmental gross profit. In most cases, the direct operating expenses will be controllable by the

Figure 21-8
Departmental Income Statement

ANDREWS HARDWARE STORE
Income Statement
(Departmental Net Income Format)
Year Ended December 31, 1984

	Tools Department	Hardware Department	Paint Department	Combined Departments
Net sales	$344,000	$443,200	$220,800	$1,008,000
Cost of goods sold	264,880	283,648	132,480	681,008
Gross profit	79,120	159,552	88,320	326,992
Operating expenses				
Selling expenses:				
Sales salaries	36,960	34,240	21,200	92,400
Advertising	11,215	10,162	8,863	30,240
Insurance	2,056	2,615	1,089	5,760
Bad debts	1,432	1,848	920	4,200
Supplies	1,200	1,100	1,500	3,800
Depreciation	1,900	1,500	1,800	5,200
Miscellaneous	1,637	2,112	1,051	4,800
Total	56,400	53,577	36,423	146,400
Administrative expenses:				
Management salaries	16,000	16,000	16,000	48,000
Building expenses	11,700	23,400	11,700	46,800
Purchasing	6,240	6,656	3,104	16,000
General office	6,480	5,670	4,050	16,200
Miscellaneous	1,978	2,552	1,270	5,800
Total	42,398	54,278	36,124	132,800
Total operating expenses	98,798	107,855	72,547	279,200
Net income (loss)	$ (19,678)	$ 51,697	$ 15,773	$ 47,792

department managers, so the departmental contribution to indirect expenses can be used effectively in responsibility accounting. The operating results of Andrews Hardware Store have been restated into the departmental contribution to indirect expenses format in Figure 21-9. Since the indirect expenses are outside the control of the department managers, they are left as common expenses that are deducted from the total departmental contribution to indirect expenses. The departmental contributions of $30,372, $115,849 and $56,811 identify the controllable profit performances of the three departmental managers.

Figure 21-9
Departmental Income Statement

ANDREWS HARDWARE STORE
Income Statement
(Departmental Contribution to Indirect Expenses Format)
Year Ended December 31, 1984

	Tools Department	Hardware Department	Paint Department	Combined Departments
Net sales	$344,000	$443,200	$220,800	$1,008,000
Cost of goods sold	264,880	283,648	132,480	681,008
Gross profit	79,120	159,552	88,320	326,992
Direct operating expenses				
Sales salaries	36,960	34,240	21,200	92,400
Advertising	5,200	2,400	5,000	12,600
Insurance	2,056	2,615	1,089	5,760
Bad debts	1,432	1,848	920	4,200
Supplies	1,200	1,100	1,500	3,800
Depreciation	1,900	1,500	1,800	5,200
Total	48,748	43,703	31,509	123,960
Departmental contribution to indirect operating expenses	30,372	115,849	56,811	203,032
Indirect operating expenses				
Advertising				17,640
Miscellaneous selling				4,800
Management salaries				48,000
Building expenses				46,800
Purchasing				16,000
General office				16,200
Miscellaneous administration				5,800
Total				155,240
Net income				$ 47,792

In Figure 21-9, we see that the Tools Department has made a contribution of $30,372 to the indirect expenses. Consequently, rather than increasing the total net income by $19,678, the elimination of the Tools Department actually would cause a decrease in net income of $30,372. This decrease in profit would occur because the two remaining departments have a combined departmental contribution to indirect expenses of $172,660 and will have to absorb all of the indirect operating expenses, amounting to $155,240. Thus, the net income would be only $17,420 in contrast to the profit of $47,792 from a three-department operation. The difference is the $30,372 contributed by the Tools Department. An alternative way to evaluate the results of eliminating the Tools Department is to consider the gross profit of $79,120 given up versus the decreased direct operating expenses of $48,748. Again, the difference is $30,372 in favor of keeping the department. The most significant point in this analysis is that profitability measurement involving allocated expenses can generate misleading information when it is applied incorrectly.

A complete analysis of the Tools Department would have to take into consideration alternative uses of the space currently occupied by it and any adverse effect on the sales of the Hardware and Paint departments from its elimination. Customers may want to shop only at a store with a complete line of hardware products, so the elimination of tools is likely to affect adversely the sales of the other two departments. Also, we have assumed that all of the direct operating expenses are avoidable expenses while all of the indirect expenses are unavoidable. Avoidable expenses are ones that can be eliminated by the termination of a department, but unavoidable expenses are those that will continue. Consequently, only the direct operating expenses can be eliminated by disposing of the Tools Department, while the indirect expenses will not change since the store will require essentially the same amount of services to support the remaining departments. In some cases, certain indirect operating expenses also may be avoidable because they can be eliminated by reducing the size of the operation.

FUNDAMENTALS OF BRANCH ACCOUNTING

Our final concern with business segmentation is a brief coverage of branch accounting procedures. As merchandising firms grow, they often open branch stores to serve new marketing territories. National and regional chain-store operations have become increasingly popular in recent years. The growth of suburban shopping centers has contributed significantly to the number of branch operations.

A branch manager is assigned to each store and usually given broad responsibilities for operating the store within the general guidelines established by top management. The branch maintains its own inventories, sells the merchandise, approves customer credit, and may even collect its own accounts receivable. A branch may obtain all of its merchandise from the home office or some of it may be purchased from outside suppliers. Regardless of how much independence a branch is given, an accounting system is needed to control the transactions between the home office and the branch store as well as to provide management with the information required to evaluate the branch's operating results.

CENTRALIZED VERSUS DECENTRALIZED ACCOUNTING

Management must decide whether the accounting for its branch operation will be accomplished with a centralized or a decentralized system. Many small merchandising firms use a centralized accounting system in which most of the records are maintained by the home office. The preparation of basic source documents such as sales invoices or summaries, payroll time cards, and purchase vouchers is the only accounting work performed by the branch. Copies of the basic documents are sent periodically to the home office for processing through the accounting system. All the journals and ledgers are maintained by the home office, which usually operates a computerized accounting system. Separate branch accounts for sales, cost of goods sold, and operating expenses are maintained in the home office general ledger. Basically, the same procedures discussed earlier for departmental accounting are used to process the accounting data and prepare timely reports with which the operating performance can be evaluated, since each branch in essence is a department.

As a system of branch operations grows, the volume of transactions and the accounting problems associated with the geographical separation of the stores force most firms to use decentralized accounting. Each branch maintains a self-contained accounting system, including an on-site computer in many large operations. The accounting principles and procedures used by each branch are basically the same as those of an autonomous store. The one exception is that a *Home Office account* is used by a branch instead of capital accounts and will show the net investment in the branch on the part of the firm. The account will be credited for cash, inventory, and other resources provided by the home office for the branch. It will be debited for cash, inventory, and other resources sent by the branch to the home office or to other branches. The Home Office account also will replace retained earnings in closing the branch books and will be credited for branch net income or debited for a net loss.

In a decentralized accounting system, a *Branch Investment account* will be maintained on the home office books to record transactions affecting a firm's investment in the branch operation. The Home Office account and the Branch Investment account are defined as *reciprocal accounts* since they basically measure the same thing and should always be equal when all the accounting is completed. The Branch Investment account is debited for cash, inventory, and other resources provided by the home office for the branch as well as the net income earned by the branch. It is credited for any cash, inventory, or other resources transferred from the branch as well as any net loss incurred by the branch.

BRANCH ACCOUNTING ILLUSTRATION

The Caine Company, with a *home office* in Chicago, operates a major department store chain. The firm recently opened its eighth *branch store* (Branch 8) in a suburban shopping center and will continue to use a decentralized accounting system because of the number of branches and the distance between the home office and the branch stores. During January 1984, the following transactions took place:

1. The home office transferred $5,000 in cash, $75,000 in inventory, and $20,000 of display equipment to the new branch store.
2. Sales for January at Branch 8 amounted to $86,500.
3. The cost of the merchandise sold by Branch 8 during January was $61,200. In addition, the operating expenses incurred by the branch were $7,890, divided as follows:

Branch manager's salary	$1,800
Sales salaries	3,800
Advertising	600
Insurance	350
Utilities	280
Depreciation—equipment	810
Other expenses	250

4. Collections on customers' accounts totaled $32,100 at Branch 8.
5. A cash transfer of $3,000 was made to the home office by Branch 8.
6. The branch books were closed at the end of January and the monthly net income was reported to the home office.

The journal entries required to account for the January transactions of the home office and its branch are shown in Figure 21-10. You should note that the two reciprocal accounts, Branch Investment 8 and Home Office, are in agreement at the end of January as follows:

Home Office Books		Branch Books	
Branch 8 Investment		**Home Office**	

100,000	3,000	3,000	100,000
17,410			17,410
117,410	3,000	3,000	117,410
Balance 114,410			114,410 Balance

CAINE COMPANY
Journal Entries for Home Office and Branch 8
Month of January 1984

Home Office Books			Branch 8 Books		
1. Branch 8 investment	100,000		Cash	5,000	
Cash		5,000	Merchandise inventory	75,000	
Merchandise inventory		75,000	Display equipment	20,000	
Display equipment		20,000	Home Office		100,000
To record transfer of assets to Branch 8.			To record assets received from home office.		
2. No entry			Accounts receivable	86,500	
			Sales		86,500
			To record January branch sales		
3. No entry			Cost of goods sold	61,200	
			Management salaries expense	1,800	
			Sales salaries expense	3,800	
			Advertising expense	600	
			Insurance expense	350	
			Utilities expense	280	
			Depreciation expense	810	
			Other expenses	250	
			Merchandise inventory		61,200
			Accrued salaries payable		5,600
			Accumulated depreciation		810
			Cash		1,480
			To record January branch cost of goods sold and operating expenses		
4. No entry			Cash	32,100	
			Accounts receivable		32,100
			To record January branch cash collections.		
5. Cash	3,000		Home office	3,000	
Branch 8 investment		3,000	Cash		3,000
To record transfer of cash from branch.			To record transfer of cash to home office.		
6. No entry			Sales	86,500	
			Cost of goods sold		61,200
			Management salaries expense		1,800
			Sales salaries expense		3,800
			Advertising expense		600
			Insurance expense		350
			Utilities expense		280
			Depreciation expense		810
			Other expenses		250
			Income summary		17,410
			To close sales and expenses to income summary		
Branch 8 investment	17,410		Income summary	17,410	
Branch 8 net income		17,410	Home office		17,410
To record branch net income			To close income summary account.		

Figure 21-10
Branch Accounting Journal Entries

GLOSSARY

AVOIDABLE COSTS OR EXPENSES. Costs or expenses that can be eliminated if a department or a product is terminated (p. 843).

BRANCH ACCOUNTING. Procedures used to account for branch operations (p. 843).

BUSINESS SEGMENTATION. The division of a business into well-defined components directed toward common goals (p. 826).

CONTROLLABLE COSTS OR EXPENSES. Costs or expenses that can be regulated or influenced at a particular level of management during a specified time period (p. 829).

COST. An economic sacrifice of resources made in exchange for a product or service (p. 826).

COST OBJECTIVE. Any activity for which separate cost measurement is performed. Examples are a department, a product, or a branch office (p. 835).

DEPARTMENTAL ACCOUNTING. Accounting procedures required to evaluate the financial performance of individual departments within an organization (p. 830).

DEPARTMENTAL CONTRIBUTION TO INDIRECT EXPENSES. The revenues of a department less its cost of goods sold and direct operating expenses (p. 840).

DEPARTMENTAL GROSS PROFIT. The revenues of a department less its cost of goods sold (p. 831).

DEPARTMENTAL NET INCOME. The revenues of a department less its cost of goods sold, its direct operating expenses, and an allocated portion of indirect expenses (p. 834).

DIRECT COSTS OR EXPENSES. Costs or expenses that can be traced to a specific cost objective (p. 835).

EFFECTIVENESS. A measure of how well a firm attains its goals (p. 824).

EFFICIENCY. Maintaining a satisfactory relationship between a firm's resource inputs and its outputs of products or services (p. 824).

EXPENSE. A cost that is expired because it no longer has future benefit (p. 826).

INDIRECT COSTS OR EXPENSES. Costs or expenses incurred for the common benefit of multiple cost objectives (p. 835).

MANAGERIAL ACCOUNTING. A branch of accounting that provides management information for planning, controlling, and decision-making (p. 823).

MANAGEMENT BY EXCEPTION. The concentration on performance results that deviate significantly from those planned (p. 825).

MANAGEMENT FUNCTIONS. The planning, organizing, directing, and controlling required to manage an organization (p. 824).

OPERATING EXPENSE ALLOCATION. A systematic and rational process used to apportion indirect expenses to departments (p. 834).

ORGANIZATION. A group of people who share common goals with a well-defined division of labor (p. 823).

RESPONSIBILITY ACCOUNTING. The accounting procedures used to evaluate the financial performance of responsibility centers (p. 828).

RESPONSIBILITY CENTER. A business segment organized as a cost center, a profit center, or an investment center so responsibility accounting can be performed (p. 828).

SERVICE DEPARTMENT. A department that provides supporting services such as personnel, advertising, accounting, maintenance, or purchasing (p. 835).

UNAVOIDABLE COSTS OR EXPENSES. Costs or expenses that will not be eliminated if a department or a product is terminated (p. 843).

VARIANCE. A measure of the difference between a planned financial performance and the actual results achieved. An example is a favorable cost variance that occurs when the actual cost is less than the amount planned. In contrast, an unfavorable cost variance exists when the actual cost exceeds the amount expected (p. 829).

DISCUSSION QUESTIONS

1. What are the basic differences between financial accounting and managerial accounting?
2. Distinguish between efficiency and effectiveness measurements. Which of the two concepts is being measured in the following?
   (a) Departmental sales salaries required for June sales in a retail store.
   (b) Actual June sales compared with those planned by a retail store.
   (c) Labor costs required to perform the laboratory tests during June in a medical clinic.
   (d) New car sales for an automobile dealership in June were 48 units. The sales manager had forecast 55 units for the month.
   (e) The labor cost per tax return prepared by a CPA firm.
3. A university basketball team is an organization. How are such managerial considerations as goals, management functions, and the role of information important to the success of the team?
4. Differentiate between a cost and an expense. What is meant by the saying, "There are different costs for different purposes?"
5. Why is a business divided into segments and how does segmentation relate to responsibility accounting?
6. Distinguish between a cost center, a profit center, and an investment center. Give an example of a business segment established as each type of responsibility center.
7. How is the term *controllable* used in responsibility accounting? Which of the following items would you expect to be controllable by the manager of the hardware department in a large discount store during a given month?
   (a) Depreciation on departmental equipment
   (b) Rent on the building in which the store is located
   (c) Cost of goods sold
   (d) Departmental sales salaries
   (e) Advertising expenses
8. Explain the concept of management by exception.

9. What is a variance in a responsibility accounting application? When does a variance require corrective action?
10. Why is departmental gross profit important in a merchandising firm?
11. How have electronic data terminals improved departmental accounting in recent years?
12. Distinguish between direct and indirect expenses. What must each be related to before the terms *direct* and *indirect* have meaning? Refer to question 7. Which of the five items are direct expenses for the hardware department? Are direct expenses always controllable expenses?
13. What is the role of a service department in a merchandising operation? Suggest the best ways to allocate the costs of the following service departments to the selling departments:
    (a) Personnel
    (b) Purchasing
    (c) Advertising
    (d) Maintenance
    (e) Janitorial
14. Identify the advantages and disadvantages of departmental income statements prepared on the basis of:
    (a) Departmental gross profit
    (b) Departmental net income
    (c) Departmental contribution to indirect expenses
15. In considering the elimination of what appears to be an unprofitable department, identify the most important considerations. How do avoidable and unavoidable expenses affect the decision? Given the following facts, should the merchandise department of the Campus Bookstore be eliminated? Why or why not?

	Merchandise Department	Book Department	Total
Sales	$500,000	$750,000	$1,250,000
Direct expenses	400,000	325,000	725,000
Indirect expenses	150,000	225,000	375,000
Operating income (loss)	($ 50,000)	$200,000	$ 150,000

16. Explain briefly what a branch operation is and why branch accounting is required.
17. Distinguish between a centralized and a decentralized branch accounting system. When are the reciprocal accounts, Home Office and Branch Investment, used and why are they necessary?

EXERCISES

Exercise 21-1 (Departmental Gross Profit)
The Klondike Store operates two departments, farm supplies and hardware. An income statement is prepared on the basis of departmental gross profit. Operating data for the year 1984 are as follows:

	Farm Supplies	Hardware	Total Store
Sales	$840,000	$640,000	$1,480,000
Gross profit %	50%	37.5%	
Operating expenses			$ 540,000

Required:

A. What is the cost of goods sold for each of the departments?

B. Prepare an income statement that emphasizes departmental gross profit. (Disregard income taxes.)

Exercise 21-2 (Departmental Contribution to Indirect Expenses)

The Read-More Bookstore operates two departments, Books and General Merchandise. During 1984, the store had the following operating results:

	Books	General Merchandise
Sales	$218,000	$420,000
Sales returns	8,000	12,000
Direct operating expenses	43,000	112,000
Gross profit % of sales	30%	40%

In addition, indirect operating expenses that are not allocated to the departments amounted to $51,200.

Required:

Prepare a departmental income statement for 1984 based on the contribution to indirect expenses approach. Use three columns for Books Department, General Merchandise Department, and Total. (Disregard income taxes.)

Exercise 21-3 (Indirect Operating Expense Allocation)

The Yares Clothing Store operates three selling departments. Certain indirect operating expenses are allocated to the selling departments as follows:

Expense	Amount	Basis of Allocation
Personnel department	$24,000	Payroll
Building rent	36,000	Square feet of floor space
Advertising	60,000	Sales
Insurance on inventory	15,000	Amount of inventory

The following information is obtained from store records for 1984:

	Dept. A	Dept. B	Dept. C
Payroll	$ 84,000	$ 60,000	$ 96,000
Square feet of floor space	3,000	3,840	5,160
Sales	225,000	187,500	337,500
Amount of inventory	52,500	40,500	57,000

Required:
Prepare a schedule allocating the indirect operating expenses to the three selling departments.

Exercise 21-4 (Indirect Operating Expense Allocation with Sales)

The Beech Variety Store allocates indirect operating expenses to its three departments on the basis of sales. In 1983, the following allocations were made:

	Dept. A	Dept. B	Dept. C	Total
Sales	$500,000	$400,000	$100,000	$1,000,000
Indirect operating expenses	240,000	192,000	48,000	480,000

Assume that Departments A and B have sales of $500,000 and $400,000, respectively, in 1984 but Department C's sales increase to $300,000 because of the popularity of a new product line. Assume further that the indirect operating expenses of $480,000 remain the same in 1984.

Required:
A. Determine the allocation of indirect operating expenses in 1984 using the same approach taken in 1983.
B. Are the results of requirement (A) logical for an equitable allocation of indirect operating expenses?

Exercise 21-5 (Elimination of a Department)

The Herff Company operates a discount store with three departments. John Herff, the president of the company, wants to eliminate Department C because it continually shows a net operating loss. During the past year (1983), the departmental operating performances were as follows:

	Dept. A	Dept. B	Dept. C
Sales	$400,000	$240,000	$160,000
Cost of goods sold	240,000	156,000	120,000
Gross profit	160,000	84,000	40,000
Direct expenses	40,000	24,000	20,000
Indirect expenses	70,000	42,000	28,000
Net income (loss)	$ 50,000	$ 18,000	$ (8,000)

In analyzing these operating results, the company's accountant determines that advertising expenses amounting to $4,000 are the only indirect operating expenses that can be avoided if Department C is eliminated. All direct expenses are avoidable.

Required:
What would be the effect on the company's profits of eliminating Department C? (Disregard income taxes.)

Exercise 21-6 (Branch Accounting)

At the end of 1984, the Bloomington Branch and Home Office accounts of the Village Department Store were as follows:

Home Office Records
Bloomington Branch

Date	Transactions	Dr	Cr	Balance
12/1	Beginning balance			116,400
12/10	Merchandise shipped to branch	16,200		132,600
12/27	Cash received from branch		4,500	128,100
12/28	Fixtures sent to branch	3,600		131,700

Bloomington Branch Records
Home Office

Date	Transactions	Dr	Cr	Balance
12/1	Beginning balance			116,400
12/10	Merchandise from home office		16,200	132,600
12/27	Cash sent to home office	4,500		128,100
12/31	December net income		9,600	137,700

Required:

Prepare the journal entries required in the home office records and branch records to reconcile the Bloomington Branch and Home Office accounts as of December 31, 1984.

PROBLEMS

Problem 21-1 (Indirect Expense Allocation)

The Miles Department Store operates four departments, A–D, at its Bloomfield location. In order to prepare a departmental income statement, the store bookkeeper allocates indirect expenses with the following predetermined allocation bases:

Indirect Expense	Allocation Base	Total Amount
Rent	Relative value of square footage	$ 8,000
Personnel Department	Number of employees	12,000
Insurance	Value of inventory	5,600
Utilities	Square footage	3,200

The bookkeeper has also been provided the following data relative to the four departments:

	Dept. A	Dept. B	Dept. C	Dept. D
Square footage	700	300	400	600
Number of employees	5	4	6	5
Value of inventory	$12,000	$15,000	$6,000	$7,000

Departments A and B are located on the first floor and Departments C and D are on the second floor. The company believes the first floor is three times as valuable as the second floor for the allocation of the rent expense.

Required:
Prepare a schedule allocating the indirect expenses to the four departments.

Problem 21-2 (Departmental Contribution to Indirect Expenses)

The Netzman Electric Company, Inc., operates two departments—Appliance Sales and Bottled Gas Sales. The corporate income statement for the year ending October 31, 1984, has been prepared from the accounting records.

NETZMAN ELECTRIC COMPANY, INC.
Income Statement
Year Ended October 31, 1984

Sales	$835,000
Cost of goods sold:	
Beginning inventory	85,000
Purchases	305,000
Goods available for sale	390,000
Ending inventory	59,000
Cost of goods sold	331,000
Gross profit	504,000
Operating expenses:	
Salesmen's salaries	185,000
Advertising	62,000
Depreciation	36,000
Managerial salaries	85,000
Rent	53,000
Property taxes	12,000
Interest	38,000
Total operating expenses	471,000
Net income	$ 33,000

The corporation maintains departmental records for departmental revenue and direct expenses. The records indicate that the following percentages of each expense or revenue are directly chargeable to the departments (any balance is an indirect expense):

	Appliance Sales	Bottled Gas Sales
Purchases	60%	40%
Salesmen's salaries	53	47
Advertising	45	25
Depreciation	21	16
Property taxes	29	23
Sales	55	45

The beginning inventory for the Appliance department was $70,000 and the ending inventory was $52,000. The beginning inventory for the Bottled Gas department was $15,000 and the ending inventory $7,000.

Required:
Prepare a departmental income statement for the year ending October 31, 1984, showing each department's contribution to indirect expenses.

Problem 21-3 (Departmental Accounting)

The Celestial Limited Corporation has prepared an income statement using the departmental gross profit format for its two departments, Jewelry department and Fine China department.

CELESTIAL LIMITED CORPORATION
Income Statement
Year Ended April 30, 1984

	Jewelry	Fine China	Total
Sales	$630,000	$245,000	$875,000
Cost of goods sold	349,875	116,625	466,500
Gross profit	280,125	128,375	408,500
Operating expenses:			
Salaries			165,000
Advertising			67,000
Depreciation			46,000
Rent			24,000
Utilities			17,000
Payroll taxes			9,500
Total operating expenses			328,500
Net income			$ 80,000

The bookkeeper has been able to divide the ending balance in each expense account into three components: direct expenses chargeable to the Jewelry department, direct expenses chargeable to the Fine China department, and indirect expenses. The breakdown, presented as a percentage of the expense account balance, and the allocation bases for the indirect expenses are as follows:

Expense Item	Direct Expenses by Department		Indirect Expenses (%)	Allocation Base for Indirect Expenses
	Jewelry (%)	Fine China (%)		
Salaries	65	25	10	Sales
Advertising	40	20	40	Orders processed
Depreciation	42	30	28	Fixed asset cost
Rent	52	26	22	Space occupied
Utilities	60	20	20	Space occupied
Payroll taxes	65	25	10	Sales

The following data are also available.

	Jewelry	Fine China
Orders processed	18,423	6,141
Floor space in square feet	15,000	7,500
Fixed asset cost	$65,000	$16,250

Required:

A. Prepare a departmental income statement showing departmental contribution to indirect expenses.

B. Prepare a departmental income statement showing departmental net income.

Problem 21-4 (Elimination of a Department)

The Nykamp Furniture Showcase Company operates three departments at its Grand Rapids location—a Commercial Furniture department, a Residential Furniture department, and an Assemble-Yourself furniture department for the budget conscious. The president has prepared an income statement by department for the most recent year and for the third year in a row, the Assemble-Yourself furniture department has shown a loss. If the company president decides to eliminate the unprofitable department, 60% of the space occupied by the Assemble-Yourself furniture department will be used by the Residential Furniture department and the remaining 40% will be used by the Commercial Furniture department. The president does not believe that eliminating the third department, while at the same time enlarging the remaining two departments, will change the sales or gross profits of the Residential and Commercial departments.

The president has also provided the following information:

1. The president's salary of $75,000 per year has been allocated equally between the departments.

2. At present, there are three salesmen and a manager in the Assemble-Yourself department. If the department is eliminated, the manager would be transferred to the Commercial Furniture department and the three salesmen would be discharged. The manager's salary is $35,000 per year.
3. The utilities, rent, and insurance are allocated on the basis of square footage. The insurance would decrease $2,000 a year if the department is eliminated; the rent and utilities would not change.
4. Indirect advertising in the amount of $80,000 was allocated to the departments on the basis of sales. The direct advertising expenditures incurred by the Assemble-Yourself department would be eliminated.
5. The equipment in the Assemble-Yourself department would be transferred to the other departments—70% to the commercial furniture department and 30% to the residential furniture department.

NYKAMP FURNITURE SHOWCASE CO.
Income Statement
Year Ended December 31, 1984

	Commercial Furniture	Residential Furniture	Assemble Yourself-Furniture	Total
Sales	$850,000	$510,000	$340,000	$1,700,000
Cost of goods sold	340,000	229,500	119,000	688,500
Gross profit	510,000	280,500	221,000	1,011,500
Operating expenses:				
Salaries	160,750	82,500	89,750	333,000
Utilities	15,400	18,100	14,500	48,000
Advertising	140,000	87,000	96,000	323,000
Rent on building	28,000	37,000	25,000	90,000
Depreciation on equipment	35,000	26,000	22,000	83,000
Insurance	8,100	12,150	6,750	27,000
Total Operating Expenses	387,250	262,750	254,000	904,000
Net Income (Loss)	$122,750	$ 17,750	$ (33,000)	$ 107,500

Required:
Should the Assemble-Yourself department be eliminated? Prepare a departmental income statement reflecting the results if the department is dropped.

Problem 21-5 (Branch Accounting)
The Casaretti Candy Corporation has branch retail outlets throughout New York. In June 1984, the corporation opened a branch in Fairport and the following transactions took place during the first month of operations:

June	1	The Casaretti Candy Corporation transferred $6,500 to the Fairport branch along with $8,400 of office equipment and display cases purchased by the home office. The equipment is estimated to have a seven-year life with no salvage value and should be depreciated using the straight-line method.
	2	The branch receives $5,000 of merchandise it had ordered from an outside supplier on account.
	4	The branch received $22,000 of inventory from the home office.
	7	The branch paid the rent for June in the amount of $1,000.
	15	Branch sales for the first two weeks of June are $37,000, sales on account; $3,000 cash sales.
	16	The branch paid for the merchandise it received June 2.
	18	Branch collections of accounts receivable, $29,000.
	20	The branch paid the following bills:

Utilities		$350
Telephone		175
Salaries		12,000

	25	The branch transferred $10,000 to the home office.
	26	The branch paid the following bills:

Payroll taxes		$ 825
Insurance		1,200
Advertising		615

	28	The branch received $18,000 of inventory from the home office.
	30	Branch sales for the last two weeks of the month were: Sales on account, $25,000; cash sales, $2,600.
	30	The branch ending inventory was $7,820.
	30	The branch books were closed at the end of June and the net income was reported to the home office.

Required:
A. Record the journal entries to be made by the home office and the branch for the month of June.
B. Calculate the balance in the home office and the branch account as of June 30.

ALTERNATE PROBLEMS

Problem 21-1A (Indirect Expense Allocation)

The Van Hall Department Store is a retail outlet that has four departments. The indirect operating expenses are allocated with predetermined allocation bases as follows:

Indirect Expense	Allocation Base	Total Amount
Office expense	Number of employees	$15,500
Advertising	Sales	3,200
Rent	Relative value of square footage	25,200
Utilities	Square footage	5,600

In order to prepare a departmental income statement, the firm's accountant has compiled the following data:

	Dept. A	Dept. B	Dept. C	Dept. D ·
Number of employees	6	4	3	7
Sales	$40,000	$25,000	$15,000	$20,000
Square footage	1,500	500	1,200	800

Departments A and B are located on the first floor and Departments C and D are on the second floor. The company believes the space on the first floor is twice as valuable as the space on the second floor for the allocation of rent expense.

Required:
Prepare a schedule showing the allocation of operating expenses to the four departments.

Problem 21-2A (Departmental Contribution to Indirect Expenses)

The Tiny Tot Store operates two departments—a children's clothing department and a toy department. The bookkeeper has prepared a corporate income statement for the year ending May 31, 1984.

TINY TOT STORE
Income Statement
Year Ended May 31, 1984

Sales		$940,000
Cost of goods sold		
Beginning inventory	$105,000	
Purchases	610,000	
Goods available for sale	715,000	
Ending inventory	92,000	
Cost of goods sold		623,000
Gross profit		317,000
Operating expenses		
Salaries	125,000	
Insurance	43,000	
Advertising	45,000	
Depreciation	17,000	
Supplies	26,000	
Interest	36,000	
Total Operating Expenses		292,000
Net Income		$25,000

The beginning inventory of the children's clothing department was $43,000 and the ending inventory was $38,000. The beginning inventory for the toy department was $62,000 and the ending inventory was $54,000.

The corporate departmental records indicate that the following percentages of each expense or revenue are directly chargeable to the departments (any balance is an indirect expense):

Item	Children's Clothing Department (%)	Toy Department (%)
Sales	45	55
Salaries	21	34
Insurance	26	36
Advertising	32	43
Depreciation	23	19
Supplies	33	35
Purchases	47	53

Required:

Prepare a departmental income statement for the year ended May 31, 1984, showing each department's contribution to indirect expenses.

Problem 21-3A (Departmental Accounting)

The Flower City Cleaners has used the departmental gross profit format to prepare an income statement for its two departments, commercial linen service and household dry cleaning.

FLOWER CITY CLEANERS
Income Statement
Year Ended November 30, 1983

	Commercial Linen Service	Household Drycleaning	Total
Sales	$355,100	$174,900	$530,000
Cost of goods sold	160,600	59,400	220,000
Gross profit	194,500	115,500	310,000
Operating expenses:			
Salaries			120,000
Depreciation			22,500
Insurance			18,000
Advertising			23,000
Supplies			32,000
Utilities			19,500
Total Operating Expenses			235,000
Net Income			$75,000

The company has been able to determine the percentage of each expense category that is chargeable as direct expense to commercial linen service, as direct expense to household dry cleaning, or as indirect expense. The breakdown, presented as a percentage of the expense account balance and the allocation bases for indirect expenses are as follows:

Expense Item	Direct Expenses by Department		Indirect Expenses (%)	Allocation Base for Indirect Expenses
	Commercial (%)	Household (%)		
Salaries	55	30	15	Sales
Depreciation	46	20	34	Fixed asset cost
Insurance	52	35	13	Fixed asset cost
Advertising	32	21	47	Orders processed
Supplies	42	33	25	Cost of goods sold
Utilities	61	29	10	Space occupied

The following data are also available:

	Commercial	Household
Fixed asset cost	$94,500	$40,500
Orders processed	21,360	14,240
Floor space in square feet	7,600	1,900

Required:

A. Prepare a departmental income statement showing departmental contribution to indirect expenses.

B. Prepare a departmental income statement showing departmental net income.

Problem 21-4A (Elimination of a Department)

Mr. Sharp operates a hardware store with three departments—hardware, plumbing, and paint.

For the past three years, the paint department has shown a net loss and the owner of the store has asked you to determine whether the paint department should be eliminated. If Mr. Sharp decides to eliminate the paint department, 75% of the space occupied by the paint department will be used by the hardware department and the remaining 25% will be used by the plumbing department. Neither sales nor gross profits of the hardware or plumbing departments will change if the paint department is eliminated.

The following additional information describes the expenses currently related to the paint department:

1. The owner's salary of $30,000 has been allocated equally among the three departments.

2. At present, there is one salesperson and a manager in the paint department. If the paint department is eliminated, the manager would be transferred to the hardware department and the salesperson would be discharged. The salesperson's salary is $12,000.
3. The office expense, telephone, and supplies are allocated on the basis of sales. The supplies expense would decrease by $1,000 if the paint department is eliminated, but the office expense and telephone expense would not change.
4. The rent expense is allocated on the basis of square footage and the rent expense would not change if the paint department is eliminated.

SHARP HARDWARE STORE
Income Statement
Year Ended July 31, 1984

	Hardware	Plumbing	Paint	Total
Sales	$171,600	$92,400	$ 45,500	$309,500
Cost of goods sold	79,850	43,150	13,650	136,650
Gross profit	91,750	49,250	31,850	172,850
Operating expenses:				
Salaries	51,000	29,000	35,000	115,000
Office expenses	6,000	4,320	1,680	12,000
Telephone	2,750	1,980	760	5,490
Supplies	11,000	7,920	3,080	22,000
Rent	8,000	4,500	3,500	16,000
Total Operating Expense	78,750	47,720	44,020	170,490
Net Income (Loss)	$ 13,000	$ 1,530	$(12,170)	$ 2,360

Required:
A. Should the paint department be eliminated?
B. Prepare a departmental income statement showing the results if the department is dropped.

Problem 21-5A (Branch Accounting)
The Pannell Auto Store, Inc., opened a branch retail outlet in Sodus, New York, on April 1. The following transactions took place during the first month of operations:

April 1 The home office transferred $7,500 in cash to the Sodus branch along with $3,600 of store fixtures and equipment. The store fixtures and equipment are estimated to have a five-year life with no salvage value and should be depreciated using the straight-line method.
3 The branch received $15,000 of inventory from the home office.

5 The branch received $16,000 of inventory it had ordered from an outside supplier on account.

6 The branch paid the rent for April in the amount of $800.

9 Branch sales for the first two weeks in April: $18,000, sales on account; $5,000, cash sales.

10 The branch paid the following bills:

Utilities	$ 150
Supplies	900
Telephone	200
Salaries	4000

12 The branch paid for the inventory it received on April 5.

15 Branch collections on accounts receivable amounted to $13,000.

27 The branch received $10,000 of inventory from the home office.

29 Branch sales for the last two weeks of the month were: Sales on account of $12,000 and cash sales of $6,000.

29 The branch paid the following expenses:

Salaries	$5,000
Insurance	300

30 The branch ending inventory was $16,400.

30 The branch books were closed at the end of April and the net income was reported to the home office.

Required:

A. Record the journal entries to be made by the home office and the branch for the month of April.

B. Calculate the balance in the home office account and the branch account as of April 30.

CASE FOR CHAPTER 21

Decision Problem (Responsibility Accounting)

Anderson Automobiles, Inc. is a franchised dealership operating in the Midwest. In recent years, the firm has experienced unsatisfactory profit results because of slumping sales in the area. At the suggestion of the firm's CPA, responsibility accounting was implemented at the beginning of 1984. The following departments were organized as profit centers:

1. New car sales
2. Used car sales
3. Service—mechanical
4. Service—body shop
5. Parts and accessories

Monthly reports are prepared showing the profit results of each of the five departments. On April 20, 1984, the parts and accessories manager and the used car manager have demanded a meeting with the firm's president, Bill Anderson, to discuss the way responsibility accounting is being applied. In particular, they are protesting two policies that currently are in effect:

1. The parts and accessories department must transfer all parts and accessories internally to other departments at their original invoice cost.
2. The used car sales department is charged the full dollar amount allowed by the new car sales department on a used car traded in for a new car. In many cases, this amount exceeds the ultimate selling price of the used car. The used car sales manager tells the president about a recent case that is typical. A 1980 model automobile with a wholesale market value of $4,000 was traded in on a new car with a list price of $10,200 and a dealer cost of $8,160. An allowance of $5,440 was given on the used car to promote the deal and the customer paid cash of $4,760. Consequently, a profit of $2,040 ($5,440 + $4,760 − $8,160) was recognized by the new car sales department. The retail market value of the used car was $4,600 and it was sold at that price two weeks later. Since the used car sales department was charged $5,440 when the used car was added to inventory, it incurred a loss of $840 on the ultimate sale.

Both managers (parts and accessories as well as used car) are upset by what they consider unfair practices and violation of the basic premise of responsibility accounting.

Required:
A. Do you agree or disagree with the two managers?
B. What would you do to improve the situation, if anything?

CHAPTER 22
ACCOUNTING FOR A MANUFACTURING FIRM

OVERVIEW AND OBJECTIVES

This chapter presents the accounting fundamentals required for a manufacturing operation. When you have completed the chapter, you should understand:

- The basic nature of a manufacturing operation (pp. 865–866).
- The difference between the inventories of a manufacturing firm and a merchandising business (pp. 866–867).
- The distinction between product and period costs (pp. 867–868).
- The three manufacturing cost elements—direct materials, direct labor, and manufacturing overhead—used in a production operation (pp. 869–871).
- The basic nature of absorption costing and a cost classification based upon cost behavior (pp. 871–873).
- The preparation of an income statement for a manufacturing firm and the supporting information reported in a cost of goods manufactured statement (pp. 873–875).
- The additional accounts and accounting procedures required for a manufacturing firm (pp. 875–877).
- The use and limitations of a periodic inventory system in a manufacturing operation (pp. 876–877, 886–887).
- The role of a worksheet in a manufacturing firm and how to prepare financial statements from it (pp. 877–884).
- The problems associated with the valuation of inventories when a periodic inventory system is used by a manufacturing firm (pp. 883–886).

In earlier chapters, we have been concerned with the development of accounting fundamentals for service and merchandising firms. We purposefully have avoided manufacturing operations so far because of certain complexities associated with them. A **manufacturing firm** is the *most complete type* of business enterprise because it is involved with production, selling, and administrative functions. Manufacturers convert raw materials that they purchase into salable finished products. An automobile manufacturing firm purchases steel, aluminum, glass, and other basic materials and converts them through a production process into automobiles that are sold to the firm's franchised dealers. In contrast, the dealers are merchandisers who sell the automobiles to the public. A manufacturing firm will use most of the accounting fundamentals discussed earlier, but will require additional accounting procedures for the collection, reporting, and control of production costs.

To help you visualize what manufacturing is all about, consider the simplified production flow of Designer Jeans, Inc., a maker of high-quality jeans, shown below. The firm has two production departments, Cutting and Sewing. Skilled labor and a highly automated production process are combined to make a pair of jeans that is sold to a retail store. Raw materials (primarily denim) are purchased from an outside supplier, kept in the Stores Department, and issued as needed to the Cutting Department. In the Cutting Department, each

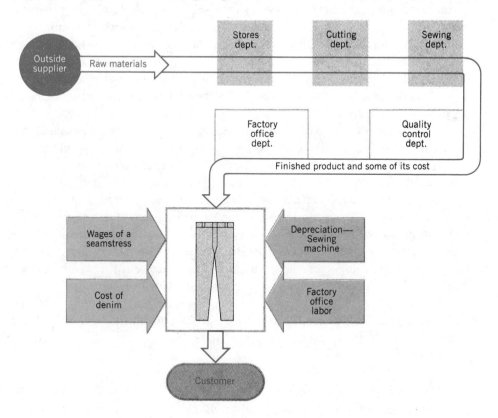

pair of jeans is cut to an appropriate size and then transferred to the Sewing Department, where the product is finished through an elaborate sewing process.

Management must be able to account for the costs incurred for the production of jeans to make such decisions as pricing the finished product and evaluating the profitability of the operation. Note that production occurs in only the two production departments, Cutting and Sewing, even though the company operates five departments in the manufacturing process. The other three departments—Stores, Factory Office, and Quality Control—are called service departments because they support the two production departments. For example, the Factory Office Department provides such services as accounting, payroll, personnel, and purchasing. Note also that selling and administrative functions are not part of the manufacturing·process. We now turn to the accounting fundamentals required for a manufacturing operation.

MANUFACTURING VERSUS NONMANUFACTURING FIRMS

Manufacturing and nonmanufacturing firms are alike in that they depend upon revenue from the products or services they sell. They also engage in many of the same selling and administrative activities such as advertising, calling on customers, issuing credit, doing clerical work, and performing general management functions. The valuation of a manufacturing firm's inventories, however, introduces some important accounting differences between it and a service entity that does not have an inventory or a merchandising enterprise that buys goods ready for resale. The cost flow associated with the manufacturing process used to convert raw materials into finished products causes more complicated accounting problems than those experienced by nonmanufacturing businesses. For example, consider the comparison of the inventory cost flows of a merchandising business and a manufacturing firm, as shown in Figure 22-1.

Three different inventory accounts must be maintained by a manufacturing firm—raw materials, work in process, and finished goods. At the end of any accounting period, the balance in each of the three inventory accounts will be reported as a current asset on the balance sheet. In contrast, a merchandising firm uses a single inventory account. A proper matching of revenue and expenses will be dependent on the accuracy with which the costs of the three inventories are accumulated throughout the production process. Costs are transferred from raw materials to work in process to finished goods and ultimately to cost of goods sold. The *three types of inventory* for manufacturing are the following.

Raw Materials. The cost of the basic materials and parts that have been purchased and are available for future conversion into salable products are classified as **raw materials** inventory. Examples are the steel, aluminum,

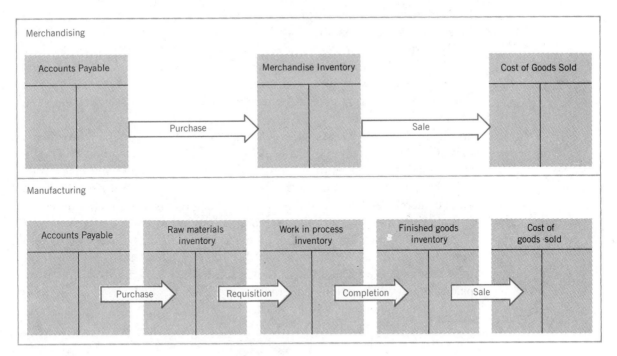

Figure 22-1
Merchandising and Manufacturing Firms Inventory Cost Flows

glass, zinc, rubber, plastics, paint, and other basic ingredients used to manufacture automobiles.

Work in Process.   The inventory that is partially finished but requires further processing before it can be sold is classified as **work in process** inventory. For example, all the automobiles placed into production on an assembly line but unfinished at the end of an accounting period will be treated as work in process inventory.

Finished Goods.   The total cost assigned during the production process to all products fully manufactured and ready for sale is classified as **finished goods** inventory. For example, the automobiles that have been completed and are awaiting delivery to the manufacturer's dealers will be shown as finished goods inventory.

PRODUCT AND PERIOD COSTS

We learned in Chapter 21 that managerial accountants classify costs in many ways. We also noted that a cost is an asset as long as it has future benefit.

Expired costs are charged to the income statement as expenses since they no longer have future benefit.

The terms *product cost* and *period cost* are particularly important in the development of a manufacturing firm's income statement. A proper *matching of revenue and expenses* must be based upon a well-defined distinction between the product and period costs. The reason is that the period in which the benefit of any cost is received is the period in which the cost should be deducted as an expense. **Product costs** can be thought of as attaching to the products since they are necessary for the physical existence of a salable product. They are inventoried as assets until the products are sold. At that point, the product costs have been consumed in the production of revenue so they are expensed on the income statement of the period. **Period costs** are identified with a specific time interval since they are not required to produce a salable product. Consequently, they are not inventoried and are charged as expenses to a period according to the matching principle discussed in Chapter 13. In most cases, this means they are expensed as they are incurred. Exceptions would be prepaid rent and depreciation. The flows of product costs and period costs through the financial statements can be illustrated as follows:

	Balance Sheet	Income Statement
	Current assets:	Sales
Product costs (as incurred) →	Inventory → (as sold)	Cost of goods sold
		Gross profit
Period costs (as incurred) ─────────────────────→		Operating expenses
		Net income

A merchandising firm's product costs will consist only of its *purchase costs*, as we have seen earlier, since the merchandise purchased is ready for resale. The purchase costs are kept in an inventory account until they are matched against revenue as cost of goods sold. All other costs, including labor, are charged to a specific period as selling or administrative expenses. A service firm such as an accounting practice or a real estate business *will not have product costs* since it does not maintain an inventory for resale. As a result, all costs are period costs because they are expensed in specific periods.

In a manufacturing firm, *all* the manufacturing cost elements that attach to products as they are being produced are treated as product costs. They are inventoried as assets until the products are sold. Then they are transferred as expenses to the cost of goods sold section of the income statement. The nonproduct or period costs chargeable to a period are classified as either selling or administrative expenses according to their functional nature and are expensed on the income statement since they are not incurred to produce a salable product. For example, advertising expense and the president's salary would be treated by a manufacturing firm as period costs. The next consideration is the identification of the manufacturing cost elements that are inventoried as product costs.

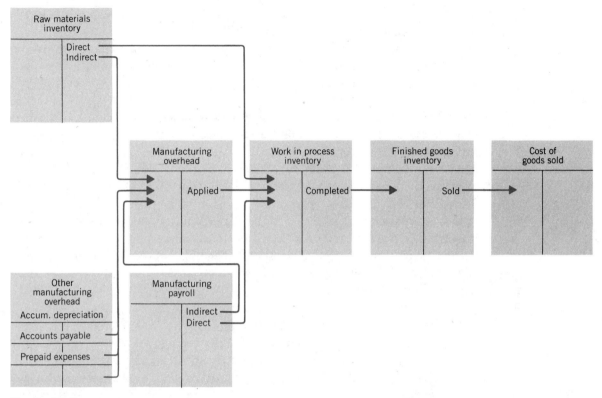

Figure 22-2
Manufacturing Cost Flow

MANUFACTURING COST ELEMENTS

The inventory cost flow of a manufacturing firm, illustrated in Figure 22-1, can be expanded to the more complete manufacturing cost flow shown in Figure 22-2. A flow of **manufacturing cost elements** is associated with the *physical flow of products* through the production process. Managerial accountants must record the manufacturing cost elements as they are incurred so they can be accumulated as assets and properly matched with revenue once the related products are sold. The cost of a finished product consists of three basic elements—*direct materials, direct labor, and manufacturing overhead.*

Direct Materials.   The raw materials directly traceable as an integral part of a finished product are called **direct materials.** The aluminum used for an automobile, the plastic used for a calculator, the crude oil used for gasoline, and the steel used for a golf club are examples of direct materials. Since direct materials physically become part of a finished product, they can be traced to the product or, in some situations, batches of products. Direct materials do not include such miscellaneous items as lubricants, glue, screws, or nails, which are treated as indirect materials and included in manufacturing overhead. It may not be possible to trace such items to the products or it may not be economically feasible to do so.

Direct Labor.   The wages paid to employees whose time and effort can be traced to the products are classified as **direct labor.** As long as the employees perform tasks that can be identified specifically with the conversion of direct materials into finished goods, the labor is a direct cost. Examples are the wages paid to welders on an automobile manufacturing assembly line. The direct labor also becomes a part of the finished product, so it can be traced to a product or batches of products. Other labor will be required to support the production process but will not be traceable to finished products. The wages or salaries paid to janitors, maintenance personnel, production supervisors, cafeteria workers, and material handlers will be classified as indirect labor and included in manufacturing overhead.

Manufacturing Overhead.   All manufacturing costs except direct materials and direct labor are included in **manufacturing overhead.** Other terms used instead of manufacturing overhead are indirect manufacturing cost, factory overhead, and factory burden. Indirect materials, indirect labor, utilities, maintenance, insurance, rent, depreciation, property taxes, and payroll taxes are examples of manufacturing overhead items. Three issues must be resolved in accounting for manufacturing overhead. First, several costs such as rent, depreciation, insurance, and real estate taxes *may be applicable in part* to manufacturing and *in part* to selling and administrative functions. Consequently, they are common costs since they are incurred for all three activities. In Chapter 21, we discussed methods that can be used to allocate indirect operating expenses to the departments of a merchandising firm. The same procedures can be utilized to distribute common costs to the manufacturing, selling, and administrative functions.

Second, manufacturing overhead is incurred in both **production** and **service departments** although products are worked on only in the production departments. The service departments provide support to the production departments with such activities as maintenance, production control, inspection, stores, and engineering. The service department overhead costs must be assigned in some way to the production departments so they ultimately can be included in the product cost. Again, the allocation procedures discussed in Chapter 21 are applicable for the apportionment of the service department costs to the production departments.

Finally, the indirect nature of manufacturing overhead (for example, property taxes) prevents it from being traced to the products in the same manner as direct materials and direct labor. Nevertheless, such items as indirect labor, rent, property taxes, insurance, and utilities are indispensable for the production process because without them manufacturing could not take place. A manufacturing firm must develop a reliable method by which the overhead costs can be assigned as product costs. Instead of tracing manufacturing overhead to the production process, the costs are applied on some basis that closely relates the costs incurred with the work performed. Commonly used bases for the application of manufacturing overhead are direct labor cost, direct labor hours, or units produced. An **overhead application rate** (also called a burden rate) is developed by dividing the total manufacturing overhead cost by the basis used to measure production activity. For example, if manufacturing overhead costs are $200,000 and direct labor hours are 50,000, an overhead application rate of $4 can be computed by dividing manufacturing overhead costs by direct labor hours ($200,000 ÷ 50,000). Manufacturing overhead will be assigned as product costs by applying the $4 rate to each direct labor hour worked during the production process. It is important to note that an overhead application rate usually is based on estimates of both manufacturing overhead cost and production activity rather than actual results. This subject is discussed in more detail in Chapter 23.

BASIC COST BEHAVIOR CONSIDERATIONS

Two product costing methods, absorption costing and variable costing, are available to a manufacturing firm. With **absorption costing,** the manufacturing costs are treated as product costs regardless of whether or not they may change in relation to production levels. Consequently, all direct materials, direct labor, and manufacturing overhead will be treated as product costs. In contrast, **variable costing,** sometimes called direct costing, recognizes *only* those manufacturing costs that change in relation to production levels as product costs. We will limit our coverage of product costing to the procedures used with absorption costing until Chapter 26, where we will discuss variable costing. Generally accepted accounting principles require the application of absorption costing for external financial reporting with the justification that all of the manufacturing cost elements needed to produce a salable product must be inventoried.

Management also will use absorption costing for many of its internal accounting applications. However, management often must evaluate the effect of changes in sales or production volume on the profits of the firm. One of the most widely used ways to classify costs in managerial accounting is by their **cost behavior,** which is the measure of how a cost will react to changes in the level of business activity. Our primary concern at this point is with the cost behavior of the manufacturing costs, although the same basic concepts also can be applied to selling and administrative expenses.

VARIABLE COST

A variable cost will vary in total amount *proportionately* with some measure of business activity such as sales dollars, units produced, or direct labor hours worked. Direct materials, direct labor, and certain manufacturing overhead items such as the electricity cost for machinery operation will be variable costs. For example, if a direct labor cost of $40 is required to produce one unit of product, the total direct labor cost will increase and decrease proportionately with the number of units produced, as illustrated in the following schedule:

Number of Units Produced	Direct Labor Cost per Unit	Total Direct Labor Cost
1	$40	$ 40
25	40	1,000
50	40	2,000
100	40	4,000

While the direct labor rate per unit is constant, the total direct labor cost varies with the level of production.

FIXED COST

A fixed cost will remain constant in total amount over a wide range of business activity. In a manufacturing operation, a fixed cost *will be the same* regardless of the amount produced. Many of the manufacturing overhead items will be fixed costs. Examples are depreciation, rent, property taxes, and supervisory salaries. While a fixed cost remains constant in total regardless of the level of activity, it will have a unit cost that varies inversely with volume. For example, a $500 monthly depreciation charge for production equipment will be constant regardless of the production level, but would change as a unit cost as follows:

Number of Units Produced	Monthly Depreciation	Depreciation per Unit
1	$500	$500
25	500	20
50	500	10
100	500	5

Since variable and fixed costs are not segregated in the product costing process with absorption costing, cost behavior information is not readily available from the accounting system. In contrast, the distinction between variable and fixed costs actually is incorporated into the formal accounting procedures with variable costing, as we will see in Chapter 26.

COST OF GOODS SOLD

The major difference between accounting for a merchandising firm and a manufacturing operation is the *calculation of cost of goods sold*. As we saw in Chapter 5, a merchandising firm calculates cost of goods sold as follows:

$$\begin{matrix} \text{Beginning merchandise} \\ \text{inventory} \end{matrix} + \begin{matrix} \text{Purchases of} \\ \text{merchandise} \end{matrix} - \begin{matrix} \text{Ending merchandise} \\ \text{inventory} \end{matrix} = \begin{matrix} \text{Cost of} \\ \text{goods sold} \end{matrix}$$

In contrast, a manufacturing operation determines cost of goods sold in the following way:

$$\begin{matrix} \text{Beginning finished} \\ \text{goods inventory} \end{matrix} + \begin{matrix} \text{Cost of goods} \\ \text{manufactured} \end{matrix} - \begin{matrix} \text{Ending finished} \\ \text{goods inventory} \end{matrix} = \begin{matrix} \text{Cost of} \\ \text{goods sold} \end{matrix}$$

At first glance, the two cost of goods sold calculations may appear to be the same, but actually they are somewhat different because of the production flow associated with manufacturing. In effect, the cost of goods manufactured in a manufacturing firm results from the conversion of raw materials to finished goods and replaces the purchases of merchandise in a merchandising enterprise. This difference carries forward into the development of an income statement.

COMPARISON OF INCOME STATEMENTS

In Figure 22-3, the cost of goods sold calculation is shown as the difference between income statements prepared for merchandising and manufacturing firms. Sales revenue, selling expenses, administrative expenses, and income taxes are treated the same, as can be seen in Figure 22-3. Again, we see that the cost of goods manufactured in the manufacturing firm's income statement replaces the purchases of the merchandising business. The next step is to identify what constitutes the cost of goods manufactured.

COST OF GOODS MANUFACTURED STATEMENT

The cost of goods manufactured can be computed as:

$$\begin{matrix} \text{Cost} \\ \text{of goods} \\ \text{manufactured} \end{matrix} = \begin{matrix} \text{Direct} \\ \text{materials} \\ \text{cost} \end{matrix} + \begin{matrix} \text{Direct} \\ \text{labor} \\ \text{cost} \end{matrix} + \begin{matrix} \text{Manufacturing} \\ \text{overhead} \\ \text{cost} \end{matrix} + \begin{matrix} \text{Beginning} \\ \text{work in} \\ \text{process} \\ \text{inventory} \end{matrix} - \begin{matrix} \text{Ending} \\ \text{work in} \\ \text{process} \\ \text{inventory} \end{matrix}$$

A MERCHANDISING FIRM Income Statement Year Ended December 31, 1984			A MANUFACTURING FIRM Income Statement Year Ended December 31, 1984		
Sales		$1,000,000	Sales		$1,000,000
Cost of goods sold:			Cost of goods sold:		
Beginning merchandise inventory	$150,000		Beginning finished goods inventory	$150,000	
Purchases of merchandise	710,000		Cost of goods manufactured (Figure 22-4)	710,000	
Goods available	860,000		Goods available	860,000	
Ending merchandise inventory	160,000		Ending finished goods inventory	160,000	
Cost of goods sold		700,000	Cost of goods sold		700,000
Gross profit		300,000	Gross profit		300,000
Operating expenses:			Operating expenses:		
Selling expenses	110,000		Selling expenses	110,000	
Administrative expenses	120,000		Administrative expenses	120,000	
Total operating expenses		230,000	Total operating expenses		230,000
Net income before taxes		70,000	Net income before taxes		70,000
Income taxes		16,000	Income taxes		16,000
Net income		$54,000	Net income		$54,000

Figure 22-3

Comparison of Income Statements

A **cost of goods manufactured statement** is prepared to show the supporting calculations for the cost of goods manufactured reported on the income statement. In Figure 22-3, the cost of goods manufactured amounts to $710,000, and the purpose of the supporting statement shown in Figure 22-4 is to provide a detailed explanation of the total. The total of the direct materials cost, the direct labor cost, and the manufacturing overhead cost represents the manufacturing costs of the period. The direct materials used totaling $142,000 are determined by adding the purchases of the period ($141,000) to the beginning materials ($48,000) and subtracting the ending materials ($47,000). You should note that the presentation of the direct materials used is basically the same as the cost of the goods sold shown on the income statement of a merchandising business. The direct labor cost amounting to $355,000 and the manufacturing overhead of $208,000 would be recorded during the period. Consequently, the total manufacturing costs for the period are $705,000.

The individual manufacturing overhead items are listed and totaled on the statement as long as they are not too numerous. If a large number of accounts are involved, they may be shown on a separate schedule to keep the cost of goods manufactured statement from being too lengthy. The beginning work in process inventory of $35,000 represents costs that have been incurred in the previous period and they are added to the manufacturing costs of the current period. Since the ending work in process of $30,000 consists of costs asso-

Figure 22-4
Cost of Goods Manufactured Statement

A MANUFACTURING FIRM
Cost of Goods Manufactured Statement
Year Ended December 31, 1984

Direct materials:		
Beginning raw materials	$ 48,000	
Purchases (net)	+ 141,000	
Raw materials available	189,000	
Ending raw materials	− 47,000	
Direct materials used		142,000
Direct labor		355,000
Manufacturing overhead:		
Indirect labor	56,000	
Supplies	5,000	
Utilities	42,000	
Rent	22,600	
Insurance	18,000	
Payroll taxes	28,400	
Depreciation	32,000	
Miscellaneous	4,000	
Total manufacturing overhead		208,000
Manufacturing costs for the period		705,000
Beginning work in process		35,000
Total work in process		740,000
Ending work in process		30,000
Cost of goods manufactured		$710,000

Mfg Sum Should equal this → (handwritten)

ciated with products that will be finished later, it must be subtracted to compute the cost of goods manufactured for the period. The cost of goods manufactured of $710,000 represents the production cost of the products that have been completed and transferred to finished goods inventory during the period. This figure is transferred to the income statement in Figure 22-3.

ACCOUNTING SYSTEM CONSIDERATIONS

A manufacturing firm's accounting system will be *more complex* than one utilized by a nonmanufacturing business because of the manufacturing cost flow illustrated in Figure 22-2. The basic accounts used for assets, liabilities, owners' equity, revenues, selling expenses, and administrative expenses in nonmanufacturing businesses also are needed in a manufacturing firm. Additional asset and income statement accounts will be required in manufacturing to accurately determine the cost of goods sold and provide management with reliable product cost information.

A manufacturing firm must decide between a periodic and perpetual inventory system in accounting for the manufacturing costs. We introduced the essential features of periodic and perpetual inventories in Chapter 5. In this chapter, we will illustrate the use of a periodic inventory approach and then extend these procedures to a perpetual inventory system in the next chapter.

PERIODIC INVENTORY SYSTEM FOR MANUFACTURING

Small manufacturing firms may be able to use a periodic inventory system if a single product or a few similar products are produced. As such, the manufacturing accounting is performed within the general accounting system by extending the basic procedures used for merchandising accounting. The additional accounts required with a periodic inventory system in a manufacturing operation are:

1. Raw materials inventory
2. Raw materials purchases
3. Work in process inventory
4. Finished goods inventory
5. Manufacturing plant and equipment
6. Manufacturing payroll
7. Manufacturing overhead
8. Manufacturing summary

Many of these accounts will be set up as control accounts supported by the detailed information of a subsidiary ledger. For example, the balance in the Manufacturing Overhead account will be the sum of the amounts recorded in subsidiary ledger accounts for such items as indirect labor, supplies, utilities, and rent.

The Manufacturing Summary account is used at the end of an accounting period to summarize the costs incurred and to determine the cost of goods manufactured. It should be kept in mind that beginning balances are carried in the three inventory accounts (raw materials, work in process, and finished goods) during an accounting period when a periodic inventory system is used. At the end of each accounting period, a physical count of raw materials, work in process, and finished goods must be made and costs must be assigned to inventory units before financial statements can be prepared. Consequently, the manufacturing cost flow shown in Figure 22-2 is not accounted for as it takes place, and the inventory cost information is made available through the closing of the accounts at the end of the period. For example, the Manufacturing Summary account would be used by A Manufacturing Firm with the information in Figures 22-3 and 22-4 as follows:

Manufacturing Summary

1984			1984		
Dec. 31	Beginning raw materials	48,000	Dec. 31	Ending raw materials	47,000
31	Purchases of raw materials	141,000	31	Ending work in process	30,000
31	Manufacturing payroll	355,000	31	Close cost of goods manufactured	710,000
31	Manufacturing overhead	208,000			
31	Beginning work in process	35,000			
		787,000			787,000

Income Summary

1984			1984		
Dec. 31	Beginning finished goods	150,000	Dec. 31	Ending finished goods	160,000
31	Cost of goods manufactured	710,000			
	Balance	700,000			

The $700,000 balance shown in the Income Summary account before the revenue, selling expenses, administrative expenses, and income taxes are closed represents the cost of goods sold and coincides with the amount shown in Figure 22-3. After the revenue and other expenses are closed to the Income Summary account, a credit balance of $54,000 will remain as the net income for the period.

The net income of $54,000 will be closed to retained earnings as a final step in the closing process. The cost of goods manufactured under a periodic inventory system usually will be calculated on a manufacturing worksheet, similar to the one introduced in Chapter 5 for a merchandising business. A description of a manufacturing worksheet and a more complete illustration of manufacturing accounting with a periodic inventory system follow.

WORKSHEET FOR A MANUFACTURING FIRM

The worksheet of a merchandising firm can be adapted easily for use by a manufacturing firm. Two additional columns are required to record the financial data reported in the cost of goods manufactured statement. The **manufacturing worksheet** of Boyles Precision Manufacturing Company, a Midwestern producer of small metal parts, is presented in Figure 22-5. The balances of the general ledger accounts are listed as a trial balance in the first two columns. The end of the period adjustments are made in the adjustments columns, and the cost of goods manufactured information is recorded in the manufacturing columns. Income statement columns and balance sheet columns are used for the data needed to prepare the two basic financial statements. As we saw in Chapter 5, a worksheet is used by a business firm to *organize* financial information in a systematic manner and to *prepare* the financial statements. It is especially important for a manufacturing operation because of the complexities associated with the production process and the additional financial data that are involved.

Once the trial balance data are entered on the worksheet, the end of the period adjustments must be made. Boyles Precision Manufacturing Company has identified the following adjustments that are required as of December 31:

1. Bad debt expense is estimated at one-half of one percent (.005) of credit sales of $1,400,000.
2. Expired insurance on manufacturing equipment currently recorded as a prepaid expense is $1,700.
3. Accrued wages amount to $8,200—distributed as $7,000 for direct labor and $1,200 for indirect labor. The associated employer payroll taxes are $574.
4. Accrued interest expense on the long-term note payable is $280.
5. Depreciation on the machinery used in manufacturing is $10,750.
6. Depreciation on the manufacturing equipment is $6,400.
7. Amortization of patents is $1,100.
8. Federal and state income tax expense amounts to $35,040.
9. An inventory of the small tools used in manufacturing was taken on December 31. Small tools amounting to $10,800 were on hand as compared with the $14,100 shown in the small tools account. Consequently, $3,300 is written off in 1984.

The debits and credits associated with the adjustments are in balance at $74,344. The amounts in the adjustments columns are combined with the amounts in the trial balance columns and the results are transferred according to their ultimate presentation in the financial statements to the manufacturing columns, income statement columns, or balance sheet columns. Those items that will appear on the cost of goods manufactured statement are shown in the manufacturing columns. All items except the ending work in process and raw materials inventories will have debit balances since they will be expensed on the statement. The beginning work in process and raw materials inventories

BOYLES PRECISION MANUFACTURING COMPANY
Manufacturing Worksheet
Year Ended December 31, 1984

Account	Unadjusted Trial Balance Dr.	Cr.	Adjustments Dr.	Cr.	Manufacturing Dr.	Cr.	Income Statement Dr.	Cr.	Balance Sheet Dr.	Cr.
Cash	24,500								24,500	
Accounts receivable	102,000								102,000	
Allowance for doubtful accounts		2,100		(1) 7,000						9,100
Inventories:										
Finished goods	210,000						210,000	201,500	201,500	
Work in process	49,000				49,000	50,700			50,700	
Raw materials	67,200				67,200	71,500			71,500	
Prepaid expenses	2,600			(2) 1,700					900	
Manufacturing machinery	86,000								86,000	
Accumulated depreciation—machinery		26,000		(5) 10,750						36,750
Manufacturing equipment	32,000								32,000	
Accumulated depreciation—equipment		11,000		(6) 6,400						17,400
Small tools	14,100			(9) 3,300					10,800	
Patents	9,600			(7) 1,100					8,500	
Accounts payable		18,000								18,000
Accrued payroll taxes		1,400		(3) 574						1,974
Notes payable (long term)		28,000								28,000
Common stock ($10 par value)		50,000								50,000
Retained earnings		316,336								316,336
Sales		1,400,000						1,400,000		
Raw materials purchases	194,600				194,600					
Freight in	2,800				2,800					
Direct labor	490,000		(3) 7,000		497,000					
Indirect labor	77,200		(3) 1,200		78,400					
Supplies	8,726				8,726					
Utilities	58,800				58,800					
Rent	31,640				31,640					
Insurance	22,120		(2) 1,700		23,820					
Payroll taxes	39,270		(3) 574		39,844					
Other expenses	5,600				5,600					
Advertising	20,800						20,800			
Sales salaries	121,520						121,520			
Other selling expenses	11,680						11,680			
Administrative salaries	156,800						156,800			
Other administrative expenses	11,200						11,200			
Interest expense	3,080		(4) 280				3,360			
Totals	1,852,836	1,852,836								
Bad debt expense			(1) 7,000				7,000			
Accrued wages payable				(3) 8,200						8,200
Accrued interest expense				(4) 280						280
Depreciation expense—machinery			(5) 10,750		10,750					
Depreciation expense—equipment			(6) 6,400		6,400					
Amortization expense—patent			(7) 1,100		1,100					
Income tax expense			(8) 35,040				35,040			
Accrued income taxes				(8) 35,040						35,040
Depreciation expense—tools			(9) 3,300		3,300					
Cost of goods manufactured						956,780	956,780			
Totals			74,344	74,344	1,078,980	1,078,980				
Net income							67,320			67,320
Totals							1,601,500	1,601,500	588,400	588,400

Figure 22-5
Manufacturing Worksheet

of $49,000 and $67,200, respectively, are entered as debit balances in the manufacturing section.

The ending work in process and raw materials inventories amounting to $50,700 and $71,500, respectively, are entered in the manufacturing credit column since they will be deducted on the cost of goods manufactured statement. They are then extended to the balance sheet debit column to be reported as assets on the balance sheet. The $956,780 figure required to balance the debits and credits in the manufacturing columns is the cost of goods manufactured for the period, which is transferred to the income statement debit column.

The beginning finished goods inventory of $210,000 is entered in the income statement debit column since it represents an addition in the determination of cost of goods sold. The ending finished goods inventory of $201,500 is entered in the income statement credit column because it will be subtracted from goods available in the determination of cost of goods sold. The figure also is entered in the balance sheet debit column to be reported as an asset on the balance sheet. The sales of $1,400,000 are recorded in the income statement credit column. The operating expenses totaling $329,000, the interest expense of $3,360, and the income tax expense amounting to $35,040 are recorded in the income statement debit column. The debit of $67,320 needed to balance the income statement columns is the annual net income, which ultimately will be closed to retained earnings. All asset, liability, and stockholders' equity items are carried forward to the balance sheet columns. Formal statements prepared by Boyles Precision Manufacturing Company from the worksheet are presented in Figures 22-6, 22-7, and 22-8.

CLOSING ENTRIES FOR A MANUFACTURING FIRM

The account balances that are used to determine the cost of goods manufactured are closed through the Manufacturing Summary account, which is then closed to the Income Summary account. Boyles Precision Manufacturing Company would require the following entries to close the account balances shown on the work sheet in Figure 22-5.

1.					
Dec.	31	Manufacturing Summary		1,078,980	
		Raw Materials Inventory			67,200
		Work in Process Inventory			49,000
		Raw Material Purchases			194,600
		Freight In			2,800
		Direct Labor			497,000
		Indirect Labor			78,400
		Supplies Expense			8,726

		Utilities Expense		58,800
		Rent Expense		31,640
		Insurance Expense		23,820
		Payroll Taxes Expense		39,844
		Other Expenses		5,600
		Depreciation Expense—Machinery		10,750
		Depreciation Expense—Equipment		6,400
		Patent Amortization Expense		1,100
		Small Tools Depreciation		3,300
		To close manufacturing accounts with debit balances.		
2. Dec.	31	Raw Materials Inventory	71,500	
		Work in Process Inventory	50,700	
		Manufacturing Summary		122,200
		To establish ending raw materials and work in process inventories.		
3. Dec.	31	Income Summary	1,534,180	
		Finished Goods Inventory		210,000
		Advertising Expense		20,800
		Sales Salaries Expense		121,520
		Other Selling Expenses		11,680
		Administrative Salaries Expense		156,800
		Other Administrative Expenses		11,200
		Interest Expense		3,360
		Bad Debt Expense		7,000
		Income Tax Expense		35,040
		Manufacturing Summary		956,780
		To close the income statement accounts with debit balances.		
4. Dec.	31	Finished Goods Inventory	201,500	
		Sales	1,400,000	
		Income Summary		1,601,500
		To establish the ending finished goods inventory and close the sales account.		
5. Dec.	31	Income Summary	67,320	
		Retained Earnings		67,320
		To close net income to retained earnings.		

You should note that all of the account balances used in the closing process are taken directly from the worksheet. The first entry includes all debit bal-

Figure 22-6
Income Statement

BOYLES PRECISION MANUFACTURING COMPANY
Income Statement
Year Ended December 31, 1984

Sales		$1,400,000
Cost of goods sold		
Beginning finished goods inventory	$ 210,000	
Cost of goods manufactured (Figure 22-7)	956,780	
Goods available	1,166,780	
Ending finished goods inventory	201,500	
Cost of goods sold		965,280
Gross profit		434,720
Operating expenses		
Selling expenses:		
Advertising	$20,800	
Sales salaries	121,520	
Bad debt expense	7,000	
Other selling expenses	11,680	
Total selling expenses	161,000	
Administrative expenses:		
Administrative salaries	156,800	
Other administrative expenses	11,200	
Total administrative expenses	168,000	
Total operating expenses		329,000
Operating income		105,720
Interest expense		3,360
Net income before tax		102,360
Income taxes		35,040
Net income		$ 67,320

ances in the manufacturing section of the worksheet. The second entry sets up the ending raw materials and work in process inventories, which are shown as credits in the manufacturing section of the worksheet. The balance left in the Manufacturing Summary account after the second closing entry is $956,780, which is the cost of goods manufactured for the period. The $956,780 balance is closed along with the other debit balances of the income statement section of the worksheet in the third closing entry. In the fourth entry, the ending finished goods inventory is established and the sales for the year are closed to income summary. The credit balance left in the Income Summary account is

Figure 22-7
Cost of Goods Man-
ufactured Statement

BOYLES PRECISION MANUFACTURING COMPANY
Cost of Goods Manufactured Statement
Year Ended December 31, 1984

Direct materials		
Beginning raw materials	$ 67,200	
Purchases	194,600	
Freight in	2,800	
Raw materials available	264,600	
Ending raw materials	71,500	
Direct materials used		$ 193,100
Direct labor		497,000
Manufacturing overhead		
Indirect labor	78,400	
Supplies	8,726	
Utilities	58,800	
Rent	31,640	
Insurance	23,820	
Payroll taxes	39,844	
Other expenses	5,600	
Depreciation expense	20,450	
Patent amortization expense	1,100	
Total manufacturing overhead		268,380
Total manufacturing costs for the period		958,480
Beginning work in process		49,000
Total work in process		1,007,480
Ending work in process		50,700
Cost of goods manufactured		$ 956,780

$67,320, which is the annual net income. The final closing entry transfers the
net income to the retained earnings account.

VALUATION OF INVENTORIES IN MANUFACTURING

When a periodic inventory system is used in a manufacturing firm such as
Boyles Precision Manufacturing Company, the three types of inventory must
be valued at the end of an accounting period before the financial statements
can be prepared. The worksheet shown in Figure 22-5 indicates that the ending
balances of raw materials, work in process, and finished goods are $71,500,

Figure 22-8
Balance Sheet

BOYLES PRECISION MANUFACTURING COMPANY
Balance Sheet
December 31, 1984

Assets			Liabilities	
Current assets:			Current liabilities:	
Cash		$ 24,500	Accounts payable	$ 18,000
Accounts			Accrued payroll	
receivable	$ 102,000		taxes	1,974
Allowance for			Accrued wages	
doubtful accounts	(9,100)	92,900	payable	8,200
Inventories			Accrued interest	
			expense	280
Finished goods	201,500		Accrued income	
			taxes	35,040
Work in process	50,700		Total current	
			liabilities	63,494
			Long term liabilities:	
Raw materials	71,500		Notes payable	28,000
Total inventories		323,700	Total liabilities	91,494
Prepaid expenses		900		
Total current assets		442,000		
Plant assets:				
Machinery	86,000			
Accumulated				
depreciation	(36,750)	49,250	Stockholders' Equity	
Equipment	32,000		Common stock ($10	
Accumulated			par value)	50,000
depreciation	(17,400)	14,600	Retained earnings	383,656
Small tools		10,800	Total stockholders'	
Patents		8,500	equity	433,656
Total assets		$525,150	Total liabilities and	
			stockholders'	
			equity	$525,150

$50,700, and $201,500 respectively. We must consider next the procedures needed to determine these ending inventory values. Remember that a periodic inventory system requires that the inventory items must be counted and costed to determine the value of the ending inventories. The valuation of the raw materials inventory is relatively straightforward because it is very similar to the procedures used for merchandise inventory. Since the inventory is in the same form in which it was purchased, a count is made and the cost is determined from original purchase invoices. A choice between the various flow assumptions (for example, FIFO or LIFO) also must be made.

The valuation of work in process and finished goods with a periodic inventory approach is more complex. As Figure 22-2 illustrates, the production flow used to convert raw materials to finished goods is a constant process. Yet we must stop the process at the end of a period for accounting purposes to count and place a value on the ending inventories without the benefit of detailed records concerning the costs incurred during production. Because of the addition of direct labor and manufacturing overhead during the period, the ending work in process and finished goods inventories are in different forms than they were at the beginning of the manufacturing process. But the question is "How much of the total manufacturing costs incurred should be assigned to the ending inventories and how much should be charged to the cost of goods manufactured?" Most manufacturing firms produce more than one product, so a unit cost of each product cannot be computed by simply dividing the total cost of goods manufactured by the number of units produced. Also, the units in work in process will be unfinished and usually are at different stages of production.

A manufacturing firm using a periodic inventory system must rely on the sound judgment of the managerial accountant and the production manager to approximate the value of the ending work in process and finished goods inventories. The amount of direct materials assignable to the ending inventory normally can be found by referring to the product specifications for the units in work in process and finished goods. Each finished product will require a certain amount of direct materials compatible with its quality level and selling price. The same product specifications will indicate how much labor cost should be required to complete a product. Based on the percentage of completion for the various products in the ending inventories, management can assign an approximate amount of labor that should have been used. Since the direct materials and direct labor are directly related to the production of products, these estimates usually are reasonably accurate in the valuation of ending inventories.

We discovered earlier that manufacturing overhead is not traceable directly to the products manufactured since it is, by definition, an indirect cost. Instead, an overhead application rate is used to assign manufacturing overhead costs to inventories. When a periodic inventory system is used, the most common practice is to express manufacturing overhead as a percentage of direct labor costs. The use of this overhead application rate is based on the assumption that the ratio of manufacturing overhead costs to direct labor costs is the same for all products produced during the period. The overhead rate is multiplied times the direct labor cost estimated for the ending work in process and finished goods inventories so manufacturing overhead cost can be charged to each of the inventories. In the Boyles Precision Manufacturing Company case, the firm incurred manufacturing overhead costs of $268,380 and direct labor amounted to $497,000. The overhead application rate is, therefore, $268,380 ÷ $497,000 or 54% of direct labor cost. Consequently, 54 cents of manufacturing overhead will be assigned as product costs for every dollar of direct labor cost. We assume that the procedures discussed in this section have been used to value Boyles Precision Manufacturing Company's ending inventories. The amounts of direct materials, direct labor, and manufacturing overhead assigned to work in process and finished goods are the following—based on management's estimates of the direct costs incurred and the use of the 54% overhead application rate:

	Direct Materials	Direct Labor	Manufacturing Overhead	Total
Work in process	$24,674	$ 16,900	$ 9,126	$ 50,700
Finished goods	46,345	100,750	54,405	201,500

LIMITATIONS OF A PERIODIC INVENTORY SYSTEM

We must emphasize that only a small manufacturing firm can utilize a periodic inventory system. Even then, the results may not be adequate to satisfy the cost information needs of management. Product costs are calculated in manufacturing for three basic purposes: *inventory valuation, income determination,* and *management decision-making applications* such as product pricing, cost control, product profitability analysis, and resource allocations. As we can see in the Boyles Precision Manufacturing Company example, the cost information will be available only at the end of an accounting period after physical inventories have been taken for raw materials, work in process, and finished goods. The cost information from a periodic inventory system will not be sufficiently timely, accurate, and detailed to serve the day-to-day needs of management except in extremely simple situations.

As we have demonstrated previously, counting and pricing an ending inventory is very time consuming—particularly for work in process and finished goods inventories. Consequently, a complete inventory usually is taken only at the end of the year despite the fact that management needs the information for decisions that must be made regularly throughout the period. We noted in the Boyles Precision Manufacturing Company example that rough approximations may be the only measures possible for the ending work in process and finished goods inventories. Any errors made with the estimates will have an adverse effect on the income reported for the period and the management decision-making process. In addition, management may have trouble controlling costs over time because the cost results are not adequately detailed. Since unit costs for each product are not computed, it will be difficult to evaluate the effect of changes in costs between periods. Management typically needs to relate the cost information to responsibility centers and to products. The use of responsibility accounting requires the determination of what costs should be as well as what they actually are. Timely reports that pinpoint the responsibility for variances between the planned and actual cost performance must be based upon a detailed description of the costs incurred.

The deficiencies of a periodic inventory system increase with the number of products and producing departments. A cost accounting system is used by many manufacturing firms to correct the deficiencies of a periodic inventory system. Cost accounting provides management with the cost information necessary to plan, control, and evaluate the performance of the production function. Perpetual inventories are maintained so the cost information is timely, accurate, and detailed. The emphasis of cost accounting is on unit cost determination for each type of product rather than the total cost of goods manufactured during the period. The two types of cost accounting systems, job order costing and process costing, are discussed in the next chapter.

GLOSSARY

ABSORPTION COSTING. The inventory valuation method used by a manufacturing firm in which all manufacturing costs are charged as product costs regardless of whether or not they may change in relation to production levels (p. 871).

COST OF GOODS MANUFACTURED STATEMENT. A detailed accounting of the manufacturing cost performance reported on the income statement of a manufacturing firm (p. 874).

COST BEHAVIOR. The measure of how a cost will react to changes in the level of business activity (p. 871).

DIRECT LABOR. Represents the wages paid to employees whose time and effort can be traced to specific products (p. 870).

DIRECT MATERIALS. Consist of the raw materials that can be traced as an integral part of a finished product (p. 869).

FINISHED GOODS. The cost of the products that have been manufactured completely and are ready for sale (p. 867).

FIXED COST. A cost that will remain constant in total amount over a wide range of business activity (p. 872).

MANUFACTURING COST ELEMENTS. The direct materials, direct labor, and manufacturing overhead required to produce a salable product (p. 869).

MANUFACTURING FIRM. A business that converts raw materials into salable products (p. 865).

MANUFACTURING OVERHEAD. All manufacturing costs except direct materials and direct labor required in the production process (p. 870).

MANUFACTURING WORKSHEET. Working papers used by a manufacturing firm to organize financial data including the manufacturing costs and to prepare financial statements (p. 878).

OVERHEAD APPLICATION RATE. A rate used to assign manufacturing overhead costs as product costs (p. 871).

PERIOD COSTS. Costs charged to the income statement of the period in which they are incurred rather than being inventoried as product costs (p. 868).

PRODUCT COSTS. Costs inventoried as assets during the production process and charged to the income statement when the related finished goods are sold (p. 868).

PRODUCTION DEPARTMENTS. Departments engaged directly in the manufacturing operation required to convert raw materials into finished goods (p. 870).

RAW MATERIALS. Represent the cost of the basic materials and parts that have been purchased by a manufacturing firm and are available for conversion into salable products (p. 866).

SERVICE DEPARTMENTS. Departments that support the production departments with such activities as maintenance, production control, and stores (p. 870).

VARIABLE COST. A cost that will vary in total amount proportionately with some measure of business activity (p. 872).

VARIABLE COSTING. The inventory valuation method used for internal reporting purposes by a manufacturing firm. Only variable manufacturing costs are charged as product costs with this method (p. 871).

WORK IN PROCESS. The inventory that has been partially converted into finished products (p. 867).

DISCUSSION QUESTIONS

1. Explain the basic differences between the inventories of a manufacturing firm and those of a merchandising enterprise. What is the effect of these differences on the income statements of the two types of businesses?
2. Distinguish between product and period costs. Identify which of the following is a product cost and which is a period cost.
   (a) Indirect materials
   (b) Depreciation—manufacturing equipment
   (c) Gas heat—sales office
   (d) President's salary
   (e) Direct labor
   (f) Insurance—factory
   (g) Sales manager's salary

(h) Production supervisor's salary

(i) Depreciation—President's car

3. What are the three manufacturing cost elements? Which of the nine items in question 2 would be classified as manufacturing cost and how would each be classified (direct materials, direct labor, or manufacturing overhead)?

4. Explain the basic difference between a fixed and a variable cost. On the basis of their most likely cost behavior, how would each of the items in question 2 be categorized (fixed or variable)?

5. Explain the basic difference between:

(a) Manufacturing costs for the period

(b) Cost of goods manufactured

(c) Cost of goods sold

6. The Merrill Company incurred the following manufacturing costs during the year:

Direct materials	$140,000
Direct labor	350,000
Manufacturing overhead	210,000

(a) Assume that the company had no work in process inventory at the beginning or end of the year. How much was the firm's cost of goods manufactured?

(b) Assume instead that the company had a work in process inventory of $20,000 at the beginning of the year but none at the end of the year. How much was the firm's cost of goods manufactured?

(c) Assume instead that the company had a work in process inventory of $20,000 at the beginning of the year and $40,000 at the end of the year. How much was the firm's cost of goods manufactured?

7. During the previous year, the cost of materials used by a manufacturing firm was $80,000. The materials inventory decreased by $9,000 during the period. What was the cost of materials purchased?

8. Explain what the balance of the Manufacturing Summary account represents before the account is closed.

9. What is the purpose of a worksheet in the accounting cycle of a manufacturing firm?

10. Why is the cost of goods manufactured entered as a credit in the manufacturing columns of a worksheet and a debit in the income statement columns?

11. Why is the beginning finished goods inventory entered as a debit in the income statement columns of a worksheet instead of in the balance sheet columns?

12. If a given cost is incurred for the common benefit of manufacturing, selling, and administrative activities, how should the amount be divided among the three?

13. The Do-Rite Company evaluates the performance of its manufacturing operation by considering controllable costs only. All direct costs are classified as being controllable and all indirect costs are considered uncontrollable. Do you agree with this approach?

14. What are the basic procedures involved when valuing inventories in a manufacturing operation with a periodic inventory system?

15. What are the limitations of a periodic inventory system used by a manufacturing firm? How would a perpetual inventory system eliminate these deficiencies?

16. What is a manufacturing overhead rate and why is it used by most manufacturing firms?

17. The Kemper Company uses a manufacturing overhead rate of 60% of direct labor cost to apply overhead to work in process inventory. If manufacturing overhead amounting to $32,520 is applied to work in process at the end of the year, what is the proper amount of direct labor charged to the inventory?

EXERCISES

Exercise 22-1 (Determining Beginning Work in Process)

The information below is taken from the financial statements of the Howard Company for the year ended December 31, 1984.

Factory overhead, 62.5% of direct labor cost	$ 90,000
Raw materials inventory, January 1, 1984	15,000
Cost of goods manufactured	409,000
Raw materials inventory, December 31, 1984	20,000
Work in process inventory, December 31, 1984	45,000
Raw materials purchased in 1984	198,000

Required:
Compute the cost of work in process inventory on January 1, 1984.

Exercise 22-2 (Valuing Manufacturing Inventories)

During 1985, the Lexington Corporation incurred the following costs in its manufacturing activities.

Direct labor	$145,000
Direct materials	197,000
Factory overhead	217,500

The company allocates overhead to its work in process inventory and finished goods inventory using an overhead rate based on direct labor costs.

Required:
A. Determine the company's overhead rate.
B. If the company's finished goods inventory of $23,000 includes $4,000 of direct material costs, determine the inventory's labor and overhead costs.
C. The company's work in process inventory amounted to $25,000. If labor costs included in the ending inventory figure amounted to $7,000, calculate the inventory's material and overhead costs.

Exercise 22-3 (Manufacturing Accounting with Missing Data)

For each company fill in the missing data. Each company is independent of the others.

Income Statement

	Company X	Company Y	Company Z
Sales	$53,000	?	$61,000
Finished goods, beginning inventory	7,000	?	15,000
Cost of goods manufactured	19,000	$40,000	?
Finished goods, ending inventory	?	15,000	21,000
Cost of Goods Sold	20,000	37,000	?
Gross profit	?	44,000	?
Operating expenses	15,000	?	23,000
Net income	?	25,000	?
Work in process, beginning inventory	?	10,500	12,000
Direct labor	7,000	15,000	21,000
Raw materials used	6,500	9,000	17,000
Manufacturing overhead	8,000	12,000	15,000
Work in process, ending inventory	9,000	?	30,000

Exercise 22-4 (Manufacturing Accounting with Missing Data)

Income statement data for the Brighton Corporation for four years are presented below.

Income Statement

	1982	1983	1984	1985
Sales	?	?	$460,000	$450,000
Finished goods, beginning inventory	$ 65,000	?	?	?
Work in process, beginning inventory	20,000	?	?	15,000
Raw materials used	89,000	$ 95,000	60,000	85,000
Direct labor	?	105,000	80,000	55,000
Manufacturing overhead	95,000	?	75,000	60,000
Work in process, ending inventory	30,000	?	?	?
Cost of goods manufactured	?	?	225,000	190,000
Finished goods, ending inventory	85,000	?	?	23,000
Cost of goods sold	291,000	289,000	242,000	?
Gross profit	275,000	?	?	210,000
Operating expenses	85,000	75,000	?	50,000
Net income	?	180,000	120,000	?

Required:

Fill in the missing data. (*Hint:* 1985 data provide information required to find 1984 unknowns)

Exercise 22-5 (Evaluating Cost Classifications)

Identify the most likely correct answer for each of the following costs as a product or period cost and as variable or fixed cost with respect to level of activity.

	Product	Period	Variable	Fixed
1. Manufacturing utilities				
2. Manufacturing supplies				
3. Direct materials				
4. President's salary				
5. Depreciation on manufacturing equipment				
6. Manufacturing rent				
7. Sales office utilities				
8. Depreciation on sales office equipment				
9. Nails used in production				
10. Maintenance contract on manufacturing equipment				

Exercise 22-6 (Evaluating the Use of Raw Materials)

The Denver Tool Company produces and sells high-quality woodworking tool sets. Each set of tools is contained in a wooden carrying case that is purchased from an outside supplier. The wooden carrying cases are held as raw materials inventory until they are placed into production and combined with the related tool sets. The production and purchasing departments have provided the following information for the month of January:

1. Beginning raw materials inventory included 950 wooden cases at a cost of $21,375.
2. The company purchased 2,000 additional cases at $22.50 each.
3. A total of 2,200 cases were transferred into production.
4. An additional 150 cases were given for promotional purposes to managers of prospective retail outlets.

Of the cases placed into production, 65% were combined with tool sets that were completed and transferred to finished goods. Of the cases transferred to finished goods during January, 70% had been sold by month-end. There was no beginning inventory of wooden cases in finished goods or in work in process.

Required:

Determine the cost of the wooden cases that would be included in the following accounts as of January 31:

A. Raw materials
B. Work in process

C. Finished goods
D. Selling expense
E. Cost of goods sold

PROBLEMS

Problem 22-1 (Fundamentals of Manufacturing Accounting)

During 1984, the Pruis Manufacturing Company incurred the following expenses in connection with its production activities:

Factory utilities	$ 30,500
Indirect labor	43,000
Raw material purchases	175,000
Direct labor	130,000
Depreciation on factory equipment	24,000
Factory rent expense	25,000
Supplies used in production	13,000
Repairs to factory equipment	27,000

The beginning and ending inventory values were:

	Beginning Inventory	Ending Inventory
Raw materials	$22,000	$19,000
Work in process	37,000	42,000
Finished goods	43,000	35,000

Required:
A. Calculate the relationship between direct labor cost and manufacturing overhead costs.
B. Prepare a cost of goods manufactured statement for the year ending December 31, 1984.
C. Prepare closing entries for the manufacturing accounts using the manufacturing summary account.
D. Prepare the entry to close the manufacturing summary account.

Problem 22-2 (Determining Cost of Goods Sold)

The treasurer of the Basset Company has compiled information concerning the company's 1984 manufacturing costs. The beginning inventories included raw materials—$96,000, work in process—$64,000, and finished goods—$118,000. The company incurred direct labor costs of $676,800 and its total cost of goods manufactured amounted to $2,410,000 for 1984. Overhead costs are assigned to work in process and finished goods using the relationship between direct labor costs and manufacturing overhead incurred. The ending inventories are comprised of the following costs:

	Raw Materials	Work in Process	Finished Goods
Raw materials	$88,000	$22,000	$30,000
Direct labor	—	22,400	26,400
Overhead costs	—	?	39,600
Total ending inventory	$88,000	?	$96,000

Required:
Prepare a schedule showing the cost of goods sold for 1984.

Problem 22-3 (Manufacturing Income Statement)

The following amounts and accounts were taken from the completed worksheet of the Webster Manufacturing Company:

Advertising	$ 42,000
Bad debt expense	11,000
Depreciation—factory machinery	15,000
Depreciation—office equipment	6,000
Direct labor	253,000
Factory utilities	10,700
Factory rent	78,000
Factory supplies	50,000
Finished goods, 1/1/86	92,000
Finished goods, 12/31/86	85,000
Freight-in	8,000
Indirect labor	54,000
Machinery repairs	14,000
Office rent	21,000
Officers' salaries	154,000
Property taxes—factory equipment	6,000
Property taxes—office equipment	13,000
Purchase discounts on raw materials	12,000
Raw materials inventory 1/1/86	44,000
Raw materials inventory 12/31/86	53,000
Raw material purchases	450,000
Sales	1,251,000
Sales returns	22,000
Sales commissions	40,000
Work in process 1/1/86	17,000
Work in process 12/31/86	21,000

Required:
Prepare an income statement and a cost of goods manufactured statement for the year ending December 31, 1986.

Problem 22-4 (Correcting a Manufacturing Income Statement)

The treasurer of the Allen Manufacturing Company hired his daughter, who had just completed her first accounting course, as summer help in the accounting department. Her first assignment was to prepare an income statement for the month of May. Applying the knowledge she had acquired in Financial Accounting I, she prepared the following statement.

ALLEN MANUFACTURING COMPANY
Income Statement
Month Ended May 31, 1985

Sales	$493,000
Operating expenses:	
Raw material purchases	97,000
Rent	62,000
Depreciation	15,000
Utilities	30,000
Direct labor	125,000
Indirect labor	23,000
Office salaries	31,000
Administrative and selling expenses	47,000
Total operating expenses	430,000
Net income	$63,000

The treasurer has decided to prepare a correct income statement and has gathered the following data:

1. The beginning and ending inventories of raw materials were $21,000 and $24,000, respectively.
2. Three of the expenses listed on his daughter's income statement were applicable to both factory operations and the selling and administrative functions. The percentages applicable to each are as follows:

	Factory Operations	Selling and Administrative
Rent	65%	35%
Depreciation	75%	25%
Utilities	60%	40%

3. The work in process and finished goods inventories were:

	May 1	May 31
Work in process	$37,000	$35,000
Finished goods	$29,000	$31,000

Required:

Prepare a corrected income statement for the month of May.

Problem 22-5 (Use of a Manufacturing Worksheet)

The unadjusted trial balance of the Summit Manufacturing Company on December 31, 1986, is presented below:

SUMMIT MANUFACTURING COMPANY
Unadjusted Trial Balance
December 31, 1986

	Debits	Credits
Cash	$ 10,000	
Accounts receivable	21,000	
Allowance for doubtful accounts		$ 1,000
Finished goods inventory, 1/1/86	35,000	
Work in process, 1/1/86	17,000	
Raw materials inventory, 1/1/86	9,000	
Prepaid insurance	3,000	
Machinery and equipment	91,000	
Accumulated depreciation		32,500
Accounts payable		19,000
Notes payable		30,000
Common stock		1,000
Retained earnings		43,600
Sales		1,080,000
Raw materials purchases	405,000	
Direct labor	244,000	
Indirect labor	63,000	
Factory supplies	34,000	
Utilities	24,500	
Rent	42,000	
Insurance	19,000	
Property taxes	9,000	
Selling expenses	37,000	
Administrative and office expenses	54,000	
Sales commissions	68,600	
Interest expense	21,000	
	$1,207,100	$1,207,100

Additional information:

1. On September 1, 1986, the company paid $3,000 for a 12-month insurance account. Prepaid insurance was debited at the time of the transaction.
2. The Machinery and Equipment account is comprised of $31,500 of office equipment and $59,500 of factory machinery. All machinery and equipment is depre-

ciated using the straight-line method with a seven-year life and no salvage value. There were no fixed assets acquisitions or disposals during 1986.

3. The inventories as of December 31, 1986 were:

Raw materials	$ 7,500
Work in process	19,000
Finished goods	40,000

4. Expenses incurred as of year-end but not yet recorded: direct labor—$6,000; indirect labor—$1,500; selling expenses—$4,700.
5. The utilities, rent, insurance, and property taxes are attributable to factory operations.
6. An additional bad debt expense of $260 is to be recognized and treated as an administrative expense.
7. Ignore federal and state income taxes.

Required:
A. Prepare a worksheet including pairs of columns for Unadjusted Trial Balance, Adjustments, Manufacturing, Income Statement, and Balance Sheet.
B. Prepare a cost of goods manufactured statement for the year ended December 31, 1986.
C. Prepare the closing entries using a manufacturing summary account.
D. Calculate the relationship between overhead and direct labor costs. Using that relationship, calculate the labor and overhead included in the ending inventories if work in process ending inventory contains $6,330 of raw materials and $9,230 of raw materials is included in the finished goods ending inventory.

ALTERNATE PROBLEMS

Problem 22-1A (Fundamentals of Manufacturing Accounting)

The following costs were incurred by the Redlands Corporation in its manufacturing activities during 1984:

Factory insurance	$ 20,000
Direct labor	120,000
Raw material purchases	153,000
Factory utilities	43,000
Repairs to factory equipment	17,000
Indirect labor	54,000
Factory supplies	34,000

The beginning and ending inventory values were:

	Beginning Inventory	Ending Inventory
Raw materials	$27,000	$24,000
Work in process	41,000	45,000
Finished goods	33,000	31,000

Required:

A. Calculate the relationship between direct labor costs and manufacturing overhead costs.

B. Prepare a cost of goods manufactured statement for the year ending December 31, 1984.

C. Prepare closing entries for the manufacturing accounts using the manufacturing summary account.

D. Prepare the entry to close the manufacturing summary account.

Problem 22-2A (Determining Cost of Goods Sold)

The Hayward Manufacturing Corporation incurred labor costs of $378,000 and its total cost of goods manufactured was $1,150,000 during 1985. The company assigns overhead costs to work in process and finished goods using the relationship between direct labor costs and manufacturing overhead incurred. The beginning inventories included raw materials—$75,000, work in process—$83,000, and finished goods—$125,000.

The ending inventories were comprised of the following costs:

	Raw Materials	Work in Process	Finished Goods
Raw materials	$80,000	$ 28,350	$41,550
Direct labor	—	25,500	41,500
Overhead costs	—	33,150	?
Total ending inventory	$80,000	$87,000	?

Required:

Prepare a schedule showing the cost of goods sold for 1985.

Problem 22-3A (Manufacturing Income Statement)

The Ontario Manufacturing Company, Inc. has compiled the following amounts and accounts for the preparation of the annual financial statements:

Work in process, 1/1/84	$27,000
Raw materials, 1/1/84	35,000
Finished goods, 1/1/84	75,000
Indirect labor	67,000
Sales commissions	137,640
Sales	1,147,000
Raw material purchases	360,000
Freight-in	15,000
Purchase discounts on raw materials	7,000
Factory rent	17,200
Advertising	25,000
Finished goods, 12/31/84	68,000
Sales returns	16,000
Factory supplies	34,500
Depreciation—office equipment	49,500

Raw materials, 12/31/84	39,000
Direct labor	197,000
Factory utilities	13,700
Officers' salaries	157,200
Work in process, 12/31/84	31,600
Factory insurance	9,100
Depreciation—factory equipment	16,100

Required:
Prepare an income statement and a cost of goods manufactured statement for the year ending December 31, 1984.

Problem 22-4A (Correcting a Manufacturing Income Statement)

Mr. Scofield has offered to perform accounting services for the manufacturing company his nephew has organized. Using his financial accounting textbook, he has prepared the following income statement.

GRANGER MANUFACTURING, INC.
Income Statement
Month Ended August 31, 1986

Sales	$45,000
Operating expenses:	
Raw material purchases	22,000
Rent	2,000
Depreciation	1,500
Insurance	900
Direct labor	12,000
Indirect labor	1,800
Administrative and selling expenses	3,100
Total operating expenses	43,300
Net income	$ 1,700

Mr. Scofield's nephew has compiled the following data in order to prepare a corrected income statement.

	Beginning Inventory	Ending Inventory
Raw materials	$2,000	$2,500
Work in process	4,300	4,700
Finished goods	1,800	2,100

Three of the expenses listed on the income statement were attributable to both factory operations and the selling and administrative functions. The percentages applicable to each are:

	Factory Operations	Selling and Administrative
Rent	70%	30%
Depreciation	80%	20%
Insurance	62%	38%

Required:

Prepare a corrected income statement for August 31, 1986.

Problem 22-5A (Use of a Manufacturing Worksheet)

The unadjusted trial balance of the Hillcrest Manufacturing Company on December 31, 1984, is presented below:

HILLCREST MANUFACTURING CO.
Unadjusted Trial Balance
December 31, 1984

	Debits	Credits
Cash	$ 14,700	
Accounts receivable	33,000	
Allowance for doubtful accounts		$ 2,700
Finished goods inventory, 1/1/84	23,000	
Work in process, 1/1/84	7,500	
Raw materials inventory, 1/1/84	3,700	
Prepaid rent	54,000	
Machinery and equipment	196,000	
Accumulated depreciation		35,000
Accounts payable		18,000
Notes payable		75,000
Common stock		40,000
Retained earnings		37,000
Sales		860,000
Direct labor	216,000	
Raw material purchases	205,000	
Indirect labor	71,000	
Factory supplies	18,000	
Utilities	56,000	
Insurance	16,300	
Selling expenses	32,000	
Administrative expenses	67,000	
Interest expense	23,000	
Rent expense	31,500	
	$1,067,700	$1,067,700

Additional information:

1. The Machinery and Equipment account is comprised of $147,000 of factory machinery and $49,000 of office equipment. All machinery and equipment is depreciated using a seven-year life, no salvage value, and the straight-line method.
2. On July 1, 1984, the company paid $54,000 for the next 12 months' rent. Prepaid rent was debited at the time of the transaction.
3. The inventories as of December 31, 1984 were:

Raw materials	$3,100
Work in Process	8,700
Finished goods	25,000

4. The utilities, rent, and insurance expenses are related to factory operations.
5. Expenses incurred as of year-end but not yet recorded are: direct labor—$4,000, indirect labor—$1,200, administrative expenses—$700.
6. Ignore federal and state income taxes.

Required:
A. Prepare a worksheet including a pair of columns for Unadjusted Trial Balance, Adjustments, Manufacturing, Income Statement, and Balance Sheet.
B. Prepare a cost of goods manufactured statement.
C. Prepare the closing entries using a manufacturing summary account.
D. Calculate the relationship between manufacturing overhead and direct labor costs. Using that relationship, calculate the labor and overhead included in the ending inventories if work in process ending inventory contains $2,400 of raw materials and $4,000 of raw materials is included in the finished goods inventory.

CASE FOR CHAPTER 22

Decision Problem (Manufacturing Accounting with Missing Records)

The Combustible Company produces a highly flammable chemical product. The company experienced a fire on April 1, 1984, that destroyed its entire work in process inventory but did not affect the raw materials or finished goods inventories because they were located elsewhere. You have been asked to assist the firm's insurance company in determining the amount of work in process inventory at the time of the fire. Combustible Company uses a periodic inventory system so perpetual records are not available.

A periodic inventory taken after the fire indicated that raw materials were valued at $60,000 and finished goods at $78,000. The company's accounting records show that the inventories as of January 1, 1984 were:

Raw materials	$20,000
Work in process	60,000
Finished goods	92,000

In addition, the accounting records indicate that the costs recorded during the first quarter of 1984 amounted to:

| Purchase of raw materials | $108,000 |
| Direct labor | 60,000 |

In the past, manufacturing overhead costs have amounted to 150 percent of direct labor.

Sales for the first quarter of 1984 amounted to $400,000. The firm's gross profit has been 40% of sales for a long time.

Required:

Prepare a report that shows:

A. The firm's cost of goods sold for the first quarter of 1984.
B. The firm's cost of goods manufactured for the first quarter of 1984.
C. The firm's work in process inventory as of March 31, 1984, broken down as direct materials, direct labor, and manufacturing overhead.

CHAPTER 23
COST ACCOUNTING SYSTEMS

OVERVIEW AND OBJECTIVES

This chapter presents the essential features of cost accounting systems. When you have completed the chapter, you should understand:

- The basic nature of a cost accounting system (pp. 903–904).
- The manufacturing operations requiring job order costing and those using process costing (pp. 904–905, 914).
- How product costs are determined with each type of cost accounting system (pp. 905–907, 914–917).
- The role of a job order cost sheet (pp. 905–906).
- The accounting procedures used in job order costing (pp. 906–914).
- The difference between actual and applied manufacturing overhead (pp. 910–913).
- How equivalent units are used in process costing (pp. 914–916).
- The role of a cost of production report (p. 916).
- The accounting procedures applied in process costing (pp. 916–921).

We demonstrated in Chapter 22 the difficulties caused by the production process and its associated cost elements in determining the cost of manufacturing specific units of output. Nevertheless, every manufacturing firm must know what it costs to produce each product so a selling price adequate to earn a satisfactory gross profit can be established. **Cost accounting** is a specialized type of accounting used by a manufacturing firm to accumulate product costs as production takes place. In contrast to the periodic inventory procedures discussed in the preceding chapter, a perpetual inventory system is maintained as a *continuous record* of the costs, and the emphasis is on the *unit cost* of the products produced rather than the total manufacturing costs of a period. Cost accounting data are collected in separate ledger accounts included in the general accounting system. The cost information, developed through cost accounting and used for both external and internal reporting, serves two basic purposes: product costing and managerial decision-making.

Product costs are used to value a manufacturing firm's work in process and finished goods inventories as well as to determine its net income periodically. Product costing on a perpetual basis eliminates the need for the rough estimates of ending inventory values used in a periodic inventory system. In addition, management requires reliable cost information on a regular basis for such decision-making functions as projecting a firm's financial performance, product pricing, product profitability analysis, production cost control, and resource allocations.

Although the emphasis of this chapter is on the use of cost accounting in a manufacturing operation, it also is applicable in many nonmanufacturing businesses such as hospitals, banks, retail stores, insurance companies, accounting firms, and construction companies. Nonmanufacturing firms use cost accounting procedures to determine the costs of performing services or activities rather than producing products. Examples are a bank costing its credit card service, an insurance company costing the policies written by its agents, a hospital costing a medical procedure, and an accounting firm costing the preparation of a corporate tax return.

The two basic types of cost accounting systems available are *job order costing* and *process costing*. The choice between the two will depend upon the nature of the manufacturing operation. When products are produced as separately identifiable units or groups of units, job order costing is appropriate. An example of a job order costing application is a publishing firm producing a textbook such as the one you are reading. If the products are manufactured on a continuous or homogeneous basis, they cannot be separated realistically, and process costing should be used. An example of a process costing application is a firm producing paint that is sold to retail stores. Product costing with both methods is an averaging procedure—although a job order unit cost usually is more accurate than a unit cost computed with process costing.

JOB ORDER COSTING

Job order costing is most appropriate when products are manufactured according to customers' orders or specifications and the identity of each job must be kept separate. A major characteristic of a manufacturing operation in which a job order costing system is appropriate is that it must have a well-defined beginning and completion time. The technique can be used to accumulate the costs of a single product (for example, a large airplane being produced) or a group of identical or similar products (for example, several dining-room tables being manufactured). Such industries as commercial printing, aerospace, shipbuilding, heavy machinery, and furniture rely on job order costing for the determination of product costs. It is also utilized by construction businesses, hospitals, repair shops, accounting firms, and motion picture companies.

CONTROL DOCUMENT—JOB ORDER COST SHEET

A control document is required with a job order cost system to accumulate the production costs and report the results to management. In job order costing, the job itself is the focal point for product cost accumulation. The control document used in job order costing, a **job order cost sheet,** has two basic purposes. It provides an *itemized listing* of all direct materials, direct labor, and manufacturing overhead charged to a job and it serves as a *subsidiary ledger* during and after the manufacturing operation. A job order cost sheet is illustrated in Figure 23-1. The information recorded on the cost sheet will be explained subsequently.

A control number is assigned to each job entered into production and is recorded on a job order cost sheet. Information concerning the customer and

Figure 23-1
Job Order Cost Sheet

Job No. 691			JOB ORDER COST SHEET					
			VILLAGE MANUFACTURING COMPANY					
Customer		Carr, Inc.						
Product		L-100		Quantity		100		
Date Started		1/12	Date Finished		1/19			

Labor			Material			Overhead	
Date	Reference	Amount	Date	Reference	Amount	Direct Labor Hours	1,350
1/12	12-30	$1,920	1/12	1126	$6,000	Overhead rate	$4.50
1/13	13-30	1,920	1/19	1198	1,500	Overhead applied	$6,075
1/14	14-30	1,920					
1/15	15-30	1,920				Summary	
1/16	16-30	1,920				Direct labor	$10,800
1/19	19-17	1,200				Direct material	7,500
						Manufacturing Overhead	6,075
						Total cost	24,375
						Unit cost	$243.75

product description is also entered before the cost sheet is filed in the work in process subsidiary ledger file. The cost sheet in Figure 23-1 indicates that Village Manufacturing Company, which produces furniture, started Job 691 on January 12 and finished it on January 19. One hundred dining-room tables were produced for the customer, Carr, Inc. The subsidiary ledger of cost sheets is controlled by the Work in Process Inventory account while production takes place. The reference columns show the original sources of data recorded in the job order cost sheet (for example, a specific labor time ticket). When direct materials are requisitioned from the storeroom for a specific job, their cost is charged to the job in the material column of the job's cost sheet. The direct labor cost required to convert raw materials to finished goods is charged to the job in the labor column of the job's cost sheet, and an appropriate amount of manufacturing overhead also is recorded on the cost sheet. When the job is completed, its total cost can be determined by adding the costs recorded in the three columns.

The manufacturing costs recorded on the job order cost sheets also must be debited periodically to the Work in Process Inventory account. At the end of a month, the sum of the costs shown on the cost sheets assigned to unfinished jobs should equal the balance in the Work in Process Inventory account after the monthly accounting is finished. When a job is completed, the costs recorded on its cost sheet are totaled and the amount debited to Finished Goods Inventory, with the same amount credited to the Work in Process Inventory account. The cost sheet then is removed from the work in process subsidiary ledger file and transferred to the finished goods subsidiary ledger file, which is controlled by the Finished Goods Inventory account in the general ledger. When a job is sold, the total cost of the job is charged to the Cost of Goods Sold account and credited to Finished Goods Inventory. The job order cost sheet is transferred to the cost of goods sold subsidiary ledger file (maintained on an annual basis) as a final step in the job order costing flow, illustrated in Figure 23-2. All aspects of the manufacturing cost flow illustrated in Figure 23-2 are accounted for perpetually as a job progresses from the raw materials stage to the point of sale.

We now turn our attention to the specific procedures required to perform job order costing with perpetual inventories. The Village Manufacturing Company's January 1984 performance will be used to illustrate the job order costing procedures.

ACCOUNTING FOR MATERIALS

The purchasing cycle discussed in Chapter 7 can be used to control the raw materials acquired. All raw materials are kept in a storeroom under the supervision of a stores manager and are issued to work in process upon receipt

Job Order Costing Flow
(General Ledger Accounts)

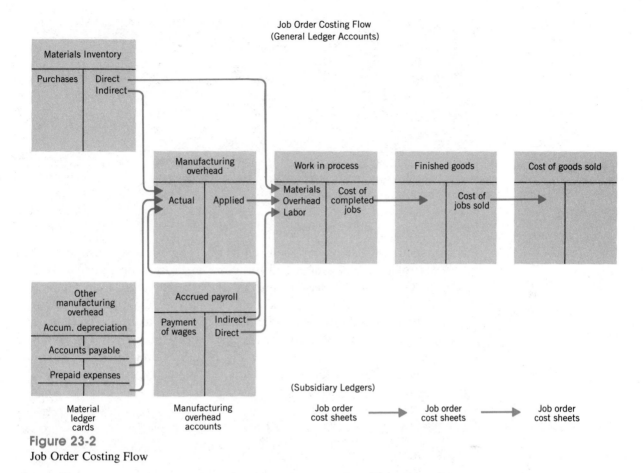

Figure 23-2
Job Order Costing Flow

of a properly prepared and authorized **materials requisition form** such as the one shown in Figure 23-3. The materials requisition form is prepared and signed by the manager responsible for the work being performed. It identifies the specific material required and shows the job or manufacturing overhead account to which it is to be charged as direct or indirect materials. The material requisition forms are sent to the accounting department at the end of each day for further processing. Figure 23-3 indicates that 250 units of raw material were charged to Job 691 at a total cost of $6,000 on January 12.

Material ledger cards such as the one presented in Figure 23-4 are maintained for each type of material used and serve as the subsidiary ledger for the Raw Materials Inventory account. The ledger cards provide perpetual inventory control with columns for receipts, issues, and a current balance. The raw materials requisitioned during an accounting period are recorded as direct materials on the job order cost sheets or as indirect materials charged to manufacturing overhead by someone in the accounting department. The $6,000 of materials requisitioned to Job 691 have been deducted in Figure 23-4 to

Figure 23-3
Material Requisition
Form

MATERIAL REQUISITION FORM		Number	1126
Job Number	691	Date	1/12
Overhead Account	—		
Authorized By	JGH		

Description	Quantity	Unit Cost	Amount
AZ 100	250	$24	$6,000

maintain a current balance of goods on hand. The costs also must be charged to the control accounts established for Work in Process Inventory and Manufacturing Overhead. We assume that Village Manufacturing Company makes all entries to the general ledger accounts at the end of the month, although they may be recorded throughout the month in other situations. The entries in the ledger cards should be made perpetually during the period. The company purchased raw materials amounting to $42,500, including $7,200 for the material in Figure 23-4, in January, so the following entry would be required:

Jan.	31	Raw Materials Inventory	42,500	
		Accounts Payable		42,500
		To record raw materials purchased during January.		

Five jobs, including Job 691, were worked on during the month and each would have a separate job order cost sheet, although we will consider only the one for Job 691. As we saw in Figure 23-1, raw materials totaling $7,500 were requisitioned for Job 691 during January. The total raw materials

Figure 23-4
Material Ledger
Card

MATERIAL LEDGER CARD
Item   AZ 100

		Received			Issued			Balance		
Date	Reference	Quantity	Unit Cost	Total Cost	Quantity	Unit Cost	Total Cost	Quantity	Unit Cost	Total Cost
1/6	18/20	300	24	$7,200				300	24	$7,200
1/12	1126				250	24	$6,000	50	24	$1,200

requisitioned for the five jobs amounted to $36,550 and those charged to manufacturing overhead were $1,680. The following journal entry would be made:

Jan.	31	Work in Process Inventory	36,550	
		Manufacturing Overhead	1,680	
		Raw Materials Inventory		38,230
		To record raw materials requisitioned		
		during January.		

ACCOUNTING FOR LABOR

A time reporting system consisting of *labor time tickets, time cards,* and a *payroll register* is used to accumulate labor costs with job order costing. A **labor time ticket** such as the one illustrated in Figure 23-5 is used to record the time spent by each employee on a specific job or an overhead assignment. A time card is utilized to control the total daily labor hours; each employee is required to clock in when work begins and clock out at the end of the day. A payroll register similar to the one discussed in Chapter 12 also is maintained as a detailed description of the manufacturing payroll—usually classified on a departmental basis.

The labor time tickets are prepared daily under the supervision of the manager responsible for the work activity. Each labor hour recorded on the time tickets is multiplied times the appropriate rate and the total cost is charged either to jobs as direct labor or to manufacturing overhead as indirect labor. In large organizations, a timekeeper may perform the clerical work associated with the tickets, which usually are in a form appropriate for computerized processing. During each day, a time ticket is prepared each time an employee changes from one job or overhead assignment to another. For example, the employee accounted for in Figure 23-5 spent eight hours on Job 691. At the end of the day, all of the time tickets are sent to the accounting department for classification as direct or indirect labor. Since labor cannot be inventoried like raw materials, the entire manufacturing payroll must be distributed each period as direct or indirect labor. Based on the time cards, Village Manufacturing Company incurred a manufacturing payroll of $48,200 during January. The labor time tickets indicate that the firm's direct labor was $42,000 (including $10,800 for Job 691) and the indirect labor amounted to $6,200. The following entry would be recorded (payroll withholdings are ignored):

Jan.	31	Work in Process Inventory	42,000	
		Manufacturing Overhead	6,200	
		Wages Payable		48,200
		To record the direct and indirect labor for		
		January.		

Figure 23-5
Labor Time Ticket

LABOR TIME TICKET				
Employee Name	J. Ford	Number		12-18
Employee Number	18	Date		1/12
Work Performed	Assembly	Job		691
Approved By	JGH	Overhead Account		—
Time Started	Time Stopped	Hours	Rate	Amount
7:00	11:00	4	$8	$32
12:00	4:00	4	8	32
Total Cost				$64

ACCOUNTING FOR MANUFACTURING OVERHEAD

The accumulation of the direct costs was basically straightforward since they could be traced to production with a materials requisition or labor time reporting system. Accounting for manufacturing overhead is more complicated because of its indirect nature and the need to accumulate costs currently in a perpetual inventory system. Accounting for the total manufacturing overhead of a given period is relatively simple. The difficult accounting problem is to relate the overhead cost to production output on some reliable basis. We learned in Chapter 22 that manufacturing overhead is a common cost incurred for the benefit of all products so it cannot be traced to production as the direct costs can be. Instead, it must be related to the jobs on some production activity basis that closely relates the *cost* to the work performed. Examples of bases used are direct labor hours, direct labor cost, machine hours, or units produced.

With a perpetual inventory system, a firm *cannot* wait until the end of an accounting period to charge the manufacturing overhead actually incurred to the jobs, since management needs the product cost information for decision-making purposes during the period. Also, fluctuations in either the amount of manufacturing overhead or the level of production activity between short time periods such as months may produce inconsistent results if actual costs and actual production activity are used. For example, assume that a highly automated toy manufacturing firm has a monthly depreciation charge for its machinery of $50,000, which must be included in the product cost. Assume further that production activity is seasonal and 25,000 units are produced in January while 100,000 units are manufactured in September. If actual manufacturing overhead and actual production activity are used, the unit cost for depreciation would be $2.00 for January and $.50 for September. In months of high production, the unit cost would be low, while in months of low production the unit cost would be high, despite the fact that the products and the manufacturing process are identical from month to month. In order to avoid these accounting problems, a predetermined overhead rate is used to apply the cost to the jobs as they are worked on. A **predetermined overhead rate** can be computed for an upcoming year based on the following fraction:

$$\frac{\text{Estimated annual manufacturing overhead cost}}{\text{Estimated annual level of production activity}} = \frac{\text{Predetermined}}{\text{overhead rate}}$$

For example, assume that Village Manufacturing Company forecasted manufacturing overhead of $270,000 for 1984 and expected to work 60,000 direct labor hours. Its predetermined overhead rate would be:

$$\frac{\$270,000}{60,000} = \$4.50 \text{ per direct labor hour}$$

Since 1,350 direct labor hours were incurred for Job 691, the manufacturing overhead applied would be $6,075—or 1,350 hours times $4.50, as shown in Figure 23-1. The amounts charged to the various job order cost sheets would be totaled and recorded in the Work in Process account with an entry as follows (a total of 5,280 direct labor hours were worked in January):

Jan.	31	Work in Process Inventory	23,760	
		Manufacturing Overhead		23,760
		To record manufacturing overhead applied during January (5,280 hours at $4.50).		

The applied manufacturing overhead is credited to the Manufacturing Overhead account. The actual manufacturing overhead incurred is debited to the same account and to subsidiary ledger accounts established for the individual overhead items such as depreciation, rent, insurance, real estate taxes, utilities, indirect material, and indirect labor. Village Manufacturing Company already has recorded $1,680 for indirect material and $6,200 for indirect labor. Additional manufacturing overhead charges for January were:

Depreciation	$8,200
Rent	2,200
Insurance	850
Real estate taxes	600
Utilities	3,470
Total	$15,320

The total actual manufacturing overhead for January, 1984 was $23,200, and the following entry would be required to record the additional charges:

Jan.	31	Manufacturing Overhead	15,320	
		Accounts Payable		5,670
		Accumulated Depreciation		8,200
		Accrued Taxes Payable		600
		Prepaid Insurance		850
		To record the balance of actual		
		manufacturing overhead for January.		

OVERAPPLIED AND UNDERAPPLIED MANUFACTURING OVERHEAD

The actual manufacturing overhead and the applied manufacturing overhead *seldom are equal* at the end of any given month. If the applied amount exceeds the actual costs, the Manufacturing Overhead account will have a credit balance so the overhead will be **overapplied.** This means that more overhead is charged to work in process than is actually incurred. When the amount applied is less than the actual costs, a debit balance will exist and manufacturing overhead will be **underapplied.** In the Village Manufacturing Company example, manufacturing overhead is overapplied by $560, since $23,760 was applied to the jobs but only $23,200 actually was incurred. Ideally, the estimates used for the predetermined overhead rate will be accurate and any balance in the Manufacturing Overhead account will be small—particularly at the end of an annual period.

At the end of the year, any over/underapplied manufacturing overhead can be subtracted from or added to the annual cost of goods sold to reconcile the actual and applied amounts. Alternatively, the difference may be disposed of by prorating it among the ending work in process inventory, ending finished goods inventory, and annual cost of goods sold. In most cases, this proration is not practical unless the difference is exceptionally large because of the accounting time required, and the adjustment is made to cost of goods sold only. On an interim basis, the balance in the Manufacturing Overhead account usually *is carried forward on the balance sheet* from month to month as an asset (underapplied) or a liability (overapplied) until the end of the year. An underapplied balance is an asset because more overhead has been incurred than the amount charged to work in process. In contrast, an overapplied balance is shown as a liability because that amount has not actually been incurred. As such, the credit balance of $560 for Village Manufacturing Company would be shown as a liability on a balance sheet prepared as of January 31, 1984. If the same condition existed at the end of the year, the overapplied balance could be closed to cost of goods sold as follows:

Dec.	31	Manufacturing Overhead	560	
		Cost of Goods Sold		560
		To eliminate overapplied manufacturing overhead for the year.		

ACCOUNTING FOR THE COMPLETION OF A JOB

When a job is completed, its costs are totaled on the job order cost sheet and transferred from Work in Process Inventory to Finished Goods Inventory. In addition, the job order cost sheet is removed from the work in process subsidiary ledger, marked "completed," and refiled in the finished goods subsidiary ledger. In order to record the completion of Job 691, Village Manufacturing Company would make the following entry:

Jan.	31	Finished Goods Inventory	24,375	
		Work in Process Inventory		24,375
		To record the completion of Job 691 and transfer it to finished goods inventory.		

ACCOUNTING FOR THE SALE OF A JOB

Since perpetual inventories are maintained with job order costing, the total costs accumulated for each job are known at the point of completion. As we see in Figure 23-1, Job 691 consisted of 100 tables produced at a unit cost of $243.75. This information is important to management for decision-making functions such as *product pricing, production performance evaluation, profitability analysis, forecasts of future operations, and cost control.* Job order costing also permits the recording of the cost of goods sold at the time of sale. For example, if Job 691 is sold on credit for $39,000, the transaction would be recorded as follows:

Jan.	31	Accounts Receivable	39,000	
		Sales		39,000
		Cost of Goods Sold	24,375	
		Finished Goods Inventory		24,375
		To record the sale of Job 691.		

The job order cost sheet for Job 691 would be removed from the finished goods subsidiary ledger, marked "sold," and transferred to the cost of goods sold subsidiary ledger as the final step in the job order costing flow. Note that the difference between the selling price of Job 691 ($39,000) and the cost of goods sold ($24,375) is the job's gross profit ($14,625).

PROCESS COSTING

Process costing is used by manufacturing firms with the *continuous production flows* usually found in mass-production industries. The homogeneity of the production output prevents the separation of units or groups of units required in job order costing. Firms producing chemicals, rubber, plastics, petroleum, and pharmaceuticals rely on process costing. The technique also can be applied to accumulate costs for a number of nonmanufacturing activities such as the services performed by a utility, mail sorting in a post office, similar condominium units built by a contractor, and check clearing in a bank. The focal point of process costing is the **processing center** in which the work is performed during a specified period of time. A process costing center can be a department, a work station, an assembly line, or a division. Output usually is measured in such units as gallons, pounds, liters, tons, barrels, or square feet. Unit costs are computed for raw materials and conversion costs in each processing center. **Conversion costs** are defined as the combined total of the direct labor and manufacturing overhead costs incurred by a processing center. In its most basic form, process costing produces an average unit cost computed as:

$$\frac{\text{Total processing center costs for a period}}{\text{Total processing center output for a period}} = \text{Average unit cost}$$

This deceptively simple computation becomes more complicated in most cases for the following reasons:

1. When a processing center has work in process at the beginning or at the end of a period, its output cannot be measured solely in terms of the units actually completed. Costs will have been incurred for any partially completed units that are part of the center's output despite the fact they are not in a finished form.

2. The manufacturing cost elements usually will not be incurred uniformly during the production process. For example, the conversion costs that consist of direct labor and manufacturing overhead typically are consumed continuously during the production process, whereas raw materials normally are added at specific points in time. Consequently, a work in process inventory may be at different stages of completion for different cost elements.

CONCEPT OF EQUIVALENT UNITS

Since any unfinished work must be costed along with the finished units, production output in a process costing system usually cannot be expressed entirely in terms of physical or whole units. Unfinished work in process inventory on hand at the end of a period will require additional work and costs in the next period. Any beginning work in process inventory will include work and costs incurred in a previous period. The partial units cannot be equated with whole units since their form obviously is not the same. **Equivalent units** are used to overcome this problem and represent the number of units that would have been produced if all the work and costs had been applied to complete units. In other words, any partially processed inventories must be *restated* to the equivalent number of finished units they would represent before they are combined with the completed units. For example, 500 units that are 50% completed are the equivalent of 250 units that are 100% finished. Since no additional work is required for the completed units, they automatically become equivalent units. Consequently, the equivalent units for a particular period will be a measure of how many whole units of production are represented by the units finished plus the units partially finished.

The stage of completion for each manufacturing cost element must be evaluated separately in the calculation of equivalent units except in the rare case where all of the manufacturing costs are incurred uniformly. To illustrate the most basic form of equivalent units, assume that there is no beginning inventory and 108,000 units are entered into production. During the period, 90,000 units are finished and 18,000 are left in the ending work in process inventory, one-third finished as far as conversion costs are concerned. The equivalent units for the conversion costs would be 96,000 as shown below (90,000 units completed plus one-third of the 18,000 unfinished). If the conversion costs for the period are $336,000, the unit conversion cost would be $3.50. Assume further that raw materials are added at the beginning of the production process at a cost of $216,000. Since the stage of completion for raw materials is 100%, their equivalent units are 108,000 and the unit cost for material is $2.00.

	Conversion Costs	Raw Materials
Production units started	108,000	108,000
Production units finished	90,000	90,000
Equivalent units in ending inventory	6,000	18,000
Total equivalent units (a)	96,000	108,000
Total cost (b)	$336,000	$216,000
Unit cost (b ÷ a)	$3.50	$2.00

A beginning work in process inventory complicates the equivalent unit computational process since some of the work will have been performed in an earlier period and part of it will occur in the current period. A flow assumption must be made for costing purposes to determine which costs are transferred out of a processing center and which are left in ending inventory. The flow assumption concept is essentially the same one discussed in Chapter 9 and usually consists of two possibilities in a process costing situation: (1) the weighted average method or (2) the FIFO method. When the weighted average method is used, the units and costs in the beginning work in process inventory are *combined* with those of the current period. In contrast, the FIFO method requires a *distinction* between the units and costs of different periods.

We will limit coverage of process costing to the weighted average method because it is the simplest and is widely used. For example, assume that the beginning work in process inventory consists of 10,000 units at the 40% stage of completion for conversion costs, 108,000 units are entered into production, 100,000 units are completed during the period, and 18,000 units are one-third finished in the ending inventory. Since we do not distinguish between the units or costs in the beginning inventory and those of the current period with the weighted average method, we will have 106,000 equivalent units for the conversion costs (100,000 plus one-third of 18,000). The percentage of completion for the beginning inventory is ignored since the units and costs of the different periods are combined. If the conversion costs in the beginning work in process inventory are $7,500 and those of the current period are $151,500, the total of $159,000 is divided by 106,000 to calculate a unit cost of $1.50.

CONTROL DOCUMENT—COST OF PRODUCTION REPORT

A **cost of production report** serves as the control document in process costing since it is used to account for the costs charged to a processing center during a specified time period. The report usually is prepared on a monthly basis, although a shorter or longer period may be chosen if the benefits exceed the costs. A cost of production report such as the one shown in Figure 23-7 on page 919 has three sections:

1. A *physical flow section* shows the number of production units for which a processing center is responsible, their stage of completion, and where they are at the end of the period.
2. A *costs to be accounted for* section identifies the manufacturing cost elements for which the processing center is accountable, the equivalent units for each cost element, and the unit costs computed.
3. A *costs accounted for* section indicates what happened to the cost elements for which the processing center is responsible in terms of finished units and those left in process at the end of the period.

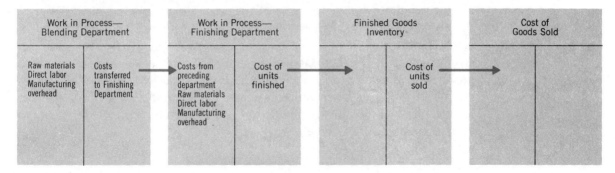

Figure 23-6
Process Costing Flow

PROCESS COSTING PROCEDURES

The flow of costs for a firm operating two departments, Blending and Finishing, with process costing is summarized in Figure 23-6. Raw materials, direct labor, and manufacturing overhead are accumulated within each processing center with procedures similar to those discussed earlier for job order costing. However, the absence of jobs simplifies the accounting significantly since costs are accumulated by processing centers instead of separate jobs. Detailed cost sheets are therefore not required. Costs are accounted for over longer periods such as a month rather than over the life of each job. Many of the employees work in only one department, so the labor time reporting requirements will be minimal. For example, a departmentalized payroll register may provide all the information required to distribute labor costs without the detail of labor time tickets. Also, the distinction between direct and indirect costs (materials and labor) required in job order costing is not necessary since the costing objective changes to a processing center. All of the material and labor costs are considered as being direct to the processing center. In some situations where manufacturing overhead and production output are relatively constant from month to month, actual overhead may be used for costing purposes rather than a predetermined overhead rate.

A Work in Process Inventory account is established for each processing center and is debited for the manufacturing costs incurred during a given period. Once the amount of each manufacturing cost is known, a total unit cost can be calculated. The total unit cost of the production output of each processing center is computed by dividing the costs accumulated for each cost element by its respective number of equivalent units and summing the resulting quotients. When multiple processing centers are involved, the *output of a given center becomes the input of a succeeding center,* costed with the total unit cost accumulated up to the point of transfer. The receiving center's Work in Process account is debited for the total cost transferred, and the transferring center's account is credited for the same amount. When the production process is completed, a Finished Goods Inventory account is debited and the final processing center's Work in Process account is credited. Cost of production reports are prepared for each processing center's periodic performance to monitor the physical flow of the production, the costs to be accounted for, and the costs accounted for.

ILLUSTRATION OF PROCESS COSTING

The Marco Chemical Company produces a single product, *Stayclean,* used for swimming-pool maintenance. Two departments, Blending and Finishing, are operated as processing centers with the output of the Blending Department becoming the input of the Finishing Department. Raw materials in chemical powder form are issued at the start of production in the Blending Department and at the end of the processing in the Finishing Department. Conversion costs (direct labor and manufacturing overhead) are incurred uniformly throughout the processing in each of the departments. The following data summarize the January, 1984 operating performance of the two departments:

Beginning Work in Process Data

	Blending Department	Finishing Department
Units in beginning inventory	8,000 gallons	10,000 gallons
Raw materials	$12,000	—
Conversion costs	$16,000	$14,500
Cost from preceding department (Blending)		$55,000

January Processing Data

	Blending Department	Finishing Department
Units started	106,000 gallons	108,000 gallons
Units finished	108,000 gallons	100,000 gallons
Units in ending inventory	6,000 gallons	18,000 gallons
Raw materials	$159,000	$160,000
Conversion costs	$424,000	$292,900
Cost from preceding department (Blending)		$594,000

The beginning and ending work in process inventories of the Blending Department are one-half and one-third complete, respectively, in terms of the conversion costs of that department. The same stages of completion prevail for the beginning and ending work in process inventories of the Finishing Department. The January cost of production reports for the two departments are shown in Figures 23-7 and 23-8, respectively. Essentially the same procedures and concepts are required to prepare either report so we will concentrate on the basic features of the cost of production report for the Finishing Department.

The physical flow schedule shows the units (gallons) for which the Finishing Department is accountable as well as their disposition. A total of 118,000 units are involved, with 100,000 completed and 18,000 remaining in the ending inventory—one-third complete. The costs to be accounted for section identifies the costs incurred for the various cost elements, their equivalent units, and the average unit cost calculations. The weighted average method is used for inventory costing. All units are finished as far as the preceding department (Blending) costs are concerned, so their equivalent units amount to 118,000. Since the raw materials are not added until the end of the process, none are

Figure 23-7
Cost of Production Report

MARCO CHEMICAL COMPANY
Blending Department
Cost of Production Report
Month Ended January 31, 1984

Physical Flow Schedule
Work in process, January 1 .... 8,000 gallons (½ complete)
Units started .... 106,000 gallons
Units finished .... 108,000 gallons
Work in process, January 31 .... 6,000 gallons (⅓ complete)

| Costs to Be Accounted For | | | | Equiv. | Unit |
Cost Element	Beginning	Current	Total	Units	Cost
Raw materials	$12,000	$159,000	$171,000	114,000	$1.50
Conversion costs	16,000	424,000	440,000	110,000	4.00
Total	$28,000	$583,000	$611,000		$5.50

Costs Accounted For
Units transferred to Finishing Department
(108,000 gal. × $5.50) $594,000
Work in process, January 31
Raw materials (6,000 gal. × $1.50) $9,000
Conversion costs (6,000 gal. × ⅓ × $4.00) .... 8,000 ... 17,000
Total $611,000

Figure 23-8
Cost of Production
Report

MARCO CHEMICAL COMPANY
Finishing Department
Cost of Production Report
Month Ended January 31, 1984

Physical Flow Schedule

Work in process, January 1	10,000 gallons (½ complete)
Units started	108,000 gallons
Units finished	100,000 gallons
Work in process, January 31	18,000 gallons (⅓ complete)

Costs to Be Accounted For

Cost Element	Beginning	Current	Total	Equiv. Units	Unit Cost
Raw materials	$ 0	$160,000	$160,000	100,000	$1.60
Conversion costs	14,500	292,900	307,400	106,000	2.90
Cost from preceding department	55,000	594,000	649,000	118,000	5.50
Total	$69,500	$1,046,900	$1,116,400		$10.00

Costs Accounted For

Units transferred to Finished Goods (100,000 gal. × $10.00)		$1,000,000
Work in process, January 31		
Raw materials	–0–	
Conversion costs (18,000 gal. × ⅓ × $2.90)	$17,400	
Cost from preceding department (18,000 gal. × $5.50)	99,000	116,400
Total		$1,116,400

---

in the ending inventory and the equivalent units are equal to those actually finished, or 100,000. The equivalent units for the conversion costs are the total of the finished units plus one-third of those in process at the end of January, or 106,000. Again, the percentage of completion for the beginning inventory is irrelevant because the weighted average method is used. Unit costs are computed by dividing the total costs accumulated for each element by their respective number of equivalent units. The total unit cost after both departments are finished with production is $10. Note that the unit cost of $5.50 incurred in the Blending Department is applied to each of the units transferred to the Finishing Department, as shown on both cost of production reports.

The final section of the report shows the accountability for the departmental cost performance. The Finishing Department has costs of $1,116,400 for which it is accountable. The units transferred to finished goods are costed at $1,000,000, and $116,400 is left in the ending inventory that will be completed in February. Note that separate computations must be made for the various cost elements in the ending inventory because of the different equivalent units and unit costs. The ending work in process inventory of $116,400 will be shown as a current asset on the balance sheet as of January 31, 1984, along with that amounting to $17,000 in the Blending Department.

We assume that 80,000 gallons of Stayclean are sold by Marco Chemical Company on credit at a price of $18 per gallon. The remaining 20,000 gallons produced during January will be left in finished goods inventory at a cost of $200,000. Essentially the same journal entries shown earlier for job order costing are made to record the work in process costs of each department. The journal entries required to transfer units from the Blending Department to the Finishing Department, record the finished goods, and record the sales for January are:

Jan.	31	Work in Process—Finishing	594,000	
		Work in Process—Blending		594,000
		To record the transfer of inventory from the Blending Department to the Finishing Department.		
		Finished Goods Inventory	1,000,000	
		Work in Process—Finishing		1,000,000
		To record the finished goods inventory.		
		Accounts Receivable	1,440,000	
		Sales		1,440,000
		Cost of Goods Sold	800,000	
		Finished Goods Inventory		800,000
		To record the sale of 80,000 gallons of product.		

GLOSSARY

CONVERSION COSTS. The combined total of direct labor and manufacturing overhead costs incurred by a processing center (p. 914).

COST ACCOUNTING. A specialized type of accounting that enables a manufacturing firm to accumulate product costs with a perpetual inventory flow (p. 903).

COST OF PRODUCTION REPORT. The control document used in process costing to account for the manufacturing costs of a processing center during a specified time period (p. 916).

EQUIVALENT UNITS. A measure of how many whole units of production are represented by the units finished plus the units partially finished in a process costing operation (p. 915).

JOB.   A product or group of products being produced when job order costing is used (p. 904).

JOB ORDER COSTING.   A cost accounting system with which costs are accumulated for a job (p. 904).

JOB ORDER COST SHEET.   The control document used with job order costing to provide a detailed listing of the manufacturing costs related to the production of a job (p. 905).

LABOR TIME TICKET.   A record of how much time an employee spends on a job or an overhead assignment (p. 909).

MATERIAL REQUISITION FORM.   A record of the amount of raw material requisitioned from the storeroom for a job or as indirect material (p. 907).

OVERAPPLIED MANUFACTURING OVERHEAD.   The excess of the manufacturing overhead applied to work in process with a predetermined rate during a given period over the actual manufacturing overhead incurred (p. 912).

PREDETERMINED OVERHEAD RATE.   The rate determined by dividing estimated manufacturing overhead for a period by some measure of the estimated production activity and used to apply overhead to work in process (p. 911).

PROCESS COSTING.   A cost accounting system with which costs are accumulated for a processing center during a specified period (p. 914).

PROCESSING CENTER.   A segment of the manufacturing operation in which costs are accumulated with process costing (p. 914).

UNDERAPPLIED MANUFACTURING OVERHEAD.   The excess of the actual manufacturing overhead incurred during a particular period over the manufacturing overhead applied to work in process (p. 912).

DISCUSSION QUESTIONS

1. What is a cost accounting system and what are its benefits?
2. How are perpetual inventories maintained with a cost accounting system?
3. Distinguish between job order costing and process costing.
4. What is a job order cost sheet?
5. Identify the basic business forms required with job order costing.
6. What is a predetermined overhead rate and why is it used by most manufacturing firms?
7. Johnson Manufacturing Company applies overhead to jobs on the basis of 60% of direct labor cost. Job 691 has been charged with $8,400 of direct labor cost and $6,200 of direct materials. If 100 units were produced in Job 691, what is the cost per unit?
8. What is underapplied manufacturing overhead? Overapplied manufacturing overhead? How would each be disposed of at the end of a period?
9. When a job order costing system is used, does indirect labor become a part of work in process inventory? Explain.
10. What type of industry is likely to use job order costing? Give some examples.

11. What type of industry is likely to use process costing? Give some examples.
12. What is meant by the average unit cost in process costing?
13. What are equivalent units and why are they necessary with process costing?
14. Decker Company began the period with no work in process inventory, started producing 75,000 units, and had 10,000 units in ending work in process inventory that were one-fourth finished in terms of conversion costs. How many equivalent units were involved for the conversion costs that are incurred uniformly throughout the process?
15. What is the role of a cost of production report? What are the three major sections of such a report?
16. Distinguish between the costs to be accounted for and the costs accounted for in a process costing application.
17. How is the cost of the ending work in process inventory computed in a cost of production report?
18. Are the accounting procedures required with process costing usually more or less detailed than those used with job order costing? Explain.

EXERCISES

Exercise 23-1 (Use of Predetermined Overhead Rates)

The estimated cost and operating data for two manufacturing companies are presented below:

	Company	
	A	**B**
Units produced	26,000	17,000
Manufacturing overhead	$ 70,200	$145,860
Direct labor hours	42,000	56,100
Direct labor cost	$190,000	$252,400

Company A applies overhead on the basis of units of production while Company B uses direct labor hours. During the past year, Company A actually produced 24,000 units and incurred overhead costs of $63,000. Company B's actual overhead costs were $150,100 and 57,000 direct labor hours were used.

Required:
A. Calculate the predetermined overhead rate of each company.
B. Determine whether the overhead was overapplied or underapplied for each company.

Exercise 23-2 (Job Order Costing Procedures)

Job order cost data for jobs 1–10 are shown below. The costs were incurred by the Carmichael Company during April and May, the firm's first two months of operations.

Job Order No.	Costs as of May 1	May Production Costs
1	$4,200	
2	3,700	
3	2,600	
4	1,900	$ 800
5	2,200	2,100
6		3,700
7		4,610
8		1,540
9		1,290
10		790

Jobs 1–3 were completed in April.
Jobs 4–7 were completed in May.
Jobs 8–10 were incomplete as of May 31.
Jobs 1, 3, 5, 7 were sold during May.

Required:
Calculate the following costs:
A. Work in process, May 1
B. Work in process, May 31
C. Finished goods, May 1
D. Finished goods, May 31
E. Cost of goods sold for May

Exercise 23-3 (Job Order Costing Procedures)

The Zeplin Furniture Company utilizes a job order cost system. The April cost and operating data were as follows:

Raw materials purchased	$143,000
Direct labor costs	148,000
Raw materials issued for production	133,000
Actual overhead incurred	111,000
(Included is depreciation of $11,000)	
Cost of goods manufactured	381,000
Machine hours	27,000
Sales on account	420,000

The company applies overhead to production at a rate of $4 per machine hour. The beginning raw materials inventory was $16,000; the beginning work in process inventory was $27,000. The beginning and ending finished goods inventories were $40,000 and $52,000, respectively.

Required:
A. Prepare journal entries to record the April transactions.
B. Was overhead overapplied or underapplied for the month of April?
C. Calculate the ending balances of raw materials and work in process. (*Hint:* Prepare T accounts for the inventory accounts.)

Exercise 23-4 (Fundamentals of Process Costing)

The Corwin Company produces a single product using several processing departments. The June cost and operating data for the first department is presented below.

Beginning work in process	–0–
Units started in Department 1	34,000
Units transferred to Department 2	28,000
Materials cost	$307,200
Conversion costs	$165,200

The work in process in Department 1 at June 30 is 25% complete as to conversion costs and two-thirds complete as to materials.

Required:
A. Calculate the equivalent units in Department 1 for materials and conversion costs.
B. Calculate the total and unit cost of goods transferred to Department 2 and the cost of work in process inventory in Department 1 at June 30.

Exercise 23-5 (Process Costing with Beginning Inventory)

The Macedon Company produces plastic novelty gifts in a single molding process department. Materials are added at the beginning of the molding process and conversion costs are incurred continuously throughout the process. As of June 1, there were 6,000 units in beginning inventory at a cost of $48,000. This cost was comprised of $30,000 for materials and $18,000 for conversion costs. The beginning inventory was 50% complete as to conversion costs.

During June, raw material costs amounted to $60,000 and conversion costs were $84,000. During the month, 12,000 units were started in the molding process and 14,000 units were transferred to finished goods. The ending inventory in the molding process was 75% complete as to conversion costs.

Required:
Calculate the cost of the units transferred from the molding department and those left in ending inventory. The Macedon Company uses the weighted average method to calculate the cost of equivalent units.

PROBLEMS

Problem 23-1 (Job Order Costing and Manufacturing Overhead)

The Woodall Company uses a job order cost system to control production costs in its two departments. The job cost card for Job 242 shows the following data:

	Department 1	Department 2
Direct labor hours	1,000	950
Direct labor cost	$4,500	$4,845
Raw materials	$3,000	$4,300
Machine hours	50	62

The company applies overhead to production on the basis of direct labor cost in Department 1 and machine hours in Department 2. The annual budget showed the following estimated production data:

	Department 1	Department 2
Direct labor hours	130,000	97,000
Direct labor cost	$ 520,000	$485,000
Machine hours	6,500	6,790
Overhead costs	$1,664,000	$156,170

Required:
A. Calculate the overhead rate for each department.
B. Calculate the total cost of Job 242.
C. If actual machine hours used in Department 2 were 6,800 and actual overhead was $160,500, was overhead overapplied or underapplied?

Problem 23-2 (Job Order Costing Procedures)

The Speculator Products Company uses a job order cost system. Cost and operating data for 1986 are as follows:

1. Total payroll incurred—$81,000, of which $21,000 was indirect labor and the remainder direct.
2. Raw materials purchased—$85,000.
3. Raw materials issued to production—$89,000; $9,000 of these materials were indirect.
4. Overhead is applied at 140% of direct labor cost.
5. Factory expenses paid:

Utilities	$12,000
Rent	24,000
Supplies	11,000
Insurance	7,000
Miscellaneous	10,000

6. Factory depreciation—$8,000.
7. Jobs completed and transferred to finished goods—$145,000.
8. Jobs with a cost of $140,000 were sold for $218,000 on account.
9. The beginning inventories for 1986 were: raw materials—$9,000; work in process—$20,000; finished goods—$5,000.

Required:
A. Prepare the journal entries to record the transactions.
B. Calculate the ending balances in raw materials, work in process, and finished goods.
C. Was overhead underapplied or overapplied for 1986?

Problem 23-3 (Journal Entries for Job Order Costing)

The Ryan Company uses a job order cost system. On January 1, 1984, job orders number 33 and 34 were in process with costs of $120 and $155, respectively. Part of the production data for January is as follows:

1. Factory payroll of $503.30 was paid. Each factory worker earns $7.00 per hour. Ignore income taxes and other payroll deductions.
2. The direct labor was distributed as follows:

Job 33	$105.00
Job 34	119.00
Job 35	129.50
Job 36	107.80
Indirect labor	42.00

3. Raw materials requisitioned were charged to the following jobs:

Job 33	$180.00
Job 34	205.00
Job 35	221.00
Job 36	195.00
General factory use	65.00

4. Additional overhead costs incurred and paid during the month—$41.00.
5. Overhead is applied at $2.10 per direct labor hour.
6. Jobs 33, 34, 35 were completed and transferred to finished goods.
7. Jobs 33 and 35 were sold at cost plus 40%.

Required:
Prepare the journal entries to record the January data.

Problem 23-4 (Process Costing Procedures)

The L. L. Frelier Company manufactures suntan lotion and utilizes a process cost accounting system. The lotion is produced in the blending department and then is transferred to the bottling department. The company assigns overhead using the relationship between direct labor costs and overhead costs. The production budget for 1986 estimated direct labor costs of $210,000, raw material usage of $350,000, and factory overhead of $336,000. The inventory balances as of October 1, 1986 were:

Raw materials	$25,000
Work in process—Blending	40,000
Work in process—Bottling	30,000
Finished Goods	19,000

During October, the following transactions took place:

1. Raw materials transferred to blending—$45,000
   Raw materials transferred to bottling—35,000
2. Direct labor costs incurred by blending—42,000
   Direct labor costs incurred by bottling—31,000
   Indirect labor—29,000
3. Other production expenses for October were:

Rent	15,000
Supplies	12,000
Utilities	21,000

Depreciation	24,000
Repairs	14,000

4. Goods with an assigned cost of $125,000 were transferred from blending to bottling.
5. Goods with an assigned cost of $205,000 were transferred from bottling to finished goods.
6. Finished goods with an assigned cost of $190,000 were sold for $228,000.
7. Raw material purchases were $70,000.
8. Overhead was applied to each department.

Required:
A. Prepare journal entries to record the October transactions. Use a single manufacturing overhead account and assume all expenses were paid when incurred.
B. Calculate the ending work in process inventory balances in each department for both raw materials and finished goods.
C. Was overhead underapplied or overapplied in October?

Problem 23-5 (Calculating Unit Costs with Process Costing)

The Monroe Brass Company produces brass products in three consecutive processes: cutting, molding, and packaging. Materials are added at two points—at the beginning of the cutting process and at the end of the packaging process. At the end of the month, 6,000 units were transferred to finished goods.

Production data in units are as follows:

	Beginning Inventory	% Complete	Units Started	Ending Inventory	% Complete
Cutting	3,000	30	11,000	4,000	25
Molding	1,500	40	?	3,500	20
Packaging	?	30	?	2,200	30

Beginning inventory costs are:

	Cutting	Molding	Packaging
Prior department	—	$17,400	$2,670
Materials	$25,500	—	—
Conversion costs	2,790	1,050	288
	$28,290	$18,450	$2,958

Production costs incurred are:

	Cutting	Molding	Packaging
Materials	$93,500	—	$ 9,000
Conversion cost	31,310	$14,175	5,040

Required:
Calculate the unit cost of production for each process. The Monroe Brass Company uses the weighted average method.

Problem 23-6 (Process Costing with Beginning Inventory)
The Browncroft Company manufactures spaghetti sauce using three processes: blending, cooking, and packaging. Materials are added continuously in the blending process and at the beginnng of the packaging process. All conversion costs are incurred continuously.

The beginning inventory costs for September are:

	Blending	Cooking	Packaging
Costs from previous departments	—	$49,800	$ 91,800
Raw materials	$ 9,600	—	10,200
Conversion costs	7,000	6,000	2,720
Total cost	$16,600	$55,800	$104,720

The production costs for September are:

	Blending	Cooking	Packaging
Raw materials	$157,200.00	—	$40,800.00
Conversion costs	114,625.00	$81,812.50	62,080.00

Production data in gallons are:

	Beginning Inventory	% Complete	Ending Inventory	% Complete	Gallons Completed and Transferred
Blending	20,000	20	15,000	30	65,000
Cooking	12,000	40	9,000	25	68,000
Packaging	17,000	20	8,000	50	77,000

Required:
A. Calculate the unit cost of the gallons completed in each of the three processes using the weighted average method.
B. Prepare a cost of production report for the September operating performance of the Blending Department.

ALTERNATE PROBLEMS

Problem 23-1A (Job Order Costing and Manufacturing Overhead)
The Humbolt Company utilizes a job order cost system to control production costs in its two departments. Manufacturing overhead is applied on the basis of machine hours

in Department A and labor cost in Department B. The data compiled for the annual budget included the following:

	Department A	Department B
Machine hours	6,300	8,200
Direct labor cost	$106,250	$174,240
Direct labor hours	12,500	19,800
Overhead costs	$170,100	$453,024

The job cost card for job 1498 shows the following data:

	Department A	Department B
Machine hours	43	49
Direct labor cost	$748	$845
Direct labor hours	88	96
Raw materials	$521	$601

Required:

A. Calculate the manufacturing overhead rate for each department.

B. Calculate the total cost of job 1498.

C. If actual labor cost used in Department B was $176,100 and actual overhead was $457,200, was manufacturing overhead overapplied or underapplied?

Problem 23-2A (Job Order Costing Procedures)

The controller of the Hoadley Company has asked you to journalize the following transactions, which took place during May, 1985. The company uses a job order cost system.

1. Raw materials purchased—$15,000.
2. Total payroll included $18,000 of direct labor and $4,000 of indirect labor.
3. Overhead is applied at 125% of direct labor cost.
4. Raw materials issued to production—$14,000 direct materials and $2,000 indirect materials.
5. Factory expenses paid:

Rent	$2,700
Supplies	3,000
Insurance	2,500
Utilities	4,200

6. Factory depreciation—$3,500.
7. Jobs completed and transferred to finished goods—$53,100.
8. Jobs with a cost of $52,000 were sold for $65,000 cash.
9. The beginning inventories included:

Raw materials	$3,500
Work in process	5,600
Finished goods	4,800

Required:
A. Prepare the journal entries to record the transactions.
B. Calculate the ending balances in work in process, raw materials, and finished goods. (*Hint:* Prepare T accounts.)
C. Was overhead underapplied or overapplied in May 1985?

Problem 23-3A (Journal Entries for Job Order Costing)

The Dayton Company accounts for its manufacturing costs using a job order cost system and has provided the following production data for part of its performance during the month of June:

1. Job order number 103 was in process as of June 1 with a cost of $85.
2. Raw materials requisitioned were charged to the following jobs:

Job 103	$70.00
Job 104	65.00
Job 105	95.00
General factory use	35.00

3. Factory payroll of $243.75 was paid. Each factory worker earns $7.50 per hour. Ignore income taxes and other payroll deductions.
4. Factory payroll was distributed as follows:

Job 103	$69.00
Job 104	81.00
Job 105	73.50
Indirect labor	20.25

5. Additional overhead costs incurred and paid during the month were $43.00.
6. Overhead is applied at $3.35 per direct labor hour.
7. Jobs 103 and 104 were completed and transferred to finished goods.
8. Job 103 was sold at cost plus 50%.

Required:
Prepare the journal entries to record the transactions.

Problem 23-4A (Process Costing Procedures)

The Country Craft Company produces quilting kits using two processes—cutting and packaging.

The company uses a process cost accounting system and overhead is assigned using the relationship between direct labor costs and overhead costs. The production budget for 1985 estimated raw material usage of $425,000, manufacturing overhead of $308,000, and direct labor costs of $220,000.

During March, the following transactions were accounted for:

1. Raw materials transferred to cutting—$25,000
   Raw materials transferred to packaging—32,000
2. Direct labor costs incurred by cutting—18,000
   Direct labor costs incurred by packaging—23,000

3. Other production expenses for March were:

Supplies	$29,000
Depreciation	18,700
Repairs	7,100
Insurance	2,000

4. Goods with an assigned cost of $70,000 were transferred from cutting to packaging.
5. Overhead was applied in each department.
6. Raw material purchases were $65,000.
7. Goods with an assigned cost of $155,000 were transferred from packaging to finished goods.
8. Finished goods with an assigned cost of $161,000 were sold for $183,500.
9. Beginning inventory as of March 1 was comprised of the following amounts:

Raw materials	$20,000
Work in process—cutting	21,000
Work in process—packaging	25,000
Finished goods	16,000

Required:
A. Prepare the journal entries to record the March transactions. Assume all expenses were paid when incurred and use a single manufacturing overhead account.
B. Calculate the ending work in process inventory balances in each department and finished goods.
C. Was overhead underapplied or overapplied in March?

Problem 23-5A (Calculating Unit Costs with Process Costing)

The Bates Company produces its products in three consecutive processes: fabricating, finishing, and packaging. Materials are added continuously in the fabricating department, at the end of the finishing department, and at the beginning of the packaging department.

Production data in units are as follows:

	Beginning Inventory	% Complete	Units Started	Ending Inventory	% Complete
Fabricating	2,000	20	10,000	3,000	30
Finishing	?	40	?	4,000	25
Packaging	1,500	25	8,000	?	20

During the month, 7,000 units were transferred to finished goods. Production costs incurred during the month are:

	Fabricating	Finishing	Packaging
Materials	$80,750	33,600	$9,600
Conversion costs	68,875	28,860	9,975

Beginning inventory costs are:

	Fabricating	Finishing	Packaging
Prior department	—	$47,250	$35,475
Materials	3,400	—	1,800
Conversion costs	2,900	4,440	525
Totals	$6,300	$51,690	$37,800

Required:
Calculate the unit cost of production for each process. The Bates Company uses the
weighted average method.

Problem 23-6A (Process Costing with Beginning Inventory)

The Brettan Company produces pewter products in three consecutive processes: molding, polishing, and packaging. Materials are added at the beginning of the molding
process and at the end of the packaging process. All conversion costs are incurred
continuously in each department.

The production data in units for May are:

	Beginning Inventory	% Complete	Ending Inventory	% Complete	Units Completed and Transferred
Molding	8,000	30	7,000	40	10,000
Polishing	6,000	20	5,000	30	11,000
Packaging	4,000	25	6,000	20	9,000

The beginning inventory costs are:

	Molding	Polishing	Packaging
Costs from previous departments	—	$20,400	$20,600
Raw materials	$12,800	—	—
Conversion costs	4,320	2,100	1,350
Totals	$17,120	$22,500	$21,950

The production costs for May are:

	Molding	Polishing	Packaging
Raw materials	$14,400	–0–	$13,500
Conversion costs	18,720	$19,775	12,420

Required:

A. Calculate the unit cost of the units completed in each department.

B. Prepare a cost of production report for the May operating performance of the packaging department.

CASE FOR CHAPTER 23

Decision Problem (Evaluating Problems with Fluctuating Unit Costs)

The Fine Toy Company produces a single product that is sold to retail stores throughout the Southeast. The demand for the toy is very seasonal, with peak retail sales in the summer months and at Christmastime. Joe O'Malley, the president of the company, is very concerned because of the variation in unit costs from quarter to quarter and wants to know whether there is a better way to determine unit product costs than the method currently being used. Unit costs are computed quarterly by dividing the total manufacturing costs for a quarter by the units produced during the quarter. The company's estimated costs and production, by quarter, for the next year are:

	First Quarter	Second Quarter	Third Quarter	Fourth Quarter
Direct materials	$ 20,000	$ 40,000	$ 20,000	$ 80,000
Direct labor	40,000	80,000	40,000	160,000
Variable manufacturing overhead	12,000	24,000	12,000	48,000
Fixed manufacturing overhead	160,000	160,000	160,000	160,000
Totals	$232,000	$304,000	$232,000	$448,000
Units produced	10,000	20,000	10,000	40,000
Unit cost	$ 23.20	$ 15.20	$ 23.20	$ 11.20

Required:

What suggestions would you make to Mr. O'Malley to improve the way the firm computes unit costs?

PART SEVEN
FINANCIAL PLANNING AND CONTROLLING OPERATIONS

CHAPTER 24
FINANCIAL PLANNING
AND CONTROL
WITH BUDGETING

OVERVIEW AND OBJECTIVES

This chapter presents the basic concepts of budgeting for a business. When you have completed the chapter, you should understand:

- The basic nature of financial planning and control (pp. 936–937).
- The importance of goal congruence for an organization (pp. 937–938).
- The benefits of budgeting (pp. 938–940).
- The significance of an accurate sales forecast (pp. 940–941).
- The steps involved in preparing a master budget (pp. 940–942).
- The preparation and use of each of the individual budgets comprising the master budget (pp. 943–955).
- The difference between an operating budget and a financial budget (pp. 941–942).
- The use of budgets for performance reporting and financial control (pp. 955–957).

A budget is a detailed plan that shows how resources are expected to be acquired and used during a specified time period. Virtually every person and every organization use some form of budget for an efficient and effective use of scarce resources. A budget prepared by a business typically is much more detailed and formalized than one used by an individual, although all budgets serve the same basic purpose. The process of preparing a budget, called budgeting, is an essential phase of managing a business in an efficient and effective manner. Budget information is utilized throughout the management process discussed in Chapter 21, although the primary application is in the planning and controlling functions.

A budget as a management tool can be compared to the architectural drawings used by a contractor to build a house. If the contractor is to build the house efficiently (with the proper amount of resources in the form of labor and materials) and effectively (so the results are compatible with the predetermined specifications), he or she must follow the blueprint drawings carefully to guide the building process from beginning to end. A budget serves management in the same manner by providing a formal plan for the firm's future course of action according to well-defined organizational goals. Initially, budgeting identifies certain financial and operating targets, which become management's goals for the future. These targets provide the direction for the firm's activities and transactions, which are expected to lead to satisfactory profit results. Then, as the actual performance occurs, it is monitored and checked against the related targets for control purposes. When significant variances between the actual and planned performances are found, they are investigated and corrected whenever possible through the responsibility accounting procedures introduced in Chapter 21. Budgeting and responsibility accounting are closely related, since the budget provides many of the performance targets used in responsibility accounting. While the primary emphasis of this chapter is on budgeting for a business, many of the concepts and procedures are useful in nonbusiness activities as well.

IMPORTANCE OF GOAL CONGRUENCE

Every organization must be certain that all of its segments work toward common goals. Since the performances of the various segments will be interrelated in many ways, each segment manager must know not only his or her own role but also how it interacts with the rest of the organization. For example, the accounting, finance, marketing, personnel, production, and purchasing functions of a manufacturing firm must be coordinated. The same is true for the agencies of a government, the services of a bank, or the departments of a hospital. Otherwise, inefficiency and ineffectiveness will develop in the allocation and utilization of scarce resources.

This coordination will not occur automatically because individuals within an organization and the organization as a whole may have different goals. For example, consider the potential conflict that could develop in a manufacturing firm from differing inventory policies of the managers responsible for production and marketing. The production manager is concerned primarily with using the manufacturing facilities efficiently and maintaining stable inventory levels. In contrast, the marketing manager is concerned primarily with having enough inventory available at all times to meet customers' demands—even if large variations in sales volume occur between periods. The stable inventory levels and fluctuating sales demand are not compatible, and a compromise becomes necessary. Without a formal coordination system, individual managers would tend to operate in different directions and in many cases against the best interests of the organization. This problem becomes increasingly difficult as an organization grows and management responsibility is delegated to more people. Goal congruence occurs when the managers of a firm accept the organizational goals as their own. The various activities of a business must be planned and controlled with the full participation and support of the managers responsible for them.

BENEFITS OF BUDGETING

Achieving satisfactory profits in today's competitive and uncertain business world is no easy matter. For example, the average profit margin for large corporations in the United States is only about 5%, which means that the typical company has approximately *five cents out of every sales dollar* with which to pay dividends, retire debt, and reinvest in the business. The profit performances of 10 large corporations biannually from 1974 to 1980 are shown in Figure 24-1 to illustrate how small corporate profits really are. The profit

Figure 24-1
Profitability Performance of 10 Large Corporations

Company	Profit Margin Percentage				Return on Total Capital Percentage			
	1974	1976	1978	1980	1974	1976	1978	1980
American Airlines	.9	2.7	4.5	def.*	2.4	5.5	8.8	def.
Chase Manhattan Corp.	4.8	3.3	4.2	4.7	8.8	5.2	7.7	11.4
Ford Motor Company	1.7	3.5	4.1	def.	5.7	12.3	16.9	def.
General Foods	3.7	4.1	3.5	3.7	10.4	14.0	13.4	13.2
Holiday Inns	3.8	3.6	5.6	7.6	6.0	5.8	8.7	12.3
IBM Corporation	14.7	14.6	14.7	13.2	19.7	19.7	22.4	20.4
Marathon Oil	6.1	5.0	4.3	4.5	16.0	14.2	10.2	13.6
Pabst Brewing	3.1	4.2	1.6	1.3	6.8	12.0	3.8	3.7
Sears Roebuck	4.8	4.2	4.7	2.2	10.8	9.5	10.5	6.5
Texas Instruments	6.1	5.6	5.6	5.3	17.4	14.3	17.5	21.1

*Indicates a net loss for the period.
Source: "Annual Report on American Industry," *Forbes* (January 1975), 1977, 1979, 1981.

margin measure is calculated by dividing net income by net sales; the return on total capital is found by dividing the total capital invested in a business (long-term debt and owners' equity) into the net income. Little room for error exists with these tight profit results, and management must do everything possible to operate efficiently and effectively. A firm's financial performance must be planned and controlled as thoroughly as possible with sound budgeting procedures if acceptable profit results are to be achieved. The major benefits of budgeting that can ultimately lead to a profitable operation are as follows:

1. It *forces* management to plan ahead and anticipate the future on a systematic basis. Most managers are very busy with their day-to-day activities and may resist formalized planning unless budgeting is part of their job. Nevertheless, every successful manager knows what he or she wants to accomplish and when it should be done. The regularity of the budgeting process forces managers to formalize their thinking and participate in the goal-setting activities of the firm.

2. It provides management with *realistic performance targets* against which actual results can be compared with responsibility accounting. Management by exception is performed by identifying significant variances that require corrective action if the firm is to achieve its goals. Consequently, the budget plays an important role in controlling the acquisition and use of resources.

3. It *coordinates* the various segments of the organization and makes each manager aware of how the different activities fit together. Goal congruence can be achieved by the unifying effect budgeting has on an organization—particularly when it is combined with responsibility accounting.

4. It serves as a *communication device* with which the various managers can exchange information concerning goals, ideas, and achievements. Since direct contact will decrease as an organization increases in size, a formal communication network is required. Budgeting enables the managers to interact and develop an awareness of how each of their activities contributes to the firm's overall operation.

5. It furnishes management with *motivation* in the form of the goals to be achieved. Few people work for the sheer joy of it; most of us need some form of stimulus to work hard and maintain an enthusiastic attitude toward our job. A properly used budget is a motivating device that provides performance targets against which actual results can be evaluated. Unfortunately, an improperly prepared budget may have an adverse effect on the motivation of managers—who may then criticize the process as being unfair. Two key aspects of a correct application of budgeting are (a) that the budgeted level of performance should be attainable with a reasonably efficient amount of effort and (b) that the managers who will be evaluated with the budget data should participate actively in their development. Man-

agers will be more highly motivated with *self-imposed* budget estimates than with ones established by someone at a higher level in the organization.

FINANCIAL PLANNING WITH BUDGETING

The primary objective of the financial planning phase of budgeting is to identify how management intends to acquire and use the firm's resources during a budget period in order to achieve organizational goals. A *master budget* consisting of several interrelated budgets provides the basis for financial planning. The major steps in developing a master budget are the following:

1. Management identifies the organizational goals for the budget period, including those that are financially oriented such as desired net income, profit margins, return on investment, liquidity, share of the market, and financial position.
2. The managers of the various responsibility centers participate in the development of the parts of the master budget for which they are accountable.
3. Sales for the budget period are forecast.
4. Cost of goods sold and operating expenses for the budget period are estimated.
5. Capital expenditures for the budget period are identified.
6. Accrual accounting is converted to a cash basis to determine cash receipts and disbursements. Any nonoperating sources or uses of cash (such as the sale of stock, issue of debt, payment of dividends, or retirement of debt) are considered.
7. A set of estimated financial statements is prepared based on the initial version of the financial performance projections.
8. The estimated financial performance results are compared with the organizational goals, and revisions are made wherever necessary to make the final version of the budget compatible with the overall goals.

SALES FORECAST

An accurate sales forecast is the cornerstone of successful budgeting since virtually everything else is dependent on it. The sales information provides the basis for preparing a sales budget, predicting cash receipts, and constructing a variety of expense budgets. At the same time, the sales forecast usually is subject to more uncertainty than any other aspect of budgeting. Unless a business firm has a large number of unfilled orders that guarantee future sales or a highly consistent demand for its products or services, sales forecasting will be complicated by the uncertainties of the future. The general economy, industry conditions, effect of proposed advertising, actions of competitors, consumer buying habits, population changes, and technological developments are factors that influence the reliability of a sales forecast.

A combination of several methods can be used to forecast sales. The most common methods are predictions by members of the sales staff, group estimates prepared by top management, and the use of statistical or mathematical techniques. The sales staff generally is aware of current market conditions and should participate actively in the preparation of the sales forecast. Field surveys can be conducted to predict revenue by products or services, geographical areas, customers, and sales representatives. In large businesses, a market research staff may be available to conduct the field studies of consumer demand and develop sales revenue estimates.

All members of the top management team—including production, finance, purchasing, and administrative officers—should collectively develop their own estimate of expected revenue based on their knowledge of the total business and the environment in which the firm will operate. In addition, a number of statistical and mathematical techniques beyond the scope of this text are available. The basic reason for using alternative forecasting methods is that they provide a check on each other and produce a compromise representing management's best estimate of sales revenue.

STRUCTURE OF THE MASTER BUDGET

The **master budget** is a set of interrelated budgets representing a comprehensive plan of action for a specified time period. A budget committee normally is appointed and given responsibility for coordinating the development of the master budget. It is typically prepared for a one-year period that coincides with a firm's calendar or fiscal year. The budget for the year should be subdivided into shorter periods such as months or quarters so that timely comparisons of actual and budgeted results can be made. Alternatively, the budget may be developed for a continuous period of 12 months or more by adding a month or in the future as the month or quarter just ended is eliminated. In any case, the budgeted targets often *must be revised* as the year progresses and new information concerning the business and its environment becomes available.

The master budget consists of two major parts, the operating budget and the financial budget. The **operating budget** is a detailed description of the revenues and costs required to achieve satisfactory profit results. The **financial budget** shows the funding and financial position needed for the planned operations. Each of the two components has several separate but interrelated budg-

Figure 24-2
Master Budget Inter-
relationships

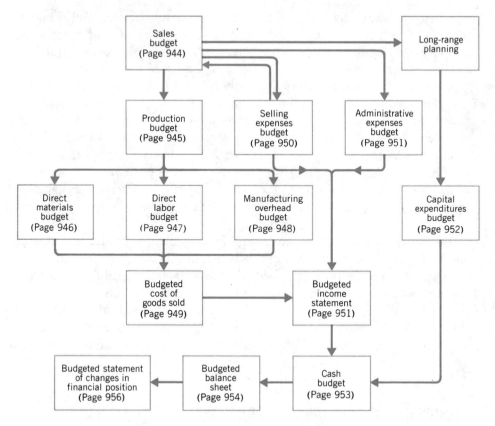

ets, such as those shown schematically in Figure 24-2 for a typical manufacturing firm. The page numbers shown refer to the presentation of the related budget in an illustration later in the chapter. Essentially, the same budgeting cycle as the one illustrated in Figure 24-2 is applicable in a nonmanufacturing business, although some of the individual budgets may differ (for example, a merchandising firm would not need a production budget). In the preparation of a master budget, a manufacturing firm will prepare the following budgets:

Operating Budget	Financial Budget
Sales budget	Capital expenditures budget
Production budget	Cash budget
Direct materials budget	Budgeted balance sheet
Direct labor budget	Budgeted statement of changes in financial
Manufacturing overhead budget	position
Cost of goods sold budget	
Selling expenses budget	
Administrative expenses budget	
Budgeted income statement	

MASTER BUDGET ILLUSTRATION

To illustrate the preparation of a master budget, we will refer to the Kort Company, which produces two types of medallions that are sold to campus bookstores. A Deluxe Medallion is larger and requires more direct labor than a Standard Medallion. Ounces of a special metal alloy are purchased by Kort Company and converted into medallions with skilled labor and a highly automated manufacturing process. The following data represent the direct costs estimated for the production of each medallion:

	Deluxe	Standard
Direct materials	2.4 ounces @ $2.50 per ounce	2.0 ounces @ $2.50 per ounce
Direct labor	2 hours @ $8.00 per hour	1 hour @ $8.00 per hour

The master budget is prepared for a calendar year and is subdivided into quarters. In the following illustration, we are concerned with a summary of the steps taken by Kort Company in the preparation of the master budget. Work in process inventories are negligible for Kort Company, so they are ignored here in order to concentrate on the basic principles of budgeting.

SALES BUDGET

As noted earlier, virtually every phase of the master budget is dependent on the sales forecast. The **sales budget** is prepared from the sales forecast. Detailed information concerning sales volume, selling prices, and sales mix is presented in the sales budget. Kort Company has used the forecasting methods discussed earlier to develop the sales budget shown in Figure 24-3. In addition, management has considered the influence of selling expenses such as advertising on the projected demand for the two products. The sales budget also furnishes the information required to prepare the cash receipts part of the cash budget shown later in Figure 24-13.

PRODUCTION BUDGET

Once the sales budget has been prepared, the production requirements for the period are determined as:

$$\begin{matrix} \text{Production} \\ \text{units} \\ \text{required} \end{matrix} = \begin{matrix} \text{Forecast} \\ \text{sales} \\ \text{units} \end{matrix} + \begin{matrix} \text{Desired ending} \\ \text{finished} \\ \text{goods} \end{matrix} - \begin{matrix} \text{Beginning} \\ \text{finished} \\ \text{goods} \end{matrix}$$

Kort Company plans its inventory level for each finished product so as to have an adequate number of units available to satisfy the expected sales demand

based on estimates

KORT COMPANY
Sales Budget
Year Ending December 31, 1984

| | Quarter | | | | Annual |
	1	2	3	4	Total
Deluxe Medallion					
Budgeted sales units *est.*	4,000	6,000	6,500	5,000	21,500
Budgeted price per unit *est.*	48	48	48	48	48
Budgeted sales dollars	$192,000	$288,000	$312,000	$240,000	$1,032,000
Standard Medallion					
Budgeted sales units	6,000	8,000	8,500	7,000	29,500
Budgeted price per unit	25	25	25	25	25
Budgeted sales dollars	$150,000	$200,000	$212,500	$175,000	$ 737,500
Total					
Budgeted sales dollars	$342,000	$488,000	$524,500	$415,000	$1,769,500

Figure 24-3
Sales Budget

for a current quarter and have enough ending inventory for future sales. The desired ending finished goods inventory for a particular quarter is set equal to the expected sales for the *first month of the succeeding quarter*. This policy has enabled the company to maintain an adequate but not excessive ending inventory in the past. For example, the desired ending inventory for Deluxe Medallions at the end of the first quarter is set equal to the sales expected for April. Since the **production budget** is developed before the budget year 1984 starts, the beginning inventory has to be estimated. The production budget for 1984 is shown in Figure 24-4.

DIRECT MATERIALS BUDGET

After the production requirements have been determined, the **direct materials budget** can be developed. Inventory level decisions again must be made by management in the preparation of the direct materials budget. Essentially the same approach used for the production budget is taken with budgeted direct materials purchases calculated as:

$$\begin{array}{ccccc} \text{Budgeted} & & \text{Budgeted} & \text{Desired} & \text{Beginning} \\ \text{purchases} & = & \text{direct} & + \text{ending} & - \text{direct} \\ \text{in units} & & \text{materials} & \text{direct} & \text{materials} \\ & & \text{usage} & \text{materials} & \end{array}$$

The direct materials required are determined initially in ounces and then converted to dollars by multiplying the ounces needed by the cost of an ounce of metal alloy. Kort Company requires 2.4 ounces of direct materials to produce one Deluxe Medallion and 2 ounces for a Standard Medallion. Each ounce costs $2.50. In Chapter 25, we will see how the prices and quantities of the resources required for production can be predetermined as standard costs. The firm also uses a one-month supply for the estimate of desired ending direct materials inventory. The total purchases of direct materials are $282,765, as shown in Figure 24-5.

DIRECT LABOR BUDGET

The **direct labor budget** is also developed from the production budget and provides important information concerning the size of the labor force that is necessary each quarter. The primary objective is to maintain a labor force large enough to satisfy the production requirements but *not so large that it results in costly idle time*. The first step in the development of the direct labor budget is to estimate the time needed to produce each type of medallion. Two hours are required for one Deluxe Medallion and one hour is needed for a Standard Medallion. The total labor hours required are computed by multiplying these hourly measures times the respective number of medallions to be produced. For the year, 74,100 direct labor hours are projected. Multiplication

Figure 24-4
Production Budget

KORT COMPANY
Production Budget
Year Ending December 31, 1984

| | Quarter | | | | Annual |
	1	2	3	4	Total
Deluxe Medallion					
Forecast sales units (Figure 24-3)	4,000	6,000	6,500	5,000	21,500
Desired ending finished goods	3,000	2,150	1,650	1,950	1,950
Total units needed	7,000	8,150	8,150	6,950	23,450
Beginning finished goods	1,350	3,000	2,150	1,650	1,350
Production required—units	5,650	5,150	6,000	5,300	22,100
Standard Medallion					
Forecast sales units (Figure 24-3)	6,000	8,000	8,500	7,000	29,500
Desired ending finished goods	2,500	3,000	2,500	2,400	2,400
Total units needed	8,500	11,000	11,000	9,400	31,900
Beginning finished goods	2,000	2,500	3,000	2,500	2,000
Production required—units	6,500	8,500	8,000	6,900	29,900

of the total direct labor hours by the hourly labor rate of $8 gives the budgeted total direct labor cost, which amounts to $592,800 for the year, as shown in Figure 24-6.

MANUFACTURING OVERHEAD BUDGET

Kort Company applies manufacturing overhead to inventory on the basis of the 74,100 budgeted direct labor hours found in the direct labor budget. Total budgeted manufacturing overhead is $518,700, so the predetermined overhead rate used for product costing purposes is $7 per direct labor hour ($518,700 ÷ 74,100). The company distinguishes between variable and fixed manufacturing overhead. As we see in Figure 24-7, variable manufacturing overhead costs total $177,840 for the year, or $2.40 per budgeted direct labor hour

Figure 24-5
Direct Materials Budget

KORT COMPANY
Direct Materials Budget
Year Ending December 31, 1984

	Quarter				Annual Total
	1	2	3	4	
Deluxe Medallion					
Production units required (Figure 24-4)	5,650	5,150	6,000	5,300	22,100
Ounces of materials per unit	2.4	2.4	2.4	2.4	2.4
Ounces of materials required	13,560	12,360	14,400	12,720	53,040
Desired ending materials	4,104	4,800	4,248	4,776	4,776
Ounces needed	17,664	17,160	18,648	17,496	57,816
Beginning materials	4,560	4,104	4,800	4,248	4,560
Purchases required—ounces	13,104	13,056	13,848	13,248	53,256
Cost per ounce	$2.50	$2.50	$2.50	$2.50	$2.50
Cost of purchases	$32,760	$32,640	$34,620	$33,120	$133,140
Standard Medallion					
Production units required (Figure 24-4)	6,500	8,500	8,000	6,900	29,900
Ounces of materials per unit	2	2	2	2	2
Ounces of materials required	13,000	17,000	16,000	13,800	59,800
Desired ending materials	5,650	5,500	4,600	4,200	4,200
Ounces needed	18,650	22,500	20,600	18,000	64,000
Beginning materials	4,150	5,650	5,500	4,600	4,150
Purchases required—ounces	14,500	16,850	15,100	13,400	59,850
Cost per ounce	$2.50	$2.50	$2.50	$2.50	$2.50
Cost of purchases	$36,250	$42,125	$37,750	$33,500	$149,625
Total purchases	$69,010	$74,765	$72,370	$66,620	$282,765

KORT COMPANY
Direct Labor Budget
Year Ending December 31, 1984

| | Quarter | | | | Annual |
	1	2	3	4	Total
Deluxe Medallion					
Production units required (Figure 24-4)	5,650	5,150	6,000	5,300	22,100
Direct labor hours per unit given	2	2	2	2	2
Total hours required	11,300	10,300	12,000	10,600	44,200
Labor rate per hour	$8.00	$8.00	$8.00	$8.00	$8.00
Direct labor cost	$ 90,400	$ 82,400	$ 96,000	$ 84,800	$353,600
Standard Medallion					
Production units required (Figure 24-4)	6,500	8,500	8,000	6,900	29,900
Direct labor hours per unit	1	1	1	1	1
Total hours required	6,500	8,500	8,000	6,900	29,900
Labor rate per hour	$8.00	$8.00	$8.00	$8.00	$8.00
Direct labor cost	$ 52,000	$ 68,000	$ 64,000	$ 55,200	$239,200
Total direct labor cost	$142,400	$150,400	$160,000	$140,000	$592,800
Total direct labor hours	17,800	18,800	20,000	17,500	74,100

Figure 24-6
Direct Labor Budget

($177,840 ÷ 74,100). The total fixed manufacturing overhead costs are $340,860 or $4.60 per budgeted direct labor hour ($340,860 ÷ 74,100). For every hour of direct labor recorded during the actual production performance, $7 will be applied for manufacturing overhead.

The fixed portion of the **manufacturing overhead budget** is determined by spreading the annual fixed costs equally over the four quarters, since we assume that Kort Company does not have any seasonal differences in its fixed costs. As a result, the fixed manufacturing costs are $85,215 per quarter. Cost behavioral analysis has shown that the variable costs fluctuate with the production level per quarter, based on the following rates:

Overhead Item	Estimated Variable Rate per Direct Labor Hour
Indirect labor	$ .30
Indirect materials	.10
Employee benefits	1.60
Utilities	.40
Total	$2.40

The direct labor hours of 17,800, 18,800, 20,000, and 17,500 for the four quarters, respectively, are multiplied by the variable rates above to determine the budgeted variable overhead costs per quarter as shown in Figure 24-7.

COST OF GOODS SOLD BUDGET

The **cost of goods sold budget** is shown in Figure 24-8. The unit costs of $36 and $20 for Deluxe and Standard Medallions, respectively, can be multiplied times the number of units sold to determine the cost of goods sold for each product. The budgeted sales units of Deluxe Medallions are 21,500, so the cost of goods sold is $774,000, while 29,500 Standard Medallions are

Figure 24-7
Manufacturing Overhead Budget

KORT COMPANY
Manufacturing Overhead Budget
Year Ending December 31, 1984

	Quarter 1	2	3	4	Annual Total
Variable Costs					
Indirect labor	$ 5,340	$ 5,640	$ 6,000	$ 5,250	$ 22,230
Indirect materials	1,780	1,880	2,000	1,750	7,410
Employee benefits	28,480	30,080	32,000	28,000	118,560
Utilities	7,120	7,520	8,000	7,000	29,640
Total	42,720	45,120	48,000	42,000	177,840
Fixed Costs					
Supervision	36,715	36,715	36,715	36,715	146,860
Property taxes	5,400	5,400	5,400	5,400	21,600
Insurance	4,200	4,200	4,200	4,200	16,800
Maintenance	9,500	9,500	9,500	9,500	38,000
Utilities	8,600	8,600	8,600	8,600	34,400
Depreciation	16,000	16,000	16,000	16,000	64,000
Other	4,800	4,800	4,800	4,800	19,200
Total	85,215	85,215	85,215	85,215	340,860
Total manufacturing overhead	$127,935	$130,335	$133,215	$127,215	$518,700
Direct labor hours	17,800	18,800	20,000	17,500	74,100
Manufacturing overhead rate per direct labor hour					$7.00

KORT COMPANY
Cost of Goods Sold Budget
Year Ending December 31, 1984

	Deluxe Medallion	Standard Medallion	Total
Beginning finished goods	$ 48,600	$ 40,000	$ 88,600
Direct materials used			
Beginning materials	$ 11,400	$ 10,375	$ 21,775
Budgeted purchases (Figure 24-5)	133,140	149,625	282,765
Ending materials	11,940	10,500	22,440
Direct materials used	132,600	149,500	282,100
Direct labor (Figure 24-6)	353,600	239,200	592,800
Manufacturing overhead (direct labor hours × $7)	309,400	209,300	518,700
Total manufacturing cost	795,600	598,000	1,393,600
Ending finished goods	70,200	48,000	118,200
Cost of goods sold	$774,000	$590,000	$1,364,000
Unit costs per product			
Direct materials	2.4 lbs. @ $2.50 = $ 6.00	2 lbs. @ $2.50 = $ 5.00	
Direct labor	2 hrs. @ $8.00 = $16.00	1 hr. @ $8.00 = $ 8.00	
Manufacturing overhead	2 hrs. @ $7.00 = $14.00	1 hr. @ $7.00 = $ 7.00	
Unit Cost	$36.00	$20.00	

Figure 24-8
Cost of Goods Sold Budget

planned at a cost of $590,000. The total budgeted cost of goods sold is $1,364,000. The same result is obtained for each product by working through the traditional form of cost of goods sold computational schedule as shown in Figure 24-8.

SELLING EXPENSES BUDGET

We noted earlier that the influence of selling expenses on the sales budget must be evaluated carefully. The management of Kort Company does this by preparing the **selling expenses budget** along with the sales budget, and the expected effect on sales from the selling effort is considered when the sales

Figure 24-9
Selling Expenses
Budget

KORT COMPANY
Selling Expenses Budget
Year Ending December 31, 1984

Selling Expenses	Quarter				Annual Total
	1	2	3	4	
Advertising	$ 4,500	$ 4,500	$ 4,500	$ 4,500	$ 18,000
Sales salaries	23,450	23,450	23,450	23,450	93,800
Travel	1,200	1,200	1,200	1,200	4,800
Entertainment	800	800	800	800	3,200
Insurance	320	320	320	320	1,280
Property taxes	380	380	380	380	1,520
Utilities	200	200	200	200	800
Depreciation	1,200	1,200	1,200	1,200	4,800
Other	100	100	100	100	400
Total	$32,150	$32,150	$32,150	$32,150	$128,600

volume is forecast. We assume for illustrative purposes that all the selling expenses are fixed and amount to $128,600 spread evenly over the four quarters. The selling expenses budget is presented in Figure 24-9.

ADMINISTRATIVE EXPENSES BUDGET

The **administrative expenses budget** provides a listing of the administrative expense estimates for the period. All the administrative expenses of Kort Company are fixed; their total is $100,004. Again, the total is spread evenly among the quarters, as shown in Figure 24-10.

BUDGETED INCOME STATEMENT

The budgeted income statement shown in Figure 24-11 is developed from the individual budgets discussed previously. At first glance, the statement may appear to be the result of simply combining the end products of the other budgets once they are available. However, remember that the basic premise of budgeting is a planned financial performance that is acceptable to management. The control feature of the budgeted statement is exercised when management compares the actual operating results with the plan. Top management starts the budgeting process by establishing certain guidelines within which

KORT COMPANY
Administrative Expenses Budget
Year Ending December 31, 1984

Administrative Expenses	Quarter				Annual Total
	1	2	3	4	
Management salaries	$21,441	$21,441	$21,441	$21,441	$ 85,764
Clerical salaries	2,500	2,500	2,500	2,500	10,000
Insurance	130	130	130	130	520
Property taxes	160	160	160	160	640
Supplies	150	150	150	150	600
Depreciation	500	500	500	500	2,000
Other	120	120	120	120	480
Total	$25,001	$25,001	$25,001	$25,001	$100,004

Figure 24-10
Administrative Expenses Budget

KORT COMPANY
Budgeted Income Statement
Year Ending December 31, 1984

	Deluxe Medallion	Standard Medallion	Total
Sales—units (Figure 24-3)	21,500	29,500	51,000
Sales—dollars (Figure 24-3)	$1,032,000	$737,500	$1,769,500
Cost of goods sold (Figure 24-8)	774,000	590,000	1,364,000
Gross profit	258,000	147,500	405,500
Operating expenses:			
Selling (Figure 24-9)			128,600
Administrative (Figure 24-10)			100,004
Total operating expenses			228,604
Net income before tax			176,896
Income tax (from tax schedule)			65,686
Net income			$ 111,210

Figure 24-11
Budgeted Income Statement

the business will plan its financial performance. These guidelines may pertain to such goals as profit margin, return on investment, share of the market, growth rate, cash flow, research and development, cost control, financial position, and productivity. The management of Kort Company included among its guidelines the goals of achieving a before-tax profit margin of 10% of sales and a before-tax return on average stockholders' equity in the range of 23 to

Figure 24-12
Capital Expenditures
Budget

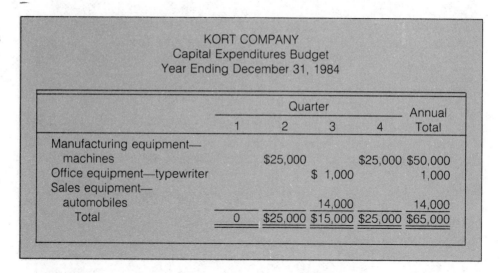

KORT COMPANY
Capital Expenditures Budget
Year Ending December 31, 1984

| | Quarter | | | | Annual |
	1	2	3	4	Total
Manufacturing equipment— machines		$25,000		$25,000	$50,000
Office equipment—typewriter			$ 1,000		1,000
Sales equipment— automobiles			14,000		14,000
Total	0	$25,000	$15,000	$25,000	$65,000

25%. The before-tax net income is budgeted at $176,896, which is about 10% of sales and an approximate 23.3% before-tax return on average stockholders' equity. The average stockholders' equity is calculated from the balance sheets presented later by adding the beginning and ending balances of stockholders' equity for the year and dividing the result by two.

CAPITAL EXPENDITURES BUDGET

The **capital expenditures budget** included in the master budget shows the acquisition of facilities and equipment planned for the period. Capital expenditures represent investments that are expected to yield benefits over a relatively long time period. Most firms, including Kort Company, prepare long-term capital expenditures budgets for periods of five or more years, so the amounts shown in Figure 24-12 would represent the current portion planned for the upcoming year. (Capital budgeting is discussed in Chapter 27.) Kort Company will finance capital expenditures of $65,000 out of operating income during 1984.

CASH BUDGET

The revenues and expenses of the operating budget must be translated into *cash receipts and cash disbursements* for financial planning purposes. The goal is to make sure that the business has sufficient liquidity to pay its bills as they come due. The **cash budget** (Figure 24-13) is used to plan an adequate but not excessive cash balance throughout the period. Excess cash can be used more productively by investing it in earning assets. A satisfactory income statement does not guarantee sufficient liquidity because of the time lags be-

KORT COMPANY
Cash Budget
Year Ending December 31, 1984

| | Quarter | | | | Annual |
	1	2	3	4	Total
Beginning cash balance	$ 62,000	$ 31,206	$ 16,606	$ 94,641	$ 62,000
Cash collections from sales of:					
Current quarter (.7)	239,400	341,600	367,150	290,500	1,238,650
Previous quarter (.3)	123,000	102,600	146,400	157,350	529,350
Total cash from sales	362,400	444,200	513,550	447,850	1,768,000
Total cash available	424,400	475,406	530,156	542,491	1,830,000
Cash disbursements:					
Direct materials purchased in:					
Current quarter (.8)	55,208	59,812	57,896	53,296	226,212
Previous quarter (.2)	13,200	13,802	14,953	14,474	56,429
Total cash for purchases	68,408	73,614	72,849	67,770	282,641
Direct labor	142,400	150,400	160,000	140,000	592,800
Manufacturing overhead	111,935	114,335	117,215	111,215	454,700
Selling expenses	30,950	30,950	30,950	30,950	123,800
Administrative expenses	24,501	24,501	24,501	24,501	98,004
Total cash for operations	378,194	393,800	405,515	374,436	1,551,945
Net cash available from operations	46,206	81,606	124,641	168,055	278,055
Capital expenditures	–0–	25,000	15,000	25,000	65,000
Cash dividends	–0–	25,000	–0–	50,000	75,000
Estimated quarterly income tax	15,000	15,000	15,000	15,000	60,000
Ending cash balance	$ 31,206	$ 16,606	$ 94,614	$ 78,055	$ 78,055

Figure 24-13
Cash Budget

tween accrual and cash accounting. An estimate of the time lag between revenue recognized and cash collections as well as that associated with expenses charged and cash payments must be considered carefully. In addition, any noncash expenses (such as depreciation) must be eliminated in the preparation of the cash budget.

Kort Company has analyzed its previous experience with cash receipts from sales and has decided that 70% of each quarter's sales should be collected currently and 30% the following quarter. Bad debts are negligible, so they are ignored. The company also projects that 80% of its materials purchases will be paid for in the quarter in which they are acquired and 20% in the following quarter. All other expenses are paid for in the quarter in which they occur. Depreciation amounting to $70,800 has been eliminated from the various budgets

Figure 24-14
Budgeted Balance Sheet

KORT COMPANY
Budgeted Balance Sheet
December 31, 1984
(With Comparative Estimates as of December 31, 1983)

	1983		1984	
Assets				
Cash	$ 62,000		$ 78,055	
Accounts receivable	123,000		124,500	
Finished goods inventory	88,600		118,200	
Raw materials inventory	21,775		22,440	
Total current assets		$295,375		$343,195
Land		110,000		110,000
Building and equipment	629,585		694,585	
Accumulated depreciation	(280,000)	349,585	(350,800)	343,785
Total assets		754,960		796,980
Liabilities				
Accounts payable		13,200		13,324
Accrued income taxes		–0–		5,686
Total current liabilities		13,200		19,010
Stockholders' Equity				
Common stock (100 shares outstanding, no par)		100,000		100,000
Retained earnings		641,760		677,970
Total stockholders' equity		741,760		777,970
Total liabilities and stockholders' equity		$754,960		$796,980

since it is a noncash expense. Kort Company expects to begin the year with $62,000 and end it with $78,055. Dividends of $75,000 will be paid during the year. An estimated tax payment of $15,000 will be paid each quarter. The remaining balance of the total tax liability shown on the income statement ($5,686) will be paid when the tax returns are filed. The cash available each quarter is within the guidelines established by management for the budget period.

BUDGETED BALANCE SHEET

Since the budget for 1984 is prepared by Kort Company before the end of 1983, the balance sheet as of December 31, 1983, must be estimated. It is shown in Figure 24-14 and provides the beginning balances for the 1984 budgeting process. Once the actual results are known, the beginning balance sheet may be revised if significant differences occur. The budgeted balance sheet for December 31, 1984, also is presented in Figure 24-14 and is the result of translating the beginning balances through the 1984 budgeting process into ending balances. For example, cash increases from $62,000 to $78,055 as a result of the cash receipts and disbursements shown in the cash budget. Accounts receivable increase from $123,000 to $124,500 because of the sales recorded but not collected. The other balances can be reconciled by referring to their respective budgets. Management must evaluate the budgeted balance sheet carefully to make sure that it reflects a sufficiently strong financial position. If the projected balance sheet is not acceptable, revisions to the budget should be made.

BUDGETED STATEMENT OF CHANGES IN FINANCIAL POSITION

The budgeted statement of changes in financial position is the final step in the preparation of the financial budget and is presented in Figure 24-15. The budgeted schedule of working capital changes also is shown in Figure 24-15. The statement of changes in financial position provides management with valuable information concerning the proposed financing and investing activities of the firm. It shows the sources of working capital, the uses of working capital, and the changes in working capital expected during the year. The increase in working capital of $42,010 can be reconciled with the changes in working capital items shown in Figure 24-15. The content and benefits of the statement were explained more fully in Chapter 19.

FINANCIAL CONTROL WITH BUDGETING

The control phase of budgeting consists of three major steps: (1) comparing the actual financial performance with the budget estimates, (2) identifying any significant variances, and (3) deciding what management action should be taken. The emphasis of budgetary control is on both efficiency and effectiveness measures. **Budget performance reports** that show significant variances between the actual and planned performance provide the feedback necessary to evaluate the financial results on the basis of management by exception. Unfavorable variances will be investigated to determine whether corrective action can be taken to improve the future performance. Even significantly large favorable variances should be evaluated to be sure the related estimates were correct. If they were too easy to attain, the estimates should be changed for the future. The performance reports are prepared for the business as a whole and for its various segments on a responsibility accounting basis. Only

Figure 24-15
Budgeted Statement
of Changes in Fi-
nancial Position

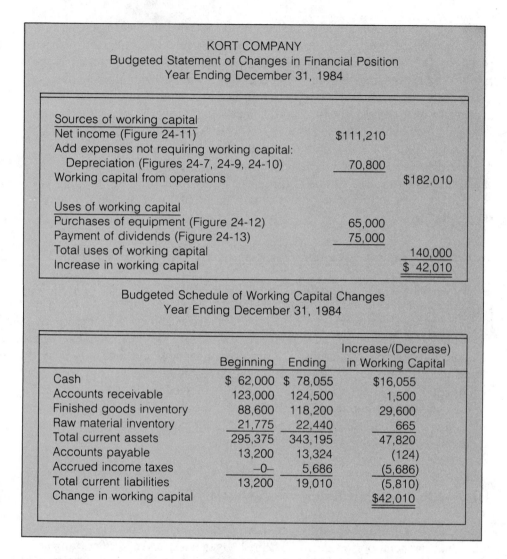

KORT COMPANY
Budgeted Statement of Changes in Financial Position
Year Ending December 31, 1984

Sources of working capital		
Net income (Figure 24-11)	$111,210	
Add expenses not requiring working capital:		
Depreciation (Figures 24-7, 24-9, 24-10)	70,800	
Working capital from operations		$182,010
Uses of working capital		
Purchases of equipment (Figure 24-12)	65,000	
Payment of dividends (Figure 24-13)	75,000	
Total uses of working capital		140,000
Increase in working capital		$ 42,010

Budgeted Schedule of Working Capital Changes
Year Ending December 31, 1984

	Beginning	Ending	Increase/(Decrease) in Working Capital
Cash	$ 62,000	$ 78,055	$16,055
Accounts receivable	123,000	124,500	1,500
Finished goods inventory	88,600	118,200	29,600
Raw material inventory	21,775	22,440	665
Total current assets	295,375	343,195	47,820
Accounts payable	13,200	13,324	(124)
Accrued income taxes	–0–	5,686	(5,686)
Total current liabilities	13,200	19,010	(5,810)
Change in working capital			$42,010

controllable revenues and costs should be included in the performance reports; it would be unfair to hold managers accountable for uncontrollable items.

To illustrate the basic format of a performance report, one prepared for the sales manager of Kort Company is shown in Figure 24-16. The report includes the controllable costs of the sales department during the first quarter. The "actual" column shows the actual costs incurred by the department, and the "budget" column contains the budget estimates for each category. The *U* indicates an unfavorable variance, while the *F* refers to a favorable variance. The sales department incurred expenses that exceeded its budget by $2,535. Unless sales are substantially higher because of the increased spending, these results will have an adverse effect on the firm's profits and will require corrective action if the financial goals of future quarters are to be achieved.

Figure 24-16
Budget Performance
Report

KORT COMPANY
Sales Department
Budget Performance Report
Quarter Ending March 31, 1984

Controllable Expenses	Budgeted	Actual	Variance
Advertising	$ 4,500	$ 5,200	$ 700 U
Sales salaries	23,450	24,550	1,100 U
Travel	1,200	1,750	550 U
Entertainment	800	980	180 U
Utilities	200	210	10 U
Other	100	95	5 F
Total	$30,250	$32,785	$2,535 U

GLOSSARY

ADMINISTRATIVE EXPENSES BUDGET.   Estimates of the administrative expenses for the budget period (p. 950).

BUDGET.   A quantitative plan showing how resources are expected to be acquired and used during a specified time period (p. 936).

BUDGETING.   The process of preparing a budget for financial planning and control (p. 936).

BUDGET PERFORMANCE REPORT.   A report showing a comparison of the actual and budgeted performance with an emphasis on any variances (p. 955).

CAPITAL EXPENDITURES BUDGET.   The acquisition of long-term assets planned during a future period (p. 952).

CASH BUDGET.   The cash receipts and disbursements expected during the budget period (p. 952).

COST OF GOODS SOLD BUDGET.   An estimate of the cost of goods sold required for the budget period (p. 948).

DIRECT LABOR BUDGET.   A projection of the direct labor needs of a budget period based on the expected production level (p. 945).

DIRECT MATERIALS BUDGET.   A projection of the direct materials that must be purchased to satisfy the production requirements of a budget period (p. 944).

FINANCIAL BUDGET.   The part of the master budget that shows the funding and financial position needed for the planned operations (p. 941).

GOAL CONGRUENCE.   The reconciliation of the goals of individual managers with those of the organization (p. 938).

MANUFACTURING OVERHEAD BUDGET.   A projection of the manufacturing overhead cost items required to support the expected production level (p. 947).

MASTER BUDGET. A set of interrelated budgets representing a comprehensive plan of action for a specified time period (p. 941).

OPERATING BUDGET. The component of the master budget that describes the revenues and costs required to achieve a satisfactory financial performance (p. 941).

PRODUCTION BUDGET. An estimate of the number of units that will be manufactured during the budget period (p. 944).

SALES BUDGET. A translation of the sales forecast for a budget period into detailed information concerning the products or services that are expected to be sold (p. 943).

SELLING EXPENSES BUDGET. Estimates of the selling expenses needed to generate the expected sales volume for the budget period (p. 949).

DISCUSSION QUESTIONS

1. Why can it be said that the budgeting process actually consists of multiple budgets?
2. How is a budget used for (a) planning, and (b) control?
3. What is goal congruence and why is it important for a business?
4. What are the benefits of budgeting?
5. What are the two major components of a master budget?
6. Why is an accurate sales forecast essential for effective budgeting? Why is it difficult to forecast sales accurately?
7. What are the most popular methods used to forecast sales?
8. Distinguish between a sales budget and a production budget.
9. What are the major purposes of an operating budget and a financial budget?
10. Why are inventory level decisions important in the budgeting process?
11. How are responsibility accounting and budgeting related?
12. The McDonald Company expects to sell 60,000 units during the upcoming year. It wants to have 12,000 units on hand at the end of the year and has 9,000 units available at the beginning of the year. How many units should the firm produce during the year?
13. Why is a reliable cash budget required even with an accurate prediction of a business's income statement performance?
14. You recently overheard a local businesswoman say, "My business involves too many uncertainties for budgeting to be practical." Do you agree? Explain.
15. Why is it important to distinguish between fixed and variable costs in preparing a manufacturing overhead budget?
16. How does budgeting assist management in developing its employment policies?
17. Is the budgeted income statement simply the product of combining a number of revenue and expense budgets?
18. What are the major steps in the control phase of budgeting?
19. How should management decide what costs to include in budget performance reports?

EXERCISES

Exercise 24-1 (Calculating Cash Receipts)

The Freemont Department Store's budgeted monthly gross sales for July through December are presented below. The company's experience is that 70% of the monthly sales are on credit. All payments received during the month of sale are subject to a 2% cash discount. This policy applies to both cash and credit sales. Approximately 45% of the credit sales are collected in the month of sale, 30% in the month following the sale, and 20% in the second month following the sale; 5% are never collected.

The budgeted gross sales by month are:

July	$40,000
August	60,000
September	50,000
October	55,000
November	45,000
December	65,000

Required:

Calculate the forecasted cash receipts for October, November, and December.

Exercise 24-2 (Determining Budgeted Purchases and Cash Disbursements)

The Red Creek Department Store has prepared a sales budget for the fiscal year ending April 30, 1987, and has provided the following data:

Purchases for March 1986	$180,000
Purchases for April 1986	192,000
Ending inventory—April 30, 1986	265,200
Budget sales: May 1986	300,000
June 1986	270,000
July 1986	320,000
August 1986	290,000

The cost of goods sold is 65% of sales, and it is the company policy to maintain a month-end inventory balance sufficient to meet the projected sales requirement for the following month and 40% of the sales requirements for the second following month. The company pays for 50% of its purchases in the month of purchase, 35% in the following month, and 15% in the second month following the sale.

Required:

A. Calculate the amount of purchases for May and June 1986.
B. Calculate the disbursements in May and June for merchandise purchased.

Exercise 24-3 (Preparing a Direct Labor Budget)

The Eastern Manufacturing Company maintains an ending inventory balance equal to 60% of the sales requirements of the following month. The ending inventory balance on October 31 was comprised of 540 units, and the projected unit sales for November, December, and January were 900, 960, and 700 units, respectively.

The labor requirements per unit are as follows:

	Time Required (Hours)	Rate Per Hour
Welder	3.5	$12
Assembly labor	2.7	10
Painter	5.0	7

Required:
Prepare a direct labor budget for November and December.

Exercise 24-4 (Preparing a Sales Budget)

The Lighthouse Company has asked each production manager to prepare a sales budget for 1984. In reviewing the actual sales data for the previous year, the managers agreed that the number of units of product A sold in 1984 should represent a 15% increase over 1983 sales, product B unit sales should increase 5%, while product C sales in units should decrease 4%. The managers' projections took into consideration the general economic conditions and the anticipated changes in selling prices. The selling price for product A and B will increase 10% while the selling price of product C will drop 5%. The percentage of each product's sales occurring in a given quarter are:

	First Quarter	Second Quarter	Third Quarter	Fourth Quarter
Product A	25%	30%	15%	30%
Product B	20%	25%	35%	20%
Product C	30%	20%	25%	25%

The actual 1983 product sales data were:

	Unit Selling Price	Total Sales
Product A	$14	$329,000
Product B	9	162,000
Product C	12	252,000

Required:
Prepare a sales budget for 1984 containing projected dollar sales by quarter. Round all calculations to the nearest dollar.

Exercise 24-5 (Evaluating Future Cash Flow)

The Hofman Company is preparing a cash budget for May, 1984 and has provided the following information:

1. Seventy percent of each month's sales are on account, with 79% of the accounts being collected in the month of sale. The remaining accounts are collected the following month.
2. The cost of goods sold equals 65% of sales. Sixty percent of all purchases are paid in the month of sale and 40%, the following month.

3. The company policy is to maintain an inventory level equal to 50% of the next month's sales requirement. The requirement was met on May 1, 1984.
4. Selling and administrative expenses are budgeted at $10,000 for May. This includes $3,000 of depreciation. All selling and administrative expenses, except depreciation, are paid in the month incurred.
5. Cash balance, May 1 — $10,500

April sales	35,000
May sales	52,000
June sales	45,000
April purchases	28,275

Required:
A. Prepare a budgeted income statement for May.
B. Prepare a cash budget for May.

Exercise 24-6 (Evaluating Future Cash Flows)

The Sullivan Company has prepared a budgeted income statement for the month of June. The company pays for 60% of its merchandise purchased in the month of purchase and 40% in the month following the purchase. Seventy percent of all sales are collected in the month of sale and 30% the following month. The annual insurance premium was prepaid in February and the annual property taxes are due in November. All other cash expenses are paid currently. The company maintains a minimum cash balance of $500, and the cash balance as of June 1 was $850. A new piece of equipment costing $300 will be paid for in June.

Additional information:

May sales	$1,600
May purchases	900
June purchases	1,200

SULLIVAN COMPANY
Budgeted Income Statement
For the Month of June

Sales		$2,000
Cost of goods sold		900
Gross profit		1,100
Operating expenses:		
Insurance	$ 75	
Property taxes	90	
Rent	150	
Wages	550	
Depreciation	50	
Total expenses		915
Net income		$ 185

Required:

A. Prepare a cash budget for the month of June.

B. How much cash can the owners of the Sullivan Company withdraw during June and maintain the minimum cash balance required?

PROBLEMS

Problem 24-1 (Preparing a Sales Forecast)

The Dailey Company manufactures a line of water heaters designed for apartment use. The company markets this line in two cities—Conesus and Walworth. Approximately 60% of all new apartment complexes in the two areas will have an individual water heater installed in each apartment. They have also projected that 5% of the existing apartments will install new individual water heaters to improve existing systems or replace old individual heaters that cannot be repaired. Based on past experience, the Dailey Company anticipates it can capture 30% of the new apartment construction market and 10% of the replacement market.

The company sells two models of water heaters—the standard and the deluxe, a more energy-efficient unit. Builders will use the standard model in 70% of the apartments they construct and the deluxe model in 30%. When an existing complex installs new water heaters, it will use the standard model in 25% of the apartment units and the deluxe model in 75%.

The other information available is:

	Conesus	Walworth
Number of units to be constructed	42,000	51,000
Number of existing units	500,000	400,000
Selling price—standard	$190	$190
Selling price—deluxe	$250	$245

Required:
Prepare a sales forecast for the Dailey Company by market area.

Problem 24-2 (Preparing a Production Budget and Related Budgets)

The Ellison Company manufactures redwood patio and lawn furniture. The manager in charge of the production of picnic tables has been asked to prepare a production budget, a direct materials budget, and a direct labor budget for part of 1985 based on management's sales forecast.

The materials and labor requirements per table are:

	Quantity	Cost
Lumber	20 feet	$5.00 per foot
Stain	1 quart	$2.50 per quart
Cutting labor	3 hours	$8.00 per hour
Finishing labor	8 hours	$11.00 per hour

The company requires a finished goods ending inventory for each quarter that equals 40% of expected sales for the next quarter. Also, the ending inventory balance of direct materials should equal 30% of the next quarter's production requirements. The inventory balances on January 1, 1985 are forecasted as:

Lumber	25,200 feet
Stain	1,260 quarts
Picnic tables	1,200 units

The forecasted quarterly sales in units are:

First quarter, 1985	3,000
Second quarter, 1985	6,000
Third quarter, 1985	4,000
Fourth quarter, 1985	2,000

Required:
A. Prepare a quarterly production budget for the first three quarters of 1985.
B. Prepare a direct materials budget for the first two quarters of 1985.
C. Prepare a direct labor budget for the first two quarters of 1985.

Problem 24-3 (Preparing a Cash Budget)

The Elm Company is in the process of preparing a cash budget for the next year. The company collects 70% of its sales in the quarter the sale was made, 25% in the quarter following the sale, and the remainder in the subsequent quarter. Seventy-five percent of all purchases are paid for in the quarter in which they are purchased, with the remaining 25% paid for in the following quarter.

The selling expenses are $10,000 each quarter, plus 10% of sales. Administrative expenses are $60,000 per quarter, including $20,000 of depreciation expense. The company is planning to buy equipment during the second quarter at a cost of $12,000 and to pay a $7,000 dividend in the first quarter. The cash balance on January 1, 1984, is $11,500.

The following sales and purchases data have been compiled for the preparation of the budget:

	Sales	Purchases
Third quarter, 1983	$100,000	$40,000
Fourth quarter, 1983	90,000	36,000
First quarter, 1984	105,000	42,000
Second quarter, 1984	110,000	37,000

Required:
Prepare a cash budget by quarter and in total for the first two quarters of 1984.

Problem 24-4 (Preparing Budgeted Financial Statements)

The James Company is preparing its quarterly budget for the three months ending March 31, 1984. The information available for the budget is as follows:

1. Cash sales represent 30% of all monthly sales. Seventy percent of all credit sales are collected in the month of sale and the remainder in the month following the sale.
2. Merchandise purchases that are made on account equal 60% of the forecasted sales for that month. Sixty percent of the purchases are paid in the month of purchase, and 40% are paid the following month.
3. Ending inventory on March 31, 1984, is projected to be $23,000.
4. Equipment purchases for the first quarter are budgeted at $2,000.
5. Other quarterly expenses are budgeted as follows: utilities—$4,600; rent—$13,000; salaries—$25,000. These expenses are paid when incurred.
6. Depreciation for the first quarter will be $4,000.
7. The balance sheet as of January 1, 1984, contained the following accounts:

Cash	$ 7,100	Accumulated depreciation	$24,000
Accounts receivable	4,900	Accounts payable	2,400
Inventory	10,000	Common stock	20,500
Equipment	56,000	Retained earnings	31,100

8. Budgeted sales are: January—$52,000; February—$50,000; March—$48,000.
9. Ignore income taxes.

Required:
Prepare a budgeted income statement and a budgeted balance sheet for the quarter ending March 31, 1984.

Problem 24-5 (Comprehensive Budgeting Problem)

The Duke Company is preparing a master budget for the first quarter of 1985 and has compiled the following data:

1. The company sells a single product at a price of $13 per unit. The corporate sales forecast (in units) for the last quarter of 1984 and the first seven months of 1985 is:

	Number of Units
October	10,000
November	11,000
December	10,700
January	9,200
February	12,000
March	11,500
April	10,500
May	10,900
June	10,100
July	9,500

2. Sixty percent of the sales are collected in the month of sale, 25% the following month, and 15% in the second month following the sale.

3. There will be no beginning inventories on January 1, 1985. The ending inventory in finished goods should equal 15% of the sales requirements for the next three months, and the raw materials ending inventory should equal 40% of the next month's production requirement.
4. Ignore income taxes.
5. Eighty percent of the material purchases are paid in the quarter of purchase and 20% the following quarter. Unpaid purchases from 1984 are $55,000 as of January 1, 1985.
6. Variable selling expenses are 3% of sales. Administrative expenses are $36,000 per quarter of which $4,000 represents depreciation expense. Fixed selling expenses are $14,000 each quarter. All selling and administrative expenses are paid in the quarter in which they are incurred.
7. The product requirements are:

	Direct Material	Direct Labor
Per unit	1 lb.	.3 hours

The direct materials can be purchased for $3 a pound. The direct labor wage rate is $10 an hour. The manufacturing overhead cost amounts to $2 per unit, and all manufacturing overhead, except depreciation, is paid in the month incurred.
8. January 1, 1985, cash balance is $6,000.

Required:
A. Prepare a sales budget for the period November 1984–March 1985.
B. Determine cash collections for the first quarter.
C. Calculate the number of units produced in the first quarter of 1985.
D. Prepare a direct materials budget for the first quarter.
E. Prepare a cash budget for the first quarter.
F. Prepare a budgeted income statement for the first quarter.

ALTERNATE PROBLEMS

Problem 24-1A (Preparing a Sales Forecast)

The Cobbs Hill Corporation manufactures a line of dishwashers designed for residential use in the towns of Jenison and Southlake. Dishwashers will be installed in approximately 80% of all new residential units, and the company projects that 5% of all existing residential units will be replacing older dishwashers during the next year. Based on past experience, the company anticipates it can capture 25% of the new residential construction market and 10% of the replacement market.

The company markets two types of dishwashers—the standard and the deluxe. The standard model will be placed in 75% of new units constructed, and 25% of the builders will choose the deluxe model. Thirty percent of existing homeowners will choose the standard model to replace their older dishwashers, while 70% will choose the deluxe model.

The Cobbs Hill Corporation has compiled the following data in the preparation of a sales forecast:

	Jenison	Southlake
Number of existing units	750,000	520,000
Number of units to be constructed	10,000	8,000
Selling price—standard	$350	$355
Selling price—deluxe	$415	$425

Required:
Prepare a sales forecast for the Cobbs Hill Corporation by town.

Problem 24-2A (Preparing a Production Budget and Related Budgets)

The Essex Company manufactures upholstered furniture and is in the process of preparing a production budget, direct materials budget, and direct labor budget.

The labor and materials requirements per unit are:

Cutting labor	1 hour at $7.50 per hour
Finishing labor	2 hours at $9.00 per hour
Fabric	7 yards at $5.00 per yard
Lumber	15 feet at $6.00 per foot

The forecasted quarterly sales in units are:

First quarter, 1986	4,000
Second quarter, 1986	2,500
Third quarter, 1986	3,000
Fourth quarter, 1986	2,000

The company requires an ending inventory balance of raw materials that is equal to 10% of the next quarter's production requirements. Also, the ending inventory balance of finished goods should be equal to 20% of the next quarter's expected sales. The projected inventory balances as of January 1, 1986, are:

Fabric	2,590 yards
Lumber	5,550 feet
Finished goods	800 units

Required:
A. Prepare the quarterly production forecast for the first three quarters of 1986.
B. Prepare a direct materials budget for the first two quarters of 1986.
C. Prepare a direct labor budget for the first two quarters of 1986.

Problem 24-3A (Preparing a Cash Budget)

The Woodcliff Company wants to prepare a cash budget for the first two quarters of 1986. The company's experience is that 60% of sales will be collected during the quarter of the sale, 25% in the quarter following the sale, 10% in the second quarter following the sale, and 5% in the third quarter following the sale. The company pays for 70% of its purchases in the quarter of the purchase, and the balance is paid in the following quarter.

Selling expenses amount to $15,000 per quarter plus 15% of sales. Administrative expenses are estimated to be $40,000 per quarter, which includes $12,000 of depreciation expense. All selling and administrative expenses, except depreciation, are paid when incurred.

The company is planning to purchase equipment during the first quarter at a cost of $20,000. The company will pay off a $30,000 note, which will mature during the second quarter. The interest due at maturity will be $3,500. The company's anticipated cash balance at January 1, 1986, is $15,000.

The company's estimated sales and purchases data are as follows:

	Sales	Purchases
Second quarter, 1985	$120,000	$70,000
Third quarter, 1985	110,000	60,000
Fourth quarter, 1985	140,000	80,000
First quarter, 1986	190,000	50,000
Second quarter, 1986	130,000	60,000

Required:
Prepare a cash budget for the first two quarters of 1986, by quarter and in total.

Problem 24-4A (Preparing Budgeted Financial Statements)
The Farley Company has compiled the following data in order to prepare a quarterly budget for the three months ending June 30, 1985.

1. Merchandise purchases are made on account and monthly purchases amount to 55% of the forecasted sales for that month. Purchases are paid 70% in the month of purchase and 30% in the following month.
2. Sales on account represent 80% of all monthly sales. Sixty percent of all credit sales are collected in the month of sale and the remainder in the month following the sale.
3. Principal payments on the company's note payable to be made during the first quarter are budgeted at $5,000. Interest payments during the first quarter will be $1,200.
4. Other quarterly expenses are budgeted as follows: salaries—$100,000; rent—$10,000; insurance—$3,000. These expenses will be paid when incurred.
5. The depreciation expense per quarter is $6,000.
6. The ending inventory as of June 30, 1985, is projected to be $12,000.
7. The balance sheet as of April 1, 1985 included the following accounts:

Cash	$ 9,000
Accounts receivable	34,500
Inventory	10,000
Equipment	52,000

Accumulated depreciation	7,800
Accounts payable	18,000
Note payable	25,000
Common stock	10,000
Retained earnings	44,700

8. Budgeted sales are as follows: April—$102,000; May—$110,000; June—$115,000.

Required:
Prepare a budgeted income statement and a budgeted balance sheet for the quarter ending June 30, 1985.

Problem 24-5A (Comprehensive Budgeting Problem)

The Ott Company has asked the accounting department to prepare a master budget for the last quarter of 1985.

1. The company's single product sells for $37 a unit. The sales manager has prepared the following sales forecast (in units):

July, 1985	20,500
August, 1985	18,000
September, 1985	19,300
October, 1985	21,700
November, 1985	20,400
December, 1985	19,600
January, 1986	18,350
February, 1986	20,750
March, 1986	19,100

2. Sixty-five percent of all sales are collected in the month of sale, 20% in the following month, and 15% in the second month following the sale.
3. The beginning inventory of finished goods on October 1, 1985 will be 8,420 units. There will be no beginning raw materials inventory. The ending inventory in finished goods should equal 20% of the next two months' sales requirements. The ending inventory in raw materials should equal 30% of the production requirements for the next month.
4. Eighty percent of the purchases are paid for in the quarter of purchase and 20% in the following quarter. Unpaid purchases from the third quarter of 1985 are $285,000 as of October 1, 1985.
5. The product requirements per unit are 2.5 pounds of material A and 1.5 hours of direct labor. Material A can be purchased for $6 per pound, and the direct labor rate is $8 per hour.
6. The manufacturing overhead cost amounts to $4 per unit, and all manufacturing overhead is paid in the month incurred.
7. Fixed selling expenses are $75,000 per quarter; fixed administrative expenses are $93,000 per quarter. Fixed quarterly administrative expenses include $15,000 of depreciation expense. Variable selling expenses are 2% of sales. All selling and

administrative expenses, except depreciation, are paid in the quarter in which they are incurred.

8. Beginning cash balance as of October 1 is $10,000.
9. Ignore income taxes.

Required:

A. Prepare a sales budget for the period August–December, 1985.
B. Prepare a cash collections schedule for the fourth quarter, of 1985.
C. Calculate the number of units to be produced during the fourth quarter of 1985.
D. Prepare a direct materials budget for the last quarter of 1985.
E. Prepare a cash budget for the last quarter of 1985.
F. Prepare a budgeted income statement for the last quarter of 1985.

CASE FOR CHAPTER 24

Decision Problem (Budgeted Income Statement and Cash Budget)

The Gulfside Medical Center is located in southern Florida. During the months of December through April, the center operates an outpatient clinic for the treatment of minor illnesses and injuries. Because of the seasonal nature of tourism in the area, the clinic is closed for the remainder of the year and regular patients are treated by other departments of the center. The clinic is organized as a separate profit center with its own budget and accounting records. You have just been assigned the responsibility of preparing a budget for the clinic's next five months of operations (December–April).

You have determined from past clinic performance and discussions with center management that the following are realistic projections for the next five months of operations:

Salaries. Six people will be employed in the clinic with total monthly salaries of $23,200.

Operating expenses. Monthly operating expenses for the clinic are expected to be $6,000. Depreciation charges of $1,000 are included.

Collections. Past experience has shown that 40% of the bills are paid in cash when the services are performed. Twenty percent of the bills are on credit without insurance and are paid in the month following the service. Thirty-eight percent of the bills are on credit and are covered by insurance. They are paid two months after the service is performed, and the other 2% of the bills are never collected. The average bill per patient appointment is $25.

Payments. All salaries are paid in the month in which the services are performed. Eighty percent of the monthly cash operating expenses are paid in the same month, while 20% of them are paid in the next month.

Patient activity. The number of patient appointments expected for the period are:

December	1,100
January	2,200
February	2,600
March	3,100
April	1,500

Cash balance. The clinic will have a cash balance of $20,000 on December 1. A minimum cash balance of $2,000 is required for the clinic by the management of Gulfside Medical Center at the end of each month. Whenever the cash balance at the end of a month is below $2,000, the clinic has to borrow the required cash from the center for the next month or as long as it is required, whichever is longer, at 15% interest. Whenever the cash balance exceeds $20,000 at the end of a month, the excess is transferred to the general bank account of the center.

Required:

A. Prepare a budgeted income statement for each month during the December through April period.

B. Prepare a cash budget for each month during the December through April period.

CHAPTER 25
FLEXIBLE BUDGETS AND STANDARD COSTS

OVERVIEW AND OBJECTIVES

This chapter discusses flexible budgets and standard costs. When you have completed the chapter, you should understand:

- The basic differences between a flexible budget and a fixed budget (pp. 971–972).
- How a flexible budget is constructed (pp. 973–974).
- The use of a flexible budget for performance evaluation (pp. 974–976).
- The basic nature of standard costs and their role in financial planning and control (pp. 976–977).
- The benefits of standard costs (pp. 977–978).
- The various methods used to establish standard costs and the types of standards possible (pp. 978–979).
- The calculation of standard cost variances and their responsibility assignment within a manufacturing firm (pp. 979–983, 987–988).
- The accounting procedures required to charge standard costs to the work in process inventory and to identify cost variances with journal entries (pp. 980–982, 988).
- How a specific capacity level is chosen in the development of a predetermined overhead rate with a flexible budget (pp. 983–986).
- How standard cost variances are disposed of at the end of an accounting period (pp. 989–990).

Flexible budgets and standard costs are two important managerial accounting tools. The master budgeting procedures discussed in the preceding chapter have a potential deficiency in many applications: all budgeted costs are estimated on the basis of a *single* level of activity for sales or production. A budget of this type is called a **fixed** or **static budget** since *only one* level of activity is considered. As long as the level of activity actually achieved is approximately the same as the one planned, the fixed budget serves as a useful managerial tool. When significant differences between the actual and budgeted levels of activity take place, however, the budgets should be revised to reflect these changes. This can be done with the use of a **flexible budget,** which is a series of budgets for different levels of activity. As we will see later in this chapter, a flexible budget is particularly important for planning and controlling manufacturing overhead costs.

Standard costs are predetermined costs used as performance targets for an efficient manufacturing operation. They are analogous to other performance targets used as the basis for measuring the level of achievement in many aspects of our lives. Examples are a B+ academic performance for scholastic recognition, a par round of golf for a serious golfer, a recipe used by a restaurant to prepare a pizza, and the engineering specifications followed in the production of a calculator. Many of the performance targets required for financial planning and control will be in the form of standard costs.

PERFORMANCE EVALUATION WITH A FIXED BUDGET

As we learned in Chapter 24, the starting point in the development of a master budget is the sales forecast for the budget period. The planning phase of the management cycle is served effectively by this approach since all of the firm's activities are directed toward a common level of achievement. The production level and all budgets for manufacturing, selling, and administrative activities are based on the single estimate of sales. This is an example of a fixed budgeting approach since cost and revenue estimates are developed for only one level of activity. A potential problem with a fixed budget for control purposes is that it does not take into consideration the possibility that the sales or production goals of the firm may not be achieved. If the actual level of activity for sales or production differs *significantly* from that planned, performance evaluation is difficult to make with a fixed budget. For example, consider the comparison of the budgeted performance and the actual cost results achieved by the production department of the Naville Manufacturing Company shown in Figure 25-1.

Can we really say that the production department's actual cost performance was $64,550 less than its budget? This might be the conclusion based upon a fixed budgeting approach, although it would be erroneous. We also note that the department did not produce the 25,000 units budgeted, so all of the variable costs should automatically be lower with the 20,000 units actually produced.

Figure 25-1
Fixed Budget Performance Report

NAVILLE MANUFACTURING COMPANY
Fixed Budget Performance Report
Year Ended December 31, 1984

	Budget	Actual	Variance
Production units	25,000	20,000	5,000 U
Variable costs			
Direct materials	$125,000	$110,000	$15,000 F
Direct labor	300,000	260,000	40,000 F
Indirect materials	12,500	11,400	1,100 F
Indirect labor	18,750	16,200	2,550 F
Utilities	31,250	24,600	6,650 F
Total Variable Costs	487,500	422,200	65,300 F
Fixed costs			
Supervision	60,500	61,400	900 U
Property taxes	8,700	8,700	0
Insurance	5,200	5,300	100 U
Maintenance	4,700	4,450	250 F
Depreciation	15,300	15,300	0
Total Fixed Costs	94,400	95,150	750 U
Total Manufacturing Costs	$581,900	$517,350	$64,550 F

U indicates an unfavorable variance.
F indicates a favorable variance.

The budget estimates in Figure 25-1 simply do not reflect what costs should be for the actual units produced. We cannot compare the manufacturing costs of one production level with those of another production level and expect the results to be of any value to management. Instead, a flexible budget should be used to provide a *comparable basis* for evaluating financial performance when the actual level of activity is different from the one budgeted.

PREPARATION OF A FLEXIBLE BUDGET

A flexible budget is developed for a *range of activity* rather than for a single level. As such, a flexible budget is said to be dynamic since it enables management to *adjust the budget* to the actual level achieved. The adjusted budget will be representative of what costs should have been for the actual activity level. The initial step in the preparation of a flexible budget is to distinguish between the fixed and variable costs. The cost behavior of each cost item over past periods can be studied to see whether it changes as the activity level changes. As we learned in Chapter 22, a *variable cost* will vary in total amount proportionally with changes in volume. The variable cost rate will be constant on a per-unit basis. A *fixed cost* will remain constant in total amount over a wide range of activity but will vary inversely on a per-unit basis. We will consider procedures for analyzing the cost behavior of specific costs in Chapter 26.

In the case of Naville Manufacturing Company, three of the manufacturing overhead items—indirect materials, indirect labor, and utilities—have been classified as variable costs along with the direct materials and direct labor. The firm has established the following variable cost rates for the manufacturing cost performance:

Cost Item	Variable Cost Rate per Unit
Direct materials	$ 5.00
Direct labor	12.00
Indirect materials	.50
Indirect labor	.75
Utilities	1.25
Total	$19.50

The variable cost portion of the flexible budget will change for different levels of production, as we see in Figure 25-2. The range of production activity is from 20,000 units to 30,000 units of production. The variable cost rates are multiplied by a specific number of units to determine the expected variable costs for that level of production. The five fixed cost items remain constant over the entire range of activity (Figure 25-2). Consequently, the variable costs are the costs that ''flex'' over different levels of activity.

PERFORMANCE EVALUATION WITH A FLEXIBLE BUDGET

The use of a flexible budget for cost performance reporting makes the budget estimates and actual results comparable since they both are based on the same level of activity. Figure 25-3 presents a *flexible budget performance report* for the production department of the Naville Manufacturing Company. Instead of achieving favorable financial results that might be reported with the fixed budget shown earlier, the department *actually incurred an unfavorable variance of $32,950*. Both the budget column and the actual column in the report are based on the production level of 20,000 units. The flexible budget performance report represents a much more realistic evaluation of the departmental cost performance than the fixed budget performance report.

The variances shown in Figure 25-3 have meaning since they relate to the cost performance only. Production differences have been eliminated by adjusting the flexible budget to the level of 20,000 units. The performance report

Figure 25-2
Flexible Budget

NAVILLE MANUFACTURING COMPANY
Flexible Budget
Year Ended December 31, 1984

	Per Unit	Levels of Activity		
		20,000	25,000	30,000
Production units				
Variable costs				
Direct materials	$ 5.00	$100,000	$125,000	$150,000
Direct labor	12.00	240,000	300,000	360,000
Indirect materials	.50	10,000	12,500	15,000
Indirect labor	.75	15,000	18,750	22,500
Utilities	1.25	25,000	31,250	37,500
Total Variable Costs	19.50	390,000	487,500	585,000
Fixed costs				
Supervision		60,500	60,500	60,500
Property taxes		8,700	8,700	8,700
Insurance		5,200	5,200	5,200
Maintenance		4,700	4,700	4,700
Depreciation		15,300	15,300	15,300
Total Fixed Costs		94,400	94,400	94,400
Total Manufacturing Costs		$484,400	$581,900	$679,400

provides management with a realistic indication of the areas that should be investigated further in order to control the production costs. For example, direct materials cost and direct labor cost exceeded the budget estimates by $10,000 (10%) and $20,000 (8.3%), respectively. Corrective action will be required if future profitability goals are to be achieved.

The dynamic nature of a flexible budget permits management to adjust it to any level as long as the same cost behavioral patterns prevail. In the Naville Manufacturing Company case, the actual level of activity was the same as one of the levels in the original flexible budget (20,000 units). Even if the actual activity level is not found in the flexible budget, management easily can adjust the budget to that level. For example, if the Naville Manufacturing Company had produced 22,400 units, the budget would be adjusted to that level and the results would be compared with the associated actual costs. The variable cost rates (totaling $19.50 per unit) would be multiplied by 22,400 to determine the total variable costs, and the fixed costs would be the same as they were for the production of 25,000 units ($94,400). The total budgeted manufacturing costs for 22,400 units would be $531,200.

Figure 25-3
Flexible Budget Performance Report

NAVILLE MANUFACTURING COMPANY Flexible Budget Performance Report Year Ended December 31, 1984			
	Budget	Actual	Variance
Production units	20,000	20,000	
Variable costs			
Direct materials	$100,000	$110,000	$10,000 U
Direct labor	240,000	260,000	20,000 U
Indirect materials	10,000	11,400	1,400 U
Indirect labor	15,000	16,200	1,200 U
Utilities	25,000	24,600	400 F
Total Variable Costs	390,000	422,200	32,200 U
Fixed costs			
Supervision	60,500	61,400	900 U
Property taxes	8,700	8,700	0
Insurance	5,200	5,300	100 U
Maintenance	4,700	4,450	250 F
Depreciation	15,300	15,300	0
Total Fixed Costs	94,400	95,150	750 U
Total Manufacturing Cost	$484,400	$517,350	$32,950 U

U indicates an unfavorable variance.
F indicates a favorable variance.

USE OF STANDARD COSTS

Chapter 23 demonstrated how a cost accounting system can be used to determine the actual costs of producing a product. This information furnishes management with a *detailed record* of the manufacturing costs that are incurred in the production of a job or the operation of a processing center. The cost data are also used in the inventory-valuation and income-determination aspects of financial reporting. However, the results have serious limitations concerning the measurement of the efficiency of the manufacturing operation. Management planning must be founded on reliable projections of an efficient utilization of resources. Management control is concerned with a comparison of actual results and those planned, as we saw in the discussion of budgeting.

The limitation of historical or actual cost data is that they represent what happened, which is not necessarily what should have happened. Consequently, it is difficult to determine a reliable performance measurement base with historical cost data. Are the costs too high? If so, who is responsible? How can they be reduced? Are the costs representative of the future? These typical questions are difficult to answer with historical cost data. Efficiency evaluations are limited to historical comparisons such as unit costs from month to month and to management's judgment about what costs should be. The problem with trend analysis is that there is no guarantee that the operation was efficient to begin with, so it may be meaningless to compare the costs of one period with those of another period. In addition, difficulties will be encountered in assessing the impact of changes in 'such factors as the volume of production, wage rates, product quality levels, productivity, raw materials prices, and the cost of overhead items. Management judgment about what costs should be is hindered by the same limitations.

If a manufacturing firm is to operate efficiently, it must be certain that economical amounts of resource inputs are utilized in the production of its products. This is true for both job order and process costing operations. Standard costs are carefully predetermined measures of what costs should be to produce a product or perform an operation in accordance with management's planned performance. They serve as benchmarks against which the actual performance can be evaluated realistically. While our primary concern in this chapter is the application of standard costs in manufacturing firms, they also are used in a wide range of other businesses such as hospitals, restaurants, accounting firms, banks, and automobile service centers. In practice, standard costing is potentially applicable whenever the activities of a business are repetitive.

In a manufacturing operation, standards are used to plan and control direct materials, direct labor, and manufacturing overhead. The objective is to establish a standard cost for each unit of product by predetermining the cost per unit of the direct materials, direct labor, and manufacturing overhead required to produce it. Both the per-unit dollar amounts that should be incurred for the three manufacturing cost elements and the quantity of each that should be used are identified. The standard direct materials cost consists of a standard price per unit of material multiplied by the standard number of units to be used. Likewise, the standard direct labor cost is composed of a standard labor rate per hour multiplied by the standard number of hours required. The standard amount of manufacturing overhead for a product is found by multiplying a predetermined overhead rate by some measure of standard production activity such as standard direct labor hours. The predetermined overhead rate is essentially the same as the one introduced in Chapter 23 with an actual cost accounting system.

BENEFITS OF STANDARD COSTS

The most important *benefits* of standard costs are the following:

1. Standard costs provide *reliable estimates* for the planning phase of budgeting. We noted in Chapter 24 that accurate projections for direct materials, direct labor, and manufacturing overhead are necessary to perform effective budgeting. Since standard costs are carefully predetermined costs, they provide the best basis for estimating future cost performance. Consequently, standard costs contribute significantly to the planning function of management.

2. Standard costs serve as *targets* in the application of responsibility accounting to evaluate performance and to control manufacturing costs. The standard costs represent measures of what costs should be, so any variances between them and the actual costs incurred can be investigated for potential corrective action. Cost control does not necessarily mean minimizing costs, but it does mean keeping them within acceptable limits. Responsible managers receive periodic reports that reveal any significant variances through the application of management by exception.

3. Standard costs can be used for inventory valuation with cost savings in the recordkeeping function. The inventories are maintained on the basis of standard costs without the detailed accounting of the actual costs needed in an actual costing system. Since the standard costs are predetermined costs, they are used to record the materials, labor, and manufacturing overhead as production takes place. A reconciliation of the actual costs is made at the end of an accounting period with variance analysis, thus eliminating much of the detailed accounting work and clerical cost incurred during the period.

4. Standard cost information is available on a timely basis for managerial decision-making. Management must make decisions regularly concerning such activities as product pricing, product profitability analysis, departmental performance evaluation, and utilization of resources. Standard costs can be used in many cases without waiting for the results of the actual performance.

5. Standard costs make employees *more aware of costs* and their impact on the operation. Most employees will not be trained accountants and will be more concerned with operating procedures than with the costs associated with them. Since the standard costs represent what costs should be, they make the employees more cost and time conscious, thus promoting an efficient use of resources. An incentive wage system, tied in with standard costs, can be implemented to increase the benefits from cost awareness further.

ESTABLISHING STANDARD COSTS

Standard costs are made up of a quantity and a unit cost. For example, the production of one finished product may require five pounds of direct materials at a cost of $2 per pound. The standard direct materials cost would be $10 per finished unit. Product specifications must be considered carefully in the establishment of standard costs to ensure that desired quality levels are maintained. Standard costs usually are established with one or some combination of the following three methods: an engineering approach, analysis of historical performance data, and management judgment concerning future operating conditions. Time studies, work sampling, and synthesizing procedures are examples of engineering techniques that can be used to develop standards. Their major purpose is to determine economical quantities of material and labor on a scientific basis. For example, a time study may be performed to determine the best combination of labor steps needed for a particular job. Historical cost data should not be ignored in the development of standard costs even though they may have the deficiencies mentioned earlier. The most recent past, in particular, can provide valuable insights into what can be expected in the future. Finally, management judgment concerning future performance must be weighed heavily. The managers responsible for the various activities are the persons closest to the day-to-day operations, so their opinions and knowledge must be considered. This is particularly important whenever external influences such as union negotiations for wage rates and market conditions for materials prices are involved. In many businesses, a standards committee is formed and given the responsibility to coordinate the development and revision of standard costs.

Management also must decide what type of standards the firm will use. The choice between ideal standards and attainable standards depends upon *how demanding* management wants the planned performance to be. **Ideal standards** require the highest possible level of effort if they are to be achieved. Consequently, they represent maximum efficiency and do not consider allowances for such factors as waste, spoilage, fatigue, work interruptions, and human error. Few businesses use ideal standards since they will produce significant variances from all but the very best performances and may discourage average or above-average workers from trying to achieve them.

Attainable standards are the preferred type because they represent targets that can be achieved with a reasonably efficient effort. As such, they are difficult but possible to attain and include allowances for departures from maximum efficiency. Once the standards are established, they should be reviewed regularly and revised whenever necessary to coincide with internal and external changes. For example, in inflationary times, material price standards will be changed frequently to keep pace with market conditions.

STANDARD COST VARIANCES

Standard cost variances arise when actual costs are different from standard costs. The cost variances enable management to evaluate the efficiency of the manufacturing operation and to improve the cost performance whenever necessary. *Standard cost variance analysis* is used to determine the amount of any difference between actual and standard costs as well as to discover what caused the deviation. When the actual costs exceed the standard costs, a variance is *unfavorable*. A *favorable* variance occurs when the actual costs are less than the standard costs.

Standard costs can be used for analytical purposes only or can be incorporated into the formal accounting system. When they are used only for analytical purposes, standard cost variances are shown on management performance reports used to control manufacturing costs. As such, they are not recorded in the general ledger. The more complete treatment is to establish cost variance accounts that are used to accumulate any differences between the actual and standard cost performance in the general ledger. When the cost variances are recognized in the general ledger, the costs charged to inventories and ultimately to cost of goods sold are standard costs rather than the actual costs incurred. An unfavorable variance will have a debit balance since it is in essence an *added cost*. A favorable variance will have a credit balance because it represents a *reduced cost*. In the following discussion of specific standard cost variances, we assume that standard costs and the related variances are recorded within the accounting system. To illustrate standard cost variances, we will refer to the Jackson Manufacturing Company's cost performance for January 1984. The company has predetermined the following standard costs for the production of one drum of Clean-up, an industrial cleaning compound that is the only product produced by the firm:

Standard costs for one unit of product (drum of Clean-up):

Direct materials—4 pounds @ $8.00	$32.00
Direct labor—2 hours @ $8.50	17.00
Manufacturing overhead—2 hours @ $7.00	14.00
Standard cost per drum	$63.00

The firm plans to produce one unit of product at a total cost of $63. During the month of January, the actual manufacturing costs incurred in the production of 4,100 drums were:

Actual costs for January:

Direct materials—17,200 pounds @ $8.50	$146,200
Direct labor—8,100 hours @ $8.70	70,470
Manufacturing overhead:	
Variable overhead cost—18,200	
Fixed overhead cost—45,100	
Total overhead cost	63,300
Total actual manufacturing costs for January	$279,970

The first step in variance analysis is to compare the actual costs incurred to produce 4,100 units of product with the standard costs that should have been incurred. Any difference will be a total cost variance that can be explained by a combination of material variances, labor variances, and manufacturing overhead variances. The total cost variance is computed as follows:

Total actual costs for January	$279,970
Total standard costs for January	
(4,100 units × $63)	258,300
Total unfavorable cost variance	$ 21,670

The next step is to identify the sources of the unfavorable cost variance of $21,670 incurred during January.

MATERIAL VARIANCE ANALYSIS

Any difference between the actual material cost and the standard material cost can be explained by a combination of a material price variance and a material quantity variance. The **material price variance** is the difference between the standard material price and the actual material price multiplied by the actual units of material purchased or used. It is used to *evaluate the performance* of the purchasing department and to *measure the effect* of price increases or decreases on the firm's profit results. Frequently, an unfavorable material price variance is not controllable because of changes in market prices. The **material quantity variance** is the difference between the standard amount of material allowed for production and the actual amount used multiplied by the standard price of material. It will provide a measure of a production department's efficiency in utilizing direct materials and will be the responsibility of the manager in charge of the related manufacturing activity. The material variances can be computed and journalized as follows:

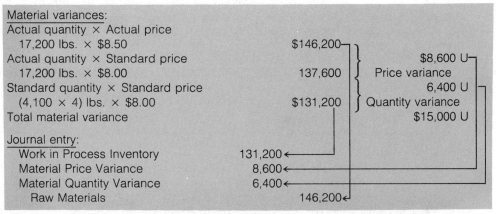

The *U* indicates an unfavorable variance. Since the actual cost of materials used exceeded the standard amount allowed by $15,000, an unfavorable total material variance was incurred. The material price variance was the result of a $.50-per-pound deviation from standard times 17,200 pounds, or $8,600. The production of 4,100 units of product called for only 16,400 standard pounds of material in contrast with the 17,200 pounds used. The difference of 800 pounds multiplied by the standard price of $8 indicates an unfavorable quantity variance of $6,400. Note that in the journal entry for material, the work in process inventory has been charged for standard material price and quantity with the two variances isolated for performance evaluation. Both unfavorable variances will require further investigation and corrective action if future profit goals are to be achieved.

LABOR VARIANCE ANALYSIS

A deviation between the actual direct labor cost and the standard labor cost can be divided into a labor rate variance and a labor efficiency variance. A **labor rate variance** is the difference between the standard labor rate and the actual labor rate multiplied times the actual hours worked. In many cases, standard labor rates are determined through a collective bargaining agreement according to employees' *experience, skills,* and *seniority*. In other situations, the rates are established by the personnel department in conjunction with higher management. Consequently, the responsibility for a labor rate variance must be assigned carefully. The manager in charge of the production performance will be accountable for scheduling workers with the correct wage rates to specific jobs. If an employee earning a wage rate different from the standard rate specified is assigned to a job, a labor rate variance—controllable by the related manager—will arise. The **labor efficiency variance** is the difference between the standard labor hours allowed and the actual hours used multiplied by the standard labor rate. The labor efficiency variance is used to measure the productivity of the labor force in achieving production results, so it will be the responsibility of the manager in charge of the manufacturing operation. The labor variances can be calculated and journalized in the following ways:

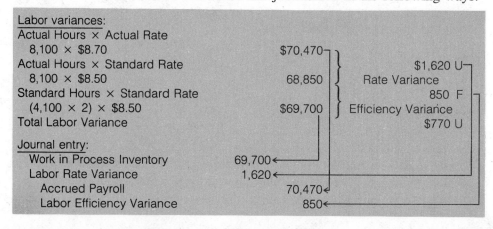

Again, the *U* indicates an unfavorable variance while the *F* identifies a favorable one. The labor rate variance is unfavorable because the actual rate exceeded the standard rate by $.20 per hour times 8,100 hours. In contrast, the labor efficiency variance is favorable, since 8,100 actual hours of labor were required for the production output when the standard hours allowed were 8,200. Each of the 100 hours below standard saved the firm $8.50 for a total of $850. The journal entry for labor also charges standard rate and hours to the work in process inventory, so it can be maintained purely on the basis of standard costs. Management will have to look at both labor variances to determine what corrective action is required. In doing so, any interrelationship between the two variances must be considered carefully. For example, the favorable efficiency variance may have occurred because highly skilled workers who can complete the job faster were used. This, in turn, may have caused the unfavorable rate variance because the highly skilled labor costs more than the standard rate.

STANDARD APPLICATION OF MANUFACTURING OVERHEAD

In effect, the predetermined overhead rate discussed in Chapter 23 is a standard cost. When the rate is applied to the actual direct labor hours worked, the charge to work in process is a *partial standard cost*. The standard amount of manufacturing overhead in a standard cost system is determined by multiplying the predetermined overhead rate times some measure of standard production activity such as standard direct labor hours, standard direct labor cost, or standard machine hours. For example, the standard cost information presented earlier for the Jackson Manufacturing Company indicates that the predetermined rate is $7 and that two standard direct labor hours per drum of Cleanup are required. The standard amount of overhead is therefore $14 for each finished unit. In a standard cost system, the actual hours worked are not considered in the application of manufacturing overhead since the applied overhead should not vary from the standard amount just because the actual and standard labor hours are different.

FLEXIBLE BUDGET FOR MANUFACTURING OVERHEAD

When we introduced the concept of a predetermined overhead rate in Chapter 23, we assumed for illustrative purposes that the consideration of one level of production activity was sufficient. As a result, we used a fixed budgeting approach we now know to be of limited value, because actual cost results can be compared only with budget estimates for the single level of activity. A flexible budget can be prepared for manufacturing overhead to avoid the limitations of a fixed budget. A distinction between variable and fixed costs is made and the budget is prepared for a range of production levels so management can evaluate the impact of attaining an activity level different from the one planned. The production activity levels are based on the same measure of standard production used to apply the overhead. Whenever the standard production performance is different from that planned, management can easily adjust to the change by revising the original budget. The budgeted fixed overhead costs for the standard production level attained will be the same as those in the original budget, but the budgeted variable overhead cost will change. A manufacturing overhead flexible budget for the Jackson Manufacturing Company is shown in Figure 25-4. The budget represents the January portion of the annual flexible budget used by the firm to calculate a predetermined overhead rate and to provide a comparative basis for cost performance evaluation with variance analysis. Standard direct labor hours are used to measure the level of production and range from 7,000 to 10,000 for the budget period. Four production levels are budgeted as percentages of maximum capacity at 70%, 80%, 90%, and 100%. *Maximum capacity* is the measure of the highest production level a firm can achieve with its existing physical facilities and organizational structure. The variable overhead costs change at a rate of $2 per standard direct labor hour within the budgeted range of activity. The fixed costs remain constant at $45,000. As a result, the total manufacturing overhead at any level of activity can be calculated with the following formula:

Manufacturing overhead = $45,000 + $2 (Standard direct labor hours)

Since a range of production activity is considered in the flexible budget, a single level of production must be selected for the calculation of the predetermined overhead rate. The choice of a specific production level is important because different overhead rates will be computed for different levels of production. These differences are caused by the fact that the fixed costs per standard direct labor hour decrease as the number of hours increases. The following schedule illustrates the effect of cost behavior on the calculation of a predetermined overhead rate from the flexible budget of Jackson Manufacturing Company:

		70%	80%	90%	100%
Standard direct labor hours	(A)	7,000	8,000	9,000	10,000
Variable overhead cost	(B)	$14,000	$16,000	$18,000	$20,000
Fixed overhead cost	(C)	45,000	45,000	45,000	45,000
Total overhead cost	(D)	59,000	61,000	63,000	65,000
Variable overhead rate per hour	(B ÷ A)	2.00	2.00	2.00	2.00
Fixed overhead rate per hour	(C ÷ A)	6.43	5.63	5.00	4.50
Total overhead rate per hour	(D ÷ A)	$ 8.43	$ 7.63	$ 7.00	$ 6.50

Figure 25-4
Manufacturing Over-
head Flexible
Budget

JACKSON MANUFACTURING COMPANY
Manufacturing Overhead Flexible Budget
Month of January, 1984

	Per hour		Normal Capacity		
Percentage of capacity		70	80	90	100
Units of production		3,500	4,000	4,500	5,000
Standard direct labor hours		7,000	8,000	9,000	10,000
Budgeted manufacturing overhead					
Variable costs					
Indirect materials	$ .20	$ 1,400	$ 1,600	$ 1,800	$ 2,000
Maintenance	1.10	7,700	8,800	9,900	11,000
Utilities	.70	4,900	5,600	6,300	7,000
Total Variable Costs	2.00	14,000	16,000	18,000	20,000
Fixed costs					
Supervision		9,500	9,500	9,500	9,500
Insurance		3,000	3,000	3,000	3,000
Property taxes		9,300	9,300	9,300	9,300
Supplies		2,200	2,200	2,200	2,200
Rent		6,000	6,000	6,000	6,000
Depreciation		15,000	15,000	15,000	15,000
Total Fixed Costs		45,000	45,000	45,000	45,000
Total Manufacturing Overhead		$59,000	$61,000	$63,000	$65,000
Predetermined overhead rate per standard direct labor hour ($63,000 ÷ 9,000 hours)					$7.00

As a result, the total overhead rate decreases from $8.43 per hour to $6.50 per hour as the capacity increases from 70% to 100%. If the correct production level is not selected at the beginning of the period, the *wrong amount of overhead* will be applied to work in process even if the actual cost performance is equal to its related budget estimates. For example, if Jackson Manufacturing Company selects its predetermined overhead rate from the maximum capacity level, the fixed portion of the rate will be $4.50. If the firm only works 8,000 standard direct labor hours, the fixed overhead applied will be $36,000 (8,000 × $4.50) despite the fact that the budgeted fixed costs were $45,000. The variable costs do not cause the same problem since they automatically adjust to the level of 8,000 standard direct labor hours, with the applied amount and budgeted amount being equal at $16,000 (8,000 × $2). The following four concepts of capacity can be considered for the choice of a production level within a flexible budget:

1. **Maximum capacity.** Highest level of production activity possible if optimal operating conditions exist with no delays, material shortages, or maintenance problems.
2. **Practical capacity.** Maximum capacity less reasonable allowances for departures from an optimal performance.
3. **Expected capacity.** Level of production activity expected for a specific year, given the firm's operating conditions and market demand for its products.
4. **Normal capacity.** The average annual production activity that will satisfy the market demand over a relatively long time, such as a three- to five-year period.

Since sales demand is ignored with maximum and practical capacities, they are not popular methods for predetermining a manufacturing overhead rate. If the sales volume does not fluctuate significantly from year to year, expected capacity and normal capacity will be approximately equal. Most accountants believe that normal capacity produces the *most accurate* manufacturing overhead rate when significant fluctuations in sales volume occur between years. The longer period will *normalize* the fluctuations between years and provide more consistent overhead application rates. We assume that Jackson Manufacturing Company uses normal capacity for the calculation of the predetermined overhead rate and that it amounts to 9,000 standard direct labor hours for the month of January. Consequently, the predetermined overhead rate is $7, as shown in Figure 25-4 and in the standard cost information presented earlier. The rate consists of $2 for the variable costs and $5 for the fixed costs. Each time a standard direct labor hour is recorded, $7 will be applied to the work in process inventory for manufacturing overhead.

UNDERAPPLIED AND OVERAPPLIED OVERHEAD

The difference between the actual manufacturing overhead and the standard amount applied to production is an overapplied or underapplied variance. If the actual overhead exceeds the amount applied, the result is an underapplied variance. In contrast, an overapplied variance exists when the standard amount of overhead applied to the work in process inventory during the period exceeds the actual overhead incurred. An underapplied condition is *unfavorable* because the cost of the inventory is understated while the reverse is true (*favorable*) for an overapplied situation. In order to control manufacturing overhead costs, management needs to be able to identify the sources underlying any difference between the actual and applied overhead just as it did with materials and labor.

OVERHEAD VARIANCE ANALYSIS

The division of the total overhead variance for analytical purposes is analogous to the variance analysis discussed earlier for materials and labor, when a total variance was separated into *price* and *quantity components*. While manufacturing overhead variances can be computed in several ways, we will restrict our attention in this text to a *two-variance approach* consisting of a controllable variance and a capacity variance. A **controllable variance** is the difference between the actual manufacturing overhead costs and the manufacturing overhead budgeted for the standard production activity level attained. The actual overhead costs will be recorded in the general ledger during an accounting period and the budgeted overhead will be determined by adjusting the flexible budget to the standard production level of the period. The controllable variance is a measure of management's efficiency in utilizing the manufacturing overhead costs and will be the responsibility of the manager in charge of the related manufacturing operation.

A **capacity variance** is the difference between the manufacturing overhead budgeted for the standard production activity level attained and the standard amount of overhead applied to the work in process inventory during the period. The capacity variance is also called a volume variance or denominator variance because it results from using the estimated level of activity rather than the actual level as the denominator in calculating the predetermined overhead rate. As pointed out earlier, the fixed overhead costs applied will not equal those budgeted when the standard production activity level attained differs from the original capacity level budgeted. Therefore, a capacity variance is the result of absorbing the budgeted fixed overhead costs over a different production level. It is an important measure of the cost of capacity available but not utilized. For example, in the Jackson Manufacturing Company case, management's goal was to operate at a normal capacity of 9,000 standard direct labor hours but only 8,200 standard direct labor hours were recorded. Consequently, the fixed cost portion of the predetermined overhead rate ($5) was not adequate to absorb all of the budgeted fixed overhead costs ($45,000). The reasons for the idle capacity may range from manufacturing problems to a lack of sales orders. As a result, either the production department or the sales department may be responsible for a capacity variance, depending on the circumstances.

The controllable variance and the capacity variance for the Jackson Manufacturing Company can be computed and journalized as follows:

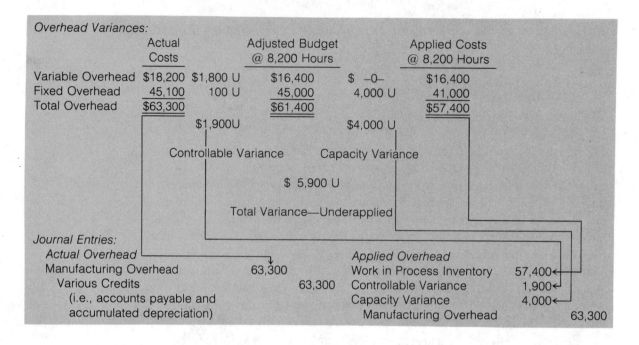

Overhead Variances:

	Actual Costs		Adjusted Budget @ 8,200 Hours		Applied Costs @ 8,200 Hours
Variable Overhead	$18,200	$1,800 U	$16,400	$ –0–	$16,400
Fixed Overhead	45,100	100 U	45,000	4,000 U	41,000
Total Overhead	$63,300		$61,400		$57,400

$1,900U — Controllable Variance

$4,000 U — Capacity Variance

$ 5,900 U

Total Variance—Underapplied

Journal Entries:

Actual Overhead			*Applied Overhead*	
Manufacturing Overhead	63,300		Work in Process Inventory	57,400
Various Credits		63,300	Controllable Variance	1,900
(i.e., accounts payable and			Capacity Variance	4,000
accumulated depreciation)			Manufacturing Overhead	63,300

An unfavorable controllable variance of $1,900 was incurred because the actual variable overhead and the actual fixed overhead exceeded the budget by $1,800 and $100, respectively. The unfavorable controllable variance of $1,900 can be analyzed in more detail for each of the cost items involved, by developing the report shown in Figure 25-5. The unfavorable capacity variance of $4,000 was the result of working 8,200 standard direct labor hours instead of the 9,000 hours representing normal capacity. The 800-hour difference multiplied times the fixed cost rate of $5 per hour is equal to the capacity variance. The sum of the two overhead variances is equal to the amount of underapplied manufacturing overhead or $5,900. Again, notice that the work in process inventory is charged with the standard overhead costs only, which are calculated by multiplying the predetermined rate of $7 times the standard direct labor hours of 8,200, or a total of $57,400.

RECAP OF VARIANCES

Earlier we noted that the actual manufacturing costs for Jackson Manufacturing Company exceeded the standard costs by $21,670. Having computed the six variances attributable to the manufacturing cost performance, we can divide the total variance as follows for further investigation with management by exception:

Unfavorable material price variance	$ 8,600
Unfavorable material quantity variance	6,400
Unfavorable labor rate variance	1,620
Favorable labor efficiency variance	(850)
Unfavorable controllable variance	1,900
Unfavorable capacity variance	4,000
Total manufacturing cost variances	$21,670

JACKSON MANUFACTURING COMPANY
Controllable Variance Report
Month Ended January 31, 1984

	Budget*	Actual	Controllable Variance
Variable overhead costs			
Indirect materials	$ 1,640	$ 1,690	$ 50 U
Maintenance	9,020	10,150	1,130 U
Utilities	5,740	6,360	620 U
Total	16,400	18,200	1,800 U
Fixed costs			
Supervision	9,500	9,500	—
Insurance	3,000	3,000	—
Property taxes	9,300	9,300	—
Supplies	2,200	2,300	100 U
Rent	6,000	6,000	—
Depreciation	15,000	15,000	—
Total	45,000	45,100	100 U
Total Manufacturing Overhead	$61,400	$63,300	$1,900 U

*Adjusted budget for 8,200 standard direct labor hours.
U Indicates an unfavorable variance.

Figure 25-5
Controllable Variance Report

DISPOSITION OF COST VARIANCES

When cost variances are recorded in general ledger accounts as they were in the Jackson Manufacturing Company illustration, their balances at the end of an accounting period must be disposed of in the preparation of financial statements. Cost variances normally are allowed to accumulate for external reporting from month to month since unfavorable variances in one month often are offset with favorable variances of another month. For interim reporting purposes, they are shown on the balance sheet with an unfavorable variance as an asset and a favorable variance as a liability. At the end of the year, relatively small balances in the variance accounts are adjusted to cost of goods sold in the income statement. When the variances are significant, they should be prorated to the work in process inventory, finished goods inventory, and cost of goods sold because only actual costs can be used with generally accepted accounting principles.

The treatment of standard cost variances for internal reporting purposes is somewhat different. Since the standard costs represent management's goals for a specific period, it is customary to report the variances to management as they occur. This is accomplished by adjusting each period's cost of goods sold in the income statement prepared for management. For example, assume that Jackson Manufacturing Company sold all 4,100 drums of Clean-up that it produced in January. The cost of goods sold section of a monthly income statement prepared for management would show the following:

Standard cost of goods sold (4,100 units @ $63)		$258,300
Plus unfavorable cost variances:		
Material price variance	8,600	
Material quantity variance	6,400	
Labor rate variance	1,620	
Controllable variance	1,900	
Capacity variance	4,000	
Less favorable cost variances:		
Labor efficiency variance	(850)	21,670
Actual cost of goods sold		$279,970

GLOSSARY

ATTAINABLE STANDARDS. Performance targets that can be achieved with a reasonably efficient effort (p. 979).

CAPACITY VARIANCE. The difference between the budgeted manufacturing overhead cost for the standard production activity level attained and the standard amount of overhead applied to the work in process inventory (p. 987).

CONTROLLABLE VARIANCE. The difference between the budgeted manufacturing overhead cost for the standard production activity level attained and the actual overhead costs for the period (p. 987).

EXPECTED CAPACITY. The level of production activity expected for a specific year, given the firm's operating conditions and market demand for its products (p. 986).

FIXED (STATIC) BUDGET. A budget prepared for only one level of activity (p. 972).

FLEXIBLE BUDGET. A series of budgets prepared for a range of business activity (p. 972).

IDEAL STANDARDS. Performance targets that can be achieved only with an optimal performance (p. 979).

LABOR EFFICIENCY VARIANCE. The difference between the standard labor hours allowed for production and the actual hours used multiplied by the standard labor rate. It is used to measure the productivity of the labor force (p. 982).

LABOR RATE VARIANCE. The difference between the standard labor rate and the actual labor rate multiplied by the actual hours worked. It is used to measure how well the firm stayed within its labor rate limits (p. 982).

MATERIAL PRICE VARIANCE. The difference between the standard material price and the actual material price multiplied by the actual units of material purchased or used. It is used to measure the performance of the purchasing department and evaluate the effect of price changes on profits (p. 981).

MATERIAL QUANTITY VARIANCE. The difference between the standard amount of material allowed for production and the actual material used multiplied by the standard price of material. It is used to measure the efficiency of material utilization (p. 981).

MAXIMUM CAPACITY. The highest level of production activity possible if optimal conditions exist (p. 986).

NORMAL CAPACITY. The average annual production activity that will satisfy the market demand over a relatively long time, such as a three- to five-year period. It is the most popular choice of capacity for the calculation of a predetermined manufacturing overhead rate (p. 986).

PRACTICAL CAPACITY. The maximum production capacity of a firm less reasonable allowances for departures from an optimal performance (p. 986).

STANDARD COSTS. Carefully predetermined costs that should be incurred to produce a product or perform an operation. They are used to plan and control a firm's financial performance and are especially important in a manufacturing firm (p. 972).

STANDARD COST VARIANCES. The difference between standard costs and actual costs, which can be used in the application of management by exception (p. 979).

DISCUSSION QUESTIONS

1. Differentiate between a fixed budget and a flexible budget.
2. What is the deficiency of a fixed budget for performance evaluation purposes?
3. What are the major steps involved in the preparation of a flexible budget?
4. "The flexible aspect of a flexible budget consists of variable costs." Do you agree? Explain.
5. "Fixed costs are not important in the use of a flexible budget." Do you agree? Explain.
6. What is a standard cost?
7. What is wrong with comparing actual performance with past performance to evaluate a firm's efficiency?

8. What are the benefits of standard costs?
9. How are standard costs established?
10. Distinguish between ideal and attainable standards.
11. Who is usually responsible for a material price variance? A material quantity variance?
12. Who is usually responsible for a labor rate variance? A labor efficiency variance?
13. The Balton Company has a standard labor rate of $8.60 per hour. Each of its finished products requires 4 hours of labor. During July, 5,200 units are produced with 22,800 labor hours and a labor cost of $202,920. What is the total labor cost variance? How much of it is attributable to labor rate? Labor efficiency?
14. What is a controllable overhead variance? A capacity variance?
15. Why is the determination of a specific capacity level important in the application of manufacturing overhead with a flexible budget?
16. Explain the following terms:
    (a) Maximum capacity
    (b) Practical capacity
    (c) Expected capacity
    (d) Normal capacity
17. The Colt Company uses normal capacity measured in standard direct labor hours to apply manufacturing overhead. During 1984, normal capacity was 10,000 standard direct labor hours while the standard direct labor hours allowed for the production level achieved amounted to 9,600. Actual hours worked amounted to 10,200. The predetermined overhead rate was $6.00, of which $2.00 was variable. How much overhead was applied to work in process? What was the capacity variance?
18. Explain the basic difference in disposing of standard cost variances in internal reports as compared with the treatment of them for external reporting.

EXERCISES

Exercise 25-1 (Computing Material Price and Quantity Variances)
The Monroe Company uses a standard cost system that specifies that 30 board-feet of lumber at $3.50 per board-foot should be used to manufacture one office desk. The company used 9,900 board-feet of lumber to produce 300 desks. The total purchase price of the materials used in production was $33,660.

Required:
Calculate the material price and quantity variances.

Exercise 25-2 (Computing Labor Rate and Efficiency Variances)
The Darlington Company has decided that the labor standards for each unit produced are 3 hours of assembly labor at $3.75 per hour and 2.5 hours of finishing labor at $4.50 per hour. During May, the company produced 700 units using 1,890 hours of

assembly labor and 2,100 hours of finishing labor. The company's direct labor payroll was $7,182 for assembly labor and $9,555 for finishing labor.

Required:
Calculate the labor rate and efficiency variances for the assembly labor and the finishing labor.

Exercise 25-3 (Computing Overhead Controllable and Capacity Variances)

The Grafton Company manufactures washing machines and applies manufacturing overhead using standard direct labor hours. The company estimated that it would use 30,000 standard direct labor hours to produce 6,000 washing machines during 1985. At this level of production, the company has budgeted variable overhead to be $120,000 and fixed overhead at $67,500. Actual production for 1985 was 6,200 units, and the actual overhead incurred was $191,300, of which $124,300 was variable overhead.

Required:
Calculate the manufacturing overhead controllable variance and capacity variance.

Exercise 25-4 (Evaluating Labor Efficiency and Overhead Capacity Variances)

The following six independent companies apply fixed manufacturing overhead on the basis of direct labor hours. For each company, the budgeted standard direct labor hours used to calculate the fixed overhead application rate, the actual direct labor hours incurred, and the standard direct labor hours allowed for the actual production are presented below.

Company	Budgeted Direct Labor Hours	Actual Direct Labor Hours	Standard Direct Labor Hours
Thread Company	12,000	10,500	11,000
Needle Company	16,000	15,300	16,000
Stitch Company	13,000	14,000	14,500
Berry Company	10,000	11,000	10,200
City Company	11,000	10,000	10,000
Country Company	15,000	15,500	15,500

Required:
For each company, indicate whether there would be a favorable or unfavorable capacity variance. Also specify whether the company incurred a favorable or unfavorable labor efficiency variance.

Exercise 25-5 (Basic Concepts of a Flexible Budget)

The Ramsey Company has prepared cost estimates within a relevant range of 10,000 to 12,000 direct labor hours.

	Fixed Costs	Variable Cost per Direct Labor Hour
Maintenance	$3,000	$.25
Depreciation	5,000	—
Supplies	700	.45
Utilities	1,500	.15
Rent	2,000	—
Insurance	3,000	—
Indirect labor	6,000	.75

Required:

A. Prepare a flexible overhead budget for 10,000, 11,000, and 12,000 direct labor hours.

B. Calculate the fixed and variable manufacturing overhead rate if 10,000 direct labor hours are the normal capacity.

C. Calculate the fixed and variable overhead rate if 12,000 direct labor hours are the normal capacity. Round all calculations to the nearest hundredths.

Exercise 25-6 (Preparing a Flexible Budget Performance Report)

The Fairhaven Company applies manufacturing overhead on the basis of units produced and has prepared the following flexible budget.

Number of units	8,000	9,000	10,000
Indirect labor	$ 7,600	$ 8,100	$ 8,600
Supplies	5,700	5,850	6,000
Utilities	10,100	10,350	10,600

At a production level of 9,000 units, the fixed overhead rate is $.40 per unit for indirect labor, $.50 per unit for supplies, and $.90 per unit for utilities. During the preceding year, the company produced 8,700 units and the actual overhead costs incurred included indirect labor—$8,000; supplies—$5,790; and utilities—$10,315.

Required:

Prepare a flexible budget performance report for the Fairhaven Company.

PROBLEMS

Problem 25-1 (Use of a Flexible Budget Performance Report)

The Todd Company has prepared a fixed budget performance report for the year ending December 31, 1985:

	Budget	Actual	Variance
Units of production	35,000	37,000	2,000 U
Manufacturing costs			
Direct materials	$227,500	$246,790	$19,290 U
Direct labor	288,750	303,770	15,020 U
Manufacturing overhead			
Variable costs			
Indirect labor	56,700	62,530	5,830 U
Supplies	19,950	18,500	1,450 F
Repairs	11,550	13,320	1,770 U
Total variable overhead	88,200	94,350	6,150 U
Fixed costs			
Insurance	4,000	4,200	200 U
Rent	12,000	12,000	–0–
Depreciation	10,000	10,000	–0–
Supervisory salaries	21,000	21,500	500 U
Total Fixed Overhead	47,000	47,700	700 U
Total Manufacturing Overhead	135,200	142,050	6,850 U
Total Manufacturing Costs	$651,450	$692,610	$41,160 U

Required:

Prepare a flexible budget performance report.

Problem 25-2 (Evaluating Variances from Standard Costs)

The RTB Company had a total favorable direct labor variance of $220 for the month of April. The standard labor wage rate was $6, but due to a recent pay increase the labor rate variance for April was $260, unfavorable. The actual hours of direct labor used in production were 520. The company's total direct material variance for April was $80, unfavorable, and the material quantity variance was $300, unfavorable. The actual cost of the materials used in production was $3,080; the standard quantity of direct materials for April's production was 1,000 pounds.

Required:

Calculate the actual labor wage rate per unit and the standard direct labor hours allowed for the units produced. Also determine the standard price, the actual price, and the actual number of pounds for the materials used in production.

Problem 25-3 (Determining Standard Cost Variances)

The Heiting Company uses a standard cost system for planning and control and has prepared the following budgets.

	75%	90%
Capacity	75%	90%
Production in units	3,000	3,600
Manufacturing overhead		
Variable		
Indirect labor	$9,750	$11,700
Supplies	2,190	2,628
Repairs	630	756
Utilities	1,080	1,296
Fixed		
Rent	9,000	9,000
Insurance	5,000	5,000
Property taxes	3,000	3,000
Depreciation	1,720	1,720

The standard cost data for the company's product is:

Direct labor—4 hours at $8 per hour

Direct materials—20 pounds at $2 per pound

Manufacturing overhead—4 hours at $ _?_ per hour. The company uses normal capacity of 90% for the calculation of the predetermined overhead rate.

The company operated at 75% of capacity and produced 3,000 units. The actual costs were:

Direct labor: 12,200 hours at $7.80 per hour	$ 95,160
Direct materials: 59,700 pounds at $2.10 per pound	125,370
Rent	9,000
Insurance	5,000
Property taxes	3,000
Depreciation	1,720
Indirect labor	9,810
Supplies	2,130
Repairs	540
Utilities	1,200

Required:

A. Calculate the predetermined overhead rate. In your calculations of the fixed and variable overhead rate per hour, use four decimal places.

B. Calculate the price (rate) and quantity (efficiency) variances for material (labor).

C. Compute the controllable and capacity variances for manufacturing overhead.

Problem 25-4 (Calculating Standard Cost Variances)

The R.M.N. Company has provided the following information regarding the company's only product:

Standard direct materials cost	$1.35 per pound
Standard direct labor cost	$4.20 per hour
Standard hours of direct labor per unit	3 hours
Standard quantity of materials per unit	5 pounds
Variable overhead per direct labor hour	$3.00
Budgeted production in units	6,000
Fixed overhead per direct labor hour	$1.50

During the preceding month, the actual production was 6,300 units. The company purchased and used 32,000 pounds of material at a cost of $1.25 per pound. The average wage paid for the 19,000 hours of direct labor was $4.40 per hour. The actual variable manufacturing overhead was $58,900, and the actual fixed manufacturing overhead was $27,200.

Required:
A. Compute the material price and quantity variances and the labor rate and efficiency variances.
B. Calculate the overhead controllable and capacity variances.

Problem 25-5 (Accounting for Variances from Standard Performance)

The JoJo Company has predetermined the following standard costs needed to produce one product and recorded the actual unit costs incurred during the preceding month. The actual production was 2,400 units; budgeted production was normal capacity of 2,500 units. The firm uses normal capacity to calculate its predetermined overhead rate.

	Standard Cost	Actual Cost
Materials	7 feet @ $6.30 per yard	6.8 feet @ $6.45 per yard
Labor	3.2 hours @ $5.20 per hour	3.4 hours @ $5.10 per hour
Variable overhead	3.2 hours @ $4.10 per hour	3.4 hours @ $4.25 per hour
Fixed overhead	3.2 hours @ $1.20 per hour	3.4 hours @ $1.20 per hour

Required:
A. Calculate the labor rate and efficiency variances.
B. Calculate the material price and quantity variances.
C. Calculate the overhead controllable and capacity variances.
D. Prepare journal entries to record the variances and costs incurred in the Work in Process account for materials, labor, and manufacturing overhead.

ALTERNATE PROBLEMS

Problem 25-1A (Use of a Flexible Budget Performance Report)

Fritz's Supply Company has prepared the following fixed budget performance report for the year ending July 31, 1984.

	Budget	Actual	Variance
Units of production	15,000	13,000	2,000 U
Manufacturing costs			
Direct material	$135,000	$120,250	$14,750 F
Direct labor	105,000	89,700	15,300 F
Manufacturing overhead			
Variable costs			
Indirect labor	15,000	13,650	1,350 F
Supplies	22,500	22,750	250 U
Repairs	11,250	11,700	450 U
Total Variable Overhead	48,750	48,100	650 F
Fixed costs			
Depreciation	3,000	3,100	100 U
Insurance	1,000	800	200 F
Rent	5,000	5,000	—
Salaries	7,000	7,200	200 U
Total Fixed Overhead	16,000	16,100	100 U
Total Manufacturing Cost	$304,750	$274,150	$30,600 F

Required:

Prepare a flexible budget performance report that corrects the deficiencies of the report shown above.

Problem 25-2A (Evaluating Variances from Standard Costs)

The Corning Company had a total unfavorable material cost variance of $300. The material price variance was $200, unfavorable. The standard cost of material was $2 per pound, and the total standard cost of the materials for May's production was $3,900. The company's total direct labor variance was $100, unfavorable. The actual cost of labor was $8,625, and the actual labor rate was $11.50. The labor efficiency variance was $275, favorable.

Required:

Calculate the standard direct labor hours for the units produced, the actual number of direct labor hours incurred, and the standard labor rate. Also calculate the actual quantity of materials used in production, the actual unit price of the materials, and the standard quantity of materials allowed for the production level achieved.

Problem 25-3A (Determining Standard Cost Variances)

The Hodge Company has prepared the following summarized manufacturing overhead budget using a standard cost system.

Capacity	90%	95%
Production in units	18,000	19,000
Manufacturing overhead		
Variable	$124,200	$131,100
Fixed	85,500	85,500

The standard cost data for the company's only product are:

Direct material	15 pounds at $4 per pound
Direct labor	6 hours at $12 per hour
Manufacturing overhead	6 hours at $1.90 per hour

The company uses normal capacity of 95% for the calculation of the predetermined overhead rate. The company actually operated at 90% of capacity, producing 18,000 units and incurring the following costs:

Direct material: 288,000 pounds at $3.90 per pound	$1,123,200
Direct labor: 104,400 hours at $12.10 per hour	1,263,240
Variable manufacturing overhead	128,000
Fixed manufacturing overhead	85,500

Required:
A. Calculate the efficiency (quantity) and rate (price) variances for labor and material.
B. Calculate the controllable and capacity variances for manufacturing overhead.

Problem 25-4A (Calculating Standard Cost Variances)

The Seneca Company produced 3,800 units during the previous month. The company had purchased and used 31,160 pounds of material at a cost of $3.60 per pound. The actual variable manufacturing overhead was $78,700, and the actual fixed manufacturing overhead was $45,100. The company used 14,820 hours of direct labor, and the actual wage rate was $7.30 per hour.

The company's standard costs for the product are:

Standard quantity of direct materials per unit	8 pounds
Standard hours of direct labor per unit	4 hours
Standard direct material cost per pound	$3.70
Standard direct labor rate per hour	7.10
Variable overhead per direct labor hour	5.00
Fixed overhead per direct labor hour	3.00
Budgeted production in units	4,000

Required:
A. Calculate the material price and quantity variances.
B. Calculate the labor rate and efficiency variances.
C. Calculate the manufacturing overhead controllable and capacity variances.

Problem 25-5A (Accounting for Variances from Standard Performance)

The Placid Company has compiled the following data for the standard costs and actual costs incurred during production in the preceding month:

	Standard Cost	Actual Cost
Labor	5.4 hours at $8.00 per hour	5.2 hours at $8.20 per hour
Material	4.3 pounds at $5.10 per pound	4.6 pounds at $4.90 per pound
Variable overhead	5.4 hours at $3.50 per hour	5.2 hours at $3.75 per hour
Fixed overhead	5.4 hours at $1.60 per hour	5.2 hours at $1.60 per hour

The actual production was 5,100 units; budgeted production was normal capacity of 5,000 units. The firm uses normal capacity to calculate the predetermined overhead rate.

Required:
A. Calculate the material price and quantity variances.
B. Calculate the labor rate and efficiency variances.
C. Calculate the overhead controllable and capacity variances.
D. Prepare journal entries to record the variances and costs incurred in the Work in Process account for materials, labor, and manufacturing overhead.

CASE FOR CHAPTER 25

Decision Problem (Establishing the Basis for Standard Labor Hours)

The Cardwell Company produces several models of robots that are used to manufacture automobiles. The firm has been in existence for only five years and has experienced significantly higher production costs during the past three years. A job order cost system using actual cost data has been used to accumulate product costs. The president of the firm, Bill Cardwell, has an engineering background. He has analyzed the cost data from the performance of the past three years and is alarmed because labor costs have increased 50% during that period. In turn, the company's profits declined by 80%.

Mr. Cardwell hired an engineering consulting firm to evaluate the labor cost performance and establish labor standards for the future. In analyzing the report prepared by the engineering consulting firm, the president notes the following times required by several workers to perform a certain operation in the production of a particular robot:

Worker	Time Required (Hours)
J. Jones	5.5
H. Herff	5.5
J. Alkins	5.5
R. Merden	5.8
D. Madden	6.2
B. Kulsrod	6.2
V. Bingley	6.2

D. Douglas	6.6
B. Jordan	7.2
S. Burns	7.3
Average	6.2

In addition, the president is further confused because the engineering consulting firm has informed him that the operation in question should be performed in five hours if ideal operating conditions and labor efficiency existed. The firm's cost accountant advises the president that the standard labor quantity should be 5.5 hours for the operation. However, the production manager involved says that the average amount of labor (6.2 hours) should be used as the standard. The president believes that the choice of an appropriate labor standard for this operation is an important decision because the same thinking will be used for all production operations in order to control future labor costs.

Required:

A. What is the difference between an ideal standard cost and an attainable standard cost?

B. What should be established as the standard quantity of labor in this case? Why?

PART EIGHT
BUSINESS DECISION
MAKING

CHAPTER 26
COST-VOLUME-PROFIT RELATIONSHIPS

OVERVIEW AND OBJECTIVES

This chapter covers the subject of cost-volume-profit relationships. When you have completed the chapter, you should understand:

- The importance of cost behavioral analysis for managerial accounting applications (pp. 1005–1009).
- The basic techniques used to determine linear cost functions (pp. 1009–1011).
- The significance of the relevant range (pp. 1007–1008).
- The benefits of a contribution margin-oriented income statement (pp. 1011–1013).
- The basic differences between absorption costing and variable costing income statements (pp. 1013–1017).
- The benefits and limitations of variable costing (p. 1018).
- The manner in which profit goals can be achieved by a business with cost-volume-profit analysis (pp. 1019–1024).
- The calculation and application of break-even sales (pp. 1020–1022, 1027–1028).
- The use of a cost-volume-profit chart to evaluate the profitability of different levels of business activity (pp. 1021–1022).
- The evaluation of changes in such factors as selling price, sales volume, sales mix, and costs with cost-volume-profit analysis (pp. 1024–1027).

In Chapter 24, we emphasized the importance of a planned profit performance. Management is constantly faced with decisions concerning *selling prices, sales volume, sales mix,* and *costs* in the search for the combination of these factors that will produce acceptable profits. To find the right combination, management must be able to evaluate the effect on net income of interrelationships among the four factors. **Cost-volume-profit (CVP) analysis** is an important managerial accounting technique used to determine how costs and profits are affected by changes in the level of business activity. It can assist in answering such questions as:

1. What is the firm's break-even point—the sales level at which the business will neither earn a profit nor incur a loss?
2. What will be the impact on sales volume and profit of increasing advertising expenses?
3. What level of sales must be achieved to earn a desired amount of net income?
4. If selling prices are increased or decreased, what will be the effect on sales volume?
5. If a variable cost such as direct labor is eliminated and replaced with a fixed cost such as machinery depreciation, what would be the impact on profits?
6. How much additional sales volume is required to offset a pending increase in direct materials cost by a vendor?
7. If additional plant capacity is acquired at a higher level of fixed manufacturing overhead cost, what will happen to net income?
8. What is the most profitable sales mix?

When the cost behavioral concepts introduced in Chapter 22 are combined with information concerning selling prices, sales volume, and sales mix, the effect of a change in the level of business activity can be evaluated effectively with CVP analysis. Thus, knowledge about cost behavioral patterns is an integral part of CVP analysis. Many manufacturing firms develop the cost data required for CVP analysis within the accounting system by using the variable costing method of product costing (also introduced in Chapter 22) rather than the absorption costing method we have been concerned with so far in our discussion of manufacturing accounting.

COST BEHAVIORAL ANALYSIS REVISITED

Chapter 22 introduced the concept of cost behavior, which is the measure of how a cost will respond to changes in the level of business activity. Several types of cost behavior are possible, but the three most important ones for CVP analysis are variable costs, fixed costs, and mixed costs. Recall that a variable cost will *vary in total amount proportionately* with some measure of activity or volume such as sales dollars, products produced, or direct labor hours. In contrast, a fixed cost will *remain constant in total amount* over a wide range of activity. A third type of cost behavior is a mixed cost (sometimes called a semi-variable cost), which contains both fixed and variable cost components.

The managerial accountant must be able to evaluate each cost item incurred by the firm to determine the cost function that best describes the item's cost behavior. In its most basic form, a **cost function** is a relationship between cost as a dependent variable and some measure of activity or volume as an independent variable. In more advanced cases (which are beyond the scope of this text), more than one independent variable can be considered.

An important aspect of CVP analysis is that all cost functions are assumed to be **linear** (in the form of a straight line) so the rate of change is constant and easy to predict. As such, the cost function used in CVP analysis can be expressed as a linear equation, as follows:

$$y = a + bx$$

where: y = the total cost

a = the y intercept or the fixed portion of the total cost

b = the slope of the cost function or the variable cost rate

x = the measure of activity or volume such as sales dollars,

units produced, or direct labor hours

This basic equation was used for the development of the manufacturing overhead flexible budget in Chapter 25, where y was equal to the manufacturing overhead cost, a was $45,000, b was $2, and x represented standard direct labor hours. The three basic cost functions can be graphed as shown in Figure 26-1. Unfortunately, many firms experience some costs that are not exactly variable and others that are not exactly fixed over the entire range of business activity possible. In order to understand and justify how managerial accountants treat the more complex cost behavioral patterns in the application of CVP analysis, we must first consider some of the complications associated with variable and fixed cost behavior.

Figure 26-1
Three Basic Cost
Functions

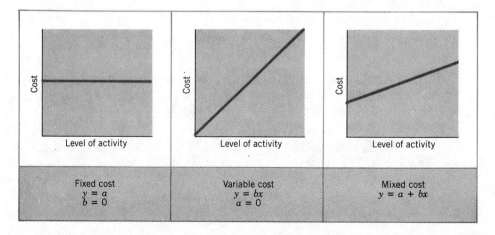

Fixed cost	Variable cost	Mixed cost
$y = a$	$y = bx$	$y = a + bx$
$b = 0$	$a = 0$	

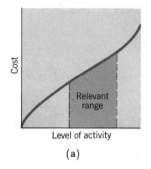

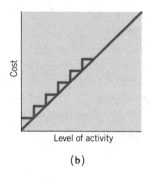

Figure 26-2
Curvilinear and Step
Cost Functions

VARIABLE COST BEHAVIOR

Few variable costs behave exactly as linear functions with constant slopes over all levels of activity. Two notable exceptions, a *curvilinear function* and a *step function,* are found in many businesses. A graphic version of each of these cost functions is shown in Figure 26-2. The curvilinear variable cost shown in graph (*a*) is the result of what economists describe as economies and diseconomies of scale. At extremely low levels of activity, a firm does not have sufficient volume to take advantage of such factors as automation and the specialization of labor. Consequently, the variable cost function increases at an increasing rate. When unusually high levels of activity are achieved, inefficiencies and bottlenecks occur so a variable cost again increases at an increasing rate. Within the shaded area of graph (*a*), the cost function is approximately linear because the rate of increase is relatively constant. The shaded area of the graph is called the **relevant range,** which is the range of activity within which a firm expects to operate. The relevant range concept is important for CVP analysis because it permits a linearity assumption for curvilinear variable costs within the specified limits of activity.

A step cost function such as the one exhibited in graph (*b*) will be incurred for some variable cost items because they cannot be purchased in divisible units. For example, labor services generally are acquired on the basis of 40 hours per week. The associated costs cannot be inventoried for future use since they must be utilized or lost as each workday passes. Consequently, each worker's wages represent a step in the cost function shown in graph (*b*). The cost function increases abruptly as an additional worker is hired to satisfy the needs of a higher level of activity. Again, the managerial accountant converts the step function into a linear function, as shown in graph (*b*) by connecting the points representing the highest level of activity for each step. The justification for the conversion is that the business will want to fully utilize the labor cost for any given step by attaining the highest level of activity possible.

Figure 26-3
Fixed Cost Function

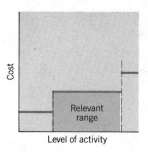

FIXED COST BEHAVIOR

The relevant-range concept also permits management to assume that the total fixed costs will remain constant over a range of activity. In reality, the total fixed costs may change over a complete range of activity in wide steps, as shown in Figure 26-3. Many fixed costs are defined as **discretionary fixed costs** because they can be reduced or discontinued by management if adequate time is available. At low levels of activity, management may decide to reduce or eliminate such activities as advertising, research and development, and employee training programs. At an extremely low level of activity such as one caused by a prolonged strike, drastic measures may be necessary to eliminate all but the committed fixed costs through layoffs and curtailments. The **committed fixed costs** are required even if the operation is shut down temporarily. They consist of such items as depreciation, property taxes, insurance, and top management salaries.

At an extremely high level of activity, added capacity will be necessary to satisfy the market demand for the firm's products or services, so fixed costs such as depreciation and managerial salaries will increase. Again, the relevant-range concept permits management to ignore the low and high levels by concentrating on the normal range of operation. Within the relevant range, the fixed costs will remain constant in total amount.

MIXED COST BEHAVIOR

As we can see in Figure 26-1, a mixed cost contains *both* fixed and variable components. Consequently, a mixed cost increases or decreases linearly with changes in activity but has a positive amount at zero activity. The fixed portion of a mixed cost represents the minimum cost of obtaining a service, while the variable element is the result of a change in activity. For example, the rental of an automobile will be a mixed cost when a fixed amount per day and a certain rate per mile are charged. Other examples of mixed costs in some cases are utilities, maintenance, sales salaries, employees' insurance, and office machine rental.

COST BEHAVIORAL ANALYSIS OF MIXED COSTS

For mixed costs to be planned and controlled, they must be divided into their fixed and variable components. A number of techniques based on the equation $y = a + bx$ can be used for the separation of mixed costs. The three most popular techniques are *visual fit of a scatter diagram, high–low method,* and *linear regression analysis*. All three techniques are based on the collection of historical data that represent the mixed costs incurred at different levels of activity. The objective is to develop a cost function that best reflects the cost behavior pattern of the mixed costs. As a simplified example, assume that a manufacturing firm has experienced the following maintenance costs and machine hours during the past 12 months:

Month	Maintenance Costs	Machine Hours
January	$27,550	2,920
February	28,600	3,625
March	31,680	4,380
April	33,350	4,752
May	36,000	5,986
June	37,700	7,250
July	41,760	8,640
August	38,610	7,150
September	36,250	6,525
October	34,560	5,720
November	30,030	5,005
December	29,930	4,350

The monthly maintenance costs can be plotted as a function of machine hours, as shown in Figure 26-4. The visual fit of a scatter diagram method is applied by drawing a straight line through the relationships of the dependent and independent variables. The straight line through the points representing the various relationships of maintenance costs and machine hours is chosen as the best visual fit by the person performing the analysis. This means that the differences between the scatter points and the straight line are minimal compared with other lines that might be drawn through the scatter diagram. The fixed portion of maintenance costs is determined by extending the line to the vertical axis and amounts to approximately $20,000.

The variable costs can be found for any given number of machine hours by subtracting the fixed costs of $20,000 from the total costs related to that level of activity. For example, total maintenance costs of $35,000 are estimated for 6,000 machine hours, so the variable costs would be $15,000 ($35,000 less

Figure 26-4
Scatter Diagram—
Maintenance Costs

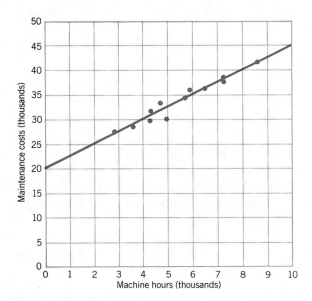

$20,000). In turn, the variable cost rate is approximately $2.50 ($15,000/6,000). Consequently, the maintenance cost function is equal to $20,000 plus $2.50 per machine hour. While the visual fit method often provides a useful estimation technique, it is dependent on the judgment of the person performing the analysis and therefore is subject to significant error.

The high–low method is a quantitative technique that can be used to estimate a mixed cost function. As long as the costs at the highest level of activity and those at the lowest level are representative of the straight line that best describes a cost function, they provide useful information for cost estimation. The high–low method is based on the procedure used to determine the slope of any linear function because it compares the cost at the highest level of activity with the cost at the lowest level. The difference in cost caused by variable costs is divided by the difference in activity to find the variable cost rate. Once the variable costs for a given level of activity are known, they can be subtracted from the total costs to determine the fixed costs. This method must be used carefully, however, since the high and low points in many cases will not represent the true cost function. The high–low method can be applied to the maintenance cost data as follows:

	Maintenance Cost	**Machine Hours**
High	$41,760	8,640
Low	27,550	2,920
Difference	$14,210	5,720

Variable cost rate = $14,210 ÷ 5,720 = $2.484 per hour
Fixed costs = $41,760 − (2.484 × 8,640)
= $20,298

The results of using the visual fit technique and high–low method in this case are approximately the same. The weaknesses of these two cost estimation approaches can be eliminated by applying linear regression analysis to find the straight line that best fits the points on a scatter diagram. The technique is beyond the scope of this text but is described in introductory statistics text books. If linear regression analysis had been used, the estimated cost function would have been:

$$\text{Maintenance costs} = \$19{,}645 + (\$2.568 \times \text{Machine hours})$$

In this example, the two less accurate estimation techniques produced approximately the same cost function as the more sophisticated one, but this will not always be the case.

COST BEHAVIOR AND THE INCOME STATEMENT

The primary concern in CVP analysis and many other managerial accounting applications is an income statement expected in the future. To project a future earnings performance, management must be able to evaluate how *costs and profits will fluctuate* with changes in sales volume. Unfortunately, the conventional income statement discussed in earlier chapters will be of limited value in predicting cost-volume-profit relationships. In a conventional income statement, costs are classified by business function (manufacturing, selling, administrative) without any consideration of the cost behavior involved. While such a statement may be very factual concerning the historical earnings performance of a specific period, it will not indicate what should happen to costs and profits with a different sales volume in the future. For example, consider the conventional income statement of the Butler Manufacturing Company shown in Figure 26-5.

The firm earned net income of $120,000, which was 12% of sales. Suppose management expects sales to increase by $200,000 to $1,200,000, or 20%, in 1985 because more units will be sold and wants to predict the related net income. Can management simply multiply the projected sales revenue of $1,200,000 by the profit margin of 12% to predict a 1985 net income of $144,000 (which also would be a 20% increase)? The answer is *no;* many of the costs involved will be fixed and will not change with the increase in sales volume as long as the firm remains within the relevant range. We know from our discussion of absorption costing in Chapter 22 that fixed manufacturing overhead costs will be included in the cost of goods sold section of the income statement because they are assigned to the products during the production operation. We also know that the selling and administrative expenses typically will be both fixed and variable. Even if the Butler Manufacturing Company were a retailing business, its operating expenses most likely would be partially fixed and partially variable.

Figure 26-5
Income Statement

BUTLER MANUFACTURING COMPANY
Income Statement
Year Ended December 31, 1984

	Amount	Percentage
Sales	$1,000,000	100
Cost of goods sold	520,000	52
Gross profit	480,000	48
Operating expenses		
Selling expenses	200,000	20
Administrative expenses	160,000	16
Total operating expenses	360,000	36
Net income	$ 120,000	12

To eliminate the deficiency of a conventional income statement, many businesses construct the statement on the basis of cost behavior. Here, the emphasis is on the **contribution margin**—sales revenue less all variable costs. The **contribution margin rate** is found by dividing the contribution margin by sales. The contribution margin represents the amount of sales revenue available first to absorb the fixed costs and then to contribute toward profit. Since only the variable costs are deducted to calculate the contribution margin, it will vary directly as a fixed percentage with sales volume. Before an income statement emphasizing the contributed margin can be prepared, each cost item must be analyzed carefully with the procedures discussed earlier in this chapter to determine its cost behavior. We assume that the cost behavioral classifications shown in Figure 26-6 have been developed for the Butler Manufacturing Company.

The information contained in the revised income statement in Figure 26-6 will enable management to evaluate the effect on net income of a change in sales volume. If sales of $1,200,000 are expected, the resulting net income can be computed as follows:

Projected contribution margin ($1,200,000 × .4)	$480,000
Fixed costs	280,000
Net income	$200,000
Net income as a percentage of sales	16.7

The net income projected for 1985 is $200,000 and is a higher percentage of sales than that of 1984 because the fixed costs remain at $280,000. Only the variable costs have increased on the basis of 60% of sales. Thus, the

Figure 26-6
Income Statement

BUTLER MANUFACTURING COMPANY
Income Statement
Year Ended December 31, 1984

	Amount	Percentage
Sales	$1,000,000	100
Variable cost of goods sold	400,000	40
Variable operating expenses	200,000	20
Contribution margin	400,000	40
Fixed costs		
Manufacturing	120,000	12
Operating	160,000	16
Total fixed costs	280,000	28
Net income	$120,000	12

contribution margin in dollars increases from $400,000 to $480,000, but as a percentage of sales remains constant at 40%. Alternatively, the increase in net income of $80,000 can be computed by multiplying the sales increase of $200,000 by the contribution margin rate of .40. An income statement that emphasizes the contribution margin will be used for internal purposes only and will provide the basis for CVP analysis. Since a manufacturing firm can develop an income statement of this type with variable costing rather than the absorption costing method with which we have been concerned in previous chapters, let us turn to a brief coverage of variable costing before proceeding with the subject of CVP analysis.

VARIABLE COSTING

We learned in Chapter 22 that absorption costing must be used for external reporting purposes because generally accepted accounting principles require both fixed and variable manufacturing overhead to be absorbed as product costs. However, we have demonstrated that management often needs income statement information that is useful in predicting the impact of changes in sales volume on the costs and profits of a firm. This information is difficult, if not impossible, to obtain with absorption costing since there is no clear-cut distinction between fixed and variable costs. **Variable costing** is an alternative product costing method that can be used for internal reporting purposes to overcome the deficiencies of absorption costing. Variable costing eliminates the problems associated with unit fixed costs that vary inversely with production volume, since the fixed manufacturing costs are treated as period, rather than product costs. Three major steps are involved in the application of variable costing:

1. All costs—manufacturing, selling, and administrative—are analyzed carefully to determine which are fixed and which are variable. A mixed cost is separated into its fixed and variable parts.
2. Variable manufacturing costs—direct materials, direct labor, and variable manufacturing overhead—are assigned as product costs. Therefore, work in process, finished goods, and cost of goods sold will be valued on the basis of the costs that vary proportionately with volume.
3. All fixed manufacturing costs, as well as the selling and administrative expenses, are treated as period costs and charged to the income statement of the period in which they are incurred. The variable selling and administrative expenses are separated, however, from the fixed selling and administrative expenses for presentation on the income statement. The variable selling and administrative expenses are deducted along with the variable cost of goods sold to determine the contribution margin of a period. In contrast, the fixed selling and administrative expenses are subtracted (along with the fixed manufacturing overhead costs) from the contribution margin to determine the net income of a period.

An income statement developed with variable costing has the same basic format as the one shown in Figure 26-6. The only difference may be the presentation of a **manufacturing margin,** which is optional and is the difference between sales revenue and the variable cost of goods sold. The **manufacturing margin rate** is the manufacturing margin expressed as a percentage of sales. Proponents of variable costing support its format on the premise that it distinguishes between the *costs of doing business* (the variable costs deducted to determine the contribution margin) and the *costs of being in business* (the fixed costs subtracted from the contribution margin). The costs of doing business will rise and fall as the level of business activity increases and decreases. In contrast, the costs of being in business represent capacity costs that will occur regardless of the volume of business achieved.

RECONCILING VARIABLE COSTING AND ABSORPTION COSTING NET INCOME

The major difference between variable costing and absorption costing is the timing of the fixed manufacturing costs as deductions on the income statement. The variable costing method charges the fixed manufacturing costs to the income statement as they are incurred. Absorption costing applies the fixed manufacturing costs to the products produced during a period so they are deducted from the income statement when the products are sold. The amount of fixed manufacturing costs left on the balance sheet at the end of a given period will be in proportion to the number of units left in the ending inventory.

When sales and production volumes are equal, inventories do not increase or decrease, so the same amount of fixed manufacturing costs will be charged to the income statement with both methods. Consequently, the net income with variable costing will be equal to the net income with absorption costing. If sales and production volumes are different, variable costing net income and absorption costing net income also will be different. When production exceeds sales, part of the fixed manufacturing costs inventoried with absorption costing will be deferred in inventory to a future period. As a result, absorption-costing net income will be greater than variable-costing net income. In contrast, variable-costing net income will be higher than that of absorption costing when sales exceed production. This is caused by the fact that, as inventory is depleted, fixed manufacturing costs of a previous period will be combined with those of the current period with absorption costing.

ILLUSTRATION OF VARIABLE COSTING

The basic difference between variable costing and absorption costing can be illustrated by preparing income statements with each method. To do so, the January and February operating performance of the Component Company, a West Coast electronics manufacturer, is utilized:

Sales in units	40,000 in January
	50,000 in February
Production in units	50,000 in January
	40,000 in February
Inventory at January 1	none
Selling price per unit	$20.00
Variable manufacturing costs per unit	$5.00
Variable selling and administrative expenses per unit	$2.00
Fixed manufacturing overhead costs per month	$400,000
Fixed selling and administrative expenses per month	$80,000

A comparison of income statements prepared with absorption costing and variable costing is presented in Figure 26-7. In January, production exceeded sales by the 10,000 units transferred to ending inventory at a cost of $130,000 with absorption costing. The variable costs in the ending inventory are $50,000 (10,000 units $\times$ $5) and the balance of $80,000 represents fixed manufacturing costs (1/5 of $400,000). Net income with absorption costing is greater than that of variable costing by the same $80,000 since one-fifth of the fixed manufacturing costs is deferred from the January income statement. In contrast, the total fixed manufacturing costs of $400,000 are charged to the January income statement with variable costing. The situation is reversed in February, when sales exceed production by 10,000 units. The fixed manufacturing costs charged to the income statement under absorption costing are $400,000 for February plus the $80,000 balance carried forward from January. Again, the fixed manufacturing costs shown on the variable costing income statement are $400,000, so its net income is $80,000 higher than the net income with absorption costing. During the two-month period, sales and production both equal 90,000 units, so the total net income is $210,000 with either method.

In Figure 26-7, the variable costing net income moves in the same direction as sales. The manufacturing margin (sales less the variable cost of goods sold) is a constant percentage of sales (75% in this case). The contribution margin

Figure 26-7
Absorption Costing
and Variable Costing

COMPONENT COMPANY
Comparison of Income Statements
Absorption Costing and Variable Costing

	January	February	Total
Absorption Costing			
Sales	$800,000	$1,000,000	$1,800,000
Cost of goods sold (1)	520,000	730,000	1,250,000
Gross profit	280,000	270,000	550,000
Selling and administrative expenses			
(2)	160,000	180,000	340,000
Net income	$120,000	$ 90,000	$210,000
(1) Cost of goods sold			
Beginning inventory	–0–	130,000	–0–
Production costs			
(50,000 × $5) + $400,000 =	650,000		
(40,000 × $5) + $400,000 =		600,000	
Total			1,250,000
Ending inventory (1/5)	130,000	–0–	–0–
Cost of goods sold	520,000	730,000	1,250,000
(2) Selling and administrative expenses			
(40,000 × $2) + 80,000	160,000		
(50,000 × $2) + 80,000		180,000	

Figure 26-7
Continued

Variable Costing			
Sales	$800,000	$1,000,000	$1,800,000
Cost of goods sold (3)	200,000	250,000	450,000
Manufacturing margin	600,000	750,000	1,350,000
Variable selling and administrative			
expenses (4)	80,000	100,000	180,000
Contribution margin	520,000	650,000	1,170,000
Fixed costs			
Manufacturing	400,000	400,000	800,000
Selling and administrative	80,000	80,000	160,000
Net income	$ 40,000	$ 170,000	$ 210,000

(3) Cost of goods sold			
Beginning inventory		–0–	50,000
Production costs			
(50,000 × $5)		250,000	
(40,000 × $5)			200,000
Ending inventory	(1/5)	50,000	–0–
Cost of goods sold		200,000	250,000

(4) Variable selling and administrative		
expenses		
(40,000 × $2)	80,000	
(50,000 × $2)		100,000

also is a *constant* 65% of sales. Consequently, management can easily predict the impact of a change in sales volume on net income because of the linear relationships involved. When sales increased by $200,000 from January to February, the increase in net income of $130,000 is logical because of the following computation:

$$\begin{array}{ccc} \text{Increase in} \\ \text{sales volume} \end{array} \times \begin{array}{c} \text{Contribution} \\ \text{margin rate} \end{array} = \begin{array}{c} \text{Increase in} \\ \text{net income} \end{array}$$
$$\$200,000 \quad \times \quad .65 \quad = \quad \$130,000$$

However, the absorption costing results are much more difficult to interpret and explain. Despite the fact that sales increased by $200,000 in February, the net income actually was $30,000 lower than that of January. The basic reason for these inconsistent results is the fact that net income with absorption costing is *affected by changes in inventory* (sales not equal to production) because of the absorption of fixed manufacturing costs as product costs. As such, absorption-costing net income is a function of both sales and production as compared to variable-costing net income, which is a function of sales only.

BENEFITS AND LIMITATIONS OF VARIABLE COSTING

Many manufacturing firms use variable costing for internal reporting purposes during an accounting period and convert to absorption costing at the end of the period by adding fixed manufacturing costs to inventories and to cost of goods sold. The primary benefits and limitations of variable costing must be evaluated carefully so it can be used properly.

Benefits of Variable Costing

1. Variable costing forces management to evaluate the cost behavioral pattern of each cost item.
2. The information needed for CVP analysis can be obtained directly from the income statement rather than from special analysis independent of the income statement.
3. The effect of fixed costs on profits is emphasized because the total fixed costs are treated as period costs and are reported in one place on the income statement rather than being scattered throughout the statement.
4. Variable costing provides the basis for the preparation of a flexible budget in which variable and fixed costs are separated.
5. Since variable costs and fixed costs are divided, variable costing assists management in such decision-making activities as profit planning, cost control, pricing, and resource allocations.

Limitations of Variable Costing

1. The separation of many cost behavioral patterns into variable and fixed elements is very difficult, and the results are only approximations at best.
2. Variable costing is not acceptable for financial reporting or income tax reporting.
3. Variable costing may give the misleading impression that only the variable costs must be considered in pricing decisions. In the long run, both variable and fixed costs must be recovered before net income can be earned. As we shall see in Chapter 27, short-run pricing may be based on variable costing.
4. Balance sheet inventories valued with variable costing will be understated, so working capital will be lower than it would be with absorption costing.

ASSUMPTIONS OF COST-VOLUME-PROFIT ANALYSIS

Now that we have considered the basic aspects of a contribution-margin oriented income statement, we can turn to the following assumptions underlying CVP analysis:

1. The unit sales price remains constant.
2. All costs can be identified as variable or fixed costs with a reasonable amount of accuracy.
3. Variable costs will change proportionately with volume.
4. The fixed costs will remain constant.
5. Efficiency will remain unchanged.
6. Whenever more than one product is sold, total sales will be in some predictable proportion or sales mix.
7. Variable costing will be used or, if absorption costing is used, the number of units sold will be equal to the number of units produced.

PROFIT PLANNING WITH CVP ANALYSIS

As indicated earlier, CVP analysis is used by management to evaluate the interrelationships of selling price, sales volume, sales mix, and costs so acceptable profits can be earned. Profit goals are established during the budgeting process and are reevaluated continuously during the budget period. In order to plan profits, management must estimate the selling price of each product, the variable costs required to produce and sell it, and the fixed costs expected for a given period. This information is combined with estimates concerning the expected sales volume and sales mix. The variable costing concepts discussed previously provide the foundation for profit planning with CVP analysis. The coverage of CVP analysis that follows refers to the operating performance of the Stabilizer Company, which began manufacturing a single model of cross-country skis on January 1, 1983, in a Midwestern plant. A condensed income statement for the firm's first year of operation is shown below:

	Amount	Percentage
Sales (8,000 units @ $50)	$400,000	100.0
Variable cost of goods sold	240,000	60.0
Manufacturing margin	160,000	40.0
Variable selling and administrative expenses	40,000	10.0
Contribution margin	120,000	30.0
Fixed costs		
Manufacturing	110,000	27.5
Selling and administrative	40,000	10.0
Net income (loss)	($30,000)	(7.5)

BREAK-EVEN ANALYSIS

Break-even analysis is the typical starting point for CVP analysis. The **break-even point** is the sales volume at which revenues and total costs are equal, with no net income or loss. Net income is earned above the break-even point; a net loss is incurred below it. Both the variable and fixed costs are covered by sales revenue at the break-even point. While a break-even point is not a desired performance target because of the lack of profit, it does indicate the level of activity necessary to avoid a loss. As such, the break-even point represents a target of the minimum sales volume that must be achieved by a business. In addition, break-even analysis provides valuable information concerning the impact of cost behavioral patterns at different sales levels. We will see later that the basic procedures of break-even analysis can be extended to plan for a *desired amount of profit* and to evaluate the *margin of safety* associated with the expected sales volume.

BREAK-EVEN EQUATION

The break-even point can be determined mathematically or graphically and can be expressed in either sales units or sales dollars. Mathematically, the basic variable costing income statement format can be stated as:

$$\text{Sales} = \text{Variable costs} + \text{Fixed costs} + \text{Net income}$$

At the break-even point, the net income obviously is zero. To illustrate the use of the equation, consider the financial data presented earlier for the Stabilizer Company. The firm operated below its break-even point in 1983 because it incurred a net loss of $30,000. Note that fixed costs were $150,000 and variable costs were 70% of sales: ($240,000 + $40,000) ÷ $400,000, or $35 per unit ($280,000 ÷ 8,000). The break-even sales (S) can be determined as:

$$S = .7S + \$150,000$$
$$.3S = \$150,000$$
$$S = \$500,000$$

The break-even sales dollars can be converted to sales units of 10,000 by dividing $500,000 by $50, the selling price. Alternatively, the equation can be established as:

$$\$50S = \$35S + \$150,000$$
$$\$15S = \$150,000$$
$$S = 10,000 \text{ units}$$

The break-even sales in units can be converted to sales dollars of $500,000 by multiplying 10,000 units by the selling price of $50. With either approach, the analysis indicates that the Stabilizer Company must increase its sales level by 25% to $500,000 or 10,000 pairs of skis in order to break even.

CONTRIBUTION MARGIN APPROACH

Remember that the contribution margin is found by subtracting all variable costs from sales. The contribution margin rate or percentage is determined by dividing the contribution margin by sales. The contribution margin is shown on the left side of both of the above equations. In the first equation, $.3S$ expresses the contribution margin as a percentage of sales (30%), while $15S$ in the second equation shows the contribution margin as a dollar amount. When the contribution margin was stated as a percentage, the break-even point was calculated in sales dollars. However, the use of the contribution margin measured as dollars resulted in a break-even point in sales units. Instead of using the equations, a contribution margin approach can be utilized as:

$$\frac{\text{Break-even}}{\text{sales}} = \frac{\text{Fixed costs}}{\text{Contribution margin \%}} = \frac{\$150,000}{.3} = \$500,000$$

or

$$\frac{\text{Break-even}}{\text{sales}} = \frac{\text{Fixed costs}}{\text{Unit contribution margin}} = \frac{\$150,000}{\$15} = 10,000 \text{ units}$$

GRAPHIC APPROACH

For visual purposes, the break-even point can be plotted on a **cost-volume-profit chart** such as the one shown in Figure 26-8 for the Stabilizer Company. In addition to the break-even point, the profitability of various revenue and cost relationships over a range of volume can be evaluated. The vertical scale of the chart represents dollars of revenues and costs in thousands, while the volume of units in thousands is measured along the horizontal axis. The steps used to prepare this cost-profit-volume chart are:

1. Plot the revenue line, which begins at the origin and increases at the rate of $50 per unit.
2. Plot the variable cost function, which begins at the origin and increases at the rate of $35 per unit.
3. Plot the fixed cost line, which begins at $150,000 and runs parallel to the variable cost function.

The chart indicates that the Stabilizer Company's break-even point is $500,000 in sales or 10,000 units—the results obtained with the mathematical approach

Figure 26-8
Stabilizer Company
Cost-Volume-Profit
Chart

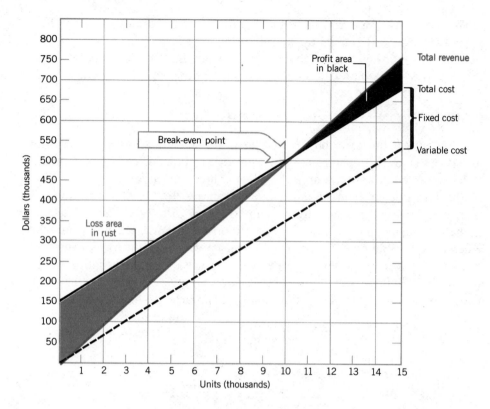

earlier. The profit or loss anticipated for any sales volume can be found on the chart. If the company does not achieve sales of $500,000, it will incur an operating loss (the rust area). A profit will be earned when sales exceed $500,000 (the black area). By comparing the variable costs with revenue, the contribution margin in dollars also can be determined at any sales volume from the cost-volume-profit chart. For example, the contribution margin at the break-even point is the $150,000 needed to cover the fixed costs.

MARGIN OF SAFETY CONCEPT

An important extension of the break-even point is its use to determine a firm's **margin of safety**—the amount by which sales can decrease before a loss occurs. The margin of safety is the excess of actual or expected sales over the break-even sales. A large margin of safety is an indication that a business can absorb a significant decline in sales volume without incurring a loss. For example, assume that the management of the Stabilizer Company expects sales of $600,000 in 1984 without any change in its break-even point of $500,000. Its margin of safety for 1984 would be $100,000.

TARGET NET INCOME

The basic procedures of break-even analysis also can be used to determine the sales volume needed to *earn a desired net income*. A profit goal can be expressed as a fixed amount of net income or as a percentage of sales. In either case, the basic income statement equation presented earlier is used to find the sales volume required for the desired profit. Assume that management of the Stabilizer Company wants to earn a net income before tax of $60,000 in 1984 and expects the same selling price and costs as those experienced in 1983. The necessary sales target can be computed as:

S = Sales target

S = Variable costs + Fixed costs + Target net income before tax

S = .7S + $150,000 + $60,000

.3S = $210,000

S = $700,000 or 14,000 units

With the sales of $700,000, the following income statement shows that net income before tax will be $60,000:

Sales (14,000 units @ $50)	$700,000
Variable costs (14,000 @ $35)	490,000
Contribution margin	210,000
Fixed costs	150,000
Net income before tax	$ 60,000

Alternatively, assume that management's goal is to achieve before-tax profits that are 10% of sales. The equation required to determine the sales target is:

S = Sales target

S = .7S + $150,000 + .1$S$

.2S = $150,000

S = $750,000 or 15,000 units

Again, an income statement can be prepared to prove that a sales level of $750,000 will produce a before-tax profit equaling 10% of sales:

Sales (15,000 units @ $50)	$750,000	
Variable costs (15,000 units @ $35)	525,000	
Contribution margin	225,000	10%
Fixed costs	150,000	
Net income before tax	$ 75,000	

Many firms choose to define their profit target as net income after tax, in which case an additional computation is required to determine the net income before tax. To do so, the after-tax net income is divided by the factor (1 − tax rate). For example, assume that the Stabilizer Company's profit goal for 1984 is to earn after-tax net income of $42,000 with a tax rate of 30%. The required sales volume can be calculated as follows:

$$S = \text{Variable costs} + \text{Fixed costs} + \text{Target net income before tax}$$

$$S = .7S + \$150{,}000 + [\$42{,}000/(1 - .3)]$$

$$.3S = \$150{,}000 + \$60{,}000$$

$$.3S = \$210{,}000$$

$$S = \$700{,}000 \text{ or } 14{,}000 \text{ units}$$

Alternatively, the income before tax can be calculated as follows:

$$X = \text{Income before tax}$$

$$.3X = \text{Tax}$$

$$X - .3X = \text{Income after tax}$$

$$X - .3X = \$42{,}000$$

$$.7X = \$42{,}000$$

$$X = \$60{,}000$$

Then, the $60,000 can be inserted into the equation to solve for S, the sales volume required to earn an after-tax profit of $42,000.

It should be noted that the sales level necessary to achieve the after-tax net income goal is the same as that found earlier for a before-tax net income target of $60,000 since $42,000 ÷ .7 = $60,000.

EVALUATING THE IMPACT OF CHANGE

Once the cost-volume-profit relationships are known, management can use the information to find the combination of revenue and costs that will produce acceptable profits. CVP analysis is particularly important to management during the budgeting process, when various alternative strategies regarding the future financial performance must be evaluated. Effective profit planning must be concerned with the impact on profits of: (1) changes in selling prices; (2) changes in sales volume; (3) changes in sales mix; (4) changes in variable costs; and (5) changes in fixed costs. To illustrate the CVP analysis used to evaluate potential changes, we will continue to use the 1983 financial data of the Stabilizer Company. Management undoubtedly would be dissatisfied with its first-year financial results since a net loss of $30,000 occurred. Assume that the initial version of the 1984 budget has been prepared with the 1983 selling prices and costs, but sales volume is expected to increase by 2,000 units. As a result, the following income statement is projected without any additional changes:

Sales (10,000 @ $50)	$500,000
Variable costs (10,000 @ $35)	350,000
Contribution margin	150,000
Fixed costs	150,000
Net income	$ –0–

While the projected performance is better than the results of 1983, it is not acceptable to management because the firm will only operate at break-even sales. Consequently, the firm is considering a number of changes and will apply CVP analysis to evaluate their impact on profits. We will consider each of these changes independently, although they would be evaluated concurrently in a real-life situation.

CHANGE IN SELLING PRICE

The sales manager of the Stabilizer Company estimates that a price reduction of *10%* will increase the number of units sold by *20%*, from 10,000 units to 12,000 units. If this happens, the impact on break-even sales and net income is:

$$S = \text{Break-even sales}$$
$$\$45S = \$35S + \$150,000$$
$$\$10S = \$150,000$$
$$S = 15,000 \text{ units or } \$675,000$$

Sales (12,000 × $45)	$540,000
Variable costs (12,000 × $35)	420,000
Contribution margin	120,000
Fixed costs	150,000
Net income (loss)	($30,000)

Despite the fact that sales revenue would increase by $40,000 with this proposal, the firm would incur a net loss of $30,000 instead of operating at break-even. The reason is the $5 loss of contribution margin per unit, which is not offset by selling 2,000 additional units. The break-even point also increases from $500,000 to $675,000, so this change would not produce favorable results for the firm.

CHANGE IN VARIABLE COSTS

The firm's production manager believes that changes in the manufacturing process will make labor utilization more efficient and reduce the variable costs by *$5 per unit*. The impact on the break-even sales and net income would be:

$$S = \text{Break-even sales}$$

$$\$50S = \$30S + \$150,000$$

$$\$20S = \$150,000$$

$$S = 7,500 \text{ units or } \$375,000$$

Sales (10,000 units @ $50)	$500,000
Variable costs (10,000 units @ $30)	300,000
Contribution margin	200,000
Fixed costs	150,000
Net income	$ 50,000

The improved efficiency will increase the firm's profits by $50,000 because the contribution margin per unit will be $20 instead of $15. In addition, the break-even point is reduced from 10,000 units to 7,500 units.

CHANGE IN FIXED AND VARIABLE COSTS

The management of the firm is considering changing the method of compensating its sales manager, whose 1983 salary was based on a commission of 10% of sales. Instead of the commission, management is proposing to pay the person a fixed sum of *$40,000* per year. Without the commission, the variable costs will be 60% (70% less 10%) and the contribution margin 40%. The effect on the firm's break-even point and net income would be:

$$S = \text{Break-even sales}$$

$$S = .6S + \$190,000$$

$$.4S = \$190,000$$

$$S = \$475,000$$

Sales (10,000 units @ $50)	$500,000
Variable costs (10,000 units @ $30)	300,000
Contribution margin	200,000
Fixed costs	190,000
Net income	$ 10,000

The net income is increased by $10,000 with this proposed change because the total contribution margin increases by $50,000 (10,000 units times $5 per unit) while the fixed costs increase by only $40,000.

CHANGE OF FIXED COSTS AND SALES VOLUME

Another proposal being considered by the management of the Stabilizer Company is an advertising campaign that would cost the firm *$30,000* per year. Management estimates that sales will increase by 30%, from 10,000 units to 13,000 units, as a result of the additional advertising. The new break-even point and net income would be:

$$S = \text{Break-even sales}$$
$$\$50S = \$35S + \$180,000$$
$$\$15S = \$180,000$$
$$S = 12,000 \text{ units or } \$600,000$$

Sales (13,000 @ $50)	$650,000
Variable costs (13,000 @ $35)	455,000
Contribution margin	195,000
Fixed costs	180,000
Net income	$ 15,000

 The break-even point would increase by 2,000 units because an additional contribution margin of $30,000 (2,000 units @ $15 per unit) is necessary to cover the proposed advertising expenditures. Since the sales are expected to increase by 3,000 units, the projected net income will be $15,000—the result of earning a contribution margin of $15 for each of the 1,000 units above the break-even point.

EXTENSION TO MULTIPLE PRODUCTS

In the Stabilizer Company illustration, we considered cost-volume-profit analysis with only one product. Earlier we stated as a basic assumption of CVP analysis that total sales must be in *some predictable proportion or sales mix* whenever more than one product is sold. CVP analysis is performed by a multiproduct firm with a weighted average contribution margin for a given sales mix. For example, assume that the Stabilizer Company can produce and sell two models of cross-country skis with the following data:

	Standard Model	Deluxe Model
Selling price	$50	$80
Variable costs	35	48
Contribution margin	$15	$32
Contribution margin %	30	40

The fixed costs are $184,000 and the firm's product mix is four Standard Models for each Deluxe Model. The weighted average contribution margin per unit would be $18.40, computed as follows:

Total contribution margin for 5 units of product ($15 × 4) + ($32 × 1)	= $92.00
Divided by number of units	5.00
Average contribution margin per unit	= $18.40

Thus, the break-even sales with the two products would be:

S = Break-even sales

$$S = \frac{\text{Fixed costs}}{\text{Weighted average contribution margin per unit}}$$

$$S = \frac{\$184,000}{\$18.40}$$

S = 10,000 units

Since the sales mix is 4 Standard Models for 1 Deluxe Model, the 10,000 units will be divided into 8,000 Standard Models and 2,000 Deluxe Models ($\frac{4}{5}$ × 10,000 = 8,000 Standard Models and $\frac{1}{5}$ × 10,000 = 2,000 Deluxe Models). The break-even income statement will be:

	Standard Model	Deluxe Model	Total
Sales—units	8,000	2,000	10,000
Sales—dollars	$400,000	$160,000	$560,000
Variable costs	280,000	96,000	376,000
Contribution margin	120,000	64,000	184,000
Fixed costs			184,000
Net income			$ –0–

This same weighted average contribution margin approach can be used to determine break-even sales or plan profits in any multiproduct firm as long as the sales mix can be predicted.

GLOSSARY

BREAK-EVEN POINT. The sales volume at which revenues and total costs are equal with no net income or loss (p. 1020).

COMMITTED FIXED COSTS. Fixed costs that are required even if the operation is shut down temporarily (p. 1008).

CONTRIBUTION MARGIN. The sales revenue less all variable costs (p. 1012).

CONTRIBUTION MARGIN RATE. The contribution margin expressed as a percentage of sales (p. 1012).

COST BEHAVIOR. How a cost responds to changes in the level of business activity (p. 1005).

COST FUNCTION. The relationship between a cost as a dependent variable and some measure of the level of business activity as an independent variable (p. 1006).

COST-VOLUME-PROFIT (CVP) ANALYSIS. A managerial accounting technique used to evaluate how costs and profits are affected by changes in the level of business activity (p. 1005).

COST-VOLUME-PROFIT CHART. A graphic display of the break-even point as well as the net income or loss for a range of activity (p. 1021).

DISCRETIONARY FIXED COSTS. Fixed costs that can be reduced or discontinued by management if adequate time is available (p. 1008).

LINEARITY ASSUMPTION. A key assumption of CVP analysis that all revenue and costs will behave as straight-line functions (p. 1006).

MANUFACTURING MARGIN. The sales revenue less the variable cost of goods sold (p. 1014).

MANUFACTURING MARGIN RATE. The manufacturing margin expressed as a percentage of sales (p. 1014).

MARGIN OF SAFETY. The amount by which sales can decrease before a loss results (p. 1022).

MIXED COST. A cost that has both a variable component and a fixed component (p. 1005).

RELEVANT RANGE. The range of activity within which a business expects to operate and incur variable costs with constant slopes as well as fixed costs that are constant in total amount (p. 1007).

VARIABLE COSTING. The product costing technique used for internal reporting in which only the variable manufacturing costs are inventoried (p. 1013).

DISCUSSION QUESTIONS

1. Why is cost-volume-profit analysis such an important managerial accounting subject?
2. Identify the major characteristics of a:
   (a) Variable cost
   (b) Fixed cost
   (c) Mixed cost
3. Explain what is meant by the relevant range concept. How does this concept contribute to the linearity of cost functions?
4. What is a cost function and how does a linear cost function respond to changes in activity?
5. Differentiate between a variable cost that actually is a curvilinear function and one that is a step function. How is the treatment of each one as a linear function justified?
6. Distinguish between a discretionary fixed cost and a committed fixed cost. Give an example of each.

7. The Hi-Lo Company wants to estimate the cost behavior of its manufacturing supplies. Selected data are as follows:

Manufacturing Supplies	Production Level
$23,280	4,320 hours
$20,880	3,120 hours

   Using these data, estimate the cost behavior of manufacturing supplies.

8. What is the basic limitation of the income statement format used for external reporting in projecting a firm's future profitability?

9. What is the contribution margin? Why is it an important managerial accounting measure?

10. What are the major characteristics of variable costing? How does it differ from absorption costing?

11. How can variable-costing net income and absorption-costing net income be reconciled for a given accounting period?

12. What are the benefits and limitations of variable costing?

13. The Peek Company uses variable costing for internal reporting and absorption costing for external reporting. During the previous year, the firm produced 60,000 units and sold 75,000 units. The variable costs required to manufacture one unit were $2.20 and the fixed costs were $6.00 per unit. Which of the two methods, variable costing or absorption costing, would report the highest net income? By how much based on the facts given?

14. What are the basic assumptions underlying cost-volume-profit analysis?

15. Define the following terms:
   (a) Break-even point
   (b) Break-even equation
   (c) Cost-volume-profit chart
   (d) Margin of safety

16. How can break-even analysis be extended to determine the sales volume required to earn a desired net income?

17. The Fox Corporation sells a product for $20. Variable costs are $12 per unit and fixed costs are $24,000 per month.
   (a) What is the firm's break-even point?
   (b) If the firm wants to earn a before-tax profit of $6,000 per month, how many units must be sold?
   (c) If the firm wants to earn a before-tax profit of 16% of sales, what sales volume is necessary?

18. In recent years, the airlines have received a great deal of publicity with their "no frills" air fares. Since these fares are discounted significantly, how can they be justified on the basis of cost-volume-profit relationships?

19. What are the major changes that must be evaluated to find the combination of revenue and costs that will produce acceptable profits?

20. What is meant by the weighted average contribution margin when CVP is applied to multiple products?

EXERCISES

Exercise 26-1 (High–low Method and Cost Behavior)

The Nyhof Company rents a copy machine for which it pays a per-copy charge and a fixed annual rental fee. The company has estimated that the cost per copy is $.0985 if 80,000 copies are made during a year. If the company makes 125,000 copies per year the copy cost is $.076.

Required:
A. Calculate the variable rate per copy and the fixed annual rental fee.
B. What total cost would the company incur if the company makes 110,000 copies during a year?

Exercise 26-2 (Evaluating Mixed Costs with the High–low Method)

The Kuipers Company has compiled total manufacturing overhead costs at the company's high and low levels of activity, which are 120,000 machine hours and 80,000 machine hours, respectively. The total manufacturing overhead, which includes variable costs, mixed costs, and fixed costs, was $320,000 for 120,000 machine hours and $240,000 for 80,000 machine hours. The company has determined that at the 80,000 machine hour activity level, the total factory overhead can be broken down into the following components:

Fixed costs	$ 60,000
Variable costs	96,000
Mixed costs	84,000
	$240,000

Required:
A. Compute the fixed and the variable portion of the mixed costs. The variable portion should be expressed as a rate per machine hour.
B. What should be the total factory overhead cost for 100,000 machine hours?

Exercise 26-3 (Absorption Costing Versus Variable Costing)

During 1985, the Scofield Company manufactured 2,000 units and compiled the following data:

Direct materials per unit	$15
Direct labor per unit	$10
Variable manufacturing overhead per unit	$7
Selling price per unit	$40
Fixed selling and administration expenses	$3,000
Fixed manufacturing overhead	$10,000

There was no beginning inventory in 1985 and 1,700 units were sold during the year.

Required:
A. Calculate the unit cost under absorption costing.
B. Calculate the unit cost under variable costing.
C. Calculate the net income for 1985 under absorption costing.
D. Calculate the net income for 1985 under variable costing.
E. Reconcile the net income under absorption and variable costing.
F. Calculate the break-even point in terms of units.

Exercise 26-4 (Evaluating Changes with CVP Analysis)
The Bentley Company sells its only product at a price of $200 per unit. Variable expenses are $150 per unit and total fixed expenses are $225,000. Average annual sales are 15,000 units. Calculate the company's net income under each of the following independent situations.

1. Variable expenses increase 20%.
2. Sales volume decreases 20%.
3. Fixed costs increase 20%.
4. Sales price increases 20%.
5. Sales price increases 20%, variable expenses increase 20%, sales volume decreases 20%, and fixed costs decrease 20%.

Exercise 26-5 (Evaluating CVP Relationships)
Information for four independent companies is presented below.

1. Company A has a product that sells for $40 and is produced at a variable cost of $30 per unit. The variable costs can be reduced 20% by installing a new piece of equipment. Installation of the new equipment will increase fixed costs from the present level of $52,000 to $76,800. Calculate the present break-even point and the new break-even point if the equipment is installed.
2. Company B wishes to attain a before-tax net income equal to 35% of sales revenue. Variable expenses are 47.5% of sales and fixed expenses are $262,500. Calculate the dollar amount of sales necessary to achieve the profit goal.
3. Company C incurs variable costs of $15 per unit for a product that has a selling price of $25. If the break-even point is $80,000 of annual sales, what are the company's annual fixed costs?
4. Company D has annual fixed costs of $90,475. The variable costs are $3.30 per unit and the break-even point is 19,250 units. Calculate the selling price per unit.

Exercise 26-6 (Cost-volume-profit Analysis with Two Products)
The Mooring Company sells two products, A and B. During 1982, fixed costs were $5,202 and sales were in the ratio of six units of product A to each four units of product B. Product A sells for $31 each and the variable costs are $22 per unit. Product B sells for $40 each and the variable costs are $28 per unit.

Required:
A. Compute the break-even point in total units and the number of units of each product that must be sold at the break-even point.

B. How many units of product A and product B must the company sell to achieve a before-tax net income of $10,000? Round all calculations to the nearest unit.

PROBLEMS

Problem 26-1 (Absorption Costing Versus Variable Costing)

The Ada Company has prepared income statements for the past three years under absorption costing for external reporting purposes. The company applies fixed manufacturing costs to the units of production on the basis of the actual production for that year. The total fixed manufacturing costs are $28,800 and the contribution margin is 25%. The company's selling and administrative expense is a mixed cost. The company's unit sales and production data for the past three years are:

	1986	1987	1988
Sales	12,000	15,000	12,000
Production	15,000	16,000	12,000

The income statements under absorption costing are:

	1986	1987	1988
Sales	$480,000	$600,000	$480,000
Beginning inventory	–0–	92,760	123,200
Cost of goods manufactured	463,800	492,800	376,800
Less: Ending inventory	92,760	123,200	125,600
Cost of goods sold	371,040	462,360	374,400
Gross profit	108,960	137,640	105,600
Selling and administrative expenses	22,000	25,000	22,000
Net income	$ 86,960	$112,640	$ 83,600

Required:

A. Calculate the fixed manufacturing overhead rate that was used to apply overhead in each year.

B. Calculate the variable selling and administrative expense per unit sold.

C. Prepare income statements for the three years using variable costing. Assume a FIFO inventory flow.

Problem 26-2 (Performing CVP Analysis)

The Racine Company has provided the following production and sales information:

Machine time per unit	3 hours at $4 per hour
Direct labor	1 hour at $8 per hour
Direct materials	2 pounds at $5 per pound
Sales commissions	10% of the retail price
Retail selling price	$60
Other fixed costs	$62,400

The company sells its product only at a discount of 20% of the retail price to distributors.

Required:

A. Calculate the company's break-even point.

B. Calculate the number of units that must be sold to achieve a before-tax profit of $15,000.

C. Would it be better if the company sold 6,000 units with a retail price of $60 each or 8,000 units with a retail price of $55?

D. If the company spends an additional $12,000 on fixed advertising costs, what level of dollar sales must be attained to earn a before-tax net income of $15,000? Assume that there has been no change in the sales price.

E. Assume that income taxes are 40%. How much additional advertising can be incurred at a sales level of 8,000 units if the company is still to earn an after-tax net income of $15,000?

Problem 26-3 (Evaluating Alternatives with CVP Analysis)

The Brunsting Company has prepared an income statement for the past fiscal year.

Sales (25,000 units)		$1,000,000
Cost of sales		
Direct materials	$237,500	
Direct labor	375,000	
Variable overhead	112,500	
Fixed overhead	50,000	775,000
Gross profit		225,000
Variable selling expenses	75,000	
Fixed selling and administrative expenses	20,000	95,000
Net income before taxes		130,000
Income taxes (40%)		52,000
Net income		$ 78,000

Required:

Consider each of the following independent situations:

A. If the company desires to attain an after-tax net income of $120,000, what is the dollar level of sales necessary to reach its goal?

B. If the company's sales volume increases by 10% as a result of increasing fixed selling expenses by $15,000 and variable selling expenses by $.50 per unit, what is the company's after-tax net income?

C. If direct material costs increase 10%, direct labor costs increase 15%, variable overhead costs increase 8%, and fixed overhead increases by $5,000, how many units must be sold to earn an after-tax net income of $78,000? Round your calculations to the nearest unit.

D. If the changes in part (C) occur and the sales volume is 25,000 units, what is the selling price needed to achieve an after-tax profit of $120,000?

Problem 26-4 (Performing CVP Analysis with Multiple Products)

The Lucky Company has provided the following per-unit cost and sales data for 1984:

	Product			
	A	**B**	**C**	**D**
Selling price	$ 30	$ 35	$ 20	$ 15
Direct labor	8	10	8	5
Direct materials	12	10	5	3
Variable manufacturing overhead	3	4	2	1
Variable selling expenses	1	2	1	1
Units sold in 1984	10,000	12,500	7,500	20,000
Budgeted 1985 unit sales	17,500	21,000	7,000	24,500

The company's fixed manufacturing overhead costs are $44,000 per year, and the annual fixed selling and administrative costs are $10,450. Round all calculations to the nearest unit.

Required:

A. Calculate the break-even point for 1984 and 1985 in total units and the number of units of each product that will be sold at the break-even point.

B. Calculate the number of units of each product that would have had to be sold in 1984 to achieve an after-tax net income of $217,800. The company's tax rate is 40%.

C. Calculate the number of units of each product that would have to be sold in 1985 to achieve an after-tax net income of $217,800. Round all calculations to the nearest unit.

Problem 26-5 (Evaluating the Impact of Change with CVP)

The CSN Company has prepared its 1985 income statement, which is presented below. The company is evaluating four independent situations and has asked for your assistance.

Sales (20,000 units)	$80,000
Variable expenses	46,000
Contribution margin	34,000
Less fixed expenses	28,000
Net income	$ 6,000

Required:

A. If a new marketing method would increase variable expenses, increase sales units 10%, decrease fixed costs 5%, and increase net income by 25%, what would be the company's break-even point in terms of dollar sales if it adopts this new method? Assume that the sales price per unit would not be changed.

B. If sales increase 30% in the next year and net income increases 150%, did the manager perform better or worse than expected in terms of net income? Assume that there was adequate capacity to meet the increased volume without increasing fixed costs.

C. If variable costs would decrease 20% per unit due to a change in the quality of direct materials and sales would decrease 10% in spite of increasing advertising costs $10,000, should the company make the change in the materials used in production?

D. If the company hires an additional salesperson at a salary of $6,375, how much must sales increase in terms of dollars to maintain the company's current net income?

ALTERNATE PROBLEMS

Problem 26-1A (Absorption Costing Versus Variable Costing)

The Maquelin Company prepares income statements under absorption costing for external reporting purposes but uses variable costing for managerial decision making. The company applies the annual fixed manufacturing overhead cost of $42,000 to the units of production on the basis of actual production for that year. The company's only product has a contribution margin of 30%, and the selling and administrative expense is a mixed cost. The income statements, under absorption costing, for the past three years are:

	1984	1985	1986
Sales	$360,000	$360,000	$270,000
Beginning inventory	–0–	36,000	37,000
Cost of goods manufactured	252,000	222,000	162,000
Less: Ending inventory	36,000	37,000	20,250
Cost of goods sold	216,000	221,000	178,750
Gross profit	144,000	139,000	91,250
Selling and administrative expense	79,500	79,500	61,500
Net income	$ 64,500	$ 59,500	$ 29,750

The company's unit sales and production data for the past three years are:

	1984	1985	1986
Sales	12,000	12,000	9,000
Production	14,000	12,000	8,000

Required:

A. Calculate the fixed manufacturing overhead rate used to apply overhead in each year.

B. Calculate the variable selling and administrative expense per unit sold.

C. Prepare income statements for the three years using variable costing. Assume a FIFO inventory flow.

Problem 26-2A (Performing CVP Analysis)

The Greenbriar Company has provided the following production and sales information:

Direct materials	4 pounds at $3 per pound
Direct labor	2 hours at $7 per hour

Machine time	1 hour at $3 per hour
Sales commissions	10% of the retail price
Retail selling price	$50
Other fixed costs	$240,000

Required:

A. Calculate the company's break-even point.

B. If the company desires to attain a before-tax profit of $40,000, calculate the number of units the company must sell to reach its goal.

C. In order to maximize the company's before-tax profit, should the company sell 20,000 units with a retail price of $50 each or 14,000 units at $60 each?

D. If the company increases fixed costs by $60,000, what level of dollar sales must be attained to earn a before-tax income of $40,000? The sales price and variable costs per unit will not change.

E. If the company's income tax rate is 20%, how much additional fixed cost can the company incur at a sales level of 20,000 units and still maintain an after-tax net income of $40,000?

Problem 26-3A (Evaluating Alternatives with CVP Analysis)

The Cook Company has prepared the following income statement for the previous year:

Sales (18,000 units)		$1,080,000
Cost of sales		
Direct materials	$306,000	
Direct labor	324,000	
Variable manufacturing overhead	126,000	
Fixed manufacturing overhead	54,000	810,000
Gross profit		270,000
Variable selling expenses	72,000	
Fixed selling and administrative expenses	86,000	158,000
Net income before taxes		112,000
Income taxes (40%)		44,800
Net income		$ 67,200

Required:

Consider each of the following independent situations:

A. What is the dollar level of sales necessary to attain an after-tax net income of $126,000?

B. If the company increases fixed selling expenses by $5,000 and variable selling expenses by $4 per unit, unit sales are expected to increase by 20%. Calculate the company's after-tax net income with these changes.

C. If direct labor costs increase 10%, direct material costs increase 5%, variable manufacturing overhead increases 20%, and fixed manufacturing overhead increases $10,000, how many units must be sold to maintain an after-tax income of $67,200? Round your calculations to the nearest unit.

D. If the changes in requirement (C) prevail, what should be the new selling price if the sales volume is 20,000 units and the company wants to achieve an after-tax net income of $90,000?

Problem 26-4A (Performing CVP Analysis with Multiple Products)

The Lanark Company has compiled the following sales and per unit cost data:

	Product			
	A	**B**	**C**	**D**
Selling price	25	30	40	20
Direct labor	9	10	12	6
Direct materials	5	5	8	4
Variable manufacturing overhead	2	3	4	2
Variable selling expense	1	2	2	2
Units sold in 1986	8,000	14,000	12,000	6,000
Budgeted 1987 unit sales	12,500	15,000	17,500	5,000

The company's fixed manufacturing and administrative costs are $214,200. The company's tax rate is 40%.

Required:
A. Calculate the number of units of each product that will be sold at the break-even point for 1986 and 1987.
B. Calculate the number of units of each product that would have had to be sold in 1986 to achieve an after-tax net income of $61,200.
C. Calculate the number of units of each product needed to earn an after-tax net income of $94,500 in 1986.

Problem 26-5A (Evaluating the Impact of Change with CVP)

The JHN Company has prepared the following income statement for the previous fiscal year:

Sales (6,500 units)	$130,000
Variable expenses	74,750
Contribution margin	55,250
Less fixed expenses	48,100
Net income	$ 7,150

Required:
Answer the following questions for each of the four independent situations:

A. If the company's president is considering increasing his salary by $10,200, how much must dollar sales increase to maintain the company's current net income?
B. If the company decreases sales commissions, variable expenses would decrease by 10%. The company believes that unit sales would decrease 5%, due to the loss of sales representatives, even though the company plans to increase its advertising budget by $5,000. Should the company decrease the sales commissions?
C. If the company changes its production and marketing techniques, it is projected

that variable expenses will increase 10%, fixed expenses will decrease 15%, and sales will increase 20%. Calculate the company's break-even point in terms of sales dollars if the new strategy is adopted. Assume that the sales price per unit would not be changed. Round your answer to the nearest dollar.

D. If the company's net income increases 250% next year due to a 28% increase in sales, did the company perform better or worse than expected? Assume that the company has adequate capacity to meet the increased volume without increasing fixed costs.

CASE FOR CHAPTER 26

Decision Problem (CVP Analysis and Variable Costing)

The Delmono Company, located in the northern part of California, produces and sells a selection of medium-priced bottled wines. The firm has been in operation for 10 years but has not been able to achieve profit results that are acceptable to its president and majority stockholder, William Delmono. These results have occurred despite the fact that sales demand for the product in recent years has been increasing and production last year was very near the limit of the firm's capacity of 1,000,000 bottles per year. The firm's most recent income statement, prepared with absorption costing, shows the following operating results:

Sales (980,000 bottles @ $4)		$3,920,000
Cost of goods sold		
Beginning inventory (10,000 bottles @ $3.60)	36,000	
Production cost (985,000 bottles @ $3.60)	3,546,000	
Total	3,582,000	
Ending inventory (15,000 bottles @ $3.60)	54,000	
Cost of goods sold		3,528,000
Gross profit		392,000
Selling and administrative expenses		340,000
Net income before tax		$ 52,000

The president has hired you to find ways to improve the firm's profitability. Your first step is to evaluate the cost behavioral patterns involved as follows:

Production costs:
 Variable—$2.00 per bottle
 Fixed—$1,576,000 for 985,000 bottles, or $1.60 per bottle
Selling and administrative expenses:
 Variable—$.10 per bottle sold
 Fixed—$242,000

Required:
A. Prepare an income statement for the firm using variable costing.
B. Why is the net income in requirement (A) different from that shown earlier with absorption costing?

C. What is the firm's break-even point in bottles? Dollars?
D. The company's marketing manager believes that a $20,000 increase in advertising expenses will result in sales of 1,000,000 bottles. Should this decision be made?
E. In addition to the $20,000 in advertisting expenses, the firm can increase its capacity to 1,200,000 bottles per year by increasing the fixed manufacturing costs by $360,000. There will not be any change in the variable manufacturing costs or selling and administrative expenses. What would be the effect on the firm's break-even point? Assuming all 1,200,000 bottles can be sold, what would be the effect on the firm's net income?

CHAPTER 27
MANAGERIAL ACCOUNTING AND DECISION - MAKING

OVERVIEW AND OBJECTIVES

This chapter describes the role of managerial accounting in decision-making. When you have completed the chapter, you should understand:

- The nature of decision-making (pp. 1041–1042).
- The major steps in the decision-making process (pp. 1042–1043).
- The application of differential analysis to choices between alternative courses of action (pp. 1043–1044).
- How to evaluate special orders, make or buy decisions, and joint product costs (pp. 1045–1049).
- The essential features of product-mix decisions (pp. 1049–1050).
- How to use return on investment and residual-income analysis (pp. 1050–1052).
- The use of contribution margin variance analysis (pp. 1053–1054).
- The basic nature of capital budgeting (pp. 1054–1055).
- The use of cash flows in capital budgeting decisions (pp. 1055–1056).
- The application of three capital budgeting methods—payback period, return on average investment, and discounted cash flows (pp. 1056–1060).

We saw in Chapter 21 that managers make decisions continuously as they *plan activities, organize resources, direct operations,* and *control performance*. The managerial accounting topics covered in previous chapters assist management in making decisions, either directly or indirectly. This chapter deals specifically with the subject of decision-making and the kind of accounting information required for the decision-making process. **Decision-making** involves a choice between alternative courses of action, and the alternative chosen is usually selected on the basis of some measure of profitability or cost savings. What products to produce, how to produce them, how to sell them, what price to charge, how to allocate resources, and whether or not to expand production capacity are examples of business decisions. While all business decisions are future-oriented, some will have longer-term implications than others. In general, the quality of decision-making is highly dependent on the quality of the information available to the decision-maker. Good information leads to good decisions, while bad information leads in the opposite direction. A discussion of the role of accounting information in decision-making must be preceded by a basic understanding of the decision-making process used by managers.

BASICS OF MANAGERIAL DECISION-MAKING

Business decisions range from the routine and repetitive to the complex and nonrecurring. Except for the simplest cases, managerial decision-making is both an art and a science because a combination of qualitative (subjective) and quantitative (objective) factors enter the picture. Such qualitative factors as public image, social responsibility, competitive reaction, management intuition, and employee attitudes often have an important bearing on a decision. At the same time, management will attempt to structure a decision-making situation in quantitative terms whenever possible so a choice can be made on a systematic basis. Managerial accounting provides most of the quantitative information (revenues, costs, invested capital, and operating statistics) required to evaluate alternative courses of action.

While there is no universal way managers make decisions, the **decision-making process** in general consists of these four steps:

1. Definition of the problem
2. Selection of alternative courses of action
3. Obtaining relevant information
4. Making a decision

In the problem-definition phase of decision-making, a manager should develop a complete understanding of the problem that must be solved and the objective he or she wants to accomplish. The problem should be identified precisely, and all pertinent facts associated with it interpreted carefully. This first step is essential because the other phases of the decision-making process depend on it. If the problem is incorrectly defined, time and resources will be wasted by ineffective decision-making.

The second step is the selection of the possible alternative courses of action. In some cases, only two alternatives are considered. For example, a firm may decide whether to produce a certain part needed in the production process or to purchase it. More complex decisions involve more than two alternatives. The major consideration when numerous alternatives are possible is to limit the analysis to a manageable number of alternatives, but still find a satisfactory solution. For example, a medical clinic may be trying to decide what kind of computer to install for data processing. Rather than consider every computer manufacturer, the clinic will consider only those companies known for their expertise in the health care field.

The third step in the decision-making process is the collection of information by means of which the various alternatives can be evaluated. Only *relevant* information should be considered—information useful in influencing the decision. All irrelevant information should be discarded, but both qualitative and quantitative information should be gathered. Some of the information will be internal to the business, some external. Whenever the information is the result of past performance, it should be recast as a projection of what is expected or desired in the future.

Once the pertinent facts have been thoroughly analyzed, a decision is made. The final choice among alternative courses of action is the one the decision-maker believes will lead to the desired objective identified in the problem-definition step. In many cases, a **decision model** (a formalized method for evaluating alternatives) is used as an aid in the selection process. The cost-volume-profit analysis methods discussed in Chapter 26 are examples of decision models that can be used to evaluate the profitability of various alternatives. Other decision models based on mathematical or statistical procedures are also available for decision-making in well-structured situations.

DIFFERENTIAL ANALYSIS

Differential analysis, also called **incremental analysis,** is a decision model that can be used to evaluate the differences in revenue and costs for alternative courses of action. The costs considered are not necessarily those used in conventional financial reporting. As noted earlier, there are different costs for different purposes. For decision-making purposes, relevant costs, differential costs, unavoidable costs, sunk costs, and opportunity costs are important classifications. **Relevant costs** are expected future costs, which will differ among alternatives. The difference between the relevant costs of two or more alternatives is called a **differential cost.** For example, if a production manager is deciding which of two machines to buy, direct labor cost may or may not be relevant. If the same skilled labor with an hourly rate of $12 is required to operate either machine, the cost is not relevant. However, if one machine requires less skill with a $10-per-hour operator, the labor cost is relevant and the differential cost is $2 per hour.

All costs are relevant in decision-making except the unavoidable costs; they will be the same regardless of the alternative selected. **Unavoidable costs** are either future costs that will not differ between alternatives (the $12 direct labor cost needed for both machines in the example above) or sunk costs. **Sunk costs** are not relevant in decision-making because they have already been incurred and cannot be changed. An example is the book value of an item of equipment a business is trying to decide whether or not to replace. Assume that the equipment does not have any residual value. If the item is replaced, the book value will be written off in the period of disposal. If it is kept, the same amount will be depreciated over the remaining life of the asset. Consequently, the book value will be expensed in either case so it is a sunk cost.

An **opportunity cost** is the potential benefit forgone by rejecting one alternative while accepting another. Opportunity costs are not found in the general ledger but are considered either formally or informally as part of virtually every decision. For example, if a student decides to attend summer school instead of accepting a job that will pay $2,200, the true cost of attending school is more than books, tuition, and housing. The opportunity cost of attending summer school is $2,200. As a business example, if a firm is considering the investment of working capital in land to be held for future expansion, the income that will be lost from an alternative investment such as a bank certificate of deposit will be an opportunity cost associated with the land acquisition.

The concepts of relevancy and differential also can be applied to revenues. **Relevant revenues** are those that will differ between alternatives; **differential revenue** is the difference between the relevant revenues of two or more alternatives. Whenever there are no relevant revenues (meaning that the differential revenue is zero) for a given decision, the selection between alternatives is made on the basis of the lowest cost. For an example of relevant revenue, assume that a firm is considering the addition of a new product to utilize available production capacity. Two choices are being evaluated: cross-country skis or downhill skis. The projected revenue with cross-country skis is $286,000 while that of downhill skis is $326,000, or a differential revenue of $40,000. The related costs also would be considered if they are relevant.

Differential analysis can assist management in making several types of business decisions. We used differential analysis without identifying it as such in Chapter 21 when we considered a department's contribution to indirect expenses in evaluating whether or not to discontinue the Tools Department. Other examples are: Should a special order be accepted? Should a product or product line be discontinued? Is it better to produce or to purchase a part needed in manufacturing? Does a product need further processing or is it ready to sell? Should a fixed asset be replaced? In the following sections, we will consider the application of differential analysis to some of these decisions.

EVALUATION OF A SPECIAL ORDER

Business firms often must decide whether or not to accept a special order, usually at a price lower than its normal selling price. The long-term pricing policy of any business must be based on a consideration of all costs incurred if the firm is to be profitable. When idle capacity exists, however, a special order may be attractive even though a lower-than-normal selling price is involved. Differential analysis can be applied to evaluate the differential revenue and costs associated with a special order. (Remember that a pricing decision based on differential analysis is valid for a one-time order but normally not for a firm's regular line of business.)

To illustrate a decision concerning a special order, let us refer to the Western Hardball Company, a manufacturer of baseballs sold with a Western label to discount stores. The company has the capacity to produce 100,000 baseballs per month, although the sales forecast for January is only 60,000 units because of seasonal demand for the product. An exporter located in Miami has offered to purchase 10,000 baseballs at a price of $1.90 each for distribution in a South American country. The normal selling price per baseball is $2.50. The variable costs required to produce a baseball are $.80 and the monthly fixed production costs are $84,000. No additional selling and administrative expenses will be required with the order, but there will be a setup cost of $5,000 for a special label that must be imprinted on each baseball. Should the offer be accepted? If the decision is made on the basis of the average production cost per baseball with the order, the offer will be rejected because the $1.90 price is less than the average cost of $2.07 ($.80 + $89,000/70,000). However, the average cost of production is irrelevant, as shown by differential analysis:

	Without Order	With Order	Differential Analysis	
Sales 60,000 @ $2.50	$150,000	$150,000		
10,000 @ $1.90		19,000	$19,000	(Differential Revenue)
Variable costs				
60,000 @ $.80	48,000	48,000		
10,000 @ $.80		8,000	(8,000)	(Differential Costs)
Fixed costs—regular	84,000	84,000		
—setup		5,000	(5,000)	(Differential Costs)
Gross profit	$ 18,000	$ 24,000	$ 6,000	

The firm's profit will be $6,000 higher with the offer even though the price is lower than normal. As long as the company does not have a better alternative use of the production capacity and is certain that the special offer will not have an adverse effect on its regular business, the offer should be accepted.

EVALUATION OF A MAKE OR BUY DECISION

Most manufacturing firms use many component parts in the assembly of their finished products. The parts can be produced by the manufacturer or purchased from an outside source. An automobile manufacturer may produce its own engines but purchase tires. In turn, certain parts of the engine (such as nuts and bolts) may be acquired from other manufacturers. Whenever a manufacturing firm has the production capacity and expertise to produce a given part, the decision to make it or buy it should be based on the relevant costs of each alternative. Differential analysis can be used to evaluate the relevant costs of making or buying a part. For example, assume that the Beech Company has been operating at 75% of capacity and has been paying $8 each to purchase a small gear used in its production process. A forecast of the future indicates that regular production will remain at approximately 75% of capacity. As a means of utilizing some of the unused capacity, the firm is considering the possibility of producing 20,000 gears instead of purchasing them. Based on the firm's normal product-costing approach with absorption costing, the following costs are estimated for 20,000 gears:

Direct materials	$ 42,000
Direct labor	73,000
Variable manufacturing overhead	20,000
Fixed manufacturing overhead	55,000
Total costs	$190,000
Cost of each gear (20,000 gears)	$9.50

At first glance, it may appear that the cost of producing a gear exceeds the purchase price by $1.50 ($9.50 less $8.00). However, differential analysis requires a review of the manufacturing costs to determine which actually are avoidable if the gears are purchased. Assume that this has been done and the direct materials, direct labor, variable manufacturing overhead, and fixed manufacturing overhead of $5,000 can be eliminated by purchasing the gears. Fixed manufacturing overhead of $50,000 will be incurred whether the gears are produced or purchased, so it is not a relevant cost. Differential analysis shows:

	Make the Gears	Buy the Gears	Differential Analysis
Direct materials	$ 42,000		$42,000
Direct labor	73,000		73,000
Variable manufacturing overhead	20,000		20,000
Fixed manufacturing overhead	55,000	$ 50,000	5,000
Purchase costs (20,000 @ $8)		160,000	(160,000)
Total costs	$190,000	$210,000	($20,000)

The relevant costs of producing the gears are $140,000 ($42,000 + $73,000 + $20,000 + $5,000), or $7 per unit. Therefore, a cost savings of $1 per unit ($8 less $7) will result if the firm produces the gears—for a total cost savings of $20,000. The firm also should consider any alternative uses of the unused capacity with a contribution margin in excess of $20,000, since they would generate even higher profits than the production of gears. Also, the desire to control the quality of the gears internally may be an important factor in the analysis. In addition, any potential adverse effect on the business relationship with the outside supplier of the gear—who may provide other components used in the production process—must be evaluated carefully.

TREATMENT OF JOINT PRODUCT COSTS

Many manufacturing firms produce several products from common raw materials or the same production process. For example, an oil refinery may produce gasoline, fuel oil, kerosene, lubricating oils, naphtha, and paraffin from crude oil. Chemical, lumber, mining, and meatpacking industries are others in which it is not possible to produce a single product without producing other products. These multiple products are called **joint products;** the common costs required to produce them before they are identifiable as separate units of output are termed **joint product costs.** The point in the production process at which the joint products become separate products is called the **split-off point.** Some of the products may be in salable form at the split-off point while others may require further processing before they can be sold. Graphically, the production flow of a manufacturing firm with two products (A and B) that are salable at the split-off point and one product (C) that must be processed further is:

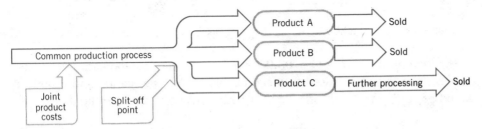

In the treatment of joint product costs, a distinction must be made between the valuation of inventories and decision-making concerning the point at which the products should be sold. Joint product costs are common costs that must be allocated to the individual products involved to value inventories for financial reporting purposes. The most common practice is to allocate joint product costs on the basis of the product's relative sales value. Assume that a chemical company produces 12,000 gallons of Alodane and 6,000 gallons of Balodane while incurring joint product costs of $108,000. Alodane sells for $8 per gallon and Balodane sells for $9 per gallon. Therefore, the sales of Alodane are $96,000 and the sales of Balodane are $54,000, for total sales of $150,000. Using the relative sales value method, the joint product costs of $108,000 would be assigned to the two products as follows:

$$\text{Alodane} \quad \frac{\$96,000}{\$150,000} \times \$108,000 = \$ 69,120$$

$$\text{Balodane} \quad \frac{\$54,000}{\$150,000} \times \$108,000 = \underline{\$ 38,880}$$

Total joint costs $\underline{\underline{\$108,000}}$

The allocation of joint product costs must be performed so that the production costs can be divided between inventories and the cost of goods sold. However, like any cost allocation procedure, the results must be interpreted carefully since they are only approximations of the true costs of producing individual products.

Managers often must decide whether to sell a joint product at the split-off point or to process it further. Joint product costs are irrelevant in such decisions since they are *sunk costs* and should not be allocated to the joint products involved for decision-making purposes. Instead, differential analysis should be used to evaluate the relevant costs and revenues. For example, assume that the two products Alodane and Balodane can either be sold at the split-off point for $8 and $9 per gallon, respectively, or can be processed further and subsequently sold. The following data are relevant:

Product	Selling Price per Gallon at Split-off Point	Further Processing Costs per Gallon	Selling Price per Gallon after Further Processing
Alodane	$8.00	$4.00	$14.00
Balodane	$9.00	$7.00	$15.50

The joint product costs of $108,000 are ignored because they are sunk costs. Alodane would be processed further and sold for $14 per gallon and Balodane would be sold at the split-off point for $9 because of this differential analysis:

Product	Differential Revenue with Further Processing	Differential Cost of Further Processing	Profit (Loss) of Further Processing
Alodane	$6.00 ($14.00 less $8.00)	$4.00	$2.00
Balodane	$6.50 ($15.50 less $9.00)	$7.00	($ .50)

The gross profit earned by selling Alodane after further processing and Balodane at the split-off point would be $66,000 [(12,000 × $14) + (6,000 × $9) − (12,000 × $4) − $108,000]. This is $24,000 higher than the gross profit of \$42,000 (\$150,000 − \$108,000) that would be earned by selling both products at the split-off point. The reason is the additional income of \$24,000 (12,000 × \$2) earned by the further processing of Alodane.

PRODUCT-MIX DECISIONS

Any business that sells more than one product must continuously evaluate the profitability of the various products to determine the most profitable product mix. In most cases, this cannot be done by simply selecting the products with the highest individual contribution margins because *scarce resources and other limiting factors* are characteristic of virtually every business. For example, a manufacturing firm will have a limited amount of production capacity as measured by direct labor hours or machine hours. In a department store, the limitation is the amount of floor space available. These limitations are called *constraints,* and management's job is to maximize the use of them. The most profitable product mix should be determined in these situations by relating the contribution margin of each product to the constraints of the firm. For example, consider a company that produces and sells two types of furniture—tables and chairs—with these selling prices and variable costs:

	Table	Chair
Selling price	\$30	\$24
Variable costs	15	18
Contribution margin	\$15	\$ 6
Contribution margin %	50	25

At first glance, a table appears to be the most profitable and management might be tempted to produce as many tables as can be sold. Assume, however, that the same machines are used to produce both products and only 60,000 machine hours are available each month. Six machine hours are required to produce a table, two machine hours for each chair. If an unlimited number of either product can be sold, only chairs should be produced because they are more profitable on the basis of contribution margin per machine hour:

	Table	Chair
Contribution margin per machine hour	$\frac{\$15}{6} = \$2.50$	$\frac{\$6}{2} = \$3.00$

By producing a maximum of 30,000 chairs (60,000/2), the total contribution margin earned will be \$180,000 (30,000 chairs × \$6 or 60,000 hours × \$3). It is unlikely, however, that an unlimited number of chairs can be sold since the market usually imposes constraints that must be recognized in product-mix decisions. For example, a minimum number of tables may have to be produced to satisfy the needs of customers who want to buy both tables and chairs. In addition, the maximum number of chairs that can be sold may be less than 30,000. Other constraints such as limited raw materials and direct labor hours also may require consideration in the analysis. In most cases, more than two products must be evaluated, so the determination of the most profitable product mix is a complex decision. Linear programming is a mathematical tool that can be used to overcome the complexities of multiple constraints and multiple products. The subject of linear programming, which is a series of algebraic manipulations, is beyond the scope of this text but is described in most quantitative business analysis textbooks.

RETURN ON INVESTMENT ANALYSIS

In Chapter 20, we showed how the rate of return on certain measures of investment can be used as important evaluations of a business firm's profitability. When **return on investment (ROI) analysis** is combined with the business segmentation topics discussed in Chapter 21, management has an effective means of deciding which segments of the business are most profitably using their resources. Recall from Chapter 21 that a responsibility center can be established as an *investment center* if the manager of that center has control of the revenue, costs, and resources invested. ROI analysis can be applied to such investment centers as divisions, product lines, plants, and retail stores with this formula:

$$\text{ROI} = \text{Margin earned} \times \text{Turnover of assets}$$

$$= \frac{\text{Net operating income}}{\text{Sales}} \times \frac{\text{Sales}}{\text{Operating assets}}$$

Since sales obviously cancel out in the ROI computation, the same result can be found by dividing net operating income by operating assets. The expanded version of ROI shown above is preferred by most managers because it emphasizes the fact that ROI is actually a function of two variables, *margin earned* and *turnover of assets*. To achieve a desired ROI, management must control both of these variables. Improvements in ROI can be achieved by *increasing sales, reducing costs,* or *reducing assets.* Net operating income typically is income before interest expense and taxes in ROI analysis. The interest expense is eliminated because it is considered a return to creditors for the assets they have provided. Operating assets are usually defined as the average of the annual beginning and ending asset balances. All productive assets—cash, accounts receivable, inventories, and fixed assets—are included. To illustrate the application of ROI analysis, the G & P Company operates two divisions as investment centers. Top management wants to know which of the two earned the highest ROI during the past year so it can decide which segment of the business to expand in the future. The following data indicate that the Personal Products Division has a higher ROI than the Cleaning Products Division even though it is much smaller:

		Personal Products Division	Cleaning Products Division
Net income before taxes	(a)	$ 420,000	$ 880,000
Interest expense	(b)	30,000	44,000
Net operating income	(c = a + b)	450,000	924,000
Sales	(d)	3,600,000	8,400,000
Average operating assets	(e)	2,400,000	6,000,000
Margin earned	(c ÷ d)	12.5%	11.0%
Turnover of assets	(d ÷ e)	1.5	1.4
ROI	(c ÷ e)	18.75%	15.4%

The Cleaning Products Division has a lower margin earned and a lower turnover of assets than the Personal Products Division. As a result, the Cleaning Products Division's ROI is only 15.4% compared with 18.75% for the Personal Products Division. Future expansion should take place in the Personal Products Division and resources might be moved to it from the Cleaning Products Division. If a higher ROI is to be achieved, the divisions will have to increase sales, reduce costs, or reduce operating assets.

RESIDUAL-INCOME ANALYSIS

An alternative way to evaluate the performance of an investment center is by applying residual-income analysis. **Residual income** is the net operating income earned in excess of a certain minimum rate of return on operating assets. When residual income is used to evaluate performance, the objective is to maximize the amount of residual income rather than the return on investment. The advantage of residual-income analysis is that it prevents the possibility of a segment manager rejecting an opportunity to earn a return on investment acceptable to the firm as a whole but below the ROI of his or her investment center. For example, assume that the G & P Company has decided that a minimum ROI of 12% is acceptable. Since the Personal Products Division has an ROI of 18.75%, its manager may reject an opportunity to earn 15% with a new product even though it is acceptable to the firm because the division's ROI will decrease. The residual-income approach would charge the division manager only 12% so all projects with a return in excess of 12% will be accepted. The major limitation of the residual-income approach is that it is difficult to compare the performance of business segments of different sizes with it since the larger segments will have more residual income than the smaller ones. Nevertheless, it is useful for evaluating the profitability of specific profit results. The following analysis illustrates the application of the residual-income approach to the G & P Company's performance:

		Personal Products Division
Average operating assets	(a)	$2,400,000
Minimum return at 12%	(b=.12a)	288,000
Net operating income	(c)	450,000
Residual income	(c−b)	$ 162,000

TRANSFER PRICING DECISIONS

One of the most important considerations in performance evaluation with either ROI or residual-income analysis is the firm's transfer pricing policy. **Transfer pricing** refers to the prices charged by one segment of a decentralized firm for products or services transferred to another segment. For example, the Delco Electronics Division of General Motors Corporation provides radios for the Oldsmobile Division. The key question is "What prices should be charged for such interdivisional transfers?" Since both the buyer and the seller are segments of the same organization, the transactions will not be independent, as they are with external sources. The most basic form of transfer price is the transferring segment's *cost,* which we used in the process-costing illustration in Chapter 23. There, the Finishing Department was charged for the full cost of the products transferred from the Blending Department. However, one of the main objectives in a decentralized organization is to achieve a certain amount of autonomy for each of the segments. The use of a cost-based transfer price does not provide any profit incentive for the transferring segment. Performance evaluation of the various segments based on ROI or residual income will consequently be impossible.

Some form of *market price* is typically used to provide the profit incentive needed for segment-performance measurement. If the product or service being transferred has a market price determinable from external sources, it can be used. Otherwise a *negotiated price* may be determined by bargaining between the buying division and selling division as an amount equitable to both parties. Some firms use a *cost-plus basis* for transfer pricing in which the price is set at the transferring segment's cost plus a fixed amount or a certain percentage of cost. Several other transfer pricing methods are available and are discussed in most cost accounting textbooks.

CONTRIBUTION MARGIN VARIANCE ANALYSIS

Another important managerial decision-making technique is **contribution margin variance analysis.** When carefully planned profits are not achieved, management needs information concerning the causes so it can decide who and what are to blame. Contribution margin variance analysis enables management to evaluate why the contribution margin of a given period is different from that planned in the budget, or from that of a previous period. Essentially the same analysis can be applied to differences in gross profit instead of contribution margin. Since the contribution margin is the difference between sales and the variable costs, any change in it will be due to one or a combination of the following:

1. A variation of selling price per unit sold
2. A variation of the number of units sold
3. A variation of the mix or combination of units sold
4. A variation of the variable costs of producing and selling each unit

To illustrate the fundamentals of contribution margin variance analysis, we will consider a firm that sells only one product. This means that the firm cannot incur a sales mix variance, a subject deferred to more advanced accounting textbooks. Assume that the management of the ITL Company has received the following income-statement information showing the actual contribution margin earned from the sales of a single model of calculator during the year compared with the one budgeted:

	Budget	Actual	Variance
Sales—units	21,000	22,000	1,000 F
Sales—dollars	$1,008,000	$990,000	$18,000 U
Variable costs	735,000	814,000	79,000 U
Contribution margin	$ 273,000	$176,000	$97,000 U

Management wants an explanation of why the actual contribution margin was $97,000 lower than the budgeted contribution margin despite the fact that the actual number of calculators sold exceeded those budgeted by 1,000. Three separate variances—selling price, sales volume, and cost—must be computed to determine the causes of the unfavorable contribution margin variance of $97,000. This is accomplished by considering only one factor at a time while holding the other two constant.

SELLING PRICE VARIANCE

The budgeted selling price was $48 per unit $\left(\dfrac{\$1,008,000}{21,000}\right)$ but the actual selling price was only $45 per unit $\left(\dfrac{\$990,000}{22,000}\right)$. The selling price variance is unfavorable and is computed by multiplying the difference of $3 per unit times the 22,000 units actually sold. The result is an unfavorable selling price variance of $66,000.

SALES VOLUME VARIANCE

A favorable sales volume variance was incurred because the actual units sold (22,000) were 1,000 units more than those budgeted (21,000). The additional units would cause both sales revenue and the cost of goods sold to increase, so the net effect is a higher contribution margin. The budgeted contribution margin per unit was $13 $\left(\dfrac{\$273,000}{21,000} \right)$, thus the favorable sales volume variance was 1,000 times $13, or $13,000.

COST VARIANCE

The budgeted variable costs for each unit were $35 $\left(\dfrac{\$735,000}{21,000} \right)$, whereas the actual costs were $37 $\left(\dfrac{\$814,000}{22,000} \right)$. As a result, the actual costs per unit were $2 higher than expected. The $2-per-unit deviation is multiplied by the 22,000 units sold to compute an unfavorable cost variance of $44,000.

The algebraic summation of the three variances should equal the unfavorable contribution margin variance of $97,000. The unfavorable variances for selling price ($66,000) and cost ($44,000) less the favorable sales volume variance ($13,000) equals $97,000. These variances will be reported to the managers responsible for the related financial performance so corrective action can be taken wherever possible to improve the future profitability of the operation.

CAPITAL BUDGETING

The types of managerial decisions considered so far in this chapter have been primarily short-term oriented. **Capital budgeting,** which involves the planning and financing of capital investments such as the replacement of equipment, expansion of production facilities, and introduction of a new product line, is another important area of managerial decision-making. These decisions are concerned with a current expenditure that will pay for itself and yield an acceptable rate of return over a relatively long period of time. As such, capital budgeting decisions are critical to the long-term profitability of a firm since they will determine its capacity to do business. Capital budgeting decisions must be considered carefully by top management for several reasons:

1. They involve large sums of money.
2. The resources invested are committed for a long time period.
3. They cannot be reversed easily since the investment becomes a sunk cost that can be recovered only through the productive use of the related assets.
4. Since they are long-term oriented, substantial risk is involved because of such uncertainties as economic conditions, technological developments, consumer preferences, and social responsibilities.
5. In many cases, the success or failure of a firm may be dependent on a single decision.

A number of methods are available to management for the evaluation of capital expenditures. In fact, entire books have been written about the subject of capital budgeting—which can involve many sophisticated techniques. As a result, we will be forced to limit our coverage of capital budgeting to three fundamental methods: *payback period, return on average investment,* and *discounted cash flows*.

To illustrate the three capital budgeting methods, assume that the Carson Company is evaluating the possibility of producing a new product, which will require the acquisition of a new machine. The machine will cost $81,000, including installation and transportation charges. It has a useful life of 10 years and an estimated residual value of $9,000. The company estimates that the new product will increase its annual net income by $10,800, computed as:

Estimated sales of new product		$50,000
Estimated costs and expenses:		
Manufacturing costs, including depreciation of $7,200	$25,000	
Selling and administrative expenses	5,000	30,000
Estimated before tax income		20,000
Income taxes at 46%		9,200
Estimated net income		$10,800

USE OF CASH FLOWS

Most capital budgeting methods use *cash flows* to evaluate the return from an investment. The analysis involves a cash outlay made currently to obtain net cash flows (cash receipts in excess of cash disbursements or cost savings) from the investment in future years. An exception to the use of cash flows is the return on average investment method, which we will discuss later. The basic reason for using cash flows instead of accounting net income to measure the return from an investment is the time value of money, a concept introduced in the appendix to Chapter 17. The cash received from an investment today is worth more than the same amount of cash received next month or next year. Since net income is based on accrual accounting, it does not necessarily reflect the flow of cash in and out of the business.

For simplicity, we assume that the Carson Company will receive the revenue from the new product in cash, and all costs other than depreciation will be paid in cash. When complete accrual accounting is involved, the procedures discussed in Chapter 19 can be used to convert net income to net cash flow.

DEPRECIATION AS A TAX SHIELD

The net cash flow expected by the Carson Company is $18,000 per year. Annual depreciation of $7,200 has been computed with the straight-line method $\left(\dfrac{\$81,000 - \$9,000}{10}\right)$. Since the depreciation expense does not require a cash outlay, it must be added to the net income after tax to determine the net cash flow of $18,000. Alternatively, the $18,000 net cash can be computed as ($50,000 − $17,800 − $5,000 − $9,200). Although the depreciation expense does not involve a cash outflow, it is deductible in determining taxable income. Consequently, it reduces the cash outflow by the amount deducted multiplied by the tax rate ($7,200 × .46 = $3,312). The depreciation deduction is called a **tax shield** because it is a tax-deductible expense that saves the firm $3,312 in income taxes. This means that the cash outlay for income taxes would have been $3,312 higher without depreciation because it would have been computed as ($50,000 − $22,800) times .46, or $12,512 instead of $9,200.

PAYBACK PERIOD

The **payback period** is the length of time required to recover the cost of an investment from the net cash flows it generates; this is the period of time needed for an investment to pay for itself. The payback period is simple to compute and easy to understand. Use of the shortest payback period possible often is desirable for two reasons: (1) The sooner the cash is recovered, the sooner it can be reinvested in other productive assets, something particularly important in times of high inflation. (2) A quick payback period may reduce the risk of the investment since uncertainty usually increases with the passage of time. A primary disadvantage of the method is that it ignores the total life of the investment. An investment selected because of its short payback period may therefore be less profitable over its entire life than an alternative invest-ment with a longer payback period and total life. Nevertheless, many firms use the method to make a final choice among alternatives when other methods of evaluation indicate they are equally attractive. The payback period in the Carson Company's decision is computed as:

$$\text{Payback period} = \frac{\text{Initial cost of investment}}{\text{Annual net cash flows}}$$

$$= \frac{\$81,000}{\$18,000} = 4.5 \text{ years}$$

As a result, it will take 4.5 years to recover the initial investment of $81,000.

RETURN ON AVERAGE INVESTMENT

The **return on average investment** is a rough approximation of an invest-ment's profitability. It is calculated by dividing the average annual net income after tax from an investment by the average investment. When straight-line depreciation is used, the book value of an asset decreases uniformly over its life. As a result, the average investment is computed as:

$$\text{Average investment} = \frac{\text{Initial cost} + \text{Residual value}}{2}$$

When the residual value is zero, the average investment is simply the initial cost divided by two. The return on average investment for the Carson Com-pany's proposed machine is:

$$\text{Return on average investment} = \frac{\text{Average net income}}{\text{Average investment}} = \frac{\$10,800}{\$45,000} = 24\%$$

The 24% return would be compared with the returns of alternative invest-ments and with the minimum return required by management to determine whether it should be accepted. In addition, the risk associated with each al-ternative must be evaluated carefully. Most businesses using the return on average investment method rank all of the investments according to their returns and risks. Available resources are committed to those investments with an acceptable combination of returns and risks.

The proponents of this method support it on the premise that it follows the income statement in measuring the return on an investment. The $10,800 used in the example is the estimate of annual net income rather than the estimated net cash flows. The method is widely used to rank alternative investments because it is easy to use and understand. Unlike the payback-period method, the return on average investment method does consider the profitability of an investment over its useful life. However, it has a serious weakness: *it does not consider the time value of money*. The use of the average annual net income ignores the timing of cash receipts and disbursements. Consequently, the net cash flow from an investment's last year of life is valued the same as that of its first year. In addition, the method does not distinguish between an investment requiring an immediate payment of cash and one that will be paid for in the future. Since cash available in the current year clearly is worth more than cash available in the distant future, the time value of money should be taken into consideration with effective capital budgeting.

DISCOUNTED CASH FLOWS

Discounted cash flows can be used to compare the cost of an investment with the present value of the net cash flows expected from it in the future. As we have seen with the other two capital budgeting methods, the cash flows associated with an investment occur at different times. For example, the Carson Company is considering an investment of $81,000 in current dollars, which will yield expected future cash flows of $18,000 for each of 10 years and $9,000 from the disposal value at the end of the tenth year. In making any investment decision, the expected future cash flows must be compared with the amount of the investment required to obtain them. The objective is to return the amount invested as well as earn a satisfactory return on the investment. As we demonstrated in the appendix to Chapter 17, however, a dollar expected in the future is not equivalent to a dollar held today because of the time value of money. Consequently, the expected future cash flows from an investment can be compared with the investment only when *both* are measured in *equivalent* dollars. This can be accomplished by discounting the future dollars to their present value. Present value in general is the equivalent dollar value today of a known future amount, given a certain discount rate and time period of receipt or payment.

In a capital budgeting application, the present value of the expected future cash flows is the amount a business will pay today to receive those future amounts over a fixed time period with a given discount rate. The use of present value analysis in capital budgeting is essentially the same as its application to the pricing of long-term bonds, discussed in Chapter 17.

A popular discounted cash flow technique is the **net present value method.** By discounting the expected future cash flows into present value terms, they can be compared directly with the investment cost. The discount rate chosen for the discounting process is the firm's required rate of return on its investments, often called the cost of capital. **Cost of capital** is the firm's cost of obtaining funds in the form of debt or owners' equity. As long as an investment offers a rate of return higher than the cost of capital, it should be accepted, because the return will exceed the cost of the funds used to finance it. This will occur when the *net present value,* which is the difference between the discounted expected future net cash flows and the cost of the investment, is positive (discounted expected future cash flows exceed the cost of the investment). In contrast, a negative net present value indicates that an investment should be rejected, since the discounted expected future net cash flows are less than the investment cost. In such cases, the cost of the investment will exceed its return to the firm. If the net present value of an investment is zero, management will be indifferent about accepting or rejecting it.

To illustrate the net present value method, assume that the management of the Carson Company requires a return in excess of 16%. The expected future cash flows can be discounted by one of two approaches. They can be discounted year by year, using the present value of $1 table as shown in Figure 27-1. The factors shown in the third column are from the present value of $1 table (Table 17-3) presented in the appendix to Chapter 17 on page 698. Alternatively, the expected future net cash flow of $18,000 per year can be discounted using the present value of an annuity of $1 table (16% and 10 periods) since the amount received is the same each year. Again, the present value of an annuity of $1 is presented in the appendix to Chapter 17 as Table 17-4 on page 700. Then the disposal value of $9,000 would be discounted using the present value of $1 table (16% and 10 periods). This must be done since the $9,000 disposal value will not be received for 10 years. The alternative treatment would be determined as follows:

Present value of expected annual cash flows ($18,000 × 4.8332)	$86,998
Present value of expected disposal value ($9,000 × .2267)	2,040
Total present value of expected future cash flows	89,038
Cost of initial investment	81,000
Net present value	$ 8,038

Whenever the expected future cash flows are not constant each year, they must be discounted on a year-by-year basis with the present value of $1 table (Table 17-3). The machine should be purchased because the investment has a net present value of $8,038. The total present value of $89,038 represents the maximum amount the Carson Company could pay and still earn the required 16%. However, it can make the investment for only $81,000. As a result, the actual rate of return is significantly higher than the minimum of 16% required. Another discounted cash flow technique called the internal rate of return method can be used to determine the actual rate of return for the machine (approximately 18.5%). The **internal rate of return** is defined as the interest rate that will discount the future cash flows so their present value is exactly equal to the cost of the investment. It should be noted in Figure 27-1 that the $18,000 expected annual cash flow is worth less and less in present value terms as time passes. If an interest rate higher than 16% had been used, the total present

Figure 27-1
Analysis of Investment in Machine

Year	Expected Net Cash Flow	Present Value of $1 at 16%	Present Value of Net Cash Flow
1	$18,000	.8621	$15,518
2	18,000	.7432	13,377
3	18,000	.6407	11,533
4	18,000	.5523	9,941
5	18,000	.4761	8,570
6	18,000	.4104	7,387
7	18,000	.3538	6,368
8	18,000	.3050	5,490
9	18,000	.2630	4,734
10	18,000	.2267	4,080
10	9,000	.2267	2,040
Total present value of cash flows			$89,038
Cost of initial investment			81,000
Net present value			$ 8,038

value of the cash flows would have been lower than $89,038. In contrast, a lower interest rate would have produced a total present value of the cash flows in excess of $89,038. An inverse relationship will exist between the interest rate chosen and the present value of future net cash flows, which means that a business will be willing to pay less for an investment when it requires a higher return on the investment.

GLOSSARY

CAPITAL BUDGETING. The planning and financing of capital investments (p. 1054).

CONTRIBUTION MARGIN VARIANCE ANALYSIS. A technique used to evaluate the difference between the actual contribution margin for a given period and the contribution margin budgeted for the same period or one for a previous period (p. 1053).

COST OF CAPITAL. A firm's cost of obtaining funds in the form of debt or owners' equity (p. 1058).

DECISION-MAKING. Making a choice among alternative courses of action (p. 1041).

DECISION-MAKING PROCESS. Defining the problem, selecting alternative courses of action, obtaining relevant information, and arriving at a decision (p. 1042).

DECISION MODEL. A formalized method for evaluating alternative courses of action (p. 1043).

DIFFERENTIAL ANALYSIS (INCREMENTAL ANALYSIS). A decision model used to evaluate the differences in relevant revenue and costs between alternative courses of action (p. 1043).

DIFFERENTIAL COSTS. The difference between the relevant costs of two alternatives (p. 1043).

DIFFERENTIAL REVENUE. The difference between the relevant revenue of two alternatives (p. 1044).

DISCOUNTED CASH FLOWS. Capital budgeting method used to compare the cost of an investment with the present value of the net cash flows expected from it in the future (p. 1058).

INTERNAL RATE OF RETURN. The interest rate that will discount the net cash flows from an investment so their present value is exactly equal to the cost of the investment (p. 1059).

JOINT PRODUCTS. More than one product produced from common raw materials or the same production process (p. 1047).

JOINT PRODUCT COSTS. Common costs required to produce joint products before they are identifiable as separate units (p. 1047).

NET PRESENT VALUE METHOD. A capital budgeting method used to discount future net cash flows into present value terms with the firm's cost of capital (p. 1058).

OPPORTUNITY COST. The potential benefit forgone by rejecting one alternative while accepting another (p. 1044).

PAYBACK PERIOD. The length of time required to recover the cost of an investment from the net cash flows it generates (p. 1056).

RELEVANT COSTS. Expected future costs that will differ between alternatives (p. 1043).

RELEVANT REVENUE. Expected future revenue that will differ between alternatives (p. 1044).

RESIDUAL INCOME. The net operating income earned in excess of a certain minimum rate of return on operating assets (p. 1051).

RETURN ON AVERAGE INVESTMENT. A capital budgeting method that provides a rough approximation of an investment's profitability (p. 1057).

RETURN ON INVESTMENT ANALYSIS. A technique used to evaluate the profitability of segments of a business (p. 1050).

SPLIT-OFF POINT. The point in the production process at which joint products become separate products (p. 1047).

SUNK COSTS. Costs that are not relevant in decision-making because they already have been incurred and cannot be changed (p. 1044).

TAX SHIELD. The total amount of a tax-deductible expense such as depreciation (p. 1056).

TRANSFER PRICING. The prices charged by one segment of a decentralized firm for products or services transferred to another segment (p. 1052).

UNAVOIDABLE COSTS. Either future costs that will not differ between alternatives or sunk costs (p. 1044).

DISCUSSION QUESTIONS

1. What is decision-making? What are the basic steps followed in the decision-making process?

2. You recently heard a business manager make the following comment: "Quantitative analysis may be all right for some businesses, but I'd rather make decisions based on my intuition and years of experience." Do you agree? Explain.

3. What is differential analysis?

4. Define each of the following terms:
   (a) Relevant costs
   (b) Differential costs
   (c) Unavoidable costs
   (d) Sunk costs
   (e) Opportunity costs

5. The All-Sports Company produces golf balls that are sold for $6 per dozen. Under what circumstances might the firm consider an order at a price lower than $6?

6. The Back Camper Company uses a number of parts to produce several models of campers. The company has been purchasing a certain part from another firm at a price of $106 even though it has the expertise to produce the part internally. The chief accountant has estimated that the following costs would be incurred in the production of each of the parts:

Direct costs	$ 90
Variable overhead	10
Fixed overhead	20
Total	$120

   Do you agree that the firm should buy the part based on this analysis? Explain your reasoning.

7. Define the following terms:
   (a) Joint products
   (b) Joint product costs
   (c) Split-off point for joint products

8. Why can't a firm simply select the products with the highest contribution margins to find the most profitable product mix?

9. Differentiate between return on investment analysis and residual income analysis.

10. Why are transfer pricing decisions important in evaluating the profit performance of the segments of a business?

11. Why is contribution margin variance analysis an important managerial accounting tool?

12. The budget of the Reech Company for the previous year indicated that 20,000 units of product should have been sold at a price of $15 each with unit costs of $10. Actual sales were 22,000 units at a price of $12 each with unit costs of $10. Identify the causes of the difference between actual and budgeted profits.

13. What is capital budgeting? Why are capital budgeting decisions critical to the overall success of a firm?

14. Differentiate between cash flow and net income as the terms are used in capital budgeting. Why are cash flows used in most capital budgeting models?

15. What is the payback period? What is the primary limitation of the use of the payback period in capital budgeting?
16. What are the primary advantage and disadvantage of using the return on average investment method?
17. Why are discounted cash flows the best basis with which capital budgeting decisions can be made?
18. What is a firm's cost of capital? How does it relate to capital budgeting decisions?
19. What does the term *net present value* mean?
20. Discounting future cash flows at 16% provides a lower present value than discounting them at 12%. Why?

EXERCISES

Exercise 27-1 (Evaluating a Special Order)

The May Company manufactures portable cassette players at a per unit cost of:

Direct labor	$15
Direct materials	20
Variable manufacturing overhead	12
Fixed manufacturing overhead	18
Total unit cost	$65

The company sells each casette player for $80 and is presently operating at 75% of its capacity of 50,000 units per year. The company has received a special order at a price of $53 per unit from a mail order firm for 1,000 units per month for one year only. The units sold to the mail order firm would be identical to the firm's regular players except for a special nameplate. The May Company would have to purchase a new machine for $35,000 to produce the special nameplate. The machine will have no alternative use or residual value at the end of the year. The sales by the mail order firm would not affect the company's regular sales because of the different label and markets involved.

Required:
Should the company accept the special order?

Exercise 27-2 (Evaluating a Make/Buy Decision)

The McConnell Company manufactures calculators and has always produced all necessary parts for the calculators, including the subassembly. The cost per unit of the subassembly at a production level of 50,000 units is:

Direct materials	$ 7
Direct labor	8
Variable manufacturing overhead	4
Fixed manufacturing overhead	8
Total unit cost	$27

One-fourth of the fixed manufacturing overhead is a common cost that is allocated to the subassembly production. The remaining fixed manufacturing overhead cost is direct and one-half of direct fixed overhead cost could be eliminated if the subassemblies are purchased rather than produced. An outside supplier has offered to produce and sell the McConnell Company 50,000 subassemblies at a price of $23 per unit.

Required:
A. Should the offer be accepted if there are no alternative uses for the factory space currently being used to produce the subassembly?
B. Should the offer be accepted if the factory space currently being used could be rented for $75,000 per year?

Exercise 27-3 (Differential Analysis and Joint Products)

The Lyell Company produces four joint products—A, B, C, and D—at a total cost of $75,000. The company can sell the products immediately after the split-off point for $10,000, $8,000, $9,000, and $12,000, respectively. The products also can be processed further and sold as follows:

Product	Additional Processing Costs	Sales
A	$12,000	$20,000
B	14,000	24,000
C	22,000	35,000
D	6,000	14,000

All costs after the split-off point can be eliminated for any product that is not processed beyond the split-off point.

Required:
Which products should be processed further and which should be sold at the split-off point?

Exercise 27-4 (Combining Contribution Margin and a Scarce Resource)

The Elmwood Company produces and sells four products—A, B, C, and D. The selling prices, variable costs, and number of machine hours required to produce each product are:

Product	Selling Price	Variable Costs	Machine Hours per Unit
A	$16	$10	2
B	20	8	3
C	15	10	1
D	30	14	8

The company can produce each of the four products with a single machine that has a maximum operating capacity of 2,400 hours per year.

Required:

A. How many units of each of the four products can be produced in a year if the company produces only that product?

B. Assuming the company can sell all the units it produces, which product or mix of products should be produced?

C. Assuming the firm must produce 200 units of Product A, what additional products should be produced?

Exercise 27-5 (Evaluating Profitability Performance)

The Highland Company operates four departments. The company has gathered the following departmental data:

		Cost of Goods Sold	Operating Expenses	Operating Assets Beginning Balance	Ending Balance
Department	Sales				
1	$ 40,000	$ 30,000	$ 3,000	$ 30,000	$ 40,000
2	18,000	7,000	4,700	44,000	40,000
3	300,000	250,000	39,000	180,000	260,000
4	250,000	150,000	55,200	250,000	310,000

Required:

Rank the four departments on the basis of return on investment. Assume the company requires a minimum return on the average investment in operating assets of 10% in your calculation of residual income. What is the residual income of Department 4?

Exercise 27-6 (Contribution Margin Variance Analysis)

The Elizabethian Company has prepared the following income statement information showing the actual contribution margin earned from the sale of the company's single product as compared with the budgeted performance:

	Budget	Actual	Variance
Sales—units	4,200	4,100	100 U
Sales—dollars	$386,400	$385,400	$1,000 U
Variable costs	205,800	196,800	9,000 F
Contribution margin	180,600	188,600	8,000 F

Required:

Calculate the selling price variance, the sales volume variance, and cost variance.

Exercise 27-7 (Capital Budgeting Evaluations)

The Smithville Company is evaluating three investment alternatives and has compiled the following information:

	Investment		
	A	**B**	**C**
Initial investment:	$45,638	$75,816	$41,973
Net cash inflows:			
Year: 1	$10,000	$20,000	$15,000
2	10,000	20,000	15,000
3	10,000	20,000	15,000
4	10,000	20,000	15,000
5	10,000	20,000	
6	10,000		
7	10,000		

The company requires a 12% minimum return on new investments.

Required:
A. Calculate the payback period for each investment.
B. Calculate the net present value for each of the investments.

PROBLEMS

Problem 27-1 (Evaluating a Special Order with Opportunity Costs)

The Postma Company produces flower vases. The operating results of the preceding year were:

Sales (77,000 units @ $8)	$616,000
Cost of goods sold	
Direct materials	115,500
Direct labor	154,000
Manufacturing overhead	92,400
Total	361,900
Gross profit	254,100
Selling expenses	38,500
Administrative expenses	23,100
Total operating expenses	61,600
Net income	$192,500

The company has received a special order to buy 10,000 vases at a unit cost of $6.90. Material costs per unit would not change but the labor costs for the special order would be 25% greater than normal since some overtime wages would be incurred. Fixed manufacturing overhead is 50% of the variable manufacturing overhead at the present level of production. Fixed manufacturing overhead would not change and there would be no additional variable or fixed selling expenses. The administrative expenses, which are all fixed, would increase $2,000 if the special order is accepted. Current variable selling expenses are $.20 per unit. The company has a maximum capacity of 85,000 vases so the company would have to reduce its regular sales by 2,000 units if it accepts the special order.

Required:
Should the company accept the special order?

Problem 27-2 (Evaluating a Make/Buy Decision)

The Culver Company has realized a significant increase in demand for its products and is presently producing at a full capacity level of 100,000 units. The company is considering expanding output to 125,000 units by the adoption of one of the following alternatives:

1. The additional 25,000 units could be purchased from an outside source at a price of $6 per unit.
2. The company could expand its production capacity, which would result in added direct fixed expenses of $50,000 per year.

The company's sales and cost data at the 100,000 unit level of output are:

Sales	$750,000
Direct materials	100,000
Direct labor	150,000
Variable overhead	50,000
Direct fixed overhead	250,000
Allocated fixed overhead	75,000
Net income	$125,000

Common fixed costs allocated to production would increase from $75,000 to $93,750 since the common fixed overhead is allocated on the basis of sales volume, although the firm's total common fixed costs would not increase under either alternative.

Required:
Which of the two alternatives should the company adopt?

Problem 27-3 (Differential Analysis and Joint Products)

The Bullseye Company produces two joint products, X and Y. The annual production is 10,000 units of X and 6,000 units of Y at a joint cost of $104,000. Product X can be sold for $10 per unit at the split-off point and product Y can be sold for $16 per unit. Product Y can be further processed at a cost of $2,000 into products A and B. The additional processing will produce 4,000 units of A and 2,000 units of B. The selling price of product A is $12 per unit and product B sells for $20 per unit. Product X can be processed further at an annual cost of $20,000 and sold for $20 per unit.

Required:
Which products should be sold at the split-off point and which should be processed further?

Problem 27-4 (Profitability Analysis)

The Spall Company has compiled the following budgeted data for next year's operations:

	Account Balance on 1/1	Account Balance on 12/31
Cash	$10,000	$25,000
Accounts receivable	25,000	35,000
Inventory	45,000	50,000
Plant and equipment	80,000	70,000
Accounts payable	20,000	30,000

Total fixed costs	$50,000
Variable costs per unit	$ 10
Estimated volume	10,000

Required:

A. If the company wants to earn net income that is a 15% before-tax return on its average investment in operating assets, what should be the selling price per unit? (*Hint:* Use CVP analysis)

B. If the company actually produces and sells 9,000 units at the price computed in requirement (A), what is the firm's actual rate of return on its average investment in operating assets?

C. If the company actually sells 12,000 units at a selling price of $17 per unit, what is the company's residual income assuming a minimum acceptable return on assets of 12%?

Problem 27-5 (Capital Budgeting Evaluations)

The Ontario Company is considering a project that would require the purchase of a new machine at a cost of $34,000. The new machine would have a five-year life and a residual value of $4,000. The new project would produce a net cash inflow and net income of $14,000 before depreciation on the new equipment and income taxes each year. The company's income tax rate is 50% of its before-tax net income. Consequently, the annual net income after taxes will be:

Net income before depreciation and taxes	$14,000
Depreciation (straight-line)	6,000
Income before taxes	8,000
Income taxes	4,000
Net income	$ 4,000

The company requires a rate of return of at least 12% on investments of this type.

A. What is the payback period for the machine?

B. Calculate the return on average investment for the machine.

C. Calculate the net present value of the net cash flows discounted at 12%.

ALTERNATE PROBLEMS

Problem 27-1A (Evaluating a Special Order with Opportunity Costs)

The Spring Company manufactures gas grills and is considering expanding production. A distributor has asked the company to produce a special order of 8,000 grills to be sold overseas. The grills would be sold under a different brand name and would not influence Spring Company's current sales. The plant is currently producing 95,000 units per year. The company's maximum capacity is 100,000 units per year so the company would have to reduce the production of units sold under its own brand name by 3,000 units if the special order is accepted.

The company's income statement for the previous year is presented below:

Sales (95,000 units)		$7,125,000
Cost of goods sold		
Direct materials	$2,375,000	
Direct labor	1,900,000	
Manufacturing overhead	1,425,000	5,700,000
Gross profit		1,425,000
Selling expenses	575,000	
Administrative expenses	237,500	812,500
Net income		$ 612,500

The company's variable manufacturing overhead is $10 per unit and the variable selling expense is $5 per unit. The administrative expense is completely fixed and would increase by $5,000 if the special order is accepted. There would be no variable selling expense associated with the special order and variable manufacturing overhead per unit would remain constant.

The company's direct labor cost per unit for the special order would increase 5% while direct material cost per unit for the special order would increase 10%. Fixed manufacturing overhead and fixed selling expense would not change.

Required:
If the distributor has offered to pay $67 per unit for the special order, should the company accept the offer?

Problem 27-2A (Evaluating a Make/Buy Decision)

The Fairfax Company produces air compressors. The motors for the compressors are purchased directly from an outside supplier at a cost of $46 each. The company has some factory space that it currently rents to a firm as warehouse space. The annual rental income is $50,000. If the company decides to manufacture the motors, it would have to purchase a new machine at a cost of $75,000. The new equipment would enable the firm to produce its annual requirement of 5,000 motors and would have no residual value at the end of a five-year useful life. In addition, the company has compiled the following per unit costs, which do not reflect the cost of the new machine:

Direct labor	$12
Direct materials	15
Variable manufacturing overhead	8
Fixed manufacturing overhead—direct	2
Fixed manufacturing overhead—allocated	5
Total	$42

Required:
Should the firm make or buy the motors for the air compressors?

Problem 27-3A (Differential Analysis and Joint Products)

The Curme Chemical Company produces two products, A and B at a joint cost of $24,000. The company can sell 8,000 units of product A for $2 per unit or the units can be processed further at a cost of $10,000 to produce 3,000 units of product X, 4,000 units of product Y, and 1,000 units of product Z. The unit selling prices for products X, Y, and Z are $3, $2, and $4, respectively. The company can sell 5,000 units of product B or they can be processed further to produce 2,000 units of product C and 3,000 units of product D. The additional processing to produce products C and D will cost $3,000. The per unit selling prices are product B—$3; product C—$5; product D—$3.

Required:

Which of the products should be sold at the split-off point and which should be processed further?

Problem 27-4A (Profitability Analysis)

The Fly-By-Night Company, an overnight package delivery service, wants to maintain a 20% before-tax return on the average investment in operating assets. The operating assets totaled $800,000 on January 1 and are estimated to be $840,000 on December 31. The company anticipates it will deliver 50,000 packages during the next calendar year. The variable costs per package average $5 and total fixed costs are budgeted to be $100,000.

Required:

A. What should the company charge to deliver a package in order to achieve its goal? (*Hint:* Use CVP analysis)

B. If the company actually delivers 45,000 packages at the price determined in requirement (A), what is the firm's actual rate of return on its average investment in operating assets?

C. If the company actually delivers 52,000 packages at a delivery fee of $10.40 per package, what is the company's residual income, assuming a minimum acceptable return on assets of 15%?

Problem 27-5A (Capital Budgeting Evaluations)

The Division Company is considering the purchase of a new machine. The machine would cost $62,000 and have a useful life of five years. At the end of five years, the machine could be sold for $2,000. The new machine would provide a net cash inflow and net income before depreciation and taxes of $22,000 each year. Straight-line depreciation is to be used. The company's income tax rate is 40%, and it requires a rate of return of at least 10% on investments of this type.

Required:

A. What is the payback period for the machine?

B. Calculate the return on average investment for the machine.

C. Calculate the net present value of the net cash inflows discounted at 10%

Case for Chapter 27

Decision Problem (Make or Buy Decision)

You are an accountant with the Roll-on Company, a producer of golf carts. At a recent management meeting, the vice president, Ed Rogers, has reported that the equipment used to manufacture a particular component of the golf cart is worn out and will have to be replaced. It has no residual value. Alternatively, he informs the other managers at the meeting that the company could consider purchasing the component from an outside supplier and not replacing the equipment that is used for the components only.

The president of the company has listened to Mr. Rogers' report and has asked you to develop an analysis of the costs associated with the two alternatives, making or buying the component. You have accumulated the following facts:

Making the component. The new equipment required to manufacture the component has a cost of $360,000 and a five-year useful life. Straight-line depreciation is used by the company and the equipment will not have a residual value. Each year, 48,000 components are required and the firm's cost incurred to produce one unit last year were:

Direct materials		$3.30
Direct labor		4.80
Manufacturing overhead:		
Variable portion	$ .72	
Fixed portion	4.38	
Total		5.10
Total cost per unit		$13.20

Included in the fixed manufacturing costs is depreciation on the old equipment amounting to $1.08 per unit. Ed Rogers believes that the new equipment will be more efficient and will reduce direct labor cost and variable overhead cost by 25%. The direct materials cost and fixed manufacturing overhead cost other than depreciation will not change if the new equipment is acquired. The firm can produce a maximum of 72,000 components each year with the new equipment and has no other use for the space involved.

Purchasing the component. The components can be purchased from a reliable outside supplier at a price of $8.60 each. The supplier is willing to sign a contract guaranteeing that the price will be the same for five years.

Required:

A. Assuming that the company will continue to use 48,000 components each year, should the components be produced or purchased?

B. Assuming that the company will require 72,000 components each year, would your decision be different?

C. Suppose the space involved with the production of the components can be leased for five years at an annual rent of $16,000. Would this affect your decision?

D. Can you think of any nonfinancial considerations that should be analyzed in the decision to make or buy the component?

CHAPTER 28
INCOME TAXES: AN OVERVIEW

OVERVIEW AND OBJECTIVES

This chapter is an overview of federal income tax laws as they pertain to individual taxpayers and corporations. When you have completed this chapter, you should understand:

* Some basic features of the federal income tax system (pp. 1074–1076).
* The importance of tax planning (pp. 1075, 1093–1097).
* The major components of an individual tax return, such as gross income, deductions from adjusted gross income, personal deductions, personal exemptions, and tax credits (pp. 1076–1089).
* How to compute the tax liability for an individual using both tax tables and tax rate schedules (pp. 1083–1087).
* The computation of taxable income and income tax liability for a corporation (pp. 1089–1093).
* Why accounting income and taxable income may differ (pp. 1097–1099).
* How to record income tax expense when there is a timing difference between taxable income and accounting income (pp. 1097–1102).

In preceding chapters, the impact of taxes on business decisions has not been emphasized, but tax payments to various governmental bodies are a significant part of the cost of doing business. Corporations often pay 40% or more of their pretax income in income taxes alone. For example, in its 1980 annual report Johnson & Johnson reported income before taxes of $675.3 million and income tax expense of $274.6 million—40.7% of pretax income. Because of the magnitude of taxes, few business decisions are made without first considering their effect on alternative courses of action. The various taxes levied by federal, state, and local governments also have a significant effect on individuals. Although federal income tax rates vary, the minimum rate for individuals is 11% of taxable income and the maximum 50%. Planning to minimize the legal tax liability is vitally important for individual taxpayers, as it is for business.

Because of the complexity of tax rules and regulations, tax specialists are often paid to determine the tax consequences of various alternatives. To benefit fully from the advice of specialists, decision-makers must have an understanding of the structure of the tax system. A general knowledge of the tax system is needed so that decision-makers will be aware of the tax consequences of their business decisions.

This chapter discusses the basic provisions of the federal income tax laws that affect both individuals and corporations. The aspects of the federal tax laws covered incorporate the provisions of The Economic Recovery Tax Act of 1981 and The Tax Equity and Fiscal Responsibility Act of 1982. Federal income tax laws are emphasized because they have the greatest impact on personal and business income and because the tax laws of states are generally modeled after the federal statutes. Although the state tax rates are modest compared to federal rates, they do increase the total tax burden and cannot be ignored in tax planning.

A BRIEF HISTORY OF FEDERAL INCOME TAXATION

Federal income taxes were first collected to help finance the American Civil War. However, in the late 1800s the Supreme Court ruled the tax unconstitutional because it was levied in proportion to the income of individuals rather than in proportion to a census, as permitted by the Constitution. In 1913, Congress enacted the first permanent income tax law after the Sixteenth Amendment to the Constitution was ratified. The amendment gave Congress the power to levy and collect taxes on incomes without regard to a census. Since passing the 1913 law, Congress has enacted numerous other tax laws, compiled in the **Internal Revenue Code.**

The U.S. Treasury Department, operating through an agency called the Internal Revenue Service (IRS), is responsible for administering and enforcing the income tax laws. The IRS, with Treasury Department approval, periodically issues regulations that reflect its interpretations of these laws. The ultimate interpretation of the tax laws, however, lies with the federal court system, which handles disputes between the IRS and taxpayers.

The original purpose of the income tax was to raise revenue. Although that is still the primary purpose, Congress has also used its taxing authority to accomplish other economic and social goals such as attaining full employment, providing an incentive to small businesses, providing economic stimulation to certain industries or the national economy, redistributing national income, and controlling inflation.

SOME FEATURES OF THE FEDERAL INCOME TAX SYSTEM

Before looking at some of the specific tax provisions related to computing taxable income for individuals and businesses, it will be helpful to discuss some of the basic features of the federal income tax system.

CLASSIFICATIONS OF TAXABLE ENTITIES

For purposes of federal income tax, there are four classifications of taxable entities: individuals, corporations, estates, and trusts. Each must file a tax return and pay taxes on taxable income. (Here we will limit our discussion to individual and corporate taxes. Taxation of estates and trusts is covered in more advanced courses.)

A single proprietorship or a partnership is recognized as a separate business entity for accounting purposes, but they are not subject to tax as separate taxable entities. Instead, a sole proprietor must include the income or loss from a business in his or her individual tax return. A partnership must file an information return showing the results of operations and a computation of how the income or loss is allocated to each partner. In turn, the partners must include their share of the income or loss in their respective individual tax returns. Remember that the income of a sole proprietorship or the allocable share of income of a partnership is taxed directly to the individual owners whether or not it is actually withdrawn from the business.

A corporation, on the other hand, is a separate taxable entity that must file a tax return and pay a tax on its taxable income. When after-tax income is distributed to stockholders, dividends in excess of an excluded amount must be included as income in the stockholders' individual tax returns. This taxing of income when it is earned by the corporation and again when it is distributed to the stockholders has led to the assertion that corporate income is subject to double taxation.

Corporations that satisfy certain criteria can avoid the direct tax on the corporate income by electing to be considered a **Subchapter S Corporation,** a corporation treated similar to a partnership for tax purposes. One of the basic conditions for Subchapter S treatment is that the number of stockholders cannot exceed a specified maximum (at this time the number is 25). The election is thus generally available only to relatively small businesses.

RELATIONSHIP TO GENERALLY ACCEPTED ACCOUNTING PRINCIPLES

Congress, as noted earlier, has used the income tax system for two purposes: to raise revenue and to implement certain economic and social policies. To accomplish these purposes, Congress has enacted an increasingly complex and ever-changing set of tax laws under which taxable income is based on objectives and rules that are sometimes different from the generally accepted accounting principles applied in determining **accounting income.** Furthermore, a taxpayer often is permitted to use one accounting method for tax purposes and another for accounting purposes. Consequently, taxable income often does not equal accounting income.

THE ROLE OF TAX PLANNING

Income taxes are usually a significant factor in evaluating alternative courses of action. **Tax planning** or **tax avoidance** involves evaluating the impact of alternative courses of action on taxable income. The objective is to structure business and personal transactions in such a way that the tax liability is minimized legally. In most business decisions, however, the tax factor is only one variable and should be considered in the light of other objectives. For example, the owners of a new business should evaluate the tax consequences of incorporating versus forming a partnership since each alternative will have a different effect on the amount of taxable income allocable to the owners. Regardless of the tax impact, however, other factors such as the cost of incorporating, the fact that partners have unlimited liability, and the amount of funds needed should also be considered and may be more important than the tax implications of the decision. Regardless of other considerations, implementing the alternative that produces the lowest legal tax liability is the goal of tax planning.

   Tax evasion, in contrast, is the deliberate misstatement of a tax liability by failing to report income received or by claiming fraudulent deductions. For example, taxes are evaded when interest, tips, and gains on the sale of investments are not reported; excessive depreciation is deducted; and a contribution to a charitable organization is deducted but not made. Tax evasion is illegal and the penalties for evasion can be severe.

CASH BASIS VERSUS ACCRUAL BASIS

The *accrual basis* of accounting described throughout the preceding chapters is used by most businesses. Under this method, revenues are recognized when a sale is made or services are rendered, and expenses are recognized when used in the production of revenue, regardless of when cash is received or paid. Any taxpayer (other than an individual whose only income is salary) who maintains a set of accounting records can also elect to use the accrual basis for tax purposes. When inventories are a significant factor in the calculation of net income, the accrual basis is required for purchases and sales figures.

The *cash basis* of accounting—revenues recognized when cash is received and expenses or deductions claimed when cash is paid—is used by most individuals not engaged in a business and by businesses that do not have significant inventories, a method therefore widely used by service businesses. For income tax purposes, the cash basis is primarily modified in two ways. First, revenue is reported as income when it is available to the taxpayer, called **constructive receipt** in tax terms. Interest credited to a savings account is taxable even though it was not withdrawn by the taxpayer. Second, the cost of acquiring a depreciable asset with an estimated useful life longer than one year cannot be deducted in full in the year of purchase but must be depreciated over its estimated useful life.

A taxpayer who engages in a business and also has other sources of income such as salaries, rental income, and interest may elect to report the business income on the accrual basis but other income and deductions on a cash basis. Although the cash basis is simple to use and requires a minimum of record-keeping, its major advantage often is that it permits a taxpayer greater flexibility in tax planning. When this method is used, generally a taxpayer may legally control receipts for services performed and payments for deductible items. A doctor may purposely delay billing patients until after year-end, or reasonable amounts of office supplies may be purchased in advance and deducted in the current tax year. Thus, income tax liability is deferred until the next period.

In most cases, transactions for a service firm are in cash. However, receipt of noncash items for services rendered must be included at their fair value for income tax purposes. To illustrate a noncash transaction, assume that an accountant agrees to maintain the accounting records and prepare the tax returns for a dentist in exchange for dental care for his family. Both the accountant and the dentist have taxable income measured by the fair value of the services received by each party. The dentist also has a deduction for the accounting services received. If the accountant fails to report the value of the dental services received, he or she could be charged with income tax evasion and be subject to possible penalties.

TAX CONSIDERATIONS FOR INDIVIDUALS

Tax returns are filed on forms provided by the federal government. Although the listing of specific data in a form varies from time to time, the general approach to computing taxable income for an individual taxpayer is shown in Figure 28-1. Ordinarily, tax returns for individuals must be filed within 3½ months after the close of the tax year. Most individuals are on a calendar year and therefore must file their individual returns by April 15.

Total Income (broadly defined)		$81,420
Less: Exclusions from income		1,180
Gross income for tax purposes		80,240
Less: Deductions from gross income		7,000
Adjusted gross income		73,240
Less: Deductions from adjusted gross income		
Itemized deductions	$16,760	
Less: Zero bracket amount	3,400	$13,360
Exemptions	4,000	17,360
Taxable income		$55,880
Gross tax liability from tax tables or tax rate		
schedules		$13,602
Less: Tax credits	100	
Tax prepayments	13,180	13,280
Net tax liability (or refund)		$ 322

Figure 28-1
Approach to Determining Taxable Income for an Individual Taxpayer

Note in Figure 28-1 that there are three classifications of subtraction in deriving the net tax liability: exclusions, deductions, and credits. **Exclusions** are items that are omitted from the tax computation altogether. In most cases, exclusions are not listed in the tax return because they are not part of the tax concept of income. In contrast, a **deduction** is an item that reduces the amount of income subject to tax, whereas a **tax credit** is a direct reduction in the amount of tax liability.

TOTAL INCOME, EXCLUSIONS, AND GROSS INCOME

The starting point for computing an individual's tax liability is the determination of all income that was recognized during the tax year. Not all income is included in the tax concept of gross income. **Gross income** for tax purposes is defined as all income not specifically excluded by law, IRS regulations, or court decisions. Examples of items to be included in gross income and items excluded from gross income are shown in Figure 28-2.

Note in Figure 28-2 that certain types of income are exempt from taxation. In addition, there are specific exclusions and deductions provided for by law that affect other types of income. For example, $100 received for wages, tips, or interest increases taxable income by $100, whereas corporate dividends received in the amount of $100 ($200 if a married couple files a joint return) or less are excluded from taxable income. In addition, certain income items receive favorable tax treatment by qualifying for special deductions. For example, as discussed in the next section, a $100 gain on the sale of a certain type of asset held for more than one year qualifies for a $60 deduction that is

Figure 28-2
Examples of Items Included in the Sections of an Individual's Tax Return

These items represent general rules and are subject to certain exceptions.

Items Excluded from Gross Income	Items Included in Gross Income
Interest on state and municipal bonds	Wages and salaries
Certain life insurance proceeds	Bonuses
Social security benefits	Interest on savings account
Scholarship not requiring a service from the recipient	Severance pay
	Gambling gains
Group health and accident insurance premiums paid by an employer	Corporate dividends in excess of $100*
	Tips for services rendered
Corporate dividends up to $100* per person	Rents
	Royalties
Gifts	Vacation payments
Inheritance	Business income from sole proprietorship
Accident and disability benefits	Allocable share of partnership income
Return of capital as opposed to income	Prizes
	Proceeds from lotteries
	Gains from sale or exchange of real estate, investments, and other property

*$200 for a married couple filing a joint return.

not subject to tax. This means that taxable income will be increased by only $40. Thus the nature of the income item can have a significant impact on the tax liability.

Capital Gains and Losses

Gains or losses from the sale of capital assets receive special tax treatment. **Capital assets** are defined in the Internal Revenue Code as any item of property except (1) inventories, (2) trade accounts and notes receivable, (3) land, buildings, and equipment used in a trade or business, and (4) certain intangible assets such as copyrights and literary works or artistic compositions. Stock and bond investments, a personal residence, an automobile, and a coin collection are examples of capital assets that may be held by an individual. Although depreciable and real property used in a trade or business [see (3) above] are not capital assets, such assets may be treated as capital assets under certain conditions.

When a capital asset is sold, the gain or loss reported is the difference between the selling price and the ''basis'' of the asset. Determining the basis of the asset for tax purposes may be complex, but in general it is the asset's cost or cost less depreciation taken on the asset in computing taxable income.

After the gain or loss is computed, the next step is to classify each sale as short-term or long-term. A gain or loss is classified as a **long-term capital gain or loss** if an asset is held more than one year and a **short-term capital gain or loss** if it is held one year or less. The long-term gains and losses are combined to obtain the **net long-term capital gain or loss.** Short-term gains and losses are combined to obtain the **net short-term capital gain or loss.** These two net amounts are combined into one amount called the *net capital gain or loss*.

Net Capital Loss. If the taxpayer has a net capital loss during a given year, the loss is offset against gross income up to $3,000 in any one year. The amount of net capital loss in excess of $3,000 can be carried forward indefinitely to be deducted in future years. In determining the amount of the offset, short-term and long-term losses receive somewhat different treatment. Net short-term losses are considered first and are offset against income on a dollar-for-dollar basis. In the case of net long-term losses, it takes $2 of loss to offset $1 of income. When a net capital loss is carried forward, the two types of loss (short-term or long-term) must be maintained separately and retain their short-term or long-term attributes.

To illustrate the treatment of capital losses, assume the following examples of reported capital gains and losses:

	Example			
	1	**2**	**3**	**4**
Net short-term capital gain (loss)	($6,000)	$4,000	($1,800)	($5,000)
Net long-term capital gain (loss)	2,000	(12,000)	(2,600)	(4,000)
Net capital gain (loss)	($4,000)	($8,000)	($4,400)	($9,000)
Deduction from income				
Net short-term capital loss	$3,000	–0–	$1,800	$3,000
Net long-term capital loss	–0–	$3,000	1,200	–0–
Total deduction	$3,000	$3,000	$3,000	$3,000
Net capital loss carryforward				
Short-term capital loss	$1,000	–0–	–0–	$2,000
Long-term capital loss	–0–	$2,000	$ 200	$4,000

In computing the net long-term capital loss deduction, $2 of loss are needed per $1 of deduction. The $3,000 deduction in Example 2 requires $6,000 of the net long-term capital loss, leaving $2,000 to be carried forward as a long-term capital loss. In Example 3, the $1,200 deduction requires $2,400 of the loss, leaving a carryforward of $200. For this reason, if a taxpayer must take a loss on a capital asset, it is advantageous to dispose of the asset before the end of the 12-month holding period to have it qualify as a short-term loss.

Net Capital Gains.   If a taxpayer's capital transactions result in a net short-term capital gain, the gain is fully taxable and it is added to ordinary income. However, when a net capital gain consists of an excess of net long-term capital gains over net short-term losses, if any, 60% of the excess is deducted in determining the taxable amount. The following examples will be used to illustrate the process just described:

	Example				
	1	2	3	4	5
Net short-term capital gain (loss)	–0–	$5,000	$5,000	($6,000)	$10,000
Net long-term capital gain (loss)	$5,000	–0–	4,000	10,000	(4,000)
Net capital gain	$5,000	$5,000	$9,000	$4,000	$6,000
Included in gross income	$5,000	$5,000	$9,000	$4,000	$6,000
Deductible in computing adjusted gross income	3,000	–0–	2,400	2,400*	–0–
Net increase in adjusted gross income	$2,000	$5,000	$6,600	$1,600	$6,000

*Note that the deduction is computed as 60% of the excess of net long-term gain over net short-term losses.

These examples illustrate the importance of the capital gain provision in tax planning. By timing the holding period for capital assets, a taxpayer can effectively reduce the tax rate on such items. If, for example, the taxpayer in Example 1 was in the 50% tax bracket, the effective tax rate on this transaction is 20% ($2,000 × 50% = $1,000 tax ÷ $5,000 gain).

DEDUCTIONS FROM GROSS INCOME

There are two classifications of deductions in Figure 28-1: (1) deductions from gross income to arrive at **adjusted gross income,** and (2) deductions from adjusted gross income to arrive at **taxable income.** As will be discussed next, the amount of certain itemized deductions made from adjusted gross income is affected by the size of adjusted gross income.

The deductions from gross income to arrive at adjusted gross income are generally of a business nature. The major deductions are:

Ordinary and necessary operating expenses of a business
Capital gains deduction (60% of net long-term capital gains)
Employee moving expenses

Outside salesperson expenses

Employee transportation expenses (excluding commuting expenses)

All reasonable employee expenses while traveling away from home

Payments to individual retirement accounts (IRA)

Payments to Keogh retirement plans

10% of income earned (up to $30,000 reduced by IRA and Keogh contributions) by the spouse with the lower income

Alimony payments

Disability income exclusion

Losses from sale or exchange of property used in a trade or business or the production of income

Generally, each item must satisfy some criterion before it is deductible, and limits are usually placed on the amount of each item that can be deducted.

DEDUCTIONS FROM ADJUSTED GROSS INCOME

The two categories of deductions from adjusted gross income are itemized deductions and exemptions.

Itemized Deductions

An individual taxpayer may deduct the sum of certain personal expenses, called itemized deductions, in excess of a specified standard deduction referred to as the zero bracket amount—the amount of income on which no tax will be paid. In recent years, the zero bracket amount has been $3,400 for a married couple filing a joint return ($1,700 per person if separate returns are filed) and $2,300 for a single person.[1] Taxpayers may elect to itemize their allowable deductions if in excess of the zero bracket amount. The taxpayer should obviously elect whichever alternative produces the greatest deduction. If deductions are itemized, sufficient records must be maintained to support the deductions.

The tax laws specify the circumstances under which an item qualifies as an itemized deduction and any limitations of the amount that may be deducted. The categories of itemized deductions are:

1. *Medical and dental expenses*. Medical and dental expenses of the taxpayer and his or her family that exceed 5% of adjusted gross income are deductible.[2]

---

[1]Beginning January 1, 1985, zero bracket amounts are scheduled to be adjusted for inflation.

[2]During 1983, medicine and drugs in excess of 1% of adjusted gross income are combined with other medical and dental expenses, and the total amount in excess of 5% of adjusted gross income is deductible. Starting in 1984, the separate 1% provision is eliminated and costs for prescription drugs and insulin can be grouped with other medical expenses. Over-the-counter drugs cannot be deducted. The 1984 law is applied in the illustration in this chapter and should be used in solving end of chapter material.

2. *Taxes.* Many state and local taxes paid are deductible, but federal taxes do not qualify as an itemized deduction. Examples are state and local income taxes, sales taxes, real estate taxes, and personal property taxes. State and local taxes on gasoline, liquor, tobacco, and most types of license fees such as marriage, driver's, and pet are not deductible.

3. *Interest.* Interest paid on almost any form of personal indebtedness is deductible.

4. *Charitable contributions.* Cash contributions to religious, charitable, educational, scientific, or literary organizations are deductible with a maximum deduction of 50% of adjusted gross income. Noncash gifts are subject to other limitations.

5. *Casualty or theft losses.* Uninsured casualty and theft losses in excess of $100 per loss are deductible to the extent they exceed 10% of adjusted gross income. A casualty is a sudden, unexpected, or unusual event such as a hurricane, flood, fire, lightning, or earthquake. Automobile accidents also qualify. Progressive damage to property caused by termites, moths, or other insects does not qualify as a casualty loss.

6. *Miscellaneous deductions.* Included in this category are allowable expenses related primarily to a taxpayer's employment or to the management of income-producing assets that are not deductible in arriving at adjusted gross income. These include:

Union dues
Safety equipment and protective clothing
Small tools and supplies needed on the job
Uniforms
Physical examinations required by employer
Educational expenses required by employer or law
Safe deposit box rental
Fees paid to have tax return prepared and for income tax advice
Subscriptions to professional journals
Dues to professional organizations

If a taxpayer elects to itemize deductions, only the excess over the zero bracket income amount may be deducted.

Exemptions

A taxpayer is entitled to deduct $1,000 from adjusted gross income for each personal exemption claimed.[3] A separate **exemption** is allowed for the taxpayer, for his or her spouse if a joint return is filed, and for each dependent.

[3]Beginning January 1, 1985, personal exemptions are scheduled to be adjusted for inflation.

Additional exemptions are allowed if the taxpayer or spouse is 65 or over or if either is blind.

To qualify as a dependent, a person must satisfy all of the following tests:

1. Have received over half of his or her support from the taxpayer.
2. Be closely related to the taxpayer or be a member of the taxpayer's household for the entire year.
3. Received less than $1,000 in income. (This test does not have to be satisfied if a taxpayer's child was under 19 at the end of the year or a full-time student for at least five months of the year.)
4. Be a citizen of the United States or a resident of the United States, Canada, or Mexico.
5. If the dependent is married, has not filed a joint return with his or her spouse.

COMPUTING THE TAX LIABILITY

Once the taxpayer's taxable income is computed, the next step is to compute the gross tax liability from the appropriate tax table or tax rate schedule. Tax tables and rate schedules are provided for single taxpayers, married taxpayers filing joint returns, married taxpayers filing separate returns, qualifying widows and widowers with dependent children, and heads of household.[4]

Tax Tables

The appropriate tax table or tax rate schedule used to determine the gross tax liability depends on the taxpayer's filing status and the amount of taxable income. Tax tables are normally used if the amount of taxable income is less than $50,000. Figure 28-3 shows part of a tax table.[5] Note that the table incorporates the zero bracket income amount. Thus, for a married couple filing jointly, the table does not show a tax liability below a taxable income of $3,400.

Tax tables may be used whether or not the taxpayer elects to itemize deductions. Two examples will be used to illustrate the determination of the gross tax liability when tax tables are applicable. First, assume that Bob and Emily Newhart filed a joint return and reported adjusted gross income of

[4]A head of household is, in general, an unmarried taxpayer who provides more than half the cost of maintaining a home (which could be a separate home) for certain qualified persons such as an unmarried child or a parent of the taxpayer.

[5]Beginning January 1, 1985, income tax brackets will be adjusted for inflation. The amount of tax shown in the tax tables and tax rate schedules will of course change as Congress enacts new legislation increasing or decreasing taxes. For example, included in the Economic Recovery Tax Act of 1981 are scheduled reductions in the individual tax rates of approximately 23% to take effect over a period of 33 months.

Tax Table
Based on Taxable Income
For persons with taxable incomes of less than $50,000.

If line 34 (taxable income) is—		And you are—				If line 34 (taxable income) is—		And you are—				If line 34 (taxable income) is—		And you are—			
At least	But less than	Single	Married filing jointly *	Married filing separately	Head of a household	At least	But less than	Single	Married filing jointly *	Married filing separately	Head of a household	At least	But less than	Single	Married filing jointly *	Married filing separately	Head of a household
		Your tax is—						Your tax is—						Your tax is—			
0	1,700	0	0	0	0	**3,000**						5,500	5,550	510	294	618	468
1,700	1,725	0	0	a2	0							5,550	5,600	519	302	627	476
1,725	1,750	0	0	5	0	3,000	3,050	100	0	189	100	5,600	5,650	528	310	635	484
						3,050	3,100	107	0	197	107	5,650	5,700	537	318	644	492
1,750	1,775	0	0	9	0	3,100	3,150	114	0	204	114	5,700	5,750	546	326	653	500
1,775	1,800	0	0	12	0	3,150	3,200	121	0	212	121						
1,800	1,825	0	0	16	0	3,200	3,250	128	0	220	128	5,750	5,800	554	334	662	508
1,825	1,850	0	0	19	0							5,800	5,850	563	342	671	515
1,850	1,875	0	0	22	0	3,250	3,300	135	0	228	135	5,850	5,900	572	350	680	523
						3,300	3,350	142	0	236	142	5,900	5,950	581	357	689	531
1,875	1,900	0	0	26	0	3,350	3,400	149	0	244	149	5,950	6,000	590	365	698	539
1,900	1,925	0	0	29	0	3,400	3,450	156	c3	252	156						
1,925	1,950	0	0	33	0	3,450	3,500	164	10	260	162	**6,000**					
1,950	1,975	0	0	36	0							6,000	6,050	599	373	709	547
1,975	2,000	0	0	40	0	3,500	3,550	172	17	268	169	6,050	6,100	608	381	719	555
2,000						3,550	3,600	180	24	276	176	6,100	6,150	617	389	730	563
						3,600	3,650	188	31	283	183	6,150	6,200	626	397	740	571
2,000	2,025	0	0	43	0	3,650	3,700	196	38	291	190	6,200	6,250	634	405	750	579
2,025	2,050	0	0	47	0	3,700	3,750	203	45	299	197						
2,050	2,075	0	0	50	0							6,250	6,300	643	413	761	587
2,075	2,100	0	0	54	0	3,750	3,800	211	52	307	204	6,300	6,350	652	421	771	594
2,100	2,125	0	0	57	0	3,800	3,850	219	59	316	211	6,350	6,400	661	429	781	602
						3,850	3,900	227	66	324	218	6,400	6,450	670	436	792	610
2,125	2,150	0	0	60	0	3,900	3,950	235	73	333	225	6,450	6,500	679	444	802	618
2,150	2,175	0	0	64	0	3,950	4,000	243	79	342	232						
2,175	2,200	0	0	67	0	**4,000**						6,500	6,550	688	452	812	627
2,200	2,225	0	0	71	0							6,550	6,600	697	460	823	635
2,225	2,250	0	0	74	0	4,000	4,050	251	86	351	238	6,600	6,650	707	468	833	644
2,250	2,275	0	0		0	4,050	4,100	259	93	360	245						

42,750	42,800	13,917	11,277	16,528	12,912	45,750	45,800	15,546	12,550	18,275	14,360	48,750	48,800	17,176	14,001	20,023	15,959
42,800	42,850	13,944	11,298	16,556	12,935	45,800	45,850	15,574	12,573	18,304	14,386	48,800	48,850	17,203	14,025	20,052	15,986
42,850	42,900	13,971	11,319	16,585	12,957	45,850	45,900	15,601	12,597	18,333	14,413	48,850	48,900	17,230	14,049	20,081	16,013
42,900	42,950	13,999	11,340	16,614	12,980	45,900	45,950	15,628	12,621	18,362	14,440	48,900	48,950	17,257	14,073	20,110	16,039
42,950	43,000	14,026	11,361	16,644	13,003	45,950	46,000	15,655	12,646	18,391	14,466	48,950	49,000	17,284	14,097	20,139	16,066
43,000						**46,000**						**49,000**					
43,000	43,050	14,053	11,383	16,673	13,026	46,000	46,050	15,682	12,670	18,421	14,493	49,000	49,050	17,312	14,121	20,168	16,093
43,050	43,100	14,080	11,404	16,702	13,048	46,050	46,100	15,709	12,694	18,450	14,520	49,050	49,100	17,339	14,146	20,198	16,119
43,100	43,150	14,107	11,425	16,731	13,071	46,100	46,150	15,737	12,718	18,479	14,546	49,100	49,150	17,366	14,170	20,227	16,146
43,150	43,200	14,134	11,446	16,760	13,094	46,150	46,200	15,764	12,742	18,508	14,573	49,150	49,200	17,393	14,194	20,256	16,173
43,200	43,250	14,161	11,468	16,789	13,116	46,200	46,250	15,791	12,767	18,537	14,600	49,200	49,250	17,420	14,218	20,285	16,199
43,250	43,300	14,189	11,489	16,818	13,139	46,250	46,300	15,818	12,791	18,566	14,626	49,250	49,300	17,447	14,242	20,314	16,226
43,300	43,350	14,216	11,510	16,847	13,162	46,300	46,350	15,845	12,815	18,595	14,653	49,300	49,350	17,475	14,267	20,343	16,253
43,350	43,400	14,243	11,531	16,877	13,185	46,350	46,400	15,872	12,839	18,624	14,680	49,350	49,400	17,502	14,291	20,372	16,279
43,400	43,450	14,270	11,553	16,906	13,207	46,400	46,450	15,899	12,863	18,654	14,706	49,400	49,450	17,529	14,315	20,402	16,306
43,450	43,500	14,297	11,574	16,935	13,230	46,450	46,500	15,927	12,888	18,683	14,733	49,450	49,500	17,556	14,339	20,431	16,333
43,500	43,550	14,324	11,595	16,964	13,253	46,500	46,550	15,954	12,912	18,712	14,760	49,500	49,550	17,583	14,363	20,460	16,359
43,550	43,600	14,352	11,616	16,993	13,275	46,550	46,600	15,981	12,936	18,741	14,786	49,550	49,600	17,610	14,388	20,489	16,386
43,600	43,650	14,379	11,637	17,022	13,298	46,600	46,650	16,008	12,960	18,770	14,813	49,600	49,650	17,637	14,412	20,518	16,413
43,650	43,700	14,406	11,659	17,051	13,321	46,650	46,700	16,035	12,984	18,799	14,840	49,650	49,700	17,665	14,436	20,547	16,439
43,700	43,750	14,433	11,680	17,081	13,344	46,700	46,750	16,062	13,009	18,828	14,866	49,700	49,750	17,692	14,460	20,576	16,466
43,750	43,800	14,460	11,701	17,110	13,366	46,750	46,800	16,090	13,033	18,858	14,893	49,750	49,800	17,719	14,484	20,605	16,493
43,800	43,850	14,487	11,722	17,139	13,389	46,800	46,850	16,117	13,057	18,887	14,920	49,800	49,850	17,746	14,509	20,635	16,519
43,850	43,900	14,515	11,744	17,168	13,412	46,850	46,900	16,144	13,081	18,916	14,946	49,850	49,900	17,773	14,533	20,664	16,546
43,900	43,950	14,542	11,765	17,197	13,434	46,900	46,950	16,171	13,105	18,945	14,973	49,900	49,950	17,800	14,557	20,693	16,573
43,950	44,000	14,569	11,786	17,226	13,457	46,950	47,000	16,198	13,130	18,974	15,000	49,950	50,000	17,828	14,581	20,722	16,599

*This column must also be used by a qualifying widow(er).

50,000 or over – use tax rate schedules

Figure 28-3
Tax Tables

The tax table is effective for a 1981 tax year. At the time this text was printed, tax tables for subsequent years were not available. The Economic Tax Recovery Act of 1981 provides for a cumulative tax rate reduction of approximately 23% through 1984. Beginning in January 1, 1985, tax tables are scheduled to be indexed to adjust for inflation.

$9,890 during the year. The Newharts claimed exemptions for two children, and their itemized deductions totaled $2,980. Because their deductions were less than the $3,400 zero bracket amount for a joint return, they would not itemize deductions. Their taxable income was $5,890 ($9,890 − $4,000) and their gross tax liability of $350 was determined directly from the tax table. (See Figure 28-3, income bracket $5,850 to $5,900.)

Now assume that the Newharts earned $53,600 and had itemized deductions of $9,620. Their tax table income would be computed as follows:

Adjusted gross income			$53,600
Less: Itemized deductions	$9,620		
Less: Zero bracket amount	3,400	$6,220	
Personal exemptions (4 × $1,000)		4,000	10,220
Taxable income			$43,380

The excess itemized deductions are subtracted to compute the tax table income because the $3,400 zero tax bracket amount is already incorporated in the tax table. The gross tax liability from the tax table in Figure 28-3 is $11,531.

Tax Rate Schedules

Taxpayers must use tax rate schedules if their taxable income equals or exceeds $50,000 or they qualify for using an alternative method to figure their tax. If they use an alternative method such as income averaging, which is discussed below, they must use the tax rate schedules even if their taxable income is less than $50,000. Tax rate schedules are shown in Figure 28-4. To illustrate the use of the tax rate schedules, assume that Bob and Emily Newhart—with two children—filed a joint return. Their taxable income was computed as follows:

Adjusted gross income			$66,380
Itemized deductions	$13,280		
Less: Zero bracket amount	3,400	$9,880	
Personal exemptions (4 × $1,000)		4,000	13,880
Taxable income			$52,500

From Schedule Y in Figure 28-4, the Newharts' gross tax liability would be computed as follows:

Tax on first $45,800	$ 9,772
Tax on the remaining income ($52,500 − $45,800 = $6,700 × 38%)	2,546
Gross tax liability	$12,318

Figure 28-4
Tax Rate Schedules

Schedule X
Single Taxpayers

Taxable Income		Tax Liability		
Over	But Not Over	Amount	Plus %	Of the Amount Over
–0–	$ 2,300	–0–	–0–	–0–
$ 2,300	3,400	–0–	11	$ 2,300
3,400	4,400	$ 121	12	3,400
4,400	6,500	241	14	4,400
6,500	8,500	535	15	6,500
8,500	10,800	835	16	8,500
10,800	12,900	1,203	18	10,800
12,900	15,000	1,581	20	12,900
15,000	18,200	2,001	23	15,000
18,200	23,500	2,737	26	18,200
23,500	28,800	4,115	30	23,500
28,800	34,100	5,705	34	28,800
34,100	41,500	7,507	38	34,100
41,500	55,300	10,319	42	41,500
55,300	81,800	16,115	48	55,300
81,800	——	28,835	50	81,800

Schedule Y
Married Taxpayers Filing Joint Returns

Taxable Income		Tax Liability		
Over	But Not Over	Amount	Plus %	Of the Amount Over
–0–	$ 3,400	–0–	–0–	–0–
$ 3,400	5,500	–0–	11	$ 3,400
5,500	7,600	$ 231	12	5,500
7,600	11,900	483	14	7,600
11,900	16,000	1,085	16	11,900
16,000	20,200	1,741	18	16,000
20,200	24,600	2,497	22	20,200
24,600	29,900	3,465	25	24,600
29,900	35,200	4,790	28	29,900
35,200	45,800	6,274	33	35,200
45,800	60,000	9,772	38	45,800
60,000	85,600	15,168	42	60,000
85,600	109,400	25,920	45	85,600
109,400	162,400	36,630	49	109,400
162,400	——	62,600	50	162,400

Tax rate schedules are effective for taxable years beginning after 1983 as passed by Congress in The Economic Recovery Tax Act of 1981. Beginning January 1, 1985, income tax brackets are scheduled to be indexed to adjust for inflation.

The 38% in this case is referred to as the **marginal tax rate** because it is the rate applied on the next dollar of income. The marginal tax rate is often used by taxpayers to identify their income tax bracket. However, because lower income levels are taxed at lower rates, the effective or average tax rate for the Newharts is 23.5% ($12,318 ÷ $52,500).

One can see the highly progressive nature of the income tax rates from the tax rate schedules. A **progressive tax** is one in which the tax rate becomes higher as the amount of taxable income increases.

Income Averaging

The law also provides a tax break to individual taxpayers who have annual income that fluctuates widely. Such taxpayers may benefit from the **income averaging** provisions, which permits them to use their lower taxable income of the preceding four years to reduce the tax rate applicable to the current year's taxable income. It is a method for determining the tax liability for the current year; the tax liability for the prior years is unaffected.

TAX CREDITS AND PREPAYMENTS

Recall that a tax credit is a reduction in the amount of tax liability computed on taxable income. A tax credit is more beneficial to a taxpayer than a deduction because it is a direct dollar-per-dollar reduction in the tax liability. In contrast, a deduction reduces the amount of income subject to tax. For example, one-half of the amounts contributed to political candidates up to a maximum of $50 ($100 on a joint return) may be taken as a credit against the tax liability. Thus, a contribution of $100 will reduce the tax liability by $50. If the $100 had been considered a deduction and a tax rate of 40% is assumed, taxes would have been reduced by only $40. Other income tax credits are available to the elderly, for child care while the taxpayer or spouse is at work, for payments of income taxes to foreign countries, for homeowners who have installed energy-saving items, and for taxpayers who have income below $10,000. Generally, there are specific limitations to each of these income tax credits.

During the tax year, income tax payments are withheld by employers from the salaries paid to employees, as we noted in Chapter 12. The amount withheld is based on the employee's earnings for the year, his or her marital status, and the number of exemptions claimed by the employee. The amount withheld must be reported to an employee by January 31 for a preceding calendar year. Taxpayers who receive income not subject to withholding generally must estimate their tax for the year and make quarterly installment payments to the IRS. The sum of the amounts withheld and the quarterly estimated payments are subtracted along with the tax credits from the gross tax liability to determine the amount of unpaid taxes due or the refund claimed at the time a tax return is filed.

THE IMPORTANCE OF THE MARGINAL TAX RATE

When considering various alternatives that will affect taxable income, it is important for individual taxpayers and other taxable entities to use the marginal tax rate in assessing the impact of taxes on their decisions. To illustrate, assume that a married couple is considering whether to invest $10,000 in a municipal bond that pays 13% nontaxable interest or invest the $10,000 in a corporate bond that pays 17% interest. The couple has taxable income of $58,000 from other sources. The after-tax cash flow from each investment can be computed as follows:

	Invest in Municipal Bonds	Invest in Corporate Bonds
Cash flow from interest	$1,300	$1,700
Less: Increase in cash outflow for taxes*	–0–	646
Net after-tax cash flow	$1,300	$1,054

$$\begin{array}{ccccc} \text{*Marginal} & & \text{Increase in} & & \text{Increase in cash} \\ \text{tax} & \times & \text{taxable} & = & \text{outflow for} \\ \text{rate} & & \text{income} & & \text{taxes} \end{array}$$

Investment in municipal bonds.	Investment in corporate bonds.
Interest of $1,300 is nontaxable income.	Interest of $1,700 is taxable income.
(38% × –0–) = –0–	(38% × $1,700) = $646

(The marginal tax rate for taxable income between $45,800 and $60,000 is 38% from Figure 28-4.)

Although the interest rate is higher on the corporate bonds, the after-tax cash flow is greater when the $10,000 is invested in municipal bonds.

The increase in taxes of $646 is verified below:

	No Additional Investment	Invest in Corporate Bonds	Difference
Taxable income before interest	$58,000	$58,000	–0–
Taxable interest	–0–	1,700	+$1,700
Taxable income	$58,000	$59,700	+ 1,700
Income tax			
Income tax on $45,800 (from Figure 28-4)	$ 9,772	$ 9,772	–0–
Income tax on amount over $45,800			
($58,000 − $45,800) × 38%	4,636		
($59,700 − $45,800) × 38%		5,282	+$ 646
Total income taxes	$14,408	$15,054	+$ 646

A similar analysis can be performed in assessing the net cost of a tax deduction that results in a decrease in taxable income. For example, the net cost of a $10,000 contribution is $5,000 for a married couple with taxable income over $162,400.

COMPUTATION OF INCOME TAX FOR A JOINT RETURN ILLUSTRATED

To illustrate the computation of the federal income tax, assume that Julie and Tom George, ages 34 and 32, respectively, file a joint tax return. They have two children who qualify as dependents. Julie George, a real estate agent, earned commissions of $22,000 and made quarterly estimated federal income tax payments of $3,900 during the year. Julie's employer does not have a retirement plan established for his employees. She therefore created her own plan by contributing $2,000 to a qualified individual retirement account. Tom George earned $50,000 during the year working as an accountant and had $9,280 withheld from his salary for federal income taxes. During the year the Georges sold a coin collection (for an $8,000 gain) they had held for five years and also disposed of a common stock investment (at a $3,000 loss) held for five months. Dividends in the amount of $2,800 were received on a jointly owned stock investment. Interest of $980 on municipal bonds was received during the year and $640 was credited to their savings account that was available for withdrawal. The itemized deductions and computation of tax shown in Figure 28-5 are self-explanatory. In Figure 28-5, the information is presented in condensed form. In practice, some of the information would have been shown in more detail and in separate schedules.

TAX CONSIDERATIONS FOR CORPORATIONS

A corporation is a separate taxable entity that must file tax returns and pay taxes on its taxable income. Corporate returns are due within 2½ months of the close of the fiscal year. Some corporations are exempt by law from taxation and other corporations, such as banks and insurance companies, are subject to special tax regulations. For corporations without special regulations, the computation of taxable income centers around an income statement similar to the one prepared for external reporting. However, the computation of taxable income can still be very complex. For this reason we will discuss only some of the major distinguishing features of the corporate tax system.

There are fewer steps in determining the taxable income of a corporation than that of an individual because there is no distinction between gross income and adjusted gross income for a corporation. Furthermore, a corporation does not itemize personal deductions or deduct personal exemptions, and there is no deduction comparable to the zero bracket amount. The steps for determining the corporate tax liability are shown in Figure 28-6.

Figure 28-5
Computation of Federal Income Tax—
Julie and Tom
George, Joint Return

Gross Income:			
Salary		$50,000	
Real estate commissions		22,000	
Dividends income	$2,800		
Less: Exclusion	200	2,600	
Capital gains:			
Net long-term capital gains	8,000		
Net short-term capital losses	3,000	5,000	
Interest received or credited to account:			
Savings accounts		640	
(Interest on municipal bonds of $980 is excluded.)			
Gross income for tax purposes			$80,240
Deductions from gross income:			
Long-term capital gains deduction (60% × $5,000 excess of net long-term capital gain over net short-term capital losses)		$ 3,000	
Contribution to individual retirement account		2,000	
10% of lower earning spouse's income reduced by IRA contribution ($22,000 − $2,000) × 10%		2,000	7,000
Adjusted gross income			73,240
Deductions from adjusted gross income:			
Itemized deductions:			
Medical and dental expenses (doctors' fees, dentists' fees, nursing services, hospital care, X-rays, medical insurance premiums, prescription drugs, eyeglasses, ambulance service, lab fees, crutches, and physical therapist)	$4,222		
Less: 5% of adjusted gross income	3,662	$ 560	
Taxes: Real estate		2,460	
General sales tax		480	
State and local income taxes		1,050	
Personal property		460	
Interest on home mortgage		6,280	
Other interest payments		2,300	
Charitable contributions		2,490	
Miscellaneous (dues to professional organizations and safety deposit box rental)		680	
Total itemized deductions		16,760	
Less: Zero bracket amount		3,400	
Excess itemized deductions		13,360	
Personal exemptions (4 × $1,000)		4,000	
Total deductions from adjusted gross income			17,360
Taxable income			$55,880

Computation of federal income tax (See Figure 28-4 for tax rate schedules.) $9,772 + 38% ($10,080)		$13,602
Less: Tax credits—Political contribution, $400 ($400 × 50% = $200; limited to $100)	$ 100	
Prepayments—Federal income tax withheld	9,280	
Estimated quarterly tax payments	3,900	13,280
Net tax liability due with tax return		$ 322

TOTAL REVENUES AND EXCLUSIONS

The first step in the computation of taxable income for a corporation is the determination of the corporation's total revenue and gains recognized during the year. Examples are revenues from the sale of goods or the performance of a service, interest and dividends on investments, gains from the sale of assets, rental receipts, and royalties. In most cases, revenues recognized for accounting purposes are also considered revenue for tax purposes. There are, however, some exceptions. For example, interest on obligations of state and local governments and life insurance proceeds received by the corporation on the death of an insured employee or officer are reported in the income statement but are excluded from gross income for tax purposes.

Total Revenues	$780,000
Less: Exclusions from revenue	32,000
Gross income	748,000
Less: Deductions from gross income	612,000
Taxable income	$136,000
Compute tax liability from rate schedule	$ 42,310
Less: Tax credits	4,200
Net tax liability	$ 38,110

Figure 28-6
Steps in Computing Corporate Tax Liability

DEDUCTIONS FROM GROSS INCOME

Most of the deductions from gross income are the usual expenses incurred by operating the corporation and producing revenue. These include cost of goods sold, selling expenses, and administrative expenses. There are certain other deductions and limitations on some expenses that are specified by law and result in a difference between accounting income and taxable income. Some of the more common differences are:

1. *Capital gains and losses.* Capital losses of a corporation cannot be offset against ordinary income; capital losses can be used to offset capital gains only. The unused portion of the loss can be carried back to the three years preceding the year of the loss and carried forward five years following the loss year. Again, however, the loss carryback and carryforward can be offset against capital gains only. If carried back, the tax liability for that year is recomputed and a refund claim filed with the IRS for the difference between the original tax and the recomputed tax. Capital gains are included in taxable income and subject to taxation at the regular tax rates. In general, if the marginal tax rate is greater than 28%, the excess of net long-term capital gains over net short-term capital losses is taxed at a maximum rate of 28%. In addition, corporations are not permitted the special long-term capital gain deduction of 60% that is available to individuals.

2. *Dividends received deduction.* A corporation is permitted a deduction of 85% of dividends received from shares of stock in other domestic corporations. The intent of this deduction is to reduce the effects of taxing three entities for the same income. That is, if the deduction was not permitted, the distributing corporation would have already paid a tax on its net income, the dividend would be taxed to the receiving corporation, and when distributed to the stockholders of the receiving corporation, another layer of tax would be imposed.

3. *Net operating loss.* A corporation is permitted to offset losses of a particular year against income of other years. Losses may be carried back to the three preceding years. The tax is recomputed and the difference between this amount and the original tax is refunded to the corporation. Any unused loss may be carried forward successively to the next 15 years following the loss year and deducted from income. A corporation can elect to forgo the carryback and only carry the loss forward.

4. *Charitable contributions.* A corporation may deduct charitable contributions but the amount is limited to 10% of taxable income before deducting any contributions and the 85% dividend-received deduction. Contributions in excess of the 10% limitation may be carried forward to the five succeeding years, subject to the 10% limitation in each year.

5. *Expenses not deductible.* Premiums paid for employees' life insurance policies under which the corporation is the named beneficiary and the amortization of goodwill are not deductible for tax purposes.

Figure 28-7
Tax Rate Schedule
for Corporations

Taxable Income		Tax Liability			Of the
Over	But Not Over	Amount	Plus	%	Amount Over
–0–	$ 25,000	–0–		15	–0–
$ 25,000	50,000	$ 3,750		18	$ 25,000
50,000	75,000	8,250		30	50,000
75,000	100,000	15,750		40	75,000
100,000	—	25,750		46	100,000

Corporation income tax rates for tax years beginning in 1983.

COMPUTING THE TAX LIABILITY

The tax liability is computed by applying the appropriate tax rate to the taxable income. The current corporation income tax rate structure is shown in Figure 28-7. The corporate tax is also a progressive tax. To illustrate the use of this schedule, a corporation with reported taxable income of $80,000 would compute its tax liability as:

Tax on first $75,000	$15,750
Tax on excess ($80,000 − $75,000 = $5,000 × 40%)	2,000
Total tax liability	$17,750

Like individuals, a corporation may qualify for certain tax credits to be deducted from the gross tax liability and must pay estimated taxes in quarterly installments.

TAX PLANNING AND BUSINESS DECISIONS

As noted before, income taxes have a significant effect on most business decisions and are often the most important factor influencing a business decision. Because of the complexity of the tax system, most firms hire a tax specialist to review tax implications of alternative courses of action and to provide guidance in arranging business transactions so that taxes are minimized legally. The following are some examples of the tax impact on alternative approaches to various business problems.

TAX IMPLICATIONS FOR THE CHOICE OF BUSINESS ORGANIZATION

One of the first decisions an owner or owners of a business must make at the time of organization is whether to operate as a corporation, a sole proprietorship, or a partnership. Because of the difference between individual and corporate tax rates and because other tax provisions vary greatly with the legal form of a business, the tax consequences should be carefully considered in making the decision. The major tax factors are:

1. A corporation is a separate taxable entity and must report and pay taxes on its income at rates ranging from 15% to 46%. Dividends paid are not a tax-deductible business expense. Furthermore, dividends above a minimal amount are taxed again to the individual stockholders when received. On the other hand, partners or sole proprietors must report business income on their individual returns when it is earned whether it is withdrawn or left in the business. Business income and dividends are taxed to individuals at rates that range from 11% to 50%.

2. Corporations may deduct, as a business expense from gross income, reasonable salaries paid to stockholders who also work for the corporation. In the case of a partnership or a sole proprietor, salaries to the owner(s) are considered an allocation of income.

As previously noted, a business may obtain the legal benefits of a corporation and still be treated similar to a partnership by electing Subchapter S Corporation status if certain criteria are satisfied.

To illustrate the impact of taxes on the form of business organization, assume that Jack Jones is going to form a business that he expects will produce an annual income of $100,000 before deducting his own salary of $60,000, a salary considered reasonable for the services he performs. There are to be no other withdrawals from the business. The corporate tax and individual tax for Jones under a corporation and sole proprietorship are compared in Figure 28-8. Under these assumed conditions, his combined tax burden is $9,872 lower ($26,550 − $16,678) if he incorporates than if he operates as a sole proprietor. This is a result of the fact that the $40,000 earnings retained in the business are taxed as ordinary income when operating as a sole proprietorship. His individual marginal tax rate on this income was higher than the marginal tax rate used to compute the corporate tax on the $40,000. If a part or all of the $33,550 corporate net income is distributed in subsequent periods, the dividends are taxable to Jones as ordinary income. Should the dividends not be withdrawn and he is later able to sell his shares of capital stock at an increased price that reflects the retained earnings, the gain will be treated as a long-term capital gain. In either case, he is able to postpone the tax on the portion of earnings retained by the corporation. A corporation, however, may be subject to a penalty tax on accumulated earnings deemed excessive and retained for the purpose of avoiding the tax on dividends.

Unfortunately, determining the tax advantage of one form of organization over another is not as straightforward as it appears from this illustration. The apparent tax advantage one form of organization may have over another can vanish with a change in such variables as the marginal tax rates of the individual and the corporation, the level of income, what constitutes a reasonable salary, and the amount of earnings retained in the business. To illustrate, the combined corporate and individual income tax is computed below, assuming that all of the corporate net income was distributed to Jones:

Taxable Income:	
Salary	$60,000
Dividends of $33,550 [see Figure 28-8] less $200 exclusion	33,350
	$93,350
Less: deductions	13,000
Taxable income	$80,350
Income tax liability:	
Individual tax:	
Tax on first $60,000	$15,168
Excess $20,350 × 42%	8,547
	$23,715
Plus the corporate tax	6,450
Combined tax liability:	$30,165

The combined tax liability is $30,165 when all of the corporate net income is distributed. The change in assumption does not affect the combined tax liability when a sole proprietorship is operated; it remains the same at $26,550 as computed in Figure 28-8. Thus, when all of the corporate net income is distributed, the lowest combined tax liability is incurred when the sole proprietorship form of organization is adopted ($26,550 compared to $30,165).

CHOICE OF FINANCING METHODS

When a corporation seeks additional funds for long-term purposes, it may obtain them by retaining working capital generated from operations, by issuing additional shares of capital stock, or by issuing long-term debt. As discussed in Chapter 17, there are a number of factors to consider in making the financing decision. In any case, a significant factor is the overall tax effect on the business and the stockholders. The tax impact of the various forms of financing varies because interest on debt is a tax-deductible expense whereas a dividend paid on capital stock is not. To illustrate this point, assume that a firm needs to raise $500,000 for plant expansion on which a return of 18% is expected.

| | Legal Form of Business Organization | |
	Corporation	Sole Proprietorship
Business income excluding salary to owner	$100,000	$100,000
Less: Salary to owner	60,000	—
Taxable income	40,000	—
Corporate tax expense		
First $25,000 ... $3,750		
Tax on excess $15,000 × 18% ... 2,700	6,450	–0–
Net income	$ 33,550	$100,000
Individual tax*	$ 10,228	$ 26,550
Tax paid by business	6,450	–0–
Combined tax	$ 16,678	$ 26,550
Individual income	$ 60,000	$100,000
Less: Itemized deductions and personal exemptions	(13,000)	(13,000)
Taxable income	$ 47,000	$ 87,000
Income tax liability		
First $45,800	$ 9,772	First $85,600 $ 25,920
Excess $1,200 × 38%	456	Excess $1,400 × 45% 630
Total	$ 10,228	$ 26,550

*From tax rate schedule in Figure 28-4, assuming a joint return and total deductions and exemptions of $13,000. Figure 28-3 would normally be used for some of these computations if a complete table was available.

Figure 28-8
Comparison of Tax Impact on Forms of Business Organization

Management is considering whether to issue shares of 12% preferred stock or borrow at a 14% rate of interest. The firm is in a 46% marginal tax bracket. The after-tax results for the two alternatives are:

	Issue Stock	Issue Bonds
Increase in earnings ($500,000 × 18%)	$90,000	$90,000
Interest expense ($500,000 × 14%)	–0–	70,000
Taxable income	90,000	20,000
Income tax expense:		
$90,000 × 46%	41,400	
$20,000 × 46%		9,200
Net income before dividends	48,600	10,800
Preferred dividends ($500,000 × 12%)	60,000	
Net income available to common stockholders	($11,400)	$10,800

Clearly, in certain situations, the tax advantage of debt encourages its use to finance a business.

OPERATING THE BUSINESS

Once the business is organized, management should use the marginal tax rate to assess the impact of taxes on alternative decisions as illustrated earlier for an individual. There are also many ways transactions can be arranged so that a favorable tax treatment is obtained legally. Primarily, these relate to the timing of transactions and to the choice of accounting methods. The latter is discussed in the final section of this chapter.

Timing of Transactions

The timing of business transactions is one of the simplest tax-planning techniques available. A company seeking to reduce taxable income can move discretionary expenses (such as routine plant and equipment maintenance) planned for the next year into the current year. Charitable contributions are another example of a discretionary expense. In addition, sales transactions near the end of the current year may be deferred until the next year. Capital assets that are to be disposed of at a gain should be held for at least 12 months if at all possible, in order to qualify for long-term capital gains treatment. The preferential treatment given capital gains is so significant that it may be beneficial to defer the sale, even if it means that a smaller gain will be realized.

REPORTING INCOME TAX EXPENSE

As mentioned earlier, there are some differences between the tax law and generally accepted accounting principles that result in differences between accounting income and taxable income. If a particular item creates a permanent difference, it will enter into the computation of either taxable income or accounting income—but not both. For example, interest received on a bond issued by a state government is reported on the books as income but not for tax purposes. Consequently, accounting income in the year the interest is accrued is greater than taxable income. In other cases, the differences will cause taxable income to exceed accounting income. For example, as noted earlier, premiums paid for life insurance policies on employees under which the corporation is the named beneficiary are not deductible in computing taxable income, but such payments are expensed for external reporting purposes.

If the difference between the amount of taxable income and accounting income is the result of a permanent difference, the income tax expense reported in the income statement will be equal to the income tax liability. In such cases the effective tax rate as a percentage of accounting income will not equal the statutory tax rate.

In contrast with permanent differences, other differences between taxable income and accounting income, called **timing differences,** arise when an item of revenue or expense enters into the computation of both taxable income and accounting income but in different periods. A timing difference may result because the timing of certain revenues and expenses, as required by tax law, differs from the timing of revenues and expenses in accordance with generally accepted accounting principles. For example, the tax law specifies that an advance receipt of rent is fully taxable in the same year, but for financial reporting purposes it is recognized as revenue as it is earned. Although the rent is reported as revenue earlier for tax purposes, the total revenue for tax and financial reporting will be the same over the rental period. The only difference is the pattern of recognizing the annual income amounts. In addition, for some items, the tax law permits a taxpayer to elect for tax purposes accounting methods that are different from those used for financial reporting purposes. For example, many firms elect to use an accelerated depreciation method in computing taxable income and the straight-line method in computing accounting income. In this case, the total depreciation recognized over the useful life of the asset will be the same for financial reporting and tax purposes, but the amount computed for each purpose each year will not be equal.

For assets placed into service after December 31, 1980, the Economic Recovery Tax Act of 1981 provides a new system for computing the amount of depreciation to be deducted each period for tax purposes. This new system has been designated the "Accelerated Cost Recovery System" or ACRS. The new law provides that the cost of such assets acquired after 1980 are to be recovered over predetermined periods that are generally shorter than the useful lives of the assets (the cost is not reduced by residual value in computing the tax deduction). The ACRS deduction is computed by applying the percentages appearing in tables provided in the law to the asset's cost. These percentages are based on an accelerated method of cost recovery and permit ½ year depreciation in the year of acquisition. For example, the ACRS provides that the cost of an automobile placed into service is to be recovered over a three-year period. The ACRS percentage table provides for a deduction of 25% of the cost in the first year, 38% in the second, and 37% in the third. However, a taxpayer may elect to use the straight-line method over the three-year period or over a specified longer recovery period.[6]

When the use of alternative accounting methods results in a timing difference, a financial accounting problem arises as to the proper measurement of the income tax expense. To illustrate the nature of this problem, assume that Ewing Oil Company purchased for $600,000 an asset that had a four-year useful life and a zero expected residual value. The company reported accounting income of $500,000 before taxes and depreciation on the new asset in each of four years. The company elected to use the straight-line method of depreciation for book purposes and the ACRS for tax purposes. The asset falls into the 3-year class under the ACRS. To simplify the tax computations, a fixed corporate tax rate of 40% is assumed. Depreciation expense under both methods, the income tax liability, and a condensed income statement for each of the four years are shown in Figure 28-9. Figure 28-9 is developed to illustrate the justification for the allocation of income taxes. As shown later, the income statement results are not in accordance with generally accepted accounting principles.

Note that the total depreciation computed over the life of the asset is the same for tax and accounting purposes. However, more depreciation is deducted under the ACRS method in the early years of the asset's useful life, which results in taxable income lower than accounting income before taxes. In later years, this reverses since less depreciation is deducted for tax purposes than for accounting purposes and taxable income exceeds accounting income before taxes. In the income statement, income tax expense reported each period is equal to the tax liability computed each period. This approach results in a fluctuating tax expense and, except for the second year, a decreasing net income even though the before-tax accounting income was the same each year. Opponents of this method contend that such results are misleading and confusing to statement readers.

In order to avoid such distortion in the income statement, *the APB concluded that income tax allocation procedures should be followed* when the difference between accounting and taxable income is caused by timing differences.[7] **Income tax allocation** procedures result in the accrual of income tax expense based on accounting income rather than on taxable income. Using tax allocation procedures, income statements for Ewing Oil Company would appear as follows:

---

[6]An election is available for a taxpayer to immediately write-off a portion of the cost of a qualified asset. This election is ignored in the illustration and problem material at the end of the chapter.

[7]Accounting Principles Board, "Accounting for Income Taxes," *APB Opinion No. 11* (New York: AICPA, 1967), par. 34.

Income Statement	Year 1	2	3	4	Total
Income before depreciation and taxes	$500,000	$500,000	$500,000	$500,000	$2,000,000
Depreciation expense	150,000	150,000	150,000	150,000	600,000
Income before taxes	350,000	350,000	350,000	350,000	1,400,000
Income tax expense (40%)	140,000	140,000	140,000	140,000	560,000
Net income	$210,000	$210,000	$210,000	$210,000	$ 840,000

Using this approach, the income tax expense for each period is computed by multiplying the pretax accounting income reported in the income statement by the tax rate. Since the tax expense does not equal the tax liability, an account

Figure 28-9
Illustration of Reporting Income Tax Expense—Income Taxes Not Allocated

	Year 1	2	3	4	Total
Depreciation Expense					
Depreciation expense—book purposes ($600,000 ÷ 4 years)	$150,000	$150,000	$150,000	$150,000	$600,000
Tax purposes	$150,000	$228,000	$222,000	–0–	$600,000

Year 1 $600,000 × 25% = $150,000
   2 $600,000 × 38% = $228,000
   3 $600,000 × 37% = $222,000
   4 $600,000 × 0% = –0–
The useful life of 3 years and rates are derived from tables provided by the Internal Revenue Service.

Income Tax Liability					
Taxable income before depreciation	$500,000	$500,000	$500,000	$500,000	$2,000,000
Depreciation expense	150,000	228,000	222,000	–0–	600,000
Taxable income	$350,000	$272,000	$278,000	$500,000	$1,400,000
Income tax liability (40%)	$140,000	$108,800	$111,200	$200,000	$560,000

Income Statement
Income tax expense is not reported in accordance with generally accepted accounting principles.

	Year 1	2	3	4	Total
Income before depreciation and taxes	$500,000	$500,000	$500,000	$500,000	$2,000,000
Depreciation expense	150,000	150,000	150,000	150,000	600,000
Income before taxes	350,000	350,000	350,000	350,000	1,400,000
Income tax expense (actual tax liability)	140,000	108,800	111,200	200,000	560,000
Net income	$210,000	$241,200	$238,800	$150,000	$840,000

called Deferred Income Tax Liability is created to balance the two, as shown in these journal entries:

Year	1	Income Tax Expense	140,000	
		Income Tax Payable		140,000
Year	2	Income Tax Expense	140,000	
		Income Tax Payable		108,800
		Deferred Income Tax Liability		31,200
Year	3	Income Tax Expense	140,000	
		Income Tax Payable		111,200
		Deferred Income Tax Liability		28,800
Year	4	Income Tax Expense	140,000	
		Deferred Income Tax Liability	60,000	
		Income Tax Payable		200,000

The four-year history of the Deferred Income Tax Liability account is:

						Balance	
Date		Description	Post Ref.	Debit	Credit	Debit	Credit
Year	1				–0–		–0–
	2				31,200		31,200
	3				28,800		60,000
	4			60,000			—

Deferred Income Tax Liability

The credit balance in the Deferred Income Tax Liability account is reported as a liability because the balance in the account represents an obligation for taxes that will be paid in future tax years when taxable income exceeds accounting income. The classification of the account as current or long-term depends on the classification of the asset or liability that gave rise to the timing difference.[8] In this illustration, the balance in the deferred income tax liability account is reported as long-term, since it results from a difference in depreciation expenses computed on an asset classified as long-term. If the difference were related to alternative methods used to account for a current asset, the deferred income tax liability account would be classified as a current liability.

In the preceding illustration, tax payments were postponed as a result of taking a deduction for tax purposes before it was recognized as an expense in the accounting records. Taxes may also be postponed if revenue is recognized for book purposes before it is subject to tax. In contrast, taxes may be prepaid

[8]*Ibid.*, par. 57 and Financial Accounting Standards Board, "Balance Sheet Classification of Deferred Income Taxes," *Statement No. 37* (Stamford: 1980), p. 2.

when expenses are recognized in computing accounting income before they are deducted in computing taxable income or when revenues are included in taxable income before they are recognized in the books. In these latter cases, taxable income is greater than accounting income, thereby creating a tax liability greater than tax expense. The excess of the tax liability over the tax expense, called Deferred Income Tax Expense, is reported as an asset in the balance sheet. The prepaid tax is then expensed when the income is reported later in the income statement.

Note in Figure 28-9 that the cumulative income tax of $560,000 is equal to the income tax liability for the four years and that the total net income is $840,000 whether income taxes were allocated or not. Why then does a company elect to use an alternative method for tax purposes? The attraction of the accelerated method for tax purposes can be shown by comparing the pattern of cash payments for taxes had the straight-line method been used for tax purposes rather than the ACRS:

Tax Payments	Straight-line	ACRS
Year 1	$140,000	$140,000
2	140,000	108,800
3	140,000	111,200
4	140,000	200,000
Total tax payments	$560,000	$560,000

Although the total tax payment is the same in both cases, the use of an accelerated depreciation method results in the postponement of a portion of the payment for income taxes in the first three years. Thus at the end of Year 2, the company has $31,200 and an additional $28,800 in Year 3 available for use in operations until it must be paid in Year 4.

The use of different methods for book and tax purposes requires keeping two sets of depreciation records. To avoid this duplication, many firms keep their accounting records on the same basis as their tax records. This practice is acceptable when the tax method does not result in a material difference from what would be reported in accordance with generally accepted accounting principles. If the difference between the two methods is material, the proper accounting method should be used for external reporting purposes.

A corporation also has a choice of selecting the method used to account for the flow of inventory costs. As you already know, during periods of rising prices the LIFO inventory method will produce lower taxable income than other methods—which partially explains the popularity of the method for tax purposes. However, tax laws require that a company using LIFO for tax purposes must also use LIFO for financial reporting purposes. A company is allowed to make a footnote disclosure of the net income computed by another cost flow method (e.g., FIFO).

GLOSSARY

ACCOUNTING INCOME.   The income amount reported for external reporting purposes (p. 1075).

ADJUSTED GROSS INCOME.   Gross income less ordinary and necessary business expenses and other deductions permitted by law (p. 1080).

CAPITAL ASSET.   Any item of property except (1) inventories, (2) trade accounts and notes receivable, (3) land, building, and equipment used in a trade or business, and (4) certain intangible assets (p. 1078).

CONSTRUCTIVE RECEIPT.   The point in time when a cash receipt is taxable because it is controlled by a taxpayer even though it is not actually received (p. 1076).

DEDUCTION.   An item that reduces an amount subject to tax (p. 1077).

EXCLUSION.   An item omitted from gross income as provided by the tax laws (p. 1077).

EXEMPTIONS.   A deduction from adjusted gross income (currently $1,000 per exemption) for each exemption claimed by a taxpayer. A separate exemption is allowed for the taxpayer, the taxpayer's spouse, and each qualified dependent (p. 1082).

GROSS INCOME.   All income not specifically excluded by law (p. 1077).

INCOME AVERAGING.   A tax provision that enables individual taxpayers to use their taxable income for the preceding four years to reduce the tax rate applicable to the current year's taxable income (p. 1087).

INCOME TAX ALLOCATION.   An accounting procedure under which the reported income tax expense is based on accounting income rather than taxable income (p. 1099).

INTERNAL REVENUE CODE.   A compilation of all current federal income tax laws (p. 1073).

ITEMIZED DEDUCTIONS.   Personal expenses that are permitted by law to be deducted from adjusted gross income in computing taxable income (p. 1080).

LONG-TERM CAPITAL GAIN OR LOSS.   A gain or loss from the sale of a capital asset held longer than one year (p. 1079).

NET CAPITAL GAIN OR LOSS.   The difference between net long-term capital gains or losses and net short-term capital gains or losses (p. 1079).

NET LONG-TERM CAPITAL GAIN OR LOSS.   The difference between long-term capital gains and long-term capital losses (p. 1079).

NET SHORT-TERM CAPITAL GAIN OR LOSS.   The difference between short-term capital gains and short-term capital losses (p. 1079).

MARGINAL TAX RATE.   The tax rate applied to the next dollar of taxable income (p. 1087).

PERMANENT DIFFERENCE.   An item that enters into the computation of accounting income or taxable income but not both (p. 1097).

PROGRESSIVE TAX.   A tax in which the tax rate increases as the level of taxable income increases (p. 1087).

SHORT-TERM CAPITAL GAIN OR LOSS.   A gain or loss from the sale of a capital asset held less than one year (p. 1079).

SUBCHAPTER S CORPORATION.   A corporation that elects to be taxed similar to a partnership when certain criteria are satisfied (p. 1074).

TAXABLE INCOME.   The amount of income on which the gross tax liability is computed (p. 1080).

TAX CREDIT.   An item that is a direct reduction in the amount of tax liability (p. 1077).

TAX EVASION.   The deliberate misstatement of taxable income, tax credits, pre-payments, and/or other taxes (p. 1075).

TAX PLANNING (TAX AVOIDANCE).   A legal means of reducing or deferring an income tax liability (p. 1075).

TIMING DIFFERENCE.   A revenue or expense item that enters into the determination of both accounting income and taxable income but in different periods (p. 1098).

ZERO BRACKET AMOUNT.   A standard deduction permitted in lieu of itemized deductions that is already incorporated in the tax tables and rate schedules (p. 1080).

DISCUSSION QUESTIONS

1. What are the four classifications of taxpayers for federal income tax purposes?
2. The taxable income of a sole proprietorship is $63,000, and the owner withdrew $35,000 during the year. How much business income must the owner report on his income tax return?
3. Explain the meaning of the expression "double taxation of corporate income."
4. Define tax planning and tax evasion.
5. How is the cash basis of accounting modified for income tax purposes?
6. What are the advantages of using the cash basis of accounting for income tax purposes?
7. An individual taxpayer has a net short-term capital loss of $1,000 and a net long-term capital loss of $2,000. What amount can be offset against the current year's ordinary income?
8. An individual taxpayer has a net short-term capital loss of $4,500 and a net long-term capital gain of $7,000.
   (a) What is the net capital gain?
   (b) What is the amount of the net increase in adjusted gross income resulting from the net capital gain?
9. Define the following terms: (a) exclusion, (b) deduction, (c) zero bracket amount, and (d) tax credit.
10. Arrange the following items in the correct order to arrive at the net tax liability or refund due for an individual taxpayer:
   (a) Tax credits
   (b) Exclusions from income

(c) Deductions from gross income
(d) Exemptions
(e) Adjusted gross income
(f) Taxable income
(g) Total income
(h) Excess itemized deductions
(i) Tax prepayments
(j) Gross income
(k) Gross tax liability

11. Does it make any difference if an item is deducted to arrive at adjusted gross income or from adjusted gross income? Why?
12. A married couple filing a joint return has taxable income of $52,000.
    (a) What is their gross tax liability?
    (b) What is the marginal tax rate?
    (c) What is their effective or average tax rate?
13. List in order the steps used to compute corporate net tax liability.
14. What are some ways in which the treatment of corporate capital gains and losses differs from the treatment of the capital transactions of individual taxpayers?
15. Differentiate between the tax treatment of the owners' salaries for a corporation and for a partnership.
16. What is the tax advantage of financing with debt rather than with stock?
17. When are income tax allocation procedures used? Why are they used?
18. Why is the balance in the Deferred Income Tax account sometimes classified as an asset and sometimes as a liability?

EXERCISES

(For the exercises and problems in this chapter, round all computations to the nearest dollar.)

Exercise 28-1 (Identifying Items of Income and Expense)
   Possible sources of income for an individual taxpayer are listed below.

1. Social security benefits
2. Lottery winnings
3. Tips
4. Royalties
5. Scholarship received for academic achievement
6. Profit from a sole proprietorship

   Possible expenses incurred by an individual taxpayer appear below.

7. Alimony payments
8. Contribution to the Salvation Army
9. Fee paid to CPA to have tax return prepared
10. Cost of marriage license

11. Payments to an individual retirement account
12. Interest paid on credit cards used for personal use

Required:

A. Determine whether each source of income should be included in gross income or excluded from gross income for tax purposes.
B. Determine whether each expense is deductible to arrive at adjusted gross income, deductible from adjusted gross income, or not deductible.

Exercise 28-2 (Capital Gains and Losses)

Each of the following independent cases summarizes an individual's capital transactions during the year.

Case	Long-term Capital Gain	Long-term Capital Loss	Short-term Capital Gain	Short-term Capital Loss
1	$4,700	$5,500	$8,500	$10,700
2	9,000	3,500	3,200	2,900
3	7,400	6,100	1,800	2,500

Required:

Assume taxable income before considering capital transactions of $40,000. For each case, determine the following:

A. Net long-term capital gain or loss
B. Net short-term capital gain or loss
C. Net capital gain or loss
D. Adjusted gross income

Exercise 28-3 (Computation of Tax Liability for an Individual)

Nancy Gonzo is single and has no dependents. She compiled the following tax-related information:

Total income	$54,670
Income tax withheld from salary	15,780
Itemized deductions	4,900
Exclusions from income	3,000
Deductions from gross income	1,200

Required:

Determine the following:

A. Taxable income
B. Gross tax liability (Use the Tax Table in Figure 28-3.)
C. Net tax liability or refund
D. Average tax rate

Exercise 28-4 (Computation of Tax Liability for a Corporation)

The records of the Anchor Corporation contain the following information:

Operating revenue	$400,000
Dividends from U.S. corporations	7,000
Net long-term capital gain	10,900
Net short-term capital loss	12,000
Operating expenses	250,000

Required:
Compute the tax liability of the Anchor Corporation.

Exercise 28-5 (Income Tax Allocation)

The records of the Toucan Corporation contain the following income tax information.

	1983	1984	1985
Actual income tax	$24,350	$25,950	$26,350
Income tax reported on the income statement	25,550	25,550	25,550

Required:
A. Prepare journal entries to record the income tax expense and liability for each of the years.
B. Post the entries to a T account entitled Deferred Income Tax Liability.

PROBLEMS

Problem 28-1 (Computation of Tax Liability for a Married Couple)

Gene and Cindy Holmquist are married and have one dependent child. They are both in their 30s. Gene is a psychologist with his own private practice. Cindy heads the public relations department of a large firm. They plan to file a joint return, and they compiled the following information to give to their accountant.

Gross revenue from Gene's practice	$107,600
Expenses of Gene's practice	66,000
Estimated tax paid by Gene	8,100
Cindy's salary	39,000
Income tax withheld from Cindy's salary	10,300
Interest earned on savings in the bank	350
Sales tax	690
Property tax	580
Inheritance received	5,000
Medical and dental expenses	4,628
Net long-term capital gains	3,000
Net short-term capital losses	4,500

Interest on home mortgage	7,800
Theft loss	470
Dividends	1,000

Required:

Compute the Holmquists' adjusted gross income, taxable income, and net income tax liability.

Problem 28-2 (Computation of Tax Liability for a Married Couple)

Roy and Tina Butler file a joint tax return. Roy is 65 and Tina is 60. They support their 21-year-old daughter who is a full-time student and who earned $1,500 during the summer. Roy is a photographer and Tina works part-time as a salesclerk. Their records contain the following information.

Roy's salary	$50,895
Tina's salary	5,690
Received a gift of cash	3,000
Interest on savings account	210
Interest on City of Phoenix bonds	130
Sold stock purchased three years ago for $6,700	4,200
Sold gold coins purchased three months ago for $3,200	3,100
Political contributions	180
Charitable contributions	1,460
Interest expense on loans	700
Medicine and drugs	395
Doctor and hospital payments	2,780
Uninsured loss from flood damage	7,360
Safe deposit box rental	40
Sales tax	510
State gas tax	90
Income tax withheld from Roy's salary	13,820
Income tax withheld from Tina's salary	410

Required:

Compute the Butler's taxable income, gross tax liability (use the Tax Table in Figure 28-3 if taxable income is covered in the table), and amount of unpaid taxes due or refund to be received.

Problem 28-3 (Type of Business Organization)

Kim Rogers and George Hayes plan on starting a business by investing equal amounts of money. They would like to organize the business as either a partnership or a corporation. They anticipate an annual net income of $80,000 before deducting their salaries of $21,000 each for services performed. Both Kim and George are single and have no dependents. Neither of them itemizes deductions. The business would be Kim's only source of income. George has income from other sources of $15,000. For this problem, use the tax rate schedules in Figure 28-4 to compute their individual income tax liability even though taxable income may be less than $50,000.

Required:

A. Assuming the business is organized as a partnership, determine the income tax liability of (1) Kim and (2) George. Profits of the partnership are shared equally.

B. Assume the business is organized as a corporation and no dividends are distributed. Allocate one-half of the corporate income tax to each owner, and determine the tax liability of (1) Kim and (2) George.

C. Assume a corporation is formed and all the net income is distributed as dividends. Allocate one-half of the corporate income tax to each owner, and determine the tax liability of (1) Kim and (2) George.

Problem 28-4 (Income Tax Allocation)

The Austin Corporation purchased a machine on January 2 for $85,000. The machine has a four-year useful life and a zero residual value. The corporation uses the ACRS of depreciation (25%, year 1; 38%, year 2; 37%, year 3) for tax purposes and the straight-line method for financial statement purposes. The corporation's annual income before depreciation and income tax is $260,000. Assume a fixed corporate tax rate of 40% and a calendar year-end.

Required:

A. Determine the taxable income and income tax liability for each of the four years.

B. For each year, determine the financial statement net income assuming that (1) actual tax liability is reported and (2) allocated income tax expense is reported.

C. Prepare journal entries to record each year's allocated tax expense and tax liability.

D. Set up a T account entitled Deferred Income Tax Liability. Post the journal entries to this account.

Problem 28-5 (Income Tax Allocation)

On July 1, 1983, Park View Development Corporation received $14,400 as advance payment for 24 months' rent. The rental period began on that date. Park View has an annual taxable income without considering the rent of $110,000. Assume a fixed corporate tax rate of 40% and a calendar year-end.

Required:

A. Compute the income tax liability for 1983, 1984, and 1985.

B. Determine the accounting net income for 1983, 1984, and 1985 assuming the actual tax liability is reported on the income statement.

C. Determine the accounting net income for each year assuming income tax allocation procedures are used.

D. Prepare journal entries to allocate the tax expense and record the tax liability.

Problem 28-6 (Tax Effects on Financing Decisions)

The Liberty Corporation needs $800,000 to introduce a new product line. The investment is expected to yield a return of 17% before taxes. The following methods of raising the capital are being considered.

1. Issue $800,000 of 10-year, 12% bonds at par.

2. Issue 8,000 shares of 9%, cumulative, nonparticipating preferred stock for $100 a share.

3. Issue 32,000 shares of common stock for $25 a share.

Liberty Corporation currently has 60,000 shares of common stock outstanding. The firm has a 46% marginal tax rate.

Required:
Determine the effect of each of the three financing methods on the income tax expense, net income, net income available to common stockholders, and earnings per share on common stock.

ALTERNATE PROBLEMS

Problem 28-1A (Computation of Tax Liability for a Married Couple)
Brian and Susan Ingstam, a married couple in their 40s, have three dependent children. They compiled the following information for use in preparing their joint return.

Brian's salary	$29,000
Income tax withheld from Brian's salary	5,900
Susan's salary	26,000
Income tax withheld from Susan's salary	5,400
Sales tax	470
Charitable contributions	150
Net long-term capital gains	3,400
Net short-term capital gains	900
Interest on home mortgage	4,000
Interest on credit cards	190
Medical and dental expenses	1,950
Interest on corporate bonds	810
Interest on municipal bonds	150
Dividends	330
Lottery winnings	200
State income tax	3,100

Required:
Compute the Ingstams' adjusted gross income, taxable income, and net tax liability. (Use the Tax Table in Figure 28-3 if taxable income is covered in the Table.)

Problem 28-2A (Computation of Tax Liability for a Married Couple)
Scott and Judy Stevens are a married couple in their 20s. They support Scott's 17-year-old sister, who lives with them. Scott is an engineer. Judy, who is blind, is a lawyer. Their records contain the following information, which may be used in preparing their joint return.

Judy's salary	$19,000
Scott's salary	46,960
Interest on savings account	140
Dividends	180

Gambling gains	1,100
Sold a painting purchased eight years ago for $3,000	7,200
Sold stock purchased four months ago for $2,600	1,900
Political contributions	200
Sales tax	440
Medical and dental expenses	4,200
Uninsured loss from automobile accident	650
Alimony payments to Scott's first wife	3,600
Subscriptions to professional journals	67
Property tax	530
Interest on home mortgage	7,050
Income tax withheld from Judy's salary	3,900
Income tax withheld from Scott's salary	10,100

Required:
Compute the Stevens' taxable income, gross tax liability, and amount of unpaid taxes due or refund to be received.

Problem 28-3A (Type of Business Organization)

Jim Brown and Al Reed have decided to start a small business. They will contribute equal amounts of capital and share profits equally. They anticipate an annual net income of $100,000 before deducting their salaries of $30,000 each, which is reasonable compensation. Jim is single with no dependents. The business will be his only source of income. Al is married and has one young child. The business and his wife's salary of $12,000 (after deducting 10% from her lower earnings) are the only sources of income to be reported on his joint return. Neither Jim nor Al itemizes deductions. Use the tax rate schedule shown in Figure 28-4 to compute their income tax liability even though taxable income may be less than $50,000.

Required:
A. Assume the business is organized as a partnership. Compute the tax liability of (1) Jim and (2) Al.
B. Assume a corporation is organized and no dividends are distributed. Allocate one-half of the corporate income tax liability to each owner, and then compute the total tax liability of (1) Jim and (2) Al.
C. Assume the business is organized as a corporation and all the net income is distributed as dividends. After allocating one-half of the corporate tax liability to each owner, compute the total tax liability of (1) Jim and (2) Al.

Problem 28-4A (Income Tax Allocation)

The Great Falls Corporation bought a new piece of equipment for $240,000 on January 4. The equipment is expected to have a useful life of four years and a zero residual value. Great Falls anticipates an annual net income before depreciation and income tax of $330,000. The company uses the ACRS of depreciation (25%, year 1; 38%, year 2; 37%, year 3) for income tax purposes and the straight-line method for financial accounting purposes. Assume a fixed corporate tax rate of 40% and a calendar year-end.

Required:

A. Compute the taxable income and income tax liability for each year of the equipment's useful life.

B. For each year, determine the financial statement net income assuming that (1) actual tax liability is reported and (2) allocated income tax expense is reported.

C. Prepare a journal entry for each year to record allocated tax expense and tax liability.

D. Set up a T account entitled Deferred Income Tax Liability. Post the journal entries to this account.

Problem 28-5A (Income Tax Allocation)

The A & F Corporation received $13,500 on October 1, 1984, as an advance payment of rent for the 18-month period beginning that day. A & F has taxable income from other sources of $70,000 per year. Assume a fixed corporate tax rate of 40% and a calendar year-end.

Required:

A. Determine A & F's income tax liability for 1984, 1985, and 1986.

B. Determine A & F's accounting net income for each of the years assuming that the actual tax liability appears on the income statement.

C. Determine the accounting net income assuming that an allocated income tax expense is reported on the income statement.

D. Prepare journal entries to record the allocated tax expense and the actual tax liability.

Problem 28-6A (Tax Effects on Financing Decisions)

Fazio Corporation would like to purchase several pieces of machinery and equipment for $450,000. Three proposals have been suggested to raise the capital.

1. Sell 50,000 shares of common stock for a total price of $450,000.
2. Sell 9,000 shares of 10% preferred stock for $50 a share.
3. Sell $450,000 of 12% bonds at par.

Fazio Corporation expects a before-tax yield on the investment of 19%. There are 75,000 shares of common stock currently outstanding. The firm has a 40% marginal tax rate.

Required:

Calculate the expected effect of each proposal on the firm's income tax expense, net income, net income available to common stockholders, and earnings per share on common stock.

CASE FOR CHAPTER 28

(Annual Report Analysis)

For this case you are to refer to the General Motors Corporation and the Modern Merchandising, Inc. annual reports presented in the Appendix to the text.

Required:

A. Compute the effective tax rate for the most recent fiscal period reported for both General Motors and Modern Merchandising.

B. In a footnote, General Motors presents a reconciliation of the statutory income tax rate of 46.0% with the consolidated effective income tax credit. What is the primary reason for the difference between the two items?

C. What is the major source of timing differences for General Motors? For Modern Merchandising?

D. What is the policy of each company with respect to accounting for the investment tax credit? (Hint: See the summary of significant accounting policies.)

E. With reference to the balance sheet of Modern Merchandising, Inc.:
   1. What was the amount of deferred tax charges on January 31, 1981?
   2. What was the amount of current tax liability on January 31, 1981?
   3. What was the amount of deferred tax credits on January 31, 1981?

APPENDIX CONSOLIDATED FINANCIAL STATEMENTS

GENERAL MOTORS CORPORATION

For Years Ended December 31, 1981 and 1980

A 1 - A 14

MODERN MERCHANDISING, INC.

For Years Ended January 31, 1981, and February 2, 1980

A 15 - A 24

MARY MOPPET'S DAY CARE SCHOOLS, INC.

For Years Ended September 30, 1981 and 1980

A 25 - A 31

GENERAL MOTORS ANNUAL REPORT 1981

CONSOLIDATED FINANCIAL STATEMENTS   General Motors Corporation and Consolidated Subsidiaries

RESPONSIBILITIES FOR FINANCIAL STATEMENTS

The following financial statements of General Motors Corporation and consolidated subsidiaries were prepared by the management which is responsible for their integrity and objectivity. The statements have been prepared in conformity with generally accepted accounting principles and, as such, include amounts based on judgments of management. Financial information elsewhere in this Annual Report is consistent with that in the financial statements.

Management is further responsible for maintaining a system of internal accounting controls, designed to provide reasonable assurance that the books and records reflect the transactions of the companies and that its established policies and procedures are carefully followed. From a stockholder's point of view, perhaps the most important feature in the system of control is that it is continually reviewed for its effectiveness and is augmented by written policies and guidelines, the careful selection and training of qualified personnel, and a strong program of internal audit.

Deloitte Haskins & Sells, independent certified public accountants, are engaged to examine the financial statements of General Motors Corporation and its subsidiaries and issue reports thereon. Their examination is conducted in accordance with generally accepted auditing standards which comprehend a review of internal accounting controls and a test of transactions. The Accountants' Report appears on page 26.

The Board of Directors, through the Audit Committee (composed entirely of non-employe Directors), is responsible for assuring that management fulfills its responsibilities in the preparation of the financial statements. The Committee selects the independent public accountants annually in advance of the Annual Meeting of Stockholders and submits the selection for ratification at the Meeting. In addition, the Committee reviews the scope of the audits and the accounting principles being applied in financial reporting. The independent public accountants, representatives of management, and the internal auditors meet regularly (separately and jointly) with the Committee to review the activities of each and to ensure that each is properly discharging its responsibilities. To ensure complete independence, Deloitte Haskins & Sells have full and free access to meet with the Committee, without management representatives present, to discuss the results of their examination, the adequacy of internal accounting controls, and the quality of the financial reporting.

Chairman

Chief Financial Officer

STATEMENT OF CONSOLIDATED INCOME

For The Years Ended December 31, 1981, 1980 and 1979
(Dollars in Millions Except Per Share Amounts)

	1981	1980	1979
Net Sales (Note 2)	$62,698.5	$57,728.5	$66,311.2
Costs and Expenses			
Cost of sales and other operating charges, exclusive of items listed below	55,185.2	52,099.8	55,848.7
Selling, general and administrative expenses	2,715.0	2,636.7	2,475.5
Depreciation of real estate, plants and equipment	1,837.3	1,458.1	1,236.9
Amortization of special tools	2,568.9	2,719.6	1,950.4
Provision for the Bonus Plan (Note 3)	—	—	133.8
Total Costs and Expenses	62,306.4	58,914.2	61,645.3
Operating Income (Loss)	392.1	(1,185.7)	4,665.9
Other income less income deductions—net (Note 4)	367.7	348.7	560.3
Interest expense (Note 1)	(897.9)	(531.9)	(368.4)
Income (Loss) before Income Taxes	(138.1)	(1,368.9)	4,857.8
United States, foreign and other income taxes (credit) (Note 6)	(123.1)	(385.3)	2,183.4
Income (Loss) after Income Taxes	(15.0)	(983.6)	2,674.4
Equity in earnings of nonconsolidated subsidiaries and associates (dividends received amounted to $189.7 in 1981, $116.8 in 1980 and $112.8 in 1979)	348.4	221.1	218.3
Net Income (Loss)	333.4	(762.5)	2,892.7
Dividends on preferred stocks	12.9	12.9	12.9
Earnings (Loss) on Common Stock	$ 320.5	($ 775.4)	$ 2,879.8
Average number of shares of common stock outstanding (in millions)	299.1	292.4	286.8
Earnings (Loss) Per Share of Common Stock (Note 7)	$1.07	($2.65)	$10.04

Reference should be made to notes on pages 20 through 26.

CONSOLIDATED BALANCE SHEET

December 31, 1981 and 1980
(Dollars in Millions Except Per Share Amounts)

ASSETS	1981	1980
Current Assets		
Cash	$ 204.1	$ 157.2
United States Government and other marketable securities and time deposits—at cost, which approximates market of $1,086.3 and $3,541.4	1,116.6	3,558.0
Accounts and notes receivable (including GMAC and its subsidiaries—$636.2 and $704.9)—less allowances	3,645.5	3,768.4
Inventories (less allowances) (Note 1)	7,222.7	7,295.0
Prepaid expenses	1,527.2	706.5
Total Current Assets	13,716.1	15,485.1
Equity in Net Assets of Nonconsolidated Subsidiaries and Associates (principally GMAC and its subsidiaries—Note 8)	3,379.4	2,899.8
Other Investments and Miscellaneous Assets—at cost (less allowances)	1,783.5	1,147.3
Common Stock Held for the Incentive Program (Note 3)	71.5	125.8
Property		
Real estate, plants and equipment—at cost (Note 9)	34,811.5	29,202.7
Less accumulated depreciation (Note 9)	16,317.4	15,217.1
Net real estate, plants and equipment	18,494.1	13,985.6
Special tools—at cost (less amortization)	1,546.6	937.4
Total Property	20,040.7	14,923.0
Total Assets	$38,991.2	$34,581.0

LIABILITIES AND STOCKHOLDERS' EQUITY	1981	1980
Current Liabilities		
Accounts payable (principally trade)	$ 3,699.7	$ 3,967.7
Loans payable (principally overseas) (Note 11)	1,727.8	1,676.5
Accrued liabilities (Note 10)	7,127.6	6,628.8
Total Current Liabilities	12,555.1	12,273.0
Long-Term Debt (Note 11)	3,801.1	1,886.0
Capitalized Leases	242.8	172.3
Other Liabilities (including GMAC of $424.0 in 1981)	3,215.1	1,482.5
Deferred Credits (principally investment tax credits)	1,456.0	952.6
Stockholders' Equity (Notes 3 and 12)		
Preferred stocks ($5.00 series, $183.6; $3.75 series, $100.0)	283.6	283.6
Common stock (issued, 304,804,228 and 298,053,782 shares)	508.0	496.7
Capital surplus (principally additional paid-in capital)	1,589.5	1,297.2
Net income retained for use in the business	15,340.0	15,737.1
Total Stockholders' Equity	17,721.1	17,814.6
Total Liabilities and Stockholders' Equity	$38,991.2	$34,581.0

Reference should be made to notes on pages 20 through 26.
Certain amounts for 1980 have been reclassified to conform with 1981 classifications.

STATEMENT OF CHANGES
IN CONSOLIDATED FINANCIAL POSITION

For The Years Ended December 31, 1981, 1980 and 1979
(Dollars in Millions)

	1981	1980	1979
Source of Funds			
Net income (loss)	$ 333.4	($ 762.5)	$2,892.7
Depreciation of real estate, plants and equipment	1,837.3	1,458.1	1,236.9
Amortization of special tools	2,568.9	2,719.6	1,950.4
Deferred income taxes, undistributed earnings of nonconsolidated subsidiaries and associates, etc.—net	(146.0)	50.4	(321.2)
Total funds provided by current operations	4,593.6	3,465.6	5,758.8
Proceeds from issuance of long-term debt	2,172.7	1,305.1	41.3
Proceeds from sale of newly issued common stock	303.6	271.9	249.9
Proceeds from disposals of property—net	217.5	261.1	166.9
Other—net	1,712.0	95.2	125.4
Total	8,999.4	5,398.9	6,342.3
Application of Funds			
Expenditures for real estate, plants and equipment	6,563.3	5,160.5	3,351.3
Expenditures for special tools	3,178.1	2,600.0	2,015.0
Dividends paid to stockholders (Note 12)	730.5	874.1	1,533.2
Investments in nonconsolidated subsidiaries and associates	321.0	4.1	542.8
Retirements of long-term debt	257.6	299.1	140.2
Total	11,050.5	8,937.8	7,582.5
Decrease in working capital	(2,051.1)	(3,538.9)	(1,240.2)
Working capital at beginning of the year	3,212.1	6,751.0	7,991.2
Working capital at end of the year	$ 1,161.0	$3,212.1	$6,751.0
Increase (Decrease) in Working Capital by Element			
Cash, marketable securities and time deposits	($ 2,394.5)	$ 728.8	($1,068.4)
Accounts and notes receivable	(122.9)	(1,262.0)	(608.3)
Inventories	(72.3)	(844.1)	520.1
Prepaid expenses	820.7	243.1	(265.9)
Accounts payable	268.0	(586.4)	115.9
Loans payable	(51.3)	(752.4)	191.1
Accrued liabilities	(498.8)	(1,065.9)	(124.7)
Decrease in working capital	($ 2,051.1)	($3,538.9)	($1,240.2)

Reference should be made to notes on pages 20 through 26.
Certain amounts for 1980 and 1979 have been reclassified to conform with 1981 classifications.

NOTES TO FINANCIAL STATEMENTS

NOTE 1. Significant Accounting Policies

Principles of Consolidation

The consolidated financial statements include the accounts of the Corporation and all domestic and foreign subsidiaries which are more than 50% owned and engaged principally in manufacturing or wholesale marketing of General Motors products. General Motors' share of earnings or losses of nonconsolidated subsidiaries and of associates in which at least 20% of the voting securities is owned is generally included in consolidated income under the equity method of accounting.

Income Taxes

Investment tax credits are deferred and amortized over the lives of the related assets. The tax effects of timing differences between pretax accounting income and taxable income (principally related to depreciation, sales and product allowances, undistributed earnings of subsidiaries and associates, and benefit plans expense) are deferred. Provisions are made for estimated United States and foreign taxes, less available tax credits and deductions, which may be incurred on remittance of the Corporation's share of subsidiaries' undistributed earnings less those deemed to be permanently reinvested. Possible taxes beyond those provided would not be material.

Inventories

Inventories are stated generally at cost, which is not in excess of market. The cost of substantially all domestic inventories was determined by the last-in, first-out (LIFO) method. If the first-in, first-out (FIFO) method of inventory valuation had been used by the Corporation for U.S. inventories, it is estimated they would be $2,077.1 million higher at December 31, 1981, compared with $1,784.5 million higher at December 31, 1980. As a result of decreases in unit sales in 1981 and 1980, certain LIFO inventory quantities carried at lower costs prevailing in prior years as compared with the costs of current purchases were liquidated. The effect of these inventory reductions was to favorably affect income (loss) before income taxes by approximately $89.2 million and $259.2 million, respectively. The cost of inventories outside the United States was determined generally by the FIFO or the average cost method.

Major Classes of Inventories

(Dollars in Millions)	1981	1980
Productive material, work in process and supplies	$4,561.5	$4,682.8
Finished product, service parts, etc.	2,661.2	2,612.2
Total	$7,222.7	$7,295.0

Depreciation and Amortization

Depreciation is provided on groups of property using, with minor exceptions, an accelerated method which accumulates depreciation of approximately two-thirds of the depreciable cost during the first half of the estimated lives of the property.

Expenditures for special tools are amortized, with the amortization applied directly to the asset account, over short periods of time because the utility value of the tools is radically affected by frequent changes in the design of the functional components and appearance of the product. Replacement of special tools for reasons other than changes in products is charged directly to cost of sales.

Pension Program

The Corporation and its subsidiaries have several pension plans covering substantially all of their employes, including certain employes in foreign countries. Benefits under the plans are generally related to an employe's length of service, wages and salaries, and, where applicable, contributions. The costs of these plans are determined on the basis of actuarial cost methods and include amortization of prior service cost over periods not in excess of 30 years from the later of October 1, 1979 or the date such costs are established. With the exception of certain overseas subsidiaries, pension costs accrued are funded within the limitations set by the Employee Retirement Income Security Act.

Product Related Expenses

Expenditures for advertising and sales promotion and for other product related expenses are charged to costs and expenses as incurred; provisions for estimated costs related to product warranty are made at the time the products are sold.

Expenditures for research and development are charged to expenses as incurred and amounted to $2,249.6 million in 1981, $2,224.5 million in 1980 and $1,949.8 million in 1979.

Foreign Exchange

Exchange and translation activity included in net income amounted to gains of $226.2 million in 1981, $164.6 million in 1980 and $86.2 million in 1979. Statement of Financial Accounting Standards (SFAS) No. 8, Accounting for the Translation of Foreign Currency Transactions and Foreign Currency Financial Statements, was applied throughout the three-year period.

Interest Cost

Total interest cost incurred in 1981, 1980 and 1979 amounted to $995.2 million, $567.1 million and $368.4 million, respectively, of which $97.3 million in 1981 and $35.2 million in 1980 was capitalized under SFAS No. 34, Capitalization of Interest Cost, which became effective in 1980.

NOTE 2. Net Sales

(Dollars in Millions)	1981	1980	1979
Net sales includes sales to:			
Nonconsolidated subsidiaries and associates	$ 130.4	$ 104.1	$ 145.8
Dealerships operating under dealership assistance plans	$1,688.9	$1,456.0	$1,853.5

Unrealized intercompany profits on sales to nonconsolidated subsidiaries and to associates are deferred.

NOTES TO FINANCIAL STATEMENTS (continued)

NOTE 3. Incentive Program

The Incentive Program consists of the General Motors Bonus Plan and the General Motors Stock Option Plans. The By-Laws provide that the Plans shall be presented for action at a stockholders' meeting at least once in every five years. The Program was last approved by stockholders at the 1977 Annual Meeting and will be submitted at the 1982 Annual Meeting.

The Corporation maintains a reserve for purposes of the Bonus Plan to which may be credited each year an amount which the independent public accountants of the Corporation determine to be 8% of the net earnings which exceed 7% but not 15% of net capital, plus 5% of the net earnings which exceed 15% of net capital, but not in excess of the amount paid out as dividends on the common stock during the year. However, for any year the Bonus and Salary Committee may direct that a lesser amount be credited. Bonus awards under the Bonus Plan and such other amounts arising out of the operation of the Program as the Committee may determine are charged to the reserve.

As a result of the low earnings in 1981 and net loss in 1980, no credits were made to the Reserve for the Bonus Plan. Accordingly, the Committee determined that there would be no bonus awards related to the years 1981 and 1980.

Under the provisions of the Program, participants receive their awards in instalments in as many as five years. If participants in the Bonus and Stock Option Plans fail to meet conditions precedent to receiving undelivered instalments of bonus awards (and contingent credits related to the Stock Option Plan prior to 1977), the amount of any such instalments is credited to income. Upon the exercise of stock options, any related contingent credits are proportionately reduced and the amount of the reduction is credited to income.

Common stock held for the Incentive Program is stated substantially at cost and used exclusively for payment of Program liabilities.

(Dollars in Millions)	1981 Shares	1981 Amount	1980 Shares	1980 Amount
Balance at Jan. 1	2,037,978	$125.8	3,108,316	$192.9
Acquired during the year	2,833	.1	9,097	.5
Sold to trustee of S-SPP	(8,224)	(.5)	(11,216)	(.6)
Delivered to participants	(855,450)	(53.9)	(1,068,219)	(67.0)
Balance at Dec. 31	1,177,137	$ 71.5	2,037,978	$125.8

Changes during 1979, 1980 and 1981 in the status of options granted under the Stock Option Plans are shown in the following table. The option prices are 100% of the average of the highest and lowest sales prices of General Motors common stock on the dates the options were granted as reported (1) on the New York Stock Exchange for options granted prior to 1976, and (2) on the Composite Tape of transactions on all major exchanges and nonexchange markets in the U.S. for options granted in 1976 and subsequent years. The options expire ten years from date of grant but are subject to earlier termination under certain conditions.

The Corporation intends to deliver newly issued stock upon the exercise of any of the options. The maximum number of shares for which additional options might be granted under the Plan was 1,904,325 at January 1, 1979, 1,582,170 at December 31, 1979, 1,230,055 at December 31, 1980 and 931,405 at December 31, 1981.

Year Granted	1973	1974	1976	1977	1978	1979	1980	1981
Option Price	$73.38	$50.00	$65.19	$66.57	$63.75	$59.50	$53.25	$50.00
Outstanding at Jan. 1, 1979	134,106	196,786	129,786	279,920	315,755	—		
Granted	—	—	—	—	—	351,940		
Terminated	(24,288)	(35,214)	(11,982)	(19,125)	(10,185)	(475)		
Outstanding at Dec. 31, 1979	109,818	161,572	117,804	260,795	305,570	351,465	—	
Granted	—	—	—	—	—	—	425,590	
Terminated	(16,764)	(18,998)	(10,764)	(23,790)	(26,190)	(20,085)	(3,410)	
Outstanding at Dec. 31, 1980	93,054	142,574	107,040	237,005	279,380	331,380	422,180	—
Granted	—	—	—	—	—	—	—	464,255
Terminated	(29,856)	(35,340)	(38,394)	(37,340)	(41,390)	(44,865)	(22,015)	(19,995)
Outstanding at Dec. 31, 1981	63,198	107,234	68,646	199,665	237,990	286,515	400,165	444,260

NOTES TO FINANCIAL STATEMENTS (continued)

NOTE 4. Other Income Less Income Deductions

(Dollars in Millions)	1981	1980	1979
Other income:			
Interest	$427.9	$392.1	$507.0
Other	123.6	81.7	72.2
Income deductions	(183.8)	(125.1)	(18.9)
Net	$367.7	$348.7	$560.3

NOTE 5. Pension Program

Total pension expense of the Corporation and its consolidated subsidiaries amounted to $1,493.8 million in 1981, $1,922.1 million in 1980 and $1,571.5 million in 1979. For purposes of determining pension expense, the Corporation uses a variety of assumed rates of return on pension funds in accordance with local practice and regulations, which rates approximated 6% in 1980 and 1979. In 1981, the assumed rate of return used in determining retirement plan costs in the United States and Canada was increased to 7%. The Corporation's independent actuary recommended this change, and other changes in actuarial assumptions, after taking into account the experience of the plans and reasonable expectations. The total effect of these changes was to reduce retirement plan costs for 1981 by $411.1 million and accordingly increase net income by $205.6 million ($0.69 per share). The following table compares accumulated plan benefits and plan net assets for the Corporation's defined benefit plans in the United States and Canada as of October 1 (generally, the plans' anniversary date) of both 1981 and 1980:

(Dollars in Millions)	1981	1980
Actuarial present value of accumulated plan benefits:		
Vested	$16,228.5	$17,438.5
Nonvested	1,890.3	2,234.1
Total	$18,118.8	$19,672.6
Market value of assets available for benefits:		
Held by trustees	$10,795.1	$10,584.6
Held by insurance companies	3,049.4	2,769.2
Total	$13,844.5	$13,353.8

The assumed rates of return used in determining the actuarial present value of accumulated plan benefits (shown in the table above) were based upon those published by the Pension Benefit Guaranty Corporation, a public corporation established under the Employee Retirement Income Security Act (ERISA). Such rates averaged approximately 10% for 1981 and 8¼% for 1980.

The Corporation's foreign pension plans are not required to report to governmental agencies pursuant to ERISA, and do not otherwise determine the actuarial value of accumulated benefits or net assets available for benefits as calculated and shown above. For those plans, the total of the plans' pension funds and balance sheet accruals, less pension prepayments and deferred charges, exceeded the actuarially computed value of vested benefits by approximately $200 million at December 31, 1981 and $215 million at December 31, 1980.

NOTE 6. United States, Foreign and Other Income Taxes (Credit)

(Dollars in Millions)	1981	1980	1979
Taxes estimated to be payable (refundable) currently:			
United States Federal	$442.9	($307.7)	$1,578.7
Foreign	62.4	56.2	412.9
State and local	41.4	(36.9)	127.9
Total	546.7	(288.4)	2,119.5
Taxes deferred—net:			
United States Federal	(829.3)	(342.2)	51.5
Foreign	(57.9)	131.9	(126.4)
State and local	(89.6)	(39.0)	7.0
Total	(976.8)	(249.3)	(67.9)
Investment tax credits deferred—net:			
United States Federal	312.6	126.0	116.5
Foreign	(5.6)	26.4	15.3
Total	307.0	152.4	131.8
Total taxes (credit)	($123.1)	($385.3)	$2,183.4

Investment tax credits entering into the determination of taxes estimated to be payable (refundable) currently amounted to $592.1 million in 1981, $350.9 million in 1980 and $290.7 million in 1979.

The deferred taxes (credit) for timing differences in 1981 consisted principally of ($546.3) million related to benefit plans expense and ($267.2) million related to sales and product allowances. The deferred taxes (credit) in 1980 consisted principally of ($232.1) million related to sales and product allowances.

Income (loss) before income taxes included the following components:

(Dollars in Millions)	1981	1980	1979
Domestic income (loss)	$288.7	($ 928.6)	$4,032.3
Foreign income (loss)	(426.8)	(440.3)	825.5
Total	($138.1)	($1,368.9)	$4,857.8

The consolidated effective income tax rate (credit) was different than the United States statutory income tax rate (credit) for the reasons set forth in the table below:

	1981	1980	1979
U.S. statutory income tax rate (credit)	(46.0%)	(46.0%)	46.0%
Investment tax credits—net	(201.8)	(12.0)	(3.4)
Foreign tax rate differential	149.6	29.0	1.5
State and local income taxes	(18.8)	(3.0)	1.5
Other adjustments	27.9	3.9	(0.7)
Consolidated effective income tax rate (credit)	(89.1%)	(28.1%)	44.9%

NOTE 7. Earnings (Loss) Per Share of Common Stock

Earnings (loss) per share of common stock are based on the average number of shares outstanding during each year. The effect on earnings (loss) per share resulting from the assumed exercise of outstanding options and delivery of bonus awards and contingent credits under the Incentive Program is not material.

NOTES TO FINANCIAL STATEMENTS (continued)

NOTE 8. General Motors Acceptance Corporation and Subsidiaries
Condensed Consolidated Balance Sheet (Dollars in Millions Except Per Share Amounts)

	1981	1980
Cash	$ 464.4	$ 473.0
Investments in Securities (market value, 1981—$1,182.3; 1980—$1,007.2)	1,245.5	1,003.0
Finance Receivables (1981—$45,543.0; 1980—$34,859.2; less unearned income: 1981—$5,389.3; 1980—$3,273.9; and allowance for financing losses: 1981—$461.2; 1980—$351.2)	39,692.5	31,234.1
Insurance Receivables, Unamortized Debt Expense, and Other Assets	446.2	336.8
Total Assets	$41,848.6	$33,046.9
Notes, Loans and Debentures Payable Within One Year (less unamortized discount)	$23,256.1	$16,814.0
Accounts Payable and Other Liabilities:		
General Motors Corporation and affiliated companies	636.2	704.9
Other	1,871.3	1,566.2
Notes, Loans and Debentures Payable After One Year (less unamortized discount)	10,676.7	9,185.8
Subordinated Indebtedness Payable After One Year (less unamortized discount)	2,173.2	2,024.1
Total Liabilities	38,613.5	30,295.0
Stockholder's Equity:		
Preferred stocks, $100 par value, redeemable at GMAC option (6% cumulative, $75.0; 7¼% cumulative, $35.0)	110.0	110.0
Common stock, $100 par value (outstanding, 1981—17,650,000 shares; 1980—14,650,000 shares)	1,765.0(1)	1,465.0
Net income retained for use in the business (net income: 1981—$365.2; 1980—$231.0; 1979—$224.1; cash dividends: 1981—$182.0; 1980—$107.0; 1979—$102.0)	1,360.1	1,176.9
Total Stockholder's Equity	3,235.1	2,751.9
Total Liabilities and Stockholder's Equity	$41,848.6	$33,046.9

(1)In January 1982, General Motors Corporation purchased an additional 4,000,000 shares of common stock for $400.0 million.

NOTE 9. Real Estate, Plants and Equipment and Accumulated Depreciation (Dollars in Millions)

	1981	1980
Real estate, plants and equipment (Note 11):		
Land	$ 350.8	$ 332.1
Land improvements	1,026.4	886.5
Leasehold improvements—less amortization	38.4	33.2
Buildings	7,159.6	6,209.4
Machinery and equipment	21,470.4	17,843.7
Furniture and office equipment	350.3	302.0
Capitalized leases	655.4	316.6
Construction in progress	3,760.2	3,279.2
Total	$34,811.5	$29,202.7
Accumulated depreciation:		
Land improvements	$ 530.8	$ 490.1
Buildings	3,409.4	3,177.2
Machinery and equipment	11,987.2	11,183.9
Furniture and office equipment	132.5	139.5
Capitalized leases	208.2	177.1
Extraordinary obsolescence	49.3	49.3
Total	$16,317.4	$15,217.1

NOTE 10. Accrued Liabilities (Dollars in Millions)

	1981	1980
Taxes, other than income taxes	$ 812.2	$ 723.9
Payrolls	1,576.2	1,667.3
Dealer and customer allowances, claims, discounts, etc.	2,685.4	2,600.0
Other	2,053.8	1,637.6
Total	$7,127.6	$6,628.8

NOTE 11. Long-Term Debt (Dollars in Millions)

GM:			1981	1980
U.S. dollars:				
13.95% Notes		1983	$ 150.0	$ —
10% Notes		1984-86	200.0	200.0
8.05% Notes		1985	300.0	300.0
12.2% Notes		1986-88	200.0	200.0
10% Notes		1991	200.0	—
8⅝% Debentures		2005	300.0	300.0
Other	4.8%	1983-2000	69.3	72.3
British pounds	14.5%	1983-87	271.7	—
Consolidated subsidiaries:				
United States dollars	12.7%	1983-91	829.9	318.0
Canadian dollars	15.7%	1985	687.9	284.4
German marks	7.0%	1983-97	248.3	—
Spanish pesetas	14.0%	1983-90	188.3	38.5
Other currencies	Various	1983-2004	270.4	180.0
Total			3,915.8	1,893.2
Less unamortized discount (principally on 10% notes due 1991)			114.7	7.2
Total			$3,801.1	$1,886.0

At year-end 1981, the Corporation and its consolidated subsidiaries had unused short-term credit lines of approximately $3.6 billion and unused long-term credit agreements of approximately $1.1 billion. Long-term debt at December 31, 1981 included approximately $660 million of short-term obligations which are intended to be renewed or refinanced under long-term credit agreements. Long-term debt (including current portion) bore interest at a weighted average rate of approximately 12.7% at December 31, 1981 and 13.5% at December 31, 1980.

In December 1981, the Corporation and a subsidiary arranged a private financing of $500 million in 10% notes due 1991, of which $400 million was outstanding at December 31, 1981. The difference between the 10% stated interest rate and the effective rate at date of issuance (15.45%) reflects the discount to be amortized over the life of the loan.

(continued)

NOTES TO FINANCIAL STATEMENTS (continued)

NOTE 11. (concluded)

An option to acquire certain real estate in 1991 was also granted. The option holder may deliver the notes in payment for the real estate.

Under the sinking fund provisions of the trust indenture for the Corporation's $300.0 million 8⅝% Debentures due 2005, the Corporation will provide an annual sinking fund of $11.8 million in each of the years 1986 to 2004, inclusive.

Maturities of long-term debt in the years 1982 through 1986 are (in millions) $186.4 (included in loans payable at December 31, 1981), $1,000.1, $305.9, $1,167.1 and $276.0. Loans payable at December 31, 1980 included $137.0 million current portion of long-term debt.

NOTE 12. Stockholders' Equity (Dollars in Millions Except Per Share Amounts)	1981	1980	1979
Capital Stock:			
Preferred Stock, without par value, cumulative dividends (authorized, 6,000,000 shares), no change during the year:			
$5.00 series, stated value $100 per share, redeemable at Corporation option at $120 per share (issued, 1,875,366 shares; in treasury, 39,722 shares; outstanding, 1,835,644 shares)	$ 183.6	$ 183.6	$ 183.6
$3.75 series, stated value $100 per share, redeemable at Corporation option at $100 per share (issued and outstanding, 1,000,000 shares)	100.0	100.0	100.0
Common Stock, $1⅔ par value (authorized, 500,000,000 shares):			
Issued at beginning of the year (298,053,782 shares in 1981, 292,472,499 in 1980 and 288,069,840 in 1979)	496.7	487.4	480.1
Newly issued stock sold under provisions of the Employe Stock Ownership Plans, Savings-Stock Purchase Programs and the Dividend Reinvestment Plan (6,750,446 shares in 1981, 5,581,283 in 1980 and 4,402,659 in 1979)	11.3	9.3	7.3
Issued at end of the year (304,804,228 shares in 1981, 298,053,782 in 1980 and 292,472,499 in 1979)	508.0	496.7	487.4
Total capital stock at end of the year	791.6	780.3	771.0
Capital Surplus (principally additional paid-in capital):			
Balance at beginning of the year	1,297.2	1,034.6	792.0
Proceeds in excess of par value of newly issued common stock sold under provisions of the Employe Stock Ownership Plans, Savings-Stock Purchase Programs and the Dividend Reinvestment Plan	292.3	262.6	242.6
Balance at end of the year	1,589.5	1,297.2	1,034.6
Net Income Retained for Use in the Business:			
Balance at beginning of the year	15,737.1	17,373.7	16,014.2
Net income (loss)	333.4	(762.5)	2,892.7
Total	16,070.5	16,611.2	18,906.9
Cash dividends:			
Preferred stock, $5.00 series, $5.00 per share	9.2	9.2	9.2
Preferred stock, $3.75 series, $3.75 per share	3.7	3.7	3.7
Common stock, $2.40 per share in 1981, $2.95 in 1980 and $5.30 in 1979	717.6	861.2	1,520.3
Total cash dividends	730.5	874.1	1,533.2
Balance at end of the year	15,340.0	15,737.1	17,373.7
Total Stockholders' Equity	$17,721.1	$17,814.6	$19,179.3

The preferred stock is subject to redemption at the option of the Board of Directors on any dividend date on not less than thirty days' notice at the redemption prices stated above plus accrued dividends.

The Certificate of Incorporation provides that no cash dividends may be paid on the common stock so long as current assets (excluding prepaid expenses) in excess of current liabilities of the Corporation are less than $75 per share of outstanding preferred stock. Such current assets (with inventories calculated on the FIFO basis) in excess of current liabilities were greater than $75 in respect of each share of outstanding preferred stock at December 31, 1981.

The overall policy with respect to the payment of dividends by consolidated subsidiaries is predicated on the laws of the respective countries in which the subsidiaries are located. Generally, dividend payments are based on accumulated earnings. In the opinion of

management, there are no restrictions on the payment of dividends by consolidated subsidiaries which would have a significant effect on the operations of the Corporation and its consolidated subsidiaries.

The equity of the Corporation and its consolidated subsidiaries in the net undistributed earnings, since acquisition, of non-consolidated subsidiaries and associates has been included in net income retained for use in the business and amounted to $1,314.3 million at December 31, 1981.

GMAC agreements with respect to outstanding subordinated indebtedness include, among other things, provisions which have the effect of limiting its payment of dividends to the Corporation. Under the most restrictive of these provisions, approximately $893.5 million of its net income retained for use in the business at December 31, 1981 was available for the payment of dividends.

NOTES TO FINANCIAL STATEMENTS (continued)

NOTE 13. Segment Reporting

General Motors is a highly vertically-integrated business operating primarily in a single industry consisting of the manufacture, assembly and sale of automobiles, trucks and related parts and accessories classified as automotive products. Because of the high degree of integration, substantial interdivisional and intercompany transfers of materials and services are made. Consequently, any determination of income by area of operations or class of products is necessarily arbitrary because of the allocation and reallocation of costs, including Corporate costs, benefiting more than one division or product.

Substantially all of General Motors' products are marketed through retail dealers and through distributors and jobbers in the United States and Canada and through distributors and dealers overseas.

To assist in the merchandising of General Motors' products, GMAC and its subsidiaries offer financial services and certain types of automobile insurance to dealers and customers.

Net sales, net income (loss), total and net assets and average number of employes in the U.S. and in locations outside the U.S. for 1981, 1980 and 1979 are summarized below. Net income (loss) is after provisions for deferred income taxes applicable to that portion of the undistributed earnings deemed to be not permanently invested, less available tax credits and deductions, and appropriate consolidating adjustments for the geographic areas set forth below. Interarea sales are made at negotiated selling prices.

1981	United States	Canada	Europe	Latin America	All Other	Total[1]
Net Sales:			(Dollars in Millions)			
Outside	$47,022.4	$4,099.2	$6,585.2	$2,730.0	$2,261.7	$62,698.5
Interarea	5,731.1	4,747.2	265.6	129.9	128.1	—
Total net sales	$52,753.5	$8,846.4	$6,850.8	$2,859.9	$2,389.8	$62,698.5
Net Income (Loss)	$ 763.3	($ 35.6)	($ 426.7)	($ 62.6)	$ 129.2	$ 333.4
Total Assets	$27,510.8	$2,772.8	$5,208.5	$2,642.8	$ 992.5	$38,991.2
Net Assets	$15,608.7	$ 832.6	$ 505.5	$ 640.7	$ 247.3	$17,721.1
Average Number of Employes (in thousands)	522	39	113	38	29	741

1980	United States	Canada	Europe	Latin America	All Other	Total[1]
Net Sales:			(Dollars in Millions)			
Outside	$41,637.4	$4,218.0	$7,437.6	$2,448.4	$1,987.1	$57,728.5
Interarea	5,287.1	3,876.7	317.5	72.3	64.3	—
Total net sales	$46,924.5	$8,094.7	$7,755.1	$2,520.7	$2,051.4	$57,728.5
Net Income (Loss)	($ 71.9)	($ 20.3)	($ 559.3)	$ 42.9	($ 150.8)	($ 762.5)
Total Assets	$25,494.2	$1,891.0	$4,319.3	$1,953.2	$1,029.9	$34,581.0
Net Assets	$15,753.6	$ 791.9	$ 670.6	$ 528.8	$ 152.0	$17,814.6
Average Number of Employes (in thousands)	517	37	125	37	30	746

1979	United States	Canada	Europe	Latin America	All Other	Total[1]
Net Sales:			(Dollars in Millions)			
Outside	$49,559.9	$4,611.8	$8,338.2	$2,023.8	$1,777.5	$66,311.2
Interarea	5,454.9	3,432.9	276.9	109.0	34.4	—
Total net sales	$55,014.8	$8,044.7	$8,615.1	$2,132.8	$1,811.9	$66,311.2
Net Income	$ 2,320.5	$ 224.1	$ 338.2	$ 14.5	$ 13.9	$ 2,892.7
Total Assets	$24,052.7	$1,884.2	$4,173.3	$1,237.9	$1,073.7	$32,215.8
Net Assets	$16,472.4	$ 754.9	$1,245.9	$ 366.8	$ 417.4	$19,179.3
Average Number of Employes (in thousands)	618	39	131	33	32	853

[1] After elimination of interarea transactions.

NOTES TO FINANCIAL STATEMENTS (concluded)

NOTE 14. Contingent Liabilities

There are various claims and pending actions against the Corporation and its subsidiaries with respect to commercial matters, including warranties and product liability, governmental regulations including environmental and safety matters, civil rights, patent matters, taxes and other matters arising out of the conduct of the business. Certain of these actions purport to be class actions, seeking damages in very large amounts. The amounts of liability on these claims and actions at December 31, 1981 were not determinable but, in the opinion of the management, the ultimate liability resulting will not materially affect the consolidated financial position or results of operations of the Corporation and its consolidated subsidiaries.

ACCOUNTANTS' REPORT

Deloitte Haskins · Sells
CERTIFIED PUBLIC ACCOUNTANTS

1114 Avenue of the Americas
New York 10036

General Motors Corporation, its Directors and Stockholders: February 8, 1982

We have examined the Consolidated Balance Sheet of General Motors Corporation and consolidated subsidiaries as of December 31, 1981 and 1980 and the related Statements of Consolidated Income and Changes in Consolidated Financial Position for each of the three years in the period ended December 31, 1981. Our examinations were made in accordance with generally accepted auditing standards and, accordingly, included such tests of the accounting records and such other auditing procedures as we considered necessary in the circumstances.

In our opinion, these financial statements present fairly the financial position of the companies at December 31, 1981 and 1980 and the results of their operations and the changes in their financial position for each of the three years in the period ended December 31, 1981, in conformity with generally accepted accounting principles applied on a consistent basis.

SUPPLEMENTARY INFORMATION

Selected Quarterly Data (Dollars in Millions Except Per Share Amounts)

	1981 Quarters				1980 Quarters			
	1st	2nd	3rd	4th	1st	2nd	3rd	4th
Net sales	$15,723.9	$18,015.1	$13,410.2	$15,549.3	$15,712.8	$13,785.5	$12,027.8	$16,202.4
Operating income (loss)	267.4	1,029.2	(959.5)	55.0	161.4 (	834.6) (	960.4)	447.9
Income (loss) before income taxes	261.5	892.4	(1,155.8) (	136.2)	173.6 (	862.3) (	1,025.6)	345.4
United States, foreign and other income taxes (credit)	130.8	446.2	(585.0) (	115.1)	60.8 (	377.6) (	386.0)	317.5
Income (loss) after income taxes	130.7	446.2	(570.8) (	21.1)	112.8 (	484.7) (	639.6)	27.9
Equity in earnings of nonconsolidated subsidiaries and associates	59.6	68.4	102.6	117.8	41.9	72.8	72.6	33.8
Net income (loss)	190.3	514.6	(468.2)	96.7	154.7 (	411.9) (	567.0)	61.7
Dividends on preferred stocks	3.2	3.3	3.2	3.2	3.2	3.3	3.2	3.2
Earnings (loss) on common stock	$ 187.1	$ 511.3	($ 471.4)	$ 93.5	$ 151.5	($ 415.2)	($ 570.2)	$ 58.5
Average number of shares of common stock outstanding (in millions)	297.2	298.2	299.2	301.6	290.2	291.5	293.1	294.8
Earnings (loss) per share of common stock*	$0.63	$1.72	($1.59)	$0.31	$0.52	($1.43)	($1.95)	$0.21
Dividends per share of common stock	$0.60	$0.60	$0.60	$0.60	$1.15	$0.60	$0.60	$0.60
Stock price range**								
High	$56.13	$58.00	$53.13	$46.50	$55.75	$49.50	$58.88	$54.13
Low	$43.88	$51.38	$42.63	$33.88	$44.00	$39.50	$46.38	$40.38

*Includes favorable (unfavorable) effects on EPS of revisions to pension plans in 1981 (second quarter—$0.33, third quarter—$0.20, fourth quarter—$0.16), reductions in accruals due to salaried policy modifications in the fourth quarter of 1981—$0.25, and foreign exchange/translation activity (1981: first quarter—$0.19, second quarter—$0.45, third quarter—$0.64, fourth quarter —($0.53); 1980: first quarter—$0.27, second quarter—($0.41), third quarter—$0.21, fourth quarter—$0.56).
**The principal market is the New York Stock Exchange and prices are based on the Composite Tape. As of December 31, 1981, there were 1,122,167 holders of record of common stock.

The consolidated effective income tax rate (credit) for the fourth quarter of 1981 was higher than would be expected as a result of the combination of the high level of U.S. investment tax credits and the low level of earnings.

The consolidated effective income tax rates varied from the U.S. statutory income tax rate (credit) in the first and third quarters of 1980 due principally to a combination of lower earnings and the continuing high level of U.S. investment tax credits. The consolidated effective income tax rate for the 1980 fourth quarter was higher than would be expected due to the adjustment of the estimated annual effective tax rate, used throughout the year, as a result of increased losses at overseas subsidiaries where no applicable tax credits were currently available, coupled with additional U.S. income taxes due to improved U.S. performance during the quarter.

Selected Financial Data (Dollars in Millions Except Per Share Amounts)

	1981	1980	1979	1978	1977
Net sales	$62,698.5	$57,728.5	$66,311.2	$63,221.1	$54,961.3
Earnings (loss) on common stock	$ 320.5	($ 775.4)	$ 2,879.8	$ 3,495.1	$ 3,324.6
Dividends on common stock	717.6	861.2	1,520.3	1,712.6	1,944.8
Net income (loss) retained in the year	($ 397.1)	($ 1,636.6)	$ 1,359.5	$ 1,782.5	$ 1,379.8
Earnings (loss) on common stock—per share	$1.07	($2.65)	$10.04	$12.24	$11.62
Dividends on common stock—per share	2.40	2.95	5.30	6.00	6.80
Net income (loss) retained in the year—per share	($1.33)	($5.60)	$ 4.74	$ 6.24	$ 4.82
Average shares of common stock outstanding (in millions)	299.1	292.4	286.8	285.5	286.1
Dividends on capital stock as a percent of net income	219.1%	N.A.	53.0%	49.2%	58.7%
Expenditures for real estate, plants and equipment	$ 6,563.3	$ 5,160.5	$ 3,351.3	$ 2,695.5	$ 1,833.0
Expenditures for special tools	$ 3,178.1	$ 2,600.0	$ 2,015.0	$ 1,826.7	$ 1,775.8
Working capital	$ 1,161.0	$ 3,212.1	$ 6,751.0	$ 7,991.2	$ 7,668.2
Total assets	$38,991.2	$34,581.0	$32,215.8	$30,598.3	$26,658.3
Long-term debt and capitalized leases	$ 4,043.9	$ 2,058.3	$ 1,030.8	$ 1,124.5	$ 1,201.2

EFFECTS OF INFLATION ON FINANCIAL DATA

Inflation remains the nemesis of the orderly conduct of business. Its adverse ramifications are dramatized when the effects of inflation are taken into account in the evaluation of comparative financial results.

The accompanying Schedules display the basic historical cost financial data adjusted for general inflation (constant dollar) and also for changes in specific prices (current cost) for use in such evaluation. The Schedules are intended to help readers of financial data assess results in the following specific areas:

    a. The erosion of general purchasing power,
    b. Enterprise performance,
    c. The erosion of operating capability, and
    d. Future cash flows.

In reviewing these Schedules, the following comments may be of assistance in understanding the reasons for the different "income" amounts and the uses of the data.

Financial statements—historical cost method

The objective of financial statements, and the primary purpose of accounting, is to furnish, to the fullest extent practicable, objective, quantifiable summaries of the results of financial transactions to those who need or wish to judge management's ability to manage. The data are prepared by management and audited by the independent public accountants.

The present accounting system in general use in the United States and the financial statements prepared by major companies from that system were never intended to be measures of relative economic value, but instead are basically a history of transactions which have occurred and by which current and potential investors and creditors can evaluate their expectations. There are many subjective, analytical, and economic factors which must be taken into consideration when evaluating a company. Those factors cannot be quantified objectively. Just as the financial statements cannot present in reasonable, objective, quantifiable form all of the data necessary to evaluate a business, they also should not be expected to furnish all the data needed to evaluate the effect of inflation on a company.

Data adjusted for general inflation—constant dollar method

Financial reporting is, of necessity, stated in dollars. It is generally recognized that the purchasing power of a dollar has deteriorated in recent years, and the costs of raw materials and other items as well as wage rates have increased and can be expected to increase further in the future. It is not as generally recognized, however, that profit dollars also are subject to the same degree of reduction in purchasing power. Far too much attention is given to the absolute level of profits rather than the relationship of profits to other factors in the business and to the general price level. For example, as shown in Schedule A, adjusting the annual amount of sales and net income (loss) to a constant 1967 dollar base, using the U.S. Bureau of Labor Statistics' Consumer Price Index for Urban Consumers (CPI-U), demonstrates that constant dollar profits have not increased in recent years in line with the changes in sales volume. This is reflected in the general decline in the net income (loss) as a percent of sales over that period as well as the decrease in the dividends paid in terms of constant dollars of purchasing power.

The constant dollar income statement contains only two basic adjustments. Most importantly, the provision for depreciation is recalculated. Historical dollar accounting understates the economic cost of plant and equipment consumed in production because the depreciation charge is based on the original dollar cost of assets acquired over a period of years. Constant dollar depreciation restates such expense based on asset values adjusted to reflect increases in the CPI-U subsequent to acquisition or construction of the related plant and equipment. In addition to recalculating depreciation expense, cost of goods sold is adjusted to reflect changes in the CPI-U for the portion of inventories not stated on the last-in, first-out (LIFO) basis in the conventional financial statements. Other items of income and expense are not adjusted because they generally reflect transactions that took place in 1981 and, therefore, were recorded in average 1981 dollars.

Data adjusted for changes in specific prices—current cost method

Another manner in which to analyze the effect of inflation on financial data (and thus the business) is by adjusting the historical cost data to the current costs for the major balance sheet items which have been accumulated through the accounting system over a period of years and which thus reflect different prices for the same commodities and services.

The purpose of this type of restatement is to furnish estimates of the effect of price increases for replacement of inventories and property on the potential future net income of the business and thus assess the probability of future cash flows. Although these data may be useful for this purpose, they do not reflect specific plans for the replacement of property. A more meaningful estimate of the effect of such costs on future earnings is the estimated level of future capital expenditures which is set forth on page 16 in the Financial Review: Management's Discussion and Analysis.

Summary

In the accompanying Schedules, the effects of the application of the preceding methods on the last five years' and the current year's operations are summarized. Under both the constant dollar and the current cost methods, the net income of General Motors is lower (or the net loss is higher) than that determined under the historical cost method. This means that business, as well as individuals, is affected by inflation and that the purchasing power of business dollars also has declined. In addition, the costs of maintaining the productive capacity, as reflected in the current cost data (and estimate of future capital expenditures), have increased, and thus management must seek ways to cope with the impact of inflation through accounting methods such as the LIFO method of inventory valuation, which matches current costs with current revenues, and through accelerated methods of depreciation.

Another significant adjustment is the restatement of stockholders' equity—the investment base. The adjustment for general inflation puts all the expenditures for these items on a consistent purchasing power basis—the average 1967 dollar. This adjustment decreases the historical stockholders' equity, as represented by net assets in Schedule A, of about $17.7 billion at December 31, 1981 to a constant dollar basis of $10.2 billion. In other words, the $17.7 billion represented in the financial statements has only $10.2 billion of purchasing power expressed in 1967 dollars. The net assets adjusted for specific prices, as shown in Schedule A, amounted to $10.4 billion at December 31, 1981. This is $0.2 billion higher than that shown on a constant dollar basis due to the fact that the CPI-U index is accelerating more rapidly than the indices of specific prices applicable to General Motors.

Finally, it must be emphasized that there is a continuing need for national monetary and fiscal policies designed to control inflation and to provide adequate capital for future business growth which, in turn, will mean increased productivity and employment.

SCHEDULE A

Comparison of Selected Data Adjusted for Effects of Changing Prices
(Dollars in Millions Except Per Share Amounts)
Historical cost data adjusted for general inflation (constant dollar) and changes in specific prices (current cost). (A)

	1981	1980	1979	1978	1977
Net Sales—as reported	$62,698.5	$57,728.5	$66,311.2	$63,221.1	$54,961.3
—in constant 1967 dollars	23,017.1	23,390.8	30,501.9	32,354.7	30,281.7
Net Income (Loss)—as reported	$ 333.4	($ 762.5)	$ 2,892.7	$ 3,508.0	$ 3,337.5
—in constant 1967 dollars	(305.8)(B)	(1,023.8)	817.0	1,384.5	1,580.9
—in current cost 1967 dollars	(252.8)(B)	(829.5)	829.5		
Earnings (Loss) per share of common stock—as reported	$1.07	($2.65)	$10.04	$12.24	$11.62
—in constant 1967 dollars	(1.04)(B)	(3.52)	2.83	4.83	5.50
—in current cost 1967 dollars	(0.86)(B)	(2.86)	2.87		
Dividends per share of common stock—as reported	$2.40	$2.95	$5.30	$6.00	$6.80
—in constant 1967 dollars	0.88	1.20	2.44	3.07	3.75
Net income (loss) as a percent of sales—as reported	0.5%	(1.3%)	4.4%	5.5%	6.1%
—in constant 1967 dollars	(1.3)	(4.4)	2.7	4.3	5.2
—in current cost 1967 dollars	(1.1)	(3.5)	2.7		
Net income (loss) as a percent of stockholders' equity—as reported	1.9%	(4.3%)	15.1%	20.0%	21.2%
—in constant 1967 dollars	(3.0)	(9.4)	6.7	11.2	13.1
—in current cost 1967 dollars	(2.4)	(7.3)	6.4		
Net assets at year-end—as reported	$17,721.1	$17,814.6	$19,179.3	$17,569.9	$15,766.9
—in constant 1967 dollars	10,247.2	10,887.6	12,163.4	12,351.3	12,041.4
—in current cost 1967 dollars	10,450.9	11,377.2	12,982.7		
Unrealized gain from decline in purchasing power of dollars of net amounts owed	$ 241.3	$ 182.3	$ 83.8		
Excess of increase in general price level over increase in specific prices of inventory and property	$ 619.0	$ 689.2	$ 221.8		
Market price per common share at year-end—unadjusted	$38.50	$45.00	$50.00	$53.75	$62.88
—in constant 1967 dollars	14.13	18.23	23.00	27.51	34.64
Average Consumer Price Index	272.4	246.8	217.4	195.4	181.5

(A) Adjusted data have been determined by applying the Consumer Price Index — Urban to the data with 1967 (CPI-100) as the base year. Depreciation has been determined on a straight-line basis for this calculation.

(B) These amounts will differ from those shown for constant dollar and current cost in Schedule B because a different base year (1981) has been used in Schedule B in order to illustrate the effect of changing prices in an alternative form.

SCHEDULE B

Schedule of Income Adjusted for Changing Prices
For The Year Ended December 31, 1981
(Dollars in Millions Except Per Share Amounts)

	As Reported in the Financial Statements (Historical Cost)	Adjusted for General Inflation (1981 Constant Dollar)	Adjusted for Changes in Specific Prices (1981 Current Cost)
Net Sales	$62,698.5	$62,698.5	$62,698.5
Cost of sales	55,185.2	55,766.5	55,413.5
Depreciation and amortization expense	4,406.2	4,991.6	5,200.1
Other operating and nonoperating items—net	2,896.8	2,896.8	2,896.8
United States and other income taxes (credit)	(123.1)	(123.1)	(123.1)
Total costs and expenses	62,365.1	63,531.8	63,387.3
Net Income (Loss)	$ 333.4	($ 833.3)(A)	($ 688.8)(A)
Earnings (Loss) per share of common stock	$1.07	($2.83)(A)	($2.35)(A)
Unrealized gain from decline in purchasing power of dollars of net amounts owed		$ 657.3	$ 657.3
Excess of increase in general price level over increase in specific prices of inventory and property			$ 1,686.2 (B)

(A) These amounts will differ from those shown for constant dollar and current cost in Schedule A because a different base year (1967) has been used in Schedule A in order to illustrate the effect of changing prices in an alternative form.

(B) At December 31, 1981, current cost of inventory was $9,299.8 million and current cost of property (including special tools), net of accumulated depreciation and amortization, was $28,710.8 million. The current cost of property owned and the related depreciation and amortization expense were calculated by applying (1) selected producer price indices to historical book values of machinery and equipment and (2) the Marshall Valuation Service index to buildings, and the use of assessed values for land.

MODERN MERCHANDISING, INC.

For Years Ended January 31, 1981, and February 2, 1980

Consolidated Balance Sheets
Modern Merchandising, Inc. and Subsidiaries

Assets	January 31, 1981	February 2, 1980
Current Assets:		
Cash (Note D)	$ 11,160,529	$ 10,018,805
Accounts receivable, less allowance for doubtful accounts of $515,000 and $378,000, respectively	20,461,898	22,187,065
Merchandise inventories	147,418,894	199,328,595
Prepaid expenses and other current assets	7,740,826	5,827,525
Total Current Assets	186,782,147	237,361,990
Property and Equipment, net (Notes C, D and H):		
Owned property and equipment, less accumulated depreciation of $17,215,797 and $12,613,547, respectively	45,237,013	38,235,945
Leased property under capital leases, less accumulated amortization of $17,013,327 and $12,159,768, respectively	86,599,943	75,425,413
	131,836,956	113,661,358
Other Assets:		
Intangibles arising on consolidation, less accumulated amortization of $1,807,991 and $1,501,302, respectively	10,717,684	11,024,373
Deferred tax charges	1,495,980	1,159,976
Miscellaneous	1,613,451	1,979,770
	13,827,115	14,164,119
	$332,446,218	$365,187,467
Liabilities and Stockholders' Equity		
Current Liabilities:		
Notes payable (Note D):		
Bank	$ 7,000,000	$ 57,500,000
Commercial paper		19,502,200
Other		412,837
Accounts payable	55,314,361	36,114,304
Checks outstanding, net	18,792,759	9,908,852
Taxes on income:		
Current	1,787,840	4,877,343
Deferred	3,666,000	1,992,000
Other current liabilities	14,028,130	14,922,704
Dividends payable	413,945	
Current portion of long-term debt (Notes D and H)	7,338,316	4,465,233
Total Current Liabilities	108,341,351	149,695,473
Long-Term Debt:		
Notes and contracts payable (Note D)	31,681,310	36,940,672
Obligations under capital leases (Note H)	95,211,378	81,998,389
10% subordinated debentures (Note D)	3,283,793	3,581,547
	130,176,481	122,520,608
Lease Commitments (Note H)		
Stockholders' Equity (Notes D and E):		
Common stock, par value $.01 a share, authorized 20,000,000 shares; issued and outstanding 8,278,799 and 8,104,549; respectively	82,788	81,044
Additional paid-in capital	28,596,066	26,893,362
Retained earnings	65,249,532	65,996,980
	93,928,386	92,971,386
	$332,446,218	$365,187,467

See notes to consolidated financial statements.

Consolidated Statements of Earnings

Modern Merchandising, Inc. and Subsidiaries

	Fiscal year ended		Seven months ended
	January 31, 1981	February 2, 1980	February 3, 1979
Revenues	**$678,758,905**	$678,819,697	$360,702,282
Costs and Expenses:			
Cost of sales	518,309,182	516,737,129	266,876,913
Selling, general and administrative	138,919,610	123,962,552	61,012,155
Interest on borrowings	11,286,981	8,378,267	3,260,940
Interest on capitalized leases	8,657,240	6,629,095	2,806,935
Gain on insurance recovery (Note G)	(686,675)		
	676,486,338	655,707,043	333,956,943
Earnings Before Taxes on Income	2,272,567	23,112,654	26,745,339
Taxes on Income (Note F)	961,000	10,373,000	12,801,000
Net Earnings	$ 1,311,567	$ 12,739,654	$ 13,944,339
Net Earnings per Common and Common Equivalent Share	$.15	$1.52	$1.66
Weighted Average Number of Common and Common Equivalent Shares Outstanding	8,479,856	8,399,488	8,423,754

See notes to consolidated financial statements.

Consolidated Statements of Stockholders' Equity

Modern Merchandising, Inc. and Subsidiaries

	Common stock	Additional paid-in capital	Retained earnings
Balances at July 1, 1978	$80,469	$26,673,853	$42,215,355
Adjustment for the cumulative effect of applying retroactively the new method of accounting for vacation pay (net of income taxes of $630,000)			(641,048)
Balances at July 1, 1978, as adjusted	80,469	26,673,853	41,574,307
Issuance of common shares under exercise of stock options and warrants, 25,872 shares	259	109,460	
Cash dividends declared—$.13 per share			(1,048,205)
Net earnings for the period			13,944,339
Balances at February 3, 1979	80,728	26,783,313	54,470,441
Issuance of common shares under exercise of stock options and warrants, 31,600 shares	316	110,049	
Cash dividends declared—$.15 per share (Note E)			(1,213,115)
Net earnings for the year			12,739,654
Balances at February 2, 1980	81,044	26,893,362	65,996,980
Issuance of common shares under exercise of stock options and warrants, 46,045 shares	461	453,988	
Issuance of common shares to employee stock ownership plan	1,283	1,248,716	
Cash dividends declared—$.25 per share (Note E)			(2,059,015)
Net earnings for the year			1,311,567
Balances at January 31, 1981	$82,788	$28,596,066	$65,249,532

See notes to consolidated financial statements.

Consolidated Statements of Changes
in Financial Position
Modern Merchandising, Inc. and Subsidiaries

	Fiscal year ended		Seven months ended
	January 31, 1981	February 2, 1980	February 3, 1979
Source of Working Capital:			
Operations:			
Net earnings	$ 1,311,567	$ 12,739,654	$ 13,944,339
Depreciation and amortization	10,640,970	8,597,448	3,733,860
Deferred taxes on income	(336,004)	519,204	(486,000)
	11,616,533	21,856,306	17,192,199
Increase in obligations under capital leases	16,085,066	23,027,383	13,436,858
Issuance of common shares to employee stock ownership plan	1,249,999		
Proceeds from long-term borrowings	669,312	15,413,268	7,006,396
Common stock issued	454,449	110,365	109,719
Proceeds from disposal of property and equipment	417,885	113,291	1,862,909
Decrease in other assets	366,319	(847,498)	(100,562)
	30,859,563	59,673,115	39,507,519
Application of Working Capital:			
Additions to leased property under capital leases	16,028,089	23,048,160	13,540,802
Additions to owned property and equipment	12,899,675	15,114,047	9,584,523
Current maturities and payments on long-term debt	9,128,505	9,796,197	1,155,861
Net assets of purchased subsidiary (Note B)		2,863,765	
Cash dividends declared	2,059,015	1,213,115	1,048,205
	40,115,284	52,035,284	25,329,391
(Decrease) Increase in Working Capital	$ (9,225,721)	$ 7,637,831	$ 14,178,128
Changes in Components of Working Capital:			
Increase (decrease) in current assets:			
Cash	$ 1,141,724	$ 4,553,744	$ 170,891
Accounts receivable	(1,725,167)	10,209,637	(1,326,661)
Merchandise inventories	(51,909,701)	67,799,153	(21,108,221)
Prepaid expenses and other current assets	1,913,301	(3,278,128)	5,211,187
	(50,579,843)	79,284,406	(17,052,804)
Decrease (increase) in current liabilities:			
Notes payable	70,415,037	(47,402,465)	7,746,997
Accounts payable	(19,200,057)	(16,867,786)	33,108,999
Checks outstanding, net	(8,883,907)	(4,454,030)	(5,454,822)
Taxes on income	1,415,503	1,657,564	(3,479,456)
Other current liabilities	894,574	(2,786,277)	(118,364)
Dividends payable	(413,945)	403,847	(81,964)
Current portion of long-term debt	(2,873,083)	(2,197,428)	(490,458)
	41,354,122	(71,646,575)	31,230,932
(Decrease) Increase in Working Capital	$ (9,225,721)	$ 7,637,831	$ 14,178,128

See notes to consolidated financial statements.

Notes to Consolidated Financial Statements
Modern Merchandising, Inc. and Subsidiaries
Fiscal Years Ended January 31, 1981 and February 2, 1980, and Seven
Months Ended February 3, 1979

A. Summary of significant accounting policies:

Consolidation:
The consolidated financial statements include the accounts of the Company and its subsidiaries after elimination of all material intercompany balances and transactions.

Change in year-end:
Effective February 3, 1979, the Company changed its fiscal year-end from the Saturday closest to June 30 to the Saturday closest to January 31.

Merchandise inventories:
Merchandise inventories are stated at the lower of cost (first-in, first-out) or market.

Property and depreciation:
Owned property and equipment are stated at cost. Depreciation is computed using principally the straight-line method, based on the following estimated useful lives: buildings—to a maximum of 45 years, leasehold improvements—the shorter of the estimated useful lives or the lease period of the respective depreciable assets and equipment—3 to 15 years.
Leased property under capital leases are capitalized based on the present value of future lease obligations and are amortized using the straight-line method over the life of the lease.

Intangibles:
Intangibles arising on consolidation represent the excess of cost over the net assets of acquired companies, less amortization using the straight-line method over periods not exceeding 40 years.

Taxes on income:
Provision is made for deferred income taxes and deferred tax charges applicable to timing differences between financial and tax reporting. These timing differences consist primarily of certain inventories of subsidiaries being valued for income tax purposes using the last-in, first-out (LIFO) method, differences between book and tax methods of depreciation and lease accounting and a subsidiary's change from the cash basis to accrual basis method of income tax reporting.
The Company records the investment tax credit as a reduction of federal income taxes in the year eligible equipment purchases are placed in service.

Preopening costs:
Preopening costs of catalog showroom stores are charged against operations as incurred.

Earnings per share:
Net earnings per common and common equivalent share are based upon the weighted average number of common and common equivalent shares outstanding during the respective periods. Common equivalent shares represent the dilutive effect of stock options and warrants. Assuming full dilution, the net earnings per share would be substantially the same.

B. Acquisition:
Effective May 5, 1979, the Company acquired all of the outstanding stock of Leeds Holding, Inc., a catalog showroom holding company, for $2,475,000 in cash and a $7,500,000 promissory note payable in five annual principal installments of $1,500,000 which commenced in May, 1980 and bears interest at the rate of 8½% per annum. The acquisition has been accounted for as a purchase. The earnings of Leeds Holding, Inc. have been included in the consolidated financial statements since the effective date of acquisition.
Pro forma results of operations as though Leeds Holding, Inc. had been combined with the Company for the entire seven months ended February 3, 1979 and fiscal year ended February 2, 1980 are as follows:

(Unaudited)	Fiscal year ended February 2, 1980	Seven months ended February 3, 1979
Revenues	$685,354,000	$383,730,000
Net earnings	12,919,000	14,913,000
Net earnings per common and common equivalent share	$1.54	$1.77

C. Owned property and equipment:

	January 31, 1981	February 2, 1980
Cost:		
Land	$ 5,727,386	$ 4,162,839
Buildings	10,969,236	8,355,858
Leasehold improvements	10,510,405	9,919,038
Equipment	32,625,547	28,266,274
	59,832,574	50,704,009
Less accumulated depreciation	17,215,797	12,613,547
	42,616,777	38,090,462
Construction in progress	2,620,236	145,483
	$45,237,013	$38,235,945

Depreciation expense was $5,480,722 and $4,571,301 respectively, for the fiscal years ended January 31, 1981 and February 2, 1980 and $2,036,303 for the seven months ended February 3, 1979.

D. Debt:

On January 31, 1981, the Company had available annually renewable, unsecured seasonal lines of bank credit totaling $78,500,000, of which $71,500,000 was unused. Borrowing under these lines is at the prime interest rate. In compensation for the line of credit arrangements with the banks, the Company was expected to and did maintain average compensating balances of approximately $9,900,000 during the year ended January 31, 1981 and $3,900,000 during the year ended February 2, 1980. These balances, which have no restrictions on withdrawals, served as part of the Company's operating cash balance and, at certain banks, served additionally as compensation for account handling and other services. There are no significant commitment fees connected with these seasonal lines of bank credit.

Notes and contracts payable consist of:

	January 31, 1981	February 2, 1980
Promissory notes, 9.125%, due in semi-annual installments of $1,700,000	$15,300,000	$17,000,000
Promissory note, 8.5%, due in annual installments of $1,500,000	6,000,000	7,500,000
Industrial revenue bond, 7.375%, due in April, 2004 and requiring annual sinking fund payments of $390,000 commencing April, 1990	5,900,000	5,900,000
Promissory note, 8.5%, due in annual installments of $300,000	2,100,000	2,400,000
Building mortgages, 9.875% and 9.125%, due in monthly installments of $20,635, including interest, through August, 2002 and $12,159 through December, 2009	2,337,180	2,359,906
Industrial revenue bonds, 7.375%, due in October, 2003 and requiring annual sinking fund payments of $130,000 commencing October, 1989	2,000,000	2,000,000
Industrial revenue bonds, 5.5% and 6.5%, due in installments of $500,000 in 1987 and in 2007	1,000,000	1,000,000
Other notes and contracts payable	1,270,511	855,307
	35,907,691	39,015,213
Less current portion	4,226,381	2,074,541
	$31,681,310	$36,940,672

The most restrictive long-term debt agreements of the Company contain provisions (1) limiting additional funded debt, security interests and other indebtedness or guarantees by the Company; (2) requiring the maintenance of $87,500,000 of tangible net worth; (3) requiring the maintenance of net working capital at a level at least 150% of total funded debt, as defined, and a ratio of current assets to current liabilities of 120% on the last day of the first and third fiscal quarters and 140% on the last day of the second and fourth fiscal quarters, and (4) imposing certain restrictions on the payment of cash dividends upon common shares. Approximately $27,000,000 of retained earnings were available for dividends at January 31, 1981.

Owned property and equipment carried at approximately $9,130,000 at January 31, 1981 is pledged as collateral under the notes and contracts payable.

The 10% subordinated debentures are due June 1, 1987 and require an annual sinking fund payment of $500,000 which began June 1, 1979. The debentures are subordinate to notes and contracts payable and short-term notes payable and were redeemable beginning June 1, 1979 at their principal amount through operation of a sinking fund. The debentures are also callable at the option of the Company at prices ranging downward from 107.8%.

Aggregate long-term debt maturities and sinking fund requirements, excluding lease obligations, are as follows for each of the next five years ending in:

1982	$4,655,450
1983	5,829,761
1984	5,692,614
1985	5,705,825
1986	4,219,468

Interest expense on debt was as follows:

	Fiscal year ended		Seven months ended
	January 31, 1981	February 2, 1980	February 3, 1979
Capital lease obligations	$ 8,657,240	$ 6,629,095	$2,806,935
Long-term debt, including $64,850, $96,726 and $96,726 of amortization of debt discount, respectively	3,726,051	3,575,676	1,620,181
Short-term debt	7,560,930	4,802,591	1,640,759
	$19,944,221	$15,007,362	$6,067,875

E. Stockholders' equity and stock options:

Due to the change in year end, the fourth quarter dividend declaration for the fiscal year ended February 2, 1980 was not made until after year end. Subsequent to that date, cash dividends of $.05 per share, or $405,352, were declared.

In 1972, the Company adopted a qualified stock option plan and reserved 250,000 shares for issuance thereunder. Options are granted at not less than 100% of market value and are exercisable within five years after grant. Any options still outstanding on May 21, 1981 become non-qualified under the Tax Reform Act of 1976.

In December 1976, the Company granted a non-qualified stock option for 20,000 shares at $12.13 per share. The option became exercisable on date of grant and expires in December 1981.

In August 1980, the Company granted a non-qualified stock option for 10,000 shares at $14.50 per share. The option became exercisable on date of grant and expires in August 1985.

At January 31, 1981, 405,921 shares of common stock were reserved for exercise of common stock warrants at $4.20 per share which expire June 1, 1982.

Additional data about stock options is summarized as follows:

	Number of shares	Option price (1)	
		Per share	Total
Stock options outstanding:			
At July 1, 1978	104,439	$ 2.00 -$12.69	$1,011,591
Granted	2,000	15.25	30,500
Cancelled	(1,626)	2.00	(3,252)
Exercised	(10,162)	2.00 - 12.69	(43,737)
At February 3, 1979	94,651	2.00 - 15.25	995,102
Granted	10,290	13.75	141,488
Cancelled	(5,100)	12.69 - 13.75	(67,894)
Exercised	(15,400)	2.00 - 12.69	(42,330)
At February 2, 1980	84,441	3.55 - 15.25	1,026,366
Granted	15,000	14.50	217,500
Cancelled	(2,251)	3.55 - 12.69	(26,266)
Exercised	(35,645)	3.55 - 13.75	(410,769)
At January 31, 1981	61,545	$12.13 -$15.25	$ 806,831

(1) Option price is the same as the market price in all cases above except for the shares exercised and is the average of the bid and asked prices on the over-the-counter market or the closing price on the New York Stock Exchange on the date granted. Options were exercised at a market price of $10.75 to $15.00 and aggregated $495,269 in the fiscal year ended January 31, 1981, $12.25 to $14.88 and aggregated $216,788 in the fiscal year ended February 2, 1980 and $13.88 to $18.25 and aggregated $151,305 during the seven months ended February 3, 1979.

F. Taxes on income:

	Fiscal year ended		Seven months ended
	January 31, 1981	February 2, 1980	February 3, 1979
Current:			
Federal	$ (739,000)	$ 7,694,000	$11,020,000
State	513,000	941,000	1,796,000
	(226,000)	8,635,000	12,816,000
Deferred:			
Federal	1,068,000	1,487,000	(13,000)
State	119,000	251,000	(2,000)
	1,187,000	1,738,000	(15,000)
Provision for taxes on income	$ 961,000	$10,373,000	$12,801,000

The principal items creating timing differences for which deferred tax charges (credits) on income are provided are:

LIFO method of valuing certain inventories of subsidiaries	$ 1,562,000	$ 1,979,000	
Amortization and interest on leases capitalized for financial statement purposes in excess of related rent	(1,233,000)	(915,000)	$ (422,000)
Excess of tax depreciation over book depreciation	828,000	854,000	249,000
Cash basis income tax reporting for a subsidiary	(73,000)	(71,000)	(81,000)
Other	103,000	(109,000)	239,000
	$ 1,187,000	$ 1,738,000	$ (15,000)

A reconciliation of the expected federal income taxes at ordinary rates with the provision for income taxes is as follows:

Computed expected federal income tax expense	46.0%	46.0%	48.0%
State and city income taxes, net of federal tax benefit	14.2	2.8	3.0
Investment and jobs tax credits	(25.3)	(4.3)	(2.8)
Amortization of intangibles arising on consolidation	6.2	.6	.3
Other	1.2	(.2)	(.6)
Provision for taxes on income	42.3%	44.9%	47.9%

G. Gain on insurance recovery:

On May 9, 1980, the Company's Minnetonka, Minnesota showroom was destroyed by fire. A gain of $686,675, less taxes of $371,000, was recognized in the fourth quarter of the year ended January 31, 1981 from the business interruption insurance proceeds and the excess of insurance proceeds over the related book value of inventory and property and equipment destroyed in the fire.

H. Leases:

Substantially all of the Company's showrooms are leased under leases with initial terms of 25 years and usually provide for one or more five-year renewal options. Certain of these leases include provisions for rent in addition to minimum annual rentals based on certain contingencies, such as sales performance.

Leased assets included in the accompanying balance sheets are as follows:

	January 31, 1981	February 2, 1980
Buildings	$ 96,997,478	$ 84,349,822
Equipment	6,615,792	3,235,359
	103,613,270	87,585,181
Less accumulated amortization	(17,013,327)	(12,159,768)
	$ 86,599,943	$ 75,425,413

Several of the Company's showrooms, currently carried at $5,745,000, are leased under industrial revenue bonds expiring through 2003. The Company can purchase the facilities for nominal amounts at the expiration of the bonds.

Amortization of property under capital leases was $4,853,559 and $3,659,926 respectively, for the fiscal years ended January 31, 1981 and February 2, 1980 and $1,460,571 for the seven months ended February 3, 1979.

Rental expense was as follows:

	Fiscal year ended		Seven months ended
	January 31, 1981	February 2, 1980	February 3, 1979
Minimum rentals— operating leases	$4,655,745	$4,433,403	$2,238,000
Contingent rentals— all leases	301,565	360,725	210,000
	$4,957,310	$4,794,128	$2,448,000

Sublease rentals were not material.

Minimum future obligations on leases in effect at January 31, 1981 that had initial noncancellable lease terms in excess of one year are as follows for the years ending in:

	Capital leases	Operating leases
1982	$ 11,994,481	$ 2,128,428
1983	12,043,469	2,034,842
1984	12,060,217	1,854,014
1985	11,620,865	1,558,328
1986	11,193,885	1,351,046
Later	167,456,695	12,174,703
Total minimum obligation	226,369,612	$21,101,361
Less amount representing interest	128,475,368	
Present value of net minimum obligation	97,894,244	
Less current portion	2,682,866	
Long-term obligation at January 31, 1981	$95,211,378	
Long-term obligation at February 2, 1980	$81,998,389	

Subsequent to January 31, 1981 the Company has entered into additional showroom leases covering land and buildings. The aggregate minimum annual rental commitments under these leases are estimated to be approximately $630,000 with the lease periods extending through 2011.

I. Accounting for vacation pay:

Prior to 1980, the Company accounted for vacation pay as an expense when paid; whereas, in the fourth quarter of the year ended January 31, 1981, the Company began accounting for vacation pay as earned. The new method of accounting was adopted to conform to Statement of Financial Accounting Standards No. 43, "Accounting for Compensated Absences." The accounting change decreased net earnings and net earnings per common and common equivalent share for the year ended January 31, 1981 by $93,000 and $.01, respectively.

The cumulative effect of this change, net of applicable income tax benefit, has been applied retroactively to June 29, 1975 retained earnings. Net earnings for the periods subsequently ended have not been restated since the effect of the change in these periods is not material.

J. Incentive compensation and stock ownership plan:

The Company has a management incentive plan which provides for incentive payments to certain members of the management group. Payments under the plan are determined under a formula whereby the participants receive a graduated percentage of base compensation upon the Company's attaining a specified level of performance in earnings per share. For the seven month period ended February 3, 1979, a total of $453,000 was accrued under the plan for all management participants. For the fiscal years ended January 31, 1981 and February 2, 1980, no incentive payments were accrued.

The Company has an employee stock ownership plan covering most employees. Contributions to the plan are made at the discretion of the Board of Directors with the maximum contribution in any one year being the maximum amount deductible for federal income taxes. Costs and expenses include approximately $293,000, $1,450,000 and $550,000 for contributions to the plan for the fiscal years ended January 31, 1981 and February 2, 1980 and for the seven months ended February 3, 1979, respectively.

K. Segment information:

The Company is principally engaged in the business of selling general merchandise through catalog showrooms and in the business of publishing merchandise catalogs.

Information on the Company's business segments is as follows:

(in thousands)	Fiscal year ended January 31, 1981	Fiscal year ended February 2, 1980	Seven months ended February 3, 1979
Revenues from unaffiliated companies:			
Catalog Showrooms	$646,908	$630,947	$329,892
Catalog publishing	31,851	47,873	30,810
Total	$678,759	$678,820	$360,702
Intersegment revenues—			
Catalog publishing	$ 11,467	$ 11,118	$ 5,701
Operating earnings:			
Catalog showrooms	$ 20,330	$ 33,536	$ 28,255
Catalog publishing	5,080	7,296	6,207
Total	25,410	40,832	34,462
General corporate expenses	(3,193)	(2,712)	(1,649)
Interest expense	(19,944)	(15,007)	(6,068)
Earnings before taxes on income	$ 2,273	$ 23,113	$ 26,745
Identifiable assets:			
Catalog showrooms	$317,848	$350,252	$240,371
Catalog publishing	2,070	3,226	3,766
Corporate	12,528	11,709	9,123
Total	$332,446	$365,187	$253,260
Depreciation and amortization:			
Catalog showrooms	$ 10,530	$ 8,478	$ 3,687
Catalog publishing	73	54	17
Corporate	38	65	30
Total	$ 10,641	$ 8,597	$ 3,734
Capital expenditures—			
Catalog showrooms	$ 28,928	$ 38,162	$ 23,125

Operating earnings include total revenues less all costs and expenses directly related to the segment involved. Intersegment sales are made at approximate cost.

Identifiable assets are those used by the segment involved. Corporate assets consist principally of cash and owned property and equipment.

L. Quarterly financial information (unaudited):
(in thousands, except per share data)

	Fiscal year ended January 31, 1981			
	13 weeks ended May 3, 1980	13 weeks ended Aug. 2, 1980	13 weeks ended Nov. 1, 1980	13 weeks ended Jan. 31, 1981
Revenues	$127,978	$128,243	$158,012	$264,526
Cost of sales	96,770	96,886	119,869	204,784
Earnings (loss) before taxes on income	(6,147)	(4,825)	(151)	13,396
Taxes (benefit) on income	(2,889)	(2,268)	(71)	6,189
Net earnings (loss) (Notes G and I)	(3,258)	(2,557)	(80)	7,207
Net earnings (loss) per common and common equivalent share	$(.39)	$(.30)	$(.01)	$.85

	Fiscal year ended February 2, 1980			
	13 weeks ended May 5, 1979	13 weeks ended Aug. 4, 1979	13 weeks ended Nov. 3, 1979	13 weeks ended Feb. 2, 1980
Revenues	$116,630	$123,498	$172,472	$266,220
Cost of sales	87,750	92,105	130,091	206,791
Earnings before taxes on income	630	581	7,541	14,361
Income taxes	315	266	3,544	6,248
Net earnings	315	315	3,997	8,113
Net earnings per common and common equivalent share	$.04	$.04	$.48	$.96

Cost of sales for the interim periods presented above are determined on a basis of historical gross margins for each subsidiary adjusted to reflect current market conditions. Any difference between historical gross margins and actual gross margins are recorded in the quarter in which a physical inventory is performed. Physical inventories were performed and differences reflected in January 1981 and 1980, respectively.

M. Supplementary financial data on the effects of changing prices (unaudited):

Rapidly changing prices have had an increased impact on the Company in recent years. Inflation affects the Company in many ways—particularly the costs of acquiring inventory and the costs of replacing property and equipment. The Company's ability to react to inflation depends on, among other things, its ability to compensate for cost increases with increased sales prices, and its method of financing the enterprise.

In 1979, the Financial Accounting Standards Board issued Statement No. 33, *Financial Reporting and Changing Prices,* which established standards for reporting supplementary information concerning the effects of inflation. The Statement requires that selected financial data be restated to reflect the effects of general inflation (constant dollar) and changes in specific prices (current cost). The information included in the accompanying tables has been prepared on a reasonable basis and in a manner consistent with the requirements of the Statement, however, numerous judgmental decisions and assumptions are involved, particularly with respect to the current cost data, which, by its nature, is highly subjective. It should, therefore, be recognized that the data is most meaningful when used for the purpose of identifying relationships and trends within and between periods and that the dollar amounts shown are estimates as opposed to precise measurements.

Constant dollar accounting represents a method of reporting financial data in dollars having the same general purchasing power. As required by the Statement, this has been accomplished by adjusting the historical costs of inventories and property and equipment by the percentage change in the Consumer Price Index—All Urban Consumers since the dates the assets were acquired. As a result of the restatement process, these balances are expressed in a common unit of measure which is the average purchasing power of the dollar for 1980.

Under the current cost method, historical amounts are restated to reflect changes in the prices of the specific goods and services the Company uses. As a result, the current cost of inventories and property and equipment represents the number of dollars required to acquire assets having the same service potential as the assets that are actually owned. With respect to inventories, this has been accomplished by adjusting historical costs through the use of internally generated indexes based on the average age of the inventories at year-end.

The current cost of major items of property and equipment was determined primarily based on estimates of the cost of replacing existing capacity based on the assumed manner in which this would most likely take place were it necessary to do so. These amounts were obtained through the use of modeling, quotations, and various other sources. The current cost of other assets not specifically priced was determined through the use of appropriate government indexes, especially certain components of the Producers' Price Index.

Under both methods, depreciation and amortization expense have been adjusted based on the restated asset values using the same methods and lives used in the primary financial statements. Cost of sales has also been adjusted to reflect a charge for inflation for the period inventory was held prior to sale. No other items of revenue or expense were adjusted.

The gain from decline in purchasing power of net monetary amounts owed results from the decline in the general purchasing power of the dollar. While these gains do not represent the receipt of cash for reinvestment or distribution through dividends, they represent an economic benefit to the Company which results from the fact that the dollars used to pay the Company's liabilities during the year were worth less than the dollars represented by the original obligations. A similar benefit results from liabilities incurred but not yet paid at year-end since the dollars used to satisfy them will also be worth less than those represented by the actual obligations.

Statement No. 33 does not permit the restatement of income tax expense to reflect the effects of increased costs under the constant dollar and current cost methods because such increases are not deductible for income tax purposes. Accordingly, income taxes have been reflected at their historical cost amounts.

Condensed consolidated statement of earnings adjusted for inflation

Fiscal Year Ended January 31, 1981 (in thousands, except per share data)

	As reported in financial statement	Adjusted for changes in consumer price index (constant dollars)	Adjusted for changes in specific prices (current costs)
Revenues	$678,759	$678,759	$678,759
Costs:			
Cost of sales	518,309	539,155	537,662
Other operating expenses	147,843	147,843	147,843
Depreciation and amortization	10,334	13,341	12,646
Earnings (loss) before taxes on income	2,273	(21,580)	(19,392)
Taxes on income	961	961	961
Net earnings (loss)	$ 1,312	$(22,541)	$(20,353)
Net earnings (loss) per common and equivalent share	$.15	$(2.66)	$(2.40)
Net assets at end of year	$ 93,928	$138,282	$144,426
Purchasing power gain on net monetary items		$ 24,385	$ 24,385
Increase in specific prices (current cost) of inventories and property and equipment held during the year (a)			$ 27,973
Effect of increase in general price level			39,878
Excess of increase in general price level over increase in the specific prices			$(11,905)

(a) At January 31, 1981 current cost of inventory was $156,968 and current cost of property and equipment, net of accumulated depreciation, was $172,786.

Summary of supplementary financial data

Five years ended January 31, 1981
(in thousands, except per share data) (a)

	Fiscal Year Ended Jan. 31, 1981	Feb. 2, 1980	Seven Months Ended Feb. 3, 1979	Fiscal Year Ended July 1, 1978	July 2, 1977
Revenues					
As reported	**$678,759**	$678,820	$360,702	$453,343	$334,386
As adjusted	**678,759**	768,628	449,265	600,584	473,282
Earnings (loss) from continuing operations:					
As reported	**1,312**	12,740			
Constant dollar	**(22,541)**	3,055			
Current cost	**(20,353)**	(15,002)			
Earnings (loss) from continuing operations per common share:					
As reported	**.15**	1.52			
Constant dollar	**(2.66)**	.36			
Current cost	**(2.40)**	(1.79)			
Net assets at year-end:					
As reported	**93,928**	92,971			
Constant dollar	**138,282**	138,251			
Current cost	**144,426**	163,236			
Excess of increase in specific prices over increase in the general price level	**(11,905)**	23,602			
Gain from decline in purchasing power of net amounts owed	**24,385**	27,799			
Cash dividends per common share	**.25**	.17	.16	.18	.15
Market price per share at year-end	**11.12**	14.64	17.57	19.67	19.00
Average consumer price index	**249.1**	220.0	200.6	187.6	175.8

(a) All amounts are expressed in average fiscal 1981 dollars.

Stockholders and Board of Directors
Modern Merchandising, Inc.
Minneapolis, Minnesota

We have examined the consolidated balance sheets of Modern Merchandising, Inc. and subsidiaries as of January 31, 1981 and February 2, 1980, and the related statements of earnings, stockholders' equity and changes in financial position for each of the two years in the period ended January 31, 1981 and the seven months ended February 3, 1979. Our examinations were made in accordance with generally accepted auditing standards and, accordingly, included such tests of the accounting records and such other auditing procedures as we considered necessary in the circumstances.

In our opinion, the consolidated financial statements referred to above present fairly the financial position of Modern Merchandising, Inc. and subsidiaries at January 31, 1981 and February 2, 1980, and the results of their operations and the changes in their financial position for each of the two years in the period ended January 31, 1981 and the seven months ended February 3, 1979, in conformity with generally accepted accounting principles applied on a consistent basis after restatement for the change, with which we concur, in the method of accounting for vacation pay as described in Note I to the financial statements.

Touche Ross + Co.
Certified Public Accountants

Minneapolis, Minnesota
April 28, 1981

MARY MOPPET'S DAY CARE SCHOOLS, INC.

For Years Ended September 30, 1981 and 1980

BALANCE SHEETS

	September 30,	
	1981	**1980**
ASSETS		
CURRENT ASSETS:		
Cash, including certificates of deposit of $100,000 in 1981	$ 220,098	$ 92,471
Franchise contracts receivable (Note A)	27,500	123,000
Notes and other receivables, less allowance for doubtful accounts		
of $3,100 and $60,600	329,839	242,553
School properties under development (Note A)	20,973	240,346
Prepaid expenses and other assets	102,610	79,555
Refundable income taxes (Note A)	25,620	77,994
TOTAL CURRENT ASSETS	726,640	855,919
NOTES RECEIVABLE, less current portion included		
above (Note C)	171,051	268,862
PROPERTY AND EQUIPMENT - net (Notes A, B and D)	633,206	602,048
INTANGIBLES (Note A):		
Deferred Company operated school development costs, less		
accumulated amortization of $22,822 and $21,360	56,483	41,634
Excess of cost over net assets of reacquired school franchises,		
less accumulated amortization of $93,379 and $48,652	405,590	445,843
	462,073	487,477
	$1,992,970	$2,214,306
LIABILITIES AND STOCKHOLDERS' EQUITY		
CURRENT LIABILITIES:		
Notes payable to bank (Note C)	$ 52,620	$ 163,575
Accounts payable	48,287	57,527
Accrued expenses	104,670	51,328
Other liabilities	10,500	24,992
Dividends payable	58,411	58,411
Current portion of long-term debt	60,883	47,418
TOTAL CURRENT LIABILITIES	335,371	403,251
LONG-TERM DEBT, less current portion included above (Note D)	459,792	485,898
DEFERRED FRANCHISE FEES, net of deferred costs of $3,476		
and $3,715 (Note A)	31,523	158,285
DEFERRED INCOME TAXES (Note A)	36,147	25,050
DEFERRED INCOME	34,650	32,541
COMMITMENTS AND CONTINGENCIES (Notes E and J)		
STOCKHOLDERS' EQUITY:		
Preference stock, no par value:		
Authorized, 100,000 shares — none issued		
Common stock, par value $.10 a share:		
Authorized, 1,100,000 shares		
Issued, 408,018 (Note F)	40,802	40,802
Additional paid-in capital	600,357	600,357
Retained earnings	529,494	543,288
Less: Common stock in Treasury, 42,952 shares at cost	(75,166)	(75,166)
	1,095,487	1,109,281
	$1,992,970	$2,214,306

STATEMENTS OF EARNINGS
STATEMENTS OF STOCKHOLDERS EQUITY

	Years ended September 30,	
	1981	**1980**
EARNINGS		
REVENUES (Note A):		
Initial franchise fees	$ 80,000	$ 216,600
Franchise royalties and services	519,249	483,347
Child care fees from Company schools	1,483,786	1,133,361
Net (loss) from sale of school properties developed	(5,197)	(11,042)
Other	291,545	216,584
	2,369,383	2,038,850
COSTS AND EXPENSES:		
Cost of franchises sold	42,581	116,882
Franchise service costs	101,705	137,247
Operating costs and expenses of Company schools	1,512,152	1,179,593
Administrative and general	596,292	499,405
Interest, net of $4,234 capitalized in 1980	55,847	46,282
Bad debts expense (Note J)	87,000	9,000
	2,395,577	1,988,409
(LOSS) EARNINGS BEFORE INCOME TAXES	(26,194)	50,441
INCOME TAXES (CREDIT) (Note G)	(12,400)	10,400
NET (LOSS) EARNINGS	($ 13,794)	$ 40,041
(LOSS) EARNINGS PER COMMON SHARE (based on weighted average shares outstanding)	($.04)	$.11

STOCKHOLDERS' EQUITY	Common stock	Additional paid-in capital	Retained earnings	Treasury stock
BALANCE, OCTOBER 1, 1979	$40,802	$600,357	$561,658	$75,166
NET EARNINGS			40,041	
DIVIDEND DECLARED — $.16 per share			(58,411)	
BALANCE, SEPTEMBER 30, 1980	40,802	600,357	543,288	75,166
NET LOSS			(13,794)	
BALANCE, SEPTEMBER 30, 1981	$40,802	$600,357	$529,494	$75,166

STATEMENTS OF CHANGES IN FINANCIAL POSITION

	Years ended September 30,	
	1981	**1980**
SOURCE OF FUNDS:		
Cash provided from operations:		
Net earnings (loss)	($ 13,794)	$ 40,041
Non-cash items:		
Depreciation and amortization	147,688	99,024
Funds provided from operations	133,894	139,065
Carrying amount of Company constructed schools sold	955,368	401,531
Decrease in franchise contracts receivable	95,500	88,850
Increase in current and deferred income taxes	63,471	
Loan proceeds	45,500	324,804
Decrease in notes and other receivables	10,525	110,869
Increase in dividends payable		58,411
Increase in short-term borrowings		29,775
Other — net	36,598	45,301
	1,340,856	1,198,606
APPLICATION OF FUNDS:		
Land acquired and construction costs of school properties	735,995	419,231
Decrease in deferred franchise fees	126,762	81,763
Additions to property and equipment	122,349	171,437
Decrease in notes payable to bank	110,955	
Payments on long-term debt	58,141	76,650
Additions to intangible assets	35,972	439,808
Increase (decrease) in prepaid expenses and other assets	23,055	(29,535)
Decrease in current and deferred income taxes		91,997
Common stock dividends		58,411
	1,213,229	1,309,762
INCREASE (DECREASE) IN CASH	$ 127,627	($ 111,156)

See notes to financial statements.

NOTES TO FINANCIAL STATEMENTS

A. **Summary of Significant Accounting Policies:**

Franchise fees and related costs are deferred and recognized in operations when the related franchise school is opened.

Generally, the Company agrees to assist a franchisee in locating and negotiating a building lease. If, after a period of twelve months such a lease has not been obtained, the Company will pay the franchisee interest at 8% per annum on the initial payments made and such monies become refundable after twenty-four months.

Intangibles consist of the excess of costs over the net assets acquired on franchise schools repurchased, reacquired franchise areas and deferred Company operated school development costs.

The excess of cost over the net assets acquired on franchised schools repurchased which is not allocated to a reacquired franchise area, is being amortized to operations over the remaining life of the respective building leases using the straight-line method. The remaining lives of the building leases range from seven to nineteen years.

Costs associated with reacquired franchise areas are being amortized to operations over a five-year period using the straight-line method.

NOTES TO
FINANCIAL STATEMENTS CONT.

The first several months of school operations are of a developmental nature and directly benefit future operations. Accordingly, the first six months' operating results are deferred and amortized to future operations over a three-year period using the straight-line method.

School properties under development consist of land and construction in process related to school buildings. The buildings are being constructed for franchise or Company operated schools which upon completion the Company generally intends to sell to third party investors.

Net gains from the sale of franchise school properties developed are recognized when the down payment requirements of the AICPA publication "Accounting for Profit Recognition on Sales of Real Estate" are met. Net gains on the sale and leaseback of Company school properties developed are deferred and amortized over the lease term. If these Company schools are subsequently sold as franchises and the Company is released from primary liability under the lease, any unamortized gain is recognized in operations at that time.

Royalty revenues are due from franchisees under the provisions of the franchise agreements. Franchisees pay a monthly royalty of 6% of their monthly gross income, but not less than $100 per month. Such amounts are reflected in operations as earned.

Gain on Company schools sold as franchises arises when schools are sold for amounts in excess of the normal franchise fee. The excess of the sales price over the normal franchise fees less the carrying amount of any related intangible assets is recorded as a gain on Company schools sold as franchises. That portion of the sales prices applicable to the normal franchise fee is recorded as initial franchise fees and the carrying amount of any related assets sold are recorded as cost of franchises sold.

Property and equipment is recorded at cost. Depreciation and amortization is provided on the straight-line basis over the following estimated useful lives:

Buildings	20 to 30 years
Leasehold improvements	Lesser of term of lease or life of asset (3 to 15 years)
Furniture and equipment	3 to 10 years

Expenditures for repairs and maintenance are charged to operations as incurred. Expenditures for betterments or renewals are capitalized.

Deferred income taxes are provided for timing differences between amounts reported in the financial statements and tax returns. Such timing differences arise from the use for income tax purposes of the percentage of completion method of accounting for franchise fees and related franchise costs, the use of accelerated depreciation, the immediate recognition of gains on the sale and leaseback of school properties sold and the expensing of amounts incurred for Company operated school development costs.

Investment tax credits are used to reduce the income tax provision in the year such credits become available as credits for income tax purposes (flow-through method).

Certain account balances have been restated at September 30, 1980 to be consistent with account presentation at September 30, 1981.

B. **Property and Equipment:**

Property and equipment includes:

	September 30,	
	1981	1980
Property leased to others:		
Land	$ 34,000	$ 34,000
Buildings	121,933	121,933
	155,933	155,933
Less accumulated depreciation	27,644	23,105
	128,289	132,828
Property and equipment:		
Land	108,148	108,148
Buildings and leasehold improvements	220,607	211,353
Furniture and equipment	392,566	311,447
	721,321	630,948
Less accumulated depreciation and amortization	216,404	161,728
	504,917	469,220
	$633,206	$602,048

C. **Notes Payable to Bank:**

Notes payable to bank at September 30, 1981 represent borrowings under the Company's line of credit. The maximum level of bank borrowings during the year ended September 30, 1981 was approximately $256,200. These obligations bear interest at 1½% above the prevailing prime rates (19.5% at September 30, 1981). The average amount of outstanding loans during the period amounted to approximately $153,000 and the weighted average interest rate, computed on monthly outstanding loan balances, amounted to approximately 18%. The Company has $447,380 of unused lines of credit at September 30, 1981.

At September 30, 1981, borrowings under these

NOTES TO
FINANCIAL STATEMENTS cont.

agreements are collaterlized by a note receivable having a carrying amount of approximately $93,000.

D. Long-Term Debt:
Long-term debt consists of the following:

	September 30,	
	1981	**1980**
10.0% promissory note, due in monthly installments of $3,953, including interest, through January, 1985, collateralized by equipment and intangible assets having a carrying amount of approximately $311,021	$249,629	$270,932
10.0% note, due in monthly installments of $1,136, including interest, through February, 2001, collateralized by land and buildings having a carrying amount of approximately $154,000	116,558	118,434
9.5% promissory note, due in monthly installments of $904, including interest, through March, 1998, collateralized by land and buildings having a carrying amount of approximately $106,327	90,312	92,470
15.0% promissory note, due in monthly installments of $745, including interest, through October, 1983, collateralized by equipment having a carrying amount of approximately $8,685 and all future receivables of the Roswell, New Mexico schools	15,370	21,499
Equipment contracts at rates from 9.75% to 18%, due in monthly installments through January, 1984, collateralized by equipment having a carrying amount of approximately $60,990	47,608	24,120
Promissory notes at rates from 8% to 11%, due in monthly installments through January, 1982	1,198	5,861
	520,675	533,316
Less current portion	60,883	47,418
	$459,792	$485,898

Aggregate annual principal payments applicable to long-term debt for each of the five years subsequent to September 30, 1981 are:

1982 $61,000 .... 1984 $36,000
1983 60,000 .... 1985 38,000
1986 and thereafter $326,000

E. Leased Assets and Commitments:
The Company reports in its financial statements as operating leases, certain leases which meet the capital lease criteria of Statement of Financial Accounting Standards No. 13 "Accounting for Leases" except that they were entered into prior to the effective date of the statement. The statement was effective for lease agreements entered into on or after January 1, 1977, and by fiscal 1982 its provisions will have to be applied retroactively by the Company by restating its financial statements. Certain leases in effect at September 30, 1981 and September 30, 1980, which are now being accounted for as operating leases, will be classified and accounted for as "capital leases" under Statement No. 13. If the Company had accounted for such leases as capital leases, assets would have increased by $427,000 and $469,000, and liabilities would have increased by $607,000 and $606,000 at September 30, 1981 and September 30, 1980, respectively.

The effect of such treatment would have decreased earnings before income taxes for the year ended September 30, 1981 and September 30, 1980 by $18,000 and $17,000, respectively.

At September 30, 1981, minimum future rentals on operating leases, and operating leases defined as capital leases in accordance with Statement No. 13 are as follows:

	Operating defined as capital	Operating
1982	$ 122,000	$ 360,000
1983	122,000	356,000
1984	122,000	356,000
1985	122,000	356,000
1986	122,000	356,000
1987 — later years	680,000	3,873,000
Total minimum lease payments	1,290,000	5,657,000
Less:		
Sublease rentals	154,000	
Amount representing interest	683,000	2,569,000
Aggregate minimum net lease payments		$3,088,000
Present value of net minimum lease payments	$ 453,000	

NOTES TO
FINANCIAL STATEMENTS CONT.

Operating lease commitments during 1981 increased substantially over the prior year due to the addition of five leases related to Company schools opened or acquired during the current year, and the escalation of rental payments in accordance with existing lease agreements.

Rent expense for the periods indicated is as follows:

	Years ended September 30,	
	1981	1980
Operating leases defined as capital leases	$118,926	$116,090
Operating leases	300,172	165,824
	$419,098	$281,914

Most of the leases required the Company to pay taxes, insurance and maintenance costs and provide for rental adjustments every three to five years based on the consumer price index.

The Company is contingently liable as guarantor on building leases of seventeen franchisee operated schools with total annual rentals of $162,000 and remaining terms of four to eighteen years.

On November 7, 1978, the Company's Board of Directors granted to the wife of the president of the Company the option to require the Company to repurchase all shares of the Company's stock owned by the president upon his death at book value. The liability is currently fully funded by life insurance on the life of the president payable to the Company.

F. Common Stock:

In 1979, the Company adopted a new restricted Stock Option Plan for key employees which permits the granting of options for up to 35,000 common shares. No options have been granted under the plan.

G. Income Taxes:

Income tax expense consists of the following:

	Years ended September 30,	
Taxes currently payable:	1981	1980
Federal	($14,000)	$ 4,700
State		(1,200)
Investment tax credits	(7,700)	(7,300)
Deferred taxes	9,300	14,200
	($12,400)	$10,400

The Company's effective tax rates differed from statutory rates for the following reasons:

	Years ended September 30,	
	1981	1980
Taxes computed at statutory rates	($12,000)	$23,200
State income taxes — net of federal benefit		(700)
Officer's life insurance	7,700	12,200
Investment tax credit	(7,700)	(7,300)
Rates at less than statutory rate	(100)	(17,000)
Other	(300)	
Income tax provision	($12,400)	$10,400

H. Related Party Transactions:

Rental payments approximating $29,000 annually on two Company schools are paid to two landlords who are directors of the Company. The rental payments are comparable to those paid to unrelated parties.

I. Principal Business Segment Information:

The Company is presently managed and accounted for in two industry segments for both operating and segment reporting purposes.

The number of franchises sold, reacquired and schools opened during each of the years ended September 30, 1981 and 1980 is summarized as follows:

	1981	1980
Franchise contracts signed	1	3
Franchises reacquired:		
Operating	2	7
Franchise schools opened	2	7
Company schools opened	1	2

Revenues and operating earnings of the Company by principal business segments for each of the two years ended September 30, 1981 and 1980 set forth below, have been prepared in accordance with Statement No. 14 of the Financial Accounting Standards Board. The Company has no intersegment sales.

Operating earnings represents revenues less costs and expenses before deductions for interest, corporate expenses and income taxes.

NOTES TO FINANCIAL STATEMENTS CONT.

	Years ended September 30,	
	1981	**1980**
Revenues:		
Franchise operations	$ 599,249	$ 699,947
Company school operations	1,483,786	1,133,361
Other	286,348	205,542
	$2,369,383	$2,038,850
Operating earnings:		
Franchise operations	$ 454,964	$ 445,818
Company school operations	(28,366) (	38,232)
Other	81,024	64,313
	507,622	471,899
Interest	55,847	46,282
General corporate expense	477,969	375,176
(Loss) earnings before income taxes	($ 26,194)	$ 50,441

Additional information with respect to business segments is set forth below:

Year ended September 30, 1981

Segment	Assets at year end	Amortization and depreciation	Capital expenditures
Franchise operations	$ 529,017	$	$
Company school operations	737,926	77,599	111,351
Other	243,242	8,423	735,995
	1,510,185	86,022	847,346
Corporate	482,785	61,666	9,080
	$1,992,970	$147,688	$856,426

Year ended September 30, 1980

Segment	Assets at year end	Amortization and depreciation	Capital expenditures
Franchise operations	$ 652,920	$	$
Company school operations	739,623	61,413	142,753
Other	405,093	7,050	419,231
	1,797,636	68,463	561,984
Corporate	416,670	30,561	28,684
	$2,214,306	$99,024	$590,668

J. Contingencies:

During the current fiscal year, the Company has written-off accounts and notes receivable from two franchisees that have abandoned their franchise schools. The franchisees declared bankruptcy subsequent to September 30, 1981 and it is management's opinion that the collectibility is doubtful. The Company is currently operating one school as a Company operated school and the others have ceased operating.

The Company is involved in litigation as a plaintiff in several suits with franchisees. The revenues of prior years of two of these franchisees have been reviewed and it appears that royalties were underpaid and that the franchisees are liable to the Company for approximately $49,000. These amounts have not been received by the Company as of the date of our report. Under Statement of Financial Accounting Standards No. 5 "Accounting for Contingencies", these amounts are not includable in income until received.

ACCOUNTANTS REPORT

Board of Directors and Stockholders
Mary Moppet's Day Care Schools, Inc.
Scottsdale, Arizona

We have examined the balance sheets of Mary Moppet's Day Care Schools, Inc. as of September 30, 1981 and 1980, and the related statements of earnings, stockholders' equity and changes in financial position for the years then ended. Our examinations were made in accordance with generally accepted auditing standards and, accordingly, included such tests of the accounting records and such other auditing procedures as we considered necessary in the circumstances.

In our opinion, the financial statements referred to above present fairly the financial position of Mary Moppet's Day Care Schools, Inc. at September 30, 1981 and 1980, and the results of its operations and the changes in its financial position for the years then ended, in conformity with generally accepted accounting principles applied on a consistent basis.

Phoenix, Arizona
December 11, 1981

Touche Ross & Co.

INDEX

Numbers in **boldface** refer to pages in the glossary.

AAA, 13
Absorption costing, 871–873, **887,** 1011–1016
Accelerated Cost Recovery System (ACRS), 1099–1102
Accelerated depreciation method:
  defined, 420, **428**
  illustrated
    double-declining balance, 419–420
    sum-of-years'-digits, 417–418
    timing difference related to tax returns, 1099–1102
Account:
  balance, 45, 169
  chart of accounts, 51–52
  closing of, 160–169
  contra account, 103
  defined, 45, **76**
  forms of, 46, 47
  nominal, 96–97, 160
  permanent, 96–97, 160
  recording business transactions, 45–46
  sequence and numbering, 51–52
  T account, 45
  titles of individual accounts, 46–51
Account balance:
  defined, 45, **76**
  normal, 54
Account form (balance sheet), 115, **123**
Accounting:
  accrual basis, 26, 94–97, 1075–1076
  cash basis, 94, 1075–1076
  characteristics of, 5–6
  defined, 5, **27**
  need for, 4, 5
  profession, 8–12
  recording and reporting, 7–8
  using, 6–7
Accounting changes, *see* Change in accounting principles
Accounting cycle:
  complete cycle, 149
  defined, 43, **77**
  end of period, 97–121, 141–185
  steps during period, 43–44
Accounting entity, 502, **523**
  see also Business entity concept
Accounting equation, 16, **27**
Accounting income, 1075, **1103**

Accounting information:
  characteristics of, 5–6
  recording, 7–8
  using, 6–7
Accounting machine, 267, **272**
Accounting model (equation):
  defined, 16, 17
  effect of transactions, 22–27
  expanded for owner's equity accounts, 50
Accounting period, 43, **77**
Accounting principle, 12, **27**
  See also Generally accepted accounting principles
Accounting Principles Board, 12
  Opinions:
    No. 10, 508
    No. 11, 1099
    No. 12, 423
    No. 15, 629
    No. 16, 732, 725, 728
    No. 17, 454
    No. 18, 707
    No. 19, 754
    No. 20, 422, 510, 627
    No. 21, 413, 661
    No. 22, 511
    No. 29, 446, 448
    No. 30, 622, 625
Accounting Research Bulletins, 12
  No. 43, 705
  No. 45, 506
Accounting Review, 13
Accounting system:
  defined, 246, **272**
  EDP, 268–272
  manual, 250–266
Account payable:
  accounting for, 348
  defined, 17, **27,** 348, **351**
Account receivable:
  accounting for, 333–341
  defined, 25, **27,** 333, **351**
  uncollectible accounts, 334–341
Accounts control, 251–252
ACRS, 1099–1102
Accrual basis of accounting, 26, 94–97, 1075–1076
Accruals:
  defined, 98, **123**

entries in subsequent periods, 176–177
see also Adjusting entries
Accrued expenses, 98, 105–108
Accrued revenue, 98, 109
Accumulated depreciation:
 computing depreciation, 416–420
 defined, 103, **123**
 exchange of assets, 446–449
 not cash, 423–424
 retirement of plant asset, 443–446
Acid test ratio (quick ratio), 797–**798**
Activity accounting, 904
Adjusted gross income, 1080, **1103**
Adjusted Trial Balance, 109, **124**
Adjusting entries:
 accruals, 98, 105–109
 deferrals, 97–98, 98–105
 defined, 97, **124**
 necessity of, 97
 prepaid expenses, 97, 98–104
 preparation from worksheet, 157–160
 unearned revenue, 98, 104–105
 unrecorded expenses, 98, 105–108
 unrecorded revenue, 98, 109
 worksheet, 151–153, 157–160
Administrative expenses, 206, **228**
Administrative expenses budget, 950, **957**
Aging of accounts receivable, 336, **351**
AICPA, 8, 12
All financial resources approach:
 defined, 754, **770**
 illustrated, 755–771
Allocating expenses, 835–840, 870
Allowance for Uncollectible Accounts, 335, **352**
American Accounting Association (AAA), 13
American Institute of Certified Public Accountants (AICPA),
  8, 12
Amortization:
 bond investment, 713–715
 bonds payable, 659–664, 669–672
 copyright, 455
 defined, 454, **460**
 franchises, 457–458
 goodwill, 458–459
 leaseholds, 456–457
 patent, 454–455
 trademarks, 455–456
Analysis of variances, 829–830, 956, 972–976, 979–990
Annual budget, 941
Annual report, 43, **77**
Asset, 17, **27**
Attainable standards, 979, **990**
Audit, 9, **27**
Authorized stock, 587, **598**

Average cost:
 defined, 371, **391**
 perpetual inventory system, 367, 371
Avoidable costs (expenses), 843, **847**, 1046

Bad debts expense:
 accounting for, 335–341
 defined, 334, **352**
Balance:
 account, 45
 adjusted, 109
 normal, 54
 trial, 70
Balance sheet:
 account form, 115
 classified, 115
 consolidated, 718–725
 constant dollar, 516–517
 current cost, 518–521
 defined, 16, **27**
 preparation:
  from trial balance, 116
  from worksheet, 156–158
 report form, 115
Balance sheet equation (accounting equation), 17, 50
Bank reconciliation:
 defined, 302, **316**
 preparation, 302–308
Bank statement
 defined, 300, **316**
 illustrated, 300–302
Base period, 790
Batch processing, 270, **272**
Beginning inventory, 216, **228**
Board of Directors, 584
Bond (bond payable):
 adjusting entries, 665–666
 bond sinking fund, 668–669
 classification of, 653–654
 computing issue price, 656–659
 conversion, 667–668
 defined, 650, 652, **676**
 effective interest method of amortization, 669–672
 issued at discount, 659–661, 670–671
 issued between interest payment dates, 664–665
 issued at par value, 654–656
 issued at premium, 661–664, 671–672
 retirement, 667
 why issue, 650–652, 1095–1097
Bond indenture, 652
Bond investment:
 long-term, 712–716
 temporary, 705

Bond sinking fund:
  defined, 668, **676**
  illustrated, 668–669
Bonus:
  defined, 554, **563**
  to new partner, 555–556
  to old partner, 554–555
Bookkeeping machine,. 267, **272**
Book of original entry (journals), 54, **77**
Book value:
  for decision making, 1044
  per common share:
    computing, 597–598
    defined, 597, **598**
  plant asset, 104, **124,** 419, **428**
Branch accounting, 843–846, **847**
Branch operations, 843
Break even analysis, 1020–1022
Break even point, 1020–1022, **1028**
Budget:
  administrative expenses, 950, **957**
  balance sheet, 954
  capital expenditures, 952, **957**
  cash, 952, **957**
  cost of goods sold, 948, **957**
  defined, 10, 936, **957**
  direct labor, 945, **957**
  direct materials, 944, **957**
  income statement, 950
  manufacturing overhead, 946
  production, 943, **958**
  sales, 943, **958**
  selling expenses, 949, **958**
  statement of changes in financial position, 955
Budgeting, 936, **957**
Budget performance report, 955–957, **957**
Buildings, 48, **409**
Business combination:
  accounting for, 716–730
  defined, 726, **731**
  types of, 726
Business document, 44, **77**
Business entity concept, 20, **27,** 502
Business forms (documents), 247
Business goals, 824
Business organizations, 14–15, 177–180, 1093–1095
Business segmentation, 826, **847**

Calendar year firm, 44, **77**
Callable bond, 654, **676**
Callable preferred stock, 594–595
Call provision, 594, **598**
Canceled checks, 301, **316**
Capacity, 825, 986

Capacity variance, 987–988, **990**
Capital, 17, 50
  see also Owner's equity
Capital asset, 1078–1080, **1103**
Capital budgeting:
  defined, 1054, **1060**
  discounted cash flows, 1058–1060
  payback period, 1056–1057
  return on average investment, 1057–1058
Capital expenditures, 424, **429,** 952, 1054–1055
Capital expenditures budget, 952, **957**
Capital gains and losses:
  corporations tax returns, 1092
  individual tax returns, 1078–1080
Capital lease, 674, **676**
Capital statement:
  defined, 19, 120
  preparation from worksheet, 156–157
Capital stock, *See* Common stock
Carrying value of bonds, 659, **676**
CASB, 14
Cash, defined, 47, 289, **317**
Cash basis of accounting, 94, 1075–1076
Cash budget, 952, **957**
Cash discount, 208, **228**
Cash disbursements journal, 262–265, **272**
Cash flow analysis, 1055–1056
Cash flow statement:
  defined, 764, **770**
  preparation of statement, 769–770
  provided by operations, 766–769
Cash receipts journal, 259–262, **272**
Cash short and over account, 297
Casualty or theft losses itemized, deductions, 1082
Centralized branch accounting, 844
Certificate in Management Accounting (CMA), 14
Certified Public Accountant (CPA), 8, **27**
Change in accounting principle:
  accounting for, 626–628
  defined, 626, **633**
  depreciation, 422
Charge, 45, **77**
Charitable contributions itemized, deductions, 1082, 1092
Chart of accounts, 51, **77**
Check register:
  defined, 315, **317**
  use of, 315–316
Classified balance sheet, 115, **124**
Closing entries:
  defined, 160, **186**
  illustrated, 160–169
  merchandising firm, 223–225
CMA, 14
Collateral, 650, **676**

Committed fixed costs, 1008, **1028**
Common size statements, 791, **802**
Common stock:
    accounting for issue of, 587–591
    defined, 587–**598**
    investment in, 705–712, 716–730
    issue for cash, 588, 589
    issue for noncash assets, 589–590
    no-par, 590–591
    outstanding, 588
    par value, 587–588
    retirement, 615
Comparative statements, 787, **802**
Complex capital structure, 629, **633**
Composite-rate depreciation:
    defined, 449, **460**
    illustrated, 449–451
Compound interest, 690
Compound journal entry, 55, **77**
Computer, 268–272, 832
Computerized accounting, 271–272
Computer program, 270, **272**
Computer programmer, 270, **272**
Conservatism:
    applied to inventory, 376
    defined, 376, **392**, 512, **523**
Consignee, 366, **392**
Consignment, 365, **392**
Consignor, 366, **392**
Consistency principle:
    accounting principle, 510, **523**
    change in accounting principle, 626, **633**
    inventory methods, 376, **393**
Consolidated finance statements:
    balance sheet, 718–725
    defined, 717, **731**
    conditions for preparation, 729–730
    income statement, 725–726
    preparation of, 716–730
    purchase *vs.* pooling of interests, 726–729
Constant dollar accounting, 514, **523**
Constructive receipt, 1076, **1103**
Consumer Price Index, 513
Contingent liability, 346, **352**
Continuous budget, 941
Contra account, 103, **124**
Contributed capital, defined, 178, **186**, 586, **598**
Contribution margin, 1012, **1028**
Contribution margin rate, 1012, **1028**
Contribution margin variance analysis, 1053–1054, **1060**
Contribution margin-weighted average, 1027–1028
Controllable costs (expenses), 829, **847**
Controllable variance, 987–988, **990**
Control account, 251, **273**

Controller, 10, **28**, 585
Controlling operations, 825, 955–957, 971–990
Conversion costs, 914, **921**
Convertible bond:
    defined, 654, **676**
    illustrated, 667–668
Convertible preferred stock, 595–596
Copyright, 455, **460**
Corporate charter, 582, **599**
Corporation:
    accounting for, 178–180, 578–598, 612–633
    advantages of, 579–581
    book value, 597–598
    capital stock, 587–591
    capital stock subscription, 596–597
    contributed capital, 586
    defined, 15, **28**, 579
    disadvantages, 581
    dividends, 591–596
    forming corporation, 582
    legal capital, 587
    nonprofit, 579
    nonpublic (closely held), 579
    preferred stock, 593–596
    profit, 579
    public, 579
    retained earnings, 586
    stock dividend, 617–619
    stockholders' equity, 586
    stock retirement, 615–616
    stock split, 619–620
Cost, 826, **847**
    expired, 95
    principle, 20, 23, **28**, 505, **523**
    unexpired, 95
Cost accounting, 10, **28**, 903, **921**
Cost Accounting Standards Board (CASB), 14
Cost behavior, 871, **887**, 1005, **1029**
Cost center, 828
Cost function, 1006, **1029**
Cost method of accounting for stock investments:
    defined, 717, **731**
    illustrated, 717–709
Cost objective, 835, **847**
Cost of capital, 1058, **1060**
Cost of goods manufactured, 873
Cost of goods manufactured statement, 874, **887**
Cost of goods sold, 206, **228**, 873
Cost of goods sold budget, 948, **957**
Cost principle, 20, 23, **28**, 505, **523**
Cost of production report, 916, **921**
Cost-volume-profit (CVP) analysis, 1005, 1018–1028, **1029**
Cost-volume-profit chart, 1021–1022, **1029**
Coupon (bearer) bond, 654, **676**

Coupon rate (nominal or stated rate), 653, **676**
CPA, 8, **27**
Credit:
    balance sheet accounts, 52–53
    defined, 45, **77**
    income statement accounts, 53–54
Creditor, 17, **28, 49, 77**
Credit period, 208, **228**
Credit terms, 208, **228**
Crossfooting, 153, **186**
Cumulative preferred stock, 593, **599**
Current assets, 117, **124**
Current liabilities, 119, **124**
Current ratio, 796, **797**
Current replacement cost (current cost):
    current value, 518–521
    defined, 519, **524**
Current-value accounting (current-cost accounting), 514, **523**

Data processing, 268, **273,** 832–833
Debenture bond (unsecured bond), 653, **676**
Debit:
    balance sheet accounts, 52–53
    defined, 45, **77**
    income statement accounts, 53–54
Debtors, 48, **77**
Debt to total assets, 800
Decentralized branch account, 844
Decision making, 825–826, 1041, **1060**
Decision-making process, 1042–1043, **1060**
Decision model, 1043, **1060**
Declining-balance method, 419–420
Deduction:
    from adjusted gross income, 1081–1082
    defined, 1077, **1103**
    from gross income, 1080–1081
    itemized deductions, 1081
Deferrals, defined, 98, **124**
    see also Adjusting entries
Deferred revenue, 351, **352**
Deficit (corporation):
    corporation, 587, **599**
    partnership capital interest, 561, **563**
Denominator variance, 987–988, **990**
Department analysis sheets, 832–833
Departmental accounting, 830, **847**
Departmental contribution to indirect expenses, 840–843, **847**
Departmental expense allocation, 835–840
Departmental gross profit, 831–834, **847**
Departmental net income, 833–840, **847**
Dependent, 1083
Depletion:
    defined, 451, **460**
    natural resources, 451–452

Depreciation:
    adjusting entry, 102–104
    comparison of methods, 420–421
    composite rate, 449–451
    defined, 102, **124,** 414, **429**
    depreciation methods, 416–420
    double declining-balance method, 419–420
    factors in computing, 414–416
    income tax purposes, 421–422
    reporting in statements, 423
    revision of depreciation rates, 422
    straight-line method, 416–417
    sum-of-years'-digits method, 417–418
    units of production method, 417
Differential analysis, 1043, **1060**
Differential costs, 1043, **1061**
Differential revenue, 1044, **1061**
Digital computer, 269, **273**
Direct cost (expense), 834–835, **847**
Direct costing, 871–873, **888,** 1013–1018, **1029**
Direct labor, 870, **887**
Direct labor budget, 945, **957**
Direct materials, 869, **887**
Direct materials budget, 944, **957**
Direct write-off method, 341, **352**
Directing operations, 825
Discontinued operations, 841–843
Discount:
    bond:
        amortization, 659–661, 670–671
        defined, 653, **676**
    notes, 345, **352**
Discounted cash flow, 1058–1060, **1061**
Discount period:
    notes, 345, **352**
    sale of inventory, 208, **229**
Discretionary fixed costs, 1008, **1029**
Dishonored note, 344, **352**
Disposal of business segment, 622–623
Dividend:
    cash, 591–594
    deduction on tax return, 1078, 1092
    defined, 179, **186,** 591, **599**
    liquidating, 591
Dividends in arrears, 593, **599**
Dividend yield (ratio), 795–796
Double declining-balance depreciation
    defined, 419, **429**
    illustrated, 419
Double-entry, 27, **29**
Drawing account:
    closing of, 168–169
    defined, 50
Dun & Bradstreet, Inc., 786

Earnings per share:
  complex capital structure, 629
  computing, 628–630
  defined, 628, **633**
  fully-diluted, 629
  primary, 629
  ratio to analyze profitability, 794–795
Economic Recovery Tax Act of 1981, 1073
Effective interest method (bonds), 669–672
Effectiveness, 824, **847**
Efficiency, 824, **847**
Electronic data processing, 268, **273,** 832–833
Elimination of unprofitable department, 841–843
Employee earnings record, 483–484, **488**
Employee's withholding allowance certificate (Form W-4),
  473, 477–479, **488**
Employer's quarterly federal tax return (Form 941), 486–487,
  488
Ending inventory, 216, **229**
Endorsement, 333, **352**
Equipment:
  defined, 48, **409**
  depreciation, 414–421
  exchange (trade-in), 446–449
  records, 426–428
  repairs, 425–426
  retirement, 443–444
  sale, 444–446
Equity method of accounting for stock investments:
  defined, 707, **731**
  illustrated, 709–711
Equivalent units, 914–916, **921**
Errors, discovery and correction of, 71–73
Estimated useful life:
  defined, 102, **124**
  plant assets, 415
Exclusion, 1077, **1103**
Exemptions, 1082–1083, **1103**
Expected capacity, 986, **990**
Exenditure, 410, **429**
Expense:
  accrual basis, 95–96
  cash basis, 94
  closing, 164–165
  defined, 19, **29,** 51, 826, **847**
  matching, 509–510
Expense recognition principle, 25, **29,** 509–510
Expired cost, 102, **124,** 826
External transactions, 42, 77
Extraordinary item:
  accounting for, 624–626
  defined, 624, **633**
Extraordinary repairs, 425–426

Face value, bonds issued at, 652, 654–656
Factory burden (factory overhead), 870–871, **888,** 910–913,
  917, 947–948, 983–988
FASB, 13, 29
Favorable variances, 829, 956, 982–983
Federal depository bank, 487
Federal Fair Labor Standards Act, 475, **489**
Federal Insurance Contribution Act (FICA), 476, **489**
Federal Unemployment Tax Act (FUTA), 480, **489**
Federal unemployment taxes, 480–481, **489**
FICA taxes, 476–477, **489**
File, 271, **273**
Financial Accounting Standards Board (FASB), 13, 29
  see also Statements of Financial Accounting Standards
Financial budget, 941–942, **957**
Financial statements:
  defined, 7
  preparation of, 15–19
Financial statement analysis:
  horizontal analysis, 787–790
  limitations of, 801–802
  need for, 786
  objectives, 786–787
  ratio, 791–801
  trend analysis, 790
  vertical analyses, 791
Finished goods (inventory), 867, 885, **887,** 913, 921
Finished goods inventory account, 876
First-In, First-Out (FIFO):
  defined, 369, **393**
  periodic inventory system, 369–370, 373–374
  perpetual inventory system, 381, 383–386
Fiscal year, 43, **77**
Fixed assets, 409, **429**
  see also Plant assets
Fixed budget, 971–973, **990**
Fixed cost, 872, **887,** 984–985, 1008
Flexible budget, 972, 974–976, 983–985, **990**
FOB destination, 209, **229,** 365, **393**
FOB shipping point, 209, **229,** 365, **393**
Footing, 46, **77,** 153, **186,**
Forecasting, 940–941
Foreign Corrupt Practices Act, 291–292
Franchise, 457, **460**
Fraud-payroll, 473
Freight-In (Transportation-In), 212, **229**
Freight-Out (delivery expense), 209, **229**
Full costing, 871–873, **887,** 1011–1016
Full disclosure principle, 511, **524**
Fully diluted earnings per share, 629, **633**
Funded plan, 675, **676**
Funds, 747, 770
Future value:

ordinary annuity, 694–696
single amount, 691–694
tables, 693, 695

GAAP, *see* Generally Accepted Accounting Principles (GAAP)
General accounting system, 823, 876
General journal (two column journal):
  defined, 55, **77**
  illustrated, 55–57, 265–266
  posting, 57
General ledger:
  after closing process, 169–174
  defined, 45, **77**
  illustrated, 67–70, 251–252
  posting, 57
Generally Accepted Accounting Principles (GAAP), 12
  business entity concept, 20, 502
  consistency, 376, 393, 510, 523, 623, 626
  conservatism, 512
  cost principle, 21, 505
  defined, 12, **27**, 501, **524**
  expense recognition principle, 25, 509–510
  full-disclosure, 511
  going concern assumption, 21, 96, 502–503
  materiality, 511–512
  monetary unit, 504
  objectivity principle, 21, 504–505
  relationship to Internal Revenue Code, 1074–1076, 1097–1102
  revenue recognition principles, 25, 505–506
  source of, 12–14, 501–502
  stable-dollar assumption, 21–22
  time period assumption, 96, 503–504
General partnership, 544, **563**
General price level:
  constant dollar, 515–518
  defined, 513, **524**
General price level change, 513, **524**
Goal congruence, 937–938, **957**
Going concern assumption, 21, **29**, 96, 503, **524**
Goods available for sale, 216, **229**
Goods in process, 867, 885–886, **888,** 908–909, 911
Goodwill:
  computing, 458–460
  defined, 458, 460
Governmental accounting, 11
Gross earnings, 475, **489**
Gross income, 1077, 1080, **1103**
Gross invoice method, 208, **229**
Gross profit (gross margin) on sales, 206, **229,** 831–832
Gross profit method:
  defined, 390, **393**
  illustrated, 390–391

Hardware, 270, **273**
  high-low method, 1010
  historical costs, 976–977, 979
Head of household, 1083
Horizontal analysis:
  defined, 787, **802**
  illustrated, 787–790

Ideal standards, 979, **991**
Idle capacity, 987
Imputing interest, 413, **429**
Inadequacy, 415, **429**
Income averaging, 1087, **1103**
Income statement:
  consolidated, 725–726
  constant dollar, 517–518
  current value, 518–521
  defined, 18, **29**
  departmental contribution to indirect expenses, 840–843
  departmental gross profit, 831–832, 833
  departmental net income, 833–834, 840–841
  manufacturing firm, 873–874, 882, 1012–1013, 1011–1017
  merchandising firm, 206, 225, 873–874
  multiple step, 225
  preparation from trial balance, 114
  preparation from worksheet, 156–157
  single-step, 112–114
  special items, 623, 631
Income summary, 160–169
Income tax allocation:
  defined, 1099, **1103**
  depreciation timing difference, 1099–1102
  illustrated, 1098–1102
  Permanent differences, 1097
  Timing difference, 1098
Income taxes:
  cash basis *vs.* accrual basis, 1075–1076
  choice of business, 1093–1095
  choice of financing methods, 1095–1097
  classification of taxable entities, 1074
  corporations, 1089–1102
  income tax allocation, 1097–1102
  individuals, 1076–1089
  installment method, 508
  merchandise inventory, 372–376, 1102
  operating the business, 1097
  plant assets, 441–442, 449, 1098–1102
  reporting income tax expense, 1097–1102
  tax planning and business decisions, 1093–1097
  timing difference, 1097–1099
Incorporators, 582, **599**
Incremental analysis, 1043, **1060**
Incremental costs, 1043, **1061**

Indenture, 652, **676**
Indirect cost (expense), 835, **847,** 870–871
Indirect labor, 870, 907, 909, 917
Indirect materials, 870, 907, 917
Inflation:
    accounting for, 513–523
    constant dollar, 515–518
    current value, 518–521
    defined, 513, **524**
    FASB requirements, 521–523
Installment method, 508, **524**
Intangible asset:
    copyright, 455
    defined, 119, **124,** 453, **460**
    franchises, 457–458
    goodwill, 458–459
    leasehold, 456–457
    patent, 454–455
    trademarks, 455–456
Interest:
    compound, 690
    computing, 108, 342
    defined, 341, 352
    future value:
        of ordinary annuity, 694–696
        of single amount, 691–694
    imputing interest, 413
    present value:
        of ordinary annuity, 699–700
        of single amount, 696–699
    simple, 690
Interest itemized deduction, 1082
Interim statements:
    defined, 44, **77,** 175, **186**
    preparation without closing, 175–176
Internal accounting, 823, **847**
Internal auditing:
    defined, 11, **29**
    part of internal control, 295
Internal control:
    accounting system, 248
    administrative controls, 290–291
    control of cash disbursements, 297–308
    control of cash receipts, 295–297
    defined, 290, **317**
    design of, 290–300
    payroll, 473–474
Internal Revenue Code, 1073, **1103**
Internal rate of return, 1059, **1061**
Internal transactions, 42, **77**
Inventory, *see* Merchandise inventory
Inventory turnover, 799–800
Inventory valuation problems-manufacturing, 883–887
Investee company, 707, **731**

Investment center, 828, 1050
Investments:
    bonds, 712–716
    classification of, 704
    common stock, 707–712
    consolidated statements, 716–730
    equity method, 709–710
    income taxes, 1088
    long-term, 706–730
    temporary, 704–706
Investor company, 707, **731**
Invoice, 308, **317**
Itemized deductions, 1080, **1103**

Job, 904, **922**
Job completion, 913
Job order accounting, 904–914
Job order costing, 905, **922**
Job order cost sheet, 905–906
Job sale, 913–914
Joint products, 1047, **1061**
Joint product costs:
    defined, 1047, **1061**
    inventory valuation, 1047–1048
    relative sales value, 1047–1048
    relevant costs, 1048–1049
Journal of Accountancy, 12
Journal entry, 55, **77**
Journalizing, 55, **77**

Labor cost, 870, 909–910, 917, 945–947, 982–983
Labor efficiency variance, 982–983, **991**
Labor incentive plan, 978
Labor rate variance, 982–983, **991**
Labor time ticket, 909–910, **922**
Labor variances, 982–983
Land:
    cost of, 411
    defined, 48
    lump sum acquisition, 412
Land improvements, 411
Last-In, First-Out (LIFO):
    defined, 370, **393**
    periodic inventory system, 370–371, 374–375
    perpetual inventory system, 381–382, 383–386
LCM, *see* Lower of Cost-or-Market (LCM) rule
Lease:
    capital, 673–675
    defined, 456, **460,** 673, **676**
    operating, 675
Leasehold:
    accounting for, 456–457
    defined, 456, **460**
Leasehold Improvements, 457, **460**

Ledger, *see* General ledger
Legal capital, 587
Lessee, 456, **460**
Lessor, 456, **460**
Leverage, 650, **676**
Liabilities:
    accrued, 105–108
    classification, 348
    contingent, 346
    current, 348–351
    defined, 17, **29**
    long-term, 648–675
Limited partnership, 544, **563**
Linearity assumption, 1006, **1029**
Liquidating dividend, 591, **599**
Liquidation, partnership:
    defined, 559, **563**
    illustrated, 559–562
Liquidity, 115, **124,** 787, **802**
Long-term debt, 119–120
    current portion of, 119
Long-term investments, defined, 118, **124,** 706, **731**
    see also Investments
Long-term liabilities, 120, **124**
Lower of cost or market (LCM) rule:
    defined, 376, **393**
    illustrated, 376–379
Lump-sum acquisition:
    apportioning cost, 412
    defined, 412, **429**

Make or buy decisions, 1046–1047
Maker, 341, **352**
Management Accounting, 14
Management advisory services, 9–10
Management decision making, 825–826, 1042–1043
Management by exception, 825, **847,** 939, 955–956, 978
Management functions, 824–825, **847**
Managerial accounting, 823, **847**
Manual accounting system, 250–266
Manufacturing accounting:
    accounts required, 876
    defined, 865
    Inventory valuation problems, 883–887
    periodic and perpetual, 876, 887
    procedures required, 866–871, 875–883
Manufacturing cost elements, 869–871, **887**
Manufacturing firm, 865–866, **888**
Manufacturing margin, 1014, **1029**
Manufacturing margin rate, 1014, **1029**
Manufacturing overhead, 870–871, **888,** 910–913, 917, 947–948, 983–988
Manufacturing overhead budget, 947–948, **957**

Manufacturing overhead subsidiary accounts, 876
Manufacturing worksheet, 877–880
Marginal tax rate, 1088–1089, **1103**
Margin of safety, 1022, **1029**
Marketable securities, *see* Temporary investments
Market rate (effective rate, yield):
    defined, 656, **676**
    determination of bond issue price, 656–658
Marshall, John (Chief Justice), 579
Master budget, 941–942, **958**
    illustrated, 943–955
Matching principle:
    accrual basis of accounting, 95–96
    adjusting entries, 97
    defined, 94, **124,** 509–510, **524**
Materiality, 511, **524**
Material ledger cards, 907–908
Material price variance, 981–982, **991**
Material quantity variance, 981–982, **991**
Material requisition form, 907–908, **922**
Material requisition process, 907
Materials, 869, **887**
Material variances, 981–982
Maturity date, 342, **352,** 652, **676**
Maturity value, 342, **352**
Maximum capacity, 986, **991**
Medical and dental expense itemized deduction, 1081
Merchandise inventory:
    consignment, 365–366
    cost flow methods, 368–386
    defined, 205, **229**
    determining cost, 366–367
    error correction, 386–388
    gross profit method, 390–391
    income taxes, 372–376, 1102
    lower of cost or market, 376–379
    net realizable value, 379–380
    periodic inventory system, 215–220
    perpetual inventory system, 210–215
    retail inventory method, 389–390
    taking physical count, 364
    transfer of ownership, 365–366
Microcomputer, 268
Minicomputer, 268
Minimum wage rate, 475
Minority interest:
    defined, 720, **731**
    illustrated, 720–722
Mixed cost, 1005, 1008–1011, **1029**
Monetary items, 515, **524**
Monetary unit principle, 504, **524**
Money, 6
Moody's Investors Service, 786
Mortgage, 673, **676**

Mortgage note payable:
    accounting for, 673
    defined, 49, 650, **676**
Moving average:
    defined, 383, **393**
    perpetual inventory system, 383
Multiple product CVP, 1027–1028
Multiple-step income statement, 225, **229**
Mutual agency, 544, **563**

National Association of Accountants (NAA), 14
Natural business year, 43, **77**
Natural resources, 451–453
Negotiable instrument, 333, **352**
Net capital gain or loss, **1103**
    net capital gain, 1080
    net capital loss, 1079–1080
Net income (earnings or profit), 19, **29**, 51, **77**, 476–479, **489**
Net invoice method, 227, **229**
Net long-term capital, gain or loss, 1079–1080, **1103**
Net loss, 19, **29**, 51, **78**
Net operating loss, 1092
Net present value, 1058–1060, **1061**
Net realizable value:
    current value accounting, 519
    defined, 379, **393**, 519, **524**
    valuation of inventory, 379–380
Net short-term capital gain or loss, 1079–1080, **1103**
Nominal accounts, 96–97, 160
Noncumulative preferred stock, 594, **599**
Nonmonetary items, 516, **524**
Nonprofit corporation, 579, **599**
Nonpublic (closely held) corporation, 579, **599**
Nonsufficient funds check (NSF), 302, **317**
No-par stock, 590, **599**
Normal account balance, 54, **78**
Normal capacity, 986, **991**
Normal operating cycle, defined, 117, **124**
Note payable, 49
    defined, 49, 348, **352**
    exchange for fixed asset, 412–414
Note receivable:
    accounting for, 341–347
    defined, 47, 333, **352**
    discounting, 345–347
    dishonored, 344–345
    end of period adjustment, 347

Objectivity principle, 21, **29**, 504, **524**
Obsolescence, 415, **429**
Online processing, 270, **273**
Operating budget, 941–942, **958**
Operating expense allocation, 834–840, **847**
Operating lease, 675, **677**

Operating loss, **1092**
Opportunity cost, 1044, **1061**
Ordinary repairs and maintenance, 425
Organization, 823, **847**
Organization costs, 582, **599**
Organizing, 825
Outstanding checks, 302, **317**
Overapplied manufacturing overhead, 912, **922**, 986
Overhead application rate, 871, 885–886, **888**, 910–911, 946–948, 983–986
Owners' equity:
    closing, 168–169
    defined, 17, **29**
    elements of, 49–51

Paid Vouchers File, 315, **317**
Parent Company, 716, **731**
Partnership:
    admission of new partner, 553–556
    allocation of profit or loss, 548–552
    characteristics of, 543–545
    defined, 14, **29**, 543, **563**
    financial statements, 552
    formation of, 546–548
    liquidation, 559–562
    withdrawal of partner, 556–559
Partnership agreement (partnership contract, articles of partnership):
    defined, 545, **563**
    need for, 545–546
Partnership formation, 547–548
Partnership liquidation, 559–562
Partnership-profit and loss agreement:
    fixed ratio, 549
    interest, salaries, 550–522
    ratio of capital balances, 549
Par value (face value, principle, maturity value):
    bonds issued at: 654–656
    defined, 652, **677**
Patent:
    accounting for, 454–455
    defined, 454, **460**
Payables:
    accounting for, 347–351
    accounts payable, 348
    classification of, 348
    end of period adjustment, 350–351
    other current liabilities, 351
    short-term note payable, 348–350
Payback period, 1056–1057, **1061**
Payee, 341, **352**
Payout ratio, 796
Payroll accounting, 473–488
Payroll bank account, 474, 484–485, **489**

Payroll fraud, 473
Payroll register, 482, **489**
Payroll taxes, 476–481, **489**
Pension plan, 675, **677**
Percentage-of-completion method, 506, **524**
Period budget, 941
Period costs, 868, **888**
Periodic inventory system:
  contrasted to perpetual, 218–220
  cost flow methods, 368–373, 383–386
  defined, 215, **229**
  illustrated, 215–218
  manufacturing firm, 876–877, 886–887
  worksheet, 220–225
Permanent (real) accounts, defined, 97, **124**, 160
Permanent difference, 1097, **1103**
Perpetual inventory system:
  contrasted to periodic, 218–220
  cost flow methods, 380–386
  defined, 210, **229**
  illustrated, 210–215
  manufacturing firm, 887, 903–907, 917–918
  worksheet, 220–225
Petty cash fund:
  accounting for, 298–300
  defined, 298, **317**
Petty cash receipt, 298, **317**
Physical inventory, 214, **229**
Planning, 824–825, 839–840, 1019–1027
Plant assets:
  capital and revenue expenditures, 424–425
  construction for own use, 411
  defined, 118, **124**
  depreciation, 414–421
  determining cost of, 410–411
  exchange of notes, 412–414
  exchange (trade-in), 446–449
  income tax, 421–422, 449, 1099–1102
  lump sum acquisition, 412
  records, 426–428
  repairs, 425–426
  retirement, 443–444
  sale, 444–446
  trade-in:
    dissimilar assets, 448–449
    similar assets, 446–447
    tax rules, 449
Point of sale accounting, 832–833
Pooling of interests:
  compared to purchase, 726–729
  defined, 727, **731**
  illustrated, 727–729
Portfolio, 705, **731**
Post-closing trial balance, 174, **186**

Posting, 57, **78**
Posting reference, 57
Practical capacity, 986, **991**
Predetermined overhead rate, 910–911, **922**, 94
  983–986
Preemptive right, 584, **599**
Preferred stock:
  asset preference, 594
  callable, 594–595
  convertible, 595–596
  defined, 593, **600**
  dividend, 593–594
Premium, bond:
  amortization, 661–664, 671–672
  defined, 653, **677**
Prepaid expenses, 48, 97, 98–104
Present value:
  ordinary annuity, 699–700
  single amount, 696–699
  Tables, 698, 700
Price-earning rates, 795
Primary earnings per share, 629, **633**
Principal, 342, **352**
Prior period adjustment:
  defined, 632, **633**
  recording and reporting, 630–632
Proceeds, 345, **352**
Process costing, 914, **922**
  illustration, 918–921
Processing center, 914, **922**
Process or sell decision, 1048–1049
Product costs, 868, **888**
Production budget, 943–945, **958**
Production capacity, 986
Production departments, 865, 870, **888**
Profit center, 824
Profit corporation, 579, **600**
Progressive tax, 1087, **1103**
Promissory note, 341, **352**
Proprietorship, 17
Protest fee, 346, **352**
Proxy statement, 584, **600**
Public accounting, 8–10
Public corporation, 579, **600**
Purchase, 216, **229**
Purchase discounts, 208, **229**
Purchase method:
  compared to pooling, 726–729
  defined, 726, **732**
  illustrated, 717–726
Purchase order, 308, **317**
Purchase returns and allowances, 217, **229**
Purchase requisition, 308, **317**
Purchases journal, 256–258, **273**

Purchasing power, 513, **524**
Purchasing power gain (loss), 515, **524**

Quick ratio (acid test ratio), 797–798

Rate of return:
  on common stockholders' equity, 793–794
  on total assets, 792–793
Ratio:
  analyze liquidity, 796–800
  analyze profitability, 792–796
  analyze solvency, 800–801
  computing, 791
  defined, 791, **802**
  limitations of, 801
  see also specific ratios
Raw materials (inventory), 866, 888
Real accounts, 96–97, 160
Realization principle, 25, **29**, 515, **525**
Receivables:
  accounting for, 332–347
  aging of, 337
  classification of, 333
  defined, 332
  uncollectible accounts, 334–341
    allowance method, 335–341
    direct write-off, 341
Receivable turnover, 798–799
Receiving report, 310, 317
Registered bond, 653, **677**
Relevant costs, 1043, 1045–1046, **1061**
Relevant range, 1007–1008, **1029**
Relevant revenue, 1044–1045, **1061**
Repairs (plant asset), 425–426
Replacement cost, 519
Report form (balance sheet), 115, **124**
Residual income, 1051–1052, **1061**
Residual value, 415, **429**
Responsibility accounting, 828–830, 848
Responsibility center, 828, **848**
Retail inventory method:
  defined, 389, **393**
  illustrated, 389–390
Retained earnings:
  defined, 178, **186,** 586, **600**
  restrictions, 620–621
Return on average investment, 1057–1058, **1061**
Return on investment analysis, 1050–1051, **1061**
Return on sales, 794
Revenue:
  accrual basis, 95
  cash basis, 94
  closing of, 164
  defined, 18, **29,** 50

Revenue expenditure, 425, **429**
Revenue recognition principle, 25, **29,** 515, **525**
Reversing entries:
  defined, 180, **186**
  illustrated, 180–183
Robert Morris and Associates, 786

Salary, 63, 475, **489**
Sales, 206, **229**
Sales budget, 943–944, **958**
Sales discount, 208, **229**
Sales forecast, 940–941
Sales journal, 253–256, **273**
Sales mix decisions, 1049–1050
Sales returns and allowances, 207, **230**
Secretary, corporate, 585
Secured (mortgage) bond, 653, **677**
Securities and Exchange Commission (SEC), 13
Segment of a business, 622, **633**
Selling expense, 206, **230**
Selling expenses budget, 949–950, **958**
Serial bonds, 654, **677**
Service department, 835, 839, **848,** 866, 870, **888**
Shareholder, 15, **29**
Short-term capital gain or loss, 1079–1080, **1104**
Simple interest, 690
Single proprietorship, 14, **29**
Sinking fund, bond, 668–670
Slide, 72, **78**
Software, 270, **273**
Solvency, 787, **802**
Source of funds:
  current operations, 750–752
  defined, 748, **771**
  illustrated, 748–750
  other sources, 752
Special journal, 252–253, **273**
Special order evaluation, 1045
Specific identification:
  defined, 368, **393**
  periodic inventory system, 368–369, 373
  perpetual inventory system, 381
Specific price change, 513, **525**
Split-off point, 1047, **1061**
Stable-dollar assumption, 21, **29**
Standard & Poor's Corporation, 786
Standard costs:
  benefits, 977–978
  defined, 972, **991**
  establishing, 978–979
  use, 976–977
Standard cost variances, 979–990
Standard labor cost, 977, 982–983
Standard manufacturing overhead, 977, 983–988

Standard materials cost, 977, 981–982
Statement of changes in financial position, 746–766
Statement of partners' capital, 552, **563**
Statement of retained earnings, 179
Statements of Financial Accounting Standards, 13
    No. 2, 454
    No. 4, 626, 667
    No. 12, 705
    No. 13, 674
    No. 16, 630
    No. 33, 521
    No. 34, 411
    No. 45, 1101
State unemployment taxes, 480–481, **489**
Static budget, 972–973
Stock, *see* Common stock; Preferred stock
Stock dividend, 617, **633**
Stockholders, 583–584
Stockholders' equity:
    defined, 586
    illustration, 586, 622
Stock split, 619, **633**
Straight-line amortization:
    bond investment, 713–715
    bonds payable, 659–664
Straight-line depreciation:
    defined, 416, **429**
    illustrated, 416–417
Subchapter S Corporation, 543, 1074, 1093–1095, **1104**
Subsidiary company, 717, **732**
Subsidiary ledger, 251–252, **273**
Summarization, 6
Sum-of-year's-digits depreciation
    defined, 417, **429**
    illustrated, 417–418
Sunk costs, 1044, **1061**
Systems, *see* Accounting system
Systems analysis, 249, **273**
Systems design, 249–250, **273**
Systems implementation, 250, **273**

T account, 45, **78**
Taxable income, 1080, **1104**
Tax accounting, 11
Tax credit, 1077, 1087, **1104**
Tax Equity and Fiscal Responsibility Act of 1982, 1073
Taxes itemized deduction (income tax return), 1082
Tax evasion, 1075, **1104**
Tax planning, 1075, **1104**
Tax rate schedules, 1085–1087
Tax shield, 1056, **1061**
Tax tables, 1083–1085
Temporary (nominal) accounts:
    closing, 160–169

    defined, 97, **125**
Temporary investments:
    accounting for, 704–706
    defined, 704, **732**
Term bonds (ordinary bonds), 654, **677**
Time card, 909
Time period assumption:
    accrual basis, 96
    defined, 43, **78**, 503, **525**
Times interest earned, 801
Timesharing-computer, 268
Time studies, 979
Timing difference, 1098, **1104**
Trade discounts, 209, **230**
Trade receivables, 333, **352**
Transactions:
    analysis, 52, 57–67
    business transactons, 5
    defined, 5, 29
    external, 5, 42, 77
    internal, 5, 42, 77
    types of, 5, 42
Transfer pricing, 1052, **1061**
Transposition, 72, **78**
Treasurer, 585
Treasury stock:
    accounting for, 613–615
    defined, 612, **633**
Trend analysis, 790
Trial balance, 70, **78**
Trustee, 653, **677**

Unavoidable cost (expense), 843, **848,** 1044–1046, **1061**
Uncollectible accounts, 334–341
Underapplied manufacturing overhead, 912, **922,** 986
Underwriter, 653, **677**
Unearned revenue, 49, 98, 104–105
Unexpired cost, 95, **125**
Unfavorable variance, 829, 955–957, 972–973, 981–989
Uniform Partnership Act (UPA), 542, **563**
Units-of-production depreciation:
    defined, 417, **429**
    illustrated, 417
Unlimited liability, 544, **563**
Unpaid vouchers file, 314, **317**
Unprofitable department analysis, 840–843
Unsecured note payable, 649, **677**
Useful life, 415, **429**
Use of funds:
    defined, 748, **771**
    illustrated, 748–750, 752–753

Variable costs, 872, **888,** 946–948, 973–975, 1005, 1007, 1026

Variable costing, 871–873, **888**, 1013–1018, **1029**
Variances:
  accounting for, 980
  analysis of, 981–983, 987–988
  defined, 829, **848**
  disposition of, 989–990
  labor, 982–983
  manufacturing overhead, 987–988
  material, 981–982
Vertical analysis, 791, **802**
Volume variance, 987–988, **990**
Voucher, 312, **317**
Voucher register, 313, **317**
Voucher system:
  defined, 308, **317**
  design of, 308–316

Wage, 63
Wage and tax statement (Form W-2), 486, **489**
Wages, 475, **489**
Weighted average:
  defined, 371, **393**
  periodic inventory system, 371, 375

Withdrawal, *see* Drawing account
Withholding, 476–480
Withholding allowance, 477–478, **489**
Withholding table, 477–478, **489**
Work in process (inventory) 867, 885–886, **888**, 908–909, 911
Working capital:
  computation of changes in working capital, 759–760
  defined, 115, **124**, 747, **771**
  illustrated, 755–764
  preparation of statement, 764
  worksheet, 760–764
Worksheet:
  defined, 150, **186**
  illustrated, 150–156
  manufacturing, 877–879
  merchandising firm, 220–225
W-2 form, 486, **489**

Zero bracket amount:
  defined, 1080, **1104**
  illustrated, 1083–1087, 1090